W9-ARY-586

SPARKNOTES™

SPARKNOTES®

10 practice tests for the SAT*

Spark Publishing
A Division of Barnes & Noble
120 Fifth Avenue
New York, NY 10011
www.sparknotes.com

ISBN-13: 978-1-4114-0467-0
ISBN-10: 1-4114-0467-X

Printed and bound in Canada.

15 14 13 12 11 10

Contents

HOW TO USE THIS BOOK

TAKE PRACTICE TEST. SCORE PRACTICE TEST. Repeat ten times. Come test day, you'll be a lean, mean test-taking machine. You'll also be exhausted and frustrated.

A better method is to take, score, and review each practice test *before* moving on to the next test. This way, you can identify and target your weaknesses—and you can conquer them before you take another test. If you take the time to study up on your weak spots, you'll see improvement from one practice test to the next. You'll also gain confidence for test day.

You can use this book in several ways:

- To simulate the real SAT experience
- To identify your weaknesses and prioritize your study time
- To get more practice on specific sections or questions
- To set a target score

PRACTICING WITH PRACTICE TESTS

Studying practice tests is a powerful SAT prep tool. That's why we give you access to an additional 3 practice tests online at **http://testprep.sparknotes.com/upgrade/sat**.

Below, we explain step-by-step exactly how to do it yourself.

Control Your Environment

You should do everything in your power to make every practice test you take feel like the real SAT. The more your practice resembles the real thing, the more helpful it is.

- Take a timed test. Don't give yourself any extra time. Be as strict as the proctor administering the test will be. If you have to go to the bathroom, let the clock keep running. That's what'll happen on the test day.
- Take the test in a single sitting. Training yourself to endure roughly four-and-a-half hours of test-taking is part of your preparation.
- Take the test without distractions. Don't take the practice test in a room with lots of people walking through it. Go to a library, your bedroom, an empty classroom—anywhere quiet.

Simulating the real SAT experience as closely as possible during your study time will ensure that there will be no surprises to distract you on test day. Understanding what you're in for on test day will give you the focus and calm you'll need to reach your target score.

Score Your Practice Test

After you take a practice test, score it and see how you did. However, when you do your scoring, don't just tally up your raw score. As part of your scoring, you should also keep a list of every question you got wrong and every question you skipped. This list will be your guide when you study your test.

The College Board will score your real test using the following formula:

$$\#\text{ of questions you got correct} - \frac{\#\text{ of questions you got wrong}}{4} = \text{raw score}$$

Your raw score then gets plotted on a curve, along with the raw scores of every other test-taker. All of these raw scores are eventually assigned to a number between 200 and 800. That number is your scaled score. Since the SAT has three sections, 2,400 is the perfect scaled score.

The ten practice tests in this book come with a chart that shows you how to translate your raw score into a scaled score.

Study Your Practice Test

After grading your test, you should have a list of the questions you answered incorrectly or skipped. Studying your test involves using this list and examining each question you answered incorrectly, figuring out why you got the question wrong, and understanding what you could have done to get the question right.

The practice tests in our books were specifically designed to help you study. Each question is categorized by its major subject, such as geometry; by its specific subject, such as circles; and by its difficulty level, such as medium. The answers also provide full explanations of each question so you can identify and focus on your specific weaknesses.

Why Did You Get It Wrong?

There are four reasons why you might have gotten an individual question wrong:

1. You thought you solved the answer correctly, but you actually didn't.
2. You managed to eliminate some answer choices and then guessed among the remaining answers. Sadly, you guessed wrong.
3. You knew the answer but made a careless error.
4. You left it blank.

You should know which of these reasons applies to each question you got wrong. Once you figure out why you got a question wrong, you need to figure out what you could have done to get the question right.

Reason 1: Lack of Knowledge

A question answered incorrectly for reason 1 pinpoints a weakness in your knowledge. Discovering this kind of error gives you the opportunity to fill the void in your knowledge base and eliminate future errors on the same question type.

For example, if the question you got wrong refers to factoring quadratics, don't just work out how to factor that *one* quadratic. Take the chance to go over the fundamental techniques that allow you to factor *all* quadratics.

Remember, you will not see a question exactly like the question you got wrong. But you probably will see a question that covers the same topic as the practice question. For that reason, when you get a question wrong, don't just figure out the right answer to the question. Study the broader topic that the question tests.

Reason 2: Guessing Wrong

If you guessed wrong, review your guessing strategy. By thinking in a critical way about the decisions you made while taking the practice test, you can train yourself to make quicker, more decisive, and better decisions.

Did you guess smartly? Did you eliminate answers you knew were wrong? Could you have eliminated more answers? If yes, why didn't you? Remember: if you can eliminate even one of the five answer choices, you've reduced the number of choices from five to four and increased your odds of getting the question right. And you should always guess on math grid-in questions, because there's no penalty for wrong answers on those questions.

If you took a guess and chose the incorrect answer, don't let that discourage you from guessing. The SAT is almost an entirely multiple-choice test, which means the answer is right there in front of you. If you eliminated at least one answer, you followed the right strategy by guessing even if you got the question wrong. Review the answer choices for every question—even those you answered correctly. Figuring out why certain answer choices are wrong will help you identify other wrong answers on future SAT questions.

Reason 3: Carelessness

Here it might be tempting to say to yourself, "Oh, I made a careless error," and assure yourself you won't do that again. Unacceptable! You made that careless mistake for a reason, and you should figure out why. Getting a question wrong because you didn't know the answer reveals a weakness in your knowledge about the test. Making a careless mistake represents a weakness in your test-taking method.

To overcome this weakness, you need to approach it in the same critical way you would approach a lack of knowledge. Study your mistake. Retrace your thought process on the problem and pinpoint the origin of your carelessness: If you pin down your mistake, you are less likely to repeat it.

Reason 4: Leaving the Question Blank

It's also a good idea to study the questions you left blank on the test, since those questions constitute a reservoir of lost points. A blank answer results from one of two situations:

1. A total inability to answer a question.
2. A lack of time.

If you were totally unable to answer a question, you must either learn the material or at least try to identify a way you could have eliminated an answer choice in order to turn the guessing odds in your favor. Always guess if you can eliminate at least one answer choice.

If you left an answer blank because of time constraints, look over the question and see whether you think you could have answered it correctly. If you could have, then you know you need to speed up as much as possible without making more careless errors. If you couldn't have answered it correctly, then you've just identified a weakness waiting to be overcome.

TEST-TAKING STRATEGIES

BEFORE DIVING INTO OUR GLOBAL test-taking strategies, let's define some terms. We'll use an example from the multiple-choice portion of the Writing section:

6. Eager to pass his final exams, studying was the student's top priority.

(A) studying was the student's top priority.
(B) the student made studying his top priority.
(C) the top priority of the student was studying.
(D) the student's top priority was studying.
(E) studying was the top priority for the student.

The stuff that follows the number is called the **question**. The lettered options are the **answer choices**. Only one of the answer choices is correct. The other four answer choices are called **distractors** because that is exactly what they are designed to do—*distract* attention from the correct answer.

In Reading Passages and Improving Paragraphs, you'll also have **passages** that provide information. In those question types, more than one question is tied to a passage.

A **section** refers to a Critical Reading, Writing, or Math timed section that usually contains a mix of various question types.

BOMBING RUNS

The key to tackling any standardized test is managing your time so you can answer as many questions correctly as possible. On just about every test you take in school, you start at number 1, work on it until you come up with an answer, go to number 2, do the same, and so on. This method is *death* on the SAT, and here's why. Imagine two test-takers, Jack and Jill, who have identical skill levels. Each test-taker has the ability to answer every question on the SAT correctly. Generally, every ten questions appear in the following order of difficulty:

Question Number	Difficulty Level
1	Difficult
2	Easy
3	Difficult
4	Easy
5	Difficult
6	Medium
7	Easy
8	Easy
9	Medium
10	Difficult

Jack follows human nature. He starts at the first question and works his way through the questions in the order in which they are presented, spending as much time to get an answer as is necessary. Jack runs out of time after question 6, but he gets all six questions correct.

Jill, however, flies **Bombing Runs**. She scans the questions and completes the set in the following order:

Question Number	Order in Which Jill Attempts Question	Difficulty Level
1	7th	Difficult
2	1st	Easy
3	8th	Difficult
4	2nd	Easy
5	9th	Difficult
6	5th	Medium
7	3rd	Easy
8	4th	Easy
9	6th	Medium
10	10th	Difficult

Here's how Bombing Runs work: Jill does all the easy questions first, then goes back and does all the medium questions, and finally attempts the hard questions. Jill—who has the exact same skill levels as Jack—has enough time to attempt every question and gets all 10 points. Jill bombs the easy targets first, then the medium ones, and finally the hard ones.

Jill's got the right idea. Fly Bombing Runs to distribute your knowledge across a section as efficiently as possible.

Order of Difficulty

Easy, medium, difficult—what do these terms really mean? Well, there are several ways of understanding difficulty on the SAT.

First, a question's difficulty is a statistical quality based on the test-takers who encountered that question on an experimental section. A geometry question can be considered hard if only those students who tend to score high in the Math section answer it correctly.

The questions in Sentence Completion sets and multiple-choice Math sections are set up by order of difficulty, whereas the other sections mix these questions up. More difficult questions tend to have more seductive distractors.

But you're an individual, and just because *most* test-takers found a question easy (or difficult) doesn't mean that *you* will. When you fly Bombing Runs and skip around in a section, your personal determination of a question's difficulty based on your experience and practice is what counts, not its statistical difficulty level. Difficulty is *not* an essential feature of a question.

The take-home message here is not to worry too much about how the SAT orders the questions. What counts is *your* order of difficulty.

We illustrate this in the chart below. Jack and Jill have equivalent overall general skill levels—over a full test, they'll score the same—but more realistically, they have different specific skill levels. For example, Jack is better at geometry. Jill shines in word problems. Assume Jack and Jill are taking the same test but categorize the difficulty of each question differently, as follows:

Question Number	Jack's Determination of Difficulty Level	Jill's Determination of Difficulty Level
1	Difficult	Easy
2	Easy	Medium
3	Difficult	Easy
4	Easy	Easy
5	Difficult	Medium
6	Medium	Difficult
7	Easy	Medium
8	Easy	Medium
9	Medium	Difficult
10	Difficult	Difficult

As long as both Jack and Jill fly Bombing Runs, given that their overall skill levels are the same, we can assume they'll each answer all ten questions correctly, although they'll attempt them in different orders, based on their own personal determination of difficulty level:

Question Number	Jack's Difficulty Level	Order in Which Jack Attempts Question	Jill's Difficulty Level	Order in Which Jill Attempts Question
1	Difficult	7th	Easy	1st
2	Easy	1st	Medium	4th
3	Difficult	8th	Easy	2nd
4	Easy	2nd	Easy	3rd
5	Difficult	9th	Medium	5th
6	Medium	5th	Difficult	8th
7	Easy	3rd	Medium	6th
8	Easy	4th	Medium	7th
9	Medium	6th	Difficult	9th
10	Difficult	10th	Difficult	10th

Do the questions in order of difficulty from easiest (for you) to hardest (for you). Ignore the order in which the questions are presented. Smart test-takers fly Bombing Runs based on their personal determination of difficulty.

Section-Level Bombing Runs

We've been talking about flying Bombing Runs on groups of questions, but you can also apply this strategy to an entire timed section. This strategy works especially well on the Critical Reading section. A typical Critical Reading section includes Sentence Completions, Short Reading Passages, and Long Reading Passages. Let's say you encountered a Critical Reading section made up of the following:

- 10 sentence completions
- 1 short reading passage on humanities with two questions
- 1 short reading passage on science with two questions
- 1 long fiction passage with nine questions

Because all questions are worth the same amount of points, always do the lowest investment questions first. Here's how you'd fly a Bombing Run on this section:

- Do the sentence completions first. They require a far lower time investment than the reading passages.
- Next, tackle the short reading passages. They require less of an investment than the long passages. If you're into science, do that one first. If not, do the humanities one first.
- Tackle the long reading passage last, making sure to fly a Bombing Run within the questions.

The same idea applies to the Math section. If you know you're good at geometry, word problems, or data analysis, do those questions first.

Knowing When to Bail

If a question starts eating up a lot of time, you have to overcome your desire to finish at all costs. If you're taking too much time on a question, you'll eventually have to let go and move on. Questions are each worth 1 point. You get no extra credit for taking five minutes to answer the hardest question on the test. Instead, you'll end up with 1 point and less time for all the easier questions.

Bailing can mean a couple of things:

- Stopping work on that question completely and moving on to another question. You'll go back to it later if you have time.
- Eliminating one or more answer choices, guessing from the remaining, and moving on.

Keep a clock going in the back of your head as you work through a section. It doesn't pay to be too nutty about exact amounts of time, but if you're pushing two minutes for any question, you should be looking for a parachute—a way to bail out.

Think of it this way: don't be a drum machine or metronome, counting out exact packets of time per question. Be more like a real human drummer, keeping time loosely. Through practice, you'll get a sense of how long it normally takes you to answer a question. Eventually, you will have the time constraints running in the back of your mind, but your focus will be on the question at hand, not the clock.

ACCURACY

Managing your time efficiently is only one part of the equation. Once you've got a plan, you need execute that plan with accuracy. The more accurate you are, the more points you earn on the SAT. Here are some general tips that you should always keep in mind.

Have an Idea of the Answer Before You Look at Any Answer Choices

Remember, in multiple-choice questions, four answer choices are *distractors*. Do *not* simply let the answer choices guide your thought. Attack each question with some idea of the correct answer. The methods you'll use for coming up with your own answer will differ for each question type.

Avoid Carelessness

Speed is only part of the goal on the SAT. Speed balanced with accuracy is the full goal. In general, the less you do in your head and the more explicit you make your approach to every question, the less careless you'll be. If you're solving a math question, take the time to write out all your steps. Even an easy question can become a real challenge if you try to keep all the steps in your head.

In almost every situation, you'll also want to take a split-second and ask yourself, "Is my answer reasonable?" If not, chances are you made a careless mistake in solving the question.

Give the Question What It Wants

This may seem most applicable to Math, but it's actually applicable to the entire test. In Math, you can be sure that a multistep question will include a distractor that lists a key number you need to find the ultimate result. For example, if a question asks you to solve for $x + 1$, you can be sure that the value of x will be one of the distractors. When you come up with an answer, make sure it's what the question is asking for. Usually on the SAT, you have to perform one final step to convert the number you've come up with into the number the question asks for.

All of Critical Reading—Sentence Completions and Reading Passages—tests your reading *in context*. So you may find distractors that are correct outside of the specific context but are actually incorrect in the question. For example, on some vocabulary questions, the correct answer is usually a second or third meaning of the word. The context of the question determines which meaning is appropriate.

The Writing section is also context-dependent. You either identify an error (Identifying Sentence Errors) or identify an error and fix it (Improving Sentences and Paragraphs) according to the context of the sentence or sentences. Even the essay follows this guideline—one of the only ways to get a zero on the essay is not to address the issue presented in the prompt.

Educated Guessing

The SAT does *not* have a guessing penalty. What it does have is a **wrong-answer penalty**. The SAT is set up to cancel out random guessing, not educated guessing.

Here's an illustration. Imagine a ten-question group on the SAT. Each question has five answer choices, A through E. Let's say you simply fill in the bubble sheet randomly. For every question you get right, you get a point. For every question you get wrong, you lose a quarter-point. What would happen?

Question	Right Answer	Your Random Guess	Right/Wrong	Points Gained or Lost
1	D	A	Wrong	–1/4
2	C	B	Wrong	–1/4
3	B	C	Wrong	–1/4
4	A	D	Wrong	–1/4
5	D	D	Right	+1
6	D	A	Wrong	–1/4
7	E	B	Wrong	–1/4
8	E	C	Wrong	–1/4
9	C	C	Right	+1
10	A	E	Wrong	–1/4
			Total Wrong	–2
			Total Right	+2
			Net Gain	0

In a five-answer multiple-choice question, the chance of getting the question correct by random guessing is 1 in 5. The chance of getting the question incorrect is 4 in 5. Therefore, you have a 1-in-5 chance of getting 1 point and a 4-in-5 chance of losing $^1/_4$ of a point. Although you gained 2 points for the two correct answers, you lost 2 points for the eight incorrect answers ($8 \times {}^1/_4 = 2$).

Educated guessing is all about earning a net gain of points on the test. Every time you eliminate even *one* answer choice as being most likely incorrect and guess from what remains, you are nudging your net points higher and higher.

For example, let's say that in ten questions, you eliminated two answer choices as wrong for each question. Instead of having a 1-in-5 chance of answering a question correctly, you now have a 1-in-3 chance. Similarly, instead of having a 4-in-5 chance of answering a question incorrectly, you have a 2-in-3 chance. What would happen to your net points?

- 10 questions × $\frac{1}{3}$ chance of guessing correctly = $\frac{10}{3}$ = $3\frac{1}{3}$ questions answered correctly. $3\frac{1}{3}$ questions answered correctly × 1 point for a correct answer = $3\frac{1}{3}$ points.
- 10 questions × $\frac{2}{3}$ chance of randomly guessing incorrectly = $\frac{20}{3}$ = $6\frac{2}{3}$ questions answered incorrectly. $6\frac{2}{3} \times -\frac{1}{4}$ points for an incorrect answer = $-1\frac{2}{3}$ points.
- $3\frac{1}{3}$ points + $-1\frac{2}{3}$ points = $1\frac{2}{3}$ net points.

Instead of netting zero points, you've netted almost 2 points—*without knowing the correct answer to any of the ten questions.*

As you can see, educated guessing is critical to raising your score. Think of it this way: There are a certain number of questions you can answer correctly even if you've never seen the SAT before, and that number increases as you become familiar with the test.

However, you put a "glass ceiling" on your score potential if you refuse to guess when you've eliminated one or more choices as being most likely incorrect. You must use educated guessing to increase your score.

CONQUERING TEST-TAKING ANXIETIES

THE BEST WAY TO TACKLE YOUR ANXIETY is to practice, practice, practice. That's why you bought this book, right? The more familiar you are with the SAT, and the more you know what to expect, the more comfortable you'll feel on test day. To help you get familiar with the SAT, we've gathered together some anti-anxiety strategies. Read on—and feel the anxiety melt away.

SET A TARGET SCORE

Concrete goals are better than vague hopes. Here's a vague hope: "I want to do really well on the SAT." Okay. Go study everything. In contrast, here's a concrete goal: "I want to raise my score on the SAT Math section by 40 points." If you want to raise your score on the SAT Math section by 40 points, you have to take the following three steps:

- Study the particular math concepts that give you trouble.
- Leave fewer questions blank.
- Pick up your pace.

Concrete goals allow you to come up with a specific plan. This will make the time you spend preparing for the SAT much more efficient, leaving you more time to enjoy your life.

When setting a target score, be honest and realistic. Base your target score on the range that the schools you want to go to will expect. A good target score should be 50–100 points above the average for those schools. You can also gauge your target score by your first practice test. If you score a 500 on the Math section of the first practice test, don't set your target score at 750. You'll just get frustrated and you won't know where to focus your preparation time. Instead, your target should be about 50 points higher on each section than your score on your first practice test. That may not seem like much, but 50 points on each section of the test will raise your total score by 150 points!

If You Reach Your Target Score . . .

Give yourself a cookie or, if you're a health freak, a carrot. But just because you've hit your target score doesn't mean you should stop working. In fact, you should view reaching your target score as proof that you can do better than that score: set a new target 50–100 points above your original, pick up your pace a little bit, and skip fewer questions.

Slow and steady beats the test. By working to improve bit by bit, you'll integrate your knowledge of how to take the test and the subjects the test covers without burning out. If you can handle working just a little faster without becoming careless and losing points, your score will certainly go up. If you meet your new target score again, rinse and repeat.

PREP YOURSELF FOR TEST DAY

Begin getting up early on weekends if you don't normally do so. Get your body in that habit—it helps. As far as specific foods go, the simple truth of nutrition is to eat balanced meals. Don't alter your food intake radically unless you eat only junk food. Get your gut used to a nutritious morning meal.

If your test site isn't at a familiar location, take a drive one morning to see how to get there and how much traffic there is. Don't leave finding the site to the day of the test. Who needs that kind of pressure?

The Day Before the Test

Our advice for the day before the test is:

- Don't do any SAT prep work!
- Don't do any SAT prep work!
- Don't do any SAT prep work!

Whatever factoid you might gain the night before will be more than outweighed by the anxiety you'll be producing. Watch a movie. Hang out with friends. Read a book. Play a video game. Go for a run. Do something other than studying for the SAT.

Run through the following checklist and put everything in your bag or backpack the night before so you won't have to worry about it in the morning:

- Timepiece
- Approved calculator with fresh batteries
- Backup approved calculator with fresh batteries
- More fresh batteries
- At least four sharpened No. 2 pencils
- A small pencil sharpener
- An extra big eraser that really works
- A photo ID
- Your admissions ticket
- A snack
- Tissues, even if you're not sniffly
- Layers, in case it's cold in the room
- A portable CD player or iPod, if you think music will calm or focus you during breaks

Remember:

- You can't use an alarm during the test.
- You can't eat or drink during the test inside the testing room.
- You can't bring in any scratch paper, notes, books, highlighters, pens, protractors, etc. Check out the full list of accepted and prohibited materials at **http://collegeboard.com/student/testing/sat/testday/bring.html**.
- You can't use your iPod or CD player inside the test room.
- You must turn off your cell phone.
- Go to bed at your usual time. If you can't fall asleep, don't worry about it. Worrying is what keeps you awake. Try some deep-breathing exercises and realize that no matter how little sleep you end up getting, you'll be revved up for the test, come morning.

On Test Day

Here's what you need to do:

- Wake up early enough to eat your normal nutritious breakfast and relax. You should be able to go through your usual routine without feeling rushed and still have enough time to get to the test site at least 30 minutes early. You'll want to avoid, if possible, the unforeseen disasters of traffic or other wacky delays.
- Do not drink a lot of caffeine. Drink whatever amount you're used to, if you drink any at all. Caffeine is a diuretic—you don't want to take bathroom breaks during the test or feel distracted by having to go and not wanting to take a break.
- Grab your prepacked bag and go.
- Once you arrive at the test site, be selfish. Do whatever you need to do to put yourself in the proper mindset. Talk to friends, listen to music, be by yourself. Do whatever relaxes you.
- When the test starts, stay calm. Trust your preparation and effort. It will pay off. Focus completely on the test. Drown out all other sensory input, aside from your timepiece. Don't even think about how you're doing or scoring—just do it. You are an efficient, savvy, test-taking machine. Take control of that test.

GETTING ONLINE

If you haven't visited our website, what are you waiting for? Get thee online, and go to **http://testprep.sparknotes.com/upgrade/newsat** to take a free diagnostic SAT test. Our powerful test software will pinpoint your problem areas and help you overcome your weaknesses. Based on your diagnostic test, we will build you a personalized study plan that links to the SAT topics you need to review. SparkNotes' SAT website also provides the following features:

- Three more SAT tests—*free*. This book gives you access to three SAT practice tests online. So log on, take a practice test, and score higher.
- Searchable versions of our *SAT Power Tactics*, SAT Vocabulary novels, and the *SparkNotes Guide to the SAT*, our guide to everything you need to know about the SAT.
- A free PDF list of 1,000 of the most frequently tested SAT vocabulary words.
- Message boards where you can chat about your anxieties and share study tips with fellow test-takers.

REGISTERING FOR THE SAT

You have a few options:

- Register online at **http://collegeboard.com/student/testing/sat/reg.html**.
- Register by mail by getting the official Registration Bulletin at your high school's guidance office.

Taking the SAT will cost you $41.50. Financial aid is available for qualified students. You can find information on getting a fee waiver at **http://collegeboard.com/student/testing/sat/calenfees/feewaivers.html**.

You can also find information on special circumstances for test-takers on the general College Board registration site.

Good luck!

THE SAT ESSAY

A "GREAT SAT ESSAY" AND A "GREAT ESSAY" ARE *not* the same thing. Truly great essays take hours or even days to plan, research, and write. The SAT essay can't take more than twenty-five minutes.

The College Board knows that twenty-five minutes isn't enough time for anyone, anywhere, to write a genius essay. Forget genius. Forget about trying to write an essay that changes the world. When the SAT directions say to you, "Here's twenty-five minutes, write an essay," what they're really saying is: "Write a *standard* essay that does exactly what we want."

To give the SAT what it wants, you need to have a very firm essay-writing strategy in place before you sit down to take the test. You then need to apply that strategy to whatever topic the SAT essay gives you. In this chapter, we teach you a strategy for writing a great SAT essay that works every time, on any topic. It all starts with fast food.

THE FAST FOOD ESSAY

One of the best things about fast food is not just that it's quick, but that it's *consistent*. Walk into a McDonald's in Tosserdorf, Germany, and a Big Mac is still a robust, comforting Big Mac, just like at home. What makes fast food so consistent? Restaurants like McDonald's use the same ingredients and preparation methods at every location.

To write a top-notch SAT essay every time, you need to think about fast food. In fact, you need to write a *fast food essay*. Just like the fast food chains, you need to know three things:

- Your customers
- Your ingredients
- How to put the ingredients together

KNOW YOUR CUSTOMERS

After you finish taking the SAT, your essay is scanned into a computer, uploaded to a secure website, and graded on computer screens at remote locations by "essay-graders." These essay-graders are usually English teachers, writing teachers, or graduate students in the humanities who have been hired and trained to grade SAT essays by the company that makes the SAT.

Every essay is actually read by two graders. Each grader is instructed to spend no more than *three minutes* reading an essay before giving it a score on a scale of 1 to 6.

The two grades are then added together to make up your entire essay subscore, which ranges from 2 to 12. (If two graders come to wildly different scores for an essay, like a 2 and a 5, another is brought in.)

So the essay-graders are your *customers*. You want to give them an essay that tastes just like what they're expecting. How are *you* supposed to know what *they're* expecting? You can learn exactly what SAT essay-graders expect by looking at two very important guidelines: the actual SAT essay directions and the grading criteria that the SAT gives its graders.

The SAT* Essay Directions

The first thing you should *not* do when writing your SAT essay is read the directions. Don't waste your time. Instead, read the directions now and make sure you understand them.

> The essay gives you an opportunity to show how effectively you can develop and express ideas. You should, therefore, take care to develop your point of view, present your ideas logically and clearly, and use language precisely.
>
> Your essay must be written on the lines provided on your answer sheet—you will receive no other paper on which to write. You will have enough space if you write on every line, avoid wide margins, and keep your handwriting to a reasonable size. Remember that people who are not familiar with your handwriting will read what you write. Try to write or print so that what you are writing is legible to those readers.
>
> You have twenty-five minutes to write an essay on the topic assigned below. DO NOT WRITE ON ANOTHER TOPIC. AN OFF-TOPIC ESSAY WILL RECEIVE A SCORE OF ZERO.

We've translated these directions into a list of Dos and Don'ts to make all the rules easier to grasp:

DO	DON'T
Write only on the given topic as directed.	Write on a topic that relates vaguely to the one given.
Take a clear position on the topic.	Take a wishy-washy position or try to argue two sides.
Write persuasively to convince the grader.	Write creatively or ornately just to show off.
Include reasons and examples that support your position.	Include examples not directly related to your position.
Write with correct grammar and spelling.	Forget to proof your work for spelling and grammar mistakes.
Write as clearly as possible.	Use too many fancy vocabulary words or overly long sentences.
Write specifically and concretely.	Be vague or use generalizations.
Write more than one paragraph.	Put more importance on length than on quality.
Write only on the given lined paper.	Make your handwriting too large or you'll sacrifice space.
Write as neatly as possible in print or cursive.	Write in cursive if you can print. Print is much easier to read.

* SAT test directions selected from the SAT Reasoning Test. Reprinted by permission of the College Board, the copyright owner.

The Grader's Instructions

Essay-graders must refer to a set-in-stone list of criteria when evaluating each essay and deciding what grade (1 through 6) it deserves. The following chart is our explanation of the grading criteria that the SAT gives the graders.

Score	Description of Essay
6	A 6 essay is *superior* and demonstrates a *strong and consistent* command of the language throughout the entire essay, with at most a few small errors. A 6 essay: • shows a firm grasp of critical thinking and takes a powerful and interesting position on the topic • supports and develops its position with appropriate and insightful examples, arguments, and evidence • is tightly organized and focused, with a smooth and coherent progression of ideas • demonstrates a facility with language through the use of descriptive and appropriate vocabulary • intelligently varies sentence structure • contains, at most, a few errors in grammar, spelling, and punctuation
5	A 5 essay is *strong* and demonstrates a *generally consistent* command of language throughout the entire essay, with no more than a few significant flaws and errors. A 5 essay: • shows well-developed critical thinking by taking a solid position on the topic • supports and develops its position on the topic with appropriate examples, arguments, and evidence • is organized and focused and features a coherent progression of ideas • demonstrates competence with language by using appropriate vocabulary • uses varied sentence structure • contains few errors in grammar, spelling, and punctuation
4	A 4 essay is *competent* and demonstrates a basic *command* of the language throughout the entire essay. A 4 essay: • shows adequate critical thinking by taking a position on the topic and supporting that position with generally appropriate examples, arguments, and evidence • is mostly organized and focused, with a progression of ideas that is mostly coherent • demonstrates inconsistent facility with language and uses mostly appropriate vocabulary • uses some variation in sentence structure • contains some errors in grammar, spelling, and punctuation

Score	Description of Essay
3	A 3 essay shows *developing competence* and contains *one or more* of the following: • some critical thinking skills, as demonstrated by its position on the topic • inadequate support or development of its position based on deficiencies in examples, arguments, or evidence presented • lapses in organization and focus, including ideas that are not always coherent • a capacity for competent use of language, with occasional use of vague or inappropriate vocabulary • only minor variation in sentence structure • a variety of errors in grammar, spelling, and punctuation
2	A 2 essay is *seriously flawed* and demonstrates a *poor command* of the language throughout the entire essay. A 2 essay contains *one or more* of the following: • poor critical thinking skills as shown by an inconsistent or unclear position on the topic • insufficient support for the position on the topic as a result of faulty or nonexistent examples, arguments, and evidence • weak organization and focus, including ideas that are frequently incoherent • poor language skills through use of limited or wrong vocabulary • errors in sentence structure • errors in grammar, spelling, punctuation, and other rules of writing that make the meaning hard to understand
1	A 1 essay is *profoundly flawed* and demonstrates a *very poor command* of the language throughout the entire essay. A 1 essay contains *one or more* of the following: • no position on the topic, or almost no support or development of the position • poor organization and focus that makes the essay incoherent • numerous vocabulary errors • fundamental errors in sentence structure • errors in grammar, spelling, and punctuation that make parts of the essay unintelligible
0	Essays written on a topic other than the one assigned will receive a score of zero.

KNOW YOUR INGREDIENTS

To write a tasty SAT essay, you've got to know the necessary ingredients. The different grades of 1 to 6 are based on the quality of your essay in four fundamental categories:

1. **Positioning:** the strength and clarity of your stance on the given topic
2. **Examples:** the relevance and development of the examples you use to support your argument

3. **Organization:** the organization of each of your paragraphs and of your essay overall
4. **Command of language:** sentence construction, grammar, and word choice

Now you know your customers, and you know what they want. We'll spend the rest of this chapter teaching you precisely how to give it to them.

Positioning

SAT essay topics are always really, really broad. We're talking "the big questions of life" broad. A typical SAT essay topic gives you a statement that addresses ideas like *the concept of justice, the definition of success*, or *the importance of learning from mistakes.*

The broad nature of SAT topics means you'll never be forced to write about topical or controversial issues of politics, culture, or society (unless you want to—and we'll talk about whether you *should* want to a little later). But the broadness of the topics also means that with a little thought you can come up with plenty of examples to support your position on the topic.

Philosophers take years to write tomes on the topics of *justice* or *success*. On the SAT, you get twenty-five minutes. Given these time constraints, the key to writing a great SAT essay is to take a strong position on an extremely broad topic. You need to select your position strategically. To do this, follow a two-step strategy:

- Rephrase the prompt.
- Choose your position.

It's time to learn how to take a stand. Here's a sample essay topic for the SAT:

> Think carefully about the issue presented in the following excerpt and the assignment below.
>
> "It is a mistake to suppose that men succeed through success; they much oftener succeed through failures. Precept, study, advice, and example could never have taught them so well as failure has done."
> —Samuel Smiles, Scottish author (1812–1904)
>
> **Assignment:** Is there truly no success like failure? Plan and write an essay in which you develop your point of view on this issue. Support your position with reasoning and examples taken from your reading, studies, experience, or observations.

Rephrase the Prompt

Rephrase the prompt in your own words and make it more specific. If you rephrase the statement "Is there truly no success like failure?" you might come up with a question like "Can failure lead to success by teaching important lessons that help us avoid repeating mistakes in the future?"

In addition to narrowing down the focus of the broad original topic, putting the SAT essay question into your own words makes it easier for you to take a position confidently, since you'll be proving your own statement rather than the more obscure version put forth by the SAT.

Choose Your Position

Once you've rephrased the topic, agree with it or disagree with it. On the twenty five-minute fast food essay, your job is to agree or disagree. It's that simple.

You may have qualms or otherwise "sophisticated" thoughts at this point. You may be thinking, "I could argue the 'agree' side pretty well, but I'm not sure that I 100 percent believe in the agree side because. . . ." Drop those thoughts. Remember, you're not going to have a week to write this essay. You need to keep it simple. Agree or disagree, then come up with the examples that support your simple stand.

Examples

To make an SAT essay really delicious, you've got to load it up with excellent examples. Just coming up with any three examples that fit a basic position on a broad topic is not going to cut it. But there are two things that *do* make excellent SAT examples stand out from the crowd:

- **Specific examples**
- **Variety of examples**

Specific Examples

Good examples discuss specific events, dates, or measurable changes over time. Another way to put this is: you have to be able to talk about things that have happened in detail.

Just as bricks hold up a building, detailed facts support an argument. There are literally millions of good, potential examples for every position you might choose. You need to choose examples that you know a lot about in order to be specific. Knowing a lot about an example means you know more than just the basic facts. You need to be able to use all the detailed facts about your example, such as dates and events, to show how your example proves your argument.

This one-two punch—a solid example and details that use the example to prove your argument—makes the difference between a good SAT essay example and a great one.

Variety of Examples

The other crucial thing about SAT essay examples is how much ground they cover. Sure, you could come up with three examples from your personal life about how you learned from failure. But you're much more likely to impress the grader and write a better essay if you use a broad range of examples from different areas: history, art, politics, literature, science, and so on. That means when you're thinking up examples, you should consider as wide a variety as possible, as long as all of your examples remain closely tied to proving your argument.

To prove the position that "there's no success like failure," you might choose one example from history, literature, and business or current events. Here are three examples that you might choose from those three areas:

- **History:** the Americans' victory over the British in the Revolutionary War
- **Literature:** Dickens's success in writing about the working class based on his years spent in poverty as a child laborer
- **Business or Current Events:** the JetBlue airline succeeding by learning from the mistakes of its competitors

A broad array of examples like those will provide a more solid and defensible position than three examples drawn from personal experience or from just one or two areas.

Organization

No matter what topic you end up writing about the organization of your essay should be the same. That's right, the same. If you're asked to write about whether "there's no success like failure" or about the merits of the phrase "progress always comes at a cost," the *structure* of your essay should be almost identical. The SAT is looking for those standard ingredients, and the structure we're about to explain will make sure those ingredients stand out in your essay.

So what's this magical essay structure? Well, it's back to the trusty fast food analogy: a good SAT essay is a lot like a triple-decker burger.

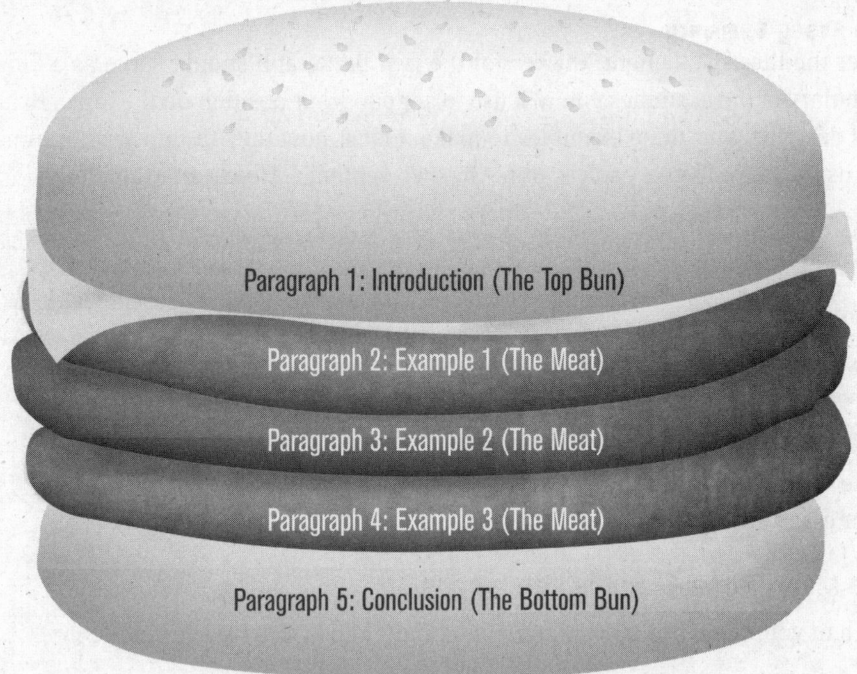

No matter what the topic is, what you feel about it, or which examples you choose, always follow this five-paragraph structure on your SAT essay. The first and last paragraphs are your essay's introduction and conclusion; each of the middle three paragraphs discusses an example that supports and illustrates your argument. That's it.

Just as important as the organization of your entire essay is the organization within each of the five paragraphs. Let's take a closer look at each paragraph next.

The Top Bun: Introduction

The introduction to an SAT essay has to do three things:

- Grab the grader's attention.
- Explain your position on the topic clearly and concisely.
- Transition the grader smoothly into your three examples.

To accomplish these three goals, you need three to four sentences in your introduction. These three to four sentences will convey your thesis statement and the overall map of your essay to the grader.

The Thesis Statement

The thesis statement is the first sentence of your essay. It identifies where you stand on the topic and should pull the grader into the essay. A good thesis statement is strong, clear, and definitive. A good thesis statement for the essay topic, "Is there truly no success like failure?" is:

> Learning from the lessons taught by failure is a sure route to success.

This thesis statement conveys the writer's position on the topic boldly and clearly. In only a few words, it carves out the position that the essay will take on the very broad, vague topic: learning from failure yields success.

The Essay Summary

After the thesis statement, the rest of the first paragraph should serve as a kind of summary of the examples you will use to support your position on the topic. Explain and describe your three examples to make it clear how they fit into your argument. It's usually best to give each example its own sentence. Here's an example:

> The United States of America can be seen as a success that emerged from failure: by learning from the weaknesses of the Articles of Confederation, the founding fathers were able to create the Constitution, the document on which America is built. Google Inc., the popular Internet search engine, is another example of a success that arose from learning from failure, though in this case Google learned from the failures of its competitors. Another example that shows how success can arise from failure is the story of Rod Johnson, who started a recruiting firm that rose out of the ashes of Johnson's personal experience of being laid off.

Three sentences, three examples. The grader knows exactly what to expect from your essay now and is ready to dive in.

The Meat: Three-Example Paragraphs

Each of your three example paragraphs should follow this basic format:

- Each paragraph should be four to five sentences long.
- The first sentence should be the topic sentence, which serves as the thesis statement of the paragraph. It explains what your example is and places it within the context of your argument.
- The next three to four sentences are for developing your example. In these sentences you show how your example supports your essay thesis statement through specific, concrete discussion of facts and situations.

For now we're just going to show you one "meat" paragraph. As we continue through the chapter, you'll see several more: some that are good, some that are bad. This one is good:

> The United States, the first great democracy of the modern world, is also one of the best examples of a success achieved by studying and learning from earlier failures. After just five years of living under the Articles of Confederation, which established the United States of America as a single country for the first time, the states realized that they needed a new document and a new, more powerful government. In 1786, the Annapolis convention was convened. The result, three years later, was the Constitution, which created a more powerful central government while also maintaining the integrity of the states. By learning from the failure of the Articles, the founding fathers created the founding document of a country that has become both the most powerful country in the world and a beacon of democracy.

The best meat paragraphs on the SAT essay are specific. The SAT's essay directions say it loud and clear: "Be specific." In its topic sentence, this paragraph states that the United States is one of the great examples of "a success achieved by studying and learning from failures." It then uses the specific example of the Articles of Confederation, the Annapolis convention, and the Constitution to prove its position. It's specific throughout and even includes a few dates.

Transitions Between Meat Paragraphs

Your first meat paragraph dives right into its thesis statement, but the second and third meat paragraphs need transitions. The simplest way to build these transitions is to use words like *another* and *finally*. That means your second meat paragraph should start with a transitional phrase, such as "Another example ..."

A slightly more sophisticated way to build transitions is to choose examples from different sources, such as from history and business. If the first paragraph is about a political instance of learning from failure and the second is from business, make that fact clear in your transition: "As in politics, learning from failure is a means to gaining success in business. Take the case of ..."

The Bottom Bun: Conclusion

The conclusion of your essay should accomplish two main goals:

- Recap your argument while broadening it a bit.
- Expand your position. Look to the future.

To accomplish these two goals, your conclusion should contain three to four sentences.

Recap Your Argument

The recap is a one-sentence summary of what you've already argued. As in the thesis statement, the recap should be straightforward, bold, and declarative. By "broadening" your argument, we mean that you should attempt to link your specific examples to wider fields, such as politics, business, and art. Here's a recap example:

> The examples of the Constitution, Rod Johnson, and Google make it clear that in the realms of politics and business, the greatest successes arise from careful considerations of the lessons of failure.

Expand on Your Position

The last two or three sentences of the essay should take the argument you just recapped and push it a little further. One of the best ways to push your argument further is to look to the future and think about what would happen if the position that you've taken in your essay could be applied on a broader scale. Here's an example:

> Failure is often seen as embarrassing, something to be denied and hidden. But as the examples of the U.S. Constitution, Google, and Rod Johnson prove, if an individual, organization, or even a nation is strong enough to face and study its failure, then that failure can become a powerful teacher. As the examples of history and business demonstrate, if everyone had the courage and insight to view failure as a surefire way to learn from mistakes, success would be easier to achieve.

The bottom bun wraps up the entire SAT essay. And there you have it! If you follow the template we just provided and break down the essay into its core ingredients, your SAT essay will be strong, clear, and easy to write.

The Universal SAT Essay Template

To make sure you really understand the organization of a fast food essay, we created a chart that sums it all up. Here's the SAT essay outline you should use, no matter what topic you get or what position you take:

	Length	Purpose
The Introduction		
Thesis Statement	1 sentence	Describe your argument clearly and concisely.
Essay Summary	3 sentences	Lay out the three examples you will use to support your thesis statement.
Example Paragraph 1		
Topic Sentence	1 sentence	Describe your example and fit it into the context of your overall thesis statement.
Example Development	3–4 sentences	Use specific facts to show how your example supports your argument. Be as specific as possible.
Example Paragraph 2		
Topic Sentence	1 sentence	Describe your example and fit it into the context of your overall thesis. Provide a transition from the previous example paragraph.
Example Development	3–4 sentences	Use specific facts to show how your example supports your argument. Be as specific as possible.
Example Paragraph 3		
Topic Sentence	1 sentence	Describe your example and fit it into the context of your overall thesis. Provide a transition from the previous paragraph.
Example Development	3–4 sentences	Use specific facts to show how your example supports your argument. Be as specific as possible.
The Conclusion		
Recap	1 sentence	Summarize your argument and examples, and link the examples to broader things like politics, history, art, or business.
Expand Your Argument	2–3 sentences	Expand your position by contemplating what would happen in the world if people (or nations, or businesses) followed the argument you make in your essay.

Command of Language

Taking a clear position and defending it with solid, detailed examples is a strong start to a successful SAT essay. But the essay-graders also care about the mechanics of your writing, which we call your "command of language." Think of your command of language as your fast food essay's Special Sauce—it's the sprinkling of perfect word choice, grammar, sentence structure, and spelling that must ooze through your entire essay. An SAT essay with a clear position and strong examples won't get a perfect score without the Special Sauce, so pay close attention to these three facets of your essay (the actual SAT essay-grading guidelines mention them specifically):

- Variation in sentence structure
- Word choice
- Grammar and spelling

Variation in Sentence Structure

> Sentence structure is very important. Sentence structure, if done well, can keep your readers engaged and help make your essay exciting and easier to read. Sentence structure, if it is monotonous and unchanging, can make your essay sound boring and unsophisticated. Sentence structure is important on the SAT essay. Sentence structure is also important in essays you write for school.

Did you notice how dull that entire last paragraph became after the first two sentences? That's because every one of those sentences not only started in the same way but also had the same straight-ahead plodding rhythm.

Now go back and look at the earlier sample meat paragraph on the Constitution. Notice how the various sentences start differently and also have different internal rhythms. These variations in sentence structure keep the writing vibrant and interesting. Focus on changing the structure of your sentences as you write the essay. You don't have to invert every clause, but you should be careful not to let a few sentences in a row follow the same exact structure. You've got to mix it up. Here's the boring first paragraph of this section rewritten with varied sentence structure:

> Sentence structure is very important. Varying the structure of your sentences keeps your reader engaged and makes your writing easier to read and more exciting. Monotonous and repetitive sentence structure can make your essay sound boring and unsophisticated. Mixing up your sentence structure is crucial on the SAT essay—it's also important to consider when writing essays for school.

Much easier to read and far less repetitive, right?

Transition Between Sentences

One great way to vary your sentence structure while increasing the logical flow of your essay is to use transitions. Transitions provide the context your readers need to understand the flow of your argument. They're words, phrases, or sentences that take readers gently by the hand, leading them through your essay. Here are some different kinds of transitions you can use to spice up your sentence structure:

- **Showing Contrast:** *Katie likes pink nail polish.* In contrast, *she thinks red nail polish looks trashy.*
- **Elaborating:** *I love sneaking into movies.* Even more than that, *I love trying to steal candy while I'm there.*
- **Providing an Example:** *If you save up your money, you can afford pricey items.* For example, *Patrick saved up his allowance and eventually purchased a sports car.*
- **Showing Results:** *Manuel ingested nothing but soda and burgers every day for a month.* As a result, *he gained ten pounds.*
- **Showing Sequence:** *The police arrested Bob at the party.* Soon after, *his college applications were all rejected,* and eventually *Bob drifted into a life of crime.*

Overly Complex Sentences

Sometimes students think writing long complicated sentences will impress teachers. It's doubtful, and it definitely won't impress essay-graders. Keep your sentences short and simple. Complex sentences are difficult to understand, and your SAT essays should be as clear and easy to read as possible.

We could fill an entire book with rules about creating simple and succinct prose. In fact, we did: *SparkNotes Ultimate Style* is our concise guide to grammar, usage, and style. Check it out online at www.sparknotes.com/writing/style. Here, though, we'll just give you two handy rules to simplify the sentences that you write on the SAT essay:

1. Never write a sentence that contains more than three commas. Try to avoid sentences with more than two commas (unless you need to include a list).
2. Never write a sentence that takes up more than three lines of SAT essay paper.

Those rules are certainly not foolproof, but abiding by them will keep you from filling your SAT essay with overly complex sentences and will ultimately make your essay easier to understand.

Word Choice

When students see that "word choice" plays a part in their essay score, they think it means that they have to use tons of sophisticated vocabulary words in order to score well. That belief is wrong and potentially damaging to your SAT essay score. If you strain to put big fancy words into your essay, you're bound to end up misusing those words. And misusing a sophisticated word is a worse offense than not using one at all.

Word choice doesn't mean that you have to go for the big word every time. It means you should go for the *proper* word, the best word, the word that makes your essay as clear as possible. Let's look at part of the paragraph about the Constitution:

> The United States, the first great democracy of the modern world, is also one of the best examples of a success achieved by studying and learning from earlier failures. After just five years of living under the Articles of Confederation, which established the United States of America as a single country for the first time, the states realized that they needed a new document and a new, more powerful government. In 1786, the Annapolis convention was convened. The result, three years later, was the Constitution, which created a more powerful central government while also maintaining the integrity of the states. By learning from the failure of the Articles, the founding fathers created the founding document of a country that has become both the most powerful country in the world and a beacon of democracy.

This is 6-level writing, but it isn't teeming with five-syllable words. What the paragraph does is use every single word correctly. When it does reach for an uncommon word, like *beacon*, it uses the word appropriately and effectively. Now *that's* good word choice.

So don't try to use a word unless you know what it means. Don't go throwing around tough words in the hopes that you're going to use it correctly and impress your reader. The likelihood is that you're going to use the word incorrectly and give the grader a bad impression. Instead, keep it simple and stick to words you know well.

Grammar and Spelling

A few grammar or spelling mistakes sprinkled throughout your essay will not destroy your score. The essay-graders understand that you're bound to make minor mistakes in a rushed twenty-five-minute essay.

Graders are instructed to look out for patterns of errors. If a grader sees that your punctuation is consistently wrong, that your spelling of familiar words is often incorrect, or that you write run-on sentences again and again, that's when your score will suffer. You need to be able to write solid grammatical sentences to score well on the essay.

KNOW HOW TO PUT THE INGREDIENTS TOGETHER

By now you know all of the ingredients you should use, and you've mastered the template you should follow to write a great SAT essay. Next you need to learn the writing process that will empower you to put it all together into a top score–worthy essay every time. Follow the five steps we describe next and you'll be on your way to a 6.

Five Steps to a 6

Step 1	Understand the topic and take a position.	1 minute
Step 2	Brainstorm examples.	2–3 minutes
Step 3	Create an outline.	3–4 minutes
Step 4	Write the essay.	15 minutes
Step 5	Proof the essay.	2 minutes

Step 1: Understand the topic and take a position. (1 minute)

The first thing you must do before you can even think about your essay is read the topic very carefully. Here's the sample topic we use throughout this section:

Think carefully about the issue presented in the following excerpt and the assignment below.

"There's no success like failure."

Assignment: Is there truly no success like failure? Plan and write an essay in which you develop your point of view on this issue. Support your position with reasoning and examples taken from your reading, studies, experience, or observations.

Make sure you understand the topic thoroughly by making it your own. To do that, use the two strategies we discussed in the Ingredients section:

- **Rephrase the Prompt.** "Failure can lead to success by teaching important lessons that help us avoid repeating mistakes in the future."
- **Choose Your Position.** (In our example, we agree with the topic.)

That's it. One step down, four more to go.

Step 2: Brainstorm examples. (2–3 minutes)

Your position is that you agree with the statement that "failure can lead to success by teaching important lessons that help us avoid repeating mistakes in the future." Terrific.

Brainstorming, or thinking up examples to support your position, is the crucial next step. Plenty of SAT-takers will succumb to the temptation to plunge straight from Step 1 into writing the essay (Step 4). Skipping the brainstorming session will leave you with an opinion on the topic but with no clearly thought-out examples to prove your point. You'll write the first thing that comes to mind, and your essay will probably derail. So even though you feel the time pressure, don't skip brainstorming.

Brainstorming seems simple. You just close your eyes and scrunch up your face and THINK REALLY HARD until you come up with some examples. But, in practice, brainstorming while staring at a blank page under time pressure can be intimidating and frustrating. To make brainstorming less daunting and more productive, we've got two strategies to suggest.

Brainstorm by Category

The best examples you can generate to support your SAT essay topic will come from a variety of sources, such as science, history, politics, art, literature, business, and personal experience. So brainstorm a list split up by category. Here's the list we brainstormed for the topic, "There's no success like failure."

Current Events	Failure of 9/11 security led to the creation of Homeland Security
Science	Babies learn to walk only after trying and failing time and again
History	??? Can't think of one
Politics	The U.S. Constitution was written only after the failure of the Articles of Confederation
Art	??? Can't think of one
Literature	James Joyce became a writer only after failing as a singer
Personal Experience	Rod Johnson (your uncle) realized the need for a placement agency in South Carolina after getting laid off
Business	Google watched the failures of its competitors and learned to improve its Internet business model and technology

Let's say you took three minutes and came up with a list of eight categories like ours, and you got examples for five of them. That's still great. That means your next step is to choose the top three of your five potential examples.

Prepare Ahead of Time

You could also do some brainstorming ahead of time. Brainstorming ahead of time can be a great method because it gives you time to do more than just brainstorm. You can actually prepare examples for each of the seven categories we've brainstormed above in our chart. You could, for instance, read up about various scientists, learning about their successes, their failures, the impact of their discoveries (positive and negative), and memorize dates, events, and other facts.

The risk of planning ahead is that you can get stuck with a topic on the SAT to which all your knowledge about scientists just isn't applicable. This is somewhat of a risk, but because the SAT essay topics are so broad, you can often massage your examples to fit. Preparing ahead of time will pay off if you develop a few examples that you know a lot about for the essay. But it could backfire if it winds up that you absolutely cannot use the examples you prepared. Then you'll have to resort to thinking up examples on the spot. If you don't want to risk wasting time preparing ahead of time, don't. It's up to you.

Choose Your Top Three

When you go through your brainstormed and pre-prepared examples to decide which three you should actually use, you need to keep three things in mind:

1. Which examples can you be most specific about?
2. Which examples will give your essay the broadest range?
3. Which examples are not controversial?

The first two reasons are pretty straightforward: specificity and variety in your examples will help you write the strongest essay. The point about controversy is a bit subtler.

Staying away from very controversial examples ensures that you won't accidentally offend or annoy your grader, who, if annoyed, might then be more inclined to lower your grade. For instance, the 9/11 example from our brainstormed list should be cut. The event is too full of unresolved issues to serve as a suitable essay topic, and the last thing you want to do is upset or offend your grader.

Here's another example. Let's say that you're not so certain if that story about James Joyce being a singer is even really true and that you think lots of test-takers might go for the babies walking example. That would mean you decide to keep the examples about the Constitution, Google, and the story of Rod Johnson. What if instead of referring to Rod Johnson as your enterprising uncle, you portray him as a businessman you read about in an esteemed publication recently? Transform your personal experience and make it seem like an actual example from current events. The SAT essay-graders care much more about how well you write and how intelligently you can use examples to back up your position than they care about the truth of what you say in examples drawn from personal experience.

That means you've narrowed down your brainstormed topics to the top three. Next up: outlining.

Step 3: Create an outline. (3–4 minutes)

After brainstorming comes writing an outline. On fast food essays like the SAT essay, which rewards standard conformity much more than it does creativity, organizing your ideas in outline form and then sticking to that outline is crucial. Though you may feel that you're wasting your time, we guarantee that the four or five minutes that you invest in writing an outline will *definitely* be paid back when you write the essay.

Writing the Outline

Since your outline is a kind of bare-bones "map" of your essay, the outline should follow our Universal SAT Essay Template. Here's a summary of the template:

PARAGRAPH	PURPOSE	WHAT IT SHOULD CONTAIN
1	Introduction	Thesis statement; state examples
2	Example 1	Topic sentence for example 1; explain example 1
3	Example 2	Topic sentence for example 2; explain example 2
4	Example 3	Topic sentence for example 3; explain example 3
5	Conclusion	Thesis rephrased in a broader way; expand position

As you write the outline, remember that your goal is to generate ideas. Your outline need not be articulate or even comprehensible to anyone other than you. But your outline must contain all the essential raw material that will become your thesis statement, topic sentences, and concluding statement when you write your essay.

As you sketch out your outline, consider where you want each example to go. We suggest that you put what you consider to be your strongest example first, followed by the second strongest, and then the least strong. We suggest this because the essay is a timed section, and if for some reason you run out of time and can only fit two example paragraphs between your intro and conclusion, they might as well be your best two examples.

Here's a sample outline we've written based on the topic and examples we have already discussed. Notice that we've placed our examples in strongest to weakest order starting in paragraph 2.

PARAGRAPH 1: INTRODUCTION	Failure can lead to success teaching lessons, learning mistakes. Three examples: (1) U.S. Constitution and Articles failure, (2) failed dot-coms lead to more successful online businesses, (3) guy who started successful recruiting business after getting laid off.
PARAGRAPH 2: EXAMPLE 1 (BEST)	U.S. Constitution developed by studying the failures of previous document, Articles of Confederation. By studying failures U.S. became true revolutionary democracy.
PARAGRAPH 3: EXAMPLE 2 (NEXT BEST)	Google studied competitors' struggles, came up with better technological solution and better business model. Since failure is good teacher, intelligent companies look for failure everywhere, even in rivals, to learn and evolve.
PARAGRAPH 4: EXAMPLE 3 (NEXT BEST)	Johnson founded job placement agency based on difficulties finding a new job after getting laid off. Studied his failure, found problems lay with system, not with him.
PARAGRAPH 5: CONCLUSION	Failure often seen as embarrassing. People try to hide it. But if you or society take responsibility for it, study it, history shows failure leads to success for everyone.

Your outline does not have to be written in complete sentences. Notice how in the example above we drop verbs and write in a note-taking style. Feel free to write just enough to convey to yourself what you need to be able to follow during the actual writing of your essay. Once you have the outline down on paper, writing the essay becomes more a job of polishing language and ideas than creating them from scratch.

Step 4: Write the essay. (15 minutes)

Writing the essay consists of filling out your ideas by following your outline and plugging in what's missing. That adds up to only about ten more sentences than what you've jotted down in your outline, which should already contain a basic version of your thesis statement, one topic sentence for each of your three examples, and a conclusion statement that ties everything together. All together your essay should be about fifteen to twenty sentences long.

As you write, keep these three facets of your essay in mind:

- Organization
- Development
- Clarity

Following your outline will make sure you stick to the Universal SAT Essay Template. That means *organization* shouldn't be a problem.

As far as *development* goes, you should make sure that every sentence in the essay serves the greater goal of proving your thesis statement. Every sentence should also build on the supporting examples you presented in the intro and in the topic sentences of each example paragraph. You should make sure that you are *specific* with your examples: give dates, describe events in detail, and so on.

By *clarity*, we mean the simplicity of the language that you use. That involves spelling and grammar, but it also means focusing on varying sentence length and structure as well as including a few well-placed vocabulary words that you definitely know how to use correctly.

Do not break from your outline. Never pause for a digression or drop in a fact or detail that's not entirely relevant to your essay's thesis statement. You're serving fast food, and fast food always sticks to the core ingredients and the universal recipe.

If You Run Out of Time

If you're running out of time, don't fret. Instead, here's what you should do: drop one of your example paragraphs. You can still get a decent score, possibly a 4 or 5, with just two. Three examples are definitely the strongest and safest way to go, but if you just can't get through three, take your two best examples and go with them. Just be sure to include an introduction and a conclusion in every SAT essay.

The Finished Essay: Our Example

Here is an example of a complete SAT essay. It's based strictly on the outline we built in step 3 of our Five Steps to a 6, with a focus on clear simple language and the occasional drop of Special Sauce.

> Learning the lessons taught by failure is a sure route to success. The United States of America can be seen as a success that emerged from failure: by learning from the weaknesses of the Articles of Confederation, the founding fathers were able to create the Constitution, the document on which America is built. Google Inc., the popular Internet search engine, is another example of a success that arose from learning from failure, though in this case Google learned from the failures of its competitors. Another example that shows how success can arise from failure is the story of Rod Johnson, who started a recruiting firm that arose from Johnson's personal experience of being laid off.
>
> The United States, the first great democracy of the modern world, is also one of the best examples of a success achieved by studying and learning from earlier failures. After just five years of living under the Articles of Confederation, which established the United States of America as a single country for the first time, the states realized that they needed a new document and a new, more powerful government. In 1786, the Annapolis convention was convened. The result, three years later, was the Constitution, which created a more powerful central government while also maintaining the integrity of the states. By learning from the failure of the Articles, the founding fathers created the founding document of a country that has become both the most powerful country in the world and a beacon of democracy.
>
> Unlike the United States, which had its fair share of ups and downs over the years, the Internet search engine company Google has suffered few setbacks since it went into business in the late 1990s. Google has succeeded by studying the failures of other companies in order to help it innovate its technology and business model. Google identified and solved the problem of assessing the quality of search results by using the number of links pointing to a page as an indicator of the number of people who find the page valuable. Suddenly, Google's search results became far more accurate and reliable than those from other companies, and now Google's dominance in the field of Internet search is almost absolute.
>
> The example of Rod Johnson's success also shows how effective learning from mistakes and failure can be. Rather than accept his failure after being laid off, Johnson decided to study it. After a month of research, Johnson realized that his failure to find a new job resulted primarily from the inefficiency of the local job placement agencies, not from his own deficiencies. A month later, Johnson created Johnson Staffing to correct this weakness in the job placement sector. Today Johnson Staffing is the largest job placement agency in South Carolina and is in the process of expanding into a national corporation.
>
> Failure is often seen as embarrassing, something to be denied and hidden. But as the examples of the U.S. Constitution, Google, and Rod Johnson prove, if an individual, organization, or even a nation is strong enough to face and study its failure, then that failure can become a powerful teacher. The examples of history and business demonstrate that failure can be the best catalyst of success, but only if people have the courage to face it head on.

Now it's time to move on to the final step of our Five Steps to a 6—proofing your essay.

Step 5: Proof the essay. (2 minutes)

Proofing your essay means reading through your finished essay to correct mistakes or to clear up words that are difficult to read. If you don't have two minutes after you've finished writing the essay (step 4), spend whatever time you do have left proofing. Read over your essay and search for rough writing, bad transitions, grammatical errors, repetitive sentence structure, and all that Special Sauce stuff. The SAT explicitly says that handwriting will not affect your grade, but you should also be on the lookout for instances in which bad handwriting makes it look as if you've made a grammatical or spelling mistake.

If you're running out of time and you have to skip a step, proofing is the step to drop. Proofing is important, but it's the only one of the Five Steps to a 6 that isn't absolutely crucial.

A SAMPLE SAT ESSAY

Below is our sample essay question, which is designed to be as close as possible to an essay question that might appear on the SAT. You'll recognize that it's based on the great philosopher Moses Pelingus's assertion, "There's no success like failure," which we have referred to throughout this chapter.

This particular essay topic presents you with a very broad idea and then asks you to explain your view and back it up with concrete examples. Not every SAT essay topic will take this form, but every SAT essay question will require you to take a position and defend it with examples.

Here's the sample prompt again:

> Think carefully about the issue presented in the following excerpt and the assignment below.
>
> "There's no success like failure."
>
> **Assignment:** Is there truly no success like failure? Plan and write an essay in which you develop your point of view on this issue. Support your position with reasoning and examples taken from your reading, studies, experience, or observations.

Below we provide an example of a 6 essay, complete with a brief evaluation according to three sets of criteria:

- Our four essential essay ingredients
- The SAT grader's checklist
- A checklist based on our Universal SAT Essay Template

As you read the essay, note that we have marked certain sentences and paragraphs to illustrate where and how the essay does or does not abide by our Universal SAT Essay Template.

A 6 Essay

Learning the lessons taught by failure is a sure route to success. (THESIS STATEMENT) The United States of America can be seen as a success that emerged from failure: by learning from the weaknesses of the Articles of Confederation, the founding fathers were able to create the Constitution, the document on which America is built. (BEST SUPPORTING EXAMPLE [1]) Google Inc., the popular Internet search engine, is another example of a success that arose from learning from failure, though in this case Google learned from the failures of its competitors. (NEXT BEST SUPPORTING EXAMPLE [2]) Another example that shows how success can arise from failure is the story of Rod Johnson, who started a recruiting firm that arose from Johnson's personal experience of being laid off. (NEXT BEST SUPPORTING EXAMPLE [3])

The United States, the first great democracy of the modern world, is also one of the best examples of a success achieved by studying and learning from earlier failures. (TOPIC SENTENCE FOR EXAMPLE 1) After just five years of living under the Articles of Confederation, which established the United States of America as a single country for the first time, the states realized that they needed a new document and a new more powerful government. In 1786, the Annapolis convention was convened. The result, three years later, was the Constitution, which created a more powerful central government while also maintaining the integrity of the states. By learning from the failure of the Articles, the founding fathers created the founding document of a country that has become both the most powerful country in the world and a beacon of democracy. (FOUR DEVELOPMENT SENTENCES TO SUPPORT EXAMPLE 1)

Unlike the United States, which had its fair share of ups and downs over the years, the Internet search engine company Google Inc. has suffered few setbacks since it went into business in the late 1990s. (TOPIC SENTENCE FOR EXAMPLE 2) Google has succeeded by studying the failures of other companies in order to help it innovate its technology and business model. Google identified and solved the problem of assessing the quality of search results by using the number of links pointing to a page as an indicator of the number of people who find the page valuable. Suddenly, Google's search results became far more accurate and reliable than those from other companies, and now Google's dominance in the field of Internet search is almost absolute. (THREE DEVELOPMENT SENTENCES TO SUPPORT EXAMPLE 2)

The example of Rod Johnson's success as an entrepreneur in the recruiting field also shows how effective learning from mistakes and failure can be. (TOPIC SENTENCE FOR EXAMPLE 3) Rather than accept his failure after being laid off, Johnson decided to study it. After a month of research, Johnson realized that his failure to find a new job resulted primarily from the inefficiency of the local job placement agencies, not from his own deficiencies. A month later, Johnson created Johnson Staffing to correct this weakness in the job placement sector. Today Johnson Staffing is the largest job placement agency in South Carolina, and is in the process of expanding into a national corporation. (FOUR DEVELOPMENT SENTENCES TO SUPPORT EXAMPLE 3)

Failure is often seen as embarrassing, something to be denied and hidden. But as the examples of the U.S. Constitution, Google, and Rod Johnson prove, if an individual, organization, or even a nation is strong enough to face and study its failure, then that failure can become a powerful teacher. (THESIS STATEMENT REPHRASED IN BROADER WAY THAT PUSHES IT FURTHER) The examples of history and business demonstrate that failure can be the best catalyst of success, but only if people have the courage to face it head on.

Why This Essay Deserves a 6

First, we need to assess whether this essay contains the four essential ingredients of a great SAT essay. Here they are, just to refresh your memory:

1. Positioning: the strength and clarity of the position on the given topic
2. Examples: the relevance and development of the examples used to support your argument

3. Organization: the organization of each paragraph and of the essay overall
4. Command of language: sentence construction, grammar, and word choice

This essay serves up all four SAT essay ingredients. It takes a very strong and clear stance on the topic in the first sentence and sticks to it from start to finish. It uses three examples from a very diverse array of disciplines—from Internet technology to history and politics to a profile of an entrepreneur—and it never veers from using these examples to support the thesis statement's position. The organization of the essay follows our Universal SAT Essay Template perfectly, both at the paragraph level (topic sentences and development sentences) and at the overall essay level (intro, three meaty example paragraphs, and a strong conclusion). The command of language remains solid throughout. The writer does not take risks with unfamiliar vocabulary but instead chooses a few out of the ordinary words like *beacon*, *deficiencies*, and *innovate* that sprinkle just the right amount of Special Sauce throughout the essay. Sentence structure varies often, making the entire essay more interesting and engaging to the grader. Finally, no significant grammar errors disrupt the overall excellence of this SAT essay.

Here's a quick-reference chart that takes a closer look at this 6 essay based on the actual SAT's evaluation criteria for graders and based on our Universal SAT Essay Template.

SAT CRITERIA FOR LEVEL-6 ESSAYS	YES OR NO?
Consistently excellent, with at most a few minor errors	YES
Takes a clear position on the topic and uses insightful relevant examples to back it up	YES
Shows strong overall organization and paragraph development	YES
Demonstrates a superior command of language, as shown by varied sentence structure and word choice	YES
OUR UNIVERSAL SAT ESSAY TEMPLATE CRITERIA	**YES OR NO?**
Thesis statement in first sentence of paragraph 1	YES
Three examples listed in paragraph 1 in order from best to worst	YES
Topic sentence for example in paragraph 2	YES
3–4 development sentences to support paragraph 2's example	YES
Topic sentence for example in paragraph 3	YES
3–4 development sentences to support paragraph 3's example	YES
Topic sentence for example in paragraph 4	YES
3–4 development sentences to support paragraph 4's example	YES
Conclusion paragraph contains rephrased thesis statement	YES
About 15 sentences total	YES

Now on to the practice tests!

SAT PRACTICE TEST 1

SAT* Reasoning Test—General Directions

Timing

- You will have 3 hours and 20 minutes to work on this test. (On the actual SAT, you would have 3 hours and 45 minutes to complete ten sections, one of which would be unscored and experimental.)
- There are nine separately timed sections:
  - ➤ One 25-minute essay
  - ➤ Five other 25-minute sections
  - ➤ Two 20-minute sections
  - ➤ One 10-minute section
- You may work on only one section at a time.
- The supervisor will tell you when to begin and end each section.
- If you finish a section before time is called, check your work on that section. You may NOT turn to any other section.
- Work as rapidly as you can without losing accuracy. Don't waste time on questions that seem too difficult for you.

Marking Answers

- Carefully mark only one answer for each question.
- Make sure each mark is dark and completely fills the circle.
- Do not make any stray marks on your answer sheet.
- If you erase, do so completely. Incomplete erasures may be scored as intended answers.
- Use only the answer spaces that correspond to the question numbers.
- Use the test book for scratchwork, but you will not receive credit for anything written there.
- After time has been called, you may not transfer answers to your answer sheet or fill in circles.
- You may not fold or remove pages or portions of a page from this book, or take the book or answer sheet from the testing room.

Scoring

- For each correct answer to a question, you receive one point.
- For questions you omit, you receive no points.
- For a wrong answer to a multiple-choice question, you lose one-fourth of a point.
  - ➤ If you can eliminate one or more of the answer choices as wrong, you increase your chances of choosing the correct answer and earning one point.
  - ➤ If you can't eliminate any choice, move on. You can return to the question later if there is time.
- For a wrong answer to a "grid-in" math question, you don't lose any points.
- The essay is scored on a 1 to 6 scale by two different readers. The total essay score is the sum of the two readers' scores.
- An off-topic or blank essay will receive a score of zero.

---

* SAT test directions selected from the SAT Reasoning Test. Reprinted by permission of the College Board, the copyright owner.

SAT PRACTICE TEST 1 ANSWER SHEET

SECTION 2

1. Ⓐ Ⓑ Ⓒ Ⓓ Ⓔ	7. Ⓐ Ⓑ Ⓒ Ⓓ Ⓔ	13. Ⓐ Ⓑ Ⓒ Ⓓ Ⓔ	19. Ⓐ Ⓑ Ⓒ Ⓓ Ⓔ
2. Ⓐ Ⓑ Ⓒ Ⓓ Ⓔ	8. Ⓐ Ⓑ Ⓒ Ⓓ Ⓔ	14. Ⓐ Ⓑ Ⓒ Ⓓ Ⓔ	20. Ⓐ Ⓑ Ⓒ Ⓓ Ⓔ
3. Ⓐ Ⓑ Ⓒ Ⓓ Ⓔ	9. Ⓐ Ⓑ Ⓒ Ⓓ Ⓔ	15. Ⓐ Ⓑ Ⓒ Ⓓ Ⓔ	21. Ⓐ Ⓑ Ⓒ Ⓓ Ⓔ
4. Ⓐ Ⓑ Ⓒ Ⓓ Ⓔ	10. Ⓐ Ⓑ Ⓒ Ⓓ Ⓔ	16. Ⓐ Ⓑ Ⓒ Ⓓ Ⓔ	22. Ⓐ Ⓑ Ⓒ Ⓓ Ⓔ
5. Ⓐ Ⓑ Ⓒ Ⓓ Ⓔ	11. Ⓐ Ⓑ Ⓒ Ⓓ Ⓔ	17. Ⓐ Ⓑ Ⓒ Ⓓ Ⓔ	23. Ⓐ Ⓑ Ⓒ Ⓓ Ⓔ
6. Ⓐ Ⓑ Ⓒ Ⓓ Ⓔ	12. Ⓐ Ⓑ Ⓒ Ⓓ Ⓔ	18. Ⓐ Ⓑ Ⓒ Ⓓ Ⓔ	24. Ⓐ Ⓑ Ⓒ Ⓓ Ⓔ

SECTION 3

1. Ⓐ Ⓑ Ⓒ Ⓓ Ⓔ	6. Ⓐ Ⓑ Ⓒ Ⓓ Ⓔ	11. Ⓐ Ⓑ Ⓒ Ⓓ Ⓔ	16. Ⓐ Ⓑ Ⓒ Ⓓ Ⓔ
2. Ⓐ Ⓑ Ⓒ Ⓓ Ⓔ	7. Ⓐ Ⓑ Ⓒ Ⓓ Ⓔ	12. Ⓐ Ⓑ Ⓒ Ⓓ Ⓔ	17. Ⓐ Ⓑ Ⓒ Ⓓ Ⓔ
3. Ⓐ Ⓑ Ⓒ Ⓓ Ⓔ	8. Ⓐ Ⓑ Ⓒ Ⓓ Ⓔ	13. Ⓐ Ⓑ Ⓒ Ⓓ Ⓔ	18. Ⓐ Ⓑ Ⓒ Ⓓ Ⓔ
4. Ⓐ Ⓑ Ⓒ Ⓓ Ⓔ	9. Ⓐ Ⓑ Ⓒ Ⓓ Ⓔ	14. Ⓐ Ⓑ Ⓒ Ⓓ Ⓔ	19. Ⓐ Ⓑ Ⓒ Ⓓ Ⓔ
5. Ⓐ Ⓑ Ⓒ Ⓓ Ⓔ	10. Ⓐ Ⓑ Ⓒ Ⓓ Ⓔ	15. Ⓐ Ⓑ Ⓒ Ⓓ Ⓔ	20. Ⓐ Ⓑ Ⓒ Ⓓ Ⓔ

SECTION 4

1. Ⓐ Ⓑ Ⓒ Ⓓ Ⓔ	7. Ⓐ Ⓑ Ⓒ Ⓓ Ⓔ	13. Ⓐ Ⓑ Ⓒ Ⓓ Ⓔ	19. Ⓐ Ⓑ Ⓒ Ⓓ Ⓔ
2. Ⓐ Ⓑ Ⓒ Ⓓ Ⓔ	8. Ⓐ Ⓑ Ⓒ Ⓓ Ⓔ	14. Ⓐ Ⓑ Ⓒ Ⓓ Ⓔ	20. Ⓐ Ⓑ Ⓒ Ⓓ Ⓔ
3. Ⓐ Ⓑ Ⓒ Ⓓ Ⓔ	9. Ⓐ Ⓑ Ⓒ Ⓓ Ⓔ	15. Ⓐ Ⓑ Ⓒ Ⓓ Ⓔ	21. Ⓐ Ⓑ Ⓒ Ⓓ Ⓔ
4. Ⓐ Ⓑ Ⓒ Ⓓ Ⓔ	10. Ⓐ Ⓑ Ⓒ Ⓓ Ⓔ	16. Ⓐ Ⓑ Ⓒ Ⓓ Ⓔ	22. Ⓐ Ⓑ Ⓒ Ⓓ Ⓔ
5. Ⓐ Ⓑ Ⓒ Ⓓ Ⓔ	11. Ⓐ Ⓑ Ⓒ Ⓓ Ⓔ	17. Ⓐ Ⓑ Ⓒ Ⓓ Ⓔ	23. Ⓐ Ⓑ Ⓒ Ⓓ Ⓔ
6. Ⓐ Ⓑ Ⓒ Ⓓ Ⓔ	12. Ⓐ Ⓑ Ⓒ Ⓓ Ⓔ	18. Ⓐ Ⓑ Ⓒ Ⓓ Ⓔ	24. Ⓐ Ⓑ Ⓒ Ⓓ Ⓔ

SECTION 5

1. Ⓐ Ⓑ Ⓒ Ⓓ Ⓔ	3. Ⓐ Ⓑ Ⓒ Ⓓ Ⓔ	5. Ⓐ Ⓑ Ⓒ Ⓓ Ⓔ	7. Ⓐ Ⓑ Ⓒ Ⓓ Ⓔ
2. Ⓐ Ⓑ Ⓒ Ⓓ Ⓔ	4. Ⓐ Ⓑ Ⓒ Ⓓ Ⓔ	6. Ⓐ Ⓑ Ⓒ Ⓓ Ⓔ	8. Ⓐ Ⓑ Ⓒ Ⓓ Ⓔ

	9	10	11	12	13
/	⊘ (col. 3)	⊘ (col. 3)	⊘ (col. 3)	⊘ (col. 3)	⊘ (col. 3)
.	⊙ ⊙ ⊙ ⊙	⊙ ⊙ ⊙ ⊙	⊙ ⊙ ⊙ ⊙	⊙ ⊙ ⊙ ⊙	⊙ ⊙ ⊙ ⊙
0	— ⓪ ⓪ ⓪	— ⓪ ⓪ ⓪	— ⓪ ⓪ ⓪	— ⓪ ⓪ ⓪	— ⓪ ⓪ ⓪
1	① ① ① ①	① ① ① ①	① ① ① ①	① ① ① ①	① ① ① ①
2	② ② ② ②	② ② ② ②	② ② ② ②	② ② ② ②	② ② ② ②
3	③ ③ ③ ③	③ ③ ③ ③	③ ③ ③ ③	③ ③ ③ ③	③ ③ ③ ③
4	④ ④ ④ ④	④ ④ ④ ④	④ ④ ④ ④	④ ④ ④ ④	④ ④ ④ ④
5	⑤ ⑤ ⑤ ⑤	⑤ ⑤ ⑤ ⑤	⑤ ⑤ ⑤ ⑤	⑤ ⑤ ⑤ ⑤	⑤ ⑤ ⑤ ⑤
6	⑥ ⑥ ⑥ ⑥	⑥ ⑥ ⑥ ⑥	⑥ ⑥ ⑥ ⑥	⑥ ⑥ ⑥ ⑥	⑥ ⑥ ⑥ ⑥
7	⑦ ⑦ ⑦ ⑦	⑦ ⑦ ⑦ ⑦	⑦ ⑦ ⑦ ⑦	⑦ ⑦ ⑦ ⑦	⑦ ⑦ ⑦ ⑦
8	⑧ ⑧ ⑧ ⑧	⑧ ⑧ ⑧ ⑧	⑧ ⑧ ⑧ ⑧	⑧ ⑧ ⑧ ⑧	⑧ ⑧ ⑧ ⑧
9	⑨ ⑨ ⑨ ⑨	⑨ ⑨ ⑨ ⑨	⑨ ⑨ ⑨ ⑨	⑨ ⑨ ⑨ ⑨	⑨ ⑨ ⑨ ⑨

	14	15	16	17	18
/	⊘ (col. 3)	⊘ (col. 3)	⊘ (col. 3)	⊘ (col. 3)	⊘ (col. 3)
.	⊙ ⊙ ⊙ ⊙	⊙ ⊙ ⊙ ⊙	⊙ ⊙ ⊙ ⊙	⊙ ⊙ ⊙ ⊙	⊙ ⊙ ⊙ ⊙
0	— ⓪ ⓪ ⓪	— ⓪ ⓪ ⓪	— ⓪ ⓪ ⓪	— ⓪ ⓪ ⓪	— ⓪ ⓪ ⓪
1	① ① ① ①	① ① ① ①	① ① ① ①	① ① ① ①	① ① ① ①
2	② ② ② ②	② ② ② ②	② ② ② ②	② ② ② ②	② ② ② ②
3	③ ③ ③ ③	③ ③ ③ ③	③ ③ ③ ③	③ ③ ③ ③	③ ③ ③ ③
4	④ ④ ④ ④	④ ④ ④ ④	④ ④ ④ ④	④ ④ ④ ④	④ ④ ④ ④
5	⑤ ⑤ ⑤ ⑤	⑤ ⑤ ⑤ ⑤	⑤ ⑤ ⑤ ⑤	⑤ ⑤ ⑤ ⑤	⑤ ⑤ ⑤ ⑤
6	⑥ ⑥ ⑥ ⑥	⑥ ⑥ ⑥ ⑥	⑥ ⑥ ⑥ ⑥	⑥ ⑥ ⑥ ⑥	⑥ ⑥ ⑥ ⑥
7	⑦ ⑦ ⑦ ⑦	⑦ ⑦ ⑦ ⑦	⑦ ⑦ ⑦ ⑦	⑦ ⑦ ⑦ ⑦	⑦ ⑦ ⑦ ⑦
8	⑧ ⑧ ⑧ ⑧	⑧ ⑧ ⑧ ⑧	⑧ ⑧ ⑧ ⑧	⑧ ⑧ ⑧ ⑧	⑧ ⑧ ⑧ ⑧
9	⑨ ⑨ ⑨ ⑨	⑨ ⑨ ⑨ ⑨	⑨ ⑨ ⑨ ⑨	⑨ ⑨ ⑨ ⑨	⑨ ⑨ ⑨ ⑨

SAT PRACTICE TEST 1 ANSWER SHEET

SECTION 6			
1. Ⓐ Ⓑ Ⓒ Ⓓ Ⓔ	10. Ⓐ Ⓑ Ⓒ Ⓓ Ⓔ	19. Ⓐ Ⓑ Ⓒ Ⓓ Ⓔ	28. Ⓐ Ⓑ Ⓒ Ⓓ Ⓔ
2. Ⓐ Ⓑ Ⓒ Ⓓ Ⓔ	11. Ⓐ Ⓑ Ⓒ Ⓓ Ⓔ	20. Ⓐ Ⓑ Ⓒ Ⓓ Ⓔ	29. Ⓐ Ⓑ Ⓒ Ⓓ Ⓔ
3. Ⓐ Ⓑ Ⓒ Ⓓ Ⓔ	12. Ⓐ Ⓑ Ⓒ Ⓓ Ⓔ	21. Ⓐ Ⓑ Ⓒ Ⓓ Ⓔ	30. Ⓐ Ⓑ Ⓒ Ⓓ Ⓔ
4. Ⓐ Ⓑ Ⓒ Ⓓ Ⓔ	13. Ⓐ Ⓑ Ⓒ Ⓓ Ⓔ	22. Ⓐ Ⓑ Ⓒ Ⓓ Ⓔ	31. Ⓐ Ⓑ Ⓒ Ⓓ Ⓔ
5. Ⓐ Ⓑ Ⓒ Ⓓ Ⓔ	14. Ⓐ Ⓑ Ⓒ Ⓓ Ⓔ	23. Ⓐ Ⓑ Ⓒ Ⓓ Ⓔ	32. Ⓐ Ⓑ Ⓒ Ⓓ Ⓔ
6. Ⓐ Ⓑ Ⓒ Ⓓ Ⓔ	15. Ⓐ Ⓑ Ⓒ Ⓓ Ⓔ	24. Ⓐ Ⓑ Ⓒ Ⓓ Ⓔ	33. Ⓐ Ⓑ Ⓒ Ⓓ Ⓔ
7. Ⓐ Ⓑ Ⓒ Ⓓ Ⓔ	16. Ⓐ Ⓑ Ⓒ Ⓓ Ⓔ	25. Ⓐ Ⓑ Ⓒ Ⓓ Ⓔ	34. Ⓐ Ⓑ Ⓒ Ⓓ Ⓔ
8. Ⓐ Ⓑ Ⓒ Ⓓ Ⓔ	17. Ⓐ Ⓑ Ⓒ Ⓓ Ⓔ	26. Ⓐ Ⓑ Ⓒ Ⓓ Ⓔ	35. Ⓐ Ⓑ Ⓒ Ⓓ Ⓔ
9. Ⓐ Ⓑ Ⓒ Ⓓ Ⓔ	18. Ⓐ Ⓑ Ⓒ Ⓓ Ⓔ	27. Ⓐ Ⓑ Ⓒ Ⓓ Ⓔ	

SECTION 7			
1. Ⓐ Ⓑ Ⓒ Ⓓ Ⓔ	6. Ⓐ Ⓑ Ⓒ Ⓓ Ⓔ	11. Ⓐ Ⓑ Ⓒ Ⓓ Ⓔ	16. Ⓐ Ⓑ Ⓒ Ⓓ Ⓔ
2. Ⓐ Ⓑ Ⓒ Ⓓ Ⓔ	7. Ⓐ Ⓑ Ⓒ Ⓓ Ⓔ	12. Ⓐ Ⓑ Ⓒ Ⓓ Ⓔ	17. Ⓐ Ⓑ Ⓒ Ⓓ Ⓔ
3. Ⓐ Ⓑ Ⓒ Ⓓ Ⓔ	8. Ⓐ Ⓑ Ⓒ Ⓓ Ⓔ	13. Ⓐ Ⓑ Ⓒ Ⓓ Ⓔ	18. Ⓐ Ⓑ Ⓒ Ⓓ Ⓔ
4. Ⓐ Ⓑ Ⓒ Ⓓ Ⓔ	9. Ⓐ Ⓑ Ⓒ Ⓓ Ⓔ	14. Ⓐ Ⓑ Ⓒ Ⓓ Ⓔ	19. Ⓐ Ⓑ Ⓒ Ⓓ Ⓔ
5. Ⓐ Ⓑ Ⓒ Ⓓ Ⓔ	10. Ⓐ Ⓑ Ⓒ Ⓓ Ⓔ	15. Ⓐ Ⓑ Ⓒ Ⓓ Ⓔ	

SECTION 8			
1. Ⓐ Ⓑ Ⓒ Ⓓ Ⓔ	5. Ⓐ Ⓑ Ⓒ Ⓓ Ⓔ	9. Ⓐ Ⓑ Ⓒ Ⓓ Ⓔ	13. Ⓐ Ⓑ Ⓒ Ⓓ Ⓔ
2. Ⓐ Ⓑ Ⓒ Ⓓ Ⓔ	6. Ⓐ Ⓑ Ⓒ Ⓓ Ⓔ	10. Ⓐ Ⓑ Ⓒ Ⓓ Ⓔ	14. Ⓐ Ⓑ Ⓒ Ⓓ Ⓔ
3. Ⓐ Ⓑ Ⓒ Ⓓ Ⓔ	7. Ⓐ Ⓑ Ⓒ Ⓓ Ⓔ	11. Ⓐ Ⓑ Ⓒ Ⓓ Ⓔ	15. Ⓐ Ⓑ Ⓒ Ⓓ Ⓔ
4. Ⓐ Ⓑ Ⓒ Ⓓ Ⓔ	8. Ⓐ Ⓑ Ⓒ Ⓓ Ⓔ	12. Ⓐ Ⓑ Ⓒ Ⓓ Ⓔ	16. Ⓐ Ⓑ Ⓒ Ⓓ Ⓔ

SECTION 9			
1. Ⓐ Ⓑ Ⓒ Ⓓ Ⓔ	5. Ⓐ Ⓑ Ⓒ Ⓓ Ⓔ	9. Ⓐ Ⓑ Ⓒ Ⓓ Ⓔ	13. Ⓐ Ⓑ Ⓒ Ⓓ Ⓔ
2. Ⓐ Ⓑ Ⓒ Ⓓ Ⓔ	6. Ⓐ Ⓑ Ⓒ Ⓓ Ⓔ	10. Ⓐ Ⓑ Ⓒ Ⓓ Ⓔ	14. Ⓐ Ⓑ Ⓒ Ⓓ Ⓔ
3. Ⓐ Ⓑ Ⓒ Ⓓ Ⓔ	7. Ⓐ Ⓑ Ⓒ Ⓓ Ⓔ	11. Ⓐ Ⓑ Ⓒ Ⓓ Ⓔ	
4. Ⓐ Ⓑ Ⓒ Ⓓ Ⓔ	8. Ⓐ Ⓑ Ⓒ Ⓓ Ⓔ	12. Ⓐ Ⓑ Ⓒ Ⓓ Ⓔ	

SECTION 1

ESSAY

Time—25 minutes

The essay gives you an opportunity to show how effectively you can develop and express ideas. You should, therefore, take care to develop your point of view, present your ideas logically and clearly, and use language precisely.

Your essay must be written on the lines provided on your answer sheet—you will receive no other paper on which to write. You will have enough space if you write on every line, avoid wide margins, and keep your handwriting to a reasonable size. Remember that people who are not familiar with your handwriting will read what you write. Try to write or print so that what you are writing is legible to those readers.

You have twenty-five minutes to write an essay on the topic assigned below. DO NOT WRITE ON ANOTHER TOPIC. AN OFF-TOPIC ESSAY WILL RECEIVE A SCORE OF ZERO.

Think carefully about the issue presented in the following excerpt and the assignment below.

> Wealthier nations are often called on to provide aid to poorer countries undergoing a crisis caused by a natural disaster such as an earthquake, typhoon, or tsunami.

Assignment: Should a wealthier nation always provide aid to a poorer country? If so, how much should a wealthy nation give? Plan and write an essay in which you develop your point of view on this issue. Support your position with reasoning and examples taken from your reading, studies, experiences, or observations.

DO NOT WRITE YOUR ESSAY IN YOUR TEST BOOK. You will receive credit only for what you write on your answer sheet.

BEGIN WRITING YOUR ESSAY ON THE ANSWER SHEET.

IF YOU FINISH BEFORE TIME IS CALLED, YOU MAY CHECK YOUR WORK ON THIS SECTION ONLY.
DO NOT TURN TO ANY OTHER SECTION IN THE TEST.

SECTION 1—ESSAY

Time—25 minutes

SECTION 1—ESSAY

Time—25 minutes

SECTION 2

Turn to Section 2 of your answer sheet to answer the questions in this section.

Time—25 Minutes
24 Questions

Directions: For each question in this section, select the best answer from among the choices given and fill in the corresponding oval on the answer sheet.

Each sentence below has one or two blanks, each blank indicating that something has been omitted. Beneath the sentence are five words or sets of words labeled A through E. Choose the word or set of words that, when inserted in the sentence, best fits the meaning of the sentence as a whole.

Example:

Eliza felt ----- when her boss asked her to work seven weekends in a row but ----- when her work earned her a promotion.

(A) enervated . . weakened
(B) depressed . . intellectual
(C) advantageous . . salacious
(D) angry . . shopworn
(E) irate . . elated   

1. Theo's elaborate plans for his girlfriend's birthday party were really just a ----- to disguise his intention to propose to her in front of her family and friends.

(A) muse
(B) boon
(C) ruse
(D) memento
(E) negotiation

2. Even though the industry attempts to give the impression that fashion is a continuously evolving art form, most trends are ----- and brought out for the public after they have been ----- from view long enough to have been forgotten.

(A) invented . . evaporated
(B) salvaged . . presented
(C) destroyed . . inspected
(D) recycled . . hidden
(E) reused . . regenerated

3. Despite MacArthur's insistence that he was putting into place ----- institutions in Japan following that country's defeat in World War II, many found the general's actions to be ironically ----- in nature.

(A) egalitarian . . plebeian
(B) dominating . . selfish
(C) eccentric . . awkward
(D) safer . . freewheeling
(E) democratic . . dictatorial

4. The recent discovery of a miniature-sized human suggests that ancient bipedal life was ----- and did not necessarily follow a linear path to develop the into Homo sapiens we are accustomed to seeing today.

(A) finalized
(B) diverse
(C) fastidious
(D) enormous
(E) rabid

5. The choreographer understood that his pieces affected the audience -----—that is, they impacted people's instincts and senses in a way that was difficult to describe with language and logic.

(A) licentiously
(B) viscerally
(C) laconically
(D) acrobatically
(E) rationally

6. During the Elizabethan Renaissance, the Protestant Church insisted that the Bible be written in ----- English, so that even a commoner could understand the word of God, whereas the Catholic Church printed no such texts and recited the scriptures in Latin.

(A) appreciative
(B) pellucid
(C) intricate
(D) amiable
(E) nascent

GO ON TO THE NEXT PAGE

SECTION 2

7. The audience responded to the performance with ----- applause, confirming the critic's assertion that this revival of the play had finally ----- the essence of the author's intent.

(A) enthusiastic . . resisted
(B) thunderous . . captured
(C) tepid . . affirmed
(D) mannered . . released
(E) adequate . . confined

8. In the court hearing, it was finally revealed that the child's ----- had caused the nanny to leave her two famous employers, and not the divorcing couple's ----- as the press had speculated.

(A) petulance . . acrimony
(B) insistence . . harmony
(C) boorishness . . pulchritude
(D) iniquity . . exigency
(E) whimsy . . altercations

GO ON TO THE NEXT PAGE

SECTION 2

Directions: Each passage below is followed by questions based on its content. Answer the questions on the basis of what is stated or implied in each passage and in any introductory material that may be provided.

Questions 9–10 are based on the following passage.

Daylight savings time was initiated in an attempt to better utilize the available daylight at any given time during the year. In the spring, Americans set their clocks forward an hour. In the fall, they turn the clock back one hour. By coinciding "morning" with the rising sun, people are not forced to turn on their lights and therefore waste precious electricity. In adhering to daylight savings, the Department of Transportation has shown that Americans are able to cut total energy consumption by 1 percent per day. Daylight savings time also has safety benefits. By making sure commuters are able to travel during light hours, fewer accidents are likely to occur as a result of drivers being unable to see the road or each other.

9. According to the passage, what was the primary impetus behind instituting daylight savings time?

(A) Agreeing to cooperate with other countries that had adopted daylight savings time
(B) The conservation of energy
(C) The health benefits of exposure to the sun
(D) Keeping "morning" consistent across the country
(E) Making sure the roads are safe during the day

10. The phrase "coinciding 'morning' with the rising sun" most likely means which of the following as it is used in the passage?

(A) Resetting the clock every day so the sun rises at the same time
(B) Checking the weather before determining the time
(C) Making sure adults wake up at the same time everyday
(D) Making sure that children can see when they go to school
(E) Making sure that "morning" always occurs when the sun is rising

Questions 11–12 are based on the following passage.

Among the many quiet dangers for homeowners are termites whose primary source of food is wood, and who can silently destabilize the walls of an ordinary home. This danger can be avoided, however, by remaining watchful. The first obvious sign of termites is termites themselves—winged insects all emerging from the same location. Second, mud protruding from the floor or between cracks in a wall can signal the presence of termites, who use the mud to construct tubes through which they can then cross open areas not sheltered by wood.

11. This passage would most likely appear in which of the following type of publication?

(A) A pamphlet for new homeowners
(B) A brochure about pesticide
(C) A science magazine
(D) A newsletter for science teachers
(E) A research journal for chemists

12. It is implied that termites construct mud tubes because

(A) they eat mud in addition to wood
(B) they like to hide from homeowners
(C) they do not like to cross the open air unprotected
(D) they do not fly unless they have to
(E) they are careless

GO ON TO THE NEXT PAGE

SECTION 2

Directions: The passages below are followed by questions based on their content; questions following a pair of related passages may also be based on the relationship between the paired passages. Answer the questions on the basis of what is stated or implied in the passages and in any introductory material that may be provided.

Questions 13–24 are based on the following passages.

The following passages were adapted from articles published in two academic journals in 1999. Both articles discuss the Elgin Marbles, *which were once situated on the Parthenon in Athens, before being moved to the British Museum in London in the late nineteenth century.*

Passage 1

Imagine in the year 479 B.C. that you are a proud Greek leader who has just defeated the Persians at the Battle of Marathon. You want to do something to celebrate the successful defense of your people, and, because you are a shrewd leader, you want to begin to focus the energies of your people toward the future—toward cultural riches and successes. Not unlike today's business leaders who routinely donate their earnings to medical research, the construction of buildings, and the support of the arts, Pericles, the famed leader of the ancient Greek world, decided that he would bring culture and pride to the capital of Greece—the city Athens. One of the structures to emerge from this remarkable period of cultural flowering was the Parthenon, a temple seated high up on a hill known as the Acropolis. The Parthenon was a rectangular building, with two rows of columns circling the perimeter. The roof was sloped, with the result that either end had a triangular shape sitting atop the columns. To decorate the Parthenon, artists were hired to sculpt three sets of sculptures: the metopes, friezes, and pediments.

The metopes are individual sculptures sculpted in relief. Originally, there were ninety-two metopes, thirty-two on each of the longer sides of the Parthenon and fourteen on the ends. The metopes were located just above the outside row of columns and generally featured Greek heroes in mythical battles. The north side, for example, showed violent scenes from the great Greek myth, the Trojan War. The south side depicted battles between such mythical creatures as the centaurs and Amazons.

The friezes were 160 meters long and placed above the inner row of columns. These sculptures are less violent in nature and portray a showy, festive procession of people and animals on their way to the Panathenaea festival.

The pediment statues sat on top of the triangular space, on either end of the temple. Sadly, the pediments have been so greatly destroyed over time that we can only surmise what must have once been there. The Greek writer Pausanias, who wrote circa A.D. 150, tells us that the east pediment depicted the glorious birth of the goddess Athena, patron goddess of the city of Athens, as she is born from the head of her father, the god Zeus. The western pediment, according to Pausanias, showed us Athena and the sea god Poseidon struggling for control over the land of Attica.

The marbles are magnificent to behold, and all the more humbling when we consider their age. The metopes, with their depiction of war, capture fluidity—you can almost see the muscles of the horses ripple, their manes whip in the wind. The artists were so expert in their craft that the scene truly seems to flow from body to body, as though we are not looking at a solid piece of marble but at a moment in time, a freeze frame from a movie about a war. Likewise, the friezes capture the stateliness of a procession. It is not hard to imagine the sense of wonder and pride that ancient Athenians felt when they saw these friezes. The Parthenon was meant to reflect the glory of old Athens and to inspire its people. They would have recognized the stories and characters depicted and would have been proud that these images were a product of their own culture.

Oddly enough, the *Elgin Marbles*, those artifacts of a world disappeared, don't even reside in Greece. In fact, their very name, "Elgin," is not even Greek at all. Lord Elgin was a Scottish earl who traveled to Greece during the early nineteenth century on the recommendation of his doctor. Britain was in the grip of a Romantic revival, its populace obsessed with all things from the ancient world. Lord Elgin decided to "rescue" the pieces of the Parthenon that had fallen to the ground and to remove any other pieces of the Parthenon that he thought might fall in the future. Never mind that some of the pieces shattered as they were lowered to the ground. All in all he was able to remove enough marble to fill one hundred boxes and ship these stolen goods to England. Some of the pieces were lost at sea. Others were stolen by members of Napoleon's fleet before being returned to Elgin. Eventually the pieces were assembled in the British Museum.

Over the past few years, the cry to return the *Elgin Marbles* to Greece has grown louder. The arguments that were it not for the British, the *Elgin Marbles* might have been destroyed by the Turks and Greeks who warred during the nineteenth century, and later by the pollution that has suffocated the city of Athens, seem unconvincing. It is not as though the British even took particularly good care of the marbles: they have been scrubbed and rescrubbed to the point of damage, because English Victorian tastes preferred statues to be pure white. The Greek plan to build a special museum to house the marbles, near the Parthenon where the sculptures originally resided, should be taken up with haste. The marbles are part of the Greek heritage and should be returned to the people whom Pericles hoped to inspire over two millennia ago.

GO ON TO THE NEXT PAGE

SECTION 2

Passage 2

Much ink has been spilled over the *Elgin Marbles*, currently housed in the British Museum in London. Certainly the marbles deserve the great deal of attention they receive. They are stunning to behold, situated in a large rectangular room that roughly conveys the dimensions of the Parthenon and thus the effect that the sculptures would have had on a viewer from the ancient world. Certainly the British Museum has not failed to capitalize on the marbles' appeal: the room is routinely rented out for corporate events or cocktail parties during which the wealthy can sip champagne amid the ruffling manes and tails of horses now over 2,000 years old.

Over the years, the taking of the marbles from Greece to England has become the subject of many a poet, artist, activist, politician, and moralist. Even the poet Lord Byron was moved to insult Lord Elgin. In a poem titled "Childe Harold," Byron wrote, "Dull is the eye that will not weep to see Thy walls defac'd, thy mouldering shrines removed, By British hands." In 1999 clamor over the subject seemed to reach a new decibel level, with the European Union suggesting England return the marbles and American president Bill Clinton offering to mediate. Once again, the sad history of the marbles was revisited, with England insisting it had really saved the marbles from certain destruction during Greece's recent unstable history and questioning what kind of a precedent the return of the marbles would set for other museums housing works of foreign origin, while Greece insisted that England had not so much "cleaned" the marbles as "scraped" and therefore destroyed them.

Recently, however, the debate has taken a legalistic turn. It is difficult, after all, in this modern world to appeal to one's morals alone as a stimulus for action. The English insist that Lord Elgin only took possession of the marbles because the Ottomans who were in control of Greece at the time gave him permission to do so. The Ottomans were only too pleased to give the marbles to England because of incidents taking place hundreds of kilometers away: the French, who had controlled Egypt, had recently been defeated by the English. The Ottomans hoped to retrieve control over Egypt, now that the French were gone, and gave away the marbles as a sort of good faith gift. The French had been trying for years to get their hands on the Parthenon's treasures. If this is true, and the English are able to produce a document proving that the Ottomans consciously gave away the marbles, then the matter may be tied up in courts and in negotiations for many more years.

13. In Passage 1, line 4, "shrewd" most nearly means

(A) cutting
(B) wise
(C) critical
(D) exemplary
(E) useful

14. In lines 6–8 ("Not unlike . . . arts"), the author notes that business leaders routinely use their wealth for all of the following EXCEPT

(A) promoting education
(B) researching medical cures
(C) building new structures
(D) supporting the arts
(E) constructing buildings

15. In line 43, the author mentions the fluidity of the marbles to show

(A) the confusing subject matter of the marbles
(B) what must have been placed in the pediments of the temple
(C) how the procession depicted in the friezes must have been boring in contrast to the metopes
(D) how much marble was used to finish the Parthenon
(E) how expertly carved and therefore inspiring the marbles must have been to ancient Greeks

16. The author's tone in lines 31–40 could most accurately be described as

(A) wistful
(B) admiring
(C) angry
(D) frustrated
(E) neutral

17. In lines 74–76 ("The pollution . . . marbles"), the author suggests that the pollution of Athens is not a sufficient reason to prevent the return of the marbles to Greece because

(A) the pollution in Athens has improved
(B) the marbles would be housed inside and not exposed to the elements
(C) the marbles are durable and could easily withstand pollution
(D) the English have not really cleaned the marbles as they claim to have
(E) the air in London is also polluted

18. The word "heritage" in line 81 most closely means

(A) lineage
(B) pride
(C) history
(D) art
(E) loot

GO ON TO THE NEXT PAGE

SECTION 2

19. The author of Passage 2 argues that

(A) it is difficult to know what Pericles would have wanted for the marbles and the Parthenon
(B) there may be legal reasons why the *Elgin Marbles* should stay in the British Museum
(C) the marbles should be returned to Greece on moral grounds alone
(D) the return of the *Elgin Marbles* to Greece would set a precedent for other museums to return stolen artifacts
(E) the *Elgin Marbles* need to be returned to Greece as soon as possible

20. In lines 84–110 ("Much ink . . . them"), the author's attitude toward the marbles is revealed to be

(A) generally positive
(B) gently amused
(C) highly annoyed
(D) easily dismissive
(E) unnaturally bombastic

21. In lines 90–94, the author's tone in regard to cocktail parties is

(A) enthusiastically excited
(B) mildly skeptical
(C) deeply disappointed
(D) characteristically blasé
(E) tentatively approving

22. The author quotes the poem of Lord Byron in lines 99–100 to

(A) showcase the broad artistic talent of the British people
(B) demonstrate one of the many ways in which England was undergoing a romantic revival
(C) highlight the praise that Lord Elgin received from his peers
(D) warn other looters from removing artifacts from their natural habitat
(E) emphasize how much controversy the presence of the *Elgin Marbles* in Britain has generated over the years

23. In paragraph 7, the author of Passage 1 insists that the *Elgin Marbles* should be returned to England because

(A) they would be better protected in Greece than in England
(B) Pericles would have wanted modern Greeks to enjoy the marbles as part of their cultural past
(C) the marbles can only be full appreciated when viewed in their original spots on the Parthenon
(D) the marbles may not last forever if they remain in the British Museum
(E) the presence of the marbles in Athens would significantly improve tourist traffic to Greece.

24. Reading the sentence "It is difficult, after all, in this modern world to appeal to one's morals alone as a stimulus for action." (lines 111–113), the author of Passage 1 would most likely

(A) strongly agree
(B) strongly disagree
(C) ask for further clarification of what is mean by morals
(D) apply one set of morals to the English and another to the Greeks
(E) remain indifferent

S T O P

IF YOU FINISH BEFORE TIME IS CALLED, YOU MAY CHECK YOUR WORK ON THIS TEST ONLY. DO NOT TURN TO ANY OTHER SECTION IN THIS TEST.

SECTION 3

Turn to Section 3 of your answer sheet to answer the questions in this section.

Time—25 Minutes
20 Questions

Directions: For this section, solve each problem and decide which is the best of the choices given. Fill in the corresponding oval on the answer sheet. You may use any available space for scratchwork.

Notes:

1. The use of a calculator is permitted. All numbers used are real numbers.
2. Figures that accompany problems in this test are intended to provide information useful in solving the problems. They are drawn as accurately as possible EXCEPT when it is stated in a specific problem that the figure is not drawn to scale. All figures lie in a plane unless otherwise indicated.
3. Unless otherwise specified, the domain of any function f is assumed to be the set of all real numbers x for which $f(x)$ is a real number.

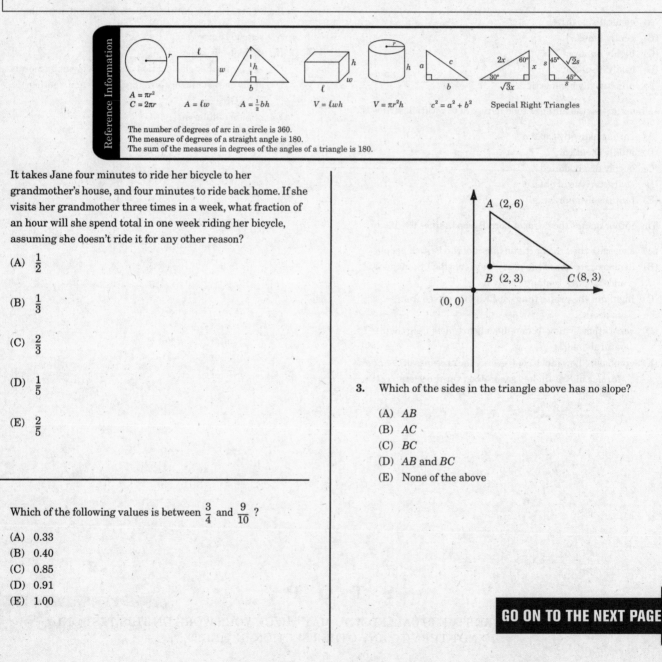

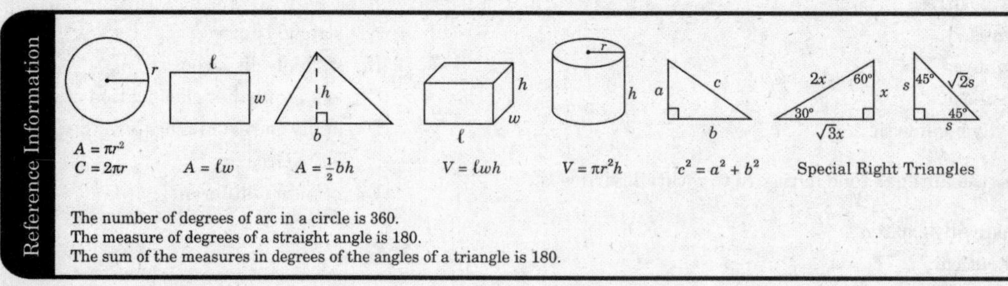
Reference Information
$A = \pi r^2$
$C = 2\pi r$
$A = \ell w$
$A = \frac{1}{2}bh$
$V = \ell wh$
$V = \pi r^2 h$
$c^2 = a^2 + b^2$
Special Right Triangles
The number of degrees of arc in a circle is 360.
The measure of degrees of a straight angle is 180.
The sum of the measures in degrees of the angles of a triangle is 180.

1. It takes Jane four minutes to ride her bicycle to her grandmother's house, and four minutes to ride back home. If she visits her grandmother three times in a week, what fraction of an hour will she spend total in one week riding her bicycle, assuming she doesn't ride it for any other reason?

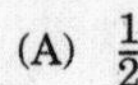

(A) $\frac{1}{2}$

(B) $\frac{1}{3}$

(C) $\frac{2}{3}$

(D) $\frac{1}{5}$

(E) $\frac{2}{5}$

2. Which of the following values is between $\frac{3}{4}$ and $\frac{9}{10}$?

(A) 0.33
(B) 0.40
(C) 0.85
(D) 0.91
(E) 1.00

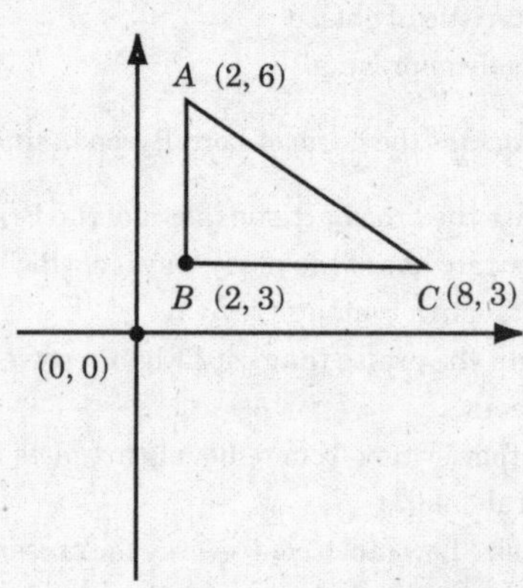
A (2, 6)
B (2, 3)
C (8, 3)
(0, 0)

3. Which of the sides in the triangle above has no slope?

(A) AB
(B) AC
(C) BC
(D) AB and BC
(E) None of the above

GO ON TO THE NEXT PAGE

SECTION 3

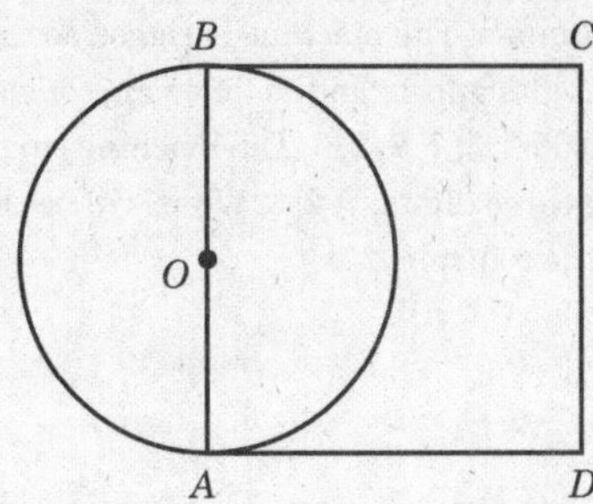

4. In the figure above, square $ABCD$ is inscribed in the circle with center O. If the area of the square is 16, what is the radius of the circle?

(A) 1
(B) 2
(C) 4
(D) 8
(E) 16

5. If a and b are integers, and $b \neq 0$, then $\frac{a}{b}$ is an integer.

Which of the following values of a and b proves that the statement above is true?

(A) $a = 1, b = 4$
(B) $a = 2, b = 4$
(C) $a = 4, b = 3$
(D) $a = 4, b = 1$
(E) $a = 2, b = 3$

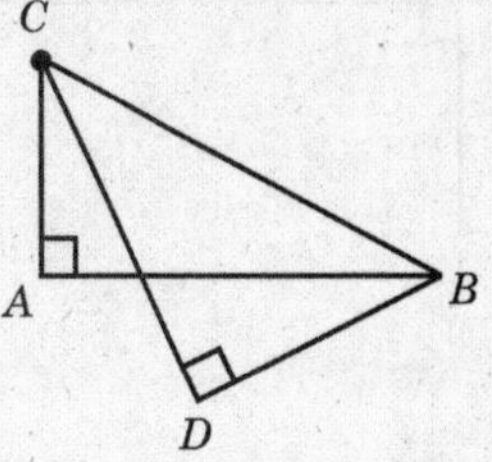

6. Line segment CB is equal to which of the following?

(A) $AC^2 + AB^2$
(B) $CD^2 + DB^2$
(C) $\sqrt{AC^2 + BC^2}$
(D) $\sqrt{CD^2 + DB^2}$
(E) $\sqrt{AB^2 + CD^2}$

7. Three winners of a reality TV show are to share a grand prize totaling $1,000,000. The prize is to be shared in the ratio 7:2:1. What is the amount of the largest share?

(A) $7,000,000
(B) $700,000
(C) $70,000
(D) $7,000
(E) $700

8. If $2 + y - |3 - 6| = 4$, then what is the value of y?

(A) –1
(B) 1
(C) 5
(D) 9
(E) 11

GO ON TO THE NEXT PAGE

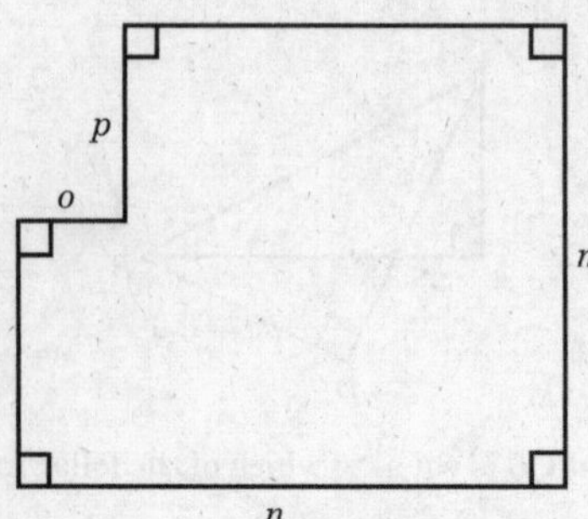

9. Which of the following is equal to the perimeter of the figure above?

(A) $2(m + n)$
(B) $2(m + n) - (o + p)$
(C) $m + n + (m - p) + (n - o)$
(D) $m + n + 2p + o$
(E) $m + n + o + p$

10. If $2a + 5b = 5$ and $a = 10 - 10b$, then what is $\frac{a}{b}$?

(A) 0
(B) 1
(C) 2
(D) 3
(E) 5

11. A square sheet of paper with area 49 is to be folded in half to make a rectangle. What is the perimeter of this rectangle?

(A) 3.5
(B) 7
(C) 14
(D) 21
(E) 28

12. A machine has three small windows, each of which displays a single digit number. The machine is rigged so that in each window, the digits appear in the following consistent and repeating pattern: 3, 7, 9, 2, 5. The machine currently displays the following three digits: 7, 2, 3. What will be the sum of the digits on the next display?

(A) 8
(B) 12
(C) 21
(D) 26
(E) 957

13. Which of the following could be the sum of a prime number and its factors?

(A) 15
(B) 16
(C) 17
(D) 18
(E) 19

GO ON TO THE NEXT PAGE

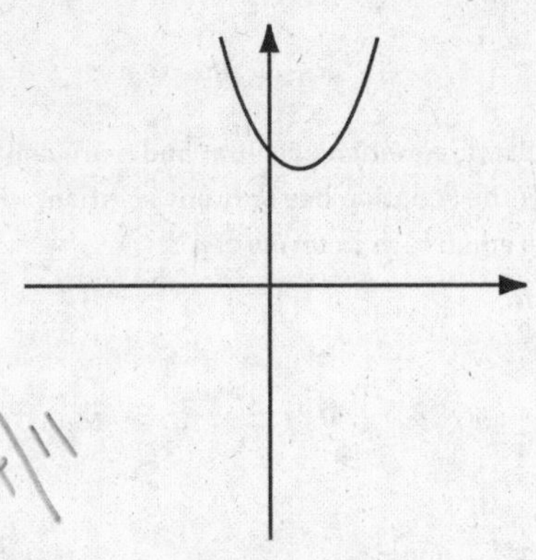

14. The figure above is a representation of the equation $y = 3x^2 - 2x + 4$. Which of the following diagrams could be a depiction of the equation $y = 3x^2 - 2x - 4$?

(A) 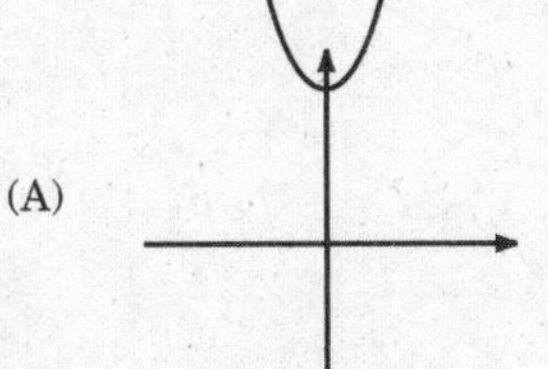

(B) 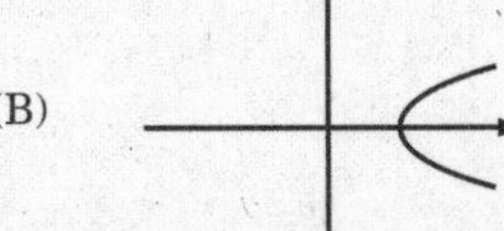

(C) 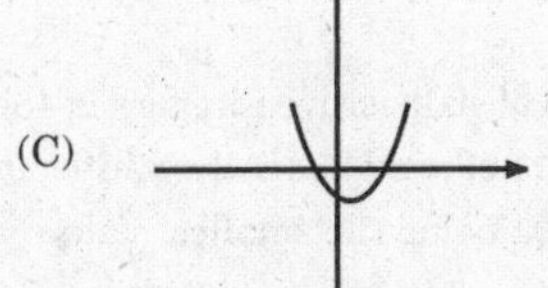

(D) 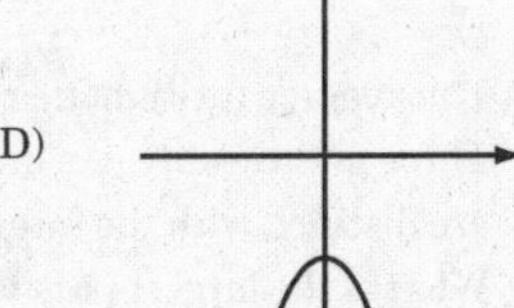

(E) 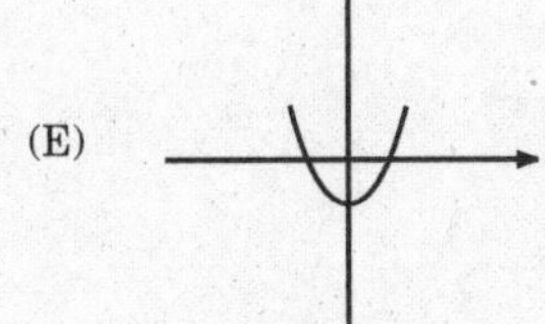

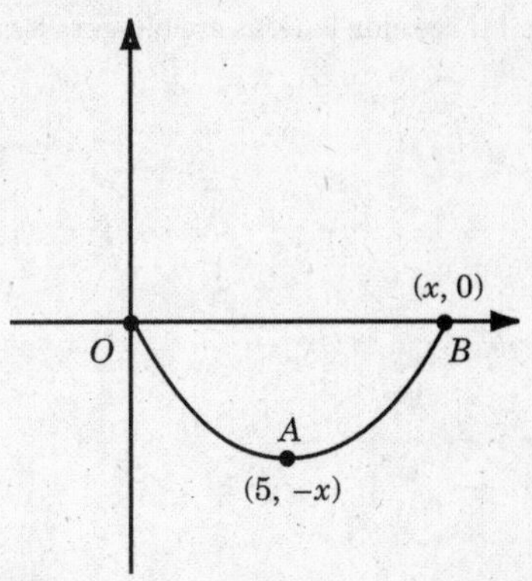

15. In the figure above, A is the midpoint of arc OB. What is the x-coordinate of the point on the semicircle that is the farthest from the origin?

(A) 9
(B) 10
(C) 11
(D) 12
(E) 13

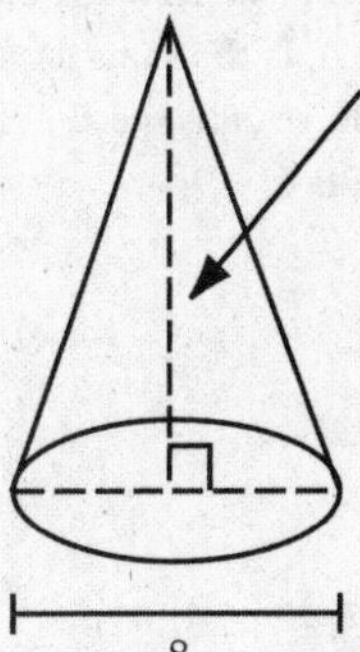

16. The figure above shows a right circular cone with the diameter of the base and the height as marked. If the sides of the cone are to be extended, keeping the proportions intact, so the new base of the cone has a diameter of 12, what will be the height?

(A) 3
(B) 4.5
(C) 6
(D) 7.5
(E) 9

GO ON TO THE NEXT PAGE

SECTION 3

17. What is the maximum possible perimeter of an isosceles triangle if all three side lengths are integers less than 10 ?

(A) 24
(B) 25
(C) 26
(D) 27
(E) 30

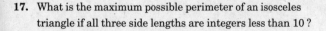

18. The ninth grade at Emerson High has had four tests in their history class. The average (arithmetic mean) of John's test scores, 83, 93, 71, and A, is the same as the average of Jeff's test scores, which were 100, 82, 83, and B. What is the difference between scores A and B ?

(A) 12
(B) 14
(C) 16
(D) 18
(E) 20

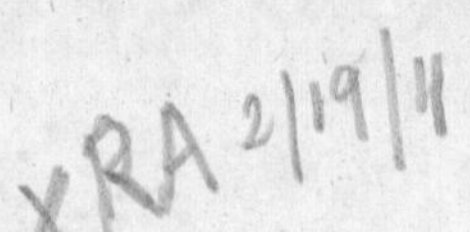

$$mx^2 + nx + 16 = 0$$

19. In the quadratic equation above, m and n are nonzero real numbers. If the equation has only one solution, which of the following is equal to m in terms of n ?

(A) $m = \frac{n}{2}$

(B) $m = \frac{n}{4}$

(C) $m = \frac{n}{16}$

(D) $m = \frac{n^2}{16}$

(E) $m = \frac{n^2}{64}$

20. The average (arithmetic mean) of six positive integers is 450. Three of these integers are 201, 202, and 203. All six integers are distinct, with the integer 201 being the smallest value. What is the largest possible value of the three remaining integers?

(A) 204
(B) 205
(C) 206
(D) 1,685
(E) 2,700

S T O P

IF YOU FINISH BEFORE TIME IS CALLED, YOU MAY CHECK YOUR WORK ON THIS TEST ONLY.
DO NOT TURN TO ANY OTHER SECTION IN THIS TEST.

SECTION 4

Turn to Section 4 of your answer sheet to answer the questions in this section.

Time—25 Minutes
24 Questions

Directions: For each question in this section, select the best answer from among the choices given and fill in the corresponding oval on the answer sheet.

Each sentence below has one or two blanks, each blank indicating that something has been omitted. Beneath the sentence are five words or sets of words labeled A through E. Choose the word or set of words that, when inserted in the sentence, <u>best</u> fits the meaning of the sentence as a whole.

<u>Example</u>:

Eliza felt ----- when her boss asked her to work seven weekends in a row but ----- when her work earned her a promotion.

(A) enervated . . weakened
(B) depressed . . intellectual
(C) advantageous . . salacious
(D) angry . . shopworn
(E) irate . . elated   

1. Although young students often find Shakespeare's poetry to be -----, scholars and experts find his work -----, extremely clear, and vivid.

(A) confusing . . impenetrable
(B) entertaining . . delightful
(C) metaphoric . . trite
(D) enchanting . . sensible
(E) oblique . . lucid

2. The scene outside the window was of a -----; wind stirred the litter on the streets into a conical -----, which seemed intent on destroying anything in its path.

(A) maelstrom . . whirlpool
(B) conflagration . . whirlwind
(C) nuisance . . gust
(D) hurricane . . serenity
(E) paradise . . placebo

3. Though the trees looked -----, foresters knew that it was only a matter of time before the invisible fungus ----- the park.

(A) healthy . . rejuvenated
(B) pallid . . destroyed
(C) verdant . . decimated
(D) monstrous . . uplifted
(E) fresh . . reinstated

4. Expert mushroom pickers rely on such ----- characteristics as smell, feel, and color to distinguish between edible and highly toxic varieties.

(A) salacious
(B) salient
(C) salivating
(D) solipsistic
(E) solicitous

5. Known for their ----- yet ----- children, the MacAfees were a colorful if somewhat disruptive presence at all neighborhood parties.

(A) principled . . moralistic
(B) precocious . . charming
(C) imaginative . . somnolent
(D) dire . . exigent
(E) attractive . . engaging

GO ON TO THE NEXT PAGE

SECTION 4

Directions: The passages below are followed by questions based on their content; questions following a pair of related passages may also be based on the relationship between the paired passages. Answer the questions on the basis of what is stated or implied in the passages and in any introductory material that may be provided.

Questions 6–9 are based on the following passages.

Passage 1

People all over the world yearn for the comforts of the developed world. And who can blame them? In the wealthiest countries, the infant mortality rate, for example, is very low. When we consider how someone living in the sixteenth century could expect that only one of his children would survive to adulthood, we are fortunate to live in a time when most children will outlive their parents. In fact, adults also live their full life spans in developed countries, because they have access to good, cheap food and expert medical care. Modernity is the salvation of all people who suffer.

Passage 2

The modern world has not brought the benefits its architects had hoped for. Modern medicine has become costly and is in danger of becoming the privileged benefit for a select few in society. Cheap food has led to obesity in our culture, with the result that for the first time, we can expect to see a generation of adults live shorter and sicklier lives than their parents. Doctors also are starting to rethink the mechanized, austere care they give that was long the hallmark of modern medicine. In developing countries, for example, new mothers have always known that by placing a premature infant on their chests, they would be able to transfer healthy, nurturing bacteria to the tiny baby's skin.

6. The description of modern medicine as a "privileged benefit for a select few in society" (lines 13–14) in Passage 2 is an example of

(A) metaphor
(B) simile
(C) paradox
(D) extremism
(E) irony

7. How would you describe the attitudes of the authors of these two passages toward the modern world?

(A) The author of Passage 1 is dispassionate, whereas the author of Passage 2 is disapproving.
(B) The author of Passage 1 is praising, whereas the author of Passage 2 is insulted.
(C) The author of Passage 1 is charmed, whereas the author of Passage 2 is bored.
(D) The author of Passage 1 is celebratory, whereas the author of Passage 2 is skeptical.
(E) The author of Passage 1 is cautious, whereas the author of Passage 2 is exuberant.

8. All of the following words are ways to describe the modern world as it is depicted in the two passages EXCEPT

(A) promising
(B) over-hyped
(C) disappointing
(D) wonderful
(E) intentional

9. The author of the second passage would most likely use all of the following evidence to disprove the statement in the first passage that the modern world is "the salvation of all people who suffer" (lines 9–10) EXCEPT

(A) it is universally acknowledged that the best physicians always graduate from medical schools in the West
(B) the current generation of children will live shorter lives due to complications from obesity
(C) Second-World medical care for premature infants is just as good, and much cheaper, than expensive first-world medicine
(D) cheap food in the first world has led to overeating
(E) only the rich can afford the best medical care in the first world

GO ON TO THE NEXT PAGE

SECTION 4

Directions: Each passage below is followed by questions based on its content. Answer the questions on the basis of what is stated or implied in each passage and in any introductory material that may be provided.

Questions 10–15 are based on the following passage.

A naturalist discusses a diverse geographical region.

The Great Basin is a geographically impressive region, encompassing some 500,000 kilometers, most of which is situated in the state of Nevada. The area received its name from the explorer John C. Fremont, who realized that all water draining into the area from nearby mountain lakes did not drain into the ocean but instead was contained in this vast stretch of land. The water collects in shallow mud lakes, salt flats, and marshes before evaporating into the dry desert air. In fact, the Great Basin is not just one large basin but is made up of many small ones, each of which is separated by a range of mountains. A drive through the landscape thus takes the viewer through a repeating pattern of basin and range.

In fact, a first-time visitor might be tempted to think that the Great Basin and range is monotonous and uninteresting. To a biologist, or even an amateur naturalist, however, nothing could be further from the truth. The Great Basin is often compared to the ocean, which, at first glance, appears to have very little life beneath its surface. Some of the mountains reach 12,000 to 13,000 feet in elevation, thereby isolating the "basins" on either side. In return, the basins effectively turn the "ranges" into biological islands, with the result that one set of mountains may support a unique species of plant or animal. Further, the Great Basin is also a desert, receiving fewer than 10 inches of rain per year. Most of this precipitation comes in the form of snow, which settles on the taller mountain peaks. These factors have forced plants to find specialized ways to survive.

One such fascinating plant is the bristlecone pine (*Pinus aristata*), which is also the official state tree of Nevada. Bristlecone pines are widely considered to be the oldest living things in the world. They survive by growing slowly, into a characteristic gnarled shape. Some years, the pines do not even grow a full ring, due to the harsh conditions of their particular environment. Because of this slow growth, however, the wood becomes very dense and is resistant to insects and rot. In 1964, the park service cut down a bristlecone pine, before the Great Basin Park was established, and discovered that the tree was over 4,900 years old. The park service later admitted to the error, and bristlecone pines have been protected ever since.

Another interesting plant is the big sagebrush, which is visible throughout each valley. The roots of the big sagebrush may grow as large as 90 feet in circumference, allowing the plant to tap as much water as possible, even when the rains are scarce. The leaves are also hairy, preventing moisture from evaporating in the heat. Because plants like the big sagebrush have found ingenious ways to adapt to such harsh conditions, a variety of animals are able to use these plants as their habitat.

10. Which of the following statements can be inferred from lines 3–8 ("The area . . . air")?

(A) Every river will lead to the ocean.
(B) Water in the Great Basin will shift from basin to basin.
(C) John C. Fremont made a mistake in naming the Great Basin.
(D) Not all water drains out to the ocean.
(E) There are many basins in the world.

11. The term "monotonous" in line 14 most nearly means

(A) boring
(B) changing
(C) cold
(D) unusual
(E) noisy

12. Which of the following is NOT a function of the use of the word "ocean" in line 17?

(A) To suggest that the Great Basin contains biological surprises below the surface
(B) To demonstrate how mountain ranges function as small islands
(C) To highlight the great wealth of life in the Great Basin
(D) To account for the presence of marine animals in the Great Basin
(E) To demonstrate how the Great Basin might seem empty of life but is not

13. It is implied that the protection of the bristlecone pine was in part due to

(A) Washington's sudden interest in preserving the legacy of the West
(B) the park service unwittingly destroying an extremely old—and therefore rare—life-form
(C) the realization that insects are dependent on the Bristlecone pine as a major food source
(D) a response to a fire that nearly decimated the bristlecone population
(E) a desire to protect the Great Basin from an influx of tourists

GO ON TO THE NEXT PAGE

14. What new information will the author most likely discuss next?

(A) The complex root system of the big Sagebrush
(B) The formation of rings in the bristlecone pine
(C) The naming of the Great Basin
(D) Some of the animals who live in the Great Basin
(E) Unfortunate actions taken by the park service

15. Which of the following best sums up the themes of the passage so far?

(A) How plants adapt to extreme conditions
(B) The discovery of a rare land formation
(C) How states choose their official plants
(D) An unusual landscape and its inhabitants
(E) The interrelation between humans and the environment

GO ON TO THE NEXT PAGE

SECTION 4

Questions 16–24 are based on the following passage.

A retiring and successful opera singer remembers her initial impressions when she left her native Japan as a student to travel to New York to study at the famed Julliard School.

My first glimpse of the city that was to become my home both terrified and inspired me. I saw it first from the air. The man seated next to me, aware that this was my virgin trip both in an airplane and abroad, suggested that I look out my window. New York was below me, with its iconic skyscrapers glinting in the fading sunlight. The impression seized my adolescent imagination and failed to let go. It had been an arduous journey. We had flown first from Tokyo to Hawaii, then to San Francisco, then to Chicago, and finally to New York. I would not see my parents for a year, when I would reverse this journey—even longer because the airplane would battle the jet streams, which would be pulsing in the exact opposite direction I wanted to go. For better or for worse, this steel and glass city below me would be my home.

I was quite surprised to discover that the city was an entirely different creature from the inside than the outside. Of course, this is true of many things, especially people, who would learn this lesson more completely than I, a creature of the stage, accustomed to donning a wig, makeup, and costume to convince people that I was actually a gypsy or a courtier from a long since vanished kingdom? Inside New York, I found the city to be a labyrinth, with none of the order it pretends to have from the air. True, the streets were arranged along the pattern of a grid, but at any moment I might be accosted by a homeless man begging for change (something I never saw in my native country) or a woman might rudely push herself in front of me to capture a vacant taxi.

I would say now that two things shocked me the most. The first was the unpredictability of language. In Japan I had seen dubbed versions of American films (*East of Eden* and *Miracle on 34th Street* come to mind). In those movies, the actors had lived in purely American settings with white actors all enunciating in perfect, if at that time unintelligible, English. (I later did manage to become fluent.) But in New York it was never that my taxi driver, Laundromat manager, makeup counter girl, or bank teller would speak English as a native. In some respects this was comforting, for I could expect some sympathy from a newly arrived immigrant, such as myself, to take the time to decipher my miming or my insecure and therefore imperfect uses of the language. At other times, I found myself as puzzled by accents as by turns of phrases.

By far the most challenging aspect of my first year abroad involved a seemingly incurable matter: I was constantly hungry. In my early days in New York, I valiantly tried to order food from the menu of diners, for my classmates were able to do so with great enthusiasm and certitude and seemed not at all to be confused by the myriad items listed on those great white sheets of paper bound in plastic. The waiters, likewise, were impatient with clients who took too much time deciding what to eat, as I often did. But my stomach, accustomed to a milder diet of rice, fish, and soy, soon grew frustrated with my attempts to acclimate to pastrami and cheese. Remember too in those days Japanese food was hardly the craze it is today, and there were few places I could go for home-style nourishment. So it was that I focused the bulk of my energy not on eating or understanding what was happening around me, but on that very thing for which I had crossed such a great distance in the first place: my music.

16. The word "virgin" in line 3 most nearly means

(A) unblemished
(B) luxury
(C) static
(D) first
(E) tardy

17. From the passage, it is possible to infer that, at the time of the incidents described, the narrator was

(A) a young woman
(B) a successful singer
(C) a tourist
(D) a thief
(E) a flight attendant

18. The narrator would not see her family for a year because

(A) travel was expensive
(B) it was difficult and far to travel home
(C) her family did not know where she was
(D) transcontinental flights were rare at the time
(E) she did not like to travel

19. In lines 15–21, the metaphor comparing cities to people does all of the following EXCEPT

(A) demonstrate how people have a tendency to dress up in New York
(B) show how a change in perspective can make the same landscape look different
(C) show that the aerial, ordered view of the city from the airplane did not match the author's experience on the ground
(D) reinforce that things are not necessarily as they seem
(E) show how the author became adept at pretending to be someone she was not when performing on the stage

GO ON TO THE NEXT PAGE

20. The author mentions movies in lines 27–30 ("I would say . . . mind") in order to

(A) assure the reader of her early fluency with English
(B) tell the reader how she was first introduced to American English
(C) share how she was first inspired to become a performer
(D) confirm how her expectations of America were met when she finally reached New York
(E) lament the unrealistic portrayal of America in films

21. The reference to ordering food in diners in lines 44–45 suggests that

(A) the author enjoyed her meals in the diner
(B) prior to coming to New York, the author had never eaten in a diner before
(C) the other students were more sophisticated than she
(D) teachers insisted that children learn to eat in diners before traveling
(E) there were no Japanese restaurants in New York at the time the author arrived

22. The word "myriad" in line 46 most nearly means

(A) paper
(B) appetizing
(C) great variety of
(D) sweltering
(E) bewildering

23. The author points out the modern day Japanese food "craze" in lines 51–52 in order to

(A) celebrate the popularization of her native culture
(B) question an appropriate diet for an immigrant
(C) decry the lack of good nutrition in New York
(D) emphasize how alienating her experiences were
(E) lament that diners have given way to Japanese restaurants

24. The tone of this passage can best be described as

(A) nostalgic and slightly amused
(B) reflective and saddened
(C) serene and awestruck
(D) dismissive and annoyed
(E) neutral and detached

S T O P

IF YOU FINISH BEFORE TIME IS CALLED, YOU MAY CHECK YOUR WORK ON THIS TEST ONLY. DO NOT TURN TO ANY OTHER SECTION IN THIS TEST.

SECTION 5

Turn to Section 5 of your answer sheet to answer the questions in this section.

Time—25 Minutes
18 Questions

Directions: For this section, solve each problem and decide which is the best of the choices given. Fill in the corresponding oval on the answer sheet. You may use any available space for scratchwork.

Notes:

1. The use of a calculator is permitted. All numbers used are real numbers.
2. Figures that accompany problems in this test are intended to provide information useful in solving the problems. They are drawn as accurately as possible EXCEPT when it is stated in a specific problem that the figure is not drawn to scale. All figures lie in a plane unless otherwise indicated.
3. Unless otherwise specified, the domain of any function f is assumed to be the set of all real numbers x for which $f(x)$ is a real number.

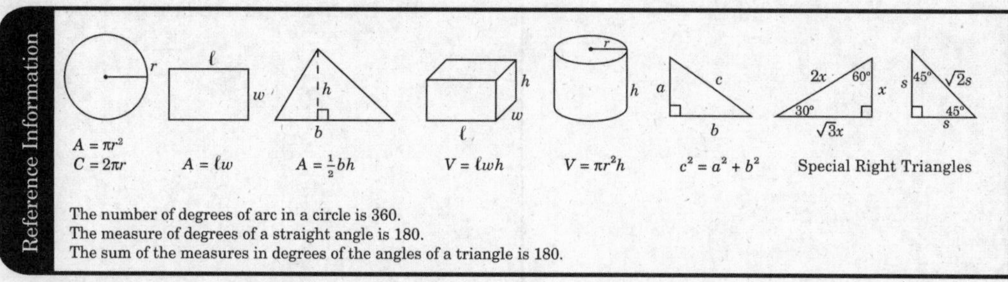

Reference Information
$A = \pi r^2$
$C = 2\pi r$
$A = \ell w$
$A = \frac{1}{2}bh$
$V = \ell wh$
$V = \pi r^2 h$
$c^2 = a^2 + b^2$
Special Right Triangles
The number of degrees of arc in a circle is 360.
The measure of degrees of a straight angle is 180.
The sum of the measures in degrees of the angles of a triangle is 180.

1. A study of the Patterson Municipal Library found that nearly 25 percent of its library books are returned late each month. If the library loaned 2,376 books last month, about how many were returned tardy this month?

   (A) 594
   (B) 1,188
   (C) 1,578
   (D) 1,782
   (E) 2,376

2. If $x^2 - 20 = -x$, what are two possible values of x ?

   (A) 4 and –4
   (B) –4 and –5
   (C) 4 and –5
   (D) 4 and 5
   (E) –4 and 5

3. Sixty percent of 30 is the same as 25 percent of what number?

   (A) 18
   (B) 36
   (C) 48
   (D) 72
   (E) 90

4. If a and b are constants and $x^2 + ax + 22$ is equal to $(x + 11)(x + b)$, then what is the value of b for all values of x ?

   (A) 2
   (B) 3
   (C) 11
   (D) 13
   (E) 22

GO ON TO THE NEXT PAGE

SECTION 5

NUMBER OF TOY BOATS PRODUCED

Factory A	
Factory B	
Factory C	

= 200,000 boats

5. According to the chart above, what is the average number of toy boats produced by all three factories?

(A) 200,000
(B) 600,000
(C) 800,000
(D) 900,000
(E) 1,200,000

6. For which of the following sets of numbers is the mean greater than the mode?

(A) (1, 2, 3, 4, 4)
(B) (1, 1, 1, 2, 3)
(C) (1, 1, 1, 1, 1)
(D) (–1, 1, 2, 2, 3)
(E) (1, 1, 2, 2, 2)

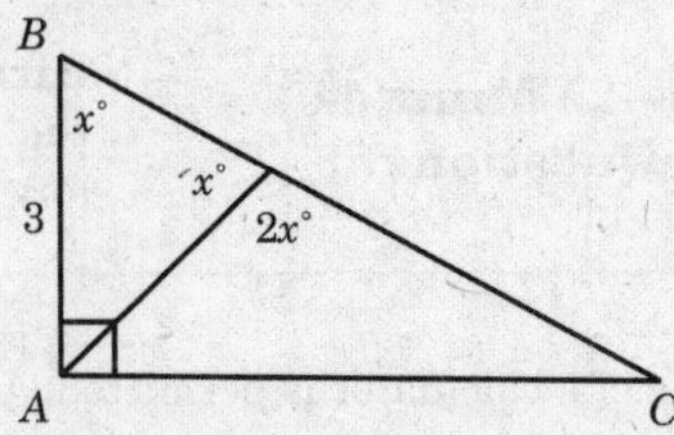

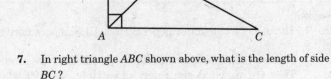

7. In right triangle ABC shown above, what is the length of side BC ?

(A) 3
(B) 4
(C) 5
(D) 6
(E) It cannot be determined from the information given.

8. Which of the following is an expression for 13 less than the difference between x and 5 ?

(A) $13 - x - 5$
(B) $x - 12$
(C) $5x - 13$
(D) $(x - 5) - 13$
(E) $5 - 13 - x$

GO ON TO THE NEXT PAGE

SECTION 5

Directions: For Student-Produced Response questions 9–18, use the grids on the answer sheet.

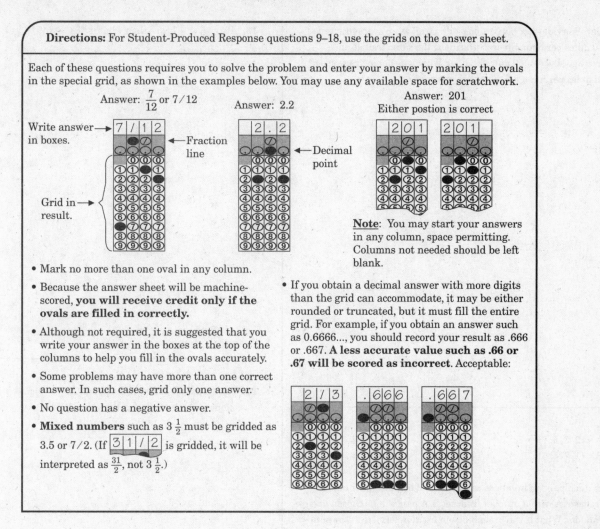

Each of these questions requires you to solve the problem and enter your answer by marking the ovals in the special grid, as shown in the examples below. You may use any available space for scratchwork.

Answer: $\frac{7}{12}$ or 7/12 Answer: 2.2

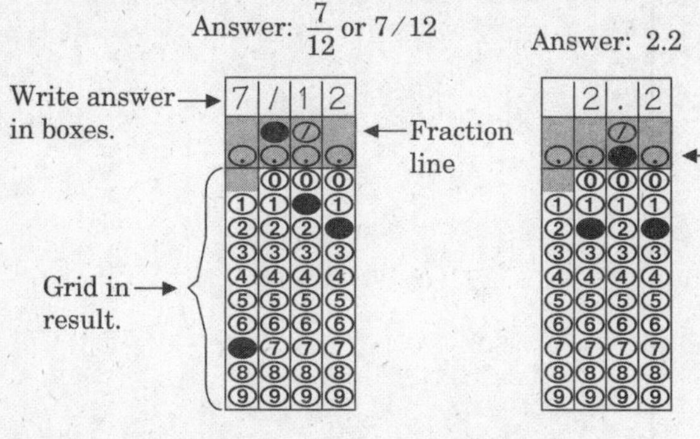

Answer: 201
Either postion is correct

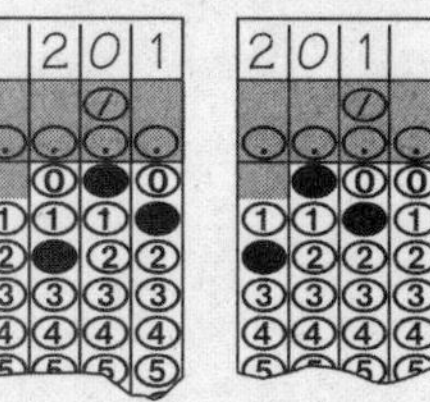

Note: You may start your answers in any column, space permitting. Columns not needed should be left blank.

- Mark no more than one oval in any column.
- Because the answer sheet will be machine-scored, **you will receive credit only if the ovals are filled in correctly.**
- Although not required, it is suggested that you write your answer in the boxes at the top of the columns to help you fill in the ovals accurately.
- Some problems may have more than one correct answer. In such cases, grid only one answer.
- No question has a negative answer.
- **Mixed numbers** such as $3\frac{1}{2}$ must be gridded as 3.5 or 7/2. (If 3 1 / 2 is gridded, it will be interpreted as $\frac{31}{2}$, not $3\frac{1}{2}$.)
- If you obtain a decimal answer with more digits than the grid can accommodate, it may be either rounded or truncated, but it must fill the entire grid. For example, if you obtain an answer such as 0.6666..., you should record your result as .666 or .667. **A less accurate value such as .66 or .67 will be scored as incorrect**. Acceptable:

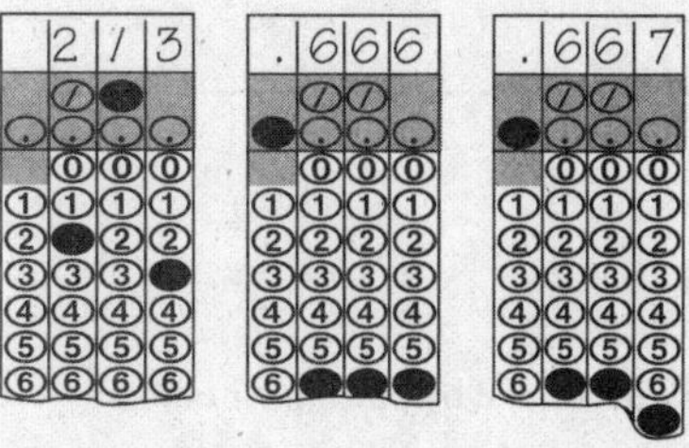

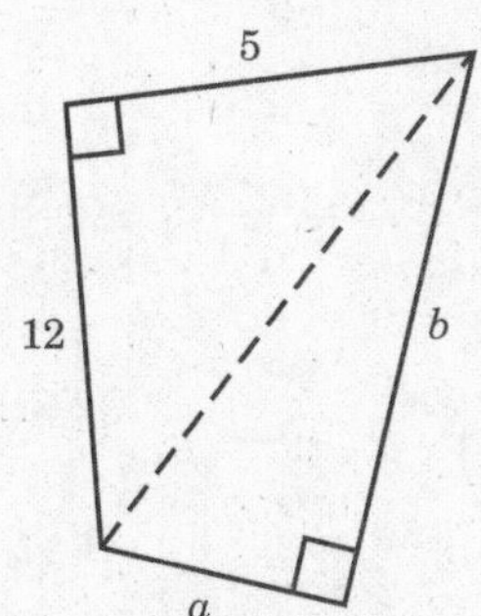

Note: Figure not drawn to scale.

9. In the figure above, what is the value of $a^2 + b^2$?

10. A brand new flat-screen TV costs $4,000. Josephine was able to find this TV on sale for 15 percent off. She waited one more week, and the same TV was again reduced, this time by 25 percent. What amount, in dollars, did Josephine save off of the original cost by waiting for the extra reduction?

GO ON TO THE NEXT PAGE

11. Caroline rides her horse along a dirt trail at an average speed of 20 miles per hour. She returns along the same trail at an average speed of 30 miles an hour. What was her average speed, in miles per hour, for the entire journey?

12. A = (2, 3, 5, 7)
B = (1, 2, 4, 5)

Sixteen pairs of numbers will be formed by pairing a number from set A with a number from set B. A pair will be chosen at random. What is the probability, in fraction form, that the sum of the pair of numbers will be even?

13. If $*r* = (r-1)\sqrt{r}$, then what is $*81* - *49*$?

14. Line v passes through the points $R(-1, -3)$ and $S(f, 6)$. If the slope is $\frac{3}{2}$, then what is the value of f ?

GO ON TO THE NEXT PAGE

SECTION 5

15. The sum of five consecutive integers is equal to their product. What is the sum of these integers?

16. In a plane, lines are drawn through a given point O so that the measure of each nonoverlapping angle formed around point O is 45 degrees. How many different lines are there?

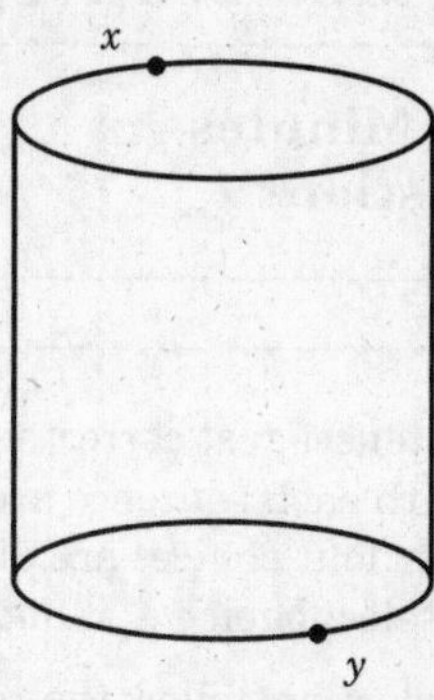

17. The figure above shows a cylinder with a radius of 3 and a height of 8. Points x and y lie on the circumference of the cylinder. What is the greatest possible distance between points x and y if a straight line were drawn to connect the two points?

18. A coin with two faces is tossed three times. What is the possibility that the coin will land with the same face up all three times?

S T O P

IF YOU FINISH BEFORE TIME IS CALLED, YOU MAY CHECK YOUR WORK ON THIS TEST ONLY. DO NOT TURN TO ANY OTHER SECTION IN THIS TEST.

SECTION 6

Turn to Section 6 of your answer sheet to answer the questions in this section.

Time—25 Minutes
35 Questions

Directions: For each question in this section, select the best answer from among the choices given.

The following sentences test correctness and effectiveness of expression. Part of each sentence or the entire sentence is underlined; beneath each sentence are five ways of phrasing the underlined material. Choice A repeats the original phrasing; the other four choices are different. If you think the original phrasing produces a better sentence than any of the alternatives, select choice A; if not, select one of the other choices.

In making your selection, follow the requirements of standard written English; that is, pay attention to grammar, choice of words, sentence construction, and punctuation. Your selection should result in the most effective sentence—clear and precise, without awkwardness or ambiguity.

Example:
In the poem "Ulysses" by Alfred, Lord Tennyson, the speaker says, "I cannot rest from travel," instead, he will live life to the fullest.

(A) "I cannot rest from travel," instead,
(B) "I cannot rest from travel"; instead,
(C) "I cannot rest from travel" instead,
(D) "I cannot rest from travel," upon which
(E) "I cannot rest from travel,"

1. More and more people are attending college, but the cost at the country's most elite institutions have gone up so much that fewer and fewer families can afford to pay tuition without some aid.

(A) have gone up so much that fewer and fewer families can afford to pay tuition without some aid
(B) has gone up so much that fewer and fewer families can afford to pay tuition without some aid
(C) having gone up so much, fewer and fewer families can afford to pay tuition without some aid
(D) going up so much, fewer and fewer families can afford to pay tuition without some aid
(E) in going up so much, fewer and fewer families can afford to pay tuition without some aid

2. Raining as it had not done in the past 30 years.

(A) Raining
(B) Raining heavily
(C) It rained
(D) In raining
(E) As it rained

3. The Mediterranean diet is considered to be among the world's healthiest and Mediterranean people live for a long time and the food is also tasty.

(A) The Mediterranean diet is considered to be among the world's healthiest and Mediterranean people live for a long time and the food is also tasty.
(B) The Mediterranean diet, considered to be among the world's healthiest because Mediterranean people live for a long time, is also tasty.
(C) Because the Mediterranean diet is considered to be among the world's healthiest, Mediterranean people live for a long time and the food is also tasty.
(D) Although the Mediterranean diet is considered to be among the world's healthiest, Mediterranean people live for a long time and the food is also tasty.
(E) Although the Mediterranean diet is considered to be among the world's healthiest, Mediterranean people live for a long time because the food is tasty.

GO ON TO THE NEXT PAGE

SECTION 6

4. Oily fish like mackerel and salmon are high in omega fatty acids, these acids help prevent the development of cancer.

(A) these acids
(B) those acids
(C) which
(D) however these acids
(E) because

5. The amaryllis, with its brightly colored red flower and long green leaves, has, like the poinsettia, come to be a potent symbol of the Christmas season.

(A) with its brightly colored red flower and long green leaves, has, like the poinsettia,
(B) with their brightly colored red flower and long green leaves, has, like the poinsettia,
(C) like the poinsettia with its brightly colored red flower and long green leaves, has
(D) has, with its brightly colored red flower and long green leaves like the poinsettia,
(E) has brightly colored red flower and long green leaves like the poinsettia,

6. Modern-day furniture must be practical in addition to being simple enough to fit in with pieces already present in a home.

(A) in addition to being simple enough
(B) as well as being as simple enough
(C) and simple enough
(D) and to be simple enough
(E) and being simple enough

7. Edward Hopper's paintings are known for their depicting humble landscapes and the subtle effects of light.

(A) their depicting humble landscapes and the subtle effects of light.
(B) depicting humble landscapes and the subtle effects of light.
(C) his depicting humble landscapes and the subtle effects of light.
(D) his depicting humble landscapes and their subtle effects of light.
(E) depicting humble landscapes and their containing subtle effects of light.

8. Universally considered one of the best books of the year, the reading public enthusiastically embraced Jonathan Franzen's novel *The Corrections*.

(A) the reading public enthusiastically embraced Jonathan Franzen's novel *The Corrections*.
(B) the Jonathan Franzen's novel *The Corrections*, was enthusiastically embraced by the reading public.
(C) *The Corrections*, by Jonathan Franzen, the reading public enthusiastically embraced novel.
(D) *The Corrections*, by Jonathan Franzen, generated an enthusiastic embrace from the reading public.
(E) *The Corrections* was enthused by an embrace from the public.

9. When the filmmakers sought to bring a modern-day version of the story of Grendel to the screen, they wanted to bring the palpable terror of the story, but were not trying to show its datedness.

(A) they wanted to bring the palpable terror of the story, but were not trying to show its datedness.
(B) and they wanted to bring the palpable terror of the story, but not to try to show its datedness.
(C) and they were wanting to bring the palpable terror of the story, but not trying to show its datedness.
(D) and they wanted to bring the palpable terror of the story, not trying to show its datedness.
(E) they wanted to bring the palpable terror of the story without showing its datedness.

GO ON TO THE NEXT PAGE

10. The rise in the popularity of video games is attributed not only to advances in technology, but it is also because game makers are trying to create games that reach a broader audience.

(A) not only to advances in technology, but it is also because game makers are trying to create games that reach a broader audience
(B) not only to advances in technology but also for game makers trying to create games that reach a broader audience
(C) not only because of advances in technology, but it is also because game makers are trying to create games that reach a broader audience
(D) not only due to advances in technology but also because the game makers are trying to create games that reach a broader audience
(E) not only to advances in technology but also to game makers' attempts to create games that reach a broader audience

11. While vacationing in Mexico, paintings of native Indians for sale were discovered by Jillian who was pleased to buy several of these native pieces to add to her growing collection of more formal paintings at home.

(A) paintings of native Indians for sale were discovered by Jillian who was pleased to buy several of these native pieces
(B) paintings of native Indians discovered by Jillian for sale were bought
(C) several native pieces of paintings of native Indians for sale were discovered and bought by Jillian
(D) Jillian was pleased to discover paintings by native Indians for sale and bought several of these native pieces
(E) Jillian, pleased to discover paintings by native Indians for sale, and buying several of these native pieces

GO ON TO THE NEXT PAGE

SECTION 6

Directions: For each question in this section, select the best answer from among the choices given.

The following sentences test your ability to recognize grammar and usage errors. Each sentence contains either a single error or no error at all. No sentence contains more than one error. The error, if there is one, is underlined and lettered. If the sentence contains an error, select the one underlined part that must be changed to make the sentence correct. If the sentence is correct, select choice E. In choosing answers, follow the requirements of standard written English.

Example:

The other (A) delegates and him (B) immediately (C) accepted the resolution drafted by (D) the neutral states. No error (E)

Ⓐ ● Ⓒ Ⓓ Ⓔ

12. Although (A) privatizing social security is an attractive idea to many people, (B) they (C) may open the way for many people to lose valuable funds should (D) the stock market crash. No error (E)

13. Renowned (A) for their (B) displays of wealth and exclusivity, the stores of Fifth Avenue in New York City showcases (C) merchandise from most of the world's most (D) expensive shops. No error (E)

14. The (A) town of Fremont have (B) eagerly (C) embraced the municipal law requiring all homes to be outfitted (D) with free access to DSL. No error (E)

15. Many American (A) knitters find it easier to (B) hold a ball of yarn in their right hand and not by holding (C) it in their left hand in the manner of (D) continental knitters. No error (E)

16. With (A) a childhood spent in Africa, England, and the Bahamas, Ross was (B) clearly the more cosmopolitan (C) of all of the children in the group (D). No error (E)

17. Although nostalgic historians decry (A) the harshness of modern day lighting as opposed (B) to gaslight who (C) had a romantic yellow cast, they (D) fail to take into consideration the health hazard that gas presented in old homes. No error (E)

18. The noisome (A) quality of most stereo users (B) is a frustration for apartment dwellers who come (C) home seeking peace and quiet and not the intrusion of someone else's (D) musical tastes. No error (E)

19. Even friends of the couple were shocked (A) by the announced separation, swearing that (B) the twosome had always been (C) loyal, loving, and they enjoyed (D) shared activities. No error (E)

20. It is difficult for my twin brother Ted and I (A) to clearly (B) articulate our differences, but (C) we have always had a strong sense of being unique (D) individuals. No error (E)

21. *The Tale of Genji,* often considered the world's (A) first authentic literary novel, represented (B) a story that was (C) as intriguing for its scandalous plot as (D) it was for its psychological exploration of the characters' inner lives. No error (E)

22. Protests for (A) the labor tactics of the national (B) chain of grocery stores forced (C) corporate heads to reconsider (D) their policies toward their employees. No error (E)

GO ON TO THE NEXT PAGE

SECTION 6

23. The (A) number of accidents along the ill-fated expressway obviated (B) the need for the city council to build safer (C) ways for (D) pedestrians to cross traffic. No error (E)

24. The entire crop of oranges, except (A) for one orchard located on the side of a hill, were (B) decimated (C) by a frost that struck early in the winter and lasted for (D) three days. No error (E)

25. Visitors to Scotland are (A) always charmed by the friendliness of its (B) people and the romantic, sweeping (C) landscape of the northern (D) Highlands. No error (E)

26. Enthusiasts of fall foliage are so (A) passionate about viewing (B) the changing colors that hardly no (C) means of charting the color progression is not employed (D). No error (E)

27. The large (A) enormous cost of putting a pool in one's backyard has recently (B) been made (C) all the worse by the fact that water has started to become a scarce (D) commodity. No error (E)

28. Some critics prefer the inherent artistry of (A) ballet, whereas (B) others are more (C) enthusiastic about its technical perfection (D). No error (E)

29. A basic (A) law states that (B) ignorance is no reason for people to fail to comply (C) by (D) the law. No error (E)

GO ON TO THE NEXT PAGE

SECTION 6

Directions: The following passage is an early draft of an essay. Some parts of the passage need to be rewritten.

Read the passage and select the best answers for the questions that follow. Some questions are about particular sentences or parts of sentences and ask you to improve sentence structure or word choice. Other questions ask you to consider organization and development. In choosing answers, follow the requirements of standard written English.

Questions 30–35 are based on the following essay, a response to a writing assignment on health issues.

(1) *It can be very difficult for a person who wants to be healthy to know how to incorporate the latest health warnings into your daily routine; one is always receiving contradictory news.* **(2)** *Just when a particular food is targeted as being unhealthy, like eggs or red meat, an opposing view is released.* **(3)** *In other words, it seems like even the doctors aren't sure what they recommend.* **(4)** *They contradict themselves all the time.* **(5)** *Even healthy foods, like water, have been touted as miracles, as though there isn't enough water you can drink, but then later, doctors have said that too much water can cause serious health problems.*

(6) *Another thing that complicates the debate is the fact that food has changed greatly over the past fifty years.* **(7)** *For example, take meat.* **(8)** *Animals are raised differently now.* **(9)** *Incidentally, cattle were free to roam on the plains, nourished by natural grass and water.* **(10)** *Now, many animals are raised in small pens and forced to eat food that is full of antibiotics and other chemicals.* **(11)** *Fish, which can be a strong source of calcium and essential acids, are also raised in farms with water that might be polluted.* **(12)** *Some feel that the positive benefits of these food sources, then, are negated by their unnatural habitats, and the toxins they pass on to the human digestive system.*

(13) *Probably the most important thing for people to do, because they are faced with so much conflicting information, is to eat in moderation.* **(14)** *It is by deriving the health benefits of a number of nutritious foods, people have the greatest chance of staying healthy.*

30. What is the best revision of sentence 1 (reproduced below)?

It can be very difficult for a person who wants to be healthy to know how to incorporate the latest health warnings into your daily routine; one is always receiving contradictory news.

(A) (As it is now)
(B) It can be very difficult for a person who wants to be healthy to know how to incorporate the latest health warnings into their daily routine; one is always receiving contradictory news.
(C) It can be very difficult for one who wants to be healthy to know how to incorporate the latest health warnings into your daily routine; you are always receiving contradictory news.
(D) For one who wants to be healthy; one is always receiving contradictory news.
(E) Because one is always receiving contradictory news, it can be difficult to know how to incorporate the latest health warnings into one's daily routine.

31. Which of the following is LEAST essential to the first paragraph?

(A) Sentence 1
(B) Sentence 2
(C) Sentence 3
(D) Sentence 4
(E) Sentence 5

32. Which of the following is the best way to combine sentences 7 and 8?

(A) (As it is now)
(B) Animals are raised differently, so as a result, meat, for example, has changed.
(C) Meat, for example, has changed, because animals are raised very differently now.
(D) Because animals are raised differently, for example, so is meat different.
(E) Because, for example, animals are raised differently, so has meat changed.

GO ON TO THE NEXT PAGE

SECTION 6

33. Which of the following would be the best replacement for "incidentally" at the beginning of sentence 9?

(A) Perhaps
(B) Oddly
(C) Because
(D) Although
(E) Once

34. Which of the following is a strategy used by the writer?

(A) Noting how food has changed over history
(B) Citing numerous examples of harmful food
(C) Detailing the confusion people feel
(D) The first person
(E) Parenthetical clauses

35. How could sentence 14 (reproduced below) best be rewritten?

It is by deriving the health benefits of a number of nutritious foods, people have the greatest chance of staying healthy.

(A) (As it is now)
(B) By deriving the health benefits of a number of nutritious foods, then people have the greatest chance of staying healthy.
(C) It is by deriving the health benefits of a number of nutritious foods that people have the greatest chance of staying healthy.
(D) Deriving the health benefits of a number of nutritious foods, people have the greatest chance of staying healthy.
(E) Through the health benefits of a number of nutritious foods, then people have the greatest chance of staying healthy.

S T O P

IF YOU FINISH BEFORE TIME IS CALLED, YOU MAY CHECK YOUR WORK ON THIS TEST ONLY.
DO NOT TURN TO ANY OTHER SECTION IN THIS TEST.

SECTION 7

Turn to Section 7 of your answer sheet to answer the questions in this section.

Time—20 Minutes
19 Questions

Directions: For each question in this section, select the best answer from among the choices given and fill in the corresponding oval on the answer sheet.

Each sentence below has one or two blanks, each blank indicating that something has been omitted. Beneath the sentence are five words or sets of words labeled A through E. Choose the word or set of words that, when inserted in the sentence, best fits the meaning of the sentence as a whole.

Example:

Eliza felt ----- when her boss asked her to work seven weekends in a row but ----- when her work earned her a promotion.

(A) enervated . . weakened
(B) depressed . . intellectual
(C) advantageous . . salacious
(D) angry . . shopworn
(E) irate . . elated   

1. Opera, the dramatic presentation of song, celebrates the ----- qualities of the human voice merged with a capacity for ----- interpretation of music.

(A) cavernous . . simple
(B) sonorous . . artistic
(C) sympathetic . . rhythmic
(D) enormous . . concerned
(E) rabid . . strenuous

2. Some critics prefer the ----- quality of Johnny Hodges's smoky tone, whereas others admire his technical -----.

(A) sensuous . . laziness
(B) uneven . . prowess
(C) redundant . . ability
(D) alluring . . finesse
(E) engaging . . ineptitude

3. The ----- restoration of the frescos in the chapel was marred by complaints from the academic community, who found the touched-up portraits too colorful and therefore -----.

(A) completed . . garish
(B) smooth . . minute
(C) torpid . . accentuated
(D) spectacular . . finished
(E) remarkable . . highlighted

4. The human mind seems to be uniquely adjusted to allow a ----- existence; people all over the world are able to keep secrets and live double lives.

(A) solicitous
(B) unctuous
(C) duplicitous
(D) riotous
(E) malodorous

5. The author Tom Wolfe made waves in the 1970s when he ----- the lack of fiction addressing serious social issues.

(A) embellished
(B) intuited
(C) expounded
(D) decried
(E) admired

6. Though no journal has ever printed these claims, scientists have long ----- acknowledged that the common house cat is the most ----- of animals and is therefore nearly impossible to use as a subject for scientific experiments, because it will not behave in a consistent fashion.

(A) emphatically . . agreeable
(B) enthusiastically . . recalcitrant
(C) comically . . regenerative
(D) patriotically . . remunerative
(E) tacitly . . unpredictable

GO ON TO THE NEXT PAGE

SECTION 7

Directions: The passage below is followed by questions based on its content. Answer the questions on the basis of what is stated or implied in the passage and in any introductory material that may be provided.

Questions 7–19 are based on the following passage.

The passage below is excerpted from an essay written by a scholar who has devoted the past twenty or so years of his life to the study of Shakespeare.

The relationship between the author and his work is very much in vogue these days. Critics and interviewers alike may make mention of certain details of an author's life in the same passage in which they critique the actual work. As a result, even in the academy, students read texts looking for hints as to the artist's true intent, or for clues to a secret, a skeleton in the closet.

What are we to make of this interest in not only the artist's work but also his personal life? It is tempting to decry how quick readers are to want to break down the suspension of disbelief. What happened to the days when readers were thrilled to read a book and content just to be immersed in a fictional world? Now, readers want to know everything about a writer and how her sensibilities might have helped construct a character, a situation, or a broken heart. Have we become so cynical a people that we are not content to let a book rest on its merits alone? Judging from the plethora of biographies that are printed on Austen, Brontë, and even Shakespeare year after year, the public is still not tired of looking for hints into the personal lives of the artists who gave us Elizabeth Bennet, Jane Eyre, and Falstaff. But does uncovering some new detail—how Austen was not actually a quiet spinster but enjoyed a romance with an Irish clergyman, for example—really heighten the merits of a work of art itself? Are we so starved for entertainment that we must pry into the artists' lives, as if by knowing the story behind the story, we will be afforded some extra thrill not found in fiction alone? As a writer myself, I might have argued along these lines in years past. More recently, I have begun to rethink this ossified position.

Shakespeare should be the ideal candidate of the author who leaves us with little personal information but with an enormous body of work to titillate our senses and challenge our very perception of the world. And yet, by exploring the few known facts about him, we are able to glean a deeper understanding of his work and therefore more fully appreciate the weight of his dramas. For example, Shakespeare's dramas are often rife with the suffocation of personal terror. Desdemona lives in fear of who has framed her. Romeo and Juliet harbor a secret love. Macbeth must battle invisible forces. Certainly, the Elizabethan Age in which Shakespeare lived is regarded as a more humanistic time than Elizabeth's half-sister Queen Mary's reign some years before, in which people were forced to prove their allegiance to the Catholic Church. Yet, the Elizabethan Era was still a time of quiet fears. Initially, Queen Elizabeth did not wish to subject her people to the same grueling hurdles of proving personal faith and allegiance to the crown. But, as incidents of treason did reveal that there were some in the populace who had a greater allegiance to Rome than to their queen, Elizabeth was forced to hunt for traitors and to brutally execute them in a public display; the heads of prominent noblemen were placed on spears on the London Bridge for the people of London to see, so others would keep their behavior in check and their fate would not be as gruesome.

Shakespeare, scholars now agree, was most likely a Catholic. And while it is difficult to ascertain the degree to which he was committed to this faith and to Rome itself, he must have been aware of the brutal fate that would befall those who did not outwardly show adherence to Protestantism. There are numerous reasons why we assume today that he was a Catholic. Certainly, his family came from Catholic stock—his maternal grandfather was a devout Catholic. We have reports of a bricklayer retiling Shakespeare's natal home and discovering a document hidden in the rafters in which John Shakespeare, William's father, writes that he secretly swears his devotion to the pope. If this is true, then William must constantly have been aware of the effort and personal strain needed to create a safe, double life in Elizabethan England where the hunt was always on for traitors.

How does knowing this small bit of information help us when we read Shakespeare's dramas today? On a general level, we can understand even more deeply the allure of the world of the stage to a young, talented, and somewhat secretive man. In the theater, William Shakespeare, born of a family of modest means, could impersonate a nobleman, and, in fact, it was his very success in the theater that afforded him the chance to successfully apply for a coat of arms so that he might die and be buried as a gentleman. In plays, nothing is necessarily as it seems: ghosts appear, people lie, kings act like fools. The theater is a safe way to show openly what one might not be able to demonstrate upon the street.

There are also deeper resonances. Hamlet, the eponymous star of Shakespeare's great play, seems to wrestle with Catholicism and Protestantism, never fully allying himself to either faith. This internal struggle heightens the character's vacillation. Desdemona's terror and innocence must mirror the fear that Shakespeare either witnessed or experienced himself. The failure of the Church in the form of the friar sent to rescue Romeo and Juliet from their doom must also be a reflection of the disappointment Shakespeare's contemporaries felt in their faith to rescue them from death.

These close readings of Shakespeare's life and work help us to more fully appreciate his genius. Clearly, it can indeed be instructive to learn something about the hands and hearts that

GO ON TO THE NEXT PAGE

fashion all great works of art. But we must not make the reverse assumption that a lively personal and inner life will manifest itself into great art. Ultimately, the very forces that are required to produce a work of genius remain a mystery. And it is perhaps this single fact that continues to prompt leagues of readers and scholars to dig even deeper to uncover one single cause of talent.

7. Which of the following statements best describes the author's attitude toward readers as stated in lines 7–15 ("What . . . merits alone")?

(A) Knowing the biography of a writer can help a reader better understand a book.
(B) It is unfortunate that readers are unwilling to let a work of art rest on its own laurels but want to know more about the person who created it.
(C) It is important to preserve as much biographical information about an author as possible.
(D) Letters have often been a primary source of information for scholars who write biographies about famous writers.
(E) Most great writers have struggled with questions of religion.

8. Which of the following best expresses the meaning of the word "ossified" in line 27?

(A) hardened
(B) awkward
(C) liberal
(D) perplexing
(E) wonderful

9. By saying that Shakespeare "should be the ideal candidate of the author who leaves us with little personal information" (lines 28–29), the author means that

(A) Shakespeare intentionally erased personal information from the historic record
(B) in Shakespeare we have the opportunity to test the idea that not knowing much biographical information about a writer doesn't take away from fully appreciating an author's work
(C) scholars should not dig through the remaining material about Shakespeare's life to try to understand his personality
(D) it is frustrating for readers to have so little information about who Shakespeare was as a person
(E) too much time has passed for us to ever fully appreciate or understand Shakespeare

10. The author mentions *Romeo and Juliet* in order to

(A) show that Shakespeare could write drama and comedy
(B) insist that *Romeo and Juliet* is an example of a humanistic drama
(C) illustrate how Shakespeare could understand the tensions of young love
(D) counter the idea that Shakespeare created original characters
(E) demonstrate an example of two characters who live with a secret love and fear

11. According to the author of the passage, the heads displayed on London Bridge were intended to evoke which emotion in the population of London?

(A) Intensity
(B) Sadness
(C) Submission
(D) Faith
(E) Awe

12. The author uses the term "gruesome" in line 50 to do which of the following?

(A) Emphasize how frightening the Elizabethan era could be
(B) Prove that Shakespeare must have been Catholic
(C) Illustrate a real life moment that appears in Shakespeare's plays
(D) Question the effectiveness of Elizabeth's methods
(E) Sympathize with the beheaded nobles

13. The author's tone in lines 1–27 ("The relationship . . . position") can best be described as

(A) elated
(B) skeptical
(C) cynical
(D) disinterested
(E) thoughtful

14. The word "allure," as used in line 67, is closest in meaning to which of the following?

(A) Complexity
(B) Trap
(C) Simplicity
(D) Attraction
(E) Conventionality

GO ON TO THE NEXT PAGE

SECTION 7

15. The author mentions Shakespeare's application for a coat of arms and burial as a gentleman in lines 71–72 to outline

(A) Shakespeare's firm disdain for the royalty
(B) how Shakespeare's fortunes declined in old age
(C) the manner in which Shakespeare gradually became concerned with shallow pursuits
(D) one way in which his life on the stage—acting as a gentleman—translated to real life
(E) argue for a redefinition of what makes a gentleman

16. In lines 80–81 ("Desdemona's terror . . . himself"), the author draws a parallel between

(A) the sameness to each of Shakespeare's plays
(B) the fears of Shakespeare's characters and his own personal terror
(C) the themes of Shakespeare's plays and the plight of modern man
(D) the characters Hamlet and Desdemona
(E) the nobility and the commoners

17. In the final paragraph, the author of the essay concludes that

(A) we should never try to understand a writer's background
(B) one can never really know an author's true intention
(C) the best scholars will always look at a book for biographical information about its author
(D) it is unfortunate that readers are eager to understand the private lives of artists
(E) it is impossible to ever pinpoint exactly how a genius is created

18. In the essay, the author is primarily concerned with

(A) how Shakespeare's works have been able to last so long
(B) how to use biography when reading a literary work
(C) the progress of one writer's career
(D) how works of theater are sometimes overlooked in favor of books
(E) how drama is always more effective than comedy

19. According to the passage, what's the relationship between an inner life and great art?

(A) If an author has an exciting inner life, he or she will produce great art.
(B) If an author has a boring inner life, he or she will produce great art.
(C) The production of great art destroys the possibility of having a rich inner life.
(D) The connection between an inner life and great art is unknown.
(E) There is no connection between an inner life and great art.

S T O P

IF YOU FINISH BEFORE TIME IS CALLED, YOU MAY CHECK YOUR WORK ON THIS TEST ONLY.
DO NOT TURN TO ANY OTHER SECTION IN THIS TEST.

SECTION 8

Turn to Section 8 of your answer sheet to answer the questions in this section.

Time—20 Minutes
16 Questions

Directions: For this section, solve each problem and decide which is the best of the choices given. Fill in the corresponding oval on the answer sheet. You may use any available space for scratchwork.

Notes:

1. The use of a calculator is permitted. All numbers used are real numbers.

2. Figures that accompany problems in this test are intended to provide information useful in solving the problems. They are drawn as accurately as possible EXCEPT when it is stated in a specific problem that the figure is not drawn to scale. All figures lie in a plane unless otherwise indicated.

3. Unless otherwise specified, the domain of any function f is assumed to be the set of all real numbers x for which $f(x)$ is a real number.

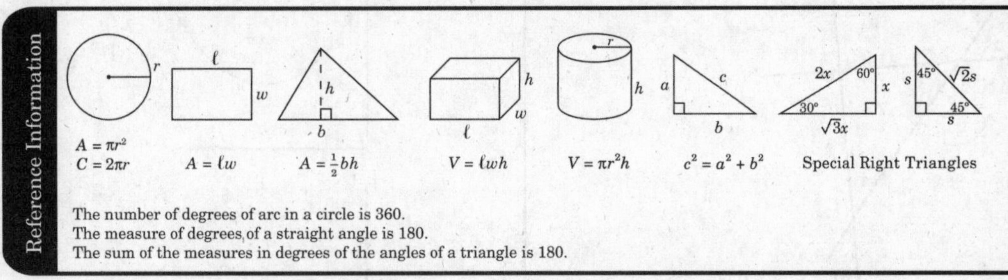

Reference Information
$A = \pi r^2$
$C = 2\pi r$
$A = \ell w$
$A = \frac{1}{2}bh$
$V = \ell wh$
$V = \pi r^2 h$
$c^2 = a^2 + b^2$
Special Right Triangles
The number of degrees of arc in a circle is 360.
The measure of degrees of a straight angle is 180.
The sum of the measures in degrees of the angles of a triangle is 180.

1. Janna has a $20 bill in her purse. She needs to buy shampoo, which costs $4.95; toothpaste, which costs $2.79; a toothbrush, which costs $.89; and soap, which costs $3.89. Approximately how much change should she expect to receive?

(A) $3
(B) $7
(C) $11
(D) $16
(E) $17

2. What number increased by 6 equals the product of that number and 4 ?

(A) –2
(B) –1
(C) 0
(D) 1
(E) 2

3. If 32 is divided by 13, what are the positive factors of its remainders?

(A) (1, 2)
(B) (1, 2, 3)
(C) (1, 13)
(D) (1, 2, 13)
(E) (1, 3)

4. If $a + b + c = 5$ and $c - b = 2$, then what is the value of $a + 2b$?

(A) –3
(B) –1
(C) 0
(D) 3
(E) 5

GO ON TO THE NEXT PAGE

SECTION 8

5. Mrs. Perkins is on a budget. She has exactly 7 outfits; 2 black, 1 white, 1 pink, 1 yellow, 1 red, and 1 gray. Assuming that there are exactly 20 working days in a month and Mrs. Perkins consistently rotates her wardrobe according to the pattern above, how many times will she wear the pink outfit in one month?

(A) 1
(B) 2
(C) 3
(D) 4
(E) 5

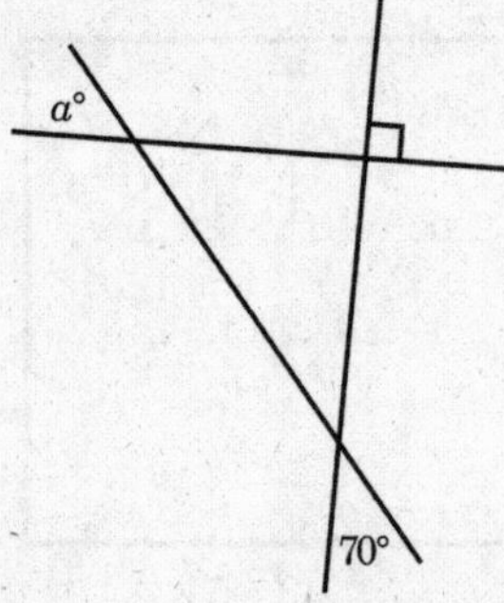

6. According to the figure above, what is the value of $3a$?

(A) 20
(B) 30
(C) 60
(D) 70
(E) 90

7. Let x^* be defined for all positive integers x by the equation $x^* = \sqrt[3]{x} - \sqrt{x}$. If $x > 1$, what is the least possible value of x such that x is an even integer?

(A) 16
(B) 25
(C) 36
(D) 64
(E) 72

8. A tropical island experiences a gradual rise in temperature during the summer months, then a gradual shift to a cooling period that peaks around December. Which of the following graphs could represent the island's temperature over the course of a year?

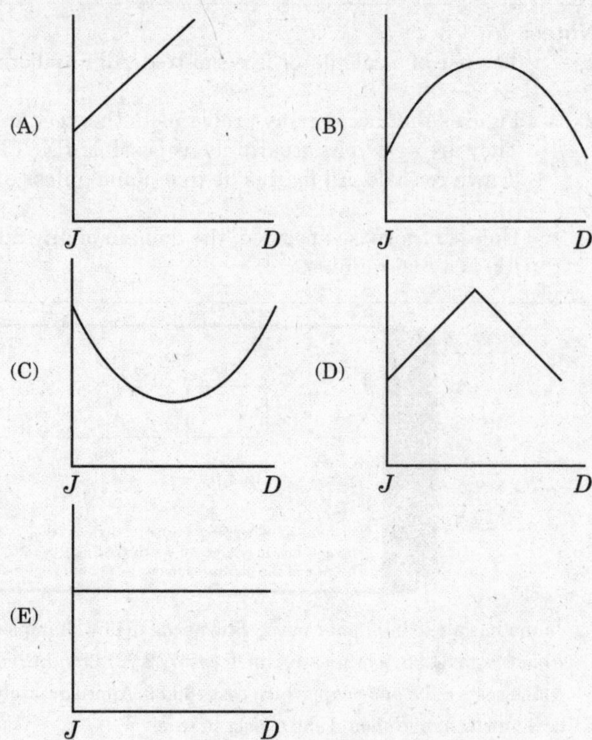

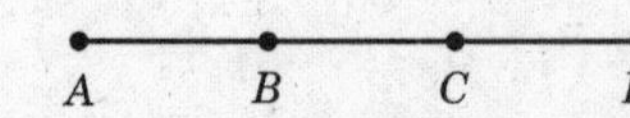

Note: Figure not drawn to scale.

9. In the line segment above, segment $CD < BC$ and $AB = BD$. Which of the following statements is true?

(A) Segment BC is equal to AB.
(B) Point B is the midpoint of line segment $ABCD$.
(C) Segment CD plus AB equals BC.
(D) Point C is the midpoint of line segment $ABCD$.
(E) Segment CD equals segment AB.

GO ON TO THE NEXT PAGE

SECTION 8

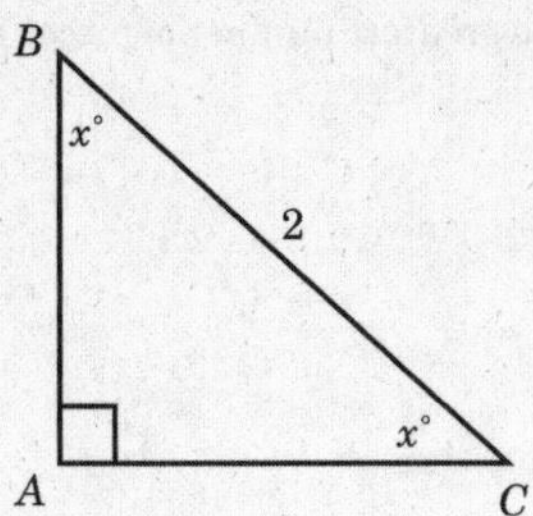

10. In the figure above, what is the value of side AB ?

(A) 2
(B) $2\sqrt{2}$
(C) $\sqrt{2}$
(D) $\sqrt{3}$
(E) $2\sqrt{3}$

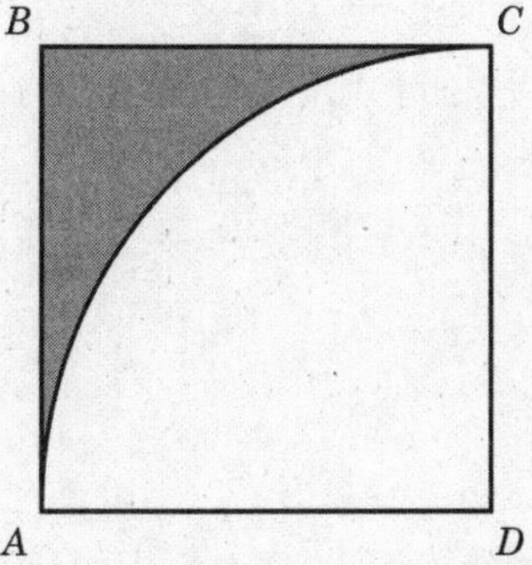

11. In the figure above, a quarter circle is inscribed in a square. The perimeter of the circle is 36π. What is the perimeter of the shaded region?

(A) $9 + 9\pi$
(B) $18 + 9\pi$
(C) $36 + 9\pi$
(D) $18 + 36\pi$
(E) $36 + 36\pi$

12. In a certain fishing village, sardines are caught at an average rate of x sardines per minute, where $x > 0$. At this rate, how many sardines will be caught in y hours, assuming $y > x$?

(A) $\frac{x60}{y}$

(B) $\frac{y60}{x}$

(C) $\frac{x}{y}$

(D) $60xy$

(E) $xy - 60$

13. For all $x \neq 5$, the expression $\frac{2x^2 + 8x - 10}{x^2 - 25} =$

(A) $\frac{2x+1}{x+5}$

(B) $\frac{x-1}{x-5}$

(C) $\frac{2x-1}{x+5}$

(D) $\frac{2x-2}{x-5}$

(E) $\frac{x-1}{x+5}$

GO ON TO THE NEXT PAGE

SECTION 8

14. If $x^2 + y^2 = -2xy$, what is the value of $x + y$?

(A) -1
(B) 0
(C) 1
(D) 2
(E) 3

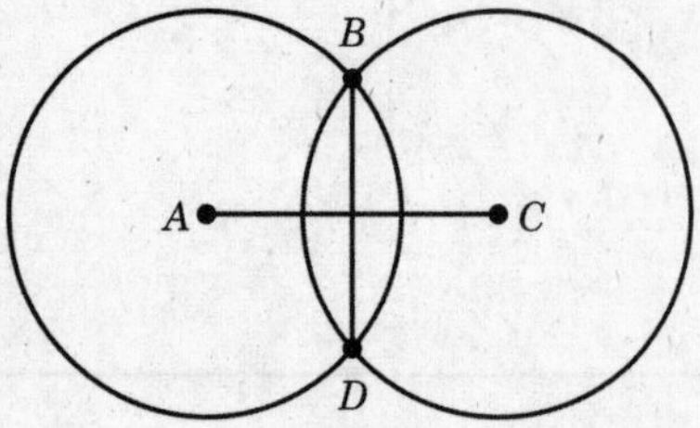

15. In the figure above, the diameter of each circle is 10, and line segment BD is 6. What is the length of line segment AC ?

(A) 6
(B) 7
(C) 8
(D) 9
(E) 10

16. A perfectly spherical scoop of ice cream is to be divided by three cuts. What is the greatest number of pieces that can result from this division?

(A) 3
(B) 4
(C) 6
(D) 7
(E) 8

S T O P

IF YOU FINISH BEFORE TIME IS CALLED, YOU MAY CHECK YOUR WORK ON THIS TEST ONLY. DO NOT TURN TO ANY OTHER SECTION IN THIS TEST.

SECTION 9

Turn to Section 9 of your answer sheet to answer the questions in this section.

Time—10 Minutes
14 Questions

Directions: For each question in this section, select the best answer from among the choices given.

The following sentences test correctness and effectiveness of expression. Part of each sentence or the entire sentence is underlined; beneath each sentence are five ways of phrasing the underlined material. Choice A repeats the original phrasing; the other four choices are different. If you think the original phrasing produces a better sentence than any of the alternatives, select choice A; if not, select one of the other choices.

In making your selection, follow the requirements of standard written English; that is, pay attention to grammar, choice of words, sentence construction, and punctuation. Your selection should result in the most effective sentence—clear and precise, without awkwardness or ambiguity.

Example:

In the poem "Ulysses" by Alfred, Lord Tennyson, the speaker says, "I cannot rest from travel," instead, he will live life to the fullest.

(A) "I cannot rest from travel," instead,
(B) "I cannot rest from travel"; instead,
(C) "I cannot rest from travel" instead,
(D) "I cannot rest from travel," upon which
(E) "I cannot rest from travel,"

1. Denise must choose a dress that is traditional, modern, or find one that is romantic.

(A) or find one that is romantic
(B) or finding a romantic one
(C) or romantic
(D) or romance
(E) or a romantic one

2. Thomas had just finished putting the groceries away when the telephone rings.

(A) when the telephone rings
(B) when the telephone rang
(C) when the telephone is ringing
(D) and then the telephone is ringing
(E) and then there is the telephone ringing

3. In perhaps almost as much time as it might have taken to finish doing the laundry, Lawrence complained about his chores.

(A) In perhaps almost as much time as it might have taken to finish doing the laundry,
(B) In as much time as it would have taken to finish the laundry,
(C) In almost as much time as doing the laundry perhaps might have taken,
(D) Taking as much time as doing the laundry might even have perhaps,
(E) Taking perhaps as much time as the laundry might have,

4. The PR agent released news of the famous couple's split on a Friday, when most magazine editors were going out of the office, at home or on vacation.

(A) going out of the office, at home, or on vacation
(B) going out of the office, or at home, or on vacation
(C) out of the office, at home, or on vacation
(D) going out of the office, or going home, or on vacation
(E) out of the office, going home or leaving for vacation

5. Though the city inspected the property on which the development was going to be built, it did not foresaw that the nearby hillside would weaken and slip in the following year's rainstorm.

(A) it did not foresaw that the nearby hillside would weaken and slip in the following year's rainstorm
(B) it did not foresaw that the nearby hillside weakened and slipped in the following year's rainstorm
(C) it did neither foresaw that the nearby hillside would weaken nor slip in the following year's rainstorm
(D) it do not foresee that the nearby hillside will weaken and slip in the following year's rainstorm
(E) it did not foresee that the nearby hillside would weaken and slip in the following year's rainstorm

GO ON TO THE NEXT PAGE

SECTION 9

6. To lose weight, it is important to watch your diet, <u>and, too, you must get plenty of exercise</u>.

(A) and, too, you must get plenty of exercise
(B) and also you must exercise
(C) and get plenty of exercise
(D) and in addition you must get plenty of exercise
(E) and also you must get plenty of exercise

7. Because the dress is lined with pockets of down, <u>they cannot very easily be hemmed</u>.

(A) they cannot very easily be hemmed
(B) it cannot very easily be hemmed
(C) they cannot all that easily be hemmed
(D) it cannot be hemmed easy
(E) they cannot be hemmed

8. There is always a conflict between people who believe good fiction is accessible and people who think it is for the elite<u>, this discussion is probably going to go on indefinitely</u>.

(A) this discussion is probably going to go on indefinitely
(B) ; this discussion is probably going to go on indefinitely
(C) and this discussion is probably going to go on indefinite
(D) this discussion is going on and on indefinitely
(E) , but this discussion is probably going to go on indefinitely

9. Aunt Petunia gave <u>Roderick and I</u> a set of walkie-talkies to share on our birthday.

(A) Roderick and I
(B) to Roderick and I
(C) Roderick and me
(D) for Roderick and me
(E) to Roderick and to me

10. The dancers onstage wore brilliantly colored costumes, <u>and their shoes were bright too</u>.

(A) and their shoes were bright too
(B) and bright shoes
(C) and they were also wearing bright shoes
(D) and shoes that were bright
(E) and their shoes, too, were bright

11. When cooking a steak, it is important to not only take into consideration the quality of meat, <u>but you have to pay attention to the temperature too</u>.

(A) but you have to pay attention to the temperature too
(B) but the temperature too
(C) but one has to pay attention to the temperature too
(D) also, however, the temperature must be paid attention to
(E) but also the temperature

12. By buying the new desk, <u>a better use of time was made by Gordon when he worked</u>.

(A) a better use of time was made by Gordon when he worked
(B) a use of time was better made by Gordon when he worked
(C) Gordon was working with a better use of his time
(D) working was made better by Gordon using his time
(E) Gordon was better able to make use of his time

13. In giving the diary to Mike for safekeeping, Georgia was showing her faith in <u>him</u>.

(A) him
(B) he
(C) his
(D) himself
(E) their

14. <u>Reading the satellite photographs, the hurricane's path was easily predicted and scientists could warn the residents of the towns that lay in its path.</u>

(A) Reading the satellite photographs, the hurricane's path was easily predicted and scientists could warn the residents of the towns that lay in its path.
(B) Reading the satellite photographs, the hurricane's path could warn the residents of the towns and was easily predicted by the scientists.
(C) Reading the satellite photographs, the hurricane's path, in the way of towns, could be predicted by scientists who could warn.
(D) Reading the satellite photographs, scientists could predict the hurricane's path and warn the residents of the towns that lay in its path.
(E) Reading the satellite photographs, scientists could warn the residents of the towns that lay in its path and predict the hurricane.

S T O P

IF YOU FINISH BEFORE TIME IS CALLED, YOU MAY CHECK YOUR WORK ON THIS TEST ONLY. DO NOT TURN TO ANY OTHER SECTION IN THIS TEST.

PRACTICE TEST 1 EXPLANATIONS

PRACTICE TEST 1 ANSWERS

Question Number	Answer	Right	Wrong
Section 2			
1	C		
2	D		
3	E		
4	B		
5	B		
6	B		
7	B		
8	A		
9	B		
10	E		
11	A		
12	C		
13	B		
14	A		
15	E		
16	A		
17	D		
18	C		
19	B		
20	A		
21	B		
22	E		
23	B		
24	B		
Section 3			
1	E		
2	C		
3	A		
4	B		
5	D		
6	D		
7	B		
8	C		
9	A		
10	A		
11	D		
12	C		
13	A		
14	C		
15	B		
16	B		
17	D		
18	D		
19	E		
20	D		
Section 4			
1	E		
2	A		
3	C		
4	B		
5	B		
6	D		
7	D		

Question Number	Answer	Right	Wrong
Section 4, continued			
8	E		
9	A		
10	D		
11	A		
12	D		
13	B		
14	D		
15	D		
16	D		
17	A		
18	B		
19	A		
20	B		
21	B		
22	C		
23	D		
24	A		
Section 5			
1	A		
2	C		
3	D		
4	A		
5	D		
6	B		
7	D		
8	D		
9	169		
10	1450		
11	24		
12	1/2		
13	384		
14	5		
15	0		
16	4		
17	10		
18	1/4, .25		
Section 6			
1	B		
2	C		
3	B		
4	C		
5	A		
6	C		
7	B		
8	D		
9	E		
10	E		
11	D		
12	C		
13	C		
14	B		
15	C		
16	C		

Question Number	Answer	Right	Wrong
Section 6, continued			
17	C		
18	A		
19	D		
20	A		
21	E		
22	A		
23	B		
24	B		
25	E		
26	C		
27	A		
28	D		
29	D		
30	E		
31	D		
32	C		
33	E		
34	A		
35	C		
Section 7			
1	B		
2	D		
3	A		
4	C		
5	D		
6	E		
7	B		
8	A		
9	B		
10	E		
11	C		
12	A		
13	E		
14	D		
15	D		
16	B		

Question Number	Answer	Right	Wrong
Section 7, continued			
17	E		
18	B		
19	D		
Section 8			
1	B		
2	E		
3	B		
4	D		
5	C		
6	C		
7	D		
8	B		
9	B		
10	C		
11	C		
12	D		
13	D		
14	B		
15	C		
16	E		
Section 9			
1	C		
2	B		
3	B		
4	C		
5	E		
6	C		
7	B		
8	B		
9	C		
10	B		
11	E		
12	E		
13	A		
14	D		

CALCULATING YOUR SCORE

Writing Section Raw Score

A. Essay Score (from 1–6) ______ A

B. Section 6 Multiple Choice: ______ no. correct − (______ no. incorrect ÷ 4) = ______ B

C. Section 9 Multiple Choice: ______ no. correct − (______ no. incorrect ÷ 4) = ______ C

D. Unrounded Multiple-Choice Score (B + C) ______ D

E. Total Rounded Multiple-Choice Raw Score
(Rounded to the nearest whole number) ______ E

F. Writing Multiple-Choice Subscore
(See the Writing Multiple-Choice conversion table on the following pages) ______ Writing MC Score

G. Total Scaled Score
(See the Writing conversion table on the following pages) ______ SAT Writing Score

Math Section Raw Score

A. Section 3 Raw Score: ______ no. correct − (______ no. incorrect ÷ 4) = ______ Subtotal A

B. Section 5 Raw Score: ______ no. correct ______ Subtotal B

C. Section 8 Raw Score: ______ no. correct − (______ no. incorrect ÷ 4) = ______ Subtotal C

D. Total Unrounded Raw Score
(Total A + B + C) ______ D

E. Total Rounded Raw Score (Rounded to the nearest whole number) ______ E

F. Scaled Score
(See the conversion table on the following pages) ______ SAT Math Score

Critical Reading Section Raw Score

A. Section 2 Raw Score: ______ – (______ ÷ 4) = ______

no. correct | no. incorrect | A

B. Section 4 Raw Score: ______ – (______ ÷ 4) = ______

no. correct | no. incorrect | B

C. Section 7 Raw Score: ______ – (______ ÷ 4) = ______

no. correct | no. incorrect | C

D. Total Unrounded Raw Score
(Total A + B + C)

______
D

E. Total Rounded Raw Score
(Rounded to the nearest whole number)

______
E

F. Scaled Score
(See the conversion table on the following pages)

______
SAT Critical Reading Score

CONVERTING YOUR RAW SCORES

Raw Score	Critical Reading Scaled Score	Math Scaled Score
67	800	
66	790	
65	770	
64	760	
63	750	
62	740	
61	720	
60	710	
59	700	
58	690	
57	680	
56	670	
55	670	
54	660	800
53	650	780
52	640	760
51	640	740
50	630	730
49	620	710
48	610	700
47	610	690
46	600	670
45	590	660
44	590	650
43	580	650
42	580	640
41	570	630
40	560	620
39	560	610
38	550	600
37	540	590
36	540	590
35	530	580
34	530	570
33	520	560
32	510	560
31	510	550
30	500	540
29	500	530
28	490	520
27	480	520
26	480	510
25	470	500
24	470	490
23	460	490
22	450	480
21	450	470
20	440	460
19	430	460

Raw Score	Critical Reading Scaled Score	Math Scaled Score
18	430	450
17	420	440
16	410	430
15	410	430
14	400	420
13	390	410
12	380	400
11	380	390
10	370	380
9	360	380
8	350	370
7	340	360
6	330	340
5	320	330
4	310	320
3	300	310
2	280	290
1	270	280
0	250	260
–1	250	250
–2	240	240
–3	230	230
–4	220	220
–5	210	210
–6	200	200

Writing Subscores

- **Essay Subscore:** Subtotal A from Writing Score (page 86)
- **Multiple-Choice Subscore:** Calculate by plugging in Subtotal E from your writing score (page 86) into the score conversion table below

Raw Score	Multiple-Choice Subscore	Raw Score	Multiple-Choice Subscore
49	80	30	59
48	79	29	58
47	77	28	57
46	76	27	56
45	75	26	55
44	74	25	54
43	72	24	53
42	71	23	52
41	70	22	51
40	69	21	51
39	68	20	50
38	67	19	49
37	66	18	48
36	65	17	47
35	64	16	46
34	63	15	45
33	62	14	44
32	61	13	43
31	60	12	42

Raw Score	Multiple-Choice Subscore	Raw Score	Multiple-Choice Subscore
11	41	2	32
10	40	1	30
9	39	0	29
8	38	−1	27
7	37	−2	25
6	36	−3	24
5	35	−4	23
4	34	−5	22
3	33	−6	21

Writing Scaled Score

MC raw score	Essay Score					
	6	5	4	3	2	1
49	800	790	780	770	720	700
48	790	780	760	730	700	680
47	780	770	750	720	690	670
46	770	760	740	710	680	660
45	770	750	740	700	670	650
44	760	750	730	690	660	640
43	750	740	710	680	650	630
42	750	730	700	670	640	620
41	740	730	690	660	630	610
40	740	720	690	650	620	600
39	740	710	680	640	610	590
38	730	700	670	630	610	590
37	720	690	660	630	600	580
36	710	680	650	620	590	570
35	710	680	640	610	580	560
34	700	670	640	600	570	550
33	690	660	630	590	560	540
32	680	650	620	580	560	540
31	670	640	610	580	550	530
30	660	630	600	570	540	520
29	650	630	590	560	530	510
28	640	620	590	550	520	510
27	640	610	580	540	510	490
26	630	600	570	530	500	490
25	620	590	560	520	500	480
24	610	580	550	510	490	470
23	600	570	540	510	480	460
22	590	570	530	500	470	450
21	590	570	530	500	470	450
20	580	560	520	490	460	440
19	570	550	520	480	450	430
18	570	540	520	470	440	420
17	560	530	510	460	430	420
16	550	520	500	450	430	410
15	540	510	490	450	420	400
14	530	500	480	440	410	390
13	520	500	470	430	400	380
12	510	490	460	420	390	370

Writing Scaled Score

MC raw score	Essay Score					
	6	5	4	3	2	1
11	510	480	450	410	380	360
10	500	470	450	400	370	350
9	490	460	440	390	360	350
8	480	450	430	390	360	340
7	470	440	420	380	350	330
6	460	430	410	370	340	320
5	450	430	400	360	330	310
4	450	420	390	350	320	300
3	440	410	390	340	310	290
2	430	400	380	330	300	280
1	420	380	370	320	290	270
0	400	370	350	310	280	260
–1	380	360	340	290	270	260
–2	370	340	320	270	260	250
–3	360	330	310	260	250	240
–4	350	320	290	250	240	230
–5	340	310	280	240	230	220
–6	340	310	280	240	220	210

SECTION 2: CRITICAL READING

Sentence Completions

1. **C** One-Word/One-Way *Easy*

The words *really just* and *disguise* are good clues to tell you that Theo is up to something. A good prediction for the blank would be a word like "cover." The only word that fits is *ruse,* **C**.

2. **D** Two-Word/Two-Way *Easy*

The words *even though* are a strong clue, indicating that the sentence is going to contain a contrast. The first blank has to be the opposite of *continuously evolving*. A good prediction would be "old." Eliminate **A**, **B**, and **C**. In the second blank, you need a word that says something like "hidden from view." Only **D** fits.

3. **E** Two-Word/Two-Way *Medium*

Despite is a strong clue, indicating that the sentence is going to contain a contrast. On the one hand, General MacArthur put some kind of institutions into place, but people view his actions to contrast his stated intent. **B** and **C** are awkward and don't fit the meaning of the sentence. **A** is wrong, because *egalitarian* and *plebeian* don't have a real contrast. The word *freewheeling* in **D** makes no sense. But in **E** the words *democratic* and *dictatorial* fit the inherent contrast in the sentence.

4. **B** One-Word/One-Way *Medium*

The word in the first blank defines *ancient bipedal life*. The word you are looking for roughly means "did not necessarily follow a linear path." A good prediction would be a word like "varied" or *diverse*, **B**. The word *rabid*, **E**, means "raging or uncontrollable," and *fastidious*, **C**, means "extremely neat and tidy."

5. **B** One-Word/One-Way *Medium*

The correct word will mean *impacted people's instincts*. In other words, **D** and **E**, *acrobatically* and *rationally*, cannot be the correct answer. *Licentiously*, **A**, means "without moral discipline." *Laconically*, **C**, means "using few words," which might be tempting, except that it does not capture the idea of a performance that impacts *instincts*. Only *viscerally*, **B**, which means "instinctively," fits the sentence.

6. **B** One-Word/One-Way *Difficult*

The Bible, according to the sentence, was written so that *even a commoner could understand the word of God*. In other words, the Bible must have been written "simply" and "clearly," which is what *pellucid*, **B**, means. Watch out for *intricate*, **C**, which means "complex" and for *nascent*, **E**, which means "newly created."

7. **B** Two-Word/Two-Way *Difficult*

The audience either has demonstrated positive or negative *applause*. A couple of little words in the sentence give a strong indication as to what kind of applause this is: the words *finally* and *confirming* seem to tell us that the applause was "positive." Eliminate **C**, **D**, and **E**. Now take the second blank. The applause is "positive," so the play must be doing something equally positive, like "fulfilling," the author's original intent. **B** must be the answer.

8. **A** Two-Word/Two-Way *Difficult*

The nanny has *left her former employer*. Whatever happened in the *famous couples'* house, it wasn't good. If you can't predict the exact meaning of the first word, you can at least figure out that it is a negative word. Unfortunately, this only enables you to eliminate **E**. The press, however, thinks that the famous couple lost their nanny because of the couple's behavior—"negative" behavior. At this point you can eliminate **B**, because *harmony* is not a negative word. If you cannot determine the answer now, you should at least attempt to guess. *Pulchritude* in **C** means "beauty," so eliminate it. *Exigency*, **D**, means "pressing" or "urgent." This leaves us with *acrimony*, in **A**, which means "bitterness."

Short Reading Passages

9. **B** Main Idea *Easy*

The first sentence of the paragraph tells you quite clearly that *Daylight savings time was initiated in an attempt to better utilize the available daylight*. In other words, daylight savings time was instituted to help people use energy and daylight in a more efficient way, **B**. The *health benefits* of the sun, **C**, and making *roads safer*, **E**, are byproducts of the instituting daylight savings but did not actually prompt the decision to adopt it.

10. **E** Specific Information *Medium*

A is tricky, because daylight savings does include resetting the clock, but, according to the passage, people only reset their clocks twice a year, not every day. Eliminate **A**. Daylight savings also has nothing to do with the *weather*, **B**. The passage does state that daylight savings is intended to *coincide 'morning' with the rising sun.* Only **E** restates this idea.

11. **A** Themes and Arguments *Easy*

The tone of the pamphlet is factual and contains numerous warnings. However, it does not contain any highly technical information that would appear in a science journal. Eliminate **C**, **D**, and **E**. The warnings, however, do indicate that the text might have been written to help someone be aware of the dangers of termites. The opening lines, *among the many quiet dangers for homeowners*, tell you who the intended audience might be—homeowners.

12. **C** Implied Information *Medium*

Take a look at the lines discussing mud tubes. *Termites . . . use the mud to construct tubes through which they cross open areas not sheltered by wood.* The clues are a little bit hidden but are still there if you look closely. The termites travel through the tubes when they need to cross areas that aren't *sheltered*. In other words, the tubes provide shelter for termites when they can't find it elsewhere. Clearly, termites like to cross open air with some kind of protection, **C**. Nothing in the passage indicates that termites actually like to *eat mud*, **A**. Also, homeowners do on occasion see termites, which counters the idea that termites are actually trying to hide, **B**.

Paired Reading Passages

13. **B** Words in Context *Easy*

The text makes it pretty clear that Pericles is a wise leader. He had the ability to lead the Greeks to beat the Persians, and he was able to construct the Parthenon. You are looking for a positive word. Eliminate **A**. *Critical*, **C**, is a rather negative word that doesn't capture the greatness of Pericles. The word *useful*, **E**, doesn't quite capture the spirit of the opening lines. Certainly Pericles was useful, but he was much more than that. He was a great leader. You might be tempted by *exemplary*, **D**, because Pericles certainly could have served as a leader for others. But you really want a word that captures his intelligence and foresight. Only *wise*, **B**, fits.

14. **A** Specific Information *Medium*

A quick look at the passage should reveal that businessmen do support everything listed among the answer choices, except for *education*, **A**.

15. **E** Themes and Arguments *Easy*

The opening lines of the third paragraph sum up the author's point: *The marbles are magnificent to behold, and all the more humbling when we consider their age.* In other words, the author is impressed by the marbles and believes that we should be too. The detail about the *fluidity* is one example of just how the marbles are impressive, **E**. **A** is wrong, because the author makes it clear that the ancient Greeks would have understood the meaning of the sculptures. **B** is wrong, because the author is describing the metopes, not the pediments in the third paragraph. **C** and **D** mention information not discussed in the passage.

16. **A** Attitude or Tone *Medium*

The word *sad* gives you a pretty strong clue as to the tone: the author is clearly "upset." He is definitely not *neutral*, **E**. Watch out for *frustrated*, **D**, and *angry*, **C**, which are a little too strong for the author. Sure, he's upset, but he isn't railing against the forces of history. Beware of **B**, as well. The author might have sounded *admiring* in the previous paragraph, but that is not the case here. Eliminate **B**. Only *wistful*, **A**, works.

17. **D** Implied Information *Medium*

The author states that the pollution of Athens as a reason to avoid the return of the marbles is *unconvincing*. He then goes on to write: *It is not as though the British even took particularly good care of the marbles. They have been scrubbed and rescrubbed to the point of damage, because English Victorian tastes preferred statues to be pure white.* In other words, the English did not take particularly good care of the marbles and only damaged their surface. **D** is therefore correct. The information in **A**, **C**, and **E** is never stated.

18. **C** Words in Context *Medium*

Reread the sentence in which the word *heritage* appears: *The marbles are part of Greek heritage and should be returned to the people whom Pericles hoped to inspire over two millennia ago.* A good prediction for the word *heritage* would be something like "past" or "tradition." The word *lineage*, **A**, means "ancestry." That's a close fit, but you really want a word that is closer in meaning to "past," as the marbles aren't physically the ancestors of modern day Greeks. *Pride*, **B**, is a positive word in keeping with the tone of the sentence, but it does not fit logically. Ditto for **D** and **E**. Only *history*, **C**, really works.

19. **B** Themes and Arguments *Medium*

The first and second sentences of the third paragraph reveals how the author of this second passage differs slightly from the author of the first passage: *Recently, however, the debate has taken a legalistic turn. It is difficult, after all, in this modern world to appeal to one's morals alone as a stimulus for action.* The author is stating that there are legal reasons why the marbles might need to be returned to Greece, **B**. Watch out for **C**, which directly contradicts the author's point of view. The author states quite clearly that *it is difficult, after all, in this modern world to appeal to one's morals alone as a stimulus for action*.

20. **A** Attitude or Tone *Medium*

The author doesn't praise or defend the *Elgin Marbles* as vehemently as the author of Passage 1 sets out to do. However, the author does say, *They are stunning to behold*. From this, you can deduce that the author does like the marbles and is impressed by them. Eliminate **C**, **D**, and **E**, which are too negative. **B** doesn't quite get the tone right, because the author isn't actually *amused* by the marbles. The correct answer must be **A**.

21. **B** Attitude or Tone *Medium*

Take a look at the lines in which the cocktail parties are discussed: *Certainly the British Museum has not failed to capitalize on the marbles' appeal. The room is routinely rented out for corporate events or cocktail parties during which the wealthy can sip champagne amid the ruffling manes and tails of horses now over 2,000 years old.* The inclusion of words like *mildly* and *routinely* tells us that the author is slightly uncertain of the benefits of having cocktail parties. He is definitely not in favor of them, so eliminate **A** and **E**. He isn't really *blasé* or dismissive of the idea, so eliminate **D**. He is also not highly upset; so eliminate **C**. Only *skeptical*, **B**, fits.

22. **E** Technique *Difficult*

The whole point of paragraph 2 is to emphasize how much controversy the marbles has caused over the years. The author writes, *Even the poet Lord Byron was moved to insult Lord Elgin.* In other words, Byron's poetry is included to demonstrate how upset people were about the marbles—**E**. **A** and **D** mention information that the author does not discuss in the passage. While the author does discuss the *romantic revival* in Britain later in Passage 1, it is not mentioned in Passage 2, so eliminate **B**. **C** is the exact opposite of the information in the passage.

23. **B** Themes and Arguments *Difficult*

The last line of Passage 1 states that *The marbles are part of the Greek heritage and should be returned to the people whom Pericles hoped to inspire over two millennia ago.* In other words, Pericles hoped to inspire the Greeks, and the author assumes that he would still want to inspire modern Greeks as well as the ancient ones. **B** is therefore the answer. **A** and **C** may seem tempting, but they contain information that is never overtly stated in the passage. The author never mentions an increase in tourist traffic, **E**.

24. **B** Relating Two Passages *Difficult*

The author of the first passage generally makes the claim that the marbles should be returned to Greece, because this is what Pericles would have wanted—it is simply the right thing to do. In other words, the author of Passage 1 *would* consider moral values a good enough reason to send the marbles to their country of origin. Thus, we can assume that the author of Passage 1 would strongly disagree with the author of Passage 2, making **B** the correct answer.

SECTION 3: MATH

Multiple Choice

1. **E** Numbers & Operations: Fractions *Easy*

Jane spends a total of 8 minutes riding her bike to and from her grandmother's house. If she goes to her grandmother's house 3 times a week, this means she rides her bike for a total of 24 minutes out of the week. There are 60 minutes in an hour. The number 24 is $\frac{2}{5}$ of 60, making **E** the correct answer.

2. **C** Numbers & Operations: Basic Operations *Easy*

This problem is simple if you know how to convert fractions into decimals. You should know that the decimal 0.33 roughly equals a third, so it is too small to be the answer. **B** is also too small. On the other hand, **D** and **E** are too large. **C** must be the correct answer.

3. **A** Geometry: Angles and Lines *Easy*

A line has no slope if it is parallel to the y-axis. You know that line AB is parallel to the y-axis because both points A and B have the same x-coordinate. The answer must be AB, or **A**.

4. **B** Geometry: Polygons *Easy*

If the area of the square is 16, then the length of one side is 4. This means that the diameter of the circle is 4, and that the radius, which is half of the diameter, is 2.

5. **D** Numbers & Operations: Basic Operations *Easy*

This problem is testing your knowledge of integers. An integer is a whole number; therefore, no fraction can be an integer. Plugging in the numbers given in the answer choices, you should see pretty quickly that the only set that will yield a whole number is **D**.

6. **D** Geometry: Polygons *Medium*

Do you remember the rules regarding the Pythagorean theorem? In a right-angle triangle, the sum of the legs squared will equal the hypotenuse squared. Notice that side CB is the hypotenuse of both triangles ABC and CDB. This means that:

$$AC^2 + AB^2 = CB^2\text{, which means that } \sqrt{AC^2 + AB^2} = \sqrt{CB^2}$$

and that

$$CD^2 + DB^2 = CB^2\text{, which means that } \sqrt{CD^2 + DB^2} = \sqrt{CB^2}$$

The only answer choice that fits these conditions is **D**.

7. **B** Numbers & Operations: Ratios *Medium*

According to the problem, the prize money will be divided into a ratio of 7:2:1. The largest portion of the prize will be 7 times larger than the smallest one. Adding up all the pieces of the ratio, you will see that the total prize will be divided into 10 "units": $7 + 2 + 1 = 10$. That means that the smallest portion will be $100,000. Now, multiply this amount by 7 to learn that the largest amount will be $700,000, or **B**.

8. **C** Algebra: Basic Operations *Medium*

This problem is testing your knowledge of absolute value, which is the positive value of any number. Take a look at the equation:

$$2 + y - |3 - 6| = 4$$

First, focus on the numbers between the absolute value signs.

$$|3 - 6|$$

Simplify: $|-3|$

Now, since we are dealing with absolute value, the number must be positive. Simplifying further, we have:

$$2 + y - 3 = 4$$
$$y - 1 = 4$$
$$y = 5$$

9. **A** Geometry: Polygons *Medium*

Notice that the figure has right angles. You know right away that the figure will include the side lengths m and n, but you need to account for the other four sides. The top piece will equal the length of n with o subtracted. The left-most side will equal m minus p. You will also need to add o and p. Putting all this together you have:

$$m + n + (n - o) + (m - p) + o + p$$

Simplify, noticing that the o's and p's are cancelled out

$$2m + 2n$$

Simplify further:

$$2(m + n)$$

10. **A** Algebra: Solving Equations *Medium*

This is a system of equations problem, where you need to solve for variables a and b. Begin by simplifying

$$a = 10 - 10b$$

Substitute:

$$2a + 5b = 5$$
$$2(10 - 10b) + 5b = 5$$
$$20 - 20b + 5b = 5$$
$$-15b = -15$$
$$b = 1$$

Now, solve for a:

$$a = 10 - 10b$$

Plug in the value for b:

$$a = 10 - 10b$$
$$a = 10 - 10(1)$$
$$a = 0$$

Don't forget to do the final step:

$$\frac{a}{b} = \frac{0}{1}$$

11. **D** Geometry: Polygons *Medium*

If the area of the square is 49, you know that one side of the square is 7. Now, the square is supposed to be folded in half. This would give you a rectangle with two lengths of 7 and two sides that are half this length, 3.5 each. Adding up all three sides, you have the following:

$$7 + 7 + 3.5 + 3.5 = 21$$

12. **C** Data Analysis, Statistics & Probability: Logic *Medium*

This problem may seem confusing at first. Just take it a piece at a time. The first window displays the number 7. You know, from the problem, that the next digit after 7 will be 9. That is the first number. In the next window, you have a 2. On the next round, that number 2 will turn to 5. Finally, the number 3, in the third window, will turn into a 7. Adding up all three new numbers, we have:

$$9 + 5 + 7 = 21$$

13. **A** Numbers & Operations: Factors and Multiples *Medium*

A prime number is a number that can only be divisible by 1 and itself. Start by checking prime numbers in order. The first prime number is 2. Its factors are 2 and 1. Adding these up, we get 5. This is not among the answer choices. The next prime number is 3. Adding the factors—3 and 1—we have a total of 7, which is still not among our answer choices. The next prime number is 5. Adding the factors, we have $5 + 5 + 1 = 11$. Still no answer choice. Next, try 7. We have $7 + 7 + 1 = 15$. Bingo! Here is our answer—**A**. None of the other answer choices can possibly work.

14. **C** Geometry: Coordinate Geometry *Difficult*

This problem is fairly straightforward if you recognize that the two equations are essentially the same. The only difference is that the *y*-coordinate in the second equation is lower than the first equation. In other words, the graph undergoes a shift along the *y*-axis. The correct answer must be **C**.

15. **B** Geometry: Coordinate Geometry, Circles *Difficult*

Another way to ask this problem would be: what is the value of *x*? Notice that *x* is the coordinate that is farthest from the origin. Notice, also, that you are told this is a semicircle. In other words, the distance from the origin to *x* is the diameter of the semicircle. You also know that the *x*-coordinate of point *A* is the radius. Since the value of the *x*-coordinate of point *A* is 5, this means that the diameter is 10.

16. **B** Geometry: Geometric Visualizations *Difficult*

The cone currently has a diameter of 8 and a height of 3. The radius is therefore 4. The new diameter is going to be 12, or a radius of 6. The new radius is therefore going to be $\frac{1}{2}$ larger than the original one. The height will also be $\frac{1}{2}$ larger.

$$3(1.5) = 4.5$$

17. **D** Geometry: Triangles *Difficult*

An isosceles triangle by definition has two sides and two angles that are equal in length. But before you choose **C** $(9 + 9 + 8 = 26)$ and move on, you need to remember that all equilateral triangles are also isosceles triangles. That means that the three sides could add up to 27 $(9 + 9 + 9)$, or **D**.

18. **D** Data Analysis, Statistics & Probability: Statistical Analysis *Difficult*
The word *average* means the sum of all terms divided by the number of terms. You are told that the medians of the two boys' scores are equal. Using this information, you can set up the following equation:

$$\frac{83 + 93 + 71 + A}{4} = \frac{100 + 82 + 83 + B}{4}$$

$$\frac{247 + A}{4} = \frac{265 + B}{4}$$

Multiply both sides by 4, and simplify further:

$$247 + A = 265 + B$$
$$A = B + 18$$

19. **E** Algebra: Binomials and Quadratics *Difficult*
If there is only one solution for this quadratic equation, then you know that the quadratic equation is the result of a binomial multiplied by itself. Substituting in the letter a, we have the following solution:

$$(ax + 4)(ax + 4)$$
$$a^2x^2 + 4ax + 4ax + 16$$
$$a^2x^2 + 8ax + 16$$

Now, looking at the original equation, we can set up the following equations:

$$mx^2 = a^2x^2, \text{ and } nx = 8ax$$

Simplify further:

$$m = a^2, \text{ and } n = 8a$$

How would you make n equal to m? First you would divide both sides by 8, then square both sides.

$$\frac{n}{8} = \frac{8a}{8}$$
$$\frac{n}{8} = a$$
$$\frac{n^2}{64} = a^2$$

20. **D** Data Analysis, Statistics & Probability: Statistical Analysis *Difficult*
If there are 6 numbers total, then you can multiply their average by 6 to find the sum of all the numbers. $6(450) = 2{,}700$. You are then asked to find the largest possible value for the remaining numbers, assuming that 201 is the smallest value and that all numbers are distinct integers. The best way to make the remaining number as large as possible is to make the other numbers as small as possible. Subtract the sum of the three numbers you do know from 2,700.

$$2{,}700 - 201 - 202 - 203 = 2{,}094$$

The next possible value for one of the 6 new numbers is 204. Subtracting 204 from 2,094, you find:

$$2{,}094 - 204 = 1{,}890$$

The next smallest possible number is 205.

$$1{,}890 - 205 = 1{,}685$$

SECTION 4: CRITICAL READING

Sentence Completions

1. **E** Two-Word/Two-Way *Medium*

The second blank is probably the easiest one to predict first. You are told that scholars find Shakespeare's work to be *extremely clear and vivid*. You are looking for a word that means "clear" for the second blank. Eliminate **A**, **B**, and **C**. The word *although* at the beginning of the sentence signals that students don't find Shakespeare's poetry to be *remotely clear*. The answer must be **E**.

2. **A** Two-Word/One-Way *Medium*

The semicolon midway through the sentence tells you that the first blank will be defined by subsequent wording—that is, *wind stirred the litter on the streets*. In other words, the scene outside the window shows some kind of a "storm." Eliminate **C** and **E**. Watch out for *conflagration* in **B**—*conflagration* is an enormous fire. Eliminate **B**. Now that we know the scene outside the window shows a "storm," what can we expect the litter to have been stirred into? A *whirlpool*, **A**, or a *serenity*, **D**? Certainly the idea of a *serenity* contrasts with the whole point of the sentence. The correct answer must be **A**.

3. **C** Two-Word/Two-Way *Medium*

The word though tells you that there is an inherent contrast in the sentence. Even though the forest appears one way, an invisible fungus is actually doing something to the trees. What would be a good prediction for the second blank? Well, you know that an invisible fungus would harm the trees in some way. A good prediction for the second blank is "harmed." Since the first half of the sentence must contrast with the idea of a "harmed" park, you can predict that the trees appear "healthy." The correct answer is **C**, with *verdant* meaning "extremely green" and *decimated* meaning "destroyed." Watch out for *pallid*, **B**, which means "pale" and *rejuvenated*, **A**, which means "revitalized."

4. **B** One-Word/One-Way *Medium*

All of the answers contain similar sounding words, so you must use your ability to decode the sentence to find the correct answer. *Mushroom pickers rely* on certain kinds of *characteristics* to tell the difference between edible and poisonous mushrooms. The examples given are *smell, feel, and color*. A good prediction would be the word "particular" or "distinguishing." Even if you couldn't come up with a good prediction, however, you could eliminate some of the answer choices right away. *Salacious*, **A**, means "slanderous," and definitely doesn't make sense. *Salivating*, **C**, might have seemed tempting because you might "salivate" over something that tastes good, but mushroom pickers rely on more than taste to figure out which mushrooms are good or bad. *Solipsistic*, **D**, refers to the theory that "the only thing knowable is the self," and *solicitous*, **E**, means "polite." Only *salient*, **B**, meaning "defined and particular," fits the sentence.

5. **B** Two-Word/Two-Way *Easy*

The McAfees sure sound like an interesting family. They are *colorful and disruptive*, and you can assume that their children will be the same. You are looking for two words that mirror the description of the McAfees to apply to the children, but which also have an inherent contrast in them—the word *yet* separates the two words describing the children. Rule out **A** and **D**, which are too negative and which don't really provide a contrast. **E** also doesn't fit: although the words are complimentary, *attractive* and *engaging* don't require the word *yet* to separate them. In **C**, *imaginative* and *somnolent*, meaning "sleep inducing," you might see a contrast, but the word *somnolent* doesn't really have any place in the sentence, because nowhere does the sentence imply that the McAfees put people to sleep. In **B**, however, *precocious* means "showing unusually early maturity, sometimes to the point of irritation," and *charming* means "engaging." Here there is a very slight contrast, and yet the two words taken together paint a positive picture of the McAfee children.

Paired Reading Passages

6. **D** Technique *Easy*

The author isn't saying that modern medicine is definitely a benefit for a privileged few, but he is saying that medicine is in *danger* of becoming a privileged benefit. In other words, the lines *the privileged benefit for a select few in society* represent an "extreme case scenario," or **D**. Remember, a simile is a comparison between two things joined together by the words *like* or *as*. A metaphor is like a simile, except it does not use *like* or *as*.

7. **D** Relating Two Passages *Easy*

Read the two passages and assign a tone to the two authors. The first author seems to say that the modern world is a purely wonderful thing. The author of the second paragraph is less enthusiastic. In other words, author 1 is positive and author 2 is negative. You can easily eliminate **A**, **B**, and **E**. The author of the second passage doesn't really sound *bored*, **C**; he just sounds mildly negative. The correct answer must be **D**.

8. **E** Specific Information *Easy*

The key to answering this question lies in having a clear sense of the two authors' tones. The first author praises the modern world—eliminate **A** and **D**. The second author is unhappy with the modern world—eliminate **B** and **C**. The word *intentional*, **E**, means "doing on purpose," and just doesn't fit the context of either paragraph.

9. **A** Relating Two Passages *Medium*

You want to find the answer choice that would not disprove the statement in the first passage that *modernity is the salvation of all people who suffer.* In other words, you want to find the answer choice that would weaken the second author's assertion that the modern world is overrated. Most of the answer choices strengthen the second author's position. Take **B**, for example, which states that the current generation of wealthier people will live shorter lives than their parents due to obesity. This fact, if true, will only strengthen the author's point of view. Ditto for most every other answer choice except for **A**. If it could be proved that the best doctors all come from the modern world thereby showing a benefit of the first world, then the second author's opinion would be weakened.

Long Reading Passages

10. **D** Implied Information *Medium*

Reread the lines in the question: *The area received its name from the explorer John C. Fremont, who realized that all water draining into the area from nearby mountain lakes did not drain into the ocean but instead was contained in this vast stretch of land. The water collects in shallow mud lakes, salt flats, and marshes before evaporating into the dry desert air.* What can you infer? You know that the Great Basin was so named because the water that runs down from mountains sits in the desert and doesn't go out to sea. This idea is in direct contrast to **A**, so rule that choice out. Watch out for **B** and **C**, which mention terms used in these lines but are not facts actually supported by the passage. Where does it say, for example, that Fremont made a mistake? This is also true of **E**. The passage never mentions the number of basins that exist in the world. However, you do know that the water that goes to the basin stays there, never making it to the ocean. Therefore you can infer that not all rivers run to the ocean.

11. **A** Words in Context *Medium*

As with all vocab-in-context questions, reread the lines surrounding the word you want to define: *In fact, a first-time visitor might be tempted to think that the Great Basin and range is monotonous and uninteresting.* The word *uninteresting* provides you with a clue: the basin and range might seem uninteresting to someone seeing it for the first time. The correct definition of monotonous will be negative. Rule out **B** and **D**. The word *noisy*, **E**, doesn't fit the context of the sentence, as sound is not discussed. Neither is temperature, so rule out **C**. The word *boring*, **A**, however, fits in with *uninteresting*. This is your answer.

12. **D** Themes and Arguments *Medium*

Take a look at how the word *ocean* is used in the passage: *The Great Basin is often compared to the ocean, which, at first glance, appears to have very little life beneath its surface. Some of the mountains reach 12,000 to 13,000 feet in elevation, thereby isolating the "basins" on either side. In return, the basins effectively turn the "ranges" into biological islands, with the result that one set of mountains may support a unique species of plant or animal.* The author's whole point in this paragraph is to show how much life exists in the Great Basin, despite the fact that a first-time visitor might mistake the region as being boring. The word *ocean* is used as a metaphor—like the ocean, which might seem empty on the surface, the Great Basin also contains many forms of life. However, the author is not trying to make the point that the Great Basin contains any marine animals.

13. **B** Implied Information *Medium*

The author states, *In 1964, the park service cut down a bristlecone pine, before the Great Basin Park was established, and discovered that the tree was over 4,900 years old. The park service later admitted to the error, and bristlecone pines have been pro-*

tected ever since. In other words, the park service started protecting the bristlecone pines after realizing they had cut down a very old tree, **B**. Watch out for **A** and **E**, which introduce information not discussed in the passage. **C** directly contradicts information contained in the passage: few insects are able to penetrate the pines' bark.

14. **D** Themes and Arguments *Medium*

To determine what the author will discuss next, take a look at the last sentence of the passage: *Because plants like the big sagebrush have found ingenious ways to adapt to such harsh conditions, a variety of animals are able to use these plants as* their *habitat.* In paragraph 2, the author made the point that the Great Basin is full of life. He then went on to discuss some of the plants. The last lines introduce the concept of animals, so it is a safe bet to assume he will switch his discussion to animal life, **D**. All of the other answer choices have already been discussed earlier in the passage.

15. **D** Main Idea *Medium*

This question is essentially a main idea question: the test makers are checking to see if you understand the large point of the passage. Basically, the whole passage is about the Great Basin and some of the life forms it supports. Moreover, the author makes the point that the Great Basin is a somewhat unusual place. The answer choice that best restates this idea is **D**. **A** mentions plants, but that is only one focus of the passage. The discovery of the Great Basin, **B**, is also a small detail within the passage. Ditto for **C**. **E** introduces information not discussed in the passage.

16. **D** Words in Context *Easy*

Take a look at the words surrounding the vocabulary word in question: *My first glimpse of the city that was to become my home both terrified and inspired me. I saw it first from the air. The man seated next to me, aware that this was my virgin trip both in an airplane and abroad, suggested that I look out my window.* From these lines, you can deduce that this is the first airplane trip that the narrator has ever taken. We don't know if the trip is late, or *tardy*, **E**, and we don't know if it is a *luxury*, **B**. It is, however, definitely a *first* trip, **D**. Watch out for *unblemished*, **A**, which is a secondary definition for the word *virgin*, meaning, "not destroyed."

17. **A** Implied Information *Easy*

The introductory lines to the passage tell us that the memoir is written by a woman looking back on her life as a student, or *young woman*, **A**. At the time of the events described in the memoir, she is not yet successful, ruling out **B**. She is also not a *tourist*, **C**, but a student. She is certainly not a thief, **D**. Although the narrator does describe her airplane flight, she is not a flight attendant, **E**.

18. **B** Specific Information *Difficult*

Look at the lines where the author discusses traveling home to see her family: *We had flown first from Tokyo to Hawaii, then to San Francisco, then to Chicago, and finally to New York. I would not see my parents for a year, when I would reverse this journey—even longer because the airplane would battle the jet streams, which would be pulsing in the exact opposite direction I wanted to go.* Sound complicated? The author had to travel on numerous planes just to make it to New York. She would not go home for a year, at which time the journey would be even *longer*. From this, you can pretty much assume that the trip is too long and difficult for her to make repeatedly: **B**. The other answers mention information that is not stated in the passage.

19. **A** Technique *Difficult*

Look at the opening lines to the second paragraph: *I was quite surprised to discover that the city was an entirely different creature from the inside than the outside.* This is the key to understand the author's main point: things on the inside are not necessarily the same as they are on the outside. The author then goes on to talk about how the ordered city of New York she saw from the air did not match the tangled streets as she saw them from ground level. She then carries the metaphor even further, pointing out that people on the stage act differently that they might in real life. This is an example of an "extended metaphor." The only answer choice that contains information not included in the passage is **A**. Nowhere does the author talk about how people in New York dress. It might be true that New Yorkers dress up, but the author does not mention it in her memoir.

20. **B** Themes and Arguments *Medium*

You are asked to account for why the author included the following lines: *In Japan, I had seen dubbed versions of American films (*East of Eden *and* Miracle on 34th Street *come to mind)*. The author is telling us that her first impression of English came to her through movies. Although she eventually became fluent in English, this did not happen early in her stay in New York, so rule out **A**. Although the author did become a performer, she is not describing what inspired her to do so, so **C** is therefore wrong. **D** directly contradicts the author's point: her expectations about New York were not met at all. New York turned out to be very different from the America she had seen in the movies. **E** is an exaggeration. Although the America portrayed in the movies is different from the actual country, the author does not actually *lament* this difference; she is merely *shocked* by it.

21. **B** Implied Information *Difficult*

About diners, the author writes, *I was constantly hungry. In my early days in New York, I valiantly tried to order food from the menu of diners, for my classmates were able to do so with great enthusiasm and certitude and seemed not at all to be confused by the myriad items listed on those great white sheets of paper bound in plastic.* While her classmates were not confused by diners, the author was. From this we can deduce that eating in diners was a new experience for the writer. Hence, **B** is the correct answer. We don't really know if she *enjoyed her meals*, **A**, or we know that there were few *Japanese restaurants*, so **E** is wrong. Although the other students were more comfortable in the diner, nothing suggests that the author found them more *sophisticated*, **C**.

22. **C** Words in Context *Difficult*

What is it about the diner menus that is so confusing to the author? While her classmates were not confused by the items listed on those *great white sheets of paper*, the author was very clearly confused. Why? Because of the *myriad*—or "great many"—items listed. You might have been tempted by *appetizing*, **B**. The items on the menu might very well have seemed tempting, but the point is that the author was confused by the menu because of how much it listed, not because it all looked good to eat. You might also have been tempted by *bewildering*, **E**, because the author states very clearly that she was confused. However, *bewildering* is not a possible definition of *myriad*.

23. **D** Technique *Difficult*

The author writes, *Remember too, in those days Japanese food was hardly the craze it is today, and there were few places I could go for home-style nourishment.* The entire point of these lines—and in fact of this paragraph—is just how hungry and alienated the young opera singer felt. She might very well be happy now that Japanese food is so popular, but her whole point is that it was not popular then, so eliminate **A**.

24. **A** Attitude or Tone *Difficult*

The key to understanding the overall tone of the passage lies in understanding the author's point of view. A retired opera singer is remembering her experiences as a young person and the difficulties she faced. Some of the time, she seems even a little bit amused by her lack of experience. The very fact that she is looking back on the past should tell you that she is being nostalgic, **A**. She is certainly not *neutral*, **E**—this is not a parade of facts but of personal experiences. She is also not angry or *dismissive*, **D**. Watch out for **B**: although the word *reflective* might appear tempting, the author isn't really *saddened*.

SECTION 5: MATH

Multiple Choice

1. **A** Numbers & Operations: Percents *Easy*

The question is essentially asking you to determine 25 percent of 2,376. Use your calculator to solve the problem, or work it out on paper.

$$(.25)(2{,}376) = 594$$

2. **C** Algebra: Binomials and Quadratics *Easy*

This problem is checking to see if you know how to factor a quadratic equation and solve for the variables.

$$x^2 - 20 = -x$$

Make sure all the variables are on the same side:

$$x^2 + x - 20 = 0$$

Now simplify:

$$(x+5)(x-4) = 0$$
$$x = 4,\ -5$$

3. **D** Numbers & Operations: Percents *Easy*

Translate this word problem into an equation:

$$(.60)(30) = (.25)x$$

Now simplify and solve:

$$18 = (.25)x$$
$$\frac{18}{.25} = x$$
$$x = 72$$

4. **A** Algebra: Binomials and Quadratics *Easy*

Notice the positive signs in the factors of the quadratic equation. First, factor the quadratic equation:

$$x^2 + ax + 22$$
$$(x + 11)(x + 2)$$

You now know that b must equal 2.

5. **D** Data Analysis, Statistics & Probability: Statistical Analysis *Easy*

To find the average, you will need to take the sum of all values, and then divide by the number of values. Since there are three factories—Factory A, Factory B, and Factory C—this means that you will divide by 3. Now you need to find the sum. To do this, you will need to convert the chart with the boats into actual numbers. According to the chart, one image of a boat is 200,000 actual boats. This means that you have the following:

$$\text{Factory A} = 3 \text{ boats} = 3(200{,}000) = 600{,}000$$
$$\text{Factory B} = 6 \text{ boats} = 6(200{,}000) = 1{,}200{,}000$$
$$\text{Factory C} = 4.5 \text{ boats} = 4.5(200{,}000) = 900{,}000$$

Add all three values and divide by 3:

$$\frac{600{,}000 + 1{,}200{,}000 + 900{,}000}{3} = 900{,}000$$

6. **B** Data Analysis, Statistics & Probability: Statistical Analysis *Medium*

The mean is the average of all numbers in a set. The mode is the number that occurs most frequently in a set. When there is no number that occurs most frequently, there is no mode. Take a look at each of the sets.

A. (1, 2, 3, 4, 4)
The mode is 4 because it occurs more than once.

The average is $1 + 2 + 3 + 4 + 4 = \frac{14}{5} = 2.8$

In this case, the median, 2.8, is not larger than the mode, 4, and therefore **A** is not the answer.

B. (1, 1, 1, 2, 3)
The mode is 1 because it occurs most often.

The average is $1 + 1 + 1 + 2 + 3 = \frac{8}{5} = 1.6$

In this case, the mean, 1.6, is larger than the mode, 1, and therefore **B** is the answer. You do not need to keep looking.

7. **D** Geometry: Triangles *Medium*

Begin answering this question by taking note of all the information you are given. You know, for example, that angles x and $2x$ must equal 180 degrees, since there are always 180 degrees in a straight line.

$$x + 2x = 180$$
$$3x = 180$$
$$x = 60$$

Now you know that angle B is 60 degrees. Since you know that angle A is 90 degrees, you can solve for angle C, which will be 30 degrees. Lo and behold, you learn that you are dealing with a special right triangle. Remember, in a 30-60-90 triangle, the sides are always in the ratio of x, $x\sqrt{3}$, $2x$. Since side AB, opposite the 30-degree angle, is 3, you know that side BC, the hypotenuse, will be twice this value, or 6.

8. **D** Numbers & Operations: Basic Operations *Medium*

This is a translation problem, requiring you to keep careful track of all the bits and pieces of information. Start with *13 less*. Be careful—you are going to take 13 away from *some other value*.

$$-\ 13$$

Now, you want to know 13 less than what? Than the difference between x and 5.

$$(x - 5) - 13$$

If you got the order of subtraction wrong, you might have been tempted by **A**.

Grid-Ins

9. **169** Geometry: Triangles *Medium*

This problem warns you right away that the figure is not drawn to scale, so you can guesstimate the answer. However, you should see that you are dealing with two right angle triangles stuck together. Remember, with any right angle triangle, the sum of the squares of both sides of the triangle equals the square of the third side. This means that both triangles share a hypotenuse. In other words:

$$a^2 + b^2 = 5^2 + 12^2$$

Before you start plugging in numbers, however, it would be helpful if you remembered the Pythagorean triplet of 5, 12, and 13. This means that the hypotenuse of both triangles will be 13. Just remember, though, that the problem is asking you for the *squared* value of the hypotenuse.

$$13^2 = 169$$

10. **$1,450** Numbers & Operations: Percents *Easy*

Be sure you take this percent problem a step at a time. The flat-screen TV starts out at $4,000. First, the price is reduced by 15 percent.

$$\$4,000 - (.15) =$$
$$\$4,000 - \$600 = \$3,400$$

So, the price has gone down to $3,400. But we're not finished yet! Now the TV is reduced by another 25 percent. Remember; you want to subtract 25 percent from the new price.

$$\$3,400 - (.25)(\$3,400) =$$
$$\$3,400 - \$850 = \$2,550$$

At this point you might be tempted to put $2,550 in as your answer. But read the question carefully: it asks you to determine *how much Josephine saved*. You have one more step. Take the original price, minus the final price, to determine the total savings.

$$\$4{,}000 - \$2{,}550 = \$1{,}450$$

11. **24** Numbers & Operations: Ratios *Medium*

Make sure you don't just average the two speeds together and write down 25 as your answer. With average-rate problems, you have to be on the lookout. Remember, she spends *more time* going at a slower rate than she does at a faster rate. To make this problem easy, pick a value for the number of miles she rides—say 60 miles. Now, look at the formula.

$$\text{Distance} = (\text{rate})(\text{time})$$

Let's figure out how much time she spends at the first rate.

$$\begin{aligned} \text{Distance} &= (\text{rate})(\text{time}) \\ 60 &= 20t \\ 3 &= t \end{aligned}$$

In other words, she spends 3 hours going one way. Now, find the time she travels for the other speed.

$$\begin{aligned} \text{Distance} &= (\text{rate})(\text{time}) \\ 60 &= 30t \\ 2 &= t \end{aligned}$$

She spends 2 hours going the other way. Now you are ready to find the average speed.

$$\text{Average distance} = (\text{total rate})(\text{total time})$$

$$\text{Average rate} = \frac{\text{Total distance}}{\text{Total time}}$$

$$\text{Average rate} = \frac{120 \text{ miles}}{5 \text{ hours}}$$

$$\text{Average rate} = 24 \text{ miles/hour}$$

12. **1/2** Data Analysis, Statistics & Probability: Probability *Medium*

There are 16 possible combinations of integers by choosing two numbers—one from set A and the other from set B. You are asked to determine the possibility of finding an even sum. The formula for determining the possibility of an event is:

$$\frac{\text{Number of desirable outcomes}}{\text{Number of possible outcomes}} = \text{Probability}$$

First, you have to determine the total number of possible outcomes, which you know is 16. Now, you have to figure out how many of the sums would be even:

$$2 + 2 = 4 \qquad 5 + 1 = 6$$
$$2 + 4 = 6 \qquad 5 + 5 = 10$$
$$3 + 1 = 4 \qquad 7 + 1 = 8$$
$$3 + 5 = 8 \qquad 7 + 5 = 12$$

There are 8 possible solutions that would be even. Now, we can plug in the values to determine the probability.

$$\frac{8}{16} = \text{Probability}$$

So you have a probability of $\frac{1}{2}$ of choosing an even sum. Make sure you put the answer in fraction form as the question asks you to.

13. **384** Algebra: Absolute Value and Exponents *Medium*

This is simply an algebra problem disguised as a symbolism problem. Plug in the values given to find the answer.

$$*r* = (r-1)\sqrt{r}$$

$$*81* - *49*$$
$$(81-1)\sqrt{81} - (49-1)\sqrt{49}$$
$$80(9) - 48(7)$$
$$720 - 336$$
$$384$$

14. **5** Geometry: Coordinate Geometry *Difficult*

To find the slope in any line, you want to find the change in the y-coordinates over the change in x-coordinates. Using this, and the information given in the problem, we can set up the following equation:

$$\frac{\text{Change in } y\text{-coordinates}}{\text{Change in } x\text{-coordinates}} = \text{slope}$$

$$\frac{6-(-3)}{f-(-1)} = \frac{3}{2}$$
$$\frac{6+3}{f+1} = \frac{3}{2}$$
$$\frac{9}{f+1} = \frac{3}{2}$$

Now, cross-multiply:

$$2(9) = 3(f+1)$$
$$18 = 3f + 3$$
$$15 = 3f$$
$$f = 5$$

15. **0** Numbers & Operations: Basic Operations *Difficult*

There is only one combination of integers for which the sum and product could be the same. If you had difficulty determining what those numbers could be, it might help if you remember that 0 multiplied by any other numbers is 0. If you figured out this much, then you would know that the numbers in question are –2, –1, 0, 1, 2

$$-2 + -1 + 0 + 1 + 2 = 0$$
$$(2)(1)(0)(1)(2) = 0$$

Now that you are sure of the integers, make sure you answer the question correctly: you are asked to find the sum of the numbers, which is 0.

16. **4** Geometry: Geometric Visualizations *Difficult*

This is a visualization problem that will be made easier for you if you draw the figures on a sheet of paper. You are asked to determine how many lines you will need to draw to form 45-degree angles around point *O*.

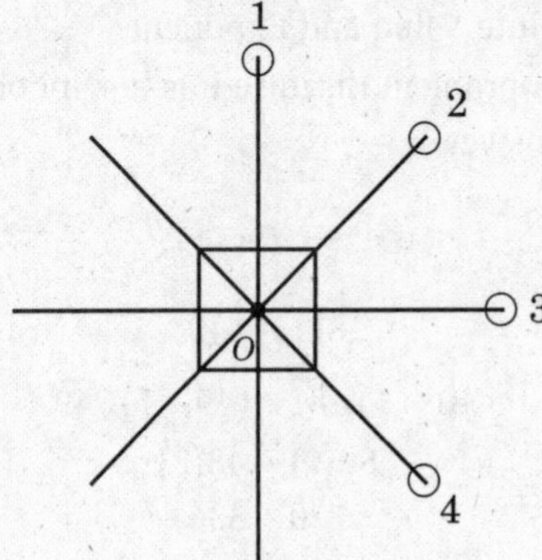

You can see that you will need to draw exactly 4 lines.

17. **10** Geometry: Solids *Difficult*

Always make sure that you draw in values when they are given in a problem but not present on the diagram. You are asked to find the greatest possible distance between points *x* and *y*. The best way to make these points as far away as possible from each other would be if they formed a diagonal across the center of the cylinder. Now, you should notice that these points do in fact form a right-angle triangle.

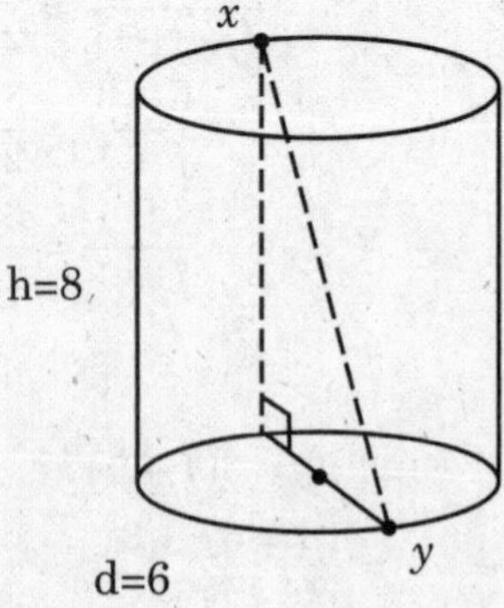

Further, if the radius is 3, then the diameter is 6. Right away you should recognize that this is a Pythagorean triplet, and that the hypotenuse of the triangle—the distance between points *x* and *y*—is 10.

18. **1/4, .25** Data Analysis, Statistics & Probability: Probability *Medium*
The probability of a series of events occurring can be found if you take the probability of one event times each subsequent event. In the case of the coin, each time it is tossed, you have a $\frac{1}{2}$ chance that the coin will land face up.

$$\left(\frac{1}{2}\right)\left(\frac{1}{2}\right)\left(\frac{1}{2}\right) = \frac{1}{8}$$

Because there are two faces, we need to multiply $\frac{1}{8}$ by 2 to get $\frac{1}{4}$. The same face can be achieved two different ways, as heads or tails, but the remaining two flips must be the same as the first flips.

SECTION 6: WRITING

Improving Sentences

1. **B** Subject-Verb Agreement *Easy*
This question is checking your ability to identify subject and verb agreement. The subject in the second clause of the sentence is *cost*, while the verb, as the sentence originally appears, is *have*. However, *cost* is a singular noun and requires a singular verb. The word *has*, in **B**, would fix this problem. Beware of the word *institutions* in the original clause. Because it is plural, it might have fooled you into thinking that the sentence contained no error. The word *institutions* is part of the prepositional phrase modifying *at the country's most elite institutions* and therefore cannot be the subject of the sentence.

2. **C** Fragments *Easy*
This sentence is a fragment. Each sentence must have a clear subject and verb. In this case, the sentence might have sounded funny to you, because it has a verb, *raining*, but no clear subject. To make the sentence complete, you will need to add a subject, as **C** does by using the pronoun *it*, and by changing the verb from *raining* to *rained*. None of the other answer choices would make this sentence complete.

3. **B** Wordiness *Easy*
This sentence suffers from the curse of being excessively wordy and redundant. There is no need for the presence of the word *and* twice in the sentence. Also, the words *the food* are redundant: it is clear that the subject of the sentence is *Mediterranean food* and that the rest of the sentence is just providing more information about this subject. **C** is problematic, because it implies that the population of the Mediterranean *live a long time* simply because the *food is considered healthy*. Logically, things need to be the other way around—with the health of the food affecting people's longevity. **D** and **E** introduce a contrast with the word *although*, but this changes the meaning of the original sentence. **B**, however, solves the original problem by making some of the modifying information, *considered to be among the world's healthiest because the population of the Mediterranean people live for a long time*, into a dependent clause.

4. **C** Run-Ons *Medium*
This is a classic run-on sentence with two independent clauses stuck together. To make the sentence grammatically accurate, one of the clauses would need to be

made dependent on the other. **A** and **B** simply keep the problem intact, so eliminate these. **D**, in using the word *however*, introduces the idea of a contrast, which changes the meaning of the sentence. **E**, *because*, doesn't fix the problem. **C**, however, makes the second half of the sentence dependent on the first and is therefore correct.

5. **A** No Error *Medium*

There is no error here. If you chose **B**, watch out that you didn't make the mistake of assuming that *amaryllis* was plural and required the plural pronoun *their*.

6. **C** Parallelism *Medium*

When you are describing an object with a list of adjectives, the modifiers should all be in the same form. Here, the sentence is describing *modern-day furniture*. The first adjective is straightforward: *practical*. The second adjective, however, includes the unnecessary prepositional phrase, *in addition to*. To make the adjectives parallel, you will need to remove these extraneous words, which **C** does very nicely. All of the other answer choices continue to complicate the sentence.

7. **B** Pronouns *Medium*

This sentence might have just "sounded" wrong to you, because it included the pronoun *their*. Watch out for **C** and **D**, which introduce the pronoun *his*. This is tricky. Hopper's paintings are known for depicting two things: *humble landscapes* and the *subtle effects of light*. In other words, it isn't Edward Hopper himself who depicts these things, but his *paintings*.

8. **D** Misplaced Modifiers *Difficult*

Be careful here. It isn't the *reading public* that was *universally considered one of the best books of the year*, it was *Jonathan Franzen's novel* The Corrections. This sentence contains the classic error of a misplaced modifier. **B** makes things worse by putting the article *the* in front of *Jonathan Franzen*. **C** and **E** start to correct the problem by putting the modified noun in the correct location, however, both phrases are awkward and clunky. Only **D** really solves the problem.

9. **E** Parallelism *Medium*

This is an excessively wordy sentence, which probably sounded strange to your ear. Remember, whenever you make a list of items, you want to keep those items in parallel form, which is what **E** accomplishes. The other answer choices maintain the level of redundancy and confusion.

10. **E** Coordination and Subordination *Difficult*

The words *not only* and *but also* are always joined together. The items that they are comparing must be kept in parallel form. The first item being compared is *to advances in technology.* Now, watch what happens to the second item being compared: *but it is also because game makers are trying to create games that reach a broader audience.* The two items being compared are not parallel because the second item introduces the subject *it is.* The correct answer choice will take all of the information in the second item being compared and make it mimic the form of the first item. Take a look at **E**, which turns *but it is also because game makers are trying to create games that reach a broader audience* into *but also to game makers' attempts to create games that reach a broader audience.* **C** and **D** are wordy, since they introduce the words *because* and *due to* respectively. **B** is clumsy, because it uses the phrase *but also for*.

11. **D** Misplaced Modifiers *Difficult*

The way the sentence was originally written makes it sound as though the paintings were vacationing in Mexico. Actually, it was Jillian who was in Mexico. The correct answer choice will thus move Jillian next to the introductory modifying clause. This narrows down the choices to **D** and **E**. However, if you read **E** back into the sentence, you will see that the end trails off, and it does not form a complete sentence. **D** must be the right answer, and it is.

Identifying Sentence Errors

12. **C** Pronouns *Easy*

Every pronoun must refer back to one clear noun. What is it that might *open the way for many people to lose valuable funds*? Privatizing social security. Notice that this is a singular verb and not a plural verb. The pronoun *they*, then, cannot be correct. The verb *should* is in the correct form.

13. **C** Subject-Verb Agreement *Easy*

This question is testing your knowledge of subject-verb agreement. The subject of the sentence is *stores*, which is plural. This means that the pronoun *their*, **A**, is correct. However, the verb *showcases* is incorrect, because it is in the form necessary to agree with a singular subject. Your subject, *stores*, is plural.

14. **B** Subject-Verb Agreement *Easy*

Here is a another question testing your knowledge of subject-verb agreement. The subject, *town*, is singular and requires a singular verb. However, the verb *have* is plural. This is incorrect and is therefore the answer to the question. The phrase *to be outfitted* is correct.

15. **C** Parallelism *Easy*

Items being compared should always be placed in parallel form. Look at the two things being compared: *to hold a ball of yarn* and *not by holding*. You should notice that these two verbs are not in the same form. The first verb contains the preposition *to*:—*to hold*. The second verb contains an ending of *-ing*:—*holding*.

16. **C** Faulty Comparison *Easy*

Be careful when you are comparing items. When you are comparing two things, the most extreme item will be "better" or "more." However, when comparing more than two things, you will need to use the superlative—the most or the best—to distinguish the items. In this case, Ross is part of a group of children. Therefore, he should be the *most* cosmopolitan, not the *more*.

17. **C** Pronouns *Easy*

The pronoun *who* can only refer to people. In this case, the sentence is trying state that gaslight *had a romantic yellow cast*, but it makes the mistake of using the pronoun *who* at the start of the modifying clause. Since gaslight is a thing, not a person, this is an error.

18. **A** Wrong Word *Easy*

Here you have a classic misuse of vocabulary words. The word *noisome* might look like it has something to do with sound since it starts with *nois*, and the sentence deals with the noisiness of stereos. However, the word *noisome* actually means "foul smelling," and is used incorrectly here.

19. **D** Parallelism *Medium*

Items in a list must always be placed in parallel form. The couple in the sentence is described by these three characteristics: *loyal, loving, and they enjoyed.* Notice that the first two items in this list are adjectives, whereas the third introduces the pronoun *they.* To be correct, the third item in the list would need to be placed in adjectival form, or *content with*.

20. **A** Pronouns *Medium*

It is a common problem these days for people to make mistakes in using the pronouns *I* and *me.* In this particular sentence, the pronoun *I* is used incorrectly. The sentence is making the case that *it is difficult for . . . me*. Whenever a pronoun is the object of a preposition, it must be placed in its objective case.

21. **E** No Error *Medium*

There is no error in this sentence. The items being compared are in parallel form and are correct.

22. **A** Idioms *Medium*

The SAT will occasionally test your knowledge of idioms. In this sentence, you are being tested on the difference between a *protest for* and a *protest against* something. The sentence tells us that corporate heads *reconsidered* their tactics. This would lead us to conclude that the protests were *against* the corporate heads, not *for* them.

23. **B** Wrong Word *Difficult*

Here we have another vocab question. The word *obviated* does not mean "to make obvious," though it might sound like it to you. In reality, the verb to *obviate* means "to deny." And yet the sentence pretty clearly needs a verb that means something like "to make obvious." The word *obviate* is therefore out of place here.

24. **B** Subject-Verb Agreement *Medium*

Beware of sentences in which the subject and verb are separated from each other by a number of intervening clauses and phrases. Here, the subject of the sentence is *crop*, which takes a singular verb. However, the verb phrase *were decimated* is plural. Here is your error.

25. **E** No Error *Medium*

This sentence contains no error. The adjectives *romantic* and *sweeping* are correctly separated by a comma.

26. **C** Double Negative *Medium*

Words like *hardly* and *scarcely* function as negatives in the English language. On the SAT, a sentence should not contain a double negative—that is, a sentence should never have two negatives side by side. In this particular sentence, the phrase *hardly no* is a double negative and is therefore incorrect.

27. **A** Redundancy *Difficult*
It is not necessary for a sentence to contain two adjectives that mean the same thing. This particular sentence starts out with the words *large* and *enormous*, which are not both required for the sentence to be clear. One of the words, therefore, should be cut.

28. **D** Parallelism *Difficult*
There are two things being compared here: the *artistry* of ballet and the *technical perfection [of ballet]*. Remember, when comparing two items in a list, the items must be in parallel form. In this particular sentence, matters are made complicated by the inclusion of the pronoun *its* just before *technical perfection*. For this sentence to be correct, the pronoun would need to be removed.

29. **D** Parallelism *Difficult*
This sentence is testing your knowledge of the idiom *to comply with*.

Improving Paragraphs

30. **E** Sentence Revision *Difficult*
The original sentence is unnecessarily wordy. The best way to fix the sentence would be to make one of the independent clauses dependent, using a word like "because" or the words "due to." **B** and **C** do not resolve this problem. **D** just sounds vague and leaves out necessary information. **E**, however, resolves the problem nicely.

31. **D** Sentence Revision *Difficult*
Before you get rid of a sentence, make sure that the sentence is unnecessary and/or repeats vital information that is stated somewhere else. In sentence 3, the author has written the following: *In other words, it seems like even the doctors aren't sure what they recommend.* The information contained in sentence 4, *they contradict themselves all the time,* essentially just repeats what was already stated in sentence 3.

32. **C** Sentence Combination *Difficult*
You definitely don't want to leave sentences the way they are now. They sound clunky and don't flow as well as the other sentences do. Eliminate **A**. Watch out for **B** and **E**, which are excessively wordy and take away from the clarity of the original sentences. **D** isn't bad, but it sounds very awkward with the phrase *for example* stuck in the middle. Only **C** sounds like a credible rewriting of the original sentences.

33. **E** Sentence Revision *Medium*
The word *incidentally* is used when an author is throwing in an extra piece of information that is interesting but not necessarily essential to an argument he is making. In this case, the idea that cattle were *once free to roam* the plains is very pertinent to the story's overall arc. Clearly, *incidentally* does not really fit the sentence. The author is not trying to make a contrasting point, so eliminate **A** and **D**. He or she is also not introducing any strange information, so eliminate *oddly,* **B**. The word

because can only be used to introduce a dependent clause. A dependent clause cannot stand alone and must be attached to an independent clause. If you added *because* to the start of sentence 8, it would be incomplete. Only *once*, **E**, helps strengthen the sentence.

34. **A** Essay Analysis *Difficult*

The author doesn't cite numerous examples of harmful food. He or she only mentions the idea that fish might carry pollutants. Get rid of **B**. The author does not use the pronoun *I*, so eliminate **D**. There are definitely no parentheses anywhere in the passage, so **E** must be wrong. While he makes the point that people are confused, he does not describe in great detail the manner in which they are confused, **C**. He does, however, go on to describe how food has changed over time.

35. **C** Sentence Revision *Difficult*

There is a linking word missing between the two halves of this sentence. **C** corrects this problem by introducing the conjunction *that*. **E** starts off well enough with the preposition *through*, but it gets awkward by also using *then*. **B** is plagued with a similar problem. **D** is wrong because people don't actually derive any health benefits unless they start eating a variety of foods.

SECTION 7: CRITICAL READING

Sentence Completions

1. **B** Two-Word/One-Way *Easy*

The words *dramatic* and *celebrates* clue you in to the meaning of the missing words. The first blank is definitely going to be a positive word. Also, the phrased *merged with* tells you that the two words are going to have to compliment each other. A good prediction for the first blank might be "beautiful" or even "dramatic." Eliminate **E**, *rabid*, which means "overly aggressive." For the second blank, you will also need a word that means something along the lines of "beautiful" or "dramatic." Eliminate **A**, **C**, and **D**. You might have fallen for **C**, because it included the word *rhythmic*, and music does tend to have rhythm. However, taken together, the words *sympathetic* and *rhythmic* do not capture the idea that opera actually *celebrates* song.

2. **D** Two-Word/Two-Way *Easy*

The word *whereas* signals a contrast in this sentence. Some people prefer one aspect of Johnny Hodges playing, whereas others admire another quality. The words *smoky tone* tell you that the first blank means something like "smoky" and "attractive." Eliminate **B** and **C**. The big clue for the second blank is the word *technical*. Whatever it is that people also admire about Johnny Hodges, it must be a positive quality, but it must also compliment *technical*. The only word that fits is *finesse*, which means "skill," **D**. Watch out for *prowess*, **B**, which also means "skill."

3. **A** Two-Word/Two-Way *Medium*

The second blank is probably the easier one to predict first. You are told that the academics consider the paintings to be *too colorful*. A good prediction would be "overdone." The only words that really fit are **A** and **C**. Now focus on the first blank. This is a harder word to predict. You are told that the restoration of the frescoes is *marred*, which means the completion is "dirtied" or made "less satisfying" somehow. In other words, what would have been a "good" restoration is made "less satisfying," because the frescoes are *too colorful*. **A** must be the right answer.

4. **C** One-Word/One-Way *Medium*

The semicolon signals to you that the missing word will be defined in the sentence. In fact, you are told that *people all over the world are able to keep secrets and double lives*. A good prediction for the blank would have been "secretive," which is what *duplicitous*, **C**, means. The word *unctuous*, **B**, means "oily." *Malodorous*, **E**, means "having a bad smell."

5. **D** One-Word/One-Way *Difficult*

Tom Wolfe had something to say about *the lack of fiction addressing serious social issues*. We can guess that he was upset about this *lack*, and therefore the word in the blank will have a negative meaning. If you noticed that **D**, *decried*, has the prefix *de*, you might have been able to choose this answer choice on that basis alone. The word *intuited*, **B**, means "to determine or make a decision using intuition." *Embellished*, **A**, means to "make more ornate." And *expounded*, **C**, means "to describe in great detail."

6. **E** Two-Word/Two-Way *Difficult*

Start with the second blank first. The common house cat *will not behave in a consistent fashion*. If this is true, then what kind of an animal is the house cat? It is definitely not a good candidate for scientific experiments. A good prediction for the second blank would be "bad." At this point you can eliminate **A**, **C**, and **D**. Now, be careful with the first blank. The sentence tells you that *no journal has ever printed these claims*. In other words, scientists have not declared to the world that the house cat makes a terrible test subject. They have *tacitly*, or "quietly," understood, the truth about cats.

Long Reading Passage

7. **B** Attitude or Tone *Easy*

Take a look at the second sentence of the second paragraph in the passage: *It is tempting to decry how quick readers are to want to break down the suspension of disbelief*. After some introductory lines, during which the author points out how popular it is these days for people to want to know about the personal lives of artists, the author goes on to say that it is a shame that readers have a tendency to do so. **A** does present information the author states, but only much later in the passage. **D** and **E** are superficially related to the passage—the author does discuss a letter and religion—but these choices present points of view not really discussed in the passage. While the author might agree with **C**, we don't really know, because he never really states this.

8. **A** Words in Context *Medium*

Here are the lines in question: *As a writer myself, I might have argued along these lines in years past. More recently, I have begun to rethink this ossified position*. The words *more recently* signal that the author has started to rethink his original position. In other words, he has started to reconsider his "hardened" or "calcified" original stance.

9. **B** Implied Information *Easy*
First, take a look at the lines that the author references: *Shakespeare should be the ideal candidate of the author who leaves us with little personal information but with an enormous body of work to titillate our senses and challenge our very perception of the world.* Now, take a look at the very next sentence: *And yet, by exploring the few known facts about him, we are able to glean a deeper understanding of his work and therefore more fully appreciate the weight of his dramas.* The author is saying that we can in fact better understand Shakespeare's works if we know more about his personal life and times. **B** restates this position. You could have automatically eliminated **A**, because the information contained there is not stated in the passage. **C** states a position that is in direct opposition to the author's point of view.

10. **E** Themes and Arguments *Medium*
Whenever you are asked to identify the purpose of a detail in a passage, make sure you understand the whole point of the paragraph in which it appears. In this case, the author makes the following point in paragraph 3: *For example, Shakespeare's dramas are often rife with the suffocation of personal terror.* The whole point of this paragraph is to demonstrate ways in which Shakespeare's characters lived with terror. This idea is restated in **E**. **D** contains information not stated in the passage. Although it is true that Shakespeare could *understand young love*, **C**, and had the ability to write both *comedy and tragedy*, **A**, these are not reasons why the author mentions Romeo and Juliet in this particular paragraph.

11. **C** Specific Information *Medium*
Be careful here. Although it might, on the surface, seem that the main reason to *display heads* would be to terrify people, the author makes a different, subtle point. He writes that the presence of heads was meant to ensure that *others would keep their behavior in check*. In other words, people were not necessarily supposed to be afraid of the queen but to see the heads and to behave, or display *submission*. *Sadness*, **B**, might have been a secondary emotion, but it is not one the author discusses. This is also true of *awe*, **E**.

12. **A** Themes and Arguments *Medium*
Here is another purpose of detail question. You are asked to determine why the author chose the word *gruesome*. Remember, the correct answer to a purpose of detail question is always heavily dependent on the author's point in the paragraph in question. Here, in paragraph 3, the author is making the point that people during Shakespeare's time lived with a great deal of *terror*. In other words, the author uses the word *gruesome* to *emphasize how frightening the Elizabethan era could be.* While the author does eventually discuss Shakespeare's possible Catholicism, **B**, this detail is not mentioned in paragraph 3.

13. **E** Attitude and Tone *Medium*
Correctly answering tone questions requires you to understand the author's point of view and what he or she is trying to accomplish. In this case, the author makes the point that although he didn't used to believe it was important to know about a writer to understand her work, in the case of Shakespeare, it is certainly true that understanding the Bard's life can give us greater appreciation of his work. In other words, the author is exploring a point of view and trying to prove it. The tone of the passage is generally neutral. He does not really attack anyone—except at the beginning

where he questions the motives of readers—nor does he unnecessarily praise anyone. The correct answer choice will reflect this neutral position. You can easily eliminate **A**, **C**, and **D** on this basis alone. While the opening lines of the passage may display some *skepticism*, **B**, the rest of the passage is really very *thoughtful*, **E**.

14. **D** Words in Context *Difficult*

The author has just made the point that Shakespeare was probably born a Catholic in a time when Catholicism was not necessarily tolerated. He then goes on to write, *On a general level, we can understand even more deeply the allure of the world of the stage to a young, talented, and somewhat secretive man. In the theater, William Shakespeare, born of a family of modest means, could impersonate a nobleman . . .* In other words, being on stage would hold an *attraction*, **D**, for Shakespeare, who could pretend to be something he was not. **B**, *trap*, and *conventionality*, **E**, are very much the opposite of *allure* and don't fit the sentence at all.

15. **D** Specific Information *Difficult*

The author makes the point that Shakespeare was free to portray anything he wanted on stage. He then goes on to say, *In the theater, William Shakespeare, born of a family of modest means, could impersonate a nobleman, and, in fact, it was his very success in the theater that afforded him the chance to successfully apply for a coat of arms so that he might die and be buried as a gentleman.* In other words, after pretending to be a nobleman on the stage, Shakespeare was able to become one in real life. **D**, *one way in which his life on the stage—acting as a gentleman—translated to real life*, makes the same point. **C** contains a hint of judgment, but the author never condemns Shakespeare as being *shallow*. **B** is the opposite: Shakespeare couldn't have become a gentleman if his *fortunes declined*.

16. **B** Technique *Difficult*

Take a look at the lines in question: *Desdemona's terror and innocence must mirror the fear that Shakespeare either witnessed or experienced himself.* Remember, the whole point of this paragraph is to show how the emotions of the outside world—terror—are mirrored in Shakespeare's plays. In other words, Desdemona's fear must, according to the author, have been a reflection of Shakespeare's own. If you understood the point of the paragraph, then you would not have been tempted by **E**, which makes a parallel, but not the correct one.

17. **E** Specific Information *Medium*

The end of this essay takes a somewhat lively turn. After discussing Shakespeare and the times in which he lived, the author states: *And it is perhaps this single fact that continues to prompt leagues of readers and scholars to dig even deeper to uncover one single cause of talent.* In other words, no matter how much we know about an author's life, it will always be difficult to determine exactly how a genius is created, **E**. **D** restates an idea that appeared at the beginning of the passage. **A** restates an idea that is in opposition to the author's: he does, eventually, agree that knowing about a writer's life can enhance our understanding of his work.

18. **B** Main Idea *Medium*

This question is basically a main idea question disguised by tricky wording. You are supposed to determine what the main concern of the author is. Although the passage does cover a great deal of territory, the main idea is still set out in the first few lines. The author wants to discuss how knowing about a particular author's life can help us to more fully appreciate his work, and the author explores this idea by examining the life of Shakespeare—hence **B** as the correct answer. Watch out for **A**: the author doesn't really analyze why Shakespeare's works have a lasting impact, but rather how Shakespeare's personal life informed his writings. **C** is also tricky, because the passage discusses much more than how Shakespeare's career progressed.

19. **D** Specific Information *Medium*

This question tests how well you've understood the information presented in the passage. In the final paragraph, the author states, *But we must not make the reverse assumption that a lively personal and inner life will manifest itsself into great art.* Eliminate **A**. In the next sentence, the author continues, *Ultimately, the very forces that are required to produce a work of genius remain a mystery*. In other words, we don't know the connection between an inner life and great art, or **D**.

SECTION 8: MATH

Multiple Choice

1. **B** Numbers & Operations: Basic Operations *Easy*

This is an estimate question. You should round each of the values up or down to their nearest whole value.

$4.95 → $5.00
$2.79 → $3.00
$0.89 → $1.00
$3.89 → $4.00
Total: $13.00

If Janna has a $20 bill in her pocket to start out with, then she will have about $7.00 left over after she is done shopping.

2. **E** Numbers & Operations: Basic Operations *Easy*

Translate this problem into an equation, substituting x for "that number."

$$x + 6 = 4x$$

Now, solve:

$$6 = 3x$$
$$2 = x$$

3. **B** Numbers & Operations: Divisibility and Remainders *Easy*

First, you have to figure out what the remainder will be if you divide 32 by 13. You may find this problem easier to do on scratch paper than with your calculator. 13 will go into 32 two times evenly, with a remainder of 6. Now, you must list the factors of 6:

(1, 2, 3)

4. **D** Algebra: Systems of Equations *Easy*

The best way to solve algebra problems when there does not seem to be a clear path to take is to look at the information given and ask yourself, "What *can* I do?" Since you are supposed to solve for a value that includes variables a and b but not c, it might be a good idea to substitute the second equation into the first one. First, rewrite the second equation so you know the value of c:

$$c - b = 2$$
$$c = 2 + b$$

Now, substitute and solve:

$$a + b + c = 5$$
$$a + b + 2 + b = 5$$
$$a + 2b + 2 = 5$$
$$a + 2b = 3$$

5. **C** Data Analysis, Statistics & Probability: Permutations and Combinations *Easy*

Poor Mrs. Perkins! She has exactly 7 outfits (make sure you noted that she had 2 black ones), which she must repeat in order. If she repeats everything in a consistent order, you want to know how many times she must wear the pink outfit. First, divide 20 by 7. You will see that 7 goes into 20 two times, with a remainder of 6. So far, the pink outfit will appear exactly 2 times. Now, you need to see which outfits will be used on the remaining 6 days. Since the pink outfit will be worn on the fourth day of the 6 remaining days, you know that Mrs. Perkins can be expected to be seen in her pink outfit exactly 3 times in a 20-day period.

6. **C** Geometry: Angles and Lines *Medium*

The angle opposite the 70-degree angle will also measure 70 degrees. The angle opposite the right-angle mark will measure 90 degrees. Since there are always 180 degrees in a triangle, you know that the angle opposite angle A will measure 20. But be careful. You are asked to find the value of 3 times A.

$$3(20) = 60$$

7. **D** Algebra: Functions *Medium*

The best way to solve this problem is to start with the answer choices. Start with **A**, and plug the values into the formula:

$$x* = \sqrt[3]{x} - \sqrt{x}$$
$$16* = \sqrt[3]{16} - \sqrt{16}$$

You can stop your work here, because there is no integer value for the cube root of 16, and the problem expressly asks you to find an integer. Try the next answer choice:

$$x* = \sqrt[3]{x} - \sqrt{x}$$
$$25* = \sqrt[3]{25} - \sqrt{25}$$

Again, there is no cube root integer for 25.

$$x* = \sqrt[3]{x} - \sqrt{x}$$
$$36* = \sqrt[3]{36} - \sqrt{36}$$

No cube root that is an integer again.

$$x* = \sqrt[3]{x} - \sqrt{x}$$
$$64* = \sqrt[3]{64} - \sqrt{64}$$
$$64* = 4 - 8$$
$$64* = -4$$

This is an integer, and we have found the correct answer.

8. **B** Data Analysis, Statistics & Probability: Graphs, Charts, and Tables *Medium*

You are told that the temperature on this tropical island peaks during the summer, then gradually goes back down. The correct answer choice will therefore have a slight climbing curve before it descends. This is exactly what is portrayed in **B**. **E** is problematic because it shows a straight line, and therefore static temperature. Notice that **C** is the opposite of what you are looking for.

9. **B** Geometry: Angles and Lines *Medium*

If *AB* is equal to *BD*, then point *B* must be the midpoint of the line segment. Don't be fooled by the diagram: note that it is not drawn to scale. None of the other answer choices fits the information you are given. If the problem is still difficult, redraw the line segment, following the information you are given.

10. **C** Geometry: Triangles *Medium*

The two *X* angles tell you that you are dealing with an isosceles triangle with angles measuring 45, 45, and 90 degrees. These kinds of triangles have sides that are always in a ratio of x, x, $x\sqrt{2}$. The longest side, $x\sqrt{2}$, is always opposite the hypotenuse. In this problem, however, the hypotenuse is 2. To find the length of the legs of the triangle, you will need to divide 2 by $\sqrt{2}$.

$$\frac{2}{\sqrt{2}}$$

Since you can't leave a radical in the denominator, you will need to find a way to rewrite the value:

$$\frac{2}{\sqrt{2}}(1) = \frac{2}{\sqrt{2}}\left(\frac{\sqrt{2}}{\sqrt{2}}\right) = \frac{2\sqrt{2}}{2} = \sqrt{2}$$

11. **C** Geometry: Circles *Medium*

The perimeter of the shaded region is going to include two sides of the square and one-quarter of the total perimeter of the circle. We are told that the perimeter of the circle is 36π. One-quarter of this perimeter would therefore be 9π. Now you need to find the length of the side of the square. Since the perimeter of the circle is 36π, and you know that the formula for finding the perimeter of a circle is $2\pi r$, where r is the radius, you know that the radius of the circle is 18. Since the radius of the circle is also the side of the square, you know that two sides of the square would equal 36. The final perimeter of the shaded area is thus $36 + 9\pi$.

12. **D** Algebra: Ratios *Medium*

Sardines are caught at a rate of *x* sardines per minute:

$$\frac{x \text{ sardines}}{1 \text{ minute}}$$

The problem then asks you to determine how many sardines are caught in *y* hours. You will need to convert minutes to hours. There are 60 minutes in an hour; so $60x$ sardines are caught in one hour. To find the number of sardines caught in *y* hours, multiply $60x$ by *y*.

13. **D** Algebra: Binomials and Quadratics *Medium*

Whenever you see a quadratic equation on the SAT, your first impulse should be to factor.

$$\frac{2x^2 + 8x - 10}{x^2 - 25}$$

$$\frac{(2x-2)(x+5)}{(x+5)(x-5)}$$

$$\frac{(2x-2)}{(x-5)}$$

14. **B** Algebra: Binomials and Quadratics *Difficult*

Not sure where to start? As with all SAT questions that initially seem confusing, begin by doing what you can with the problem. In this case, try rearranging the problem:

$$x^2 + y^2 = -2xy$$
$$x^2 + y^2 + 2xy = 0$$
$$x^2 + 2xy + y^2 = 0$$

At this point, it should be very clear that you can factor the problem:

$$(x + y)(x + y) = 0$$

Since both the factors are the same, and since multiplied together they equal 0, you know that the sum of *x* and *y* must be 0.

15. **C** Geometry: Circles *Difficult*

The diameter of the circles is 10, but the circles have been smushed together to the point that it is hard to know the length of *AC* exactly. You know already that the length of *AC* must be shorter than 10, since the circles overlap. You can eliminate **E**. You are also told that line segment *BD* is equal to 6. Notice anything? If you were to draw in a midpoint on *BD* and call it *O*, then the length of *BO* would be 3, and *OD* would also be 3. Notice that line *BD* is also perpendicular to *AC*. If you drew a line from point *B* to point *A*, you would have a right-angle triangle. Further, line *AB* is the radius of the circle. You already know that the diameter of the circle is 10, which makes the radius 5. You are dealing with a Pythagorean triplet! Now you know that side *AO* must be the leg of a triangle and must measure 4. This makes the entire length of *AC* 8.

16. **E** Geometry: Geometric Visualizations *Difficult*
Try to visualize: the first cut would yield 2 pieces. The second cut would slice these 2 cuts in half, giving you 4 pieces. The final cut would then divide these 4 pieces in half, giving you a total of 8 pieces.

SECTION 9: WRITING

Improving Sentences

1. **C** Parallelism *Easy*
Items in a list must be placed in parallel form. In this case, you have two adjectives describing Denise's dress—*traditional* and *modern*. But the third adjective includes the verb *find*. To make this sentence grammatically correct, you will need to remove the verb *find*, and just have the word *romantic* in adjective form alone, which is precisely what **C** accomplishes.

2. **B** Tense *Easy*
Here you are being tested on your ability to recognize correct verb tense. Thomas *had just finished* with the groceries. In other words, his activities took place in the past. The verb *rings*, however, is in the present tense. To be correct, the verb *rings* must be placed in its past tense—*rang*. Notice that all of the incorrect answer choices leave the verb *rings* in the wrong tense.

3. **B** Redundancy *Easy*
This sentence suffers from an extreme case of wordiness. Further, the sentence compares two activities—*doing the laundry* and complaining. When two items are being compared in a sentence, they must be placed in parallel form. The first item, however, is written like this: *it might have taken to finish doing the laundry*. The second item is written as follows: *complained about his chores*. To be correct, the verb phrase *might have taken to finish doing the laundry* must be placed in the simple past tense. **B** corrects this error.

4. **C** Parallelism *Easy*
Here we have three items in a list: *going out of the office, at home, or on vacation*. Notice that the first item in the list contains the verb *going*, whereas the other items have no verbs at all. In order to be correct, all the items in the list must be in the same form: they must all contain either verbs or a prepositional phrase. **C** solves this problem.

5. **E** Tense *Medium*
The verb in the underlined portion of the sentence reads *foresaw*. However, the earlier part of the sentence reads as follows: *though the city inspected the property on which the development was going to be built*. The sentence is trying to make the point that the city did not see *at the time of development* that the hill was going to collapse. In other words, the verb *foresaw* must be rewritten as *foresee*, as in **E**.

6. **C** Parallelism *Medium*

When you make lists of items in a sentence, they must be written in parallel form. The items being compared are *to watch your diet*, and *too, you must get plenty of exercise*. Notice how the second item contains the pronoun *you*. For these items to be parallel, the pronoun *you* must either be in both halves of the list or in neither, as is the case with **C**.

7. **B** Pronouns/Other *Medium*

A pronoun must always refer to one clear antecedent, and it must agree with the antecedent in number. Here, the pronoun *they* refers to the *dress*. However, notice that *dress* is singular, and that the pronoun *they* is plural. The correct answer will replace *they* with *it*. Watch out for **D**, which misuses the word *easy*. You need an adverb, *easily*, to modify the verb *hemmed*.

8. **B** Run-Ons *Medium*

Here we have a classic run-on sentence. In a sentence with more than one clause, there can only be one complete sentence. The other clause or clauses must be made dependent on the independent clause. To combine these two sentences—*There is always a conflict between people who believe good fiction is accessible and people who think it is for the elite* and *this discussion is probably going to go on indefinitely*—you will either need to add a conjunctive word like "and," "but," or "because," or combine the sentences with a semicolon, as in **B**. Watch out for **C**, which puts the adverb *indefinitely* in its adjective form, *indefinite*, which is incorrect.

9. **C** Pronouns *Medium*

Be careful here. Aunt Petunia gave the walkie-talkies to *Roderick* and to *me*, not *I*. A pronoun must always be in the objective case after a preposition. **E** gets the pronoun right but unnecessarily complicates matters by including the preposition *to* twice.

10. **B** Parallelism *Medium*

The dancers wore two things: *brilliantly colored costumes* and *their shoes were bright too*. Notice, however, that these two items are not written in parallel form. The second item in the list includes the pronoun *their* and adds the adverb *too* at the end of the sentence. To be correct, the sentence should read, *The dancers onstage wore brilliantly colored costumes and bright shoes*, **B**.

11. **E** Idioms *Difficult*

The words *not only* and *but also* always go together. In this case, if you look at the original sentence, you see the words *not only take into consideration*. This means that the rest of the sentence should contain the phrase *but also*, and yet it does not. **E** fixes this error.

12. **E** Misplaced Modifiers *Difficult*

The way the sentence reads initially, it sound as though *a better use of time* was able to *buy the desk*. This doesn't make logical sense. We know that it is *Gordon* who bought the desk. This sentence contains the classic error of a misplaced modifier. To be correct, the sentence must make clear that it is *Gordon* who bought the desk. **E** fixes the problem. **C** does move *Gordon* closer to the modifying phrase, but the verb phrase *was working* is in the wrong tense.

13. **A** No Error *Difficult*

There is no error here. The pronoun *him* is in the objective case, as it needs to be following a preposition. Watch out for **B**, which puts the pronoun in the subjective case of *he*.

14. **D** Misplaced Modifiers *Difficult*

As it is originally worded, the sentence sounds as though the *hurricane* was *reading the photographs*, which makes no logical sense. Clearly, it is the *scientists* who read the photographs. The correct answer choice will move the word *scientists* immediately after the introductory modifying phrase. Although both **D** and **E** accomplish this, **E** sounds muddled, and the pronoun *its* is vague.

SAT PRACTICE TEST 2

SAT* Reasoning Test—General Directions

Timing

- You will have 3 hours and 20 minutes to work on this test. (On the actual SAT, you would have 3 hours and 45 minutes to complete ten sections, one of which would be unscored and experimental.)
- There are nine separately timed sections:
  - One 25-minute essay
  - Five other 25-minute sections
  - Two 20-minute sections
  - One 10-minute section
- You may work on only one section at a time.
- The supervisor will tell you when to begin and end each section.
- If you finish a section before time is called, check your work on that section. You may NOT turn to any other section.
- Work as rapidly as you can without losing accuracy. Don't waste time on questions that seem too difficult for you.

Marking Answers

- Carefully mark only one answer for each question.
- Make sure each mark is dark and completely fills the circle.
- Do not make any stray marks on your answer sheet.
- If you erase, do so completely. Incomplete erasures may be scored as intended answers.
- Use only the answer spaces that correspond to the question numbers.
- Use the test book for scratchwork, but you will not receive credit for anything written there.
- After time has been called, you may not transfer answers to your answer sheet or fill in circles.
- You may not fold or remove pages or portions of a page from this book, or take the book or answer sheet from the testing room.

Scoring

- For each correct answer to a question, you receive one point.
- For questions you omit, you receive no points.
- For a wrong answer to a multiple-choice question, you lose one-fourth of a point.
  - If you can eliminate one or more of the answer choices as wrong, you increase your chances of choosing the correct answer and earning one point.
  - If you can't eliminate any choice, move on. You can return to the question later if there is time.
- For a wrong answer to a "grid-in" math question, you don't lose any points.
- The essay is scored on a 1 to 6 scale by two different readers. The total essay score is the sum of the two readers' scores.
- An off-topic or blank essay will receive a score of zero.

SAT PRACTICE TEST 2 ANSWER SHEET

SECTION 2

1. Ⓐ Ⓑ Ⓒ Ⓓ Ⓔ	7. Ⓐ Ⓑ Ⓒ Ⓓ Ⓔ	13. Ⓐ Ⓑ Ⓒ Ⓓ Ⓔ	19. Ⓐ Ⓑ Ⓒ Ⓓ Ⓔ
2. Ⓐ Ⓑ Ⓒ Ⓓ Ⓔ	8. Ⓐ Ⓑ Ⓒ Ⓓ Ⓔ	14. Ⓐ Ⓑ Ⓒ Ⓓ Ⓔ	20. Ⓐ Ⓑ Ⓒ Ⓓ Ⓔ
3. Ⓐ Ⓑ Ⓒ Ⓓ Ⓔ	9. Ⓐ Ⓑ Ⓒ Ⓓ Ⓔ	15. Ⓐ Ⓑ Ⓒ Ⓓ Ⓔ	21. Ⓐ Ⓑ Ⓒ Ⓓ Ⓔ
4. Ⓐ Ⓑ Ⓒ Ⓓ Ⓔ	10. Ⓐ Ⓑ Ⓒ Ⓓ Ⓔ	16. Ⓐ Ⓑ Ⓒ Ⓓ Ⓔ	22. Ⓐ Ⓑ Ⓒ Ⓓ Ⓔ
5. Ⓐ Ⓑ Ⓒ Ⓓ Ⓔ	11. Ⓐ Ⓑ Ⓒ Ⓓ Ⓔ	17. Ⓐ Ⓑ Ⓒ Ⓓ Ⓔ	23. Ⓐ Ⓑ Ⓒ Ⓓ Ⓔ
6. Ⓐ Ⓑ Ⓒ Ⓓ Ⓔ	12. Ⓐ Ⓑ Ⓒ Ⓓ Ⓔ	18. Ⓐ Ⓑ Ⓒ Ⓓ Ⓔ	24. Ⓐ Ⓑ Ⓒ Ⓓ Ⓔ

SECTION 3

1. Ⓐ Ⓑ Ⓒ Ⓓ Ⓔ	6. Ⓐ Ⓑ Ⓒ Ⓓ Ⓔ	11. Ⓐ Ⓑ Ⓒ Ⓓ Ⓔ	16. Ⓐ Ⓑ Ⓒ Ⓓ Ⓔ
2. Ⓐ Ⓑ Ⓒ Ⓓ Ⓔ	7. Ⓐ Ⓑ Ⓒ Ⓓ Ⓔ	12. Ⓐ Ⓑ Ⓒ Ⓓ Ⓔ	17. Ⓐ Ⓑ Ⓒ Ⓓ Ⓔ
3. Ⓐ Ⓑ Ⓒ Ⓓ Ⓔ	8. Ⓐ Ⓑ Ⓒ Ⓓ Ⓔ	13. Ⓐ Ⓑ Ⓒ Ⓓ Ⓔ	18. Ⓐ Ⓑ Ⓒ Ⓓ Ⓔ
4. Ⓐ Ⓑ Ⓒ Ⓓ Ⓔ	9. Ⓐ Ⓑ Ⓒ Ⓓ Ⓔ	14. Ⓐ Ⓑ Ⓒ Ⓓ Ⓔ	19. Ⓐ Ⓑ Ⓒ Ⓓ Ⓔ
5. Ⓐ Ⓑ Ⓒ Ⓓ Ⓔ	10. Ⓐ Ⓑ Ⓒ Ⓓ Ⓔ	15. Ⓐ Ⓑ Ⓒ Ⓓ Ⓔ	20. Ⓐ Ⓑ Ⓒ Ⓓ Ⓔ

SECTION 4

1. Ⓐ Ⓑ Ⓒ Ⓓ Ⓔ	7. Ⓐ Ⓑ Ⓒ Ⓓ Ⓔ	13. Ⓐ Ⓑ Ⓒ Ⓓ Ⓔ	19. Ⓐ Ⓑ Ⓒ Ⓓ Ⓔ
2. Ⓐ Ⓑ Ⓒ Ⓓ Ⓔ	8. Ⓐ Ⓑ Ⓒ Ⓓ Ⓔ	14. Ⓐ Ⓑ Ⓒ Ⓓ Ⓔ	20. Ⓐ Ⓑ Ⓒ Ⓓ Ⓔ
3. Ⓐ Ⓑ Ⓒ Ⓓ Ⓔ	9. Ⓐ Ⓑ Ⓒ Ⓓ Ⓔ	15. Ⓐ Ⓑ Ⓒ Ⓓ Ⓔ	21. Ⓐ Ⓑ Ⓒ Ⓓ Ⓔ
4. Ⓐ Ⓑ Ⓒ Ⓓ Ⓔ	10. Ⓐ Ⓑ Ⓒ Ⓓ Ⓔ	16. Ⓐ Ⓑ Ⓒ Ⓓ Ⓔ	22. Ⓐ Ⓑ Ⓒ Ⓓ Ⓔ
5. Ⓐ Ⓑ Ⓒ Ⓓ Ⓔ	11. Ⓐ Ⓑ Ⓒ Ⓓ Ⓔ	17. Ⓐ Ⓑ Ⓒ Ⓓ Ⓔ	23. Ⓐ Ⓑ Ⓒ Ⓓ Ⓔ
6. Ⓐ Ⓑ Ⓒ Ⓓ Ⓔ	12. Ⓐ Ⓑ Ⓒ Ⓓ Ⓔ	18. Ⓐ Ⓑ Ⓒ Ⓓ Ⓔ	24. Ⓐ Ⓑ Ⓒ Ⓓ Ⓔ

SECTION 5

1. Ⓐ Ⓑ Ⓒ Ⓓ Ⓔ	3. Ⓐ Ⓑ Ⓒ Ⓓ Ⓔ	5. Ⓐ Ⓑ Ⓒ Ⓓ Ⓔ	7. Ⓐ Ⓑ Ⓒ Ⓓ Ⓔ
2. Ⓐ Ⓑ Ⓒ Ⓓ Ⓔ	4. Ⓐ Ⓑ Ⓒ Ⓓ Ⓔ	6. Ⓐ Ⓑ Ⓒ Ⓓ Ⓔ	8. Ⓐ Ⓑ Ⓒ Ⓓ Ⓔ

9				10				11				12				13			
		/				/				/				/				/	
.	.	.	.	.	.	.	.	.	.	.	.	.	.	.	.	.	.	.	.
	0	0	0		0	0	0		0	0	0		0	0	0		0	0	0
1	1	1	1	1	1	1	1	1	1	1	1	1	1	1	1	1	1	1	1
2	2	2	2	2	2	2	2	2	2	2	2	2	2	2	2	2	2	2	2
3	3	3	3	3	3	3	3	3	3	3	3	3	3	3	3	3	3	3	3
4	4	4	4	4	4	4	4	4	4	4	4	4	4	4	4	4	4	4	4
5	5	5	5	5	5	5	5	5	5	5	5	5	5	5	5	5	5	5	5
6	6	6	6	6	6	6	6	6	6	6	6	6	6	6	6	6	6	6	6
7	7	7	7	7	7	7	7	7	7	7	7	7	7	7	7	7	7	7	7
8	8	8	8	8	8	8	8	8	8	8	8	8	8	8	8	8	8	8	8
9	9	9	9	9	9	9	9	9	9	9	9	9	9	9	9	9	9	9	9

14				15				16				17				18			
		/				/				/				/				/	
.	.	.	.	.	.	.	.	.	.	.	.	.	.	.	.	.	.	.	.
	0	0	0		0	0	0		0	0	0		0	0	0		0	0	0
1	1	1	1	1	1	1	1	1	1	1	1	1	1	1	1	1	1	1	1
2	2	2	2	2	2	2	2	2	2	2	2	2	2	2	2	2	2	2	2
3	3	3	3	3	3	3	3	3	3	3	3	3	3	3	3	3	3	3	3
4	4	4	4	4	4	4	4	4	4	4	4	4	4	4	4	4	4	4	4
5	5	5	5	5	5	5	5	5	5	5	5	5	5	5	5	5	5	5	5
6	6	6	6	6	6	6	6	6	6	6	6	6	6	6	6	6	6	6	6
7	7	7	7	7	7	7	7	7	7	7	7	7	7	7	7	7	7	7	7
8	8	8	8	8	8	8	8	8	8	8	8	8	8	8	8	8	8	8	8
9	9	9	9	9	9	9	9	9	9	9	9	9	9	9	9	9	9	9	9

SAT PRACTICE TEST 2 ANSWER SHEET

SECTION 6			
1. Ⓐ Ⓑ Ⓒ Ⓓ Ⓔ	10. Ⓐ Ⓑ Ⓒ Ⓓ Ⓔ	19. Ⓐ Ⓑ Ⓒ Ⓓ Ⓔ	28. Ⓐ Ⓑ Ⓒ Ⓓ Ⓔ
2. Ⓐ Ⓑ Ⓒ Ⓓ Ⓔ	11. Ⓐ Ⓑ Ⓒ Ⓓ Ⓔ	20. Ⓐ Ⓑ Ⓒ Ⓓ Ⓔ	29. Ⓐ Ⓑ Ⓒ Ⓓ Ⓔ
3. Ⓐ Ⓑ Ⓒ Ⓓ Ⓔ	12. Ⓐ Ⓑ Ⓒ Ⓓ Ⓔ	21. Ⓐ Ⓑ Ⓒ Ⓓ Ⓔ	30. Ⓐ Ⓑ Ⓒ Ⓓ Ⓔ
4. Ⓐ Ⓑ Ⓒ Ⓓ Ⓔ	13. Ⓐ Ⓑ Ⓒ Ⓓ Ⓔ	22. Ⓐ Ⓑ Ⓒ Ⓓ Ⓔ	31. Ⓐ Ⓑ Ⓒ Ⓓ Ⓔ
5. Ⓐ Ⓑ Ⓒ Ⓓ Ⓔ	14. Ⓐ Ⓑ Ⓒ Ⓓ Ⓔ	23. Ⓐ Ⓑ Ⓒ Ⓓ Ⓔ	32. Ⓐ Ⓑ Ⓒ Ⓓ Ⓔ
6. Ⓐ Ⓑ Ⓒ Ⓓ Ⓔ	15. Ⓐ Ⓑ Ⓒ Ⓓ Ⓔ	24. Ⓐ Ⓑ Ⓒ Ⓓ Ⓔ	33. Ⓐ Ⓑ Ⓒ Ⓓ Ⓔ
7. Ⓐ Ⓑ Ⓒ Ⓓ Ⓔ	16. Ⓐ Ⓑ Ⓒ Ⓓ Ⓔ	25. Ⓐ Ⓑ Ⓒ Ⓓ Ⓔ	34. Ⓐ Ⓑ Ⓒ Ⓓ Ⓔ
8. Ⓐ Ⓑ Ⓒ Ⓓ Ⓔ	17. Ⓐ Ⓑ Ⓒ Ⓓ Ⓔ	26. Ⓐ Ⓑ Ⓒ Ⓓ Ⓔ	35. Ⓐ Ⓑ Ⓒ Ⓓ Ⓔ
9. Ⓐ Ⓑ Ⓒ Ⓓ Ⓔ	18. Ⓐ Ⓑ Ⓒ Ⓓ Ⓔ	27. Ⓐ Ⓑ Ⓒ Ⓓ Ⓔ	

SECTION 7			
1. Ⓐ Ⓑ Ⓒ Ⓓ Ⓔ	6. Ⓐ Ⓑ Ⓒ Ⓓ Ⓔ	11. Ⓐ Ⓑ Ⓒ Ⓓ Ⓔ	16. Ⓐ Ⓑ Ⓒ Ⓓ Ⓔ
2. Ⓐ Ⓑ Ⓒ Ⓓ Ⓔ	7. Ⓐ Ⓑ Ⓒ Ⓓ Ⓔ	12. Ⓐ Ⓑ Ⓒ Ⓓ Ⓔ	17. Ⓐ Ⓑ Ⓒ Ⓓ Ⓔ
3. Ⓐ Ⓑ Ⓒ Ⓓ Ⓔ	8. Ⓐ Ⓑ Ⓒ Ⓓ Ⓔ	13. Ⓐ Ⓑ Ⓒ Ⓓ Ⓔ	18. Ⓐ Ⓑ Ⓒ Ⓓ Ⓔ
4. Ⓐ Ⓑ Ⓒ Ⓓ Ⓔ	9. Ⓐ Ⓑ Ⓒ Ⓓ Ⓔ	14. Ⓐ Ⓑ Ⓒ Ⓓ Ⓔ	19. Ⓐ Ⓑ Ⓒ Ⓓ Ⓔ
5. Ⓐ Ⓑ Ⓒ Ⓓ Ⓔ	10. Ⓐ Ⓑ Ⓒ Ⓓ Ⓔ	15. Ⓐ Ⓑ Ⓒ Ⓓ Ⓔ	

SECTION 8			
1. Ⓐ Ⓑ Ⓒ Ⓓ Ⓔ	5. Ⓐ Ⓑ Ⓒ Ⓓ Ⓔ	9. Ⓐ Ⓑ Ⓒ Ⓓ Ⓔ	13. Ⓐ Ⓑ Ⓒ Ⓓ Ⓔ
2. Ⓐ Ⓑ Ⓒ Ⓓ Ⓔ	6. Ⓐ Ⓑ Ⓒ Ⓓ Ⓔ	10. Ⓐ Ⓑ Ⓒ Ⓓ Ⓔ	14. Ⓐ Ⓑ Ⓒ Ⓓ Ⓔ
3. Ⓐ Ⓑ Ⓒ Ⓓ Ⓔ	7. Ⓐ Ⓑ Ⓒ Ⓓ Ⓔ	11. Ⓐ Ⓑ Ⓒ Ⓓ Ⓔ	15. Ⓐ Ⓑ Ⓒ Ⓓ Ⓔ
4. Ⓐ Ⓑ Ⓒ Ⓓ Ⓔ	8. Ⓐ Ⓑ Ⓒ Ⓓ Ⓔ	12. Ⓐ Ⓑ Ⓒ Ⓓ Ⓔ	16. Ⓐ Ⓑ Ⓒ Ⓓ Ⓔ

SECTION 9			
1. Ⓐ Ⓑ Ⓒ Ⓓ Ⓔ	5. Ⓐ Ⓑ Ⓒ Ⓓ Ⓔ	9. Ⓐ Ⓑ Ⓒ Ⓓ Ⓔ	13. Ⓐ Ⓑ Ⓒ Ⓓ Ⓔ
2. Ⓐ Ⓑ Ⓒ Ⓓ Ⓔ	6. Ⓐ Ⓑ Ⓒ Ⓓ Ⓔ	10. Ⓐ Ⓑ Ⓒ Ⓓ Ⓔ	14. Ⓐ Ⓑ Ⓒ Ⓓ Ⓔ
3. Ⓐ Ⓑ Ⓒ Ⓓ Ⓔ	7. Ⓐ Ⓑ Ⓒ Ⓓ Ⓔ	11. Ⓐ Ⓑ Ⓒ Ⓓ Ⓔ	
4. Ⓐ Ⓑ Ⓒ Ⓓ Ⓔ	8. Ⓐ Ⓑ Ⓒ Ⓓ Ⓔ	12. Ⓐ Ⓑ Ⓒ Ⓓ Ⓔ	

SECTION 1
ESSAY

Time—25 minutes

The essay gives you an opportunity to show how effectively you can develop and express ideas. You should, therefore, take care to develop your point of view, present your ideas logically and clearly, and use language precisely.

Your essay must be written on the lines provided on your answer sheet—you will receive no other paper on which to write. You will have enough space if you write on every line, avoid wide margins, and keep your handwriting to a reasonable size. Remember that people who are not familiar with your handwriting will read what you write. Try to write or print so that what you are writing is legible to those readers.

You have twenty-five minutes to write an essay on the topic assigned below. DO NOT WRITE ON ANOTHER TOPIC. AN OFF-TOPIC ESSAY WILL RECEIVE A SCORE OF ZERO.

Think carefully about the issue presented in the following excerpt and the assignment below.

> Dictators of rogue nations often threaten or appeal to the leaders of wealthier, more democratic nations.

Assignment: How should a democratic nation deal with the dictator of a foreign country? Is it best to give in to some of the dictators' demands or to take a hard-and-fast "no yielding" policy? Cite specific examples from your own knowledge of the world, reading, and personal experience to craft an essay addressing this subject.

DO NOT WRITE YOUR ESSAY IN YOUR TEST BOOK. You will receive credit only for what you write on your answer sheet.

BEGIN WRITING YOUR ESSAY ON THE ANSWER SHEET.

IF YOU FINISH BEFORE TIME IS CALLED, YOU MAY CHECK YOUR WORK ON THIS SECTION ONLY. DO NOT TURN TO ANY OTHER SECTION IN THE TEST.

SECTION 1—ESSAY

Time—25 minutes

SECTION 1—ESSAY

Time—25 minutes

SECTION 2

Turn to Section 2 of your answer sheet to answer the questions in this section.

Time—25 Minutes
24 Questions

Directions: For each question in this section, select the best answer from among the choices given and fill in the corresponding oval on the answer sheet.

Each sentence below has one or two blanks, each blank indicating that something has been omitted. Beneath the sentence are five words or sets of words labeled A through E. Choose the word or set of words that, when inserted in the sentence, best fits the meaning of the sentence as a whole.

Example:

Eliza felt ----- when her boss asked her to work seven weekends in a row but ----- when her work earned her a promotion.

(A) enervated . . weakened
(B) depressed . . intellectual
(C) advantageous . . salacious
(D) angry . . shopworn
(E) irate . . elated   

1. Pianist Art Tatum's hearing was so ----- that he could distinguish the difference between a penny and a dime hitting a hard surface.

(A) acute
(B) erratic
(C) trusting
(D) simpering
(E) false

2. Because jade is such a hard substance, the ancient Chinese believed it had the ability to ----- immortality upon humans and keep their physical bodies intact.

(A) reprove
(B) bestow
(C) enact
(D) surmise
(E) retract

3. It would have been helpful for Jane to display even a ----- of respect for her boss, for a modest display of gratitude might have helped ----- her position in the company.

(A) glimmering . . eject
(B) scent . . save
(C) notice . . object
(D) tissue . . hold
(E) modicum . . retain

4. As an old man, Uncle Percy had a reputation for being -----. As a young man, however, he was known to be quite -----.

(A) cantankerous . . moody
(B) benign . . generous
(C) obstreperous . . charming
(D) grumpy . . parsimonious
(E) gregarious . . fastidious

5. Many found the prize-winning novel to be ----- and could not see past its hyped-up sentimentality to the sensitive observations it contained about daily life.

(A) regenerative
(B) mawkish
(C) blissful
(D) desiccated
(E) dithering

6. While the public often ----- the plethora of negative ads that appear every election year, research shows that such questionable tactics have a strong ability to sway voters' opinions and to win votes for the more ----- candidate.

(A) deplores . . submissive
(B) amuses . . vacillating
(C) lauds . . aggressive
(D) decries . . belligerent
(E) appreciates . . youthful

GO ON TO THE NEXT PAGE

SECTION 2

7. The onstage persona of the ballerina as ----- and vulnerable is an illusion. In reality, tremendous strength and ----- must go into each performance.

   (A) ethereal . . stamina
   (B) gaunt . . negotiation
   (C) fiery . . suppleness
   (D) wafting . . ineptitude
   (E) opprobrious . . talent

8. Any foray into fiction worthy of publication will need to ensure that the text is not -----, for editors and readers alike are all searching for something new, something unusual.

   (A) ribald
   (B) florid
   (C) fecund
   (D) hackneyed
   (E) unusual

GO ON TO THE NEXT PAGE

SECTION 2

Directions: Each passage below is followed by questions based on its content. Answer the questions on the basis of what is stated or implied in each passage and in any introductory material that may be provided.

Questions 9–10 are based on the following passage.

Nearly everyone has a personality quirk or two that may become accentuated as they grow older. Most people, however, are so socialized that they are unwilling or even afraid to act on wild impulses or flights of fancy. But some people seem to have those quirks in spades and are often referred to as "eccentrics." Is eccentricity a medical condition that can be diagnosed and cured? Some scientists don't think so. It has often been noted that eccentrics tend to live longer and live free from stress, because they do not bend to the social pressures to conform. Eccentrics also have a strong inner life, questioning ideas and pursuing specialized interests. As a result, they are less dependent on material goods and other generally accepted comforts.

9. The author implies that eccentrics suffer from less stress (lines 8–9) because

(A) they do not work and therefore do not have to worry about their jobs
(B) they are mentally ill and are unaware of the world around them
(C) they are highly controlled individuals who rarely make societal missteps
(D) they act on wild impulses
(E) they do not worry about fitting in with other people

10. According to the passage, all of the following characterize eccentrics EXCEPT

(A) suffering from less stress
(B) relying on material goods for comfort
(C) questioning ideas
(D) acting on wild impulses
(E) pursuing individual interests

Questions 11–12 are based on the following passage.

Long before the Egyptians built their famed pyramids, the ancient Sumerians constructed similar structures known as "ziggurats." But whereas a pyramid tends to be triangular in shape, with smooth walls and a square base, the ziggurat is tier-shaped, like the layers of a wedding cake, with a base that is circular, rectangular, or square. The Sumerians, who lived in present-day Iraq, built the ziggurats from sun-baked clay and fired clay bricks lined the outside face. Often, these facing bricks were painted with a glaze and may have been assembled in a specific pattern to depict religious symbolism. Unlike the Egyptian pyramids, ziggurats were not tombs, but rather houses for the gods. Only priests were allowed to enter the ziggurats, and as a result of their contact with deities, priests became highly influential members of Sumerian society.

11. A ziggurat is different from a pyramid, because it

(A) does not ascend toward the sky
(B) has not survived to modernity
(C) was built with sophisticated machinery
(D) may have a circular base
(E) is not made of brick

12. In the passage, the author implies that

(A) ziggurats eventually became tombs for influential priests
(B) the Egyptians learned how to build ziggurats from the Sumerians
(C) only highly regarded individuals could enter the ziggurat
(D) a drought brought down the Sumerian Empire
(E) the Sumerians learned about their gods' existence because they built ziggurats

GO ON TO THE NEXT PAGE

SECTION 2

Directions: The passages below are followed by questions based on their content; questions following a pair of related passages may also be based on the relationship between the paired passages. Answer the questions on the basis of what is stated or implied in the passages and in any introductory material that may be provided.

Questions 13–24 are based on the following passages.

The following passages were adapted from articles published in two academic journals in 1999. Both articles discuss the development of language in human beings.

Passage 1

Have you ever wondered how human beings are able to acquire language? All across the globe, children are born without speaking a word, and yet, from culture to culture, they are able to begin speaking on relatively the same timetable. There is even evidence that children are able to understand language before they are able to speak: little children often respond to commands and names before they themselves are able to construct intelligible sentences. How does this happen? The linguist Noam Chomsky posited the idea in the 1960s that human beings possess a "deep structure" that leaves us hardwired not just for thought, but also for language, though he sees the two things as very different. In fact, it is a capacity for language that makes human beings unique. It is simply, in Chomsky's words, what we are "good at." While other animals demonstrate a capacity for flying, with an innate understanding of shifting winds and changing angles, humans are able to master increasingly complex levels of language to express a seemingly endlessly complex series of thoughts.

One of Chomsky's main ideas included that of "universal grammar," the idea that there is an embedded structure of language within the brain. The scientist Stephen Pinker, at MIT, carried this idea even further, suggesting that there is a language "instinct." According to Pinker, evolution has hardwired the brain with the capacity to develop sophisticated language. How this "instinct" or "universal grammar" takes on its particular form depends on where a child is raised and to what language she is exposed. In North America, for example, a child will learn English if this is the language that surrounds her. In China, she will learn Chinese. Interestingly, even children who are born deaf can and will develop the capacity for language. A recent study of eight deaf children with hearing parents showed that the children developed a sophisticated gestural language—far more complex than the simple movements their parents had developed to communicate with their children. And, also interestingly, in each case, the children did not communicate through a random series of gestures, but through an actual language. That is, they used sentences with set rules and set patterns, one of the hallmarks of language. There is some evidence, however, that children must be exposed to language before puberty. If not, the capacity to develop language and to adhere to the rules of grammar diminishes. There have been examples of "wild" children raised without exposure to the human voice. Upon being introduced to society post-puberty, these children never truly learn to articulate complex ideas.

Language also has the ability to develop and change, suggesting that its very structure is malleable. Animals seem to communicate to each other through behavior or through a limited set of noises. Unlike animal noises, language is able to evolve. Every year, news outlets cover the newest additions to the world's dictionaries. Words like *internet* and *blog* are among the latest to be added to the list of acceptable words. Consider too that a computer is incapable of speaking with a higher level of language than a three-year-old. There is no mechanism that can reproduce the impressive facility with which humans use language.

When it comes to the question of exactly how humans develop language, scientists are on much less certain footing. How, for example, does a small child develop a vocabulary of 60,000 words in the space of a few years? An adult could certainly not master this many words without some great effort. How does a child learn to distinguish without error the difference between a cup, a saucer, a fork, and a knife on a table? To take matters one step further, how does a child know that a large four-legged expandable table in the dining room requires the same name, *table,* as the small round table in the kitchen? Clearly, when we learn words, we do not just learn a definition but something of the function of each word, its texture, and its malleability. When thought of this way, language seems like a nearly impossible thing to teach to a computer, and we have not even yet started to discuss the complex rules surrounding grammar acquisition. This complexity, in part, is what prompts scientists to propose the idea of the language instinct: each new child must be born with some sort of ability to put all of the information floating around in the noisy world together to develop a capacity for language. The brain can't just be a blank slate ready to receive large amounts of information that it learns to order over time. If this were true, then a computer could learn to talk. So too, supposedly, could animals.

In fact, no one has successfully taught an animal to talk, though there have been efforts over the years. Scientists such as Chomsky pooh-pooh this kind of attempt, pointing out that humans are able to suspend themselves in hang-gliders, but this does not really mean that they have learned to fly. Similarly, animals, such as dogs, might learn to respond to vocal commands, but this does not mean they have learned speech and that we are going to be able to explore a dog's emotional life and experiences

GO ON TO THE NEXT PAGE

in detail. Much has been made about the ability of chimps to speak using symbols or hand gestures. But scientists are highly skeptical of these claims. They point out that chimps do not learn to put words together in grammatically ordered ways, and their speech is a jumble of words and sounds. And, as we all learned in grade school science, an animal will learn to press any combination of buttons if a treat will appear at the end of the lesson.

In the end, although we continue to learn more about language, its real mysteries must remain so. Perhaps the best we can hope for at this point is to more fully appreciate our faculties as humans and to respect each other as a result.

Passage 2

Humans have always been fascinated by animals. We suspect we have much in common with them, and yet we have always thought of ourselves as superior. At the same time, many childhood stories depict the friendship between a child and another animal, raising suspicion that we feel we have much to learn from our mammalian brethren. And, for centuries, people have enjoyed living with animals for companionship.

Of all the mammals on the earth, however, perhaps none is quite as compelling to us as the primate. We find them fascinating because they resemble us in so many ways, with their humanlike faces, their nimble hands, and familiar, familial behavior. If we have any cousins in the animal kingdom, they are primates, and recent DNA tests do confirm that the chimpanzee is our closest living relative. Exactly where in the history of evolution our paths diverged is unclear, but it is certain that once upon a time our ancestors lived together quite intimately.

So perhaps it is understandable that we have a strong desire to teach these primates to talk. The reasons are many. We might learn something about language—about the capacity for language—and consequently ourselves, if we are able to communicate with chimpanzees. The early part of the twentieth century saw so-called scientists attempt to teach chimps to speak. Even very young animals, however, were unable to manipulate their lips and palates to produce the wide variety of sounds that constitute words. The average human can distinguish between such sounds as "pa" and "ba," but minute differences seem to be impenetrable for other animals. Creative scientists insisted that the chimps were actually saying, "Mama" or "Papa," but, over time, such claims have been dismissed.

Other scientists are skeptical, noting that the chimp "men" may have had a propensity for fighting. Also, when training chimps, scientists often use food as a reward for a successful "communication." Might a chimp not learn, then, that by putting together random words, he will be able to receive a treat? Orrin's report might well be like an astrological report or fortune cookie: the information is vague enough that, with some effort on the part of the scientist, it might seem as though it relates to very real events.

The debate about training animals to speak will no doubt persist for many more generations. Until there is some kind of agreed upon test that can be administered to check an animal's ability to communicate, and whose results can be duplicated, there will no doubt continue to be those convinced that animals can speak, and those convinced that they cannot. But we must admire the drive of scientists who continue to pursue this unique avenue of study. If we ever were able to find a way to actually communicate with chimps or any other primate, it might dispel the notion once and for all that language is a kind of divine gift bestowed on humans, as encapsulated in such theories as the "language instinct" or "deep structure" that are appealing to contemporary scientists, but which eventually raise more questions than they answer. To really understand language, scientists must strive to decode the manner in which it is acquired and teach other animals or computers to communicate in the same way. Believing that language is a mystical gift seems to be sloppy science. Certainly, once upon a time, humans found flight to be a mystifying phenomenon, judging from the number of old religions and cultures that imbued birds with magical properties. But, over time, humans have understood the physics and mechanics behind flight, and it is just a matter of time before the mysteries of language are similarly decoded.

13. In line 14, the author of Passage 1 uses the example of flying to suggest that

(A) humans are naturally gifted in language, just as other animals are gifted in flight
(B) humans have learned to fly, just as other animals have learned to speak
(C) the traits of some animals are gifts that will never be understood
(D) language is as mysterious a gift as flight
(E) by better understanding flight, we will better understand how language developed in humans.

14. In line 20, the word "embedded" most nearly means

(A) fixed
(B) rigged
(C) buried
(D) asleep
(E) cancelled

GO ON TO THE NEXT PAGE

SECTION 2

15. The author of Passage 1 mentions deaf children in lines 29–36 ("Interestingly, even . . . language") in order to show that

(A) the development of language is limited only to certain children in certain parts of the world
(B) very small babies are not able to understand human speech
(C) if deaf children can learn to speak, so can primates
(D) language cannot be learned by humans beyond a specific age
(E) all children, whether hearing or not, develop language if exposed to it at a young age

16. All of the following are referred to in Passage 1 as evidence of a language instinct EXCEPT

(A) the malleability of language to absorb new words
(B) the ability of other animals to learn language
(C) the explosion of vocabulary words in small children
(D) the capability of even hearing-impaired children to communicate
(E) the capacity for children in different countries to learn different languages on roughly the same timetable.

17. In lines 66–69 ("When thought . . . acquisition"), the author of Passage 1 implies that a computer cannot be taught language, because it

(A) requires too much programming to account for all of the intricacies of grammar
(B) does not have original thoughts
(C) cannot learn to answer questions
(D) cannot grasp the many meanings behind a word or a word's texture, malleability, and attributes
(E) does not distinguish between the many idioms contained in language

18. In lines 106–107 ("because they . . . behavior"), the author of Passage 2 states that we find primates compelling, because

(A) we consider ourselves superior to other animals
(B) they are the only animals capable of learning language
(C) results of DNA tests state that chimps share our DNA
(D) they look and behave very similarly to us
(E) they are amusingly clumsy

19. In context, "impenetrable" (line 123) most nearly means

(A) impassable
(B) immortal
(C) inimitable
(D) indigenous
(E) impudent

20. According to the author of Passage 2, true proof of a chimp's ability to communicate will only be known when

(A) skeptical scientists will open their minds
(B) scientists teaching chimps to speak use more trustworthy methods of instruction
(C) humans learn to communicate via the language of chimps
(D) chimps stop communicating as a way to get food
(E) a chimp can be tested via some test with results that can be repeated

21. The author of Passage 1 would most likely read the closing paragraph of Passage 2 and state that

(A) the ability of humans to fly like birds proves that all animals can teach their gifts to each other
(B) just because humans have learned to fly in airplanes does not mean that they have obtained the gift of flight matching the skill of birds
(C) in order to teach animals how to speak, scientists may need to find new ways to teach language
(D) flight and language are not analogous and do not belong in the same discussion
(E) language is infinitely more complex than flight

22. The author of Passage 2 regards the idea of a "language instinct" (line 146) as

(A) unscientific and smacking of divine intervention
(B) a way to explain the sudden proliferation of words in a three-year-old
(C) proof that chimps will never really learn to speak
(D) the only logical explanation behind the mysterious properties of human language
(E) a logical departing point for setting up the prerequisites for a test to see if chimps can communicate

GO ON TO THE NEXT PAGE

SECTION 2

23. The authors of Passage 1 and Passage 2 agree that

(A) teaching primates language will invariably deepen our understanding of how the mind works
(B) the components of all animal gifts can be dissected, understood, and taught
(C) if humans are able to learn to fly, then other animals should be able to learn to speak
(D) so far, proven attempts to teach chimps to speak have failed
(E) in order to acquire language, animals must have a hardwired "instinct" in their brains

24. The argument made by the author of Passage 1 would be strengthened if which of the following were true?

(A) It is discovered that the ability to learn language is linked to part of DNA particular to humans.
(B) Humans are able to understand the language of chimps using specially modulated equipment.
(C) A hearing-impaired child raised without any contact with human beings until she is an adult cannot learn to express her thoughts through language.
(D) Very young chimps are able to learn to speak provided they are raised exclusively by humans.
(E) A newly programmed computer is able to communicate on the level of a four-year-old human child.

S T O P

IF YOU FINISH BEFORE TIME IS CALLED, YOU MAY CHECK YOUR WORK ON THIS TEST ONLY. DO NOT TURN TO ANY OTHER SECTION IN THIS TEST.

SECTION 3

Turn to Section 3 of your answer sheet to answer the questions in this section.

Time—25 Minutes
20 Questions

Directions: For this section, solve each problem and decide which is the best of the choices given. Fill in the corresponding oval on the answer sheet. You may use any available space for scratchwork.

Notes:

1. The use of a calculator is permitted. All numbers used are real numbers.
2. Figures that accompany problems in this test are intended to provide information useful in solving the problems. They are drawn as accurately as possible EXCEPT when it is stated in a specific problem that the figure is not drawn to scale. All figures lie in a plane unless otherwise indicated.
3. Unless otherwise specified, the domain of any function f is assumed to be the set of all real numbers x for which $f(x)$ is a real number.

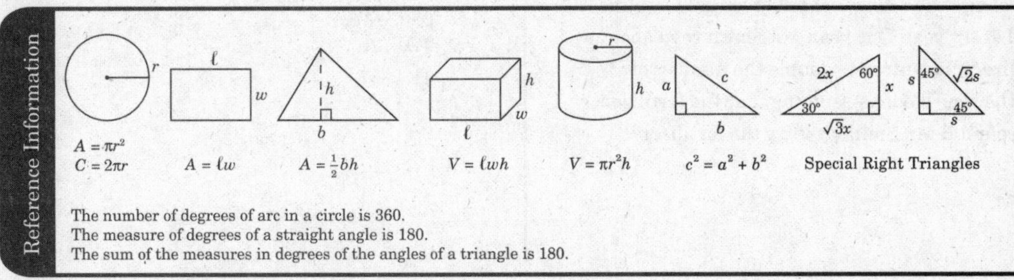

1. If $3y - 7 = 20$, what is the value of $2y + 1$?

(A) 13
(B) 15
(C) 17
(D) 19
(E) 21

2. There are 7 shelves on a bookshelf. If one hardback book is roughly the size of two paperback books, and each shelf can hold approximately 45 paperback books, then which of the following could be the total number of books to be shelved on and completely fill this particular bookcase?

(A) 285 paperbacks and 15 hardbacks
(B) 315 paperbacks and 12 hardbacks
(C) 15 paperbacks and 315 hardbacks
(D) 15 paperbacks and 285 hardbacks
(E) 150 paperbacks and 165 hardbacks

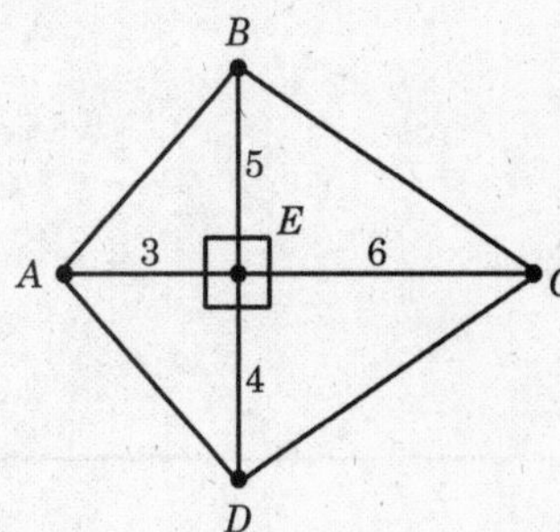

3. In the figure above, which of the following triangles will have the largest area?

(A) *BEC*
(B) *ABE*
(C) *AED*
(D) *DEC*
(E) *BDC*

GO ON TO THE NEXT PAGE

SECTION 3

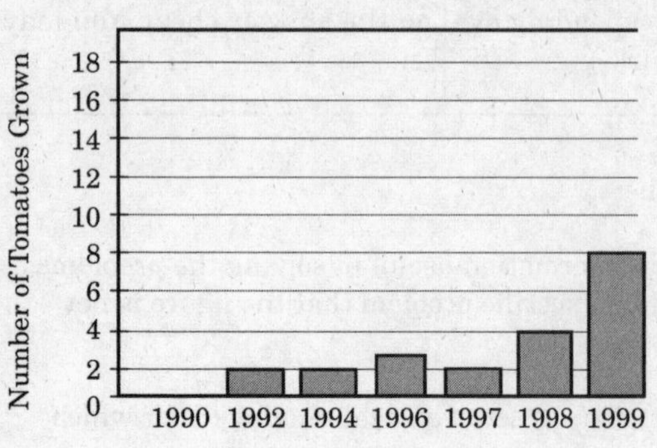

4. The figure above shows the number of tomatoes grown in the Smith's backyard every year. One year, Mr. Smith read about a new kind of fertilizer guaranteed to double the number of tomatoes grown the year before. Assuming that the fertilizer works, in which year did Mr. Smith *first* try the fertilizer?

(A) 1995
(B) 1996
(C) 1997
(D) 1998
(E) 1999

5. The average of three numbers is 22. The average of two of those numbers is also 22. What is the value of the third number in the original three?

(A) 20
(B) 21
(C) 22
(D) 23
(E) 24

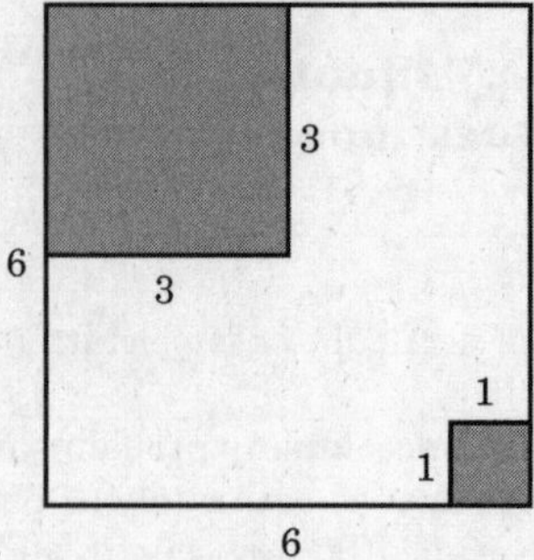

6. In the figure above, what is the area of the unshaded region?

(A) 10
(B) 16
(C) 20
(D) 26
(E) 27

7. If $fghi < 0$, and $fhij = 2$, then which of the following must be true?

(A) $f = 0$
(B) $i = 0$
(C) $g < 1$
(D) $fhi < 1$
(E) j is an integer

GO ON TO THE NEXT PAGE

SECTION 3

8. According to one popular diet, in a 2,500-calorie-filled day, one-fourth of the calories should come from fat. One-fifth of the remaining calories should come from meat. One-half of the remaining calories should come from whole grains. The remaining number of calories should come from fruit. What fraction of the total number of calories should come from fruit?

(A) $\frac{6}{7}$

(B) $\frac{3}{8}$

(C) $\frac{4}{5}$

(D) $\frac{1}{2}$

(E) $\frac{3}{10}$

---

9. If $4^{2x+1} = 8^2$, then what is the value of x?

(A) –1
(B) 0
(C) 1
(D) 2
(E) 3

---

10. If 7 less than 2 times a certain number is 2 less than the number, what is the number?

(A) 2
(B) 3
(C) 4
(D) 5
(E) 6

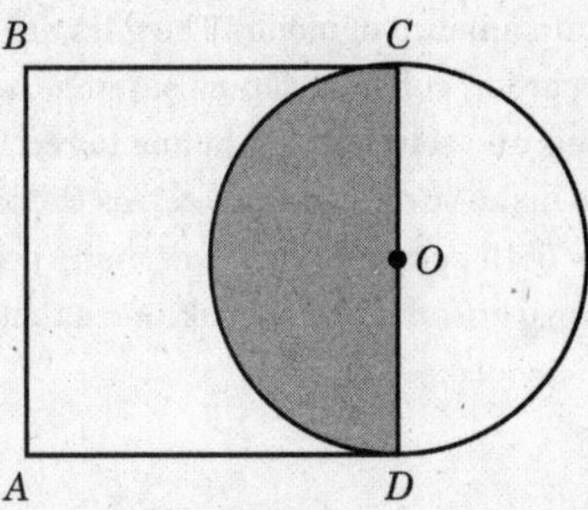

11. In the diagram above, figure *ABCD* is a square, bisecting circle with center *O*. If the length of one side of the square is 4, what is the perimeter of the shaded region?

(A) 2
(B) 4
(C) 2π
(D) $4 + 4\pi$
(E) $4 + 2\pi$

---

x	$f(x)$
0	2
1	3
2	6
3	11
4	18

12. The table above shows some values for the function *f*. If *f* is a linear function, which of the following could be the equation for *f*?

(A) $f(x) = x^2 + 2$
(B) $f(x) = x^2 + 1$
(C) $f(x) = 2x + 1$
(D) $f(x) = 2x + 2$
(E) $f(x) = 2x - 2$

GO ON TO THE NEXT PAGE

SECTION 3

13. A department store is giving away free gifts to customers who spend a certain amount of money. The gifts are given away in the following order: cubic zirconium earrings, scarf, lipstick, socks, tote bag, and tiara. Meg is in line to receive her free gift. She wants to make sure that she receives the tiara. If she is currently the 55th person in line, how many people will she need to allow go ahead of her to make sure that she receives the tiara?

(A) 3
(B) 4
(C) 5
(D) 6
(E) 7

14. In the *xy*-plane, the equation of line *a* is $y = 3x - 2$. If line *b* is the reflection of line *a* in the *x*-axis, what is the equation of line *b* ?

(A) $y = 3x + 2$
(B) $y = -3x - 2$
(C) $y = -3x + 2$
(D) $y = 3x - 1$
(E) $y = 3x + 1$

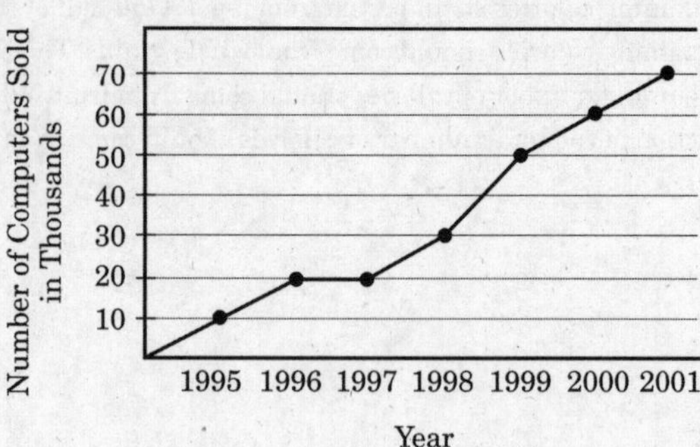

15. The figure above shows the number of computers sold by Macro Computers every year. According to the chart, the computers sales in the year 2000 were what percent higher than the computers sales in 1996 ?

(A) 50
(B) 100
(C) 150
(D) 200
(E) 300

16. Which of the following has an area equivalent to a circle with an area 36π ?

(A) A triangle with height 6π and base 6
(B) A triangle with height 12 and base 3π
(C) A square with side 6
(D) A rectangle with base 1 and height 36
(E) A rectangle with base 4 and height 9π

GO ON TO THE NEXT PAGE

SECTION 3

17. If $3a = \frac{2b+1}{5}$, then what is the value of b in terms of a ?

(A) $15a - 1$

(B) $\frac{3a-6}{2}$

(C) $\frac{15a-1}{2}$

(D) $\frac{15a-6}{2}$

(E) $\frac{15}{2a-1}$

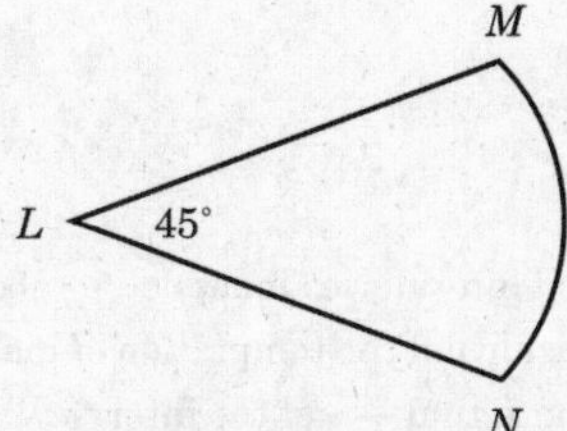

18. In the figure above, MN is the arc of a circle with center L. If the area of the sector is 8π, what is the length of arc MN ?

(A) 2π
(B) 8π
(C) 16π
(D) 24π
(E) 64π

19. There are 150 more crates of yellow grapefruit than red grapefruit in the back of Sam's vegetable shop. If there are r crates of red grapefruit, then, in terms of r, what fraction of the grapefruit crates in the back of Sam's shop are red?

(A) $\frac{150}{r+150}$

(B) $\frac{r}{r+150}$

(C) $\frac{r}{2r+150}$

(D) $\frac{150}{r+150}$

(E) $\frac{2r}{r+150}$

20. $\begin{array}{r} 73 \\ +\ \underline{EM} \\ GG5 \end{array}$

In the correctly worked problem above, which of the following could be the sum of G and M ?

(A) 1
(B) 2
(C) 3
(D) 4
(E) 5

S T O P

IF YOU FINISH BEFORE TIME IS CALLED, YOU MAY CHECK YOUR WORK ON THIS TEST ONLY. DO NOT TURN TO ANY OTHER SECTION IN THIS TEST.

SECTION 4

Turn to Section 4 of your answer sheet to answer the questions in this section.

Time—25 Minutes
24 Questions

Directions: For each question in this section, select the best answer from among the choices given and fill in the corresponding oval on the answer sheet.

Each sentence below has one or two blanks, each blank indicating that something has been omitted. Beneath the sentence are five words or sets of words labeled A through E. Choose the word or set of words that, when inserted in the sentence, best fits the meaning of the sentence as a whole.

Example:

Eliza felt ----- when her boss asked her to work seven weekends in a row but ----- when her work earned her a promotion.

(A) enervated . . weakened
(B) depressed . . intellectual
(C) advantageous . . salacious
(D) angry . . shopworn
(E) irate . . elated   

1. The neighborhood is often cited as a(n) ----- for other communities to follow: it is racially integrated, has a low crime rate, and possesses some of the ----- schools in the entire city.

(A) model . . finest
(B) tower . . dirtiest
(C) example . . swarthiest
(D) nadir . . best
(E) prototype . . cheapest

2. The failure of soccer to ----- the American sports-watching audience has always been a ----- to European countries whose members are avid enthusiasts of the intricate game.

(A) enervate . . disappointment
(B) interest . . boon
(C) augment . . priority
(D) dominate . . credo
(E) electrify . . mystery

3. Plate tectonics, now widely accepted by geologists as a fundamental truth behind the formation of land masses and continents, was once regarded with great -----.

(A) allegiance
(B) fortitude
(C) skepticism
(D) veracity
(E) centrism

4. The community ----- that their nationally recognized aquarium was the first to contain a healthy, live great white shark and basked in the praise heaped upon them by local and distant media outlets.

(A) surmised
(B) resumed
(C) spoiled
(D) rejoiced
(E) undulated

5. While a talented interviewer must be ----- about a great many subjects, he must avoid the temptation of making his own well roundedness the actual ----- of the interview.

(A) knowledgeable . . beatitude
(B) androgynous . . aim
(C) hounded . . celebrity
(D) conversant . . spectacle
(E) florid . . emphasis

GO ON TO THE NEXT PAGE

SECTION 4

Directions: Each passage below is followed by questions based on its content. Answer the questions on the basis of what is stated or implied in each passage and in any introductory material that may be provided.

Questions 6–7 are based on the following passage.

The development of the health food industry in many ways mirrors the country's growing concern with fitness and physical appearance. During the 1970s, joggers, weightlifters, and alfalfa sprouts were seen as the obsessions of cuckoo-headed individuals focusing on niche activities or, worse, hobbies bordering on craziness. But the people who pounded the pavement in their sneakers and measured their calories during each meal are the ones who paved the way for what is a multimillion-dollar industry now. Diet books routinely hit the bestseller list, and clothing companies run neck and neck to try to convince consumers that their latest shoe will enhance performance and lead to weight loss. Every year it seems that some new food is heralded for its nearly miraculous ability to cure any ill. Indeed, what was once seen as a fad has now fully become entrenched as part of our society's general culture.

6. Which of the following is the author most likely to add to the list in lines 3–4?

(A) Seeing every hit movie
(B) Assessing the caloric value of every meal
(C) Vacationing at the latest "in" spot
(D) Emulating a neighbor's hobbies
(E) Decorating a house according to the tastes of the time

7. The last sentence of the passage serves to

(A) confirm how what was once seen as an oddity has become the norm
(B) contradict the opening sentence of the passage
(C) reinforce a long-held idea
(D) pose questions about the accuracy of the author's argument
(E) predict a future trend

Questions 8–9 are based on the following passage.

Studying this ancient tomb through the lens of economics raises new questions. In the past, we have focused purely on the personalities of the people buried inside or on the aesthetic value of the artwork. Now we can ask more fundamental questions. How much did it cost, for example, to build such a structure? When we marvel at its scale, we must ask ourselves what the cost would be to create a similar building today using modern-day tools. The ancient kingdom of China had at its disposal a seemingly endless supply of laborers, who worked for almost nothing. Given this surplus of labor, it's likely that the planners involved in deciding what the structure would look like spent more time calculating what was technologically possible.

8. What would most likely appear immediately before this paragraph?

(A) An introduction to the basic schematics of the tomb in question
(B) A review of general principles of economics
(C) A diagram of the tomb
(D) Illustrations of the frescoes inside the tomb
(E) A complete catalogue of the objects retrieved by archaeologists

9. This passage would most likely appear in

(A) an art book
(B) a pamphlet selling art restoration materials
(C) a table of expenses
(D) a personal journal
(E) a scholarly journal

GO ON TO THE NEXT PAGE

SECTION 4

Questions 10–18 are based on the following passage.

In this passage, an art dealer recalls how he built his collection into the treasure trove it is today.

There are those who consider the world of art dealing to be full of tricksters, high-stakes investors, and fraud. The number two crime currently handled by the FBI is that of art theft; and every year we are treated to a story about a theft from a museum, and every month smaller collections are raided and relieved of their treasures. But the world of art dealing has never really been so glamorous or shady for me.

I began dealing art out of the simplest of motives. My grandfather had always had a strong interest in the East, and I was treated at an early age to pictures of jades and ceramics. These images made a strong impression on me, and I will never forget an early visit to the Metropolitan Museum of Art in New York where I learned that the glossy images captured in those books also existed in real life. When I learned that a person such as myself could actually buy an object, I became even more interested in pursuing a life of collection. Before long, I was visiting museums and auctions, befriending collectors happy to share their knowledge with a young and eager person. When I was twenty-one, my grandfather took me on a trip to Asia, and it was there that I purchased my first painting and my first collection of jade figures.

A life of collection, however, does not feed a family. I learned quickly that if I was really going to immerse myself in the world of art every minute of my waking life, I would have to sell some of the pieces I owned in order to feed my habit and pay for such mundane costs as food and a mortgage. And this was how I got my start, slowly at first, buying a piece here and there, and quietly and patiently building my clientele. As tastes changed, I was forced to adapt my collection. So too did the quality and type of object available for sale. In the late seventies, for example, a neolithic stoneware pot from China was quite rare and valuable. Today, these pots are ubiquitous and have lost their value, disproving the old adage that art is a great investment that will only increase with time.

Since I did not set out to join the world of Asian art because I wanted or even expected to make money through investments, I have found over time that my favorite clients are those who are motivated by the same drive that I am: they simply love good art. I am always happy to spend an afternoon with a client who is captured by the virtuosity of a sinewy piece of jade as it twists and turns to reveal the milky outline of a cow or perhaps a mother bird and her chick. Certainly the artists who created these wonders did so out of a desire to tantalize the eye, and it would do me no good not to appreciate those who can see the splendor of a small piece of art.

I am sometimes asked for advice as to how one should commence building a collection. Of foremost importance, I am now convinced, is not necessarily the age or potential value of a piece, but the fact that it is something one truly appreciates. It is necessary too to educate oneself, to learn how to distinguish between the different dynasties, in the case of Chinese painting, for example. But I strongly believe that art is meant to be lived with, not trapped inside the case of a museum, and it does no one any good to purchase something if it does not have the ability to transmit joy on a daily basis. Life can be full of drudgery, after all, and everyone needs a quiet spot in a room filled with light or beauty to spruce up the day.

10. The narrator suggests that he began his career as an art dealer because

(A) it was part of the family business
(B) he needed a way to make money
(C) he enjoyed spending time with objects of art
(D) art dealing can be a highly lucrative business
(E) he liked spending time in museums

11. The contrast mentioned in lines 22–26 ("A life . . . mortgage") is best described in which terms?

(A) Strong-mindedness versus yielding to temptation
(B) Idealistic yearnings versus practical matters
(C) A desire to acquire material possessions versus altruism
(D) Sincerity versus nonchalance
(E) Stubbornness versus verisimilitude

12. The word "ubiquitous" as it is used in this passage in line 32 most nearly means

(A) untidy
(B) collectible
(C) scattered
(D) omnipresent
(E) cluttering

GO ON TO THE NEXT PAGE

13. Which of the following best compares clients who would buy the art mentioned in lines 30–31 ("In the late . . . art") with the clients described in lines 37–38 ("I have found . . . art")?

(A) The former are motivated by material concerns, whereas the latter are inspired by personal passion.
(B) The former are cynical, whereas the latter are idealistic.
(C) The former are humble and respectful, whereas the latter are dismissive.
(D) The former are retaliatory, whereas the latter are laudatory.
(E) The former are interested in the practical issues of building a collection, whereas the latter are content to admire one.

14. The word "adage," as it is used in this passage in line 33, most nearly means

(A) proverb
(B) rule
(C) preemption
(D) premonition
(E) exception

15. In line 40, the author refers to the "virtuosity of a sinewy piece of jade" in order to

(A) question the techniques used to produce small masterpieces
(B) highlight the degree to which he holds art in high esteem
(C) pinpoint the qualities that most make a work of art saleable
(D) emphasize how the value of a piece can rise with good craftsmanship
(E) detail his favorite pieces in his collection

16. In lines 42–45 ("Certainly . . . art"), the narrator makes the assumption that

(A) the artist would be pleased to see a high value assigned to his creation
(B) he knows for what purpose the artist originally created his work
(C) he can understand the amount of work that goes into producing each piece
(D) his best customers are aware of the level of craftsmanship required to carve jade
(E) the market for art objects will always increase

17. In the closing paragraph, the author refers to art as

(A) a futile occupation for all but the most serious collectors
(B) an intellectually challenging and satisfying endeavor
(C) an emotional haven from an otherwise troubling world
(D) a hobby only for the strong at heart
(E) the preoccupation of idealists

18. The passage serves mainly to

(A) stimulate lively debate about the value of art in the modern world
(B) dispel some misconceptions about the illegality of the art trade
(C) recount past triumphs in art sales
(D) affirm a strongly-held belief about the appropriate way to approach art
(E) predict the next wave of hit art objects

GO ON TO THE NEXT PAGE

SECTION 4

Questions 19–24 are based on the following passage.

In this passage, a scholar examines the relevance of a modern cultural phenomenon to a classic of contemporary literature.

Reality television is very much with us these days, with its broad displays of public romances and rejection as well as feats of supposed daring. Critics find reality TV to be unabashedly bad. "Where is the art?" they cry. Television, after all, was initially used as a means of entertainment, in which the world could share in its appreciation of a culture's self-expression. For the first time, all people across America could watch the same jokes and punch lines unfold at the same time, or share in the hysteria that surrounded the arrival of the Beatles. Reality television, say critics, has none of these cultural touch points.

But, of course, the very fact that so many tune their television sets every week to various reality programs suggests that we as a people are very much captivated by what we see on these shows. In part this must be because, as Americans, we are democratic by nature and believe that anyone should have the right to participate in the grand world of television. We do not like the idea that an overarching power structure is set on determining who will become a star and who will not. It is important for us to feel that we can relate to our cultural heroes, and so perhaps it is not really a surprise that we now have shows set up to attract "ordinary" people and to turn these citizens into stars. But really, this phenomenon is not as original as we might think.

All reality television shows involve a highly ritualized scenario. A group of people get together and compete against each other in tasks set forward by a producer. There are winners and losers. The reaction of both sets of people is captured on film and generally edited down to a two-second sound bite. From this little bit of speech, we, the audience, make snap judgments about the person: whether they have a good attitude, whether they have learned anything from their ordeals, etc. In his 1965 book *The Magus*, John Fowles uses a similar setup to create one of the great works of twentieth-century fiction. In the book, a young man, Nico, travels to Greece, where he plans to become a teacher. While there, he meets the mysterious Mr. Conchis, who proceeds to put Nico through a series of elaborate "tests." Nico realizes that he is participating in a game. He meets the beautiful Julie, who pretends that she is a ghost from the past. Later, Nico learns that Julie has a twin sister, and, by coordinating appearances and reappearances, Julie and her sister are temporarily able to fool Nico into believing they are ghosts. Once Nico determines that he is not dealing with spirits, the game with Mr. Conchis continues, culminating in a final scene in which Nico is confronted by ghosts from his past.

All this might sound vaguely familiar to the serious reader of fiction. One remembers Mr. Scrooge sent off to visit the Ghosts of Christmas Past and Present. Murder mysteries often send their heroes through a series of tests, which end with the capture of a villain. Mr. Fowles acknowledges that his work was inspired by the Greek mysteries, yearly rituals that involved initiates proceeding through a predetermined set of experiences and that existed over a millennia ago. At the end of the mysteries, the initiates were said to emerge "changed" in some fundamental way. In our modern life, we have very few remnants of such mysteries. Baptism, confirmation, and modern weddings are the last vestiges of such ancient rituals.

The human animal, however, has not changed much over the last millennia, if we are to believe scientists. So, although our surroundings have changed, our need to experience raw emotion in a ritualized context free from any true threat of violence remains the same. Mr. Fowles exploited this desire to great effect in *The Magus*. So perhaps we should not wonder at the sight of ordinary people on television traipsing through a series of tests and professing to have been permanently altered as they emerge on the other side.

19. In line 4 ("Where is . . . cry"), the author uses an example of

(A) irony
(B) rhetorical questioning
(C) cynicism
(D) metaphor
(E) analysis

20. In line 9, the author mentions the Beatles in order to

(A) question the usefulness of reality television
(B) convince readers that television should primarily be used for elevating people's aesthetic tastes
(C) praise a great touch point of twentieth-century popular culture
(D) suggest that not all art is created equal
(E) provide an example for a mass cultural moment in which the entire public was able to share

GO ON TO THE NEXT PAGE

SECTION 4

21. The author refers to the fact that "Americans are democratic by nature" in lines 14–15 to suggest

(A) a reason for the popularity of reality television
(B) a reason for the success of television in the modern home
(C) that not all people have equal opportunity to appear on reality television shows
(D) that the use modern media as a source of education is not best for children
(E) that television is not available in countries ruled by dictatorship

22. In lines 31–43, the author discusses the book *The Magus,* by John Fowles, as

(A) an example of the superiority of fiction over television
(B) a fictionalized representation of the drama that also takes place in a reality show
(C) a successful attempt to merge ancient ritual with the modern condition
(D) a characterization of a self-absorbed young man named Nico
(E) the extreme to which modern writers have had to go to maintain their audience

23. The reference to the ancient Greek mysteries in line 49 serves to reinforce the point that

(A) modern day fiction writers like John Fowles must turn to the past to write masterpieces
(B) there are no ghosts in real life, although we may enjoy them in works of fiction
(C) humans have always had a desire to process their emotional and spiritual growth through set, ritualized conditions
(D) the historical roots of drama
(E) ancient Greeks were able to function as a society without television for entertainment

24. The word "exploited" as it is used in line 60 most nearly means

(A) brow-beaten
(B) misappropriated
(C) embarrassed
(D) used
(E) teased

S T O P

IF YOU FINISH BEFORE TIME IS CALLED, YOU MAY CHECK YOUR WORK ON THIS TEST ONLY.
DO NOT TURN TO ANY OTHER SECTION IN THIS TEST.

SECTION 5

Turn to Section 5 of your answer sheet to answer the questions in this section.

Time—25 Minutes
18 Questions

Directions: For this section, solve each problem and decide which is the best of the choices given. Fill in the corresponding oval on the answer sheet. You may use any available space for scratchwork.

Notes:

1. The use of a calculator is permitted. All numbers used are real numbers.
2. Figures that accompany problems in this test are intended to provide information useful in solving the problems. They are drawn as accurately as possible EXCEPT when it is stated in a specific problem that the figure is not drawn to scale. All figures lie in a plane unless otherwise indicated.
3. Unless otherwise specified, the domain of any function f is assumed to be the set of all real numbers x for which $f(x)$ is a real number.

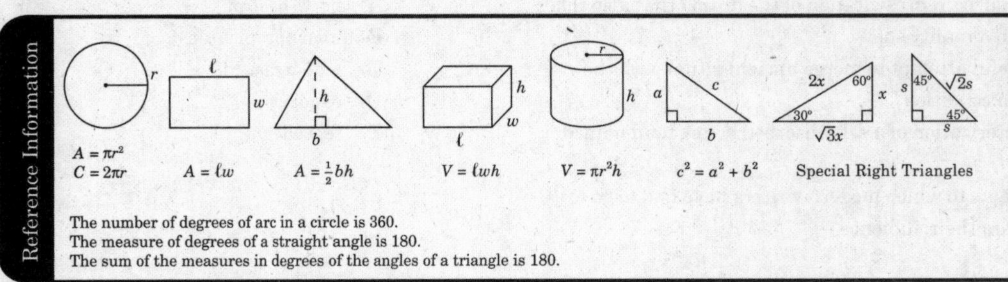
Reference Information
$A = \pi r^2$
$C = 2\pi r$
$A = \ell w$
$A = \frac{1}{2}bh$
$V = \ell wh$
$V = \pi r^2 h$
$c^2 = a^2 + b^2$
Special Right Triangles
The number of degrees of arc in a circle is 360.
The measure of degrees of a straight angle is 180.
The sum of the measures in degrees of the angles of a triangle is 180.

1. If $2y + \frac{1}{y} = 6 + \frac{1}{3}$, then y can equal which of the following?

(A) 1
(B) 2
(C) 3
(D) 4
(E) 6

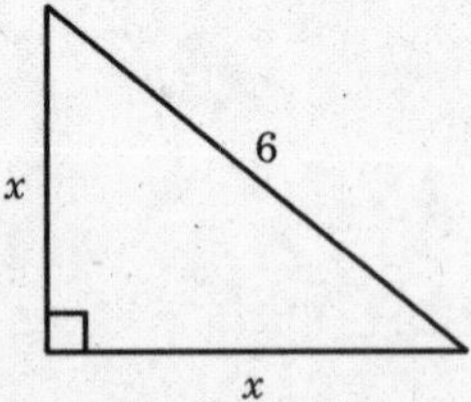
6
x
x

2. In the right triangle above, what is the value of x ?

(A) 36
(B) 18
(C) $6\sqrt{2}$
(D) $3\sqrt{2}$
(E) $2\sqrt{2}$

3. Which of the following is the smallest prime number?

(A) –2
(B) –1
(C) 0
(D) 1
(E) 2

GO ON TO THE NEXT PAGE

SECTION 5

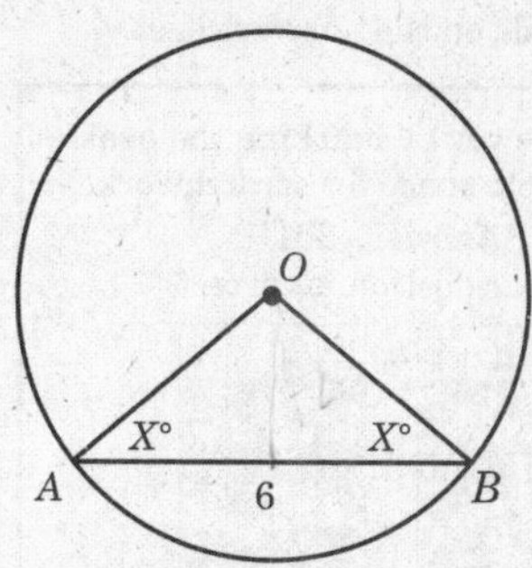

4. In the figure above, triangle AOB is inscribed in a circle with the center O, where base AB of the triangle measures 6. If the area of the triangle is 12, what is the perimeter of the circle?

(A) 25π
(B) 10π
(C) 6π
(D) 5π
(E) 4π

5. Two six-sided die, each with sides numbered 1 through 6, are thrown. Out of the distinct possible number combinations, if the resulting digits are multiplied together, what is the probability that the resulting number will be larger than 15 ?

(A) $\frac{1}{6}$

(B) $\frac{1}{9}$

(C) $\frac{1}{3}$

(D) $\frac{1}{4}$

(E) $\frac{1}{2}$

a	b
4	11
5	14
6	17
7	c

6. If the table above shows a relationship in which a is directly proportional to b, which of the following could be the value of c ?

(A) 18
(B) 19
(C) 20
(D) 21
(E) 22

7. Sara's cellphone plan costs n cents per minute for the first 100 minutes. After that, calls drop to 2 cents less a minute. In terms of n, how much money in dollars will Sara have to pay if she uses her cell phone for 300 minutes?

(A) $100n + 200(n - 2)$
(B) $3n - 4$
(C) $\frac{3n-4}{100}$
(D) $300n - 400$
(E) $\frac{4n}{100}$

8. In the following equation

$$\frac{(a)(b)}{(b)(c)} = -\frac{3}{2}$$

which of the following could be the value of a ?

(A) 2
(B) 1
(C) 0
(D) –5
(E) –6

GO ON TO THE NEXT PAGE

SECTION 5

Directions: For Student-Produced Response questions 9–18, use the grids on the answer sheet.

Each of these questions requires you to solve the problem and enter your answer by marking the ovals in the special grid, as shown in the examples below. You may use any available space for scratchwork.

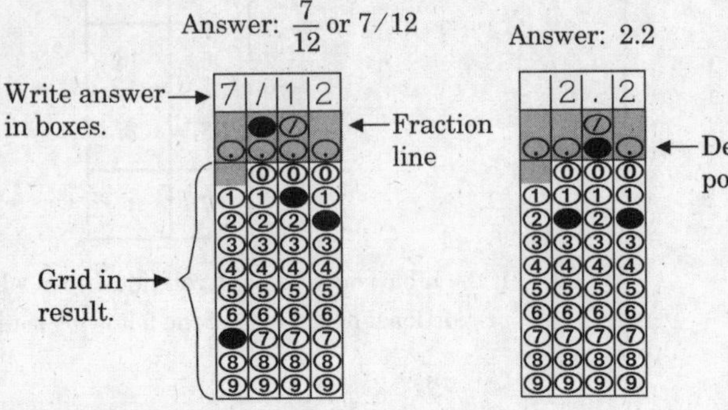

Note: You may start your answers in any column, space permitting. Columns not needed should be left blank.

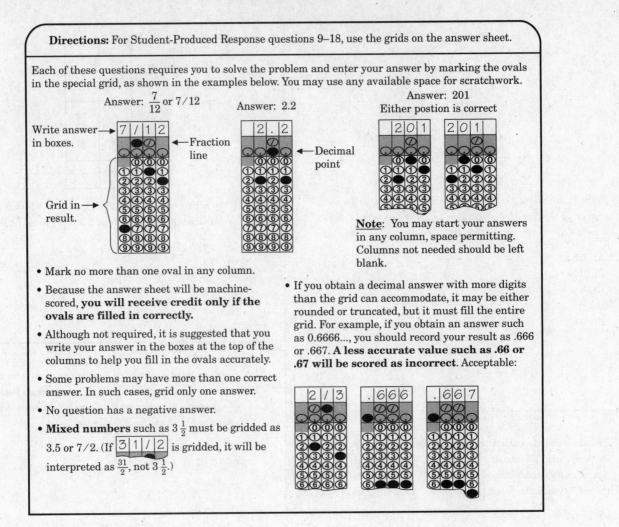

- Mark no more than one oval in any column.
- Because the answer sheet will be machine-scored, **you will receive credit only if the ovals are filled in correctly.**
- Although not required, it is suggested that you write your answer in the boxes at the top of the columns to help you fill in the ovals accurately.
- Some problems may have more than one correct answer. In such cases, grid only one answer.
- No question has a negative answer.
- **Mixed numbers** such as $3\frac{1}{2}$ must be gridded as 3.5 or 7/2. (If 3 1 / 2 is gridded, it will be interpreted as $\frac{31}{2}$, not $3\frac{1}{2}$.)
- If you obtain a decimal answer with more digits than the grid can accommodate, it may be either rounded or truncated, but it must fill the entire grid. For example, if you obtain an answer such as 0.6666..., you should record your result as .666 or .667. **A less accurate value such as .66 or .67 will be scored as incorrect**. Acceptable:

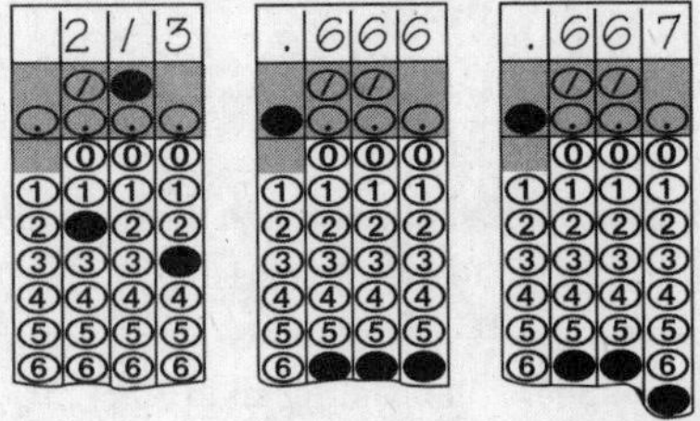

9. If $3m = 19 - n$ and $2m + 5n = 30$, then what is the value of m ?

10. A TV show ran its pilot and charged companies $1,500 per commercial spot. After the third episode, the TV show had become so popular that it raised its rates by 30 percent. How much did companies have to spend per commercial spot for the fourth episode?

GO ON TO THE NEXT PAGE

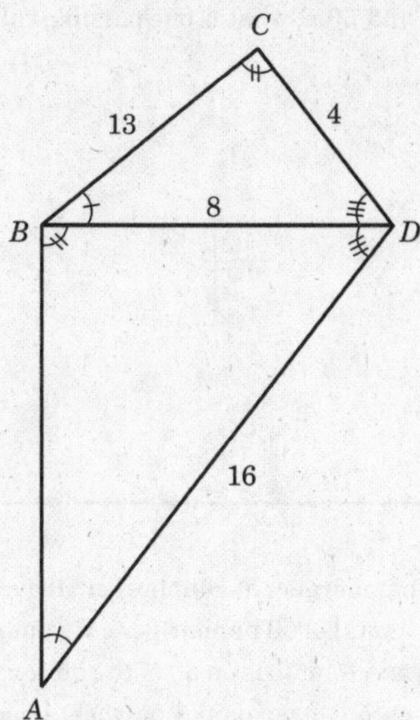

Note: Figure not drawn to scale.

11. In the figure above, what is the value of side AB ?

12. The sum of seven consecutive positive integers equals 1,505. What is the second smallest of these integers?

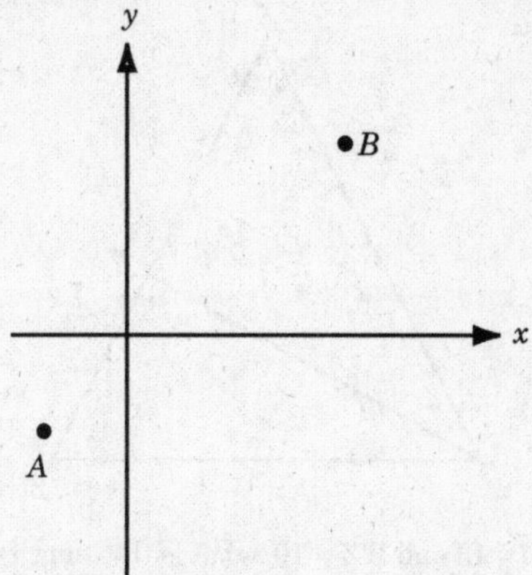

13. In the figure above, what is the distance between points A (–2, –1) and B (4, 5) ?

14. Five curios are to be arranged on a shelf that has exactly 5 display spots. How many different ways are there to arrange the curios?

GO ON TO THE NEXT PAGE

SECTION 5

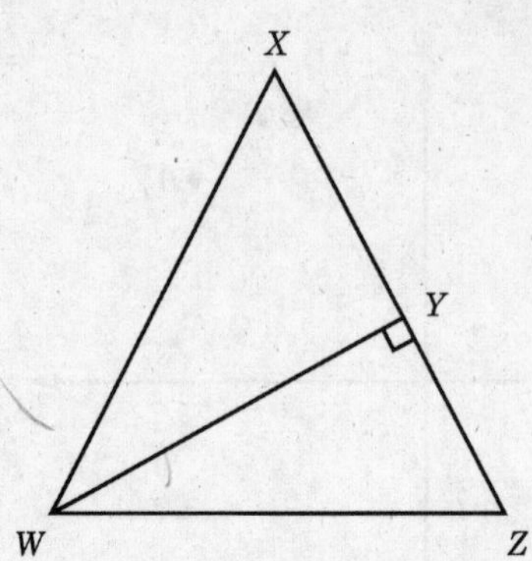

15. If $WX = XZ = 13$ and $WZ = 10$, what is the length of WY?

16. For all nonzero numbers c and k, $c*k$ is defined as $c*k = (c^2 + kx + 3) \div ck$. What is the value of x for $2*-1$ if $2*-1 = 1$?

17. The diameter of a circle is an integer. If the area of the circle is between 30π and 50π, what is one possible value of the radius?

18. Jonah makes hamburgers at Hamburger Heaven. At lunchtime, he assembled a total of 50 hamburgers. He put onions on 24 of those burgers and tomatoes on 30 of the burgers. If 22 had both onions and tomatoes, how many sandwiches had neither onions nor tomatoes?

S T O P

IF YOU FINISH BEFORE TIME IS CALLED, YOU MAY CHECK YOUR WORK ON THIS TEST ONLY.
DO NOT TURN TO ANY OTHER SECTION IN THIS TEST.

SECTION 6

Turn to Section 6 of your answer sheet to answer the questions in this section.

Time—25 Minutes
35 Questions

Directions: For each question in this section, select the best answer from among the choices given.

The following sentences test correctness and effectiveness of expression. Part of each sentence or the entire sentence is underlined; beneath each sentence are five ways of phrasing the underlined material. Choice A repeats the original phrasing; the other four choices are different. If you think the original phrasing produces a better sentence than any of the alternatives, select choice A; if not, select one of the other choices.

In making your selection, follow the requirements of standard written English; that is, pay attention to grammar, choice of words, sentence construction, and punctuation. Your selection should result in the most effective sentence—clear and precise, without awkwardness or ambiguity.

Example:

In the poem "Ulysses" by Alfred, Lord Tennyson, the speaker says, "I cannot rest from travel," instead, he will live life to the fullest.

(A) "I cannot rest from travel," instead,
(B) "I cannot rest from travel"; instead,
(C) "I cannot rest from travel" instead,
(D) "I cannot rest from travel," upon which
(E) "I cannot rest from travel,"

1. The cat was about to be fed, this was when it was starting to meow loudly to demand attention.

(A) this was when it was starting
(B) when it was then starting
(C) when it started
(D) and then it was starting
(E) by then it had started

2. Revving his engine and sliding around on the ice, the attempt to get out of the snowbank by Jordan alerted us to come help dig him out.

(A) the attempt to get out of the snowbank by Jordan alerted us to come help dig him out
(B) the alerting of Jordan that he was in a snowbank made us come to help dig him out
(C) we were alerted to come help Jordan get out of the snowbank
(D) Jordan's alerting us to attempt to get him out of the snowbank and we came to dig him out
(E) Jordan attempted to get out of the snowbank, alerting us to come help dig him out

3. Joseph, Jerome, and Moe were all stunned to see each other at the writer's conference, especially because he had not been to such a meeting in many years.

(A) he had not been to such a meeting in many years
(B) it had been many years since he had been to such a meeting
(C) it had been years since such a meeting had been attended by him
(D) Jerome had not been to such a meeting in many years
(E) Jerome had for many years not attended such a meeting as this one

GO ON TO THE NEXT PAGE

SECTION 6

4. By hanging the abstract painting upside down, the children of the heiress revealed their ignorance of the painting's true value, this was how the art dealer was able to buy the priceless painting for a bargain.

(A) this was how the art dealer was able to buy the priceless painting for a bargain
(B) and this was how the art dealer was able to buy the priceless painting for a bargain
(C) this being how the art dealer, for a bargain, was able to buy the priceless painting
(D) the painting was bought for a bargain by the priceless art dealer
(E) a bargain was paid for by the art dealer who bought the painting instead of paying a price

5. In learning to cook, it is important not only to master basic techniques, but you really have to learn the basic properties of each ingredient.

(A) but you really have to learn
(B) then again you must learn
(C) but also to learn
(D) it is also important to learn
(E) you must not forget to learn

6. Traveling to foreign countries, in addition to being stimulating to the imagination and to the senses, also inspires travelers to question aspects of personal character or culture that are taken for granted at home.

(A) also inspires travelers to question aspects of personal character or culture that are taken for granted at home
(B) is also inspiring to travelers for questioning aspects of personal character or culture that are taken for granted at home
(C) but also, for questioning aspects of personal character or culture taken for granted at home, is also inspiring
(D) it is also inspiring for travelers to question aspects of personal character or culture that are taken for granted at home
(E) it can also inspire travelers to question aspects of personal character or culture that are taken for granted at home

7. The punch-card method of voting on a ballot most ensures that they cannot cheat you of your vote.

(A) ensures that they cannot cheat you of your vote
(B) ensures that you will not be cheated of your vote
(C) likely will be the one method that will ensure they cannot cheat you of your vote
(D) often ensures that you won't be cheated of your vote
(E) easily will ensure that you, compared to other voters, will not be cheated out of your own vote

8. Although purists disagree, it is difficult to conclusively decide that sushi made in Japan is always better than American efforts to be creative with the same ingredients.

(A) better than American efforts to be creative with the same ingredients
(B) better than those ingredients assembled in America
(C) better than efforts at being creative with American ingredients
(D) better than sushi made in America
(E) better than those American efforts at being creative with ingredients

9. The term *fierce* in dance applying to dancers able to express themselves in a visceral manner that moves an audience.

(A) applying to dancers able to express themselves in a visceral manner that moves an audience
(B) applies to dancers able to express themselves in a visceral manner that moves an audience
(C) is applying to dancers able to express themselves in a visceral manner that moves an audience
(D) is for dances who are applying dance in a visceral manner that expresses the movement of an audience
(E) in applying to dancers able to express themselves in a visceral manner that moves an audience

10. The medical properties of coffee are well documented, Indians used it to give them extra courage and strength before battle.

(A) , Indians used it to give them extra courage and strength before battle
(B) , used as it was by Indians for extra courage and strength before battle
(C) ; Indians used it to give them extra courage and strength before battle
(D) which was used by Indians to give them extra courage and strength before battle
(E) for the Indians using it to give them extra courage and strength before battle

11. Forgetting that it had been defrosted, Jennifer went about preparing an entirely new meal for dinner.

(A) Forgetting that it had been defrosted,
(B) Forgetting that she had defrosted it,
(C) Forgetting that she had defrosted the meatloaf,
(D) Because she was forgetting to defrost the meatloaf,
(E) Because she had forgotten to defrost it,

GO ON TO THE NEXT PAGE

SECTION 6

Directions: For each question in this section, select the best answer from among the choices given.

The following sentences test your ability to recognize grammar and usage errors. Each sentence contains either a single error or no error at all. No sentence contains more than one error. The error, if there is one, is underlined and lettered. If the sentence contains an error, select the one underlined part that must be changed to make the sentence correct. If the sentence is correct, select choice E. In choosing answers, follow the requirements of standard written English.

Example:

The other (A) delegates and him (B) immediately (C) accepted the resolution drafted by (D) the neutral states. No error (E)

12. Accomplished New York chef Daniel Bouley regularly (A) visits (B) small, ethnic restaurants and (C) serve unusual dishes whose basic (D) flavors and seasonings he can copy. No error (E)

13. The couple, by studying the plot lines that (A) generated the highest sales, were (B) able to craft (C) an unusual romance novel that sold for (D) a six-figure price. No error (E)

14. The fleet (A) of yachts, after undergoing a series of retro fittings, was (B) able to become (C) the faster (D) team in the relay race. No error (E)

15. After considering (A) the ramifications of a lengthy trial, the parties on both (B) sides agreed to (C) a settlement to spare themselves (D) any more discomfort. No error (E)

16. It (A) is often said nothing can prepare one for parenthood, and (B) this is really true when you (C) consider that (D) being a parent is a singular experience. No error (E)

17. The better (A) way to eat a burger is (B) with your hands instead of using (C) a knife and fork or (D) a spoon. No error (E)

18. Failing (A) to find work on Broadway, the young choreographer supported (B) himself (C) by choreographing music videos, cabaret shows, and he also did some opera dance sequences (D). No error (E)

19. Japanese prints, the (A) development of paint in tubes, and (B) the Industrial Revolution are all forces which has (C) contributed to (D) the Impressionist painting movement. No error (E)

20. Because she was so tired, Charlene laid (A) down for a nap and immediately went (B) into (C) a deep restful (D) sleep. No error (E)

21. If there is one thing that we will learn (A) in the 1990s about (B) basking in the sun, it is that the sun's (C) rays can cause irreversible (D) damage leading to cancer. No error (E)

22. The critic, interviewed on a reputable TV program, posited (A) the idea that (B) attending graduate school may make young writers run the risk (C) of becoming an unimaginative drone (D). No error (E)

23. The journalist was certain that the government's declaration of the crisis in the African countries were planned (A) to deflect criticism from (B) other unpopular (C) government (D) policies. No error (E)

24. Workers at the popular zoo were shocked when the usually docile (A) lion attacked the visiting celebrity in a manner that (B) can only (C) be described as ferociously (D). No error (E)

GO ON TO THE NEXT PAGE

SECTION 6

25. After deciding to send garbage trucks to pick up trash after midnight, city officials <u>grudgingly</u> (A) admitted their plan a failure when residents <u>unanimously</u> (B) complained of <u>excessive</u> (C) noise and repeatedly interrupted <u>nights</u> (D) of sleep. <u>No error</u> (E)

26. The Japanese diet has long been noted for its <u>association with</u> (A) longevity <u>but only lately</u> (B) <u>has</u> (C) scientific studies shown specifically why the many dishes are <u>so</u> (D) salubrious. <u>No error</u> (E)

27. Using the myths of numerous cultures to support his claim, scholar Joseph Campbell <u>posited</u> (A) the idea that <u>there is</u> (B) a universal <u>approach to</u> (C) storytelling <u>across</u> (D) all cultures. <u>No error</u> (E)

28. Aware of the need to finish her speech on time, the actress <u>hurriedly</u> (A) thanked her family and friends for their <u>support with</u> (B) her during the many years she <u>worked for</u> (C) little <u>or</u> (D) no recognition. <u>No error</u> (E)

29. <u>Comparing to</u> (A) other writers of the same age and the same <u>amount of</u> (B) critical acclaim, the author <u>received</u> (C) <u>a substantially</u> (D) larger advance. <u>No error</u> (E)

GO ON TO THE NEXT PAGE

SECTION 6

Directions: The following passage is an early draft of an essay. Some parts of the passage need to be rewritten.

Read the passage and select the best answers for the questions that follow. Some questions are about particular sentences or parts of sentences and ask you to improve sentence structure or word choice. Other questions ask you to consider organization and development. In choosing answers, follow the requirements of standard written English.

Questions 30–35 are based on the following passage.

(1) *Many people wonder how they can effect positive change in their government why so much seems to be out of their control.* **(2)** *Oftentimes the decisions made in Washington seem very far away from the effects of ordinary people.* **(3)** *There is also a lot of cynicism in society.* **(4)** *Sometimes it can seem like the only intelligent thing to do in a world where there is so much unfairness is to just assume the worst.* **(5)** *But I don't subscribe to this attitude.* **(6)** *I believe that there are ways we can make good changes happen in government.*

(7) *The Jersey girls are one such inspiring example.* **(8)** *They are four widows who lost their husbands in September 11, 2001.* **(9)** *The women banded together and went repeatedly to Washington, D.C., to petition for changes to be made to our nation's security.* **(10)** *The media gave them a lot of coverage because they admired the changes they were trying to make.* **(11)** *So it was the women and the media together that got the proposed changes lots of attention.* **(12)** *Under pressure, government officials were forced to release previous classified information.* **(13)** *They also made a lot of changes to the structure of government.*

(14) *The Jersey girls are inspiring to me because they really show how four ordinary people can take on government.* **(15)** *We would never forget that government is by the people for the people.* **(16)** *Change is difficult, but it is not impossible.*

30. In context, which of the following revisions is necessary in sentence 1 (reproduced below)?

Many people wonder how they can effect positive change in their government why so much seems to be out of their control.

(A) Replace "why" with "when".
(B) Delete "many".
(C) Replace "their" with "them".
(D) Insert "are" before "wonder".
(E) Delete "so".

31. What should be done with sentence 2 (reproduced below)?

Oftentimes the decisions made in Washington seem very far away from the effects of ordinary people.

(A) (As it is now)
(B) Insert the word "do" after "people".
(C) Delete the word "very".
(D) Change the word "effects" to "lives".
(E) Insert the words "that are" before "made".

32. Which of the following is best to add before sentence 7 (reproduced below)?

The Jersey girls are one such inspiring example.

(A) (As it is now)
(B) You can rarely find any good news in the newspaper.
(C) If we search the newspaper, we can find examples of ordinary people doing amazing things to inspire us.
(D) It is difficult to count on ordinary citizens to accomplish anything extraordinary in life.
(E) Where does it say that we should stay cynical throughout our entire lives?

33. Which of the following is the best version of sentence 10 (reproduced below)?

The media gave them a lot of coverage because they admired the changes they were trying to make.

(A) (As it is now)
(B) In admiring the women, they consequently gave the Jersey girls a lot of coverage for the changes.
(C) The media admired the changes the women, who were trying to make changes and consequently much coverage was given to them.
(D) There was the media admiring and giving coverage to the women making the changes.
(E) The media admired the changes the women were trying to make and consequently gave the Jersey girls a lot of coverage.

GO ON TO THE NEXT PAGE

SECTION 6

34. What should be done with sentence 11 (reproduced below)?

So it was the women and the media together that got the proposed changes lots of attention.

(A) (As it is now)
(B) Delete the entire sentence.
(C) Replace the word "women" with "them".
(D) Delete the word "that".
(E) Add the words "and lots" after "lots".

35. In context, which of the following most logically replaces "would" in sentence 15 (reproduced below)?

We would never forget that government is by the people for the people.

(A) Should
(B) Will
(C) Won't
(D) Wouldn't
(E) Shouldn't

S T O P

IF YOU FINISH BEFORE TIME IS CALLED, YOU MAY CHECK YOUR WORK ON THIS TEST ONLY. DO NOT TURN TO ANY OTHER SECTION IN THIS TEST.

SECTION 7

Turn to Section 7 of your answer sheet to answer the questions in this section.

Time—20 Minutes
19 Questions

Directions: For each question in this section, select the best answer from among the choices given and fill in the corresponding oval on the answer sheet.

Each sentence below has one or two blanks, each blank indicating that something has been omitted. Beneath the sentence are five words or sets of words labeled A through E. Choose the word or set of words that, when inserted in the sentence, best fits the meaning of the sentence as a whole.

Example:

Eliza felt ----- when her boss asked her to work seven weekends in a row but ----- when her work earned her a promotion.

(A) enervated . . weakened
(B) depressed . . intellectual
(C) advantageous . . salacious
(D) angry . . shopworn
(E) irate . . elated   

1. Scientific discoveries like rubber and penicillin are often considered examples of ----- because scientists discovered them by accident.

(A) serendipity
(B) plenitude
(C) efficiency
(D) emergency
(E) alacrity

2. The development of the internet ----- many people to act as their own travel agents and to ----- the rewards of competing low fares.

(A) prompted . . suffer
(B) allowed . . elaborate
(C) maneuvered . . enjoy
(D) enabled . . reap
(E) dispelled . . fix

3. Even though Louis Armstrong and Duke Ellington both participated in the development of jazz, their styles were very ----- and their contributions -----.

(A) distinct . . similar
(B) unrelated . . alike
(C) individual . . noncompeting
(D) metaphoric . . akin
(E) opposite . . . analogous

4. While the high school class prayed in the hospital chapel, convinced that their wishes could will their ailing classmate to health, doctors were less -----.

(A) pellucid
(B) abashed
(C) insufferable
(D) munificent
(E) sanguine

5. Some find the actor's antics to be charming, whereas others, far from finding him eccentric, consider his comments and behavior a(n) -----.

(A) discursive
(B) effrontery
(C) approbation
(D) inebriation
(E) paragon

6. The youth was skeptical of his parents' repeated attendance at costly social functions whose sole purpose was purported to be fundraising for charities, for, in other areas of their family life, his parents were quite -----.

(A) legislative
(B) penurious
(C) imperious
(D) salacious
(E) inchoate

GO ON TO THE NEXT PAGE

SECTION 7

Directions: The passage below is followed by questions based on its content. Answer the questions on the basis of what is stated or implied in the passage and in any introductory material that may be provided.

Questions 7–19 are based on the following passage.

The following is a fictional account written by a young author. The setting is on a Native American reservation in the Southwest.

When Jim arrived to our *hogan* in his pickup truck, we proceeded slowly to the front door, perhaps a few minutes slower than Jim would expect. It was not in our nature to hurry. Greeting the white man had not usually yielded an exchange that any of us had enjoyed. Sometimes, as was the case a couple of years ago when a movie producer showed up and asked us how we would like to portray actual Indians in a movie about a guy shell-shocked from the Civil War and who is transplanted to a fort out west, we had had moments of excitement. But the moments rarely lasted. We did have fun for the few months that we played Indians, however. Since none of the producers spoke Hopi, we were free to substitute a few slang words into our dialogue, and I've never had as much fun as the time I and the tribe watched the movie together for the first time and saw my father, who had a small starring role, refer to the Civil War hero as a "ground squirrel." The producers never did know why we were laughing so much! But back to the story about Jim.

My first impression of him was of a man who looked lost. His eyes were glassy, and a little vacant, but not like those people who seem who think they have gone all deep and meaningful because they join an alternative religion or think they can invoke our ancestors. His eyes were empty of the kind of sureness that anchors most white men to their world. I thought to myself when I saw Jim, "Here is the loneliest man in the world." And just as quickly I put the thought out of my mind because I had already made up my mind not to like him, and if I felt any sympathy toward him, I might find myself down the path to empathy.

The older men in the tribe were not as closed minded as I. They knew Jim from many years ago they said. They greeted him in an alarmingly friendly way, and I locked eyes with not a few of the men my age who were immediately worried about this fraternization. It might be up to us, we said to one another with glances, to protect the tribe from the invasion of more white men. We who had grown up on the res knew how troublesome it could be to have too many white people show up, treating us as though we were objects in a museum, our way of life, our sadness, our humiliation on display for a photograph. How, I wondered to myself, could my own father be so friendly with Jim out there on the dusty street, when, just a few days ago when my father had been herding cattle across a dirt road, he had come across a camper full of Japanese tourists who had immediately started snapping pictures of him as he sat on his horse, bandana across his mouth? "I put my hand up like this," my father had said to us as he had told the story, his palm flexed flat against my eyes. "That's all the picture they got."

My father called me over to meet Jim.

"This is my oldest," my father said proudly. "I call him Tino."

"Pleased to meet you," Jim said.

I nodded.

Jim tilted his head back and his eyes scanned the sky. While he was craning his head up like this, we all had a good look at him, at the *bolo* around his neck, the worn jeans, the cracked cowboy boots. Only later did I realize that he had looked to the sky at that moment precisely because he knew we needed to look at him. I, and the other young guys, had all made the mistake of thinking that he merely wanted to indulge himself and drink in our clear sky.

"I hear you been practicing the hoop dance," he said to me.

"He's pretty good," my father said smiling, and I hated the way that he seemed to be trying so hard to be ingratiating, as though Jim's approval was something I should be proud to have.

"It was your grandfather who taught the hoop dances to me," Jim drawled slowly. "Maybe that's why you're drawn to it. Heck of a dancer, your granddad."

I swallowed and looked at my father, who looked back at me with a twinkle in his eye that only a family member like me could detect. I became annoyed, realizing that my father was enjoying my discomfort. I shrugged. "I watched a few videotapes. That's all," I said.

"Jim took those videotapes," my father said to me. "Back in the thirties."

Jim said traced a semicircle in the dirt with his toe and did a few steps. I watched this lonely, strange outcast of a man suddenly turn into a lithe eagle, then limp as though he had hurt his wing, and then turn again as though the wound had mended. "Out of practice a little," he said sheepishly. Sweat had started to accumulate in his armpits and I thought to myself that I should get Jim some water. "Anyway, shouldn't do some sacred dance like this out in the parking lot."

"We'll go to the *kiva*," my father said. When he saw me vacillating, my father spoke to me in Hopi. His words were sharp, though outwardly his face was calm and his eyes smiling. "This man is the only man now who can teach us how to dance. Our own people were foolish, forgetting our ways. You're the one who has always said you wanted to learn to dance."

I swallowed my pride and followed the men to the *kiva*.

res—reservation

bolo—a Southwestern tie piece made of silver and leather and fastened around the neck

hogan—a Native American dwelling

kiva—a ceremonial house

GO ON TO THE NEXT PAGE

SECTION 7

7. Lines 16–17 ("The producers . . . Jim") serve what purpose in the overall story?

(A) They emphasize the author's feeling of alienation.
(B) They highlight the tragedy of the author's life.
(C) They provide biographical information about Jim.
(D) They are an example of irony.
(E) They are a momentary digression.

8. The narrator feels that he and Jim are different in that

(A) the former enjoys the company of strangers and the latter is uncomfortable around them
(B) the former is an accomplished dancer whereas the latter struggles with the steps
(C) the former is close to his father whereas the latter is not
(D) the former is a part of his community and the latter seems not to truly fit in anywhere
(E) the former enjoys performing in films whereas the latter eschews popular culture

9. The narrator and the other young men his age are similar in that they

(A) are suspicious of Jim's motives
(B) enjoy the clear sky of the reservation
(C) rarely venture off the reservation
(D) tire of the stories their ancestors have told them
(E) are tired of the dry earth and hot sun

10. The word "fraternization" in line 32 most nearly means

(A) sharing
(B) amusement
(C) friendliness
(D) impoverishment
(E) enmity

11. In paragraph 3, the words "humiliation on display" serve to highlight which of the following?

(A) The amusement with which the narrator views tourists
(B) The strong suspicion that the narrator and others feel toward any white man
(C) The tenacity the narrator and his father have in the face of adversity
(D) The resignation the narrator feels toward Jim's arrival
(E) The enjoyment that the narrator feels in posing for photographs

12. Lines 37–43 ("How, I . . . mouth") indicate that the narrator's father feels toward Jim

(A) an irrepressible rejoicing
(B) a neutral coolness
(C) a general amusement
(D) an unusual acceptance and openness
(E) a deep-seated suspicion

13. In lines 53–56 ("Only . . . sky"), the narrator suggests that Jim is

(A) envious of the beauty of the reservation
(B) fully aware of the discomfort he has unwittingly provoked
(C) unable to afford better clothing
(D) uncomfortable around the narrator
(E) covetous of the videotapes that the narrator has been watching

14. In lines 71–77 ("Jim . . . water") the author's attitude switches from

(A) deep suspicion to subtle concern
(B) unfettered curiosity to deep intrigue
(C) quiet impassiveness to resignation
(D) cheerful acceptance to euphoria
(E) weariness to complete exhaustion

15. The author implies that his father has a "twinkle" in line 65 because

(A) the father is emotional over Jim's presence at the *hogan*
(B) the father is overcome by the heat
(C) the father is disturbed by his son's behavior
(D) the father is amused by his son's surprise
(E) the father wishes he could learn the hoop dances too

16. In lines 72–74 ("I . . . had mended") the author characterizes Jim's actions using which of the following literary techniques?

(A) Simile
(B) Metaphor
(C) Anthropomorphism
(D) Irony
(E) Poetic license

GO ON TO THE NEXT PAGE

SECTION 7

17. In lines 79–84 ("'We'll . . . dance'"), it is implied that the author's attitude toward the Jim has shifted from

(A) pity to empathy
(B) fear to bravery
(C) concern to ire
(D) happiness to exaltation
(E) uncertainty to openness

18. In line 80, the word "vacillating" most nearly means

(A) tilting
(B) questioning
(C) hesitating
(D) smoothing
(E) smiling

19. It is strongly implied that which of the following will happen next in the story?

(A) Jim will leave the reservation, not wishing to disturb the tribe.
(B) Jim will collapse in the heat.
(C) Jim will notice an eagle in the sky.
(D) Jim will teach the narrator how to dance.
(E) Jim will be required to change his shoes.

S T O P

IF YOU FINISH BEFORE TIME IS CALLED, YOU MAY CHECK YOUR WORK ON THIS TEST ONLY. DO NOT TURN TO ANY OTHER SECTION IN THIS TEST.

SECTION 8

Turn to Section 8 of your answer sheet to answer the questions in this section.

Time—20 Minutes
16 Questions

Directions: For this section, solve each problem and decide which is the best of the choices given. Fill in the corresponding oval on the answer sheet. You may use any available space for scratchwork.

Notes:

1. The use of a calculator is permitted. All numbers used are real numbers.
2. Figures that accompany problems in this test are intended to provide information useful in solving the problems. They are drawn as accurately as possible EXCEPT when it is stated in a specific problem that the figure is not drawn to scale. All figures lie in a plane unless otherwise indicated.
3. Unless otherwise specified, the domain of any function f is assumed to be the set of all real numbers x for which $f(x)$ is a real number.

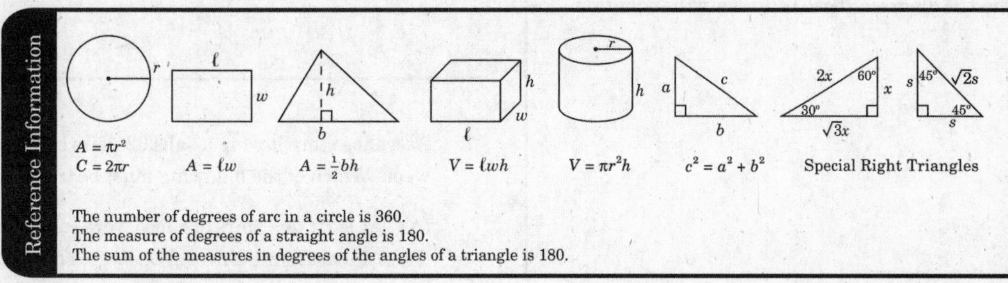

Reference Information
$A = \pi r^2$
$C = 2\pi r$
$A = \ell w$
$A = \frac{1}{2}bh$
$V = \ell wh$
$V = \pi r^2 h$
$c^2 = a^2 + b^2$
Special Right Triangles
The number of degrees of arc in a circle is 360.
The measure of degrees of a straight angle is 180.
The sum of the measures in degrees of the angles of a triangle is 180.

1. If $3b = 18$ and $ab = 2$, then what is the value of a ?

(A) 12

(B) 6

(C) 3

(D) $\frac{1}{3}$

(E) $\frac{1}{4}$

2. A unicycle wheel covers 2.5 feet each time it makes a complete revolution. At this rate, how many revolutions will it take for the wheel to cover 7 feet?

(A) 1

(B) 2

(C) $2\frac{1}{5}$

(D) $2\frac{1}{2}$

(E) $2\frac{4}{5}$

3. If $\frac{3n}{m} = \frac{1}{3}$, what is the value of $\frac{n}{m}$?

(A) $\frac{1}{9}$

(B) $\frac{1}{3}$

(C) 1

(D) 3

(E) 9

GO ON TO THE NEXT PAGE

SECTION 8

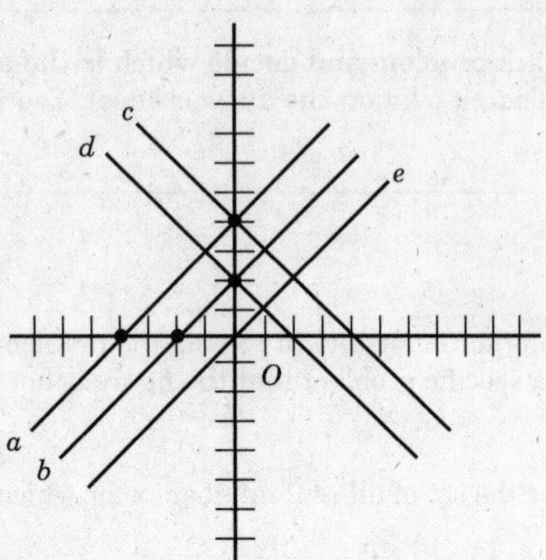

4. Which of the lines in the diagram above represents the equation $y = x + 2$?

(A) Line a
(B) Line b
(C) Line c
(D) Line d
(E) Line e

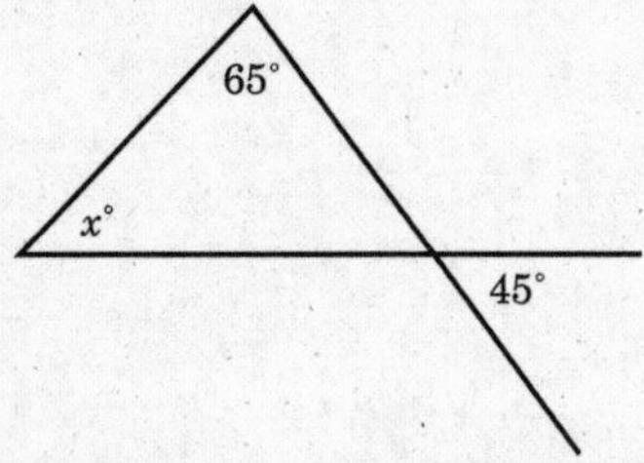

5. In the figure above, what is the value of x?

(A) 45
(B) 60
(C) 70
(D) 80
(E) 85

6. Jennifer is building a quilt by nestling progressively larger pieces around a central square. The length of each piece of the quilt is twice the size of the piece before it. For example, if a piece of quilt is 12 inches, this means that the piece before it must be 6 inches. If the most recent piece she put on the quilt was 18 inches in length, what was the length of the piece 4 pieces before?

(A) 1.125
(B) 2.25
(C) 4.5
(D) 9
(E) 12

7. At a shoe store having a sale, 32 pairs of shoes were sold in a week. Which of the following must be true?

(A) At least five pairs of shoes were sold on one day.
(B) At least four pairs of shoes were sold on Monday.
(C) At least three pairs of shoes were sold on each day.
(D) At least one pair of shoes was sold on each day.
(E) At least two pairs of shoes were sold on each day.

8. If points X and Y have the coordinates (–10, –4) and (6, 10) respectively, which are the coordinates for the midpoint of XY?

(A) (–4, 6)
(B) (4, 6)
(C) (–4, –6)
(D) (2, 3)
(E) (–2, 3)

GO ON TO THE NEXT PAGE

SECTION 8

9. If $a^2 + b^2 = 250$, and $ab = 117$, then what is the value of $(a + b)^2$?

(A) 81
(B) 117
(C) 169
(D) 484
(E) 637

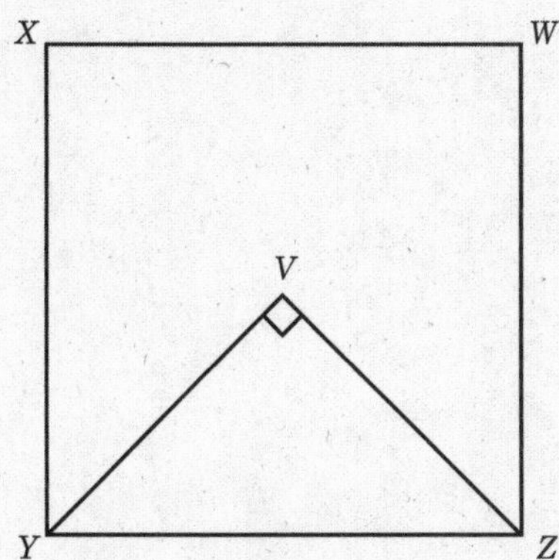

Note: Figure not drawn to scale.

10. In the figure above, triangle VYZ is a right triangle with legs of length 3 and 7. What is the area of square $WXYZ$?

(A) 58
(B) $4\sqrt{58}$
(C) $\sqrt{58}$
(D) $4\sqrt{21}$
(E) 21

11. If 20 percent of 60 percent of a certain positive number is equivalent to 120 percent of y percent of the same positive number, what is the value of y ?

(A) 1
(B) 10
(C) 20
(D) 60
(E) 120

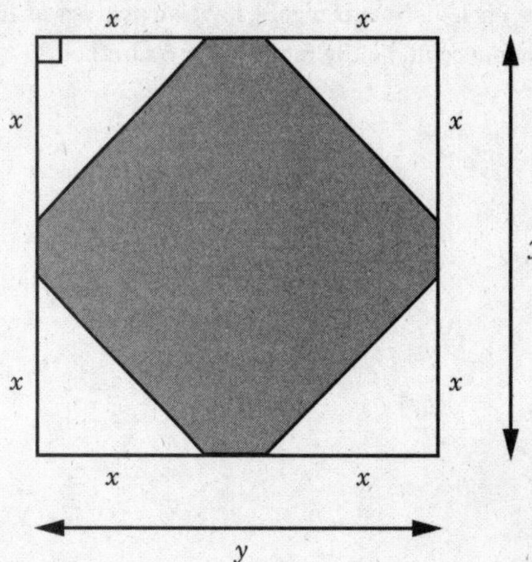

12. What is the area of the shaded region above?

(A) $4y^2 - 4x^2$
(B) $2y^2 - x^2$
(C) $2x^2$
(D) $y^2 - 4x^2$
(E) $y^2 - 2x^2$

13. If $-3 < x < 7$ and $-5 < y < 5$, which of the following best describes the range of possible values for $x - y$?

(A) $-2 < x - y < 12$
(B) $-2 < x - y < 2$
(C) $-8 < x - y < 12$
(D) $2 < x - y < 12$
(E) $-12 < x - y < 8$

GO ON TO THE NEXT PAGE

SECTION 8

14. The average of 5 numbers is 3 larger than its mode. Three of the numbers, each distinct integers, have an average of 10. Which of the following could be the mode of the 5 numbers?

(A) 3
(B) 5
(C) 11
(D) 16
(E) 30

15. If $(x+4)^{\frac{1}{2}} = (x+4)^{-\frac{1}{2}}$, then what is the value of x?

(A) 4, –4
(B) –4
(C) 4
(D) 3
(E) –3

16. For how many different positive integer values of d does $(dx-4)^2 = 0$ have integer solutions?

(A) 0
(B) 1
(C) 2
(D) 3
(E) 4

S T O P

IF YOU FINISH BEFORE TIME IS CALLED, YOU MAY CHECK YOUR WORK ON THIS TEST ONLY.
DO NOT TURN TO ANY OTHER SECTION IN THIS TEST.

SECTION 9

Turn to Section 9 of your answer sheet to answer the questions in this section.

Time—10 Minutes
14 Questions

Directions: For each question in this section, select the best answer from among the choices given.

The following sentences test correctness and effectiveness of expression. Part of each sentence or the entire sentence is underlined; beneath each sentence are five ways of phrasing the underlined material. Choice A repeats the original phrasing; the other four choices are different. If you think the original phrasing produces a better sentence than any of the alternatives, select choice A; if not, select one of the other choices.

In making your selection, follow the requirements of standard written English; that is, pay attention to grammar, choice of words, sentence construction, and punctuation. Your selection should result in the most effective sentence—clear and precise, without awkwardness or ambiguity.

Example:

In the poem "Ulysses" by Alfred, Lord Tennyson, the speaker says, "I cannot rest from travel," instead, he will live life to the fullest.

(A) "I cannot rest from travel," instead,
(B) "I cannot rest from travel"; instead,
(C) "I cannot rest from travel" instead,
(D) "I cannot rest from travel," upon which
(E) "I cannot rest from travel,"

1. A number of the childhood possessions of former First Lady Jacqueline Kennedy Onassis, including her books and toys, selling off at auction.

(A) selling off at auction
(B) will be sold off at auction
(C) are selling off at auction
(D) are being selling off at auction
(E) to be sold off at auction

2. As pet owners, cats should only receive food that contains essential nutrients, and not chemical byproducts.

(A) As pet owners, cats should only receive food
(B) As pet owners, cats should only be receiving food
(C) As pet owners, receiving food, cats should only be fed food
(D) As pet owners, food should only be served to
(E) As pet owners, people should only feed cats food

3. Compiling a list of excellent twenty-first-century fiction stacked books by her night stand so the critic could easily refer to plot lines for her list.

(A) stacked books by her night stand so the critic could easily refer to plot lines for her list
(B) stacking by her night stand so the critic could easily refer to plot lines for her list
(C) the critic stacked books by her night stand so she could easily refer to plot lines for her list
(D) the books, stacked by her night stand for the critic who was compiling her list of plotlines
(E) the books are stacked by the critic on the night stand compiling her list

4. Storm watchers are people who are motivating out of a desire to see a tornado in action whipping across the prairie.

(A) who are motivating out of a desire
(B) who are motivated out of a desire
(C) motivating out of a desire
(D) with a motivating desire for
(E) out of a desire to motivate

GO ON TO THE NEXT PAGE

SECTION 9

5. The career of writer John Steinbeck is multifaceted, beginning with his early works that focus on the plight of ordinary people and culminating in pieces suffused with a nostalgia for prewar days.

(A) culminating in pieces suffused with a nostalgia for prewar days
(B) which are culminating in pieces suffused with a nostalgia for prewar days
(C) culminating and suffusing pieces with a nostalgia for prewar days
(D) that have culminated in pieces suffused with a nostalgia for prewar days
(E) where there is a culmination in pieces suffused with a nostalgia for prewar days

6. We could not make our travel plans to see the great Greek ruins in Libya until the travel sanctions are lifting.

(A) until the travel sanctions are lifting
(B) until the travel sanctions were lifting
(C) until the travel sanctions lift
(D) until the travel sanctions had lifted
(E) until the travel sanctions lifted

7. To ensure that small children will successfully mature to adulthood, it is the doctor and the parents who will make certain that the youngsters receive the necessary vaccinations.

(A) it is the doctor and the parents who will
(B) doctors and parents must
(C) doctors and the parents are
(D) the doctor and the parents who will
(E) the doctor and the parents are both the ones

8. A private shipping company is the fastest, most efficient, and reliable way to send a prized package, but using the post office will be the cheaper method.

(A) will be the cheaper method
(B) would be the cheaper method
(C) is the cheapest method
(D) would be the cheap method
(E) is the cheap method

9. Jade is one of the toughest substances known to humankind—on a scale of 1 to 10, with 10 being a diamond, jade measures a 7.

(A) on a scale of 1 to 10, with 10 being a diamond, jade measures a 7
(B) on a scale of 1 to a diamond at 10, jade is measuring a 7
(C) measuring on a scale of 1 to 10, with 10 being a diamond, jade measures a 7
(D) there is, on a scale of 1 to 10, with 10 being a diamond, jade measures a 7
(E) jade measures a 7 on a scale of 1 to 10, with 10 being a diamond, and that is how it measures

10. Known for their salubrious qualities, people concerned with healthy eating like to get a good dose of berries for their antioxidants.

(A) people concerned with healthy eating like to get a good dose of berries for their antioxidants
(B) concerning healthy eating, people like to get a good dose of berries for their antioxidants
(C) berries being consumed by people concerned with healthy eating and antioxidants
(D) berries are consumed by people who like to get a good dose of antioxidants
(E) berries are for people concerned with healthy eating and getting a good dose of antioxidants

11. Plans for the new shopping center indicates that there will be a surplus of parking for even the heaviest shopping days.

(A) indicates that there
(B) indicate that there
(C) are indicating that there
(D) is indicated that there
(E) will indicate that there

GO ON TO THE NEXT PAGE

12. No one knows where Chelsy got her talent for painting, but from an early age she had an aptitude at drawing figures and convincing portraits.

(A) an aptitude at drawing figures and convincing portraits
(B) an aptitude in drawing figures and convincing portraits
(C) an aptitude at drawing figures and convinced portraits
(D) an aptitude against drawing figures and convincing portraits
(E) an aptitude for drawing figures and convincing portraits

13. Standing in line at the grocery store, Justin always takes a sneak peak at the tabloids, he just can't help but be curious about the gossip.

(A) Standing in line at the grocery store, Justin always takes a sneak peak at the tabloids, he just can't help but be curious about the gossip.
(B) Standing in line at the grocery store, Justin always takes a sneak peak at the tabloids, somehow he just can't help but be curious about the gossip.
(C) Standing in line at the grocery store, Justin always takes a sneak peak at the tabloids, can't help but be curious about the gossip.
(D) Standing in line at the grocery store, Justin always takes a sneak peak at the tabloids; he just can't help but be curious about the gossip.
(E) Standing in line at the grocery store, Justin always takes a sneak peak at the tabloids, he just is not helping but be curious about the gossip.

14. Even though the coastline sits on a tectonic plate and is always subject to violent earthquakes, warnings for tsunami and other earthquake-related dangers are posted at every beach.

(A) Even though the coastline sits on a tectonic plate and is always subject to violent earthquakes, warnings for tsunami and other earthquake-related dangers are posted at every beach.
(B) Therefore the coastline sitting on a tectonic plate and is always subject to violent earthquakes, warnings for tsunami and other earthquake-related dangers are posted at every beach.
(C) Because the coastline sits on a tectonic plate and is always subject to violent earthquakes, warnings for tsunami and other earthquake-related dangers are posted at every beach.
(D) Instead of the coastline sits on a tectonic plate and is always subject to violent earthquakes, warnings for tsunami and other earthquake-related dangers are posted at every beach.
(E) Inasmuch as the coastline sits on a tectonic plate and is always subject to violent earthquakes, warnings for tsunami and other earthquake-related dangers are posted at every beach.

S T O P

IF YOU FINISH BEFORE TIME IS CALLED, YOU MAY CHECK YOUR WORK ON THIS TEST ONLY.
DO NOT TURN TO ANY OTHER SECTION IN THIS TEST.

PRACTICE TEST 2

EXPLANATIONS

PRACTICE TEST 2 ANSWERS

Question Number	Answer	Right	Wrong
Section 2			
1	A		
2	B		
3	E		
4	C		
5	B		
6	D		
7	A		
8	D		
9	E		
10	B		
11	D		
12	C		
13	A		
14	A		
15	E		
16	B		
17	D		
18	D		
19	C		
20	E		
21	B		
22	A		
23	D		
24	A		
Section 3			
1	D		
2	A		
3	E		
4	D		
5	C		
6	D		
7	B		
8	E		
9	C		
10	D		
11	E		
12	A		
13	C		
14	C		
15	D		
16	E		
17	C		
18	A		
19	C		
20	C		
Section 4			
1	A		
2	E		
3	C		
4	D		
5	D		
6	B		
7	A		
Section 4, continued			
8	A		
9	E		
10	C		
11	B		
12	D		
13	A		
14	A		
15	B		
16	B		
17	C		
18	D		
19	B		
20	E		
21	A		
22	B		
23	C		
24	D		
Section 5			
1	C		
2	D		
3	E		
4	B		
5	C		
6	C		
7	B		
8	E		
9	5		
10	1950		
11	26		
12	213		
13	8.49		
14	120		
15	9.23		
16	9		
17	6, 7		
18	18		
Section 6			
1	C		
2	E		
3	D		
4	B		
5	C		
6	A		
7	B		
8	D		
9	B		
10	C		
11	C		
12	C		
13	B		
14	D		
15	E		
16	C		

Question Number	Answer	Right	Wrong	Question Number	Answer	Right	Wrong
Section 6, continued				**Section 7, continued**			
17	A			17	E		
18	D			18	C		
19	C			19	D		
20	A			**Section 8**			
21	A			1	D		
22	D			2	E		
23	A			3	A		
24	D			4	B		
25	E			5	C		
26	C			6	A		
27	E			7	A		
28	B			8	E		
29	A			9	D		
30	A			10	A		
31	D			11	B		
32	C			12	E		
33	E			13	C		
34	B			14	B		
35	A			15	E		
Section 7				16	D		
1	A			**Section 9**			
2	D			1	B		
3	C			2	E		
4	E			3	C		
5	B			4	B		
6	B			5	A		
7	E			6	D		
8	D			7	B		
9	A			8	C		
10	C			9	A		
11	B			10	D		
12	D			11	B		
13	B			12	E		
14	A			13	D		
15	D			14	C		
16	B						

CALCULATING YOUR SCORE

Writing Section Raw Score

A. Essay Score (from 1–6) ______ A

B. Section 6 Multiple Choice: ______ no. correct − (______ no. incorrect ÷ 4) = ______ B

C. Section 9 Multiple Choice: ______ no. correct − (______ no. incorrect ÷ 4) = ______ C

D. Unrounded Multiple-Choice Score (B + C) ______ D

E. Total Rounded Multiple-Choice Raw Score
(Rounded to the nearest whole number) ______ E

F. Writing Multiple-Choice Subscore
(See the Writing Multiple-Choice conversion table on the following pages) ______ Writing MC Score

G. Total Scaled Score
(See the Writing conversion table on the following pages) ______ SAT Writing Score

Math Section Raw Score

A. Section 3 Raw Score: ______ no. correct − (______ no. incorrect ÷ 4) = ______ Subtotal A

B. Section 5 Raw Score: ______ no. correct ______ Subtotal B

C. Section 8 Raw Score: ______ no. correct − (______ no. incorrect ÷ 4) = ______ Subtotal C

D. Total Unrounded Raw Score
(Total A + B + C) ______ D

E. Total Rounded Raw Score (Rounded to the nearest whole number) ______ E

F. Scaled Score
(See the conversion table on the following pages) ______ SAT Math Score

Critical Reading Section Raw Score

A. Section 2 Raw Score: ______ (no. correct) – (______ (no. incorrect) ÷ 4) = ______ A

B. Section 4 Raw Score: ______ (no. correct) – (______ (no. incorrect) ÷ 4) = ______ B

C. Section 7 Raw Score: ______ (no. correct) – (______ (no. incorrect) ÷ 4) = ______ C

D. Total Unrounded Raw Score
(Total A + B + C)

______ D

E. Total Rounded Raw Score
(Rounded to the nearest whole number)

______ E

F. Scaled Score
(See the conversion table on the next page)

______ SAT Critical Reading Score

CONVERTING YOUR RAW SCORES

Raw Score	Critical Reading Scaled Score	Math Scaled Score
67	800	
66	790	
65	770	
64	760	
63	750	
62	740	
61	720	
60	710	
59	700	
58	690	
57	680	
56	670	
55	670	
54	660	800
53	650	780
52	640	760
51	640	740
50	630	730
49	620	710
48	610	700
47	610	690
46	600	670
45	590	660
44	590	650
43	580	650
42	580	640
41	570	630
40	560	620
39	560	610
38	550	600
37	540	590
36	540	590
35	530	580
34	530	570
33	520	560
32	510	560
31	510	550
30	500	540
29	500	530
28	490	520
27	480	520
26	480	510
25	470	500
24	470	490
23	460	490
22	450	480
21	450	470
20	440	460
19	430	460

Raw Score	Critical Reading Scaled Score	Math Scaled Score
18	430	450
17	420	440
16	410	430
15	410	430
14	400	420
13	390	410
12	380	400
11	380	390
10	370	380
9	360	380
8	350	370
7	340	360
6	330	340
5	320	330
4	310	320
3	300	310
2	280	290
1	270	280
0	250	260
–1	250	250
–2	240	240
–3	230	230
–4	220	220
–5	210	210
–6	200	200

Writing Subscores

- **Essay Subscore:** Subtotal A from Writing Score (page 178)
- **Multiple-Choice Subscore:** Calculate by plugging in Subtotal E from your writing score (page 178) into the score conversion table below

Raw Score	Multiple-Choice Subscore
49	80
48	79
47	77
46	76
45	75
44	74
43	72
42	71
41	70
40	69
39	68
38	67
37	66
36	65
35	64
34	63
33	62
32	61
31	60

Raw Score	Multiple-Choice Subscore
30	59
29	58
28	57
27	56
26	55
25	54
24	53
23	52
22	51
21	51
20	50
19	49
18	48
17	47
16	46
15	45
14	44
13	43
12	42

Raw Score	Multiple-Choice Subscore	Raw Score	Multiple-Choice Subscore
11	41	2	32
10	40	1	30
9	39	0	29
8	38	–1	27
7	37	–2	25
6	36	–3	24
5	35	–4	23
4	34	–5	22
3	33	–6	21

Writing Scaled Score

MC raw score	Essay Score					
	6	5	4	3	2	1
49	800	790	780	770	720	700
48	790	780	760	730	700	680
47	780	770	750	720	690	670
46	770	760	740	710	680	660
45	770	750	740	700	670	650
44	760	750	730	690	660	640
43	750	740	710	680	650	630
42	750	730	700	670	640	620
41	740	730	690	660	630	610
40	740	720	690	650	620	600
39	740	710	680	640	610	590
38	730	700	670	630	610	590
37	720	690	660	630	600	580
36	710	680	650	620	590	570
35	710	680	640	610	580	560
34	700	670	640	600	570	550
33	690	660	630	590	560	540
32	680	650	620	580	560	540
31	670	640	610	580	550	530
30	660	630	600	570	540	520
29	650	630	590	560	530	510
28	640	620	590	550	520	510
27	640	610	580	540	510	490
26	630	600	570	530	500	490
25	620	590	560	520	500	480
24	610	580	550	510	490	470
23	600	570	540	510	480	460
22	590	570	530	500	470	450
21	590	570	530	500	470	450
20	580	560	520	490	460	440
19	570	550	520	480	450	430
18	570	540	520	470	440	420
17	560	530	510	460	430	420
16	550	520	500	450	430	410
15	540	510	490	450	420	400
14	530	500	480	440	410	390
13	520	500	470	430	400	380
12	510	490	460	420	390	370

Writing Scaled Score

MC raw score	Essay Score 6	5	4	3	2	1
11	510	480	450	410	380	360
10	500	470	450	400	370	350
9	490	460	440	390	360	350
8	480	450	430	390	360	340
7	470	440	420	380	350	330
6	460	430	410	370	340	320
5	450	430	400	360	330	310
4	450	420	390	350	320	300
3	440	410	390	340	310	290
2	430	400	380	330	300	280
1	420	380	370	320	290	270
0	400	370	350	310	280	260
−1	380	360	340	290	270	260
−2	370	340	320	270	260	250
−3	360	330	310	260	250	240
−4	350	320	290	250	240	230
−5	340	310	280	240	230	220
−6	340	310	280	240	220	210

SECTION 2: CRITICAL READING

Sentence Completions

1. **A** One-Word/One-Way *Easy*

Art Tatum is able to hear the difference between *a penny and a dime*. In other words, his hearing is really "good" or maybe really "precise." The word *acute*, **A**, means "precise." Watch out for *erratic*, **B**, which means "uneven."

2. **B** One-Word/One-Way *Easy*

Jade is a strong substance that the *Chinese believed* could help *keep their physical bodies intact*. In other words, the Chinese believed that *jade* had the ability to "give" or *bestow*, **B**, *immortality*. The word *retract*, **E**, means the opposite of bestow, "to take from."

3. **E** Two-Word/One-Way *Easy*

The word *modest* tells you that Jane should have shown a "small" bit of respect for her boss. Cross out **B**, **C**, and **D**. Now, if she had shown the "small" amount or *modicum* of respect, she might have been able to "keep," or *retain*, her position in the company.

4. **C** Two-Word/One-Way *Medium*

The word *however* tells you that there is a contrast in the way Uncle Percy behaved as a young man versus how he behaved as an old man. *Obstreperous* and *charming*, **C**, is the best answer here. *Gregarious* and *parsimonious*, **E**, are positive and negative words, respectively. However, they don't really contrast each other. *Gregarious* means "friendly and outgoing," and *parsimonious* means "stingy."

5. **B** One-Word/One-Way *Medium*

The novel contains *hyped-up sentimentality*. In other words, even though it did *sensitively* treat its subject matter, it also seemed "overly emotional," or *mawkish*, **B**. *Desiccated*, **D**, means "dried out."

6. **D** Two-Word/Two-Way *Medium*

The negative campaign ads have the ability to *sway voters*. So, even though people "don't like" or "decry" the negative ads, they are "effective." Eliminate **B**, **C**, and **E**. Also, the negative ads have the ability to *win* more votes for the more "aggressive" or *belligerent* candidate.

7. **A** Two-Word/Two-Way *Difficult*

The word describing the *ballerina* must agree with the word *vulnerable*. Eliminate **B**, **C**, and **E**. The second blank must agree with the word *strength*. The answer must be **A**. Watch out for *opprobrious*, **E**, which means "stubborn."

8. **D** One-Word/Two-Way *Difficult*

The new work of fiction must be *new* and *unusual*. In other words, it cannot be "boring and predictable." Only **D**, *hackneyed*, matches this prediction. *Fecund*, **C**, means "fertile." *Florid*, **B**, means "with a flourish and great ornamentation."

Short Reading Passages

9. **E** Implied Information *Easy*

The passage states that eccentrics do not suffer from stress, because *they do not bend to the social pressures to conform*. **E** best restates this idea. **A** contains information never discussed in the passage. Watch out for **B**, which directly contradicts the author's point of view.

10. **B** Specific Information *Medium*

You are looking for the only answer choice that contains information not stated in the passage. The only answer choice that fits is **B**. In fact, the author states that eccentrics in general don't crave material goods.

11. **D** Specific Information *Easy*

You are told that a *ziggurat is tier-shaped, like the layers of a wedding cake, with a base that is circular, rectangular, or square*. On the other hand, a pyramid tends to have a *square base*. **C** and **E** contain information not stated in the passage.

12. **C** Implied Information *Easy*

Try answering this question by crossing off the answer choices that are wrong one at a time. Nowhere does the author state that ziggurats became tombs, so eliminate **A**. We are not told anything about how the Egyptians learned to build ziggurats, **B**, or a drought, **D**. The author also does not discuss how the Sumerians learned about gods, **E**.

Paired Reading Passages

13. **A** Themes and Arguments *Medium*

Look at the lines surrounding those referenced in the question: *In fact, it is a capacity for language that makes human beings unique. It is simply, in Chomsky's words, what we are "good at." While other animals demonstrate a capacity for flying, with an innate understanding of shifting winds and changing angles, humans are able to master increasingly complex levels of language to express a seemingly endlessly complex series of thoughts.* In other words, to paraphrase Chomsky, language is what "we are good at," or a talent which humans uniquely possess, **A**. **B** is directly opposite Chomsky's point of view.

14. **A** Words in Context *Easy*

Look at the sentence in which the word *embedded* appears: *One of Chomsky's main ideas included that of "universal grammar," the idea that there is an embedded structure of language within the brain.* In other words, Chomksy believes that there is a "set" *structure of language* in the brain. The best definition is the word *fixed*, **A**. Watch out for *rigged*, **B**, which implies that someone has modified the brain, and *buried*, **C**, which implies that the language structure is hiding beneath something.

15. **E** Specific Information *Medium*

The whole point of the second paragraph is that the brain contains a predetermined mechanism for acquiring language. The author then goes on to give several examples of why this is true, including the fact that deaf children, once exposed to language, are able to acquire it. **A** and **B** contain information directly contradicted in the passage. Watch out for **D**, which is stated in the passage but does not have anything to do with this particular paragraph.

16. **B** Specific Information *Difficult*

B should stand out to you because it is directly contradicted in the passage: the author goes to great length to state that animals cannot learn language. All the other answer choices are evidence for why there is a language instinct, as argued by the passage.

17. **D** Specific Information *Difficult*

Look at the lines surrounding the discussion of the computer: *Clearly, when we learn words, we do not just learn a definition but something of the function of each word, its texture, and its malleability. When thought of this way, language seems like a nearly impossible thing to teach to a computer, and we have not even yet started to discuss the complex rules surrounding grammar acquisition.* In other words, there is much more to learning language than understanding the definition of a word or if it is a noun, adjective, etc. Only **D** restates this idea.

18. **D** Specific Information *Easy*

Look at what the author of Passage 2 says about primates: *We find them fascinating because they resemble us in so many ways, with their human-like faces, their nimble hands, and familiar, familial behavior.* In other words, we can't help but notice that they look and act like us, **D**. **C** does contain information contained in the passage, but it is not a reason why we are fascinated by primates.

19. **C** Words in Context *Medium*

Look at the words surrounding the word *impenetrable*: *The average human can distinguish between such sounds as "pa" and "ba," but such minute differences seem to be impenetrable for other animals. Creative scientists insisted that the chimps were actually saying, "Mama" or "Papa," but, over time, such claims have been dismissed.* The chimps are not able to make the sounds "pa" and "ba." In other words, speech is not something they can imitate, so it is *inimitable*, **C**.

20. **E** Specific Information *Medium*

Take a look at these lines in the last paragraph of Passage 2: *Until there is some kind of agreed upon test that can be administered to check an animal's ability to communicate, and whose results can be duplicated, there will no doubt continue to be those convinced that animals can speak, and those convinced that they cannot.* In other words, we won't know whether animals can really talk until there is a test that everyone agrees on, **E**.

21. **B** Relating Two Passages *Medium*

The author of Passage 1 doesn't believe that animals can really learn to *talk*. He also paraphrases Noam Chomsky, stating that just because humans can learn to ride in a hang glider does not mean that humans can really fly. Conversely, chimps may be able to make some approximation of speech, but they can't really ever learn to talk, making **B** the correct answer. Watch out for **D** and **E**, which express opinions not contained in the passage.

22. **A** Specific Information *Medium*

Take a look at the lines surrounding the idea of the language instinct as discussed by the author of Passage 2: *If we ever were able to find a way to actually communicate with chimps or any other primate, it might dispel the notion once and for all that language is a kind of divine gift bestowed on humans, as encapsulated in such theories as "language instinct" or "deep structure" that are appealing to contemporary scientists, but which eventually raise more questions than they answer. To really understand language, scientists must strive to decode the manner in which it is acquired and teach other animals or computers to communicate in the same way. Believing that language is a mystical gift seems to be sloppy science.* Clearly, the author of Passage 2 does not have a very high opinion of the concept of the language instinct. You need to find an answer choice that expresses a negative point of view—**A**.

23. **D** Relating Two Passages *Medium*

The only thing that the two authors really agree on is that thus far chimps have not learned to speak. The author of Passage 1 would definitely not agree with **A**. In fact, he believes the opposite. The author of Passage 1 would definitely not agree with **B** and **C**. The author of Passage 2, who is not a fan of the concept of the language instinct, would not agree with **E**. Only **D** works.

24. **A** Themes and Arguments *Difficult*

Passage 1 ends with the idea that language must be the unique trait of humans. This idea would be strengthened if there were some scientific proof that language really does belong to humans alone, which is exactly what **A** accomplishes. **B** and **D** don't strengthen the argument at all. In fact, they weaken it.

SECTION 3: MATH

Multiple Choice

1. **D** Algebra: Basic Operations *Easy*

First, solve for y:

$$3y - 7 = 20$$
$$3y = 27$$
$$y = 9$$

Now, solve for the equation you are given:

$$2y + 1 =$$
$$2(9) + 1 = 19$$

2. **A** Numbers & Operations: Factors and Multiples *Easy*

One shelf can hold 45 paperback books, for a total of 315 paperbacks for the 7 shelves. Since 2 paperback books equal 1 hardback, you know that one shelf can hold 22.5 hardback books for a total of 157.5 hardback books. The correct answer will hold some combination of these values. Take the answer choices one by one. In **A**, you are given 285 paperbacks and 15 hardbacks, where 15 hardbacks equal 30 paperbacks. Adding 285 and 30, you have a total of 315 paperbacks—the exact total number of books you need to fill the shelves.

3. **E** Geometry: Triangles *Easy*

The formula for area of a triangle is one-half base times height. Take the areas one at a time:

BEC	.5(5)(6)	=	15
ABE	.5(3)(5)	=	7.5
AED	.5(3)(4)	=	6
DEC	.5(4)(6)	=	12
BDC	.5(9)(6)	=	27

Triangle *BDC*, or **E**, is the answer.

4. **D** Data Analysis, Statistics & Probability: Graphs, Charts, and Tables *Easy*

You are looking for the first year in which Mr. Smith's tomatoes doubled in size. Notice that in 1997 the Smiths had 2 tomatoes, but in 1998 they had 4. This is the first year that the number of tomatoes doubled. Watch out for **B**, because the tomatoes only go from 2 to 3.

5. **C** Data Analysis, Statistics & Probability: Logic *Medium*

If the average of 3 numbers is 22, you know that the sum of the numbers is 66. Now, if the average of 2 of the numbers is also 22, then you know that the sum of 2 of the numbers is 44. Subtracting 44 from 66 leaves you with 22—the third number.

6. **D** Geometry: Polygons *Easy*

The area of the entire square is 36. Now, you need to subtract the area of the two shaded regions. The first one is a square with dimensions 3 and 3 for a total area of 9. The second square has dimensions 1 and 1 for a total area of 1. Now, subtract these two areas from 36:

$$36 - 9 - 1 = 26$$

7. **B** Algebra: Solving Equations *Easy*

You know that *fghi* is negative. This means that at least one of the variables is a negative number. You are then told that *fhij* is equal to 2. Both equations have *fhi* in common. If *fhi* is positive, you know that *g* is negative. However, *fhi* could also be negative, making *g* positive. Eliminate **C** and **D**. Further, you know that *f* cannot equal 0. If it did, the first equation would also equal 0. Eliminate **A**. Now, could *j*? Look at the following:

$$fhij = 2$$
$$j = \frac{2}{fhi}$$

Now, if *fhi* equals 4, then *j* is a fraction. Therefore, *j* does not need to be an integer.

The only thing you do know is that *i* cannot equal 0. If it did, *fghi* would not be negative, and *fhij* would not equal 2.

8. **E** Numbers & Operations: Fractions *Easy*

Out of a 2,500-calorie diet, one-fourth of the calories, or 625 calories, should come from fat. This leaves us with 1,875 calories. One-fifth of the remaining calories should come from meat. Since one-fifth of 1,875 equals 375, we are left with 1,500 calories. Now, one-half of the remaining calories should come from vegetables, and you will be left with only 750 calories to spend, all of which should be spent on fruit. To find what fraction of the original total number of calories should be devoted to fruit, set up the following fraction:

$$\frac{\text{Number of calories for fruit}}{\text{Total number of calories}} = \frac{750}{2,500} = \frac{3}{10}$$

9. **C** Algebra: Absolute Value and Exponents *Medium*

Make the bases of both exponents equal:

$$4^{2x+1} = 8^2$$
$$2^{2(2x+1)} = 2^{2(3)}$$

Now, set the exponents equal to each other:

$$2(2x+1) = 2(3)$$
$$4x + 2 = 6$$
$$4x = 4$$
$$x = 1$$

10. **D** Numbers & Operations: Basic Operations *Medium*

Translate the text into an equation, where *x* stands in for "a certain number."

First, translate 7 less than 2 times a certain number:

$$2x - 7$$

Now, this is equal to 2 less than that number:

$$2x - 7 = x - 2$$
$$2x = x - 2 + 7$$
$$2x = x + 5$$
$$x = 5$$

11. **E** Geometry: Polygons *Medium*

The perimeter of the shaded region will be equal to one-half of the perimeter of the circle, plus one side of the square. One side of the square is equal to the diameter of the circle. If one side of the square is 4, then you know that the entire perimeter of the circle is 4π. Now, you only want one half of the perimeter, or 2π. The perimeter of the shaded region is therefore $4 + 2\pi$.

12. **A** Algebra: Functions *Medium*

You are looking for the answer choice that, when the values from the x column are inputted, yields the value in the $f(x)$ column. Try the answer choices one by one:

$f(x) = x^2 + 2$	$f(0) = 0^2 + 2$	$= 2$
	$f(1) = 1^2 + 2$	$= 3$
	$f(2) = 2^2 + 2$	$= 6$
	$f(3) = 3^2 + 2$	$= 11$
	$f(4) = 4^2 + 2$	$= 18$

All the values fit, therefore **A** must be the correct answer. No other equation will work.

13. **C** Data Analysis, Statistics & Probability: Logic *Medium*

The gifts are given out in a repeating pattern of 6. If Meg is fifty-fifth in line, she will receive the earrings. Meg, however, wants the tiara. She needs to let people go ahead of her so that she becomes the sixtieth person in line. Then, she will receive the tiara.

14. **C** Geometry: Coordinate Geometry *Medium*

The reflection of line a will be its opposite. Only **C** shows this relationship.

15. **D** Data Analysis, Statistics & Probability: Graphs, Charts, and Tables *Medium*

There were 60,000 computers sold in 2000. In 1996, 20,000. This means that 40,000 more computers were sold in 2000 than in 1996. Since 40,000 is 200 times the value of 20,000, the correct answer must be **D**.

16. **E** Geometry: Polygons *Medium*

Take the answer choices one at a time:

A triangle with height 6π and base 6	$(6\pi)(6)(.5)$	$= 18\pi$
A triangle with height 12 and base 3π	$(3\pi)(12)(.5)$	$= 18\pi$
A square with side 6	$(6)(6)$	$= 36$
A rectangle with base 1 and height 36	$(1)(36)$	$= 36$
A rectangle with base 4 and height 9π	$(4)(9\pi)$	$= 36\pi$

17. **C** Algebra: Solving Equations *Medium*

Rewrite the equation, solving for b:

$$3a = \frac{2b+1}{5}$$
$$5(3a) = 2b + 1$$
$$15a = 2b + 1$$
$$15a - 1 = 2b$$
$$\frac{15a - 1}{2} = b$$

18. **A** Geometry: Circles *Difficult*

Angle *MLN* is 45 degrees, $\frac{1}{8}$ of the entire circle. If you knew the circumference of the entire circle, then you could take $\frac{1}{8}$ of this to find the length of the arc. You are told that the area of the sector is 8π. Since the sector is $\frac{1}{8}$ of the entire circle, you know that the area of the entire circle would be 64π. Since the formula for the area of a circle is $A = \pi r^2$, you can find the radius.

$$64\pi = \pi r^2$$
$$64 = r^2$$
$$8 = r$$

Now, find the perimeter:

$$P = 2\pi r$$
$$P = 2\pi 8$$
$$P = 16\pi$$

Now, take $\frac{1}{8}$ of this to find the length of the arc:

$$\frac{16\pi}{8} = 2\pi$$

19. **C** Algebra: Solving Equations *Difficult*

To find the fraction, first determine the total number of grapefruits. If there are r crates of red grapefruit, and there are 150 more yellow grapefruits then red, then you know that there are $r + 150$ yellow grapefruits. The total number of grapefruits is therefore:

$$r + r + 150 = 2r + 150$$

Now, take the number of red grapefruits and place this in the numerator:

$$\frac{r}{2r + 150}$$

20. **C** Numbers & Operations: Logic *Difficult*

You will need to find the values for G and M. Looking at the problem, you know that 7 + E = a two-digit number. In other words, you know that 7 + E must equal at least 10. However, 7 + E must equal a number where both digits are the same. If E is a single digit, the only value that GG could equal is 11. Further, you know that 3 + M = 5. If M is a single digit, it must equal 2.

$$M + G = 2 + 1 = 3$$

SECTION 4: CRITICAL READING

Sentence Completions

1. **A** Two-Word/One-Way *Easy*

The neighborhood has some very good qualities going for it. The sentence even tells you that the neighborhood is one to *follow*. A good prediction for the first blank would be something like "model" or "example." Rule out **B** and **D**. Now, since the neighborhood is so good, you can bet that it has some of the "best" or *finest*, **A**, schools in the city. Only **A** matches both predictions.

2. **E** Two-Word/One-Way *Easy*

Soccer has *failed* to "capture" the attention of the American audience. Eliminate **A** and **C**. Now, how would the failure of soccer to "something" the Americans seem to Europeans, who *are avid enthusiasts*? It would seem like a *mystery*.

3. **C** One-Word/Two-Way *Medium*

Currently, plate tectonics is an accepted truth in science. The word *once* tells you that plate tectonics was originally viewed as the very opposite of the truth: people were very uncertain about it. *Skepticism*, **C**, best fits in the blank. Watch out for **D**. *Veracity* means "truth" and is the opposite of what you are looking for.

4. **D** One-Word/One-Way *Medium*

The community is clearly pretty happy that they are housing a *great white shark*—otherwise they would not *bask* in the media attention. The word that best fits the blank, therefore, is *rejoiced*, **D**.

5. **D** Two-Word/Two-Way *Difficult*

The interviewer is *well rounded*. A good guess for the first blank would therefore be something like "balanced." Eliminate **B**, **C**, and **E**. However, he has to avoid making his *well roundedness* "the center" of a conversation. The answer must be **D**.

Short Reading Passages

6. **B** Themes and Arguments *Medium*

The lines in question contain the following items in the list: *joggers*, *weightlifters*, and *alfalfa sprouts*. These are all the interests of early adopters of the health food craze. You will want to pick the one thing from the list that people interested in health food would have been interested in too. Only **B** offers something that health food nuts would have been interested in doing.

7. **A** Technique *Medium*

Here is the last sentence: *Indeed, what was once seen as a fad has now fully become entrenched as part of our society's general culture.* In other words, something that was disregarded as a fad is now important, which is what **A** states.

8. **A** Themes and Arguments *Difficult*

The passage begins referring to *this ancient tomb*. We can assume that the paragraph before would give more information about the tomb, or at least would introduce it. The passage does not start with a diagram or with illustrations, but with definite text.

9. **E** Themes and Arguments *Medium*

Since the passage refers to economics and to *studying*, we can assume that it is scholarly in nature. The passage is too scholarly to be a mere journal entry, and it clearly attempts to address an audience. It cannot be a pamphlet selling restoration materials as this does not match the scope of the passage.

Long Reading Passages

10. **C** Implied Information *Medium*

The author describes why he became a dealer in the second paragraph. Look at the first sentence: *I began dealing art out of the simplest of motives.* He then goes on to discuss his early years in the art world. He went on a trip, he studied his grandfather's books, etc. In other words, he was just naturally drawn into the art world, because it interested him.

11. **B** Technique *Easy*

Here are the lines in question: *A life of collection, however, does not feed a family. I learned quickly that if I was really going to immerse myself in the world of art every minute of my waking life, I would have to sell some of the pieces I owned in order to feed my habit and pay for such mundane costs as food and a mortgage.* In other words, although it may be wonderful to work with art objects, enjoying them alone will not pay the bills. One must earn money. In other words, an enjoyment of art objects is *idealistic*, but working is *practical*.

12. **D** Words in Context *Easy*

Look at the lines surrounding *ubiquitous*: *In the late seventies, for example, a neolithic stoneware pot from China was quite rare and valuable. Today, these pots are ubiquitous and have lost their value, disproving the old adage that art is a great investment that will only increase with time.* These pots are described as once having been rare, but they are not now. In other words, *ubiquitous* means something like "not rare." *Omnipresent*, which means "present everywhere," is the word that best matches this prediction.

13. **A** Themes and Arguments *Difficult*

The lines in question are as follows: *Since I did not set out to join the world of Asian art because I wanted or even expected to make money through investments, I have found over time that my favorite clients are those who are motivated by the same drive that I am: they simply love good art.* So, on the one hand we have collectors motivated by a desire to buy something expensive, and on the other we have people who are motivated by a love of good art. **A** best restates this difference.

14. **A** Words in Context *Easy*

Look at the sentence containing the word *adage*: *Today, these pots are ubiquitous and have lost their value, disproving the old adage that art is a great investment that will only increase with time.* A good prediction would be a word like "saying," or *proverb*.

15. **B** Themes and Arguments *Medium*

In paragraph 4, the author states that he likes clients who love art the way he does. He then goes on to commend the artists who created the greatest pieces. In other words, he mentions the properties of a good piece of jade to highlight how much he likes it—how he *holds it in esteem*. He is much less concerned with *value* or *sale* prices, **C** and **D**.

16. **B** Implied Information *Easy*

In the lines in question, the author states: *Certainly the artists who created these wonders did so out of a desire to tantalize the eye, and it would do me no good not to appreciate those who can see the splendor of a small piece of art.* The author makes the assumption that the artists who created the jade and other pieces did so in order to create beauty and please the viewer. In other words, the author makes the assumption that he knows why the artist has created his pieces.

17. **C** Specific Information *Easy*

Here are the closing lines of the passage: *But I strongly believe that art is meant to be lived with, not trapped inside the case of a museum, and it does no one any good to purchase something if it does not have the ability to transmit joy on a daily basis. Life can be full of drudgery after all, and everyone needs a quiet spot in a room filled with light or beauty to spruce up the day.* The author is making the point that art makes our lives beautiful. The rest of life can be hard and ugly, but art makes the difficult times more bearable.

18. **D** Main Idea *Medium*

The passage is a memoir in which the author details how he came to be a dealer and what he believes to be the proper way to integrate art into life. He is not discussing modern art, **A**. He barely mentions the illegal art trade, **B**. He is much less concerned with sales than with appreciation, **C**. He is also not interested in the *next wave*, **E**.

19. **B** Technique *Medium*

In these lines we read the following: *"Where is the art?" they cry.* This is a particular kind of question used by essayists and is commonly referred to as a *rhetorical question*, **B**.

20. **E** Themes and Arguments *Easy*

Here are the sentences: *Television, after all, was initially used as a means of entertainment, in which the world could share in its appreciation of a culture's self-expression. For the first time, all people across America could watch the same jokes and punch lines unfold at the same time, or share in the hysteria that surrounded the arrival of the Beatles.* The author is discussing how television made it possible for all Americans to share in one culture. The Beatles are one example of a moment that people were able to share.

21. **A** Themes and Arguments *Medium*
Read the following lines: *In part this must be because, as Americans, we are democratic by nature and believe that anyone should have the right to participate in the grand world of television.* In other words, because Americans believe in democracy, so they want everyone to have the chance to participate in television fame. This conviction helps to explain why reality television is so popular.

22. **B** Specific Information *Medium*
In the third paragraph, the author describes how the ritualized setting of reality shows preexisted, in books. He writes, *In his 1965 book* The Magus, *John Fowles, uses a similar setup to create one of the great works of twentieth-century fiction.* In other words, *The Magus* is an example of a book that creates such a ritualized space.

23. **C** Themes and Arguments *Medium*
Here are the lines about the mysteries: *Mr. Fowles acknowledges that his work was inspired by the Greek mysteries, yearly rituals that involved initiates proceeding through a predetermined set of experiences and that existed over a millennia ago.* The author is pointing out that even further back than Mr. Fowles's book, we have evidence of similarly ritualized entertainment.

24. **D** Words in Context *Medium*
Here are the lines in which the word *exploited* is used: *So, although our surroundings have changed, our need to experience raw emotion in a ritualized context free from any true threat of violence remains the same. Mr. Fowles exploited this desire to great effect in his book* The Magus. In other words, Mr. Fowles used the idea of ritual in his book. Since the book was discussed as a great example of twentieth-century fiction, it doesn't make sense that Mr. Fowles would have *brow-beaten* or *misappropriated* the idea.

SECTION 5: MATH

Multiple Choice

1. **C** Algebra: Solving Equations *Easy*
Solve for *y:*

$$2y + \frac{1}{y} = 6 + \frac{1}{3}$$

You can pretty much tell right away that y must be 3 in order for both sides of the equation to be equal.

2. **D** Geometry: Triangles *Medium*
This is an isosceles triangle. Since it is also a right triangle, you know that the unmarked angles are both 45 degrees. In a 45-45-90 degree triangle, sides are always in the ratio of $x{:}x{:}x\sqrt{2}$. In other words, a leg of such a triangle is the hypotenuse

divided by $\sqrt{2}$. Since we are told that the hypotenuse is 6, you can divide this by $\sqrt{2}$ to find the leg. However, you can't leave the $\sqrt{2}$ in the denominator; you must rationalize:

$$\frac{6}{\sqrt{2}}\left(\frac{\sqrt{2}}{\sqrt{2}}\right)$$

$$\frac{6(\sqrt{2})}{2}$$

$$3\sqrt{2}$$

3. **E** Numbers & Operations: Basic Operations *Easy*

Prime numbers cannot be negative or 0. The integer 1 is not prime either. The smallest prime number is always 2.

4. **B** Geometry: Circles *Medium*

To find the perimeter of the circle, you need its diameter or radius. A look at the problem should tell you that you will need to use the information about the triangle to find the radius. You are told that line segment *AB* is 6 and that the area of the triangle is 12. Further, this is an isosceles triangle, although we don't know the value of angle *O*. You can however, find the height of the triangle:

$$A = \frac{bh}{2}$$
$$A = \frac{6h}{2}$$
$$24 = 6h$$
$$h = 4$$

Now, you can draw the height of the triangle down to the base. The height will bisect the base, forming two smaller triangles, each with a base of 3 and a height of 4. Following the rule of special triangles, you know that the hypotenuse, or lines *BA* and *BC*, measures 5. You now have the radius of the circle.

Now, solve for the perimeter:

$$P = 2\pi r$$
$$P = 2\pi 5$$
$$P = 10\pi$$

5. **C** Data Analysis, Statistics & Probability: Probability *Medium*

To find the probability, you want to take the number of desired outcomes and place this over the number of possible outcomes. Take a look at the following:

1 × 1 = 1	2 × 3 = 6	3 × 6 = 18
1 × 2 = 2	2 × 4 = 8	4 × 4 = 16
1 × 3 = 3	2 × 5 = 10	4 × 5 = 20
1 × 4 = 4	2 × 6 = 12	4 × 6 = 24
1 × 5 = 5	3 × 3 = 9	5 × 5 = 25
1 × 6 = 6	3 × 4 = 12	5 × 6 = 30
2 × 2 = 4	3 × 5 = 15	6 × 6 = 36

There are a total of 21 distinct possible number combinations. Of these, 7 will be higher than 12.

$$\frac{7}{21} = \frac{1}{3}$$

6. **C** Algebra: Functions *Medium*

You will need to figure out the function that turns the values in column a to the values in column b. Essentially, $3a - 1 = b$. Therefore, if a is equal to 7, c will equal the following:

$$3(7) - 1 = 20$$

7. **B** Algebra: Absolute Value and Exponents *Difficult*

For the first 100 minutes, Sara's cellphone plan is n cents per minute. This can be expressed as:

$$100n$$

After that, the cellphone costs 2 cents less per minute. Since Sara is using her phone for a total of 300 minutes, you know that she will spend 200 minutes at this second rate:

$$200(n - 2)$$

Adding this together you have:

$$100n + 200(n - 2)$$

Now, simplify:

$$100n + 200n - 400$$
$$300n - 400$$

One more step. You are asked to find the amount she spends in dollars. The above value is in cents. You must divide the simplified equation by 100:

$$\frac{300n - 400}{100} = 3n - 4$$

8. **E** Numbers & Operations: Ratios *Medium*

The b's in this equation cancel, leaving you with:

$$\frac{a}{c} = \frac{-3}{2}$$

You know that a must be a multiple of 3. The only possible answer is **E**.

Grid-Ins

9. **5** Algebra: System of Equations *Medium*

First, solve for n:

$$3m = 19 - n$$
$$n = 19 - 3m$$

Now, substitute:

$$2m + 5n = 30$$
$$2m + 5(19 - 3m) = 30$$
$$2m + 95 - 15m = 30$$
$$-13m = -65$$
$$m = 5$$

10. **1950** Numbers & Operations: Percents *Easy*

The commercials increased by 30 percent. You need to find 30 percent of $1,500 and add this to $1,500:

$$.3(\$1{,}500) = \$450$$

Now, add this value to $1,500:

$$\$1{,}500 + \$450 = \$1{,}950$$

11. **26** Geometry: Triangles *Medium*

The problem shows you that the triangles *BCD* and *ABD* are similar: their angles and sides are in direct proportion to each other. Side *CD* is opposite angle *B*. Angle *B* is the same as angle *A*. Note that side *CD* is one half of *BD*, so you know that the sides of triangle *BCD* will all be one half the sides of triangle *ABD*. Now, side *AB* is opposite angle *BDA*, which is the same value as angle *BDC*. Since side *BC* is 13, side *AB* must be 26.

12. **213** Numbers & Operations: Basic Operations *Medium*

You need to find seven consecutive integers that add up to 1,505. The easiest way to do this is to divide 1505 by 7 to find the median of the seven integers.

$$1505 \div 7 = 215$$

OK, so now you know that 215 is the fourth number in the series of consecutive integers, so you can easily construct the list of all seven:

212, 213, 214, 215, 216, 217, 218

Remember, you're asked to find the second smallest of these numbers, or 213.

13. **8.49** Geometry: Triangles *Medium*

Turn *AB* into the hypotenuse of a right triangle, with point *C* as the right angle. Using the coordinate information you are given, you know that *AC* measures 6 and *CB* measures 6. You have an isosceles right triangle. In an isosceles right triangle the sides are in a ratio of $x{:}x{:}x\sqrt{2}$. In this case, you know that one leg measures 6, so the hypotenuse must be $6\sqrt{2}$, or 8.49.

14. **120** Data Analysis, Statistics & Probability: Permutations and Combinations *Difficult*

You are asked to find the total number of possibilities, if there are 5 items to be displayed:

$$(5)(4)(3)(2)(1) = 120$$

15. **9.23** Geometry: Triangles *Medium*

Note that *WY* is perpendicular to side *XZ*. In other words, *WY* measures the height of the triangle if you turn the sheet of paper on its side and make *XZ* the base of the triangle. If you *knew* the area of the triangle, you could use this information to solve for *WY*. As it happens, you can *find* the area of the triangle. You know that sides *WX* and *XZ* are equal, so this is an isosceles triangle. If you draw a line down from *X* to base *WZ*, it will bisect triangle *WXZ* into two right angle triangles, each with a base of 5 and a hypotenuse of 13. Use the Pythagorean theorem to find the value of the height:

$$a^2 + b^2 = c^2$$
$$5^2 + b^2 = 13^2$$
$$25 + b^2 = 169$$
$$b^2 = 169 - 25$$
$$b^2 = 144$$
$$b = 12$$

Now, find the area:

$$A = \frac{bh}{2}$$
$$A = \frac{(10)(12)}{2}$$
$$A = 60$$

Now, using this information, solve for *WY*:

$$A = \frac{bh}{2}$$
$$60 = \frac{13(WY)}{2}$$
$$2(60) = 13(WY)$$
$$120 = 13(WY)$$
$$\frac{120}{13} = (WY)$$

16. **9** Algebra: Binomials and Quadratics *Medium*

Plug in the values for *c* and *k*:

$$c * k = (c^2 + kx + 3) \div ck$$
$$2 * (-1) = (2^2 + (-1)x + 3) \div 2(-1)$$
$$2 * (-1) = (4 - x + 3) \div -2$$
$$2 * -1 = \frac{(7 - x)}{-2}$$
$$1 = \frac{(7 - x)}{-2}$$
$$-2 = 7 - x$$
$$-9 = -x$$
$$9 = x$$

17. **6, 7** Geometry: Circles *Difficult*

The diameter of the circle has to be an integer. If the area must be larger than 30π, then the first possible radius for the circle is 6, since the diameter would be 12, an integer, and the area of such a circle would be 36π, which is between 30π and 50π. The only other possibility would be 7, which would yield an area of 49π.

18. **18** Data Analysis, Statistics & Probability: Logic *Difficult*

There are 50 hamburgers total. Twenty-two of these have both onions and tomatoes. However, you are told that there are 24 total burgers with onions. This means that, aside from the 22 just discussed, there are 2 more burgers with onions. So far we have accounted for a total of 24 burgers. However, the problem also states that 30 burgers have tomatoes. Since 22 burgers have onions and tomatoes, we know that there are 8 more burgers with only tomatoes. Adding 8 to 24, we have a total of 32 burgers with either just onions, just tomatoes, or both. This means that there are 18 burgers that have neither.

SECTION 6: WRITING

Improving Sentences

1. **C** Tense *Easy*

The verb phrase *this was when it was starting* does not match the verb phrase in the beginning of the sentence, *was about to be fed*. Also, beginning the second half of the sentence with *this* reads like a run-on sentence. **C** nicely rewrites the sentence so that the whole idea is consistent and in the past tense.

2. **E** Misplaced Modifiers *Easy*

As the sentence reads now, it sounds as though the *attempt* is *revving his engine* and attempting to *get out of the snowbank*. Logically, however, you know that it is Jordan who is struggling. You need to rewrite the sentence so *Jordan* appears right after the comma.

3. **D** Pronouns *Easy*

There are three men going to the conference: *Joseph, Jerome, and Moe*. The pronoun *he* does not agree with this plural number. Worse, the use of *he* does not make it clear exactly who had not been to a meeting in many years. Scanning the answer choices, you should see Jerome's name pop out. Eliminate **A**, **B**, and **C**. **E** is far too wordy, so the correct answer is **D**.

4. **B** Run-On *Medium*

The entire sentence is a run-on. Either one clause needs to be made dependent on the other, or you need to join the two clauses with a conjunction. **B** solves the problem by using the conjunction *and*.

5. **C** Coordination and Subordination *Medium*

The words *not only* are always joined with *but also*, which is missing in this sentence. **C** restores the connection.

6. **A** No Error *Medium*

There is no error here, so the correct answer is **A**.

7. **B** Pronouns *Medium*
This sentence includes the pronoun *they*, which is vague—exactly to whom does *they* refer? **B** makes it clear that *you* are the one who will not be cheated and removes the pronoun *they*.

8. **D** Parallelism *Medium*
Remember, when you compare two things in a sentence, they must be in the same form, and the sentence must make a logical connection. Here, the sentence is comparing *sushi made in Japan* to *American efforts to be creative.* These are not logical comparisons. **D** corrects the comparison.

9. **B** Subject-Verb Agreement *Medium*
The verb *applying* robs the sentence of a clear verb. Every sentence must have a main subject and verb and this sentence does not. **B** correctly fixes the problem, whereas the others confuse the logic of the sentence.

10. **C** Run-On *Medium*
Here we have a run-on sentence, which must be fixed either by combining both clauses with semicolons or by connecting them with a conjunction. **C** puts the semicolon into place.

11. **C** Misplaced Modifiers *Difficult*
The original sentence does not make clear *what* had been defrosted. The correct answer choice will introduce a word that makes clear what *Jennifer* forgot. **C** does this by inserting the word *meatloaf*. However **D** is wrong, because the verb tense *was forgetting* is incorrect.

Identifying Sentence Errors

12. **C** Subject-Verb Agreement *Easy*
Something sounds funny when you read this sentence out loud. The verb *serve* definitely sounds bizarre, but you can't change it because it is not underlined. Further, the sentence doesn't make sense. As it reads now, it sounds as though *Bouley* is the one who serves the dishes, but it should be *the restaurant* that does so. If you replaced *and* with *that,* the sentence would be logically correct.

13. **B** Subject-Verb Agreement *Easy*
Always be suspicious when the subject and verb are separated by a modifying clause. In this case the subject is *couple,* and the verb is *were*. However, *couple* is a collective noun that needs a singular verb—*was*.

14. **D** Faulty Comparison *Easy*
When three or more items are being compared, you need to use the superlative form. However, in this sentence, we have *faster*, which is the comparative form. To be correct, *faster* should be *fastest*.

15. **E** No Error *Easy*

There is no error here. The subjects and verbs all agree, and the pronouns are in the proper case.

16. **C** Pronouns *Medium*

It is incorrect to switch between *one* and *you*; a sentence must use one of these pronouns consistently. Since the sentence contains *one*, and this pronoun is not underlined, the underlined pronoun *you* must be the error.

17. **A** Faulty Comparison *Medium*

When two items are being compared, you may use the comparative form. However, if more than two items are being compared, you need to use the superlative. Here you are comparing the best way to eat a burger: by hand, with a knife and fork, or with a spoon. That's three ways. The word *better*, in this case, should be *best*.

18. **D** Parallelism *Medium*

Items in a list need to be in the same form. Here you have three items: *music videos, cabaret shows, and he also did some opera dance sequences.* The first two items are nouns, but the third item includes a pronoun, *he*. You need to put the third item in the same form as the first two—*opera dance sequences*.

19. **C** Subject-Verb Agreement *Medium*

The subject is a compound subject made up of three things: *Japanese prints, the development of paint in tubes, and the Industrial Revolution.* This plural subject requires a plural verb. However, in this sentence you have the verb phrase *has contributed to*, which implies the singular. To be correct, *has contributed to* would need to read *have contributed to*.

20. **A** Tense *Medium*

The correct verb should be *lay*, not *laid*. The past tense of *lie* is *lay*.

21. **A** Tense *Medium*

The *1990s* are in the past, not the future. Therefore, the verb *will learn* is in the wrong tense. To be correct, the tense should should be *learned*.

22. **D** Subject-Verb Agreement *Medium*

It is the *writers*, which is plural, who may turn *into a drone*. However, *drone* is singular. To be correct, *drone* should be *drones*.

23. **A** Subject-Verb Agreement *Medium*

The subject *declaration* is paired with the verb phrase *were planned*. However, *declaration* is singular, whereas the verb phrase *were planned* is plural. Remember, the subject and verb must agree in number. To be correct, *were planned* must be changed to *was planned*.

24. **D** Adverbs and Adjectives *Medium*

Adverbs modify verbs, while adjectives modify nouns. The *lion attacked the celebrity* in a *manner* that was *ferociously*. In this case, *ferociously* is supposed to modify the noun *manner*. However, *ferociously* is an adverb while *manner* is a noun. To be correct, *ferociously* needs to be changed to its adjective form, which is *ferocious*.

25. **E** No Error *Medium*
There is no error here. All subjects and verbs agree and modifiers are in their correct form.

26. **C** Subject-Verb Agreement *Medium*
Watch out for the following inverted subject and verb: *has scientific studies.* Note that the subject, *scientific studies,* is plural whereas the verb, *has,* is singular. Remember, subject and verb must agree in number. To be correct, the verb *has* needs to be changed to *have*.

27. **E** No Error *Medium*
There is no error here. All modifiers are in their correct form and all subjects and verbs agree.

28. **B** Idioms *Difficult*
The phrase *support for* is an idiomatic expression. However, here, the word *support* is followed by the preposition *with.* To be correct, *with* would need to be replaced by *of.*

29. **A** Idioms *Difficult*
The word *comparing* is in the wrong form. It should read *compared to.* This is the error.

Improving Paragraphs

30. **A** Sentence Revision *Medium*
In the sentence as it reads now, the word *why* does not really make sense. People are concerned about *how they can effect positive change* so much seems out of control. **A** corrects this error.

31. **D** Sentence Revision *Medium*
The word *effects* seems out of place here. It is the "lives" of ordinary people that are very far away from Washington, not the *effects*.

32. **C** Essay Analysis *Easy*
The passage now reads: *The Jersey girls are one such inspiring example.* The words *are one such* imply that the sentence is referring back to an example. However, there is no sentence preceding sentence 7 that makes it clear what kind of an example we are supposed to think about. **C** corrects this problem.

33. **E** Sentence Revision *Medium*
Look at the sentence in its original form: *The media gave them a lot of coverage because they admired the changes they were trying to make.* The problem here is that the pronoun *they* is very vague. Does *they* refer to the media or the women? **E** clears up this ambiguity.

34. **B** Sentence Revision *Medium*

Look at the sentence in context: ***(9)*** *The women banded together and went repeatedly to Washington, D.C., to petition for changes to be made to our nation's security.* ***(10)*** *The media gave them a lot of coverage because they admired the changes they were trying to make.* ***(11)*** *So it was the women and the media together that got the proposed changes lots of attention.* Sentence 11 is unnecessary, because it repeats information already contained in the passage.

35. **A** Sentence Revision *Medium*

The author wants to make the point that it is important not to forget that *government is by the people for the people*. This is an imperative, and the verb *would* should be changed to *should* to emphasize the point.

SECTION 7: CRITICAL READING

Sentence Completions

1. **A** One-Word/One-Way *Easy*

You are looking for a word that means *accident*, because the substances, like rubber, were discovered by accident. *Serendipity* is the best fit.

2. **D** Two-Word/One-Way *Easy*

The word *rewards* tells you that a good prediction for the second blank would be something like "to get." Eliminate **A**, **B**, and **E**. Now, if people are now able to reap the rewards, they probably "acted" as their own travel agents. Only **D** fits both predictions and blanks.

3. **C** Two-Word/Two-Way *Easy*

Even though tells you that there is a contrast. So, although both participated in jazz, you can assume that they are somehow different. A good prediction for the first blank is therefore "different." Eliminate **D**. The conjunction *and* tells you that the second blank will also mean something like "different." **C** must be the correct answer.

4. **E** One-Word/Two-Way *Medium*

The students are trying to help heal a friend. The word *however* tells you that the doctors are not particularly hopeful about the fate of the friend. A good prediction would be "optimistic."

5. **B** One-Word/Two-Way *Difficult*

The actor is *eccentric*—that is, he behaves "oddly." Some people find this *charming*. The word *whereas* tells you that other people don't find this behavior charming at all. You need a word in the blank that means something like "insult."

6. **B** One-Word/Two-Way *Difficult*

On the one hand, the boy's parents like to go to lots of expensive parties that are aimed at fundraising. The words *for in other areas of life* tell you that the boy's parents behave differently when they aren't attending these functions. How do the parents behave? Well, since they spend a lot to go the parties, you can assume they don't spend a lot in other areas of their lives. A good prediction for the blank would be "cheap."

Long Reading Passage

7. **E** Themes and Arguments *Medium*

Here are the lines in question: *The producers never did know why we were laughing so much! But back to the story about Jim.* The author will ultimately discuss his suspicion about Jim and reveal the reason why Jim has arrived to see the tribe. But, in the opening paragraph, the author meanders away from this subject to describe a completely different visit. In other words, these lines are a *digression*, or wandering away, from the subject of the passage.

8. **D** Specific Information *Medium*

The author writes the following: *His eyes were empty of the kind of sureness that anchors most white men to their world. I thought to myself when I saw Jim, "Here is the loneliest man in the world."* In other words, the man, Jim, doesn't really seem to fit in anywhere. The narrator, however, has a clear sense of who he is and feels that he belongs with his tribe.

9. **A** Specific Information *Medium*

The narrator writes this about the young men in the group: *I locked eyes with not a few of the men my age who were immediately worried about this fraternization. It might be up to us, we said to one another with glances, to protect the tribe from the invasion of more white men.* In other words, the narrator is deeply suspicious of why Jim has come to the tribe.

10. **C** Words in Context *Medium*

Be sure you read the lines around the immediate ones quoted to you: *The older men in the tribe were not as closed minded as I. They knew Jim from many years ago, they said. They greeted him in an alarmingly friendly way, and I locked eyes with not a few of the men my age who were immediately worried about this fraternization.* The phrase *this fraternization* refers back to the fact that the older men are being friendly with Jim. A good synonym for fraternization would be *friendliness*.

11. **B** Themes and Arguments *Medium*

The whole purpose of the third paragraph is to highlight the degree to which the narrator and the other young Native American men are suspicious of Jim. All details in this focused paragraph help to reaffirm this idea.

12. **D** Implied Information *Easy*

Here are the lines in question: *How, I wondered to myself, could my own father be so friendly with Jim out there on the dusty street, when, just a few days ago when my father had been herding cattle across a dirt road, he had come across a camper full of Japanese tourists who had immediately started snapping pictures of him as he sat on his horse, bandana across his mouth?* In other words, the narrator's father is very friendly to Jim, and the narrator contrasts his father's behavior toward Jim with the way his father behaved toward a group of tourists.

13. **B** Implied Information *Easy*

The narrator writes, *Only later did I realize that he had looked to the sky at that moment precisely because he knew we needed to look at him. I, and the other young guys, had all made the mistake of thinking that he merely wanted to indulge himself and drink in our clear sky.* In other words, although the author initially assumes that Jim is behaving selfishly, but later realizes that Jim is fully aware of the discomfort that he is causing the young men.

14. **A** Attitude or Tone *Medium*

The author is very clearly uncomfortable around Jim until the moment when Jim begins to dance. Then the author feels concern that he should give Jim a glass of water. We can see that the narrator has gone from feeling deeply suspicious of Jim to feeling concern.

15. **D** Implied Information *Medium*

Here are the lines describing the father's twinkle: *I swallowed and looked at my father, who looked back at me with a twinkle in his eye that only a family member like me could detect. I became annoyed, realizing that my father was enjoying my discomfort.* The father is enjoying the son's discomfort—he is amused by the fact that his son is so surprised.

16. **B** Technique *Medium*

Here are the lines in question: *I watched this lonely, strange outcast of a man suddenly turn into a lithe eagle, then limp as though he had hurt his wing, and then turn again as though the wound had mended.* The author compares Jim to an eagle. Because the author does not use the words *like* or *as*, you know this is a metaphor.

17. **E** Technique *Medium*

The author follows the two men to the *kiva*. It is clear that his suspicion of Jim has started to fade by the story's end. He has, in other words, gone from suspicion to a kind of openness.

18. **C** Words in Context *Medium*

Here is the sentence with the word *vacillating*: *When he saw me vacillating, my father spoke to me in Hopi.* At this point, the father goes on to say something that convinces the young man to go to the *kiva*. Before these words, the young man was not going to go the *kiva*, but his father convinced him. In other words, the man was "hesitating."

19. **D** Implied Information *Medium*

The men have gone off to the *kiva*, where Jim is going to demonstrate more of the eagle dance. The father tells the narrator in Hopi that the narrator will need Jim to learn how to do all the dances. In other words, we can assume that Jim will be teaching others how to dance.

SECTION 8: MATH

Multiple Choice

1. **D** Algebra: Solving Equations *Easy*

First, solve for b:

$$3b = 18$$
$$b = 6$$

Now, substitute the value for b in the second equation:

$$ab = 2$$
$$6a = 2$$
$$a = \frac{1}{3}$$

2. **E** Algebra: Solving Equations *Easy*

If the wheel covers 2.5 feet with one turn, you know that it will cover 5 feet with 2 turns:

$$2(2.5) = 5$$

Now, you need to add another 2 feet to the value above. The question is really what fraction of 2.5 the number 2 is:

$$2 = x2.5$$
$$.8 = x \quad \text{or} \quad \frac{4}{5} = x$$

The wheel will therefore make 2 full turns, plus $\frac{4}{5}$ of one turn.

3. **A** Algebra: Solving Equations *Easy*

Simplify, multiplying both sides by 3:

$$(3)\frac{3n}{m} = \frac{1}{3}(3)$$
$$\frac{9n}{m} = 1$$
$$\frac{n}{m} = \frac{1}{9}$$

4. **B** Geometry: Coordinate Geometry *Easy*

The y-intercept is 2. Eliminate **A**, **C**, and **E**. The x-intercept is –2. The answer must be **B**.

5. **C** Geometry: Triangles *Medium*

The angle opposite the 45-degree angle must also be 45 degrees. Since there are always 180 degrees in a triangle, you can use the following equation to solve for x:

$$45 + x + 65 = 180$$
$$110 + x = 180$$
$$x = 70$$

6. **A** Numbers & Operations: Statistical Analysis *Medium*

The current piece is 18 inches. One piece before would be half of this, or 9. Two pieces before would be half of 9, or 4.5. Three pieces before would be half of 4.5, or 2.25. Four pieces before would be half of 2.25, or 1.125.

7. **A** Data Analysis, Statistics & Probability: Permutations and Combinations *Medium*

Take these questions one at a time. Must 5 shoes have been sold on one day, **A**? One day must have at least 5, because there is no way that one day can not have at least 5. Must 4 shoes have been sold on Monday? Not necessarily. Were at least 3 shoes sold each day? Not necessarily. One day could have sold 1 pair of shoes, and the rest of the shoes could have been divided over the other days. The same applies to **D** and **E**.

8. **E** Geometry: Coordinate Geometry *Medium*

There is no reason to sketch this problem. Simply average the x-coordinates and y-coordinates to find your answer.

9. **D** Algebra: Binomials and Quadratics *Medium*

First, simplify $(a + b)^2$:

$$(a + b)^2$$
$$a^2 + 2ab + b^2$$

Now, rewrite:

$$(a^2 + b^2) + (2ab)$$

You already know that $a^2 + b^2 = 250$, and $ab = 117$. So, plug in and solve:

$$(a^2 + b^2) + (2ab)$$
$$250 + 2(117)$$
$$484$$

10. **A** Geometry: Triangles *Medium*

If the right triangle has legs of 3 and 7, you can use this information to find the hypotenuse, which, conveniently, is a leg of the square:

$$a^2 + b^2 = c^2$$
$$3^2 + 7^2 = c^2$$
$$9 + 49 = c^2$$
$$58 = c^2$$
$$\sqrt{58} = c$$

Now, the area of the square is equal to c^2, which you already know is 58.

11. **B** Algebra: Percents *Medium*

Translate the text to an equation, using x for "a number:"

$$\frac{(20)}{(100)}\frac{(60)}{(100)}(x) = \frac{(120)}{(100)}(x)(y)$$
$$(.12)x = (1.2)xy$$

You can divide both sides of the equation by x:

$$.12 = 1.2y$$
$$.10 = y$$

12. **E** Geometry: Polygons *Medium*

The overall figure is a square. Notice that there are four unshaded triangles. If you subtract the area of the unshaded triangles from the square, you will be left with the area of the shaded region. Note that one side of the square is y. Since the area of a square is one side squared, you know that the area of the square is y^2. Now look at the triangles. The base and height of each triangle is x, with a right angle in the corner. Now, find the area of one of these triangles.

$$A = \frac{bh}{2}$$
$$A = \frac{(x)(x)}{2}$$
$$A = \frac{x^2}{2}$$

Now, there are four of these triangles:

$$\left(\frac{x^2}{2}\right)(4) = 2x^2$$

So, the area of the unshaded region is:

$$y^2 - 2x^2$$

13. **C** Algebra: Inequalities *Medium*

In order to find the range of possibilities, you need to make the difference of $x - y$ as small as possible and as large as possible. First, try to make $x - y$ as small as possible. To make this small, you will need to make x as small as possible and y as large as possible. Looking at the values given, make $-3 < x$ and $y < 5$. In this case, the difference would be $-8 < x - y$. Now, to make the difference as large as possible, you will need to make x as large as possible and y as small as possible. To do this, you will need $x < 7$ and $-5 < y$. The difference would then yield $x - y < 12$.

14. **B** Data Analysis, Statistics & Probability: Statistical Analysis *Difficult*

The average of the three numbers is 10, which means that the sum is 30. Since these three numbers are distinct, none of them can be the mode. Now, take the answer choices one at a time, starting with **A**. If 3 is the mode, that means it must appear most frequently in the set—at least twice. So, the sum of all five numbers, if **A** is the answer, would be 30 + 3 + 3 = 36. However, the average of these five numbers is 7.2, and you are told that the average will be 3 larger than the mode. This is not the answer. Now, look at **B**. If the mode is 5, then the sum of all 5 numbers will be 30 + 5 + 5 = 40, and the average is 8. Here is your answer; the number 8 is 3 larger than 5.

15. **E** Algebra: Absolute Value and Exponents *Difficult*

Simplify the problem:

$$(x+4)^{\frac{1}{2}} = (x+4)^{-\frac{1}{2}}$$
$$\sqrt{x+4} = \frac{1}{\sqrt{x+4}}$$

Cross multiply:

$$(\sqrt{x+4})(\sqrt{x+4}) = 1$$
$$x+4 = 1$$
$$x = -3$$

16. **D** Algebra: Binomials and Quadratics *Difficult*

First, simplify:

$$(dx-4)^2 = 0$$
$$(dx-4)(dx-4) = 0$$

Set one binomial equal to 0 and solve:

$$(dx-4) = 0$$
$$dx = 4$$
$$x = \frac{4}{d}$$

Now, x will only be an integer if d equals 1, 2, or 4. That's three different possibilities.

SECTION 9: WRITING

Improving Sentences

1. **B** Subject-Verb Agreement *Easy*

This sentence lacks a strong main verb. Only **B** fixes this problem. The other answers are either vague or fail to correct the weak main verb.

2. **E** Misplaced Modifiers *Easy*

The way this sentence reads originally, it sounds as though *cats* are *pet owners*, but this does not make sense. Clearly, *people* are pet owners. **E** puts the noun *people* in the correct place, directly after the modifying clause.

3. **C** Misplaced Modifiers *Easy*

This sentence sounds as though the *stacked books* are responsible for compiling a list of *twenty-first-century fiction*. And yet, it is not possible for books to do such a thing—people must do so. **C** puts the noun *critic* in the correct location.

4. **B** Tense *Easy*

The word *motivating* is in the wrong tense. It should read *motivated*, to modify the noun *people*.

5. **A** No Error *Easy*

There is no error here. All verbs are in the correct tense, pronouns are in the correct form, and subjects and verbs agree.

6. **D** Tense *Easy*

The verb phrase *are lifting* probably sounds strange to you. That's because it is not in the past tense. *We* can't *make travel plans* until the *sanctions are lifted*—that is, until the lifting of the sanctions has happened and now is in the past.

7. **B** Wordiness *Medium*

This sentence contains the unnecessary inclusion of the pronoun *it*. You need to remove this and clarify who *will make certain*. Clearly, it is *doctors and parents* who are responsible.

8. **C** Faulty Comparison *Medium*

You can only use the word *the* in front of the superlative form of an adjective. For example it is correct to say *the cheapest* but not to say *the cheaper*.

9. **A** No Error *Medium*

There is no error here. The dash is appropriate, and the comparisons are in the correct form.

10. **D** Misplaced Modifiers *Medium*

The way the sentence reads originally, it sounds as though *people* are known for their healthy qualities, but it is the *berries* that are known for their healthiness. **D** resolves this problem.

11. **B** Subject-Verb Agreement *Medium*

Subjects and verbs must always agree. In this case, the subject is *plans*, which is plural, and the verb *indicates* is singular. To be correct, the verb *indicates* must be converted to its plural form, *indicate*.

12. **E** Idioms *Medium*

This sentence tests your knowledge of idioms. The word *aptitude* means "ability" or "talent." Used in a sentence, the word *aptitude* always goes with the preposition *for*. In this sentence, we see that Chelsy has an *aptitude at*. **E** corrects this error.

13. **D** Run-On *Medium*

Here you have a run-on sentence. To correct it, you will need to either make one clause dependent on the other or combine both sentences with a semicolon, which is precisely what **D** accomplishes.

14. **C** Coordination and Subordination *Medium*

The words *even though* imply a contrast. However, there is a clear causal relationship between the *tsunami warnings* and the beach's placement on a *tectonic plate*. The word *because* fixes this problem by showing that there is a causal relationship.

SAT PRACTICE TEST 3

SAT* Reasoning Test—General Directions

Timing

- You will have 3 hours and 20 minutes to work on this test. (On the actual SAT, you would have 3 hours and 45 minutes to complete ten sections, one of which would be unscored and experimental.)
- There are nine separately timed sections:
  - ➤ One 25-minute essay
  - ➤ Five other 25-minute sections
  - ➤ Two 20-minute sections
  - ➤ One 10-minute section
- You may work on only one section at a time.
- The supervisor will tell you when to begin and end each section.
- If you finish a section before time is called, check your work on that section. You may NOT turn to any other section.
- Work as rapidly as you can without losing accuracy. Don't waste time on questions that seem too difficult for you.

Marking Answers

- Carefully mark only one answer for each question.
- Make sure each mark is dark and completely fills the circle.
- Do not make any stray marks on your answer sheet.
- If you erase, do so completely. Incomplete erasures may be scored as intended answers.
- Use only the answer spaces that correspond to the question numbers.
- Use the test book for scratchwork, but you will not receive credit for anything written there.
- After time has been called, you may not transfer answers to your answer sheet or fill in circles.
- You may not fold or remove pages or portions of a page from this book, or take the book or answer sheet from the testing room.

Scoring

- For each correct answer to a question, you receive one point.
- For questions you omit, you receive no points.
- For a wrong answer to a multiple-choice question, you lose one-fourth of a point.
  - ➤ If you can eliminate one or more of the answer choices as wrong, you increase your chances of choosing the correct answer and earning one point.
  - ➤ If you can't eliminate any choice, move on. You can return to the question later if there is time.
- For a wrong answer to a "grid-in" math question, you don't lose any points.
- The essay is scored on a 1 to 6 scale by two different readers. The total essay score is the sum of the two readers' scores.
- An off-topic or blank essay will receive a score of zero.

SAT PRACTICE TEST 3 ANSWER SHEET

SECTION 2

1. Ⓐ Ⓑ Ⓒ Ⓓ Ⓔ	7. Ⓐ Ⓑ Ⓒ Ⓓ Ⓔ	13. Ⓐ Ⓑ Ⓒ Ⓓ Ⓔ	19. Ⓐ Ⓑ Ⓒ Ⓓ Ⓔ
2. Ⓐ Ⓑ Ⓒ Ⓓ Ⓔ	8. Ⓐ Ⓑ Ⓒ Ⓓ Ⓔ	14. Ⓐ Ⓑ Ⓒ Ⓓ Ⓔ	20. Ⓐ Ⓑ Ⓒ Ⓓ Ⓔ
3. Ⓐ Ⓑ Ⓒ Ⓓ Ⓔ	9. Ⓐ Ⓑ Ⓒ Ⓓ Ⓔ	15. Ⓐ Ⓑ Ⓒ Ⓓ Ⓔ	21. Ⓐ Ⓑ Ⓒ Ⓓ Ⓔ
4. Ⓐ Ⓑ Ⓒ Ⓓ Ⓔ	10. Ⓐ Ⓑ Ⓒ Ⓓ Ⓔ	16. Ⓐ Ⓑ Ⓒ Ⓓ Ⓔ	22. Ⓐ Ⓑ Ⓒ Ⓓ Ⓔ
5. Ⓐ Ⓑ Ⓒ Ⓓ Ⓔ	11. Ⓐ Ⓑ Ⓒ Ⓓ Ⓔ	17. Ⓐ Ⓑ Ⓒ Ⓓ Ⓔ	23. Ⓐ Ⓑ Ⓒ Ⓓ Ⓔ
6. Ⓐ Ⓑ Ⓒ Ⓓ Ⓔ	12. Ⓐ Ⓑ Ⓒ Ⓓ Ⓔ	18. Ⓐ Ⓑ Ⓒ Ⓓ Ⓔ	24. Ⓐ Ⓑ Ⓒ Ⓓ Ⓔ

SECTION 3

1. Ⓐ Ⓑ Ⓒ Ⓓ Ⓔ	6. Ⓐ Ⓑ Ⓒ Ⓓ Ⓔ	11. Ⓐ Ⓑ Ⓒ Ⓓ Ⓔ	16. Ⓐ Ⓑ Ⓒ Ⓓ Ⓔ
2. Ⓐ Ⓑ Ⓒ Ⓓ Ⓔ	7. Ⓐ Ⓑ Ⓒ Ⓓ Ⓔ	12. Ⓐ Ⓑ Ⓒ Ⓓ Ⓔ	17. Ⓐ Ⓑ Ⓒ Ⓓ Ⓔ
3. Ⓐ Ⓑ Ⓒ Ⓓ Ⓔ	8. Ⓐ Ⓑ Ⓒ Ⓓ Ⓔ	13. Ⓐ Ⓑ Ⓒ Ⓓ Ⓔ	18. Ⓐ Ⓑ Ⓒ Ⓓ Ⓔ
4. Ⓐ Ⓑ Ⓒ Ⓓ Ⓔ	9. Ⓐ Ⓑ Ⓒ Ⓓ Ⓔ	14. Ⓐ Ⓑ Ⓒ Ⓓ Ⓔ	19. Ⓐ Ⓑ Ⓒ Ⓓ Ⓔ
5. Ⓐ Ⓑ Ⓒ Ⓓ Ⓔ	10. Ⓐ Ⓑ Ⓒ Ⓓ Ⓔ	15. Ⓐ Ⓑ Ⓒ Ⓓ Ⓔ	20. Ⓐ Ⓑ Ⓒ Ⓓ Ⓔ

SECTION 4

1. Ⓐ Ⓑ Ⓒ Ⓓ Ⓔ	7. Ⓐ Ⓑ Ⓒ Ⓓ Ⓔ	13. Ⓐ Ⓑ Ⓒ Ⓓ Ⓔ	19. Ⓐ Ⓑ Ⓒ Ⓓ Ⓔ
2. Ⓐ Ⓑ Ⓒ Ⓓ Ⓔ	8. Ⓐ Ⓑ Ⓒ Ⓓ Ⓔ	14. Ⓐ Ⓑ Ⓒ Ⓓ Ⓔ	20. Ⓐ Ⓑ Ⓒ Ⓓ Ⓔ
3. Ⓐ Ⓑ Ⓒ Ⓓ Ⓔ	9. Ⓐ Ⓑ Ⓒ Ⓓ Ⓔ	15. Ⓐ Ⓑ Ⓒ Ⓓ Ⓔ	21. Ⓐ Ⓑ Ⓒ Ⓓ Ⓔ
4. Ⓐ Ⓑ Ⓒ Ⓓ Ⓔ	10. Ⓐ Ⓑ Ⓒ Ⓓ Ⓔ	16. Ⓐ Ⓑ Ⓒ Ⓓ Ⓔ	22. Ⓐ Ⓑ Ⓒ Ⓓ Ⓔ
5. Ⓐ Ⓑ Ⓒ Ⓓ Ⓔ	11. Ⓐ Ⓑ Ⓒ Ⓓ Ⓔ	17. Ⓐ Ⓑ Ⓒ Ⓓ Ⓔ	23. Ⓐ Ⓑ Ⓒ Ⓓ Ⓔ
6. Ⓐ Ⓑ Ⓒ Ⓓ Ⓔ	12. Ⓐ Ⓑ Ⓒ Ⓓ Ⓔ	18. Ⓐ Ⓑ Ⓒ Ⓓ Ⓔ	24. Ⓐ Ⓑ Ⓒ Ⓓ Ⓔ

SECTION 5

1. Ⓐ Ⓑ Ⓒ Ⓓ Ⓔ	3. Ⓐ Ⓑ Ⓒ Ⓓ Ⓔ	5. Ⓐ Ⓑ Ⓒ Ⓓ Ⓔ	7. Ⓐ Ⓑ Ⓒ Ⓓ Ⓔ
2. Ⓐ Ⓑ Ⓒ Ⓓ Ⓔ	4. Ⓐ Ⓑ Ⓒ Ⓓ Ⓔ	6. Ⓐ Ⓑ Ⓒ Ⓓ Ⓔ	8. Ⓐ Ⓑ Ⓒ Ⓓ Ⓔ

9				10				11				12				13			
		/				/				/				/				/	
.	.	.	.	.	.	.	.	.	.	.	.	.	.	.	.	.	.	.	.
	0	0	0		0	0	0		0	0	0		0	0	0		0	0	0
1	1	1	1	1	1	1	1	1	1	1	1	1	1	1	1	1	1	1	1
2	2	2	2	2	2	2	2	2	2	2	2	2	2	2	2	2	2	2	2
3	3	3	3	3	3	3	3	3	3	3	3	3	3	3	3	3	3	3	3
4	4	4	4	4	4	4	4	4	4	4	4	4	4	4	4	4	4	4	4
5	5	5	5	5	5	5	5	5	5	5	5	5	5	5	5	5	5	5	5
6	6	6	6	6	6	6	6	6	6	6	6	6	6	6	6	6	6	6	6
7	7	7	7	7	7	7	7	7	7	7	7	7	7	7	7	7	7	7	7
8	8	8	8	8	8	8	8	8	8	8	8	8	8	8	8	8	8	8	8
9	9	9	9	9	9	9	9	9	9	9	9	9	9	9	9	9	9	9	9

14				15				16				17				18			
		/				/				/				/				/	
.	.	.	.	.	.	.	.	.	.	.	.	.	.	.	.	.	.	.	.
	0	0	0		0	0	0		0	0	0		0	0	0		0	0	0
1	1	1	1	1	1	1	1	1	1	1	1	1	1	1	1	1	1	1	1
2	2	2	2	2	2	2	2	2	2	2	2	2	2	2	2	2	2	2	2
3	3	3	3	3	3	3	3	3	3	3	3	3	3	3	3	3	3	3	3
4	4	4	4	4	4	4	4	4	4	4	4	4	4	4	4	4	4	4	4
5	5	5	5	5	5	5	5	5	5	5	5	5	5	5	5	5	5	5	5
6	6	6	6	6	6	6	6	6	6	6	6	6	6	6	6	6	6	6	6
7	7	7	7	7	7	7	7	7	7	7	7	7	7	7	7	7	7	7	7
8	8	8	8	8	8	8	8	8	8	8	8	8	8	8	8	8	8	8	8
9	9	9	9	9	9	9	9	9	9	9	9	9	9	9	9	9	9	9	9

SAT PRACTICE TEST 3 ANSWER SHEET

SECTION 6

1. Ⓐ Ⓑ Ⓒ Ⓓ Ⓔ	10. Ⓐ Ⓑ Ⓒ Ⓓ Ⓔ	19. Ⓐ Ⓑ Ⓒ Ⓓ Ⓔ	28. Ⓐ Ⓑ Ⓒ Ⓓ Ⓔ
2. Ⓐ Ⓑ Ⓒ Ⓓ Ⓔ	11. Ⓐ Ⓑ Ⓒ Ⓓ Ⓔ	20. Ⓐ Ⓑ Ⓒ Ⓓ Ⓔ	29. Ⓐ Ⓑ Ⓒ Ⓓ Ⓔ
3. Ⓐ Ⓑ Ⓒ Ⓓ Ⓔ	12. Ⓐ Ⓑ Ⓒ Ⓓ Ⓔ	21. Ⓐ Ⓑ Ⓒ Ⓓ Ⓔ	30. Ⓐ Ⓑ Ⓒ Ⓓ Ⓔ
4. Ⓐ Ⓑ Ⓒ Ⓓ Ⓔ	13. Ⓐ Ⓑ Ⓒ Ⓓ Ⓔ	22. Ⓐ Ⓑ Ⓒ Ⓓ Ⓔ	31. Ⓐ Ⓑ Ⓒ Ⓓ Ⓔ
5. Ⓐ Ⓑ Ⓒ Ⓓ Ⓔ	14. Ⓐ Ⓑ Ⓒ Ⓓ Ⓔ	23. Ⓐ Ⓑ Ⓒ Ⓓ Ⓔ	32. Ⓐ Ⓑ Ⓒ Ⓓ Ⓔ
6. Ⓐ Ⓑ Ⓒ Ⓓ Ⓔ	15. Ⓐ Ⓑ Ⓒ Ⓓ Ⓔ	24. Ⓐ Ⓑ Ⓒ Ⓓ Ⓔ	33. Ⓐ Ⓑ Ⓒ Ⓓ Ⓔ
7. Ⓐ Ⓑ Ⓒ Ⓓ Ⓔ	16. Ⓐ Ⓑ Ⓒ Ⓓ Ⓔ	25. Ⓐ Ⓑ Ⓒ Ⓓ Ⓔ	34. Ⓐ Ⓑ Ⓒ Ⓓ Ⓔ
8. Ⓐ Ⓑ Ⓒ Ⓓ Ⓔ	17. Ⓐ Ⓑ Ⓒ Ⓓ Ⓔ	26. Ⓐ Ⓑ Ⓒ Ⓓ Ⓔ	35. Ⓐ Ⓑ Ⓒ Ⓓ Ⓔ
9. Ⓐ Ⓑ Ⓒ Ⓓ Ⓔ	18. Ⓐ Ⓑ Ⓒ Ⓓ Ⓔ	27. Ⓐ Ⓑ Ⓒ Ⓓ Ⓔ	

SECTION 7

1. Ⓐ Ⓑ Ⓒ Ⓓ Ⓔ	6. Ⓐ Ⓑ Ⓒ Ⓓ Ⓔ	11. Ⓐ Ⓑ Ⓒ Ⓓ Ⓔ	16. Ⓐ Ⓑ Ⓒ Ⓓ Ⓔ
2. Ⓐ Ⓑ Ⓒ Ⓓ Ⓔ	7. Ⓐ Ⓑ Ⓒ Ⓓ Ⓔ	12. Ⓐ Ⓑ Ⓒ Ⓓ Ⓔ	17. Ⓐ Ⓑ Ⓒ Ⓓ Ⓔ
3. Ⓐ Ⓑ Ⓒ Ⓓ Ⓔ	8. Ⓐ Ⓑ Ⓒ Ⓓ Ⓔ	13. Ⓐ Ⓑ Ⓒ Ⓓ Ⓔ	18. Ⓐ Ⓑ Ⓒ Ⓓ Ⓔ
4. Ⓐ Ⓑ Ⓒ Ⓓ Ⓔ	9. Ⓐ Ⓑ Ⓒ Ⓓ Ⓔ	14. Ⓐ Ⓑ Ⓒ Ⓓ Ⓔ	19. Ⓐ Ⓑ Ⓒ Ⓓ Ⓔ
5. Ⓐ Ⓑ Ⓒ Ⓓ Ⓔ	10. Ⓐ Ⓑ Ⓒ Ⓓ Ⓔ	15. Ⓐ Ⓑ Ⓒ Ⓓ Ⓔ	

SECTION 8

1. Ⓐ Ⓑ Ⓒ Ⓓ Ⓔ	5. Ⓐ Ⓑ Ⓒ Ⓓ Ⓔ	9. Ⓐ Ⓑ Ⓒ Ⓓ Ⓔ	13. Ⓐ Ⓑ Ⓒ Ⓓ Ⓔ
2. Ⓐ Ⓑ Ⓒ Ⓓ Ⓔ	6. Ⓐ Ⓑ Ⓒ Ⓓ Ⓔ	10. Ⓐ Ⓑ Ⓒ Ⓓ Ⓔ	14. Ⓐ Ⓑ Ⓒ Ⓓ Ⓔ
3. Ⓐ Ⓑ Ⓒ Ⓓ Ⓔ	7. Ⓐ Ⓑ Ⓒ Ⓓ Ⓔ	11. Ⓐ Ⓑ Ⓒ Ⓓ Ⓔ	15. Ⓐ Ⓑ Ⓒ Ⓓ Ⓔ
4. Ⓐ Ⓑ Ⓒ Ⓓ Ⓔ	8. Ⓐ Ⓑ Ⓒ Ⓓ Ⓔ	12. Ⓐ Ⓑ Ⓒ Ⓓ Ⓔ	16. Ⓐ Ⓑ Ⓒ Ⓓ Ⓔ

SECTION 9

1. Ⓐ Ⓑ Ⓒ Ⓓ Ⓔ	5. Ⓐ Ⓑ Ⓒ Ⓓ Ⓔ	9. Ⓐ Ⓑ Ⓒ Ⓓ Ⓔ	13. Ⓐ Ⓑ Ⓒ Ⓓ Ⓔ
2. Ⓐ Ⓑ Ⓒ Ⓓ Ⓔ	6. Ⓐ Ⓑ Ⓒ Ⓓ Ⓔ	10. Ⓐ Ⓑ Ⓒ Ⓓ Ⓔ	14. Ⓐ Ⓑ Ⓒ Ⓓ Ⓔ
3. Ⓐ Ⓑ Ⓒ Ⓓ Ⓔ	7. Ⓐ Ⓑ Ⓒ Ⓓ Ⓔ	11. Ⓐ Ⓑ Ⓒ Ⓓ Ⓔ	
4. Ⓐ Ⓑ Ⓒ Ⓓ Ⓔ	8. Ⓐ Ⓑ Ⓒ Ⓓ Ⓔ	12. Ⓐ Ⓑ Ⓒ Ⓓ Ⓔ	

SECTION 1

ESSAY

Time—25 minutes

The essay gives you an opportunity to show how effectively you can develop and express ideas. You should, therefore, take care to develop your point of view, present your ideas logically and clearly, and use language precisely.

Your essay must be written on the lines provided on your answer sheet—you will receive no other paper on which to write. You will have enough space if you write on every line, avoid wide margins, and keep your handwriting to a reasonable size. Remember that people who are not familiar with your handwriting will read what you write. Try to write or print so that what you are writing is legible to those readers.

You have twenty-five minutes to write an essay on the topic assigned below. DO NOT WRITE ON ANOTHER TOPIC. AN OFF-TOPIC ESSAY WILL RECEIVE A SCORE OF ZERO.

Think carefully about the issue presented in the following excerpt and the assignment below.

> The wealthy members of our society donate large sums of money to further the arts. Recently a wealthy donor gave $20 million to set up a temporary art exhibit in the park of a major city. The exhibit was to last for three weeks only. Critics noted that the money would have been better spent improving conditions of the poor or at the very least providing poor children with a much-needed outlet in art classes.

Assignment: Should the wealthy donate large sums of money to temporary art exhibits? What guidelines should donors follow when giving away their money? Cite specific examples from your own knowledge of the world and personal experience to craft an essay addressing this subject.

DO NOT WRITE YOUR ESSAY IN YOUR TEST BOOK. You will receive credit only for what you write on your answer sheet.

BEGIN WRITING YOUR ESSAY ON THE ANSWER SHEET.

IF YOU FINISH BEFORE TIME IS CALLED, YOU MAY CHECK YOUR WORK ON THIS SECTION ONLY. DO NOT TURN TO ANY OTHER SECTION IN THE TEST.

SECTION 1—ESSAY

Time—25 minutes

SECTION 1—ESSAY

Time—25 minutes

SECTION 2

Turn to Section 2 of your answer sheet to answer the questions in this section.

Time—25 Minutes
24 Questions

Directions: For each question in this section, select the best answer from among the choices given and fill in the corresponding oval on the answer sheet.

Each sentence below has one or two blanks, each blank indicating that something has been omitted. Beneath the sentence are five words or sets of words labeled A through E. Choose the word or set of words that, when inserted in the sentence, best fits the meaning of the sentence as a whole.

Example:

Eliza felt ----- when her boss asked her to work seven weekends in a row but ----- when her work earned her a promotion.

(A) enervated . . weakened
(B) depressed . . intellectual
(C) advantageous . . salacious
(D) angry . . shopworn
(E) irate . . elated     ●

1. The writer followed the magazine's guidelines that no piece should be too ----- and took out all references to any scandalous or potentially upsetting material.

(A) silent
(B) skeptical
(C) prompt
(D) domineering
(E) sensational

2. Farmers were ----- to see how the yearly appearance of locusts was even worse this year, for it meant that the crops would be nearly decimated by the summer's end.

(A) elated
(B) preempted
(C) disconsolate
(D) hesitant
(E) reluctant

3. Scholars now assert that many ancient rituals originally considered to be the ----- beliefs of a tribe were actually understood to be -----, and that these past peoples were not nearly as superstitious as was once believed.

(A) sincere . . doctrine
(B) devout . . metaphoric
(C) trifles . . representative
(D) musings . . allegorical
(E) dogma . . fixed

4. Trent is bombastic, always ----- and making other people feel -----.

(A) pontificating . . irrelevant
(B) dozing . . miniscule
(C) ranting . . inspired
(D) plotting . . tendentious
(E) boasting . . elevated

5. Just as a person's surroundings often reflect his or her individual tastes and preferences, dogs ----- their owners in both temperament and behavior. This is perhaps not surprising if we consider that dogs are often ----- as man's best friend.

(A) reflect . . derided
(B) genuflect . . moderated
(C) mirror . . referred to
(D) resemble . . convicted
(E) obey . . chronicled

6. The wealthy young heiress courted ----- as a form of exposure, for in truth she had little talent save for her ability to stir controversy, though she craved the attention she saw heaped on other entertainers known for true -----.

(A) adulation . . talent
(B) pragmatism . . praise
(C) flattery . . soliloquies
(D) notoriety . . accomplishments
(E) infamy . . lassitude

GO ON TO THE NEXT PAGE

SECTION 2

7. My great-aunt Jessamine was known for being susceptible to -----. All you had to do to curry favor with her was to sing her praises.

(A) insomnia
(B) rapprochement
(C) sedition
(D) floridity
(E) blandishments

8. The author has often been considered -----, for his characters abuse each other, and his stories have few humanistic moments of compassion or transcendence.

(A) misanthropic
(B) sectarian
(C) facile
(D) histrionic
(E) obsequious

GO ON TO THE NEXT PAGE

SECTION 2

Directions: Each passage below is followed by questions based on its content. Answer the questions on the basis of what is stated or implied in each passage and in any introductory material that may be provided.

Questions 9–10 are based on the following passage.

That Wellington defeated Napoleon cannot be denied, yet there are some historians who question the means by which this conquest was accomplished. It is a popular English view to assume that the Battle of Waterloo is England's finest moment, in which the brilliant general-tactician outwitted his enemy. But some nineteenth-century historians questioned this assumption, insisting that Napoleon may well have suffered from a mysterious bout of the flu, which slowed down the speed at which his own deft mind could issue orders to a loyal army or that a mysterious, and some say mythical, ditch engulfed his army and left him defenseless.

9. In line 5, the author implies that the English won the Battle of Waterloo due to

(A) complete accident
(B) excellent strategies
(C) preordained fate
(D) inclement weather
(E) superior equipment

10. The author mentions the flu in line 8 to

(A) challenge a long-held belief
(B) raise the possibility that Napoleon was not defeated after all
(C) illustrate some possible alternative explanations for Napoleon's defeat
(D) insist that Wellington was a superior tactician to Napoleon
(E) highlight the differences between the English and French armies

Questions 11–12 are based on the following passage.

I bristle when I hear people speak of the conformity of all Asian people, as though we are interchangeable, our individuality a stilted thing. And yet a part of me, a quiet part that is only vocal among other Chinese friends, understands what it is that non-Asian people see. There were often times in my youth when I felt unable to express myself in the brash manner of Americans. Their constant declarations of "I feel this" or "I feel that" struck me as abrasive. I had learned to interact with the world in a different way. If my mother was happy, then so was I. If my father was displeased with my grades, then I was sad.

11. The passage suggests that the narrator understands the observations of non-Asians as depicted in lines 4–10 ("understands what . . . sad") because

(A) she is deeply concerned with how her mother will react to her memoir
(B) she is able to perceive the universal qualities which unite all people
(C) she is unable to express herself among others like her
(D) she recalls a childhood in which her emotional reactions depended on the feelings of others
(E) she herself is not Asian

12. This passage is primarily concerned with the author's

(A) historical analysis of a long-held bias
(B) dismissal of an anachronistic attitude
(C) admission and explanation of a personal trait
(D) concern for the welfare of a neglected group
(E) views on rearing small children

GO ON TO THE NEXT PAGE

SECTION 2

Directions: The passages below are followed by questions based on their content; questions following a pair of related passages may also be based on the relationship between the paired passages. Answer the questions on the basis of what is stated or implied in the passages and in any introductory material that may be provided.

Questions 13–24 are based on the following passages.

The passages below address the topic of modernity. Both passages are adapted from essays in scholarly journals.

Passage 1

We all have a sense of modernity and what it entails. Some people emphasize wealth that accumulates in countries and others creative developments in the spheres of science and the arts. But modernity is difficult to actually describe. Is a modern country rich? At first glance you might be inclined to answer in the affirmative, but then remember a country like the United Arab Emirates, which is certainly rich in dollar numbers but hardly a modern country: nearly 90 percent of its labor force, for example, is imported from other countries. We can hardly think of a modern nation as one that is unable to employ its own people. Contrast this example with the countries of Europe, impoverished after World War II. As poor as countries like England and France might have been at the end of this war, one would have considered preposterous the notion that they were not at the forefront of all that was and would be later termed "modern."

Until the last fifty years, scholars had a very brief set of characteristics required to deem a nation with the title of "modern." All that was needed, these scholars insisted, was that a country be primarily of Anglo-Saxon origin and imbued with the values of Christianity. Not surprisingly, the very people who came up with these criteria also shared these characteristics. Notwithstanding, the obvious racist overtones that such judgments belied, scholars also believed that certain belief systems, such as Confucianism, which has shaped much of East Asia, were incompatible with the development of capitalism and therefore, modernity. Chief amongst these critics' concerns was the idea that to become a fully modern nation, a country must pass through certain stages, including feudalism.

All this changed in the last thirty years as Japan rose to become a truly international player. Few could have predicted in 1945, at the end of World War II, that Japan, a defeated, impoverished, starving nation would soon become the world's second strongest economy. The biases against Japan were many: its population was not creative, people conformed too easily, and everything it created was derivative. But once the wealth, health, and fortunes of its people reached a fever pitch, the truth could not be ignored: Japan had become a competitive modern nation. Scholars raced to explain this behavior: Japan had gone through a period of feudalism similar to the one experienced in Europe. Confucianism was very similar to Protestantism—both valued hard work, self-sacrifice, and community values. Japan might not innovate anything, but it was certainly adept at improving the creations of the West. Japan was seen as an exception.

But today new countries are rising in strength and again threatening our understanding of what it means to be modern. Smaller nations, such as Singapore and South Korea, are developing strong economies, and yet these nations have not experienced feudalism. Rather, they have been small, backwater nations, colonized by the imperial powers of China and Japan. So what accounts for their development, and how are we able to predict, and then nurture, other countries on to greater fortune? The truth may only become known to us as more countries in more unpredictable corners of the world uncover their talents and rise to join the ranks of the other world leaders. The invisible hand that characterized Adam Smith's imagination may well apply to the development of nations.

Passage 2

That there is a divergence of opinion on the merits of Second and Third World countries emulating the cultures of the Western world is tacitly understood by all but the least sensitive of social critics and historians. Still, most who work in the arena of global development want all people to have access to the very best of what westernization has to offer: good medicine, clean water, and an abundant food supply. Yet, although everyone agrees on which countries are modernized (America is, Nairobi is not, for example), no one can really agree on exactly how these countries arrived at their present exalted state, much less what an undeveloped nation would need to do to climb up a notch.

Certainly money alone is not the key, nor is a strong central government. There are numerous examples of countries rich in resources—Egypt comes to mind—but which have failed to share the wealth with its people. And then there are authoritarian governments like North Korea that rule with an iron fist while their people starve. Clearly a new definition is needed. One that, like the very idea of modernity, allows for a degree of elusiveness. And certainly the most modern nations have a degree of elasticity about them: just when you take a snapshot of American society, for example, things have changed and once-cherished truths are discarded.

I would like to put forward the idea that modernity is really defined by a country whose population develops and continues to acquire increasingly complex skills. Nothing else can account for

GO ON TO THE NEXT PAGE

the rapid gains of a hardworking country in such a short amount of time and for the breathtaking manner in which the most advanced countries are able to continuously reinvent themselves.

But how to help a nation develop its skills? Certainly, for those nations that currently lag behind, there is no choice but to subject their culture to the influence of a nation that is more advanced. There is nothing new in this idea. The Chinese influenced the Japanese, the Egyptians the Greeks and the English the Americans. Skills, institutions, and attitudes must be transferred as well. Once enough time has passed, the dominating country can release its influence. When we look at the "5 Tigers," the small East Asian countries with developing economies, we see that they are all emulating the successes of Japan.

13. In lines 4–9 of Passage 1, the author suggests that "wealth" is

(A) not enough to characterize a modern country
(B) an exception to the rule of what makes a nation modern
(C) a basic characteristic of all modern nations
(D) one of the elusive qualities of Second World countries
(E) a goal for which all leaders striving to modernize their countries should aspire

14. In line 14 of Passage 1, "preposterous" most nearly means

(A) outdated
(B) doubtful
(C) insulting
(D) laughable
(E) tricky

15. In lines 18–20 ("All that . . . Christianity"), the author of Passage 1 considers that the characteristics used to determine which nations could become modern were primarily motivated by

(A) history
(B) taste
(C) evidence
(D) practicality
(E) race

16. All of the following are referred to in Passage 1 as reasons for Japan's success in the modern world EXCEPT

(A) the hardworking nature of the Japanese people
(B) the direct involvement of the United States in reconstructing Japan after the war
(C) Japan was an exception to the rule of how a country could become modern
(D) its people have the ability to improve upon innovations
(E) the population was willing to sacrifice personal goals for the good of the country

17. Which of the following, if true, would most directly support the view described in lines 55–57 ("The invisible . . . nations")?

(A) In order to understand how to modernize a country, scholars must begin to adopt a new understanding of what it means to be "modern."
(B) We may know a modern country when we see it, but we are unlikely to see future modern countries emerging.
(C) A comprehensive study of the fastest modernizing nations can find no universal character traits shared by all.
(D) Scholars have probably made mistakes when assuming that Japan is a modern nation.
(E) The most modern countries do not need to advertise their success and may therefore be overlooked when the lists of modern countries are tabulated.

18. In context, "divergence" (line 58) most nearly means

(A) detour
(B) roadway
(C) assumption
(D) disagreement
(E) concord

19. In lines 72–74 ("and then . . . starve"), the author uses the example of North Korea to illustrate that

(A) it is imperative not to use race as a qualifying trait for defining a modern country
(B) a strong central government is not necessarily indicative of a modern nation
(C) shared culture between nations does not indicate which will be modern
(D) a country's proximity to a wealthy nation does not determine modernity
(E) countries may be resistant to developing along the path to modernity

20. According to the author of Passage 2, a modern country is one that is defined by which of the following?

I. A work force with varied, desirable skills
II. Abundant natural resources
III. The ability to adapt to new demands

(A) I only
(B) II only
(C) II and III
(D) I and II
(E) I and III

GO ON TO THE NEXT PAGE

SECTION 2

21. Which would best illustrate the definition of a modern country as stated by the author of Passage 2?

(A) A country whose population is highly educated in a variety of industries with a proven ability to retrain to meet new economic and industrial demands
(B) A country rich in a natural resource that is highly desirable to the rest of the world
(C) A country with a motivated work force willing to travel to other countries to take on undesirable jobs
(D) A country with a strong central government capable of regulating all trade
(E) A country with high personal wealth

22. The author of Passage 2 would make what assumption about European countries discussed in lines 11–15 ("Contrast . . . 'modern'") in Passage 1?

(A) The large variety of natural resources Europe retained after the war assured their place as a world leader.
(B) The European countries may have suffered damage in the war, but the workforce remained skilled and flexible.
(C) The strong influx of foreign workers to Europe after the war made it possible for European manufacturing to recover.
(D) The leadership of the United States enabled Europe to bounce back more quickly after the end of the war.
(E) The shared racial traits of Europeans made it easier for them to band together to recover at the war's end.

23. Passage 1 and Passage 2 share a general tone of

(A) apparent dissatisfaction
(B) intellectual detachment
(C) personal remorse
(D) deep nostalgia
(E) open aggression

24. Both authors agree on which of the following?

(A) Modernity cannot be so easily described.
(B) Colonialism has been healthy for some cultures.
(C) A list of modern countries must include Japan.
(D) World leaders must resist the urge to send workers overseas.
(E) Confucianism is a good indicator of a potential to modernize.

S T O P

IF YOU FINISH BEFORE TIME IS CALLED, YOU MAY CHECK YOUR WORK ON THIS TEST ONLY. DO NOT TURN TO ANY OTHER SECTION IN THIS TEST.

SECTION 3

Turn to Section 3 of your answer sheet to answer the questions in this section.

Time—25 Minutes
20 Questions

Directions: For this section, solve each problem and decide which is the best of the choices given. Fill in the corresponding oval on the answer sheet. You may use any available space for scratchwork.

Notes:

1. The use of a calculator is permitted. All numbers used are real numbers.
2. Figures that accompany problems in this test are intended to provide information useful in solving the problems. They are drawn as accurately as possible EXCEPT when it is stated in a specific problem that the figure is not drawn to scale. All figures lie in a plane unless otherwise indicated.
3. Unless otherwise specified, the domain of any function f is assumed to be the set of all real numbers x for which $f(x)$ is a real number.

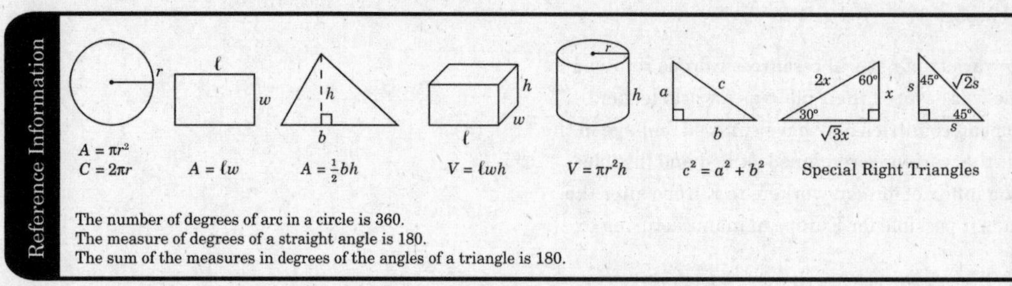

Reference Information
$A = \pi r^2$
$C = 2\pi r$
$A = \ell w$
$A = \frac{1}{2}bh$
$V = \ell wh$
$V = \pi r^2 h$
$c^2 = a^2 + b^2$
Special Right Triangles
The number of degrees of arc in a circle is 360.
The measure of degrees of a straight angle is 180.
The sum of the measures in degrees of the angles of a triangle is 180.

1. If $6a - 1 > 11$, which of the following can be the value of a ?

(A) -2
(B) -1
(C) 1
(D) 2
(E) 3

2. If $5^{3x} = 125$, then $x = ?$

(A) 0
(B) 1
(C) 2
(D) 5
(E) 25

3. How much less than $x - 5$ is $x - 8$?

(A) 5
(B) 3
(C) -3
(D) -5
(E) -8

GO ON TO THE NEXT PAGE

4. Which of the following shapes, if folded up, could represent a box with a lid and a total volume of 80 ?

(A)

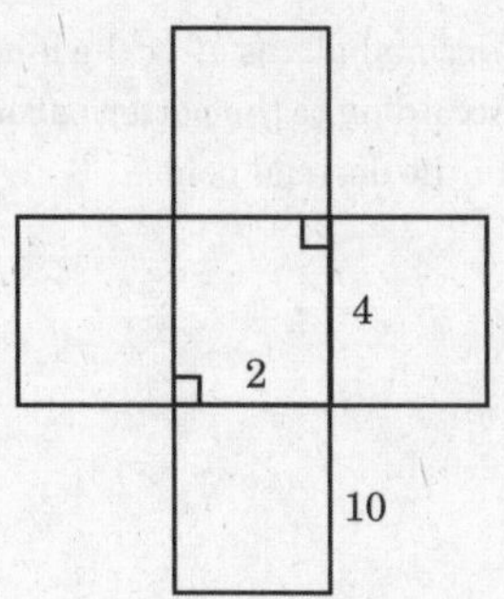

(B)

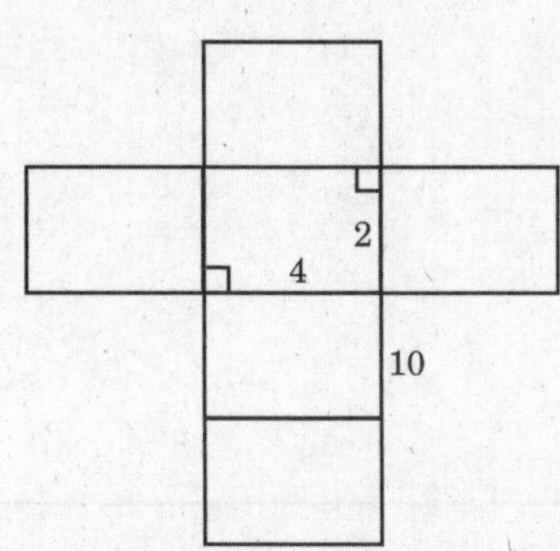

(C)

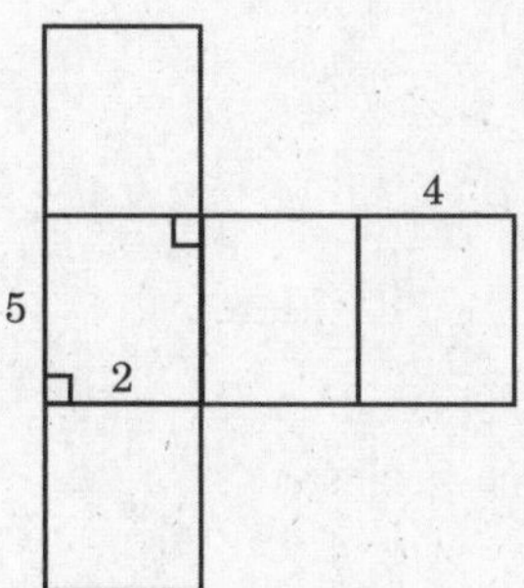

(D)

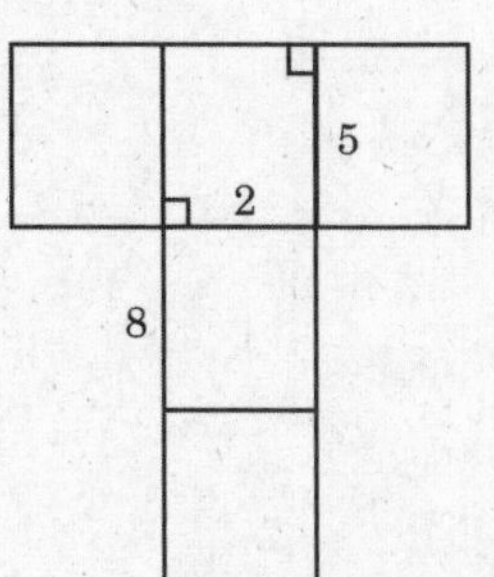

(E)

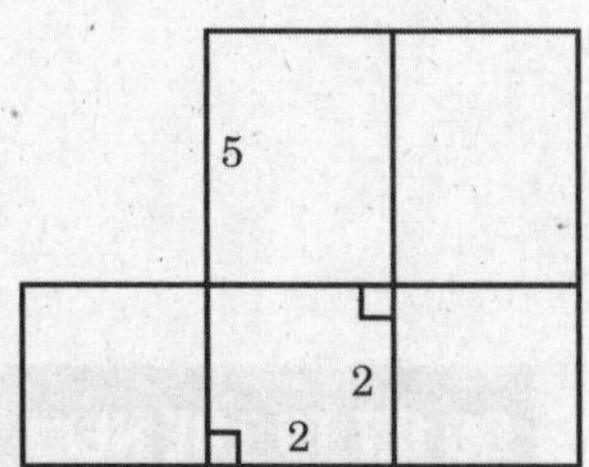

5. The figure below represents a diamond with each corner labeled A through F. The distance along one line segment is always 1. For example, the distance from A to B is 1. The distance from A to C, if one travels through point B, is 2. How many different paths are there of length 3 if one starts at point A and travels to point C ?

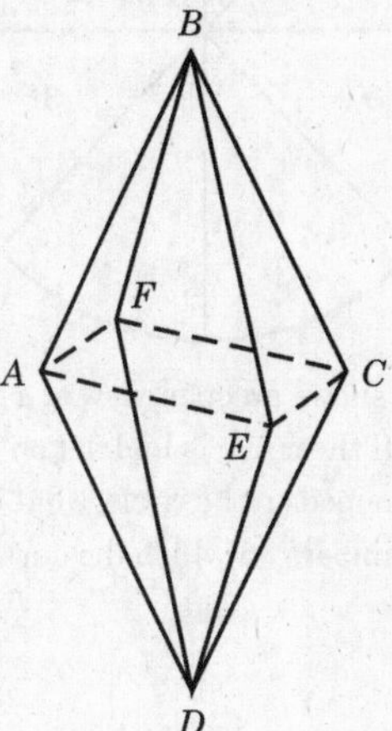

(A) 8
(B) 6
(C) 4
(D) 3
(E) 2

6. If $\frac{2}{5}$ of w is 20, what is $\frac{6}{5}$ of w ?

(A) 125
(B) 100
(C) 80
(D) 60
(E) 50

GO ON TO THE NEXT PAGE

SECTION 3

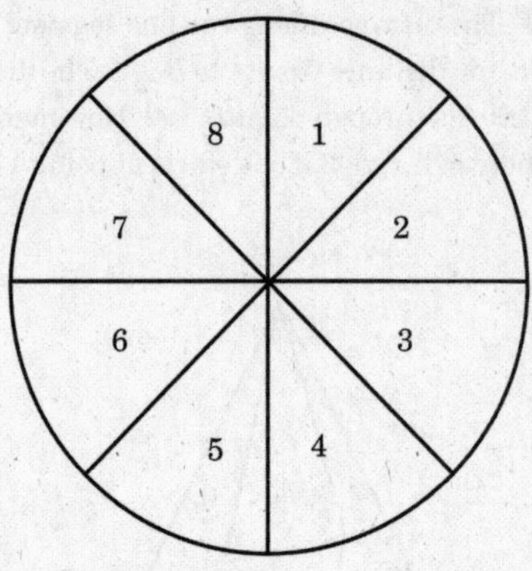

7. The figure above shows an open view of a circle divided into 8 even quadrants. If the circle is laid flat on the ground and two darts are to be dropped on the circle, what is the probability that the sum of the numbers on which the darts are dropped will be 10 or higher?

(A) $\frac{1}{12}$

(B) $\frac{2}{3}$

(C) $\frac{2}{9}$

(D) $\frac{5}{6}$

(E) $\frac{4}{9}$

---

8. If x and y are even integers, which of the following must also be an even integer?

I. xy
II. $y(x - 1)$
III. $(x + 1)(y - 1)$

(A) I only
(B) II only
(C) III only
(D) I and II
(E) I and III

6.78367347836734

9. In the number above, the decimal places after the initial digit 6 repeat as demonstrated. According to the pattern above, what will be the 100th digit after the decimal point?

(A) 7
(B) 8
(C) 3
(D) 6
(E) 4

---

10. If $f(x) = \frac{5^{2x} - 5^{x}}{x}$ then $f(2) = ?$

(A) 625
(B) 500
(C) 425
(D) 300
(E) 125

GO ON TO THE NEXT PAGE

SECTION 3

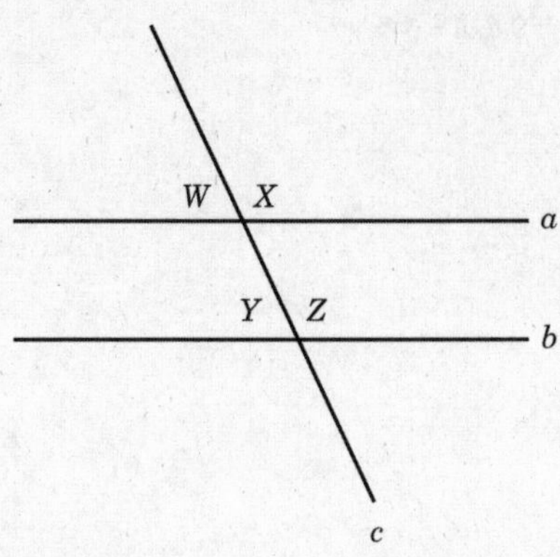

Note: Figure not drawn to scale.

11. In the figure above, line a is parallel to line b. Which of the following must be true?

(A) $W = Z$
(B) $W + Y = 180$
(C) $X + Y = 180$
(D) $X > 90$
(E) $W + Z = 180$

12. In the xy-plane, the line with equation $y = 6x + 18$ crosses the x-axis at the point with coordinates (m, n). What is the value of m ?

(A) −6
(B) −3
(C) 3
(D) 6
(E) 18

13. The test scores for 10 students in Mrs. Miller's class are 87, 92, 93, 76, 85, 99, 75, 82, 82, and one score she cannot read in her grade book. If the mode of the scores is 82 and the missing test score is definitely not 82, then the missing test score could be all of the following EXCEPT

(A) 95
(B) 69
(C) 78
(D) 81
(E) 87

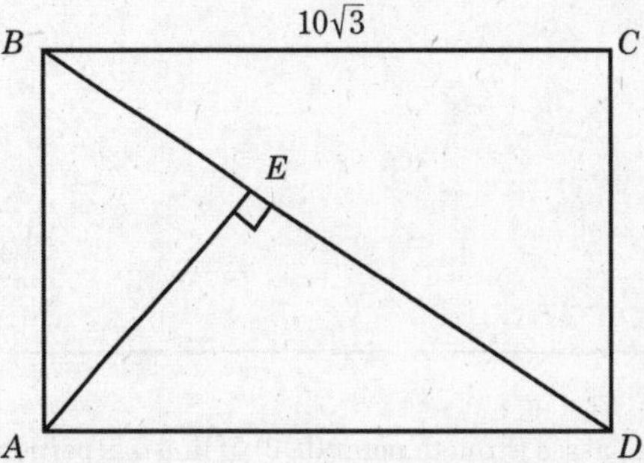

Note: Figure not drawn to scale.

14. In the figure above, rectangle $ABCD$ is divided into two small triangles by line segment BD. Triangle ABD in turn is divided into two even smaller triangles by line segment AE. If angle BAE measures 60 degrees, what is the perimeter of the shape $ABEDC$?

(A) $30\sqrt{3} + \frac{10\sqrt{3}}{3}$
(B) $30\sqrt{3} + 10$
(C) $60 + 20\sqrt{3}$
(D) $75 + 15\sqrt{3}$
(E) $20 + 20\sqrt{3}$

GO ON TO THE NEXT PAGE

SECTION 3

15. A "bridge" is said to be the ratio between a number and its largest prime factor. Which of the following is the bridge for the number 68 ?

(A) 2
(B) 4
(C) 17
(D) 34
(E) 68

16. Line a passes through point (0, 0). If line b is perpendicular to line a and has a negative slope, which of the following must be true?

(A) Line b has a positive y-intercept.
(B) Line a has a negative slope.
(C) Line a has a positive slope.
(D) Line b passes through point (0, 0).
(E) Line b has a negative x-intercept.

17. Let the operation & be defined by $x \& y = \frac{xy}{x-3}$. What is the value of y if $9 \& 5 = 5 \& y$?

(A) 60
(B) 6
(C) 3
(D) –30
(E) –60

18. Sam's CDs is having a sale. The first two CDs are bought at full price, or n dollars a piece. The next CD is a dollars less than the full price. After that, all CDs are b dollars. If Jill bought x number of CDs total, which of the following represents the total amount she spent at this sale?

(A) $3n - a + b(x - 3)$
(B) $3n - a + bx$
(C) $3n + b(x - a)$
(D) $2n + a + bx$
(E) $2n - a + b(x - 3)$

GO ON TO THE NEXT PAGE

SECTION 3

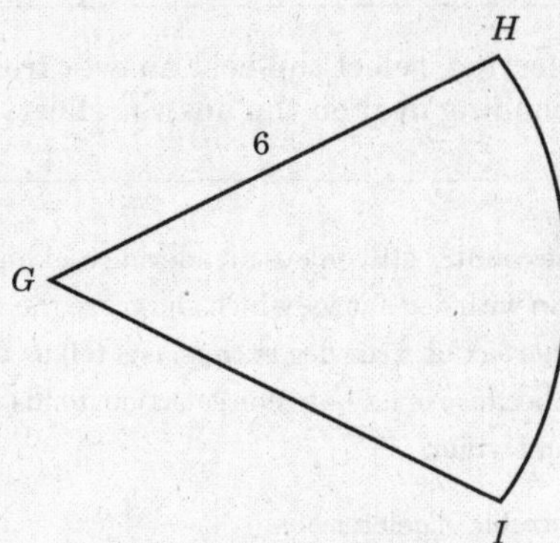

19. In the figure above, HI is the arc of circle with center G. If the area of sector GHI is 6π, then what is the measure of angle HGI?

(A) 30
(B) 45
(C) 60
(D) 90
(E) 120

20. A certain color of paint, called "ritz," contains a ratio of 35 parts blue paint for every 65 parts red. To make the color "retro," the color blue must be 20 percent of the total solution. How many parts of red must be added to "ritz" in order to turn it into "retro"?

(A) 20
(B) 35
(C) 65
(D) 70
(E) 75

S T O P

IF YOU FINISH BEFORE TIME IS CALLED, YOU MAY CHECK YOUR WORK ON THIS TEST ONLY.
DO NOT TURN TO ANY OTHER SECTION IN THIS TEST.

SECTION 4

Turn to Section 4 of your answer sheet to answer the questions in this section.

Time—25 Minutes
24 Questions

Directions: For each question in this section, select the best answer from among the choices given and fill in the corresponding oval on the answer sheet.

Each sentence below has one or two blanks, each blank indicating that something has been omitted. Beneath the sentence are five words or sets of words labeled A through E. Choose the word or set of words that, when inserted in the sentence, best fits the meaning of the sentence as a whole.

Example:

Eliza felt ----- when her boss asked her to work seven weekends in a row but ----- when her work earned her a promotion.

(A) enervated . . weakened
(B) depressed . . intellectual
(C) advantageous . . salacious
(D) angry . . shopworn
(E) irate . . elated     ●

1. On our trip to Australia, we confirmed that the sea turtle hatching is a ----- event, for we were only able to see it at night.

(A) diurnal
(B) resplendent
(C) emaciated
(D) nocturnal
(E) decadent

2. The closing of the two suburban fire departments sparked a vociferous ----- that was only ----- when the mayor agreed to reopen them.

(A) jubilation . . soothed
(B) rebellion . . assuaged
(C) debate . . accelerated
(D) denial . . modified
(E) conflagration . . intensified

3. Though the country still enjoys an adoring and highly ----- relationship with dog shows, which showcase the very epitome of genetic perfection, true dog enthusiasts tell us that it is the mutt that, because of its ----- gene selection, tends to be smarter, stronger, and wilier.

(A) pleasurable . . deleterious
(B) benign . . malignant
(C) censorious . . mutated
(D) adoring . . flaccid
(E) fawning . . varied

4. The actor worked hard to portray an outward face that the press generally described as -----, though friends and those who composed his inner circle believed him to be down to earth and a very easy-to-grasp presence in their lives.

(A) specious
(B) affable
(C) mercurial
(D) untoward
(E) debased

5. A film critic must always balance his negative criticism with constructive comments and not with -----, for otherwise his audience will begin to believe that his barbs are the result of a personal desire to sound -----, and not out of love for the craft or interest in its development as an art form.

(A) irony . . pretentious
(B) sarcasm . . erudite
(C) adulation . . snide
(D) reflection . . incensed
(E) barbs . . elated

GO ON TO THE NEXT PAGE

SECTION 4

Directions: The passages below are followed by questions based on their content; questions following a pair of related passages may also be based on the relationship between the paired passages. Answer the questions on the basis of what is stated or implied in the passages and in any introductory material that may be provided.

Questions 6–9 are based on the following passages.

Passage 1

Students of poetry can't help but pick up a slim volume of Shelley or Keats and long for the days when these poets were alive and writing in the fever of romanticism that gripped all of England. Then poets were heroes, admired for their imaginations and feted and treated as dignitaries—fawning that today is reserved for celebrities of dubious talent. How it must have been to wait with bated breath for the latest volume of poetry and to have lived in a time when readers were demanding in their tastes. Publishers too understood their readers' needs and only printed those works that met the high bar of critical taste. These days when poetry is given short shrift on the shelves of large conglomerate bookstores in favor of books whose plots are as healthy and as rewarding as saccharine sweets, it behooves us to remember the days when poetry was recognized as a great art.

Passage 2

It's tempting to think that the past is better than the present. Reading history, we can sift through facts, letting our attention rest only on those details we find most pleasing. Scanning the volumes of "great literature" that sit on the shelves of most erudite people, it is tempting too to assume that the writers of the past turned out masterpiece after masterpiece, but the truth is that much waste has been forgotten, committed to the dustbin of memory. We must also remember, when we think of the ballyhoo that surrounded the publication of a new slim volume of poetry, that this book of verse was for a very specific audience: the same audience that wrote reviews, dined in one another's houses, and tried to inspire artists. Today our education system, our social circles, and our readership have become much more diverse, and far less class based. We should expect the books published today to be more varied as well.

6. Unlike Passage 2, the tone of Passage 1 is more

(A) derogatory than adamant
(B) wistful than practical
(C) nostalgic than damning
(D) prepossessing than mannered
(E) willful than charmed

7. Both passages address

(A) ways to read poetry successfully
(B) the manner in which new books should be promoted
(C) appropriate methods of judging quality literature
(D) the popularity of past writers
(E) how to view the success of literature of the past

8. The author of Passage 1 would most likely respond in what way to the last line of Passage 2?

(A) The mass education of the population has diluted the quality of good writing.
(B) In another fifty years, the books of today will be weeded down to only a remembered few.
(C) The abundance of books does not make up for the fact that the quality of good writing has subsided.
(D) Reading has always been the pastime of a privileged minority.
(E) Publishers are less able to pick surefire hits than they were in the past.

9. The author of Passage 2 would respond to lines 1–6 ("Students of . . . talent") in Passage 1 with which of the following observations?

(A) Writers of the past were simply better skilled compared to today's artists.
(B) Television has largely replaced reading as the entertainment medium of choice.
(C) We should not be surprised that the quality of books has subsided.
(D) History has selected the few books which we remember, giving us the false impression that the past harbored works of seamless quality.
(E) Children are not taught to read and enjoy books at an early enough age.

GO ON TO THE NEXT PAGE

SECTION 4

Directions: Each passage below is followed by questions based on its content. Answer the questions on the basis of what is stated or implied in each passage and in any introductory material that may be provided.

Questions 10–15 are based on the following passage.

The passage below is taken from the memoir of a young Mexican-American physician who grew up in northern California.

When I come home now to visit my parents I am always elated by the sight of the artichoke fields lining the two-lane highway. I pass over a small river, often almost dry, then onto a dirt road leading to our home. Friends from college are often stunned to see where I grew up. Our house is the faded red of a true farm barn, raised on stilts to avoid the few times in the past couple of decades that the previously mentioned river has swelled up through the carefully maintained artichoke fields to become a sea.

When I bring friends to see my parents, they are invariably stunned.

"You grew up *here*?" they ask.

These kinds of comments used to rankle me. I always assumed that friends were talking about the decidedly modest accommodations in which I spent my formative years. The "house" really qualifies as nothing more than a shack, though it does have indoor plumbing of a kind and electricity and heat. My father has worked hard to insulate and improve our home over the years, but it is all a far cry from the modern California homes in which most of my friends grew up. Our poverty was also of the flagrant kind, clearly visible from the highway. We could not mask our modest situation. My parents spoke little English, though they had learned enough to find steady work after we were legally able to work in this country. Unlike other American families, who I have since learned struggle far more than I thought they did in the early years when we first arrived here from Mexico, we did not hide our poverty by paying for electronics and cars and dinners out on the town. My mother walked to the grocery store—a five-minute trek—and my brother and I borrowed books from the library.

This kind of "poverty" is actually a richness in many parts of Mexico, where plenty of people don't even have a toilet in the house. When we moved here, we made the mistaken assumption that we were kings. This illusion was dispelled when I started going to school and saw the casual, brash, and confident way in which so many kids interacted with each other, careless with their clothes and their possessions. Some of my other Mexican friends tried to emulate this kind of confident behavior, which, unbeknownst to them, made them seem like caricature Mexicans, arriving in America with machismo, making fools of themselves. I was a quieter type of person, focused on my studies, privately suffering the feeling that I would never fit in, would never be able to offer the kind of materialistic-based friendship that seemed to be the norm here. I could never say, "Hey, want to come and play with my Atari?"

I am less judgmental of my friends now. For one thing, I have plenty of friends, most of whom I met in college where my ethnic identity and personal story became something of an attractive combination: here I was, an authentic Latino success story, ready to be embraced into the mainstream fold. Now when I travel south to visit my parents, I can see a little of what my friends see. When they say to me, "You grew up *here*?" I imagine they are responding to the pure bucolic beauty of my home. The ocean is a few minutes' walk away. I can fish for dinner in the river, then roast it outside on a grill my father made for me. The grocery store is only minutes away, but is hidden from view by a thicket of tall willow trees. This home is a wonder for my friends, who only know me now as an accomplished physician, a man of science. Since they know my story, they are not shocked by the modest conditions in which my parents continue to live. Rather, they are stunned to see vestiges of my childhood—a youth spent in the proximity of nature and her gentle gifts.

10. In lines 9–14 ("When I . . . years"), the author characterizes his friends' comments as being

(A) shock mixed with judgment
(B) awe mixed with shame
(C) annoyance mixed with resolution
(D) amusement mixed with denial
(E) guilt mixed with agony

11. The phrase "we could not mask our modest situation" in lines 20–21 is included to

(A) emphasize the degree to which the narrator grew up poor
(B) highlight the lack of shame the narrator felt as a child
(C) suggest the unapologetic manner in which the narrator interacted with the world
(D) point out the lengths to which the narrator went to try to hide his poverty at school
(E) decry the degree to which society judges others on surface alone

GO ON TO THE NEXT PAGE

SECTION 4

12. The narrator's observation in lines 23–25 ("Unlike other . . Mexico") suggests that

(A) the United States is not at all the bastion of wealth that the narrator expected it to be when he arrived with his family
(B) although the narrator may have thought his family was the only one with financial difficulties, he learned that others face them as well
(C) the children at school who offered to share their Atari video game sets may have been lying about the existence of such expensive toys
(D) the struggle to adapt to life in America is universal for all people
(E) other children would have been happy to come to the narrator's home and eat fish for dinner

13. In lines 45–49 ("I am less . . . fold"), the narrator suggests that

(A) he has learned why he judged his impoverished upbringing so harshly
(B) his success as a doctor has made up for his difficult early years
(C) he was guilty of the same judgmental behavior that he anticipated from his schoolmates as a child
(D) he may never learn to adapt to living in America
(E) he greatly prefers the friends he made in college to those of his childhood years

14. For the narrator, a significant aspect of his appreciation for his home occurs when

(A) he becomes a doctor
(B) he grows homesick in college
(C) he returns to see his home flooded
(D) his father insulates the house
(E) he is able to see it as a physically beautiful place

15. By the end of the passage, the author's tone has become

(A) regretful
(B) nostalgic
(C) angry
(D) dissatisfied
(E) ironic

GO ON TO THE NEXT PAGE

SECTION 4

Questions 16–24 are based on the following passage.

The domestic house cat has a long and distinguished history. In true catlike fashion, it has crept up behind the dog, that holder of the title "Man's Best Friend," and in recent years has surpassed all things canine to become America's most popular household pet. Cats, their owners claim, are superior pets that are able to take care of themselves, are clean, and do not smell. The ancient people of the world must have concurred, since they began domesticating the cat at an early moment in history.

Recently, in a small grave on the island of Cyprus, scientists unearthed the carefully preserved skeleton of a cat buried next to a figure—whether man or woman is difficult to tell—who is also buried in ceremonial fashion, with offerings of polished stone and flint. Scientists assume that the cat and the human were buried together because of their proximity and positioning. The grave seems to pay tribute to the person's high status, lending credence to the idea that the cat too might have played a significant role in the lives of the people on the island of Cyprus. Certainly the date of the grave, the ninth millennium B.C., coincides with the rapid spreading of agriculture, when humans finally learned to cultivate grain for themselves. The development of farming meant that people no longer needed to exclusively hunt for their meals, but could instead say in one place. Baskets and pots of grain, however, would have attracted mice, and that alone could have inspired intrepid humans to befriend the cat. It should also be noted that cats are not native to Cyprus, so this particular cat—or its ancestors—must have been physically brought to the island.

The world also knows of the love the Egyptians had for their cats. If a cat died, its owner in ancient Egypt might shave off her eyebrows to signify her grief. By 1500 B.C., it became illegal to kill a cat, and murderers were put to death. The Egyptians also had a goddess named Bastet who was believed to bestow fertility and good luck. Her body was human, but her head was that of a cat.

Scientists now believe that most domestic cats were descended from an animal living in a desert. In fact, cats widely prefer warm spaces and are happy to sit in patches of sunlight. They are also highly dormant for large portions of the day, behavior that is typical of creatures accustomed to hot temperatures. It has also been noted that the domestic cat has a fondness for burying its feces in sand. Presumably, its ancestors lived in an area with a high abundance of sand, such as a desert.

In the Middle Ages, the cat experienced a decrease in popularity. Many scholars now believe that the anti-cat attitudes actually contributed to the vast number of people who died because of the plague. When the Black Plague initially began to kill so many people, the pope was moved to declare that the illness must be the work of the devil. Because the cat was free to roam at night, when presumably the devil was also on the move, the pope declared that the cat was in league with the devil. The fact that witches were known to consort with cats also contributed to this misconception. As a result, numerous cats were captured and killed. Sadly, however, the lack of cats meant that the rat population was able to careen out of control: rats were responsible for helping to spread the disease. It is thus interesting to note how the rise and fall of fashions can influence not just our interests but our health.

16. The author's general purpose in this passage is to

(A) convey information
(B) question a long-held belief
(C) challenge cherished opinions
(D) propose a new theory
(E) lament the loss of a figure of importance

17. As used in context, the word "concurred" in line 7 most nearly means

(A) adapted
(B) assaulted
(C) ambushed
(D) agreed
(E) applied

18. The author mentions that cats are not native on the island of Cyprus, lines 24–26 ("It should . . . island"), in order to

(A) suggest that scientists are suspicious about the presence of cats in the grave site
(B) strengthen the idea that cats must have been domesticated
(C) propose scholars revisit the origin of cats
(D) recommend that a new theory about the earliest date of domestication be considered
(E) highlight the importance of cats protecting humans from mice

19. Which of the following is not provided as evidence that cats have descended from a creature adapted to the desert?

(A) Cats like to sleep for long hours of the day
(B) Cats primarily eat meat
(C) Cats prefer heat
(D) Cats like to bury their waste in sand
(E) Cats are attracted to patches of sunlight

GO ON TO THE NEXT PAGE

SECTION 4

20. Which of the following, if true, would weaken the author's argument in lines 51–53 ("Sadly . . . the disease")?

(A) Humans had feared cats for many centuries before the Black Plague.
(B) Some humans had positive relationships with cats.
(C) Cats were only introduced to Europe at the dawn of the new millennium.
(D) Cats do not enjoy the taste of rats, preferring mice instead.
(E) Cats were needed to kill mice who were eating grain.

21. The argument in the fifth paragraph (lines 41–55) is built on

(A) proven scientific fact
(B) the opinion of a minority
(C) the passions of a persuasive group
(D) a passive audience
(E) historical information mixed with supposition

22. Cats were directly involved in the development of the Black Plague, according to the author in lines 46–53 ("Because the . . . disease") specifically because

(A) they were in league with the devil
(B) they were disliked by most plague victims
(C) the pope declared them evil
(D) they only hunted at night
(E) they were not as popular as dogs

23. The final line of the passage suggests a sense of

(A) empowerment
(B) bemusement
(C) crypticism
(D) agony
(E) sadness

24. The overall tone of the passage is

(A) neutral
(B) caring
(C) disarming
(D) electric
(E) avowed

S T O P

IF YOU FINISH BEFORE TIME IS CALLED, YOU MAY CHECK YOUR WORK ON THIS TEST ONLY. DO NOT TURN TO ANY OTHER SECTION IN THIS TEST.

SECTION 5

Turn to Section 5 of your answer sheet to answer the questions in this section.

Time—25 Minutes
18 Questions

Directions: For this section, solve each problem and decide which is the best of the choices given. Fill in the corresponding oval on the answer sheet. You may use any available space for scratchwork.

Notes:

1. The use of a calculator is permitted. All numbers used are real numbers.
2. Figures that accompany problems in this test are intended to provide information useful in solving the problems. They are drawn as accurately as possible EXCEPT when it is stated in a specific problem that the figure is not drawn to scale. All figures lie in a plane unless otherwise indicated.
3. Unless otherwise specified, the domain of any function *f* is assumed to be the set of all real numbers *x* for which *f*(*x*) is a real number.

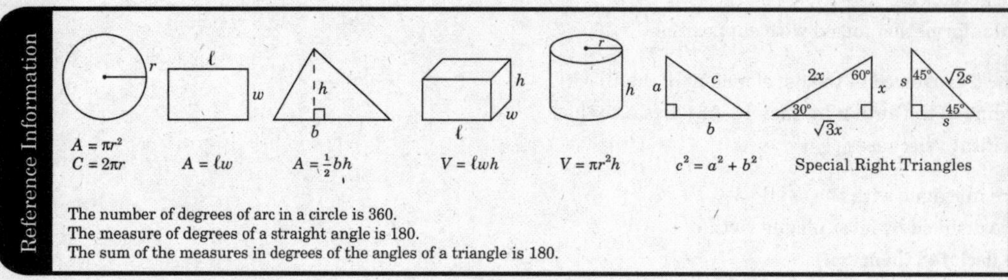

$$\frac{5x-1}{4} = 6$$

1. What is the value of x?

(A) 2
(B) 4
(C) 5
(D) 6
(E) 7

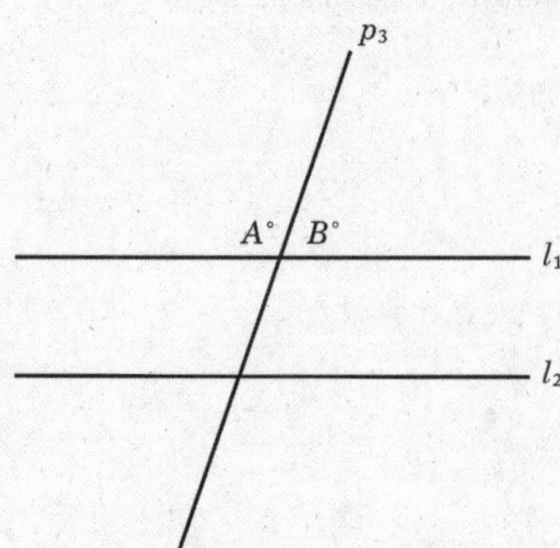

Note: Figure not drawn to scale.

2. In the figure above, angles A and B together equal 180 degrees if

(A) A is less than 90 degrees
(B) A is more than 90 degrees
(C) line 3 is parallel to line 1
(D) B is greater than 90 degrees
(E) lines 1 and 2 are parallel

GO ON TO THE NEXT PAGE

SECTION 5

KIMBALL PET ADOPTION CENTER

	Adopted	Not Adopted	Total
Cats	3,842	1,689	
Dogs			4,891
Total	5,997		

3. According to the figure above, how many dogs are not adopted?

(A) 2,736
(B) 3,842
(C) 5,997
(D) 10,422
(E) 12,366

---

4. A yarn store calculates the amount of money it makes, M, using the following function to average out the varying costs of different kinds of yarn, where y represents the number of skeins of yarn sold: $M(y) = 5y - 25$. If on a given day, the store sold 15 skeins of yarn, how much money did the store make?

(A) 5
(B) 25
(C) 30
(D) 50
(E) 74

5. If $a = bc$ and $ce = \frac{d}{b}$, then a is also equal to which of the following?

(A) $\frac{d}{e}$
(B) bce
(C) de
(D) $\frac{a}{c}$
(E) cd

---

6. The ratio of black cups to white cups in a crate of dishes is $\frac{4}{5}$. All of the following could be the total number of cups in the crate EXCEPT

(A) 9
(B) 18
(C) 26
(D) 36
(E) 45

GO ON TO THE NEXT PAGE

7. A certain knitting pattern calls for 6 stitches to the inch, which helps the knitter determine how many stitches total there will need to be for one row on a needle. For example, the total width of the finished piece must be 16 inches, so the knitter will need to have 96 stitches in one row ($6 \times 16 = 96$). However, the knitter wants to use a yarn that will only yield 4 stitches to the inch. How many stitches will she need in one row to maintain a width of 16 inches?

(A) 4
(B) 6
(C) 16
(D) 64
(E) 96

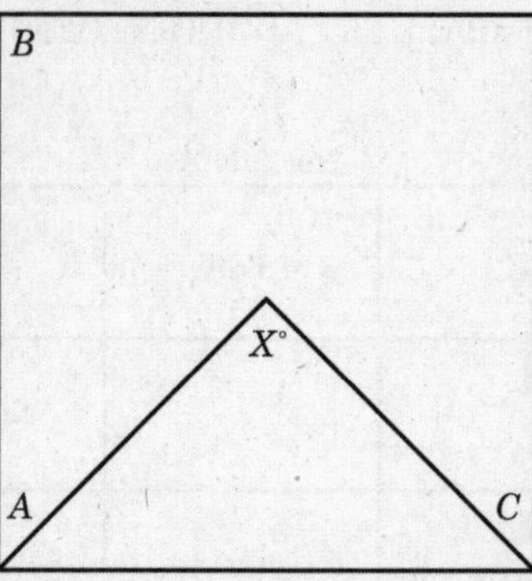

8. The figure above shows a square with angle A, and a triangle with one angle marked $X°$. Which of the following is the equivalent of angle $X°$?

(A) $2B - C$
(B) $A + C$
(C) $B - A - C$
(D) $2C + B$
(E) $2B - C - A$

GO ON TO THE NEXT PAGE

SECTION 5

Directions: For Student-Produced Response questions 9–18, use the grids on the answer sheet.

Each of these questions requires you to solve the problem and enter your answer by marking the ovals in the special grid, as shown in the examples below. You may use any available space for scratchwork.

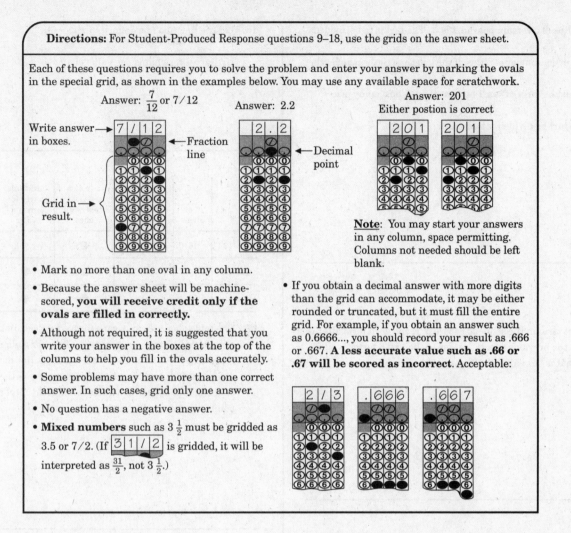

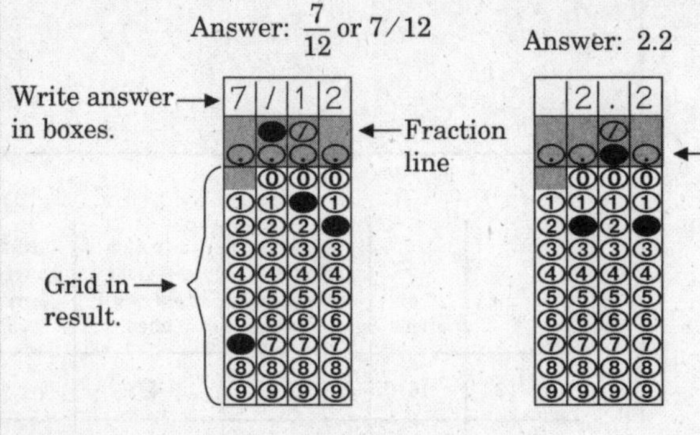

Note: You may start your answers in any column, space permitting. Columns not needed should be left blank.

- Mark no more than one oval in any column.
- Because the answer sheet will be machine-scored, **you will receive credit only if the ovals are filled in correctly.**
- Although not required, it is suggested that you write your answer in the boxes at the top of the columns to help you fill in the ovals accurately.
- Some problems may have more than one correct answer. In such cases, grid only one answer.
- No question has a negative answer.
- **Mixed numbers** such as $3\frac{1}{2}$ must be gridded as 3.5 or 7/2. (If 3 1 / 2 is gridded, it will be interpreted as $\frac{31}{2}$, not $3\frac{1}{2}$.)
- If you obtain a decimal answer with more digits than the grid can accommodate, it may be either rounded or truncated, but it must fill the entire grid. For example, if you obtain an answer such as 0.6666..., you should record your result as .666 or .667. **A less accurate value such as .66 or .67 will be scored as incorrect**. Acceptable:

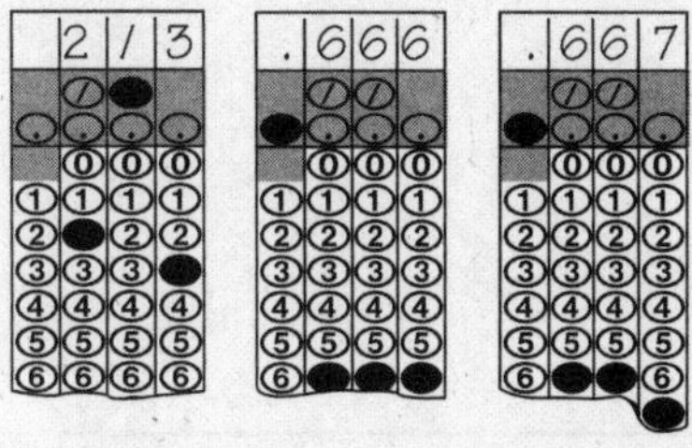

9. If $z^4 = 121$, what is the value of $3z^4$?

10. The point on a number line that is exactly midway between 11 and 2 is separated by how much from the first point or 2 ?

11. What is the smallest possible perimeter of a triangle whose distinct sides each are a prime number?

12. If $a^2 - b^2 = 21$ and $a - b = 3$, then what is the value of a ?

GO ON TO THE NEXT PAGE

SECTION 5

13. The radius of a certain pear tart is $\frac{6}{\pi}$. The tart is to be divided into an even number of slices. If the length of the crust of each slice must be larger than 1 but less than 3, how many pieces can the tart be divided into?

$$x, 4x \ldots$$

14. The first term in the sequence above is x, and each term after is 4 times the previous one. If the sum of the first 6 terms is 4,095, then what is the value of x?

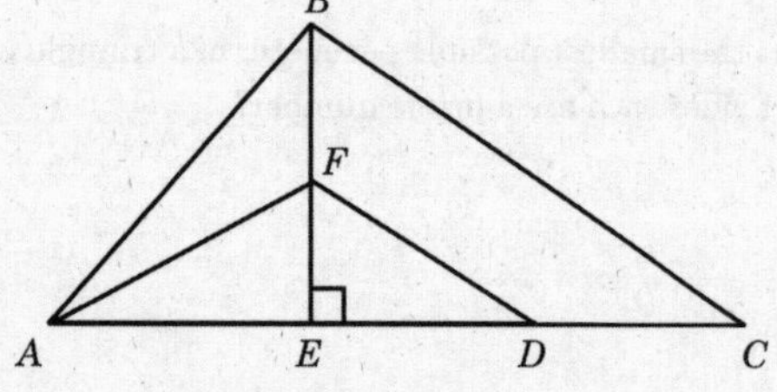

Note: Figure not drawn to scale.

15. In the figure above, the ratio of BF to BE is 1 to 4. If the area of triangle ABC is 12 and the area of triangle AFD is 6, what is the ratio of side AD to side AC?

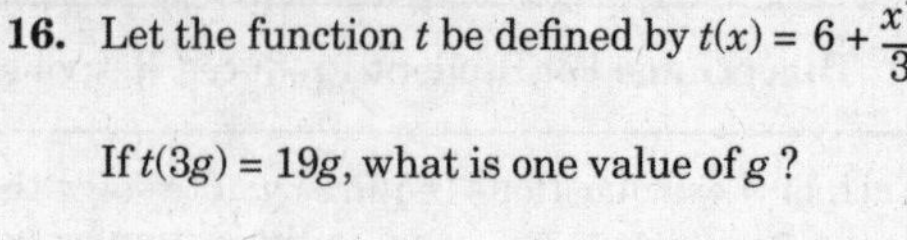

16. Let the function t be defined by $t(x) = 6 + \frac{x^2}{3}$

If $t(3g) = 19g$, what is one value of g?

	# of aliens	x points given for every $2x$ alien	$2x$ points given for every x alien	$3x$ points given for every x alien	$5x$ points given for every x alien
Quest 1	16	●	●		
Quest 2	25		●	●	
Quest 3	50		●	●	●

17. The table above shows a certain chart for calculating the number of points a gamer receives for killing aliens in a video game. The dots on the chart indicate scenarios in which points can be earned. Assuming that this chart shows the total number of aliens that appear in a game, what is the total number of points a gamer could ever hope to score?

18. An actress keeps all of her awards on a shelf. There are 5 awards total. She wants to keep the most prestigious award in the center spot on her shelf but likes to rearrange the other 4 statues. Assuming she keeps the statues in a line, what is the total number of possible arrangements of her awards?

S T O P

IF YOU FINISH BEFORE TIME IS CALLED, YOU MAY CHECK YOUR WORK ON THIS TEST ONLY. DO NOT TURN TO ANY OTHER SECTION IN THIS TEST.

SECTION 6

Turn to Section 6 of your answer sheet to answer the questions in this section.

Time—25 Minutes
35 Questions

Directions: For each question in this section, select the best answer from among the choices given.

The following sentences test correctness and effectiveness of expression. Part of each sentence or the entire sentence is underlined; beneath each sentence are five ways of phrasing the underlined material. Choice A repeats the original phrasing; the other four choices are different. If you think the original phrasing produces a better sentence than any of the alternatives, select choice A; if not, select one of the other choices.

In making your selection, follow the requirements of standard written English; that is, pay attention to grammar, choice of words, sentence construction, and punctuation. Your selection should result in the most effective sentence—clear and precise, without awkwardness or ambiguity.

Example:

In the poem "Ulysses" by Alfred, Lord Tennyson, the speaker says, "I cannot rest from travel," instead, he will live life to the fullest.

(A) "I cannot rest from travel," instead,
(B) "I cannot rest from travel"; instead,
(C) "I cannot rest from travel" instead,
(D) "I cannot rest from travel," upon which
(E) "I cannot rest from travel,"

1. For the past few years, more Americans are traveling to the Caribbean than they went to Europe.

(A) they went to Europe.
(B) to Europe.
(C) they are going to Europe.
(D) in Europe.
(E) toward Europe.

2. The emphasis on whole grains and organic meat has become increasingly popular in the United States, they are much healthier than food sprayed with pesticides.

(A) , they are much healthier than food sprayed with pesticides
(B) , and they are much healthier than food sprayed with pesticides
(C) , but they are much healthier than food sprayed with pesticides
(D) , because they are much healthier than food sprayed with pesticides
(E) , where they are much healthier than food sprayed with pesticides

3. The snow outside is not falling as heavily as last week.

(A) as last week
(B) as last week's
(C) as the last week
(D) as the week last
(E) as it did last week

4. During the planning phases, the design team studied numerous photos and art books and they therefore searched for inspiration.

(A) and they therefore searched for inspiration
(B) in searching inspiration
(C) in searching for inspiration
(D) to search inspiration
(E) in an inspiration search

5. Consulting with her entire family for a suitable gift, they decided she should make something by hand.

(A) they decided she should make something by hand
(B) she decided to make something by hand
(C) deciding to make something by hand
(D) and they decided she should make something by hand
(E) it was decided by them she should make something by hand

GO ON TO THE NEXT PAGE

SECTION 6

6. In deciding where the next Olympics was to take place, the committee considered the city's capacity for athletes and guests, the popularity of the host country, and they also wondered about how much money the city had to spend.

(A) the city's capacity for athletes and guests, the popularity of the host country, and they also wondered about how much money the city had to spend
(B) the city's capacity for athletes and guests, the popularity of the host country, and also wondered about how much money the city had to spend
(C) the city's capacity for athletes and guests, the popularity of the host country, and the amount of money the city had to spend
(D) the city's capacity for athletes and guests, the popularity of the host country, and wondering about how much money the city had to spend
(E) the city's capacity for athletes and guests, the popularity of the host country, and then the money the city had to spend

7. Traditional Aran knitting, which involves numerous cables and twists in the yarn to add extra heft and thus warmth to a sweater, originated on the isle of Aran off the coast of Scotland.

(A) which involves numerous cables and twists in the yarn to add extra heft and thus warmth to a sweater,
(B) which involving numerous cables and twists in the yarn to add extra heft and thus warmth to a sweater,
(C) which involves not only numerous cables and twists in the yarn to add extra heft and thus warmth to a sweater,
(D) which is involving numerous cables and twists in the yarn to add extra heft and thus warmth to a sweater,
(E) which involves numerous cables and twists in the yarn and, thus, adding extra heft and thus warmth to a sweater,

8. Driving through the state of Nevada after a ten-year absence, Las Vegas was, after ten years, clearly visible to Les as the fastest growing city in the United States.

(A) Las Vegas was, after ten years, clearly visible to Les as the fastest growing city in the United States
(B) Las Vegas clearly seeing to Les as the fastest growing city in the United States
(C) Las Vegas was clearly visible as the fastest growing city in the United States to Les
(D) Les clearly saw that Las Vegas was the fastest growing city in the United States
(E) Las Vegas, to Les, was clearly visible as the fastest growing city in the United States

9. With an ability to evoke the whims of kings, the passions of youth, and also an ability to express himself through deep poetic metaphor, Shakespeare continues to inspire scholars and readers alike.

(A) With an ability to evoke the whims of kings, the passions of youth, and also an ability to express himself through deep poetic metaphor,
(B) With an ability to evoke the whims of kings, the passions of youth, and also expressing himself through deep poetic metaphor,
(C) With an ability to evoke the whims of kings, the passions of youth, and he also expresses himself through deep poetic metaphor,
(D) With an ability to evoke the whims of kings, the passions of youth, and the deepest poetic metaphor,
(E) With an ability to evoke the whims of kings, the passions of youth, and he can express himself through deep poetic metaphor,

10. The settings of John Steinbeck's stories changed many times over the years, first his stories were set in California, then Mexico, and then he moved them out to the East Coast.

(A) first his stories were set in California, then Mexico, and then he moved them out to the East Coast.
(B) starting in California, then moving to Mexico, and then moving to the East Coast.
(C) first setting his stories were set in California, then choosing Mexico, and then he moved them out to the East Coast.
(D) first his stories were set in California, then Mexico, and then he moving to the East Coast.
(E) first setting in California, then Mexico, and then setting in the East Coast.

GO ON TO THE NEXT PAGE

11. <u>While university professors are often under tremendous pressure to publish as much scholarly material as possible,</u> for the reputation of an institution depends on the public's perception of the faculty as productive and influential.

(A) While university professors are often under tremendous pressure to publish as much scholarly material as possible,
(B) Because university professors are often under tremendous pressure to publish as much scholarly material as possible,
(C) Although university professors are often under tremendous pressure to publish as much scholarly material as possible,
(D) Why university professors are often under tremendous pressure to publish as much scholarly material as possible,
(E) University professors are often under tremendous pressure to publish as much scholarly material as possible,

GO ON TO THE NEXT PAGE

SECTION 6

Directions: For each question in this section, select the best answer from among the choices given.

The following sentences test your ability to recognize grammar and usage errors. Each sentence contains either a single error or no error at all. No sentence contains more than one error. The error, if there is one, is underlined and lettered. If the sentence contains an error, select the one underlined part that must be changed to make the sentence correct. If the sentence is correct, select choice E. In choosing answers, follow the requirements of standard written English.

Example:

The other (A) delegates and him (B) immediately (C) accepted the resolution drafted by (D) the neutral states. No error (E)

Ⓐ ● Ⓒ Ⓓ Ⓔ

12. Heralded (A) as the (B) first reusable spacecraft, NASA's space shuttle has inspired (C) countless numbers of young people to became (D) astronauts. No error (E)

13. The radio program began (A) an intense attempt to (B) attract younger (C) listeners by choosing topics that (D) would be of interest to young adults. No error (E)

14. Neither the media or (A) the young actor's parents could believe (B) the trouble the young performer got into, (C) so wholesome (D) was his image. No error (E)

15. Although (A) the scientist was able to re-create (B) only (C) part of the experiment, he was fairly confident that one day he will manage (D) to perform the entire thing. No error (E)

16. Due (A) to the tremendous variety that (B) goes into (C) making each quilt, it is virtually impossible for any two to be similar, making each piece one of its (D) kind. No error (E)

17. The modern age of machines and mass automation has prompted (A) hip-hop dancers to observe (B) the robotic capabilities of the body and to display (C) these movements through (D) dance. No error (E)

18. Already convinced that she wins (A) the beauty pageant, the young (B) girl acted like a star to the great (C) annoyance of the other contestants and (D) the judges alike. No error (E)

19. In more (A) modern cities which (B) have the benefit of extensive urban planning, streets are (C) wide enough to accommodate cars, and sidewalks provide (D) pedestrians with a safe place to walk. No error (E)

20. The club's (A) president read the roster and (B) found that all members were (C) present, and accumulated (D) for. No error (E)

21. The statue, said to have been carved (A) by one of the Greek artists who (B) followed Alexander the Great on their (C) quest to conquer the ancient world, bears (D) distinctly classical features. No error (E)

22. It (A) is easier to complete a job on time by (B) concentrating and working quickly than to scattering (C) attention and thus work slowly. (D) No error (E)

23. Alex did not despair when (A) he was laid off (B) by his company; instead, (C) he took his savings and began (D) to travel the world. No error (E)

GO ON TO THE NEXT PAGE

SECTION 6

24. The Native American (A) had no chemical dyes originally: they used (B) extracts from (C) different kinds of plants to make (D) dyes for their blankets. No error (E)

25. There was great enthusiasm of (A) the town when (B) it was announced (C) that a major movie studio would be using (D) the downtown area to film a movie. No error (E)

26. Intending to reward Charles and I (A) for recognition of our work with (B) young teens, the foundation presented us both (C) with a check to help defray (D) the cost of college tuition. No error (E)

27. The journalist highlighted the difficulty that ensures (A) when a news service is (B) dependent on a dearth of (C) real journalists trained to ask (D) difficult questions. No error (E)

28. The legitimacy of the art exhibit featuring numerous small statues of dogs was called (A) into question when (B) the leading art critic pointed out that (C) it (D) were all made in China. No error (E)

29. Because (A) we had not added the correct (B) proportion of ingredients, the cake did not set proper (C), and we had to throw it out and start all over (D). No error (E)

GO ON TO THE NEXT PAGE

SECTION 6

Directions: The following passage is an early draft of an essay. Some parts of the passage need to be rewritten.

Read the passage and select the best answers for the questions that follow. Some questions are about particular sentences or parts of sentences and ask you to improve sentence structure or word choice. Other questions ask you to consider organization and development. In choosing answers, follow the requirements of standard written English.

Questions 30–35 are based on the following passage.

(1) *The dog may be man's best friend, but he can also be the source of discomfort.* **(2)** *Dogs have a tendency to attract many pests, like fleas and ticks and just bathing them won't be enough to get rid of them all.* **(3)** *It's not surprising that many people keep their dogs outside in the back yard where the fleas and pests are kept out of the way.* **(4)** *These days dogs can come inside because of new medications.*

(5) *One particularly strong medicine is systemic.* **(6)** *This means it goes throughout the dog's body.* **(7)** *Whenever a flea or some other undesirable insect lands on the dog's fur, it is immediately killed by the medicine.* **(8)** *Once a month, the owner just has to remember to put on the medication.*

(9) *If you do find that you have fleas and can't get rid of them and they are in your house, you should do the following.* **(10)** *First, vacuum twice a day, using a powerful vacuum.* **(11)** *A strong one is the best.* **(12)** *Second, make sure you throw away the vacuum bag so the fleas don't crawl out of the vacuum and back into your house.* **(13)** *Third, make sure your pets are treated.* **(14)** *Fleas can cause animals to scratch their fur.* **(15)** *When this happens, they open up sores on their skin.* **(16)** *Left untreated, these sores can get infected, causing even greater problems for the dog.* **(17)** *And you will keep your dog your best friend.*

30. Which of the following is the best way to revise sentence 2 (reprinted below)?

Dogs have a tendency to attract many pests, like fleas and ticks and just bathing them won't be enough to get rid of them all.

(A) Dogs have a tendency to attract many pests, like fleas and ticks, and bathing alone won't be enough to get rid of all these bugs.
(B) Dogs have a tendency to attract many pests, and bathing alone won't be enough to get rid of all these pests, which are usually in the form of fleas and ticks.
(C) Fleas and ticks have a tendency to be attracted to dogs, whose bathing alone won't get rid of everything.
(D) Bathing alone won't be enough to get ride of the fleas and ticks that, attracted to dogs, will adhere to them.
(E) By bathing, fleas and ticks can't be gotten rid of to the dogs they are attracted to.

31. Which of the following if inserted before sentence 4 would make the passage more logical?

(A) Besides,
(B) Initially,
(C) Therefore,
(D) However,
(E) Generally,

32. Which of the following is the best way to combine sentences 5 and 6 to improve their flow?

(A) Remove the period and add a semicolon.
(B) Join the two sentences with the conjunction "but".
(C) Join the two sentences with the conjunction "and".
(D) Add the word "thereby" between the two sentences.
(E) Join the two sentences with a comma and replace "means" with "meaning".

33. What should be done with sentence 11?

(A) (As it is now)
(B) Replace the word "strong" with "powerful".
(C) Add the words "The best thing is" to the beginning.
(D) Add the words "and most efficient" at the end.
(E) Delete it.

34. Which of the following is the best rewritten version of sentence 15 (reprinted below)?

When this happens, they open up sores on their skin.

(A) (As it is now)
(B) When this is happening, opening up sores on their skin.
(C) When this happens, dogs open up sores on their skin.
(D) When it happens, the dogs are opening up sores on its skin.
(E) When happening, dogs open up sores on skin.

GO ON TO THE NEXT PAGE

SECTION 6

35. Which of the following changes made to the final sentence would give the passage a better sense of closure?

(A) Add the words "for a long time" to the end of the sentence.
(B) Remove the word "and" and add "By caring for your pet and home in this manner," to the beginning.
(C) Switch the position of last two sentences.
(D) Replace the word "best" with "better".
(E) Replace the word "you" with "one".

S T O P

IF YOU FINISH BEFORE TIME IS CALLED, YOU MAY CHECK YOUR WORK ON THIS TEST ONLY. DO NOT TURN TO ANY OTHER SECTION IN THIS TEST.

SECTION 7

Turn to Section 7 of your answer sheet to answer the questions in this section.

Time—20 Minutes
19 Questions

Directions: For each question in this section, select the best answer from among the choices given and fill in the corresponding oval on the answer sheet.

Each sentence below has one or two blanks, each blank indicating that something has been omitted. Beneath the sentence are five words or sets of words labeled A through E. Choose the word or set of words that, when inserted in the sentence, best fits the meaning of the sentence as a whole.

Example:

Eliza felt ----- when her boss asked her to work seven weekends in a row but ----- when her work earned her a promotion.

(A) enervated . . weakened
(B) depressed . . intellectual
(C) advantageous . . salacious
(D) angry . . shopworn
(E) irate . . elated    Ⓓ ●

1. Mike lamented the fact that his sister was always so -----, for she seemed to like to disagree for the sake of disagreement alone.

(A) complicit
(B) caring
(C) conformist
(D) corollary
(E) contrary

2. The editor was ----- by all her novelists for her ability to ----- every story's true drama and embellish this tension through careful pruning of sentences.

(A) adored . . mull
(B) despised . . focus
(C) venerated . . muddle
(D) beloved . . pinpoint
(E) ignored . . intern

3. Though many ----- the increasing commercialization of holidays like St. Valentine's Day, others ----- the chance to celebrate their loved ones on a publicly acknowledged day.

(A) decry . . denounce
(B) celebrate . . laud
(C) abhor . . ignore
(D) fete . . assume
(E) lament . . appreciate

4. The house on the hill is truly -----. With thirty-six rooms and four stories, we have never seen anything larger in the neighborhood.

(A) seismic
(B) plaintive
(C) bombastic
(D) monstrous
(E) penurious

5. Marketers began a campaign to introduce new writers via paperback under the ----- that readers would be more willing to purchase a lighter, cheaper book from an unknown writer than plunk down substantial money for a hardback.

(A) assumption
(B) predilection
(C) discourse
(D) divinity
(E) pandemonium

6. A good judge must be a highly developed person, with a strong internal sense of -----, and yet he or she must not be without compassion, for in weighing the fate of a criminal, a judge must on occasion use his or her fount of compassion to render judgment and ----- the temptation to right personal wrongs by judging the external world too harshly.

(A) ethics . . eschew
(B) opinions . . exasperate
(C) morals . . clinch
(D) denial . . digression
(E) bias . . embrace

GO ON TO THE NEXT PAGE

SECTION 7

Directions: The passage below is followed by questions based on its content. Answer the questions on the basis of what is stated or implied in the passage and in any introductory material that may be provided.

Questions 7–19 are based on the following passage.

This scholarly article discusses the ways critics categorize music.

Somewhere in the early twentieth century, the path of music underwent a split. The long expansive symphonic creations of the masters Mahler and Wagner gave way to a new kind of music in the New World, first called "jass," and later termed "jazz." This in turn gave birth to "rhythm and blues" and finally to "rock," which today is housed under the umbrella term "pop," short for popular. Walk into a record store and Mahler's Eighth Symphony will most certainly not be housed under the "pop" label, for that German master's compositions, although certainly well regarded among classical aficionados, is anything but popular. "Popular" music, that is, music that appeals to the masses, is an entirely different entity. It generates the people who create and promote it unprecedented sums of money. It has the ability to draw people together in large numbers, where, once assembled, the audience enjoys a powerful experience that many sociologists liken to a religious movement. The power of pop music, then, is a power indeed.

What are we to make of this power in our midst? Certainly there are those for whom the term "popular" is derogatory, implying that because something appeals on a broad level, it cannot contain any germ of quality. This is, of course, a very class-based idea. It perpetuates the myth that only a talented few in any society have the mental apparatus to fully appreciate a complex work of art. For others, art must be simple and easily penetrated, thus rendering it boring and uninspiring to that talented percent who, scholars argue, ultimately decide what in our cultural arsenal will be worth keeping and what will be worth discarding. Some will immediately remind us that many of the most well-remembered artists were in fact quite popular in their day. The old saw about Shakespeare writing for the masses and for kings and queens is often pulled out at this juncture, and although Shakespeare was certainly no musician, his ideal as the "popular artist of critical acclaim" certainly does fit the bill.

I would argue that to even begin to approach music as either "high" or "low" misses the point of music entirely. Terming art as "high" tells us a great deal about how people relate to one another and how they wish to regard each other. But it doesn't tell us anything about the art itself. History shows how art—again, the old Shakespeare example—can go from being in the domain of the popular to becoming the championed cause of an elite few. But this, again, reveals more about social forces than it does about anything intrinsic within art.

If we want to understand how or why this division occurs, I would argue that certainly it is useful to take a look at social strata. But it is also helpful to take a look at why we even have music in our lives—that is, to actually consider the function of music as art and the role it actually plays in our lives as it moves through our societal constructs. Consider, for example, the case of protest music. It is often lamented that the kind of socially conscious music that was so popular in the 1960s and 1970s is sadly lacking now. But, by its very nature, protest music challenges us, and it is intended to be difficult, thought-provoking music. What is generally termed pop music, however, is not intended to give rise to our intellectual functions or to present us with moral quandaries. It is music to be enjoyed. Presumably, we have this music in our lives because we need to be removed from the more ordinary world. In other words, pop music is not the creation of inane minds for the consumption of those who are even more vapid. Rather, it has a specific function generated out of a very specific need as experienced by a modern population.

I have said before that the division of "high" and "low" culture tells us more about the people who inhabit such a divided world than about the art of the world itself. In future studies, it would be interesting for scholars to learn how the musical tastes of a given class of people correlate to the particular stresses of their lives. Who, for example, most strongly feels a need to be removed from the drudgery of day to day life to the ease of a rhythmic and thus escapist piece of pop? Who, on the other hand, welcomes, and in fact even desires, the inherent challenge of socially conscious music?

7. In line 2, the term "split" refers to

(A) the divergence of symphonic music and jazz
(B) the division between socially popular music and critically acclaimed music
(C) the popularity of brass instruments over string instruments
(D) the focus on symphonic structure over modal composition
(E) the migration of composers from Europe to America

8. As used in line 10, "aficionados" most nearly means

(A) addicts
(B) enthusiasts
(C) practitioners
(D) repairmen
(E) amateurs

GO ON TO THE NEXT PAGE

SECTION 7

9. The reference to "sums of money" in line 13 conveys what impression about the power of pop music?

(A) It is successful because it is a new form of entertainment.
(B) It is the first art form able to take advantage of mass communication and distribution.
(C) It has the ability to sway and enrich people in a manner not seen in the past.
(D) It is inherently substandard to other forms of music because of its commercial character.
(E) It is uniquely positioned to appeal to people across the continents.

10. The author uses the term "class-based" in lines 21–22 to

(A) suggest that a new definition of "high" and "low" art is needed
(B) defend the talented percentile who are trying to purge society of "low art"
(C) imply that not all art is created equal
(D) promote the work of "low artists" as needing the attention of skilled critics
(E) suggest that the terms "low art" and "high art" reveal more about the class of the critics than of the art itself

11. The term "apparatus" is used in line 23 to characterize a person's

(A) functionality
(B) mendacity
(C) tenacity
(D) acuity
(E) propensity

12. The author is aware that some might respond to his use of Shakespeare in lines 30–33 ("The old . . . bill") by pointing out that Shakespeare

(A) was wildly successful both critically and popularly
(B) is not a musician and therefore not a suitable topic of discussion
(C) was admired by paupers and statesman alike
(D) lived too long ago to be relevant to the conversation
(E) desperately courted popular attention

13. The author's attitude toward a discussion of music as either "low" or "high" can best be described as

(A) offensive
(B) distraught
(C) skeptical
(D) admiring
(E) bland

14. The author responds to the idea of "low" and "high" music by

(A) proposing another methodology of examining music
(B) suggesting parallels between music and literature
(C) reinforcing the difference between "high" and "low" art
(D) asking how music makes people feel
(E) challenging mainstream ideas of "high" music

15. According to the passage, protest music is no longer popular because of which of the following reasons?

I. There is not the same social change sweeping the country at present as existed in the 1960s and 1970s.
II. Music is currently playing a different social role than it did in the past.
III. Most people want to hear music that is transporting.

(A) I
(B) II
(C) III
(D) I and II
(E) II and III

16. In paragraph 4 (lines 43–60), the author uses which of the following to outline his case?

(A) Irrefutable fact
(B) Personal opinion and observation
(C) Secondary sources
(D) Careful reevaluation
(E) Ironic description

17. In line 58, "inane" is best understood to mean

(A) empty
(B) amusing
(C) fabricated
(D) sad
(E) simple

GO ON TO THE NEXT PAGE

SECTION 7

18. The "specific function" (line 59) is best defined as

(A) the role that music plays in reflecting the tastes of various classes
(B) the ability of music to transport its listener to a less stressful, more enjoyable setting
(C) the function of critics in helping society determine good art from bad
(D) the job of different players within a particular performance piece
(E) the place of class within discussions of music

19. In the last lines, the author hints that he will discuss which of the following in a subsequent, but not printed, paragraph?

(A) The divergence between popular opinion and critical theory
(B) The distance between protest music and popular music
(C) The connection between manual labor and white collar labor
(D) The relationship between critic and class
(E) The correlation between class and taste in music

S T O P

IF YOU FINISH BEFORE TIME IS CALLED, YOU MAY CHECK YOUR WORK ON THIS TEST ONLY. DO NOT TURN TO ANY OTHER SECTION IN THIS TEST.

SECTION 8

Turn to Section 8 of your answer sheet to answer the questions in this section.

Time—20 Minutes
16 Questions

Directions: For this section, solve each problem and decide which is the best of the choices given. Fill in the corresponding oval on the answer sheet. You may use any available space for scratchwork.

Notes:

1. The use of a calculator is permitted. All numbers used are real numbers.
2. Figures that accompany problems in this test are intended to provide information useful in solving the problems. They are drawn as accurately as possible EXCEPT when it is stated in a specific problem that the figure is not drawn to scale. All figures lie in a plane unless otherwise indicated.
3. Unless otherwise specified, the domain of any function f is assumed to be the set of all real numbers x for which $f(x)$ is a real number.

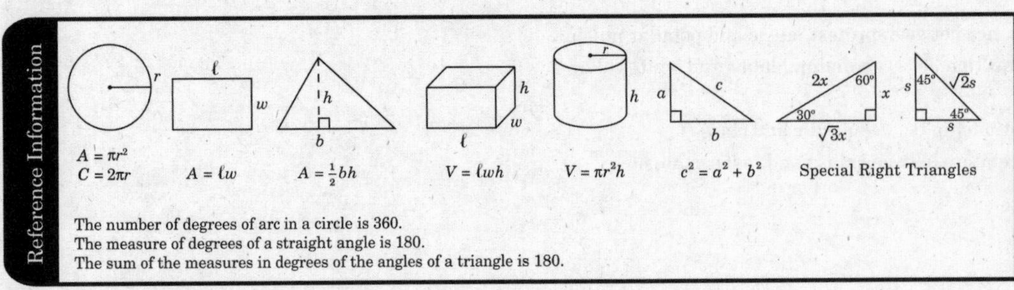

Reference Information
$A = \pi r^2$
$C = 2\pi r$
$A = \ell w$
$A = \frac{1}{2}bh$
$V = \ell wh$
$V = \pi r^2 h$
$c^2 = a^2 + b^2$
Special Right Triangles
The number of degrees of arc in a circle is 360.
The measure of degrees of a straight angle is 180.
The sum of the measures in degrees of the angles of a triangle is 180.

1. Which of the following is the graph of a linear function with a positive slope and a negative y-intercept?

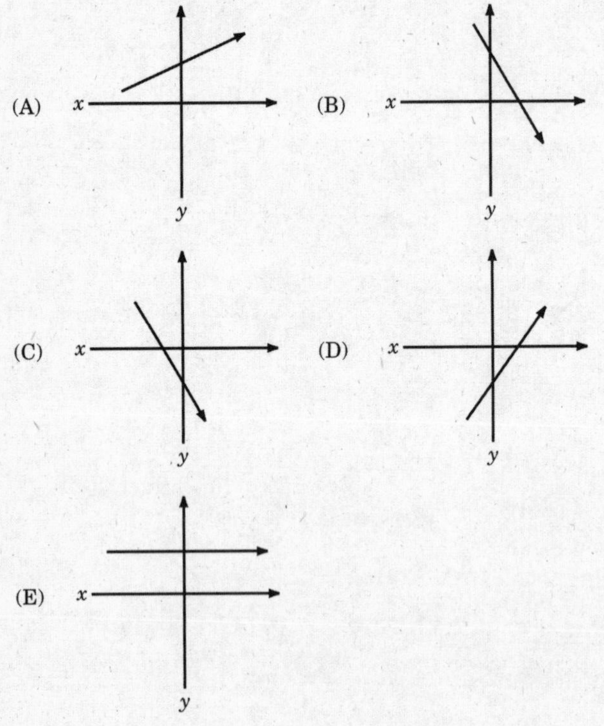

2. Genevieve has a basket of presents, with an equal number of blue packages and red packages. She hands out 6 blue packages and is left with 2 times as many red packages as blue. How many packages total did she have originally?

(A) 3
(B) 6
(C) 9
(D) 12
(E) 24

GO ON TO THE NEXT PAGE

SECTION 8

3. Julie is at the grocery store. She spends $1.89 for soap, $2.20 for razors, $5.59 for shampoo, and $3.35 for batteries. If she intends to pay with a $20 bill, approximately how much can she expect to receive in change?

(A) $4
(B) $5
(C) $6
(D) $7
(E) $8

4. If the average of 5 numbers is 100, and 2 of the numbers are 90 and 80, which of the following could be the mode of all the numbers if none of the numbers can be smaller than 80 or larger than 120 ?

(A) 65
(B) 70
(C) 75
(D) 110
(E) 150

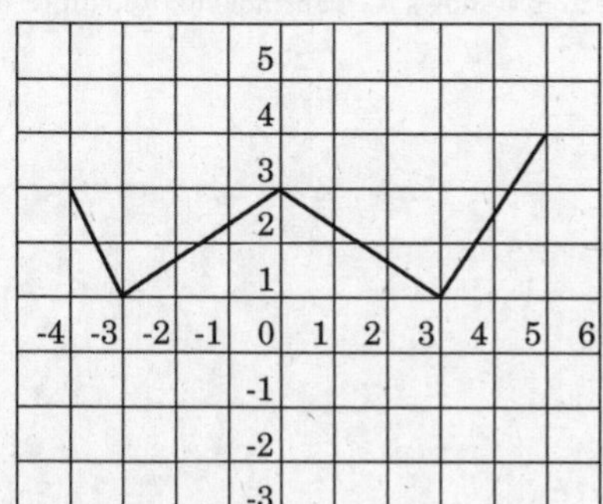

5. The figure above shows the graph of the function m. Which of the following is closest to $m(4)$?

(A) 1
(B) 2
(C) 2.5
(D) 3
(E) 3.5

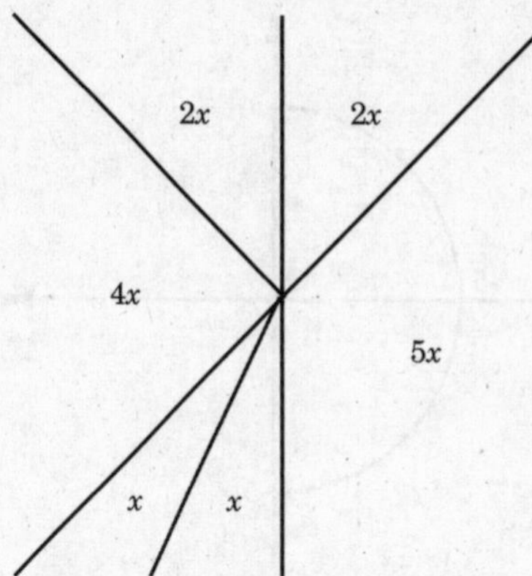

6. In the figure above, six line segments meet at a point to form six angles. What is the value of x ?

(A) 15
(B) 24
(C) 48
(D) 72
(E) 96

7. The variables a, b, and c stand for positive integers. If $a^b = 9$, and $c^b = 8b$, then what is the value of $a + b + c$?

(A) 2
(B) 3
(C) 4
(D) 5
(E) 9

GO ON TO THE NEXT PAGE

SECTION 8

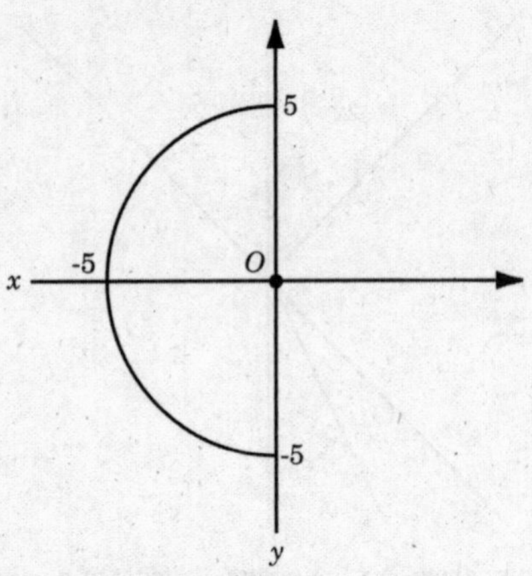

8. In the semicircle above, the center is at (0, 0). Which of the following are y-coordinates of two points on this semicircle whose x-coordinates are equal?

(A) (0, –5)
(B) (4, –4)
(C) (1, –3)
(D) (2, –4)
(E) (3, –5)

9. If q is an integer and 2 is the remainder when $2q + 5$ is divided by 3, then q could be which of the following?

(A) 2
(B) 3
(C) 5
(D) 6
(E) 7

10. Set A is made up of consecutively spaced integers. If the first term is 4 and the last term is 253, how many terms are there total?

(A) 247
(B) 248
(C) 249
(D) 250
(E) 251

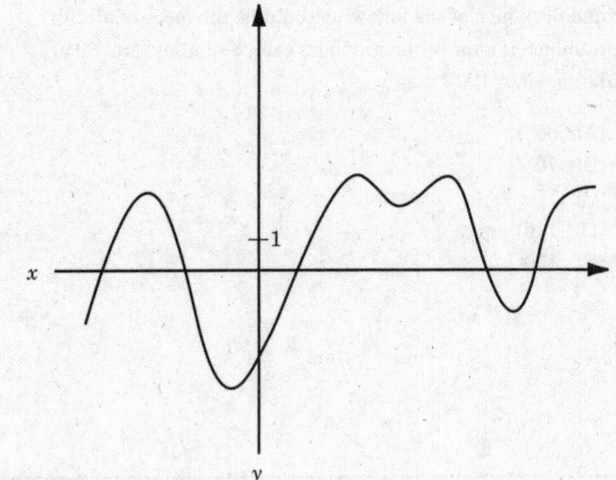

11. The figure above shows $f(x)$. For how many values does $f(x)$ equal 1 ?

(A) 0
(B) 1
(C) 2
(D) 4
(E) 5

GO ON TO THE NEXT PAGE

SECTION 8

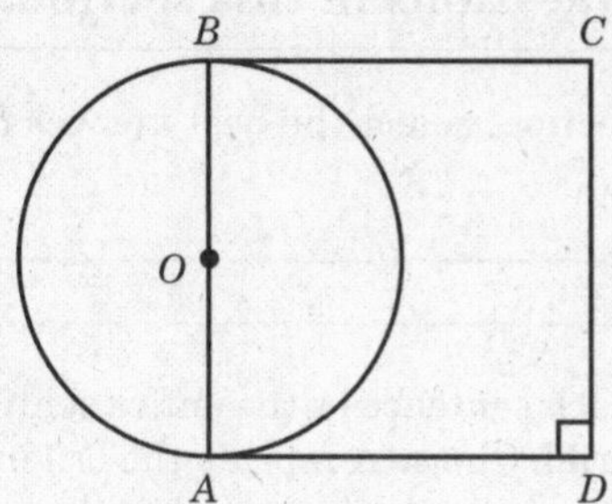

12. In the figure above, square *ABCD* overlaps circle with center *O*. If the area of the circle is 36π, then what is the length of diagonal *AC*?

(A) 6

(B) $6\sqrt{2}$

(C) $12\sqrt{2}$

(D) $18\sqrt{2}$

(E) 36

13. The price of a sofa was accidentally decreased by 20 percent. Then, a salesclerk marked up the price by 30 percent. By what percent has the sofa's price changed?

(A) Decreased by 4 percent
(B) Decreased by 10 percent
(C) Decreased by 20 percent
(D) Increased by 4 percent
(E) Increased by 10 percent

14. If a number is divisible by the first 5 positive odd integers, the number must be divisible by all of the following EXCEPT

(A) 9
(B) 15
(C) 18
(D) 21
(E) 63

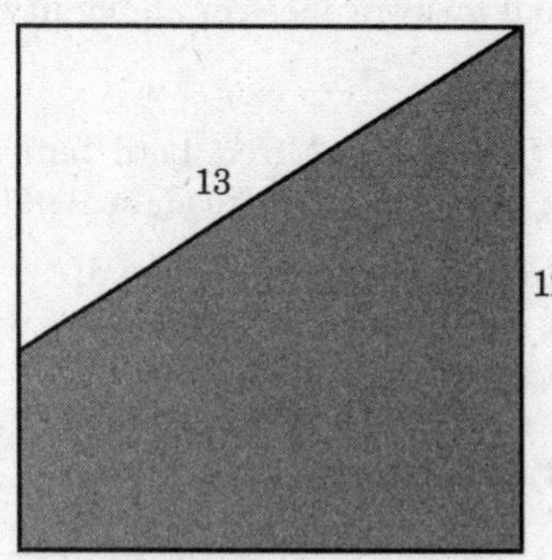

Note: Figure not drawn to scale.

15. In the square above, what is the area of the shaded region?

(A) 30
(B) 60
(C) 81
(D) 114
(E) 144

16. If $xy^2z^3 < 0$, which of the following must be negative?

(A) w
(B) y
(C) xy
(D) yz
(E) xz

S T O P

IF YOU FINISH BEFORE TIME IS CALLED, YOU MAY CHECK YOUR WORK ON THIS TEST ONLY. DO NOT TURN TO ANY OTHER SECTION IN THIS TEST.

SECTION 9

Turn to Section 9 of your answer sheet to answer the questions in this section.

Time—10 Minutes
14 Questions

Directions: For each question in this section, select the best answer from among the choices given.

The following sentences test correctness and effectiveness of expression. Part of each sentence or the entire sentence is underlined; beneath each sentence are five ways of phrasing the underlined material. Choice A repeats the original phrasing; the other four choices are different. If you think the original phrasing produces a better sentence than any of the alternatives, select choice A; if not, select one of the other choices.

In making your selection, follow the requirements of standard written English; that is, pay attention to grammar, choice of words, sentence construction, and punctuation. Your selection should result in the most effective sentence—clear and precise, without awkwardness or ambiguity.

Example:

In the poem "Ulysses" by Alfred, Lord Tennyson, the speaker says, "I cannot rest from travel," instead, he will live life to the fullest.

(A) "I cannot rest from travel," instead,
(B) "I cannot rest from travel"; instead,
(C) "I cannot rest from travel" instead,
(D) "I cannot rest from travel," upon which
(E) "I cannot rest from travel,"

1. Anticipating the then future day when humans would be able to communicate via small handheld devices, the producers of *Star Trek* showing their crew speak through small cellphonelike objects.

(A) showing their crew speak through small cellphonelike objects
(B) to show their crew speak through small cellphonelike objects
(C) is showing their crew speak through small cellphonelike objects
(D) showed their crew as speaking through small cellphonelike objects
(E) shown their crew speak through small cellphonelike objects

2. Lady Murasaki, writer of the world's first psychological novel, and she remains a mystery to even the most diligent biographers today.

(A) and she remains a mystery to even the most diligent biographers today
(B) remains a mystery to even the most diligent biographers to this day
(C) remaining a mystery to even the most diligent biographers today
(D) to this day she remains a mystery to even the most diligent biographers today
(E) and remaining a mystery to even the most diligent biographers today

3. Eccentricity cannot always be equated with social awkwardness, for although the former often goes hand in hand with an original, creative mind, the latter correlates to people who may have a serious chemical imbalance.

(A) for although the former often goes hand in hand with an original, creative mind, the latter
(B) for the former often going hand in hand with an original, creative mind, the latter
(C) because the former is hand in hand with an original, creative mind, and the latter
(D) although the former often going with an original, creative mind, the latter
(E) although the former often going hand in hand with an original, creative mind, the latter

4. Friends should provide a sympathetic ear but also be willing to speak a mind to any false steps they may see you make.

(A) be willing to speak a mind to any false steps
(B) be willing to speak a mind by any false steps
(C) be willing to speak a mind about any false steps
(D) be willing to speak up a mind about any false steps
(E) be willing to speak their mind about any false steps

GO ON TO THE NEXT PAGE

SECTION 9

5. Soap opera writers are often under tremendous pressure concocting elaborate plot scenarios intended to keep viewers watching week after week.

   (A) concocting elaborate plot scenarios intended
   (B) to concoct elaborate plot scenarios intended
   (C) for concocting elaborate plot scenarios intended
   (D) in concocting elaborate plot scenarios intended
   (E) concocted elaborate plot scenarios intended

6. The train operators insisted for collecting the full fare of the passengers despite the three-hour delay and subsequent late arrival.

   (A) operators insisted for collecting the full fare of the passengers despite
   (B) operators insisted for collecting the full fare from the passengers although
   (C) operators insisted on collecting the full fare of the passengers despite
   (D) operators insisted as to collecting the full fare of the passengers despite
   (E) operators, insisting for collecting the full fare from the passengers, despite

7. Neither the doctors who made it their job to predict the course of oncoming flus or their counterparts overseas accurately foresaw the intensity of that winter's virulent flu strains.

   (A) or their counterparts overseas
   (B) nor their counterparts overseas
   (C) or also their counterparts overseas
   (D) but also their counterparts overseas
   (E) or his counterpart overseas

8. Although younger knitters are able to appreciate the patterns of such distinguished designers as Di Gilpin, they prefer, understandably, the more fitted and therefore modern structured designs of Delphine Wilson.

   (A) Although younger knitters are able to appreciate the patterns of such distinguished designers as Di Gilpin, they prefer, understandably, the more fitted and therefore modern structured designs of Delphine Wilson.
   (B) Although younger knitters, in appreciating the patterns of such distinguished designers as Di Gilpin, they are prefering, understandably, the more fitted and therefore modern structured designs of Delphine Wilson.
   (C) Younger knitters are able to appreciate the patterns of such distinguished designers as Di Gilpin, and they therefore prefer, understandably, the more fitted and therefore modern structured designs of Delphine Wilson.
   (D) Because younger knitters are able to appreciate the patterns of such distinguished designers as Di Gilpin, they prefer, understandably, the more fitted and therefore modern structured designs of Delphine Wilson.
   (E) Although younger knitters are able to appreciate the patterns of such distinguished designers as Di Gilpin, they, however, are preferring, understandably, the more fitted and therefore modern structured designs of Delphine Wilson.

9. The view from the top floors of the luxury apartment complex will soon be obscured by the development bars sunlight from reaching the windows.

   (A) bars sunlight from reaching the windows
   (B) barring sunlight from reaching the windows
   (C) and bars sunlight from reaching the windows
   (D) which is barring sunlight from reaching the windows
   (E) for bars sunlight from reaching the windows

10. Preparing for the summer, the air conditioners were installed by the apartment owners who wanted to be able to keep the indoor climate controlled during the hottest days.

   (A) the air conditioners were installed by the apartment owners who wanted to be able to keep
   (B) the air conditioners were installed by the apartment owners wanting to be able to keep
   (C) the apartment owners installed the air conditioners to keep
   (D) and wanting the air conditioners installed, the apartment owners keeping
   (E) and the air conditioners are installed by the apartment owners who wanted to be able to keep

GO ON TO THE NEXT PAGE

SECTION 9

11. It is debatable that people can become truly well-rounded individuals, one always has more strengths in one area of life over another.

(A) one always has more strengths in one area of life over another
(B) one has more strengths in one area of life over the other area
(C) one is always stronger over another area of life
(D) because people are always stronger in one area of life than another
(E) you are always stronger in one area of life over another

12. By incorrectly entering a check mark in the wrong box, a mistake was made, and the voter was forced to ask for a new ballot.

(A) mistake was made, and the voter
(B) the voter made a mistake and
(C) mistakes were made, and the voter
(D) the voter was mistaken and
(E) mistakes were made by the voter

13. To win the pageant, the contestants must possess not only great beauty but also the ability to speak coherently as well.

(A) the contestants must possess not only great beauty but also the ability to speak coherently as well
(B) the contestants must possess not only great beauty but also the ability to speak coherently
(C) the contestants must possess great beauty in addition to the ability to speak coherently as well
(D) the contestants must not only possess great beauty but also in speaking coherently as well
(E) the contestants are possessing great beauty but also possessing the ability to speak coherently as well

14. The bookstore houses many tomes that, although not on national bestseller lists, the local content makes them attractive to tourists momentarily passing through the area.

(A) the local content makes them attractive to tourists momentarily passing through the area
(B) containing the content that makes them attractive to tourists momentarily passing through the area
(C) the local content is making them attractive to tourists momentarily passing through the area
(D) contain local content that is attractive to tourists momentarily passing through the area
(E) the local content making them attractive to tourists momentarily passing through the area

S T O P

IF YOU FINISH BEFORE TIME IS CALLED, YOU MAY CHECK YOUR WORK ON THIS TEST ONLY.
DO NOT TURN TO ANY OTHER SECTION IN THIS TEST.

PRACTICE TEST 3 EXPLANATIONS

PRACTICE TEST 3 ANSWERS

Question Number	Answer	Right	Wrong
Section 2			
1	E		
2	C		
3	B		
4	A		
5	C		
6	D		
7	E		
8	A		
9	B		
10	C		
11	D		
12	C		
13	A		
14	D		
15	E		
16	B		
17	C		
18	D		
19	B		
20	E		
21	A		
22	B		
23	B		
24	C		
Section 3			
1	E		
2	B		
3	B		
4	B		
5	C		
6	D		
7	E		
8	D		
9	B		
10	D		
11	E		
12	B		
13	E		
14	D		
15	B		
16	C		
17	C		
18	A		
19	C		
20	E		
Section 4			
1	D		
2	B		
3	E		
4	C		
5	B		
6	B		
7	E		
Section 4, continued			
8	C		
9	D		
10	A		
11	A		
12	B		
13	C		
14	E		
15	B		
16	A		
17	D		
18	B		
19	B		
20	D		
21	E		
22	C		
23	B		
24	A		
Section 5			
1	C		
2	E		
3	A		
4	D		
5	A		
6	C		
7	D		
8	B		
9	363		
10	4.5		
11	15		
12	5		
13	5, 6, 7, 8, 9, 10, 11		
14	3		
15	4/6, 2/3, .666, .667		
16	1/3, 6		
17	665		
18	24		
Section 6			
1	B		
2	D		
3	E		
4	C		
5	B		
6	C		
7	A		
8	D		
9	D		
10	B		
11	E		
12	D		
13	E		
14	A		

Question Number	Answer	Right	Wrong	Question Number	Answer	Right	Wrong
Section 6, continued				**Section 7, continued**			
15	D	___	___	16	B	___	___
16	D	___	___	17	A	___	___
17	E	___	___	18	B	___	___
18	A	___	___	19	E	___	___
19	E	___	___	**Section 8**			
20	D	___	___	1	D	___	___
21	C	___	___	2	E	___	___
22	C	___	___	3	D	___	___
23	E	___	___	4	D	___	___
24	A	___	___	5	C	___	___
25	A	___	___	6	B	___	___
26	A	___	___	7	E	___	___
27	A	___	___	8	B	___	___
28	D	___	___	9	D	___	___
29	C	___	___	10	D	___	___
30	A	___	___	11	E	___	___
31	D	___	___	12	C	___	___
32	E	___	___	13	D	___	___
33	E	___	___	14	C	___	___
34	C	___	___	15	D	___	___
35	B	___	___	16	E	___	___
Section 7				**Section 9**			
1	E	___	___	1	D	___	___
2	D	___	___	2	B	___	___
3	E	___	___	3	A	___	___
4	D	___	___	4	E	___	___
5	A	___	___	5	B	___	___
6	A	___	___	6	C	___	___
7	A	___	___	7	B	___	___
8	B	___	___	8	A	___	___
9	C	___	___	9	B	___	___
10	E	___	___	10	C	___	___
11	D	___	___	11	D	___	___
12	B	___	___	12	B	___	___
13	C	___	___	13	B	___	___
14	A	___	___	14	D	___	___
15	E	___	___				

CALCULATING YOUR SCORE

Writing Section Raw Score

A. Essay Score (from 1–6) ______ A

B. Section 6 Multiple Choice: ______ no. correct – (______ no. incorrect ÷ 4) = ______ B

C. Section 9 Multiple Choice: ______ no. correct – (______ no. incorrect ÷ 4) = ______ C

D. Unrounded Multiple-Choice Score (B + C) ______ D

E. Total Rounded Multiple-Choice Raw Score
(Rounded to the nearest whole number) ______ E

F. Writing Multiple-Choice Subscore
(See the Writing Multiple-Choice conversion table on the following pages) ______ Writing MC Score

G. Total Scaled Score
(See the Writing conversion table on the following pages) ______ SAT Writing Score

Math Section Raw Score

A. Section 3 Raw Score: ______ no. correct – (______ no. incorrect ÷ 4) = ______ Subtotal A

B. Section 5 Raw Score: ______ no. correct ______ Subtotal B

C. Section 8 Raw Score: ______ no. correct – (______ no. incorrect ÷ 4) = ______ Subtotal C

D. Total Unrounded Raw Score
(Total A + B + C) ______ D

E. Total Rounded Raw Score (Rounded to the nearest whole number) ______ E

F. Scaled Score
(See the conversion table on the following pages) ______ SAT Math Score

Critical Reading Section Raw Score

A. Section 2 Raw Score: ______ − (______ ÷ 4) = ______
no. correct — no. incorrect — A

B. Section 4 Raw Score: ______ − (______ ÷ 4) = ______
no. correct — no. incorrect — B

C. Section 7 Raw Score: ______ − (______ ÷ 4) = ______
no. correct — no. incorrect — C

D. Total Unrounded Raw Score
(Total A + B + C) ______
D

E. Total Rounded Raw Score
(Rounded to the nearest whole number) ______
E

F. Scaled Score
(See the conversion table on the following pages) ______
SAT Critical Reading Score

CONVERTING YOUR RAW SCORES

Raw Score	Critical Reading Scaled Score	Math Scaled Score
67	800	
66	790	
65	770	
64	760	
63	750	
62	740	
61	720	
60	710	
59	700	
58	690	
57	680	
56	670	
55	670	
54	660	800
53	650	780
52	640	760
51	640	740
50	630	730
49	620	710
48	610	700
47	610	690
46	600	670
45	590	660
44	590	650
43	580	650
42	580	640
41	570	630
40	560	620
39	560	610
38	550	600
37	540	590
36	540	590
35	530	580
34	530	570
33	520	560
32	510	560
31	510	550
30	500	540
29	500	530
28	490	520
27	480	520
26	480	510
25	470	500
24	470	490
23	460	490
22	450	480
21	450	470
20	440	460
19	430	460

Raw Score	Critical Reading Scaled Score	Math Scaled Score
18	430	450
17	420	440
16	410	430
15	410	430
14	400	420
13	390	410
12	380	400
11	380	390
10	370	380
9	360	380
8	350	370
7	340	360
6	330	340
5	320	330
4	310	320
3	300	310
2	280	290
1	270	280
0	250	260
–1	250	250
–2	240	240
–3	230	230
–4	220	220
–5	210	210
–6	200	200

Writing Subscores

- **Essay Subscore:** Subtotal A from Writing Score (page 262)
- **Multiple-Choice Subscore:** Calculate by plugging in Subtotal E from your writing score (page 262) into the score conversion table below

Raw Score	Multiple-Choice Subscore	Raw Score	Multiple-Choice Subscore
49	80	30	59
48	79	29	58
47	77	28	57
46	76	27	56
45	75	26	55
44	74	25	54
43	72	24	53
42	71	23	52
41	70	22	51
40	69	21	51
39	68	20	50
38	67	19	49
37	66	18	48
36	65	17	47
35	64	16	46
34	63	15	45
33	62	14	44
32	61	13	43
31	60	12	42

Raw Score	Multiple-Choice Subscore	Raw Score	Multiple-Choice Subscore
11	41	2	32
10	40	1	30
9	39	0	29
8	38	–1	27
7	37	–2	25
6	36	–3	24
5	35	–4	23
4	34	–5	22
3	33	–6	21

Writing Scaled Score

MC raw score	Essay Score					
	6	5	4	3	2	1
49	800	790	780	770	720	700
48	790	780	760	730	700	680
47	780	770	750	720	690	670
46	770	760	740	710	680	660
45	770	750	740	700	670	650
44	760	750	730	690	660	640
43	750	740	710	680	650	630
42	750	730	700	670	640	620
41	740	730	690	660	630	610
40	740	720	690	650	620	600
39	740	710	680	640	610	590
38	730	700	670	630	610	590
37	720	690	660	630	600	580
36	710	680	650	620	590	570
35	710	680	640	610	580	560
34	700	670	640	600	570	550
33	690	660	630	590	560	540
32	680	650	620	580	560	540
31	670	640	610	580	550	530
30	660	630	600	570	540	520
29	650	630	590	560	530	510
28	640	620	590	550	520	510
27	640	610	580	540	510	490
26	630	600	570	530	500	490
25	620	590	560	520	500	480
24	610	580	550	510	490	470
23	600	570	540	510	480	460
22	590	570	530	500	470	450
21	590	570	530	500	470	450
20	580	560	520	490	460	440
19	570	550	520	480	450	430
18	570	540	520	470	440	420
17	560	530	510	460	430	420
16	550	520	500	450	430	410
15	540	510	490	450	420	400
14	530	500	480	440	410	390
13	520	500	470	430	400	380
12	510	490	460	420	390	370
11	510	480	450	410	380	360

Writing Scaled Score

MC raw score	Essay Score					
	6	5	4	3	2	1
10	500	470	450	400	370	350
9	490	460	440	390	360	350
8	480	450	430	390	360	340
7	470	440	420	380	350	330
6	460	430	410	370	340	320
5	450	430	400	360	330	310
4	450	420	390	350	320	300
3	440	410	390	340	310	290
2	430	400	380	330	300	280
1	420	380	370	320	290	270
0	400	370	350	310	280	260
–1	380	360	340	290	270	260
–2	370	340	320	270	260	250
–3	360	330	310	260	250	240
–4	350	320	290	250	240	230
–5	340	310	280	240	230	220
–6	340	310	280	240	220	210

SECTION 2: CRITICAL READING

Sentence Completions

1. **E** One-Word/One-Way *Easy*

The magazine states that no piece should be "something." A good prediction here would be "scandalous," based on the clue contained in the sentence. Looking at the answer choices, the only one that fits is *sensational,* **E**.

2. **C** One-Word/One-Way *Easy*

The *locusts* are bad news. You know that the locusts will have *decimated* or "destroyed" nearly everything by the end of last summer. From this you can deduce that the farmers are not at all happy about the locusts. They are, in fact, *disconsolate,* **C**.

3. **B** Two-Word/One-Way *Medium*

The clue word here is *superstitious*. Apparently, *these past peoples* are not actually as *superstitious as was once believed.* In other words, a good prediction for the first blank would be something close to *superstitious* or "highly religious;" *devout* will work. Eliminate **C** and **D**. The second blank would be a contrast to *superstitious*: *these people* were actually "something other than *superstitious* or *metaphoric.*" **B** must be your answer.

4. **A** Two-Word/Two-Way *Medium*

Bombastic implies that a person or thing is boastfully ostentatious and therefore frustrating. You know that the first word must be something like "bragging." Eliminate **B** and **D**. Now, how would a "bragging" or *pontificating* person make others feel? Mostly likely "annoyed" and "unimportant." **A**, *irrelevant,* fits.

5. **C** Two-Word/One-Way *Medium*

Key words here are *reflect* and *temperament*. The words *just as* also tell you that *dogs*, like houses, tend to *reflect* a person. A good prediction for the first blank would be something like "reflect." Eliminate **B** and **E**. Now, for the second blank, you are looking for a word that continues the idea that dogs resemble their masters. The correct answer must therefore be choice **C**, or *referred to*.

6. **D** Two-Word/One-Way *Medium*

The words *stir controversy* tell you what kind of talent the *wealthy young heiress* has: she stirs up trouble. A good prediction for the first blank would be a word that agrees with the idea of *controversy*. Eliminate **A**, **B**, and **C**. A synonym for *controversy* could be *notoriety*. On the other hand are entertainers known for something else, and a good prediction would be "talent," or *accomplishment*. The correct answer must be **D**.

7. **E** One-Word/One-Way *Difficult*

In order to *curry favor* with Aunt Jessamine, all you have to do is *sing her praises*. In other words, you just have to "praise her excessively." The word *blandishments*, **E**, fits this prediction and is the correct answer. *Floridity* means "excessive decoration."

8. **A** One-Word/One-Way *Difficult*

You are looking for a word to describe the author. You are told that his characters *abuse each other* and his stories have few moments that are *humanistic*. You can guess that the author, therefore, is someone who is very negative. In fact, he is cruel to people, or *misanthropic*, **A**.

Short Reading Passages

9. **B** Implied Information *Difficult*

Here are the lines in question: *It is a popular English view to assume that the Battle of Waterloo is England's finest moment, in which the brilliant general-tactician outwitted his enemy.* In other words, the English general was "smart" and used "good tactics" to defeat his enemy. This is essentially what is stated in **B**.

10. **C** Themes and Arguments *Medium*

The last lines of the passage put forward ideas for why Napoleon may have lost to Wellington. The detail about the *flu* is one such possible explanation, so the purpose of this detail is to offer an alternative explanation.

11. **D** Implied Information *Easy*

Here are the lines surrounding the author's description of how she reacts emotionally to certain settings: *And yet a part of me, a quiet part that is only vocal among other Chinese friends, understands what it is that non-Asian people see. There were often times in my youth when I felt unable to express myself in the brash manner of Americans.* In other words, she too feels certain ways depending on how other people feel.

12. **C** Main Idea *Medium*

A good start here is to determine the tone of the author's passage. She is not really criticizing or praising anything, so you can eliminate **B** and **D**. At the same time, this is a somewhat heartfelt passage and can't really be described as neutral, so eliminate **A**. The passage is really a very personal admission and an exploration of feelings.

Paired Reading Passages

13. **A** Implied Information *Medium*

Take a look at the lines referenced in the question: *Is a modern country rich? At first glance you might be inclined to answer in the affirmative, but then remember a country like the United Arab Emirates, which is certainly rich in dollar numbers but hardly a modern country: nearly 90 percent of its labor force, for example, is imported from other countries.* In other words, a rich country is not necessarily modern.

14. **D** Words in Context *Medium*

Look at the lines using the word *preposterous*: *As poor as countries like England and France might have been at the end of this war, one would have considered preposterous the notion that they were not at the forefront of all that was and would be later termed "modern."* In other words, even though England and France were poor, it is "ridiculous" to assume that they were not modern. A good match is *laughable*, **D**.

15. **E** Specific Information *Medium*

Take a look at the lines referenced: *All that was needed, these scholars insisted, was that a country be primarily of Anglo-Saxon origin and imbued with the values of Christianity.* In other words, countries that were white and Christian stood the best chance of being "modern." Another way of stating this is to say that *race* determined the title of modernity.

16. **B** Specific Information *Medium*

All of the answer choices are mentioned in the passage except for the role of the United States in reconstructing Japan. The correct answer must therefore be **B**.

17. **C** Themes and Arguments *Medium*

The author has spent this passage trying to understand how and why countries become modern and what characterizes them. In the referenced lines he says, *The invisible hand that characterized Adam Smith's imagination may well apply to the development of nations.* In other words, it isn't really clear what causes countries to modernize. If it were discovered that no one clear set of characteristics unites all "modern" countries, then the author's opinion would gain support.

18. **D** Words in Context *Medium*

Look at how the word *divergence* is used: *That there is a divergence of opinion on the merits of Second and Third World countries emulating the cultures of the Western world is tacitly understood by all but the least sensitive of social critics and historians.* In other words, there is a split of opinion. Not everyone agrees. The closest definition is **D**, *disagreement*.

19. **B** Themes and Arguments *Medium*

Take a look at the lines referenced and also at the surrounding material: *Certainly money alone is not the key, nor is a strong central government. There are numerous examples of countries rich in resources—Egypt comes to mind—but which have failed to share the wealth with its people. And then there are authoritarian governments, like North Korea that rule with an iron fist while their people starve.* North Korea is used as an example of a country that *rules with an iron fist* yet whose people *starve*—a country with a strong central government whose people suffer. Again, we have an example of a country which fails to fit the bill of modernity.

20. **E** Specific Information *Medium*

Take the Roman numerals one at a time. First, the author asks you to consider a workforce with varied skills. Look at paragraph 2, specifically the following lines: *I would like to put forward the idea that modernity is really defined as a country whose population develops and continues to acquire increasingly complex skills.* The correct answer must contain I, so eliminate **B** and **C**. Now look at II. The author does not mention natural resources, so the correct answer will not contain II. Eliminate **D**. Finally, evaluate III. Look at the conclusion of the paragraph: *Nothing else can account for the rapid gains of a hardworking country in such a short amount of time and for the breathtaking manner in which the most advanced countries are able to continuously reinvent themselves.* In other words, a modern country is one in which people are able to adapt. The correct answer must contain III. The answer must be **E**.

21. **A** Specific Information *Medium*

Remember the author's definition of a modern country: *I would like to put forward the idea that modernity is really defined by a country whose population develops and continues to acquire increasingly complex skills. Nothing else can account for the rapid gains of a hardworking country in such a short amount of time and for the breathtaking manner in which the most advanced countries are able to continuously reinvent themselves.* Only **A** restates this idea.

22. **B** Relating Two Passages *Medium*

The author of Passage 2 bases his whole attitude on the idea that a modern country is one that is skilled and flexible, **B**.

23. **B** Relating Two Passages *Difficult*

Both passages, although putting forward personal opinions, are very detached and intellectual. Neither author is attempting to be too persuasive, positive, or negative. Only **B** captures this tone. The other answer choices are far too emotional.

24. **C** Relating Two Passages *Medium*

Both countries include Japan on their list of nations that have modernized. They don't agree with anything else on the list. The author of Passage 2 does put forth a list of what characterizes a modern nation, so **A** can't be correct. Neither authors agree with the ideas put forth in **B** or **D**.

SECTION 3: MATH

Multiple Choice

1. **E** Algebra: Inequalities *Medium*

Simplify:

$$6a - 1 > 11$$
$$6a > 12$$
$$a > 2$$

The correct answer must be greater than 2, and only 3, or **E**, fits the possibility.

2. **B** Algebra: Absolute Value and Exponents *Easy*

Simplify:

$$5^{3x} = 125$$
$$5^{3x} = 5^3$$

Now, set the exponents in their own equation:

$$3x = 3$$
$$x = 1$$

3. **B** Numbers & Operations: Solving Equations *Easy*

One way to do this problem is to plug in values. Let's say that $x = 10$. In this case, x minus 5 would equal 5, and x minus 8 would equal 2. In other words, x minus 8 would be 3 less than x minus 5.

4. **B** Geometry: Geometric Visualizations *Easy*

Only **B** works here. The other shapes will not give a box with a lid with the correct volume.

5. **C** Geometry: Geometric Visualizations *Medium*

Counting up the paths, there are four that will give you a length of 3. They are:

AB to *BE* to *EC*
AB to *BF* to *FC*
AD to *DE* to *EC*
AD to *DF* to *FC*

6. **D** Algebra: Solving Equations *Easy*

First, solve for w:

$$\frac{2}{5}w = 20$$
$$2w = 5(20)$$
$$2w = 100$$
$$w = 50$$

Next, substitute:

$$\frac{6}{5}w = \frac{6}{5}(50) = 6(10) = 60$$

7. **E** Geometry: Circles *Medium*

First, find the total number of sums:

$1 + 1, 1 + 2, 1 + 3, 1 + 4, 1 + 5, 1 + 6, 1 + 7, 1 + 8 = 8$ sums
$2 + 2, 2 + 3, 2 + 4, 2 + 5, 2 + 6, 2 + 7, 2 + 8 = 7$ sums
$3 + 3, 3 + 4, 3 + 5, 3 + 6, 3 + 7, 3 + 8 = 6$ sums
$4 + 4, 4 + 5, 4 + 6, 4 + 7, 4 + 8 = 5$ sums
$5 + 5, 5 + 6, 5 + 7, 5 + 8 = 4$ sums
$6 + 6, 6 + 7, 6 + 8 = 3$ sums
$7 + 7, 7 + 8 = 2$ sums
$8 + 8 = 1$ sums

Total of 36 sums

Now, you want to know how many will be larger than 10. There are 16. The ratio of $\frac{16}{36}$ reduces to $\frac{4}{9}$.

8. **D** Algebra: Substitution *Medium*

Plug in numbers. Say that $x = 2$ and $y = 4$.

$xy = (2)(4) = 8$, which is an even number. Eliminate **B** and **C**.
$y(x - 1) = 4(2 - 1) = 4(1) = 4$. Eliminate **A**.
$(x + 1)(y - 1) = (2 + 1)(4 - 1) = 3(3) = 9$. Eliminate **E**.

9. **B** Numbers & Operations: Sequences *Medium*

This number shows a repeating patter of 7. You want to know where in this repeating pattern of 7 the 100th digit falls. First divide 100 by 7. You will have a remainder of 2. This means that the 100th digit will fall 2 places into the repeating pattern of 7, or the number 8.

10. **D** Algebra: Absolute Value and Exponents *Medium*

Plug the number 2 into the function:

$$f(x) = \frac{5^{2x} - 5^x}{x}$$
$$f(2) = \frac{5^{2(2)} - 5^2}{2}$$
$$f(2) = \frac{5^4 - 5^2}{2}$$
$$f(2) = \frac{625 - 25}{2}$$
$$\frac{600}{2} = 300$$

11. **E** Geometry: Angles and Lines *Medium*

Only **E** can be correct here. You know that angles X and Z are equal to each other. You also know that line a must equal 180 degrees, because all straight lines are 180 degrees. Substituting in angle Z for angle X, you can add this value to W to find 180 degrees.

12. **B** Geometry: Coordinate Geometry *Medium*

To find the coordinate where the line crosses the x-axis, set y equal to 0:

$$0 = 6(x) + 18$$
$$0 = 6x + 18$$
$$-18 = 6x$$
$$-3 = x$$

13. **E** Data Analysis, Statistics & Probability: Statistical Analysis *Medium*

The mode of the test scores is 82. However, the missing test score cannot be 82. The mode means that the score appears most frequently in the list of scores, and no other number can appear as frequently. In this case, the mode 82 appears twice. All of the other scores must therefore appear only one time. Since 87, **E**, already appears in the list, this cannot be the missing score, because it would mean that 82 is no longer the mode.

14. **D** Geometry: Triangles *Medium*

If angle *BAE* measures 60 degrees, then you know that angle *EAD* measures 30 degrees. You also know that angle *ADE* measures 60 degrees, and angle *BDC* measures 30 degrees. Right triangles with angles measuring 30:60:90 degrees have sides in a ratio of $x:x\sqrt{3}:2x$. Since side *BC*, $10\sqrt{3}$, is opposite the 30 degree angle, you know that side *CD* measures $10\sqrt{3}(\sqrt{3})$, or 30. Now, if side *BA* measures 30, then, using triangle *BAE* with angles 30:60:90 as a reference, side *AE* measures 15. Using this, then, as a reference, and looking at triangle *ADE* with angles 30:60:90, you know that side *ED* measures $5\sqrt{3}$. Adding all this together we have:

$$30 + 30 + 15 + 10\sqrt{3} + 5\sqrt{3}$$
$$75 + 15\sqrt{3}$$

15. **B** Numbers & Operations: Factors and Multiples *Medium*

You want to find the largest prime factor of 68. This would be 17. Now, you are told to find the ratio of the original number to this factor.

$$\frac{\text{Original Number}}{\text{Largest Prime factor}} = \frac{68}{17} = 4$$

16. **C** Geometry: Coordinate Geometry *Medium*

The only thing you know about line b is that it is perpendicular to the line a, and that line b has negative slope. This means that line a must have a positive slope.

17. **C** Algebra: Functions *Medium*

Simplify:

$$x \,\&\, y = \frac{xy}{x-3}$$
$$9 \,\&\, 5 = 5 \,\&\, y$$
$$\frac{9(5)}{9-3} = \frac{5y}{5-3}$$
$$\frac{45}{6} = \frac{5y}{2}$$
$$90 = 6(5y)$$
$$90 = 30y$$
$$3 = y$$

18. **A** Algebra: Substitution *Difficult*

The first two CDs Jill buys cost n. That's a total of $2n$. After that, a CD is a dollars less, or $n - a$. After that, a CD is b dollars. Now, Jill bought x CDs total. The first three CDs are going to cost a different price than anything afterward. You should differentiate between $x - 3$ (the rest of the CDs), which will be sold at a rate of b, and the first three CDs:

$$2n + n - a + (x - 3)b$$
$$3n - a + b(x - 3)$$

19. **C** Geometry: Circles *Difficult*

If you know what fraction of the entire area of the circle the sector is, then you know what fraction of 360 degrees, or the total measure of the circle, the central angle is. You are told that area of the sector is 6π. You are also given the radius—6. This would make the entire area 36π. This means that the sector is $\frac{1}{6}$ the area of the entire circle. You now know that the angle must also be $\frac{1}{6}$ of the entire measure of the circle, or, 60 degrees.

20. **E** Numbers & Operations: Percents *Difficult*

Let's say there are 100 parts total of the paint. First, there are 35 parts blue and 65 parts red. Now, you want to make the paint so that the blue is 20 percent of the entire mix. How many parts total would you need for 35 to be 20 percent of the total?

$$35 = .2(x)$$
$$x = 175$$

In other words, another 75 parts of red must be added for the blue to become 20 percent of the new mixture.

SECTION 4: CRITICAL READING

Sentence Completions

1. **D** One-Word/One-Way *Medium*

You can only see the turtles hatching *at night*. This means they are engaging in a *nocturnal* activity. Something that is *diurnal* occurs in a day, in a twenty-four-hour period.

2. **B** Two-Word/One-Way *Medium*

The *closing* sparked something that was *vociferous*, or extremely noisy. You can bet, therefore, that people were not particularly happy about the closing. Eliminate **A** and **E**. *Rebellion* will work in the context of the sentence. At the end of the sentence, you are told that the mayor has reopened the stations. You can assume, then, that the noisy protest was "quieted" or *assuaged* once the houses were reopened, and the answer must be **B**.

3. **E** One-Word/Two-Way *Difficult*

The word *adoring* tells you that people enjoy a "positive" *relationship* with dog shows. Eliminate **B** and **C**. Although the word *benign* means "harmless," you are really looking for a word that is strongly positive, such as *fawning*. Now, the meaning of second blank is hinted at very strongly by the use of the word *mutt*, which by definition is a dog that is a mix of different breeds. In other words, the mutt has a "mixed" or *varied* gene selection. The answer must be **E**.

4. **C** One-Word/Two-Way *Difficult*

The actor's *outward* face is the opposite of someone who is *down to earth and a very easy-to-grasp presence*. The best fit here is the word *mercurial*, **C**, which means "rapid and quick changing of mood." Watch out for *specious*, which means "having the ring of truth but actually false."

5. **B** Two-Word/Two-Way *Difficult*

A film critic must make sure that he does not give the opposite of *constructive criticism*. What would be a good opposite? Try something like "insults" or "harsh criticism." Eliminate **C** and **D**. If the critic does not give the opposite of "harsh criticism," then the *audience* might think the critic is motivated by something other than *love for the craft*, such as wanting to sound smarter, or *erudite*.

Paired Reading Passages

6. **B** Relating Two Passages *Easy*

The author of Passage 1 remembers the days when poetry was highly regarded. She longs for those days and is sad that they have passed. The author of the second passage is skeptical about this kind of longing. A good contrast, then, would be *wistful* versus *practical*, or **B**.

7. **E** Relating Two Passages *Medium*

Both passages talk about the literature of the past. Whereas the author of first passage longs for those days, the author of the second passage is a little more practical about how we have come to view these past days. However, both passages are indeed linked by a desire to look at literature's glorious past, or **E**.

8. **C** Relating Two Passages *Medium*

Here are the last lines of Passage 2: *Today our education system, our social circles, and our readership have become much more diverse and far less class based. We should expect the books published today to be more varied as well.* Now, remember, the author of Passage 1 is convinced that the literature of the past is infinitely superior to the literature of the present. This is essentially the opinion restated in choice **C**. Watch out for **B** and **D**, which restate opinions of the author of Passage 2.

9. **D** Relating Two Passages *Easy*

Here are the lines referenced in the question: *Students of poetry can't help but pick up a slim volume of Shelley or Keats and long for the days when these poets were alive and writing in the fever of romanticism that gripped all of England. Then poets were heroes, admired for their imaginations and feted and treated as dignitaries—fawning that today is reserved for celebrities of dubious talent.* The author clearly believes that the good old days are far better than the ones we live in today when it comes to questions of literature. But the author of Passage 2 says, *but the truth is that much waste has been forgotten, committed to the dustbin of memory.* In other words, according to the author of Passage 2, lots of really bad literature from the past has been discarded. This viewpoint is reflected in **D**.

Long Reading Passages

10. **A** Specific Information *Medium*

Here are the lines in question: *When I bring friends to see my parents, they are invariably stunned. "You grew up* here*?" they ask. These kinds of comments used to rankle me.* So, on the one hand, the friends are stunned. Digging deeper, we realize that the friends are surprised, the author believes, because they cannot believe the degree of poverty in which the young doctor lived. In other words, their comments display both *shock* and *judgment*, **A**.

11. **A** Themes and Arguments *Medium*

This is a purpose of detail question, in which you are asked to understand why the author has included a specific detail in her or his writing. Here are the surrounding lines and the line in question: *Our poverty was also of the flagrant kind, clearly visible from the highway. We could not mask our modest situation.* In other words, the author is saying that he grew up desperately poor, so poor, in fact, that he could not hide his condition. In other words, the line in question is used to emphasize just how poor the author really was.

12. **B** Implied Information *Medium*

Here are the lines in question: *Unlike other American families, who I have since learned struggle far more than I thought they did in the early years when we first arrived here from Mexico, we did not mask our poverty by paying for electronics and cars and dinners out on the town.* The author is stating that he grew up poor, but he has since learned, he claims, that others grew up struggling with their finances as well. The Americans who seemed so well off had their own financial troubles.

13. **C** Implied Information *Easy*
Here are the lines in question: *I am less judgmental of my friends now. For one thing, I have plenty of friends, most of whom I met in college.* The author implies that he was judgmental of his schoolmates, just as he feared they judged him.

14. **E** Specific Information *Medium*
The author describes his different viewpoint of his home as follows: *I imagine they are responding to the pure bucolic beauty of my home. The ocean is a few minutes' walk away. I can fish for dinner in the river, then roast it outside on a grill my father made for me.* He specifically states that he finds his childhood home beautiful and loves the fact that it is surrounded by nature. Although it is true that he went to college and that he became a doctor, he specifically mentions the beauty of his home, so **E** must be the answer.

15. **B** Attitude and Tone *Medium*
The author's final sentences are filled with great admiration and a bit of longing for his childhood home. This kind of yearning is a good example of *nostalgia*, or **B**. He most certainly is not negative about his home, so you can eliminate **A** and **D**.

16. **A** Main Idea *Medium*
This is a very practical passage in which the author sets out information for the reading public. It is not a persuasive passage, attempting to sway the audience. Likewise, it is not a negative passage that criticizes anyone or anything. It is a neutral passage, conveying information, making **A** the answer.

17. **D** Words in Context *Easy*
Here are the lines surrounding the question: *Cats, their owners claim, are superior pets, able to take care of themselves, are clean, and do not smell. The ancient people of the world must have concurred since they began domesticating the cat at an early moment in history.* A good prediction for this word would be "agreed." The ancient people would agree with modern people that cats make good pets.

18. **B** Themes and Arguments *Easy*
In discussing the cat on Cyprus, the author writes, *baskets and pots of grain, however, would have attracted mice, and that reason alone could have inspired intrepid humans to befriend the cat. It should also be noted that cats are not native to Cyprus, so this particular cat must have been physically brought to the island.* In other words, the cat found in the burial ground was not a natural inhabitant of the island and must have been domesticated, **B**.

19. **B** Specific Information *Medium*
This question is essentially asking you about the content of paragraph 4. All of the answer choices mention characteristics discussed in this paragraph, except for **B**. Although it is true that cats primarily *eat meat*, this is not a characteristic of animals uniquely suited for the desert.

20. **D** Themes and Arguments *Difficult*

Here are the lines in question: *Sadly, however, the lack of cats meant that the rat population was able to careen out of control: rats were responsible for helping to spread the disease.* The author is making the claim that it is because of rats that the plague spread so fluidly throughout the Old World. If it were proven that cats don't actually like to eat rats, and therefore don't hunt rats, then the decreased cat population could not be blamed for the spread of rats and thus the plague, **D**.

21. **E** Technique *Medium*

The entire last paragraph discusses the role of cats in the Old World. The author points out that the decline in cat popularity might have contributed to the rise of the plague. In other words, the author is mostly citing historic evidence, while also putting forward a hypothesis about causes of the spread of the plague. The correct answer must be **E**.

22. **C** Specific Information *Easy*

The author states that *the pope declared that the cat was in league with the devil* and therefore evil. The author then supposes that the decline in cat population contributed to the rise in rat population: *Sadly, however, the lack of cats meant that the rat population was able to careen out of control: rats were responsible for helping to spread the disease*, **C**.

23. **B** Attitude or Tone *Medium*

In the last line, the author writes, *It is thus interesting to note how the rise and fall of fashions can influence not just our interests but our health.* The line is a bit of a throwaway, an ironic observation about how the popularity of pets can influence a nation's health. The observation is a bit amused, or bemused, **B**.

24. **A** Attitude or Tone *Medium*

Despite the final line of the passage, which is somewhat amused and personal, the overall purpose of this passage is to convey information and to remain *neutral*, **A**.

SECTION 5: MATH

Multiple Choice

1. **C** Algebra: Solving Equations *Easy*

Simplify:

$$\frac{5x-1}{4} = 6$$
$$5x - 1 = 6(4)$$
$$5x - 1 = 24$$
$$5x = 25$$
$$x = 5$$

2. **E** Geometry: Angles and Lines *Easy*

The only way that angles *A* and *B* can equal 180 degrees is if lines 1 and 2 are parallel. You must be careful here. Never assume that because two lines look parallel, they really are. Always check to see if a figure is drawn to scale or not.

3. **A** Data Analysis, Statistics & Probability: Graphs, Charts, and Tables *Easy*

Work through the chart carefully, filling in all of the categories. If there are 3,842 cats adopted, and a total of 5,997 animals adopted, you can subtract 3,842 from 5,997 to find the total number of dogs adopted. There are 2,155 dogs adopted. From here, you can determine the number of dogs that are not adopted. Since there are a total of 4,891 dogs, and you just learned that 2,155 dogs are adopted, you can subtract 2,155 from 4,891 to determine how many dogs were not adopted: 4,891 – 2,155 = 2,736.

4. **D** Algebra: Substitution *Easy*

Don't be fooled by the wordiness of this problem. It is essentially an algebra problem. Plug in the value 15 for *y* to solve the equation:

$$M(y) = 5y - 25$$
$$M(15) = 5(15) - 25$$
$$M(15) = 75 - 25$$
$$M(15) = 50$$

5. **A** Algebra: Substitution *Medium*

Take a look at the second equation and simplify:

$$ce = \frac{d}{b}$$
$$c = \frac{d}{be}$$
$$bc = \frac{d}{e}$$

Now, if $bc = \frac{d}{e}$ and if $a = bc$, then you know that a also equals $\frac{d}{e}$.

6. **C** Numbers & Operations: Ratios *Medium*

The total number of cups must be a multiple of the number 9, since 4 and 5 added together equals 9. The only answer choice listed that is not a multiple of 9 is 26, or **C**.

7. **D** Numbers & Operations: Ratios *Medium*

This problem is wordy and essentially checks your understanding of how to translate text into math. It is not as hard as it sounds. You want to know how many stitches are necessary to create a width of 16 inches if 4 stitches equal 1 inch. To do this, simply multiply:

(number of inches desired)(number of stitches for one inch) = total number of stitches required

$$(16)(4) = 64$$

8. **B** Geometry: Triangles *Difficult*

You are told that this figure is a square, with angle *b*. In other words, angle *B* equals 90 degrees. You know that 90 – *A* will equal one corner of the triangle. Similarly, 90 – *C* will equal the other corner of the triangle. If you subtract these two angles from 180, the total number of degrees in a triangle, you will get the value for angle x:

$$x = 180 - \{(90 - A) + (90 - C)\}$$
$$x = 180 - (90 - A + 90 - C)$$
$$x = 180 - 90 + A - 90 + C$$
$$x = A + C$$

Grid-Ins

9. **363** Algebra: Absolute Value and Exponents *Easy*

Don't bother trying to find the value of z. It isn't an integer. All you need to do is some quick multiplication and substitution:

$$z^4 = 121$$
$$3z^4 = (3)(121)$$
$$3z^4 = 363$$

10. **4.5** Geometry: Lines and Angles *Easy*

To find the midpoint, first add the terms together and divide by 2:

$$\frac{11+2}{2} = \frac{13}{2} = 6.5$$

Now, you know that the midpoint of 2 and 11 is 6.5. Don't forget, now, to determine the difference between 6.5 and 2:

$$6.5 - 2 = 4.5$$

11. **15** Geometry: Geometric Visualizations *Difficult*

Remember, the sum of any two sides of a triangle must be larger than the third side. This eliminates the consecutive prime numbers 1 and 2. However, the prime numbers 3, 5, and 7 fit the bill. 3 + 5 is greater than 7. 5 + 7 is greater than 3. And 3 + 7 is greater than 5. Adding 3, 5, and 7 together, we have a perimeter of 15.

12. **5** Algebra: Substitution *Medium*

Work with the information given to find the answer to the question:

$$a^2 - b^2 = 21$$
$$(a + b)(a - b) = 21$$

Now, substitute:

$$(a + b)(a - b) = 21$$
$$(a + b)(3) = 21$$
$$(a + b) = 7$$

Now, solve for a:

$$a - b = 3$$
$$a + b = 7$$

Adding these together you have:

$$2a = 10$$
$$a = 5$$

13. **5, 6, 7, 8, 9, 10, 11** Geometry: Circles *Medium*

First, find the circumference of the tart:

$$\text{Circumference} = 2\pi r$$

$$\text{Circumference} = (2)(\pi)\left(\frac{6}{\pi}\right)$$

$$\text{Circumference} = 12$$

The length of the edge of each slice must be larger than 1, but less than 3. The tart can be cut into 11 slices at most. It must be cut into at least 5 slices.

14. **3** Numbers & Operations: Sequences *Medium*

Each term is 4 times the previous term. All 6 terms will be:

$$x + 4x + 16x + 64x + 256x + 1{,}024x$$

Now, put these terms in an equation:

$$x + 4x + 16x + 64x + 256x + 1,024x = 4,095$$
$$1,365x = 4,095$$
$$x = 3$$

15. **4/6, 2/3, .666, .667** Geometry: Triangles *Medium*

If the ratio of *BF* to *BE* is 1 to 4, then you know that *BF* measures a multiple 1, and *FE* measures a multiple of 3. For the sake of convenience, let us say that *BF* measures 1 exactly, and *FE* measures 3 exactly. Now, remember the formula for the area of a triangle is $A = \frac{bh}{2}$. You already know the height of large triangle *ABC*. Now, let's find the base, or side *AC*:

$$A = \frac{bh}{2}$$
$$12 = \frac{b4}{2}$$
$$2(12) = b4$$
$$24 = b4$$
$$6 = b$$
$$6 = AC$$

Now, find the length of *AD*, or the base of triangle *AFD*:

$$A = \frac{bh}{2}$$
$$6 = \frac{b3}{2}$$
$$12 = b3$$
$$4 = b$$
$$AD = 4$$

The ratio of *AD* to AC is 4 to 6, or $\frac{2}{3}$.

16. **1/3, 6** Algebra: Functions *Difficult*

Plug the information into the equation and simplify.

$$t(x) = 6 + \frac{x^2}{3}$$
$$t(3g) = 6 + \frac{(3g)^2}{3}$$
$$19g = 6 + \frac{9g^2}{3}$$
$$19g = 6 + 3g^2$$
$$0 = 3g^2 - 19g + 6$$
$$0 = (3g - 1)(g - 6)$$
$$g = \frac{1}{3} \text{ or } 6$$

17. **665** Data Analysis, Statistics & Probability: Graphs, Charts, and Tables *Difficult*

The total number of points can be gained if the gamer finishes all three quests. Take the chart a step at a time to tabulate the number of points.

In quest 1, the gamer gets x points for every $2x$ aliens killed. According to the chart, there are a total number of 16 aliens. Since it takes 2 aliens to earn every 1 point, you know that a gamer can get *8 possible points*.

In quest 1, the gamer also gets $2x$ points for every x alien. In other words, the gamer gets twice as many points for each alien killed. Since there are 16 aliens, the gamer can get *32 possible points*.

In quest 2, the gamer also gets $2x$ points for every x alien. In other words, the gamer gets twice as many points for each alien killed. Since there are 25 aliens, the gamer can get *50 possible points*.

In quest 2, the gamer can also get $3x$ points for every x aliens. Since there are 25 aliens, the author can get *75 points*.

In quest 3, the gamer also gets $2x$ points for every x alien. In other words, the gamer gets twice as many points for each alien killed. Since there are 50 aliens, the gamer can get *100 possible points*.

In quest 3, the gamer can also get $3x$ points for every x aliens. Since there are 50 aliens, the author can get *150 points*.

In quest 3, the gamer can also get $5x$ points for every x aliens. Since there are 50 aliens, the author can get *250 points*.

Now, add up all the points: 8 + 32 + 50 + 75 + 100 + 150 + 250 = 665

18. **24** Data Analysis, Statistics & Probability: Permutations and Combinations *Difficult*

If the center award must be kept in one position, you are essentially asked to find the total number of combinations of only 4 awards:

$$(4)(3)(2)(1) = 24$$

SECTION 6: WRITING

Improving Sentences

1. **B** Parallelism *Easy*

In a comparison, the two things being compared must be in parallel form, which is not the case here. The first thing being compared is *to the Caribbean.* The second thing being compared is *they went to Europe.* Notice that the pronoun *they* is intruding in this sentence. **B** fixes this problem.

2. **D** Run-Ons *Easy*

This is a run-on sentence in which two complete clauses are put together. This is incorrect. You must make one of the sentences dependent on the other, or separate the sentences by a semicolon. **D** fixes this problem.

3. **E** Parallelism *Easy*

Two items being compared must be in parallel form. The first item being compared is *is not falling*. The second item being compared is *as last week.* Notice that this second item lacks a verb, which exists in the first item. **E** corrects this problem by inserting the verb *did.*

4. **C** Wordiness *Easy*

The underlined portion of this sentence sounds strange and unnecessarily wordy. Explicitly, the pronoun *they* sounds very awkward: *and they therefore searched for inspiration.* **C** fixes this problem by jettisoning the pronoun and putting the verb *search* in its correct form.

5. **B** Misplaced Modifiers *Medium*

This sentence suffers from a misplaced modifier. *They* did not consult with her *entire family—she* is the one who consulted with the family. **B** corrects this error by moving *she* next to the modifying clause.

6. **C** Parallelism *Easy*

Items in a list must appear in parallel form. Take a look at the items in a list here: *the city's capacity for athletes and guests, the popularity of the host country, and they also wondered about how much money the city had to spend.* Notice that the third item in the list includes the pronoun *they*, which is not included in the first two items. **C** fixes this problem.

7. **A** No Error *Easy*

There are no errors here. The subjects and verbs agree, and all phrases are in the proper form.

8. **D** Misplaced Modifiers *Easy*

The way the sentence originally reads, it sounds as though *Las Vegas* were driving through the *state of Nevada*, and yet this is not logically possible. It is *Les* who does the driving. **D** fixes this problem by placing *Les* right next to the modifying clause.

9. **D** Parallelism *Medium*

Items in a list must be expressed in parallel form. Here are the items in the list: *an ability to evoke the whims of kings, the passions of youth, and also an ability to express himself through deep poetic metaphor.* Notice that the last item in the list includes the pronoun *himself*. **D** fixes this problem by removing the verb.

10. **B** Parallelism *Medium*

Items in a list must be placed in parallel form. Here are the items in a list: *set in California, then Mexico, and then he moved them out to the East Coast.* Notice that the last item in the list includes the pronoun *he* and the verb *moved*. **B** fixes this problem by placing the last item in the list in the same form as the other two items.

11. **E** Coordination and Subordination *Medium*

The conjunction *while* makes the first clause dependent and implies that there is a contrast in the sentence. However, the sentence does not really contain any kind of contrast, but rather shows a logical flow of ideas. **E** fixes this problem by removing the conjunction *while*.

Identifying Sentence Errors

12. **D** Tense *Easy*

Notice that the verb *became* is in the wrong tense. It should be *become*.

13. **E** No Error *Easy*

There is no error here. All subjects and verbs agree, and all words are in their proper form.

14. **A** Coordination and Subordination *Easy*

The words *neither* and *nor* must always go together. And yet here we have the conjunction *or* following *neither*. To be correct, *or* would need to be replaced by *nor*.

15. **D** Tense *Easy*

Here we have a problem with verb tense. The verb phrase *will manage* implies the future. However, you know from an earlier, non-underlined part of the sentence, *was able*, that the sentence needs to be in the past tense.

16. **D** Idioms *Easy*

This sentence contains the phrase *one of its kind*. The correct idiomatic expression is *one of a kind*.

17. **E** No Error *Medium*

There is no error here. All subjects and verbs agree, all verbs are in the correct tense, and all words are in the correct format.

18. **A** Tense *Easy*

The sentence is supposed to be in the past tense. You know this because of the use of the verb *acted*, which is not underlined. This means that the verb *wins*, which is in the present tense, is incorrect. To be correct, the verb *wins* should read *won* or *had won*.

19. **E** No Error *Easy*

There is no error here. All subjects and verbs agree, all verbs are in the correct tense, and all words are in the correct format.

20. **D** Wrong Word *Medium*

The word *accumulated*, which means "amassed" or "adding up to," is used incorrectly here. The correct term the author hopes to use is *accounted for*.

21. **C** Pronouns *Medium*

The pronoun *their,* which modifies *quest*, refers to *Alexander the Great*. However, Alexander the Great is one person, not two. Therefore, the pronoun *their* should actually be replaced by the pronoun *his*.

22. **C** Tense *Medium*

The verb *scattering* is in the wrong tense here. It should read *scatter*, following the infinitive preposition of *to*.

23. **E** No Error *Medium*

There is no error here. All subjects and verbs agree, all verbs are in the correct tense, and all words are in the correct format.

24. **A** Pronouns *Medium*

Notice that the pronoun *their* appears throughout the sentence, implying that the subject must be plural. You also know this because the pronoun *their* is not underlined and therefore cannot be changed. However, notice that the subject of the sentence, *the Native American*, is singular. To be correct, the sentence would need to start with *the Native Americans*.

25. **A** Idioms *Medium*

This sentence tests your knowledge of idiomatic expressions. The sentence currently reads *enthusiasm of,* and yet the correct form of this expression is *enthusiasm for*.

26. **A** Pronouns *Medium*

This sentence tests a commonly made error. The pronoun *I* can only be used when *I* is the subject of the sentence. However, here, the pronoun *I* should be in its objective form because the foundation wants to reward *Charles and me*.

27. **A** Wrong Word *Medium*

This sentence contains an incorrectly used word. The sentence means to say that difficulty *ensues,* or occurs. Instead, the word *ensures* is incorrectly used.

28. **D** Pronouns *Difficult*

The pronoun *it* is singular. However, the pronoun *it* is supposed to refer back to the *dogs,* which is plural. To be correct, the pronoun *it* would need to be replaced by the pronoun *they*.

29. **C** Adverbs and Adjectives *Difficult*

Here we have an adjective when we really need an adverb. The word *proper* is supposed to modify the verb *set*. However, to be correct, the adjective *proper* should actually be in its adverbial form, which is *properly*.

Improving Paragraphs

30. **A** Sentence Revision *Easy*

The pronoun *them* as it is used in this original sentence is not clear. Does *them* refer to the *dogs* or the *bugs*? The sentence in **A** corrects this problem.

31. **D** Sentence Revision *Medium*

Something seems to be missing between sentences 3 and 4. In sentence 3 we are introduced to the idea that dogs must live outdoors. Then, all of the sudden, in sentence 4, the dogs are allowed to come indoors. You need some kind of connector word to link these two sentences together. The word *however*, in **D**, solves this problem.

32. **E** Sentence Revision *Medium*

Here are sentences 5 and 6: *One particularly strong medicine is systemic. This means it goes throughout the dog's body.* You can see that the sentences sound rather choppy. It would be a good idea to combine the sentences, giving the passage greater flow. **E** accomplishes this nicely.

33. **E** Sentence Revision *Medium*

Take a look at sentence 11 and its context: *First, vacuum twice a day, using a powerful vacuum. A strong one is the best. Second, make sure you throw away the vacuum bag so the fleas don't crawl out of the vacuum and back into your house.* Notice that sentence 11 is actually unnecessary. Sentence 10 already makes the point that you will want to use a strong vacuum. The best thing to do is to eliminate sentence 11.

34. **C** Sentence Revision *Medium*

Here is the original sentence: *When this happens, they open up sores on their skin.* The problem, however, is that it is not clear who or what opens up sores on the skin. **C** solves this ambiguity.

35. **B** Sentence Revision *Easy*

Here are the final two sentences: *Left untreated, these sores can get infected, causing even greater problems for the dog. And you will keep your dog your best friend.* Notice that there is a gap in logic between these two sentences. On the one hand, the passage discusses the sores. But then the passage then ends rather abruptly with the dog as best friend. To read clearly and logically, there needs to be some kind of logical connection between these two disparate ideas, which is exactly what **B** accomplishes.

SECTION 7: CRITICAL READING

Sentence Completions

1. **E** One-Word/One-Way *Easy*

Mike's sister seems to *like to disagree for the sake of disagreement alone*. In other words, his sister is a very "disagreeable" person. **E**, *contrary*, matches this prediction.

2. **D** Two-Word/One-Way *Medium*

This is a sentence in which it is probably easier to predict the charge of the missing words than the exact words themselves. Overall, the sentence gives you the idea that the editor is liked by her writers: the first blank is a positive word. Eliminate **B** and **E**. Now, whatever the editor does to her authors' work, she makes it better. **D** is the only answer that fits these criteria.

3. **E** Two-Word/Two-Way *Medium*

The second blank is probably easier to predict first. It is a positive word: people "like" *the chance to celebrate their loved ones on a publicly acknowledged day*. Eliminate choices **A**, **C**, and **D**. The word *though* at the beginning of the sentence tells you that there is a contrast, however; some people don't like *Valentine's Day*. **E** is the answer.

4. **D** One-Word/One-Way *Medium*

The house is described as very large, with many rooms and four stories. In other words, a good prediction for the missing word is something like "huge." **D**, *monstrous*, means exactly that.

5. **A** One-Word/One-Way *Medium*

You are looking for a word that agrees with the idea that book buyers would be *more willing to purchase a lighter, cheaper book*. In other words, you are looking for a word that means something like "the supposition" or "the belief." **A** is your answer.

6. **A** Two-Word/Two-Way *Difficult*

The first blank must be a positive word that agrees with *highly developed person*. Eliminate **D** and **E**. Now, what would such a person do with *the temptation to right personal wrongs by judging the external world too harshly?* A good judge would "reject" this temptation, or *eschew* it, **A**.

Long Reading Passage

7. **A** Words in Context *Medium*

Take a look at the way in which the word *split* is used in the passage: *Somewhere in the early twentieth century, the path of music underwent a split. The long expansive symphonic creations of the masters Mahler and Wagner gave way to a new kind of music in the New World, first called "jass," and later termed "jazz."* The author is making the point that music took different paths, or diverged. On the one hand, we have symphonic music; on the other hand, we have the development of jazz. **A** restates this division.

8. **B** Words in Context *Easy*

Here is the sentence used in context: *Walk into a record store and Mahler's Eighth Symphony will most certainly not be housed under the "pop" label, for that German's master's compositions, while certainly well regarded among classical aficionados, is anything but popular.* Here we are told that Mahler's compositions are liked by *classical aficionados* but are not *popular* with other people. In other words, Mahler *is* popular with *classical* "lovers," or *enthusiasts*. **B** is the best answer.

9. **C** Themes and Arguments *Medium*

In discussing pop music, the author writes: *It generates the people who create and promote it unprecedented sums of money.* Notice that the author uses the word *unprecedented*, which means "never before seen." **C** restates this idea.

10. **E** Themes and Arguments *Difficult*

Here are the lines surrounding the use of the term *class-based*: *What are we to make of this power in our midst? Certainly there are those for whom the term "popular" is derogatory, implying that because something appeals on a broad level, it cannot contain any germ of quality. This is, of course, a very class-based idea. It perpetuates the myth that only a talented few in any society have the mental apparatus to fully appreciate a complex work of art.* Here the author is saying that by using the terms *high* and *low* art, a critic is revealing more about his views of class than his views of the quality of art. **E** best restates this idea.

11. **D** Specific Information *Medium*

Here is the sentence in which the word *apparatus* is used: *It perpetuates the myth that only a talented few in any society have the mental apparatus to fully appreciate a complex work of art.* In other words, the author is trying to say that only "intelligent" people can appreciate a *complex work of art.* So, the word *apparatus* is referring to a person's "intelligence" or *acuity*, **D**.

12. **B** Themes and Arguments *Medium*

Take a look at how the author uses Shakespeare: *the old saw about Shakespeare writing for the masses and for kings and queens is often pulled out at this juncture, and although Shakespeare was certainly no musician, his ideal as the "popular artist of critical acclaim" certainly does fit the bill.* Here we are reading a passage about music, and yet the author pulls out Shakespeare, who was a writer. The author is aware of the fact that people might not feel that Shakespeare fits into a discussion of music, and even says as much. **B** points out this potential problem.

13. **C** Attitude and Tone *Medium*

This question tests your overall understanding of the author's point of view. He is not sure that the division of music into "high" and "low" classes is really appropriate and says as much. His attitude, therefore, is one of skepticism.

14. **A** Specific Information *Difficult*

After discussing the idea of *high* and *low* art, the author says the following: *If we want to understand how or why this division occurs, I would argue that certainly it is useful to take a look at social strata. But it is also helpful to take a look at why we even have music in our lives, that is, to actually consider the function of music as art and the role it actually plays in our lives as it moves through our societal constructs.* In other words, the author puts forward another way to look at music, which is the point that **A** makes.

15. **E** Specific Information *Medium*

Take a look at the lines describing protest music: *But, by its very nature, protest music challenges us, and it is intended to be difficult, thought-provoking music. What is generally termed pop music, however, is not intended to give rise to our intellectual functions or to present us with moral quandaries. It is music to be enjoyed.* The author is making two points. First, he says that protest music is challenging. Then, he goes on to say that most people don't want to be challenged when they listen to music. He does not, however, mention sweeping social changes. Roman numeral I, therefore, cannot be part of the correct answer.

16. **B** Themes and Arguments *Medium*

What kind of information goes into this paragraph? The author says things like, *I would argue . . .* or *Presumably, we have this music in our lives.* It cannot really be said that the author is citing fact. He is using a lot of his own observations and trying to persuade the reader of his opinion. The answer must be **B**.

17. **A** Words in Context *Medium*

Look at the way the word *inane* is used in the passage: *In other words, pop music is not the creation of inane minds for the consumption of those who are even more vapid.* The word *vapid* means "dull" and "stupid." So, the author is saying that pop music is not for "stupid" people. A good prediction for the word *inane* is "stupid," or intellectually *empty*, **A**.

18. **B** Specific Information *Medium*

Here are the lines surrounding the term in question: *Presumably, we have this music in our lives because we need to be removed from the more ordinary world. In other words, pop music is not the creation of inane minds for the consumption of those who are even more vapid. Rather, it has a specific function generated out of a very specific need as experienced by a modern population.* The author is making the point that pop music is not *vapid*, or "stupid and empty." Instead, pop music is supposed to remove us *from the ordinary world*. **B** restates this idea.

19. **E** Technique *Medium*

The author ends the passage by saying that it would be interesting to see what kinds of musical tastes correlate to what kinds of members of society. He says, *Who, for example, most strongly feels a need to be removed from the drudgery of day to day life to the ease of a rhythmic and thus escapist piece of pop? Who, on the other hand, welcomes, and in fact even desires, the inherent challenge of socially conscious music?* The author is implying that it is worth taking a look at which classes enjoy which kinds of music, or **E**.

SECTION 8: MATH

Multiple Choice

1. **D** Geometry: Coordinate Geometry *Easy*

You want a line that is positive: it must slope up toward the upper right corner. Eliminate **B**, **C**, and **E**. You are also told that the line has a negative *y* intercept, so the correct answer must be **D**, since **A** shows a positive *y*-intercept.

2. **E** Numbers & Operations: Substitution *Easy*

Genevieve gives 6 total packages away and still has some left. Eliminate **A** and **B**, because these totals are too small. **C** can also be eliminated. Genevieve starts with an equal number of red and blue packages, so **C** can't work as the original number—9 can't be divided into 2 integers.

D is also too small. If Genevieve had started with 12 presents, she'd have 6 red and 6 blue. After she gave away 6 blue packages she'd have no blue packages left. **E** is the only choice that works.

3. **D** Numbers & Operations: Basic Operations *Easy*

Round all of the values:

$1.89 = $2.00
$2.20 = $2.00
$5.59 = $6.00
$3.35 = $3.00
Total = $13.00

Julie can expect to get around $7.00 back.

4. **D** Data Analysis, Statistics & Probability: Statistical Analysis *Easy*

You are asked to find the mode of all the numbers. This means that you must have at least one number appear twice. However, all of the remaining numbers must be larger than 80, but smaller than 120. You can immediately eliminate **A**, **B**, and **C** as being too small. **E** is too large. The correct answer must be **D**.

5. **C** Algebra: Coordinate Geometry *Easy*

Check to see where the *y*-coordinate is if the *x*-coordinate is 4. You can see that it is around 2.5.

6. **B** Geometry: Circles *Medium*

All angles around a point add up to 360 degrees. Add the values of the angles together to solve for *x*:

$$x + x + 5x + 2x + 2x + 4x = 360$$
$$15x = 360$$
$$x = 24$$

7. **E** Algebra: Absolute Value and Exponents *Medium*

All the numbers must be positive integers. Take the equations a step at a time:

$$a^b = 9$$

If all variables are integers, then $a = 3$ and $b = 2$.

Now look at the following:

$$c^b = 8b$$
$$c^2 = 8(2)$$
$$c^2 = 16$$
$$c = 4$$

Now, add up the variables:

$$a + b + c = 2 + 3 + 4 = 9$$

8. **B** Geometry: Coordinate Geometry *Medium*

The coordinates revolve around the origin *O*, or points (0, 0). The points will be symmetrical, and only **B** presents coordinates that are symmetrical.

9. **D** Algebra: Absolute Value and Exponents *Medium*

Work backwards starting with **C**:

$$2q + 5$$
$$2(5) + 5 = 15$$
$$\frac{15}{3} = 5 \text{ with a remainder of } 0$$

Try **D**:

$$2q + 5$$
$$2(6) + 5 = 17$$
$$\frac{17}{3} = 5 \text{ with a remainder of } 2$$

10. **D** Numbers & Operations: Sets *Medium*

To count the number of terms in a set, subtract the smallest number from the largest and add 1:

$$253 - 4 + 1 = 250$$

11. **E** Geometry: Coordinate Geometry *Medium*

You want to see at how many points the line will have a *y*-coordinate of 1. A careful look will tell you that the line will cross these points five times.

12. **C** Geometry: Circles *Medium*

If the area of the circle is 36π, then you know that the diameter of the circle is 12:

$$A = \pi r^2$$
$$36\pi = \pi r^2$$
$$36 = r^2$$
$$6 = r$$
$$12 = d$$

The number 12 is also the measure of one side of the square. Notice too that *ABC* forms an isosceles right triangle, whose sides must be in a ratio of $x{:}x{:}x\sqrt{2}$. Since you know that the legs of such a triangle are 12, simply multiply 12 by $\sqrt{2}$ to find the hypotenuse, or $12\sqrt{2}$.

13. **D** Numbers & Operations: Percents *Medium*
Begin by choosing the number 100 for the price of the sofa. First, the price of the sofa is decreased by 20 percent. This means that the sofa price goes from 100 to 80. Now, the price of the soft goes up by 30 percent. Be careful here: you want to increase 80 by 30 percent of 80, or 24. The new price is 104. This means that the sofa price has increased by 4 percent.

14. **C** Numbers & Operations: Factors and Multiples *Medium*
What are the first five positive odd integers?

1, 3, 5, 7, and 9

The prime factors are 3, 3, 5, and 7 for a total of 315. All of the numbers listed divide evenly into 315, except for **C**.

15. **D** Geometry: Polygons *Medium*
To answer this question, you need to find the area of the square and subtract the area of the unshaded region. You know that the area of the square is 144, because 12 squared is 144. Now, find the area of the unshaded region. Notice that this unshaded region is a triangle with a side of 12 and another side of 13. The missing leg is 5, because of the special Pythagorean triplet: 5-12-13. The area of this triangle is 30. Subtracting 30 from 144, we get a total of 114.

16. **E** Algebra: Absolute Value and Exponents *Difficult*
You have to find what is reliably negative in this problem. You know that y^2 must be positive, because anything square is positive. It is an open question if z^3 is positive or negative, because if z is positive, then z^3 is positive, but if z is negative, then z^3 is negative. The only thing that you know is that xz will be negative, since overall xy^2z^3 is negative, and you have already determined that y^2 is positive.

SECTION 9: WRITING

Improving Sentences

1. **D** Tense *Easy*
Here we have a problem with verb tense. The verb *showing* makes the sentence into a fragment. **D** corrects this problem.

2. **B** Coordination and Subordination *Easy*
The presence of the conjunction *and* is awkward, keeping this sentence from being complete. To be correct, either the conjunction *and* needs to be removed or another part of the sentence needs to be turned into an independent clause. **B** fixes the problem by removing the word *and*.

3. **A** No Error *Medium*

There is no error here. All subjects and verbs agree, and other parts of speech are used correctly.

4. **E** Idioms *Easy*

This sentence tests your knowledge of idioms. The sentence incorrectly says *speak a mind* when the correct usage would be *speak their mind.*

5. **B** Tense *Easy*

This sentence is incorrect because the verb *concocting* needs to be in its infinitive form, *to concoct*, as in **B**.

6. **C** Idioms *Easy*

Here we have a misused idiomatic expression. The verb *insisted* needs to go with the preposition *on* and not *for*. **C** corrects this error.

7. **B** Coordination and Subordination *Easy*

The word *neither* must always be paired with the conjunction *nor*. However, here, the sentence matches up *neither* with the conjunction *or*. **B** corrects this error.

8. **A** No Error *Medium*

There is no error here. All subjects and verbs agree, and other parts of speech are used correctly.

9. **B** Verb Tense *Medium*

The verb *bars* here is in the incorrect form. It should read *barring*, as in **B**.

10. **C** Misplaced Modifier *Medium*

Here we have an example of a misplaced modifier. The way the sentence reads originally, it sounds as though the *air conditioners* are *preparing for the summer*, and yet this does not really make any sense. It must be the *apartment owners* who are preparing for the summer. **C** puts the noun *apartment owners* in the correct position.

11. **D** Coordination and Subordination *Medium*

Here we have two independent clauses stuck together. To be grammatically correct, you need for once sentence to be made dependent on the other, or both sentences need to be joined together by a semicolon. **D** fixes the problem by making the second clause dependent on the first.

12. **B** Misplaced Modifier *Medium*

The way the sentence reads now it sound as though *a mistake* was responsible for *entering a check mark in the wrong box.* But this makes little sense. Clearly it is *the voter* who made the error. **B** fixes this problem by placing *the voter* in close proximity to the modifying clause.

13. **B** Coordination and Subordination *Medium*

When two things are being joined by the connectors "not only" and "but also" they must appear in parallel form. On the one hand we have *great beauty*, but on the other hand we have *the ability to speak coherently as well.* Notice that the words *as well* are extraneous and unnecessary. **B** corrects this problem.

14. **D** Subject Verb Agreement *Difficult*

All sentences must contain a main verb, and yet in this sentence the main verb is clearly missing. To fix this, the noun *local content* must be moved to later in the sentence, and *containing* must be turned into a main verb of *contain*. This is precisely what **D** accomplishes.

SAT PRACTICE TEST 4

SAT* Reasoning Test—General Directions

Timing

- You will have 3 hours and 20 minutes to work on this test. (On the actual SAT, you would have 3 hours and 45 minutes to complete ten sections, one of which would be unscored and experimental.)
- There are nine separately timed sections:
  - ➤ One 25-minute essay
  - ➤ Five other 25-minute sections
  - ➤ Two 20-minute sections
  - ➤ One 10-minute section
- You may work on only one section at a time.
- The supervisor will tell you when to begin and end each section.
- If you finish a section before time is called, check your work on that section. You may NOT turn to any other section.
- Work as rapidly as you can without losing accuracy. Don't waste time on questions that seem too difficult for you.

Marking Answers

- Carefully mark only one answer for each question.
- Make sure each mark is dark and completely fills the circle.
- Do not make any stray marks on your answer sheet.
- If you erase, do so completely. Incomplete erasures may be scored as intended answers.
- Use only the answer spaces that correspond to the question numbers.
- Use the test book for scratchwork, but you will not receive credit for anything written there.
- After time has been called, you may not transfer answers to your answer sheet or fill in circles.
- You may not fold or remove pages or portions of a page from this book, or take the book or answer sheet from the testing room.

Scoring

- For each correct answer to a question, you receive one point.
- For questions you omit, you receive no points.
- For a wrong answer to a multiple-choice question, you lose one-fourth of a point.
  - ➤ If you can eliminate one or more of the answer choices as wrong, you increase your chances of choosing the correct answer and earning one point.
  - ➤ If you can't eliminate any choice, move on. You can return to the question later if there is time.
- For a wrong answer to a "grid-in" math question, you don't lose any points.
- The essay is scored on a 1 to 6 scale by two different readers. The total essay score is the sum of the two readers' scores.
- An off-topic or blank essay will receive a score of zero.

SAT PRACTICE TEST 4 ANSWER SHEET

SECTION 2

1. Ⓐ Ⓑ Ⓒ Ⓓ Ⓔ	7. Ⓐ Ⓑ Ⓒ Ⓓ Ⓔ	13. Ⓐ Ⓑ Ⓒ Ⓓ Ⓔ	19. Ⓐ Ⓑ Ⓒ Ⓓ Ⓔ
2. Ⓐ Ⓑ Ⓒ Ⓓ Ⓔ	8. Ⓐ Ⓑ Ⓒ Ⓓ Ⓔ	14. Ⓐ Ⓑ Ⓒ Ⓓ Ⓔ	20. Ⓐ Ⓑ Ⓒ Ⓓ Ⓔ
3. Ⓐ Ⓑ Ⓒ Ⓓ Ⓔ	9. Ⓐ Ⓑ Ⓒ Ⓓ Ⓔ	15. Ⓐ Ⓑ Ⓒ Ⓓ Ⓔ	21. Ⓐ Ⓑ Ⓒ Ⓓ Ⓔ
4. Ⓐ Ⓑ Ⓒ Ⓓ Ⓔ	10. Ⓐ Ⓑ Ⓒ Ⓓ Ⓔ	16. Ⓐ Ⓑ Ⓒ Ⓓ Ⓔ	22. Ⓐ Ⓑ Ⓒ Ⓓ Ⓔ
5. Ⓐ Ⓑ Ⓒ Ⓓ Ⓔ	11. Ⓐ Ⓑ Ⓒ Ⓓ Ⓔ	17. Ⓐ Ⓑ Ⓒ Ⓓ Ⓔ	23. Ⓐ Ⓑ Ⓒ Ⓓ Ⓔ
6. Ⓐ Ⓑ Ⓒ Ⓓ Ⓔ	12. Ⓐ Ⓑ Ⓒ Ⓓ Ⓔ	18. Ⓐ Ⓑ Ⓒ Ⓓ Ⓔ	24. Ⓐ Ⓑ Ⓒ Ⓓ Ⓔ

SECTION 3

1. Ⓐ Ⓑ Ⓒ Ⓓ Ⓔ	6. Ⓐ Ⓑ Ⓒ Ⓓ Ⓔ	11. Ⓐ Ⓑ Ⓒ Ⓓ Ⓔ	16. Ⓐ Ⓑ Ⓒ Ⓓ Ⓔ
2. Ⓐ Ⓑ Ⓒ Ⓓ Ⓔ	7. Ⓐ Ⓑ Ⓒ Ⓓ Ⓔ	12. Ⓐ Ⓑ Ⓒ Ⓓ Ⓔ	17. Ⓐ Ⓑ Ⓒ Ⓓ Ⓔ
3. Ⓐ Ⓑ Ⓒ Ⓓ Ⓔ	8. Ⓐ Ⓑ Ⓒ Ⓓ Ⓔ	13. Ⓐ Ⓑ Ⓒ Ⓓ Ⓔ	18. Ⓐ Ⓑ Ⓒ Ⓓ Ⓔ
4. Ⓐ Ⓑ Ⓒ Ⓓ Ⓔ	9. Ⓐ Ⓑ Ⓒ Ⓓ Ⓔ	14. Ⓐ Ⓑ Ⓒ Ⓓ Ⓔ	19. Ⓐ Ⓑ Ⓒ Ⓓ Ⓔ
5. Ⓐ Ⓑ Ⓒ Ⓓ Ⓔ	10. Ⓐ Ⓑ Ⓒ Ⓓ Ⓔ	15. Ⓐ Ⓑ Ⓒ Ⓓ Ⓔ	20. Ⓐ Ⓑ Ⓒ Ⓓ Ⓔ

SECTION 4

1. Ⓐ Ⓑ Ⓒ Ⓓ Ⓔ	7. Ⓐ Ⓑ Ⓒ Ⓓ Ⓔ	13. Ⓐ Ⓑ Ⓒ Ⓓ Ⓔ	19. Ⓐ Ⓑ Ⓒ Ⓓ Ⓔ
2. Ⓐ Ⓑ Ⓒ Ⓓ Ⓔ	8. Ⓐ Ⓑ Ⓒ Ⓓ Ⓔ	14. Ⓐ Ⓑ Ⓒ Ⓓ Ⓔ	20. Ⓐ Ⓑ Ⓒ Ⓓ Ⓔ
3. Ⓐ Ⓑ Ⓒ Ⓓ Ⓔ	9. Ⓐ Ⓑ Ⓒ Ⓓ Ⓔ	15. Ⓐ Ⓑ Ⓒ Ⓓ Ⓔ	21. Ⓐ Ⓑ Ⓒ Ⓓ Ⓔ
4. Ⓐ Ⓑ Ⓒ Ⓓ Ⓔ	10. Ⓐ Ⓑ Ⓒ Ⓓ Ⓔ	16. Ⓐ Ⓑ Ⓒ Ⓓ Ⓔ	22. Ⓐ Ⓑ Ⓒ Ⓓ Ⓔ
5. Ⓐ Ⓑ Ⓒ Ⓓ Ⓔ	11. Ⓐ Ⓑ Ⓒ Ⓓ Ⓔ	17. Ⓐ Ⓑ Ⓒ Ⓓ Ⓔ	23. Ⓐ Ⓑ Ⓒ Ⓓ Ⓔ
6. Ⓐ Ⓑ Ⓒ Ⓓ Ⓔ	12. Ⓐ Ⓑ Ⓒ Ⓓ Ⓔ	18. Ⓐ Ⓑ Ⓒ Ⓓ Ⓔ	24. Ⓐ Ⓑ Ⓒ Ⓓ Ⓔ

SECTION 5

1. Ⓐ Ⓑ Ⓒ Ⓓ Ⓔ	3. Ⓐ Ⓑ Ⓒ Ⓓ Ⓔ	5. Ⓐ Ⓑ Ⓒ Ⓓ Ⓔ	7. Ⓐ Ⓑ Ⓒ Ⓓ Ⓔ
2. Ⓐ Ⓑ Ⓒ Ⓓ Ⓔ	4. Ⓐ Ⓑ Ⓒ Ⓓ Ⓔ	6. Ⓐ Ⓑ Ⓒ Ⓓ Ⓔ	8. Ⓐ Ⓑ Ⓒ Ⓓ Ⓔ

9				10				11				12				13			
		/				/				/				/				/	
.	.	.	.	.	.	.	.	.	.	.	.	.	.	.	.	.	.	.	.
	0	0	0		0	0	0		0	0	0		0	0	0		0	0	0
1	1	1	1	1	1	1	1	1	1	1	1	1	1	1	1	1	1	1	1
2	2	2	2	2	2	2	2	2	2	2	2	2	2	2	2	2	2	2	2
3	3	3	3	3	3	3	3	3	3	3	3	3	3	3	3	3	3	3	3
4	4	4	4	4	4	4	4	4	4	4	4	4	4	4	4	4	4	4	4
5	5	5	5	5	5	5	5	5	5	5	5	5	5	5	5	5	5	5	5
6	6	6	6	6	6	6	6	6	6	6	6	6	6	6	6	6	6	6	6
7	7	7	7	7	7	7	7	7	7	7	7	7	7	7	7	7	7	7	7
8	8	8	8	8	8	8	8	8	8	8	8	8	8	8	8	8	8	8	8
9	9	9	9	9	9	9	9	9	9	9	9	9	9	9	9	9	9	9	9

14				15				16				17				18			
		/				/				/				/				/	
.	.	.	.	.	.	.	.	.	.	.	.	.	.	.	.	.	.	.	.
	0	0	0		0	0	0		0	0	0		0	0	0		0	0	0
1	1	1	1	1	1	1	1	1	1	1	1	1	1	1	1	1	1	1	1
2	2	2	2	2	2	2	2	2	2	2	2	2	2	2	2	2	2	2	2
3	3	3	3	3	3	3	3	3	3	3	3	3	3	3	3	3	3	3	3
4	4	4	4	4	4	4	4	4	4	4	4	4	4	4	4	4	4	4	4
5	5	5	5	5	5	5	5	5	5	5	5	5	5	5	5	5	5	5	5
6	6	6	6	6	6	6	6	6	6	6	6	6	6	6	6	6	6	6	6
7	7	7	7	7	7	7	7	7	7	7	7	7	7	7	7	7	7	7	7
8	8	8	8	8	8	8	8	8	8	8	8	8	8	8	8	8	8	8	8
9	9	9	9	9	9	9	9	9	9	9	9	9	9	9	9	9	9	9	9

SAT PRACTICE TEST 4 ANSWER SHEET

SECTION 6			
1. Ⓐ Ⓑ Ⓒ Ⓓ Ⓔ	10. Ⓐ Ⓑ Ⓒ Ⓓ Ⓔ	19. Ⓐ Ⓑ Ⓒ Ⓓ Ⓔ	28. Ⓐ Ⓑ Ⓒ Ⓓ Ⓔ
2. Ⓐ Ⓑ Ⓒ Ⓓ Ⓔ	11. Ⓐ Ⓑ Ⓒ Ⓓ Ⓔ	20. Ⓐ Ⓑ Ⓒ Ⓓ Ⓔ	29. Ⓐ Ⓑ Ⓒ Ⓓ Ⓔ
3. Ⓐ Ⓑ Ⓒ Ⓓ Ⓔ	12. Ⓐ Ⓑ Ⓒ Ⓓ Ⓔ	21. Ⓐ Ⓑ Ⓒ Ⓓ Ⓔ	30. Ⓐ Ⓑ Ⓒ Ⓓ Ⓔ
4. Ⓐ Ⓑ Ⓒ Ⓓ Ⓔ	13. Ⓐ Ⓑ Ⓒ Ⓓ Ⓔ	22. Ⓐ Ⓑ Ⓒ Ⓓ Ⓔ	31. Ⓐ Ⓑ Ⓒ Ⓓ Ⓔ
5. Ⓐ Ⓑ Ⓒ Ⓓ Ⓔ	14. Ⓐ Ⓑ Ⓒ Ⓓ Ⓔ	23. Ⓐ Ⓑ Ⓒ Ⓓ Ⓔ	32. Ⓐ Ⓑ Ⓒ Ⓓ Ⓔ
6. Ⓐ Ⓑ Ⓒ Ⓓ Ⓔ	15. Ⓐ Ⓑ Ⓒ Ⓓ Ⓔ	24. Ⓐ Ⓑ Ⓒ Ⓓ Ⓔ	33. Ⓐ Ⓑ Ⓒ Ⓓ Ⓔ
7. Ⓐ Ⓑ Ⓒ Ⓓ Ⓔ	16. Ⓐ Ⓑ Ⓒ Ⓓ Ⓔ	25. Ⓐ Ⓑ Ⓒ Ⓓ Ⓔ	34. Ⓐ Ⓑ Ⓒ Ⓓ Ⓔ
8. Ⓐ Ⓑ Ⓒ Ⓓ Ⓔ	17. Ⓐ Ⓑ Ⓒ Ⓓ Ⓔ	26. Ⓐ Ⓑ Ⓒ Ⓓ Ⓔ	35. Ⓐ Ⓑ Ⓒ Ⓓ Ⓔ
9. Ⓐ Ⓑ Ⓒ Ⓓ Ⓔ	18. Ⓐ Ⓑ Ⓒ Ⓓ Ⓔ	27. Ⓐ Ⓑ Ⓒ Ⓓ Ⓔ	

SECTION 7			
1. Ⓐ Ⓑ Ⓒ Ⓓ Ⓔ	6. Ⓐ Ⓑ Ⓒ Ⓓ Ⓔ	11. Ⓐ Ⓑ Ⓒ Ⓓ Ⓔ	16. Ⓐ Ⓑ Ⓒ Ⓓ Ⓔ
2. Ⓐ Ⓑ Ⓒ Ⓓ Ⓔ	7. Ⓐ Ⓑ Ⓒ Ⓓ Ⓔ	12. Ⓐ Ⓑ Ⓒ Ⓓ Ⓔ	17. Ⓐ Ⓑ Ⓒ Ⓓ Ⓔ
3. Ⓐ Ⓑ Ⓒ Ⓓ Ⓔ	8. Ⓐ Ⓑ Ⓒ Ⓓ Ⓔ	13. Ⓐ Ⓑ Ⓒ Ⓓ Ⓔ	18. Ⓐ Ⓑ Ⓒ Ⓓ Ⓔ
4. Ⓐ Ⓑ Ⓒ Ⓓ Ⓔ	9. Ⓐ Ⓑ Ⓒ Ⓓ Ⓔ	14. Ⓐ Ⓑ Ⓒ Ⓓ Ⓔ	19. Ⓐ Ⓑ Ⓒ Ⓓ Ⓔ
5. Ⓐ Ⓑ Ⓒ Ⓓ Ⓔ	10. Ⓐ Ⓑ Ⓒ Ⓓ Ⓔ	15. Ⓐ Ⓑ Ⓒ Ⓓ Ⓔ	

SECTION 8			
1. Ⓐ Ⓑ Ⓒ Ⓓ Ⓔ	5. Ⓐ Ⓑ Ⓒ Ⓓ Ⓔ	9. Ⓐ Ⓑ Ⓒ Ⓓ Ⓔ	13. Ⓐ Ⓑ Ⓒ Ⓓ Ⓔ
2. Ⓐ Ⓑ Ⓒ Ⓓ Ⓔ	6. Ⓐ Ⓑ Ⓒ Ⓓ Ⓔ	10. Ⓐ Ⓑ Ⓒ Ⓓ Ⓔ	14. Ⓐ Ⓑ Ⓒ Ⓓ Ⓔ
3. Ⓐ Ⓑ Ⓒ Ⓓ Ⓔ	7. Ⓐ Ⓑ Ⓒ Ⓓ Ⓔ	11. Ⓐ Ⓑ Ⓒ Ⓓ Ⓔ	15. Ⓐ Ⓑ Ⓒ Ⓓ Ⓔ
4. Ⓐ Ⓑ Ⓒ Ⓓ Ⓔ	8. Ⓐ Ⓑ Ⓒ Ⓓ Ⓔ	12. Ⓐ Ⓑ Ⓒ Ⓓ Ⓔ	16. Ⓐ Ⓑ Ⓒ Ⓓ Ⓔ

SECTION 9			
1. Ⓐ Ⓑ Ⓒ Ⓓ Ⓔ	5. Ⓐ Ⓑ Ⓒ Ⓓ Ⓔ	9. Ⓐ Ⓑ Ⓒ Ⓓ Ⓔ	13. Ⓐ Ⓑ Ⓒ Ⓓ Ⓔ
2. Ⓐ Ⓑ Ⓒ Ⓓ Ⓔ	6. Ⓐ Ⓑ Ⓒ Ⓓ Ⓔ	10. Ⓐ Ⓑ Ⓒ Ⓓ Ⓔ	14. Ⓐ Ⓑ Ⓒ Ⓓ Ⓔ
3. Ⓐ Ⓑ Ⓒ Ⓓ Ⓔ	7. Ⓐ Ⓑ Ⓒ Ⓓ Ⓔ	11. Ⓐ Ⓑ Ⓒ Ⓓ Ⓔ	
4. Ⓐ Ⓑ Ⓒ Ⓓ Ⓔ	8. Ⓐ Ⓑ Ⓒ Ⓓ Ⓔ	12. Ⓐ Ⓑ Ⓒ Ⓓ Ⓔ	

SECTION 1

ESSAY

Time—25 minutes

The essay gives you an opportunity to show how effectively you can develop and express ideas. You should, therefore, take care to develop your point of view, present your ideas logically and clearly, and use language precisely.

Your essay must be written on the lines provided on your answer sheet—you will receive no other paper on which to write. You will have enough space if you write on every line, avoid wide margins, and keep your handwriting to a reasonable size. Remember that people who are not familiar with your handwriting will read what you write. Try to write or print so that what you are writing is legible to those readers.

You have twenty-five minutes to write an essay on the topic assigned below. DO NOT WRITE ON ANOTHER TOPIC. AN OFF-TOPIC ESSAY WILL RECEIVE A SCORE OF ZERO.

Think carefully about the issue presented in the following excerpt and the assignment below.

> Traditionally the term "leader" has been applied to those who lead others by inspiring them or by enabling them to accomplish great tasks. But one of the most important challenges that leaders face is determining when to take a risk. Sometimes leadership requires willingness to risk taking action even when the outcome is uncertain. We should consider those who do so true leaders.

Assignment: Should leaders be defined as people who are willing to take risks that others lack the foresight to take? Plan and write an essay in which you develop your point of view on this issue. Support your position with reasoning and examples taken from your reading, studies, experience, or observations.

DO NOT WRITE YOUR ESSAY IN YOUR TEST BOOK. You will receive credit only for what you write on your answer sheet.

BEGIN WRITING YOUR ESSAY ON THE ANSWER SHEET.

IF YOU FINISH BEFORE TIME IS CALLED, YOU MAY CHECK YOUR WORK ON THIS SECTION ONLY. DO NOT TURN TO ANY OTHER SECTION IN THE TEST.

SECTION 1—ESSAY

Time—25 minutes

SECTION 1—ESSAY

Time—25 minutes

SECTION 2

Turn to Section 2 of your answer sheet to answer the questions in this section.

Time—25 Minutes 24 Questions	**Directions:** For each question in this section, select the best answer from among the choices given and fill in the corresponding oval on the answer sheet.

Each sentence below has one or two blanks, each blank indicating that something has been omitted. Beneath the sentence are five words or sets of words labeled A through E. Choose the word or set of words that, when inserted in the sentence, <u>best</u> fits the meaning of the sentence as a whole.

<u>Example</u>:

Eliza felt ----- when her boss asked her to work seven weekends in a row but ----- when her work earned her a promotion.

(A) enervated . . weakened
(B) depressed . . intellectual
(C) advantageous . . salacious
(D) angry . . shopworn
(E) irate . . elated

1. After Sally's brother ----- that he had only been joking, Sally finally agreed to ----- him.

(A) explained . . absolve
(B) proved . . incriminate
(C) denied . . forgive
(D) accepted . . believe
(E) argued . . understand

2. Although the weather forecast ----- rain this week, the weather ----- expectations and remained pleasant.

(A) expected . . upheld
(B) anticipated . . rejected
(C) predicted . . defied
(D) doubted . . met
(E) explored . . confirmed

3. The experiences in Arthur Wainwright's supposed autobiography were entirely fabricated, showing that he preferred ----- over -----.

(A) fantasy . . fact
(B) truth . . fiction
(C) fables . . narrative
(D) mystery . . reality
(E) stories . . myths

4. The bidder offered an exorbitant price for the painting in an aggressive move to ----- her competition.

(A) provoke
(B) distract
(C) inform
(D) eliminate
(E) appease

5. The scholarly journal required Lance to condense his article substantially, but the special-interest publication did not require any ----- of his piece.

(A) retraction
(B) expansion
(C) abridgement
(D) examination
(E) review

6. The entrepreneurs forged ahead fearlessly, focused only on their goal of innovation; through their ----- they became-----, people who bring about major change.

(A) audaciousness . . mercenaries
(B) diffidence . . initiators
(C) reticence . . oracles
(D) courage . . skeptics
(E) intrepidity . . harbingers

GO ON TO THE NEXT PAGE

SECTION 2

7. The software is used by nearly every practitioner in the industry; because of its ------, it must be learned by anyone wishing to work in this field.

(A) ubiquity
(B) diligence
(C) scarcity
(D) dispensability
(E) omnipotence

8. Biologists argue that before this species is ------, or completely destroyed, we should attempt to ------ it through conservation measures.

(A) established . . negate
(B) annihilated . . reduce
(C) aggrandized . . restore
(D) extirpated . . preserve
(E) propagated . . obliterate

GO ON TO THE NEXT PAGE

SECTION 2

Directions: Each passage below is followed by questions based on its content. Answer the questions on the basis of what is stated or implied in each passage and in any introductory material that may be provided.

Questions 9–10 are based on the following passage.

Jurgis was like a boy, a boy from the country. He was the sort of man the bosses like to get hold of, the sort they make it a grievance if they cannot get hold of. When he was told to go to a certain place, he would go there on the run. When he had nothing to do for the moment, he would stand round fidgeting, dancing, with the overflow of energy that was in him. If he were working in a line of men, the line always moved too slowly for him, and you could pick him out by his impatience and restlessness. That was why he had been picked out on one important occasion; for Jurgis had stood outside of Brown and Company's "Central Time Station" not more than half an hour, the second day of his arrival in Chicago, before he had been beckoned by one of the bosses. Of this he was very proud, and it made him more disposed than ever to laugh at the pessimists. In vain they would all tell him that there were men in that crowd from which he had been chosen who had stood there a month—yes, many months—and not been chosen yet. "Yes," he would say, "but what sort of men? Broken-down tramps and good-for-nothings, fellows who have spent all their money drinking, and want to get more for it. Do you want me to believe that with these arms"—and he would clench his fists and hold them up in the air, so that you might see the rolling muscles—"that with these arms people will ever let me starve?"

9. In lines 19–22 ("Do you want . . . starve"), Jurgis's question primarily conveys his

(A) hope that work conditions will improve
(B) frustration that bosses continually overlook him
(C) confidence in his ability to be hired for jobs
(D) impatience with having to wait to be chosen
(E) criticism of the other workers waiting to be hired

10. The "pessimists" referred to in line 14 would most likely include

(A) analysts who studied economic indicators
(B) bosses who felt that wages were too high
(C) men who were physically strong like Jurgis
(D) wives of workers with large families
(E) workers who were rarely hired for jobs

Questions 11–12 are based on the following passage.

The rocks contained on the Earth and within the Earth's crust can be divided into three different types. The first type of rock is known as igneous rock and is produced from hot lava that has solidified. A second type of rock, sedimentary rock, is created through the compaction of sediments that are deposited by wind or water. Finally, the third type of rock is known as metamorphic rock. As the name implies, metamorphic rock is created through a transformational process known as metamorphism.

Metamorphism changes existing rock into metamorphic rock through the application of intense heat and pressures deep beneath the Earth's crust. Metamorphic rocks may start as igneous rocks, sedimentary rocks, or even other types of metamorphic rocks. The metamorphic process changes these types of rocks into metamorphic rocks through one of three channels. The first of these, contact metamorphism, involves very high temperatures that cause the preexisting rock to melt and recrystallize. The second type of metamorphic process, regional metamorphism, occurs when intense pressures affect a wide area of rock at deep levels within the Earth. The third type of metamorphism, dynamic metamorphism, occurs as a result of the movement of stone upon stone.

11. The opening paragraph primarily serves to

(A) establish the author's expertise regarding geology
(B) explain a viewpoint that the author will refute
(C) introduce a topic that will be discussed in greater depth
(D) provide a description of three processes of metamorphism
(E) demonstrate why understanding rock formation is important

12. The author's tone in the passage might best be described as

(A) brazen
(B) tentative
(C) enthusiastic
(D) argumentative
(E) neutral

GO ON TO THE NEXT PAGE

SECTION 2

Directions: The passages below are followed by questions based on their content; questions following a pair of related passages may also be based on the relationship between the paired passages. Answer the questions on the basis of what is stated or implied in the passages and in any introductory material that may be provided.

Questions 13–24 are based on the following passages.

The following passages discuss two different models of foreign policy behavior by nation-states: the deterrence model and the spiral model. Both models attempt to account for state behavior by explaining key assumptions about state motivations and interests. Passage 1 is written by a supporter of the deterrence model view. Passage 2 is written by a spiral model theorist.

Passage 1

The deterrence model has been the predominant model employed by theorists examining international behavior, particularly since the origin of the cold war. This model derives from historical interpretations of international relations as "power politics," which have been expounded since the time of Thucydides. In his book *The Peloponnesian War*, Thucydides recounts ancient examples demonstrating the significance of power politics for state behavior. The premise of this approach is that "might makes right." Thucydides emphasizes this premise through a quote that has become a slogan of power politics: "The strong do as they will, and the weak do as they must."

The deterrence model views aggressive foreign policy behavior as the dependent variable to be explained by its theory. Its focus is on examining why states tend to behave aggressively toward each other in political and military dynamics. Proponents of the model argue that the level of aggression in state foreign policy is itself affected by the level of innate aggression in state ideology. This view predicts that a state with a high level of aggression inherent in its national ideology will display highly aggressive foreign policy behavior, whereas a less ideologically aggressive state will produce policies designed to maintain the status quo. The deterrence model does argue, however, that the impact of a highly aggressive state ideology may be tempered by high levels of force and threats on the part of defending states. These high levels of force and threats serve to deter the expansive state's aggressive intent by making the costs of aggression appear to be prohibitively high. The deterrence model therefore prescribes that nations utilize threats and force to counteract the aggressive ideologies of opponent states and to discourage their opponents' belligerent intentions.

Historical justification for the deterrence model approach draws largely from the Allied experience with Nazi Germany before World War II. Prior to the war, Allied leaders hoped to avoid conflict by appeasing Hitler and meeting his demands. It was hoped in the "appeasement" camps that Hitler's aims for Germany were limited and that his expansionistic designs could be curtailed with the concession of particular targeted territories. British prime minister Neville Chamberlain attempted to stave off war through the signing of the Munich Pact with Germany in 1937, which forced Czechoslovakia to cede their Sudetenland territory to Nazi control. This acquisition by Germany proved to be the harbinger of Hitler's unlimited ambition; once the European leaders gave in to certain demands, the Nazi grab for power accelerated and Hitler's true intentions were revealed. In hindsight, it is clear that the Allied appeasement policy encouraged Nazi expansionism by showing the Germans that Britain and France would back down and comply with German requests.

This grave historical lesson has provided deterrence model theorists with very clear guidelines for dealing with potentially aggressive adversaries. Rather than making the mistake of appeasing an adversary that might perceive conciliation as weakness, policy-makers are advised to maintain a forceful posture in response to potential threats. With truly aggressive states, demonstrations of military might are the only effective approach for deterring military action and ultimately avoiding war.

Passage 2

One significant weakness of the deterrence model view of state behavior is its reliance on a single historical example to determine the course of current action. Overemphasis of the Nazi Germany case study has caused deterrence model theorists to operate from a narrow framework that ignores the motivations of genuinely peace-seeking states. Like the deterrence model, the spiral model view of state politics attempts to explain the outcome of aggressive foreign policies. However, the spiral model also focuses on explaining cases in which force and threats do not curtail aggressive intentions but rather serve to exacerbate them.

The spiral model view arose out of revisionist attempts during the 1960s to understand the actions of the Soviet Union. It has also been heavily influenced by scholarship regarding the outbreak of World War I. Spiral model theorists argue that European countries prior to World War I were highly affected by a pervasive foreign policy mindset known as the "cult of the offensive." During the early 1900s, because of advances in military firepower, it was widely accepted that offensive strategies would prevail in any armed conflict. Thus, states that

GO ON TO THE NEXT PAGE

were not innately aggressive began to develop offensive foreign policy positions simply out of the fear that not doing so would make them vulnerable to attack. The "cult of the offensive" mindset led relatively peaceful states to become increasingly antagonistic in response to threats they perceived from other nations. The hostile dynamics eventually spiraled into a war that could have been averted with less aggression and more conciliatory approaches.

Based on evidence from the experience of World War I, the spiral model views aggressive foreign policy as caused by states' reactions to the forceful policies of other states. These foreign policies are interpreted by the status-quo states as hostile in nature. States with nonaggressive ideologies may often develop aggressive policies in the face of force and threats by other states in the system, because these nations are unable to accurately perceive opponents' threatening policies as defensive in nature. A state's inability to correctly perceive the defensive intentions of other states is a key intervening variable that can influence status quo-oriented states to develop aggressive foreign policies.

When faced with a potentially threatening competitor, then, it is of crucial importance to examine the state's intentions without merely assuming expansionistic aims. The case of Nazi Germany illustrates the utility of force and threats for dealing with a belligerent adversary, but this case does not encompass all potential dynamics between states. Contrary to the deterrence model view that force discourages aggression, the pre–World War I case documents how force by one state can generate conflict in states reacting out of fear. Far from asserting that all states are status-quo–oriented entities, however, the spiral model approach advocates that policy-makers differentiate between aggressive and nonaggressive states by carefully analyzing the states' intentions. Such analysis will enable decision-makers to assess when forceful postures may be beneficial and when they may disrupt a fragile peace.

13. The authors of both passages would most likely agree that

(A) policy-makers should learn from history in developing current strategies
(B) policy-makers should react forcefully when faced with perceived threats
(C) decision-makers tend to make political mistakes that cannot be repaired
(D) historical experiences offer few lessons for present-day leaders
(E) the study of previous wars should be restricted to the twentieth century

14. In Passage 1, *The Peloponnesian War* is presented as an example of

(A) a treaty that required Czechoslovakia to cede the Sudetenland
(B) a text that demonstrates the dynamics of power politics
(C) a conflict that spiraled out of control
(D) a war in which leaders believed that offensive strategies were militarily superior
(E) a study that reveals the importance of balancing power with democratic principles

15. The author of Passage 1 implies that force and threats will deter an expansive state's aggressive intent (lines 24–27) ("These high . . . high") if

(A) these actions allow the state to evaluate its adversary's leadership
(B) these actions convey a willingness to negotiate before declaring battle
(C) these actions reveal to the state that its opponent is too weak to resist
(D) these actions convince the state that it would lose an armed conflict
(E) these actions show the state that its adversaries are reasonable

16. The author of Passage 1 asserts that the Allied leaders' motives for appeasing Hitler (lines 33–34) ("Prior to . . . demands") were based on a

(A) commitment to react passively
(B) belief in Hitler's vulnerability
(C) desire to avoid war
(D) fear of Czechoslovakian revolt
(E) distrust of Germany's political system

17. Which of the following is most similar to the approach to foreign policy suggested in lines 49–51 ("This grave . . . adversaries")?

(A) A business learning from past business mistakes
(B) A computer program tallying survey responses
(C) A seminar teaching important skills
(D) A website providing easy navigation
(E) A machine ceasing to work if one part breaks

GO ON TO THE NEXT PAGE

SECTION 2

18. In line 67, the word "exacerbate" serves to emphasize the

(A) futility of attempts at ensuring a peaceful outcome to state conflict
(B) necessity of using force and threats to deter an apparently aggressive state
(C) dissolution of the cult of the offensive once World War I leaders realized its flaws
(D) potential danger of enacting forceful policies against adversaries that are not innately aggressive
(E) importance of developing guidelines for ambiguous foreign policy situations

19. In line 76, "prevail" most nearly means

(A) grow more complex
(B) develop
(C) win
(D) exist
(E) backfire

20. The author of Passage 2 suggests that "the case of Nazi Germany" (line 98) is

(A) highly illustrative for foreign policy decision-making and cannot be overemphasized
(B) pertinent only in situations where a country's motive is nonexpansionistic
(C) relevant particularly for understanding the causes of World War I
(D) helpful for understanding not just foreign policy matters but also economic issues
(E) not representative of every possible foreign policy scenario that a state may encounter

21. The recommendation that policy-makers "maintain a forceful posture in response to potential threats" (lines 53–54) would most likely be discredited by the author of Passage 2 on the grounds that

(A) force and threats are necessary if a state wishes to avoid appearing weak to its adversaries
(B) theorists since the time of Thucydides have emphasized the importance of understanding power politics
(C) European countries are the countries most likely to be faced with the threat of war
(D) forceful postures can cause conflicts to spiral out of control if the states involved do not have innately aggressive intentions
(E) major conflicts that might lead to global wars are relatively infrequent

22. The author of Passage 2 would defend the appeasement supporters mentioned in lines 34–37 ("It was hoped . . . territories") because they

(A) did not take the time to familiarize themselves with the Nazi form of government
(B) realized that Hitler could not be satisfied and thus refused to give in to his demands
(C) planned their response to Hitler carefully before agreeing to sign the Munich Pact
(D) collaborated with Hitler in the development of a policy that was acceptable to both sides
(E) intended through their actions to avoid provoking Germany and precipitating war

23. The author of Passage 1 would most likely view the evidence from World War I described in lines 69–74 ("It has also been . . . the offensive") as

(A) confusing, because of its failure to explain German motivations
(B) helpful as a background for understanding German actions before World War II
(C) beneficial with respect to its impact on leaders' understanding of history
(D) particularly significant in helping states determine how to assess other states' intentions
(E) less relevant to policy formation than the experience of World War II

24. Which contrast best describes how the author of each passage views the implementation of force and threats in dealing with perceived aggressive adversaries?

(A) As wasteful in Passage 1; as useful in Passage 2
(B) As instructional in Passage 1; as frivolous in Passage 2
(C) As fundamentally necessary in Passage 1; as potentially dangerous in Passage 2
(D) As usually wise in Passage 1; as usually advisable in Passage 2
(E) As entirely optional in Passage 1; as always required in Passage 2

S T O P

IF YOU FINISH BEFORE TIME IS CALLED, YOU MAY CHECK YOUR WORK ON THIS TEST ONLY.
DO NOT TURN TO ANY OTHER SECTION IN THIS TEST.

SECTION 3

Turn to Section 3 of your answer sheet to answer the questions in this section.

Time—25 Minutes
20 Questions

Directions: For this section, solve each problem and decide which is the best of the choices given. Fill in the corresponding oval on the answer sheet. You may use any available space for scratchwork.

Notes:

1. The use of a calculator is permitted. All numbers used are real numbers.
2. Figures that accompany problems in this test are intended to provide information useful in solving the problems. They are drawn as accurately as possible EXCEPT when it is stated in a specific problem that the figure is not drawn to scale. All figures lie in a plane unless otherwise indicated.
3. Unless otherwise specified, the domain of any function f is assumed to be the set of all real numbers x for which $f(x)$ is a real number.

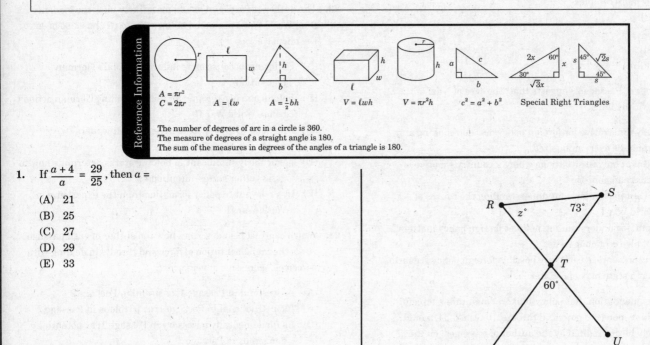

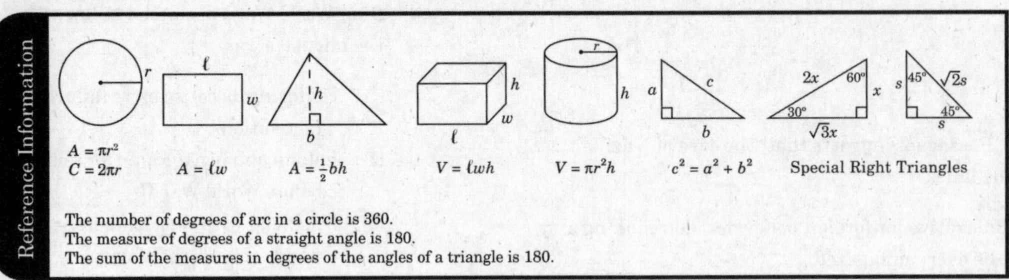

Reference Information

The number of degrees of arc in a circle is 360.
The measure of degrees of a straight angle is 180.
The sum of the measures in degrees of the angles of a triangle is 180.

1. If $\frac{a+4}{a} = \frac{29}{25}$, then $a =$

(A) 21
(B) 25
(C) 27
(D) 29
(E) 33

PETS AT AN ANIMAL SHELTER

	Male	Female	Total
Cats	a	b	m
Dogs	c	d	n
Total	j	k	p

2. In the table above, each letter represents the number of pets in that category. Which of the following must be equal to p ?

(A) $a + d$
(B) $m + k$
(C) $c + d$
(D) $c + d + n$
(E) $a + b + c + d$

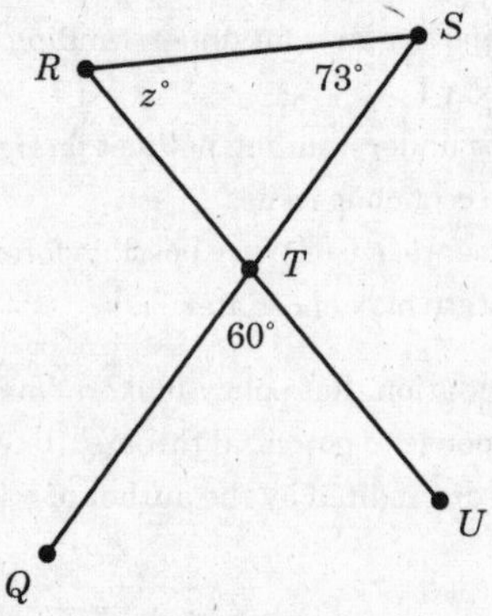

3. In ΔRST above, what is the value of z ?

(A) 27
(B) 35
(C) 47
(D) 60
(E) 120

GO ON TO THE NEXT PAGE

4. Scott's car broke down and it will cost \$1,500 to fix it. A newer car with better gas mileage, costing \$4,000, will save Scott \$50 per month in gas costs. If Scott buys the new car, in m months he will have saved an amount equal to the difference between the cost of the new car and the cost of fixing the old one. What is the value of m ?

(A) 15
(B) 30
(C) 45
(D) 50
(E) 80

5. The area of square *WXYZ* is 4 times the area of square *QRST*. If the area of square *QRST* is 16 square centimeters (cm), what is the length of one side of square *WXYZ* ?

(A) 4 cm
(B) 8 cm
(C) 16 cm
(D) 32 cm
(E) 64 cm

6. A wind turbine completes 50 revolutions per minute at a constant speed. If the turbine runs continuously for 24 hours each day, approximately how many days will it take the turbine to complete 864,000 revolutions?

(A) 12
(B) 120
(C) 1,200
(D) 12,000
(E) 120,000

7. If the average (arithmetic mean) of s and $2s$ is 15, what is the value of s ?

(A) 5
(B) 7.5
(C) 10
(D) 12.5
(E) 15

8. In a geometric sequence of terms, there is a constant ratio between consecutive terms. If the sixth term of a certain geometric sequence with a constant ratio of 2 is 288, what is the first term of the sequence?

(A) 4
(B) 6
(C) 9
(D) 12
(E) 14

9. If $2g + 4h = g + 3$, what is h in terms of g ?

(A) $3 - g$
(B) $3 - 4g$
(C) $4(g + 3)$
(D) $\frac{3-g}{4}$
(E) $\frac{3}{4}(g+1)$

GO ON TO THE NEXT PAGE

SECTION 3

10. If q is a positive integer, let $\rightarrow q$ be defined as the set of all positive factors of q. Which of the following sets contains all of the numbers found in all three of the sets $\rightarrow 3$, $\rightarrow 5$, and $\rightarrow 10$?

(A) $\rightarrow 320$
(B) $\rightarrow 627$
(C) $\rightarrow 925$
(D) $\rightarrow 1,250$
(E) $\rightarrow 1,500$

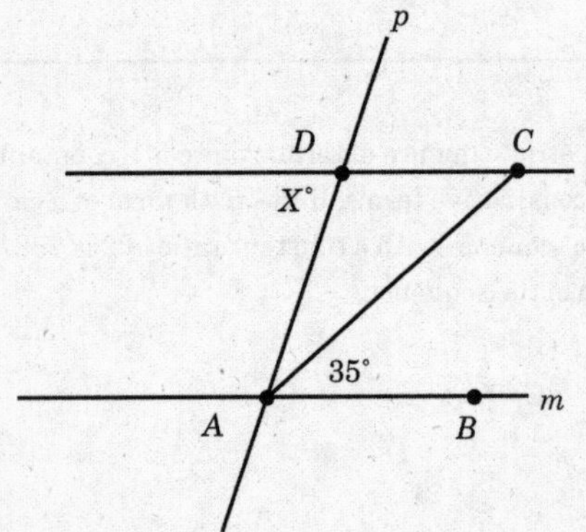

Note: Figure not drawn to scale.

11. In the figure above, line l is parallel to line m. Lines l and m are crossed by transversal p. If AC bisects $\angle DAB$, what is the value of X?

(A) 35°
(B) 70°
(C) 90°
(D) 105°
(E) 145°

12. If z is a positive integer, what is the least value of z for which $\sqrt{\frac{7z}{4}}$ is an integer?

(A) 7
(B) 10
(C) 28
(D) 96
(E) 112

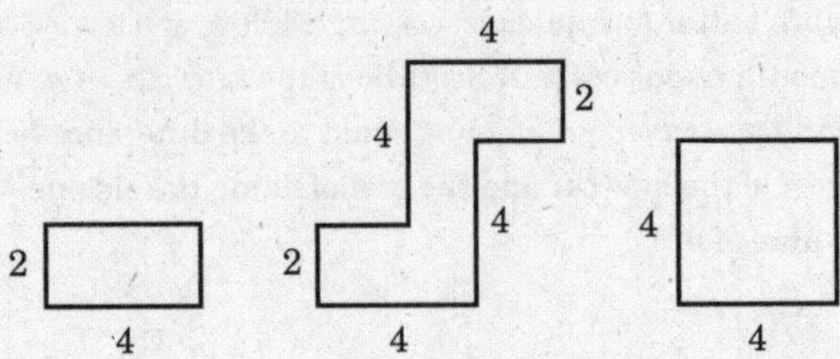

13. The figures above represent three pieces of fabric. All of the angles of the fabric pieces are right angles, all short sides have length 2, and all long sides have length 4. Which of the following patterns could be made from only the three pieces of fabric without overlapping or cutting them?

I.

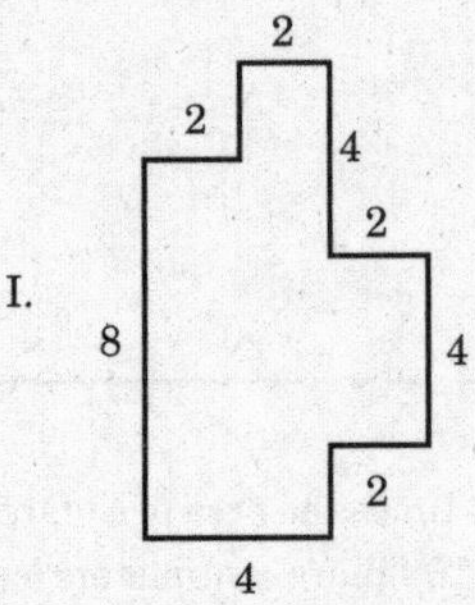

II.

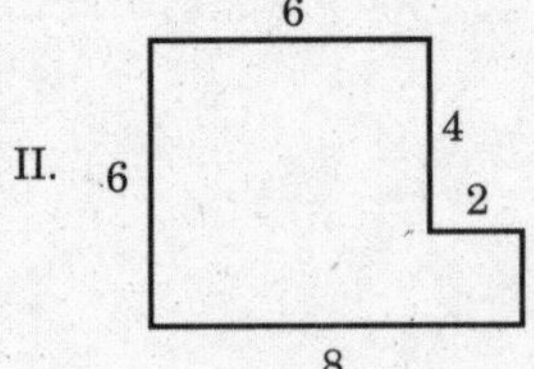

III.

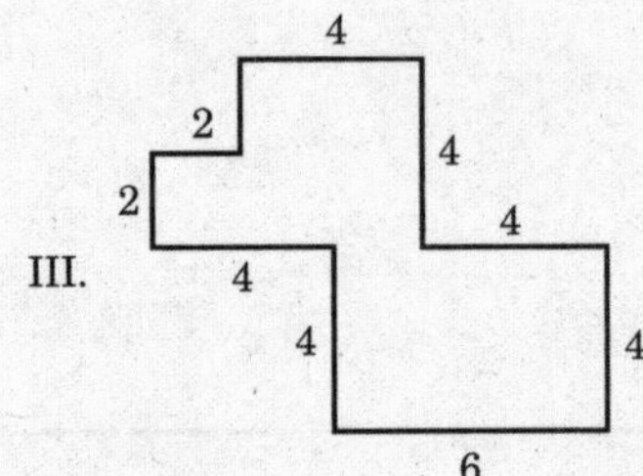

(A) None
(B) I only
(C) II only
(D) III only
(E) I and II

GO ON TO THE NEXT PAGE

SECTION 3

14. How many integers greater than 25 and less than 35 are each the product of at least two identical prime numbers?

(A) Zero
(B) One
(C) Two
(D) Three
(E) Four

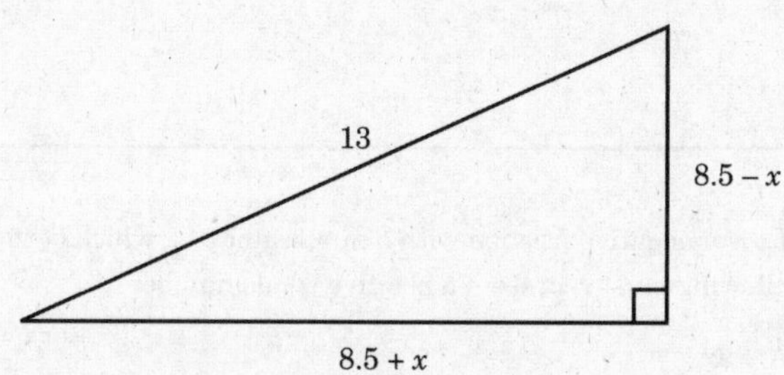

Note: Figure not drawn to scale.

15. The figure above is a right triangle. What is the value of $72.25 - x^2$?

(A) 60
(B) 85
(C) 96.75
(D) 122.50
(E) 169

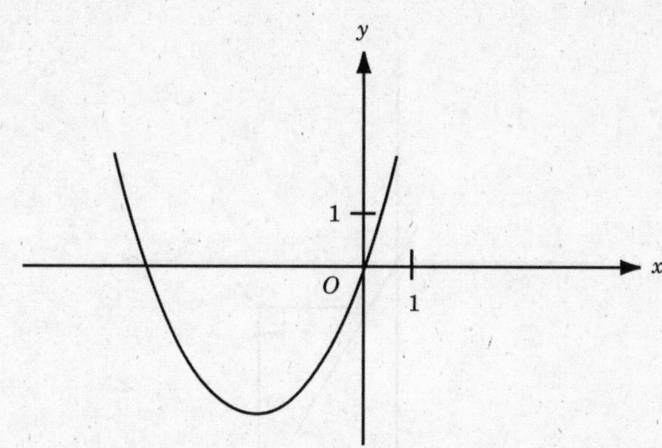

16. The figure above shows the graph of a quadratic function g whose minimum value is $g(-2)$. If $g(b) = 2$, which of the following could be the value of b?

(A) 1
(B) 0
(C) –2
(D) –3
(E) –4

17. If b and d are constants and $x^2 + bx + 6$ is equivalent to $(x + 2)(x + d)$, what is the value of b?

(A) 2
(B) 3
(C) 5
(D) 6
(E) It cannot be determined from the information given.

GO ON TO THE NEXT PAGE

SECTION 3

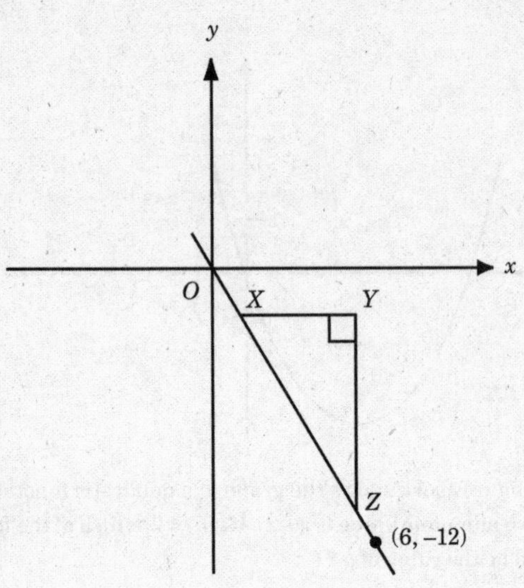

Note: Figure not drawn to scale.

18. In the figure above, if the legs of triangle *XYZ* are parallel to the *xy*-plane's axes, which of the following could be the lengths of the sides of triangle *XYZ* ?

(A) 2, 4, and $\sqrt{20}$
(B) 2, 4, and 10
(C) 3, $3\sqrt{3}$, and 6
(D) 5, 12, and 13
(E) 5, 10, and $6\sqrt{5}$

19. Let the function *j* be defined by $j(x) = 4x + 3$. If $\frac{1}{3}j(\sqrt{r}) = 3$ what is the value of *r* ?

(A) $\frac{4}{\sqrt{3}}$

(B) $\frac{3}{4}\sqrt{3}$

(C) $\frac{6}{4}$

(D) $\frac{9}{4}$

(E) 3

20. If *x* is a negative fraction with a numerator of 1, which of the following must represent a positive whole number?

(A) $3x$

(B) x^2

(C) $\frac{1}{2}(-x^2)$

(D) $4x^3$

(E) x^{-2}

S T O P

IF YOU FINISH BEFORE TIME IS CALLED, YOU MAY CHECK YOUR WORK ON THIS TEST ONLY. DO NOT TURN TO ANY OTHER SECTION IN THIS TEST.

SECTION 4

Turn to Section 4 of your answer sheet to answer the questions in this section.

Time—25 Minutes
24 Questions

Directions: For each question in this section, select the best answer from among the choices given and fill in the corresponding oval on the answer sheet.

Each sentence below has one or two blanks, each blank indicating that something has been omitted. Beneath the sentence are five words or sets of words labeled A through E. Choose the word or set of words that, when inserted in the sentence, best fits the meaning of the sentence as a whole.

Example:

Eliza felt ----- when her boss asked her to work seven weekends in a row but ----- when her work earned her a promotion.

(A) enervated . . weakened
(B) depressed . . intellectual
(C) advantageous . . salacious
(D) angry . . shopworn
(E) irate . . elated    

1. Left-brain activity requiring language is -----, or known to the thinking mind.

(A) fascinating
(B) subterranean
(C) conscious
(D) thoughtful
(E) hasty

2. Because of his in-depth background and ----- qualifications, Kevin was ----- by his company to a chief executive position.

(A) inferior . . chosen
(B) serious . . created
(C) extensive . . promoted
(D) impressive . . overlooked
(E) scientific . . interpreted

3. Samantha's artwork met with a uniform reception: laudatory reactions from art fans and ----- from several art journals.

(A) critiques
(B) comments
(C) kudos
(D) rejections
(E) apologies

4. Sloan House fabrics have a characteristic ----- whose texture enables people to ----- the fabrics even in poor lighting.

(A) smoothness . . feel
(B) odor . . smell
(C) pallor . . wash
(D) sheen . . notice
(E) weave . . recognize

5. The confession by Julian that he had embezzled company funds was such a shocking ----- that employees of the company discussed it for weeks.

(A) admission
(B) exhibition
(C) conflagration
(D) turmoil
(E) confrontation

GO ON TO THE NEXT PAGE

SECTION 4

Directions: The passages below are followed by questions based on their content; questions following a pair of related passages may also be based on the relationship between the paired passages. Answer the questions on the basis of what is stated or implied in the passages and in any introductory material that may be provided.

Questions 6–9 are based on the following passages.

Passages 1 and 2 deal with arguments regarding the study of ancient languages.

Passage 1

One is sometimes tempted to think that all learning is as repulsive to youth as the multiplication table is to Marjorie Fleming, though Fleming's frustration may be due in great part to the mechanical methods with which multiplication is taught. "I am now going to tell you," Fleming writes, "the horrible and wretched plague that my multiplication table gives me; you can't conceive it. The most maddening thing is 8 times 8 and 7 times 7; it is what nature itself can't endure." Is not Greek, or even Latin, yet more unendurable than poor Marjorie's task?

I am familiar with the arguments for making the study of Greek especially a matter of choice or chance. I admit their plausibility and the honesty of those who urge them. I should be willing also to admit that the study of the ancient languages without the hope or the prospect of going on to apply them in some way would be useful only as a form of intellectual gymnastics. Even so, the ancient languages would be as serviceable as higher mathematics are to most of us. But I think that a wise teacher should adapt his or her tasks to the highest, and not the lowest, capacities of the taught. For those of lower capacities also, the teachings would not be wholly without benefit.

One of the arguments against the compulsory study of Greek is that it is wiser to give our time to modern languages and modern history than to dead languages and ancient history. This argument, I think, involves a verbal fallacy. Only those languages can properly be called "dead" in which nothing living has been written. If the classic languages are dead, they yet speak to us, and with a clearer voice than that of any living tongue.

Passage 2

Most of us function in society perfectly well without any knowledge of ancient languages whatsoever. What percentage of our population, after all, has any skills in Greek or Latin? Yet, our technological development continues to forge ahead even despite our inability to read ancient texts in their original tongues. The Greek- or Latin-based terminology that some of us do use is typically learned through rote memorization rather than by acquiring a deeper understanding of the language, and that level of knowledge seems perfectly sufficient for common use. A background in Latin, for instance, might help a medical student to understand the meaning of medical terms with Latin roots, but this level of understanding is not necessary for the student's success in medical school or even within the medical profession. All that is required is simple memorization of the terms.

Furthermore, it is difficult and time-consuming to learn an ancient language in today's society, and this time is spent with little payoff. Students' learning must progress through memorization only; unlike with living languages, there are no communities using the language to help improve a student's levels of understanding and fluency. After putting in considerable work to learn the language, the student must then face the fact that the impact of the learning is minimal, because there are so few practical applications available for those who do know these "dead" languages. Basically, a Greek or Latin scholar has the option of either teaching the language or translating ancient texts, many of which have already been translated and re-translated.

6. Which best expresses the relationship between Passage 2 and Passage 1?

(A) Passage 2 advocates specific policies designed to redress the problems outlined in Passage 1.
(B) Passage 2 presents a case study that tests the theory outlined in Passage 1.
(C) Passage 2 provides a critique of the scholars who reached the conclusions described in Passage 1.
(D) Passage 2 provides an alternative theoretical model to the model presented in Passage 1.
(E) Passage 2 provides counterarguments to the argument made in Passage 1.

7. Both authors would most likely agree with which of the following statements?

(A) Multiplication tends to be easier to learn than ancient languages, such as Greek or Latin.
(B) The study of ancient languages is valuable, even if these languages have no practical application.
(C) Very few members of the general public have any knowledge of ancient languages.
(D) Learning an ancient language, such as Latin or Greek, can be difficult for students.
(E) Most youths dislike studying and aren't interested in learning ancient languages.

GO ON TO THE NEXT PAGE

SECTION 4

8. The author of Passage 1 would most likely react to the description in Passage 2 of ancient languages as "dead" (line 51) by

(A) considering the description and exploring our understanding of how "dead" languages can best be preserved
(B) disagreeing with the description and explaining why these languages can still be considered "living"
(C) ridiculing the description on the grounds that the author who created it has no qualifications for assessing languages
(D) agreeing with the description and going on to argue that "dead" languages should not be studied
(E) criticizing this description because it neglects to identify the "dead" languages by name

9. Lines 44–47 ("Students' learning . . . fluency") highlight a contrast between

(A) arguments for learning versus not learning ancient languages
(B) processes for improving a student's fluency level in ancient versus living languages
(C) methods available for learning ancient versus living languages
(D) techniques for memorizing the vocabulary of ancient versus living languages
(E) qualities of students who tend to study by speaking versus memorizing languages

GO ON TO THE NEXT PAGE

SECTION 4

Directions: Each passage below is followed by questions based on its content. Answer the questions on the basis of what is stated or implied in each passage and in any introductory material that may be provided.

Questions 10–15 are based on the following passage.

This passage is adapted from a futuristic novel regarding a trip to the center of the Earth.

In the first place, please bear in mind that I do not expect you to believe this story. Nor could you wonder had you witnessed a recent experience of mine when, in the armor of blissful and stupendous ignorance, I gaily narrated the gist of it to a Fellow of the Royal Geological Society on the occasion of my last trip to London.

You would surely have thought that I had been detected in no less a heinous crime than the purloining of the Crown Jewels from the Tower, or putting poison in the coffee of His Majesty the King.

The erudite gentleman in whom I confided congealed before I was half through—it is all that saved him from exploding—and my dreams of an Honorary Fellowship, gold medals, and a niche in the Hall of Fame faded into the thin, cold air of his arctic atmosphere.

But I believe the story, and so would you, and so would the learned Fellow of the Royal Geological Society, had you and he heard it from the lips of the man who told it to me. Had you seen, as I did, the fire of truth in those gray eyes; had you felt the ring of sincerity in that quiet voice; had you realized the pathos of it all—you, too, would believe. You would not have needed the final ocular proof that I had—the weird rhamphorhynchus-like creature which he had brought back with him from the inner world.

I came upon him quite suddenly, and no less unexpectedly, upon the rim of the great Sahara Desert. He was standing before a goat-skin tent amidst a clump of date palms within a tiny oasis. Close by was an Arab party of some eight or ten tents.

I had come down from the North to hunt lion. My party consisted of a dozen children of the desert—I was the only European. As we approached the little clump of vegetation, I saw the man come from his tent and with hand-shaded eyes peer intently at us. At the sight of me he advanced rapidly to meet us.

"A European!" he cried. "May the good Lord be praised! I have been watching you for hours, hoping against hope that THIS time there would be a European. Tell me the date. What year is it?"

And when I had told him, he staggered as though he had been struck full in the face, so that he was compelled to grasp my stirrup leather for support.

"It cannot be!" he cried after a moment. "It cannot be! Tell me that you are mistaken, or that you are but joking."

"I am telling you the truth, my friend," I replied. "Why should I deceive a stranger, or attempt to, in so simple a matter as the date?"

For some time he stood in silence, with a bowed head.

"Ten years!" he murmured, at last. "Ten years, and I thought that at the most it could be scarce more than one!" That night he told me his story—the story that I give you here as nearly in his own words as I can recall them:

"I was born in Connecticut about thirty years ago. My name is David Innes. My father was a wealthy mine owner. When I was nineteen, he died. All his property was to be mine when I had attained adulthood—provided that I had devoted the two years intervening in close application to the great business I was to inherit."

"I did my best to fulfill the last wishes of my parent—not because of the inheritance, but because I loved and honored my father. For six months I toiled in the mines and in the counting-rooms, for I wished to know every minute detail of the business."

"Then Perry interested me in his invention. He was an old fellow who had devoted the better part of a long life to the perfection of a mechanical subterranean prospector. As relaxation he studied paleontology. I looked over his plans, listened to his arguments, inspected his working model—and then, convinced, I advanced the funds necessary to construct a full-sized, practical prospector."

"I shall not go into the details of its construction—it lies out there in the desert now—about two miles from here. Tomorrow you may care to ride out and see it. Roughly, it is a steel cylinder a hundred feet long, and jointed so that it may turn and twist through solid rock if need be. At one end is a mighty revolving drill operated by an engine which Perry said generated more power to the cubic inch than any other engine did to the cubic foot. I remember that he used to claim that that invention alone would make us fabulously wealthy—we were going to make the whole thing public after the successful issue of our first secret trial—but Perry never returned from that trial trip, and I only after ten years."

"I recall as it were but yesterday the night of that momentous occasion upon which we were to test the practicality of that wondrous invention. It was near midnight when we repaired to the lofty tower in which Perry had constructed his 'iron mole,' as he was wont to call the thing. The great nose rested upon the bare earth of the floor. We passed through the doors into the outer jacket, secured them, and then passing on into the cabin, which contained the controlling mechanism within the inner tube, switched on the electric lights."

GO ON TO THE NEXT PAGE

10. The primary purpose of the passage is to

(A) describe a desert scene in detail
(B) explain a trip the narrator took to London
(C) defend an argument by another author
(D) introduce a story heard by the narrator
(E) analyze an interpretation of a fictional tale

11. The method of organization used by the author in the passage can best be summarized as

(A) first-person narrative regarding an historical event followed by third-person discussion of the event
(B) third-person account of a fictional story followed by third-person analysis of the story's themes
(C) third-person portrayal of one character's background followed by third-person portrayal of another character's experience
(D) first-person narrative from one time period followed by first-person narrative from an earlier time period
(E) first-person discussion of one family history followed by third-person discussion of the same family history

12. In line 8, "heinous" most nearly means

(A) sacred
(B) enlightening
(C) mediocre
(D) terrible
(E) unnoticeable

13. In the context of lines 17–20 ("Had you . . . would believe"), which of the following might the narrator use to further explain how he knew that the story he heard was true?

(A) The storyteller produced documents verifying his experience, so the truth of his narrative was confirmed.
(B) The storyteller spoke earnestly and without hesitation, so it was difficult to think he was sharing anything but the truth.
(C) The storyteller himself stated that he doubted the accuracy of his own recollection of the experience.
(D) Although the storyteller lost track of time, it was clear that his experience had lasted for many years.
(E) Although the storyteller spoke with shifty eyes, his voice conveyed a clear certainty.

14. The passage suggests that David Innes's willingness to work in the mines for two years arose primarily out of

(A) his desire to show his respect for his father by carrying out his wishes
(B) his need to prove to his family that he was capable of carrying on his father's legacy
(C) his commitment to following in the footsteps of his father and grandfather
(D) his intent to sell the mines for a large profit after learning about the business
(E) his desire to fulfill the requirements of receiving his inheritance

15. The tone of the passage can be described as both

(A) light and frivolous
(B) mysterious and adventuresome
(C) sarcastic and cutting
(D) serious and restrained
(E) humorous and relaxed

GO ON TO THE NEXT PAGE

SECTION 4

Questions 16–24 are based on the following passage.

This passage is adapted from a text concerning the interpretation of dreams, written by psychoanalyst Sigmund Freud. It addresses why dreams are forgotten after waking.

That a dream fades away in the morning is proverbial. It is, indeed, possible to recall it. For we know the dream, of course, only by recalling it after waking; but we very often believe that we remember it incompletely, that during the night there was more of it than we remember. We may observe how the memory of a dream which in the morning was still vivid fades in the course of the day, leaving only a few trifling remnants. We are often aware that we have been dreaming, but we do not know of what we have dreamed; and we are so well used to this fact—that the dream is liable to be forgotten—that we do not reject as absurd the possibility that we may have been dreaming even when, in the morning, we know nothing either of the content of the dream or of the fact that we have dreamed.

On the other hand, it often happens that dreams manifest an extraordinary power of maintaining themselves in the memory. I have had occasion to analyze, with my patients, dreams which occurred to them twenty-five years or more previously, and I can remember a dream of my own which is divided from the present day by at least thirty-seven years, and yet has lost nothing of its freshness in my memory. All this is very remarkable, and for the present incomprehensible.

The forgetting of dreams is treated in the most detailed manner by Strumpell. This forgetting is evidently a complex phenomenon, for Strumpell attributes it not to a single cause, but to quite a number of causes.

In the first place, all those factors which induce forgetfulness in the waking state determine also the forgetting of dreams. In the waking state, we commonly very soon forget a great many sensations and perceptions because they are too slight to remember, and because they are charged with only a slight amount of emotional feeling. This is true also of many dream-images; they are forgotten because they are too weak, while the stronger images in their neighborhood are remembered.

However, the factor of intensity is in itself not the only determinant of the preservation of dream-images; Strumpell, along with other authors (Calkins), admits that dream-images are often rapidly forgotten although they are known to have been vivid, whereas, among those that are retained in the memory, there are many that are very shadowy and unmeaning. In the waking state, one is wont to forget rather easily things that have happened only once, and to remember more readily things which occur repeatedly. Most dream-images are unique experiences, and this peculiarity would contribute towards the forgetting of all dreams equally.

Of much greater significance is a third cause of forgetting. In order that feelings, representations, ideas, and the like should attain a certain degree of memorability, it is important that they should not remain isolated, but that they should enter into connections and associations of an appropriate nature. If the words of a verse of poetry are taken and mixed together, it will be very difficult to remember them. "Properly placed, in a significant sequence, one word helps another, and the whole, making sense, remains and is easily and lastingly fixed in the memory. Contradictions, as a rule, are retained with just as much difficulty and just as rarely as things that are confused and disorderly." Now dreams, in most cases, lack sense and order. Dream-compositions, by their very nature, are insusceptible of being remembered, and they are forgotten because as a rule they fall to pieces the very next moment.

According to Strumpell, other factors, deriving from the relation of the dream to the waking state, are even more effective in causing us to forget our dreams. The forgetfulness of dreams manifested by the waking consciousness is evidently merely the counterpart of the fact already mentioned, namely, that the dream hardly ever takes over an orderly series of memories from the waking state, but only certain details of these memories, which it removes from the habitual psychic connections in which they are remembered in the waking state. The dream-composition, therefore, has no place in the community of the psychic series which fill the mind. It lacks all mnemonic aids. "In this manner the dream-structure rises, as it were, from the soil of our psychic life, and floats in psychic space like a cloud in the sky, quickly dispelled by the first breath of reawakening life." This situation is accentuated by the fact that on waking the attention is immediately besieged by the inrushing world of sensation, so that very few dream-images are capable of withstanding its force. They fade away before the impressions of the new day like the stars before the light of the sun.

Finally, we should remember that the fact that most people take but little interest in their dreams is conducive to the forgetting of dreams. Anyone who for some time applies himself to the investigation of dreams, and takes a special interest in them, usually dreams more during that period than at any other; he remembers his dreams more easily and more frequently.

16. Which of the following best describes the general organization of the passage?

(A) A description of several reasons for the occurrence of a phenomenon
(B) A philosophical discussion of motivations for different actions
(C) A moral argument designed to resolve an ethical dilemma
(D) An account of personal history that reveals aspects of social change
(E) An explanation of a theory that is supported with case studies

GO ON TO THE NEXT PAGE

SECTION 4

17. The second paragraph of the passage implies that the author believes that

(A) individuals tend to forget specific dreams but to remember strong feelings that are triggered by those dreams
(B) certain dreams are retained in the long-term memory for reasons that are not yet understood
(C) long dreams are easier to remember than dreams that last only minutes
(D) most dreams are forgotten within minutes of when we awake
(E) dreams are usually remembered only if they are related to a notable actual experience

18. In line 32, the word "weak" implies that the author

(A) once was more skilled at remembering his dreams
(B) sees dreams as reflecting our weak or strong natures
(C) views dreams as manifesting at different intensities
(D) feels self-conscious regarding his own inability to remember dreams
(E) understands dreams as the expression of weak personalities

19. The phrase "is wont to forget" (line 40) refers to the author's belief that

(A) dreamers tend to repress dreams of deprivation
(B) people never forget the details of a dream that is significant to them
(C) individuals forget singular or unique events rather easily
(D) individuals generally prefer not to remember their dreams
(E) individuals always remember significant events, however infrequent

20. In line 43, the word "peculiarity" most nearly means

(A) gift
(B) rugged nature
(C) deformity
(D) bizarre quality
(E) unusual characteristic

21. The author states that feelings and representations, such as those present in dreams "should not remain isolated" (line 48), because

(A) isolated concepts are easy to categorize and can therefore be more easily retained
(B) it is very difficult to remember them without appropriate connections and associations
(C) isolation enables these elements to retain a degree of memorability
(D) most individuals misinterpret the feelings and representations related to their dreams
(E) isolation of such concepts makes them more easily accessible to the short-term memory

22. The primary motivation behind the author's assertion that dreams "lack sense and order" (line 56) is to

(A) uncover a method for removing any measure of sense and order from dreams
(B) provide evidence for the third reason articulated in the passage concerning why dreams are forgotten
(C) prove his main point that dream interpretation is highly arbitrary and based on subjective judgment
(D) develop a dream interpretation approach that is based on feelings rather than logic
(E) help the reader understand why dreams are so difficult to interpret

23. The author's presentation is most like that of a

(A) mediator resolving standoff in a conflict
(B) motivational speaker presenting an inspiring talk
(C) debater refuting an inferior argument
(D) journalist reporting on a political news story
(E) researcher offering a scholarly analysis

24. The most pervasive explanatory strategy of the passage is the

(A) criticism of ideas presented by individuals who disagree with the author's view
(B) use of ideas and quotations from other scholars to support the author's viewpoint
(C) incorporation of personal anecdotes shared by the author's own clients
(D) reliance on fictional narratives to enhance the author's arguments
(E) use of humorous examples to entertain and engage the reader

S T O P

IF YOU FINISH BEFORE TIME IS CALLED, YOU MAY CHECK YOUR WORK ON THIS TEST ONLY.
DO NOT TURN TO ANY OTHER SECTION IN THIS TEST.

SECTION 5

Turn to Section 5 of your answer sheet to answer the questions in this section.

Time—25 Minutes
18 Questions

Directions: For this section, solve each problem and decide which is the best of the choices given. Fill in the corresponding oval on the answer sheet. You may use any available space for scratchwork.

Notes:

1. The use of a calculator is permitted. All numbers used are real numbers.
2. Figures that accompany problems in this test are intended to provide information useful in solving the problems. They are drawn as accurately as possible EXCEPT when it is stated in a specific problem that the figure is not drawn to scale. All figures lie in a plane unless otherwise indicated.
3. Unless otherwise specified, the domain of any function f is assumed to be the set of all real numbers x for which $f(x)$ is a real number.

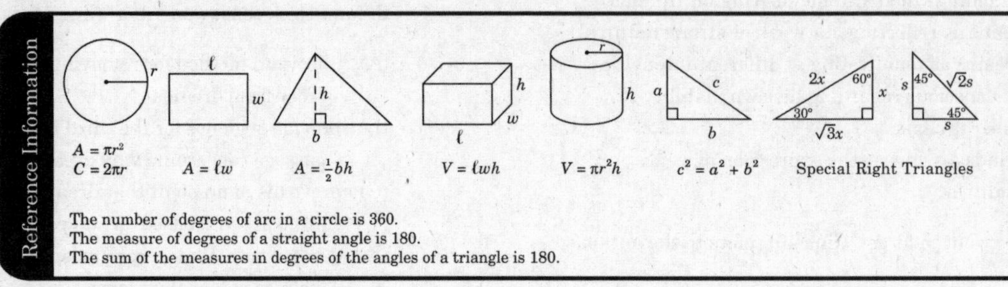
Reference Information
$A = \pi r^2$
$C = 2\pi r$
$A = \ell w$
$A = \frac{1}{2}bh$
$V = \ell wh$
$V = \pi r^2 h$
$c^2 = a^2 + b^2$
Special Right Triangles
The number of degrees of arc in a circle is 360.
The measure of degrees of a straight angle is 180.
The sum of the measures in degrees of the angles of a triangle is 180.

1. Harmon drives 120 miles in 2 hours. If his rate of speed is increased by 5 miles per hour, how many miles will Harmon drive in 3 hours at the new rate?

(A) 165
(B) 170
(C) 180
(D) 175
(E) 195

x	2	4	6	8
y	5	9	13	17

2. The table above represents a relationship between x and y. Which of the following linear equations describes the relationship?

(A) $y = x + 3$
(B) $y = x + 5$
(C) $y = 2.5x$
(D) $y = 7x$
(E) $y = 2x + 1$

GO ON TO THE NEXT PAGE

SECTION 5

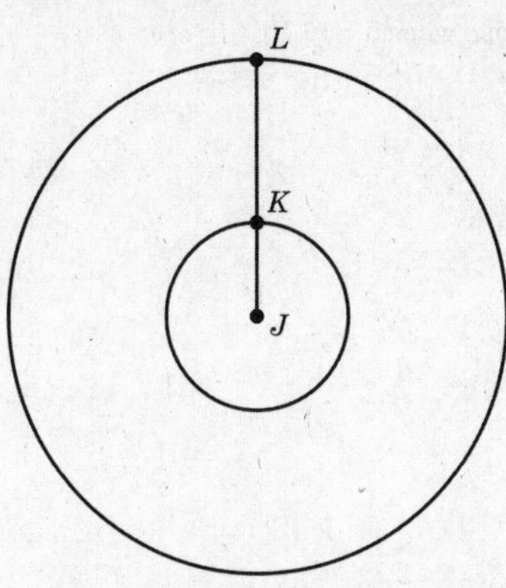

<u>Note:</u> Figure not drawn to scale.

3. In the figure above, the two circles share the same center, J, and the length of JL is 9. If the circumference of the outer circle is three times the circumference of the inner circle, what is the length of JK?

(A) $\frac{1}{3}$

(B) 1

(C) 3

(D) 4.5

(E) 6

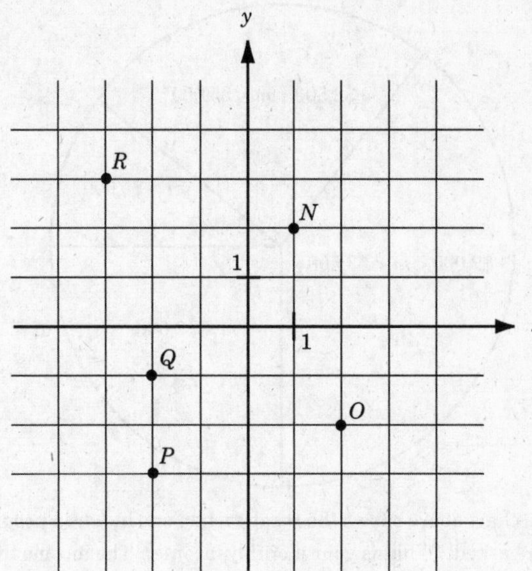

4. Which of the lettered points in the figure above has coordinates (x, y) such that $|x| + |y| = 4$?

(A) N

(B) O

(C) P

(D) Q

(E) R

GO ON TO THE NEXT PAGE

SECTION 5

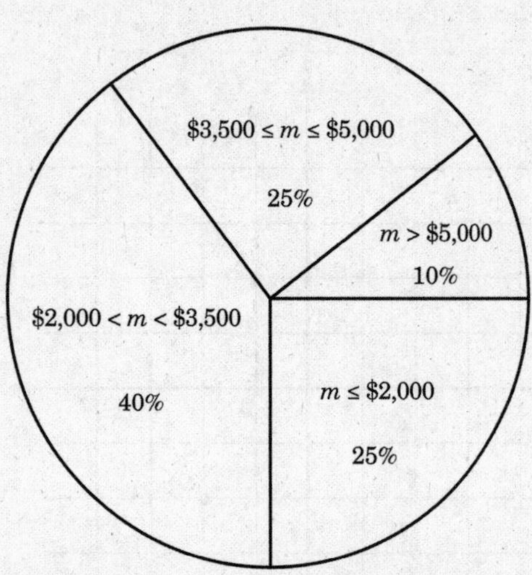

5. The chart above shows the results when one hundred people were asked, "What is your monthly income?" The income that they gave is represented by m. How many people said that their income was greater than $5,000 ?

(A) 5
(B) 10
(C) 25
(D) 40
(E) 90

6. Which of the following could be the remainders when five consecutive positive even integers are divided by 5 ?

(A) 1, 3, 4, 2, 4
(B) 1, 3, 2, 2, 4
(C) 0, 1, 2, 3, 1
(D) 0, 2, 4, 1, 3
(E) 0, 2, 4, 0, 1

7. If a is inversely proportional to b, and $a = 10$ when $b = 2$, what is the value of a when $b = 10$?

(A) $\frac{1}{10}$
(B) $\frac{1}{2}$
(C) 2
(D) 20
(E) 50

8. If $4m - n = 3p$ and $4m + 3p - n = 24$, what is the value of p ?

(A) 4
(B) 8
(C) 12
(D) 16
(E) It cannot be determined from the information given.

GO ON TO THE NEXT PAGE

SECTION 5

Directions: For Student-Produced Response questions 9–18, use the grids on the answer sheet.

Each of these questions requires you to solve the problem and enter your answer by marking the ovals in the special grid, as shown in the examples below. You may use any available space for scratchwork.

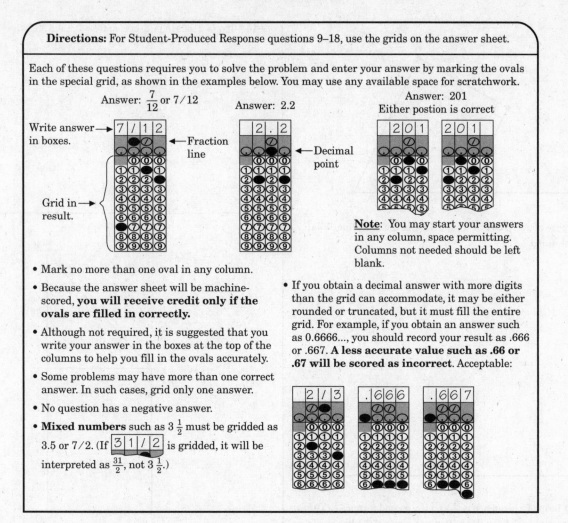

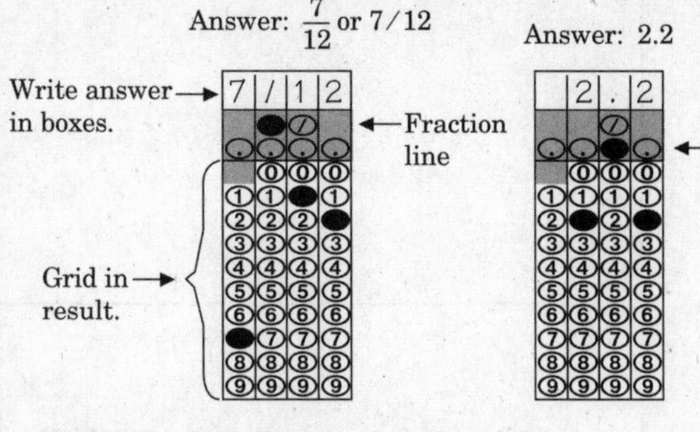

Note: You may start your answers in any column, space permitting. Columns not needed should be left blank.

- Mark no more than one oval in any column.
- Because the answer sheet will be machine-scored, **you will receive credit only if the ovals are filled in correctly.**
- Although not required, it is suggested that you write your answer in the boxes at the top of the columns to help you fill in the ovals accurately.
- Some problems may have more than one correct answer. In such cases, grid only one answer.
- No question has a negative answer.
- **Mixed numbers** such as $3\frac{1}{2}$ must be gridded as 3.5 or 7/2. (If 3 1 / 2 is gridded, it will be interpreted as $\frac{31}{2}$, not $3\frac{1}{2}$.)

- If you obtain a decimal answer with more digits than the grid can accommodate, it may be either rounded or truncated, but it must fill the entire grid. For example, if you obtain an answer such as 0.6666..., you should record your result as .666 or .667. **A less accurate value such as .66 or .67 will be scored as incorrect**. Acceptable:

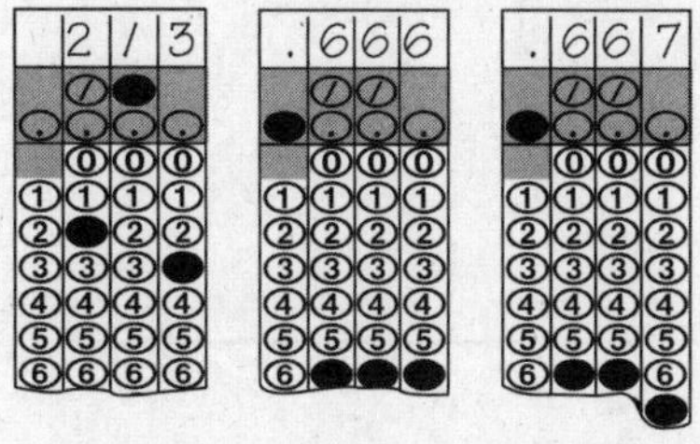

9. If $4(a + 2) = 41$, what is the value of a ?

10. Point H lies on the line defined by the equation $y + 2 = 7(x - 3)$. If the x-coordinate of H is 5, what is the y-coordinate of H ?

11. Stephanie stuffed 40 envelopes and averaged 10 envelopes per hour. If Alan stuffed envelopes at a rate of 8 per hour, how many envelopes had Alan stuffed when he had been working for the same amount of time that it took Stephanie to stuff 40 envelopes?

GO ON TO THE NEXT PAGE

SECTION 5

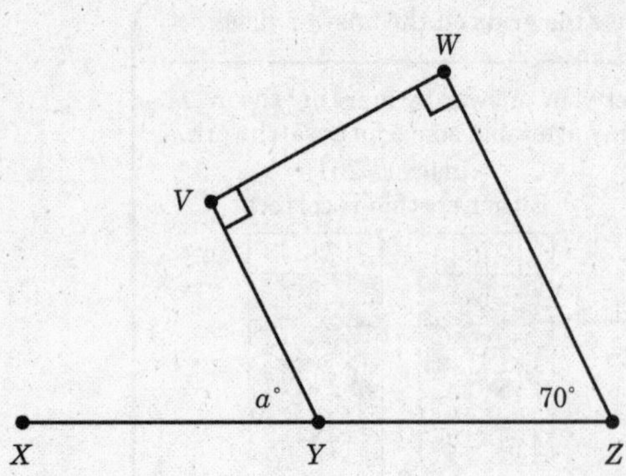

12. In the figure above, points X, Y, and Z lie on the same line. What is the value of a ?

13. The first term of a sequence is $\frac{3}{2}$ and the second term is $\frac{4}{3}$. The third term and each term thereafter is the sum of the two terms immediately preceding it. What is the value of the first term in the sequence that can be reduced to a whole number?

14. If a is $\frac{2}{3}$ of b, b is $\frac{5}{6}$ of c, and $c > 0$, then a is what fraction of c ?

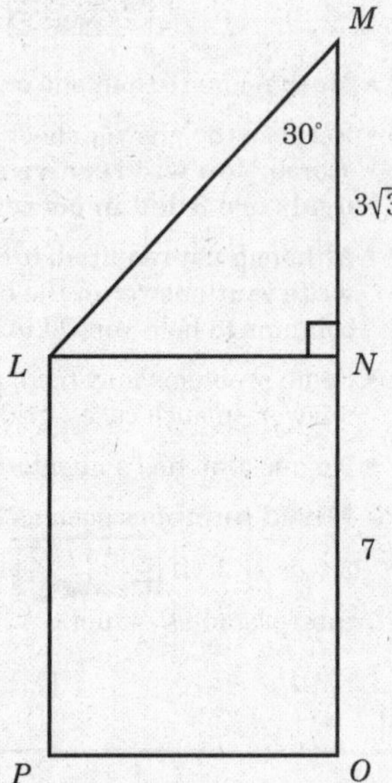

Note: Figure not drawn to scale.

15. In the figure above, $LNOP$ is a rectangle and $NO = 7$. What is the perimeter of $LNOP$?

GO ON TO THE NEXT PAGE

SECTION 5

16. In a fruit punch, the ratio by volume of fruit juice to seltzer is 4 to 5. How many gallons of fruit juice will there be in 6 gallons of this punch?

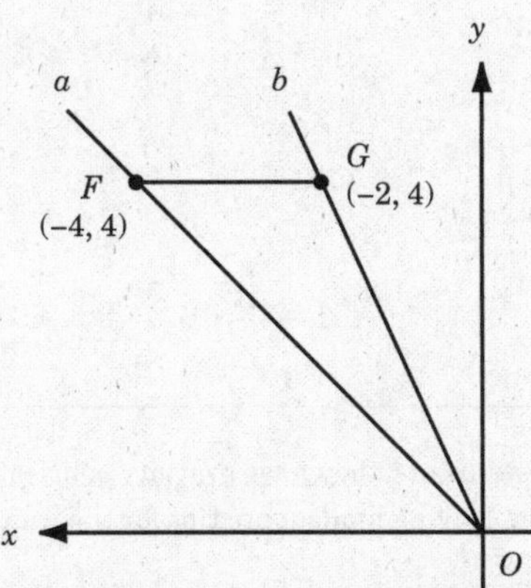

17. In the xy-plane shown above, line c (not shown) passes through O and intersects FG midway between F and G. What is the slope of line d (not shown), which is perpendicular to line c ?

CLUB DATABASE NAME SEARCH RESULTS

Letter	Number of Names Beginning with Letter
A	2,563
B	2,784
C	3,654
D	2,174
E	n

18. Marissa searched the national band club database to determine the number of student last names that began with each letter of the alphabet. The table above shows the number of student names in the database beginning with the letters A through E. If the median number of names beginning with these five letters was 2,784, and no two letters had the same number of names, what is the smallest possible value for n ?

S T O P

IF YOU FINISH BEFORE TIME IS CALLED, YOU MAY CHECK YOUR WORK ON THIS TEST ONLY. DO NOT TURN TO ANY OTHER SECTION IN THIS TEST.

SECTION 6

Turn to Section 6 of your answer sheet to answer the questions in this section.

Time—25 Minutes
35 Questions

Directions: For each question in this section, select the best answer from among the choices given.

The following sentences test correctness and effectiveness of expression. Part of each sentence or the entire sentence is underlined; beneath each sentence are five ways of phrasing the underlined material. Choice A repeats the original phrasing; the other four choices are different. If you think the original phrasing produces a better sentence than any of the alternatives, select choice A; if not, select one of the other choices.

In making your selection, follow the requirements of standard written English; that is, pay attention to grammar, choice of words, sentence construction, and punctuation. Your selection should result in the most effective sentence—clear and precise, without awkwardness or ambiguity.

Example:

In the poem "Ulysses" by Alfred, Lord Tennyson, the speaker says, "I cannot rest from travel," instead, he will live life to the fullest.

(A) "I cannot rest from travel," instead,
(B) "I cannot rest from travel"; instead,
(C) "I cannot rest from travel" instead,
(D) "I cannot rest from travel," upon which
(E) "I cannot rest from travel,"

1. Although some students thoroughly enjoyed Professor Gale's teaching style, other students being strong in their criticism of his techniques.

(A) being strong in their criticism of
(B) were strong and critical of
(C) strongly criticized
(D) strongly criticizing
(E) are strongly critical of

2. Andrew's employees, usually happy with his feedback because the comments he provides are constructive and helpful.

(A) employees, usually happy with his feedback because
(B) employees, usually happy with his feedback and
(C) employees, usually happy with his feedback when
(D) employees are usually happy with his feedback, because
(E) employees are usually happy with his feedback, although

3. Having lived in the country all her life, Celine never thought she could survive in the city.

(A) Having lived in the country all her life,
(B) Her living in the country all her life,
(C) Her having lived in the country all her life,
(D) Because living in the country all her life,
(E) Because having lived in the country all her life,

4. In many restaurants, they have gratuity policies to prevent patrons from leaving inadequate tips for the waitstaff.

(A) they have gratuity policies to prevent patrons from leaving
(B) they have gratuity policies preventing patrons from giving
(C) their gratuity policies preventing patrons from leaving
(D) gratuity policies prevent patrons from leaving
(E) gratuity policies prevent patrons from giving

5. While looking over the menu, the salmon dish with lemon butter and capers seemed most appetizing to Lorraine.

(A) the salmon dish with lemon butter and capers seemed most appetizing to Lorraine
(B) the salmon dish with a sauce of lemon butter and capers seemed to Lorraine to be most appetizing
(C) the salmon dish with lemon butter and capers was seemingly most appetizing to Lorraine
(D) Lorraine's appetite was most appealed to by the salmon dish with lemon butter and capers
(E) Lorraine found the salmon dish with lemon butter and capers to be most appetizing

GO ON TO THE NEXT PAGE

SECTION 6

6. Irish Terriers, like many other terrier breeds, are highly predatory dogs, the reason is that they were originally bred to help control pests, such as rats and moles, on large estates.

(A) dogs, the reason is that they were originally bred
(B) dogs, which were originally being bred
(C) dogs, the breeding of which was originally
(D) dogs because they were originally bred
(E) dogs, whose breeding was originally

7. Both Audrey and Allie being respected by their classmates for having provided strong leadership as class officers.

(A) Both Audrey and Allie being respected by their classmates for having provided strong leadership as class officers
(B) Both Audrey and Allie are respected by their classmates for having provided strong leadership as class officers
(C) Respected by their classmates for having provided strong leadership as class officers being both Audrey and Allie
(D) Having provided strong leadership as class officers respected by their classmates are Audrey and Allie
(E) Having provided strong respected leadership as class officers being Audrey and Allie

8. Businesses are cultivating new markets for their products, and they are turning to the internet to help them reach consumers across the globe.

(A) Businesses are cultivating new markets for their products, and they
(B) Businesses that cultivate new markets for their products, they
(C) Businesses are cultivating new markets for their products by
(D) Cultivating new markets for their products, businesses that
(E) Cultivating new markets for their products is why businesses

9. Some lawmakers believe that the penalties imposed for certain crimes should be as strict for older adolescents than they are for adults.

(A) should be as strict for older adolescents than they are for adults
(B) should be as strict for older adolescents than for adults
(C) should be as strict for older adolescents as they are for adults
(D) should be as strict for older adolescents as for those being adults
(E) should be as strict as those for older adolescents than adults

10. The reason for the success of certain entrepreneurs is that they involve careful planning and proven methods for achieving business goals.

(A) that they involve
(B) that their strategies involve
(C) because the strategies involve
(D) because of them involving
(E) they will involve

11. Normally shy and reserved, it was only when Helen started socializing with other students on campus that she realized how much she enjoyed making new friends.

(A) it was only when Helen started socializing with other students on campus that she realized how much she enjoyed making new friends
(B) when Helen started socializing with other students on campus she then realized how much she enjoyed making new friends
(C) socializing with other students on campus made Helen realize how much she enjoyed making new friends
(D) Helen did not realize how much she enjoyed making new friends until she started socializing with other students on campus
(E) the enjoyment of making new friends was unrealized by Helen until she started socializing with other students on campus

GO ON TO THE NEXT PAGE

SECTION 6

Directions: For each question in this section, select the best answer from among the choices given.

The following sentences test your ability to recognize grammar and usage errors. Each sentence contains either a single error or no error at all. No sentence contains more than one error. The error, if there is one, is underlined and lettered. If the sentence contains an error, select the one underlined part that must be changed to make the sentence correct. If the sentence is correct, select choice E. In choosing answers, follow the requirements of standard written English.

Example:

The other (A) delegates and him (B) immediately (C) accepted the resolution drafted by (D) the neutral states. No error (E)

Ⓐ ● Ⓒ Ⓓ Ⓔ

12. In the middle of the street, obvious from (A) fifty yards in either direction, is (B) rows of trees with beautiful lights and decorations provided by (C) nearly every resident of (D) the neighborhood. No error (E)

13. The films by J. Wrightman have (A) helped increasing (B) awareness about important conservation efforts that may prevent (C) the extinction of (D) endangered species. No error (E)

14. Planning (A) a surprise party and keeping it secret is (B) always a difficult endeavor, particularly if (C) the guest of honor is already suspicious and continually asks (D) questions about the event. No error (E)

15. It was expected (A) that the doctor would be able (B) to determine (C) a treatment for the patient quick (D) and with precision. No error (E)

16. Although the presenters for the conference has (A) not been finalized, it is likely that (B) the conference organizers invited several prominent (C) scholars to speak about (D) their current research. No error (E)

17. While those (A) who choreographed the piece felt frustrated (B) with the performance, the dancers themselves (C) feel (D) most satisfied with their routine. No error (E)

18. Though (A) the options presented to her (B) were (C) neither appealing or (D) encouraging, Caryn was able to make her final decision. No error (E)

19. Robert Charleson was one (A) of a small group of investigators who staked (B) their reputation (C) on finding (D) missing persons in the town of Jonesville. No error (E)

20. Before she moved away from the ocean, Denise enjoys (A) many (B) lazy days lounging on (C) the beach, watching (D) the waves, and soaking up the sun. No error (E)

21. At a college that (A) academic excellence is prized greatly, (B) scholastic prowess is (C) the surest route (D) to success. No error (E)

22. Shelby asked Tom and I (A) whether (B) we would be willing (C) to serve (D) as chaperones for the party. No error (E)

23. Something of (A) an enigma to (B) researchers, psychic experiences still confound (C) scientists and laypersons alike (D). No error (E)

GO ON TO THE NEXT PAGE

SECTION 6

24. Over the years, the residents in the village had been dedicated (A) to maintaining *bowlaka*, a system of governance in which (B) respected elders, rather than (C) the city council, run (D) local government. No error (E)

25. Listening at (A) Sharon's questions, Professor Sims had the distinct impression that (B) Sharon had studied the subject matter prior to (C) enrolling (D) in his course. No error (E)

26. The shopkeeper and his assistant, Timothy, agreed (A) completely on how to run the shop until (B) he (C) attended a management seminar and learned (D) new methods for increasing efficiency. No error (E)

27. Receiving (A) honors in each of (B) her classes, Gina is perhaps (C) the most bright (D) student in her neighborhood. No error (E)

28. Whether or not they were accomplished as singers (A), performers Randolph and Adelman have demonstrated (B) that determination was (C) a key ingredient for artistic success (D). No error (E)

29. The often illogical (A) arguments of Mayor Baldwin's critics make it impossible (B) to determine which of the critics' positions is (C) more likely (D) to influence voters in the next election. No error (E)

GO ON TO THE NEXT PAGE

SECTION 6

Directions: The following passage is an early draft of an essay. Some parts of the passage need to be rewritten.

Read the passage and select the best answers for the questions that follow. Some questions are about particular sentences or parts of sentences and ask you to improve sentence structure or word choice. Other questions ask you to consider organization and development. In choosing answers, follow the requirements of standard written English.

Questions 30–35 are based on the following passage.

(1) *Italian theorist Antonio Gramsci is probably most well known for his contributions to political philosophy.* **(2)** *His* Prison Notebooks, *written during his incarceration in Italian prisons in the 1930s, has particularly influenced modern academia's understanding of socialism, among other concepts.* **(3)** *Another important area explored by Gramsci concerns our understanding of causality, or how factors interact to create social realities.*

(4) *It can be contrasted to the traditional model of causality adopted within the natural sciences.* **(5)** *In this model, an effect is produced in a linear manner as the result of the action of some causal factor.* **(6)** *This traditional model of causality is unilateral.* **(7)** *Depicting causal relationships as operating in only one direction.* **(8)** *A factor the "independent" variable is hypothesized to produce a result the "dependent" variable.*

(9) *He accepted that one causal factor might initially produce a particular result, as the traditional model theorizes.* **(10)** *However, once this result is produced, Gramsci theorized, it develops a "life of its own" through which it then in turn impacts the independent variable.* **(11)** *In Gramsci's view, the* interaction *of these variables is significant, it is ultimately responsible for producing the reality that we perceive.* **(12)** *Gramsci was originally sentenced to 20 years in prison but died before serving his entire term.*

30. In the context of the passage, which of the following is the best way to deal with sentence 4 (reproduced below)?

It can be contrasted to the traditional model of causality adopted within the natural sciences.

(A) Delete it.
(B) Switch it with sentence 5.
(C) Change "It" to "Gramsci's work".
(D) Change "adopted" to "adapted".
(E) Insert "evidently" after "sciences".

31. What is the best way to revise the underlined portion of sentences 6 and 7 (reproduced below)?

This traditional model of causality is *__unilateral. Depicting causal relationships as operating__* *in only one direction.*

(A) unilateral because causal relationships as operating
(B) unilateral in that depiction causal relationships are operating
(C) unilateral so as to depict causal relationships as operating
(D) unilateral, depicting causal relationships as operating
(E) unilateral, it depicts causal relationships as operating

32. Which of the following is the best version of sentence 8 (reproduced below)?

A factor the "independent" variable is hypothesized to produce a result the "dependent" variable.

(A) (As it is now)
(B) Being a factor, the "independent" variable is hypothesized to produce a result the "dependent" variable.
(C) A factor the "independent" variable is hypothesized to produce as a result the "dependent" variable.
(D) A factor known as the "independent" variable is hypothesized to produce a result, known as the "dependent" variable.
(E) A factor, the "independent" variable, to produce a result, the "dependent" variable.

33. Which of the following is the best sentence to insert before sentence 9, at the beginning of the third paragraph?

(A) The traditional model of causality has been widely accepted among social scientists.
(B) Gramsci's work revises the traditional understanding of causality.
(C) Gramsci's writings were not published until after his death.
(D) The traditional model is not without its flaws, however.
(E) Gramsci's interest in understanding causality stemmed from a variety of influences.

GO ON TO THE NEXT PAGE

SECTION 6

34. Which of the following is the best version of the underlined portion of sentence 11 (reproduced below)?

In Gramsci's view, the interaction of these variables is significant, it is ultimately responsible for producing the reality that we perceive.

(A) (As it is now)
(B) as an interaction, these variables are significant and ultimately producing
(C) the interaction of these variables is significant to responsibly producing the ultimate
(D) the interaction of these variables is the significant and responsible production, ultimately, of
(E) the interaction of these variables is significant; it is ultimately responsible for producing

35. Which sentence should be omitted from the essay because it contains unrelated information?

(A) Sentence 3
(B) Sentence 5
(C) Sentence 9
(D) Sentence 10
(E) Sentence 12

S T O P

IF YOU FINISH BEFORE TIME IS CALLED, YOU MAY CHECK YOUR WORK ON THIS TEST ONLY.
DO NOT TURN TO ANY OTHER SECTION IN THIS TEST.

SECTION 7

Turn to Section 7 of your answer sheet to answer the questions in this section.

Time—20 Minutes **19 Questions**	**Directions:** For each question in this section, select the best answer from among the choices given and fill in the corresponding oval on the answer sheet.

Each sentence below has one or two blanks, each blank indicating that something has been omitted. Beneath the sentence are five words or sets of words labeled A through E. Choose the word or set of words that, when inserted in the sentence, best fits the meaning of the sentence as a whole.

Example:

Eliza felt ----- when her boss asked her to work seven weekends in a row but ----- when her work earned her a promotion.

(A) enervated . . weakened
(B) depressed . . intellectual
(C) advantageous . . salacious
(D) angry . . shopworn
(E) irate . . elated    Ⓓ ●

1. In just two days, Martin researched and reported the story -----, without so much as a suggestion from the other staff members.

(A) competitively
(B) uniquely
(C) single-handedly
(D) predictably
(E) convincingly

2. Author Mark Castillo's readers found the plot of his new book -----, but the droning nature of his writing style seemed ----- to some.

(A) confusing . . enlivening
(B) laborious . . creative
(C) foreshadowing . . unrealistic
(D) appealing . . stylistic
(E) engaging . . monotonous

3. The massage therapy program had a strong ----- component that allowed students to develop their skills through hands-on experience.

(A) verbal
(B) auditory
(C) visual
(D) intellectual
(E) kinesthetic

4. The guitarist's ----- was astonishing; his hand moved along the fretboard with great precision at lightning speed.

(A) contemplation
(B) journey
(C) passion
(D) dexterity
(E) attention

5. The lauded contributions of Sutherland Fields brought him great ----- during the early part of his political career, but, by the end of his last term in office, his widespread ----- turned supporters against him.

(A) popularity . . successes
(B) attention . . reservations
(C) respect . . efforts
(D) acclaim . . corruption
(E) notoriety . . changes

6. The director's speech on the new space program was full of -----; it implied his criticism of the initiative without stating it directly.

(A) vigor
(B) ambiguity
(C) innuendo
(D) candor
(E) fallacy

GO ON TO THE NEXT PAGE

SECTION 7

Directions: The passage below is followed by questions based on its content. Answer the questions on the basis of what is stated or implied in the passage and in any introductory material that may be provided.

Questions 7–19 are based on the following passage.

The following passage is adapted from a biology textbook that discusses the anatomy and physiology of the human eye.

It is easy to take our sense of sight for granted, since so much of our visual perception happens automatically, without our direct awareness. Though we may experience sight as an effortless phenomenon, in fact it comes about only through an intricate process of collaboration between the eye and the brain.

The human eye is structured as a spherical organ that fits in the eye sockets within the head and is attached to the brain through the optic nerve. Impulses of light enter the eye through its front opening, called the *pupil*, and travel through the lens of the eye to its rear wall, the retina. Here, the light impulse is translated into nerve impulses that travel to the brain by way of the optic nerve. The brain makes sense of the visual image for us in the final step of the process known as *sight*.

A key ingredient in the process of seeing is the presence of light, without which no sight could occur. Light itself is made up of submicroscopic particles known as *photons*, which originate in the sun and constantly bombard us. Photons are reflected by different objects in different ways; these differing methods of reflection determine how we perceive the properties of an object, such as color and texture. Photons can be reflected by a shiny surface, for instance, in a way that enables us to see our own image in the surface. When light falls on a matte surface, however, the photons comprising the light are reflected differently by the surface, and the surface appears flat and dull.

In order to process images, the human eye requires a level of light within a certain range. The light level must be high enough for the eye to perceive the object and low enough to keep the visual system from becoming overloaded. An influx of intense light that is too great for the eye to process can interfere with vision and even cause blindness.

Light intensity is particularly important for human perception of color differences. In low light, it is difficult for the eye to perceive colors and differentiate between them. We see colors best in light at medium to high levels of brightness; under these circumstances, the sensors in the retina enable us to identify colors and distinguish even subtle differences between shades.

The amount of light entering the eye is controlled by a part of the eye called the iris. The iris is the colored part of the eye encircling the pupil. It controls the intensity of light passing into the eye by expanding or contracting the diameter of the pupil. When the iris contracts the pupil, decreasing its diameter, less light flows in through the opening of the eye. By contrast, the iris expands the diameter of the pupil as necessary to allow more light in. We can see examples of pupil contraction and expansion simply by moving from a dark room to a bright one. Under low light conditions, the iris expands the diameter of the pupil to allow in enough light for perception to occur. In bright light conditions, the iris contracts the diameter of the pupil to modulate light flow and prevent visual overload.

Once the light flow is regulated by the iris and enters the eye through the pupil, it passes through a focusing device called the *lens*. The lens of the eye serves to focus incoming light on the retina. The retina, found at the back of the eye, is made up of pathways of nerve endings that are extremely light sensitive. These nerve endings take an impression of the light image in much the same way as the film of a camera. This impression is then transmitted through nerve impulses to the optical nerve, which sends the impulses to the brain.

Once visual impulses arrive at the brain, the brain then completes the staggeringly complex task of turning these visual impulses into images that we "see." The brain puts together impulses conveyed through millions of photons and translates them into comprehensible pictures. During this process, the brain must actually "flip" the images so that they appear right-side-up to us. Images are originally received through the eye in an upside-down orientation and must be inverted by the brain as they are processed.

The sense of sight provides human beings with a crucial tool for navigating through the world. Our sight enables us to perceive shapes and colors, to recognize forms and faces, and to orient ourselves spatially as well. Through the mechanism of sight, our eyes join with our brains to provide a bridge between the external world and our internal experience. We are not alone among the species that rely on sight as a survival mechanism: most living beings have some form of eyesight, and even plants have ways of sensing changes between darkness and light.

Although the size of a creature's eye is not proportional to its body size (think of flies with their large eyes, for example), the size of the eye does appear to be proportional to the *quality* of sight experienced by a human or an animal. In addition, the size of the eye also affects the level of complexity at which visual images are processed. The eye functions using only a fraction of an individual's total brain weight, leveraging brain resources to produce stunning results.

GO ON TO THE NEXT PAGE

SECTION 7

7. Two same-sized animals may have eyes of different sizes because

(A) the size of an animal's eyes is not necessarily proportional to its body size
(B) one of the animals may need to see in the dark more often than the other animal
(C) most animals have eyes that are larger than human eyes
(D) animals use their eyes to assist them in performing routine daily tasks
(E) the sense of sight is more important for helping one animal navigate through its environment than the other

8. In lines 55–56 ("These . . . camera"), the author attempts to draw a comparison between

(A) nerve endings and a camera
(B) camera film and the brain
(C) the optic nerve and camera film
(D) a camera and the retina
(E) an eye and a camera

9. The "flies" (line 78) primarily play which of the following roles in the passage?

(A) Identifying a theory
(B) Disproving an argument
(C) Illustrating a contradiction
(D) Exemplifying a point
(E) Describing an exception

10. The purpose of the third paragraph (lines 14–24) is to

(A) describe how nerve impulses travel from the optic nerve to the brain
(B) emphasize the importance of studying brain physiology
(C) explain that light is made up of tiny particles called photons
(D) critique traditional theories of eye development
(E) delineate the major components of the eye and their functions

11. The statement in lines 82–84 ("The eye . . . results") implies that

(A) the eye accomplishes a surprising amount considering that it uses relatively few brain resources
(B) the eye produces visual images that dramatically misrepresent physical reality
(C) human eyes are more impressive in their functioning than the eyes of other species
(D) human eye cells can be destroyed by excessive exposure to UV rays from the sun
(E) the eye operates independently of the brain under most conditions

12. In lines 3–5 ("Though we may . . . the brain"), the author sugests that the phenomenon of sight

(A) involves more nerve impulses for color differentiation than for spatial orientation
(B) requires complex effort on the part of both the eye and the brain
(C) varies tremendously among different species based on the eye's anatomy
(D) is less reliable than people believe it to be, because it is based on invented images
(E) starts with the regulation of light intensity by the iris of the eye

13. Which of the following situations would most likely allow for an accurate perception of color differences?

(A) Examining photographs through an infrared filter
(B) Viewing colored fabrics in a sewing room with the shades drawn
(C) Inspecting a water-color painting through a magnifying glass
(D) Reviewing paint samples near a sunny window
(E) Viewing photograph prints in an art gallery

14. The statement in lines 73–76 ("We are . . . light") implies that

(A) animals without sight are at a disadvantage in the evolutionary chain
(B) humans are unique among mammals for their reliance on sight as a survival mechanism
(C) plants can be considered to have a primitive sight mechanism
(D) humans possess more acute visual perception abilities than animals
(E) humans without sight learn to rely on their other senses more extensively

15. In lines 28–30 ("An influx . . . blindness"), the author suggests that

(A) humans require a particular quality of light in order to see most efficiently
(B) overexposure to light of extremely high intensity can severely damage the eye
(C) under correct lighting conditions, individuals can distinguish letters more easily than numbers
(D) light is comprised of tiny particles known as protons that originate in the sun
(E) the way in which a surface reflects light is determined by the number of protons contained within the light ray

GO ON TO THE NEXT PAGE

SECTION 7

16. In line 48, "modulate" most nearly means

(A) register
(B) disorient
(C) teach
(D) control
(E) separate

17. Lines 14–15 ("A key . . . occur") reveal which of the following about sight?

(A) It requires the passage of light through the retina of the eye.
(B) It occurs only in the presence of light.
(C) It is dependent upon interpretation by the brain as well as perception by the eye.
(D) It involves the processing of images that connote particular meanings.
(E) It requires greater light for color processing than for black-and-white processing.

18. The author uses the expression "staggeringly complex task" (line 60) to

(A) emphasize the brain's impressive ability to convert visual impulses into sight images
(B) highlight the scientific uncertainty regarding exactly how the brain assists in sight
(C) point out the controversy concerning how the brain transmits nerve impulses
(D) support the author's primary argument that the human brain is capable of performing very sophisticated functions
(E) refute the notion presented earlier in the passage that the brain contributes relatively little to the process of image perception

19. In lines 77–80 ("Although the size . . . an animal"), the author suggests that

(A) the size of an animal's eye is unrelated to its quality of vision
(B) animals with larger eyes experience higher quality sight than do animals with smaller eyes
(C) animals with larger bodies have bigger eyes than do animals with smaller bodies
(D) smaller-sized eyes provide animals with better visual perception than do larger-sized eyes
(E) the quality of an animal's vision is directly related to the animal's size

S T O P

IF YOU FINISH BEFORE TIME IS CALLED, YOU MAY CHECK YOUR WORK ON THIS TEST ONLY.
DO NOT TURN TO ANY OTHER SECTION IN THIS TEST.

SECTION 8

Turn to Section 8 of your answer sheet to answer the questions in this section.

Time—20 Minutes
16 Questions

Directions: For this section, solve each problem and decide which is the best of the choices given. Fill in the corresponding oval on the answer sheet. You may use any available space for scratchwork.

Notes:

1. The use of a calculator is permitted. All numbers used are real numbers.

2. Figures that accompany problems in this test are intended to provide information useful in solving the problems. They are drawn as accurately as possible EXCEPT when it is stated in a specific problem that the figure is not drawn to scale. All figures lie in a plane unless otherwise indicated.

3. Unless otherwise specified, the domain of any function f is assumed to be the set of all real numbers x for which $f(x)$ is a real number.

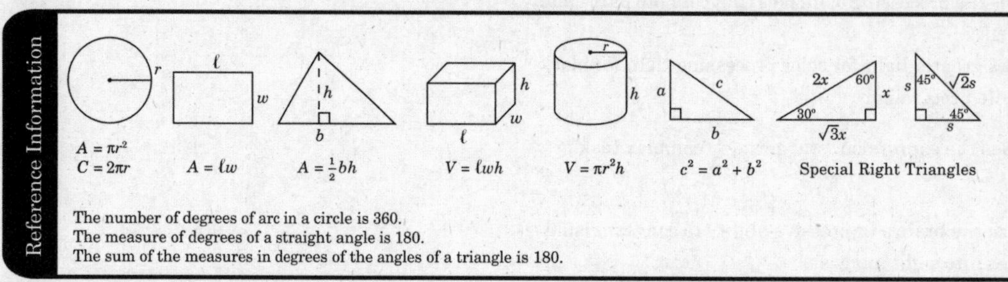
Reference Information
$A = \pi r^2$
$C = 2\pi r$
$A = \ell w$
$A = \frac{1}{2}bh$
$V = \ell wh$
$V = \pi r^2 h$
$c^2 = a^2 + b^2$
Special Right Triangles
The number of degrees of arc in a circle is 360.
The measure of degrees of a straight angle is 180.
The sum of the measures in degrees of the angles of a triangle is 180.

1. A candle manufacturer sells candles in 5 different colors and 4 different heights. How many different color-height combinations does the company sell?

(A) 20
(B) 15
(C) 10
(D) 9
(E) 1

The sum of $7a$ and 12 is equal to the product of a and $\frac{2}{3}$.

2. Which of the following equations expresses the relationship stated above?

(A) $7a = \frac{2}{3}a + 12$
(B) $12(7a) = a + \frac{2}{3}$
(C) $7(a + 12) = \frac{2}{3}a$
(D) $7a + 12 = a + \frac{2}{3}$
(E) $7a + 12 = \frac{2}{3}a$

3. This morning Richard accidentally left his jacket on one of 70 buses. It is equally likely that the jacket is on any of these 70 buses. If exactly 14 of these 70 buses are out of service today, what is the probability that the jacket will be on a bus that is out of service today?

(A) $\frac{1}{2}$
(B) $\frac{1}{3}$
(C) $\frac{1}{5}$
(D) $\frac{1}{14}$
(E) $\frac{1}{70}$

GO ON TO THE NEXT PAGE

SECTION 8

4. How many different (x, y) integer pairs satisfy the equation $\frac{x}{y} = \frac{2}{3}$?

(A) Two
(B) Four
(C) Five
(D) Six
(E) More than six

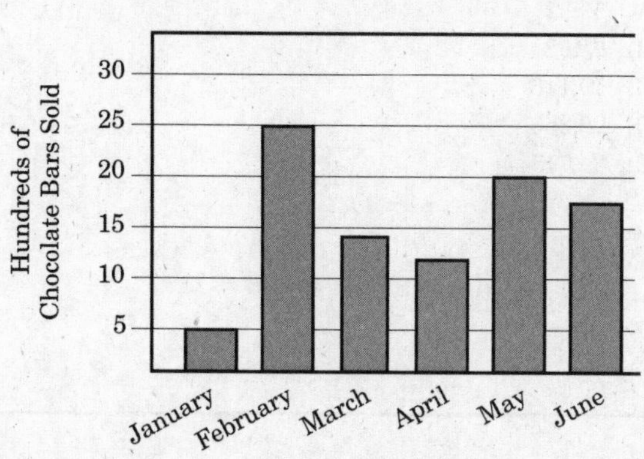

5. According to the graph above, during which of the following two-month periods did Janet's candy store sell the greatest number of chocolate bars?

(A) January and February
(B) February and March
(C) March and April
(D) April and May
(E) May and June

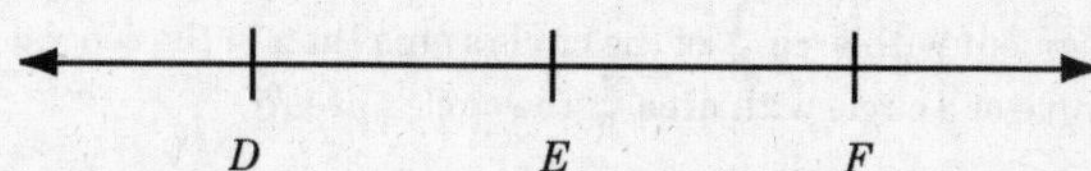

6. In the figure above, DF is 32 units in length and $DE = EF$. Point G (not shown) is on the line between E and F such that $EG = GF$. What is the unit length of DG ?

(A) 8
(B) 12
(C) 16
(D) 24
(E) 30

7. If r is a positive integer, then $(5 \times 4^{-r}) - (2 \times 4^{-r})$ must equal

(A) $\frac{3}{4}$

(B) $\frac{3}{4^r}$

(C) $\frac{3}{4^{2r}}$

(D) $\frac{7}{4^r}$

(E) $\frac{4^r}{7}$

GO ON TO THE NEXT PAGE

SECTION 8

8. How many more degrees are there in the central angle of a circle segment with area $\frac{1}{6}$ of the circle's area than in the central angle of a circle with area $\frac{1}{8}$ the circle's area?

(A) 10
(B) 15
(C) 30
(D) 45
(E) 60

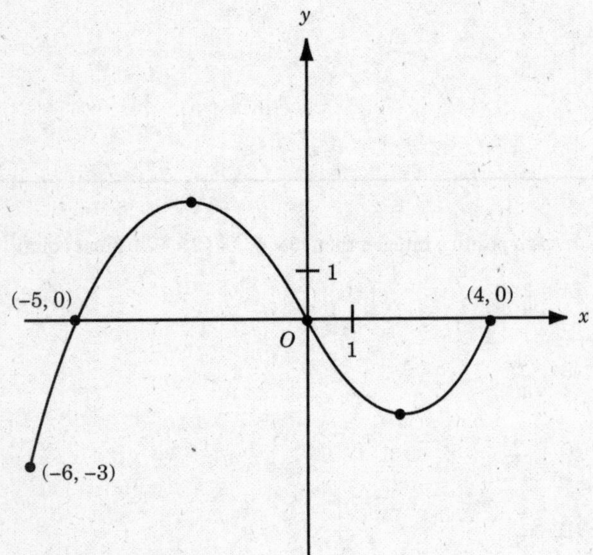

9. Based on the graph of the function f above, what are the values of x for which $f(x)$ is positive?

(A) $0 < x < 4$
(B) $-5 < x < 0$
(C) $-6 < x < -5$
(D) $-5 < x < 4$
(E) $-5 < x < 0$ and $-6 < x < -5$

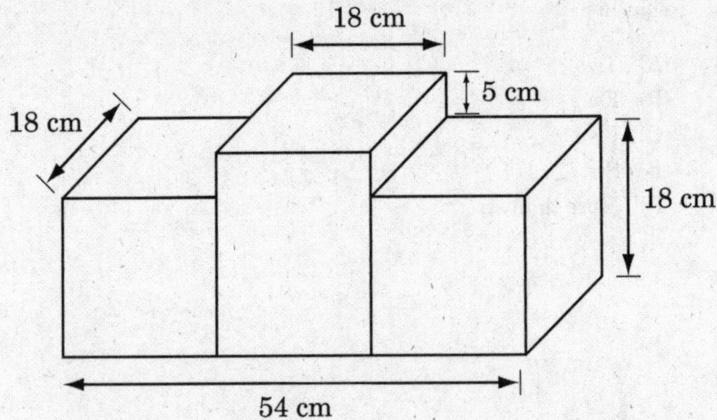

10. The figure above shows certain dimensions of a display unit constructed from three blocks of wood. The middle block is a rectangular solid, and the two outer blocks are both cubes. How many cubic centimeters of wood make up the display unit?

(A) 5,832
(B) 7,452
(C) 19,116
(D) 22,356
(E) 30,718

11. If a and b are positive integers and $27(3^a) = 3^b$, what is the value of a in terms of b?

(A) $b-3$
(B) $b-1$
(C) b
(D) $b+1$
(E) $b+3$

GO ON TO THE NEXT PAGE

SECTION 8

12. If the degree measures of the interior angles of a triangle are in the ratio 3:5:7, the measure of the smallest angle is how many degrees less than the measure of the largest angle?

(A) 12°
(B) 36°
(C) 48°
(D) 72°
(E) 84°

13. The rate for printing color posters at Lance's Copy Store is \$2.75 for the first poster and \$1.50 for each additional poster. Which of the following functions describes the cost, in dollars, to print p posters?

(A) $f(p) = 4.25p$
(B) $f(p) = 2.75 + 1.50p$
(C) $f(p) = 2.75 + 1.50(p + 1)$
(D) $f(p) = 2.75 + 1.50(p - 1)$
(E) $f(p) = 2.75p + 1.50(p - 1)$

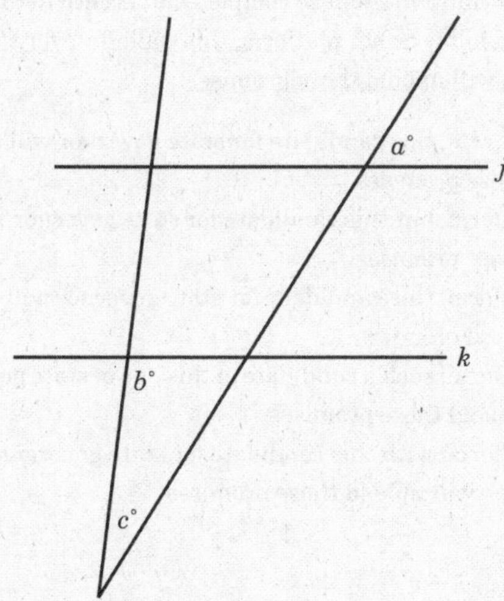

14. In the figure above, if $j \parallel k$, what does b equal in terms of a and c?

(A) $a + c$
(B) $a - c$
(C) $180 - a$
(D) $180 - a + c$
(E) $180 - a - c$

15. If $\frac{2x(x+1)^{-1}}{2x-2} = \frac{6}{j}$, and if $x \neq 1$ and $j \neq 0$, which of the following is a possible value f x?

(A) 1
(B) 2
(C) 6
(D) 12
(E) 35

16. To pay for the rental hall at a family reunion, the f family members hosting the reunion agreed to contribute equally to a rental hall that costs a total of d dollars. If n of the family members fail to contribute, which of the following represents the additional amount, in dollars, that each of the remaining family members must contribute to pay for the rental hall?

(A) $\frac{d}{f}$

(B) $\frac{d}{f-n}$

(C) $\frac{nd}{f-n}$

(D) $\frac{d(f-n)}{f}$

(E) $\frac{nd}{f(f-n)}$

S T O P

IF YOU FINISH BEFORE TIME IS CALLED, YOU MAY CHECK YOUR WORK ON THIS TEST ONLY.
DO NOT TURN TO ANY OTHER SECTION IN THIS TEST.

SECTION 9

Turn to Section 9 of your answer sheet to answer the questions in this section.

Time—10 Minutes
14 Questions

Directions: For each question in this section, select the best answer from among the choices given.

The following sentences test correctness and effectiveness of expression. Part of each sentence or the entire sentence is underlined; beneath each sentence are five ways of phrasing the underlined material. Choice A repeats the original phrasing; the other four choices are different. If you think the original phrasing produces a better sentence than any of the alternatives, select choice A; if not, select one of the other choices.

In making your selection, follow the requirements of standard written English; that is, pay attention to grammar, choice of words, sentence construction, and punctuation. Your selection should result in the most effective sentence—clear and precise, without awkwardness or ambiguity.

Example:

In the poem "Ulysses" by Alfred, Lord Tennyson, the speaker says, "I cannot rest from travel," instead, he will live life to the fullest.

(A) "I cannot rest from travel," instead,
(B) "I cannot rest from travel"; instead,
(C) "I cannot rest from travel" instead,
(D) "I cannot rest from travel," upon which
(E) "I cannot rest from travel,"

1. To emphasize customer service and to think of it that it is a critical business function is to recognize the inherent value of customer relationships and to acknowledge their role in promoting business growth.

    (A) that it is a critical business function
    (B) as a critical business function
    (C) that it must be a critical business function
    (D) as it were a critical business function
    (E) as if it were like a critical business function

2. The publicizing of positive critical reviews is one of the most important factors for the success of a theatrical production.

    (A) The publicizing of positive critical reviews is
    (B) Positive critical reviews that need to be publicized are
    (C) How positive critical reviews get to be publicized is
    (D) Publicizing positive critical reviews are
    (E) For positive critical reviews to be publicized is

3. Any politician can promise complete adherence to the policies promoted in his or her platform, this candidate for state governor will uphold those promises.

    (A) platform, this candidate for state governor will uphold those promises
    (B) platform, but this candidate for state governor will uphold those promises
    (C) platform; this candidacy for state governor will uphold those promises
    (D) platform; such a candidate of this one of state governor will uphold those promises
    (E) platform, with this candidate for state governor being one who will uphold those promises

GO ON TO THE NEXT PAGE

SECTION 9

4. Unlike Lawrence Bookman, Stanley Carp started his company with the intention of creating a business empire.

(A) Unlike Lawrence Bookman, Stanley Carp started his company with the intention of creating a business empire.
(B) Unlike Lawrence Bookman, Stanley Carp was different in that he started his company with the intention of creating a business empire.
(C) Unlike Lawrence Bookman, Stanley Carp started his company with the intention of creating a business empire and Bookman did not.
(D) Lawrence Bookman did not, but Stanley Carp's aim was to create a business empire.
(E) Different from Lawrence Bookman, for creating a business empire was the aim of Stanley Carp.

5. Ironically, one way that many teachers develop their knowledge of certain subjects is because of having taught those subjects to others.

(A) because of having taught those subjects
(B) when they taught those subjects
(C) through their teaching of those subjects
(D) by their teaching of those subjects
(E) by teaching those subjects

6. Frustrated because she had added too much oil to the batter while reviewing the recipe, the focus for Leslie now was salvaging whatever she could use of the batter.

(A) the focus for Leslie now was
(B) Leslie's focus now was
(C) Leslie now focusing on
(D) Leslie nonetheless now emphasized a focus on
(E) Leslie now focused on

7. For days, one of the festival's exhibitors were selling so many paintings that the other artists clamored to learn her sales secrets.

(A) were selling so many paintings that the other artists clamored to learn
(B) was selling so many paintings; the other artists clamored to be learning
(C) were selling so many paintings because the other artists clamored to learn
(D) was selling so many paintings that the other artists clamored to learn
(E) was selling so many paintings; so the other artists clamoring to learn

8. When Portia Richards had an internship with master Chef Juan Fernandez designed individually for her, she was mesmerized by his finesse in the kitchen, which became her greatest inspiration.

(A) which became
(B) so it was to become
(C) with the result of it becoming
(D) therefore to become
(E) as a result of it becoming

9. Even though the changes made by the editors were irreversible to the original documents, they were careful to preserve the basic arguments of the texts.

(A) Even though the changes made by the editors were irreversible to the original documents, they
(B) Even though irreversible changes to the original document were made by the editors, they
(C) Even though the editors made irreversible changes to the original documents, they
(D) Despite the fact of irreversible changes to the original documents, the editors
(E) Even considering irreversible changes to the original documents, the editors

10. The line for concert tickets started forming an entire day before the tickets went on sale; fans camped out overnight in front of the ticket office to guarantee themselves seats for the show.

(A) sale; fans camped out overnight
(B) sale, which meant fans camping out overnight
(C) sale; therefore, it meant that fans would camp out overnight
(D) sale and therefore the fans would be camping out overnight
(E) sale; with fans camping out overnight

11. Insofar as the weather was unseasonably warm, the ski slopes closed early.

(A) Insofar as the weather was
(B) With the weather that was
(C) In that there being weather that was
(D) Because there was weather being
(E) Because the weather was

GO ON TO THE NEXT PAGE

SECTION 9

12. The anthropologists found the community members equally as interesting as their laws were complex.

(A) equally as interesting as their laws were
(B) equally interesting and their laws
(C) as interesting and their laws
(D) as interesting as their laws were
(E) as interesting and their laws were

13. Although she served for two years as head of the membership committee, Laura refused to accept recognition for the expansion strategies she implemented nor otherwise taking credit for the growth of the organization.

(A) implemented nor otherwise taking credit
(B) had implemented nor otherwise did she take credit
(C) has implemented nor to have taken credit
(D) implemented or otherwise took credit
(E) had implemented or otherwise to take credit

14. The efficiency and global utilization of modern computer technology explain its indispensability for today's businesses.

(A) explain its indispensability
(B) explain their indispensability
(C) explains its indispensability
(D) is why it is indispensable
(E) are a reason for its indispensability

S T O P

IF YOU FINISH BEFORE TIME IS CALLED, YOU MAY CHECK YOUR WORK ON THIS TEST ONLY.
DO NOT TURN TO ANY OTHER SECTION IN THIS TEST.

PRACTICE TEST 4 EXPLANATIONS

PRACTICE TEST 4 ANSWERS

Question Number	Answer	Right	Wrong
Section 2			
1	A		
2	C		
3	A		
4	D		
5	C		
6	E		
7	A		
8	D		
9	C		
10	E		
11	C		
12	E		
13	A		
14	B		
15	D		
16	C		
17	A		
18	D		
19	C		
20	E		
21	D		
22	E		
23	E		
24	C		
Section 3			
1	B		
2	E		
3	C		
4	D		
5	B		
6	A		
7	C		
8	C		
9	D		
10	E		
11	B		
12	C		
13	B		
14	D		
15	A		
16	A		
17	C		
18	A		
19	D		
20	E		
Section 4			
1	C		
2	C		
3	C		
4	E		
5	A		
6	E		
7	D		
Section 4, continued			
8	B		
9	C		
10	D		
11	D		
12	D		
13	B		
14	A		
15	B		
16	A		
17	B		
18	C		
19	C		
20	E		
21	B		
22	B		
23	E		
24	B		
Section 5			
1	E		
2	E		
3	C		
4	B		
5	B		
6	D		
7	C		
8	A		
9	8.25, 33/4		
10	12		
11	32		
12	70		
13	7, 42/6		
14	5/9		
15	20		
16	24/9, 8/3, 2.67		
17	3/4, .75		
18	2785		
Section 6			
1	C		
2	D		
3	A		
4	D		
5	E		
6	D		
7	B		
8	C		
9	C		
10	B		
11	D		
12	B		
13	B		
14	E		

Question Number	Answer	Right	Wrong
Section 6, continued			
15	D		
16	A		
17	D		
18	D		
19	C		
20	A		
21	A		
22	A		
23	E		
24	E		
25	A		
26	C		
27	D		
28	C		
29	E		
30	C		
31	D		
32	D		
33	B		
34	E		
35	E		
Section 7			
1	C		
2	E		
3	E		
4	D		
5	D		
6	C		
7	A		
8	E		
9	D		
10	C		
11	A		
12	B		
13	D		
14	C		
15	B		

Question Number	Answer	Right	Wrong
Section 7, continued			
16	D		
17	B		
18	A		
19	B		
Section 8			
1	A		
2	E		
3	C		
4	E		
5	B		
6	D		
7	B		
8	B		
9	B		
10	C		
11	A		
12	C		
13	D		
14	E		
15	C		
16	E		
Section 9			
1	B		
2	A		
3	B		
4	A		
5	E		
6	E		
7	D		
8	A		
9	C		
10	A		
11	E		
12	D		
13	E		
14	A		

CALCULATING YOUR SCORE

Writing Section Raw Score

A. Essay Score (from 1–6) ______ A

B. Section 6 Multiple Choice: ______ no. correct – (______ no. incorrect ÷ 4) = ______ B

C. Section 9 Multiple Choice: ______ no. correct – (______ no. incorrect ÷ 4) = ______ C

D. Unrounded Multiple-Choice Score (B + C) ______ D

E. Total Rounded Multiple-Choice Raw Score
(Rounded to the nearest whole number) ______ E

F. Writing Multiple-Choice Subscore
(See the Writing Multiple-Choice conversion table on the following pages) ______ Writing MC Score

G. Total Scaled Score
(See the Writing conversion table on the following pages) ______ SAT Writing Score

Math Section Raw Score

A. Section 3 Raw Score: ______ no. correct – (______ no. incorrect ÷ 4) = ______ Subtotal A

B. Section 5 Raw Score: ______ no. correct ______ Subtotal B

C. Section 8 Raw Score: ______ no. correct – (______ no. incorrect ÷ 4) = ______ Subtotal C

D. Total Unrounded Raw Score
(Total A + B + C) ______ D

E. Total Rounded Raw Score (Rounded to the nearest whole number) ______ E

F. Scaled Score
(See the conversion table on the following pages) ______ SAT Math Score

Critical Reading Section Raw Score

A. Section 2 Raw Score: ______ (no. correct) – (______ (no. incorrect) ÷ 4) = ______ A

B. Section 4 Raw Score: ______ (no. correct) – (______ (no. incorrect) ÷ 4) = ______ B

C. Section 7 Raw Score: ______ (no. correct) – (______ (no. incorrect) ÷ 4) = ______ C

D. Total Unrounded Raw Score
(Total A + B + C)

______ D

E. Total Rounded Raw Score
(Rounded to the nearest whole number)

______ E

F. Scaled Score
(See the conversion table on the next page)

______ SAT Critical Reading Score

CONVERTING YOUR RAW SCORES

Raw Score	Critical Reading Scaled Score	Math Scaled Score
67	800	
66	790	
65	770	
64	760	
63	750	
62	740	
61	720	
60	710	
59	700	
58	690	
57	680	
56	670	
55	670	
54	660	800
53	650	780
52	640	760
51	640	740
50	630	730
49	620	710
48	610	700
47	610	690
46	600	670
45	590	660
44	590	650
43	580	650
42	580	640
41	570	630
40	560	620
39	560	610
38	550	600
37	540	590
36	540	590
35	530	580
34	530	570
33	520	560
32	510	560
31	510	550
30	500	540
29	500	530
28	490	520
27	480	520
26	480	510
25	470	500
24	470	490
23	460	490
22	450	480
21	450	470
20	440	460
19	430	460

Raw Score	Critical Reading Scaled Score	Math Scaled Score
18	430	450
17	420	440
16	410	430
15	410	430
14	400	420
13	390	410
12	380	400
11	380	390
10	370	380
9	360	380
8	350	370
7	340	360
6	330	340
5	320	330
4	310	320
3	300	310
2	280	290
1	270	280
0	250	260
–1	250	250
–2	240	240
–3	230	230
–4	220	220
–5	210	210
–6	200	200

Writing Subscores

- **Essay Subscore:** Subtotal A from Writing Score (page 346)
- **Multiple-Choice Subscore:** Calculate by plugging in Subtotal E from your writing score (page 346) into the score conversion table below

Raw Score	Multiple-Choice Subscore
49	80
48	79
47	77
46	76
45	75
44	74
43	72
42	71
41	70
40	69
39	68
38	67
37	66
36	65
35	64
34	63
33	62
32	61
31	60

Raw Score	Multiple-Choice Subscore
30	59
29	58
28	57
27	56
26	55
25	54
24	53
23	52
22	51
21	51
20	50
19	49
18	48
17	47
16	46
15	45
14	44
13	43
12	42

Raw Score	Multiple-Choice Subscore
11	41
10	40
9	39
8	38
7	37
6	36
5	35
4	34
3	33

Raw Score	Multiple-Choice Subscore
2	32
1	30
0	29
−1	27
−2	25
−3	24
−4	23
−5	22
−6	21

Writing Scaled Score

MC raw score	Essay Score					
	6	5	4	3	2	1
49	800	790	780	770	720	700
48	790	780	760	730	700	680
47	780	770	750	720	690	670
46	770	760	740	710	680	660
45	770	750	740	700	670	650
44	760	750	730	690	660	640
43	750	740	710	680	650	630
42	750	730	700	670	640	620
41	740	730	690	660	630	610
40	740	720	690	650	620	600
39	740	710	680	640	610	590
38	730	700	670	630	610	590
37	720	690	660	630	600	580
36	710	680	650	620	590	570
35	710	680	640	610	580	560
34	700	670	640	600	570	550
33	690	660	630	590	560	540
32	680	650	620	580	560	540
31	670	640	610	580	550	530
30	660	630	600	570	540	520
29	650	630	590	560	530	510
28	640	620	590	550	520	510
27	640	610	580	540	510	490
26	630	600	570	530	500	490
25	620	590	560	520	500	480
24	610	580	550	510	490	470
23	600	570	540	510	480	460
22	590	570	530	500	470	450
21	590	570	530	500	470	450
20	580	560	520	490	460	440
19	570	550	520	480	450	430
18	570	540	520	470	440	420
17	560	530	510	460	430	420
16	550	520	500	450	430	410
15	540	510	490	450	420	400
14	530	500	480	440	410	390
13	520	500	470	430	400	380
12	510	490	460	420	390	370

Writing Scaled Score

MC raw score	Essay Score					
	6	5	4	3	2	1
11	510	480	450	410	380	360
10	500	470	450	400	370	350
9	490	460	440	390	360	350
8	480	450	430	390	360	340
7	470	440	420	380	350	330
6	460	430	410	370	340	320
5	450	430	400	360	330	310
4	450	420	390	350	320	300
3	440	410	390	340	310	290
2	430	400	380	330	300	280
1	420	380	370	320	290	270
0	400	370	350	310	280	260
−1	380	360	340	290	270	260
−2	370	340	320	270	260	250
−3	360	330	310	260	250	240
−4	350	320	290	250	240	230
−5	340	310	280	240	230	220
−6	340	310	280	240	220	210

SECTION 2: CRITICAL READING

Sentence Completions

1. **A** Two-Word/One-Way *Easy*

In the first part of this sentence, Sally's brother tells Sally that *he had only been joking*. Then, in the second part of the sentence, Sally agrees to "forgive" her brother. The correct answer must contain two words that are consistent with "told" and "forgive." **A** is the only choice that works.

2. **C** Two-Word/Two-Way *Medium*

The first part of this sentence indicates a contrast with the second part of the sentence. The forecast called for rainy weather, but the weather stayed *pleasant* instead. **C** provides the correct missing words: the forecast "predicted" rain, but the weather "defied" expectations and remained pleasant.

3. **A** Two-Word/One-Way *Medium*

The first part of this sentence explains that Wainwright's autobiography was inaccurate and based on fictional stories. This shows that Wainwright preferred to invent experiences rather than to reveal the truth. **A** reflects this contrast.

4. **D** One-Word/One-Way *Medium*

An *exorbitant* price is a price that is very high. The bidder made such a high offer to ensure that she would out-bid her competition and acquire the painting. **D** reflects this meaning.

5. **C** One-Word/One-Way *Medium*
The scholarly article required Lance to *condense* or *shorten* his article, but the special interest publication did not require such shortening. The correct answer is a word that also means "shortening." To *abridge* is to "shorten" or "condense," so **C** fits best.

6. **E** Two-Word/One-Way *Medium*
The phrase *forged ahead fearlessly* suggests that the entrepreneurs were extremely brave. The first blank therefore means "bravery," and the second means "one who brings about change." **E** matches perfectly.

7. **A** One-Word/One-Way *Difficult*
The first part of the sentence tells us that the software is used throughout the industry. The correct answer will be a word that means "widely used." The word *ubiquitous* means "widespread," so **A** is correct.

8. **D** Two-Word/Two-Way *Difficult*
The clue to the first word is given in the phrase *or completely destroyed*. The first blank must be filled with a word that means "exterminated." The second blank must be filled with a word that means the opposite of exterminated—something similar to "conserve." **D** is the only choice that fits.

Short Reading Passages

9. **C** Implied Information *Easy*
At the end of the passage, Jurgis shows off his muscular arms and asks, *Do you want me to believe that with these arms people will ever let me starve*? By this he means that his strength is obvious and therefore that bosses will want to hire him. His question conveys his confidence in his ability to be hired, so **C** is correct.

10. **E** Implied Information *Medium*
The *pessimists* referred to in the passage are those people who believe that getting work is very difficult. These *pessimists* tell Jurgis that many men stand in the crowd for months without being hired. Among this group of people are likely to be workers who have not been chosen themselves for jobs, so **E** is correct.

11. **C** Specific Information *Difficult*
The first paragraph of the passage introduces the topic of the passage: metamorphic rocks. The next paragraph then discusses metamorphic rocks in detail, explaining how they are formed. The purpose of the first passage is to introduce a topic that will be discussed in greater detail, so **C** is correct.

12. **E** Attitude or Tone *Easy*
The author's tone in this passage is not particularly positive or negative. Instead, the tone is straightforward and explanatory. **A**, **B**, and **D** are too negative, while **C** is too positive. **E** fits best.

Paired Reading Passages

13. **A** Relating Two Passages *Medium*
Both authors agree that historical experience provides valuable information for helping to determine current policies. **A** reflects this point of agreement.

14. **B** Specific Information *Easy*
In the first paragraph of Passage 1, the author describes *The Peloponnesian War* as a text that demonstrates *the significance of power politics for state behavior*, so **B** is correct.

15. **D** Specific Information *Medium*
In the second paragraph of Passage 1, the author states that force and threats *serve to deter the expansive state's aggressive intent by making the costs of aggression appear to be prohibitively high*. If the costs of aggression are perceived to be prohibitively high, the state considering the aggression will probably conclude that it could not win an armed conflict, so it should not risk the potential losses. **D** is correct.

16. **C** Specific Information *Medium*
In the third paragraph of Passage 1, the author states, *Allied leaders hoped to avoid conflict by appeasing Hitler and meeting his demands*. The author later points out that Chamberlain attempted to *stave off war*. **C** reflects this motivation.

17. **A** Themes and Arguments *Medium*
This line from Passage 1 describes World War II as providing a *grave historical lesson*. That lesson enabled deterrence theorists to develop clear guidelines for behavior, based on past experience. This approach is most similar to a business that learns from past mistakes.

18. **D** Words in Context *Medium*
The author of Passage 2 states in the first paragraph that *the spiral model also focuses on explaining cases in which force and threats do not curtail aggressive intentions but rather serve to exacerbate them*. The word *exacerbate* means "to worsen or to make more severe." Its use in this sentence emphasizes the idea that forceful policies can actually contribute to conflict with those adversaries who are not inherently aggressive.

19. **C** Words in Context *Easy*
The passage states that before World War I, policy-makers believed that *offensive strategies would prevail in any armed conflict*. In other words, states that "went on the offense" and attacked first would "win" the conflict.

20. **E** Themes and Arguments *Medium*
The author of Passage 2 writes in the last paragraph that the *case of Nazi Germany . . . does not encompass all potential dynamics between states*. This author believes that while Nazi Germany is an important historical case study, it does not illustrate every possible foreign-policy scenario and should not be overemphasized.

21. **D** Relating Two Passages *Medium*
The author of Passage 2 explains that, in World War I, *hostile dynamics eventually spiraled into a war that could have been averted with less aggression and more conciliatory approaches*. Based on the experience of World War I, this author believes that using force can potentially be dangerous if an adversary is not innately aggressive. So **D** is correct.

22. **E** Relating Two Passages *Medium*
At the end of Passage 2, the author recommends that states refrain from assuming that other states have expansionistic aims. In order to maintain peace, this author contends, it may be necessary to forego the use of force if an adversary is merely reacting out of fear of perceived threats. This author would most likely defend the appeasement supporters, because they acted with the intention to maintain peace with Germany.

23. **E** Relating Two Passages *Difficult*
The author of Passage 1 focuses on the evidence gained from World War II. The experience of World War I is not included in this author's discussion. World War I is, however, used as a case study to support the argument in Passage 2. The author of Passage 1 would likely regard World War I as less relevant to issues of foreign policy, because that case study does not support the author's views.

24. **C** Relating Two Passages *Easy*
The deterrence model view, promoted in Passage 1, explains that the use of force is important for deterring an opponent. This author sees the use of force as fundamentally necessary. The author of Passage 2, by contrast, sees the use of force as potentially dangerous under conditions in which adversaries fear war and don't genuinely desire it. **C** captures the contrast between the two authors' views.

SECTION 3: MATH

Multiple Choice

1. **B** Numbers & Operations: Factors and Multiples *Easy*
The number 29 is a prime number. It has no factors other than 1 and 29. Therefore, the fraction $\frac{29}{25}$ cannot be reduced. In this case, $a + 4$ is equal to 29, and a is equal to 25.

2. **E** Data Analysis, Statistics & Probability: Graphs, Charts, and Tables *Easy*
The variable p represents the grand total of all pets listed in the table. There are only four categories of pets: male cats (a), female cats (b), male dogs (c), and female dogs (d). These numbers added together produce the grand total, p.

3. **C** Geometry: Triangles *Easy*
In the figure, $\angle QTU$ and $\angle RTS$ are vertical angles. This means their measures are equal. So, $\angle RTS$ measures 60°. The sum of the interior angles of a triangle is 180°. The angle marked Z equals 180° – 73° – 60°, or 47°.

4. **D** Numbers & Operations: Basic Operations *Easy*

The newer car costs $4,000. The cost to fix the old car is $1,500. The difference between these two amounts is $4,000 – $1,500, or $2,500. To find the amount of months that it will take Scott to save $2,500 in gas costs, divide $2,500 by his monthly savings, $50. It will take Scott $2,500 ÷ $50 = 50 months to save a total of $2,500 in gas costs.

5. **B** Geometry: Polygons *Easy*

If the area of square *QRST* is 16, then the area of square *WXYZ* is 4 times 16, or 64. Use the formula for an area of a square to find the length of one side of square *WXYZ*:

$$A = s^2$$
$$64 = s^2$$
$$\sqrt{64} = s$$
$$8 = s$$

6. **A** Algebra: Solving Equations *Medium*

The turbine completes 50 revolutions per minute, which is $50 \times 60 = 3{,}000$ revolutions per hour. The turbine makes $3{,}000 \times 24 = 72{,}000$ revolutions per day. To determine how many days, *d*, it takes the turbine to make 864,000 revolutions, divide 864,000 by 72,000:

$$d = \frac{864,000}{72,000}$$
$$d = 12$$

7. **C** Data Analysis, Statistics & Probability: Statistical Analysis *Medium*

The average of two numbers is equal to the sum of those numbers divided by two. Set up an equation with the average of s and $2s$ equal to 15:

$$\frac{s+2s}{2} = 15$$
$$s + 2s = 30$$
$$3s = 30$$
$$s = 10$$

8. **C** Solving Equations: Powers and Exponents *Difficult*

In the general equation $a \times r^{(n-1)} = T$, the sixth term $(T) = 288$, the constant ratio $(r) = 2$, and the number of terms in the sequence $(n) = 6$. Solve for the first term in the sequence (a):

$$a \times 2^{(6-1)} = 288$$
$$a \times 2^5 = 288$$
$$a \times 32 = 288$$
$$a = \frac{288}{32}$$
$$a = 9$$

C is correct.

9. **D** Algebra: Solving Equations *Easy*

Solve the equation for h:

$$2g + 4h = g + 3$$
$$4h = g + 3 - 2g$$
$$4h = 3 - g$$
$$h = \frac{3 - g}{4}$$

10. **E** Numbers & Operations: Factors and Multiples *Medium*

The correct answer must contain a number that is a multiple of 3, 5, and 10. Of the five numbers listed, only 1,500 fits the bill.

11. **B** Geometry: Angles and Lines *Medium*

Lines l and m are parallel lines crossed by a transversal, line p. When two parallel lines are crossed by a transversal, opposite interior angles are congruent. This means that X is equal to the measure of $\angle DAB$.

Since $\angle DAB$ is bisected by AC, we know that $\angle CAB$ is congruent to $\angle DAB$. This means that the measure of $\angle DAB$ equals $2 \times 35°$, or $70°$. Since $m\angle DAB$ is equal to X, we know that X also equals $70°$.

12. **C** Numbers & Operations: Roots and Radicals *Medium*

If $\sqrt{\frac{7z}{4}}$ is an integer, this means that $\frac{7z}{4}$ must be a perfect square. (Its square root is an integer.) Substitute each answer choice, in turn, for z, working your way up from the least value. **C** provides the least value that works: $\frac{7 \times 28}{4} = \frac{7 \times 7}{1} = 49$ (a perfect square).

13. **B** Geometry: Polygons *Medium*

The three figures can fit into all of the shapes given, but the figures only fit evenly into shape I. If the "zigzag" figure is placed into shape II, the other two figures must overlap to complete the shape. If the "zigzag" figure is placed into shape III, the other two figures cannot be added in any way that will produce the shape shown. The drawing below shows how all three figures fit evenly into shape I with no overlap:

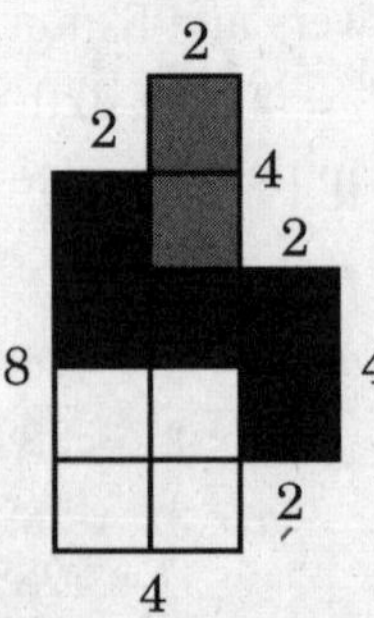

Shape I is the only shape that works, so **B** is correct.

14. **D** Numbers & Operations: Factors and Multiples *Difficult*

Determine the integers that are greater than 25 and less than 35:

26, 27, 28, 29, 30, 31, 32, 33, 34

A prime number has only one prime factor (itself), so eliminate the prime numbers 29 and 31. Factor the remaining numbers into their prime factorizations:

$$26 = 13 \times 2$$
$$27 = 3 \times 3 \times 3$$
$$28 = 7 \times 2 \times 2$$
$$30 = 5 \times 2 \times 3$$
$$32 = 2 \times 2 \times 2 \times 2 \times 2$$
$$33 = 3 \times 11$$
$$34 = 17 \times 2$$

The numbers 27, 28, and 32 each have at least two identical prime number factors. **D** is correct.

15. **A** Geometry: Triangles *Medium*

The quickest way to answer this question involves recognizing that the figure is a special right triangle, with sides in a ratio of 5:12:13. Whenever you see a hypotenuse that is a multiple of 13, check to see if the right triangle might be a 5:12:13 triangle. In this case, we can come up with a value for x such that $8.5 - x$ equals 5 and $8.5 + x$ equals 12. That value is $x = 3.5$. The 5:12:13 triangle is also produced if the value for x is -3.5.

Substitute 3.5 for x in the equation in the question:

$$\begin{aligned} 72.25 - x^2 &= 72.25 - (3.5)^2 \\ &= 72.25 - 12.25 \\ &= 60 \end{aligned}$$

This equation produces the same result if -3.5 is substituted for x.

If you didn't recognize that this was a 5:12:13 triangle, you could approach the question by using the Pythagorean theorem to solve for x:

$$\begin{aligned} a^2 + b^2 &= c^2 \\ (8.5 - x)^2 + (8.5 + x)^2 &= (13)^2 \\ [(8.5 - x)(8.5 - x)] + [(8.5 + x)(8.5 + x)] &= 169 \\ (72.25 - 17x + x^2) + (72.25 + 17x + x^2) &= 169 \\ 144.5 + 2x^2 &= 169 \\ 2x^2 &= 169 - 144.5 \\ 2x^2 &= 24.5 \\ x^2 &= \frac{24.5}{2} \\ x^2 &= 12.25 \\ x &= \sqrt{12.25} \\ x &= \pm 3.5 \end{aligned}$$

Substitute 3.5 for x in the expression $72.25 - x^2$ and solve for x. **A** is correct.

16. **A** Geometry: Coordinate Geometry *Medium*

The minimum value of this parabola is $g(-2)$. Therefore, the vertex of the parabola is some point $(-2, y)$. The parabola crosses the x-axis at the point $(0, 0)$. So, the x-coordinate of this point is exactly 2 units to the right of the x-coordinate of the vertex.

Graphs of quadratic functions are always symmetrical. The x-intercept to the left of the vertex must therefore also lie exactly 2 units to the left of the vertex. This x-intercept must have coordinates $(-4, 0)$.

We are asked to determine a possible value for b when the y-coordinate of the parabola is 2. The parabola has two points at which it passes through y-coordinates of 2. One of these is to the right of the vertex, and the other is to the left.

The parabola could possibly pass through the point (1, 2) on the right side of the vertex. None of the other values of b would work. If $b = 0$, then $y = 0$, so **B** is incorrect. The remaining answer choices all represent negative x-coordinates. The left part of the parabola crosses the x-axis at the point (–4, 0). The left part of the parabola passes through a point with y-coordinate of 2 only for values of b that are less than –4. None of the answer choices contains a negative number less than –4, so **A** is correct.

17. **C** Algebra: Binomials and Quadratics *Difficult*

Factor the expression $x^2 + bx + 6$. The first terms in each factor will be x. The last terms in each factor can be multiplied to produce 6. This means that the last terms in the factors must be either 6 and 1 or 2 and 3.

The question tells us that one of the factors is $(x + 2)$. The other factor is $(x + d)$. The only value for d that could be multiplied by 2 to produce 6 is 3. Therefore, d must equal 3.

Substitute 3 for d in the factors and multiply:

$$\begin{aligned}(x+2)(x+d) &= (x+2)(x+3)\\ &= x^2+2x+3x+6\\ &= x^2+5x+6\end{aligned}$$

The expression $x^2 + 5x + 6$ is equivalent to $x^2 + bx + 6$. The value of b is therefore 5.

18. **A** Geometry: Triangles *Difficult*

Draw a line on the graph from point (6, –12) to point (0, –12). This line is parallel to the y-axis. That means it forms a triangle that is larger than XYZ, with two legs of length 6 and 12. Use the Pythagorean theorem to find the length of the hypotenuse of this larger triangle:

$$\begin{aligned}a^2+b^2 &= c^2\\ 6^2+12^2 &= c^2\\ 36+144 &= c^2\\ 180 &= c^2\\ \sqrt{180} &= c\end{aligned}$$

The hypotenuse of the larger triangle measures $\sqrt{180}$, or $6\sqrt{5}$. The larger triangle thus has legs that are in a ratio of $6:12:6\sqrt{5}$.

Triangle XYZ has three interior angles that are congruent to the interior angles of the larger triangle. Therefore, triangle XYZ is similar to the larger triangle. This means that the lengths of its legs are in the same ratio as the lengths of the legs of the larger triangle. Look for an answer choice with legs in the same ratio as the larger triangle.

In **C** and **D**, the ratio between the two legs is not 1:2, so you can eliminate **C** and **D**. In **B**, the ratio of the hypotenuse to either leg is clearly too great, so eliminate **B**.

The legs in the triangle in **A** have a ratio of $2:4:\sqrt{20}$, or $2:4:2\sqrt{5}$. Each of the legs is exactly $\frac{1}{3}$ the side of its corresponding leg in the larger triangle. Divide the length of each leg by 3 to check this:

$$6 \div 3 = 2$$
$$12 \div 3 = 4$$
$$6\sqrt{5} \div 3 = 2\sqrt{5}$$

A represents a triangle that is similar to the larger triangle. **A** is correct.

19. **D** Algebra: Functions *Medium*

If $\frac{1}{3}j(\sqrt{r}) = 3$, this means that $j(\sqrt{r}) = 3 \times 3$, or 9. Substitute 9 in as the result of the function

$$j\left(\sqrt{r}\right) = 4\sqrt{r} + 3$$
$$9 = 4\sqrt{r} + 3$$

Now solve for r:

$$9 = 4\sqrt{r} + 3$$
$$6 = 4\sqrt{4}$$
$$\frac{6}{4} = \sqrt{r}$$
$$\left(\frac{6}{4}\right)^2 = r$$
$$\frac{36}{16} \text{ or } \frac{9}{4} = r$$

20. **E** Numbers & Operations: Powers and Exponents *Medium*

Assume that x equals $-\frac{1}{2}$. Try this value in each of the answer choices:

$$\mathbf{A} = 3x = 3\left(-\frac{1}{2}\right) = -\frac{3}{2}$$
$$\mathbf{B} = x^2 = \left(-\frac{1}{2}\right)^2 = \frac{1}{4}$$
$$\mathbf{C} = \frac{1}{2}(-x)^2 = \frac{1}{2}\left(-\frac{1}{2}\right)^2 = \frac{1}{2}\left(\frac{1}{4}\right) = \frac{1}{8}$$
$$\mathbf{D} = 4x^3 = 4\left(-\frac{1}{2}\right)^3 = 4\left(-\frac{1}{8}\right) = -\frac{1}{2}$$
$$\mathbf{E} = x^{-2} = \left(-\frac{1}{2}\right)^{-2} = \left[\frac{1}{(-\frac{1}{2})^2}\right] = \left[\frac{1}{(\frac{1}{4})}\right] = 1 \times \frac{4}{1} = 4$$

E is the only choice that produces a positive whole number. The expression x^{-2} produces a positive whole number for all negative fractions with a numerator of 1. **E** is correct.

SECTION 4: CRITICAL READING

Sentence Completions

1. **C** One-Word/One-Way *Easy*

This sentence gives the definition of the missing word. The word means *known to the thinking mind*. **C**, *conscious*, fits this meaning.

2. **C** Two-Word/One-Way *Medium*

The first part of the sentence gives us a clue to the first blank: Kevin's experience was *in-depth*, so his qualifications must have been significant as well. The second blank suggests what might happen when a person with good qualifications is recognized by his company. **C** fits best. Kevin's *extensive* qualifications earned him a promotion by his company.

3. **C** One-Word/One-Way *Difficult*

The first part of the sentence lets us know that Samantha's artwork has received a similar reception from everyone. The word *laudatory* means "congratulatory or praising"; thus, we're looking for a word that indicates a positive reaction by art journals. **C** works best.

4. **E** Two-Word/One-Way *Medium*

The word *texture* gives us a clue that the first blank has something to do with the way a fabric feels. A weave has texture, and smoothness is a particular type of texture, so **E** and **A** are possible choices. The second blank reveals that the texture enables people do something with the fabrics even in poor lighting. Poor lighting has nothing to do with whether a person can feel a fabric, but it could prevent a person from recognizing a fabric by sight. The weave of this fabric is so distinctive that people can recognize the fabric even when they can't see it very well. **E** is correct.

5. **A** One-Word/One-Way *Medium*

The word *confession* gives us a clue to the meaning of the blank. We're looking for a word that is a synonym of *confession*. **A** works best.

Paired Reading Passages

6. **E** Relating Two Passages *Medium*

Passage 2 gives reasons why we shouldn't study ancient languages, whereas Passage 1 argues that we should study ancient languages. Passage 2 presents counterarguments.

7. **D** Relating Two Passages *Medium*

The author of Passage 2 states in the second paragraph that *it is difficult and time-consuming to learn an ancient language*. The author of Passage 1 also raises a rhetorical question regarding the study of ancient languages as being *unendurable*. This question implies the author's admission that studying languages is difficult. **D** is correct.

8. **B** Relating Two Passages *Medium*

In the last paragraph of Passage 1, the author provides an argument for why the so-called "dead" languages can still be considered "living." *Only those languages can properly be called "dead,"* he writes, *in which nothing living has been written.*

9. **C** Specific Information *Medium*

The line mentioned in the question compares methods for learning ancient versus living languages. Students of ancient languages can only learn by memorizing, whereas students of living languages can learn by speaking the language with others in communities where the language is used.

Long Reading Passages

10. **D** Main Idea *Medium*

This passage introduces a story heard by the narrator. The narrator first explains how he came across the character David Innes, who revealed the story. The story is then retold in Innes's own words.

11. **D** Themes and Arguments *Medium*

The narrator starts by providing a first-person account of how he learned the story that will be revealed in the novel. Next, the story itself is presented in another first-person narrative that takes place during a time period ten years' prior to the introduction.

12. **D** Words in Context *Medium*

The word *heinous* is used in paragraph 2 to describe a type of crime, examples of which are given in the paragraph: *the purloining of the Crown Jewels from the Tower, or putting poison in the coffee of His Majesty the King.* These crimes are significant, so the meaning *terrible* fits best.

13. **B** Technique *Easy*

In the fourth paragraph, the narrator explains that the storyteller had *the fire of truth* in his eyes and a *ring of sincerity* in his voice. In the context of this explanation, the narrator might have further emphasized the earnestness of the storyteller's presentation to better support the notion that the story itself was true.

14. **A** Implied Information *Difficult*

David Innes states that he worked in the mines out of respect for his father: *I did my best to fulfill the last wishes of my parent—not because of the inheritance, but because I loved and honored my father.*

15. **B** Attitude or Tone *Medium*

With an aura of mystery, the narrator introduces a story that at first might seem too bizarre to be believed. He then introduces the character of David Innes, who begins to narrate—with a sense of adventurous spirit—the unusual tale of his trip to the center of the Earth. **B** works best.

16. **A** Themes and Arguments *Difficult*

The passage explains multiple reasons why individuals tend to forget their dreams, so **A** is correct.

17. **B** Implied Information *Medium*

The author explains in paragraph 2 that some *dreams manifest an extraordinary power of maintaining themselves in the memory*. He gives the example of one dream that he has remembered for thirty-seven years. This suggests that he believes that certain dreams can be retained in the long-term memory. The author describes this phenomenon as *incomprehensible*, which implies that, at the time of his writing, it was not understood.

18. **C** Words in Context *Easy*

At the end of paragraph 4, the author states that some dreams *are forgotten because they are too weak, while the stronger images in their neighborhood are remembered*. This contrast between weak and strong dreams suggests that the author believes that dreams manifest at different levels of intensity.

19. **C** Words in Context *Medium*

In paragraph 5, the author explains that *in the waking state, one is wont to forget rather easily things that have happened only once, and to remember more readily things which occur repeatedly*. When he states that an individual *is wont to forget*, the author means that an individual *tends* to forget events that happen only once.

20. **E** Words in Context *Medium*

In the author's view, the fact that most dreams are unique experiences seems to be a distinct defining aspect, or unusual characteristic, of dreams. *Bizarre* in **D** is too negative to represent the author's meaning. **E** works best.

21. **B** Specific Information *Medium*

The author explains in paragraph 6 that *feelings, representations, ideas, and the like . . . should not remain isolated* but instead should be presented in the context of appropriate connections and associations. Without these connections, the author argues, feelings and representations become like the verses of a piece of poetry that are scrambled up and read in random order: they are very difficult to remember. **B** is correct.

22. **B** Themes and Arguments *Difficult*

Paragraph 6 presents the third reason that dreams are often forgotten. In this paragraph, the author explains that, in order to be easily recalled, ideas must be linked by orderly connections and presented within familiar structures. Dreams by nature lack sense and order, according to the author, which provides evidence to account for why they are often forgotten.

23. **E** Attitude or Tone *Easy*

Throughout the passage, Freud offers several reasons that dreams are often forgotten after an individual wakes up. He cites the work of other authors and analyzes multiple factors affecting the outcome he explains. His presentation is therefore most like a scholarly analysis, as **E** indicates.

24. **B** Technique *Medium*

Throughout the passage, the author supplies ideas and quotations from other authors to support his own viewpoint. He particularly utilizes the work of Strumpell. **B** is correct.

SECTION 5: MATH

Multiple Choice

1. **E** Numbers & Operations: Basic Operations *Easy*

Harmon drives 120 miles in 2 hours, which means that he drives $120 \div 2 = 60$ miles per hour. If his speed is increased to 65 miles per hour, in three hours he will drive $65 \times 3 = 195$ miles.

2. **E** Algebra: Functions *Easy*

Check each answer by plugging the values for x into the equation. Determine if the resulting values for y match the values in the table. **E** is the only equation that works for every pair of values.

3. **C** Geometry: Circles *Easy*

The formula for the circumference of a circle is $C = 2\pi r$. Let the circumference of the inner circle equal $2\pi r$. The circumference of the outer circle is three times the circumference of the inner circle. Therefore, the circumference of the outer circle is $3 \times 2\pi r$. This could also be written as $2\pi \times 3r$. The radius of the outer circle is three times larger than the radius of the inner circle. The radius of the outer circle, *JL*, is 9, so the radius of the inner circle, *JK*, is 3.

4. **B** Geometry: Coordinate Geometry *Easy*

Point *O* has coordinates (2, –2). The absolute value of its *x*-coordinate, 2, is 2. The absolute value of its *y*-coordinate, –2, is also 2. These two values added together produce $2 + 2 = 4$.

5. **B** Data Analysis, Statistics & Probability: Graphs, Charts, and Tables *Medium*

The question states that 100 people were surveyed. The diagram shows that 10 percent of those surveyed reported a monthly income of more than \$5,000 ($m >$ \$5,000). Calculate 10 percent of 100:

$$100 \times 0.10 = 10 \text{ people}$$

6. **D** Numbers & Operations: Divisibility and Remainders *Difficult*

Try out each answer choice to see which one works. The question asks for consecutive positive even integers. The first even integer to produce a remainder of 0 is 10. The consecutive positive even integers starting with 10 are 10, 12, 14, 16, and 18. When 5 is divided into these numbers, the remainders are: 0, 2, 4, 1, and 3.

7. **C** Algebra: Substitution *Medium*

If a is inversely proportional to b, this means that $a = \frac{c}{b}$, where c is a constant. Use the information in the first part of the question to determine the value of the constant, c:

$$a = \frac{c}{b}$$
$$10 = \frac{c}{2}$$
$$c = 20$$

In this case, the constant, c, equals 20. The question asks you to determine the value of a when b equals 10. Substitute 10 for b and 20 for the constant, c. Then solve for a:

$$a = \frac{20}{10}$$
$$a = 2$$

8. **A** Algebra: Systems of Equations *Medium*

Solve the first equation to determine the value of n in terms of p and m:

$$4m - n = 3p$$
$$-n = 3p - 4m$$
$$n = -3p + 4m$$

Now substitute $-3p + 4m$ for n in the second equation:

$$4m + 3p - n = 24$$
$$4m + 3p - (-3p + 4m) = 24$$
$$4m + 3p + 3p - 4m = 24$$
$$6p = 24$$
$$p = 4$$

Grid-Ins

9. **8.25, 33/4** Algebra: Solving Equations *Easy*

To determine the answer, solve the equation for a:

$$4(a + 2) = 41$$
$$\frac{(a+2)}{4} = \frac{41}{4}$$
$$a + 2 = 10.25$$
$$a = 8.25 \text{ or } \frac{33}{4}$$

10. **12** Geometry: Coordinate Geometry *Easy*

Substitute 5 for x in the equation and solve for y:

$$y + 2 = 7(x - 3)$$
$$y + 2 = 7(5 - 3)$$
$$y + 2 = 7(2)$$
$$y + 2 = 14$$
$$y = 12$$

11. **32** Numbers & Operations: Basic Operations *Easy*

First, determine the number of hours that it took Stephanie to stuff 40 envelopes. She stuffed 10 envelopes per hour. Therefore, it took her $40 \div 10 = 4$ hours to stuff 40 envelopes.

Next, determine how many envelopes Alan stuffed in 4 hours. He stuffed 8 envelopes per hour. Therefore, in 4 hours, Alan stuffed $4 \times 8 = 32$ envelopes.

12. **70** Geometry: Polygons *Medium*

The figure *VWZY* is a quadrilateral. The sum of the interior angles of a quadrilateral is 360°. Use this information to find the measure of $\angle VYZ$:

$$90° + 90° + 70° + m\angle VYZ = 360°$$
$$250° + m\angle VYZ = 360°$$
$$m\angle VYZ = 110°$$

Since $\angle VYZ$ lies on a straight line with $\angle VYX$, these angles are supplementary. Their measures add up to 180°. Therefore, the value of a is $180 - 110 = 70$.

13. **7, 42/6** Numbers & Operations: Sequences *Medium*

Add the first two terms together: $\frac{3}{2} + \frac{4}{3} = \frac{17}{6}$. Add the second and third terms together: $\frac{4}{3} + \frac{17}{6} = \frac{25}{6}$. Add the third and fourth terms together: $\frac{17}{6} + \frac{25}{6} = \frac{42}{6}$, or 7.

14. **5/9** Algebra: Substitution *Medium*

Since $a = \frac{2}{3}b$, this also means that $b = \frac{3}{2}a$. We know that $b = \frac{5}{6}c$ as well. Substitute $\frac{3}{2}a$ into the second equation and solve for a:

$$b = \frac{5}{6}c$$
$$\frac{3}{2}a = \frac{5}{6}c$$
$$a = \left(\frac{2}{3}\right) \times \left(\frac{5}{6}c\right)$$
$$a = \frac{5}{9}c$$

15. **20** Geometry: Polygons *Difficult*

Triangle *LMN* is a 30-60-90 triangle. This means that its sides are in a ratio of $x{:}x\sqrt{3}{:}2x$. In this ratio, the side opposite the 60° angle is represented by $x\sqrt{3}$. The side opposite the 30° is represented by x.

In the figure, leg *MN* is opposite the 60° angle, and its length is $3\sqrt{3}$. Leg *LN* is opposite the 30° angle. Therefore, its length must be 3.

Use this length to find the perimeter of *LNOP*: $3 + 3 + 7 + 7 = 20$.

16. **24/9, 8/3, 2.67** Numbers & Operations: Fractions *Difficult*

In this punch, there are 4 parts fruit juice for every 5 parts seltzer. This makes for a total of $4 + 5 = 9$ "parts" in the mixture. There are 4 parts of fruit juice for every 9 parts of the punch. The ratio of fruit juice to punch is thus 4 to 9, or $\frac{4}{9}$.

Use this ratio to set up a proportion. Let x equal the number of gallons of fruit juice in 6 gallons of punch, and solve for x:

$$\frac{4}{9} = \frac{x}{6}$$
$$9x = 24$$
$$x = \frac{24}{9} \text{ or } \frac{8}{3}$$

17. **3/4, .75** Geometry: Angles and Lines *Difficult*

Notice that FG is horizontal (because the y-coordinates of the two endpoints are the same). Since line c intersects FG exactly midway between F and G, the xy-coordinates of that point of intersection must be (–3, 4). Use the slope formula to determine the slope of line c:

$$m = \frac{y_2 - y_1}{x_2 - x_1}$$
$$m = \frac{4 - 0}{-3 - 0}$$
$$m = -\frac{4}{3}$$

The slope of any line perpendicular to line c is $\frac{3}{4}$ (the negative reciprocal of $-\frac{4}{3}$).

18. **2785** Data Analysis, Statistics & Probability: Graphs, Charts, and Tables *Difficult*

The median of a series of numbers is the number whose value falls exactly in the middle of the set. List the numbers in the table in numerical order from smallest to largest:

2,174, 2,563, 2,784, 3,654

The number 2,784 is the median of this set, so there must be two values in the table larger than 2,784. However, the table only lists one larger value, 3,654. This means that n must also be a value that is larger than 2,784. Therefore, the smallest possible value for n is 2,785.

SECTION 6: WRITING

Improving Sentences

1. **C** Wordiness *Easy*

C provides the most concise way to phrase this sentence. It also uses an active verb, *criticized*, which most effectively expresses the action in the second part of the sentence.

2. **D** Fragments *Easy*

This sentence needs a plural verb for the subject *employees*. **D** provides the plural verb *are* while still maintaining clear meaning within the sentence. **E** doesn't work, because the word *although* suggests a contrast that doesn't make sense given the first part of the sentence.

3. **A** No Error *Medium*

The sentence is best phrased exactly as it is written. **A** is correct.

4. **D** Misplaced Modifiers *Medium*

The construction *they have gratuity policies* is incorrect in this sentence. To whom does *they* refer? **D** provides a better phrasing by explaining simply that *gratuity policies prevent patrons from leaving inadequate tips*. **E** is incorrect because *giving . . . for* is not idiomatic.

5. **E** Misplaced Modifiers *Easy*

This sentence makes it sound as if the salmon dish was *looking over the menu*. In reality, Lorraine was looking over the menu. Therefore, Lorraine needs to be in the subject position after the introductory phrase.

6. **D** Run-Ons *Easy*

This sentence contains two complete sentences joined together by only a comma. **D** corrects this problem by creating one sentence with a clear causal relationship: Irish terriers are highly predatory because they were originally bred to catch rodents.

7. **B** Fragments *Easy*

The word *being* does not work as the verb in this sentence. **B** corrects this problem by replacing *being* with the verb *are*.

8. **C** Conjunctions *Difficult*

C works best here; it is more concise and graceful than the original sentence, and it also preserves the meaning of the original.

9. **C** Idioms *Medium*

The word *than* is used incorrectly in this sentence. The word *as* should be used instead to indicate the comparison.

10. **B** Other *Medium*

In the second half of this sentence, the noun to which the word *they* refers is unclear. What exactly involves *careful planning* and *proven methods* for achieving business goals? **B** clarifies this reference by specifying that the entrepreneurs' *strategies* involve careful planning and proven methods.

11. **D** Misplaced Modifiers *Medium*

This sentence starts with the modifying phrase *normally shy and reserved*. This phrase describes Helen, so "Helen" should directly follow the phrase as the main subject of the sentence. **D** is correct.

Identifying Sentence Errors

12. **B** Subject-Verb Agreement *Easy*

The noun *rows of trees* is plural. This noun requires the plural verb *are*.

13. **B** Tense *Easy*

The gerund *increasing* should be replaced with either the infinitive form *to increase* or simply *increase*.

14. **E** No Error *Easy*

This sentence is correct as it is written. The word *endeavor* is singular, so it takes the singular verb *is*.

15. **D** Adverbs and Adjectives *Easy*

The word *quick* is used as an adverb here to describe the manner in which the doctor would determine a treatment. Adverbs usually end in *-ly*, so *quick* should be replaced with *quickly*.

16. **A** Subject-Verb Agreement *Easy*

The noun *presenters* is plural. Therefore, it should be followed by the plural verb *have*.

17. **D** Tense *Medium*

The first part of the sentence is in the past tense, as conveyed by the past tense verb *felt*. The second part of the sentence then incorrectly uses the present tense verb *feel*. This verb should be changed to the past tense *felt* as well.

18. **D** Parallelism *Easy*

The word *or* here is paired with the preceding word *neither*. But *or* goes with *either*, not *neither*. Therefore, *or* should be changed to *nor*, which goes with *neither*.

19. **C** Pronouns *Medium*

The word *investigators* is plural, and the pronoun *their* is a plural pronoun. To be consistent, the word *reputation* should be plural as well.

20. **A** Tense *Easy*

Denise enjoyed her days on the beach *before* she moved away from the ocean. So, the word *enjoys* should be changed to the past tense, *enjoyed*.

21. **A** Pronouns *Easy*

The phrase *at a college that* is clumsy in this sentence. The phrase refers to a particular place, so the word *that* should be changed to *where*.

22. **A** Pronouns *Medium*

If Shelby had asked only you, and not Tom, to do something, you wouldn't say that "Shelby asked I." Instead, you'd say, "Shelby asked me." The pronoun *me* should also be used in this case, where Tom is mentioned as well. It's correct to say, "Shelby asked Tom and me."

23. **E** No Error *Difficult*

This sentence works well as written. The phrase *something of an enigma* is used correctly here.

24. **E** No Error *Medium*

The sentence is correct as written. The noun *elders* is plural, so the plural verb *run* is OK.

25. **A** Idioms *Easy*

The phrase *listening at* is incorrect here. It should be *listening to*.

26. **C** Pronouns *Medium*

The pronoun *he* is an unclear reference in this sentence. Who took the management course, the shopkeeper or Timothy? The pronoun *he* should be changed to a more specific reference. It should be replaced with either "the shopkeeper" or "Timothy," depending on the intended meaning of the sentence.

27. **D** Other *Difficult*

The superlative *most bright* is not idomatic and should be replaced with the *brightest*.

28. **C** Tense *Difficult*

The sentence improperly mixes the present-perfect tense (*have demonstrated*) with the past tense (*was*). Since *have* is not underlined, *was* should be replaced with the present-tense verb *is*.

29. **E** No Error *Medium*

This sentence contains no errors. The phrase *often illogical arguments* is written correctly, and the arguments are plural, so they are followed by the plural verb *make*.

Improving Paragraphs

30. **C** Sentence Revision *Medium*

Sentence 4 starts with a vague pronoun reference. The use of the word *it* is confusing here; we can't be sure exactly what "it" refers to. **C** clears up this problem by replacing *It* with "Gramsci's work."

31. **D** Sentence Combination *Easy*

The word *unilateral* is modified by the phrase *depicting causal relationships as operating in only one direction*. This phrase helps define the meaning of the term *unilateral*. It should be joined to sentence 6 with a comma.

32. **D** Sentence Revision *Medium*

Sentence 8 lacks modifying words that help to differentiate the two variables. **D** corrects this problem by adding descriptive words and a comma. It clarifies the meaning of the sentence: a factor *known as* the "independent" variable is hypothesized to produce a result, *known as* the "dependent" variable.

33. **B** Sentence Addition *Medium*

The third paragraph lacks a topic sentence that will help explain what is to be discussed in the paragraph. The paragraph explains Gramsci's notion of causality and how it differs from the traditional view. **B** provides the best topic sentence for introducing this paragraph.

34. **E** Sentence Revision *Medium*

Sentence 11 contains two complete sentences joined only by a comma. The first complete sentence is, *In Gramsci's view, the interaction of these variables is significant*. The second complete sentence is, *It is ultimately responsible for producing the reality that we perceive*. These two sentences can correctly be joined with a semicolon, as **E** indicates.

35. **E** Essay Analysis *Medium*

The essay concerns Gramsci's views on causality. Specifically, it explains how Gramsci's view of causality differs from the traditional scientific view. The length of Gramsci's prison term, discussed in sentence 12, is not related to the rest of the essay.

SECTION 7: CRITICAL READING

Sentence Completions

1. **C** One-Word/One-Way *Easy*

Martin wrote the story without any help from his colleagues, so he completed the project *single-handedly*. **C** is correct.

2. **E** Two-Word/Two-Way *Medium*

The word *but* in this sentence lets us know that the words in the two blanks have contradictory or opposite meanings. The description of Castillo's writing style as *droning* suggests that the word in the second blank has a negative meaning, such as "boring." The word in the first blank must therefore be positive. **E** works best.

3. **E** One-Word/One-Way *Medium*

The second part of the sentence further explains the *massage therapy program*. We're looking for a blank that suggests a *hands-on experience*. *Kinesthetic* (which means "involving position and movement of the body") works best, so **E** is correct.

4. **D** One-Word/One-Way *Medium*

The second part of the sentence provides the meaning of the missing word. *Dexterity* means "manual skill or deftness," so **D** is correct.

5. **D** Two-Word/Two-Way *Medium*

The first part of this sentence suggests that Fields's contributions made him well respected; by the end of his career, though, something had caused him to lose support. Something like *acclaim* fits the first blank, and *corruption* fits the second—he achieved great acclaim, but his corruption later turned constituents against him.

6. **C** One-Word/One-Way *Difficult*

The last part of this sentence defines the missing word for us: it means "implied but not directly stated." An *innuendo* "suggests or insinuates meaning without stating it directly," so **C** is correct.

Long Reading Passage

7. **A** Specific Information *Easy*

The last paragraph of the passage states that *the size of a creature's eye is not proportional to its body size*. This fact explains why two same-sized animals might have eyes of different sizes.

8. **E** Implied Information *Medium*

The author draws an analogy between nerve endings on the eye's retina and the film in a camera. Extending this analogy, the eye may be compared to a camera, as **E** states.

9. **D** Technique *Easy*

In the last paragraph, the author mentions flies in order to illustrate the point that *the size of a creature's eye is not proportional to its body size.* **D** is correct.

10. **C** Specific Information *Medium*

Paragraph 3 concerns photons and their relationship to light.

11. **A** Implied Information *Medium*

The last sentence of the paragraph states that *the eye functions using only a fraction of an individual's total brain weight, leveraging brain resources to produce stunning results*. In this case, the word *stunning* is used to mean "very impressive." The eye's results are impressive considering how few brain resources the eye requires.

12. **B** Specific Information *Medium*

In paragraph 1, the author explains that *though we may experience sight as an effortless phenomenon, in fact it comes about only through an intricate process of collaboration between the eye and the brain.* This statement suggests that eye functions require significant joint action by both the eye and the brain.

13. **D** Implied Information *Medium*

Paragraph 5 states that *we see colors best in light at medium to high levels of brightness*. This suggests that a spot near a sunny window might provide optimal levels of light intensity for accurate color differentiation.

14. **C** Implied Information *Medium*

The author states, *most living beings have some form of eyesight, and even plants have ways of sensing changes between darkness and light*. This implies that plants possess some sort of sight mechanism, however primitive.

15. **B** Implied Information *Medium*

The passage states, *an influx of intense light that is too great for the eye to process can interfere with vision and even cause blindness*. Therefore, **B** is correct.

16. **D** Words in Context *Easy*

The iris contracts and expands the diameter of the pupil in order to regulate, or control, the amount of light that enters the eye.

17. **B** Specific Information *Medium*

The first sentence of paragraph 3 states, *a key ingredient in the process of seeing is the presence of light, without which no sight could occur*. Thus, the human sight system requires light in order to operate.

18. **A** Themes and Arguments *Medium*

The author states, *once visual impulses arrive at the brain, the brain then completes the staggeringly complex task of turning these visual impulses into images that we "see."* The phrase *staggeringly complex task* shows the extremely difficult nature of the work undertaken by the brain when it converts visual impulses into sight images.

19. **B** Implied Information *Medium*

In the last paragraph of the passage, the author states, *the size of the eye does appear to be proportional to the* quality *of sight experienced by a human or an animal.* This statement suggests that there is a direct relationship between size of eyes and ability to see. Therefore, animals with larger eyes have better quality vision than animals with smaller eyes.

SECTION 8: MATH

Multiple Choice

1. **A** Data Analysis, Statistics & Probability: Permutations and Combinations *Easy*

The company sells candles in 5 different colors and 4 different heights. To find the number of color-height combinations, multiply the number of different colors by the number of different heights. The company sells $5 \times 4 = 20$ different color-height combinations.

2. **E** Algebra: Solving Equations *Easy*

The sum of $7a$ and 12 can be written as $7a + 12$. The product of a and $\frac{2}{3}$ can be written as $\frac{2}{3}a$. These two expressions are equal to each other, so create an equation: $7a + 12 = \frac{2}{3}a$.

3. **C** Data Analysis, Statistics & Probability: Probability *Easy*

To find probability, divide the number of favorable outcomes by the number of possible outcomes. Richard's jacket could be on one of 70 buses. Thus, the number of possible outcomes is 70. There are 14 buses out of service today, so the number of favorable outcomes is 14. The probability that the jacket will be on a bus that is out of service today is $\frac{14}{70}$ or $\frac{1}{5}$.

4. **E** Algebra: Solving Equations *Easy*

Any fraction that can be reduced to $\frac{2}{3}$ will contain an integer pair that satisfies the equation $\frac{x}{y} = \frac{2}{3}$. The fraction $\frac{4}{6}$ for instance, contains an integer pair (4, 6) that satisfies the equation: $\frac{4}{6} = \frac{2}{3}$. The fraction $\frac{8}{12}$ also contains an integer pair (8, 12) that satisfies the equation. There are an unlimited number of possible integer pairs that satisfy the equation, so **E** is correct.

5. **B** Data Analysis, Statistics & Probability: Graphs, Charts, and Tables *Easy*
In February, Janet's candy store sold approximately 2,500 candy bars. In March, the store sold approximately 1,400 candy bars. During these two months, the store sold a total of 2,500 + 1,400 = 3,900 candy bars. This number is greater than the number of candy bars sold during any of the other two-month periods.

6. **D** Geometry: Angles and Lines *Easy*
Since the length of *DF* is 32, this means that *DE* and *EF* both measure 16. If *G* is halfway between points *E* and *F*, then *EG* is half the length of *DE*, or 8. *EF* is also 8 units long:

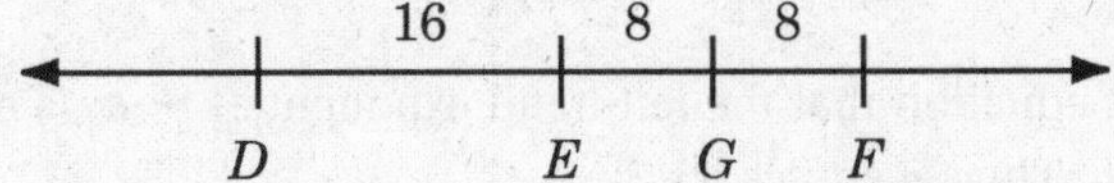

So, *DG* measures 16 + 8 = 24 units.

7. **B** Algebra: Absolute Value and Exponents *Medium*
First, factor out like terms. In this case, the term 4^{-r} is found in both parts of the expression:

$$\begin{aligned}(5 \times 4^{-r}) - (2 \times 4^{-r}) &= 4^{-r}(5-2) \\ &= 4^{-r}(3)\end{aligned}$$

Next, convert the negative exponent to a positive exponent. In this case, 4^{-r} can be converted to $\frac{1}{4^r}$:

$$\begin{aligned}4^{-r}(3) &= \frac{1}{4^r}(3) \\ &= \frac{3}{4^r}\end{aligned}$$

8. **B** Geometry: Circles *Medium*
A circle measures 360°. The central angle of $\frac{1}{6}$ of a circle measures $\frac{1}{6} \times 360° = 60°$. The central angle of $\frac{1}{8}$ of a circle measures $\frac{1}{8} \times 360° = 45°$. The difference between these two central angles is $60° - 45° = 15°$.

9. **B** Geometry: Coordinate Geometry *Medium*
In a function, the notation $f(x)$ denotes the *y*-value produced for a certain value, *x*. The question asks for all values of *x* for which $f(x)$ is positive. In other words, we're looking for all values of *x* that have positive *y*-values. On this graph, the *y*-values are only positive for *x*-values between 0 and –5. Therefore, **B** is correct.

10. **C** Geometry: Solids *Medium*
This figure is comprised of a rectangular solid and two cubes. The central rectangular solid has dimensions 18 cm × 18 cm × 23 cm, so its volume is 7,452 cm^3. The two outer cubes have dimensions 18 cm × 18 cm × 18 cm, so their volumes are each 5,832 cm^3. Add the three volumes together: 7,452 + 5,832 + 5,832 equals a total volume of 19,116 cm^3.

11. **A** Algebra: Absolute Value and Exponents *Difficult*

First, convert the terms in the equation so that they all have like bases. Two of the terms already have a base of 3. The number 27 can be converted to a number with a base of 3 as well, since 27 equals $3 \times 3 \times 3$:

$$27(3^a) = 3^b$$
$$(3^3)(3^a) = 3^b$$

Add together the exponents of terms with like bases:

$$(3^3)(3^a) = 3^b$$
$$3^{(3+a)} = 3^b$$

We see from this equation that the left-hand exponent, $3 + a$, is equal to the right-hand exponent, b. Thus, a equals $b - 3$.

12. **C** Geometry: Triangles *Medium*

Let $3x$ represent the measure of the smallest angle of the triangle. Let $5x$ represent the measure of the middle angle and $7x$ represent the measure of the largest angle. The sum of these three angles equals $180°$. We can use this information to solve for the value of x:

$$3x + 5x + 7x = 180°$$
$$15x = 180°$$
$$x = 12°$$

Therefore, the measures of the three angles are $36°$, $60°$, and $84°$. The smallest angle is $84° - 36° = 48°$ smaller than the largest angle.

13. **D** Algebra: Functions *Medium*

The first poster costs $2.75 to print. This cost can be represented by 2.75. Each poster after the first costs $1.50 to print. This cost can be represented by $1.50(p - 1)$. The term $p - 1$ is necessary here because the first poster has been accounted for by the value 2.75.

Add these terms together to create the function representing the cost of printing p posters:

$$f(p) = 2.75 + 1.50(p - 1)$$

14. **E** Geometry: Angles and Lines *Medium*

In this figure, $\angle a$ is vertical to $\angle d$, as shown:

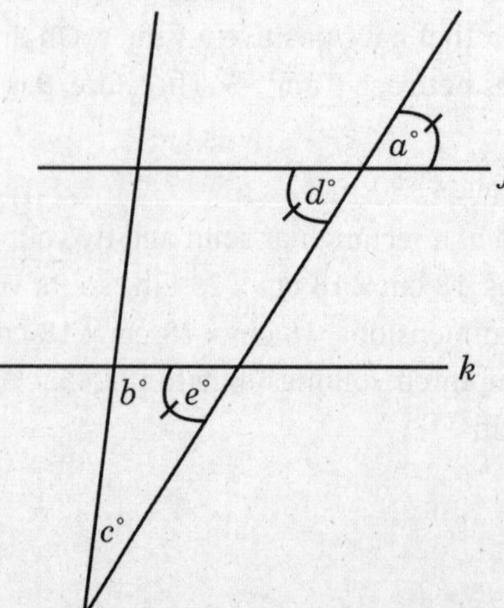

Vertical angles are congruent, so $\angle a \cong \angle d$. We know that $\angle d$ is congruent to $\angle e$, because these angles are corresponding angles in a figure where two parallel lines are crossed by a transversal. This means that $\angle a \cong \angle e$.

The sum of the measures of the interior angles of a triangle is $180°$. The three angles a, b, and c add up to 180 in degree measure. Therefore, the value of b is $180 - a - c$.

15. **C** Algebra: Solving Equations *Difficult*

First, simplify the equation. Start by factoring 2 out of the denominator of the left-hand expression:

$$\frac{2x(x+1)^{-1}}{2x-2} = \frac{6}{j}$$
$$\frac{2x(x+1)^{-1}}{2(x-1)} = \frac{6}{j}$$
$$\frac{x(x+1)^{-1}}{(x-1)} = \frac{6}{j}$$

Now, move $(x+1)^{-1}$ to the denominator of the left-hand fraction. This turns the exponent into a positive exponent. Then, combine the two binomials in the denominator:

$$\frac{x(x+1)^{-1}}{(x-1)} = \frac{6}{j}$$
$$\frac{x}{(x+1)(x-1)} = \frac{6}{j}$$
$$\frac{x}{x^2-1} = \frac{6}{j}$$

Cross-multiply and rewrite the equation in the general form $y = ax^2 + bx + c$:

$$\frac{x}{x^2-1} = \frac{6}{j}$$
$$jx = 6(x^2-1)$$
$$jx = 6x^2 - 6$$
$$0 = 6x^2 - jx - 6$$

Factor the expression $0 = 6x^2 - jx - 6$ to find possible values of x. To factor, look for pairs of numbers that multiply to produce 6. There are two possible pairs of numbers: 1 and 6 or 2 and 3. Start with the pairs 1 and 6. You'll see that the expression is indeed factorable using these two values:

$$0 = 6x^2 - jx - 6$$
$$0 = (6x+1)(x-6)$$
$$0 = (6x+1) \text{ or } 0 = (x-6)$$
$$x = -\frac{1}{6} \text{ or } x = 6$$

You've found two possible values for x. One of them, 6, is listed among the answer choices. **C** is correct.

16. **E** Algebra: Solving Equations *Difficult*

First, find the original amount that each family member agreed to pay if all family members contributed. The total cost of the rental hall is d dollars. This cost was to be split equally among f family members. If all family members contribute, each would originally need to pay $\frac{d}{f}$ dollars.

Next, find the new amount that each family member now needs to pay since some family members are not contributing. The cost of the rental hall is still d dollars. Now, however, this cost is being split among $f - n$ family members, with n representing the number of family members who do not contribute. The new amount that each family member must now pay is $\frac{d}{f-n}$ dollars.

Because there are fewer people splitting the new amount, the new amount will be larger than the original amount. The question asks for how much *more* each family member will have to pay. Subtract the original amount from the new amount:

$$\begin{aligned}\text{additional amount} &= (\text{new amount}) - (\text{original amount})\\ &= \left(\frac{d}{f-n}\right) - \left(\frac{d}{f}\right)\end{aligned}$$

Convert the fractions so that both have the same denominator:

$$\begin{aligned}\left(\frac{d}{f-n}\right) - \left(\frac{d}{f}\right) &= \left(\frac{f}{f} \times \frac{d}{f-n}\right) - \left(\frac{f-n}{f-n} \times \frac{d}{f}\right)\\ &= \left(\frac{fd}{f(f-n)}\right) - \left(\frac{d(f-n)}{f(f-n)}\right)\\ &= \frac{fd - d(f-n)}{f(f-n)}\\ &= \frac{fd - fd + nd}{f(f-n)}\\ &= \frac{nd}{f(f-n)}\end{aligned}$$

SECTION 9: WRITING

Improving Sentences

1. **B** Wordiness *Easy*

The phrasing of the underlined portion is wordy and awkward. **B** corrects this phrasing in the most concise manner, while still maintaining the meaning of the sentence.

2. **A** No Error *Easy*

The sentence is correct as written. The subject *publicizing* is singular, so it should be followed by the singular noun, *is*.

3. **B** Run-Ons *Easy*

This sentence incorrectly combines two complete sentences with only a comma. One way to correctly join two complete sentences is by using a comma *and* a coordinating conjunction, such as "and" or "but." **B** does just this.

4. **A** No Error *Easy*

This sentence works fine as is. The other revisions are either wordy or awkward, so **A** is correct.

5. **E** Wordiness *Easy*

E provides the most concise revision of this sentence. It sounds clumsy to say that teachers develop knowledge of subjects *because of having taught those subjects to others*. The revision, *by teaching those subjects*, works best.

6. **E** Misplaced Modifiers *Medium*

The original sentence makes it sound as if *the focus for Leslie* was frustrated by having *added too much oil to the batter*. In fact, Leslie herself was frustrated by this mistake. Modifying phrases should be followed directly by the nouns that they modify. **E** upholds this rule by placing the "Leslie" directly after the introductory modifying phrase.

7. **D** Subject-Verb Agreement *Easy*

The subject of this sentence is the singular noun *one of the festival's exhibitors*. It should therefore be followed by the singular verb *was*.

8. **A** No Error *Easy*

The action of this sentence takes place in the past tense, so the verb *became* is correct here.

9. **C** Misplaced Modifiers *Easy*

The subject of a modifying phrase should be the same as the subject of the main part of a sentence. In this case, *the editors* is the subject of the main part of the sentence: the editors *were careful to preserve the basic arguments of the text*. Therefore, *the editors* should also be the subject of the modifying introductory phrase. **C** provides such a revision.

10. **A** No Error *Easy*

This sentence joins two complete sentences with a semicolon. The use of the semicolon is correct here; the sentence therefore works well as written.

11. **E** Idioms *Medium*

The phrase *Insofar as* is clumsy and unnecessary here. The simple revision provided in **E** works best.

12. **D** Wordiness *Medium*

The word *equally* is redundant in this sentence. **D** eliminates this redundancy by deleting the unnecessary word, so **D** is correct.

13. **E** Parallelism *Medium*

To maintain its parallel structure, this sentence must use consistent verb forms. The first part of the sentence states that *Laura refused to accept*. The verb *to accept* is in its infinitive form, so the second verb describing her action must also be in its infinitive form: "she refused *to accept* or *to take credit*."

In addition, Laura implemented strategies before she refused to accept recognition or to take credit for her efforts. The verb *had implemented* shows that this action takes place before the other past tense action in the sentence.

14. **A** No Error *Difficult*

This sentence has a plural subject: *the efficiency and global utilization of computer technology*. In their shortest forms, the subjects are *efficiency* and *global utilization*. Both of these characteristics of computer technology explain why the technology is indispensable. The characteristics are plural, so they require the plural verb *explain*. **A** is correct.

SAT PRACTICE TEST 5

SAT* Reasoning Test—General Directions

Timing

- You will have 3 hours and 20 minutes to work on this test. (On the actual SAT, you would have 3 hours and 45 minutes to complete ten sections, one of which would be unscored and experimental.)
- There are nine separately timed sections:
  - ➤ One 25-minute essay
  - ➤ Five other 25-minute sections
  - ➤ Two 20-minute sections
  - ➤ One 10-minute section
- You may work on only one section at a time.
- The supervisor will tell you when to begin and end each section.
- If you finish a section before time is called, check your work on that section. You may NOT turn to any other section.
- Work as rapidly as you can without losing accuracy. Don't waste time on questions that seem too difficult for you.

Marking Answers

- Carefully mark only one answer for each question.
- Make sure each mark is dark and completely fills the circle.
- Do not make any stray marks on your answer sheet.
- If you erase, do so completely. Incomplete erasures may be scored as intended answers.
- Use only the answer spaces that correspond to the question numbers.
- Use the test book for scratchwork, but you will not receive credit for anything written there.
- After time has been called, you may not transfer answers to your answer sheet or fill in circles.
- You may not fold or remove pages or portions of a page from this book, or take the book or answer sheet from the testing room.

Scoring

- For each correct answer to a question, you receive one point.
- For questions you omit, you receive no points.
- For a wrong answer to a multiple-choice question, you lose one-fourth of a point.
  - ➤ If you can eliminate one or more of the answer choices as wrong, you increase your chances of choosing the correct answer and earning one point.
  - ➤ If you can't eliminate any choice, move on. You can return to the question later if there is time.
- For a wrong answer to a "grid-in" math question, you don't lose any points.
- The essay is scored on a 1 to 6 scale by two different readers. The total essay score is the sum of the two readers' scores.
- An off-topic or blank essay will receive a score of zero.

---

* SAT test directions selected from the SAT Reasoning Test. Reprinted by permission of the College Board, the copyright owner.

SAT PRACTICE TEST 5 ANSWER SHEET

SECTION 2

1. Ⓐ Ⓑ Ⓒ Ⓓ Ⓔ	7. Ⓐ Ⓑ Ⓒ Ⓓ Ⓔ	13. Ⓐ Ⓑ Ⓒ Ⓓ Ⓔ	19. Ⓐ Ⓑ Ⓒ Ⓓ Ⓔ
2. Ⓐ Ⓑ Ⓒ Ⓓ Ⓔ	8. Ⓐ Ⓑ Ⓒ Ⓓ Ⓔ	14. Ⓐ Ⓑ Ⓒ Ⓓ Ⓔ	20. Ⓐ Ⓑ Ⓒ Ⓓ Ⓔ
3. Ⓐ Ⓑ Ⓒ Ⓓ Ⓔ	9. Ⓐ Ⓑ Ⓒ Ⓓ Ⓔ	15. Ⓐ Ⓑ Ⓒ Ⓓ Ⓔ	21. Ⓐ Ⓑ Ⓒ Ⓓ Ⓔ
4. Ⓐ Ⓑ Ⓒ Ⓓ Ⓔ	10. Ⓐ Ⓑ Ⓒ Ⓓ Ⓔ	16. Ⓐ Ⓑ Ⓒ Ⓓ Ⓔ	22. Ⓐ Ⓑ Ⓒ Ⓓ Ⓔ
5. Ⓐ Ⓑ Ⓒ Ⓓ Ⓔ	11. Ⓐ Ⓑ Ⓒ Ⓓ Ⓔ	17. Ⓐ Ⓑ Ⓒ Ⓓ Ⓔ	23. Ⓐ Ⓑ Ⓒ Ⓓ Ⓔ
6. Ⓐ Ⓑ Ⓒ Ⓓ Ⓔ	12. Ⓐ Ⓑ Ⓒ Ⓓ Ⓔ	18. Ⓐ Ⓑ Ⓒ Ⓓ Ⓔ	24. Ⓐ Ⓑ Ⓒ Ⓓ Ⓔ

SECTION 3

1. Ⓐ Ⓑ Ⓒ Ⓓ Ⓔ	6. Ⓐ Ⓑ Ⓒ Ⓓ Ⓔ	11. Ⓐ Ⓑ Ⓒ Ⓓ Ⓔ	16. Ⓐ Ⓑ Ⓒ Ⓓ Ⓔ
2. Ⓐ Ⓑ Ⓒ Ⓓ Ⓔ	7. Ⓐ Ⓑ Ⓒ Ⓓ Ⓔ	12. Ⓐ Ⓑ Ⓒ Ⓓ Ⓔ	17. Ⓐ Ⓑ Ⓒ Ⓓ Ⓔ
3. Ⓐ Ⓑ Ⓒ Ⓓ Ⓔ	8. Ⓐ Ⓑ Ⓒ Ⓓ Ⓔ	13. Ⓐ Ⓑ Ⓒ Ⓓ Ⓔ	18. Ⓐ Ⓑ Ⓒ Ⓓ Ⓔ
4. Ⓐ Ⓑ Ⓒ Ⓓ Ⓔ	9. Ⓐ Ⓑ Ⓒ Ⓓ Ⓔ	14. Ⓐ Ⓑ Ⓒ Ⓓ Ⓔ	19. Ⓐ Ⓑ Ⓒ Ⓓ Ⓔ
5. Ⓐ Ⓑ Ⓒ Ⓓ Ⓔ	10. Ⓐ Ⓑ Ⓒ Ⓓ Ⓔ	15. Ⓐ Ⓑ Ⓒ Ⓓ Ⓔ	20. Ⓐ Ⓑ Ⓒ Ⓓ Ⓔ

SECTION 4

1. Ⓐ Ⓑ Ⓒ Ⓓ Ⓔ	7. Ⓐ Ⓑ Ⓒ Ⓓ Ⓔ	13. Ⓐ Ⓑ Ⓒ Ⓓ Ⓔ	19. Ⓐ Ⓑ Ⓒ Ⓓ Ⓔ
2. Ⓐ Ⓑ Ⓒ Ⓓ Ⓔ	8. Ⓐ Ⓑ Ⓒ Ⓓ Ⓔ	14. Ⓐ Ⓑ Ⓒ Ⓓ Ⓔ	20. Ⓐ Ⓑ Ⓒ Ⓓ Ⓔ
3. Ⓐ Ⓑ Ⓒ Ⓓ Ⓔ	9. Ⓐ Ⓑ Ⓒ Ⓓ Ⓔ	15. Ⓐ Ⓑ Ⓒ Ⓓ Ⓔ	21. Ⓐ Ⓑ Ⓒ Ⓓ Ⓔ
4. Ⓐ Ⓑ Ⓒ Ⓓ Ⓔ	10. Ⓐ Ⓑ Ⓒ Ⓓ Ⓔ	16. Ⓐ Ⓑ Ⓒ Ⓓ Ⓔ	22. Ⓐ Ⓑ Ⓒ Ⓓ Ⓔ
5. Ⓐ Ⓑ Ⓒ Ⓓ Ⓔ	11. Ⓐ Ⓑ Ⓒ Ⓓ Ⓔ	17. Ⓐ Ⓑ Ⓒ Ⓓ Ⓔ	23. Ⓐ Ⓑ Ⓒ Ⓓ Ⓔ
6. Ⓐ Ⓑ Ⓒ Ⓓ Ⓔ	12. Ⓐ Ⓑ Ⓒ Ⓓ Ⓔ	18. Ⓐ Ⓑ Ⓒ Ⓓ Ⓔ	24. Ⓐ Ⓑ Ⓒ Ⓓ Ⓔ

SECTION 5

1. Ⓐ Ⓑ Ⓒ Ⓓ Ⓔ	3. Ⓐ Ⓑ Ⓒ Ⓓ Ⓔ	5. Ⓐ Ⓑ Ⓒ Ⓓ Ⓔ	7. Ⓐ Ⓑ Ⓒ Ⓓ Ⓔ
2. Ⓐ Ⓑ Ⓒ Ⓓ Ⓔ	4. Ⓐ Ⓑ Ⓒ Ⓓ Ⓔ	6. Ⓐ Ⓑ Ⓒ Ⓓ Ⓔ	8. Ⓐ Ⓑ Ⓒ Ⓓ Ⓔ

9	10	11	12	13
⊘ . 0 1 2 3 4 5 6 7 8 9	⊘ . 0 1 2 3 4 5 6 7 8 9	⊘ . 0 1 2 3 4 5 6 7 8 9	⊘ . 0 1 2 3 4 5 6 7 8 9	⊘ . 0 1 2 3 4 5 6 7 8 9

14	15	16	17	18
⊘ . 0 1 2 3 4 5 6 7 8 9	⊘ . 0 1 2 3 4 5 6 7 8 9	⊘ . 0 1 2 3 4 5 6 7 8 9	⊘ . 0 1 2 3 4 5 6 7 8 9	⊘ . 0 1 2 3 4 5 6 7 8 9

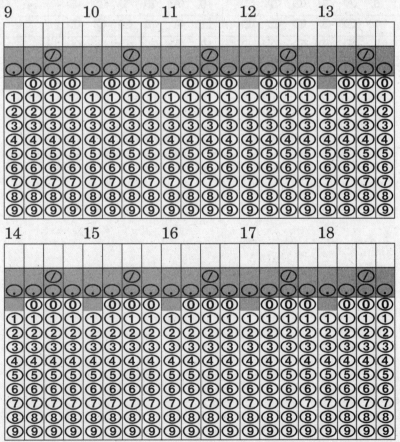

SAT PRACTICE TEST 5 ANSWER SHEET

SECTION 6			
1. Ⓐ Ⓑ Ⓒ Ⓓ Ⓔ	10. Ⓐ Ⓑ Ⓒ Ⓓ Ⓔ	19. Ⓐ Ⓑ Ⓒ Ⓓ Ⓔ	28. Ⓐ Ⓑ Ⓒ Ⓓ Ⓔ
2. Ⓐ Ⓑ Ⓒ Ⓓ Ⓔ	11. Ⓐ Ⓑ Ⓒ Ⓓ Ⓔ	20. Ⓐ Ⓑ Ⓒ Ⓓ Ⓔ	29. Ⓐ Ⓑ Ⓒ Ⓓ Ⓔ
3. Ⓐ Ⓑ Ⓒ Ⓓ Ⓔ	12. Ⓐ Ⓑ Ⓒ Ⓓ Ⓔ	21. Ⓐ Ⓑ Ⓒ Ⓓ Ⓔ	30. Ⓐ Ⓑ Ⓒ Ⓓ Ⓔ
4. Ⓐ Ⓑ Ⓒ Ⓓ Ⓔ	13. Ⓐ Ⓑ Ⓒ Ⓓ Ⓔ	22. Ⓐ Ⓑ Ⓒ Ⓓ Ⓔ	31. Ⓐ Ⓑ Ⓒ Ⓓ Ⓔ
5. Ⓐ Ⓑ Ⓒ Ⓓ Ⓔ	14. Ⓐ Ⓑ Ⓒ Ⓓ Ⓔ	23. Ⓐ Ⓑ Ⓒ Ⓓ Ⓔ	32. Ⓐ Ⓑ Ⓒ Ⓓ Ⓔ
6. Ⓐ Ⓑ Ⓒ Ⓓ Ⓔ	15. Ⓐ Ⓑ Ⓒ Ⓓ Ⓔ	24. Ⓐ Ⓑ Ⓒ Ⓓ Ⓔ	33. Ⓐ Ⓑ Ⓒ Ⓓ Ⓔ
7. Ⓐ Ⓑ Ⓒ Ⓓ Ⓔ	16. Ⓐ Ⓑ Ⓒ Ⓓ Ⓔ	25. Ⓐ Ⓑ Ⓒ Ⓓ Ⓔ	34. Ⓐ Ⓑ Ⓒ Ⓓ Ⓔ
8. Ⓐ Ⓑ Ⓒ Ⓓ Ⓔ	17. Ⓐ Ⓑ Ⓒ Ⓓ Ⓔ	26. Ⓐ Ⓑ Ⓒ Ⓓ Ⓔ	35. Ⓐ Ⓑ Ⓒ Ⓓ Ⓔ
9. Ⓐ Ⓑ Ⓒ Ⓓ Ⓔ	18. Ⓐ Ⓑ Ⓒ Ⓓ Ⓔ	27. Ⓐ Ⓑ Ⓒ Ⓓ Ⓔ	

SECTION 7			
1. Ⓐ Ⓑ Ⓒ Ⓓ Ⓔ	6. Ⓐ Ⓑ Ⓒ Ⓓ Ⓔ	11. Ⓐ Ⓑ Ⓒ Ⓓ Ⓔ	16. Ⓐ Ⓑ Ⓒ Ⓓ Ⓔ
2. Ⓐ Ⓑ Ⓒ Ⓓ Ⓔ	7. Ⓐ Ⓑ Ⓒ Ⓓ Ⓔ	12. Ⓐ Ⓑ Ⓒ Ⓓ Ⓔ	17. Ⓐ Ⓑ Ⓒ Ⓓ Ⓔ
3. Ⓐ Ⓑ Ⓒ Ⓓ Ⓔ	8. Ⓐ Ⓑ Ⓒ Ⓓ Ⓔ	13. Ⓐ Ⓑ Ⓒ Ⓓ Ⓔ	18. Ⓐ Ⓑ Ⓒ Ⓓ Ⓔ
4. Ⓐ Ⓑ Ⓒ Ⓓ Ⓔ	9. Ⓐ Ⓑ Ⓒ Ⓓ Ⓔ	14. Ⓐ Ⓑ Ⓒ Ⓓ Ⓔ	19. Ⓐ Ⓑ Ⓒ Ⓓ Ⓔ
5. Ⓐ Ⓑ Ⓒ Ⓓ Ⓔ	10. Ⓐ Ⓑ Ⓒ Ⓓ Ⓔ	15. Ⓐ Ⓑ Ⓒ Ⓓ Ⓔ	

SECTION 8			
1. Ⓐ Ⓑ Ⓒ Ⓓ Ⓔ	5. Ⓐ Ⓑ Ⓒ Ⓓ Ⓔ	9. Ⓐ Ⓑ Ⓒ Ⓓ Ⓔ	13. Ⓐ Ⓑ Ⓒ Ⓓ Ⓔ
2. Ⓐ Ⓑ Ⓒ Ⓓ Ⓔ	6. Ⓐ Ⓑ Ⓒ Ⓓ Ⓔ	10. Ⓐ Ⓑ Ⓒ Ⓓ Ⓔ	14. Ⓐ Ⓑ Ⓒ Ⓓ Ⓔ
3. Ⓐ Ⓑ Ⓒ Ⓓ Ⓔ	7. Ⓐ Ⓑ Ⓒ Ⓓ Ⓔ	11. Ⓐ Ⓑ Ⓒ Ⓓ Ⓔ	15. Ⓐ Ⓑ Ⓒ Ⓓ Ⓔ
4. Ⓐ Ⓑ Ⓒ Ⓓ Ⓔ	8. Ⓐ Ⓑ Ⓒ Ⓓ Ⓔ	12. Ⓐ Ⓑ Ⓒ Ⓓ Ⓔ	16. Ⓐ Ⓑ Ⓒ Ⓓ Ⓔ

SECTION 9			
1. Ⓐ Ⓑ Ⓒ Ⓓ Ⓔ	5. Ⓐ Ⓑ Ⓒ Ⓓ Ⓔ	9. Ⓐ Ⓑ Ⓒ Ⓓ Ⓔ	13. Ⓐ Ⓑ Ⓒ Ⓓ Ⓔ
2. Ⓐ Ⓑ Ⓒ Ⓓ Ⓔ	6. Ⓐ Ⓑ Ⓒ Ⓓ Ⓔ	10. Ⓐ Ⓑ Ⓒ Ⓓ Ⓔ	14. Ⓐ Ⓑ Ⓒ Ⓓ Ⓔ
3. Ⓐ Ⓑ Ⓒ Ⓓ Ⓔ	7. Ⓐ Ⓑ Ⓒ Ⓓ Ⓔ	11. Ⓐ Ⓑ Ⓒ Ⓓ Ⓔ	
4. Ⓐ Ⓑ Ⓒ Ⓓ Ⓔ	8. Ⓐ Ⓑ Ⓒ Ⓓ Ⓔ	12. Ⓐ Ⓑ Ⓒ Ⓓ Ⓔ	

SECTION 1

ESSAY

Time—25 minutes

The essay gives you an opportunity to show how effectively you can develop and express ideas. You should, therefore, take care to develop your point of view, present your ideas logically and clearly, and use language precisely.

Your essay must be written on the lines provided on your answer sheet—you will receive no other paper on which to write. You will have enough space if you write on every line, avoid wide margins, and keep your handwriting to a reasonable size. Remember that people who are not familiar with your handwriting will read what you write. Try to write or print so that what you are writing is legible to those readers.

You have twenty-five minutes to write an essay on the topic assigned below. DO NOT WRITE ON ANOTHER TOPIC. AN OFF-TOPIC ESSAY WILL RECEIVE A SCORE OF ZERO.

Think carefully about the issue presented in the following excerpt and the assignment below.

> The ends always justify the means.

Assignment: Does the outcome of a process always justify the method by which it was attained? Is there ever a situation in which the way a result was achieved cannot be justified despite a positive outcome? Explain your position using personal experience and current events.

DO NOT WRITE YOUR ESSAY IN YOUR TEST BOOK. You will receive credit only for what you write on your answer sheet.

BEGIN WRITING YOUR ESSAY ON THE ANSWER SHEET.

IF YOU FINISH BEFORE TIME IS CALLED, YOU MAY CHECK YOUR WORK ON THIS SECTION ONLY. DO NOT TURN TO ANY OTHER SECTION IN THE TEST.

SECTION 1—ESSAY

Time—25 minutes

SECTION 1—ESSAY

Time—25 minutes

SECTION 2

Turn to Section 2 of your answer sheet to answer the questions in this section.

Time—25 Minutes
24 Questions

Directions: For each question in this section, select the best answer from among the choices given and fill in the corresponding oval on the answer sheet.

Each sentence below has one or two blanks, each blank indicating that something has been omitted. Beneath the sentence are five words or sets of words labeled A through E. Choose the word or set of words that, when inserted in the sentence, best fits the meaning of the sentence as a whole.

Example:

Eliza felt ----- when her boss asked her to work seven weekends in a row but ----- when her work earned her a promotion.

(A) enervated . . weakened
(B) depressed . . intellectual
(C) advantageous . . salacious
(D) angry . . shopworn
(E) irate . . elated   

1. The elite marathoner astounded his critics and peers alike by ----- the long-held record of 250 miles when he ran 272 continuous miles.

(A) assuming
(B) infiltrating
(C) truncating
(D) surpassing
(E) maneuvering

2. Critics and essayists praised the new car for its -----. The vehicle represented the first practical design in a long line of cars that had previously failed to impress.

(A) expedience
(B) gestation
(C) blandishment
(D) judgment
(E) reticence

3. The new video game featured a creative premise in which a small figure uses a sticky ball to roll up objects in the home, thus creating a(n) ----- ball composed of hundreds of increasingly larger ----- objects.

(A) enormous . . celestial
(B) gargantuan . . mundane
(C) diminutive . . homely
(D) sizeable . . awkward
(E) meager . . sinister

4. Doctors once held a(n) ----- view of the ancient practice of shamanism in which spiritual figures were said to commune with the gods, but now a more ----- understanding of this, the oldest of religious traditions, has shed new light on the mind's ability to help the body heal.

(A) uncertain . . literal
(B) jaundiced . . prejudicial
(C) skeptical . . metaphoric
(D) mordant . . plebian
(E) tenuous . . admiring

5. Although the journal once had a reputation for quality and for discovering young new writers, over time it was tacitly agreed that the magazine had become a(n) ----- specimen of a former age and that its tastes had become -----.

(A) insulated . . ossified
(B) calculated . . serene
(C) open . . strict
(D) contained . . ruinous
(E) self-referential . . libertine

GO ON TO THE NEXT PAGE

SECTION 2

Directions: The passages below are followed by questions based on their content; questions following a pair of related passages may also be based on the relationship between the paired passages. Answer the questions on the basis of what is stated or implied in the passages and in any introductory material that may be provided.

Questions 6–9 are based on the following passages.

Passage 1

Of the many intellectual traditions to which we owe the ancient Greeks a debt of thanks is that of scientific inquiry. In the fifth century B.C., Leucippus of Miletus and his student Democritus of Abdera argued the case for fundamental entities, which, combined together, formed all the matter—indeed all the substances—of the world. The very word *atom* is derived from Greek and means "can't be divided." When we consider how our lives today are ruled by a mastering of the elemental nature of matter and energy, we can thank the Greeks for taking the leap of faith to even imagine such a fundamental world in the first place. For it is only by initially taking such leaps that dreams are able to make the transition from abstract idea to testable theory.

Passage 2

When we take the time to strive to understand the scientific discoveries of the last few centuries and to place them in context, we remember not to ascribe too metaphoric an understanding of the world, for in doing so, we cheapen our past accomplishments and all that we have come to know as true. I do not, for example, accept that notion that the Greeks first proposed atomic theory. To begin with, the two men whose arguments for such elemental substances are recorded in history were not taken seriously by their contemporaries. Further, their proposition did not stem from keen observation or from experiments that in any way demonstrated a deep understanding of the world beyond an intuitive hunch. The real discovery of the atomic world arose at the end of the eighteenth century, when chemists engaged in a series of experiments that tested and defined the nature of chemical substances. Here, then, are the origins of true science, of the deliberate and careful examination of the world as it is, and not a theory perpetuated from a mere "hunch."

6. Compared to the author of Passage 2, the author of Passage 1 regards the ancient Greeks with more

(A) respect
(B) certainty
(C) bemusement
(D) condescension
(E) irony

7. Unlike the author of Passage 1, the author of Passage 2 feels that the Greeks

(A) only deserve partial credit for uncovering the existence of the atom
(B) inefficiently carried out their scientific experiments
(C) did not really discover the atom
(D) were a people of great imagination
(E) struggled to take leaps of faith

8. Both authors agree about which of the following?

(A) Chemists were far more important in proposing the idea of atoms than the Greeks.
(B) The importance of experiments and testing in science was not to be underestimated.
(C) Knowledge of things on a scientific level dulls our imagination.
(D) Imagination and rigorous scientific thinking go hand in hand.
(E) The Greeks would have found proof of atoms if they had had high-tech scientific tools at their disposal.

9. The author of Passage 1 would most likely respond to lines 27–29 ("Here then . . . 'hunch'") in Passage 2 by pointing out that

(A) the historical record clearly shows that two Greek men thought up the idea of an atom
(B) the Greek origin of the word "atom" is proof enough that the Greeks invented the concept
(C) intuition alone does not offer proof of having discovered a concept
(D) it is the work of imagination to take a leap of faith to even come up with the notion of atoms, which can then be tested by the rigors of science
(E) if it weren't for the Greeks, eighteenth-century chemists would not have known to check for atoms in the first place

GO ON TO THE NEXT PAGE

SECTION 2

Directions: Each passage below is followed by questions based on its content. Answer the questions on the basis of what is stated or implied in each passage and in any introductory material that may be provided.

Questions 10–15 are based on the following passage.

The following is an excerpt of a novel written by a Latin American author describing his early life in northern California after he moved there from the Yucatan Peninsula of Mexico.

Every day we looked for wonder along the coast. Sometimes we found it in the stores our own people had created. On birthdays we bought piñatas and blindfolded ourselves to try to reach the invisible pocket of sweets buried deep beneath the papier-mâché *burro*, an animal not of this landscape, but of the one we left home. Our mother's cooking continued to enchant us, the spices welling up from the kitchen and reaching into our stomachs, sending us indoors and clambering for the magical ritual of *desayunas* or *sopas*. There, in the safety of our families, we could exchange sly jokes no *gringo* could understand, our minds lithe, witty, and observant.

There was wonder elsewhere too, and there were times when we considered that perhaps we were not so much the strangers whose job, with every passing year, it was to grow increasingly accustomed to this land of optimism and opportunity, which at times could strike us as effrontery. Perhaps instead it was our attunement to wonder in the first place which allowed us to see this ancient land anew. Perhaps, even, we were able to see this world as it was intended, if there can be one true way in which to observe the land. In the mornings we could sit on the sand cliffs near the highway, where the land was mostly made up of sand and therefore not appropriate for the elaborate, castlelike houses built further down the peninsula where the property was anchored with rich soil. Here we could watch the fog roll in and out and wonder at the celestial hand guiding this blanket across the bed of water.

Some of us learned to immerse our bodies in this water, and we wore the rubber contraptions and oxygen tanks generally rented to tourists, which in a manner of speaking, we were too. Some of our fathers had grown up on the Yucatan Peninsula and had made it a sport to descend down into the underground rivers that dotted our landscape. The ancient Maya believed that there were five levels to the earth and that the cisterns our fathers explored were in fact an actual hell, populated with ghosts and the carcasses of the dead. We did not believe in the literal presence of demons even as we sensed their inspiring or frightening presence from the stories our fathers told us about descending down wooden ladders into these pools to see the fish and roots and minerals dotting these little underwater caves. When we dipped our rubber-coated feet into the cold Pacific, we did not see the same silver fish that enchanted our fathers. For a time we saw nothing, and then, with the aid of the sun, we saw crabs, salmon, perch. These shapes flashed orange and red on hot days, then grew muted, a shade of gray against a backdrop of the deepest bluish-black. We loved the sea, but we feared it, for it is even larger than this endless land and culture.

We preferred the intimate scenes we saw in our work. We marveled at the ability of the artichoke to rejuvenate. We took a moment of pleasure in seeing the yellow mustard plants dot the highway when we traveled to work in our buses. We knew, even on days when our minds had gone numb and our imaginations no longer wandered our landscape with sentimental and romantic observations, that we were helping to keep the earth close to her intentions. It was our ability to wonder at what seemed miraculous, while the other world sped around us, that kept us attuned to work, and, despite its mundane nature, kept us proud of what we could accomplish.

10. The author opens the passage by appealing to

(A) the senses of sight and smell
(B) a sense of fairness
(C) an emotional plea
(D) an inner turmoil
(E) an idealistic hope

11. The word "wonder" (line 17) as used by the author refers to

(A) the shock of traveling home after a long time away
(B) the confusion that comes from not understanding a language
(C) the process of going from child to adult
(D) the ability to see an established landscape with unjaded eyes
(E) the changing seasons

12. In lines 20–24 ("In the . . . soil"), it is implied that the narrator and his companions sit on a piece of land that is

(A) still but exciting
(B) poor but picturesque
(C) quiet and maudlin
(D) dull and weathered
(E) wealthy but inspired

GO ON TO THE NEXT PAGE

SECTION 2

13. The author mentions the "five levels of earth" (lines 32–33) in order to

(A) explain why he will not set foot inside the Pacific Ocean
(B) contrast the benign quality of his homeland with the ocean where he lives now
(C) ridicule those who believe in superstition
(D) highlight the danger and fear that the narrator feels when he steps into the ocean
(E) draw a distinction between the wealthy and the poor

14. The author implies that he and his companions are most comfortable

(A) at the beach
(B) in other countries
(C) at school
(D) on land
(E) in the water

15. The tone at the end of the passage is

(A) regret and nostalgia
(B) resignation and optimism
(C) confusion and dread
(D) sadness and longing
(E) conceit and dismissal

GO ON TO THE NEXT PAGE

SECTION 2

Questions 16–24 are based on the following passage.

This passage is taken from a memoir written by a renowned modern dancer and choreographer.

I may be a dancer, but I do not presume to understand what dance actually is—that is, I cannot necessarily define its purpose, the reason for its continued existence. I could assume that because I am a dancer—that because I have some natural affinity for the art form—it is all the more difficult for me to analyze the exact components that have brought dance into human culture. When I was younger, I might just have accepted dance without question, but, as I grow older, I cannot help but wonder as to its overall point or purpose for modern humans. I cannot help but notice how, in societies that grow increasingly complex as ours has with whole canyons of architecture and elaborate virtual aqueducts through which money and information flow, so too has dance become a complex, profound mirror into which we can dance and see ourselves. I can only assume that dance has a purpose, inasmuch as eating and sleeping serve a function in human life, and that this purpose is to show us something of where we are in the world.

At one point I would have voiced the opinion that dance was primarily a visceral form of communication. It does not include language, and in fact the use of speech in the middle of a classical piece does not clarify the action taking place on stage but rather interrupts and confuses it. Dancers do not talk with their voices, nor do we expect them to. And yet, time and again, an audience will leave a performance feeling moved by something they have seen. There is some sort of emotion or idea being communicated in the movement on stage. As an audience member myself—for, like all good dancers, I do go to see dance as well as perform it—I can sense the effect that a performance has had. Sometimes I am left with a particular mood. Modern dance is especially good at conveying what is often called the human "condition." Some pieces simply seem to illustrate a feeling of loneliness or of deep personal struggle and persecution. In our darkest hours as humans, certainly these feelings descend upon our bodies so that we feel them physically. Who has not actually felt ill with grief? So it is no wonder that dance, that physical art form, would seek to express those emotions that are experienced internally.

But to say that dance is merely visceral, that it is experienced by the senses alone, is to discount the role that intellect might play in the construction of dance. I would argue now that dancers, like our very best actors, are not simply intuitive mimics. Dancers, like all artists, are observers. We watch for movement. Instinctively, of course, all humans do this: a thief is described as moving "furtively," and a young girl in love looks "dreamy." Dancers seek information beyond these rudimentary observations. We look to see how the way a head is tilted or arms are crossed might represent power, or dismissal. We seek to read the character in a person's gestures. A face is less important to us than it is to an actor, though we certainly like faces that convey information. But we look for the expressive power of movement and we expand it on stage. When we see someone come into our classroom, someone who is not necessarily a professional dancer, we look for signs of their profession—lawyer, accountant, or clerk. We can see who thinks too hard, who primarily uses a cerebral faculty and is thus not able to fully submit to music. We see who unthinkingly can surrender to rhythm. We see all these things, and the best of us can, on occasion, even articulate what we see.

Then there is the dance piece itself. Classical dance was very good at conveying the themes of the romantic era. We see little lithe ballerinas lifted into the air by muscular and therefore heroic men. Few of these romantic dramas focus on the psychological development of a character in adulthood—most choose to focus on the moment in which a man and a woman fall in love. It is no wonder, then, that dancers are slim and adolescent in shape, that they must have moments of great control, followed by a coltish skittishness. No wonder too that women strove to dance not just on heels, but on their toes. What great irony it is that this dancing "on pointe" requires such strength and balance and yet is meant to convey a certain lightness of being, a floating spirit.

Modern dance, by contrast, reflects our caution and even at times our discomfort with living in the world we have created. It brings in an observation of our mechanized environment, as demonstrated through the "locking" and "breaking" moves of hip-hop, which mirror the many machines that surround us and which we often take for granted. We like to show how broad and international this world has become, our steps bold in shape and influenced by the native styles of Africa and India. We like to show our internal neuroses through powerful, convoluted moves. In other words, dance is far more than a visceral form of communication: it says something very real and quantifiable. Dance is a mirror, and when we examine it, we are all able to see ourselves more clearly.

16. The first three sentences (lines 1–9) are characterized respectively by

(A) a query, a solution, and disavowal
(B) a challenge, a theory, and resolution
(C) a change of mind, confusion, and rhetorical question
(D) a theory, a contrary opinion, and disappointment
(E) a declaration, a possible explanation, and a statement of curiosity

GO ON TO THE NEXT PAGE

SECTION 2

17. In lines 11–12, the statement "whole canyons of architecture and elaborate virtual aqueducts through which money and information flow" emphasize the author's opinion that
   (A) the confusing nature of the modern world may explain why the author has difficulty understanding dance
   (B) modern dance is technically demanding and difficult for the average person
   (C) there are few narrative works of modern dance because people are less interested in the idea of "story"
   (D) the modern world is increasingly complex in the same way that dance is more and more elaborate
   (E) dance is the most refined of all arts, requiring a focus from the audience not necessary when appreciating other art forms

18. By asking, "Who has not actually felt ill with grief?" (line 34), the author means that
   (A) excessive dancing can make us feel physically sick
   (B) our emotions affect our physical bodies in addition to our mental state
   (C) most modern dance is about negative emotions
   (D) the romantics primarily saw dance as a life-affirming act
   (E) illness is part of the human condition

19. The author's point about dance as "visceral" (lines 37–39) is that
   (A) dance is primarily an instinctual art
   (B) dancers have difficulty analyzing and thinking about their performances
   (C) dance does not just come from or appeal to us on an instinctual level
   (D) dancers are essentially physical mimics
   (E) dance is full of many moments which are effective but difficult to explain

20. The author mentions "lithe ballerinas lifted into the air" (line 59) in order to convey
   (A) the strength required of male partners
   (B) a significant difference between classical dance and modern dance
   (C) one aspect of how classical dance represented the romantic period
   (D) the physical requirements of classical dancers
   (E) the visceral effect of classical dance on an audience

21. The author strongly implies that the romantic period is defined by
   (A) a desire to be ethereal and light
   (B) confusion over humanity's condition
   (C) the sense of being lost in a chasm
   (D) a longing to connect with other people
   (E) a questioning of the forces that have created the world

22. The word "mechanized" as used in line 72 most nearly means
   (A) automated
   (B) programmed
   (C) unusual
   (D) machinelike
   (E) stiff

23. The word "convoluted" as used in line 78 most nearly means
   (A) long-winded
   (B) confusing
   (C) unclear
   (D) hostile
   (E) tortuous

24. The use of the term "mirror" (line 81) at the end of the passage is an example of
   (A) irony
   (B) rhetoric
   (C) recapitulation
   (D) dissolution
   (E) sarcasm

S T O P

IF YOU FINISH BEFORE TIME IS CALLED, YOU MAY CHECK YOUR WORK ON THIS TEST ONLY. DO NOT TURN TO ANY OTHER SECTION IN THIS TEST.

SECTION 3

Turn to Section 3 of your answer sheet to answer the questions in this section.

Time—25 Minutes
20 Questions

Directions: For this section, solve each problem and decide which is the best of the choices given. Fill in the corresponding oval on the answer sheet. You may use any available space for scratchwork.

Notes:

1. The use of a calculator is permitted. All numbers used are real numbers.
2. Figures that accompany problems in this test are intended to provide information useful in solving the problems. They are drawn as accurately as possible EXCEPT when it is stated in a specific problem that the figure is not drawn to scale. All figures lie in a plane unless otherwise indicated.
3. Unless otherwise specified, the domain of any function f is assumed to be the set of all real numbers x for which $f(x)$ is a real number.

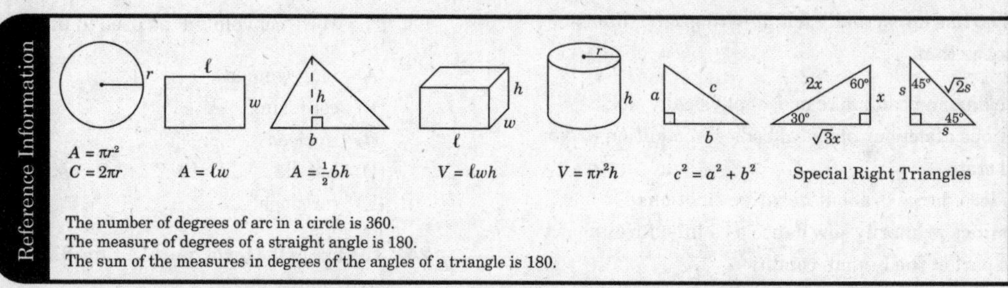
Reference Information
$A = \pi r^2$
$C = 2\pi r$
$A = \ell w$
$A = \frac{1}{2}bh$
$V = \ell wh$
$V = \pi r^2 h$
$c^2 = a^2 + b^2$
Special Right Triangles
The number of degrees of arc in a circle is 360.
The measure of degrees of a straight angle is 180.
The sum of the measures in degrees of the angles of a triangle is 180.

1. Larry went to the pet store to buy his cat some food. There were 5 "flats" of cat food. The chicken and liver flat contained 12 cans. The other 4 flats contained 10 cans each of duck pate. How many cans in all did he take home if he bought all 5 flats?

(A) 45
(B) 48
(C) 50
(D) 52
(E) 60

2. X, Y, and Z are points on a plane in that order. If YZ equals 10, and XY is one-fifth of YZ, what is the length of XZ ?

(A) 2
(B) 5
(C) 10
(D) 12
(E) 15

3. If $m + 4g = 8$, then $2m + 8g =$

(A) 16
(B) 8
(C) 4
(D) 2
(E) 1

GO ON TO THE NEXT PAGE

SECTION 3

Questions 4 and 5 refer to the diagram below.

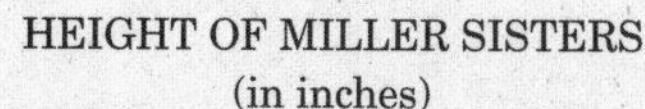

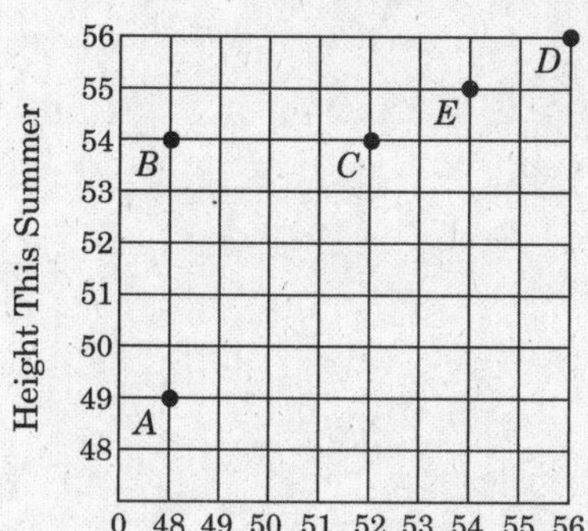

4. Above is a graph that represents the height of the five Miller sisters: Anna, Beth, Carla, Devina, and Ella. According to the graph, which sister showed the least growth between last summer and this summer?

(A) Anna
(B) Beth
(C) Carla
(D) Devina
(E) Ella

5. What is the average height of all the sisters last summer?

(A) 53
(B) 51.6
(C) 49.7
(D) 48
(E) 47.3

6. If a = –3 and b = 2, what is $\left|\frac{1}{b}+\frac{2}{a}\right|$?

(A) $-\frac{1}{6}$

(B) $-\frac{5}{6}$

(C) $\frac{1}{6}$

(D) $\frac{1}{2}$

(E) $\frac{1}{3}$

7. If $a = \frac{1}{4}$ and $b = \frac{1}{3}$, then what is the value of

$\left(\frac{1}{a}+\frac{1}{b}\right)\left(\frac{1}{a+b}\right)$?

(A) $\frac{1}{7}$

(B) $\frac{7}{12}$

(C) 4

(D) 7

(E) 12

GO ON TO THE NEXT PAGE

SECTION 3

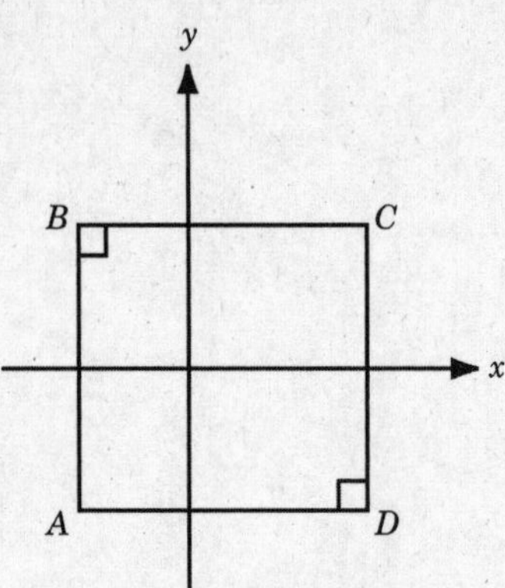

8. Figure $ABCD$ is a square with a perimeter of 20. If the x-coordinate of point A is -1, and the y-coordinate of point B is 2, then what are the coordinates of point C?

(A) (4, –2)
(B) (4, 2)
(C) (–1, 3)
(D) (3, –2)
(E) (2, 4)

x	$f(x)$
0	0
1	3
2	8
3	15
4	24

9. According to the figure above, which of the following defines f?

(A) $f(x) = x^2$
(B) $f(x) = x^2 + 2$
(C) $f(x) = x^3$
(D) $f(x) = x^2 + x$
(E) $f(x) = x^2 + 2x$

10. In j years, Jennie will be as old as her brother who is b years old. How old is Jennie now?

(A) b
(B) j
(C) $b - j$
(D) $j - b$
(E) $b + j$

B Y T E T

11. The letters above represent five blocks on Betty's shelf, currently arranged in the order above. She would like to rearrange the letters so they spell her name. The blocks are heavy, and she can only hold two at a time. Blocks can be moved only by switching two blocks. What is the least number of changes needed to spell her name correctly?

(A) 1
(B) 2
(C) 3
(D) 4
(E) 5

GO ON TO THE NEXT PAGE

SECTION 3

12. Greg is moving across country. He wants to pack his CDs into a large box with dimensions 26 centimeters by 30 centimeters by 64 centimeters. Each of his CDs measures 1 centimeter by 12 centimeters by 4 centimeters. How many CDs will fit in one large box?

(A) 19,920
(B) 1,040
(C) 520
(D) 210
(E) 48

13. If $0 < a < 1$, and $b = a^2$ and $c = \sqrt{a}$, then which of the following number lines could represent the correct ordering of points a, b, and c?

(A)
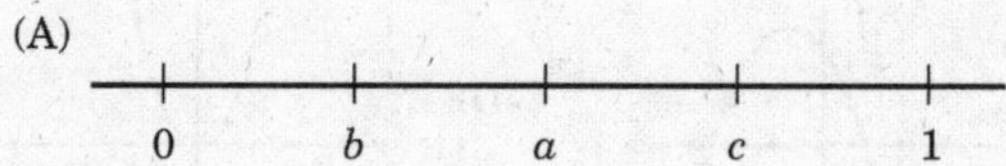

(B)
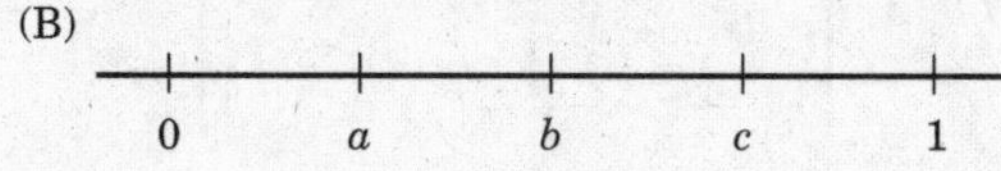

(C)
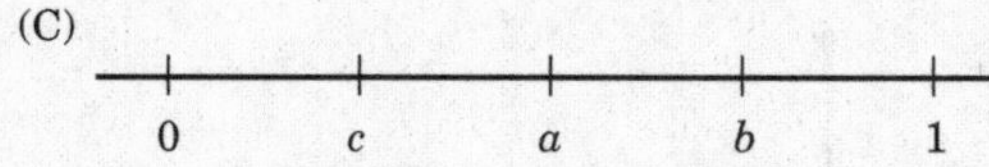

(D)
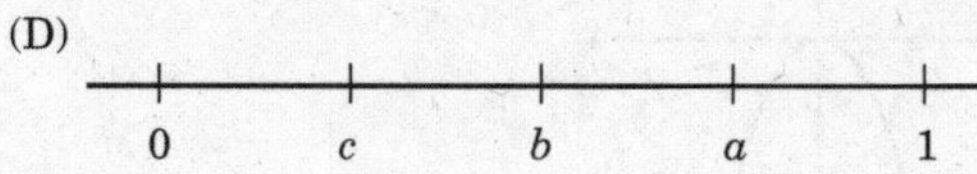

(E)
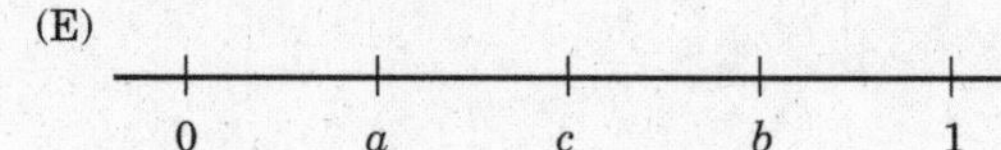

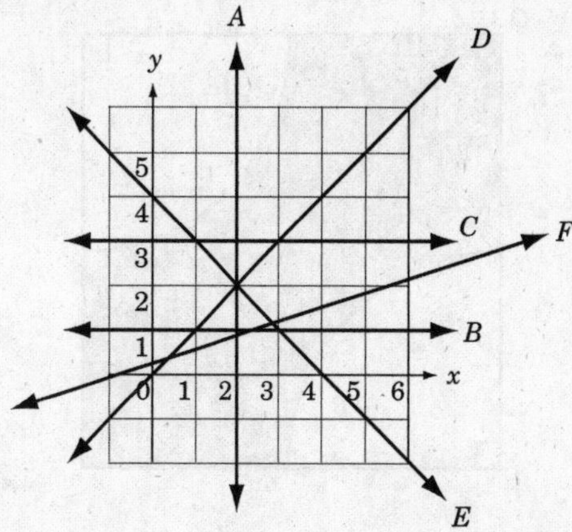

14. The figure above shows six lines. What is the mode of all the slopes?

(A) 0
(B) $\frac{1}{2}$
(C) $\frac{2}{3}$
(D) $\frac{4}{5}$
(E) 1

15. New York City is exactly 14 hours behind Tokyo. If it is 2 A.M. in New York City, for example, it is 4 P.M. in Tokyo the next day. It takes a plane 16 hours to fly from Tokyo to New York. If a plane takes off at 6 P.M. on January 23 from Tokyo, what time and date will it be in New York when the plane lands?

(A) 10 A.M. on January 24
(B) 8 A.M. on January 24
(C) 8 P.M. on January 24
(D) 6 P.M. on January 23
(E) 8 P.M. on January 23

GO ON TO THE NEXT PAGE

SECTION 3

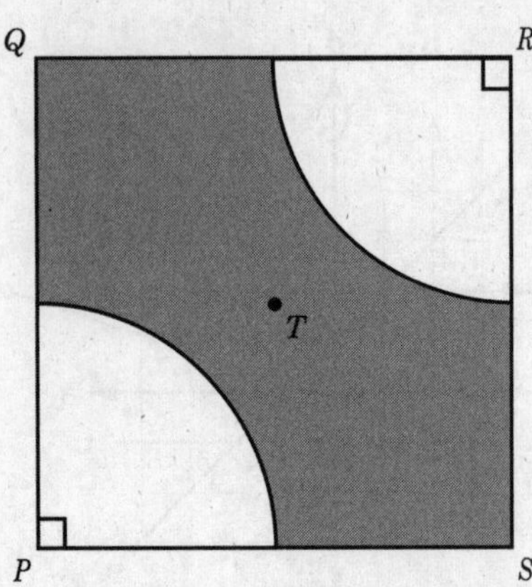

16. The figure above shows square *PQRS* with two equal quarter circles inscribed in corner *P* and corner *R*. The radius of each quarter circle measures half the side of the square. If the area of the entire square is 16, what is the area of the shaded region?

(A) 14
(B) 8
(C) $8 - 2\pi$
(D) $16 - \pi$
(E) $16 - 2\pi$

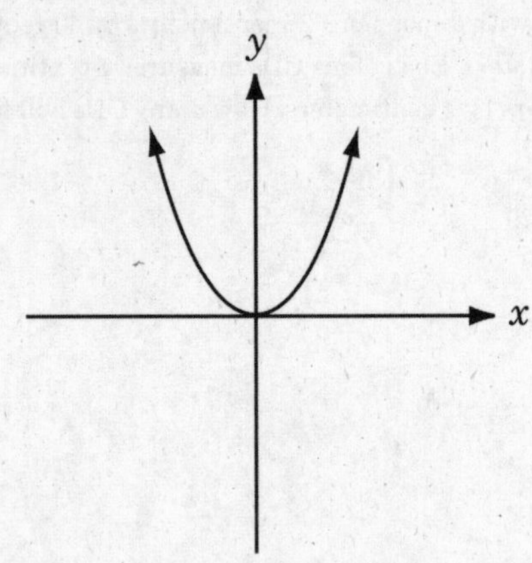

17. The figure above represents $f(x) = x^2$. Which of the following could represent $f(x) = 3x^2$?

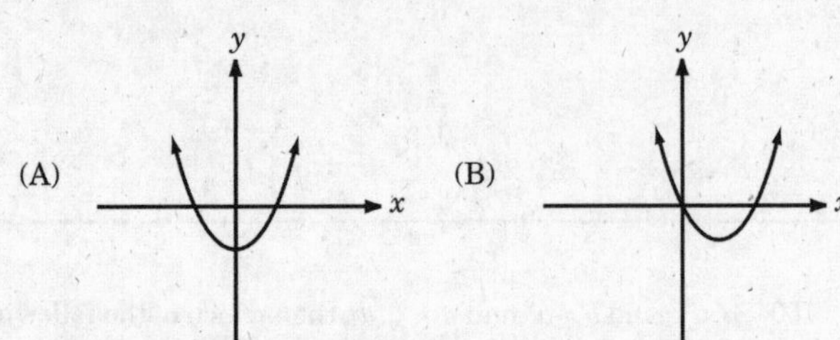

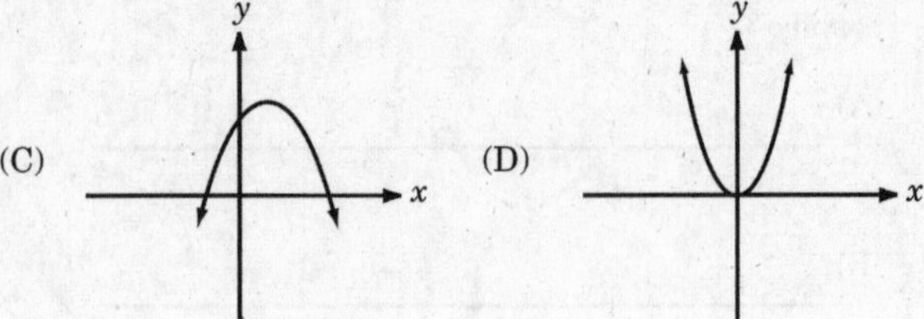

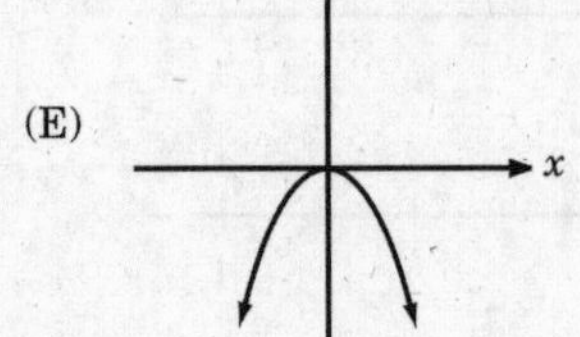

GO ON TO THE NEXT PAGE

SECTION 3

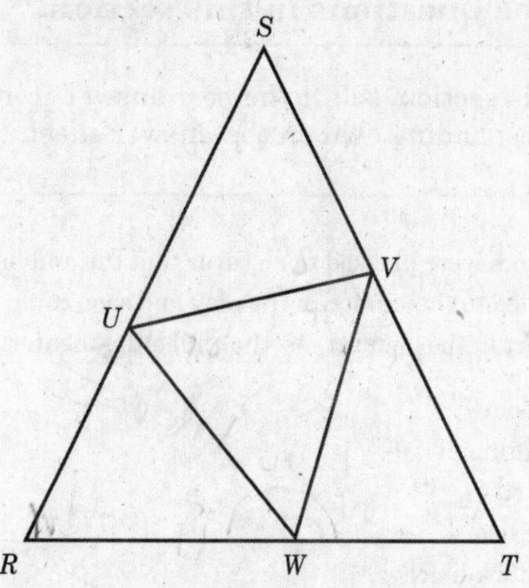

Note: Figure not drawn to scale.

18. In the figure above, $RS = ST = RT$ and $UW = VW$. If the measure of angle RWU is 50 and angle UWV is 40, then what is the measure of angle UVS ?

(A) 100
(B) 90
(C) 80
(D) 70
(E) 60

19. If the numbers w, x, y, and z are all non-zero numbers, and if $wx = yz$, then all of the following are true EXCEPT

(A) $\frac{w}{y} = \frac{x}{z}$

(B) $\frac{w}{z} = \frac{y}{x}$

(C) $\frac{wx}{y} = z$

(D) $\frac{yz}{wx} = 1$

(E) $\frac{wx}{yz} = 1$

20. If $\sqrt[3]{x} + \sqrt{x} = b$, then what is one possible value of b if b and x are both integers?

(A) 8
(B) 12
(C) 24
(D) 32
(E) 64

S T O P

IF YOU FINISH BEFORE TIME IS CALLED, YOU MAY CHECK YOUR WORK ON THIS TEST ONLY.
DO NOT TURN TO ANY OTHER SECTION IN THIS TEST.

SECTION 4

Turn to Section 4 of your answer sheet to answer the questions in this section.

Time—25 Minutes
24 Questions

Directions: For each question in this section, select the best answer from among the choices given and fill in the corresponding oval on the answer sheet.

Each sentence below has one or two blanks, each blank indicating that something has been omitted. Beneath the sentence are five words or sets of words labeled A through E. Choose the word or set of words that, when inserted in the sentence, best fits the meaning of the sentence as a whole.

Example:

Eliza felt ----- when her boss asked her to work seven weekends in a row but ----- when her work earned her a promotion.

(A) enervated . . weakened
(B) depressed . . intellectual
(C) advantageous . . salacious
(D) angry . . shopworn
(E) irate . . elated   

1. Most people are aware of the benefits of herbs, but Margo is particularly ----- about them, always proselytizing about their benefits whenever she gets the chance.

(A) sardonic
(B) rancorous
(C) tepid
(D) splendid
(E) emphatic

2. The difficulty with hurricane season lies in ----- the number of storms that will erupt and, even more challenging, determining the ----- of these extreme winds.

(A) denying . . harshness
(B) predicting . . severity
(C) assuming . . negligence
(D) ascertaining . . ineptitude
(E) anticipating . . loquaciousness

3. The actors were pleased to discover that the audience responded to the humor in the play and soon could not help but take part in the general ----- that filled the theater.

(A) gloom
(B) fulfillment
(C) mirth
(D) treacle
(E) ambivalence

4. Shannon cannot be fully blamed for her failure to perform well on the test. Though it is true that she did not study as hard as she could have, she was not responsible for the ----- information that the teacher included in the questions.

(A) exacting
(B) plentiful
(C) distracted
(D) random
(E) remarkable

5. While the songs of birds appear to be ----- —that is, birds are born with the capacity to sing—birds must, like humans, be exposed to adult versions of these complex warbles if they expect to learn to sing with fluency.

(A) innate
(B) denied
(C) appropriate
(D) learned
(E) nonsensical

6. Some called Stephen Jobs the ----- son before he returned to Apple Computer, the company he founded as a youth, after many years in which critics and fans alike thought he was wasting his talents.

(A) prodigal
(B) remunerative
(C) staid
(D) blessed
(E) dialectical

GO ON TO THE NEXT PAGE

7. The writer managed to ----- the last third of his novel after the sales department of the publishing house complained that ----- books were difficult to sell to a public hungry for abbreviated entertainment.

(A) extend . . labyrinthine
(B) truncate . . weighty
(C) aggrandize . . gargantuan
(D) amortize . . microscopic
(E) trim . . diminutive

8. The judges ruled that the opera singer's ----- to every audition made it impossible to award her first prize, for despite the singer's natural talent, a true professional would need to be relied upon to show up to every performance prepared and on time.

(A) tardiness
(B) heft
(C) precociousness
(D) lambasting
(E) shrillness

GO ON TO THE NEXT PAGE

SECTION 4

Directions: Each passage below is followed by questions based on its content. Answer the questions on the basis of what is stated or implied in each passage and in any introductory material that may be provided.

Questions 9–10 are based on the following passage.

I was from a beige land, or should I say a bleached country, where our summers and winters were equally pale and straw colored. Imagine my surprise, then, when I spent my first year in the land I have since come to call the green isle. What glorious mornings I experienced when I first opened up the white shutters of my bedroom to face an endless expanse of green. I drank it all in. Most magical of all were the afternoons when I lazed under a tree and the sun filtered light through the leaves, whose veins spread the tissue of each leaf flat, like a hand. Then I truly felt as though I had entered into the actual color itself, for the world whirred with green, the grass beneath, the trees overhead, the light, and even the air were emerald.

9. What does the narrator mean by the comment that she was from a "bleached country" (line 1)?

(A) Her native home had an absence of green.
(B) The land around her was very white.
(C) She lived far away.
(D) The country was particularly clean.
(E) She did not like the hot summers.

10. In context, the tone of lines 9–12 ("Then I . . . emerald") is best described as one of

(A) distress and confusion
(B) wonder and pleasure
(C) hunger and longing
(D) sadness and pain
(E) nostalgia and regret

Questions 11–12 are based on the following passage.

A recent discovery of a piece of silk from 1000 B.C. in Egypt has prompted scholars to reconsider the extent to which ancient people traded with each other. It is well known that the Chinese jealously guarded the secret to the making of silk for many centuries—that is, until a Chinese princess, betrothed to a Central Asian prince, went to her new home with silk worms hidden in her headdress. Once ensconced in her new home, she fed the worms mulberry leaves and apparently taught others how to boil and unravel their cocoons. It has been customary to assume that silk, therefore, did not become readily available in the ancient world until circa A.D. 200, when the Silk Road, an established trading route, enabled silk to travel from China to the Roman Empire and then later, when the aforementioned princess revealed the secrets of silk, to be mass-produced in the West. This new discovery of silk in northern Africa, however, suggests that silk was traveling along the Silk Road much earlier than expected. One explanation for this is that the silk traveled in a relay: surely no one merchant would have traveled the entire distance from ancient China to Egypt. Rather, it is likely that the silk passed through many hands before coming to its final resting place.

11. A major assumption of this passage that weakens the author's argument is that

(A) silk was desired in Rome
(B) the Chinese intentionally guarded the secret to making silk
(C) silk was eventually mass-produced in the West
(D) a trader in 1000 B.C. could not have traveled from China all the way to Egypt
(E) the silk from 1000 B.C. was correctly dated using scientific means

12. The author's tone in the final sentence is best described as

(A) annoyed
(B) neutral
(C) resistant
(D) encouraged
(E) knowing

GO ON TO THE NEXT PAGE

SECTION 4

Directions: The passages below are followed by questions based on their content; questions following a pair of related passages may also be based on the relationship between the paired passages. Answer the questions on the basis of what is stated or implied in the passages and in any introductory material that may be provided.

Questions 13–24 are based on the following passages.

These two passages, written in the 1990s, address the ways in which we have come to understand creativity. The first passage is written by an expert in the field of organizational behavior. The second is written by a venerated poet, with a career spanning more than fifty years.

Passage 1

In my thirty years as an expert in the field of organizational behavior, it has become apparent to me that to be prepared to embrace the many changes happening around us now, and which will persist well into the new millennium, individuals functioning within an organization must be encouraged to think and act creatively. We no longer live in a world in which the country with the greatest natural resources will outwit all others. Instead, it is our people and our talents that will ensure our survival and our ability to surmount any obstacle. In a recently televised documentary, the president of Chase Manhattan Bank was asked why he had amassed the largest corporate collection of modern and contemporary art. To paraphrase, he replied that part of his aim as CEO was to provide his employees with an environment that clearly championed the imagination and provided a creative approach to solving problems. In other words, by surrounding workers with obvious expressions of creativity, employees will naturally be inspired to do the same in their jobs.

What do we mean when we speak of creativity? The word "create" comes from Latin and means "to bring forth." We generally think of artists as being creative and judge their level of creativity by the products that they produce. Reconfiguring this definition so that it applies to those who work in fields outside of the fine arts, but who are nevertheless clearly creative, may seem a bit of a challenge. One definition for this elusive term is, to quote the writer Haefele, the "ability to formulate new combinations from two or more concepts already in the mind." Think of any great work of art, for example, and there are precedents, though these notable influences do not in and of themselves equal the quality of what we would term "great." Any organization—be it a governmental office or small home business—must, in order to compete, embrace this kind of thinking. How else is a technology company going to create new products? How else can a local fire department learn to better respond to emergency calls?

There are some who would protest that creativity is an innate trait that cannot be taught. But numerous studies show us that naturally creative people share a definable and quantifiable set of characteristics, much the same as professional athletes are defined in similar ways across different sporting categories. Among the traits defining creative people we see a broad range of interests, a natural impulse to take risks, strong motivation and a desire for recognition, a willingness to act independently and to tolerate ambiguity, and strong faith in oneself as a creative entity. It stands to reason that if these traits repeatedly define a creative person, then an organization can reinforce these character traits.

I have found, in my research, that creative organizations, like creative individuals, also share recurring traits. Such institutions encourage all members to participate in the making of decisions, upending the notion that all companies are filled with drones who must do a manager's bidding. Naturally, this means that the leadership encourages employees to think creatively. Since creativity will by definition upend long-held beliefs, a creative organization must be prepared to be flexible to adopt new ideas. And finally, to be truly creative, an organization must itself believe at its core that people are creative and can be nurtured to develop this creativity.

Passage 2

"Unleash Your Inner Artist!" proclaims the title of a book in the airport bookstore. "Be a Poet on the Job!" declares another. The last title in particular rankles me. I am perhaps sensitive to this notion because I am a poet and, if I am to believe the honors given to me, a well-established one at that. I must hasten now to say that I am not for bandying about my accomplishments, but I do hope that I can use the position bestowed on me to say something of importance. Specifically, I worry that in our age of instant fame and advertised accolades, we are dangerously tempted to throw around the titles of "artist" and "poet." Once upon a time these titles meant something, distinguished the hobbyist from the true practitioner, and yet, in this age of hyper-democratization, we seem intent on trying to find all possible applications for these terms, even when reason tells us that we should stop.

I say all this with a kind of sick realization that there will be those who immediately assume I am championing the kind of elitism that our forefathers fought to quell. This is not my intention at all. Let me be clear and repeat myself: I am not suggesting that art should belong to the lofty few. However, if art is to have any relevance to the ordinary man or woman, then it should be distinguishable *as* art, and not as the personal, therapeutic expressions of a person who, though well meaning, does not possess the skill to create something of true artistic merit. When I think of the artists I have known and respected, I remember their strength of will, their individuality, and their admirable ability to exist in a fluid world. These were people

GO ON TO THE NEXT PAGE

SECTION 4

guided by a relentless desire for personal exploration and expression and therefore able to take risks and have a unique worldview. To put it more bluntly, an artist has a truly unusual take on things and is always dissatisfied with institutions, no matter how they pander, and will never parrot the *supposed* attitudes of the individual.

Speaking of individualism is always tricky in America. Our national character is founded on the mythology of the individual, the belief that one person can make a difference. And I am patriotic enough, and a good enough student of history, to know that, in fact, an individual can change some of the currents rustling through history. But it is ludicrous to assume that every individual life burns with the same unusual flame and flair or that all lives, if given the proper encouragement, will reveal what is profound. Such thinking is dangerous, cheapens true art, and damages those who are misled.

I realize, of course, that I can say all this safely hidden away inside the walls of an institution that survives on the donations of corporations and wealthy individuals. As such, my life is dependent on that singular institution we call capitalism. It seems ungrateful of me to insult its desire to consider itself a creative engine. Perhaps the solution is to call for some kind of moderation. Let poets be poets. Let corporate heads be corporate heads. Both may be creative in their own ways. But only one is a poet.

13. In line 3, the word "embrace" most nearly means

(A) hug
(B) accept
(C) attract
(D) assume
(E) engage

14. The author of Passage 1 believes that artists are, according to lines 19–24 ("We . . . challenge").

(A) uniquely deserving of the title "poet"
(B) a template upon which to base all creativity
(C) often underrepresented
(D) only one example of the creative personality
(E) losing their positions of importance in the academy or university

15. The term "precedents" in line 27 refers to

(A) the act of giving up in the face of trying circumstances
(B) an artist's most distinctive work
(C) something that predates and influences the creation of a new work
(D) the very definition of "greatness"
(E) something an artist creates to inspire others

16. The author of Passage 1 uses lines 43–44 ("It stands . . . traits") to

(A) denote a contradiction in terms
(B) convince the reader that a certain course of action is plausible
(C) emphasize the impossibility of a situation
(D) mask a call for sympathy
(E) imply that her research is essentially futile

17. The first paragraph of Passage 2 presents

(A) mild bemusement
(B) general speculation
(C) genuine distress
(D) quiet reverence
(E) open admiration

18. The author repeats himself, in lines 73–74 ("Let me be . . . few") because he is concerned that the reader will

(A) take his prejudices into consideration
(B) know that he is undermining himself
(C) try to uncover his own creativity
(D) try to read more books
(E) consider him a snob

19. The term "supposed" (line 86) is used to

(A) soften the blow of the author's criticism
(B) suggest that the author might be persuaded to think differently
(C) heighten the tension between the author and reader
(D) distinguish between those who are truly original and those who are imitative
(E) exonerate the author for his elitism

20. The attitudes toward creativity in the corporation reflected by the authors of Passage 1 and Passage 2, respectively, are

(A) enthusiastic support and skepticism
(B) blithe dismissal and vitriol
(C) generous support and championing
(D) mild acceptance and negligible interest
(E) feigned superiority and advocacy

GO ON TO THE NEXT PAGE

21. What would the author of Passage 2 most likely say about the proposal in Passage 1, lines 43–44 ("It stands . . . traits")?

(A) It is impossible to delineate the characteristics that artists share.
(B) A real artist will immediately rebel against any institution, even one purported to nurture creativity.
(C) Creativity is a poorly understood and therefore not a teachable phenomenon.
(D) Corporations must move quickly to adopt creativity-fostering tactics.
(E) More people than ever have become creative.

22. The author of Passage 1 would most likely argue that the criticism of "hyper-democratization" (line 67) reflected by the author of Passage 2

(A) is a clear-cut example of elitism
(B) detracts from the author's argument
(C) is only applicable to artists and poets
(D) fails to take into consideration the competitive demands on organizations
(E) does not exist outside the academy

23. How would the author of Passage 1 respond to lines 98–101 ("I realize . . . capitalism") of Passage 2?

(A) Poets and corporations may have little in common but should be supportive of each other nonetheless.
(B) Individuals will not be prompted to think creatively unless they believe that all people have a creative potential.
(C) Creativity can flourish outside the academy.
(D) The survival of the poet in the academy is in part dependent on the ability of the corporation to thrive.
(E) A poet in the academy has no hope of understanding the pressures placed on contemporary organizations.

24. The authors of Passage 1 and Passage 2 agree that artists and poets possess all of the following traits EXCEPT

(A) a unique view on the world
(B) an ability to thrive in an undefined space
(C) a unique type of creativity
(D) the ability to express themselves
(E) an ability to take risks

S T O P

IF YOU FINISH BEFORE TIME IS CALLED, YOU MAY CHECK YOUR WORK ON THIS TEST ONLY.
DO NOT TURN TO ANY OTHER SECTION IN THIS TEST.

SECTION 5

Turn to Section 5 of your answer sheet to answer the questions in this section.

Time—25 Minutes
18 Questions

Directions: For this section, solve each problem and decide which is the best of the choices given. Fill in the corresponding oval on the answer sheet. You may use any available space for scratchwork.

Notes:

1. The use of a calculator is permitted. All numbers used are real numbers.
2. Figures that accompany problems in this test are intended to provide information useful in solving the problems. They are drawn as accurately as possible EXCEPT when it is stated in a specific problem that the figure is not drawn to scale. All figures lie in a plane unless otherwise indicated.
3. Unless otherwise specified, the domain of any function f is assumed to be the set of all real numbers x for which $f(x)$ is a real number.

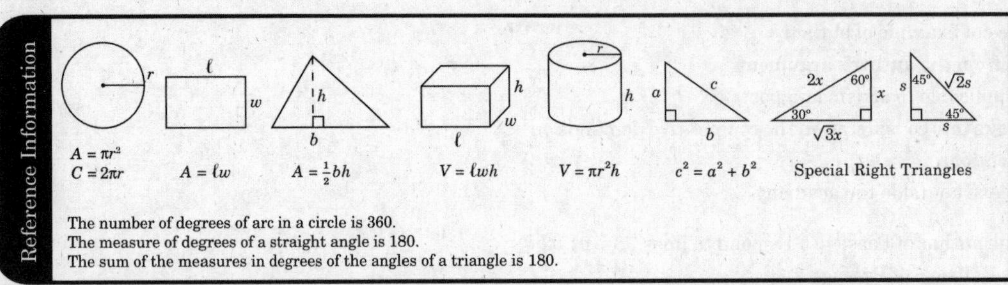
Reference Information
$A = \pi r^2$
$C = 2\pi r$
$A = \ell w$
$A = \frac{1}{2}bh$
$V = \ell wh$
$V = \pi r^2 h$
$c^2 = a^2 + b^2$
Special Right Triangles
The number of degrees of arc in a circle is 360.
The measure of degrees of a straight angle is 180.
The sum of the measures in degrees of the angles of a triangle is 180.

1. If $a = b - c$, $b = 4c$, and $c = 3$, what is a?

   (A) −9
   (B) 3
   (C) 4
   (D) 6
   (E) 9

2. If the town bank, b, is smaller than the grocery store, g, but larger than the fire department, f, then which of the following is true?

   (A) $g < b < f$
   (B) $f < b < g$
   (C) $b < f < g$
   (D) $g < f < b$
   (E) $f < g < b$

3. Theresa and her mother both went shopping. Theresa bought one bag of dry goods, and her mother bought one bag of groceries. If the sum of their purchases is \$58, what is the average cost, in dollars, of one bag?

   (A) 14
   (B) 29
   (C) 58
   (D) 87
   (E) 116

4. Let T be the set of all integers that can be written as $x^2 - 2$ where x is a positive integer. All of the following are in T EXCEPT

   (A) −2
   (B) −1
   (C) 2
   (D) 7
   (E) 14

GO ON TO THE NEXT PAGE

SECTION 5

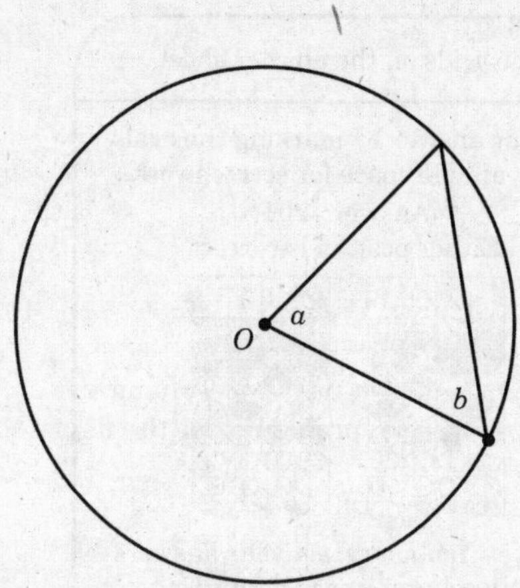

5. In the figure above, point O is the center of the circle. If $b = 70$ degrees, what is the value of a ?

(A) 20
(B) 30
(C) 40
(D) 50
(E) 60

6. All of the following are evenly divisible by 4 EXCEPT

(A) 36
(B) 56
(C) 76
(D) 86
(E) 96

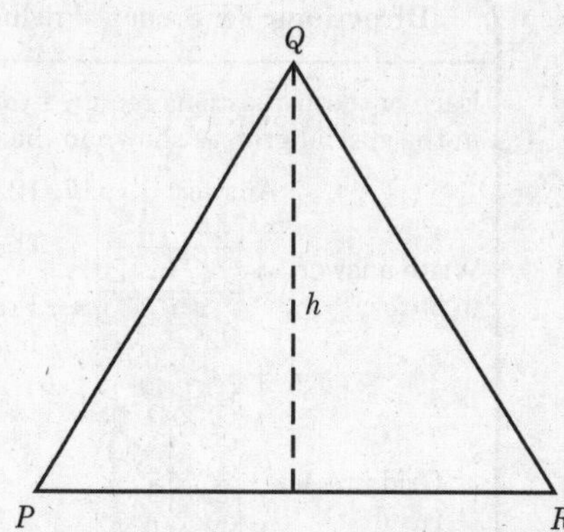

7. In triangle PQR above, the height is marked h as shown. If the area of the triangle is $\frac{2h^2}{5}$, then what is the value of the base PR in terms of h ?

(A) h
(B) $5h$
(C) $4h$
(D) $\frac{4}{5}h$
(E) $\frac{5}{4}h$

8. If $\frac{x^{\frac{1}{3}}}{4}$ is equal to an integer, which of the following could be x ?

(A) 1
(B) 4
(C) 16
(D) 24
(E) 64

GO ON TO THE NEXT PAGE

SECTION 5

Directions: For Student-Produced Response questions 9–18, use the grids on the answer sheet.

Each of these questions requires you to solve the problem and enter your answer by marking the ovals in the special grid, as shown in the examples below. You may use any available space for scratchwork.

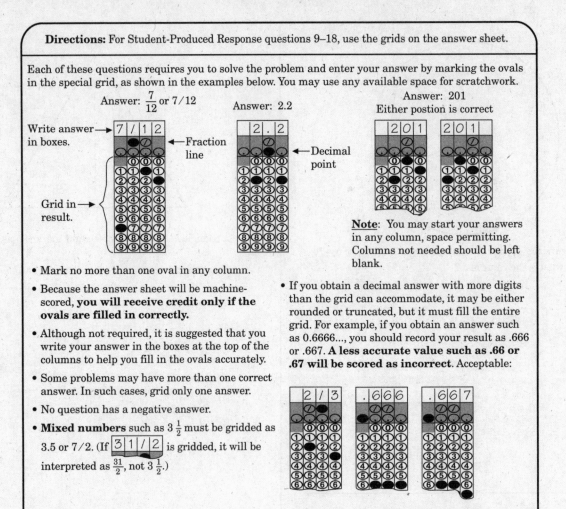

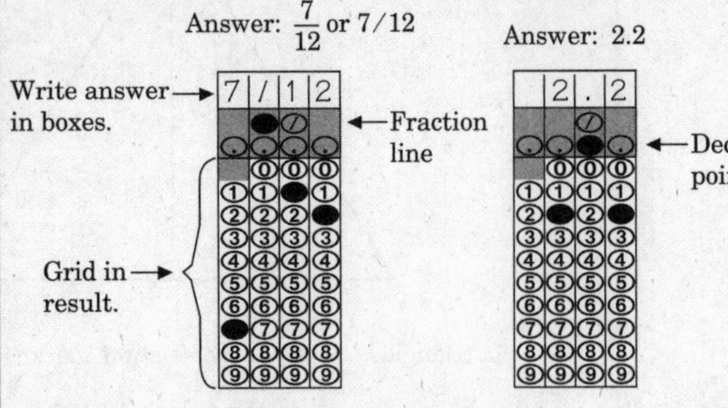

Note: You may start your answers in any column, space permitting. Columns not needed should be left blank.

- Mark no more than one oval in any column.
- Because the answer sheet will be machine-scored, **you will receive credit only if the ovals are filled in correctly.**
- Although not required, it is suggested that you write your answer in the boxes at the top of the columns to help you fill in the ovals accurately.
- Some problems may have more than one correct answer. In such cases, grid only one answer.
- No question has a negative answer.
- **Mixed numbers** such as $3\frac{1}{2}$ must be gridded as 3.5 or 7/2. (If 3 1 / 2 is gridded, it will be interpreted as $\frac{31}{2}$, not $3\frac{1}{2}$.)
- If you obtain a decimal answer with more digits than the grid can accommodate, it may be either rounded or truncated, but it must fill the entire grid. For example, if you obtain an answer such as 0.6666..., you should record your result as .666 or .667. **A less accurate value such as .66 or .67 will be scored as incorrect**. Acceptable:

9. What is the greatest three-digit integer that has a factor of 7 ?

10. A perfume mixture calls for 30 pounds of lavender for 4 bottles. How many pounds of lavender are required to make 10 bottles?

11. When an odd integer x is increased by $3x$, the result is between 20 and 35. What is the value of x ?

GO ON TO THE NEXT PAGE

SECTION 5

12. A rectangular park is to be enclosed by a fence. The area of the rectangular park is 7,500 meters. If the length of one side of the park is 600 meters, how many meters of fence are required to cover the entire perimeter of the park?

13. A school ordered $900 worth of school t-shirts. Some of the t-shirts cost $5 and some cost $10. If the school ordered the same number of $5 t-shirts as $10 t-shirts, how many total shirts were ordered?

14. If $5(a^2 - b^2) = 100$ and $a - b = 4$, then what is the value of $a + b$?

15. In a coordinate system, the center of a circle has coordinates (7, 10) and the circle touches the y-axis at one point only and the x-axis not at all. What is the diameter of the circle?

	Total Owned	# Found by ASPCA
Cats	1,400	100
Dogs	1,200	120

16. In a certain town, the ASPCA strongly advises pet owners to tag their dogs and cats. A recent study showed that 70 percent of cat owners and 70 percent of dog owners actually tag their pets. Of the pets found by the ASPCA, 80 percent are tagged and returned to their owners. What percent of non-tagged pets are found by the ASPCA?

GO ON TO THE NEXT PAGE

SECTION 5

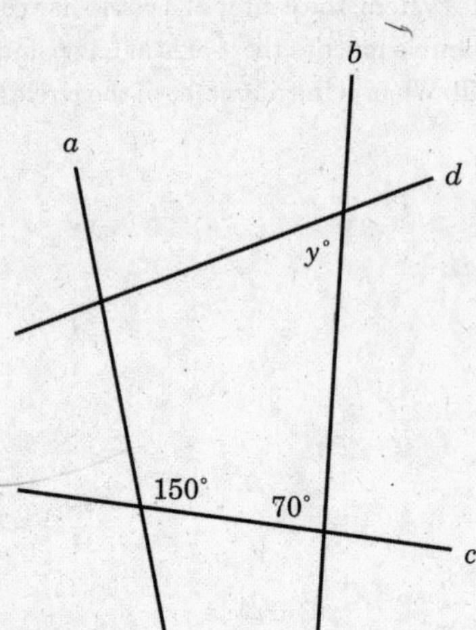

17. In the figure above, if the angle (not shown) where lines a and b intersect is one half as large as the angle (also not shown) where lines d and c intersect, what is the value of y ?

18. Points A, B, C, and D lie on a line in that order. If $AB : AD = 1:4$ and $AC : AD = 1:2$, what is the value of $CD : AD$?

S T O P

IF YOU FINISH BEFORE TIME IS CALLED, YOU MAY CHECK YOUR WORK ON THIS TEST ONLY. DO NOT TURN TO ANY OTHER SECTION IN THIS TEST.

SECTION 6

Turn to Section 6 of your answer sheet to answer the questions in this section.

Time—25 Minutes
35 Questions

Directions: For each question in this section, select the best answer from among the choices given.

The following sentences test correctness and effectiveness of expression. Part of each sentence or the entire sentence is underlined; beneath each sentence are five ways of phrasing the underlined material. Choice A repeats the original phrasing; the other four choices are different. If you think the original phrasing produces a better sentence than any of the alternatives, select choice A; if not, select one of the other choices.

In making your selection, follow the requirements of standard written English; that is, pay attention to grammar, choice of words, sentence construction, and punctuation. Your selection should result in the most effective sentence—clear and precise, without awkwardness or ambiguity.

Example:

In the poem "Ulysses" by Alfred, Lord Tennyson, the speaker says, "I cannot rest from travel," instead, he will live life to the fullest.

(A) "I cannot rest from travel," instead,
(B) "I cannot rest from travel"; instead,
(C) "I cannot rest from travel" instead,
(D) "I cannot rest from travel," upon which
(E) "I cannot rest from travel,"

1. The latest Hong Kong film was so popular, it prompted critics proclaiming the end of the foreign film as the predilection only of the elite.

(A) it prompted critics proclaiming the end of the foreign film as the predilection only of the elite
(B) it prompted critics who were proclaiming the end of the foreign film as the predilection only of the elite
(C) it prompted critics in proclaiming the end of the foreign film as the predilection only of the elite
(D) it prompted critics to proclaim the end of the foreign film as the predilection of the elite
(E) it prompted critics proclaimed the end of the foreign film as the predilection only of the elite

2. The tsunami started in a corner of the India Ocean before rolling across the continent, destroying resorts, snapping power lines, washing out highway overpasses, and it also displaced many people.

(A) it also displaced many people
(B) displacing many people
(C) also displaced many people
(D) it was displacing many people
(E) also displaces many people

3. As I entered the cabin of the plane, bound for my hometown in California, a passenger is waving to say hello and I realized it was my next-door neighbor.

(A) is waving to say hello
(B) was waving to say hello
(C) waving to say hello
(D) wave to say hello
(E) waved to say hello

4. Sharon believed that nothing was more better than a scoop of lemon sorbet on a hot day.

(A) was more better than
(B) will be more better
(C) is going to be better than
(D) has been more good
(E) was better than

GO ON TO THE NEXT PAGE

SECTION 6

5. I was initially confused by the sandwich maker in the shop when he asked me about wanting oil and vinegar dressing or mustard and mayonnaise.

(A) about wanting oil and vinegar dressing or mustard and mayonnaise
(B) about my wanting oil and vinegar dressing or mustard and mayonnaise
(C) whether I wanted oil and vinegar dressing or mustard and mayonnaise
(D) whether or not I was wanting oil and vinegar dressing or mustard and mayonnaise
(E) if I was wanting oil and vinegar dressing or mustard and mayonnaise

6. The storm having been stopped, the hikers on the birding expedition stopped to admire the rainbow across the valley.

(A) The storm having been stopped
(B) With the storm having stopped
(C) In stopping the storm
(D) When the storm stopped
(E) Once stopping the storm

7. If eating vegetables and fruits really wards off cancer or doesn't remains unproven, but certainly ingesting a variety fresh greens is the best way for the body to absorb vitamins.

(A) If eating vegetables and fruits really wards off cancer or doesn't
(B) That eating vegetables and fruits really wards cancer
(C) Whether eating vegetables and fruits really wards off cancer or doesn't
(D) The eating vegetables and fruits really wards off cancer or does not do so
(E) Eating vegetables and fruits wards off cancer or really doesn't

8. Because we did not check the parking rules for that end of the street, even so our car was impounded and we had to pay a fee to retrieve it.

(A) even so our car
(B) and then our car
(C) therefore our car
(D) our car
(E) why our car

9. Underwater for so long, the ancient vessel had developed a protective layer of algae that needed to be replicated to keep the ship intact when it was raised to the surface.

(A) had developed a protective layer of algae
(B) having developed a protective layer of algae
(C) once had a developed and protective layer of algae
(D) developing a protective layer of algae
(E) in developing a protective layer of algae

10. Although regarded as heretical by many of his contemporaries, most people now consider that Sigmund Freud was a well-intentioned person who took the emotional problems of his subjects seriously.

(A) most people now consider that Sigmund Freud was a well-intentioned person
(B) most people are considering that Sigmund Freud was a well-intentioned person
(C) Sigmund Freud is now considered a well-intentioned person
(D) Sigmund Freud was now considered a well-intentioned person
(E) Sigmund Freud has now been considered a well-intentioned person

11. Throughout the island of Japan, ancient festivals are reenacted that express the age-old desire to see a bountiful harvest, though nowadays a food shortage is not seen as a likely tragedy.

(A) though nowadays a food shortage is not seen as a likely tragedy
(B) though nowadays a food shortage will not be as a likely tragedy
(C) though a food shortage, these days, is not seen as a likely tragedy
(D) though not a likely tragedy, a food shortage is nowadays
(E) though nowadays a food shortage will not be seen as a likely tragedy

GO ON TO THE NEXT PAGE

SECTION 6

Directions: For each question in this section, select the best answer from among the choices given.

The following sentences test your ability to recognize grammar and usage errors. Each sentence contains either a single error or no error at all. No sentence contains more than one error. The error, if there is one, is underlined and lettered. If the sentence contains an error, select the one underlined part that must be changed to make the sentence correct. If the sentence is correct, select choice E. In choosing answers, follow the requirements of standard written English.

Example:

The other delegates and him immediately
A B C
accepted the resolution drafted by the
D
neutral states. No error
E

Ⓐ ● Ⓒ Ⓓ Ⓔ

12. Longer trips to foreign countries are preferable if one really
A
wants to get to know a culture, but for many longer trips are not
as practical than shorter ones because working people have so
B C D
few vacation days to spend. No error
E

13. Sitting in the sun—a leisure habit which began in the postwar
A
era and which gained popularity in the 1970s and 1980s—has
B
now been discovered to be a harmful activity that damages cells
C
and in some instances causes irreparable damage. No error
D E

14. Because subtleties of taste and seasoning are so important in
A
the highest forms of cooking, many executive chefs insist on
B
using shallots, which have a sweeter, more gentle flavor
C
from the harshness of onions. No error
D D

15. Few arguments grow as heated as that which erupt between
A B C
family members around the dinner table during a holiday
D
repast. No error
E

16. Initially the rabbits all seemed identical, yet upon closer
A B
examination we discovered that each had its own distinct
C D
personality. No error
E

17. According to the consumer magazine, the new digital imaging
A B
software was so user-friendly, it did not require any previous
C
knowledge to similar programs. No error
D E

18. Brushing your teeth regularly is one way to avoid cavities.
A B
If you don't eat sweets is another way to ward off this unwanted
C D
condition. No error
E

19. Exhausted from a long night of studying for her finals, and then
A B
completing her tests the next morning, Adrianne finally laid
C D
down to take a nap. No error
E

20. When the coffee company became a champion of beans grown in
A B
shady patches, they inadvertently started a trend in which
C
coffee drinkers sought out coffee grown in such conditions.
D
No error
E

21. Bed bugs, which were thought to has been completely eradicated
A B
in the 1950s due to the use of DDT, have started
C
to make a comeback in the United States, alarming health
D
officials. No error
E

22. If you install an air conditioner in your window proper, then it
A
can stay there all winter and will be ready for use in the summer
B C
months when the temperature becomes unbearably hot.
D
No error
E

GO ON TO THE NEXT PAGE

SECTION 6

23. The Japanese government designates certain (A) practitioners of old crafts and arts as "living national treasures," supplying (B) these lucky individuals with a stipend to ensure that their (C) talents will be preserved (D) and not lost to the forces of modernization. No error (E)

24. The letters and journals of Jane Austen, a writer of exceptional talent and wit, was (A) mostly destroyed by her family and friends who (B) wanted to protect (C) the privacy of their dear friend and (D) relative. No error (E)

25. One's appreciation for any art form, be it dance, music, or (A) writing, is always deeper if one has made (B) an effort to understand (C) the degree of skill that goes into producing a finished work as (D) if one is an audience member with no familiarity with the creative process. No error (E)

26. Learning (A) healthy eating habits and appropriate portion size is very (B) important to the person who attempt (C) to make a serious effort to lose (D) weight. No error (E)

27. For we (A) humanistic people, the very (B) idea of war is something abhorrent, and we find it difficult to discuss (C) war without imagining (D) the great human costs it causes. No error (E)

28. We could believe (A) neither the scale of the damage the earthquake caused or (B) the unprecedented media attention it generated when (C) news crews from every outlet flew to the small Pacific Island to survey (D) the destruction. No error (E)

29. Inside the piggy bank is (A) ten dollars in pennies and (B) fifty dollars in nickels, making it a virtual (C) treasure trove for the day when we finally (D) decide to crack it open. No error (E)

GO ON TO THE NEXT PAGE

SECTION 6

Directions: The following passage is an early draft of an essay. Some parts of the passage need to be rewritten.

Read the passage and select the best answers for the questions that follow. Some questions are about particular sentences or parts of sentences and ask you to improve sentence structure or word choice. Other questions ask you to consider organization and development. In choosing answers, follow the requirements of standard written English.

Questions 30–35 are based on the following passage, taken from an essay on bed bugs.

(1) *You are probably familiar with the saying, "Good night. Sleep tight. Don't let the bed bugs bite."* **(2)** *You probably wondered at one point what a bed bug looked like and what the saying was all about.* **(3)** *Maybe, for example, you might have thought, as I did, that a bed bug was large and perhaps even enormous.* **(4)** *Recently, I had the unpleasant experience of waking up every morning to mysterious, itchy welts on my body.* **(5)** *Whatever it was, it was biting me at night when I was unaware and leaving me alone in the morning.*

(6) *I started researching the kinds of insects that could be biting me, looking for signs.* **(7)** *I knew I was not dealing with mosquitoes, because they don't fly around during the winter, and I ruled out mites, because I didn't find their telltale red bodies on my sheets.* **(8)** *I read about bed bugs, which are supposedly making a comeback after years of near extinction.* **(9)** *I still didn't believe that was the problem.* **(10)** *Then I found a bug in my bed and cross-referenced the picture to a bed bug on the internet.* **(11)** *I was able to identify it due to a picture online.*

(12) *You wouldn't believe the fuss finding a bed bug caused.* **(13)** *We had to throw out my metal frame and buy a new mattress.* **(14)** *The new bed meant I had to rearrange everything in my room, but, on the upside, I feel as if my new room is better organized.* **(15)** *And I know I won't get bitten at night!*

30. In context, which of the following is the best version of sentence 3 (reproduced below)?

Maybe, for example, you might have thought, as I did, that a bed bug was large and perhaps even enormous.

(A) (As it is now)
(B) Perhaps you have thought, as I did, that a bed bug was large—even enormous.
(C) Maybe you might have thought, as I did, that a bed bug was large and perhaps even enormous.
(D) Perhaps you were thinking like me that a bed bug was large and enormous.
(E) You might, like me, have been thinking about the bed bug as a large and perhaps even enormous thing.

31. Of the following, which is the best version of the underlined portion of sentence 5 below?

<u>Whatever it was, it</u> was biting me at night when I was unaware and leaving me alone in the morning.

(A) (As it is now)
(B) Whatever the cause, it
(C) However it was, it
(D) However the cause, it
(E) Despite whatever cause, it

32. In the first paragraph (sentences 1–5), the author is primarily

(A) setting a scene
(B) asking probing questions
(C) postulating a theory
(D) advancing a prospective solution
(E) rebutting an argument

33. Of the following, which is the best way to revise and combine the underlined portion of sentences 8 and 9 (reproduced below)?

I read about bed bugs, which are supposedly making a comeback after years of near <u>extinction. I still didn't believe</u> that was the problem.

(A) extinction. I still didn't believe
(B) extinction, therefore I still didn't believe
(C) extinction, but I still didn't believe
(D) extinction, and I still didn't believe
(E) extinction: I still didn't believe

GO ON TO THE NEXT PAGE

SECTION 6

34. Which of the following should be done with sentence 11 (reproduced below)?

I was able to identify it due to a picture online.

(A) Switch the positions of sentences 10 and 11.
(B) Add the word "fortunately" to the start.
(C) Eliminate the word "online".
(D) Eliminate it.
(E) Combine sentences 10 and 11 with the conjunction "but".

35. The primary effect of the final paragraph is to

(A) leave questions in the reader's mind
(B) draw the story to a close
(C) set up another chapter in the story
(D) persuade the reader to change her or his opinion
(E) summarize a difficult theory

S T O P

IF YOU FINISH BEFORE TIME IS CALLED, YOU MAY CHECK YOUR WORK ON THIS TEST ONLY. DO NOT TURN TO ANY OTHER SECTION IN THIS TEST.

SECTION 7

Turn to Section 7 of your answer sheet to answer the questions in this section.

Time—20 Minutes
19 Questions

Directions: For each question in this section, select the best answer from among the choices given and fill in the corresponding oval on the answer sheet.

Each sentence below has one or two blanks, each blank indicating that something has been omitted. Beneath the sentence are five words or sets of words labeled A through E. Choose the word or set of words that, when inserted in the sentence, best fits the meaning of the sentence as a whole.

Example:

Eliza felt ----- when her boss asked her to work seven weekends in a row but ----- when her work earned her a promotion.

(A) enervated . . weakened
(B) depressed . . intellectual
(C) advantageous . . salacious
(D) angry . . shopworn
(E) irate . . elated   

1. After the success of Margaret Atwood's *The Handmaid's Tale*, publishers and readers ----- the particular pleasures of Canadian literature and the literary tradition of the great north was -----.

(A) rejected . . freed
(B) discovered . . born
(C) assumed . . questioned
(D) dictated . . stayed
(E) enforced . . scaled

2. In addition to ----- the professional accomplishments of potential employees, corporations are now often ----- standardized test scores as part of their initial screening process when scanning resumes.

(A) anticipating . . dismissing
(B) corrupting . . studying
(C) evaluating . . assessing
(D) scheduling . . creating
(E) assuming . . following

3. The new zoo will only feature those animals born in captivity. The founders have made it very clear that they do not wish to ----- animals from nature and stick them in the confines of a pen.

(A) pilfer
(B) distinguish
(C) ramble
(D) replace
(E) connect

4. A singer like Frank Sinatra is difficult to categorize. Some say he was a mere singer of pop tunes, but others point to his classic jazz and show-tune recordings and suggest he was an artist of great -----.

(A) mediocrity
(B) somnolence
(C) distraction
(D) range
(E) pomposity

5. Scholars often note that ancient Greek plays demonstrate an astute understanding of human nature and that these works of art seem to ----- the modern discipline of psychology, which seeks to explain human motivation.

(A) predispose
(B) preempt
(C) prefabricate
(D) presage
(E) preclude

6. Many congressional debates seem to center around the opposing viewpoints that the general population must assume ----- for its actions regardless of innate circumstances and the idea that many are born without ----- and are therefore deserving of a compassionate helping hand.

(A) responsibility . . consumption
(B) deflection . . bias
(C) accountability . . destitution
(D) prominence . . sheltering
(E) liability . . privilege

GO ON TO THE NEXT PAGE

SECTION 7

Directions: The passage below is followed by questions based on its content. Answer the questions on the basis of what is stated or implied in the passage and in any introductory material that may be provided.

Questions 7–19 are based on the following passage.

John Steinbeck (1902–1968), an American writer, received the Nobel Prize in 1968. He was known for his portrayal of ordinary people and their struggles to survive in a cruel world, as well as their redemption through humor and nature.

When John Steinbeck received the Nobel Prize for literature some six years before his death, the best of his work was already behind him. The books for which he is most known today—*The Grapes of Wrath*, *Of Mice and Men*, and *East of Eden,* among others—were written in a feverishly productive period when he was in his thirties and forties. By the time Steinbeck was in his sixties, he had moved to the East Coast and married his third wife. Though he had a few notable creative efforts, including *The Winter of Our Discontent*, his later books never again scaled the same critical heights as his earlier efforts. One has the sense that, far away from the western landscape he so dearly loved, Steinbeck was simply not able to conjure up the stories that had so inspired him in his youth. In reading a book like *Travels with Charley*, one has the sense that the world had changed after the end of the Second World War and that Steinbeck's artist's eye was less attuned to the new world.

One area in which critics have been upset with Steinbeck is his depiction of female characters, and one wonders if Steinbeck were alive today what Steinbeck would think of the proliferation of female novelists and the demands of a female readership, eager to see its gender portrayed in all its complexity, if he were alive today. We have in Steinbeck's books a few types of women: repressive mothers/wives, purely angelic young women, and witchlike temptresses. In *East of Eden*, for example, the narrator even goes so far as to describe one character, Cathy, as having been born "lacking" a crucial element of human nature—a conscience. Throughout the novel, Cathy performs acts of great selfishness and cruelty, causing harm to the men who innocently fall in love with her. When these same men, in turn, are cruel to others, Steinbeck asks us to understand and forgive them. In the end, it is through the love of an unrealistically "whole" and "pure" female character named Abra that the men are redeemed. But Cathy is not forgiven. She is instead as Steinbeck portrayed her: an incomprehensible cipher, something less than human. As a result, readers often find Cathy a dissatisfying character because they cannot believe in her and her lack of any humanity.

Diehard supporters of Steinbeck might point to Abra as evidence that Steinbeck did not dislike all women. There is also the mother character in *The Grapes of Wrath,* who is almost primal in her desire to keep her family intact. The difficulty, scholars and critics assert, is that such characters are almost placeholders within the drama of Steinbeck's books. Nowhere do we learn why Abra is so motivated to be "good." Nowhere do we learn of the mother's feelings in *The Grapes of Wrath*. The inner lives and torments of the male characters are revealed, whereas the women's are left bare.

Very few of Steinbeck's female characters are educated, intelligent women. The ones who are smart, such as the schoolteacher in *East of Eden*, are doomed to lives of spinsterhood or are too smart for their own good and consequently become evil, as in the case of the Cathy character. Other female characters are childish and simple and, as such, cause harm to men. Few women look at the world in a contemplative, complex fashion, trying to determine how best to make a living. Few women are written with a sympathetic hand.

Why did Steinbeck write his women in such a fashion? Obviously every novelist has a particular point of view which is revealed through his art, and Steinbeck is no exception. But a study of his life shows that he might very well have been predisposed to view female characters differently. His sister was a schoolteacher, and his mother an educated, efficient woman who believed in her son's talent. Steinbeck seems to have had numerous female friends, particularly in his formative years before he wrote his first published novel, *Cup of Gold*. He also married three talented women. His first wife, Carol, was a clever and accomplished poet who edited and tightened many of her husband's early books. In fact, many have long suspected that the decline in quality of Steinbeck's writing was because his later pieces lacked her magic touch. Steinbeck must have known his work gleamed under his wife's fingers, for he dedicated *The Grapes of Wrath* to her with the words that she had "willed" that particular novel to life.

Steinbeck's subsequent marriage to a young woman, Gwen, produced two children, but this marriage was apparently a struggle, and some have seen the evil Cathy character as a thinly veiled portrait of Gwen herself. It was only upon marrying his third wife, Elaine, that Steinbeck was able to find some semblance of calm and personal comfort. Despite this happy marriage, his best years as a writer were long behind him. One has the sense upon reading later works, such as *Travels with Charley*, that Steinbeck had ceased to be a writer projecting a deeply felt and believed vision of the world and had become instead a traveler, noting what he saw without really understanding its significance. It would be irresponsible not to note that part of what emerged in the postwar era, of course, was women's liberation.

In the end, it may be too much for any reader to ask for a writer to portray all humankind with sympathetic and complex

GO ON TO THE NEXT PAGE

wonder. Looking at Steinbeck's life, we may find plenty of reasons why he could have written his novels in a particular manner, but this, of course, does not mean that he should have. A close examination of a person's life will only yield so much useful information—and since writing is, by its nature, dependent on a writer sitting in solitude, day after day before an empty page and examining her or his imagination, we should not assume that a personal life will be reflected in the final written word.

7. The passage provides the most information about Steinbeck's
   (A) early life
   (B) relationship to his mother
   (C) uneven writing
   (D) portrayal of female characters
   (E) love of nature

8. As used in context, the word "scaled" (line 9) most nearly means
   (A) reached
   (B) elevated
   (C) sang
   (D) surmounted
   (E) rose

9. The discussion of *Travels with Charley* at the end of paragraph 1 (lines 13–16) suggests that Steinbeck
   (A) was trying to recapture his sense of the West in his later works
   (B) tried to escape the confines of the East by going on a trip
   (C) did not understand the extent to which the world had changed after 1945
   (D) knew his later works were a failure
   (E) was disappointed by the course of history

10. The author most likely mentions "the demands of a female readership, eager to see its own gender portrayed in all its complexity" (lines 20–21) to suggest that
   (A) Steinbeck could never be published as a contemporary author
   (B) if Steinbeck were writing today, women might not be so responsive to his work
   (C) the reading audience has become much more limited in its tastes
   (D) books featuring women are more popular than they once were
   (E) a contemporary editor would ask Steinbeck to change his portrayal of women

11. The discussion of Steinbeck asking readers to forgive his male characters (lines 29–30) ("When these . . . them") suggests that Steinbeck
   (A) could understand the motivations of men but could not understand those of women
   (B) did not realize that women as well as men would read his books
   (C) had no good female role models in his life
   (D) needed someone to better edit *East of Eden*
   (E) was proposing a new theory of behavior in his work

12. In context, the word "primal" (line 40) most nearly means
   (A) untamed
   (B) wild
   (C) needy
   (D) innate
   (E) suspect

13. In lines 51–54 ("Other . . . a living), the author suggest which of the following about Steinbeck?
   (A) He didn't think it was important to dramatize women.
   (B) He was unable to sympathize with the needs and inner lives of women.
   (C) He had had poor educational experiences with female teachers.
   (D) He liked to portray his relationship woes on paper.
   (E) He felt other authors portrayed women with enough sympathy.

14. In lines 56–67 ("Why did . . . books"), the author suggests that it is odd that Steinbeck did not write intelligent, educated women characters because
   (A) he liked to vary his subject matter and character types
   (B) his best works were written in his 30s and 40s
   (C) his stories were often set in gritty surroundings
   (D) he knew very few women in childhood
   (E) he was surrounded by smart, competent women his entire life

15. The "magic touch" in line 69 refers to
   (A) Carol Steinbeck's own poetry
   (B) Carol Steinbeck's ability to expertly edit her husband's works
   (C) the excellent editors in New York
   (D) the influence the western landscape had on Steinbeck's works
   (E) Steinbeck's carefully written prose

GO ON TO THE NEXT PAGE

SECTION 7

16. According to the passage (lines 69–72) ("Steinbeck must . . . life"), Steinbeck may well have been aware of the effect his wife Carol had on his writing because

(A) he admitted his later books were not as good as the earlier ones
(B) his second and third wives were not able to edit his books
(C) he recreated her as a character in his novels
(D) he later asked her to edit his final novels
(E) he credited her with having had a hand in the creation of *The Grapes of Wrath*

17. In lines 73–76 ("Steinbeck's . . . herself"), the author suggests that Steinbeck may have written the Cathy character in *East of Eden* as a purely evil character in part because

(A) he himself lacked fundamental understanding of the character
(B) he lacked the creative ability to give her character greater dimension
(C) his own personal life was full of strife
(D) his distress over his divorce from his first wife
(E) he missed his life in California

18. In lines 79–83 ("One has . . . significance"), the author apparently believes which of the following is the cause for the apparent lack of critical success of the novel *Travels with Charley*?

(A) Steinbeck was not fit to be a travel writer.
(B) Steinbeck had difficult writing while he was on the road.
(C) Steinbeck needed a better editor than he had at his disposal.
(D) Steinbeck was no longer able to clearly portray the world around him.
(E) Steinbeck's third wife prevented him from fully engaging in the craft of writing.

19. In line 85, the author mentions "women's liberation" to suggest that

(A) the world had changed significantly after the end of the Second World War
(B) fiction in the second half of the twentieth century necessarily must take women's lib into account
(C) Steinbeck's audience did not expect him to chronicle the women's movement
(D) Steinbeck's difficulty in understanding women is reflected in a lack of engagement with the social and political world
(E) women were becoming a greater force in determining which books were published and which were not

S T O P

IF YOU FINISH BEFORE TIME IS CALLED, YOU MAY CHECK YOUR WORK ON THIS TEST ONLY. DO NOT TURN TO ANY OTHER SECTION IN THIS TEST.

SECTION 8

Turn to Section 8 of your answer sheet to answer the questions in this section.

Time—20 Minutes
16 Questions

Directions: For this section, solve each problem and decide which is the best of the choices given. Fill in the corresponding oval on the answer sheet. You may use any available space for scratchwork.

Notes:

1. The use of a calculator is permitted. All numbers used are real numbers.
2. Figures that accompany problems in this test are intended to provide information useful in solving the problems. They are drawn as accurately as possible EXCEPT when it is stated in a specific problem that the figure is not drawn to scale. All figures lie in a plane unless otherwise indicated.
3. Unless otherwise specified, the domain of any function f is assumed to be the set of all real numbers x for which $f(x)$ is a real number.

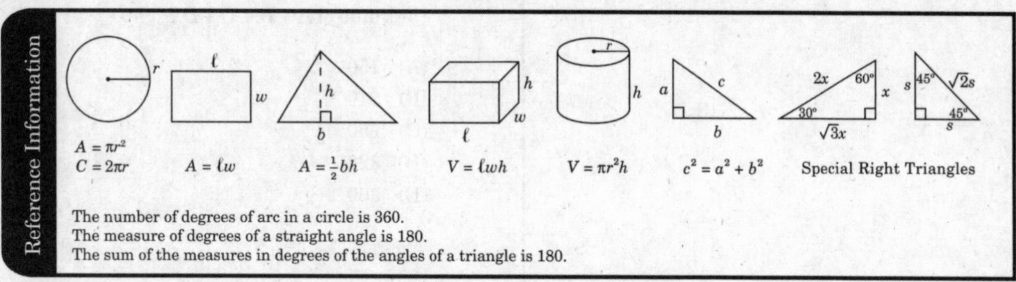

Reference Information
$A = \pi r^2$
$C = 2\pi r$
$A = \ell w$
$A = \frac{1}{2}bh$
$V = \ell wh$
$V = \pi r^2 h$
$c^2 = a^2 + b^2$
Special Right Triangles
The number of degrees of arc in a circle is 360.
The measure of degrees of a straight angle is 180.
The sum of the measures in degrees of the angles of a triangle is 180.

1. If $5(x - 2) = 30$, what is the value of x ?

(A) $\frac{5}{6}$
(B) 6
(C) 8
(D) 26
(E) 37

2. Gene has three pairs of jeans and five t-shirts. How many different combinations of shirts and jeans does he have?

(A) 7
(B) 9
(C) 12
(D) 15
(E) 20

The difference between q and r is equal to the product of a and the square of the sum of b and c.

3. Which of the following is an expression for the statement above?

(A) $q + r = a\{(b + c)^2\}$
(B) $q - r = a\{(b + c)^2\}$
(C) $q - r = ab + ac^2$
(D) $qr = a\{(b + c)^2\}$
(E) $q - r = a(b + c)$

GO ON TO THE NEXT PAGE

SECTION 8

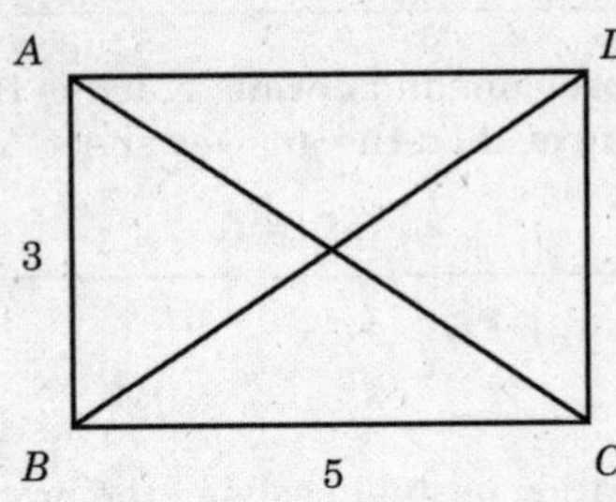

Note: Figure not drawn to scale.

4. If rectangle $ABCD$ above has a length of 5 and a height of 3, what is the product of the lengths of the diagonals AC and BD?

(A) 6
(B) 10
(C) 25
(D) 30
(E) 34

5. If $\frac{a}{4} = \frac{3a}{6y}$, then what is the value of y?

(A) 2
(B) 6
(C) 12
(D) 14
(E) 16

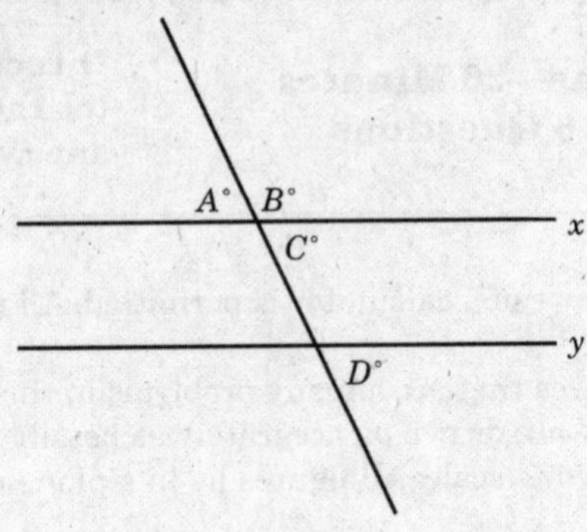

Note: Figure not drawn to scale.

6. In the figure above, lines x and y are parallel. If $d = 70$, what is the value of $A + B + C + D$?

(A) 150
(B) 210
(C) 250
(D) 320
(E) 360

7. What is the slope of a line that passes through point (3, 7) and (–1, –2)?

(A) $\frac{9}{4}$
(B) $\frac{8}{5}$
(C) $\frac{4}{9}$
(D) $\frac{3}{7}$
(E) $\frac{1}{2}$

GO ON TO THE NEXT PAGE

SECTION 8

8. The total cost c in dollars of producing a units of a certain product is given by the function $c(a) = 32a - (13a + b)$ where b is a constant. If 450 units were produced for a cost of \$75,000, what is the value of b ?

(A) 66,450
(B) 33,225
(C) 0
(D) –33,225
(E) –66,450

9. An integer between 1 and 20 multiplied by itself can end in each of the following digits EXCEPT

(A) 4
(B) 5
(C) 6
(D) 8
(E) 9

10. A gumball machine contains four types of colored gumballs: red, white, blue, and yellow. If the machine dispenses gumballs one at a time, and if the probability of receiving a red gumball is $\frac{1}{3}$, and if the probability of receiving a white gumball is $\frac{1}{8}$ and a yellow gumball is $\frac{1}{8}$, how many blue gumballs could be in the machine?

(A) 3
(B) 6
(C) 7
(D) 8
(E) 10

11. The sum of the prices of all groceries in a shopping bag is divided by the number of items, yielding a number x. What does x represent?

(A) The sum of all groceries
(B) The number of groceries
(C) The mean of the groceries
(D) The average cost of the groceries
(E) The largest price of one grocery

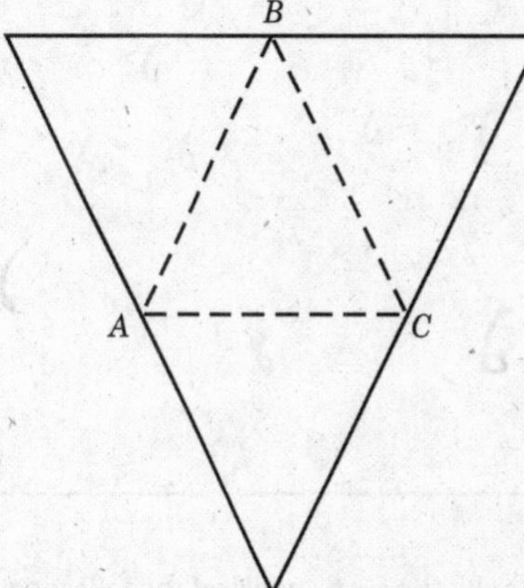

12. The figure above represents four triangles, all equal to each other. If triangle ABC is an equilateral triangle with a perimeter of 18, then what is the perimeter of the figure outlined by the solid line?

(A) 6
(B) 12
(C) 24
(D) 36
(E) 48

GO ON TO THE NEXT PAGE

SECTION 8

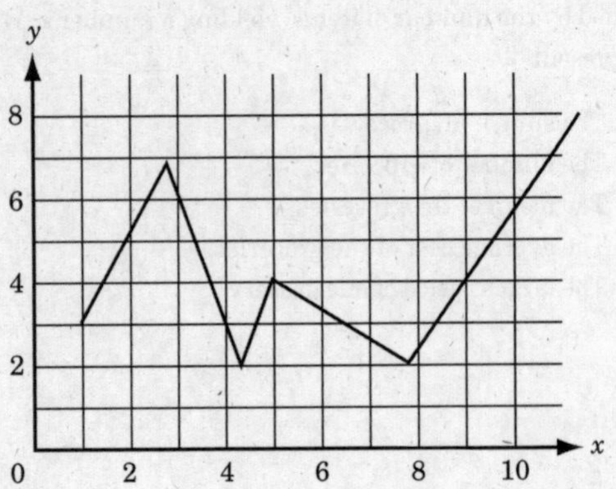

13. The graph $y = k(e)$ is shown above. If $k(1) = b$, which of the following could be the value of $k(b)$?

(A) 3
(B) 4
(C) 5
(D) 6
(E) 7

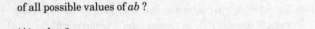

14. If $0 \le a \le 6$ and $-2 \le b \le 6$, which of the following gives the set of all possible values of ab?

(A) $ab = 6$
(B) $0 \le ab \le 36$
(C) $-12 \le ab \le 36$
(D) $-2 \le ab \le 36$
(E) $0 \le ab \le 6$

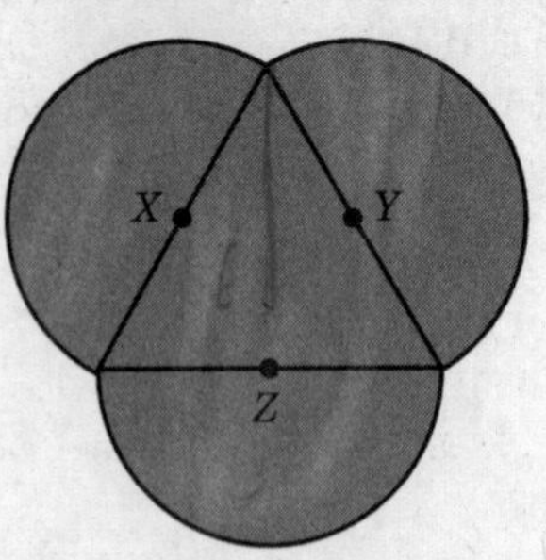

Note: Figure not drawn to scale.

15. If the semicircles with centers X, Y, and Z have areas 12.5π, 12.5π, and 32π respectively, what is the area of the shaded region?

(A) 64π
(B) $57\pi + 48$
(C) $57\pi + 64$
(D) $64\pi + 48$
(E) 57π

16. The first term in a sequence is a fraction. The second term in a sequence is 4 larger than 2 times the fraction. If $\frac{1}{x}$ is the first term of the sequence, and $x \neq 0$, what is the ratio of the first term to the second term?

(A) $\frac{1}{4x+2}$
(B) $\frac{1}{2x}$
(C) $\frac{4x+2}{1}$
(D) $\frac{1}{2x+1}$
(E) $\frac{2x+1}{2}$

S T O P

IF YOU FINISH BEFORE TIME IS CALLED, YOU MAY CHECK YOUR WORK ON THIS TEST ONLY. DO NOT TURN TO ANY OTHER SECTION IN THIS TEST.

SECTION 9

Turn to Section 9 of your answer sheet to answer the questions in this section.

Time—10 Minutes
14 Questions

Directions: For each question in this section, select the best answer from among the choices given.

The following sentences test correctness and effectiveness of expression. Part of each sentence or the entire sentence is underlined; beneath each sentence are five ways of phrasing the underlined material. Choice A repeats the original phrasing; the other four choices are different. If you think the original phrasing produces a better sentence than any of the alternatives, select choice A; if not, select one of the other choices.

In making your selection, follow the requirements of standard written English; that is, pay attention to grammar, choice of words, sentence construction, and punctuation. Your selection should result in the most effective sentence—clear and precise, without awkwardness or ambiguity.

Example:

In the poem "Ulysses" by Alfred, Lord Tennyson, the speaker says, "I cannot rest from travel," instead, he will live life to the fullest.

(A) "I cannot rest from travel," instead,
(B) "I cannot rest from travel"; instead,
(C) "I cannot rest from travel" instead,
(D) "I cannot rest from travel," upon which
(E) "I cannot rest from travel,"

1. The author suggested that for as many as thousands of years and more humans have affected their habitat through technological developments initially intended to increase the food supply.

(A) for as many as thousands of years and more
(B) for thousands of years and even more
(C) for as often as thousands of years
(D) for as many as thousands of years and more
(E) for more than a thousand years

2. The health of a child in a developing country is not as good as a child in the first world.

(A) a child in the first world
(B) like a child in the first world
(C) like the first world's child
(D) that of a child in the first world
(E) such of a child in the first world

3. Ha Jin, part of a generation of writers whose novels are set overseas, writing his first book in English even though Chinese was his native language.

(A) writing his first book in English even though Chinese was his native language
(B) wrote his first book in English even though Chinese was his native language
(C) who was writing his first book in English even though Chinese was his native language
(D) in writing his first book in English even though Chinese was his native language
(E) have been writing his first book in English even though Chinese was his native language

GO ON TO THE NEXT PAGE

SECTION 9

4. Orchestras in Europe routinely tune their instruments to a slightly higher frequency than do orchestras in the United States, <u>and there is a brighter sound as a result and not so many dark shadows</u>.

(A) and there is a brighter sound as a result and not so many dark shadows
(B) and there is a resulting brighter sound with not so many dark shadows
(C) resulting in a brighter sound and fewer dark shadows
(D) which has a brighter sound as a result and not so many dark shadows
(E) and therefore is a brighter sound as a result and not so many dark shadows

5. A surgeon must <u>have high skill and good eye-hand coordination</u> to do his or her job well.

(A) have high skill and good eye-hand coordination
(B) have highly skilled and good eye-hand coordination
(C) be of high skill and of good eye-hand coordination
(D) be highly skilled and have good eye-hand coordination
(E) being highly skilled and well eye-hand coordination

6. Because Liz was interested in Asian cultures, she made it a point to <u>live and work in both Japan and India</u> upon graduating from college.

(A) live and work in both Japan and India
(B) living and working in both Japan and India
(C) both live and work in both Japan and India
(D) go and to live and work in both Japan and India
(E) live Japan and India and work in Japan and India

7. <u>The more we complain about the level of homework</u> given by the teacher, the more you are likely to receive increasing amounts with each week.

(A) The more we complain about the level of homework
(B) With more complaining about the level of homework
(C) By complaining about the level of homework more and more
(D) In more complaining about the level of homework
(E) The more you complain about the level of homework

8. <u>Taking time to adequately prepare for the test</u> and a good night of sleep are key ingredients to doing well on an exam.

(A) Taking time to adequately prepare for the test
(B) Taking adequate time to prepare for the test
(C) Adequate preparation for a test
(D) To be adequately prepared for the test
(E) The adequate preparation for the test

9. We debated for hours whether to follow <u>our mother's suggesting</u> that we take a trip to Hawaii instead of the Bahamas, where hurricanes are more likely this time of year.

(A) our mother's suggesting
(B) our mother in suggesting
(C) mother's suggesting
(D) mother who was suggesting
(E) our mother's suggestion

10. Tabloid newspapers jumped at the news of two stars long rumored to be dating <u>who finally admitted to their relationship</u>.

(A) who finally admitted to their relationship
(B) finally admitting to their relationship
(C) who have finally admitted to their relationship
(D) finally will have been admitted to their relationship
(E) who finally have admitted to their relationship

11. Critics of the space shuttle program expressed concern <u>for the reason that there was insufficient safety testing accompanying the craft's return to space</u>.

(A) for the reason that there was insufficient safety testing accompanying the craft's return to space
(B) because of insufficient safety testing accompanying the craft's return to space
(C) over insufficient safety testing accompanying the craft's return to space
(D) due to insufficient safety testing accompanying the craft's return to space
(E) as a result of insufficient safety testing accompanying the craft's return to space

GO ON TO THE NEXT PAGE

SECTION 9

12. An art dealer suggested that California impressionist paintings had increased in value, this was due to the fact that European paintings have become prohibitively expensive and thus collectors have turned an eye toward California.

(A) this was due to the fact that European paintings have become prohibitively expensive and thus collectors have turned an eye toward California
(B) this was because European paintings have become prohibitively expensive and thus collectors have turned an eye toward California
(C) therefore European paintings have become prohibitively expensive and thus collectors have turned an eye toward California
(D) because European paintings have become prohibitively expensive and thus collectors have turned an eye toward California
(E) European paintings have become prohibitively expensive and thus collectors have turned an eye toward California

13. The teenagers who lived on the reservation where the crime occurred were upset by the enormity of the press media which covered the gory details of the tragedy.

(A) enormity of the press media which covered
(B) enormity of the media covering
(C) extensive media press which covered
(D) extensive media press covering
(E) extensive media coverage of

14. Of all the days for it to rain, Sherry thought Saturday was the worst day, because she had had plans that day that involved a party outdoors.

(A) Sherry thought Saturday was the worst day, because she had had plans that day that involved a party outdoors
(B) Sherry thought Saturday was the worst day due to plans that involved a party outdoors
(C) the weekend was the worst, involving a party outdoors for which Sherry had plans that day which
(D) Saturday was the worst, because Sherry had plans that day that involved a party outdoors
(E) Saturday for Sherry was the worst who had plans that day that involved a party outdoors

S T O P

IF YOU FINISH BEFORE TIME IS CALLED, YOU MAY CHECK YOUR WORK ON THIS TEST ONLY.
DO NOT TURN TO ANY OTHER SECTION IN THIS TEST.

PRACTICE TEST 5 EXPLANATIONS

PRACTICE TEST 5 ANSWERS

Question Number	Answer	Right	Wrong
Section 2			
1	D		
2	A		
3	B		
4	C		
5	A		
6	A		
7	C		
8	B		
9	D		
10	A		
11	D		
12	B		
13	D		
14	D		
15	B		
16	E		
17	D		
18	B		
19	C		
20	C		
21	A		
22	D		
23	E		
24	C		
Section 3			
1	D		
2	D		
3	A		
4	D		
5	B		
6	C		
7	E		
8	B		
9	E		
10	C		
11	B		
12	B		
13	A		
14	A		
15	E		
16	E		
17	D		
18	C		
19	A		
20	B		
Section 4			
1	E		
2	B		
3	C		
4	D		
5	A		
6	A		
7	B		
Section 4, continued			
8	A		
9	A		
10	B		
11	D		
12	E		
13	B		
14	D		
15	C		
16	B		
17	C		
18	E		
19	D		
20	A		
21	B		
22	D		
23	D		
24	C		
Section 5			
1	E		
2	B		
3	B		
4	A		
5	C		
6	D		
7	D		
8	E		
9	994		
10	75		
11	7		
12	1225		
13	120		
14	5		
15	14		
16	5.64		
17	30		
18	1/2, .5		
Section 6			
1	D		
2	B		
3	E		
4	E		
5	C		
6	D		
7	B		
8	D		
9	A		
10	C		
11	A		
12	B		
13	E		
14	D		
15	C		
16	E		

Question Number	Answer	Right	Wrong	Question Number	Answer	Right	Wrong
Section 6, continued				Section 7, continued			
17	D			17	C		
18	C			18	D		
19	D			19	D		
20	C			Section 8			
21	A			1	C		
22	A			2	D		
23	E			3	B		
24	A			4	E		
25	D			5	A		
26	C			6	D		
27	A			7	A		
28	B			8	E		
29	A			9	D		
30	B			10	E		
31	B			11	D		
32	A			12	D		
33	C			13	D		
34	D			14	C		
35	B			15	B		
Section 7				16	A		
1	B			Section 9			
2	C			1	E		
3	A			2	D		
4	D			3	B		
5	D			4	C		
6	E			5	D		
7	D			6	A		
8	A			7	E		
9	C			8	C		
10	B			9	E		
11	A			10	B		
12	D			11	C		
13	B			12	D		
14	E			13	E		
15	B			14	D		
16	E						

CALCULATING YOUR SCORE

Writing Section Raw Score

A. Essay Score (from 1–6) ______ A

B. Section 6 Multiple Choice: ______ no. correct – (______ no. incorrect ÷ 4) = ______ B

C. Section 9 Multiple Choice: ______ no. correct – (______ no. incorrect ÷ 4) = ______ C

D. Unrounded Multiple-Choice Score (B + C) ______ D

E. Total Rounded Multiple-Choice Raw Score
(Rounded to the nearest whole number) ______ E

F. Writing Multiple-Choice Subscore
(See the Writing Multiple-Choice conversion table on the following pages) ______ Writing MC Score

G. Total Scaled Score
(See the Writing conversion table on the following pages) ______ SAT Writing Score

Math Section Raw Score

A. Section 3 Raw Score: ______ no. correct – (______ no. incorrect ÷ 4) = ______ Subtotal A

B. Section 5 Raw Score: ______ no. correct ______ Subtotal B

C. Section 8 Raw Score: ______ no. correct – (______ no. incorrect ÷ 4) = ______ Subtotal C

D. Total Unrounded Raw Score
(Total A + B + C) ______ D

E. Total Rounded Raw Score (Rounded to the nearest whole number) ______ E

F. Scaled Score
(See the conversion table on the following pages) ______ SAT Math Score

Critical Reading Section Raw Score

A. Section 2 Raw Score: ______ (no. correct) – (______ (no. incorrect) ÷ 4) = ______ A

B. Section 4 Raw Score: ______ (no. correct) – (______ (no. incorrect) ÷ 4) = ______ B

C. Section 7 Raw Score: ______ (no. correct) – (______ (no. incorrect) ÷ 4) = ______ C

D. Total Unrounded Raw Score
(Total A + B + C)

______ D

E. Total Rounded Raw Score
(Rounded to the nearest whole number)

______ E

F. Scaled Score
(See the conversion table on the next page)

______ SAT Critical Reading Score

CONVERTING YOUR RAW SCORES

Raw Score	Critical Reading Scaled Score	Math Scaled Score
67	800	
66	790	
65	770	
64	760	
63	750	
62	740	
61	720	
60	710	
59	700	
58	690	
57	680	
56	670	
55	670	
54	660	800
53	650	780
52	640	760
51	640	740
50	630	730
49	620	710
48	610	700
47	610	690
46	600	670
45	590	660
44	590	650
43	580	650
42	580	640
41	570	630
40	560	620
39	560	610
38	550	600
37	540	590
36	540	590
35	530	580
34	530	570
33	520	560
32	510	560
31	510	550
30	500	540
29	500	530
28	490	520
27	480	520
26	480	510
25	470	500
24	470	490
23	460	490
22	450	480
21	450	470
20	440	460
19	430	460

Raw Score	Critical Reading Scaled Score	Math Scaled Score
18	430	450
17	420	440
16	410	430
15	410	430
14	400	420
13	390	410
12	380	400
11	380	390
10	370	380
9	360	380
8	350	370
7	340	360
6	330	340
5	320	330
4	310	320
3	300	310
2	280	290
1	270	280
0	250	260
−1	250	250
−2	240	240
−3	230	230
-4	220	220
−5	210	210
−6	200	200

Writing Subscores

- **Essay Subscore:** Subtotal A from Writing Score (page 430)
- **Multiple-Choice Subscore:** Calculate by plugging in Subtotal E from your writing score (page 430) into the score conversion table below

Raw Score	Multiple-Choice Subscore	Raw Score	Multiple-Choice Subscore
49	80	30	59
48	79	29	58
47	77	28	57
46	76	27	56
45	75	26	55
44	74	25	54
43	72	24	53
42	71	23	52
41	70	22	51
40	69	21	51
39	68	20	50
38	67	19	49
37	66	18	48
36	65	17	47
35	64	16	46
34	63	15	45
33	62	14	44
32	61	13	43
31	60	12	42

Raw Score	Multiple-Choice Subscore	Raw Score	Multiple-Choice Subscore
11	41	2	32
10	40	1	30
9	39	0	29
8	38	−1	27
7	37	−2	25
6	36	−3	24
5	35	-4	23
4	34	−5	22
3	33	−6	21

Writing Scaled Score

MC raw score	Essay Score					
	6	5	4	3	2	1
49	800	790	780	770	720	700
48	790	780	760	730	700	680
47	780	770	750	720	690	670
46	770	760	740	710	680	660
45	770	750	740	700	670	650
44	760	750	730	690	660	640
43	750	740	710	680	650	630
42	750	730	700	670	640	620
41	740	730	690	660	630	610
40	740	720	690	650	620	600
39	740	710	680	640	610	590
38	730	700	670	630	610	590
37	720	690	660	630	600	580
36	710	680	650	620	590	570
35	710	680	640	610	580	560
34	700	670	640	600	570	550
33	690	660	630	590	560	540
32	680	650	620	580	560	540
31	670	640	610	580	550	530
30	660	630	600	570	540	520
29	650	630	590	560	530	510
28	640	620	590	550	520	510
27	640	610	580	540	510	490
26	630	600	570	530	500	490
25	620	590	560	520	500	480
24	610	580	550	510	490	470
23	600	570	540	510	480	460
22	590	570	530	500	470	450
21	590	570	530	500	470	450
20	580	560	520	490	460	440
19	570	550	520	480	450	430
18	570	540	520	470	440	420
17	560	530	510	460	430	420
16	550	520	500	450	430	410
15	540	510	490	450	420	400
14	530	500	480	440	410	390
13	520	500	470	430	400	380
12	510	490	460	420	390	370

Writing Scaled Score

MC raw score	Essay Score					
	6	5	4	3	2	1
11	510	480	450	410	380	360
10	500	470	450	400	370	350
9	490	460	440	390	360	350
8	480	450	430	390	360	340
7	470	440	420	380	350	330
6	460	430	410	370	340	320
5	450	430	400	360	330	310
4	450	420	390	350	320	300
3	440	410	390	340	310	290
2	430	400	380	330	300	280
1	420	380	370	320	290	270
0	400	370	350	310	280	260
-1	380	360	340	290	270	260
-2	370	340	320	270	260	250
-3	360	330	310	260	250	240
-4	350	320	290	250	240	230
-5	340	310	280	240	230	220
-6	340	310	280	240	220	210

SECTION 2: CRITICAL READING

Sentence Completions

1. **D** One-Word/One-Way *Medium*

The marathoner went beyond what was expected: he *astounded his critics and peers*. You can guess that he "went beyond" the old record of 250 miles and ran 272 miles. The word *surpassed* means "to go beyond."

2. **A** One-Word/One-Way *Medium*

Critics and essayists like the car. Previously, you are told that *cars failed to impress*. But this one clearly has "impressed." The car, therefore, must possess some kind of positive quality. The only word that fits is *expedience*, **A**.

3. **B** Two-Word/One-Way *Medium*

The video game ball rolls up objects from around the house, so you can assume that it's gathering "everyday" objects. The sentence also tells you that the ball will be composed of things that are *increasingly larger*. In other words, the end result will give you a ball that is "very big." Eliminate **C** and **E**. Since the huge ball is made up of "everyday things," the correct choice must be **B**.

4. **C** Two-Word/Two-Way *Medium*

Doctors used to feel one way about *shamanism*, but now they feel another. The words *were said* should strongly indicate to you that the doctors didn't necessarily believe in shamanism originally. Thus, a good guess for the first blank would be a word like "not sure." Eliminate **B** and **D**. Now, however, doctors view shamanism differently. The only word that fits the second blank is *metaphoric*, **C**, which means "viewing as an analogy."

5. **A** Two-Word/Two-Way *Difficult*

Once upon a time, the journal had *a reputation* for *discovering young new writers*. The word *although* tells you that the journal no longer engages in this practice. The new tastes are going to be more "conservative." Eliminate **B**, **D**, and **E**. The first blank is then relatively straightforward: you know that the journal has now become "closed" or *insulated*. Nothing in the sentence indicates that this practice is *ruinous* or "detrimental."

Paired Reading Passages

6. **A** Relating Two Passages *Medium*

The author of Passage 1 is very clear about giving credit to the Greeks for our understanding of the atomic world. The author of Passage 2, in contrast, does not even mention the names of the men who postulated the notion of "atoms." The author of Passage 1, therefore, exhibits far more *respect* toward the Greeks than the author of Passage 2.

7. **C** Relating Two Passages *Difficult*

The author of Passage 2 very clearly states that the atom's existence was not clearly noted until the eighteenth century, when chemists began a series of experiments on the nature of substances. In other words, the author of Passage 2 does not believe that the Greeks helped to discover the existence of the atom, **C**.

8. **B** Relating Two Passages *Difficult*

Both authors do state that testing is important. In the last line of the first passage, for example, the author writes, *For it is only by initially taking such leaps that dreams are able to make the transition from abstract idea to testable theory.* The author of Passage 2 praises the eighteenth-century men who *engaged in a series of experiments*.

9. **D** Relating Two Passages *Difficult*

Here are the lines in question: *Here, then, are the origins of true science, of the deliberate and careful examination of the world as it is, and not a theory perpetuated from a mere "hunch."* Now, notice that the author of Passage 1 says the following: *For it is only by initially taking such leaps that dreams are able to make the transition from abstract idea to testable theory.* In other words, although it is true that the Greeks used their rational intuition to conjure up the idea of the atom, the author of Passage 1 feels that they couldn't have even intuited the idea of an atom without imagination. Watch out for **E**, which contains information not explicitly stated or supported in the passage.

Long Reading Passages

10. **A** Technique *Easy*

The author begins by describing the way food smells, the invisibility of the candy in the piñatas, and the way the coast appears. In other words, the author opens the passage by appealing to the senses of sight and smell.

11. **D** Words in Context *Medium*

The author states the following: *Perhaps instead it was our attunement to wonder in the first place that allowed us to see this ancient land anew, perhaps, even, we were able to see this world as it was intended, if there can be one true way in which to observe the land.* Here, the author states that he and his companions are able to see things as if perceiving them for the first time.

12. **B** Implied Information *Easy*

Here are the lines in question: *In the mornings we could sit on the sand cliffs near the highway, where the land was mostly made up of sand and therefore not appropriate for the elaborate, castlelike houses built further down the peninsula where the property was anchored with rich soil.* In other words, the author is not sitting on a piece of land that has "castlelike" houses. Instead, the houses here are the opposite—poor but picturesque.

13. **D** Themes and Arguments *Medium*

At the end of the paragraph, the author states, *These shapes flash orange and red on hot days, then grow muted, a shade of gray against a backdrop of the deepest bluish-black. We love the sea, but we fear it, for it is even larger than this endless land and culture.* Thus, the narrator loves the water but finds it frightening. The reference to water and hell underwater help to illustrate that sense of fear.

14. **D** Implied Information *Medium*

The author pretty clearly states, *We preferred the intimate scenes we saw in our work. We marvel at the ability of the artichoke to rejuvenate.* The author likes to be on land, working with the land.

15. **B** Attitude and Tone *Easy*

The end of the passage reads as follows: *It was our ability to wonder at what seemed miraculous, while the other world sped around us, that kept us attuned to work and, despite its mundane nature, kept us proud of what we could accomplish.* The work is defined as *mundane*, and yet the author is also proud of what he is able to do. He is resigned, but still optimistic.

16. **E** Technique *Medium*

In the first few lines, the author declares that although she is a dancer, she does not understand the purpose of dance. She then goes on to explain why she may not understand dance: she has an instinctive relationship to dance and therefore can't analyze it. Next she states that she cannot keep herself from wondering about the purpose of dance. First she declares her lack of understanding for dance, then poses a possible explanation, and finally she accepts her curiosity.

17. **D** Specific Information *Difficult*
Reading all the way through the lines, you find the following: *so too has dance become a complex, profound mirror into which we can dance and see ourselves.* Thus, dance is complex because the world is complex, and we can better understand ourselves through dance.

18. **B** Specific Information *Medium*
Here are the lines in question: *In our darkest hours as humans, certainly these feelings descend upon our bodies so that we feel them physically. Who has not actually felt ill with grief? So it is no wonder that dance, that physical art form, would seek to express those emotions that are experienced internally.* The author is making the point that humans not only feel painful emotions in their minds but also, on occasion, in their bodies. Dance, as a physical art form, is therefore appropriate for expressing these feelings.

19. **C** Words in Context *Medium*
Here are the lines surrounding the word *visceral*: *But to say that dance is merely visceral, that it is experienced by the senses alone, is to discount the role that intellect might play in the construction of dance. I would argue now that dancers, like our very best actors, are not simply intuitive mimics.* The author is making the point that dance is not merely visceral or instinctual. She wants to demonstrate that dance requires that dancers not just unthinkingly emote but also use their intellects to *observe* the world.

20. **C** Themes and Arguments *Medium*
Look at the lines surrounding the text: *Then there is the dance piece itself. Classical dance was very good at conveying the themes of the romantic era. We see little lithe ballerinas lifted into the air by muscular and therefore heroic men.* This is essentially a purpose of detail question, which tests your ability to spot why the author mentions a specific detail within a paragraph. Here, the author is making the point that classical dance reflected the concerns of the romantic period; *little lithe ballerinas* are a reflection of the romantic cultural ideal.

21. **A** Implied Information *Medium*
At the end of paragraph 4, the author writes, *No wonder too that women strove to dance not just on heels, but on their toes. What great irony it is that this dancing "on pointe" requires such strength and balance and yet is meant to convey a certain lightness of being, a floating spirit.* In these lines, the author draws a parallel between the tendency of ballerinas to dance on their toes in classical dance pieces and a desire to appear *light* and *floating*. Because these lines are within the context of a paragraph describing the romantic period, it is safe to assume that the author believes that *lightness*, in part, defines the romantic aesthetic.

22. **D** Words in Context *Medium*
With vocabulary-in-context questions, remember to always read the surrounding lines and try to predict what the word means. The lines surrounding the word are *It brings in an observation of our mechanized environment, as demonstrated through the "locking" and "breaking" moves of hip-hop, which mirror the many machines that surround us and which we often take for granted.* The author states that people live

in a world increasingly dominated by computers and machines. The best choice, then, for *mechanized*, is *machinelike*.

23. **E** Words in Context *Easy*

Take a look at the context of the word *convoluted*: *We like to show our internal neuroses through powerful, convoluted moves.* The correct definition will be a good companion to the word *powerful*. Eliminate **A**, **B**, and **C**. The word *hostile*, although a "powerful" word, is not an appropriate definition for convoluted, which means something closer to "twisting," "elaborate," and *tortuous*.

24. **C** Technique *Medium*

You should notice that the author used the idea of dance as a *mirror* reflecting societal conditions in her introduction. By using the idea of the mirror again in the conclusion, she is making a use of *circular imagery*, bringing her images full circle.

SECTION 3: MATH

Multiple Choice

1. **D** Algebra: Substitution *Easy*

One flat contains 12 cans of food. The other 4 flats contain 10 cans each, for a total of 40 cans. Adding 40 to 12 gives you a total of 52 cans.

2. **D** Geometry: Angles and Lines *Easy*

YZ is 10. *XY* is one-fifth of 10, or 2. Adding 10 and 2 gives you 12, the total length of *XZ*.

3. **A** Algebra: System of Equations *Easy*

The second equation is twice the first equation. If the first equation equals 8, then 2 times 8 equals 16.

4. **D** Data Analysis, Statistics & Probability: Graphs, Charts, and Tables *Easy*

According to the graph, Devina was 56 inches last summer and is still 56 inches this summer. In other words, she had a growth of 0 inches, making her the sister who showed the least growth.

5. **B** Data Analysis, Statistics & Probability: Graphs, Charts, and Tables *Easy*

Here are the 5 heights from last summer: Anna was 48 inches, Beth was 48 inches, Carla was 52 inches, Devina was 56 inches, and Ella was 54 inches. Add these up and divide by 5 to find an average of 51.6 inches.

6. **C** Algebra: Absolute Value and Exponents *Medium*

Absolute value requires that you solve for the positive value of an equation. First, simplify:

$$\left|\frac{1}{b}+\frac{2}{a}\right|$$

$$\left|\frac{1}{2}+\frac{-2}{3}\right|$$

$$\left|\frac{3}{6}+\frac{-4}{6}\right|$$

$$\left|\frac{-1}{6}\right|$$

$$\frac{1}{6}$$

7. **E** Algebra: Solving Equations *Easy*

Simplify and solve:

$$\left(\frac{1}{a}+\frac{1}{b}\right)\left(\frac{1}{a+b}\right)$$

$$\left(\frac{1}{\frac{1}{4}}+\frac{1}{\frac{1}{3}}\right)\left(\frac{1}{\frac{1}{4}+\frac{1}{3}}\right)$$

$$(3+4)\left(\frac{1}{\frac{3}{12}+\frac{4}{12}}\right)$$

$$(7)\left(\frac{1}{\frac{7}{12}}\right)$$

$$(7)\left(\frac{12}{7}\right)$$

$$12$$

8. **B** Geometry: Coordinate Geometry *Medium*

Use the information to find all the coordinates. The square must have 4 equal sides of 5, since the perimeter is 20. If x-coordinate of A is –1, then you know that points C and D both have an x-coordinate of 4 (so that sides AD and BC each measure 5). If the y-coordinate of B is 2, then the y-coordinate of C must also be 2.

9. **E** Geometry: Coordinate Geometry *Medium*

Only **E** gives you a function that yields the proper result when the values for x are plugged into the equation.

10. **C** Algebra: Substitution *Medium*

To find Jennie's age now, take her brother's age, or b, and subtract j years from it. Then try substituting values: let's say that j is 2 and b is 10. In two years, Jennie will be the same age as her brother, or 10. You know that now she is 8 years old, or 10 – 2.

11. **B** Data Analysis, Statistics & Probability: Logic *Medium*

This problem is not as difficult as it looks. By first switching the Y and the E blocks, and then switching the Y and T blocks, Betty will be able to spell her name.

12. **B** Geometry: Solids *Medium*

First, find the volume of the box: $(26)(30)(64) = 49{,}920$. Now find the volume of 1 CD: $(1)(12)(4) = 48$. Now, divide the volume of 1 CD into the volume of the large box: $(49{,}920) \div 48 = 1{,}040$.

13. **A** Geometry: Angles and Lines *Medium*

Let's say that a equals $\frac{1}{4}$. In that case, b would equal $\frac{1}{16}$ and c would equal $\frac{1}{2}$. The largest of these values is c. After that, you would have a and then b. **A** correctly represents these values on the number line.

14. **A** Geometry: Coordinate Geometry *Medium*

Notice that lines C and B have the same slope and that they are parallel to the x-axis. This means that both have a slope of 0. Since this slope occurs most frequently, it is the mode.

15. **E** Algebra: Absolute Value and Exponents *Medium*

The plan takes off from Tokyo at 6 P.M. and lands 16 hours later, at 10 A.M. the following day, Tokyo time. However, remember that New York is 14 hours behind Tokyo. So 10 A.M. in Tokyo is actually 8 P.M. the previous day in New York. As a result, the plane lands in New York at 8 P.M. on January 23.

16. **E** Geometry: Polygons *Medium*

The area of the entire square is 16, which means that one side is 4. Since the radius of each circle equals half the side of the square, you know that the radius of each circle is 2. The area of one whole circle would be 4π. However, you have two quarter-circles, or one half-circle, so the area of these two quarter-circles together is 2π. Now, simply take the area of the whole square and subtract the unshaded quarter-circles to find the area of the shaded region: $16 - 2\pi$.

17. **D** Geometry: Coordinate Geometry *Medium*

Multiplying a function by a number larger than 1 will cause the resulting graph to become taller and thinner. Notice that the origin of the graph should not change. The correct answer must be **D**.

18. **C** Geometry: Triangles *Medium*

You are told that RST is an equilateral triangle, which means that angles R, S, and T are all 60 degrees. Since you know that angle RWU is 50 degrees, you know that RUW must be *70* in order for triangle RUW to equal 180 degrees total. Since sides UW and VW are equal, angles UVW and VUW must also be equal. Since angle UWV is 40, subtract this from 180 and divide by 2 to find the measure of each remaining angle. Each angle equals 70 degrees. Now, look at angle VWT. You know that it must be 90 degrees in order for line RWT to equal 180 degrees total. This means that angle WVT

equals 30 degrees. Finally, line *ST* must equal 180 degrees. Subtract 30 and 70 from 180 to get 80 degrees for angle *UVS*.

19. **A** Numbers & Operations: Substitution *Difficult*

All the answer choices are simply rearranged versions of the original equation, $wx = yz$, following the rules of simplification. Only **A** violates the basic relationship between the letters.

20. **B** Algebra: Absolute Value and Exponents *Difficult*

If both x and b must be integers, then one possible value for x is 64.

$$\sqrt[3]{64} + \sqrt{64} = b$$
$$4 + 8 = 12$$

None of the other values can fit the criteria of both b and x being integers.

SECTION 4: CRITICAL READING

Sentence Completions

1. **E** One-Word/One-Way *Easy*

Margo is an extreme version of people who *are aware of the benefits of herbs.* In fact, she *proselytizes*, or preaches, about the benefit of herbs. A good guess for the blank would be "enthusiastic" or "crazy." The correct answer, *emphatic*, means "to place great emphasis" on something.

2. **B** Two-Word/One-Way *Easy*

The word *determining* gives you a strong clue that the first blank will be something similar. Eliminate **A** and **C**. The word *extreme* in the sentence also gives you a strong clue that the second blank will be something close to *extreme*. **B** fits the meaning of the sentence.

3. **C** One-Word/One-Way *Medium*

You are told that the play has a lot of *humor* in it. The *audience* has also *responded* to this humor, and the actors in the play have, in turn, reacted to the audience. You can therefore assume that the mood of the theater is something positive. Only *mirth*, **C**, fits the criteria.

4. **D** One-Word/Two-Way *Medium*

Shannon did not do well on her test, but, according to the sentence, she is not completely to blame. We are told that she *did not study as hard as she could have.* However, the teacher also slipped information into the test that made answering the questions all the more difficult. What kind of questions would make the test more difficult? Those which are beyond the scope of what she could have studied—in other words, *random* information.

5. **A** Two-Word/Two-Way *Medium*

The birds *are born with the capacity to sing.* You are looking for a word that matches this meaning. Only *innate*, **A**, fits.

6. **A** One-Word/One-Way *Medium*

Stephen Jobs *was wasting his talents* before he returned to Apple Computer. He was someone who wandered around acting reckless and wasteful, or *prodigal*.

7. **B** Two-Word/One-Way *Medium*

The key here is that the public likes *abbreviated entertainment*. The public likes works which are cut short. So, what would the author have to do in order to appease *the sales department*? He would have to "cut down" his novel. Eliminate **A**, **C**, and **D**. For the second blank, ask yourself what kinds of books the sales department would consider difficult to sell—those that are "too big." The correct answer must be **B**.

8. **A** One-Word/Two-Way *Medium*

A professional opera singer must show up *prepared and on time.* The *opera singer* has not received the award from the judges because, we are told, she does not act like a *professional.* In other words, she did not *show up on time*—and this *tardiness* prevented her from receiving first prize.

Short Reading Passages

9. **A** Specific Information *Easy*

Most of this paragraph is about how the narrator is delighted to be in a new place where the color is predominantly green. Prior to rhapsodizing about green, she mentions that she was from a land where summers and winters *were equally pale and straw colored.* In other words, her native land was very *beige*, and not green at all.

10. **B** Attitude or Tone *Medium*

The lines referenced are positive in tone. We are told that the *air is emerald* and that the *world whirred*. Neither of these things is literally possible. However, these words give a sense of how impressed she is by the *wonder* of the color green.

11. **D** Themes and Arguments *Medium*

Remember, the correct answer to an assumption question on the SAT will never be too far from what is actually stated in the passage. At the end of this paragraph, the author states, *surely no one merchant would have traveled the entire distance from ancient China to Egypt.* He claims it is impossible for a trader to have crossed all the way from China to Egypt. Therefore, evidence that a trader could or, in fact, did travel from China to Egypt would weaken the argument.

12. **E** Attitude and Tone *Easy*

The author rather confidently asserts that he knows how the silk from 1000 B.C. could have gone from China to Rome. His tone makes it clear that he knows what he is talking about, so he is *knowing*.

Paired Reading Passages

13. **B** Words in Context *Medium*

Take a look at the lines in question: *In my thirty years as an expert in the field of organizational behavior, it has become apparent to me that to be prepared to embrace the many changes happening around us now, and which will persist well into the new millennium, individuals functioning within an organization must be encouraged to think and act creatively.* A good prediction or substitution for the word *embrace* would be something like "to take on." The word *accept*, **B**, most nearly matches this prediction. Watch out for *hug*, **A**, which is a definition for *embrace* but does not fit the context of the sentence.

14. **D** Specific Information *Medium*

Be sure you look not only at the lines that are referenced but also at the surrounding material. The author writes, *We generally think of artists as being creative and judge their level of creativity by the products that they produce. Reconfiguring this definition so it applies to those who work in fields outside of the fine arts, but who are nevertheless clearly creative, may seem a bit of a challenge.* The author is arguing for the definition of "creativity" to be expanded to include people *other than* just artists. Thus, artists are just one example of the kinds of people who should be considered creative.

15. **C** Specific Information *Medium*

Here are the lines in question: *Think of any great work of art, for example, and there are precedents, though these notable influences do not in and of themselves equal the quality of what we would term "great."* Note the phrase *notable influences.* This is a strong clue as to the definition of *precedent.* A good prediction might be something like "preexisting thing that influences the artist."

16. **B** Themes and Arguments *Difficult*

The author's whole point in this paragraph is to convince the reader that creativity can be taught. The concluding line, therefore, is a recapitulation of this idea given after the author has presented her argument.

17. **C** Technique *Medium*

To answer this question correctly you need to understand the author's point of view. He begins by citing the titles of two books and calling their titles into question. He then goes on to say, *Once upon a time these titles meant something, distinguished the hobbyist from the true practitioner, and yet in this age of hyper-democratization, we seem intent on trying to find all possible applications for these terms, even when reason tells us that we should stop.* He is very unhappy that "creativity" has become a marketable concept. You can expect that the author will (and, in fact, he does) elaborate on his unhappiness and the reasons for it.

18. **E** Technique *Medium*

The second paragraph opens with a strong statement from the author: *I say all this with a kind of sick realization that there will be those who immediately assume I am championing the kind of elitism that our forefathers fought to quell. This is not my intention at all.* Even though the author is protesting that the terms *creativity* and *poet* are used too loosely, he does not want to be accused of elitism—he does not want to be considered a "snob." Watch out for **A**. The author does *not* want to be considered prejudicial.

19. **D** Themes and Arguments *Difficult*

In this paragraph, the author of Passage 2 is trying to distinguish between true artists and poets and those who are not artists: *To put it more bluntly, an artist has a truly unusual take on things and does not simply parrot the* supposed *attitudes of the individual.* The word *supposed* is in italics to emphasize the distinction between these two kinds of people.

20. **A** Attitude or Tone *Medium*

The author of the first passage is so supportive of creativity in the workplace that she wants CEOs to actually teach workers to think creatively. She even goes so far as to redefine what constitutes creativity and to propose a definition of the *creative organization*. The author of the second passage is upset with how broadly the terms *creative* and *poet* are used and wants to limit the usage of at least one of them. In other words, the first author is enthusiastically supportive, and the second is skeptical.

21. **B** Relating Two Passages *Difficult*

The author of Passage 1 proposes: *It stands to reason that if these traits repeatedly define a creative person, then an organization can reinforce these character traits.* The author of Passage 1 believes that it is possible to create conditions in which creativity is encourage and therefore flourishes. The author of Passage 2, however, says: *To put it more bluntly, an artist has a truly unusual take on things and is always dissatisfied with institutions, no matter how they pander, and will never parrot the* supposed *attitudes of the individual.* The author of Passage 2 is making the point that artists will always rebel against any institution, even if that institution is supporting "creativity."

22. **D** Relating Two Passages *Difficult*

The author of Passage 1 feels very strongly that modern companies must learn to embrace creativity if they are to remain competitive in the coming years. She states: *We no longer live in a world in which the country with the greatest natural resources will outwit all others. Instead, it is our people and our talents that will ensure our survival and our ability to surmount any obstacle.* Watch out for **A**. It is the author of Passage 2 who brings up the subject of elitism. Although the author of Passage 1 might find the author of Passage 2 elitist, nothing in Passage 1 actually overtly implies this.

23. **D** Relating Two Passages *Medium*

The whole point of the argument in Passage 1 is to try to help make corporations and other organizations more competitive. Note what the author of Passage 2 says in the last paragraph: *I realize, of course, that I can say all this safely hidden away inside the walls of an institution that survives on the donations of corporations and wealthy individuals. As such, my life is dependent on that singular institution we call capitalism.* The author of Passage 2 freely admits that his livelihood is dependent on the success of corporations. We can assume, therefore, that the author of Passage 1 would insist that her fate—and the fate of the corporation—is linked to that of the poet.

24. **C** Relating Two Passages *Medium*

Only the author of Passage 2 believes that artists have a unique type of creativity. He even says at the end of his passage that heads of corporations may be creative *in their own way*. The author of Passage 1, however, does not distinguish between "kinds" of creativity.

SECTION 5: MATH

Multiple Choice

1. **E** Algebra: Substitution *Easy*

Plug the values into the equations and solve:

$$c = 3$$

$$b = 4c$$
$$b = 4(3)$$
$$b = 12$$

$$a = b - c$$
$$a = 12 - 3$$
$$a = 9$$

2. **B** Numbers & Operations: Inequalities *Easy*

Take this problem a step at a time. The bank is smaller than the grocery store:

$$b < g$$

But the bank is larger than the fire department:

$$f < b$$

Putting it all together, you have the following:

$$f < b < g$$

3. **B** Algebra: Solving Equations *Easy*

To find the average of something, add the terms together, then divide by the number of terms. Since there are 2 terms, and the sum is $58, simply divide 58 by 2 to find an average of $29.

4. **A** Algebra: Solving Equations *Medium*

Since x must be a positive integer, the first possible value for x is 1. Plugging this into the equation, you can find the first possible value for T:

$$T = x^2 - 2$$
$$T = 1^2 - 2$$
$$T = -1$$

Moving along through the possible positive integers, you should find pretty quickly that the only answer choice that could not exist in T is –2 (if $x = 2$, then $T = 2$. If $x = 3$, then $T = 7$, and so on).

5. **C** Geometry: Circles *Medium*

If O is the center of the circle, then the triangle formed with O as a point of the triangle must be isosceles: the two lines radiating out from the center function as both radii and the legs of the triangle and, as such, are the same length. Since an isosceles triangle has not only two equal sides but also two equal angles, so you know that the angle above angle b is also 70 degrees. Since there are always 180 degrees in a triangle, subtract the two known angles to find the value of a, or 40.

6. **D** Numbers & Operations: Divisibility and Remainders *Medium*

All of the numbers listed are evenly divisible by 4 except for 86, which yields a remainder.

7. **D** Geometry: Triangles *Medium*

Don't be put off by the strange variables. Remember, the formula for finding the area of a triangle is $\frac{1}{2}bh$.

Plug in the values you are given into the formula:

$$\begin{aligned} \frac{2h^2}{5} &= \frac{bh}{2} \\ \frac{2h^2}{5}\left(\frac{1}{h}\right) &= \frac{bh}{2}\left(\frac{1}{h}\right) \\ \frac{2h}{5} &= \frac{b}{2} \\ \frac{2h}{5}(2) &= \frac{b}{2}(2) \\ \frac{4h}{5} &= b \end{aligned}$$

8. **E** Numbers & Operations: Exponents *Difficult*

Be careful here. You are looking for the value of x, which must yield an integer when the equation is simplified. Taking the answer choices one at a time, you will find that only one possible answer will work. Let's start with **E**:

$$\begin{aligned} \frac{x^{\frac{1}{3}}}{4} &= \frac{\sqrt[3]{x}}{4} \\ &= \frac{\sqrt[3]{64}}{4} \\ \frac{4}{4} &= 1 \end{aligned}$$

Grid-Ins

9. **994** Numbers & Operations: Factors and Multiples *Medium*

To find the answer, start with 999 and divide by 7. Then work backwards until you find an integer that is evenly divisible by 7. The number 994 is the largest three-digit integer evenly divisible by 7.

10. **75** Algebra: Ratios *Easy*

The first four bottles will require 30 pounds of lavender. The second four bottles will also require 30 pounds of lavender, for a total 60 pounds. However, you need to find enough lavender for another two bottles, or half the original ratio: you will need to add 15 more pounds of lavender, for a total of 75 pounds of lavender.

11. **7** Algebra: Solving Equations *Medium*

Translate the instructions. You are told that when x is increased by $3x$, the value must be between 20 and 35. Try substituting a few numbers:

$$x + 3x =$$
$$5 + 3(5) = 5 + 15 = 20$$
$$7 + 3(7) = 7 + 21 = 28$$
$$9 + 3(9) = 9 + 27 = 36$$

12. **1225** Geometry: Polygons *Medium*

The area of a rectangle is equal to the length times the width. Use the information given to find the dimensions of the park.

$$A = lw$$
$$7,500 = (600)(w)$$
$$12.5 = wh$$

Now, add up the dimensions of the park to find the perimeter:

$$P = 2(l) + 2(w)$$
$$P = 2(12.5) + 2(600)$$
$$P = 25 + 1,200$$
$$P = 1,225$$

13. **120** Algebra: Solving Equations *Medium*

There are x number of shirts at \$5 and also x number of shirts at \$10. Turning this into an equation we get:

$$5x + 10x = 900$$
$$15x = 900$$
$$x = 60$$

The school ordered 60 \$5-t-shirts and 60 \$10-t-shirts.

14. **5** Algebra: Substitution *Medium*

Simplify, substitute, and solve:

$$5(a^2 - b^2) = 100$$
$$5(a - b)(a + b) = 100$$
$$5(4)(a + b) = 100$$
$$20(a + b) = 100$$
$$a + b = 5$$

15. **14** Geometry: Circles *Medium*

Plot the center of the circle. The problem says that the circle can only touch the y-axis at one point. This will only work if you draw a line straight out from the center of the circle, to the y-axis. Note that this point is (0, 10). The radius will be the distance from this point to the center, or 7. The diameter is therefore 14.

16. **5.64** Data, Statistics & Probability: Graphs, Charts, and Tables *Medium*

There are 1,400 cats and 1,200 dogs total. Of these, 70 percent, or a total of 1,820 are tagged and 780 are not tagged. Of all pets, 100 cats and 120 dogs are found by the ASPCA. According to the problem, 80 percent of these found pets are tagged and returned to their owners. Eighty percent of 220 is 176, which leaves 44 pets that are not tagged. The problem asks you to determine which percentage of non-tagged pets are found. Use the formula for finding a percent: $\frac{\text{part}}{\text{whole}} \times 100$.

$$\frac{\text{Found non-tagged pets}}{\text{Total non-tagged pets}} \times (100 \text{ percent}) =$$

$$\frac{44}{780} \times (100 \text{ percent}) = (0.0564)(100 \text{ percent}) = 5.641 \text{ percent of } 780$$

17. **30** Geometry: Angles and Lines *Difficult*

Draw in the angles where *a* and *b* intersect and where *c* and *d* intersect. You are told that the angle where *a* and *b* intersect is one-half as large as the other angle. Mark the angle where *a* and *b* intersect *x* and the angle where *c* and *d* intersect 2*x*. Notice that lines *a, b,* and *c* form a triangle with angle *x*.

Now, you know that any straight line must equal 180 degrees. The angle beside the 150 angle must equal 30, and the angle beside the 70 degree angle must equal 110. Adding up 30 and 110, we find 140 degrees: angle *x* must equal 40. Angle 2*x* therefore must equal 80 degrees.

In the triangle formed by lines *c, d,* and *a*, the angle beside 150 degrees is 30. Adding 30 to 80, we have 110 degrees: the third angle must be 70 degrees. The angle beside this 70 degree angle must be 110. Since there are always 360 degrees in any quadrilateral, we can add up the three known angles to find the value of *y*:

$$110 + 150 + 70 + y = 360$$
$$330 + y = 360$$
$$y = 30$$

18. **1/2, .5** Geometry: Ratio *Difficult*

The easiest way to do this problem is to pick values for the line segments, then draw a picture of the points. Since you are dealing with a ratio of 1:4 and 1:2, it's a good idea to choose a line segment that is easily divisible by 2 and 4. Let's say that the full length of the line segment measures 12. You are told that the ratio of segment *AB* to *AD* is 1:4. If *AD* is 12, then *AB* is 3. Thus, if the ratio of *AC* to *AD* is 1:2, you know that *AC* must be 6 if *AD* is 12. You are asked to find the ratio of *CD* to *AD*. If *AC* is 6, then you know that *CD* must measure 6. The ratio of AC to AD is 6 to 12, or $\frac{1}{2}$ or 0.5.

SECTION 6: WRITING

Improving Sentences

1. **D** Tense *Easy*

The verb *proclaiming* is in the wrong tense. After the correctly used verb *prompted*, you need to use the infinitive form, *to proclaim*. **D** corrects this error.

2. **B** Parallelism *Easy*

Items in a list must be in parallel form. Here are the items in the list: *destroying resorts*, *snapping power lines*, *washing out highway overpasses*, and *it also displaced many people*. Notice that the last item in the list adds a pronoun, *it*, and puts the verb *displace* in the wrong form (*displaced*). To be correct, *it* should be deleted and the verb *displaced* should read *displacing*. **B** corrects this error.

3. **E** Tense *Medium*

The verb phrase *is turning* is in the wrong form. When a sentence begins with *as*, the two halves of the sentence must be in the same form. Notice that the sentence begins in the past tense: *As I entered the cabin of the plane*. The verb phrase *is turning* should also be in the same tense, which is **E**.

4. **E** Adverbs and Adjectives *Medium*

The comparative adjective *better* does not require the adverb *more* before it. The correct answer choice will remove this adverb.

5. **C** Idioms *Easy*

The subject of this sentence, *I*, is given a choice: the *sandwich maker* wants to know what *I* would like on the sandwich. The correct way to propose such a question, idiomatically, is to ask *whether* someone wants one thing or another.

6. **D** Passive Voice *Easy*

Always try to eliminate the passive voice from any sentence and replace it with the active voice. Here, the sentence begins with the passive voice: *having been stopped*. **D** corrects this error and changes the phrase to the active voice.

7. **B** Coordination and Subordination *Medium*

Read this sentence aloud and you will probably hear immediately how clumsy it sounds. If a sentence begins with the adverb *if*, then it should be followed by the adverb *then*. Since the non-underlined portion of the sentence does not contain the adverb *then*, you will need to find a correction that eliminates the use of the conjunction *if* altogether. **B** gets rid of the suppositional nature of this sentence and starts the sentence with the pronoun *that*.

8. **D** Coordination and Subordination *Medium*

This sentence begins with the adverb *because*, which implies a cause-and-effect action. Note, however, that the underlined portion includes the phrase *even so*, which does not imply the cause-and-effect relationship you are seeking. **D** eliminates this awkward wording and makes the cause-and-effect relationship clear.

9. **A** No Error *Medium*

This sentence tests your ability to juggle different verb tenses. Note that in the non-underlined portion of the sentence you learn that the ship *was raised to the surface* and that this action occurred in the simple past. The ship, therefore, needed to have developed a coat of algae *before* being raised. The way the sentence reads initially is correct and puts all actions in the correct tense.

10. **C** Misplaced Modifier *Medium*

The way the sentence reads in its initial state makes it sound as though *most people* were once *regarded as heretical*. This, however, does not make logical sense. Clearly it is *Sigmund Freud* who was once considered *heretical*. The correct answer will move the subject, *Sigmund Freud*, next to the modifying clause that begins the sentence. **C** accomplishes this task.

11. **A** No Error *Difficult*

Don't let the twists and turns within this sentence fool you: there is no error here. All verbs are in their correct tense, and all modifiers appropriately placed. The sentence reads logically and consistently.

Identifying Sentence Errors

12. **B** Faulty Comparison *Easy*

The comparison implied with *as* requires you to consistently use the adverb *as* and not insert the word *than*. To be correct, *than* would need to be replaced by *as*.

13. **E** No Error *Easy*

Don't be put off by the long phrase surrounded by dashes in the middle of this sentence. Such digressions are acceptable, as long as they are grammatically correct. This sentence is correct as is.

14. **D** Faulty Comparison *Easy*

When items are being compared in a sentence, they must be written in parallel form. Here two things are being compared: a *sweeter, more gentle flavor* and *from the harshness of onions*. Notice that they are not in parallel form. The first item is not underlined, but the second is. To be correct, *from the harshness of onions* would need to read *than onions' harsh flavor*.

15. **C** Pronouns *Medium*

The pronoun *that* is supposed to refer to the noun *arguments*. Notice, however, that *arguments* is plural, while the pronoun *that* is singular. This is incorrect, because the pronoun and antecedent should always agree in number. To be correct, the pronoun *that* would need to be replaced by the pronoun *those*.

16. **E** Pronouns *Easy*

Be careful here. Initially, the sentence includes a discussion of *rabbits*, which is a plural word. The sentence then switches to the pronoun *each*, signaling that the author is going to discuss the *rabbits* one by one. In other words, the author is switching to discuss the *singular* nature of the *rabbits*. The singular pronoun *its*, then, refers to the singular pronoun *each* and is therefore correct.

17. **D** Idioms *Easy*

This sentence tests your knowledge of idioms. The verb *knowledge to* is incorrect and should read *knowledge of*.

18. **C** Parallelism *Easy*

When comparing two items, it is important to make sure they are in parallel form. Here you have *brushing your teeth regularly* and *if you don't eat sweets*. Notice that the first item is not underlined, but the second is. The second item must be rewritten to match the first. To be correct, the second item should read *not eating sweets*.

19. **D** Tense *Easy*

The verb *laid* is incorrect here. It should read "Adrianne lay down to take a nap." The verb *laid* is the past tense for the verb *lay* when used passively: for example, "the book was laid on the table."

20. **C** Pronoun *Easy*

This sentence tests your ability to match a pronoun with its antecedent. The pronoun *they* refers to *company*. Notice that *they* is plural, whereas *company* is singular. You might have been tricked if you had noticed that *patches*, which appears just before *they*, is plural and thought that these two words are intended to agree with each other. They aren't. To be correct, the pronoun *they* should be changed to the pronoun *it*.

21. **A** Tense *Medium*

Be careful of verb tenses here. Also, remember that *bed bugs* is plural and thus requires a verb in the third-person plural.

22. **A** Adverbs and Adjectives *Medium*

Adjectives must modify nouns and pronouns, and adverbs must modify verbs and adjectives. Here, the adjective *proper* is supposed to modify the verb *install*. To be correct, the adjective *proper* should really read *properly*.

23. **E** No Error *Easy*

There is no error here. All subjects and verbs agree, and verbs are in their proper tense.

24. **A** Subject-Verb Agreement *Medium*

Be careful here. The verb *was* refers back to *letters and journals*, which form a plural compound subject. However, the verb *was* is singular. To be correct, the verb *was* would need to be replaced by *were*.

25. **D** Coordination and Subordination *Medium*

A comparison is being made in this sentence between *if one has made an effort to understand the degree of skill that goes into producing a finished work* and *if one is an audience member with no familiarity with the creative process*. To link these two points of comparison together, the sentence should include the comparative word *than*. However, the sentence incorrectly employs the adverb *as*.

26. **C** Subject-Verb Agreement *Medium*

The verb *attempt* is meant to go with the corresponding subject, *person*. Notice that while *person* is singular—and not underlined—the verb *attempt* is plural and is underlined. In order to be correct, these two parts of speech must agree with each other, so, the verb *attempt* should read *attempts*.

27. A Pronouns *Easy*

The preposition *for* should be followed by the objective case of any pronoun. In this sentence, however, the pronoun *for* is followed by the pronoun *we*, which is in the subjective case. To be correct, the pronoun *we* should be changed to *us*.

28. B Coordination and Subordination *Medium*

The connector *neither* must always be paired with *nor*, and *either* must always be paired with *or*. However, in this case, the sentence contains *neither* but is paired with *or*. To be correct, *or* needs to be replaced with *nor*.

29. A Subject-Verb Agreement *Medium*

The verb *is* in this sentence is meant to correspond to the compound subject *ten dollars in pennies and fifty dollars in nickels*. However, the verb *is* is singular, and the compound subject is plural. To be correct, the verb *is* would need to changed to *are*.

Improving Paragraphs

30. B Sentence Revision *Medium*

The wording of the original sentence is confusing and jumbled with too many turns of phrase. You need to simplify, which **B** does best.

31. B Sentence Revision *Easy*

The original wording of this sentence is clumsy in large part because it includes the pronoun *it* twice. Ideally, you only want to use *it* once. **B** fixes this error by replacing one of the *its* with *the cause*.

32. A Essay Analysis *Medium*

Take a look at the opening lines. The author asks a rhetorical question and invites the reader to us her or his imagination. The story then turns personal, and we suspect we will be treated to an individual's story about bed bugs. In other words, the opening lines are *setting a scene*.

33. C Sentence Revision *Easy*

There is a contrast between the two sentences. On the one hand, the author learns about bed bugs, but, on the other hand, he doesn't believe he has a problem with bed bugs. What is missing is a strong structural clue, like *but*, which shows this contrast. **C** fixes this problem.

34. D Sentence Revision *Medium*

This sentence can be eliminated because it restates information contained in the sentence directly before it.

35. B Essay Analysis *Medium*

The story ends in the final paragraph. We learn that the author was able to get rid of the bed bugs. There are no lingering questions and the author is not challenging the reader to accept any difficult opinions.

SECTION 7: CRITICAL READING

Sentence Completions

1. **B** Two-Word/One-Way *Easy*

Margaret Atwood's book saw *success*. You can assume, therefore, that her book helped to make other books "successful." A good prediction for the first blank would be "found." A good prediction for the second blank would be "begun."

2. **C** Two-Word/One-Way *Easy*

The phrase *initial screening process* is also a good clue that *corporations* are "studying" or "evaluating" their employees. Eliminate **A**, **D**, and **E**. The phrase *in addition to* tells you that the two blanks will agree with each other. The correct answer must be **C**.

3. **A** One-Word/Two-Way *Medium*

The zoo will feature animals born in *captivity*. In other words, the animals cannot have been born out in the wild. So, what is it that the *founders* want to make sure that the zoo does *not* do? They *don't* want to "capture" any animals from the wild. Only *pilfer*, "to steal," makes sense in this context.

4. **D** Two-Word/Two-Way *Medium*

Right away you are told that Frank Sinatra is *difficult to categorize*. The sentence then goes on to explain the ways in which Sinatra is hard to categorize, with some people suggesting he was a *mere singer of pop tunes*, a very dismissive comment, and others saying that Sinatra could sing more types of music and thus had great ability and talent, or *range*.

5. **D** One-Word/Two-Way *Difficult*

The sentence sets up an inherent contrast between *ancient Greek plays* and the *modern discipline of psychology*. These words make it clear that there is a difference in time: one discipline appeared before the other. Note too that whereas Greek plays show an *understanding of human nature*, psychology seeks to *explain human motivation*. In this way, the Greek plays seem to "foreshadow" psychology. **D** matches this prediction.

6. **E** Two-Word/Two-Way *Difficult*

The phrase *opposing viewpoints* should tip you off that the sentence will present two opposite points of view. The word *regardless* should also hint to you that the first blank will mean something like "responsibility." Eliminate **B** and **D**. The phrase *innate circumstances* should hint that the second blank will be a word that agrees with *innate*. A good prediction might be "wealth." The answer must be **E**.

Long Reading Passage

7. **D** Main Idea *Easy*

You only want to progress to the questions of a reading passage once you are sure you have understood the main point of the passage. This passage opens with a description of Steinbeck's career but demonstrates no conclusive point of view. The author's mission in writing this passage only becomes clear in the second paragraph, in which she writes, *One area in which critics have been upset with Steinbeck includes his depiction of female characters, and one wonders what Steinbeck would think of the proliferation of female novelists and the demands of a female readership eager to see its own gender portrayed in all its complexity.* From there, the author goes on to examine the many ways in which Steinbeck has portrayed women and speculates on the reasons for this portrayal.

8. **A** Words in Context *Medium*

Take a look at the sentence in question: *Though he had a few notable creative efforts, including* The Winter of Our Discontent, *his later books never again scaled the same critical heights as his earlier efforts.* The words *never again* hint that Steinbeck's later books didn't "gain" the same critical heights as previous books. The word *scaled* can mean several things, but, in context, it most nearly means *reached*, **A**.

9. **C** Implied Information *Medium*

Take a look at the lines in question: *In reading a book like* Travels with Charley *too, one has the sense that the world had changed after the end of the Second World War and that perhaps Steinbeck's artist's eye was less attuned to the new world in which he found himself.* The correct answer will be a statement that agrees with this sentence and does not stray too far from what the sentence actually says—**C**. Watch out for **A** and **B**, which attempt to give reasons for why Steinbeck wrote the book. The author doesn't actually speculate on any reasons. **D** and **E** are also too extreme and venture far away from the information given.

10. **B** Implied Information *Medium*

Take a look at the lines in question: *one wonders what Steinbeck would think of the proliferation of female novelists and the demands of a female readership eager to see its own gender portrayed in all its complexity.* The author of the passage is saying is that she is not sure a female reader today would be comfortable seeing women portrayed as Steinbeck showed them. The author does not make any claims about what an editor might do or if Steinbeck could even be published. She simply questions what the female readership's response would be.

11. **A** Implied Information *Medium*

The author makes the point that Steinbeck's male characters, though cruel, are to be forgiven, whereas female characters are not. She points out that Steinbeck even went so far as to suggest that a character named Cathy was born without a conscience. The author implies that, although it is possible for Steinbeck to understand the male characters' reasons for behaving poorly, it is difficult for him to understand the female characters' motivations.

12. **D** Words in Context *Easy*

Here is the sentence in question: *There is also the mother character in* The Grapes of Wrath, *who is almost primal in her desire to keep her family intact.* The mother has a desire to keep her family *intact*, and this desire is *primal*, or "basic." Another good guess that fits the context is *innate*, **D**.

13. **B** Themes and Arguments *Medium*

Take a look at the lines in question: *Other female characters are childish and simple and, as such, cause harm to men. Few women look at the world in a contemplative, complex fashion, trying to determine how best to make a living. Few women are painted with a sympathetic hand.* That last line strongly hints at the direction of the passage: the author is implying that Steinbeck did not write women sympathetically, because he could not.

14. **E** Implied Information *Medium*

Take a look at the following line: *But a study of his life shows that he might very well have been predisposed to view female characters differently.* The author then goes on to describe the women who were influential in Steinbeck's life. **E** restates this idea. Watch out for **A** and **C**, which introduce ideas not discussed in the passage.

15. **B** Themes and Arguments *Medium*

Take a look at the lines surrounding the phrase *magic touch*: *His first wife, Carol, was a clever and accomplished poet who edited and tightened many of her husband's early books. In fact, many have long suspected that the decline in quality of Steinbeck's writing was because his later pieces lacked her magic touch.* We learn here that Carol Steinbeck edited many of Steinbeck's earlier works but that she did not do so later on. This "magic touch" refers to Carol's ability to edit her husband's work.

16. **E** Implied Information *Medium*

Here are the lines being referenced: *Steinbeck must have known how his work gleamed under his wife's fingers, for he dedicated* The Grapes of Wrath *to her with the words that she had "willed" that particular novel to life.* Steinbeck credited Carol with having "willed" his great novel, and the author sees this as evidence that Steinbeck was aware of the effect his wife had on his work.

17. **C** Implied Information *Medium*

Here are the lines in question: *Steinbeck's subsequent marriage to a young woman, Gwen, produced two children, but this marriage was apparently a struggle, and some have seen the evil Cathy character as a thinly veiled portrait of Gwen herself.* The Cathy character may be seen as a "portrait," or representation, of Gwen, with whom Steinbeck experienced great unhappiness.

18. **D** Specific Information *Medium*

Read these lines carefully: *One has the sense upon reading later works, such as* Travels with Charley, *that Steinbeck has ceased to be a writer projecting a deeply felt and believed vision of the world, and has become instead a traveler, noting what he has seen without really understanding its significance.* The author thinks that Steinbeck is no longer able to understand the world around him and that his writing reflects this lack of clarity.

19. **D** Themes and Arguments *Difficult*

Take a look at the context: *One has the sense upon reading later works, such as* Travels with Charley, *that Steinbeck has ceased to be a writer projecting a deeply felt and believed vision of the world, and has become instead a traveler, noting what he has seen without really understanding its significance. It would be irresponsible not to note that part of what emerged in the postwar era, of course, was women's liberation.* First, the author says that Steinbeck failed to understand the world after the Second World War. Then the author points out that women's lib came after the end of the war. The author's whole thesis is that Steinbeck had difficulty portraying women as complex characters. The implication is that Steinbeck ceased to pay attention to the social and political changes, including the women's movement.

SECTION 8: MATH

Multiple Choice

1. **C** Algebra: Solving Equations *Easy*

Simplify and solve:

$$5(x-2)=30$$
$$x-2=6$$
$$x=8$$

2. **D** Data Analysis, Statistics & Probability: Statistical Analysis *Easy*

Multiply the number of jeans by the number of t-shirts to find the total number of combinations.

$$3 \times 5 = 15$$

3. **B** Algebra: Absolute Value and Exponents *Easy*

Take the statement one piece at a time. First, you are told to find the *difference* between q and r. *Difference* always means that you must subtract:

$$q - r$$

Eliminate **A** and **D**.

Next, you are told to find the *product* between a and the sum of the square of b and c. The word *product* means "multiply."

$$q - r = a(\text{sum of the square of } b \text{ and } c)$$

What are you supposed to multiply by a? The square of the sum of b and c. To find this, add b and c together, then square that value:

$$q - r = a\{(b + c)^2\}$$

4. **E** Geometry: Triangles *Medium*

The problem mentions a rectangle, but don't be fooled. This is a triangle problem dressed up as a rectangle problem. The diagonals are both hypotenuses of right triangles, so the Pythagorean theorem can be strutted out to determine the length of each diagonal.

$$a^2 + b^2 = c^2$$
$$3^2 + 5^2 = AC^2$$
$$9 + 25 = AC^2$$
$$34 = AC^2$$
$$\sqrt{34} = AC$$

At this point, two things can happen. You can recall that the diagonals of a rectangle are always the same length, or you can run through the Pythagorean theorem again to figure the length of BD. Either way you get $BD = \sqrt{34}$. Since the stem asks for the product of the two diagonals, you now multiply: $(AC)(BC) = (\sqrt{34})(\sqrt{34}) = 34$ and end up with **E**.

Always be on the lookout for triangles!

5. **A** Algebra: Solving Equations *Easy*

Simplify and solve:

$$\frac{a}{4} = \frac{3a}{6y}$$
$$(6y)a = 4(3a)$$
$$6y = \frac{12a}{a}$$
$$y = \frac{12}{6}$$
$$y = 2$$

6. **D** Geometry: Angles and Lines *Easy*

If angle D is 70 degrees, then you know that angles C and A are also 70 degrees because lines x and y are parallel. Since there are always 180 degrees in a straight line, and since you know that angle A is 70 degrees, angle B must be 110 degrees. Finally, add the measurements up:

$$70 + 70 + 70 + 110 = 320$$

7. **A** Geometry: Coordinate Geometry *Medium*

Use the information given to solve for the slope:

$$\text{Slope} = \frac{\text{change in } y}{\text{change in } x}$$

$$\text{Slope} = \frac{\text{change in } (7 - -2)}{\text{change in } (3 - -1)}$$

$$\text{Slope} = \frac{9}{4}$$

8. **E** Algebra: Substitution *Medium*

This is essentially an algebra problem, in which you must plug in values for the variables and solve. Here is the equation:

$$c(a) = 32a - (13a + b)$$

You are told that *450 units were produced for a cost of $75,000.* Plug in these values and solve for b:

$$\begin{aligned} c(a) &= 32a - (13a + b) \\ 75,000 &= 32(450) - [13(450) + b] \\ 75,000 &= 14,400 - (5,850 + b) \\ 75,000 &= 14,400 - 5,850 - b \\ 75,000 &= 8,550 - b \\ 66,450 &= -b \\ -66,450 &= b \end{aligned}$$

9. **D** Numbers & Operations: Basic Operations *Medium*

Any integer between 7 and 20 multiplied by itself will end in the following: 0, 1, 4, 5, 6, and 9. Take a look at the following:

$1 \times 1 = 1$	$5 \times 5 = 25$	$9 \times 9 = 81$
$2 \times 2 = 4$	$6 \times 6 = 36$	$10 \times 10 = 100$
$3 \times 3 = 3$	$7 \times 7 = 49$	$11 \times 11 = 121$
$4 \times 4 = 16$	$8 \times 8 = 64$	$12 \times 12 = 144$

And so on . . .

The answer must therefore be **D**.

10. **E** Data Analysis, Statistics & Probability: Statistical Analysis *Medium*

Remember, the formula for finding probability is the number of desired outcomes divided by the number of probable outcomes. For the purposes of this problem, you can think of this equation in the following manner:

$$\text{Probability of particular gumball color} = \frac{\text{number of desired gumballs}}{\text{number of total gumballs}}$$

You are given the probability for 3 of the gumballs. Note that the probability of receiving a red gumball is $\frac{1}{3}$. This means that the number of red gumballs placed over the number of total gumballs must reduce to a fraction of $\frac{1}{3}$. Similarly, the number of yellow gumballs or white gumballs placed over the number of total gumballs must reduce to $\frac{1}{8}$. The total number of gumballs will most likely be a multiple of 3 and 8, such as 24. In that instance, there would be 8 red gumballs.

$$\text{Probability of red gumballs} = \frac{\text{number of red gumballs}}{\text{number of total gumballs}}$$

$$\frac{1}{3} = \frac{\text{number of red gumballs}}{24}$$

$$\text{Number of red gumballs} = 8$$

Now solve for the number of yellow and white gumballs.

$$\text{Probability of white gumballs} = \frac{\text{number of white gumballs}}{\text{number of total gumballs}}$$

$$\frac{1}{8} = \frac{\text{number of white gumballs}}{24}$$

$$\text{Number of white gumballs} = 3$$

$$\text{Probability of yellow gumballs} = \frac{\text{number of yellow gumballs}}{\text{number of total gumballs}}$$

$$\frac{1}{8} = \frac{\text{number of yellow gumballs}}{24}$$

$$\text{Number of yellow gumballs} = 3$$

Total number of gumballs = red + white + yellow + blue

$$24 = 8 + 3 + 3 + \text{blue}$$
$$24 = 14 + \text{blue}$$
$$10 = \text{blue}$$

11. **D** Data Analysis, Statistics & Probability: Statistical Analysis *Medium*

This is a simple question masquerading as a more difficult one. Essentially, this problem tests your knowledge of averages. Remember the formula for finding an average:

$$\text{Average} = \frac{\text{sum of elements in a set}}{\text{number of elements in a set}}$$

Therefore, the problem has essentially asked you to solve for the average cost of the groceries.

12. **D** Geometry: Triangles *Medium*

The figure formed by the solid line is made up of the sides of the three outermost triangles in the figure. All of the triangles are equal to each other in dimension. If you are able to find the length of one side of one triangle, then you will be able to find the sides of all the other triangles.

13. **D** Data Analysis, Statistics & Probability: Graphs, Charts, and Tables *Medium*

This is a graph problem in which the y-coordinate depends on the value e. First you are told that $k(1) = b$. Therefore, when the x-coordinate is 1, the y-coordinate is a value, b. Looking at the graph, you can see that when the x-coordinate is 1, then the y-coordinate is 3. Therefore, $b = 3$. You're looking for the value of the y-coordinate when the x-coordinate is 3. Looking at the graph, you can see that the y-coordinate will be 6 when x is 3.

14. **C** Algebra: Inequalities *Difficult*

You need to find the smallest possible value for ab and the largest possible value for ab. First, make ab as small as possible. You might be tempted to multiply –2 by 0 and conclude that the smallest possible value for ab is 0. However, note that negative numbers are involved. This should alert you that ab could equal a value smaller than 0. In fact, If b equaled –2 and a equaled 6, then ab would equal –12. In other words, ab must be ≥ -12. Now, if a equaled 6, and b also equaled 6, then ab would equal 36. Thus, $-12 \leq ab \leq 36$.

15. **B** Algebra: Triangles and Circles *Difficult*

To find the area of the shaded region, you will need to find the area of the triangle. To find the area of the triangle, you need to find the base and the height. First, start with the semicircles. You are given the areas of the semicircles and can use this information to find the base and the height of the triangle:

Semicircle X

$$\text{Area} = \frac{\pi r^2}{2}$$

(Note that you have to divide the area by 2, because you are dealing with a semicircle and not a whole circle.)

$$12.5\pi = \frac{\pi r^2}{2}$$
$$25\pi = \pi r^2$$
$$5 = r$$
$$10 = d$$
$$10 = \text{length of side of triangle}$$

Since semicircle Y also has an area of 12.5π, you can assume that its radius is also 5. Now you have the length of two sides of the triangle. Next you must find the base using the information for semicircle Z:

$$\text{Area} = \frac{\pi r^2}{2}$$
$$32\pi = \frac{\pi r^2}{2}$$
$$64\pi = \pi r^2$$
$$8 = r$$
$$16 = d$$
$$16 = \text{length of base of triangle}$$

Now you have all the measurements of the triangle. To find the height, simply split this equilateral triangle into two smaller triangles, noting point *W*.

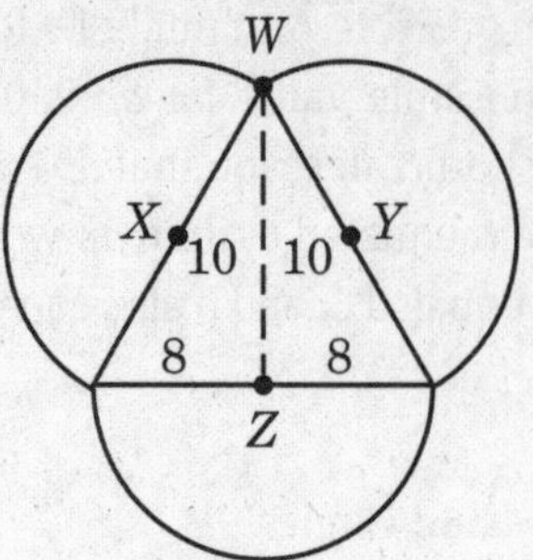

Now use the Pythagorean theorem to solve for the height:

$$a^2 + b^2 = c^2$$
$$8^2 + b^2 = 10^2$$
$$64 + b^2 = 100$$
$$b^2 = 36$$
$$b = 6$$

Now solve for the area of the triangle:

$$A = \frac{bh}{2}$$
$$A = \frac{(16)(6)}{2}$$
$$A = 48$$

Now, add all the areas together.

$$12.5\pi + 12.5\pi + 32\pi + 48$$
$$57\pi + 48$$

16. **A** Algebra: Solving Equations *Difficult*
The first term in the sequence is $\frac{1}{x}$. The second term in the sequence is 4 larger than twice the fraction, or $\frac{2}{x} + 4$. Now, set these values up in a ratio and reduce:

$$\frac{\frac{1}{x}}{\frac{2}{x}+4} = \frac{\frac{1}{x}}{\frac{2}{x}+\frac{4x}{x}} = \left(\frac{1}{x}\right)\left(\frac{x}{4x+2}\right) = \frac{1}{4x+2}$$

SECTION 9: WRITING

Improving Sentences

1. **E** Faulty Comparison *Easy*
The word *more* is used when comparing two things, and the word *many* is used when comparing more than two. It is inconsistent to use both words in one comparison. **E** corrects this error.

2. **D** Faulty Comparison *Easy*

When making a comparison, be sure you are comparing two equal things. In this case, the original sentence sounds as though *the health* of a child in a *developing country* is being compared to *a child* in the first world. To correct this error, you need to make it clear that *the health* of a child in the *developing country* is being compared to *the health* of a child in the first world.

3. **B** Subject-Verb Agreement *Easy*

Every sentence must have agreement between its subject and verb. In this case, the subject is *Ha Jin* and the verb is *writing*. However, *writing* is in the incorrect form to be a main verb and must be converted to *wrote*, as **B** does.

4. **C** Wordiness *Easy*

This sentence suffers from wordiness, including the use of the pronoun *there* when it is not necessary. **C** corrects this problem.

5. **D** Idioms *Easy*

This sentence tests your knowledge of idiomatic expressions. It is incorrect to say *have high skill*. Instead, a person *is highly skilled*, which is the correction contained in **D**.

6. **A** No Error *Easy*

This sentence contains no errors. All subjects and verbs agree and are in their correct form.

7. **E** Pronouns *Medium*

Pronoun use within a sentence must be consistent. In this case, the sentence mixes up the pronouns *we* and *you*. It can only use one of these two choices. Notice that the underlined portion of the sentence employs the pronoun *we*, and the non-underlined section employs *you*. To be correct and consistent, the underlined section should replace *we* with *you*.

8. **C** Parallelism *Medium*

Items in a list must be in parallel form. In this case, the two items in the list, *taking time to adequately prepare for the test* and *a good night of sleep*, are not in the same form. The former is an action—*taking time*—whereas the latter is a noun. **C** corrects this error by replacing *taking time* with the noun *preparation*.

9. **E** Tenses *Medium*

Here the word *suggesting* is in the incorrect form. In fact, *suggesting* should be a noun, *suggestion*, which **E** corrects.

10. **B** Pronouns *Medium*

The pronoun *who* should only be used to modify another word. In this sentence, notice that the word *who* follows the verb *dating*. However, the clause that follows *dating* does not actually modify, or provide more information about, *dating*. **B** corrects this problem by eliminating *who* and putting the verb *admit* in its correct form.

11. **C** Wordiness *Easy*

When read aloud, this sentence most likely sounds wordy and excessive to you. The phrase *for the reason that there was* adds extraneous information. It is much clearer to replace *for the reason that there was* with the preposition *over*.

12. **D** Run-Ons *Medium*

Here we have an example of a run-on sentence, in which two independent clauses are thrust together. To be correct, one of the independent clauses must be made dependent on the other or the two must be joined together by a semicolon. **D** corrects this problem.

13. **E** Wrong Word *Medium*

This sentence tests your knowledge of word usage. The word *enormity* does not mean "really enormous" or "huge" but instead means "great evil." Clearly, the author was trying to say something about the "huge" *news coverage*. **E** best corrects this error.

14. **D** Misplaced Modifiers *Medium*

The way the sentence reads now, it sounds as though *Sherry* is the day on which it is going to rain. Obviously this makes little sense: Sherry is not a day, and although you probably understand inherently what the sentence is trying convey, it is still grammatically incorrect. To be correct, the word *Saturday* must appear next to the introductory modifying clause, which **D** accomplishes.

SAT PRACTICE TEST 6

SAT* Reasoning Test—General Directions

Timing

- You will have 3 hours and 20 minutes to work on this test. (On the actual SAT, you would have 3 hours and 45 minutes to complete ten sections, one of which would be unscored and experimental.)
- There are nine separately timed sections:
  - ➤ One 25-minute essay
  - ➤ Five other 25-minute sections
  - ➤ Two 20-minute sections
  - ➤ One 10-minute section
- You may work on only one section at a time.
- The supervisor will tell you when to begin and end each section.
- If you finish a section before time is called, check your work on that section. You may NOT turn to any other section.
- Work as rapidly as you can without losing accuracy. Don't waste time on questions that seem too difficult for you.

Marking Answers

- Carefully mark only one answer for each question.
- Make sure each mark is dark and completely fills the circle.
- Do not make any stray marks on your answer sheet.
- If you erase, do so completely. Incomplete erasures may be scored as intended answers.
- Use only the answer spaces that correspond to the question numbers.
- Use the test book for scratchwork, but you will not receive credit for anything written there.
- After time has been called, you may not transfer answers to your answer sheet or fill in circles.
- You may not fold or remove pages or portions of a page from this book, or take the book or answer sheet from the testing room.

Scoring

- For each correct answer to a question, you receive one point.
- For questions you omit, you receive no points.
- For a wrong answer to a multiple-choice question, you lose one-fourth of a point.
  - ➤ If you can eliminate one or more of the answer choices as wrong, you increase your chances of choosing the correct answer and earning one point.
  - ➤ If you can't eliminate any choice, move on. You can return to the question later if there is time.
- For a wrong answer to a "grid-in" math question, you don't lose any points.
- The essay is scored on a 1 to 6 scale by two different readers. The total essay score is the sum of the two readers' scores.
- An off-topic or blank essay will receive a score of zero.

---

* SAT test directions selected from the SAT Reasoning Test. Reprinted by permission of the College Board, the copyright owner.

SAT PRACTICE TEST 6 ANSWER SHEET

SECTION 2			
1. Ⓐ Ⓑ Ⓒ Ⓓ Ⓔ	7. Ⓐ Ⓑ Ⓒ Ⓓ Ⓔ	13. Ⓐ Ⓑ Ⓒ Ⓓ Ⓔ	19. Ⓐ Ⓑ Ⓒ Ⓓ Ⓔ
2. Ⓐ Ⓑ Ⓒ Ⓓ Ⓔ	8. Ⓐ Ⓑ Ⓒ Ⓓ Ⓔ	14. Ⓐ Ⓑ Ⓒ Ⓓ Ⓔ	20. Ⓐ Ⓑ Ⓒ Ⓓ Ⓔ
3. Ⓐ Ⓑ Ⓒ Ⓓ Ⓔ	9. Ⓐ Ⓑ Ⓒ Ⓓ Ⓔ	15. Ⓐ Ⓑ Ⓒ Ⓓ Ⓔ	21. Ⓐ Ⓑ Ⓒ Ⓓ Ⓔ
4. Ⓐ Ⓑ Ⓒ Ⓓ Ⓔ	10. Ⓐ Ⓑ Ⓒ Ⓓ Ⓔ	16. Ⓐ Ⓑ Ⓒ Ⓓ Ⓔ	22. Ⓐ Ⓑ Ⓒ Ⓓ Ⓔ
5. Ⓐ Ⓑ Ⓒ Ⓓ Ⓔ	11. Ⓐ Ⓑ Ⓒ Ⓓ Ⓔ	17. Ⓐ Ⓑ Ⓒ Ⓓ Ⓔ	23. Ⓐ Ⓑ Ⓒ Ⓓ Ⓔ
6. Ⓐ Ⓑ Ⓒ Ⓓ Ⓔ	12. Ⓐ Ⓑ Ⓒ Ⓓ Ⓔ	18. Ⓐ Ⓑ Ⓒ Ⓓ Ⓔ	24. Ⓐ Ⓑ Ⓒ Ⓓ Ⓔ

SECTION 3			
1. Ⓐ Ⓑ Ⓒ Ⓓ Ⓔ	6. Ⓐ Ⓑ Ⓒ Ⓓ Ⓔ	11. Ⓐ Ⓑ Ⓒ Ⓓ Ⓔ	16. Ⓐ Ⓑ Ⓒ Ⓓ Ⓔ
2. Ⓐ Ⓑ Ⓒ Ⓓ Ⓔ	7. Ⓐ Ⓑ Ⓒ Ⓓ Ⓔ	12. Ⓐ Ⓑ Ⓒ Ⓓ Ⓔ	17. Ⓐ Ⓑ Ⓒ Ⓓ Ⓔ
3. Ⓐ Ⓑ Ⓒ Ⓓ Ⓔ	8. Ⓐ Ⓑ Ⓒ Ⓓ Ⓔ	13. Ⓐ Ⓑ Ⓒ Ⓓ Ⓔ	18. Ⓐ Ⓑ Ⓒ Ⓓ Ⓔ
4. Ⓐ Ⓑ Ⓒ Ⓓ Ⓔ	9. Ⓐ Ⓑ Ⓒ Ⓓ Ⓔ	14. Ⓐ Ⓑ Ⓒ Ⓓ Ⓔ	19. Ⓐ Ⓑ Ⓒ Ⓓ Ⓔ
5. Ⓐ Ⓑ Ⓒ Ⓓ Ⓔ	10. Ⓐ Ⓑ Ⓒ Ⓓ Ⓔ	15. Ⓐ Ⓑ Ⓒ Ⓓ Ⓔ	20. Ⓐ Ⓑ Ⓒ Ⓓ Ⓔ

SECTION 4			
1. Ⓐ Ⓑ Ⓒ Ⓓ Ⓔ	7. Ⓐ Ⓑ Ⓒ Ⓓ Ⓔ	13. Ⓐ Ⓑ Ⓒ Ⓓ Ⓔ	19. Ⓐ Ⓑ Ⓒ Ⓓ Ⓔ
2. Ⓐ Ⓑ Ⓒ Ⓓ Ⓔ	8. Ⓐ Ⓑ Ⓒ Ⓓ Ⓔ	14. Ⓐ Ⓑ Ⓒ Ⓓ Ⓔ	20. Ⓐ Ⓑ Ⓒ Ⓓ Ⓔ
3. Ⓐ Ⓑ Ⓒ Ⓓ Ⓔ	9. Ⓐ Ⓑ Ⓒ Ⓓ Ⓔ	15. Ⓐ Ⓑ Ⓒ Ⓓ Ⓔ	21. Ⓐ Ⓑ Ⓒ Ⓓ Ⓔ
4. Ⓐ Ⓑ Ⓒ Ⓓ Ⓔ	10. Ⓐ Ⓑ Ⓒ Ⓓ Ⓔ	16. Ⓐ Ⓑ Ⓒ Ⓓ Ⓔ	22. Ⓐ Ⓑ Ⓒ Ⓓ Ⓔ
5. Ⓐ Ⓑ Ⓒ Ⓓ Ⓔ	11. Ⓐ Ⓑ Ⓒ Ⓓ Ⓔ	17. Ⓐ Ⓑ Ⓒ Ⓓ Ⓔ	23. Ⓐ Ⓑ Ⓒ Ⓓ Ⓔ
6. Ⓐ Ⓑ Ⓒ Ⓓ Ⓔ	12. Ⓐ Ⓑ Ⓒ Ⓓ Ⓔ	18. Ⓐ Ⓑ Ⓒ Ⓓ Ⓔ	24. Ⓐ Ⓑ Ⓒ Ⓓ Ⓔ

SECTION 5			
1. Ⓐ Ⓑ Ⓒ Ⓓ Ⓔ	3. Ⓐ Ⓑ Ⓒ Ⓓ Ⓔ	5. Ⓐ Ⓑ Ⓒ Ⓓ Ⓔ	7. Ⓐ Ⓑ Ⓒ Ⓓ Ⓔ
2. Ⓐ Ⓑ Ⓒ Ⓓ Ⓔ	4. Ⓐ Ⓑ Ⓒ Ⓓ Ⓔ	6. Ⓐ Ⓑ Ⓒ Ⓓ Ⓔ	8. Ⓐ Ⓑ Ⓒ Ⓓ Ⓔ

9				10				11				12				13			
		/				/				/				/				/	
.	.	.	.	.	.	.	.	.	.	.	.	.	.	.	.	.	.	.	.
	0	0	0		0	0	0		0	0	0		0	0	0		0	0	0
1	1	1	1	1	1	1	1	1	1	1	1	1	1	1	1	1	1	1	1
2	2	2	2	2	2	2	2	2	2	2	2	2	2	2	2	2	2	2	2
3	3	3	3	3	3	3	3	3	3	3	3	3	3	3	3	3	3	3	3
4	4	4	4	4	4	4	4	4	4	4	4	4	4	4	4	4	4	4	4
5	5	5	5	5	5	5	5	5	5	5	5	5	5	5	5	5	5	5	5
6	6	6	6	6	6	6	6	6	6	6	6	6	6	6	6	6	6	6	6
7	7	7	7	7	7	7	7	7	7	7	7	7	7	7	7	7	7	7	7
8	8	8	8	8	8	8	8	8	8	8	8	8	8	8	8	8	8	8	8
9	9	9	9	9	9	9	9	9	9	9	9	9	9	9	9	9	9	9	9

14				15				16				17				18			
		/				/				/				/				/	
.	.	.	.	.	.	.	.	.	.	.	.	.	.	.	.	.	.	.	.
	0	0	0		0	0	0		0	0	0		0	0	0		0	0	0
1	1	1	1	1	1	1	1	1	1	1	1	1	1	1	1	1	1	1	1
2	2	2	2	2	2	2	2	2	2	2	2	2	2	2	2	2	2	2	2
3	3	3	3	3	3	3	3	3	3	3	3	3	3	3	3	3	3	3	3
4	4	4	4	4	4	4	4	4	4	4	4	4	4	4	4	4	4	4	4
5	5	5	5	5	5	5	5	5	5	5	5	5	5	5	5	5	5	5	5
6	6	6	6	6	6	6	6	6	6	6	6	6	6	6	6	6	6	6	6
7	7	7	7	7	7	7	7	7	7	7	7	7	7	7	7	7	7	7	7
8	8	8	8	8	8	8	8	8	8	8	8	8	8	8	8	8	8	8	8
9	9	9	9	9	9	9	9	9	9	9	9	9	9	9	9	9	9	9	9

SAT PRACTICE TEST 6 ANSWER SHEET

SECTION 6

1. Ⓐ Ⓑ Ⓒ Ⓓ Ⓔ	10. Ⓐ Ⓑ Ⓒ Ⓓ Ⓔ	19. Ⓐ Ⓑ Ⓒ Ⓓ Ⓔ	28. Ⓐ Ⓑ Ⓒ Ⓓ Ⓔ
2. Ⓐ Ⓑ Ⓒ Ⓓ Ⓔ	11. Ⓐ Ⓑ Ⓒ Ⓓ Ⓔ	20. Ⓐ Ⓑ Ⓒ Ⓓ Ⓔ	29. Ⓐ Ⓑ Ⓒ Ⓓ Ⓔ
3. Ⓐ Ⓑ Ⓒ Ⓓ Ⓔ	12. Ⓐ Ⓑ Ⓒ Ⓓ Ⓔ	21. Ⓐ Ⓑ Ⓒ Ⓓ Ⓔ	30. Ⓐ Ⓑ Ⓒ Ⓓ Ⓔ
4. Ⓐ Ⓑ Ⓒ Ⓓ Ⓔ	13. Ⓐ Ⓑ Ⓒ Ⓓ Ⓔ	22. Ⓐ Ⓑ Ⓒ Ⓓ Ⓔ	31. Ⓐ Ⓑ Ⓒ Ⓓ Ⓔ
5. Ⓐ Ⓑ Ⓒ Ⓓ Ⓔ	14. Ⓐ Ⓑ Ⓒ Ⓓ Ⓔ	23. Ⓐ Ⓑ Ⓒ Ⓓ Ⓔ	32. Ⓐ Ⓑ Ⓒ Ⓓ Ⓔ
6. Ⓐ Ⓑ Ⓒ Ⓓ Ⓔ	15. Ⓐ Ⓑ Ⓒ Ⓓ Ⓔ	24. Ⓐ Ⓑ Ⓒ Ⓓ Ⓔ	33. Ⓐ Ⓑ Ⓒ Ⓓ Ⓔ
7. Ⓐ Ⓑ Ⓒ Ⓓ Ⓔ	16. Ⓐ Ⓑ Ⓒ Ⓓ Ⓔ	25. Ⓐ Ⓑ Ⓒ Ⓓ Ⓔ	34. Ⓐ Ⓑ Ⓒ Ⓓ Ⓔ
8. Ⓐ Ⓑ Ⓒ Ⓓ Ⓔ	17. Ⓐ Ⓑ Ⓒ Ⓓ Ⓔ	26. Ⓐ Ⓑ Ⓒ Ⓓ Ⓔ	35. Ⓐ Ⓑ Ⓒ Ⓓ Ⓔ
9. Ⓐ Ⓑ Ⓒ Ⓓ Ⓔ	18. Ⓐ Ⓑ Ⓒ Ⓓ Ⓔ	27. Ⓐ Ⓑ Ⓒ Ⓓ Ⓔ	

SECTION 7

1. Ⓐ Ⓑ Ⓒ Ⓓ Ⓔ	6. Ⓐ Ⓑ Ⓒ Ⓓ Ⓔ	11. Ⓐ Ⓑ Ⓒ Ⓓ Ⓔ	16. Ⓐ Ⓑ Ⓒ Ⓓ Ⓔ
2. Ⓐ Ⓑ Ⓒ Ⓓ Ⓔ	7. Ⓐ Ⓑ Ⓒ Ⓓ Ⓔ	12. Ⓐ Ⓑ Ⓒ Ⓓ Ⓔ	17. Ⓐ Ⓑ Ⓒ Ⓓ Ⓔ
3. Ⓐ Ⓑ Ⓒ Ⓓ Ⓔ	8. Ⓐ Ⓑ Ⓒ Ⓓ Ⓔ	13. Ⓐ Ⓑ Ⓒ Ⓓ Ⓔ	18. Ⓐ Ⓑ Ⓒ Ⓓ Ⓔ
4. Ⓐ Ⓑ Ⓒ Ⓓ Ⓔ	9. Ⓐ Ⓑ Ⓒ Ⓓ Ⓔ	14. Ⓐ Ⓑ Ⓒ Ⓓ Ⓔ	19. Ⓐ Ⓑ Ⓒ Ⓓ Ⓔ
5. Ⓐ Ⓑ Ⓒ Ⓓ Ⓔ	10. Ⓐ Ⓑ Ⓒ Ⓓ Ⓔ	15. Ⓐ Ⓑ Ⓒ Ⓓ Ⓔ	

SECTION 8

1. Ⓐ Ⓑ Ⓒ Ⓓ Ⓔ	5. Ⓐ Ⓑ Ⓒ Ⓓ Ⓔ	9. Ⓐ Ⓑ Ⓒ Ⓓ Ⓔ	13. Ⓐ Ⓑ Ⓒ Ⓓ Ⓔ
2. Ⓐ Ⓑ Ⓒ Ⓓ Ⓔ	6. Ⓐ Ⓑ Ⓒ Ⓓ Ⓔ	10. Ⓐ Ⓑ Ⓒ Ⓓ Ⓔ	14. Ⓐ Ⓑ Ⓒ Ⓓ Ⓔ
3. Ⓐ Ⓑ Ⓒ Ⓓ Ⓔ	7. Ⓐ Ⓑ Ⓒ Ⓓ Ⓔ	11. Ⓐ Ⓑ Ⓒ Ⓓ Ⓔ	15. Ⓐ Ⓑ Ⓒ Ⓓ Ⓔ
4. Ⓐ Ⓑ Ⓒ Ⓓ Ⓔ	8. Ⓐ Ⓑ Ⓒ Ⓓ Ⓔ	12. Ⓐ Ⓑ Ⓒ Ⓓ Ⓔ	16. Ⓐ Ⓑ Ⓒ Ⓓ Ⓔ

SECTION 9

1. Ⓐ Ⓑ Ⓒ Ⓓ Ⓔ	5. Ⓐ Ⓑ Ⓒ Ⓓ Ⓔ	9. Ⓐ Ⓑ Ⓒ Ⓓ Ⓔ	13. Ⓐ Ⓑ Ⓒ Ⓓ Ⓔ
2. Ⓐ Ⓑ Ⓒ Ⓓ Ⓔ	6. Ⓐ Ⓑ Ⓒ Ⓓ Ⓔ	10. Ⓐ Ⓑ Ⓒ Ⓓ Ⓔ	14. Ⓐ Ⓑ Ⓒ Ⓓ Ⓔ
3. Ⓐ Ⓑ Ⓒ Ⓓ Ⓔ	7. Ⓐ Ⓑ Ⓒ Ⓓ Ⓔ	11. Ⓐ Ⓑ Ⓒ Ⓓ Ⓔ	
4. Ⓐ Ⓑ Ⓒ Ⓓ Ⓔ	8. Ⓐ Ⓑ Ⓒ Ⓓ Ⓔ	12. Ⓐ Ⓑ Ⓒ Ⓓ Ⓔ	

SECTION 1

ESSAY

Time—25 minutes

The essay gives you an opportunity to show how effectively you can develop and express ideas. You should, therefore, take care to develop your point of view, present your ideas logically and clearly, and use language precisely.

Your essay must be written on the lines provided on your answer sheet—you will receive no other paper on which to write. You will have enough space if you write on every line, avoid wide margins, and keep your handwriting to a reasonable size. Remember that people who are not familiar with your handwriting will read what you write. Try to write or print so that what you are writing is legible to those readers.

You have twenty-five minutes to write an essay on the topic assigned below. DO NOT WRITE ON ANOTHER TOPIC. AN OFF-TOPIC ESSAY WILL RECEIVE A SCORE OF ZERO.

Think carefully about the issue presented in the following excerpt and the assignment below.

> Do not quarrel. No one resolved to make the most of oneself can spare time for personal contention. Still less can one afford to take all the consequences, including the debasement of one's character and loss of self-control.
>
> Adapted from a letter by Abraham Lincoln to J. M. Cutts, October 26, 1863.

Assignment: Should quarrelling be avoided? Plan and write an essay in which you develop your point of view on the issue. Support your position with reasoning and examples taken from your reading, studies, experience, or observation.

DO NOT WRITE YOUR ESSAY IN YOUR TEST BOOK. You will receive credit only for what you write on your answer sheet.

BEGIN WRITING YOUR ESSAY ON THE ANSWER SHEET.

IF YOU FINISH BEFORE TIME IS CALLED, YOU MAY CHECK YOUR WORK ON THIS SECTION ONLY. DO NOT TURN TO ANY OTHER SECTION IN THE TEST.

SECTION 1—ESSAY

Time—25 minutes

SECTION 1—ESSAY

Time—25 minutes

SECTION 2

Turn to Section 2 of your answer sheet to answer the questions in this section.

Time—25 Minutes
24 Questions

Directions: For each question in this section, select the best answer from among the choices given and fill in the corresponding oval on the answer sheet.

Each sentence below has one or two blanks, each blank indicating that something has been omitted. Beneath the sentence are five words or sets of words labeled A through E. Choose the word or set of words that, when inserted in the sentence, best fits the meaning of the sentence as a whole.

Example:

Eliza felt ----- when her boss asked her to work seven weekends in a row but ----- when her work earned her a promotion.

(A) enervated . . weakened
(B) depressed . . intellectual
(C) advantageous . . salacious
(D) angry . . shopworn
(E) irate . . elated   

1. In his play *The Importance of Being Earnest*, Oscar Wilde satirizes the values of Victorian society by speaking through his characters, giving each of them sparkling ----- of great wit, wisdom, and charm.

(A) settings
(B) dialogue
(C) plots
(D) scenery
(E) actors

2. The English economist Thomas Malthus argued that resources are always limited in any society: the more abundant a society's resources, the more people that society will produce, which will eventually cause resources to become -----.

(A) plentiful
(B) irrelevant
(C) scarce
(D) unimportant
(E) critical

3. Political campaigns have become increasingly ----- policy issues; officials are elected more on the basis of personality and "likeability" than on the basis of their substantive policies.

(A) detached from
(B) concerned with
(C) authored by
(D) driven by
(E) based on

4. Despite centuries of debate, it doesn't actually matter who wrote the plays we ----- to Shakespeare; the plays exist, and they are what matter.

(A) divulge
(B) denote
(C) proscribe
(D) describe
(E) ascribe

5. -----, the silk-spinning gypsy moth, a notorious ----- that has cost untold millions of dollars to combat, was brought to America after the Civil War to boost the economy.

(A) Unfortunately . . scourge
(B) Understandably . . insect
(C) Ironically . . pest
(D) Coincidentally . . blight
(E) Predictably . . plague

6. Hawaii is the most ----- archipelago in the world; thousands of miles of ocean separate it from any other -----.

(A) famous . . island
(B) isolated . . landmass
(C) beautiful . . atoll
(D) romantic . . people
(E) dangerous . . inhabitants

GO ON TO THE NEXT PAGE

7. The reporter humiliated himself on nationwide television by ----- that he had ----- many of his award-winning stories.

(A) denying . . invented
(B) insisting . . written
(C) maintaining . . embellished
(D) ensuring . . researched
(E) admitting . . fabricated

8. Early in his career, the composer Saint-Saëns was considered to be even more of a ----- than the famously ----- Mozart, but unlike Mozart, who died at 35, Saint-Saëns never fulfilled his youthful promise, even though he outlived his predecessor by about fifty years.

(A) genius . . precocious
(B) prima donna . . foppish
(C) headache . . ebullient
(D) prodigy . . overrated
(E) failure . . fêted

GO ON TO THE NEXT PAGE

SECTION 2

Directions: Each passage below is followed by questions based on its content. Answer the questions on the basis of what is stated or implied in each passage and in any introductory material that may be provided.

Questions 9–10 are based on the following passage.

Robert Moses has done more to shape New York City than any other individual. An evangelist of the automobile and the highway, Moses's often brutal repossession of private property under the cover of "eminent domain"* has long been the subject of much controversy, especially because of its undoubtedly racist tinge. For example, Moses constructed the highways that head out from the city to Long Island with low overpasses on purpose: he wanted to ensure that public buses, which Moses assumed would be filled with what he considered to be undesirable African Americans, would be prevented from reaching the unarguably beautiful parks and beaches he had built on the Island's south coast. In this case, the design of the highways was influenced by the racism of the designer, but highways as a general technology do not, of course, necessitate such a racist deployment. Highways do, however, inherently embody a political decision (however arrived at) to privilege private over public transportation. It would seem that some aspects of the same technology are politically neutral—a nonracist would have built higher overpasses—whereas other aspects are innately political—highways, by their very nature, are built primarily for privately owned cars

* Eminent domain is the power of the state to seize private property for its own use without the owner's consent.

9. Which of the following is an irony implicit in this passage?

(A) The man who did more to shape New York City than any other individual was a racist.
(B) When it was convenient for Moses, champion of private transportation, to confiscate private property for his own uses, he did so without hesitation.
(C) Depending on which aspect of highways one wishes to consider, they can be considered either politically neutral technology or innately political technology.
(D) The parks Moses built are extremely beautiful.
(E) Technologies can embody cultural decisions.

10. The passage suggests that technology in general is

(A) always innately political
(B) never innately political
(C) sometimes innately political
(D) often innately political
(E) innately political or politically neutral

GO ON TO THE NEXT PAGE

SECTION 2

Questions 11–12 are based on the following passage.

In *Psycho* (1960), director Alfred Hitchcock fools his audience by spending the first third of the film concentrating on a diversionary plot line. The film begins with an impulsive theft of several thousand dollars by Marion Crane (played by Janet Leigh) from her office in Phoenix, Arizona. Marion's trials and tribulations in escaping Phoenix with her stolen loot and her eventual, morally laudable decision to return to Phoenix and take responsibility for her impulsive action are shown to be completely incidental to the main thrust of the movie. Perhaps the most frightening thing about *Psycho* is not *how* Leigh's character is killed (the famous "shower scene") but *why*. Leigh's character is snuffed out in the most random manner possible: she just happens to pull into the wrong motel. The psychosis of its owner, Norman Bates (played by Anthony Perkins), and his eventual unmasking, are the film's true plot lines. Unlike most other horror films, *Psycho* unravels slowly, taking its time; Hitchcock spends forty-five minutes introducing his audience to the fullness of the eventual victim's life, garnering its sympathy for her, and then, just when the audience fully identifies with her, she gets murdered by Bates. We feel the loss all the more strongly because it prevents her moral redemption; this, I believe, is what truly shocked audiences in 1960. Until *Psycho*, killing off the star of a film halfway through—let alone a star whose character has just decided to right an ethical wrong—simply wasn't done. That kind of random injustice smacked too much of reality, which, as always, is far more frightening than any film.

11. The passage suggests that the reason *Psycho* is so frightening is because

(A) Marion is brutally murdered while taking a shower
(B) Norman is irretrievably insane
(C) Marion, like many people in real life, is killed randomly and wholly undeservedly
(D) Marion deserves her fate because of her moral failings
(E) Hitchcock adopted a realistic style for the film

12. Lines 3–5 ("The film . . . Phoenix, Arizona") suggest that Marion's theft was

(A) unreflective of her basic character
(B) typical behavior for her
(C) unconnected to her eventual murder
(D) indicative of the realistic style of *Psycho*
(E) premeditated

GO ON TO THE NEXT PAGE

SECTION 2

Directions: The passages below are followed by questions based on their content; questions following a pair of related passages may also be based on the relationship between the paired passages. Answer the questions on the basis of what is stated or implied in the passages and in any introductory material that may be provided.

Questions 13–24 are based on the following passages.

These two passages are taken from papers given in the 1990s at a conference of historians that addressed the analytical concept of "mentalities." This concept was first introduced by the French philosopher and anthropologist Lucien Lévy-Bruhl as a strategy by which historians could explain behavior in past societies.

Passage 1

Lévy-Bruhl's "mentalities" are similar to other structural concepts designed to explain past human beliefs, regardless of their name. The key word here is *structural*. Like other structuralists, Lévy-Bruhl sought to lay out the structures of belief systems or thought of a given time or place. Historians who have followed Lévy-Bruhl's lead have indeed uncovered reasons for widespread belief in concepts we regard as bizarre or at least counterintuitive, such as the medieval belief in healing by the "royal touch." *Uncovered* is an apt word; many structuralist historians see themselves as "archeologists of knowledge," to borrow a phrase from another famous structural historian, Michel Foucault. They seek to explicate the "strange" that is always found in historical study, to answer that perfectly natural question that any historian asks herself at some point in her studies: "Why in the world would those people believe *that*?" An underlying assumption is that "those people" were no stupider, in the biological sense, than we are. Surely, a few hundred or even a couple of thousand of years is not enough time to make an evolutionary difference. Thus, the strangeness we often see in history must derive from cultural systems of belief—or mentalities, if you like.

What makes the mentality approach so powerful is that it forces the historian, who is herself embedded in a system of thought, to account for those aspects of past thought that strike her as against common sense. "Common sense" itself is not some natural, obvious outcome of a somehow unbiased "blank" mind confronting the world; rather, it is a label for our deepest cultural inheritances. Thus, in order to understand history from the point of view of those who made it—the "actors," as they're often called—we must understand the actors' "categories" of thought.

To return to the "royal touch": people in England and France believed that the sovereign could cure them of certain diseases simply by being touched by that sovereign. We may understand this as a collective delusion, but *they* certainly did not. So how does the concept of mentalities help us understand this collective delusion? It allows us a glimpse into the deeply held assumptions, usually never recorded in documents, which characterize a cultural unit. In this case, there was such a strong desire for, expectation of, and belief in the miraculous healing powers of the sovereign that those who were cured, post-touch, adduced their healing to that pre-existing deeply held desire. Those who were not cured, post-touch, simply concluded that they needed another touch or two. Interestingly, the royal touch was used in cases of skin ailments, mostly, which are usually self-limiting or self-correcting. But that is a modern conclusion; the point is not who is "right," "us" or "them," but how "they" understood their world. This is the power of the use of mentalities in historical research.

Passage 2

Lévy-Bruhl's "mentalities" method, like all structural methods in the historical sciences, suffers from a grave problem. No doubt, structuralist history has illuminated what was once dismissed as simply "irrational" by ignoring the question of whether we judge the actions or beliefs rational and simply studying what such widely held beliefs tell us about the culture being studied. However, the more deeply rooted the "mentality," the more problematic become such questions as, Where did it come from? How and why did it develop? How and why did it change? Structuralist approaches are excellent at explaining the mindset of a given time and place; they are quite weak when confronted with questions of historical change.

To be fair, the dichotomy of continuity and change has always dogged historians of all methodological stripes. Furthermore, it is certainly ridiculous to say that structuralist history shouldn't be done; it's been shown to be too useful and successful at rendering the strange explicable. However, if one is interested in historical *change*, mentalities won't help much.

But there are deeper problems with mentalities. First, in its original conception, it was assumed that there was a "prelogical" or "primitive" mentality with certain universal traits and a "scientific" or "modern" mentality, which was unquestionably superior. That hints at arrogance and requires a belief in cultural progress, which any historian should take to be an open question, not a fact of human nature. This dichotomy between the primitive and the modern, no doubt due to the concept's origin in turn-of-the-century anthropology, stands at the top of a very slippery slope toward racism and elitism, particularly since it surmises that history and culture progress in a linear fashion, so that each subsequent generation is smarter and more progressive than its predecessors.

Furthermore, one may very reasonably ask, by what social mechanism is a mentality maintained (setting aside questions of

GO ON TO THE NEXT PAGE

its origin and change)? The usual answer is linguistic—certain thoughts are simply not thinkable without words to describe them. One is then drawn into a chicken-and-egg debate on whether language forms thought or vice versa—or both at the same time in some kind of complex dynamic. It's a thin mechanistic reed on which to try to hang what is simply an idealistic concept, despite its usefulness in answering some historical questions.

Finally, how does one know that all members of a cultural group share *all* aspects of a mentality? How does one define that group in the first place? Everyone who speaks French? Well, until the nineteenth century, there were several types of "French" spoken throughout the region we now recognize as the French nation-state. Parisian French "won," just as Florentine Italian "won." As a famous linguist said, a language is a dialect with an army. The point here is that mentalities, like most concepts that seek to explain entire swatches of culture or history, tend to idealize—local variations are "averaged out," so to speak, and what is actually a very heterogeneous mix of ideas and beliefs becomes a monolithic "mentality" to be studied.

13. The phrase "archeologists of knowledge" (line 10) implies that structuralist historians

(A) must be trained in archeology
(B) peel back layers of inherited historical beliefs in order to uncover what the people they study actually thought
(C) study only knowledge, not actions
(D) borrowed the concept of mentalities from archeology
(E) believe that the people they study were biologically less intelligent than contemporary people are

14. In line 12, "explicate" most nearly means

(A) exemplify
(B) elude
(C) exonerate
(D) explain
(E) exhume

15. The question in line 15 ("Why . . . believe *that*?") serves to

(A) emphasize a common reaction to the strangeness that all historians encounter sooner or later
(B) express disbelief at the stupidity of historical actors
(C) prove that cultural progress has been made
(D) insinuate that primitive ideas have been rightly disregarded
(E) denounce past systems of thought

16. The author of Passage 1 mentions biological evolution in order to

(A) demonstrate that human cultural progress is due to underlying evolutionary advances
(B) dispense with the notion that the variation in human thought, belief, and action within historical time can be explained by biological evolution
(C) argue that the concept of mentalities has a scientific foundation
(D) correct a misunderstanding about the concept of mentalities
(E) foster the view that mentalities operate by an evolutionary mechanism

17. The phrase "common sense" is put in quotes in line 25 in order to

(A) emphasize that, to structuralist historians, contemporary common sense is what past systems of belief should be judged by
(B) highlight that what contemporary historians consider to be common sense is itself a reflection of those historians' mentalities or systems of belief
(C) imply that no such thing exists
(D) show that common sense has increased over time
(E) argue for a less intellectual style of historical writing

18. The discussion of the "royal touch" (lines 31–47) serves to

(A) prove how irrational historical actors were
(B) demonstrate how the movement from medieval monarchy to modern democracy constitutes a major historical change
(C) imply that structuralist history tends to yield stronger explanations when applied to historical change
(D) persuade the reader that past sovereigns had a special healing power
(E) exemplify how the concept of mentalities can illuminate a seemingly inexplicable action and belief system

19. In Passage 2, the word "rooted" in line 54 most nearly means

(A) cheered
(B) directed
(C) defeated
(D) embedded
(E) enlightened

GO ON TO THE NEXT PAGE

SECTION 2

20. The word "change" (line 65) is italicized in order to

(A) express doubt that mentalities are of much use to historians
(B) demonstrate how the concept of mentalities assumes that there is such a thing as cultural progress
(C) disprove the notion that the concept of mentalities is at its strongest when dealing with historical continuity
(D) stress that structuralist historical methods, such as mentalities, are at their weakest when applied to questions of historical change
(E) imply that questions of historical change are more important than those of historical continuity

21. The author of Passage 2 mentions that the concept of mentalities grew out of turn-of-the-century anthropology in order to

(A) show that the concept is inherently racist
(B) explain why the concept can't be applied with much success to questions of historical change
(C) warn that the dichotomy between the primitive and the modern mentality is itself a product of the mentality of a particular place and time
(D) demonstrate that the concept is historically useless
(E) exhibit the lack of a mechanism for the concept

22. In the final paragraph of Passage 2, the author argues that the concept of mentalities assumes that

(A) all people in a cultural group think and act in the same way
(B) the beliefs, thoughts, and actions of members of a cultural group are quite varied
(C) languages are higher creations than mere dialects
(D) language determines what is thinkable
(E) prelogical societies were irrational

23. Both authors would agree that the concept of mentalities

(A) is based on an explicit social mechanism
(B) suffers from its origin in turn-of-the-century anthropology
(C) is a valuable tool for historians
(D) fails to help explain the strangeness historians continually encounter in their studies
(E) tends to emphasize local variation in thought, belief, and action

24. The author of Passage 2 would respond to the lines 25–30 ("Common sense . . . of thought") in Passage 1 by saying that

(A) common sense is a natural response of the modern mentality to the natural world
(B) "actors' categories" tend to be quite similar across an entire cultural unit
(C) what the author of Passage 1 writes is entirely correct but has nothing necessarily to do with the usefulness of mentalities as an analytic concept
(D) a belief in common sense implies that the contemporary historian is intellectually superior to the historical actors she studies
(E) the entire concept of "common sense" is itself irrational

S T O P

IF YOU FINISH BEFORE TIME IS CALLED, YOU MAY CHECK YOUR WORK ON THIS TEST ONLY.
DO NOT TURN TO ANY OTHER SECTION IN THIS TEST.

SECTION 3

Turn to Section 3 of your answer sheet to answer the questions in this section.

Time—25 Minutes
20 Questions

Directions: For this section, solve each problem and decide which is the best of the choices given. Fill in the corresponding oval on the answer sheet. You may use any available space for scratchwork.

Notes:

1. The use of a calculator is permitted. All numbers used are real numbers.

2. Figures that accompany problems in this test are intended to provide information useful in solving the problems. They are drawn as accurately as possible EXCEPT when it is stated in a specific problem that the figure is not drawn to scale. All figures lie in a plane unless otherwise indicated.

3. Unless otherwise specified, the domain of any function f is assumed to be the set of all real numbers x for which $f(x)$ is a real number.

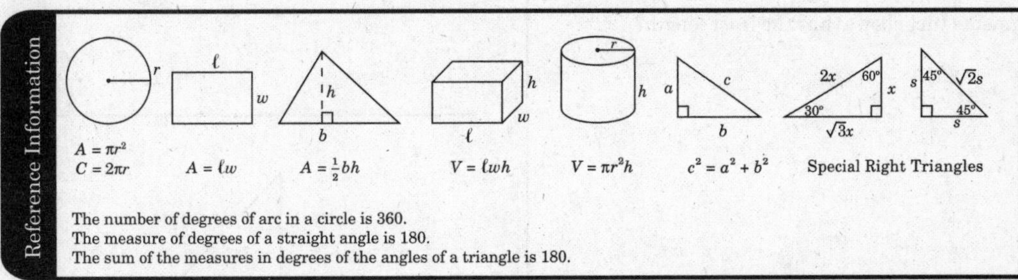
Reference Information
$A = \pi r^2$
$C = 2\pi r$
$A = \ell w$
$A = \frac{1}{2}bh$
$V = \ell wh$
$V = \pi r^2 h$
$c^2 = a^2 + b^2$
Special Right Triangles
The number of degrees of arc in a circle is 360.
The measure of degrees of a straight angle is 180.
The sum of the measures in degrees of the angles of a triangle is 180.

1. If $9x - 4 = 12$, what is the value of $9x + 4$?

(A) -12

(B) 0

(C) $\frac{4}{3}$

(D) 16

(E) 20

2. There are 30 sections of seats in a concert hall. Each section contains at least 40 seats but not more than 100 seats. Which of the following could be the number of seats in this concert hall?

(A) 1,100

(B) 2,300

(C) 3,100

(D) 3,500

(E) 4,000

GO ON TO THE NEXT PAGE

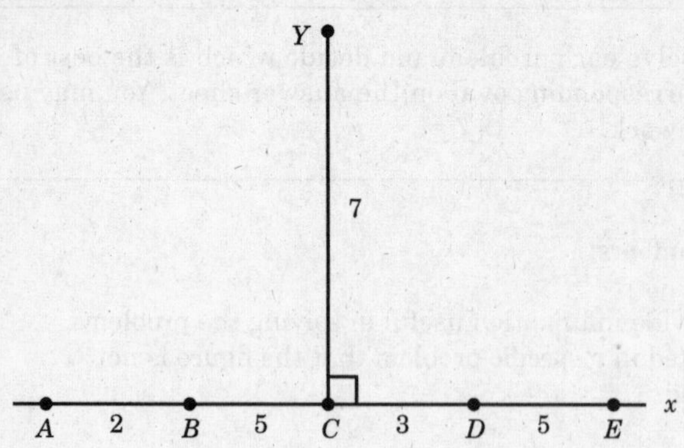

Note: Figure not drawn to scale.

3. In the figure above, YC is perpendicular to X. Which of the following line segments (not shown) has the least length?

(A) YA
(B) YB
(C) YC
(D) YD
(E) YE

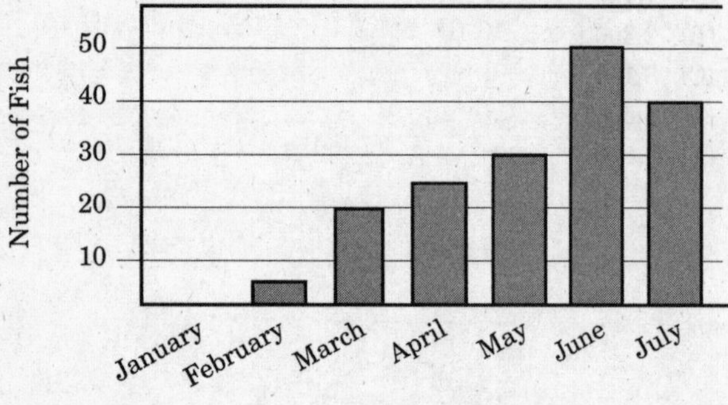

4. The graph above depicts the number of fish in an experimental fishpond by showing the total number of fish at the end of each month. The greatest increase in the number of fish in the pond occurred during which of the following months?

(A) February
(B) March
(C) April
(D) May
(E) June

5. The average (arithmetic mean) of a and b is 6 and the average (arithmetic mean) of a, b, and c is 10. What is the value of c ?

(A) 6
(B) 8
(C) 10
(D) 18
(E) 30

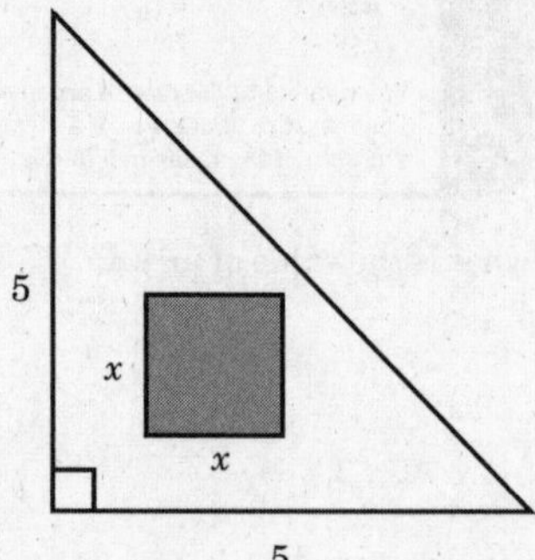

6. A small shaded square is inside a larger right isosceles triangle, as shown in the figure above. What is the area, in terms of x, of the nonshaded region?

(A) $10 - x$
(B) $10 - x^2$
(C) $12.5 - x$
(D) $12.5 - x^2$
(E) $25 - x^2$

GO ON TO THE NEXT PAGE

7. If $abce = 10$ and $abcd = 0$, which of the following must be true?

(A) $a < 1$
(B) $b < 1$
(C) $c > \frac{1}{2}$
(D) $e = 0$
(E) $d = 0$

8. During a football game, the home team scored one-fourth of its points in the first quarter, one-eighth in the second quarter, one-half in the third quarter, and the remaining points in the fourth quarter. If the total number of points scored by the home team was 56, how many points did the home team gain in the fourth quarter?

(A) 7
(B) 14
(C) 21
(D) 28
(E) 56

9. If $3^{3x} = 9^{x+1}$, what is the value of x?

(A) 0
(B) 1
(C) 2
(D) 3
(E) 4

10. If 3 less than 2 times a certain number is 4 more than the number, what is the number?

(A) 2
(B) 3
(C) 4
(D) 7
(E) 10

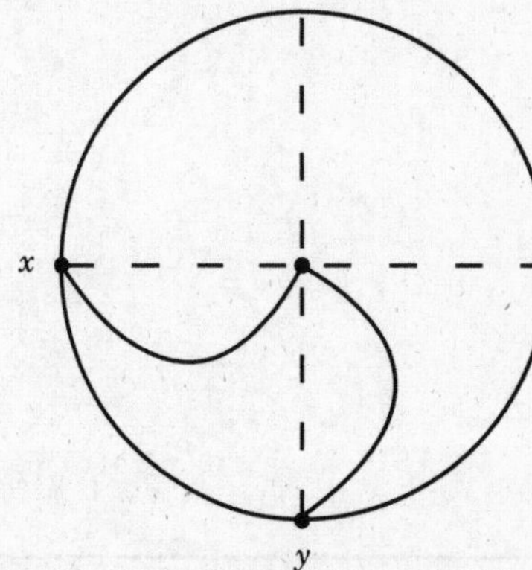

11. The circle above has a center, O, and a diameter of XY. The two semicircles have diameter OX and OY. If the area of the circle is 64π, what is the length of the path from X through O to Y?

(A) 4π
(B) 8π
(C) 16π
(D) 32π
(E) 36π

GO ON TO THE NEXT PAGE

x	$g(x)$
0	m
1	36
2	n

12. The table above shows some values for the function g. If g is a linear function, what is the value of $m + n$?

(A) 36
(B) 48
(C) 72
(D) 96
(E) It cannot be determined from the given information.

2, 6, –6, . . .

13. The first term in the sequence of numbers shown above is 2. Each even-numbered term is 4 more than the previous term and each odd-numbered term, after the first term, is –1 times the previous term. For example, the second term is 2 + 4, and the third term is -1×6 . What is the 157th term of this sequence?

(A) –6
(B) –2
(C) 2
(D) 4
(E) 6

14. In the xy-coordinate plane, the equation of a line l is $y = 3x + 2$. If line m is the reflection of line l across the x-axis, what is the equation of line m ?

(A) $y = 3x - 2$
(B) $y = -3x - 2$
(C) $y = -3x + 2$
(D) $y = -\frac{1}{3}x - 2$
(E) $y = -\frac{1}{3}x + 2$

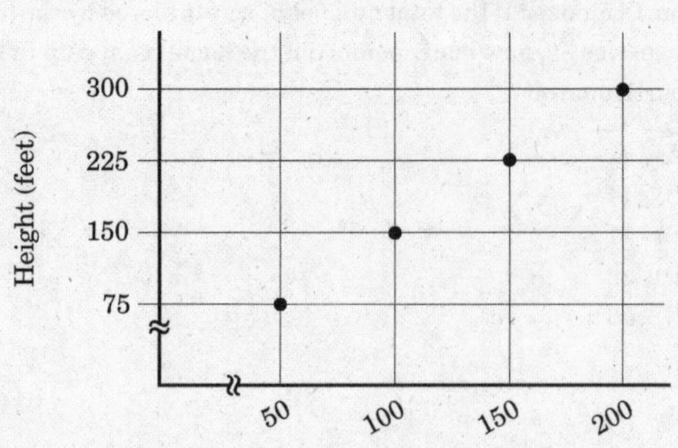

15. The graph above shows a redwood's height in feet from the age of 50 to the age of 200. The redwood's height at the age of 150 was what percent less than its height at the age of 200 ?

(A) 5
(B) 10
(C) 25
(D) 50
(E) 75

GO ON TO THE NEXT PAGE

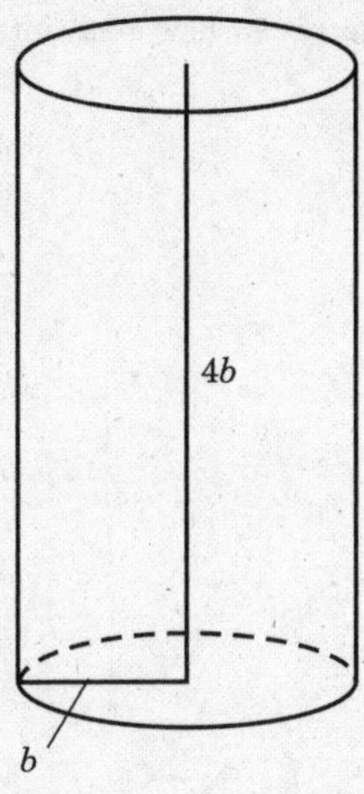

16. Which of the following has the same volume as the cylinder shown above with radius b and height $4b$?

(A) A rectangular solid with dimensions $2b$, π , $2b$
(B) A cube with edge $2\pi b$
(C) A cube with edge $2b$
(D) A rectangular solid with dimensions b, πb , $4b$
(E) A cylinder with radius $3b$ and height b

---

17. If $m - 5(2n - 4) = x$, what is $2n - 4$, in terms of m and x ?

(A) $\frac{x-m}{-5}$

(B) $\frac{x-m}{5}$

(C) $\frac{x+m}{-5}$

(D) $\frac{x+m}{5}$

(E) $\frac{xm}{5}$

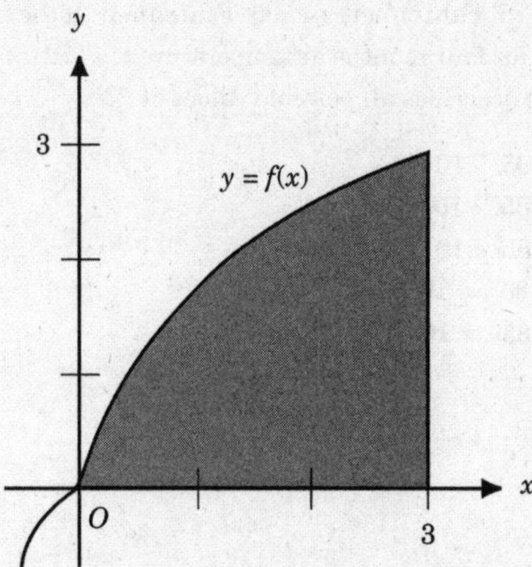

18. The shaded region in the figure above is bounded by the x-axis, the line $x = 3$, and the graph of $y = f(x)$. If the point (p, q) lies in the shaded region, which of the following must be true?

I. $p \leq 3$
II. $q > 3$
III. $q \leq f(p)$

(A) I only
(B) II only
(C) III only
(D) I and II only
(E) I and III only

GO ON TO THE NEXT PAGE

SECTION 3

19. A certain plant will survive only if kept at a temperature between 75° Fahrenheit and 95° Fahrenheit. If the plant survives for four months at temperature t, which of the following describes all possible values of t ?

(A) $|t - 85| > 10$
(B) $|t + 85| < 10$
(C) $|t - 85| < 10$
(D) $|t + 85| = 10$
(E) $|t - 85| = 10$

20. The least integer in a set of consecutive integers is –92. If the sum of these integers is 93, how many integers are in the set?

(A) 92
(B) 93
(C) 184
(D) 185
(E) 186

S T O P

IF YOU FINISH BEFORE TIME IS CALLED, YOU MAY CHECK YOUR WORK ON THIS TEST ONLY.
DO NOT TURN TO ANY OTHER SECTION IN THIS TEST.

SECTION 4

Turn to Section 4 of your answer sheet to answer the questions in this section.

Time—25 Minutes
24 Questions

Directions: For each question in this section, select the best answer from among the choices given and fill in the corresponding oval on the answer sheet.

Each sentence below has one or two blanks, each blank indicating that something has been omitted. Beneath the sentence are five words or sets of words labeled A through E. Choose the word or set of words that, when inserted in the sentence, best fits the meaning of the sentence as a whole.

Example:

Eliza felt ----- when her boss asked her to work seven weekends in a row but ----- when her work earned her a promotion.

(A) enervated . . weakened
(B) depressed . . intellectual
(C) advantageous . . salacious
(D) angry . . shopworn
(E) irate . . elated

1. The Greek term *moira* means -----, which is the notion that the human life is predestined.

(A) freedom
(B) liberty
(C) fate
(D) democracy
(E) doom

2. In the professor's brilliant lecture, the ----- of Rudyard Kipling's poems were profitably ----- the pacifism of Wilfred Owen's verse.

(A) malevolence . . compared to
(B) strenuousness . . overcome by
(C) bellicosity . . contrasted with
(D) magnificence . . undermined by
(E) naiveté . . discussed with

3. Irrationally terrified of choking, Susan didn't just chew her food, she ----- it into a fine paste before swallowing.

(A) formed
(B) flattened
(C) crushed
(D) masticated
(E) expounded

4. Unlike his brother Sam, Dave refused to ----- superiors; thus, Sam, who was more politically -----, did better in the business world than did Dave.

(A) disagree with . . tone deaf
(B) stand up to . . crafty
(C) deal with . . uninvolved
(D) kowtow to . . astute
(E) respond to . . shrewd

5. To an ear used to the smooth and ----- flow of popular music, the ----- and disordered explosiveness of Ornette Coleman's "free jazz" comes as quite a shock.

(A) unhurried . . rigid
(B) cool . . level
(C) harmonic . . understated
(D) tonal . . conventional
(E) predictable . . jagged

GO ON TO THE NEXT PAGE

SECTION 4

Directions: The passages below are followed by questions based on their content; questions following a pair of related passages may also be based on the relationship between the paired passages. Answer the questions on the basis of what is stated or implied in the passages and in any introductory material that may be provided.

Questions 6–9 are based on the following passages.

The following passages discuss the possible reasons for the delay in publication of Nicolaus Copernicus's On the Revolutions of the Celestial Spheres.

Passage 1

Nicolaus Copernicus delayed the publication of his epochal work, *On the Revolutions of the Celestial Spheres*, by at least 13 years. Some scholars claim that Copernicus had completed his famed treatise describing a heliocentric universe as many as 36 years before publication. Regardless of the actual date, the question remains: why did Copernicus delay publication? The reason is not hard to fathom. *On the Revolutions* was truly revolutionary—it was the first modern attempt to place the sun, and not the Earth, at the center of the then-known universe. This model was mathematically more elegant, a fact which was important to Copernicus who, as a follower of Pythagoras, believed that Nature had to conform to the most elegant mathematics, given that the Creator was the greatest of all mathematicians. But this model also raised deep questions about the validity of certain passages in the Bible. It's no accident that Copernicus finally published the work just before he died. He knew just how deeply his heliocentric system would upset religious orthodoxy. Unlike the future Copernicans, including Galileo, who was placed under house arrest, and Giordano Bruno, who was burned at the stake in the Campo Dei Fiori in Rome, Copernicus died naturally.

Passage 2

For a long time, historians have felt sure that Copernicus delayed publication of his classic book, *On the Revolutions of the Celestial Spheres*, because of his fear of the Church. As much as any topic in history can be considered a closed case, this seemed to be one: we all know what happened to other Copernicans—most famously Galileo and Bruno. Of course, Copernicus was no fool; he wouldn't risk the wrath of the Inquisition, and he was quite clever to die so conveniently after he finally published the work. So what's wrong with this explanation? Actually, quite a bit. Bruno was burned at the stake in 1600; Galileo was put under house arrest in 1633. Copernicus died in 1543. Unless causation works in reverse, one can't use the fates of Galileo and Bruno as evidence for Copernicus's delay in publishing. Furthermore, we know that the Inquisition didn't really start heating up (at least on such esoteric subjects as cosmology) until well after Copernicus's death. But, most important, Copernicus dedicated *On the Revolutions* to Pope Paul III. One couldn't do that without prior permission. So, how was it possible that some horrible Catholic Inquisition squelched poor Copernicus, especially when we now know that many Jesuit astronomers were quite interested in Copernicus's treatise and that that treatise was designed at least in part to be a more elegant mathematical method for calculating the movement of planets and stars, Pythagorean that Copernicus was? It's not at all clear that Copernicus actually thought that his heliocentric system was "really real," as present-day philosophers might say. Why, then, did Copernicus delay? Most likely, for the very human reason that despite all of his protestations to the contrary, he feared ridicule. The Earth moves around the sun? Ha! Any simple fool can plainly see that's not the case, whatever Copernicus's ancient views on mathematical elegance may be. Thus, Copernicus sought the highest authority in his dedication—just as Andreas Vesalius did, in the very same year *On the Revolutions* was published, for his equally radical work, *On the Structure of the Human Body*, which overturned many of the revered Roman physician Galen's ideas and for which Vesalius successfully appealed to the Holy Roman emperor Charles V for "protection" via a sanctioned dedication.

6. Both authors agree that Copernicus

(A) delayed publication of *On the Revolutions of the Celestial Spheres* because he was afraid of the Inquisition
(B) delayed publication of *On the Revolutions of the Celestial Spheres* because he was afraid of public ridicule
(C) was a Pythagorean
(D) overturned long-held beliefs about the structure of the human body
(E) was afraid to ask permission to dedicate his book to Pope Paul III

7. The author of Passage 2 most likely asks several rhetorical questions in order to

(A) cast doubt on Copernicus's heliocentric model of the universe
(B) strengthen the argument in the passage by asking and answering several key questions about the received view that Copernicus delayed publication due to fear of the Church
(C) involve the reader in the argument
(D) provoke the reader to provide answers to those questions
(E) tie Copernicus's dedication to Pope Paul III to Vesalius's dedication to Charles V

GO ON TO THE NEXT PAGE

8. The author of Passage 1 would most likely respond to the argument presented by the author of Passage 2 by arguing that

   I. Papal dedications don't necessarily entail papal understanding of the book that's being dedicated.
   II. What the author of Passage 2 interprets as "fear of ridicule" could easily be taken to be "fear of the Church."
   III. The comparison to Vesalius's work is circumstantial evidence, at best.

(A) I only
(B) II only
(C) III only
(D) I and II only
(E) I, II, and III

9. The author of Passage 2 would most likely regard the phrase "raised deep questions about the validity of certain passages in the Bible" (lines 14–15) as

(A) evidence that fear of the Church delayed Copernicus's publication of *On the Revolutions*
(B) unconnected to Vesalius's dedication of *On the Structure of the Human Body* to Charles V
(C) a distortion of Copernicus's theory
(D) assuming, without support, that the Catholic Church at the time interpreted the Bible literally
(E) not a matter of much concern to a Pythagorean

GO ON TO THE NEXT PAGE

SECTION 4

Directions: Each passage below is followed by questions based on its content. Answer the questions on the basis of what is stated or implied in each passage and in any introductory material that may be provided.

Questions 10–15 are based on the following passage.

The following passage is from a 2003 novel in which a young woman recalls a memorable Thanksgiving-night taxi ride in New York City.

It was snowing hard and we were caught unprepared. Six inches had accumulated. That may not sound like much, but in New York City, a snowfall of that usually unimpressive magnitude is always a substantial nuisance. Snowplows compound the accumulation; they had already made their initial sweep, molding the snow over parked cars, fencing in the sidewalks with two-foot-high walls. The sidewalks themselves had not yet been cleared, and when we left the restaurant, we slid down the street in our dressy shoes. Yellow taxis glided across Park Avenue. Snow continued to fall, catching the light from the streetlamps. The city was awash in white and gold.

Despite the beauty of our surroundings, we were full and tired and we wanted to go home. That is to say, we wanted to get home fast, not by subway (the definition of "slow"), but by taxi. We were caught in-between shifts; the few taxi cabs we saw were crowned with brightly lit "Off Duty" messages. But, miraculously, one off-duty cab stopped.

"Where are you going?" asked a heavily accented voice.

"Sunnyside, Queens."

"You are lucky. I live there, too, and I am going home. Come in, please!"

We climbed inside. The driver began the slow, slushy drive over the 59th Street Bridge which rose steeply into the white sky. We seemed to be driving through the air.

As usual, I became nauseated. I poked my head through the opening in the bulletproof plastic wall that separated the front seat from the back seat. I was hoping that a better view of the road would settle my stomach.

The driver had his radio tuned to what sounded like Middle Eastern music to my untutored ears. Or perhaps it was from the Subcontinent?* The driver wore a long shaggy beard, baggy clothes, and what looked to me like a turban.

As I invaded his space by leaning forward, he glanced at me from the rear view mirror. I smiled. There's nothing to fear from me, Mr. Taxi Driver, I wanted to say. But I was too tired and shy to simply communicate why I was breaking into his inner sanctum. Luckily, he took it as an invitation to converse.

"What is this thing, Thanksgiving?" he asked.

I hadn't expected to engage in conversation—New Yorkers tend to ignore their "cabbies"—but, despite my slowly subsiding nausea, a polite response seemed the least I could do, considering that he'd not only saved my husband and me from a long subway ride home, but he had also allowed me to "break the wall" that usually separates master from servant in taxicabs.

"It's a holiday," I weakly mustered.

"I know that," he retorted with a hint of don't-patronize-me in his voice. I immediately regretted my perfunctory response.

"But what *is* it?" As he spoke, he took a hand off the steering wheel and shook his fist at the sky which had quit snowing in favor of sending down sheets of freezing rain.

I began to try to explain the origin of Thanksgiving: pilgrims, Native Americans, cornbread, pumpkins.

The taxi-driver shook his head. "No, no. Who *celebrates* Thanksgiving?"

"All Americans," I replied. And then I finally understood. I set aside my nausea and engaged him in conversation.

"You have children?" I asked.

"Four."

"How old?"

"The youngest, three. The oldest, eight."

"Are they here with you?"

"No." His eyes darkened. "I work six months of the year here and save my money. Then, I take my money and go home to my wife and children."

"I'm sorry; that's gotta be tough." What else could I say?

My cabbie shrugged off both my response and his melancholy and returned, almost with relief, to his questioning.

"Do you have children?"

"Not yet," I answered. "We're thinking about it."

"What's there to think about?" our cabbie asked laughingly, and then quickly changed the subject. "So, I want to know. What is this thing about, this 'Thanksgiving'?"

"In my opinion, it's the only true American holiday."

"No religion?"

"No religion."

"Not like Christmas?"

"No. Not like Christmas. Thanksgiving is for everyone who lives in this country." I paused. "And especially for immigrants. Except for the Native Americans, all Americans are immigrants."

He smiled at this.

"What are you supposed to do on Thanksgiving?"

"You eat," I smiled. "And spend time with your family." I regretted that as soon as I had said it.

"What if you have no family close?" he asked sadly.

We were pulling up to our apartment building now. The cabbie was smiling at us. He had turned off the meter.

"No charge."

We argued; he insisted.

GO ON TO THE NEXT PAGE

SECTION 4

Once we'd gotten out of the cab, I asked, "When will you see your family again?"

"Soon, very soon. I will celebrate Thanksgiving then."

Since it seemed like the right thing to do, my husband and I both shook his hand. He smiled and waved and drove off into the icy night.

* The "Subcontinent" refers to South Asia, which is usually understood to include Pakistan, India, Bangladesh, Sri Lanka, and Myanmar.

10. The passage is narrated from the point of view of

(A) the cabbie
(B) the husband
(C) the wife
(D) an observer who knows everything about all the characters
(E) an observer who has only partial knowledge of some of the characters

11. The imagery in line 10 ("The city . . . white and gold") serves to

(A) describe the effect of the light streaming from the streetlamps through the falling snow
(B) emphasize the class differences between the American couple and the cabbie
(C) represent the action of the snowplows that are clearing the streets of freshly fallen snow
(D) symbolize the movement of the yellow taxis through the white snow
(E) signify the effect of the light emanating from the "Off Duty" messages on top of the taxis through the falling snow

12. Which of the following is the most likely purpose of the question in lines 30–31 ("Or perhaps . . . the Subcontinent?")?

(A) The wife is asking the cabbie from which part of the world the music he's playing comes from.
(B) It underscores the wife's relative ignorance about Eastern music and, by extension, Eastern cultures.
(C) The wife is asking her husband from which part of the world the music the cabbie is playing is from.
(D) It highlights her dislike of the music.
(E) It explains why her husband has dozed off.

13. In line 47, the word "perfunctory" most closely means

(A) routine
(B) cruel
(C) polite
(D) warm
(E) quick

14. The sentence in line 55 ("And then . . . finally understood") most likely refers to which of the following?

(A) The wife realizes that the cabbie is afraid of Thanksgiving.
(B) The wife realizes that the cabbie, like many immigrants, is a guest worker and probably separated from his family.
(C) The wife realizes that her nausea is irrational, and so she sets it aside with an effort of will.
(D) The wife realizes that her husband has been awake the entire time they've been in the taxi.
(E) The cabbie realizes that the wife is a little slow to understand his question.

15. The passage is best described as

(A) a series of tragic misunderstandings between members of different cultures
(B) an example of patronizing mistreatment of a foreign taxi driver by an insensitive American couple
(C) an instance of cross-cultural communication based on common human feelings
(D) a comedy of errors that focuses on cross-cultural miscommunication
(E) a satire of typical New Yorker behavior

GO ON TO THE NEXT PAGE

SECTION 4

Questions 16–24 are based on the following passage.

In this passage, a journalist discusses the phenomenon of globalization.

What is globalization? Since 1945, international trade and economic activity have greatly increased, and this increase is accelerating. Improvements in transportation, communication, and information technologies have made this accelerating increase possible by helping economic activity become increasingly rapid and inexpensive. International institutions have become more powerful at the expense of nation-state sovereignty. The World Trade Organization (WTO) regulates trade agreements among nations. The International Monetary Fund (IMF) makes loans to indebted developing nations as long as they promise to follow a "neoliberal" economic model by privatizing government-run enterprises, such as electrical power grids and water supplies; deregulating the private sector; and removing trade barriers. The World Bank makes loans to developing countries for large-scale public-works projects, as well as lends smaller amounts for social needs from the medical to the educational. A global popular culture and neoliberal consensus, both of which are largely American in origin and nature, have spread as large multinational and transnational corporations have taken advantage of freer trade and economies of scale.

The great promise of globalization—one that may still be fulfilled—is that the rising tide of economic activity would raise all boats. This has not happened. In fact, the rate of growth for the poorer half of the world's nations has been reduced by half. Aside from India and China, progress on poverty, life expectancy, infant mortality, and literacy has slowed in the poorer nations, while prosperity for most of the "First World"—Japan, the United States, and the European Union—has accelerated. Even this acceleration has not been universal within the first-world nations—especially in the United States, where the bifurcation of rich and poor has increased over the last three decades to the point that some commentators worry about the disappearance of the middle class.

Social dislocation and conflict have followed quickly on the heels of economic upheaval. Movements of people within and between countries have always occurred, but such migrations are now occurring on an order of magnitude that is truly novel. Sometime in 2004 or 2005, for the first time in human history, most of the world's population will live in cities, much of it in Dickensian poverty. Mass migration from rural to urban environments has been accompanied by a rise in emigration, legal or not, to first-world nations. These migrations have been exacerbated by the IMF's strict requirements for granting loans. As basic services (utilities, rent, education, healthcare) have become more expensive in developing nations as a result of enforced privatization and deregulation, and as local industry and agriculture have buckled under the impact of enforced trade liberalization, many in developing nations have either left their home country altogether or have been forced into a life apart from their families as "guest workers" in first-world nations, sending money home to support their families.

Traditional cultural beliefs and norms clash daily with their Euro-American counterparts, which are disseminated by transnational corporations via all media. A fundamentalist reaction in all world cultures has gathered force in the face of a perceived threat of Western dominance. International terrorism is the most militant wing of this reaction. Ironically, the most sophisticated practitioners of terror have taken full advantage of the mechanisms of globalization in order to fight the Western values they oppose. Al-Qaeda, for example, uses the internet to organize and recruit from an expanding pool of socioeconomically dislocated and disenchanted individuals, hides the movement of its members in the confusion of mass migration that no nation can control, takes advantage of deregulated capital and currency markets to raise funds, shops at semilegitimate international arms markets to acquire increasingly destructive armaments, and employs increasingly cheap transportation not only to coordinate attacks but also, infamously, as weapons of attack. Al-Qaeda is also well aware of how global media hypercoverage compounds the "terror dividend" of its attacks. It uses this fear to manipulate target nations into reacting in ways that will help Al-Qaeda spread its message. The final irony is that Al-Qaeda, unlike conventional state-sponsored terrorist groups, is itself unconnected to any one nation. Like the enterprises that spread the Western values it deplores, Al-Qaeda is essentially a decentralized, entrepreneurial transnational and multinational corporation that happens to be devoted to the production and distribution of an antiglobalist political movement.

Globalization is unstoppable. However, humanity can shape the nature of globalization, and this is the great debate that must occur within and among nations. Thus far, capital and currency exchange have been efficiently globalized. First-world nations have insisted on and received much access to developing-nation markets. The developing world, however, has begun to demand equity and parity. A consortium of developing nations, led by Brazil, walked out of a recent round of WTO negotiations to protest the refusal by the United States and the European Union to expose their agricultural products to international competition. Environmental, labor, and social justice movements are

GO ON TO THE NEXT PAGE

themselves globalizing, gaining strength through numbers. One can see the potential emergence of a global regime of collective bargaining between those groups and the IMF and WTO. Globalization may still raise all boats on a permanent surge of economic activity if the fruits of that activity can be more widely and fairly distributed and if a reasonable balance can be struck between unrestrained economic activity and labor rights, environmental preservation, and social justice. Globalization's current incarnation, however, threatens to send all boats on a race to the bottom.

16. In lines 22–23, the phrase "raise all boats" means

(A) remove all ships from dock
(B) destroy all ships
(C) benefit all parties involved
(D) arouse suspicion
(E) raise questions

17. The main purpose of the passage is to

(A) argue that globalization is a threat to equality that must be stopped
(B) present globalization as something that has caused great harm but which could benefit humanity if handled properly
(C) make the case for rich countries to send aid to poorer countries
(D) assert that globalization will usher in a new age of universal prosperity if its faults can be corrected
(E) show that economic progress in China and India has far outpaced that of the rest of the developing world

18. In the first paragraph, the author does all of the following EXCEPT

(A) link global popular culture to America
(B) pose a rhetorical question
(C) offer a positive or negative opinion on globalization
(D) connect globalization to improvements in communication
(E) make a claim about the rate of globalization

19. The irony the writer mentions in line 57 derives from which of the following factors?

(A) The fact that the movement toward globalization against which Al-Qaeda struggles is improving conditions in the very countries from which Al-Qaeda draws most of its recruits.
(B) The fact that the most sophisticated terrorist organizations are the ones most strongly opposed to Western values.
(C) The fact that terrorist groups, such as Al-Qaeda, that oppose globalization rely on the mechanisms of globalization for the growth and support of their organizational networks.
(D) The fact that as Western values are spreading throughout the world, fundamentalist movements are becoming more powerful.
(E) The fact that cheap transportation can be used as a weapon of attack as well as a way to coordinate attacks.

20. As used in line 70, the phrase "terror dividend" most nearly means

(A) the amount of money that terror attacks cost
(B) the amount of money that terror attacks produce
(C) the amount of fear apportioned out by attacks
(D) the net value of terror attacks to Al-Qaeda
(E) the amount of fear apportioned out by the media

21. In lines 85–88 ("A consortium . . . international competition"), the author mentions that Brazil and other developing nations walked out of the WTO negotiations in order to

(A) show the reader that developing nations are prepared to stand up for themselves and demand equal treatment within the emerging arena of global economic activity
(B) persuade the reader that developing nations' refusal to cooperate is one of the reasons that globalization has not ushered in an age of prosperity as had been hoped
(C) argue that American and European refusal to expose their agricultural products to international competition is a flaw in globalization's program for increasing prosperity in all nations
(D) demonstrate the futility of protesting a process that cannot be stopped once it is put in motion and that could very well benefit humanity as a whole if given a fair chance
(E) show that recent developments in the global agricultural economy are a reliable indicator of upcoming developments in the global economy as a whole

GO ON TO THE NEXT PAGE

SECTION 4

22. As used in line 98, "incarnation" most nearly means

(A) union
(B) personification
(C) lifetime
(D) doctrine
(E) version

23. The main purpose of the final paragraph is to

(A) summarize the arguments presented earlier in the passage
(B) introduce another authority's opinion on globalization
(C) suggest an alternative to globalization
(D) shows ways in which globalization could benefit all nations
(E) argue that globalization will eventually be abandoned

24. The author would be most likely to agree with which of the following statements?

(A) Increased movement of people within and between nations is a typical result of economic disorder.
(B) Growth in a nation's economy is usually accompanied by increases in that nation's rates of illiteracy and infant mortality.
(C) Globalization could probably be stopped with a concerted effort on the part of a few developing nations.
(D) Privatization and deregulation of utilities services usually reduces their costs to customers.
(E) Disenchanted people are usually less likely to be recruited by terrorist organizations.

S T O P

IF YOU FINISH BEFORE TIME IS CALLED, YOU MAY CHECK YOUR WORK ON THIS TEST ONLY. DO NOT TURN TO ANY OTHER SECTION IN THIS TEST.

SECTION 5

Turn to Section 5 of your answer sheet to answer the questions in this section.

Time—25 Minutes
18 Questions

Directions: For this section, solve each problem and decide which is the best of the choices given. Fill in the corresponding oval on the answer sheet. You may use any available space for scratchwork.

Notes:

1. The use of a calculator is permitted. All numbers used are real numbers.
2. Figures that accompany problems in this test are intended to provide information useful in solving the problems. They are drawn as accurately as possible EXCEPT when it is stated in a specific problem that the figure is not drawn to scale. All figures lie in a plane unless otherwise indicated.
3. Unless otherwise specified, the domain of any function f is assumed to be the set of all real numbers x for which $f(x)$ is a real number.

Reference Information

$A = \pi r^2$, $C = 2\pi r$ | $A = \ell w$ | $A = \frac{1}{2}bh$ | $V = \ell wh$ | $V = \pi r^2 h$ | $c^2 = a^2 + b^2$ | Special Right Triangles

The number of degrees of arc in a circle is 360.
The measure of degrees of a straight angle is 180.
The sum of the measures in degrees of the angles of a triangle is 180.

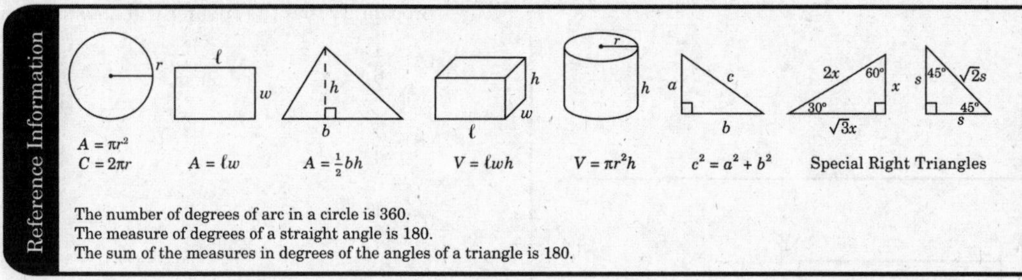

1. If $y + \frac{3}{y} = 7 + \frac{3}{7}$, then y can equal which of the following?

(A) $\frac{1}{7}$

(B) $\frac{6}{7}$

(C) 1

(D) $\frac{7}{3}$

(E) 7

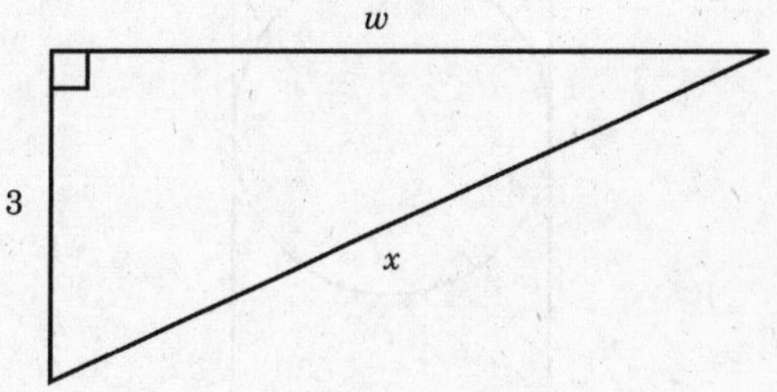

Note: Figure not drawn to scale.

2. In the right triangle above, if $w = 5$, what is the value of x ?

(A) $\sqrt{8}$ (approximately 2.83)

(B) 4

(C) $\sqrt{19}$ (approximately 4.36)

(D) $\sqrt{31}$ (approximately 5.57)

(E) $\sqrt{34}$ (approximately 5.83)

GO ON TO THE NEXT PAGE

SECTION 5

All numbers that are divisible by both 3 and 9 are also divisible by 6.

3. Which of the following numbers can be used to show that the statement above is false?

(A) 27
(B) 54
(C) 108
(D) 162
(E) 324

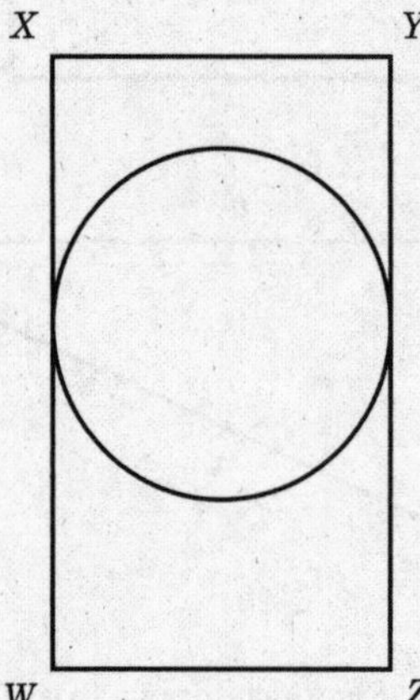

4. In the figure above, the circle is tangent to the sides XW and YZ of the 7-by-15 rectangle, $WXYZ$. What is the circumference of the circle?

(A) 3.5π
(B) 7π
(C) 7.5π
(D) 12.25π
(E) 15π

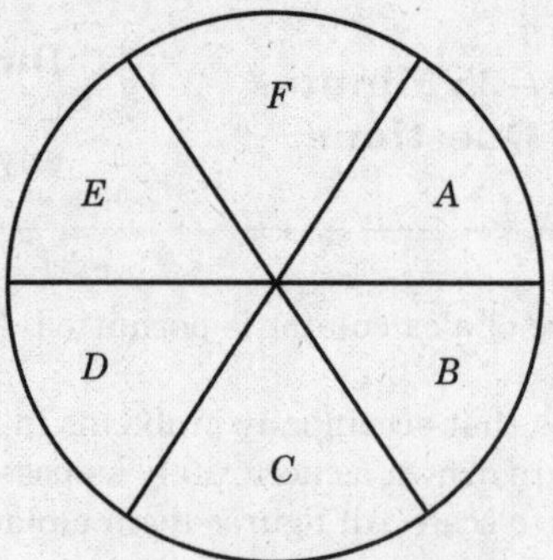

5. On the spinner shown above, a student spins the arrow once. On every spin, each of the lettered sectors has an equal probability of being the sector on which the arrow stops. What is the probability that the spinner will not stop on a consonant?

(A) $\frac{1}{6}$
(B) $\frac{1}{4}$
(C) $\frac{1}{3}$
(D) $\frac{1}{2}$
(E) 1

GO ON TO THE NEXT PAGE

SECTION 5

6. Which of the following tables shows a direct proportional relationship between a and b ?

(A)

a	b
2	4
3	9
4	16

(B)

a	b
5	20
6	24
7	28

(C)

a	b
2	4
3	5
4	6

(D)

a	b
6	12
7	21
8	32

(E)

a	b
4	8
8	12
12	16

7. Barney plows driveways for m dollars per driveway. From this amount, he spends $\frac{m}{3}$ in costs to keep his snowplowing business going. Barney saves the rest of the money. In terms of m, how many driveways will Barney have to plow in order to save $2,500 ?

(A) $\frac{m}{3{,}750}$

(B) $\frac{m}{2{,}500}$

(C) $\frac{2{,}500}{m}$

(D) $\frac{3{,}750}{m}$

(E) $3{,}750m$

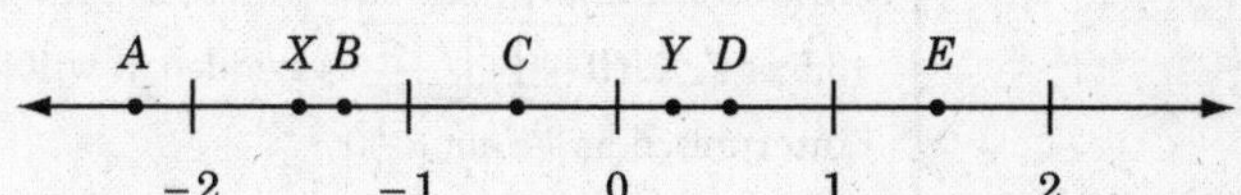

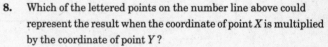

8. Which of the lettered points on the number line above could represent the result when the coordinate of point X is multiplied by the coordinate of point Y ?

(A) A

(B) B

(C) C

(D) D

(E) E

GO ON TO THE NEXT PAGE

SECTION 5

Directions: For Student-Produced Response questions 9–18, use the grids on the answer sheet.

Each of these questions requires you to solve the problem and enter your answer by marking the ovals in the special grid, as shown in the examples below. You may use any available space for scratchwork.

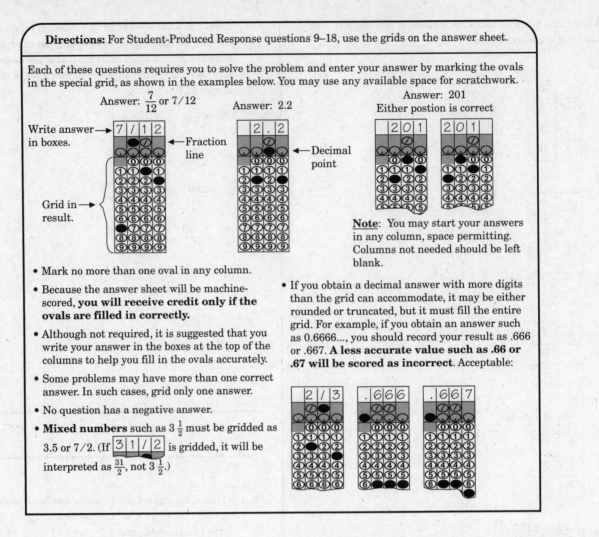

Answer: $\frac{7}{12}$ or 7/12 Answer: 2.2

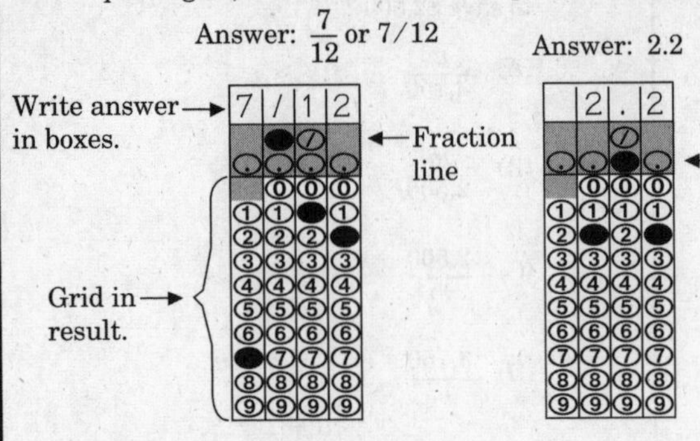

Answer: 201
Either postion is correct

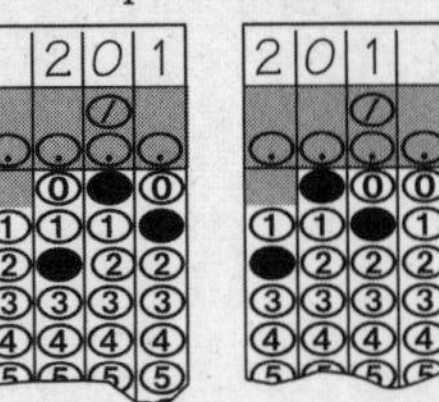

Note: You may start your answers in any column, space permitting. Columns not needed should be left blank.

- Mark no more than one oval in any column.
- Because the answer sheet will be machine-scored, **you will receive credit only if the ovals are filled in correctly.**
- Although not required, it is suggested that you write your answer in the boxes at the top of the columns to help you fill in the ovals accurately.
- Some problems may have more than one correct answer. In such cases, grid only one answer.
- No question has a negative answer.
- **Mixed numbers** such as $3\frac{1}{2}$ must be gridded as 3.5 or 7/2. (If 3 1 / 2 is gridded, it will be interpreted as $\frac{31}{2}$, not $3\frac{1}{2}$.)
- If you obtain a decimal answer with more digits than the grid can accommodate, it may be either rounded or truncated, but it must fill the entire grid. For example, if you obtain an answer such as 0.6666..., you should record your result as .666 or .667. **A less accurate value such as .66 or .67 will be scored as incorrect**. Acceptable:

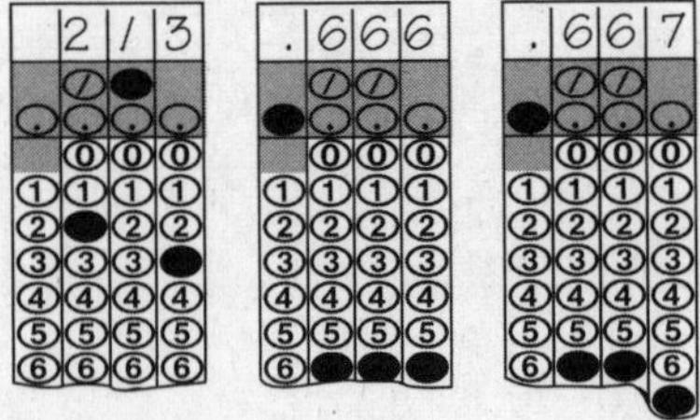

9. If $4x - 2y = 15$ and $y = x - 1$, what is the value of x ?

10. A student read an average of 10 pages an hour before taking a speed-reading class. After completing that class, the student's average reading rate increased 30 percent. How many pages per hour was the student able to read after completing the speed-reading class?

GO ON TO THE NEXT PAGE

SECTION 5

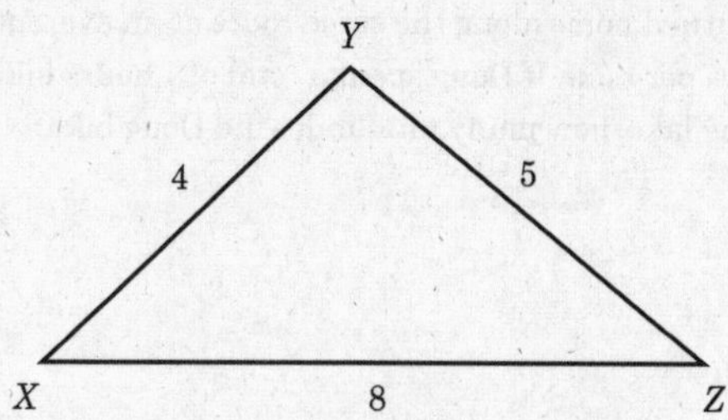

11. Each angle of ΔXYZ above has the same measure as an angle in ΔLMN (not shown). If the length of one side of ΔLMN is 40, what is one possible perimeter of ΔLMN ?

12. The sum of four consecutive integers is 1,190. What is the value of the greatest of these integers?

13. If $g(x) = 4^x - \frac{x}{4}$, then what is the value of $g(2)$?

14. Exactly five athletes are competing to be in the starting lineup on a sports team, which consists of exactly five positions. If each player can play any position, and no one player will start at more than one position, how many different assignments of players to positions are possible?

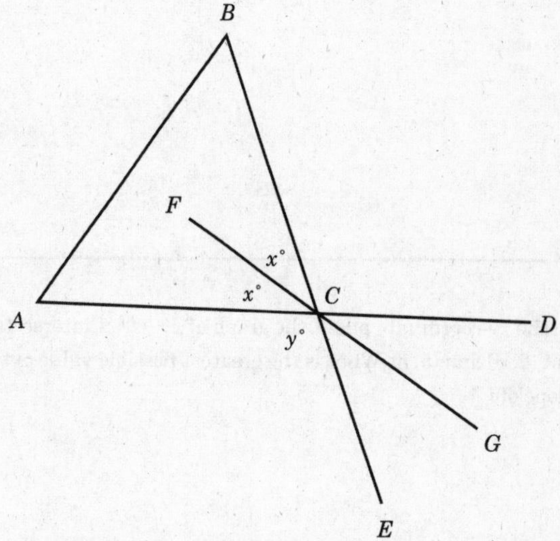

15. In the figure above, ΔABC is equilateral and FG, AD, and BE intersect at point C. What is the value of y ?

GO ON TO THE NEXT PAGE

SECTION 5

16. Let the operations ♣ and ♥ be defined for all real numbers x and y as follows:

$x ♣ y = x + 5y$
$x ♥ y = x + 3y$

If 5 ♣ $(2y) = (3y)$ ♥ 2, what is the value of y ?

17. In the xy-coordinate plane, the graph of $x = y^2 + 1$ intersects line l at $(2, q)$ and $(5, r)$. What is the greatest possible value of the slope of l ?

18. Doug biked to the lake at an average speed of 15 miles per hour. He returned home along the same route at an average speed of 10 miles per hour. If Doug spent a total of 4 hours biking to and from the lake, how many total miles did Doug bike?

S T O P

IF YOU FINISH BEFORE TIME IS CALLED, YOU MAY CHECK YOUR WORK ON THIS TEST ONLY. DO NOT TURN TO ANY OTHER SECTION IN THIS TEST.

SECTION 6

Turn to Section 6 of your answer sheet to answer the questions in this section.

Time—25 Minutes
35 Questions

Directions: For each question in this section, select the best answer from among the choices given.

The following sentences test correctness and effectiveness of expression. Part of each sentence or the entire sentence is underlined; beneath each sentence are five ways of phrasing the underlined material. Choice A repeats the original phrasing; the other four choices are different. If you think the original phrasing produces a better sentence than any of the alternatives, select choice A; if not, select one of the other choices.

In making your selection, follow the requirements of standard written English; that is, pay attention to grammar, choice of words, sentence construction, and punctuation. Your selection should result in the most effective sentence—clear and precise, without awkwardness or ambiguity.

Example:

In the poem "Ulysses" by Alfred, Lord Tennyson, the speaker says, "I cannot rest from travel," instead, he will live life to the fullest.

(A) "I cannot rest from travel," instead,
(B) "I cannot rest from travel"; instead,
(C) "I cannot rest from travel" instead,
(D) "I cannot rest from travel," upon which
(E) "I cannot rest from travel,"

1. Troy had just scored the winning touchdown and that was when he got his career-ending concussion.

(A) and that was when he got
(B) when he was hit with
(C) and then he got
(D) when he received
(E) and then he received

2. Saddled with three jobs after two of her peers had unexpectedly quit, Aimee's need for relief was great.

(A) Aimee's need for relief was great
(B) Aimee needed relief
(C) Aimee's need for relief was immense
(D) Aimee needed a great deal of assistance
(E) Aimee's need for a great deal of assistance was immediate

3. Allison, Fred, and Stephanie were swimming in the old quarry when she got a bad leg cramp and had to be rescued.

(A) when she got a bad leg cramp and had to be rescued
(B) and then she got a bad leg cramp and had to be rescued
(C) when Allison got a bad leg cramp and had to be rescued
(D) when Allison got a bad leg cramp, necessitating her subsequent rescue
(E) when the need for Allison's rescue was caused by her getting a bad leg cramp

4. By choosing only his favorites for the school play, Joe, the drama teacher, proved what many had suspected, merit played no part in landing roles in his class.

(A) , merit played no part in landing roles in his class
(B) : merit played no part in landing roles in his class
(C) : to land a role in Joe's class, merit plays no part
(D) , that merit played no part in landing roles in Joe's class
(E) : that merit played no part in landing roles in Joe's class

5. Not only can post-traumatic stress disorder plague soldiers who suffer from it, but it has a devastating affect on those soldiers' families.

(A) but it has a devastating affect on those soldiers' families
(B) but it also has a devastating effect on those soldiers' families
(C) but it also has a devastating affect on those soldiers' families
(D) but it has a devastating affect on those soldiers' families, too
(E) but it has a devastating effect on those soldiers' families, too

GO ON TO THE NEXT PAGE

SECTION 6

6. The rise of "527s"—political organizations not officially connected to particular campaigns—has been both lauded and decried by both sides of the political spectrum.

(A) has been both lauded and decried by both sides of the political spectrum
(B) has been not only lauded but also decried by both sides of the political spectrum
(C) has been lauded and decried by both sides of the political spectrum
(D) have been both lauded and decried by both sides of the political spectrum
(E) have been lauded and decried by both sides of the political spectrum

7. Archeological fieldwork is nowhere near as glamorous as they would have you believe in Hollywood films.

(A) as they would have you believe in Hollywood films
(B) as Hollywood films would have you believe
(C) as they that make Hollywood films would have you believe
(D) as that depicted in Hollywood films
(E) as they make out in Hollywood films

8. For nearly a century, physicists have been trying to reconcile quantum theory and relativity.

(A) For nearly a century, physicists have been trying to reconcile quantum theory and relativity
(B) Physicists have been trying to reconcile both quantum theory and relativity for almost a century
(C) For nearly a century, the reconciliation of quantum theory and relativity has been the task of physicists
(D) For nearly a century, quantum theory and relativity's reconciliation has been physicists' task
(E) Physicists have, for nearly a century, been trying to effect the reconciliation of quantum theory and relativity

9. The Russian author Yevgeny Zamyatin's *We* which is a chilling dystopia anticipated many of the insights in George Orwell's later and more famous novel 1984.

(A) *We* which is a chilling dystopia
(B) *We*, which is a chilling dystopia,
(C) *We*, that is a chilling dystopia,
(D) *We* that is a chilling dystopia
(E) *We* that chilling dystopia

10. For all of the twentieth century's technological progress, the fact remains that if a person living in 1800 would find daily life in 1900 far more unrecognizable than a person living in 1900 would find daily life in 2000.

(A) if a person living in 1800 would find daily life in 1900 far more unrecognizable than a person living in 1900 would find daily life in 2000
(B) a person living in 1800 would find daily life in 1900 far more unrecognizable than a person living in 1900 would find daily life in 2000
(C) if a person living in 1800 were transported to 1900, that person would find daily life far more unrecognizable than a person transported from 1900 to 2000
(D) a person living in 1900 would find daily life in 2000 more unrecognizable than a person living in 1800 would find daily life in 1900
(E) a person from 1800 would find daily life more unrecognizable than a person from 1900

11. With the fate of Europe hanging in the balance, the stand made by the British, Belgians, and French at Ypres early in World War I was truly heroic.

(A) the stand made by the British, Belgians, and French at Ypres early in World War I was truly heroic
(B) the British, Belgians, and French made a truly heroic stand at Ypres early in World War I
(C) the stand made at Ypres was truly heroic
(D) the stand made by the British, Belgians, and French at Ypres was truly heroic
(E) the British, Belgians, and French's stand at Ypres early in World War I was truly heroic

GO ON TO THE NEXT PAGE

SECTION 6

Directions: For each question in this section, select the best answer from among the choices given.

The following sentences test your ability to recognize grammar and usage errors. Each sentence contains either a single error or no error at all. No sentence contains more than one error. The error, if there is one, is underlined and lettered. If the sentence contains an error, select the one underlined part that must be changed to make the sentence correct. If the sentence is correct, select choice E. In choosing answers, follow the requirements of standard written English.

Example:

The other (A) delegates and him (B) immediately (C) accepted the resolution drafted by (D) the neutral states. No error (E)

Ⓐ ● Ⓒ Ⓓ Ⓔ

12. If a film is ever made (A) of J. R. R. Tolkien's *The Hobbit*, they'll (B) have to choose (C) whether to adopt its light tone or to continue (D) with the much darker tone of *The Lord of the Rings*. No error (E)

13. Whereas (A) the wine known as Merlot has been (B) quite popular for many years, an Australian version of Syrah, known as (C) "Shiraz," had recently been (D) gaining in popularity. No error (E)

14. Michel and Jacques decided (A) to become (B) a cultural anthropologist (C) after reading (D) Clifford Geertz's famous collection of essays *The Interpretation of Cultures*. No error (E)

15. Neither to the Americas or (A) to the lands of Christian Europe do we (B) owe the coffee house; (C) rather, it is (D) an Ottoman invention. No error (E)

16. If one forgets to bring (A) a windbreaker on a bike ride, then you risk (B) turning what should be (C) fun into (D) an ordeal. No error (E)

17. Every time you (A) set out on a hike, you should check that you have packed (B) enough food, brought (C) ample first-aid equipment, and to make sure (D) you have a map of the area in which you'll be hiking. No error (E)

18. The relatively new field of network theory has been (A) shown to underlie (B) phenomena as disparate (C) as evolutionary biology, social psychology, computer science, and (D) philosophy. No error (E)

19. Despite persistent popular misunderstanding, which seem (A) to refuse to go away, Charles Darwin never realized (B) the significance of (C) Gregor Mendel's work on genetics—in fact, (D) the term genetics wasn't coined until the early twentieth century. No error (E)

20. The work of certain (A) rock groups, such as (B) the Beatles, the Doors, and the Rolling Stones, never lose (C) its freshness, even (D) forty years later. No error (E)

21. In 1800, (A) a letter could not cross (B) Europe any faster than it will have (C) during the height of (D) the Roman Empire in the second century. No error (E)

22. Edward Tufte, a widely (A) influential statistician and graphic designer, has had (B) an impact on the visual display of quantitative information comparable to those (C) of William Strunk and E. B. White on (D) American prose style. No error (E)

GO ON TO THE NEXT PAGE

SECTION 6

23. Rock climbing, difficult though it may be (A), isn't scarcely anything (B) compared to ice climbing, which requires not only (C) special equipment but also (D) nerves of steel. No error (E)

24. As horrific as the recent earthquake-triggered (A) tsunami in the Indian Ocean was, scientists have recently discovered (B) that far more potentially devastating "megatsunamis," which can rise to (C) more than one hundred feet in height and travel dozens of miles inland, is (D) caused by massive coastal landslides. No error (E)

25. Of the (A) seven Julio-Claudian emperors (if one (B) counts Julius Caesar and Augustus), historians have (C) generally designated Caligula as worse (D). No error (E)

26. The author of the essay maintained that (A), unlike other religious texts, the Koran not only formed (B) the basis of a religion but (C) embodied (D) the highest poetic achievement in the language in which it was composed. No error (E)

27. That (A) your hard drive crashed yesterday does not pertain in (B) the fact that your (C) essay is (D) long overdue. No error (E)

28. Amazing (A) enough, after (B) a century of research scientists still (C) don't understand how water rises (D) to the top of the giant sequoias of the Pacific Northwest. No error (E)

29. The baseball team finally was (A) able to celebrate a championship after a long drought; (B) its (C) fans were (D) jubilant far into the night. No error (E)

GO ON TO THE NEXT PAGE

SECTION 6

Directions: The following passage is an early draft of an essay. Some parts of the passage need to be rewritten.

Read the passage and select the best answers for the questions that follow. Some questions are about particular sentences or parts of sentences and ask you to improve sentence structure or word choice. Other questions ask you to consider organization and development. In choosing answers, follow the requirements of standard written English.

Questions 30–35 are based on the following essay, a response to a prompt that asked writers to discuss a sport or sports.

(1) *The sport of fencing has roots that go back thousands of years.* **(2)** *The ancient Egyptians, Greeks, and Romans all practiced some form of swordsmanship to prepare men for duels and warfare.* **(3)** *Fencing in its modern form bears little relation to the types of fighting popular in these bygone civilizations.*

(4) *In the Middle Ages, the development of heavy plate armor made the sword almost useless as a weapon.* **(5)** *Gigantic broadswords are still employed, but only as crude hacking devices that hold little practical advantage over axes.* **(6)** *Plate armor was, in turn, rendered obsolete by the invention of firearms in the fifteenth century, however, and swordsmanship was resurrected as an essential tool for self-defense and warfare.*

(7) *At the beginning of the sixteenth century, swords were still heavy instruments designed for cutting and slashing.* **(8)** *The development of the modern fencing sword began later in the century with the introduction of the Italian rapier.* **(9)** *This weapon was light and slender.* **(10)** *With a sharp point that made stabbing the primary form of attack.* **(11)** *This more manageable type of sword, which could be worn at the waist without much inconvenience, allowed for the development of fencing as a pastime for wealthy gentlemen.*

(12) *In modern times, fencing is a competitive sport practiced all over the world.* **(13)** *Its emphasis on speed and agility over brute strength makes it popular with women as well as men.* **(14)** *Fencing was introduced as an Olympic sport for men in 1896, and in 1924 women fencers were allowed to compete at the Olympic level as well.* **(15)** *In recent years, fencing has become especially popular as an activity for children; its dynamic nature and low risk of injury make it an attractive alternative to boxing and other high-risk combat sports.*

30. In context, which is the most logical word to insert at the beginning of sentence 3 (reproduced below)?

> *Fencing in its modern form bears little relation to the types of fighting popular in these bygone civilizations.*

(A) Moreover,
(B) Unfortunately,
(C) Predictably,
(D) Undoubtedly,
(E) However,

31. In context, which of the following revisions needs to be made in sentence 5 (reproduced below)?

> *Gigantic broadswords are still employed, but only as crude hacking devices that hold little practical advantage over axes.*

(A) Replace "gigantic" with "huge" and leave the rest of the sentence as it is.
(B) Replace "are" with "were" and leave the rest of the sentence as it is.
(C) Replace "are" with "were" and "hold" with "held".
(D) Replace "hold" with "held" and "axes" with "axis".
(E) Replace "axes" with "axis" and leave the rest of the sentence as it is.

32. In context, which of the following topics would be the most appropriate to insert at the end of the second paragraph?

(A) A concrete example that demonstrates why swordsmanship became an essential weapon after the introduction of firearms
(B) A description of various types of plate armor
(C) An explanation of how early firearms worked
(D) A discussion of the relationship between horsemanship and swordsmanship
(E) A discussion of the invention of gunpowder

33. In context, what is the best way to deal with sentence 10 (reproduced below)?

> *With a sharp point that made stabbing the primary form of attack.*

(A) Leave it as it is now.
(B) Insert "And" before "with".
(C) Connect it to sentence 9 with a comma.
(D) Connect it to sentence 9 with a semicolon.
(E) Replace "attack" with "attacking".

GO ON TO THE NEXT PAGE

SECTION 6

34. What would be the most appropriate subject for a paragraph to insert between the third and fourth paragraphs?

(A) An examination of how fencing changed as a result of the introduction of firearms
(B) A defense of the arguments made in the third paragraph
(C) Statistics to show the increase in fencing's popularity across the world
(D) A summary of developments made in fencing between the seventeenth and twentieth centuries
(E) A summary of the points made so far

35. Of the following, which is the best way to conclude the passage?

(A) Switch the order of sentences 14 and 15.
(B) Insert the word "but" at the beginning of sentence 15.
(C) Add a sentence on the dangers of boxing.
(D) Add a sentence on the possible impact of fencing's popularity with children on the sport's future.
(E) Omit sentence 15.

S T O P

IF YOU FINISH BEFORE TIME IS CALLED, YOU MAY CHECK YOUR WORK ON THIS TEST ONLY. DO NOT TURN TO ANY OTHER SECTION IN THIS TEST.

SECTION 7

Turn to Section 7 of your answer sheet to answer the questions in this section.

Time—20 Minutes
19 Questions

Directions: For each question in this section, select the best answer from among the choices given and fill in the corresponding oval on the answer sheet.

Each sentence below has one or two blanks, each blank indicating that something has been omitted. Beneath the sentence are five words or sets of words labeled A through E. Choose the word or set of words that, when inserted in the sentence, best fits the meaning of the sentence as a whole.

Example:

Eliza felt ----- when her boss asked her to work seven weekends in a row but ----- when her work earned her a promotion.

(A) enervated . . weakened
(B) depressed . . intellectual
(C) advantageous . . salacious
(D) angry . . shopworn
(E) irate . . elated   

1. Robin wasn't a malevolent person—in fact, he was quite -----; he simply lacked tact.

(A) mean-spirited
(B) grumpy
(C) silly
(D) kind
(E) wicked

2. Despite their best intentions and efforts, the estranged couple's attempt to ----- failed.

(A) argue
(B) separate
(C) reconsider
(D) reconcile
(E) divorce

3. Scientists have long known that the subspecies *Homo sapiens neanderthalensis* coexisted with our own subspecies, *Homo sapiens sapiens*; many novelists, including William Golding, have imagined what an ----- between the two subspecies might have been like.

(A) extinction
(B) inheritance
(C) exhibition
(D) immersion
(E) encounter

4. While it has long been acknowledged that the environment is the stage upon which the human drama is acted out, a less passive role for long-term, large-scale environmental trends is becoming increasingly accepted: the natural environment actually ----- human history.

(A) shapes
(B) undermines
(C) supports
(D) exacerbates
(E) retards

5. According to T. E. Lawrence, the refusal of the British and French Armies to give heavy artillery to the Arab Revolt during World War I was ----- to ensure that the Europeans could divide up the defeated Ottoman Empire into colonies with minimal -----.

(A) conceived . . responsibility
(B) designed . . resistance
(C) decided upon . . effort
(D) concocted . . ease
(E) intended . . unfairness

6. Ever since Columbus, the Americas have been host to a highly ----- culture, mixing European, Native American, and African influences.

(A) warlike
(B) heterogeneous
(C) tolerant
(D) bigoted
(E) uniform

GO ON TO THE NEXT PAGE

SECTION 7

Directions: The passage below is followed by questions based on its content. Answer the questions on the basis of what is stated or implied in the passage and in any introductory material that may be provided.

Questions 7–19 are based on the following passage.

The following passage has been adapted from an introduction to a book by a historian of science that discusses the careers of three twentieth-century biologists: Richard Goldschmidt (1878–1958), Nikolai Kol'tsov (1872–1940), and Max Hartmann (1876–1962).

At the dawn of the twentieth century, three young biologists became friends at the Russian marine biological laboratory at Villefranche, on the French Mediterranean coast. An idyllic photograph from 1899 shows Richard Goldschmidt, Nikolai Kol'tsov, and Max Hartmann relaxing outside the laboratory. In the foreground are their collecting tools: fishing nets, wicker basket filled with collecting bottles, and ropes for hauling in the nets. Goldschmidt would later reminisce about life on the Riviera: hikes in the surrounding hills; walks to nearby Nice, with its sailors' cafes and bawdy shows; unsupervised and unstructured explorations of the marine fauna; and lunching on Russian caviar imported as biological supplies ("fish eggs") to avoid tariffs. In these charming surroundings, the three budding biologists made a pact to open an experimental biological institute. Although trained in the nineteenth-century observational traditions of morphology* and comparative anatomy, the three friends defined themselves as "experimentalists," aiming to use ideas and techniques from chemistry and physics to rejuvenate and advance biology. Plans for the institute fell through, but each biologist went on to eminent, if separate, careers. In a letter to Goldschmidt in 1922, Kol'tsov concluded: "The idea created in Villefranche has already borne good fruit! Neither the walls nor the capital nor external conditions create the scientific institute; rather it is the ideas and the specialists. Thus we all three belong to one and the same institute." But external conditions changed for the worse as the political upheavals of the 1930s engulfed each biologist in mid-career. In this decade, Kol'tsov faced Stalinism, Goldschmidt fled to the United States to escape Nazism, and Hartmann weathered the storm in Germany.

Within fifteen years of their sojourn at Villefranche, the three friends had established themselves in biology. From 1909 to 1914, Hartmann served as director of Berlin's Koch Institute. In 1914, Hartmann and Goldschmidt joined the new Kaiser Wilhelm Institute outside of Berlin in Dahlem, Goldschmidt as head of Zoological Genetics, Hartmann as head of Protozoology**. In 1916, Kol'tsov formed and headed the Institute for Experimental Biology in Moscow, which he expressly based on his youthful discussions with Goldschmidt and Hartmann at Villefranche.

These three European-born biologists exhibited many characteristics of what historians of biology have called "the mandarin style," which grew out of differences in social class, education, and professional training. Mandarin biologists absorbed the central European educational goal of Bildung, the holistic cultivation of the mind and spirit, from Gymnasia*** in the late nineteenth century. Mandarin biologists displayed a comprehensive knowledge of biology, tended to synthesize wide-ranging sets of facts and theories, were frequently interested in embryonic development, and pursued "high-culture" interests outside of science. In contrast, the mostly American-born "pragmatic" biologists tended to be specialists who felt no need to synthesize, often studied transmission genetics****, and enjoyed popular culture.

Kol'tsov, Goldschmidt, and Hartmann believed that biologists should mobilize the techniques of various biological subdisciplines to mount a concerted, synthetic attack upon the "big" theoretical problems of biology. Kol'tsov hired scientists from new fields, such as biochemistry and genetics, as well as from the old disciplines of anatomy and morphology in the hope of creating synthetic biological knowledge. What Kol'tsov attempted through his institute, Goldschmidt embodied. Goldschmidt published extensively in many fields, from experimental embryology and neurology to genetics and evolution. Furthermore, Goldschmidt periodically synthesized his wide-ranging experimental work in theoretical tomes.

Each biologist also displayed the mandarin trait of high-culture interests outside of science. Goldschmidt collected Asian art, learned several languages, and was a connoisseur of classical music. But even Goldschmidt deferred to Kol'tsov, describing him as "unbelievably cultured." Kol'tsov traveled in lofty intellectual circles—the celebrated author Maxim Gorky was a trusted friend—and wrote a book commemorating students killed during the aborted 1905 revolution. Hartmann, for his part, penned many essays on the philosophy of biology and especially criticized "American pragmatism" in biology. Kol'tsov, Goldschmidt, and Hartmann clearly typify mandarin biology. How, then, did each biologist's mandarin heritage interact with the radically different "external conditions" of the 1930s?

The culture shock Goldschmidt experienced when he moved from Berlin to Berkeley, California, in 1936 never disappeared. In Germany, Goldschmidt had headed up a major institute with Olympian status and no teaching responsibilities. In America, he was just another professor with insufficient lab space and funding. Thus deprived, Goldschmidt wrote two synthetic and heterodox books that caused a furor that resonates to the present day: *Physiological Genetics* (1938) and *The Material Basis of Evolution* (1940). In true mandarin style, Goldschmidt presented comprehensive visions of genetics and evolution that deliberately

GO ON TO THE NEXT PAGE

challenged the American biologist Thomas Hunt Morgan's pragmatic research program of transmission genetics upon which mostly Anglo-American population geneticists had based their mathematical models of evolution.

Like Goldschmidt, Kol'tsov also faced an ideological challenge, but the ideology he battled was far more dire than mere academic orthodoxy. After flourishing under Lenin's New Economic Program, Kol'tsov navigated the new ideological shoals of Stalin's "Great Break" (1929–1932) with considerable savvy, temporarily insulating his research, and that of his institute, from encroaching totalitarianism. But, by 1938, Stalin's increasing power had finally scuttled Kol'tsov's mandarin vision of his institute. Hartmann faced a situation as dangerous as Kol'tsov's, but according to eyewitnesses Hartmann openly criticized the Nazis in the halls of the Kaiser Wilhelm Institute. What needs to be explained is how Hartmann and his science weathered the Nazi storm. By comparing the different careers of Kol'tsov, Goldschmidt, and Hartmann, I hope to show how the intellectual culture forged in their youth (Kol'tsov's "institute without walls") reacted to the various cultural challenges of American pragmatism, Nazism, and Stalinism.

* Morphology is the study of physical form in living things.

** Protozoology is the study of one-celled animals.

*** Gymnasia, a German version of a Latin term, are roughly equivalent to elite private American high schools.

**** "Transmission" genetics dealt with correlating specific genes and observed traits in organisms, such as the fruit fly, and with linkage between genes on the chromosome, which formed the basis for maps of the genome.

7. In line 3, "idyllic" most nearly means

(A) nearly ideal
(B) sepia-toned
(C) typically French
(D) peacefully rustic
(E) highly active

8. Of the biologists mentioned, the passage provides the most information about

(A) Goldschmidt
(B) Hartmann
(C) Kol'tsov
(D) Morgan
(E) Anglo-American population geneticists

9. The purpose of including the quote in lines 21–25 ("The idea . . . same institute") primarily serves which of the following purposes?

(A) To foreshadow the actual establishment of a real institute by the three biologists
(B) To highlight the irony that despite Kol'tsov's belief, "external conditions" would soon affect the "institute without walls" that the three biologists had created
(C) That an outlay of capital investment was unnecessary to create an actual institute
(D) That the three biologists had moved on from marine biology to study fruit
(E) To show that the three biologists had remained friends

10. The purpose of the second paragraph is to

(A) show that the three biologists had abandoned their youthful musings on opening an institute together
(B) underscore that as the three biologists grew older, they acquiesced to the reality of constructing a career
(C) indicate that a rift had formed between Goldschmidt and Hartmann, on the one hand, and Kol'tsov, on the other hand
(D) demonstrate that the three biologists rocketed to the top of their professions
(E) emphasize how competitive the three biologists were with one another

11. The categories "mandarin" and "pragmatic" are best characterized by which of the following?

(A) They are completely discrete, with no possibility for overlap.
(B) They are totally diffuse and thus fairly useless as a means of drawing distinctions.
(C) They are roughly accurate descriptions of various styles of doing biology that can serve a useful comparative purpose.
(D) Mandarin biologists were superior to pragmatic biologists.
(E) Pragmatic biologists were superior to mandarin biologists.

GO ON TO THE NEXT PAGE

12. From lines 53–56 ("Kol'tsov, Goldschmidt . . . problems of biology"), one can infer that mandarin biologists tended to

(A) eschew synthesizing seemingly disparate facts into theories that attempted to answer the big questions in biology
(B) embrace information from diverse areas of biology and find a theoretical underpinning for this information that would illuminate long-standing problems in the field
(C) collect Asian art
(D) construct more correct theories than the pragmatic biologists
(E) break down large problems in biology into small, manageable parts, which they would then study in depth, to the exclusion of other subdisciplines of the science

13. In line 64, "tomes" most nearly means

(A) coauthored collections of essays
(B) short, popular works
(C) superficial treatments of weighty subjects
(D) weighty treatments of superficial subjects
(E) long, scholarly books

14. The purpose of the discussion in lines 65–74 ("Each biologist . . . in biology") is to

(A) show that mandarin biologists wasted precious time on nonbiological interests
(B) complete the author's argument that these three biologists typified the mandarin style
(C) emphasize the political awareness of mandarin biologists
(D) underscore the anti-American feelings of mandarin biologists
(E) demonstrate that all mandarin biologists were excellent writers

15. In line 84, "heterodox" most nearly means

(A) radical
(B) incorrect
(C) consisting of many interrelated parts
(D) unorthodox
(E) unnecessarily confrontational

16. From the discussion in lines 78–91 ("The culture . . . of evolution"), one can infer that

(A) Goldschmidt wrote two books in order to upset his American hosts
(B) Goldschmidt's lack of funding, new teaching responsibilities, and insufficient lab space most likely prevented him from continuing his experimental work and encouraged him to take the time to synthesize much of his previous work
(C) Goldschmidt and Morgan personally disliked each other
(D) Goldschmidt did not understand transmission genetics
(E) Morgan had been preventing Goldschmidt from doing research, so Goldschmidt was forced to publish theoretical books

17. Lines 94–98 ("After flourishing . . . encroaching totalitarianism") indicate that the author most likely

(A) draws a distinction between Soviet culture under Lenin and Soviet culture under Stalin
(B) morally approves of Lenin, but not of Stalin
(C) morally disapproves of Kol'tsov's political maneuvering under Stalin's ever-increasing power
(D) believes that Kol'tsov should have left the Soviet Union while he had the chance
(E) thinks that Goldschmidt and Hartmann should have come to their old friend's aid

GO ON TO THE NEXT PAGE

SECTION 7

18. The author apparently believes which of the following about the nature of science?

(A) Scientific knowledge is completely determined by external conditions.

(B) Scientific knowledge is entirely free from external political influence.

(C) Science can only flourish in democratic societies.

(D) Science is a human activity that cannot be fully understood without taking into account the external conditions in which it occurs.

(E) Scientific knowledge is no different from religious faith.

19. Lines 104–108 ("By comparing . . . Stalinism") most likely mean which of the following?

(A) The author of the article believes that American pragmatism, Nazism, and Stalinism are morally equivalent to one another.

(B) The author is interested in comparing the impact of various ideologies, regardless of their innate moral worth, on three biologists with quite similar educational backgrounds and intellectual beliefs.

(C) The author is criticizing the naïveté of Kol'tsov's belief that the three friends had created an "institute without walls."

(D) The author will likely go on to show how the entire mandarin style was doomed to failure.

(E) The author will likely go on to show how mandarin biologists tended to acquiesce to whatever the reigning ideology of their specific time and place happened to be.

S T O P

IF YOU FINISH BEFORE TIME IS CALLED, YOU MAY CHECK YOUR WORK ON THIS TEST ONLY. DO NOT TURN TO ANY OTHER SECTION IN THIS TEST.

SECTION 8

Turn to Section 8 of your answer sheet to answer the questions in this section.

Time—20 Minutes
16 Questions

Directions: For this section, solve each problem and decide which is the best of the choices given. Fill in the corresponding oval on the answer sheet. You may use any available space for scratchwork.

Notes:

1. The use of a calculator is permitted. All numbers used are real numbers.
2. Figures that accompany problems in this test are intended to provide information useful in solving the problems. They are drawn as accurately as possible EXCEPT when it is stated in a specific problem that the figure is not drawn to scale. All figures lie in a plane unless otherwise indicated.
3. Unless otherwise specified, the domain of any function f is assumed to be the set of all real numbers x for which $f(x)$ is a real number.

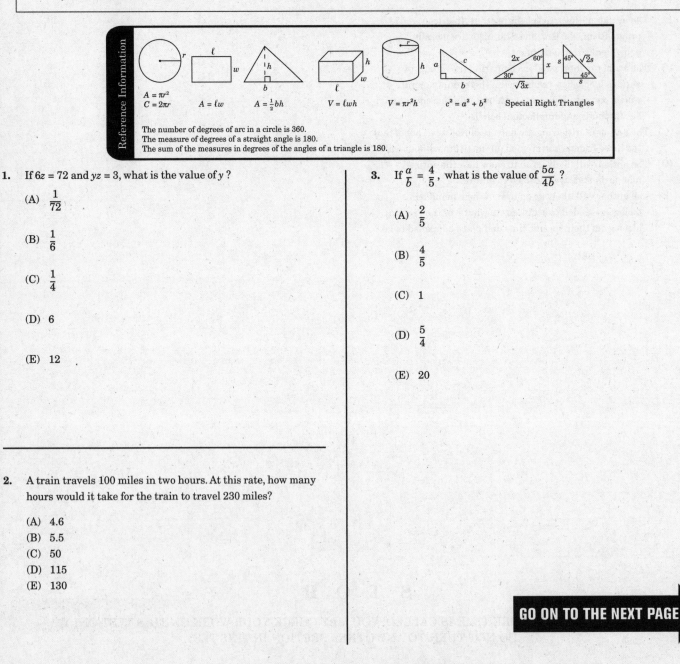

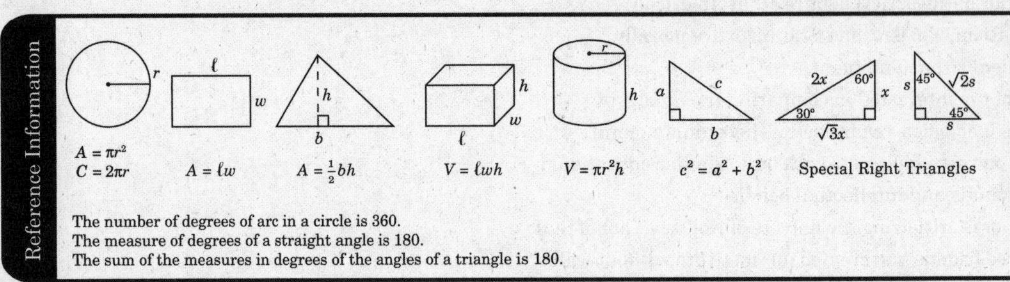

Reference Information
$A = \pi r^2$
$C = 2\pi r$
$A = \ell w$
$A = \frac{1}{2}bh$
$V = \ell wh$
$V = \pi r^2 h$
$c^2 = a^2 + b^2$
Special Right Triangles
The number of degrees of arc in a circle is 360.
The measure of degrees of a straight angle is 180.
The sum of the measures in degrees of the angles of a triangle is 180.

1. If $6z = 72$ and $yz = 3$, what is the value of y?

(A) $\frac{1}{72}$

(B) $\frac{1}{6}$

(C) $\frac{1}{4}$

(D) 6

(E) 12

2. A train travels 100 miles in two hours. At this rate, how many hours would it take for the train to travel 230 miles?

(A) 4.6
(B) 5.5
(C) 50
(D) 115
(E) 130

3. If $\frac{a}{b} = \frac{4}{5}$, what is the value of $\frac{5a}{4b}$?

(A) $\frac{2}{5}$

(B) $\frac{4}{5}$

(C) 1

(D) $\frac{5}{4}$

(E) 20

GO ON TO THE NEXT PAGE

SECTION 8

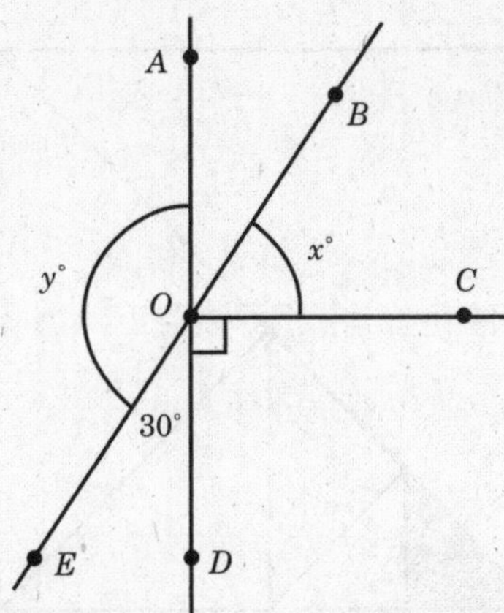

4. In the figure above, EB and DA intersect at O and OC is perpendicular to DA. What is the value of $x + y$?

(A) 30
(B) 60
(C) 90
(D) 150
(E) 210

FRIDA'S SCHEDULE

Period	Start Time	End Time
1	?	
2		
3		
4		
5		
Lunch		
6		
7		
8		3:45 P.M.

5. In Frida's class schedule above, each period is 50 minutes long. There are 5 minutes between periods. Lunch is also 50 minutes long. If eighth period ends at 3:45 P.M., at what time should first period begin?

(A) 7:15 A.M.
(B) 7:30 A.M.
(C) 7:35 A.M.
(D) 7:45 A.M.
(E) 7:50 A.M.

6. If $3y - 4$, $y + 2$, and $4y - 3$ are all integers, and $y + 2$ is the median of these integers, which of the following could be a value of y ?

(A) 2
(B) 3
(C) 4
(D) 5
(E) 6

7. A writer is selling copies of a novella on the internet. The net profit, P, in dollars, from the sale of the novella is described by the equation $P(n) = 0.8n - 100$, where n is the number of copies of the novella sold. How many copies of the novella must the writer sell in order to earn a net profit of \$10,000 ?

(A) 7,900
(B) 8,100
(C) 10,000
(D) 12,375
(E) 12,625

8. If $x^2 + y^2 = 113$ and $xy = 14$, what is the value of $(x + y)^2$?

(A) 113
(B) 127
(C) 130
(D) 141
(E) 226

GO ON TO THE NEXT PAGE

SECTION 8

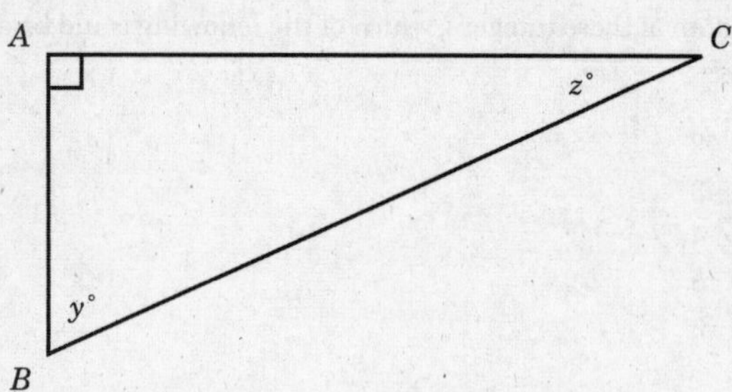

Note: Figure not drawn to scale.

9. In the right triangle above, $AB = 1$ and $AC = \sqrt{3}$. What is the value of y ?

(A) 15
(B) 30
(C) 45
(D) 60
(E) It cannot be determined from the given information.

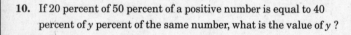

10. If 20 percent of 50 percent of a positive number is equal to 40 percent of y percent of the same number, what is the value of y ?

(A) 110
(B) 90
(C) 70
(D) 60
(E) 25

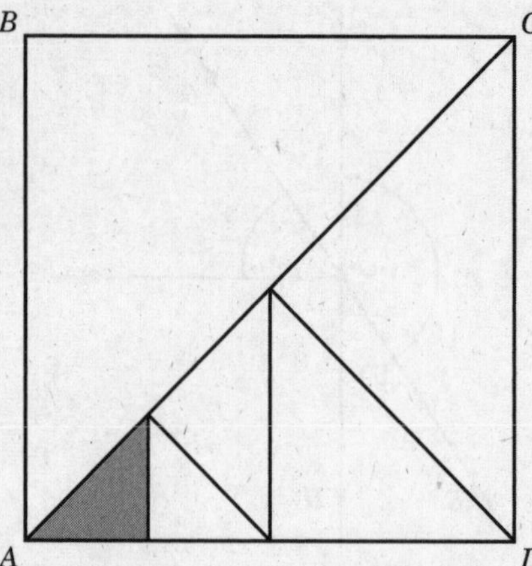

11. In the figure above, square $ABCD$ is made up of six nonoverlapping triangles. The two smallest triangles have the same area. Each of the other triangles has twice the area of the next smaller triangle. The area of the shaded triangle is what fraction of the area of square $ABCD$?

(A) $\frac{1}{64}$

(B) $\frac{1}{32}$

(C) $\frac{1}{16}$

(D) $\frac{1}{8}$

(E) $\frac{1}{6}$

12. If $3x < 2y < 0$, which of the following is the greatest?

(A) $-3x$
(B) $-(3x + 2y)$
(C) $3x$
(D) 0
(E) $2y$

GO ON TO THE NEXT PAGE

SECTION 8

13. Kyoko delivered x papers on Friday, 5 times as many papers on Saturday as on Friday, and 6 more than 3 times as many papers on Sunday as on Friday. What is the average (arithmetic mean) number of papers she delivered per day over the three days?

(A) $3x + 2$
(B) $2x + 3$
(C) $x + 1$
(D) $x + 2$
(E) x

14. If $(x - y)^{-\frac{1}{3}} = (x + y)^{\frac{1}{3}}$ which of the following must be true?

(A) $x = 0$
(B) $x + y = 1$
(C) $x - y = 1$
(D) $x^2 + 2xy + y^2 = 1$
(E) $x^2 - y^2 = 1$

15. If $|3\sqrt{x} + 9| = 15$, then x could equal which of the following?

(A) 2
(B) 6
(C) 8
(D) 24
(E) 64

16. Set A has a members and set B has b members. Set C consists of all members, c, that are common to both set A and set B ($c > 0$). Which of the following represents the number of all the members in sets A and B with the exception of those in set C?

(A) $a + b + c$
(B) $a + b - c$
(C) $a + b - 2c$
(D) $a + b + 2c$
(E) $a - b - 2c$

S T O P

IF YOU FINISH BEFORE TIME IS CALLED, YOU MAY CHECK YOUR WORK ON THIS TEST ONLY. DO NOT TURN TO ANY OTHER SECTION IN THIS TEST.

SECTION 9

Turn to Section 9 of your answer sheet to answer the questions in this section.

Time—10 Minutes
14 Questions

Directions: For each question in this section, select the best answer from among the choices given.

The following sentences test correctness and effectiveness of expression. Part of each sentence or the entire sentence is underlined; beneath each sentence are five ways of phrasing the underlined material. Choice A repeats the original phrasing; the other four choices are different. If you think the original phrasing produces a better sentence than any of the alternatives, select choice A; if not, select one of the other choices.

In making your selection, follow the requirements of standard written English; that is, pay attention to grammar, choice of words, sentence construction, and punctuation. Your selection should result in the most effective sentence—clear and precise, without awkwardness or ambiguity.

Example:

In the poem "Ulysses" by Alfred, Lord Tennyson, the speaker says, "I cannot rest from travel," instead, he will live life to the fullest.

(A) "I cannot rest from travel," instead,
(B) "I cannot rest from travel"; instead,
(C) "I cannot rest from travel" instead,
(D) "I cannot rest from travel," upon which
(E) "I cannot rest from travel,"

1. The Metropolitan Museum of Art's collection is largely combining several private collections.

(A) is largely combining several private collections
(B) combines several private collections
(C) is largely the combination of several private collections
(D) combines, in large part, several private collections
(E) for the most part is the result of the combination of several private collections

2. As students, the faculty guarantees that your final grades will be posted by private student number, not by name.

(A) As students, the faculty guarantees that your
(B) As students, your faculty guarantees that your
(C) Your faculty guarantees that as students, your
(D) The faculty guarantees that students
(E) The faculty guarantees that students'

3. Speaking on the dangerous trend of global warming, finding alternatives to the fossil fuel–based economy was urged by the world-renowned planetary scientist.

(A) finding alternatives to the fossil fuel–based economy was urged by the world-renowned planetary scientist
(B) the world-renowned planetary scientist urged that we find alternatives to the fossil fuel–based economy
(C) the world-renowned planetary scientist urged that alternatives be found by the fossil fuel–based economy
(D) finding alternatives for the fossil-fuel–based economy was urged by the world-renowned planetary scientist
(E) the world-renowned planetary scientist urged that alternatives are to be found for the fossil fuel–based economy

GO ON TO THE NEXT PAGE

SECTION 9

4. Robert Caro's multivolume biography of Lyndon Johnson begins with the geography and tenuous ecosystem of the Texas Hill Country before European settlement and, thus far, continues through Johnson's years in the Senate.

(A) begins with the geography and tenuous ecosystem of the Texas Hill Country before European settlement
(B) beginning with the geography and tenuous ecosystem of the Texas Hill Country before European settlement
(C) have begun with the geography and tenuous ecosystem of the Texas Hill Country before European settlement
(D) began with the geography and tenuous ecosystem of the Texas Hill Country before European settlement
(E) has begun with the geography and tenuous ecosystem of the Texas Hill Country before European settlement

5. Goethe, the great German polymath, not only wrote exquisite works of literature but carried out serious investigations in optics and natural history.

(A) but carried out serious investigations in optics and natural history
(B) but also carried out serious investigations in optics and natural history
(C) but additionally carried out serious investigations in optics and natural history
(D) but carried out serious investigations of optics and natural history
(E) but carried out serious investigations into optics and natural history

6. The Toyota Production System, devised by Japanese engineers in the middle of the twentieth century, has since been attempted to be transplanted to other companies with varying success.

(A) has since been attempted to be transplanted to other companies with varying success
(B) has since been attempted to be transplanted to other companies with varying degrees of success
(C) has since been transplanted to other companies with varying successes
(D) has since been transplanted to other companies who are having varying degrees of success
(E) has since been attempted at other companies with varying success

7. The eighteenth-century French philosopher Jean-Jacques Rousseau broke with the belief in technological progress so typical of his time and place in such works as *Discourse on the Origin of Inequality* and *On the Social Contract*.

(A) the belief in technological progress so typical of his time and place in such works as
(B) the belief in technological progress so typical of his time and place that was in works like
(C) his time and place's typical belief in technological progress in works such as
(D) his time and place's typical belief in technological progress in works like
(E) the technological progress so typically believed in by his time and place in works such as

8. Although currently doing booming business, the ease with which MP3s can be copied causes fears of piracy in some corporate boardrooms.

(A) the ease with which MP3s can be copied causes fears of piracy in some corporate boardrooms
(B) the ease with which MP3s can be copied has caused fears of piracy in some corporate boardrooms
(C) the ease with which MP3s can be copied has been causing fears of piracy in some corporate boardrooms
(D) MP3s are causing fears of piracy in some corporate boardrooms due to the ease with which these files can be copied
(E) MP3s have caused fears of piracy in some corporate boardrooms due to the ease with which these files can be copied

9. The English poet Alfred, Lord Tennyson once referred to Darwinian evolution as "nature, red in tooth and claw" this notion is supported by the fact that only 10 percent of sea turtles make it from their beach-borne nests to the sea, the rest falling easy prey to marauding seagulls.

(A) as "nature, red in tooth and claw" this notion is supported
(B) as "nature, red in tooth and claw," this notion is supported
(C) as "nature, red in tooth and claw"; this notion is supported
(D) as "nature, red in tooth and claw," whereas this notion is supported
(E) as "nature, red in tooth and claw," although this notion is supported

GO ON TO THE NEXT PAGE

10. Because of the advent of email, instant messaging, and other technologies, the much-vaunted paperless office is still nowhere to be found.

(A) Because of the advent of email, instant messaging, and other technologies
(B) Despite the advent of email, instant messaging, and other technologies
(C) Due to the advent of email, instant messaging, and other technologies
(D) Related to the advent of email, instant messaging, and other technologies
(E) With reference to the advent of email, instant messaging, and other technologies

11. Van Gogh is universally admired for the vibrant colors and violent brushwork of his later paintings, and his earlier works display a far darker color palette and more contained brush strokes.

(A) Van Gogh is universally admired for the vibrant colors and violent brushwork of his later paintings, and
(B) Van Gogh is universally admired for the vibrant colors and violent brushwork of his later paintings,
(C) Van Gogh is universally admired for the vibrant colors and violent brushwork of his later paintings, however
(D) Although Van Gogh is universally admired for the vibrant colors and violent brushwork of his later paintings,
(E) Despite the fact that Van Gogh is universally admired for the vibrant colors and violent brushwork of his later paintings,

12. While the *Federalist Papers*, which supported ratification of the Constitution, are well known, the equally plentiful writings against ratification, known collectively as the *Anti-Federalist Papers*, suffer from relative obscurity.

(A) While the *Federalist Papers*, which supported ratification of the Constitution, are well known,
(B) While the *Federalist Papers* that supported ratification of the Constitution are well known,
(C) Whereas the *Federalist Papers*, which supported ratification of the Constitution, are well known,
(D) Whereas the *Federalist Papers* which supported ratification of the Constitution are well known,
(E) While the *Federalist Papers*, that supported ratification of the Constitution, are well known,

13. Tourists, when confronted with an object, tend to snap away with their cameras, assuming that photographs are superior to memory and sketching embeds the object in the tourist's memory since sketching requires that the tourist stop and study the object in great detail.

(A) memory and sketching embeds the object in the tourist's memory since sketching requires that the tourist stop and study the object in great detail
(B) memory however sketching embeds the object in the tourist's memory, since sketching requires that the tourist stop and study the object in great detail
(C) memory, but, on the other hand, sketching embeds the object in the tourist's memory since sketching requires that the tourist stop and study the object in great detail
(D) memory; however, sketching embeds the object in the tourist's memory, since sketching requires that the tourist stop and study the object in great detail
(E) memory. Sketching embeds the object in the tourist's memory, since sketching requires that the tourist stop and study the object in great detail

14. Kevin and Louisa are determined to work as hard as possible in order to become a world-renowned brain surgeon.

(A) a world-renowned brain surgeon
(B) a famous brain surgeon
(C) an infamous brain surgeon
(D) world renowned brain surgeons
(E) world-renowned brain surgeons

S T O P

IF YOU FINISH BEFORE TIME IS CALLED, YOU MAY CHECK YOUR WORK ON THIS TEST ONLY. DO NOT TURN TO ANY OTHER SECTION IN THIS TEST.

PRACTICE TEST 6

EXPLANATIONS

PRACTICE TEST 6 ANSWERS

Question Number	Answer	Right	Wrong
Section 2			
1	B		
2	C		
3	A		
4	E		
5	C		
6	B		
7	E		
8	A		
9	B		
10	E		
11	C		
12	A		
13	B		
14	D		
15	A		
16	B		
17	B		
18	E		
19	D		
20	D		
21	C		
22	A		
23	C		
24	C		
Section 3			
1	E		
2	B		
3	C		
4	E		
5	D		
6	D		
7	E		
8	A		
9	C		
10	D		
11	B		
12	C		
13	C		
14	B		
15	C		
16	D		
17	A		
18	E		
19	C		
20	E		
Section 4			
1	C		
2	C		
3	D		
4	D		
5	E		
6	C		
7	B		
Section 4, continued			
8	E		
9	D		
10	C		
11	A		
12	B		
13	A		
14	B		
15	C		
16	C		
17	B		
18	C		
19	C		
20	C		
21	A		
22	E		
23	D		
24	A		
Section 5			
1	E		
2	E		
3	A		
4	B		
5	C		
6	B		
7	D		
8	C		
9	6.5, 13/2		
10	13		
11	85, 136, 170		
12	299		
13	15.5, 31/2		
14	120		
15	120		
16	1/7		
17	1		
18	48		
Section 6			
1	D		
2	A		
3	C		
4	B		
5	B		
6	D		
7	B		
8	A		
9	B		
10	B		
11	B		
12	B		
13	D		
14	C		
15	A		

Question Number	Answer	Right	Wrong	Question Number	Answer	Right	Wrong
Section 6, continued				**Section 7, continued**			
16	B	___	___	16	B	___	___
17	D	___	___	17	A	___	___
18	E	___	___	18	D	___	___
19	A	___	___	19	B	___	___
20	C	___	___	**Section 8**			
21	C	___	___	1	C	___	___
22	C	___	___	2	A	___	___
23	B	___	___	3	C	___	___
24	D	___	___	4	E	___	___
25	D	___	___	5	C	___	___
26	C	___	___	6	A	___	___
27	B	___	___	7	E	___	___
28	A	___	___	8	D	___	___
29	E	___	___	9	D	___	___
30	E	___	___	10	E	___	___
31	C	___	___	11	B	___	___
32	A	___	___	12	B	___	___
33	C	___	___	13	A	___	___
34	D	___	___	14	E	___	___
35	D	___	___	15	E	___	___
Section 7				16	C	___	___
1	D	___	___	**Section 9**			
2	D	___	___	1	D	___	___
3	E	___	___	2	E	___	___
4	A	___	___	3	B	___	___
5	B	___	___	4	A	___	___
6	B	___	___	5	B	___	___
7	D	___	___	6	E	___	___
8	A	___	___	7	A	___	___
9	B	___	___	8	D	___	___
10	D	___	___	9	C	___	___
11	C	___	___	10	B	___	___
12	B	___	___	11	D	___	___
13	E	___	___	12	C	___	___
14	B	___	___	13	D	___	___
15	D	___	___	14	E	___	___

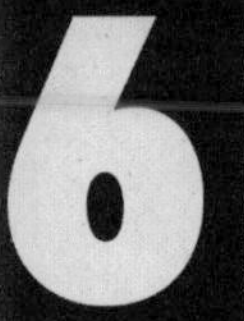

CALCULATING YOUR SCORE

Writing Section Raw Score

A. Essay Score (from 1–6) ______ A

B. Section 6 Multiple Choice: ______ (no. correct) – (______ (no. incorrect) ÷ 4) = ______ B

C. Section 9 Multiple Choice: ______ (no. correct) – (______ (no. incorrect) ÷ 4) = ______ C

D. Unrounded Multiple-Choice Score (B + C) ______ D

E. Total Rounded Multiple-Choice Raw Score
(Rounded to the nearest whole number) ______ E

F. Writing Multiple-Choice Subscore
(See the Writing Multiple-Choice conversion table on the following pages) ______ Writing MC Score

G. Total Scaled Score
(See the Writing conversion table on the following pages) ______ SAT Writing Score

Math Section Raw Score

A. Section 3 Raw Score: ______ (no. correct) – (______ (no. incorrect) ÷ 4) = ______ Subtotal A

B. Section 5 Raw Score: ______ (no. correct) ______ Subtotal B

C. Section 8 Raw Score: ______ (no. correct) – (______ (no. incorrect) ÷ 4) = ______ Subtotal C

D. Total Unrounded Raw Score
(Total A + B + C) ______ D

E. Total Rounded Raw Score (Rounded to the nearest whole number) ______ E

F. Scaled Score
(See the conversion table on the following pages) ______ SAT Math Score

Critical Reading Section Raw Score

A. Section 2 Raw Score: ______ (no. correct) – (______ (no. incorrect) ÷ 4) = ______ A

B. Section 4 Raw Score: ______ (no. correct) – (______ (no. incorrect) ÷ 4) = ______ B

C. Section 7 Raw Score: ______ (no. correct) – (______ (no. incorrect) ÷ 4) = ______ C

D. Total Unrounded Raw Score
(Total A + B + C)

______ D

E. Total Rounded Raw Score
(Rounded to the nearest whole number)

______ E

F. Scaled Score
(See the conversion table on the next page)

______ SAT Critical Reading Score

CONVERTING YOUR RAW SCORES

Raw Score	Critical Reading Scaled Score	Math Scaled Score
67	800	
66	790	
65	770	
64	760	
63	750	
62	740	
61	720	
60	710	
59	700	
58	690	
57	680	
56	670	
55	670	
54	660	800
53	650	780
52	640	760
51	640	740
50	630	730
49	620	710
48	610	700
47	610	690
46	600	670
45	590	660
44	590	650
43	580	650
42	580	640
41	570	630
40	560	620
39	560	610
38	550	600
37	540	590
36	540	590
35	530	580
34	530	570
33	520	560
32	510	560
31	510	550
30	500	540
29	500	530
28	490	520
27	480	520
26	480	510
25	470	500
24	470	490
23	460	490
22	450	480
21	450	470
20	440	460
19	430	460

Raw Score	Critical Reading Scaled Score	Math Scaled Score
18	430	450
17	420	440
16	410	430
15	410	430
14	400	420
13	390	410
12	380	400
11	380	390
10	370	380
9	360	380
8	350	370
7	340	360
6	330	340
5	320	330
4	310	320
3	300	310
2	280	290
1	270	280
0	250	260
−1	250	250
−2	240	240
−3	230	230
−4	220	220
−5	210	210
−6	200	200

Writing Subscores

- **Essay Subscore:** Subtotal A from Writing Score (page 520)
- **Multiple-Choice Subscore:** Calculate by plugging in Subtotal E from your writing score (page 520) into the score conversion table below

Raw Score	Multiple-Choice Subscore	Raw Score	Multiple-Choice Subscore
49	80	30	59
48	79	29	58
47	77	28	57
46	76	27	56
45	75	26	55
44	74	25	54
43	72	24	53
42	71	23	52
41	70	22	51
40	69	21	51
39	68	20	50
38	67	19	49
37	66	18	48
36	65	17	47
35	64	16	46
34	63	15	45
33	62	14	44
32	61	13	43
31	60	12	42

Raw Score	Multiple-Choice Subscore	Raw Score	Multiple-Choice Subscore
11	41	2	32
10	40	1	30
9	39	0	29
8	38	–1	27
7	37	–2	25
6	36	–3	24
5	35	–4	23
4	34	–5	22
3	33	–6	21

Writing Scaled Score

MC raw score	Essay Score					
	6	5	4	3	2	1
49	800	790	780	770	720	700
48	790	780	760	730	700	680
47	780	770	750	720	690	670
46	770	760	740	710	680	660
45	770	750	740	700	670	650
44	760	750	730	690	660	640
43	750	740	710	680	650	630
42	750	730	700	670	640	620
41	740	730	690	660	630	610
40	740	720	690	650	620	600
39	740	710	680	640	610	590
38	730	700	670	630	610	590
37	720	690	660	630	600	580
36	710	680	650	620	590	570
35	710	680	640	610	580	560
34	700	670	640	600	570	550
33	690	660	630	590	560	540
32	680	650	620	580	560	540
31	670	640	610	580	550	530
30	660	630	600	570	540	520
29	650	630	590	560	530	510
28	640	620	590	550	520	510
27	640	610	580	540	510	490
26	630	600	570	530	500	490
25	620	590	560	520	500	480
24	610	580	550	510	490	470
23	600	570	540	510	480	460
22	590	570	530	500	470	450
21	590	570	530	500	470	450
20	580	560	520	490	460	440
19	570	550	520	480	450	430
18	570	540	520	470	440	420
17	560	530	510	460	430	420
16	550	520	500	450	430	410
15	540	510	490	450	420	400
14	530	500	480	440	410	390
13	520	500	470	430	400	380
12	510	490	460	420	390	370

Writing Scaled Score

MC raw score	Essay Score					
	6	5	4	3	2	1
11	510	480	450	410	380	360
10	500	470	450	400	370	350
9	490	460	440	390	360	350
8	480	450	430	390	360	340
7	470	440	420	380	350	330
6	460	430	410	370	340	320
5	450	430	400	360	330	310
4	450	420	390	350	320	300
3	440	410	390	340	310	290
2	430	400	380	330	300	280
1	420	380	370	320	290	270
0	400	370	350	310	280	260
–1	380	360	340	290	270	260
–2	370	340	320	270	260	250
–3	360	330	310	260	250	240
–4	350	320	290	250	240	230
–5	340	310	280	240	230	220
–6	340	310	280	240	220	210

SECTION 2: CRITICAL READING

Sentence Completions

1. **B** One-Word/One-Way *Easy*

The correct answer must be closely associated with characters in a play and must also be capable of communicating *great wit, wisdom, and charm. Dialogue*, **B**, is the only choice to fulfill both requirements. *Actors*, **E**, is not correct, because *actors* can't be *given*.

2. **C** One-Word/One-Way *Easy*

The part of the sentence that follows the colon must be consistent in meaning with the part that precedes the colon. Therefore the correct answer must be synonymous with *limited*. Only **C** fulfills this requirement.

3. **A** One-Word/One-Way *Easy*

The two parts of this sentence (before and after the semicolon) must be consistent in meaning. The second part states, essentially, that policies are not the most critical factors in elections. The correct choice will communicate the idea of nonimportance—only **A** works.

4. **E** One-Word/Two-Way *Medium*

The *debate* in this sentence centers on the authorship credit we have given to Shakespeare. The missing word must communicate this idea. Only *ascribe*, meaning "to give credit to," works.

5. **C** Two-Word/Two-Way *Medium*

The second blank is preceded by "notorious," so the second term must have a very negative meaning. Because the sentence as a whole is communicating an unexpected outcome, the first blank must mean something like "unexpectedly." **C** fits best.

6. **B** Two-Word/One-Way *Medium*

The phrase *thousands of miles of ocean* communicates the isolation and distance of Hawaii from other lands. The first blank must mean something like "isolated," whereas the second must mean something like "land." **B** matches perfectly.

7. **E** Two-Word/One-Way *Difficult*

If the reporter humiliated himself, then he must have acted badly in regard to his *award-winning stories.* Which word pair best communicates wrongdoing within the context of the sentence? **E** does the best job—the reporter admitted that he made up the stories.

8. **A** Two-Word/One-Way *Difficult*

This sentence sets up a comparison between Mozart and Saint-Säens. The second half tells us that although both had youthful promise, only Mozart fulfilled his (even though he died young). Returning to the first half, the blanks describe how the two composers are alike—both words must communicate the idea of youthful promise. Only **A** does so.

Short Reading Passages

9. **B** Technique *Difficult*

According to the passage, Moses worshipped the privately owned automobile and reshaped New York City, often in brutal fashion, to accommodate its spread. However, when privately owned property of another kind stood in his way, Moses, champion of one type of private property, unhesitatingly used state power to undermine another type of private property. **A** is not ironic—it's a notable fact, but not particularly surprising or contrary to appearance. **C** too is not ironic. The statement simply means that perspective matters when considering complex systems, such as the interplay of politics and technology. **D** might have tempted you, but history and everyday experience are full of not particularly nice people who make beautiful things, so that's hardly an irony. **E** is only ironic if one brings in beliefs from outside of the passage at hand—namely, that technology is culturally neutral. One must always deal with the opinions expressed in the passage, regardless of whether one agrees with them.

10. **E** Implied Information *Medium*

Watch out for extreme statements; they're usually wrong. That takes care of **A** and **B. C** and **D** are off the mark, because the key point is that technologies can be *both* politically neutral *and* innately political *at the same time*, depending on one's perspective. **C** and **D** separate technology into two sets: innately political and politically neutral, which goes against the central point.

11. **C** Implied Information *Medium*

The final sentence of the passage states what the author believes is the true source of *Psycho*'s terror: the random and unjustifiable murder of Marion Crane. The movie's murder is quite like life and quite far from the usual Hollywood myths, especially at the time of the film's release.

12. **A** Implied Information *Medium*

An impulsive act is usually an out-of-character one. It is certainly the opposite of premeditated. Furthermore, the impulsivity of the act, while consistent with human nature, is not directly related in any way with the "realism" mentioned toward the end of the passage. Plus, the realism is concerned more with the unfairness of how death is distributed in the real world, not with film style *per se*. Finally, despite the fact that Marion's murder is random with respect to what Marion deserves, and grows out of her having simply made the wrong choice of motel, it is not unconnected to her theft. That theft began a chain of events that led, by chance, to her ultimate demise, so **C** is out.

Paired Reading Passages

13. **B** Implied Information *Easy*

Like actual archeologists, who dig through layers of soil in order to find the hidden structures underneath, *archeologists of knowledge* dig down through the layers of accreted historical beliefs in order to find the hidden structures of thought in past cultures.

14. **D** Words in Context *Medium*

To *explicate* is to "unravel or explain"; **D** is closest. Watch out for choices like **E**: *exhume* is included to trip up the unwary test-taker, who has read about archeology and assumes that an archeology-like word must be the answer.

15. **A** Technique *Easy*

This rhetorical question serves to link the author to his or her audience. In effect, the author is saying, "Hey, haven't we all felt this way before while doing our research? Well, here's a method that helps explain the seemingly inexplicable."

16. **B** Themes and Arguments *Medium*

The only reason the author brings up evolution is to show that it *can't* be responsible for the strangeness of belief systems in historical time (i.e., the past few thousand years), since there hasn't been enough time, biologically speaking, for much evolutionary change to have occurred.

17. **B** Technique *Difficult*

Quotation marks are often used in scholarly writing to signal to the audience that a particular concept usually taken for granted (in this case, common sense) is actually much more complex when examined more closely.

18. **E** Themes and Arguments *Difficult*

The discussion of the "royal touch" serves as an example of how the concept of mentalities has made a seemingly inexplicable belief system understandable to those outside of that belief system. The author uses this example to show how the concept of mentalities can help historians to see through the eyes of history's actors.

19. **D** Words in Context *Easy*

Like most vocabulary-in-context words, *rooted* has several meanings. **D** is the sense most applicable to this context.

20. **D** Technique *Medium*

The author's main point is that structuralist methods, like mentalities, are at their strongest when describing past systems of thought at a given time in a given place. They are at their weakest when applied to questions of historical change—the more deeply embedded the mentality, for example, the harder it is to explain how it changed or how it arose in the first place.

21. **C** Themes and Arguments *Medium*

Make sure that you pick an answer that's relevant to the portion of the passage in the question. **B** and **E** may be accurate representations of Passage 2, but neither has anything to do with the question at hand: the fact that the concept of mentalities is itself the product of a particular mentality with specific dangers.

22. **A** Specific Information *Difficult*

Here is a case in which extreme language is actually correct. The author of Passage 2 uses the extreme term *all* twice. The point is that the author of Passage 2 thinks that the concept of mentalities is far too idealizing and monolithic—it ignores diversity of thought, belief, and action in order to uncover the underlying codes of behavior in a given time and place.

23. **C** Relating Two Passages *Medium*

The author of Passage 2 is a bit more wary of mentalities, but even that author argues that the concept or approach has yielded some impressive findings. The main difference is that the author of Passage 2 thinks that the concept should be used with care to answer the appropriate kinds of historical questions—those of continuity, not of change.

24. **C** Relating Two Passages *Difficult*

The relativity of "common sense" is something about which both authors would agree. The author of Passage 1 states it outright, whereas the author of Passage 2 implies it in the third paragraph. But the point is that the author of Passage 2 would most likely agree that "common sense" is a relative concept but has little to do with the usefulness or appropriateness of mentalities as a historical concept. Passage 2 indicates that one can believe that common sense is relative without accepting mentalities in all their manifestations: monolithic, linguistically defined, carrying the baggage of an outdated anthropology, and unable to address questions of historical change.

SECTION 3: MATH

Multiple Choice

1. **E** Algebra: Substitution *Easy*

To solve this problem quickly, compare the expression to the equation. First, $9x - 4 = 12$. Second, $9x + 4$ is 8 more than the expression $9x - 4$. Therefore, $9x + 4$ must equal 8 more than $9x - 4$. Since $9x - 4 = 12$, and $12 + 8 = 20$, then $9x + 4 = 20$.

2. **B** Numbers & Operations: Sets *Easy*

The concert hall can hold a range of seats. The least it can hold is $30 \times 40 = 1{,}200$. The most it can hold is $30 \times 100 = 3{,}000$. Only **B** is within this range.

3. **C** Geometry: Triangles *Medium*

YC forms a right angle with *x*, so *YC* is the height of each right triangle formed by each of the answer choices. Because each answer choice forms the hypotenuse of the right triangle, *YC* is always going to be the shorter length.

4. **E** Data Analysis, Statistics & Probability: Graphs, Charts, and Tables *Easy*

Look for the largest jump from the previous month. Remember, this graph depicts the total number of fish at the *end* of each month. June shows the largest jump; in this graph that means that by the *end* of June—that is, during the month of June—the greatest positive increase in the number of fish occurred.

5. **D** Algebra: Systems of Equations *Medium*

Translate the words into two average equations:

(Eq. 1) $$\frac{a+b}{2} = 6$$

(Eq. 2) $$\frac{a+b+c}{3} = 10$$

Now, simplify each equation:

(Eq. 1) $$\frac{a+b}{2} = 6$$
$$a + b = 12$$

(Eq. 2) $$\frac{a+b+c}{3} = 10$$
$$a + b + c = 30$$

Finally, substitute in the numerical value of $a + b$ from equation 1 into equation 2 to find the value of *c*:

$$\begin{aligned} a + b + c &= 30 \\ (12) + c &= 30 \\ c &= 30 - 12 \\ c &= 18 \end{aligned}$$

6. **D** Geometry: Polygons *Medium*

First, find the area of the triangle, then subtract the area of the shaded square. The area of the triangle is:

$$A = \frac{1}{2}bh$$
$$A = \frac{1}{2} \times 5 \times 5$$
$$A = \frac{25}{2} = 12.5$$

The area of the square is x^2. Therefore, the correct answer is $12.5 - x^2$.

7. **E** Numbers & Operations: Sets *Medium*

If *abce* = 10, then none of these variables (*a*, *b*, *c*, or *e*) can equal 0. If *abcd* = 0, then at least one of these variables (*a*, *b*, *c*, or *d*) must equal 0. However, you already know that *a*, *b*, and *c* can't equal 0, so therefore *d* must equal 0.

8. **A** Numbers & Operations: Divisibility and Remainders *Medium*

Note that 56 is evenly divisible by the denominators of each of the fractions mentioned in the word problem: $\frac{1}{4}$, $\frac{1}{8}$, and $\frac{1}{2}$. So the problem can be quickly solved by dividing 56 by each of these denominators, adding up the total number of points yielded, and subtracting that sum from 56:

$$\frac{56}{4} = 14$$
$$\frac{56}{8} = 7$$
$$\frac{56}{2} = 28$$
$$14 + 7 + 28 = 49$$
$$56 - 49 = 7$$

9. **C** Algebra: Solving Equations *Difficult*

Plug each answer choice into the equation to see which will make both sides equal. As always, start with **C**:

$$3^{(3\times2)} = 9^{(2+1)}$$
$$3^6 = 9^3$$
$$729 = 729$$

C is correct.

10. **D** Algebra: Solving Equations *Medium*

Translate the word problem into math by writing an equation in which *x* (or whatever your favorite variable happens to be) equals "the number" and then solve for *x*:

$$2x - 3 = x + 4$$
$$(2x - 3) - x = (x + 4) - x$$
$$x - 3 = 4$$
$$x = 7$$

11. **B** Geometry: Circles *Difficult*

If the area of the circle is 64π, then its radius must be 8:

$$64\pi = \pi r^2$$
$$64 = r^2$$
$$8 = r$$

Therefore, *OY* and *OX* are also 8, and the radius of each semicircle is thus 4. A circle with radius 4 has a circumference of:

$$2\pi r = 2\pi(4)$$
$$= 8\pi$$

Since you have two half-circumferences (that is, "semicircles"), you actually have one full, smaller circle with a radius of 4. Together the semicircles form a distance of 8π.

12. **C** Algebra: Functions *Difficult*

A linear function yields a straight line that rises (or falls) at a constant rate. In this case, you know that there's a point on the line formed by this function at (1, 36). The table also shows three *x*-values: 0, 1, and 2. There is exactly one unit difference between these values, so the change in the *x*-variable is one unit for each point.

You don't know the exact change in the *y*-variable, $g(x)$, because you aren't given a specific function for the value of $g(x)$. This function could be any linear function, so the exact values of m and n can't be determined. Don't fall for **E**, however. It turns out that the sum of m and n can still be determined, even though you don't know their exact values.

To see this, choose any linear function to represent $g(x)$. If $g(x) = x + 35$, for instance, then m equals 35 and n equals 37. In this case, $m + n = 35 + 37$, or 72. Now try $g(x) = 38x - 2$. This function produces a result of $m = -2$ and $n = 74$. Again, adding $m + n$ produces $-2 + 74$, or 72. Notice that any linear function will produce a value of $m + n = 72$. Since $g(x)$ is a linear function, this means that the change between the *y*-variables will always be constant. In other words, the distance from m to 36 will always equal the distance from 36 to n. So, 36 is the midpoint between m and n. The distance between m and n will always be twice the value of the midpoint, or 72.

13. **C** Numbers & Operations: Sequences *Medium*

The term *sequence* should tip you off immediately. Surely, the SAT won't have you calculate this out to the 157th term; there's got to be a shortcut. Here it is:

First, complete the sequence, which will repeat (they always do on the SAT) and which will not be more than a handful of numbers (remember, all problems are designed to be doable in around a minute):

$$2, 6, -6, (-6 + 4 = -2), -1 \times -2 = 2$$

or

$$2, 6, -6, -2, 2$$

Once you find the first repeated digit, stop. You've got the full sequence now, which is:

$$2, 6, -6, -2$$

Now, how many terms are in this sequence? Four. Here comes the shortcut: take the number of the term for which you're supposed to find a value—157—and divide it out longhand (don't use your calculator!) by the number of terms in the sequence—4. You will get 39, with a remainder of 1.

What does this mean? It means that by the time you get to the 157th term, you will have cycled through this four-digit, repeating sequence 39 times, which will "land" you on –2. However, since you have a remainder of 1, you must move to the first digit in the sequence (which, of course, just keeps repeating). That term is 2.

14. **B** Geometry: Coordinate Geometry *Difficult*

Line m is essentially the mirror image of line l across the x-axis. This means that line m has the same "tilt" as line l but that it goes in the opposite direction. In "math-speak," line m's slope is the opposite of line l's, or –3. Line m also crosses the y-axis at a length equidistant from the origin (0, 0) as line l, but below the origin, rather than above. Since line l's y-intercept is 2, line m's is –2.

15. **C** Data Analysis, Statistics & Probability: Graphs, Charts, and Tables *Medium*

At age 150, the redwood was 225 feet tall. At age 200, it was 300 feet tall. 300 – 225 = 75 so the question then becomes: 75 is what percent of 300? In "math-speak," that's:

$$75 = \left(\frac{x}{100}\right)300$$
$$75 = \frac{300x}{100}$$
$$75 = 3x$$
$$25 = x$$

16. **D** Geometry: Solids *Difficult*

The formula for the volume of a right cylinder is $\pi r^2 h$. So, in this case:

$$\pi r^2 h = \pi \times b^2 \times 4b = 4\pi b^3$$

Only **D** gives you the same result.

17. **A** Algebra: Solving Equations *Medium*

Solve the equation for $2n - 4$:

$$m - 5(2n - 4) = x$$
$$-5(2n - 4) = x - m$$
$$2n - 4 = \frac{x - m}{-5}$$

18. **E** Geometry: Coordinate Geometry *Difficult*

Two conditions need to be filled in order for (p, q) to lie within the shaded area. First, p has to be less than or equal to 3—that is, to the left of 3. But if the only condition is $p \le 3$, then any point between on or to the left of the line $x = 3$ is fair game, all the way up to y = infinity in both directions, positive and negative. Thus, you have to limit the range of y—or, in this case, q. To do that, $q \le f(p)$.

19. **C** Algebra: Inequalities *Difficult*

The plant can survive only at a temperature between 75° Fahrenheit and 95° Fahrenheit. Therefore, the range of all possible values for t is $75 < t < 95$.

On the left side of the range, the value for t must be greater than 75, which is 85 – 10 degrees. The left side of the range can therefore be written as follows:

$$75 < t$$
$$85 - 10 < t$$
$$-10 < t - 85$$

On the right side of the range, the value for t must be less than 95, or 85 + 10 degrees. The right side of the range can therefore be written as follows:

$$t < 95$$
$$t < 85 + 10$$
$$t - 85 < 10$$

Combine the two inequalities to see that the range of values for t is $-10 < t - 85 < 10$. The absolute value of $t - 85$ will always be less than 10. **C** is correct.

20. **E** Numbers & Operations: Sets *Difficult*
Picture a number line. In the middle is zero, at the far left is –92 and at the far right is 92. If you added up all of the integers, you'd get an answer of zero. (–1 + 1 = 0, –2 + 2 = 0, and so on). However, you're told that the sum of these integers is 93 and that the integers are *consecutive.* That means that 93 has to be in the set as well, since you're told that –92 is the least integer in the set.

Now the issue is, how many integers are we dealing with here? Be careful in your counting; note how close the answer choices are. From –92 to –1 there are 92 integers. Zero is also an integer, so count that too. We're up to 93. Now, from 1 to 92 is 92 more integers. We're up to 185. However, don't forget about 93! That's the 186th integer in the set.

SECTION 4: CRITICAL READING

Sentence Completions

1. **C** One-Word/One-Way *Easy*
The missing word is described by the portion of the sentence that follows, so it must be similar in meaning to the predestination of human life. "Fate" works best. **A** and **B** mean life is not predestined, and **E** is too negative.

2. **C** Two-Word/One-Way *Easy*
The professor is talking about the poems of two authors, so the second blank must mean something like "compare" (if the poems are similar in some way) or "contrast" (if the poems are different in some way). **A** uses *compared to* but *malevolence* is not similar to *pacifism,* so this choice doesn't work. **C** uses *contrasted with,* and *bellicosity* is the opposite of *pacifism.*

3. **D** One-Word/One-Way *Medium*
Susan was so afraid of choking that she chewed her food to the point that it became a fine paste. A word like "ground" might work. **C** and **D** mean something like "grind," but only **D** refers specifically to chewing.

4. **D** Two-Word/One-Way *Medium*

Sam and Dave are opposites in this sentence. If Sam does well in the business world, he must be politically "smart" and must "cooperate with" superiors. **B**, **D**, and **E** work for the second blank, while **D** works best for the first. Note too that **A** sort of works, but ultimately **D** is the best answer—and you always should choose the best answer, as the SAT directions make clear.

5. **E** Two-Word/Two-Way *Difficult*

The first missing word is similar in meaning to "smooth" and "popular" while the second is similar in meaning to "disordered" and "explosive." Only **E** works for the second blank; this choice also works well for the first blank.

Paired Reading Passages

6. **C** Relating Two Passages *Easy*

Both authors mention Copernicus's devotion to Pythagorean principles.

7. **B** Technique *Medium*

Asking rhetorical questions and then answering them is a common technique in academic and scholarly writing.

8. **E** Relating Two Passages *Difficult*

All of the items are likely responses by the author of Passage 1 to the author of Passage 2.

9. **D** Relating Two Passages *Difficult*

D is the only choice that makes logical sense, and one doesn't need to know any history to notice this. If the Church did not interpret the Bible literally, then the new heliocentric system wouldn't cause it too much concern.

Long Reading Passages

10. **C** Technique *Easy*

The wife is the narrator—that is, the person who is telling the story.

11. **A** Technique *Easy*

The sentence just before the one quoted in the question notes that the streetlamps were shining through the snowflakes.

12. **B** Themes and Arguments *Medium*

The wife in the story isn't too familiar with Eastern or Middle Eastern music, so she can't quite place the music she's hearing or the origin of her "cabbie." This type of question is similar to a rhetorical question in nonfiction writing. In this case, the question is asked by the narrator to "herself" but also to her readers.

13. **A** Words in Context *Medium*

Perfunctory most closely means "routine."

14. **B** Themes and Arguments *Difficult*

This sentence's meaning isn't immediately obvious. You need to read on a bit, which is why this is a tougher question. It ties into one of the main plot elements in the story: this "cabbie" is separated from his family, and the tired narrator takes a while to figure out that this is likely.

15. **C** Main Idea *Medium*

The "cabbie" and the couple talk mostly about family, a universal human phenomenon that serves to bridge the cultural divide between them.

16. **C** Words in Context *Easy*

In the context of the paragraph, it is clear that the phrase *raise all boats* has nothing to do with any form of sea craft, so **A** and **B** are incorrect. As the second paragraph states, the goal of *rais[ing] all boats* has not been realized, and the rest of the paragraph clarifies this with the assertion that many developing countries and even some communities within developed nations have witnessed slower growth or actual decline during the age of globalization. Globalization has not brought positive change to all countries or even to all people within the countries it has benefited. From this, the reader can infer that *raise all boats* means "benefit all parties," so **C** is correct. **D** and **E** do not fit the context of the paragraph.

17. **B** Main Idea *Medium*

Although much of the passage is concerned with the problems caused by globalization, the final paragraph acknowledges that globalization may eventually bring positive change to the world if it is *shaped by humanity*. The most accurate description of the passage's main purpose is therefore **B**. **A** is incorrect, because it doesn't reference the author's belief that globalization can be reshaped to bring more good into the world and because it puts too much emphasis on the notion of equality. **C** and **E** are incorrect, because they focus on details mentioned in the course of the author's argument, not the argument as a whole. **D** is incorrect, because it only roughly approximates one of the author's hopes; the author believes that globalization might improve conditions around the world *if* handled properly but does not, by any means, predict a new age of universal prosperity.

18. **C** Specific Information *Difficult*

The question asks you to identify which writing strategy the author does not use in the first paragraph, so any action described in an answer choice that does refer to something in the first paragraph must be incorrect. In the final sentence, the author says that global popular culture is *largely American in origin and nature*, so **A** is incorrect. The first sentence is a rhetorical question, so **B** is incorrect. Although the author makes plenty of judgments about globalization, the author does not simply state that he or she is "for" or "against" it; the argument is far subtler than that. **C** is correct. The author connects globalization to improvements in communication in the third sentence, so **D** is incorrect. The second sentence addresses the rate of increase in international trade and economic activity, the staples of globalization, so **E** is incorrect.

19. **C** Technique *Difficult*

The adverb *ironically* is used to describe the way *the most sophisticated practitioners of terror have taken full advantage of the mechanisms of globalization*, or, in other words, the fact that the terrorist groups that oppose globalization use its mechanisms to help them accomplish their goals. **C** is thus the correct answer. Nowhere in the passage does the author suggest that the countries from which Al-Qaeda draws most of its recruits are benefiting from globalization, so **A** is incorrect. **B** is incorrect, because the author does not comment on the varying degrees to which different terrorist groups oppose Western values. The author does suggest that fundamentalist groups are growing more powerful with the spread of Western values but does not see this as ironic in any way, so **D** is incorrect. **E** is incorrect, because it describes an example of the ironic circumstances presented by the author, not the ironic circumstances in general. **E** is on the right track, but it is too specific.

20. **C** Words in Context *Medium*

Be careful—the sentence is talking about how hypermedia coverage *increases* the terror dividend of Al-Qaeda's attacks. But the phrase *terror dividend* itself refers to the terror caused by the attacks themselves.

21. **A** Specific Information *Medium*

The sixth sentence of the final paragraph, in which the author mentions Brazil and other developing nations leaving the WTO negotiations, offers an example of the phenomenon described in the fifth sentence: the developing world beginning to demand parity. **A** is therefore the correct answer. **B** is incorrect, because the author believes that developing nations' protests are something that will improve the results of globalization. American and European refusal to expose their agricultural products to international competition is what Brazil and the other countries were protesting. But the author's argument at this point in the passage is that such protests demonstrate that these less economically wealthy nations are prepared to stand up for themselves, not that American and European countries are being unfair, and thus **C** is incorrect. **D** is incorrect as well; although the author believes that globalization is unstoppable and might ultimately benefit humanity, this is not why Brazil's walkout is mentioned. **E** is incorrect, because it falls outside of the author's idea. The passage draws no connection between the agricultural economy and the economy as a whole.

22. **E** Words in Context *Medium*

In the final sentence, the author expresses the idea that while globalization could bring about positive change in the world if the changes just described came about, as things stand now, it will only benefit certain parties. In other words, the current version of globalization is only somewhat beneficial. **E** is therefore the correct answer. All the other choices offer possible meanings of "incarnation," but none of them fits the meaning of the sentence as well as **E**.

23. **D** Specific Information *Medium*

Although final paragraphs often contain summaries of arguments presented earlier, that is not the case in this passage, so **A** is incorrect. **B** is incorrect, because the author only presents one set of opinions. **C** and **E** are incorrect, because the author says that globalization is *unstoppable* in the first sentence of the last paragraph. **D** is correct, because it is the only answer that accurately describes the focus of the final paragraph:

globalization may *raise all boats* if the fruits of increased economic activity are fairly distributed.

24. **A** Themes and Arguments *Difficult*
The author notes that *social dislocation and conflict have followed quickly on the heels of economic upheaval* and that migrations are now occurring on an unprecedented scale. **A** therefore seems like a good bet, but the question asks with which statement the author would be most likely to agree. Whenever you see a question like this, remember to review all the answers, because it is possible that the author might be likely to agree with two or more statements, but one more so than the others. **B** can be eliminated—in the second paragraph the author notes that progress against illiteracy and infant mortality have slowed in poorer nations, which suggests that those nations have not experienced economic growth (the author associates economic growth with decreases in illiteracy and infant mortality). **C** is incorrect, because it directly contradicts the statement made above. Likewise, **D** and **E** contradict the evidence given in the line above. As it turns out, **A** is the only one to offer a statement with which the author might agree, so it is indeed the correct answer.

SECTION 5: MATH

Multiple Choice

1. **E** Algebra: Substitution *Easy*
The expressions on each side of the equation are exactly the same except that y stands for 7 in the first expression. Therefore, y must equal 7.

2. **E** Geometry: Triangles *Easy*
Use the Pythagorean theorem to solve for x:

$$a^2 + b^2 = c^2$$
$$3^2 + 5^2 = x^2$$
$$9 + 25 = x^2$$
$$34 = x^2$$
$$\sqrt{34} = x$$

3. **A** Numbers & Operations: Divisibility and Remainders *Easy*
The correct answer will be a number that is divisible by 3 and 9 (that is, a number that is a multiple of 3 and 9) but *not* divisible by 6 (that is, not a multiple of 6). **A**, 27, is not divisible by 6, so this answer is correct.

4. **B** Geometry: Circles *Medium*
If the circle is tangent to XW and YZ, then its diameter is equal to the entire length of the rectangle, or 7. The radius is half this, or 3.5. The circumference is therefore $2\pi r$, or $2\pi(3.5) = 7\pi$.

5. **C** Data Analysis, Statistics & Probability: Probability *Medium*
Of the six sectors, two are vowels and four are consonants. If the sector does *not* stop on a consonant, then it must stop on a vowel. The probability of this occurrence is $\frac{2}{6} = \frac{1}{3}$.

6. **B** Data Analysis, Statistics & Probability: Graphs, Charts, and Tables *Medium*

What you're being shown, in chart form, is a function. So, first figure out how each chart gets from a to b. You're looking for a chart that shows a being multiplied by a constant value to generate b. **B** shows that: in mathematical terms, it shows that $b = 4a$. If you graphed that function, you'd see a straight line sloping upward, a direct proportional relationship.

7. **D** Algebra: Solving Equations *Medium*

Barney spends one-third of his money earned per driveway $\left(\frac{m}{3}\right)$ on costs and saves the remaining two thirds $\left(\frac{2m}{3}\right)$. To find out how many driveways he must plow to save $2,500, divide the savings total by savings per driveway, then solve for m:

$$\frac{2,500}{\frac{2m}{3}} = \frac{\frac{3}{2} \times 2,500}{\frac{3}{2} \times \frac{2m}{3}} = \frac{3,750}{m}$$

8. **C** Numbers & Operations: Basic Operations *Medium*

X is negative and Y is positive, so the answer must be a negative number, which eliminates **D** and **E**. Because X and Y are both fractions, the product of X and Y will be smaller in magnitude (with the same negative sign) than X. Only **C** fits these requirements.

Grid-Ins

9. **6.5, 13/2** Algebra: Substitution *Easy*

Substitute $x - 1$ for y in the first equation and solve for x:

$$\begin{aligned} 4x - 2(x-1) &= 15 \\ 4x - 2x + 2 &= 15 \\ 2x &= 13 \\ x &= 6.5 \end{aligned}$$

10. **13** Numbers & Operations: Percents *Medium*

The original rate is 10 pages per hour. Thirty percent of this is 3 pages per hour. An *increase* of 30 percent, then, is 10 + 3 = 13 pages per hour.

11. **85, 136, 170** Geometry: Triangles *Difficult*

The side lengths in ΔXYZ are all factors of 40, so you can choose any side in the not-pictured ΔLMN, figure out the constant by which you're multiplying that side, and then do the same for the other three sides.

For example, let's say that side LM corresponds to side XY. That means that $LM = 10(XY)$, since the question says one side is 40, and XY is shown as 4. Now, multiply each side by 10 and sum them to find one potential perimeter: $5(10) = 50$, and $8(10) = 80$. Thus, $40 + 50 + 80 = 170$.

12. **299** Numbers & Operations: Sequences *Medium*

To solve, let the first integer equal x, rephrase the question as an equation, and solve for x:

$$x + (x+1) + (x+2) + (x+3) = 1,190$$
$$4x + 6 = 1,190$$
$$4x = 1,184$$
$$x = 296$$

Be careful: you're asked for the value of the greatest of these integers, which would be $x + 3$, or $296 + 3 = 299$.

13. **15.5, 31/2** Algebra: Functions *Medium*

Substituting 2 for x, you get: $4^2 - \frac{2}{4} = 16 - \frac{1}{2} = 15\frac{1}{2}$. But remember: you can't grid in mixed numbers. So convert to a decimal: 15.5.

14. **120** Numbers & Operations: Factors *Medium*

Each of the five players can play any of the five positions, but can't play more than one position at a time. So, the total number of possible combinations is: 5 possible players for the first position × 4 possible players for the second position × 3 possible players for the third position × 2 possible players for the fourth position × 1 possible player for the fifth position, or $5! = 5 \times 4 \times 3 \times 2 \times 1 = 120$.

15. **120** Geometry: Triangles *Medium*

If ΔABC is equilateral, then $\angle BCA$ is 60 degrees. Since FG bisects that angle (x° on both sides), $x = 30^\circ$. Because $x + x + y$ forms a straight line, $x + x + y = 180^\circ$. Substitute 30 for x and solve for y:

$$x + x + y = 180$$
$$30 + 30 + y = 180$$
$$60 + y = 180$$
$$y = 120$$

16 . **1/7** Numbers & Operations: Basic Operations *Medium*

Questions like this invent and define "new" operations; in this case, "clover" and "heart." The clover rule requires that you add the term before the clover to five times the term following the clover. The heart rule requires that you add the term before the heart to 3 times the term following the heart. Use these rules to rewrite the equation using "normal" operations:

$$5 + 5(2y) = 3y + 3(2)$$
$$5 + 10y = 3y + 6$$
$$10y = 3y + 1$$
$$7y = 1$$
$$y = \frac{1}{7}$$

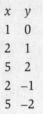

17. **1** Geometry: Coordinate Geometry *Difficult*

The best thing to do with this problem is to begin to visualize the situation. Use some simple numbers to determine the shape of the graph of $x = y^2 + 1$:

x	y
1	0
2	1
5	2
2	–1
5	–2

Now, do a quick graph of this curve, as shown below:

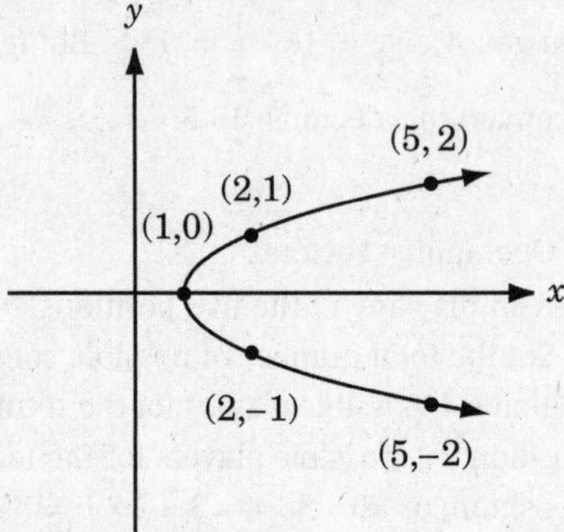

The question also tells you that a line intersects this graph at two points, $(2, q)$ and $(5, r)$. This may not seem like enough information until you look at the graph you just drew. Note how when you pick numbers clustering around zero (generally a good idea in order to generate the basic shape of a quadratic equation), you instantly start seeing 2s and 5s. What possible lines could intersect this curve at both $x = 2$ and $x = 5$? Sketch it out:

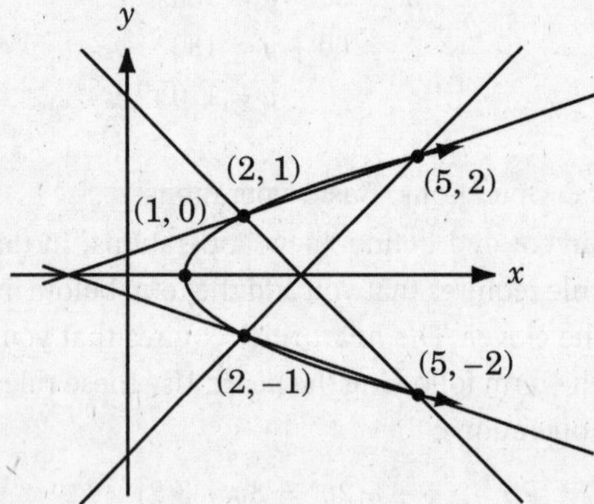

If you know that upward slanting lines have a positive slope and downward slanting lines do not, then you just need to find the slope of the steepest upward slanting line. (If you did not know this, you'd just need to find the slope of each line and pick the greatest possible value.)

The slope of the steepest upward slanting line is:

$$m = \frac{y_2 - y_1}{x_2 - x_1}$$

$$m = \frac{-1 - 2}{2 - 5}$$

$$m = \frac{-3}{-3} = 1$$

18. **48** Algebra: Solving Equations *Difficult*

What do you know and what do you need to know? Here's what you know:

- The trip to the lake had an average speed of 15 mph.
- The trip back from the lake had an average speed of 10 mph.
- The trip back and forth took 4 hours to complete.

You know you're dealing with some form of the famous distance equation: $d = rt$. You know what the total time was. You don't know what the combined rate is, and you're asked for total distance. You might think that the easiest way to solve the problem is to average the two average speeds to get 12.5 mph. Then the equation would work out this way:

$$d = rt$$

$$d = 12.5(4)$$

$$d = 50$$

But there's a problem with this answer. If it's true, then each leg of the trip (to and from the lake) was 25 miles. Check out how long it would take at the rates given to go that distance:

To the lake: $d = rt$

$$25 = 15t$$

$$1.\overline{6} = t$$

From the lake: $d = rt$

$$25 = 10t$$

$$2.5 = t$$

Those durations do not add up to 4 hours, which is what is given in the problem.

One quick way to do this problem is to use your calculator. Note that the sum of the two durations we just generated is a little above 4—actually, it's 4.167. That means that 50 is just a bit too many miles. Pick a number less than 50—how about 48? Work it out:

To the lake: $d = rt$

$$24 = 15t$$

$$1.6 = t$$

From the lake: $d = rt$

$$24 = 10t$$

$$2.4 = t$$

Now, those times add up to 4 hours, so the correct answer is 48.

SECTION 6: WRITING

Improving Sentences

1. **D** Conjunctions *Easy*

Want to score points on Improving Sentence questions? Choose the answer that makes the sentence more concise. Not that the shortest option is always correct, but it often is.

2. **A** No Error *Easy*

Here's a case in which the shortest answer *isn't* correct! Remember, you can't choose an answer choice that changes the meaning of the sentence. **B** removes the modifier of *relief*, and that's a no-no.

3. **C** Pronouns *Medium*

To which female does *she* refer? That's the problem with this sentence. **C** is the most succinct option offered to clarify this pronoun reference.

4. **B** Other *Medium*

Note that this question is about punctuation and how best to emphasize what Joe's problem is. Colons are best used in this type of situation, because they basically say, "Here's the deal: read on."

5. **B** Parallelism *Medium*

Watch out here. There are two errors in this sentence: first, *not only* lacks a "but also," and second, *affect* is not the word you need here. *Affect/effect* is often tested on the SAT, as it's often misused. Generally, *affect* is used as a verb to mean "to change," and *effect* is used as a noun to mean "result."

6. **D** Subject-Verb Agreement *Difficult*

There are two issues here. First, *527s* is clearly plural, so it should take a plural form of "to have." Second, concision, while important, does not trump the sense of the original sentence. "Both . . . and" is a specific construction that provides emphasis. Don't choose "over-edited" answer choices; maintain the intended meaning of the sentence.

7. **B** Pronouns *Medium*

To whom does *they* refer? Impossible to tell, right? This kind of language is fine for everyday speech, but not for SAT questions. Make sure all pronouns have clear antecedents.

8. **A** No Error *Difficult*

In this case, don't add the "both . . . and" construction. That changes the meaning of the sentence and is also a bit clunky. The sentence is fine as is.

9. **B** Coordination and Subordination *Difficult*

"That" vs. "which" is a perennial favorite of the SAT. Without getting into long explanations of subordinate clauses, we'll just tell you this: if you use *which*, set the which-phrase off with commas. In this case, it's clear from the sentence that the phrase *which is a chilling dystopia* modifies *we* and should thus be set off by commas.

10. **B** Wordiness *Medium*

Don't change the sense of the sentence, as some of the incorrect answers do. Also make sure to get rid of that *if*, which only confuses the sentence's meaning.

11. **B** Wordiness *Medium*

This choice is the most concise—and it preserves all of the information conveyed by the original sentence.

Identifying Sentence Errors

12. **B** Pronouns *Easy*

Who is *they*? This is the error: there isn't an antecedent for this pronoun.

13. **D** Tense *Easy*

This is the wrong tense: you want *has recently been*.

14. **C** Other *Easy*

How can *two* people, Michel and Jacques, become *one* cultural anthropologist? This is a commonly tested error on the SAT.

15. **A** Idioms *Medium*

The SAT often tests typical grammatical or idiomatic constructions that currently fall under the rules of Standard Written English. "Neither . . . nor" is a classic, and so is "not only . . . but also."

16. **B** Pronouns *Medium*

If you start with *you*, stick with *you*. If you start with *one*, stick with *one*. This sentence mixes the two, and that's a deviation from parallelism, a concept much tested on the SAT. Note that the verb *risk* is underlined too. In order to be correct, the verb would have to be changed to "one risks," just as the beginning of the sentence contains *one forgets*. This change would make the sentence parallel.

17. **D** Parallelism *Difficult*

Here's another kind of parallelism question. In a series, all the verbs should take the same form. In this case, you have two past-tense verbs, *packed* and *brought*, followed by an infinitive verb phrase, *to make sure*. That's not parallel structure.

18. **E** No Error *Difficult*

There's nothing wrong with this sentence. All verbs are in their correct forms, the subject agrees with the verb, and the items in the list are parallel.

19. **A** Subject-Verb Agreement *Medium*

This verb should be plural, since the subject, *persistent popular misunderstanding*, is singular. You wouldn't say "Fred seem sad." You'd say, "Fred seems sad." The only difference between the previous simple sentence and this question's sentence is the complexity of the subjects.

20. **C** Subject-Verb Agreement *Difficult*
The subject of this sentence is singular: *the* work *of certain rock groups*. *Work* is singular. Therefore, the verb must also be singular, or *loses*.

21. **C** Tenses *Medium*
This is the wrong tense. The Roman Empire is said to be in the past (regardless of whether any test-taker might know this—the information is there in the sentence). Therefore, the future tense can't be used here.

22. **C** Pronouns *Difficult*
Strunk and White are definitely two different people, but *those* refers to the singular word, *impact*, and should not be plural. Use "that" instead. This is a tricky one!

23. **B** Idioms *Medium*
Double negatives, like *isn't scarcely* and other similar combinations, are a no-no on the SAT. They are considered idiomatically incorrect.

24. **D** Subject-Verb Agreement *Medium*
Megatsunamis is plural, so you need a plural verb to agree. Agreement in general is a heavily tested feature of English on the SAT.

25. **D** Faulty Comparison *Medium*
Be clear on when to use comparatives (*hotter, colder, more difficult*) versus superlatives (*hottest, coldest, most difficult*). You can't use the comparative form when writing about more than two items.

26. **C** Parallelism *Difficult*
Remember to maintain parallel structure. Any time you see a "not only," you should also see a "but also"—this is an oft-tested feature of the language on the SAT.

27. **B** Idioms *Medium*
This question tests whether you know which preposition goes with the verb *pertain*. Questions like this are a matter of knowing the proper idiom. It should be "pertain to."

28. **A** Adverbs and Adjectives *Easy*
You need an adverb here: "amazingly enough . . . "

29. **E** No Error *Medium*
No problems here. Expect a few of these "No Errors" on the SAT. As you're taking the test, remember that at least some of the questions will be grammatically correct.

Improving Paragraphs

30. **E** Sentence Revision *Medium*

You need a "contrast" word here. The sense of the paragraph is that even though fencing has deep historical roots, its contemporary form deviates in some important ways from those roots.

31. **C** Sentence Revision *Medium*

Make sure that tenses don't shift within sentences. Because all of the action occurs in the past, all of the verbs should be in the past tense.

32. **A** Sentence Addition *Easy*

A claim is made at the end of the second paragraph. It would be better, and more appropriate, to include a concrete example that supports that claim before moving on, especially as it's not immediately clear why swordsmanship would have made a comeback after the introduction of firearms.

33. **C** Sentence Combination *Easy*

Turn sentence 10 into a clause of sentence 9 by connecting the two with a comma.

34. **D** Sentence Addition *Difficult*

There is a gap in the chronology here: readers would probably be interested to know what occurred between the 1600s and the 1900s. What happened to fencing during those 300 years?

35. **D** Essay Analysis *Difficult*

Again, since this passage is structured chronologically, it would make sense to end with a thought or two about fencing's future, especially since the piece discusses its popularity with young people. Where might they take the sport in the twenty-first century?

SECTION 7: CRITICAL READING

Sentence Completions

1. **D** One-Word/Two-Way *Medium*

You need a word that's the opposite of *malevolent*. If you don't know what this word means, you might still be able to infer that it's negative. Alternatively, you might have known that the prefix *mal* has a negative meaning, so you could have eliminated all but **C** and **D**. Insert those choices into the sentence, and guess from there.

2. **D** One-Word/Two-Way *Easy*

Even if you don't exactly know what *estranged* means, you can still get the sense that this couple was trying to stay together, but failed to do so. Note too that **B** and **E** are so similar that neither can possibly be right. When you find two similar answer choices, eliminate them both: the SAT is just not that subtle when it comes to shades of meaning.

3. **E** One-Word/One-Way *Easy*

If the two subspecies coexisted, they would presumably have run into each other at some point. At least that possibility exists, and the word you need is something that means "run into each other" or "meet."

4. **A** One-Word/Two-Way *Medium*

There are many clues in this sentence to help steer you to the correct answer. The introductory phrase provides a metaphor for the environment being merely the stage upon which human actors make history. Then it's mentioned that environmental trends are being granted a *less passive role*. Thus, you need a word that indicates an active role, or something like "shapes."

5. **B** Two-Word/One-Way *Difficult*

On two-blank sentence completions, take it one blank at a time. The first blank requires something like "intended." However, the second blank requires something like "difficulty." Providing your own words before looking at the answer choices will help clarify things for you. **E** works for the first blank, but not for the second. **C** works, but not nearly as well as **B**. Remember, you're supposed to pick the *best* answer. **B** gets to the point succinctly and concretely.

6. **B** One-Word/One-Way *Difficult*

The key to this sentence is that many different cultures have mixed and mingled in the Americas. You need a word that conveys this meaning. Even if you didn't know that *heterogeneous* is that word, you could have eliminated at least some of the other four on the basis that they patently do not fit the intended meaning. Don't be afraid to choose a word you don't know if you've already eliminated all the others. If you've eliminated four choices, the fifth has got to be correct.

Long Reading Passage

7. **D** Words in Context *Medium*

Don't let **A** fool you. If you're unsure of the meaning of the word in the question, treat the sentence from which it's extracted as a sentence completion: take out the word in question and ask yourself what word might accurately complete the sentence. Keep the main idea of the paragraph in mind. Clearly, this paragraph spends most of its time describing how peaceful and rustic life at the institute was for these young biologists. Using that knowledge, you can eliminate at least a few of the answer choices and guess from the rest.

8. **A** Specific Information *Medium*

This kind of question tests whether you can recognize the balance of information given in the passage. Goldschmidt comes up the most.

9. **B** Technique *Easy*

Whether in nonfiction or fiction passages, the SAT loves to make sure you can recognize irony, which is a difficult concept. The recognition of irony requires that you be able to "read between the lines" and recognize when a meaning besides the literal is meant (sometimes even the opposite of the literal meaning is the one intended to be conveyed).

10. **D** Specific Information *Medium*

These young biologists rapidly became quite powerful in their respective fields. That's the point of this short second paragraph.

11. **C** Themes and Arguments *Difficult*

If this question confused you, remember that you have some weapons in your arsenal. First, correct answers to reading questions on the SAT are usually not extreme in the sense that **A** and **B** are: *completely discrete* and *totally diffuse*. Furthermore, there's no sense that the author is judging whether one type of biologists is "better" than the other; he or she is simply stating that a difference exists, and this difference can be used in historical analysis.

12. **B** Implied Information *Difficult*

This question tests whether you understand the substantive difference between "mandarin" and "pragmatic" biologists. You are *not* expected to be familiar with these terms when you walk into the testing center, but you *are* expected to learn what they mean from the information given in the passage.

13. **E** Words in Context *Medium*

This kind of vocabulary-in-context question can be treated as a sentence completion. If you don't know what *tomes* means, you can still get to the correct answer by using context clues. First, mandarins synthesized a lot of biological information and theories, and they tried to find an underlying basis for both. Second, if Goldschmidt's work was *wide-ranging*, and if he was a mandarin, as described above and in the passage, then most likely he wrote some long books. He'd need the space! Don't hesitate to use logic to answer questions. In fact, one of the prime goals of the SAT is to encourage you to read critically and actively.

14. **B** Themes and Arguments *Medium*

A key feature of the mandarin style of biology was a tight correlation to *high-culture* pursuits. In this paragraph, the author completes the argument that these three biologists fell squarely into this mandarin category.

15. **D** Words in Context *Medium*

Remember, if you're confused by vocabulary questions, treat them as sentence completions, and pick the word that fits the sense of the sentence. In other words, eliminate those that don't and guess from the rest.

16. **B** Implied Information *Difficult*

This is an inference question. Based on the information in the passage, you can piece together that Goldschmidt, now deprived of his lofty position and apparently unlimited resources at the Kaiser Wilhelm Institute, made a virtue of that necessity and sat down to write two big, synthetic books, just as a true mandarin would.

17. **A** Themes and Arguments *Medium*

The author wouldn't mention a *"Great Break"* between Lenin and Stalin if he or she didn't draw some distinction between Soviet culture under Lenin and under Stalin. Remember, you must go with the information in the passage, regardless of whether you agree with it. The point of SAT critical reading questions are to "get the point" of the passage. Your opinion on it (if you happen to have one) is irrelevant.

18. **D** Implied Information *Difficult*
This is a fairly tough inference question. The author never comes out and says **D** (which is what makes it a tough question), but the entire thrust of the argument is that the external conditions (here, they're mostly political in one sense or another) need to be taken into account in order to understand the history of science.

19. **B** Themes and Arguments *Difficult*
Another tough question. Again, the main thrust of this question is to see whether you understand exactly what the author's argument is. It's a comparative argument: the author is not concerned with moral judgment, but rather with tracking the variation in outcomes for all three biologists' careers and ideas, given their very similar education and beginning career track and subsequent wrenching changes in the 1930s.

SECTION 8: MATH

Multiple Choice

1. **C** Algebra: Substitution *Easy*
Begin with the equation that has only one variable; use that answer to substitute into the equation with two variables:

$$6z = 72$$
$$z = 12$$
$$yz = 3$$
$$12y = 3$$
$$y = \frac{3}{12} = \frac{1}{4}$$

2. **A** Algebra: Solving Equations *Easy*
First, find the train's rate in miles-per-hour:

$$\frac{100 \text{ miles}}{2 \text{ hours}} = \frac{50 \text{ miles}}{1 \text{ hour}}$$

Next, use the equation $d = rt$ to find the number of hours (that is, t):

$$d = rt$$
$$230 = 50t$$
$$4.6 = t$$

3. **C** Numbers & Operations: Basic Operations *Easy*
This question tests your knowledge of reciprocals and operations. If $\frac{a}{b} = \frac{4}{5}$, then $\frac{5}{4} \times \frac{a}{b} = \frac{5}{4} \times \frac{4}{5} = \frac{20}{20} = 1$.

4. **E** Geometry: Angles and Lines *Medium*

If this problem confused you, remember that you should always write down what you know. Often, the next step toward the answer comes out of that exercise, which is quite brief.

Here's what you know: $x + y + 30 + 30 + 90 = 360$. How do we know that? Well, if $\angle EOD = 30$, then its opposite angle, $\angle AOB$, also has to equal 30. All of the angles added up must equal 360°. Now you just need to do the math:

$$x + y + 30 + 30 + 90 = 360$$
$$x + y + 150 = 360$$
$$x + y = 210$$

5. **C** Data Analysis, Statistics & Probability: Graphs, Charts, and Tables *Medium*

Work backward from the end time of the last period, making sure to include the five-minute break between the periods. Feel free to use the chart to write in your times as you work backward.

6. **A** Data Analysis, Statistics & Probability: Statistical Analysis *Medium*

In this case, treat each of the answer choices as a "hypothesis," and plug the number into the three expressions to see which number yields $y + 2$ as the median of the three integers.

7. **E** Algebra: Functions *Medium*

Don't let the functional notation throw you. Just substitute in 10,000 for $P(n)$ and solve:

$$P(n) = 0.8n - 100$$
$$10,000 = 0.8n - 100$$
$$10,100 = 0.8n$$
$$12,625 = n$$

8. **D** Algebra: Binomials and Quadratics *Medium*

The key to this problem is knowing how to expand $(x + y)^2$. Use FOIL to expand this expression:

$$(x + y)^2 = (x + y)(x + y) = x^2 + 2xy + y^2$$

Now take another look at the information given in the question. You're given the numerical value of all pieces of this expanded version of $(x + y)^2$: $x^2 + y^2 = 113$ and $xy = 14$. Substitute these numerical values into the expression to find the answer:

$$x^2 + 2xy + y^2 =$$
$$x^2 + y^2 + 2xy =$$
$$113 + 2(14) =$$
$$113 + 28 = 141$$

9. **D** Geometry: Triangles *Medium*

Note that even though this figure isn't drawn to scale, you're told that it's a right triangle. That should get you thinking about special right triangles, which the SAT loves. The two sides given are 1 and $\sqrt{3}$. What special right triangle has sides such as these? A 30-60-90 triangle always has the side ratio of $x{:}x\sqrt{3}{:}2x$. If x equals 1, as in this case, the other two sides would be $\sqrt{3}$ and 2. But, more importantly, the angle measurement of the side opposite $\sqrt{3}$ would have to be 60°.

10. **E** Numbers & Operations: Percents *Medium*

This is a translation problem. Translate the statement into mathematics:

English: "20 percent of 50 percent of a positive number is equal to 40 percent of y percent of the same number."

Mathematics: $(0.2)(0.5)(x) = (0.4)\left(\frac{y}{100}\right)(x)$

Once you have this equation, solve for y. Note that the xs cancel out:

$$\begin{aligned}(0.2)(0.5)(x) &= (0.4)\left(\frac{y}{100}\right)(x)\\ 0.2(0.5) &= (0.4)\left(\frac{y}{100}\right)\\ 0.1 &= \frac{0.4y}{100}\\ 10 &= 0.4y\\ 25 &= y\end{aligned}$$

11. **B** Geometry: Polygons *Difficult*

If the area of the entire square is x, and that area is divided into two equal halves six times, then the area of the shaded triangle has to be $\frac{x}{2^5} = \frac{x}{32}$. That means that whatever x may be, the area of the shaded triangle will be $\frac{1}{32}$ of x.

12. **B** Algebra: Inequalities *Medium*

The best way to do this problem is to pick a couple of easy-to-work-with numbers for x and y that fulfill the conditions of the inequality. Thus, if $3x < 2y < 0$, then you know that $3x$ and $2y$ have to be negative numbers and that $3x$ has to be less than $2y$. Try using $x = -2$ and $y = -1$. That means that $3x < 2y < 0$ becomes $3(-2) < 2(-1) < 0$, or $-6 < -2 < 0$, which fulfills the conditions of the inequality.

Before you even start plugging in your values for x and y, note that **C**, **D**, and **E** can't be correct. If you were running out of time, you could guess from the two remaining choices and move on.

Now, plug your values for x and y into the answer choices to see which yields the greatest value:

A $-3(-2) = 6$

B $-(3[-2]+2[-1]) = -(-6+-2) = -(-8) = 8$

13. **A** Data Analysis, Statistics & Probability: Statistical Analysis *Medium*

This is a translation problem. Remember that the general formula for an arithmetic mean (or average) is:

$$\frac{\text{the sum of the values}}{\text{the number of values}}$$

In this case, you have the following (we'll insert parentheses to highlight how the terms correlate with the English description in the question):

$$\frac{(x)+(5x)+(3x+6)}{3}=$$
$$\frac{x+5x+3x+6}{3}=$$
$$\frac{9x+6}{3}=$$
$$\frac{9x}{3}+\frac{6}{3}=3x+2$$

14. **E** Algebra: Absolute Value and Exponents *Difficult*

First, rewrite the equation to get rid of the negative exponent:

$$(x-y)^{-\frac{1}{3}}=(x+y)^{\frac{1}{3}}$$
$$\frac{1}{(x-y)^{\frac{1}{3}}}=(x+y)^{\frac{1}{3}}$$
$$\frac{1}{\sqrt[3]{(x-y)}}=\sqrt[3]{(x+y)}$$

Now, note the parenthetical quantities, $(x - y)$ and $(x + y)$. Look familiar? Yes, it's the expansion of the difference of two squares, and you have an answer choice that reads: $x^2 - y^2 = 1$. Use this clue to hone in on the correct answer:

$$x^2-y^2=1$$
$$(x-y)(x+y)=1$$
$$(x+y)=\frac{1}{(x-y)}$$

This has to be true in order for the cube root of those quantities to also be true.

15. **E** Algebra: Absolute Value and Exponents *Medium*

The equation $|3\sqrt{x}+9| = 15$ can equal either:

1. $3\sqrt{x}+9 = 15$, or
2. $-(3\sqrt{x}+9) = 15$

Pick one and solve, then see whether the answer shows up in the answer choices. Solve equation 1:

$$|3\sqrt{x}+9|=15$$
$$3\sqrt{x}+9=15$$
$$3\sqrt{x}=6$$
$$\sqrt{x}=2$$
$$x=4$$

That's not in the answer choices, so you have to solve equation 2:

$$|3\sqrt{x}+9|=15$$
$$-(3\sqrt{x}+9)=15$$
$$-3\sqrt{x}-9=15$$
$$-3\sqrt{x}=24$$
$$\sqrt{x}=-8$$
$$x=64$$

16. **C** Numbers & Operations: Sets *Difficult*

To visualize what's going on, draw a Venn diagram:

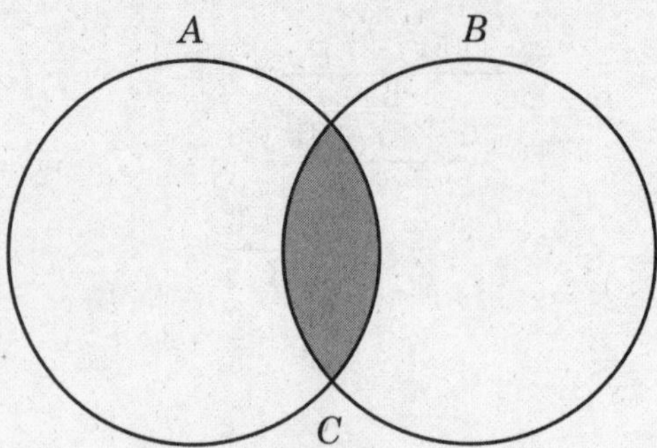

You want to account for all *a*s and *b*s that aren't also part of the shaded region. Therefore, you need to subtract the *c*s from the set *A* and from the set *B* and add the results:

$$(a - c) + (b - c) =$$
$$a - c + b - c = a + b - 2c$$

SECTION 9: WRITING

Improving Sentences

1. **D** Tenses *Easy*

This is a verb-tense question. When you see constructions like "[to be] . . . [gerund]," get suspicious. Remember that concision isn't everything on the SAT: you want to ensure that you never pick an answer that changes the meaning of the sentence by leaving out something. That's why **B** is incorrect; the sense of the Met's collection being *largely* the sum of several private collections isn't there.

2. **E** Coordination and Subordination *Medium*

The SAT loves to include needless introductory clauses in Improving Sentence questions. Furthermore, the SAT will test the plural-vs.-possessive issue most likely more than once on the test.

3. **B** Passive Voice *Easy*

Watch out for the passive voice on the SAT; it's almost always a no-no (for exceptions see the explanation to question 7 below). However, it's not uncommon to have more than one error in a sentence, nor is it uncommon for certain answer choices that seem to be fine on a quick read to actually contain a new error. (**C** has the wrong preposition: *by*). Don't fall for choices that introduce new errors, and make sure to go slowly enough not to get snagged by any distracting wrong-answer choices.

4. **A** No Error *Easy*

Remember, some of these sentences will be fine as is.

5. **B** Parallelism *Medium*

Parallel structure is well tested on the SAT. It's almost never OK to have a "not only" without a "but also."

6. **E** Wordiness *Medium*

This choice captures the meaning of the original while cutting away needless words.

7. **A** No Error *Medium*

This sentence is fine as is—even with the passive construction. Sometimes even the SAT will use a passive construction when the active equivalent is as clunky as the ones offered here.

8. **D** Tenses *Medium*

There are a couple of elements to consider here. First, when a sentence has a long introductory phrase, make sure that the actual subject that's being modified (*MP3s*) immediately follows. *The ease* is not what's currently doing booming business. Second, make sure to pick the proper tense; in this case, you want *are causing* to show that the fears of piracy are occurring right now.

9. **C** Run-Ons *Medium*

You've got a run-on sentence here. Break it up with a semicolon. A period would have been fine as well, but no choice contained one.

10. **B** Other *Difficult*

This is more a question of logic than grammar. Email and instant messaging are paperless communication technologies, but the paperless office hasn't yet arrived. You need a word that shows the contrast: *because* implies a cause-and-effect relationship not intended by this sentence.

11. **D** Conjunctions *Difficult*

This choice replaces the "weak" and in this sentence, showing more clearly the differences between Van Gogh's early and late works. **E** is unnecessarily wordy.

12. **C** Other *Difficult*

While is a time-related word that is often misused in this fashion. *Whereas* is not connected to time; it's simply a close synonym to the word "although."

13. **D** Coordination and Subordination *Difficult*

You want the semicolon version rather than the two-sentence version in **E**, because you need some contrasting element to highlight the difference between photographs and sketches.

14. **E** Other *Medium*

How can Kevin and Louisa, two people, become one world-renowned brain surgeon? Watch out for this error; maintain the proper number throughout the sentence.

SAT PRACTICE TEST 7

SAT* Reasoning Test—General Directions

Timing

- You will have 3 hours and 20 minutes to work on this test. (On the actual SAT, you would have 3 hours and 45 minutes to complete ten sections, one of which would be unscored and experimental.)
- There are nine separately timed sections:
  - ➤ One 25-minute essay
  - ➤ Five other 25-minute sections
  - ➤ Two 20-minute sections
  - ➤ One 10-minute section
- You may work on only one section at a time.
- The supervisor will tell you when to begin and end each section.
- If you finish a section before time is called, check your work on that section. You may NOT turn to any other section.
- Work as rapidly as you can without losing accuracy. Don't waste time on questions that seem too difficult for you.

Marking Answers

- Carefully mark only one answer for each question.
- Make sure each mark is dark and completely fills the circle.
- Do not make any stray marks on your answer sheet.
- If you erase, do so completely. Incomplete erasures may be scored as intended answers.
- Use only the answer spaces that correspond to the question numbers.
- Use the test book for scratchwork, but you will not receive credit for anything written there.
- After time has been called, you may not transfer answers to your answer sheet or fill in circles.
- You may not fold or remove pages or portions of a page from this book, or take the book or answer sheet from the testing room.

Scoring

- For each correct answer to a question, you receive one point.
- For questions you omit, you receive no points.
- For a wrong answer to a multiple-choice question, you lose one-fourth of a point.
  - ➤ If you can eliminate one or more of the answer choices as wrong, you increase your chances of choosing the correct answer and earning one point.
  - ➤ If you can't eliminate any choice, move on. You can return to the question later if there is time.
- For a wrong answer to a "grid-in" math question, you don't lose any points.
- The essay is scored on a 1 to 6 scale by two different readers. The total essay score is the sum of the two readers' scores.
- An off-topic or blank essay will receive a score of zero.

---

* SAT test directions selected from the SAT Reasoning Test. Reprinted by permission of the College Board, the copyright owner.

SAT PRACTICE TEST 7 ANSWER SHEET

SECTION 2

1. Ⓐ Ⓑ Ⓒ Ⓓ Ⓔ	7. Ⓐ Ⓑ Ⓒ Ⓓ Ⓔ	13. Ⓐ Ⓑ Ⓒ Ⓓ Ⓔ	19. Ⓐ Ⓑ Ⓒ Ⓓ Ⓔ
2. Ⓐ Ⓑ Ⓒ Ⓓ Ⓔ	8. Ⓐ Ⓑ Ⓒ Ⓓ Ⓔ	14. Ⓐ Ⓑ Ⓒ Ⓓ Ⓔ	20. Ⓐ Ⓑ Ⓒ Ⓓ Ⓔ
3. Ⓐ Ⓑ Ⓒ Ⓓ Ⓔ	9. Ⓐ Ⓑ Ⓒ Ⓓ Ⓔ	15. Ⓐ Ⓑ Ⓒ Ⓓ Ⓔ	21. Ⓐ Ⓑ Ⓒ Ⓓ Ⓔ
4. Ⓐ Ⓑ Ⓒ Ⓓ Ⓔ	10. Ⓐ Ⓑ Ⓒ Ⓓ Ⓔ	16. Ⓐ Ⓑ Ⓒ Ⓓ Ⓔ	22. Ⓐ Ⓑ Ⓒ Ⓓ Ⓔ
5. Ⓐ Ⓑ Ⓒ Ⓓ Ⓔ	11. Ⓐ Ⓑ Ⓒ Ⓓ Ⓔ	17. Ⓐ Ⓑ Ⓒ Ⓓ Ⓔ	23. Ⓐ Ⓑ Ⓒ Ⓓ Ⓔ
6. Ⓐ Ⓑ Ⓒ Ⓓ Ⓔ	12. Ⓐ Ⓑ Ⓒ Ⓓ Ⓔ	18. Ⓐ Ⓑ Ⓒ Ⓓ Ⓔ	24. Ⓐ Ⓑ Ⓒ Ⓓ Ⓔ

SECTION 3

1. Ⓐ Ⓑ Ⓒ Ⓓ Ⓔ	6. Ⓐ Ⓑ Ⓒ Ⓓ Ⓔ	11. Ⓐ Ⓑ Ⓒ Ⓓ Ⓔ	16. Ⓐ Ⓑ Ⓒ Ⓓ Ⓔ
2. Ⓐ Ⓑ Ⓒ Ⓓ Ⓔ	7. Ⓐ Ⓑ Ⓒ Ⓓ Ⓔ	12. Ⓐ Ⓑ Ⓒ Ⓓ Ⓔ	17. Ⓐ Ⓑ Ⓒ Ⓓ Ⓔ
3. Ⓐ Ⓑ Ⓒ Ⓓ Ⓔ	8. Ⓐ Ⓑ Ⓒ Ⓓ Ⓔ	13. Ⓐ Ⓑ Ⓒ Ⓓ Ⓔ	18. Ⓐ Ⓑ Ⓒ Ⓓ Ⓔ
4. Ⓐ Ⓑ Ⓒ Ⓓ Ⓔ	9. Ⓐ Ⓑ Ⓒ Ⓓ Ⓔ	14. Ⓐ Ⓑ Ⓒ Ⓓ Ⓔ	19. Ⓐ Ⓑ Ⓒ Ⓓ Ⓔ
5. Ⓐ Ⓑ Ⓒ Ⓓ Ⓔ	10. Ⓐ Ⓑ Ⓒ Ⓓ Ⓔ	15. Ⓐ Ⓑ Ⓒ Ⓓ Ⓔ	20. Ⓐ Ⓑ Ⓒ Ⓓ Ⓔ

SECTION 4

1. Ⓐ Ⓑ Ⓒ Ⓓ Ⓔ	7. Ⓐ Ⓑ Ⓒ Ⓓ Ⓔ	13. Ⓐ Ⓑ Ⓒ Ⓓ Ⓔ	19. Ⓐ Ⓑ Ⓒ Ⓓ Ⓔ
2. Ⓐ Ⓑ Ⓒ Ⓓ Ⓔ	8. Ⓐ Ⓑ Ⓒ Ⓓ Ⓔ	14. Ⓐ Ⓑ Ⓒ Ⓓ Ⓔ	20. Ⓐ Ⓑ Ⓒ Ⓓ Ⓔ
3. Ⓐ Ⓑ Ⓒ Ⓓ Ⓔ	9. Ⓐ Ⓑ Ⓒ Ⓓ Ⓔ	15. Ⓐ Ⓑ Ⓒ Ⓓ Ⓔ	21. Ⓐ Ⓑ Ⓒ Ⓓ Ⓔ
4. Ⓐ Ⓑ Ⓒ Ⓓ Ⓔ	10. Ⓐ Ⓑ Ⓒ Ⓓ Ⓔ	16. Ⓐ Ⓑ Ⓒ Ⓓ Ⓔ	22. Ⓐ Ⓑ Ⓒ Ⓓ Ⓔ
5. Ⓐ Ⓑ Ⓒ Ⓓ Ⓔ	11. Ⓐ Ⓑ Ⓒ Ⓓ Ⓔ	17. Ⓐ Ⓑ Ⓒ Ⓓ Ⓔ	23. Ⓐ Ⓑ Ⓒ Ⓓ Ⓔ
6. Ⓐ Ⓑ Ⓒ Ⓓ Ⓔ	12. Ⓐ Ⓑ Ⓒ Ⓓ Ⓔ	18. Ⓐ Ⓑ Ⓒ Ⓓ Ⓔ	24. Ⓐ Ⓑ Ⓒ Ⓓ Ⓔ

SECTION 5

1. Ⓐ Ⓑ Ⓒ Ⓓ Ⓔ	3. Ⓐ Ⓑ Ⓒ Ⓓ Ⓔ	5. Ⓐ Ⓑ Ⓒ Ⓓ Ⓔ	7. Ⓐ Ⓑ Ⓒ Ⓓ Ⓔ
2. Ⓐ Ⓑ Ⓒ Ⓓ Ⓔ	4. Ⓐ Ⓑ Ⓒ Ⓓ Ⓔ	6. Ⓐ Ⓑ Ⓒ Ⓓ Ⓔ	8. Ⓐ Ⓑ Ⓒ Ⓓ Ⓔ

9 10 11 12 13

14 15 16 17 18

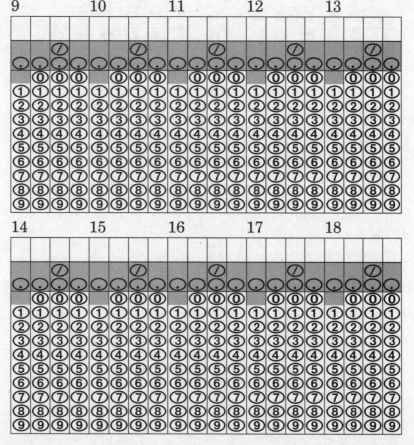

SAT PRACTICE TEST 7 ANSWER SHEET

SECTION 6

1. Ⓐ Ⓑ Ⓒ Ⓓ Ⓔ	10. Ⓐ Ⓑ Ⓒ Ⓓ Ⓔ	19. Ⓐ Ⓑ Ⓒ Ⓓ Ⓔ	28. Ⓐ Ⓑ Ⓒ Ⓓ Ⓔ
2. Ⓐ Ⓑ Ⓒ Ⓓ Ⓔ	11. Ⓐ Ⓑ Ⓒ Ⓓ Ⓔ	20. Ⓐ Ⓑ Ⓒ Ⓓ Ⓔ	29. Ⓐ Ⓑ Ⓒ Ⓓ Ⓔ
3. Ⓐ Ⓑ Ⓒ Ⓓ Ⓔ	12. Ⓐ Ⓑ Ⓒ Ⓓ Ⓔ	21. Ⓐ Ⓑ Ⓒ Ⓓ Ⓔ	30. Ⓐ Ⓑ Ⓒ Ⓓ Ⓔ
4. Ⓐ Ⓑ Ⓒ Ⓓ Ⓔ	13. Ⓐ Ⓑ Ⓒ Ⓓ Ⓔ	22. Ⓐ Ⓑ Ⓒ Ⓓ Ⓔ	31. Ⓐ Ⓑ Ⓒ Ⓓ Ⓔ
5. Ⓐ Ⓑ Ⓒ Ⓓ Ⓔ	14. Ⓐ Ⓑ Ⓒ Ⓓ Ⓔ	23. Ⓐ Ⓑ Ⓒ Ⓓ Ⓔ	32. Ⓐ Ⓑ Ⓒ Ⓓ Ⓔ
6. Ⓐ Ⓑ Ⓒ Ⓓ Ⓔ	15. Ⓐ Ⓑ Ⓒ Ⓓ Ⓔ	24. Ⓐ Ⓑ Ⓒ Ⓓ Ⓔ	33. Ⓐ Ⓑ Ⓒ Ⓓ Ⓔ
7. Ⓐ Ⓑ Ⓒ Ⓓ Ⓔ	16. Ⓐ Ⓑ Ⓒ Ⓓ Ⓔ	25. Ⓐ Ⓑ Ⓒ Ⓓ Ⓔ	34. Ⓐ Ⓑ Ⓒ Ⓓ Ⓔ
8. Ⓐ Ⓑ Ⓒ Ⓓ Ⓔ	17. Ⓐ Ⓑ Ⓒ Ⓓ Ⓔ	26. Ⓐ Ⓑ Ⓒ Ⓓ Ⓔ	35. Ⓐ Ⓑ Ⓒ Ⓓ Ⓔ
9. Ⓐ Ⓑ Ⓒ Ⓓ Ⓔ	18. Ⓐ Ⓑ Ⓒ Ⓓ Ⓔ	27. Ⓐ Ⓑ Ⓒ Ⓓ Ⓔ	

SECTION 7

1. Ⓐ Ⓑ Ⓒ Ⓓ Ⓔ	6. Ⓐ Ⓑ Ⓒ Ⓓ Ⓔ	11. Ⓐ Ⓑ Ⓒ Ⓓ Ⓔ	16. Ⓐ Ⓑ Ⓒ Ⓓ Ⓔ
2. Ⓐ Ⓑ Ⓒ Ⓓ Ⓔ	7. Ⓐ Ⓑ Ⓒ Ⓓ Ⓔ	12. Ⓐ Ⓑ Ⓒ Ⓓ Ⓔ	17. Ⓐ Ⓑ Ⓒ Ⓓ Ⓔ
3. Ⓐ Ⓑ Ⓒ Ⓓ Ⓔ	8. Ⓐ Ⓑ Ⓒ Ⓓ Ⓔ	13. Ⓐ Ⓑ Ⓒ Ⓓ Ⓔ	18. Ⓐ Ⓑ Ⓒ Ⓓ Ⓔ
4. Ⓐ Ⓑ Ⓒ Ⓓ Ⓔ	9. Ⓐ Ⓑ Ⓒ Ⓓ Ⓔ	14. Ⓐ Ⓑ Ⓒ Ⓓ Ⓔ	19. Ⓐ Ⓑ Ⓒ Ⓓ Ⓔ
5. Ⓐ Ⓑ Ⓒ Ⓓ Ⓔ	10. Ⓐ Ⓑ Ⓒ Ⓓ Ⓔ	15. Ⓐ Ⓑ Ⓒ Ⓓ Ⓔ	

SECTION 8

1. Ⓐ Ⓑ Ⓒ Ⓓ Ⓔ	5. Ⓐ Ⓑ Ⓒ Ⓓ Ⓔ	9. Ⓐ Ⓑ Ⓒ Ⓓ Ⓔ	13. Ⓐ Ⓑ Ⓒ Ⓓ Ⓔ
2. Ⓐ Ⓑ Ⓒ Ⓓ Ⓔ	6. Ⓐ Ⓑ Ⓒ Ⓓ Ⓔ	10. Ⓐ Ⓑ Ⓒ Ⓓ Ⓔ	14. Ⓐ Ⓑ Ⓒ Ⓓ Ⓔ
3. Ⓐ Ⓑ Ⓒ Ⓓ Ⓔ	7. Ⓐ Ⓑ Ⓒ Ⓓ Ⓔ	11. Ⓐ Ⓑ Ⓒ Ⓓ Ⓔ	15. Ⓐ Ⓑ Ⓒ Ⓓ Ⓔ
4. Ⓐ Ⓑ Ⓒ Ⓓ Ⓔ	8. Ⓐ Ⓑ Ⓒ Ⓓ Ⓔ	12. Ⓐ Ⓑ Ⓒ Ⓓ Ⓔ	16. Ⓐ Ⓑ Ⓒ Ⓓ Ⓔ

SECTION 9

1. Ⓐ Ⓑ Ⓒ Ⓓ Ⓔ	5. Ⓐ Ⓑ Ⓒ Ⓓ Ⓔ	9. Ⓐ Ⓑ Ⓒ Ⓓ Ⓔ	13. Ⓐ Ⓑ Ⓒ Ⓓ Ⓔ
2. Ⓐ Ⓑ Ⓒ Ⓓ Ⓔ	6. Ⓐ Ⓑ Ⓒ Ⓓ Ⓔ	10. Ⓐ Ⓑ Ⓒ Ⓓ Ⓔ	14. Ⓐ Ⓑ Ⓒ Ⓓ Ⓔ
3. Ⓐ Ⓑ Ⓒ Ⓓ Ⓔ	7. Ⓐ Ⓑ Ⓒ Ⓓ Ⓔ	11. Ⓐ Ⓑ Ⓒ Ⓓ Ⓔ	
4. Ⓐ Ⓑ Ⓒ Ⓓ Ⓔ	8. Ⓐ Ⓑ Ⓒ Ⓓ Ⓔ	12. Ⓐ Ⓑ Ⓒ Ⓓ Ⓔ	

SECTION 1

ESSAY

Time—25 minutes

The essay gives you an opportunity to show how effectively you can develop and express ideas. You should, therefore, take care to develop your point of view, present your ideas logically and clearly, and use language precisely.

Your essay must be written on the lines provided on your answer sheet—you will receive no other paper on which to write. You will have enough space if you write on every line, avoid wide margins, and keep your handwriting to a reasonable size. Remember that people who are not familiar with your handwriting will read what you write. Try to write or print so that what you are writing is legible to those readers.

You have twenty-five minutes to write an essay on the topic assigned below. DO NOT WRITE ON ANOTHER TOPIC. AN OFF-TOPIC ESSAY WILL RECEIVE A SCORE OF ZERO.

Think carefully about the issue presented in the following excerpt and the assignment below.

> Sooner or later you will always have to pick a side in an argument; you cannot always remain neutral or always act as a negotiator.

Assignment: Do we always need to choose sides in a debate? Support your position with reasoning and examples taken from your reading, studies, experience, or observations.

DO NOT WRITE YOUR ESSAY IN YOUR TEST BOOK. You will receive credit only for what you write on your answer sheet.

BEGIN WRITING YOUR ESSAY ON THE ANSWER SHEET.

IF YOU FINISH BEFORE TIME IS CALLED, YOU MAY CHECK YOUR WORK ON THIS SECTION ONLY.
DO NOT TURN TO ANY OTHER SECTION IN THE TEST.

SECTION 1—ESSAY

Time—25 minutes

SECTION 1—ESSAY

Time—25 minutes

SECTION 2

Turn to Section 2 of your answer sheet to answer the questions in this section.

Time—25 Minutes
24 Questions

Directions: For each question in this section, select the best answer from among the choices given and fill in the corresponding oval on the answer sheet.

Each sentence below has one or two blanks, each blank indicating that something has been omitted. Beneath the sentence are five words or sets of words labeled A through E. Choose the word or set of words that, when inserted in the sentence, best fits the meaning of the sentence as a whole.

Example:

Eliza felt ----- when her boss asked her to work seven weekends in a row but ----- when her work earned her a promotion.

(A) enervated . . weakened
(B) depressed . . intellectual
(C) advantageous . . salacious
(D) angry . . shopworn
(E) irate . . elated 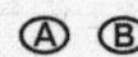   Ⓓ ●

1. Recently, scientists and doctors have concluded that people who switch to a healthy lifestyle later in life will not be able to ----- the effects of unhealthy behavior conducted in youth.

(A) counteract
(B) inspire
(C) condone
(D) express
(E) marginalize

2. In Mozart's masterpiece *The Marriage of Figaro*, the aristocracy is subtly -----, for the most high-born characters engage in the most unsavory and unappealing behavior.

(A) celebrated
(B) engaged
(C) adored
(D) mocked
(E) festooned

3. Although country A has apologized for its aggressive behavior toward country B, protests from country B continue, suggesting that the anger of the people of country B is more a ----- that population's anger against its own government than toward its neighbor.

(A) testament to
(B) consolation of
(C) predicament by
(D) contrast to
(E) argument against

4. Karnatic theory is one of the most ----- of all musical forms, using many flourishes and arresting half-tones that may strike listeners accustomed to the even tonality of Western music as -----.

(A) convoluted . . sonorous
(B) staid . . harsh
(C) ornate . . plentiful
(D) placid . . raucous
(E) complex . . discordant

5. The days where any ----- hobbyist could be hired to construct a professional website have ended, for the internet is now ----- with numerous links, data-capturing devices, and complex animated ads.

(A) casual . . devoid
(B) astute . . truncated
(C) lackadaisical . . rife
(D) practiced . . oppressed
(E) ardent . . ashen

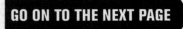

GO ON TO THE NEXT PAGE

SECTION 2

Directions: Each passage below is followed by questions based on its content. Answer the questions on the basis of what is stated or implied in each passage and in any introductory material that may be provided.

Questions 6–7 are based on the following passage.

Why did the Brontë family choose to destroy so many of Charlotte Brontë's letters? It is a great loss to scholars of literature. Charlotte's friend Mary Taylor, who lived in Australia, also chose to destroy Charlotte's letters. Fortunately, Ellen Nussey, Charlotte's childhood friend, carefully saved every one of her friend's correspondences, directly against the wishes of Charlotte's husband. And although these letters are invaluable, they are frustrating to the literary detective, for they show quiet musings of a domestic nature. In the one letter to Mary Taylor that does survive and that shows a very different Charlotte than the one Ellen knew, we see Charlotte decrying the lot of women in nineteenth-century England. It was through Mary that Charlotte was able to express her frustrated, intellectual self. Perhaps, then, this is why so many of Charlotte's letters disappeared: her family did not wish her legacy to be one of outspokenness. As a result, we have the mistaken impression of Charlotte as a quiet woman whose passion was hidden and only expressed on occasion.

6. The author suggests that Ellen Nussey's letters from Charlotte

(A) exhibit Charlotte's defiant nature
(B) show only one side of Charlotte's character
(C) may have been forged
(D) were permitted to exist by Charlotte's family because of their docile nature
(E) are useless to biographers

7. The reference to the "mistaken impression" (line 16) serves to suggest that

(A) Mary's one surviving letter gives us a false impression of Charlotte
(B) Charlotte deliberately misled Ellen Nussey
(C) letters do not give us a good picture of people's characters
(D) biographers can never reconstruct a picture of a subject
(E) we do not have a picture of the full range of Charlotte's temperament

Questions 8–9 are based on the following passage.

As an educator, I welcome the new movement among scholars to explore the voices of those previously oppressed: minorities and women. I worry, however, about the tendency to paint these people as virtuous simply as a result of their unfortunate position in society. This is not necessarily a new concept. Often in Victorian literature, one encounters the beggar with the heart of gold or the pauper who, though fallen on hard times, is infinitely more virtuous than a person of privilege. But if we are to truly examine the lives of minorities, we must do so with an open mind and paint them in all their garish colors and varying shades of virtuousness.

8. The passage suggests that minorities have sometimes been portrayed as

(A) perfect
(B) slovenly
(C) suspicious
(D) prominent
(E) propitious

9. As used in context, the word "paint" (line 9) is used as a metaphor for

(A) culture
(B) spice
(C) decoration
(D) color
(E) description

GO ON TO THE NEXT PAGE

SECTION 2

Questions 10–18 are based on the following passage.

The following was written by a scientist in 2005.

Albert Einstein once said that the entire universe could act as a magnifying lens. He meant that when we look through a telescope, objects would appear even larger to us than they actually were. Certainly we are all now familiar with the concept of the speed of light, which, while very fast, is not so fast that objects viewed in distant galaxies are now in the same shape as they were when we spied them through a telescope. In other words, when we look at galaxies, we are looking at them in a past form—it takes light that long to reach us. And now, with the benefits of recent research, we have learned that when we look at things in the galaxy through a telescope, they are of a substantially larger size than they are in reality. Apparently, Einstein was right.

In recent years, scientists have begun to build up a picture of the universe that takes into consideration the presence of dark matter and dark energy. When you look out at the night sky, either with the naked eye or through the average telescope, the stars and galaxies are only a small part of what actually exists "out there." Scientists have long theorized about the existence of dark matter, pointing out that if stars existed into infinity, there would be no "dark" patches in the sky, because every single pinpoint should be filled with the light of stars. But dark patches do exist, so something else is obviously occupying that space, something that does not have any light. This dark matter also has gravity. Some aspects of dark matter, so-called black holes, are so dense and possess gravitational fields so powerful that any nearby matter is immediately crushed and its light not allowed to escape.

Now comes word that the gravitational fields of dark matter and dark energy combine with the gravity of other heavenly bodies to act as a lens, magnifying the bodies of even more distant stars. Recently, astronomers have noted that certain photographed images of galaxies or quasars seem to be distorted into arcs or rings or even split into multiple images. Think of the way a light from a light bulb seems to blur and stretch when you place your hand in front of it, and you will have a sense of the kind of image scientists were viewing. This distortion, once faulty film and faulty tools were ruled out as culprits, seems to be caused by the gravity of galaxies between the distant stars and quasars and our position on Earth. These intermediary galaxies are called gravitational lenses. Other scientists have seen individual stars that seem to flare as their light is magnified by the gravity of a passing star. This distortion is known as "cosmic shear."

Of particular interest to scientists are quasars, which, according to the concept of cosmic shear, appear to be brighter through the lens of a telescope. Quasars are starlike bodies in young galaxies. A set of galaxies, known as the Sloan galaxies, was observed with a custom-built telescope located in New Mexico. The Sloan galaxies are estimated to be about 2.5 billion light years away. Behind these galaxies are a series of quasars, about 10 billion light years away. Initially, scientists intended to study the amount each quasar had been magnified. This proved difficult, though, because scientists do not know the exact location of each quasar and therefore do not know what size it is supposed to be. Scientists then decided to look at the number of quasars that appear around a galaxy. If the galaxy produces cosmic shear, then it would stand to reason that a large number of quasars appearing around a galaxy should correlate to the existence of a large number of quasars behind that galaxy. However, the light bending from galaxies may make a quasar "move" and appear to have a different density and placement in the sky. Scientists therefore need to examine a host of properties—including brightness and color—to determine exactly how far away a quasar actually is and by how much it has been magnified.

No one knows exactly how we stand to benefit from this information, although it does help solidify another of Einstein's arguments. The most abstract of ideas has always come into practical use much later—for example, Benjamin Franklin's dalliance with electricity once seemed the hobby of an eccentric. It was only years later that the masses were able to benefit from the discovery of electricity when gas bulbs gave way to electrical bulbs. Perhaps one day the discovery of cosmic shear will prove similarly relevant.

10. The author mentions the speed of light in line 5 to

(A) disprove one of Einstein's long-held theories
(B) suggest that science is not always accurate
(C) reprove those who purport that seeing is believing
(D) dissuade scientists from embarking on needless projects
(E) provide another example of something viewed through a telescope not reflecting an actual reality

11. The statement in lines 12–13 ("Apparently . . . right") suggests that

(A) one of Einstein's hypotheses has since been proven true
(B) Einstein correctly postulated the speed of light
(C) Einstein understood the untrustworthy nature of telescopes
(D) the hypothesized existence of quasars has been proven
(E) a dedication to proving a scientific hypothesis will always be rewarded

GO ON TO THE NEXT PAGE

SECTION 2

12. The author mentions "stars" and "galaxies" (line 18) primarily to

(A) help prove that Einstein's idea about cosmic shear was correct
(B) introduce the concept of the quasar
(C) illustrate what the naked eye can see when looking at the night sky
(D) critique the reliance of scientists on telescopes
(E) familiarize readers with the basic elements of astronomy

13. The author introduces the third paragraph with the phrase "Now comes word" (line 29) in order to

(A) show the expostulatory nature of the evidence proving cosmic shear
(B) convey a sense of how recently the evidence supporting Einstein has been discovered
(C) help readers distinguish between the speed of sound and speed of light
(D) encourage students to read science books themselves
(E) criticize scientists who were caught unaware by the news of cosmic shear

14. To help describe cosmic shear, the author uses all of the following EXCEPT

(A) analogy
(B) a visual description
(C) a scientist's point of view
(D) the role of technical tools
(E) firsthand account

15. Which of the following, if true, would undermine the information compiled about the Sloan galaxies?

(A) Light from a galaxy makes the quasar look as though it has "moved."
(B) The telescope showed pictures of quasars exhibiting cosmic shear.
(C) Objects viewed through a telescope are not necessarily how they appear in reality.
(D) The galaxies were found to be behind the quasars.
(E) Quasars look brighter than they really are when viewed behind a telescope.

16. The author mentions the "brightness and color" (line 63) of galaxies and quasars in order to

(A) account for yet another way that scientists can determine the original placement of quasars and galaxies
(B) show how impossible it is to ever determine where a quasar is located
(C) list another useful property of a telescope
(D) express how beautiful stars are when properly magnified
(E) discredit the idea that scientists can accurately measure the effect of cosmic shift on celestial bodies

17. The author mentions Benjamin Franklin's experiments with electricity in order to

(A) show an example of how the arrogance of scientists can impede the progress of meaningful research
(B) question the work of hobbyists as opposed to the work of experts
(C) demonstrate how an earlier theory of Einstein's was proven
(D) cite an example of a scientific discovery whose practical application was not obvious at the time
(E) criticize the scientists of the Sloan experiments for their negligence

18. As used in context, the word "dalliance" (line 69) most nearly means

(A) serious experiment
(B) intense interest
(C) serene faith
(D) mild flirtation
(E) bemused amusement

GO ON TO THE NEXT PAGE

SECTION 2

Questions 19–24 are based on the following passage.

The following passage is excerpted from a book on aesthetics. The author here focuses on the qualities that the Japanese people in particular find beautiful.

A writer once famously said, "If someone wishes to know the essence of the Japanese spirit, it is the fragrant cherry blossom in the early morning." It may seem flippant at first to compare an ancient culture, whose traditions have remained intact for hundreds of years, to a flower that blooms for a short period in springtime. But a closer examination of the statement reveals that it is loaded with wisdom. Indeed, the whole of Japanese aesthetics might be said to be captured in the metaphor of the cherry blossom, if we take into consideration the unique properties of that short-lived, pink-petal flower.

Central to Japanese aesthetics is the concept of *mono no aware*, or an awareness of the transience of life. From such an awareness arises a deep sense of sadness that life, and therefore beauty, are impermanent. Nothing, according to the Japanese, better captures this sense of transience than the cherry blossom, which blooms for a short period of time before dying. In fact, the beauty of the cherry blossom is made more poignant by the knowledge of its short life, and its tragic fate gives the cherry blossom even more allure. Literally thousands of poems have been written in praise of the cherry blossom in all its stages and all of its powers. The poet-nun Chiyo-ni once wrote:

Evening temple bell
Stopped in the sky
By cherry blossoms

Nature poetry exists in the West too, but it is different. Western poetry about nature is generally celebratory and generally focuses on the power of spring to express rejuvenation. The Japanese seem singularly concerned with what the passing of beauty signifies: the fact that we are all mortal, subject to the whims of fate. Closely related to *mono no aware* in Japan is the idea of *wabi-sabi*: the notion that what is imperfect is more beautiful than what is perfect. Two classic ideas are usually used to illustrate *wabi-sabi*: First, the image of a full moon covered by a small bit of cloud, which is usually regarded as lovelier than a perfectly formed sphere. The image of a cherry blossom on its way to full bloom is the second idea. The blossom just starting to decline is considered more attractive than a perfectly formed flower.

Certainly modern-day Japanese culture continues to reflect this preference. Across Japan, starting in March of each year, newscasters chart the progress of the cherry blossom, from the first blossoms in the southern island of Kyushu to the last petal in Hokkaido. Newspapers fasten onto the tiniest detail, including noting the progress of falling blossoms. When conditions are favorable, modern-day Japanese engage in the same festivities as their ancestors: they sit under the trees, admire the transient beauty, and, perhaps, recite or compose more poems to add to the seemingly infinite list of cherry blossom poems already in existence.

19. This passage is primarily concerned with the

(A) the shortcomings of what Western cultures feel is pretty
(B) the deficiency in using cherry blossoms as a metaphor for beauty
(C) exploration of what a particular culture considers beautiful
(D) a modern obsession with cherry blossoms versus an old obsession with the flowers
(E) the universality of beauty

20. As used in line 12, the word "transience" most nearly means

(A) fleeting
(B) traveling
(C) crossing
(D) unencumbered
(E) gorgeous

21. The poem cited in lines 22–24 is used as an example of how cherry blossoms

(A) are insignificant compared to a temple
(B) interrupt peaceful moments
(C) are fragile
(D) herald the start of spring
(E) have their own powerful, spiritual quality

22. The author suggests that most Western poetry differs from Japanese poetry in that Western authors emphasize

(A) distress over the fading of flowers
(B) the vibrant, life-affirming quality of nature
(C) wonder at how life has formed
(D) the sadness of the passing of seasons
(E) the human world over the natural one

GO ON TO THE NEXT PAGE

SECTION 2

23. Which of the following best expresses the concept of *wabi-sabi* as described by the author in paragraph three?

(A) A wooden box painted a smooth bright red
(B) A detailed reproduction of a bird painted on paper
(C) A symmetrically arranged bouquet of flowers
(D) A balanced display of small dishes
(E) A black glazed bowl with a scar across the center

24. In the final paragraph, the author is concerned with showing

(A) how irrelevant the cherry blossom has become to modern-day Japanese
(B) how an ancient symbol has lost its meaning in contemporary times
(C) how modern Japanese prefer modern "perfect" aesthetics to *wabi-sabi*
(D) how modern day Japanese continue the tradition of worshipping the cherry blossom
(E) how the cherry blossom has failed to mean the same thing to Americans as it does to the Japanese

S T O P

IF YOU FINISH BEFORE TIME IS CALLED, YOU MAY CHECK YOUR WORK ON THIS TEST ONLY.
DO NOT TURN TO ANY OTHER SECTION IN THIS TEST.

SECTION 3

Turn to Section 3 of your answer sheet to answer the questions in this section.

Time—25 Minutes
20 Questions

Directions: For this section, solve each problem and decide which is the best of the choices given. Fill in the corresponding oval on the answer sheet. You may use any available space for scratchwork.

Notes:

1. The use of a calculator is permitted. All numbers used are real numbers.

2. Figures that accompany problems in this test are intended to provide information useful in solving the problems. They are drawn as accurately as possible EXCEPT when it is stated in a specific problem that the figure is not drawn to scale. All figures lie in a plane unless otherwise indicated.

3. Unless otherwise specified, the domain of any function f is assumed to be the set of all real numbers x for which $f(x)$ is a real number.

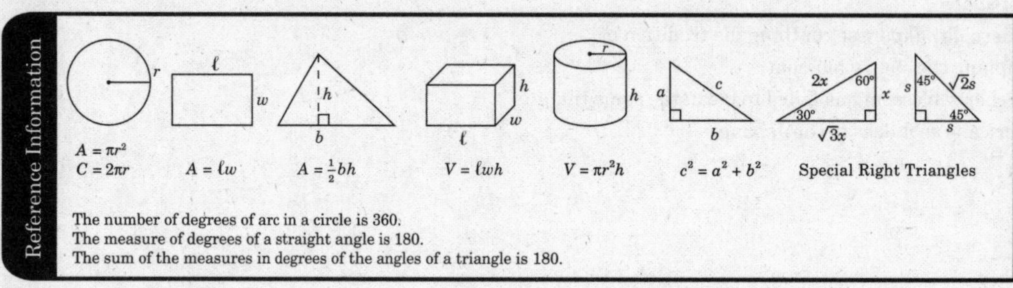

Reference Information
r
ℓ
w
h
b
w
h
ℓ
r
h
a
c
b
2x
60°
x
30°
√3x
s
45°
√2s
45°
s
A = πr²
C = 2πr
A = ℓw
A = ½bh
V = ℓwh
V = πr²h
c² = a² + b²
Special Right Triangles
The number of degrees of arc in a circle is 360.
The measure of degrees of a straight angle is 180.
The sum of the measures in degrees of the angles of a triangle is 180.

1. If $2a + 6 = 7a + 1$, what is the value of a ?

(A) 0
(B) 1
(C) 2
(D) 5
(E) 6

3, 8, 23, 68

2. The first term in the sequence above is 3, and each term after the first is determined by multiplying the preceding term by x and then subtracting y. What is the value of y ?

(A) 1
(B) 2
(C) 3
(D) 4
(E) 5

ERICA'S CLOSET

Shoes	Jeans
Sneakers	Low-rise
Sandals	Dark-rinse
Platforms	Embroidered
Flip Flops	Vintage

3. The table above shows the shoes and jeans in Erica's closet. How many different combinations of shoes and jeans type are possible?

(A) 4
(B) 8
(C) 12
(D) 16
(E) 20

GO ON TO THE NEXT PAGE

SECTION 3

4. For which of the following functions is $f(-2) > f(2)$?

(A) $f(x) = 2x^2$
(B) $f(x) = -1$
(C) $f(x) = \frac{2}{x}$
(D) $f(x) = x^2 + 2$
(E) $f(x) = -2x^3$

5. Gino's Café requires that the proportion of espresso to milk remain constant for all drinks, regardless of size. If a small latte requires 12 parts milk for every 5 parts espresso, then how many parts milk are required for an extra-large latte with 13 parts espresso?

(A) 31.2
(B) 30
(C) 25
(D) 21
(E) 20.2

6. If B is the midpoint of line segment AC, which of the following must be true?

I. $AB = \frac{AC}{2}$

II. $\frac{AB}{2} = \frac{BC}{2}$

III. $2BC = \frac{AC}{2}$

(A) I only
(B) II only
(C) I and II
(D) I and III
(E) I, II, and III

7. If $3a = 4b$, and $4b = 12c$, then what does a equal in terms of c ?

(A) $\frac{c}{8}$
(B) $\frac{c}{4}$
(C) c
(D) $4c$
(E) $12c$

8. A total of s crates of strawberries is to be transported from the farm to a distribution center. Each of the t trucks used to transport the strawberries has a maximum of c slots to hold the crates. If one truck had four empty slots and the remaining trucks were filled, which of the following best expresses the relationship between s, t, and c ?

(A) $2 + 4 = t + c$
(B) $s - 4 = tc$
(C) $tc = 4s$
(D) $s = tc - 4$
(E) $st = c - 4$

GO ON TO THE NEXT PAGE

SECTION 3

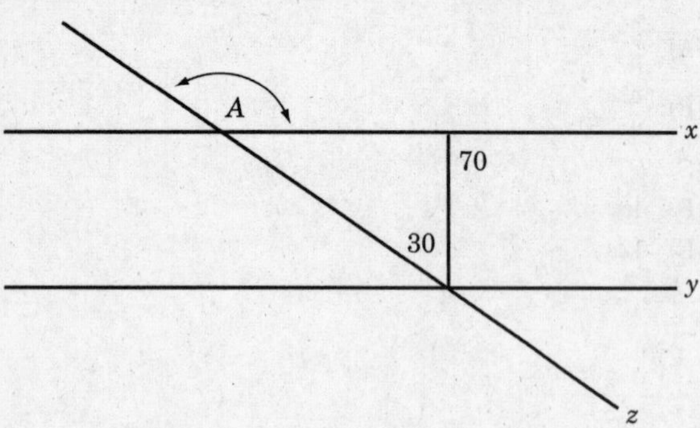

Note: Figure not drawn to scale.

9. In the figure above, lines x and y are parallel. What is the value of angle A ?

(A) 150
(B) 140
(C) 130
(D) 120
(E) 110

$$2x^3 = 2x^2$$

10. For what value of x is the statement above true?

(A) –1
(B) $-\frac{1}{3}$
(C) 0
(D) 2
(E) For no value of x

11. Miko and her mother are rolling sushi. To make sushi, a cylindrical "log" of rice is wrapped with a rectangular piece of seaweed. If the diameter of the first log of sushi is one-third the diameter of the second log of sushi, how many times longer is the second piece of seaweed than the first piece, assuming that the seaweed wraps all the way around each log with no overlapping ends?

(A) $\frac{1}{3}$
(B) 1
(C) 3
(D) 6
(E) 9

---

12. A bucket holds red balls and blue balls. The probability that a red ball is drawn at random is $\frac{5}{11}$. If a red ball is drawn first and not replaced, then what is the probability that the next ball drawn will be blue?

(A) 5
(B) 3
(C) $\frac{3}{5}$
(D) $\frac{2}{5}$
(E) $\frac{1}{3}$

---

13. The total daily cost c in dollars of producing x units of a certain product is given by the function $c(x) = x^2 - 60x + k$ where k is constant. If 30 units were produced yesterday for a total cost of \$300, what is the value of k ?

(A) 30
(B) 60
(C) 300
(D) 900
(E) 1200

GO ON TO THE NEXT PAGE

SECTION 3

14. If a and b are distinct positive integers, for how many ordered pairs (a, b) is $3a + 2b \le 8$?

(A) 0
(B) 1
(C) 2
(D) 3
(E) 4

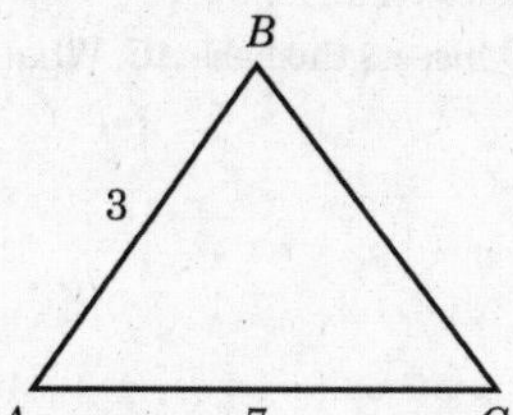

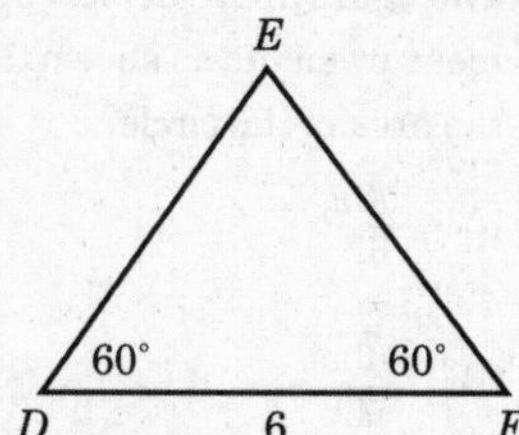

Note: Figure not drawn to scale.

15. In the triangles above, all side lengths are integer values. According to the information given, by at most which value could the perimeter of triangle DEF be greater than the perimeter of triangle ABC ?

(A) It cannot be determined by the information given
(B) 1
(C) 2
(D) 3
(E) 4

16. If a and b are consecutive even integers, where $a < b$, which of the following could be equal to b^2 ?

(A) $2a + 1$
(B) $2a^2 + 2b$
(C) $2a^2 + 2b^2$
(D) $2a + 3b^2$
(E) $2a + 3b$

17. In the xy–plane, line w passes through the origin and is perpendicular to the line $\frac{1}{3}x + y = c$ where c is constant. If the two lines intersect at the point $(a + 1, a)$, what is the x-coordinate of the point of intersection?

(A) $-\frac{1}{2}$
(B) $-\frac{3}{2}$
(C) $\frac{2}{3}$
(D) $\frac{3}{2}$
(E) $\frac{5}{2}$

GO ON TO THE NEXT PAGE

SECTION 3

18. If the sum of a and b and c is d, what is the average of $a, b, c, d,$ and e ?

(A) $\frac{d+e}{2}$

(B) $\frac{d+e}{4}$

(C) $\frac{d+e}{7}$

(D) $\frac{2d+e}{7}$

(E) $\frac{2d+2e}{7}$

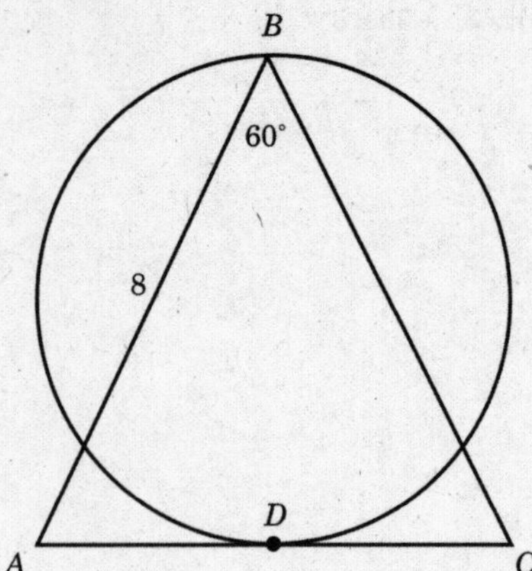

Note: Figure not drawn to scale.

19. The figure above depicts an isosceles triangle, with measurements as shown. Point D bisects the base AC. What is the area of the circle?

(A) $\frac{\sqrt{3}\pi}{32}$

(B) $\frac{\sqrt{3}\pi}{2}$

(C) $2\sqrt{3}\pi$

(D) $4\sqrt{3}\pi$

(E) 12π

20. When 17 is divided by $a + 1$, the remainder is 2. For how many values of a is this true?

(A) 0
(B) 1
(C) 2
(D) 3
(E) 4

S T O P

IF YOU FINISH BEFORE TIME IS CALLED, YOU MAY CHECK YOUR WORK ON THIS TEST ONLY. DO NOT TURN TO ANY OTHER SECTION IN THIS TEST.

SECTION 4

Turn to Section 4 of your answer sheet to answer the questions in this section.

Time—25 Minutes
24 Questions

Directions: For each question in this section, select the best answer from among the choices given and fill in the corresponding oval on the answer sheet.

Each sentence below has one or two blanks, each blank indicating that something has been omitted. Beneath the sentence are five words or sets of words labeled A through E. Choose the word or set of words that, when inserted in the sentence, <u>best</u> fits the meaning of the sentence as a whole.

<u>Example</u>:

Eliza felt ----- when her boss asked her to work seven weekends in a row but ----- when her work earned her a promotion.

(A) enervated . . weakened
(B) depressed . . intellectual
(C) advantageous . . salacious
(D) angry . . shopworn
(E) irate . . elated    Ⓓ ●

1. Formal attire at the wedding was completely -----, because neither the bride nor the groom wanted to force guests to wear anything too fancy or oppressive.

(A) discreet
(B) optional
(C) substantial
(D) celebratory
(E) felicitous

2. That we are depleting our natural resources is no longer a point of-----; all political parties and all members of government agree that something must done to expedite the search for alternative sources of energy.

(A) peroration
(B) restitution
(C) simplification
(D) adjudication
(E) contention

3. In any successful business venture, success is as dependent on ----- as it is on individual vision and drive.

(A) collaboration
(B) constitution
(C) cacophony
(D) colloquy
(E) catapulting

4. The ----- boss burst into the office at 9 A.M. on a Monday, loudly singing an obnoxious song and irritating all the employees, whom he had forced to work all weekend.

(A) beloved
(B) detested
(C) malevolent
(D) adored
(E) thrilling

5. Many independent presses ----- the favoritism that book-reviewers for big-name journals bestow on the products published by larger houses, claiming that this kind of partiality ----- the chance that new, emerging authors can reach a larger audience.

(A) rejoice . . stifles
(B) decry . . hinders
(C) celebrate . . subsumes
(D) lament . . sparks
(E) disparage . . ululate

6. People from both sides of the political spectrum admire the comedian for his -----; political loyalty does not seem to be his main motivation in poking fun at those in power who abuse their positions or embarrass themselves, but rather he delights in playful mockery.

(A) sportsmanship
(B) equanimity
(C) acumen
(D) effluvium
(E) irreverence

GO ON TO THE NEXT PAGE

SECTION 4

7. Charles Rennie Mackintosh's designs are considered ----- and -----, because he frequently adorns windows and doorways with charmingly coiled outlines of roses and fetching curls.

(A) imaginative . . stiff
(B) reductive . . smooth
(C) whimsical . . decorative
(D) polished . . faint
(E) anonymous . . specious

8. How are we to reconcile a society that possesses great ----- for the stigma of poverty and minimal personal accomplishment, yet fails to celebrate acts of ----- that help the poor to elevate their circumstances?

(A) contempt . . aggrandizement
(B) empathy . . beneficence
(C) disdain . . secession
(D) scorn . . benevolence
(E) humanity . . philanthropy

GO ON TO THE NEXT PAGE

SECTION 4

Directions: The passages below are followed by questions based on their content; questions following a pair of related passages may also be based on the relationship between the paired passages. Answer the questions on the basis of what is stated or implied in the passages and in any introductory material that may be provided.

Questions 9–12 are based on the following passages.

Passage 1

Paul Bowles once famously wrote—and here I paraphrase—that there is a difference between a true traveler and someone who simply takes trips. He meant to distinguish between those who travel to a foreign country and try to engage in the culture of the people living there in a manner that is authentic and sincere and those who do not. Sometimes, as he portrayed in his novel *The Sheltering Sky*, a true traveler will be so altered by his experiences abroad that he completely surrenders himself to the experience and returns home changed. This kind of personality is in direct opposition to the professional "visitor" who goes to a country with a checklist of foods to eat and sights to see, as though he were a bird watcher with a field guide, checking off which species he has spotted through his binoculars and returning home completely unaffected by the opportunity to have seen a world vastly different from his natural habitat, but which is still a creation of the human imagination.

Passage 2

While Europeans may still have the luxury of the six-week vacation, Americans by and large still struggle with only two or three weeks a year of so-called leisure time. Sometimes, families will try to schedule these vacations around pre-existing holidays, such as the Fourth of July or Christmas, to stretch a three- or four-day public holiday into a longer family trip. The popularity of these dates, however, means that travel costs are always driven up around this time. Others prefer to search for rest and relaxation during the off-season. But no matter how you cut it, Americans have less and less time to travel, and, as a result, travel agencies are forced to put together tours that follow an aggressive schedule of sightseeing and pre-reserved dining. In the past, no one would have dared visit Rome, Paris, and London in the space of five days, because this miniscule amount of time hardly allows one to adequately absorb the wisdom, age, and grace of these timeless cities—nor a chance to truly change as a result of travel.

9. Passages 1 and 2 both support which of the following generalizations about travelers?

(A) Americans should be given more vacation time to facilitate exploration.
(B) It is ridiculous to travel to a country with an agenda of sights to see.
(C) There are those who are personally unaffected by a trip to a foreign country.
(D) The high cost of travel prevents many from visiting countries overseas.
(E) Readers of novels have a better chance of understanding the personal benefits of travel.

10. Which of the following aspects of travel is addressed in Passage 2 but not Passage 1?

(A) The tendency of some travelers to carry checklists
(B) The scarcity of flights overseas
(C) The preference of some people to travel domestically
(D) The impact that short vacation times have on the ability to engage in leisurely travel overseas
(E) The benefits of learning a foreign language

11. Which of the following in Passage 1 could be an example of the "aggressive schedule" mentioned in Passage 2, line 28?

(A) A checklist of sights to see and foods to eat
(B) A copy of Paul Bowles's novel *The Sheltering Sky*
(C) A pair of binoculars
(D) A foreign habitat
(E) An angry tour leader

12. Passage 1 and Passage 2 both indicate that travel can be beneficial if

(A) it can be done in a cost-effective way
(B) it affects an individual in an internal, personal manner
(C) one travels off the beaten path
(D) one is not forced to travel during public holidays
(E) a tour guide is involved in the planning

GO ON TO THE NEXT PAGE

SECTION 4

Directions: The passages below are followed by questions based on their content; questions following a pair of related passages may also be based on the relationship between the paired passages. Answer the questions on the basis of what is stated or implied in the passages and in any introductory material that may be provided.

Questions 13–24 are based on the following passages.

These two passages discuss different opinions about the jazz artist Wynton Marsalis, who was recently tapped to take over the Lincoln Center jazz program. Passage 1 is excerpted from a magazine article that covers the jazz industry. Passage 2 is excerpted from a book about the history of jazz.

Passage 1

In the last few minutes of Ken Burns's wildly successful documentary on the history of jazz, the jazz trumpeter Wynton Marsalis appears on screen, beaming, trumpet in hand, there to save the day. Prior to this moment, the narrator of the documentary has informed the audience that, after 1963, jazz essentially died. For twenty years, the documentary claims, the great American art form of jazz languished—that is, until Wynton Marsalis arrived, fresh faced, charismatic, and technically fluid, to don the mantle of jazz spokesperson. Given the amount of influence Marsalis seems to have had on the documentary, this point of view is to be forgiven somewhat, particularly when we take into consideration that Ken Burns had not really listened to jazz before making the documentary. Marsalis's fingerprints are all over the documentary, shaping the arc of the story, from the focus on race relations to the aforementioned assertion that "nothing much was happening after 1963."

This criticism shows a surprising naïveté from someone who is as musically conscious and politically savvy as Marsalis. The 1960s and 1970s are generally classified in historical terms as a period of great social upheaval and change, and this restlessness is reflected in the music of these decades. From this revolutionary period, students and listeners of music have been given the spiritual cries of John Coltrane, the intricate abstraction of Ornette Coleman, the elegant chaos of Cecil Taylor, the amusing and uplifting creations of Sun Ra, and the creativity that emerged from fusion, which even Miles Davis, the great trumpeter, championed, but it is true that these periods also saw the rise of the banality of smooth jazz. It is unfortunate that Marsalis, who owes such a debt to Davis, was unable to appreciate the older trumpeter's desire to find what was current in music and to embrace it. Instead, Marsalis has become, as the critic and musician Michael Zilber said, the "Ronald Reagan of jazz," trumping a return to a gentler, quieter, and more feel-good kind of music that does not acknowledge the painful upheaval of an earlier period.

It is certainly one thing to say that, as a listener, one prefers *not* to listen to free jazz. There is such a thing as taste, and it would be inappropriate, not to mention ludicrous, to suggest that everyone should appreciate everything all the time. However, it is also unfortunate that a jazz educator, which is essentially what Wynton Marsalis is, misses the social importance of the music of the free-jazz era, the 1960s and 1970s. Just as rock music of the 1960s became so interconnected with rapid social and political change of the 1960s, so too did jazz provide creative people with an outlet to express their pain, anger, and desire for change. African-American entertainers were in a position, through free jazz, to express their spiritual longing with the precision of an auteurlike filmmaker showing her or his world view. Jazz players became something more than simple entertainers supplying the masses with dance music; they became powerful spokespeople, commenting on the human condition and railing against injustice.

Passage 2

Wynton Marsalis has, in the last twenty years, inarguably been the leading promoter of jazz. He was born in New Orleans, Louisiana, in 1961. The birthplace is important—it was in this great southern city that many say jazz was born and still retains its classical roots. His father, Ellis Marsalis, was a pianist and educator who instilled in his son the importance of practice and hard work. Legend has it that at age six, Wynton received a trumpet from his father's band leader, Al Hirt, and from then on, devoted himself to mastering this instrument, studying classical, jazz, and popular music. In 1980, Marsalis entered the prestigious Julliard School of Music and joined the famous Art Blakey in the latter's jazz group, the Messengers, with which he instantly impressed audiences and critics with his near-flawless musicianship.

As an educator, Marsalis has worked tirelessly to bring the music of his childhood to the masses. Record sales of jazz prior to Marsalis's Grammy Award–winning album in 1983 had plummeted, and if credit for a resurgence in sales is to be given to one pivotal figure, it must be given to Marsalis. Once again, audiences were able to listen to jazz music that was accessible, catchy, and uplifting. Miles Davis, Marsalis's predecessor, had turned his back on an ignorant audience, preferring instead to work with young musicians eager to hone their craft and to stretch the range of the trumpet; Davis's concern was with the music itself and not listeners. For Marsalis, both are equally important, and this is a wise position to take when we consider that music cannot survive without an audience to support it.

GO ON TO THE NEXT PAGE

SECTION 4

In 1988, Lincoln Center formed the Lincoln Center Jazz Orchestra and brought in Marsalis to head the creative effort. Like Leonard Bernstein before him, Marsalis threw himself into the opportunity, reaching out to young people, bringing new jazz players into the fold, speaking sincerely to his audience, and generally working with tireless determination to ensure that one of the greatest American musical art forms did not languish again. Of course, Marsalis has his critics. Many lament his presence on the excellent Ken Burns jazz documentary. These critics should still remember that, regardless of whether they agree with Marsalis, the trumpeter from Louisiana has still done more to help ensure the survival of jazz than anyone else—and much of that promotion has not been self-serving, but in the service of the art form itself.

13. Passage 2 is unlike Passage 1 in that it

(A) is skeptical of Marsalis's categorization of what is and what is not jazz
(B) criticizes Marsalis's ability as a trumpet player
(C) studies the history of jazz
(D) has not viewed the Ken Burns documentary
(E) demonstrates support for Marsalis's mission as an educator

14. According to the author, "Jazz languished" (line 7) because

(A) tastes had changed and people were more interested in rock and roll
(B) jazz died in 1963
(C) the audience for jazz had aged
(D) there were few players who could really play jazz
(E) no one was composing new jazz pieces

15. Lines 9–13 ("Given . . . documentary") were included to point out that

(A) Burns was naturally predisposed to like some artists over others
(B) many of the people Burns covered in his documentary had died
(C) Burns was part of the wave of people newly interested in jazz
(D) Burns was, in many ways, dependent on the knowledge of jazz "experts"
(E) most of the tracks included in the documentary were from old recordings

16. In line 24, the author of Passage 1 suggests that "the spiritual cries of John Coltrane" were strongly influenced by

(A) the political upheaval of the times
(B) a reaction to the entertainment-based jazz of the 1940s
(C) sadness over the death of Armstrong
(D) technological advances in the development of the saxophone
(E) a longing for a "savior" like Marsalis to come on the jazz scene

17. In line 52, "railing" most nearly means

(A) bordering
(B) singing
(C) protesting
(D) approving
(E) nearing

18. In Passage 2, the author mentions Marsalis's birthplace (line 54–55) primarily in order to

(A) ask the reader to sympathize with Marsalis
(B) criticize the early education Marsalis received
(C) express fascination with Marsalis's ability to travel the great distance from Louisiana to his present home in New York
(D) demonstrate how Marsalis's opinions of jazz were shaped by his childhood surroundings
(E) dispute critics' characterization of Marsalis as a "northern" jazz player

19. In line 72, the reference to "accessible" most directly implies the author's assumption that

(A) people were unable to find jazz records to buy
(B) record companies did not make many recordings
(C) music from the 1960s and 1970s had a limited appeal
(D) jazz of the 1960s and 1970s was saccharine
(E) players of earlier decades didn't care if they had an audience or not

20. In line 73, the word "predecessor" refers to

(A) the fact that Davis died before Marsalis
(B) Davis's age relative to Marsalis's, and their shared interest in the trumpet
(C) Davis's interest in classic jazz over Marsalis's interest in free jazz
(D) Marsalis's championing of instruments on the cutting edge of technology
(E) Marsalis's birthplace versus Davis's birthplace

GO ON TO THE NEXT PAGE

SECTION 4

21. The author of Passage 2 implies that Marsalis is "wise" (line 78), because

(A) he focuses on the correct aspects of jazz
(B) without an audience, musicians are unable to make any money
(C) he is fearless when it comes to self-promotion
(D) of his connection to the Ken Burns documentary
(E) he is able to teach so many young children about the importance of jazz

22. In line 82, the use of the name "Leonard Bernstein" primarily serves to emphasize that

(A) Marsalis is a devoted proselytizer and practitioner of jazz
(B) Marsalis likes to conduct his orchestra
(C) Marsalis is a fixture on the New York music circuit
(D) Marsalis's contributions to jazz are limited
(E) Marsalis continues to embrace new kinds of music

23. The authors of Passage 1 and Passage 2 both agree that

(A) Marsalis was the best spokesperson for the Ken Burns documentary
(B) Marsalis continues to define what we should all consider jazz to be
(C) Marsalis has a strong understanding of jazz music and jazz history
(D) Marsalis has a great range of taste for jazz music
(E) Marsalis is the best spokesperson for jazz alive today

24. Which of the following statements about how we are to regard jazz is supported by both passages?

(A) The period of the 1960s and 1970s understandably saw a decline in interest in jazz.
(B) To be a viable art form, that art form must have a broad audience.
(C) Matters of taste are not the same thing as matters of quality.
(D) Jazz as an art form died when Louis Armstrong did.
(E) Jazz is truly the great American musical art form.

S T O P

**IF YOU FINISH BEFORE TIME IS CALLED, YOU MAY CHECK YOUR WORK ON THIS TEST ONLY.
DO NOT TURN TO ANY OTHER SECTION IN THIS TEST.**

SECTION 5

Turn to Section 5 of your answer sheet to answer the questions in this section.

Time—25 Minutes
18 Questions

Directions: For this section, solve each problem and decide which is the best of the choices given. Fill in the corresponding oval on the answer sheet. You may use any available space for scratchwork.

Notes:

1. The use of a calculator is permitted. All numbers used are real numbers.
2. Figures that accompany problems in this test are intended to provide information useful in solving the problems. They are drawn as accurately as possible EXCEPT when it is stated in a specific problem that the figure is not drawn to scale. All figures lie in a plane unless otherwise indicated.
3. Unless otherwise specified, the domain of any function f is assumed to be the set of all real numbers x for which $f(x)$ is a real number.

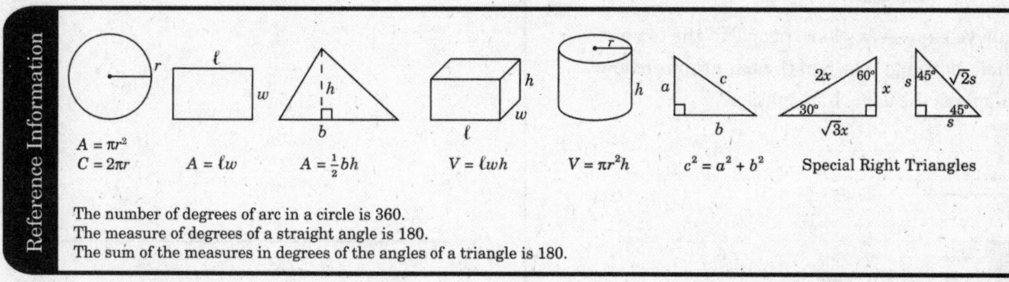

1. If $x - 1 = 7$, then what is the value of $x + 2$?

(A) 7
(B) 8
(C) 9
(D) 10
(E) 11

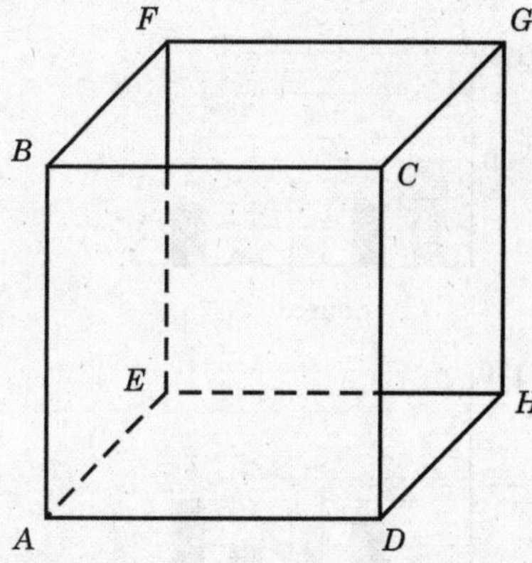

2. The figure above represents a cube. If side $AB = 5$, then all of the following also equal 5 EXCEPT

(A) AD
(B) FG
(C) GH
(D) AG
(E) AE

GO ON TO THE NEXT PAGE

SECTION 5

SOURCE OF CLOTHING PURCHASED

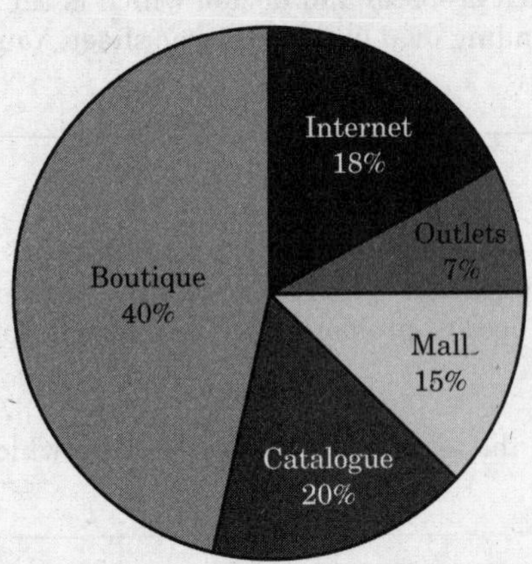

3. The circle graph above expresses where people in the town of Springfield buy their clothing. Which of the bar graphs below most accurately displays the same information?

(A)
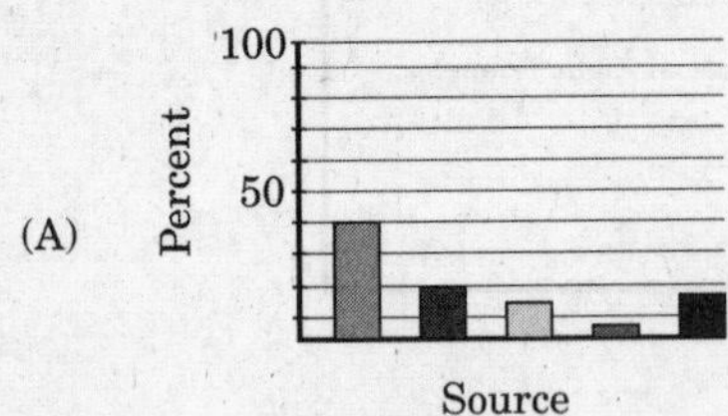

(B)
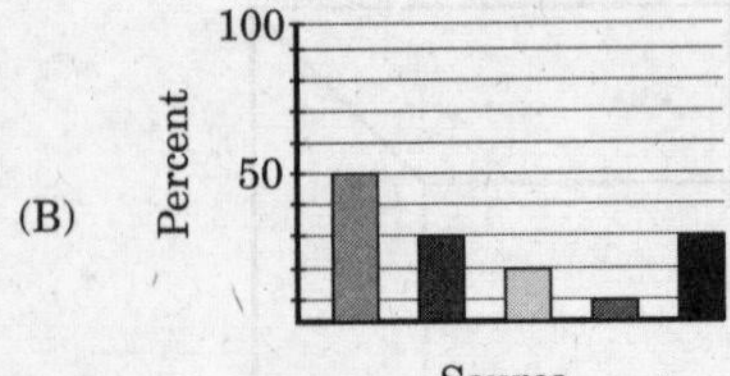

(C)
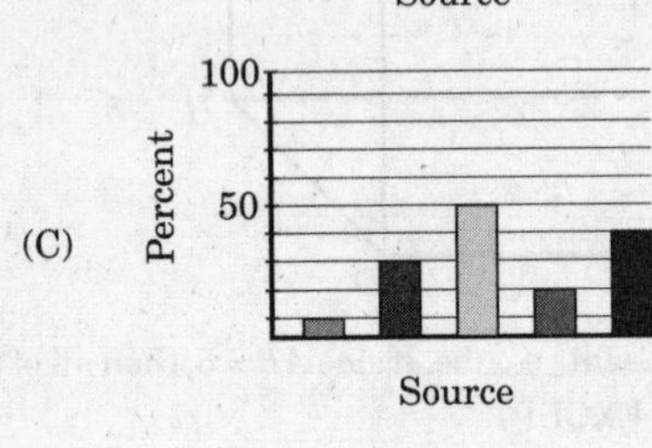

(D)
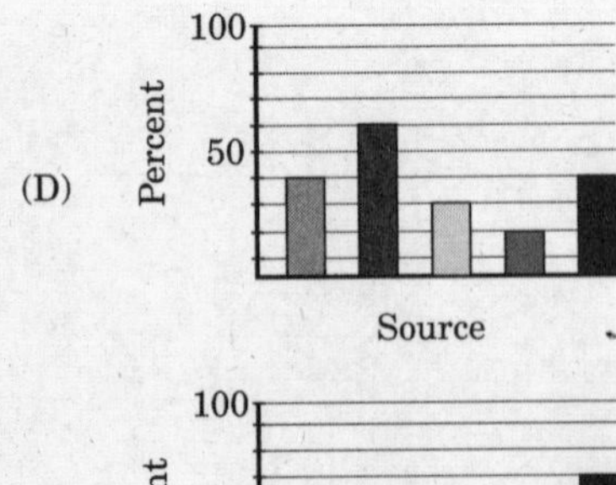

(E)
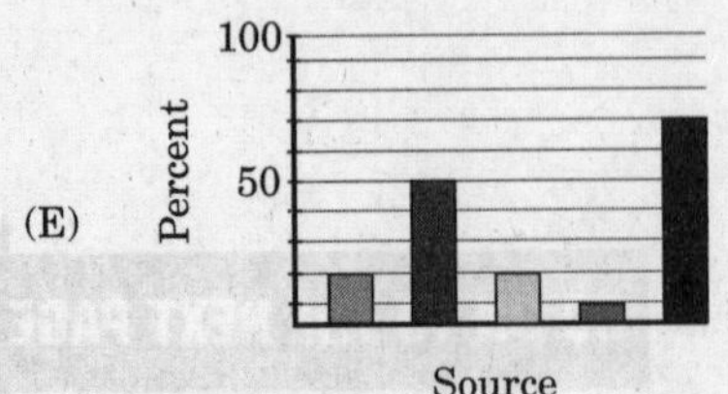

4. The denominator of a certain fraction is 8 more than the numerator. If the fraction ultimately reduces to $\frac{1}{3}$, what is the numerator of the original fraction?

(A) 1
(B) 3
(C) 4
(D) 9
(E) 12

5. If a triangle has an area of 52 and a base of 4, what is its height?

(A) 25
(B) 26
(C) 27
(D) 28
(E) 29

GO ON TO THE NEXT PAGE

SECTION 5

6. If a and b are positive and $5a^3b^2 = 125a^2$, what is $\sqrt{a}$ in terms of b ?

(A) $\frac{25}{b^2}$

(B) $\frac{5}{b}$

(C) $5b$

(D) $25b$

(E) $5b^2$

7. After a rodeo, Jimmy takes his horse and rides due west from the hitching post at a pace of 4 kilometers per hour. His friend Jerry has a slightly slower horse, which goes due south at 3 kilometers per hour. At the end of 3 hours, what is the straight line distance between Jimmy and Jerry in kilometers?

(A) 5
(B) 12
(C) 15
(D) 18
(E) 20

8. Which of the following equations could represent the equation $y = 3x^2 - 2x + 2$?

(A)

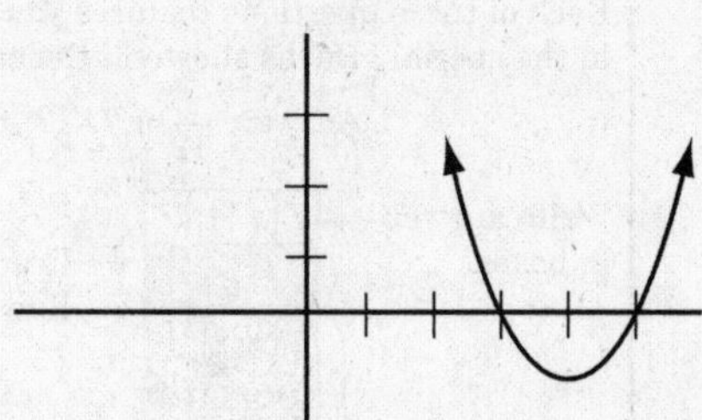

(B)

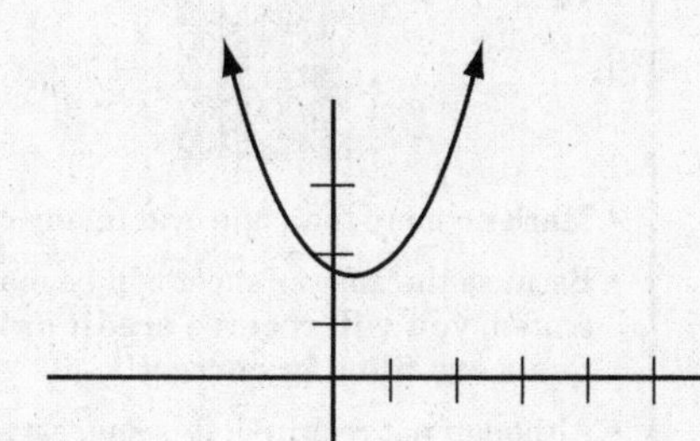

(C)

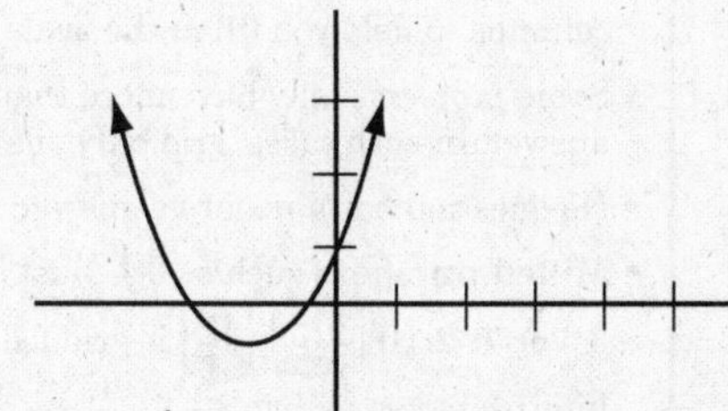

(D)

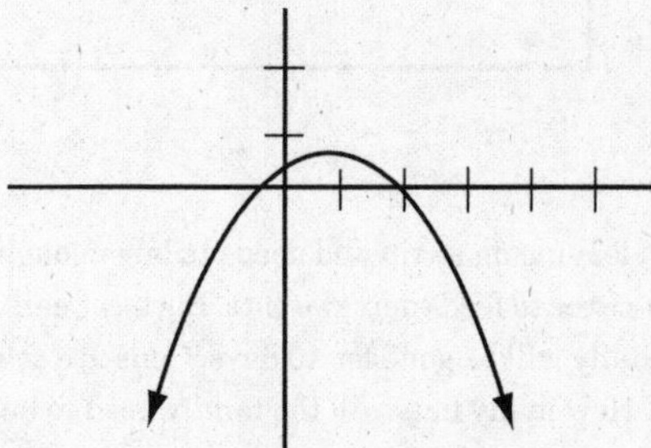

(E)

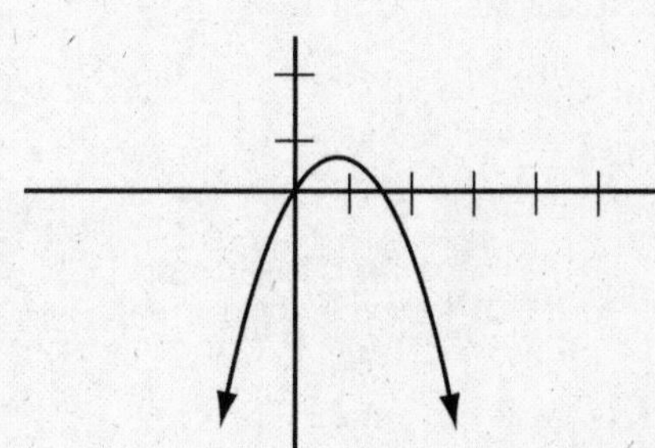

GO ON TO THE NEXT PAGE

SECTION 5

Directions: For Student-Produced Response questions 9–18, use the grids on the answer sheet.

Each of these questions requires you to solve the problem and enter your answer by marking the ovals in the special grid, as shown in the examples below. You may use any available space for scratchwork.

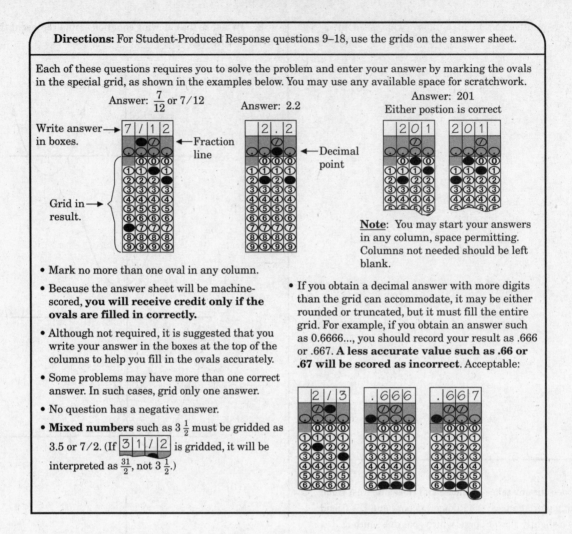

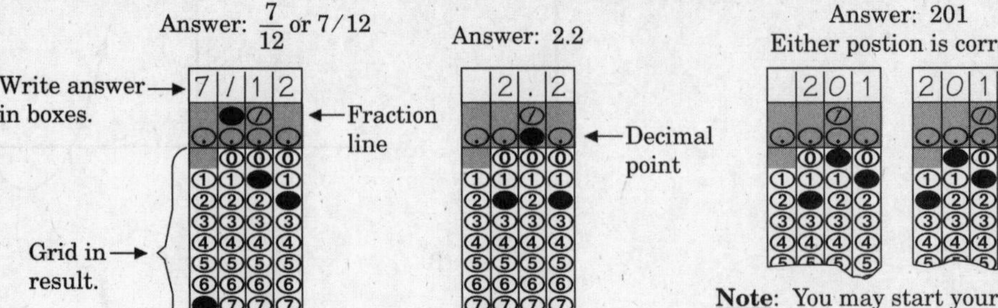

Note: You may start your answers in any column, space permitting. Columns not needed should be left blank.

- Mark no more than one oval in any column.
- Because the answer sheet will be machine-scored, **you will receive credit only if the ovals are filled in correctly.**
- Although not required, it is suggested that you write your answer in the boxes at the top of the columns to help you fill in the ovals accurately.
- Some problems may have more than one correct answer. In such cases, grid only one answer.
- No question has a negative answer.
- **Mixed numbers** such as $3\frac{1}{2}$ must be gridded as 3.5 or 7/2. (If 31/2 is gridded, it will be interpreted as $\frac{31}{2}$, not $3\frac{1}{2}$.)
- If you obtain a decimal answer with more digits than the grid can accommodate, it may be either rounded or truncated, but it must fill the entire grid. For example, if you obtain an answer such as 0.6666..., you should record your result as .666 or .667. **A less accurate value such as .66 or .67 will be scored as incorrect**. Acceptable:

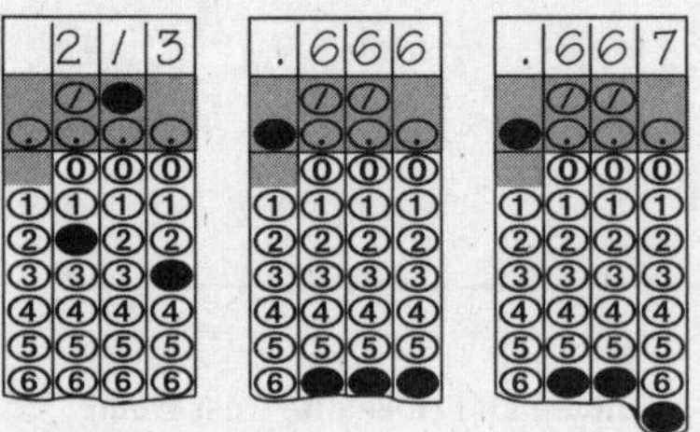

9. A family is leaving on a trip and needs to buy enough cat food for the pet-sitter to feed their two cats. Each cat eats 2 cans per day. The family will be gone for 10 days. Cans are sold in "flats" of 12 each. How many flats will the family need to buy before they leave?

$$|2 - a| = 11$$
$$|a - 4| = 9$$

10. What value of a will satisfy both equations above?

GO ON TO THE NEXT PAGE

SECTION 5

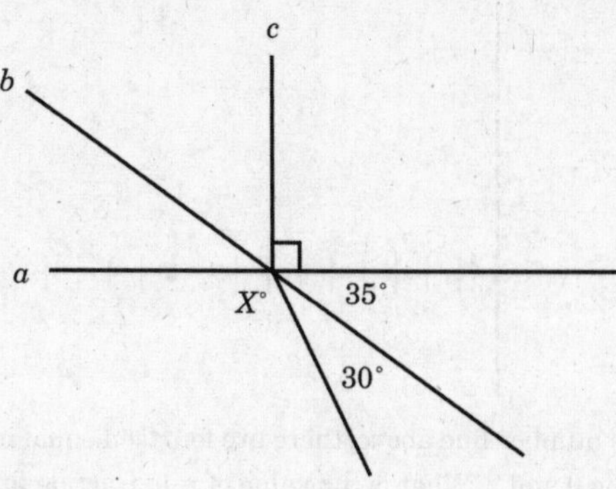

11. In the figure above, line b crosses line a. What is the value of X ?

12. The arithmetic mean of seven consecutive integers is 72. What is the smallest of these seven integers?

13. Let the function f be defined by $f(x) = 2x + 2$. If $2f(c) = 24$, what is the value of $3f(c)$?

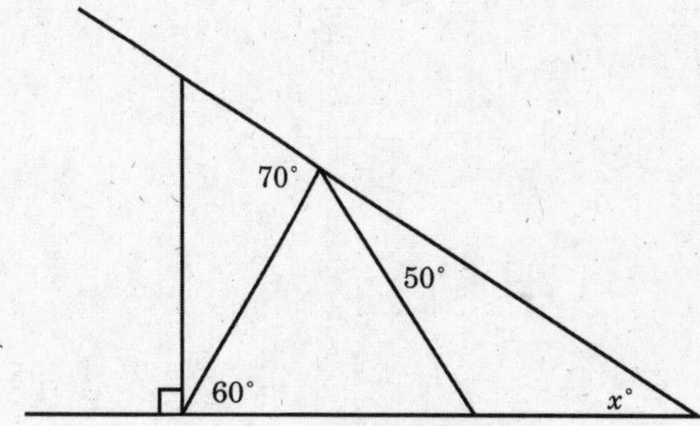

14. In the figure above, what is the value of x ?

GO ON TO THE NEXT PAGE

SECTION 5

15. A certain perfume is mixed in a 1-cup measuring cup. The perfume mixture is started with a base of lilac, which takes up $\frac{2}{3}$ of the cup. The remainder is filled with equal parts lilac, sandalwood, and honeysuckle. What fraction of the final mixture is made up of lilac?

16. If $3x + 2y$ is 200 percent of $2x$, what is the value of $\frac{x}{y}$?

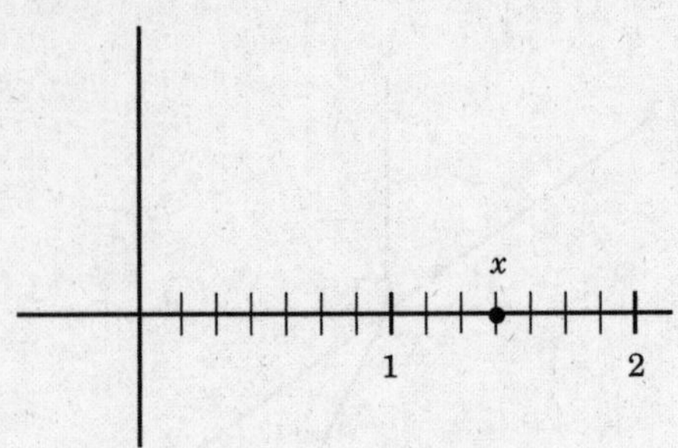

17. On the number line above, there are fourteen equal intervals between 0 and 2. What is the value of x, in fraction form?

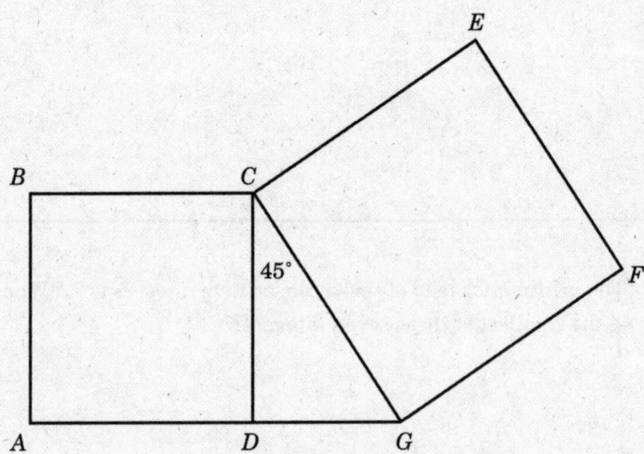

Note: Figure not drawn to scale.

18. In the figure above, $ABCD$ and $CEFG$ are squares. If the area of $CEFG$ is 64, what is the area of $ABCD$?

S T O P

IF YOU FINISH BEFORE TIME IS CALLED, YOU MAY CHECK YOUR WORK ON THIS TEST ONLY. DO NOT TURN TO ANY OTHER SECTION IN THIS TEST.

SECTION 6

Turn to Section 6 of your answer sheet to answer the questions in this section.

Time—25 Minutes
35 Questions

Directions: For each question in this section, select the best answer from among the choices given.

The following sentences test correctness and effectiveness of expression. Part of each sentence or the entire sentence is underlined; beneath each sentence are five ways of phrasing the underlined material. Choice A repeats the original phrasing; the other four choices are different. If you think the original phrasing produces a better sentence than any of the alternatives, select choice A; if not, select one of the other choices.

In making your selection, follow the requirements of standard written English; that is, pay attention to grammar, choice of words, sentence construction, and punctuation. Your selection should result in the most effective sentence—clear and precise, without awkwardness or ambiguity.

Example:

In the poem "Ulysses" by Alfred, Lord Tennyson, the speaker says, "I cannot rest from travel," instead, he will live life to the fullest.

(A) "I cannot rest from travel," instead,
(B) "I cannot rest from travel"; instead,
(C) "I cannot rest from travel" instead,
(D) "I cannot rest from travel," upon which
(E) "I cannot rest from travel,"

1. Matt having already asked Sandy to go to the prom, he was forced to reject Theresa's offer, even though he would have preferred to go with her.

(A) Matt having already asked Sandy to go to the prom, he
(B) Having already asked Sandy to go to the prom, Matt
(C) Already asking Sandy to go to the prom, he
(D) To already ask Sandy to go to the prom, Matt
(E) He, Matt, asked Sandy to go to the prom, so he

2. After visiting the temples in the sweltering afternoon heat, Jim and Nini were as drenched as though walking in the rain.

(A) as though walking
(B) as if walking
(C) as if they had walked
(D) just as though walking
(E) the same as though walking

3. The beneficial properties of dark green vegetables is increasingly gaining more scientific evidence.

(A) is increasingly gaining more scientific evidence
(B) are increasingly gaining more scientific evidence
(C) is more and more increasingly gaining more scientific evidence
(D) is increasingly gaining better scientific evidence
(E) are increasingly gaining increasingly more scientific evidence

4. The crux of the defense's argument, which was whether the defendant had been seen at the scene of the crime.

(A) argument, which was whether or not the defendant had been seen
(B) argument, which was is the defendant had been seen
(C) argument, which was that the defendant had been seen
(D) argument, was defendant seen
(E) argument was whether the defendant had been seen

5. The new commercial airplane, the first one able to seat 900 passengers, flying its maiden voyage and landed safely after four hours in the air.

(A) airplane, the first one able to seat 900 passengers, flying
(B) airplane, the first one able to seat 900 passengers, flew
(C) airplane, the first one able to seat 900 passengers, and was flying
(D) airplane, the first one able to seat 900 passengers, did the flying
(E) airplane, the first one able to seat 900 passengers, there it flew

GO ON TO THE NEXT PAGE

SECTION 6

6. The new doctor and his interns have begun to expand their expertise in neutralizing localized pain, their work in this field has been a cut above the work of most anesthesiologists.

(A) pain, their work in this field has been a cut above the work of most anesthesiologists
(B) pain; they have worked in this field a cut above the work of most anesthesiologists
(C) pain; their work in this field having been a cut above the work of most anesthesiologists
(D) pain; their work have been in this field a cut above the work of most anesthesiologists
(E) pain, for their work in this field has been a cut above the work of most anesthesiologists

7. The light seasoning and use of real meat give the gourmet cat food a flavor no feline can resist.

(A) give the gourmet cat food a flavor no feline can resist
(B) gives the gourmet cat food a flavor no feline can resist
(C) given the gourmet cat food a flavor no feline can resist
(D) giving the gourmet cat food a flavor no feline can resist
(E) give to the gourmet cat food a flavor no feline can resist

8. Possessing as he does an acerbic wit and talent for illustration, Rick is a great artist of political cartoons.

(A) Possessing as he does an acerbic wit and talent for illustration,
(B) In possession of an acerbic wit and talent for illustration,
(C) With an acerbic wit and talent for illustration,
(D) Although he has an acerbic wit and talent for illustration,
(E) Acerbically witty and talented for illustration,

9. Although never exchanging Christmas presents with her children, the eccentric artist considered such traditions materialistic and not worthy of practice.

(A) Although never exchanging Christmas presents with her children, the eccentric artist considered
(B) Despite never exchanging Christmas presents with her children, the eccentric artist considered
(C) The eccentric artist never exchanged Christmas presents with her children, although she considered
(D) The eccentric artist never exchanged Christmas presents with her children, because she considered
(E) Although never exchanging Christmas presents with her children; the eccentric artist considered

10. The song's popularity was so great and spent a week during which time it was number one on the charts.

(A) and spent a week during which time it was
(B) and spending a week during which time it was
(C) then it spent a week during which time there it was
(D) that it spent a week at
(E) that it had spent a week on

11. The reason for the video game's success is that they provide opportunities for both women and men to explore the fantastic landscape in the guise of different genders.

(A) they provide opportunities
(B) they provided opportunities
(C) it provides opportunities
(D) it was providing opportunities
(E) there were opportunities

GO ON TO THE NEXT PAGE

SECTION 6

Directions: For each question in this section, select the best answer from among the choices given.

The following sentences test your ability to recognize grammar and usage errors. Each sentence contains either a single error or no error at all. No sentence contains more than one error. The error, if there is one, is underlined and lettered. If the sentence contains an error, select the one underlined part that must be changed to make the sentence correct. If the sentence is correct, select choice E. In choosing answers, follow the requirements of standard written English.

Example:

The other [A] delegates and him [B] immediately [C] accepted the resolution drafted by [D] the neutral states. No error [E]

Ⓐ ● Ⓒ Ⓓ Ⓔ

12. Although she was never interested in politics before, Amanda Siris spending [A] an unprecedented [B] $28 million to help [C] launch a grass-roots [D] political campaign. No error [E]

13. The discussion over whether [A] the actress's award was merited or were they [B] misguided in [C] being awarded is still [D] being discussed by the press. No error [E]

14. Students which [A] require additional [B] tutoring in math should sign up for [C] office hours on the sign-up sheet posted on [D] the math teacher's office door. No error [E]

15. We were sad to cancel [A] our trip to Japan in May, because [B] we had carefully [C] reserved a hotel room, had stayed [D] there on our last trip two years ago. No error [E]

16. One difficulty the political group faced was how maintaining [A] the interest of groups at [B] the far reaches [C] of ideology while [D] courting those in the center. No error [E]

17. When [A] he is a very talented dancer, he [B] lacks the focus necessary [C] to make it through grueling [D] rehearsals and auditions. No error [E]

18. The extent to which [A] war is damaging to [B] generations is never more clearer [C] than when visiting the Vietnam War Memorial in [D] Washington, D.C. No error [E]

19. The president warned [A] that people has become [B] too dependent on [C] foreign sources of oil and that the government would need to come up [D] with a new national energy strategy. No error [E]

20. Dogs that [A] eat food which [B] contains byproducts will not be as healthy, because they are [C] made with [D] ingredients that have no nutritional benefit. No error [E]

21. This year televised [A] soccer games will use an instant replay in the assistance with [B] seeing [C] which balls are [D] out of bounds. No error [E]

22. Although the singer was [A] initially against to be interviewed [B] by the press, he quickly realized that such an interview would help [C] publicize his new record and agreed to speak [D] with the media. No error [E]

23. Although we expected the French author to be resistant to [A] the idea of her work being translated into [B] English, we later [C] learned that she was actually grateful to the translator for [D] treating her work so sensitively. No error [E]

GO ON TO THE NEXT PAGE

SECTION 6

24. Both (A) California and Tuscany are considered (B) to have Mediterranean climates, the (C) winters in Italy are longer (D). No error (E)

25. Two things contribute (A) to the excellent (B) flavor of Sheila's (C) pasta: the fresh ingredients and the way she pays (D) special attention to the timing. No error (E)

26. The number of (A) compliments that George received for his bleached teeth has calmed (B) his fears that (C) his new smile seems (D) too bright. No error (E)

27. Educators worry (A) that more young people vote for (B) the winner of the television show *American Idol* than (C) in the presidential election (D). No error (E)

28. Until it is (A) accepted as (B) a reputable, alternative form of publishing, web magazines will remain (C) secondary (D) sources. No error (E)

29. All (A) the leading scientists agree (B) that of all the possible alternative sources of (C) energy, nuclear power has the most (D) exciting future. No error (E)

GO ON TO THE NEXT PAGE

SECTION 6

Directions: The following passage is an early draft of an essay. Some parts of the passage need to be rewritten.

Read the passage and select the best answers for the questions that follow. Some questions are about particular sentences or parts of sentences and ask you to improve sentence structure or word choice. Other questions ask you to consider organization and development. In choosing answers, follow the requirements of standard written English.

Questions 30–35 are based on the following passage, taken from an essay on knitting.

(1) *Last weekend, I learned how to turn a sheep into a sweater.* **(2)** *No, I didn't actually turn the entire sheep into a sweater, but I learned how to use its wool for knitting.* **(3)** *Once a year, the Brooklyn Zoo holds a sheep-shearing demonstration, and then expert spinners take the shorn wool, clean it, and spin it.* **(4)** *Did you know that it only takes two pieces of wood or metal to start turning a skein of yarn into fabric?* **(5)** *It can be sewn together to other pieces.* **(6)** *Knitters can make up a pattern for a sweater by figuring out how wide the yarn will knit.* **(7)** *A fatter yarn will knit faster, meaning it will take less time to create a wide piece of fabric that can cover the body.* **(8)** *The woman I watched knit had learned how to do so from her grandmother, who was Scottish.* **(9)** *She was knitting a scarf that had lots of holes in the shape of leaves, she told me that this kind of knitting is called "lace knitting."*

30. The best way to describe the relationship of sentence 2 to sentence 1 is that it

(A) addresses the reader's skepticism about sentence 1
(B) directly contradicts the information in sentence 1
(C) uses a different voice than sentence 1
(D) provides a historical background for the story
(E) introduces a second narrator

31. Which of the following sentences would be most logical to insert before sentence 4?

(A) No, I didn't knit anything myself.
(B) Clearly it is impossible to knit anything unless you know how to do it.
(C) It was a very clear day that day, and I could see everything very well.
(D) My grandmother once knitted me a sweater, but I've outgrown it.
(E) Once cleaned, the wool is spun so that it resembles string, and this, in turn, is coiled into a ball or what is called a "skein."

32. In context, which is the best version of the underlined portions of sentences 4 and 5 (reproduced below)?

Did you know that it only takes two pieces of wood or metal to start turning a skein of <u>yarn into fabric? It can be sewn together to other pieces</u>.

(A) (As it is now)
(B) yarn into fabric, it can be sewn together to other pieces.
(C) yarn into fabric, which can be sewn to other pieces.
(D) yarn into fabric, although it can be sewn together to other pieces.
(E) yarn into fabric. Because it can be sewn together to other pieces.

33. In context, which of the following is the best version of the underlined portion of sentence 7 (reproduced below)?

<u>A fatter yarn will knit faster,</u> meaning it will take less time to create a wide piece of fabric that can cover the body.

(A) (As it is now)
(B) For example, a fatter yarn will knit faster,
(C) I'll bet you didn't know that a fatter yarn will knit faster,
(D) However, a fatter yarn will knit faster,
(E) Even a fatter yarn will knit faster,

34. The author uses all of the following strategies EXCEPT

(A) attempted humor
(B) familiar tone
(C) visual imagery
(D) direct quotation
(E) imaginative description

GO ON TO THE NEXT PAGE

SECTION 6

35. In context the underlined portion of sentence 9 (reproduced below) could best be revised in which of the following ways?

She was knitting a scarf that had lots of holes in the shape of leaves, she told me that this kind of knitting is called "lace knitting."

(A) (As it is now)
(B) leaves she told me
(C) leaves, she therefore told me
(D) leaves, which she told me
(E) leaves; she told me

S T O P

IF YOU FINISH BEFORE TIME IS CALLED, YOU MAY CHECK YOUR WORK ON THIS TEST ONLY. DO NOT TURN TO ANY OTHER SECTION IN THIS TEST.

SECTION 7

Turn to Section 7 of your answer sheet to answer the questions in this section.

Time—20 Minutes
19 Questions

Directions: For each question in this section, select the best answer from among the choices given and fill in the corresponding oval on the answer sheet.

Each sentence below has one or two blanks, each blank indicating that something has been omitted. Beneath the sentence are five words or sets of words labeled A through E. Choose the word or set of words that, when inserted in the sentence, best fits the meaning of the sentence as a whole.

Example:

Eliza felt ----- when her boss asked her to work seven weekends in a row but ----- when her work earned her a promotion.

(A) enervated . . weakened
(B) depressed . . intellectual
(C) advantageous . . salacious
(D) angry . . shopworn
(E) irate . . elated   

1. As outbreaks of polio are becoming increasingly frequent, health officials world-wide are doing their best to ----- third world countries to ----- immunization programs for all children.

(A) chastise . . enforce
(B) encourage . . implement
(C) push . . dismantle
(D) supply . . question
(E) hearten . . deny

2. Claire mentioned her cat's tendency to sleep between the hours of noon and 10 P.M. and to be awake thereafter as an example of how cats in the wild are actually -----.

(A) nocturnal
(B) meek
(C) diurnal
(D) bristling
(E) predatory

3. The other writers respected the older author, because she was both ----- and -----: generous with her advice and time and positive in her general outlook.

(A) redolent . . cheery
(B) obliging . . dour
(C) combative . . wan
(D) altruistic . . .sanguine
(E) accommodating . . morose

4. Some cultures look down on even the most harmless of pleasurable activities, and eating out for dinner is seen as a practice bordering on -----.

(A) platitudes
(B) synchronicity
(C) tact
(D) demolition
(E) debauchery

5. Following the country's declaration that it intended to develop nuclear weapons, its neighboring countries ----- to ----- that country for its desire to add to the pile weapons already in the nuclear arsenal.

(A) scampered . . laud
(B) languished . . fault
(C) hurried . . reprove
(D) scrutinized . . conform
(E) rationalized . . circumnavigate

6. Alternative forms of medicine frequently show no causal effect on advanced illnesses but can serve as a ----- to worried patients eager to feel as though they have some control over their lives.

(A) corollary
(B) panacea
(C) injustice
(D) preemption
(E) fluidity

GO ON TO THE NEXT PAGE

SECTION 7

Directions: The passage below is followed by questions based on its content. Answer the questions on the basis of what is stated or implied in the passage and in any introductory material that may be provided.

Questions 7–19 are based on the following passage, taken from a novel about coming of age in the suburbs.

She had impeccable timing. Which was not to say that she ever showed up when she said she would—or even called when she promised—but that she had a knack of knowing when you were in trouble but didn't know it or, more likely, when it was most inconvenient for you to be required to come to her aid. But despite this character deficiency, or perhaps even because of it, she gave the impression that life as she lived it was somehow more exciting. This is what is so attractive about people who are always in trouble. All the commotion and hollering add up to drama—real and palpable drama—instead of the stuff you see on TV where problems are tied up neatly at the end of the day.

The first time I got a whiff of what our friendship was going to be like was on a Thursday afternoon. She called me from home. We were both sixteen at the time, though she had a driver's license and I had none. Her parents worked about 300 miles from her house, and so she was frequently left alone, and that accounted for why she got a car as soon as she qualified for her license. Her family was also not very poor. I guess they figured all that money added up to something, and setting her free to care for herself didn't seem like poor parenting to them, since all of her material needs were met.

Anyway, she called me on the phone, and I was secretly thrilled. Within the school hierarchy she was someone much more popular than I, though she also had a reputation for being a little bit "wild."

("Like, how is she wild?" I would ask.

"Like, she just *is*," people would say. "Be careful."

"Yes, but what does that mean?" I would persist.

"You'll find out if you aren't careful.")

Anyway, I got on the phone and I was surprised to hear how nervous *she* sounded talking to *me*.

"I heard you don't go out on Saturdays," she said.

"Homework," I said.

"You're only young once," she insisted. "If you don't go out on some Saturdays now, you'll regret it your whole life."

"I'll regret it if my grades drop."

"Your grades won't drop," she said. "They can't. You're just like that. Your grades are like a fixed star in the universe. The essence of who you are. But I'm concerned that you don't go out on Saturdays."

As it turned out, Saturday turned out to be a pretty tame affair, with lots of driving around and stopping to talk to boys who had parked by the beach, or by the park, or other areas where teens were known to congregate. She did all the talking and I watched, and when she ran out of things to say, she blasted the radio on her car to compensate for lack of chit-chat, and she still looked pretty cool. Every now and then we would sit at a light beside another car with a young driver who was also blasting music, and then she would get tense and declare that she was going to race that driver to the next light. These kinds of declarations thrilled me and frightened me at the same time. But almost invariably, the kid at the wheel of the other car would, upon understanding her intentions, turn onto a cross-street, thereby avoiding the whole pressure to race in the first place.

Going out on Saturdays was only a small part of her agenda. I blossomed under her attention. She showed up at my house on Sunday morning and began to weed through my closet, throwing away anything that did not have style. Occasionally she would find something in my closet, and she would declare, "I don't understand why I've never seen you wear *this*." The teachers who told her she was not intelligent should have seen the fast and efficient way that she worked, running a continuous narrative the whole time. "You have to have a lot of shirts and sweaters. People don't notice when you repeat pants so much. But they notice new tops. You have to have a huge supply of tops."

Later she took me to resale shops and thrift stores where we picked for discarded fashionable items that she paid for with money of her own.

I'll never forget the day she showed up at our house one morning, on another Sunday. I had sat down to eat brunch with my family—a tradition that we loved even if other families thought us old-fashioned and quaint—and suddenly there she was in her Mercedes in our driveway, sheepishly looking through the window. I felt awkward, caught between the soothing traditions of my wholesome family and her unregulated, untamed energy. But at my mother's urging, I let her in, and my father immediately began to make extra pancakes for her while she regaled us with stories about how she had gone out to a golf course the night before and slid down one of the slopes on an ice block with a bunch of friends. I was a little jealous that I hadn't been invited, but by then I knew enough to realize that she would never invite me to something that she knew my parents would not approve of my participating in. But hearing about the story this way—in which she was the active participant—my parents were amused.

"Thank you for the pancakes," she thanked my father, like a pro. "I almost never get to eat this kind of stuff."

Later in my room, she begged me to let her take a shower and then to use what small makeup supply I had. And then it dawned on me.

"You didn't go home last night," I said.

"All-nighter," she confirmed.

GO ON TO THE NEXT PAGE

SECTION 7

"What happened?"

"Can you please just help me?" The sorrowful way she said this made me feel a little bit proud that when push came to shove, she had come to me and not to anyone else.

Whatever it was, she didn't want to say, but she went back home looking refreshed, as though nothing terrible had happened, and I thought about how it was that she managed to present the very best of herself to me, to my parents, and to her parents, and how none of us really knew what her days and nights were really like.

7. The passage is best described as

(A) a social commentary on the activities of the nouveau riche
(B) the introduction of a character as observed by a friend
(C) a warning against the effects of poor parenting
(D) a portrait of a strained and repressed individual
(E) a nostalgic depiction of how children grow to be adults

8. Lines 1–5 ("She had . . . aid") are an example of

(A) irony
(B) sarcasm
(C) metaphor
(D) simile
(E) extremity

9. The description in lines 1–11 ("She . . . the day") conveys which of the following about the female character known as "she" or "her"?

(A) shallowness
(B) disrespect
(C) foreignness
(D) introversion
(E) unpredictability

10. As contrasted with the language in the opening paragraph, the advice offered to the narrator by friends (lines 26–29) functions primarily to

(A) warn the narrator of potential trouble
(B) share in the narrator's fascination with the female character
(C) advise the narrator to continue to study hard at school
(D) egg the narrator on to do something potentially dangerous
(E) ignore the narrator and make her feel less than popular

11. As described in lines 41–44, the atmosphere on Saturday night is most nearly one of

(A) danger and excitement
(B) aloofness and coolness
(C) subtlety and wit
(D) frivolity that still seems compelling
(E) conviviality and pleasure

12. In line 55, "agenda" most nearly means

(A) description
(B) inventory
(C) plan
(D) power
(E) cajoling

13. Lines 58–60 ("Occasionally she . . . *this*") create an impression that the narrator is not

(A) happy to have her closet dissected
(B) accustomed to going shopping
(C) pleased with the mysterious female character's advice
(D) naturally comfortable with personal style and social settings
(E) going to go out this Saturday night

14. In context of the passage, the female character's statement in lines 63–65 ("'You . . . of tops'") emphasizes her

(A) stubborn tenacity
(B) overlooked intelligence
(C) general disbelief
(D) wild incoherence
(E) fantastical preoccupation

15. In line 74, the phrase "I felt awkward, caught" suggests that the narrator's delight in seeing her friend is tempered by

(A) concern that her orderly family life will be unsettled by her friend
(B) shock that the family will finally see her friend face to face
(C) embarrassment over what she is wearing
(D) desire to keep her family and social lives separate
(E) discomfort in what she is wearing

16. The narrator's reaction to the female character's story about sliding down the hill on an ice block suggests that she

(A) will later confront her new friend for an explanation as to why she, the narrator, was not included in the party the night before
(B) would not have been interested in sliding down a hill on an ice block
(C) tacitly understands the boundaries that have been set on the friendship
(D) is nervous her parents will disapprove of her friend's behavior
(E) finds her friend's story boring and uninteresting

GO ON TO THE NEXT PAGE

SECTION 7

17. The phrase "like a pro," lines 85–86, emphasizes how

(A) adept the narrator's friend is at handling adults
(B) the friend is accustomed to eating pancakes
(C) the friend tosses off generic compliments
(D) the friend hopes to come back for more pancakes again
(E) tired the friend is from her experiences the night before

18. The line "I almost never get to eat this stuff" (line 86) serves to emphasize

(A) the poor diet the friend follows
(B) the reliance that the friend has on parents other than her own to feed her
(C) the desire the friend has to be part of a normal family
(D) the lack of routine and parental involvement in the friend's life
(E) the lack of food in the friend's house

19. The friend's desire to use the shower and the narrator's closing line present a strong contrast between

(A) the values of the friend's home and the narrator's home
(B) the friend's ordered life and the fast-paced life of the narrator
(C) a desire between the friend to deepen her friendship and the narrator's resistance to do so
(D) the friend's desire for secrecy and the narrator's agreement with this point of view
(E) the friend's outward persona and internal reality

S T O P

IF YOU FINISH BEFORE TIME IS CALLED, YOU MAY CHECK YOUR WORK ON THIS TEST ONLY.
DO NOT TURN TO ANY OTHER SECTION IN THIS TEST.

SECTION 8

Turn to Section 8 of your answer sheet to answer the questions in this section.

Time—20 Minutes
16 Questions

Directions: For this section, solve each problem and decide which is the best of the choices given. Fill in the corresponding oval on the answer sheet. You may use any available space for scratchwork.

Notes:

1. The use of a calculator is permitted. All numbers used are real numbers.
2. Figures that accompany problems in this test are intended to provide information useful in solving the problems. They are drawn as accurately as possible EXCEPT when it is stated in a specific problem that the figure is not drawn to scale. All figures lie in a plane unless otherwise indicated.
3. Unless otherwise specified, the domain of any function f is assumed to be the set of all real numbers x for which $f(x)$ is a real number.

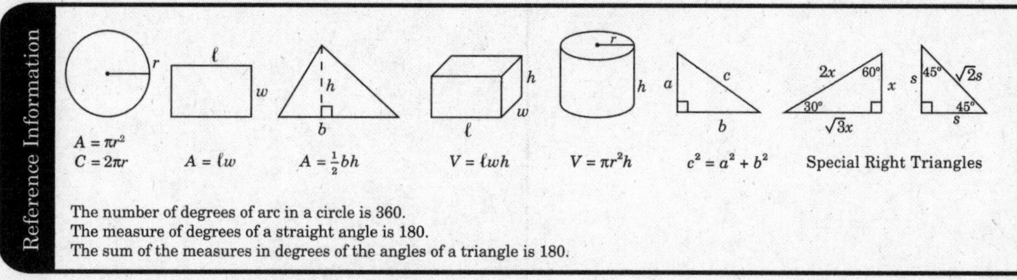
Reference Information
$A = \pi r^2$
$C = 2\pi r$
$A = \ell w$
$A = \frac{1}{2}bh$
$V = \ell wh$
$V = \pi r^2 h$
$c^2 = a^2 + b^2$
Special Right Triangles
The number of degrees of arc in a circle is 360.
The measure of degrees of a straight angle is 180.
The sum of the measures in degrees of the angles of a triangle is 180.

1. If A is the set of odd integers, B is the set of negative integers, and C is the set of integers less than 3, which of the following will be in all three sets?

(A) 3
(B) 2
(C) 1
(D) –1
(E) –2

2. If $x^2 - 7 = 57$, then $x =$

(A) 64
(B) 8
(C) 7
(D) $\sqrt{50}$
(E) $\sqrt{7}$

3. In a survey, 25 doctors suggested that people who suffer from a certain condition take medicine Y, while 14 doctors suggested that people who suffer from the same condition take medicine Z. The rest of the doctors surveyed abstained from recommending a particular medicine. If there were 45 doctors in the survey, what is the ratio of doctors who abstained from recommending medicine to the entire number of survey participants?

(A) $\frac{1}{45}$
(B) $\frac{2}{15}$
(C) $\frac{14}{45}$
(D) $\frac{5}{9}$
(E) $\frac{29}{45}$

GO ON TO THE NEXT PAGE

SECTION 8

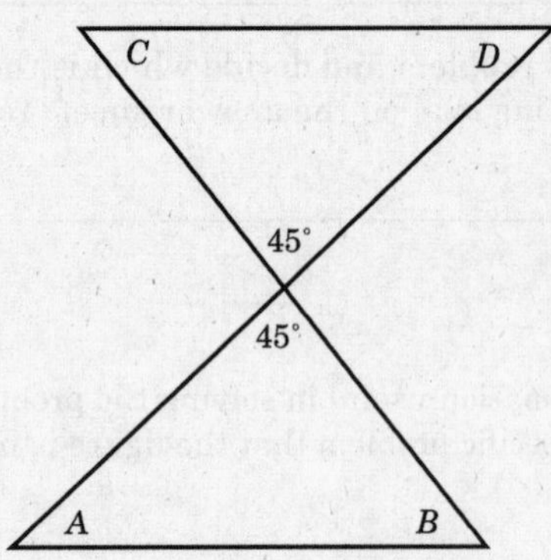

Note: Figure not drawn to scale.

4. In the figure above, what is the value of $A + B + C + D$?

(A) 45
(B) 90
(C) 180
(D) 270
(E) 360

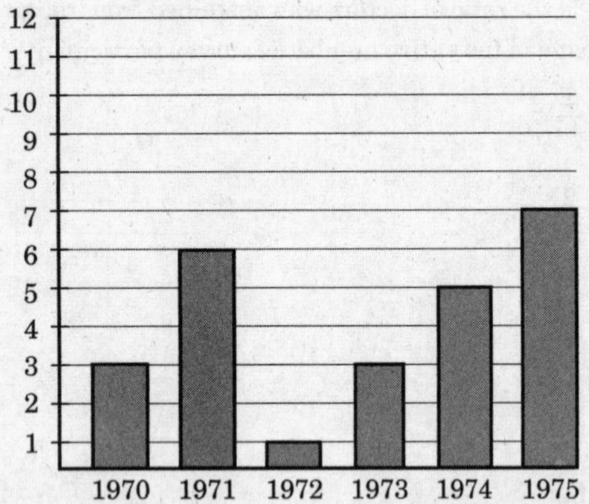

5. According to the graph above, between which consecutive years did the number of inches of rain change the most?

(A) 1970–1971
(B) 1971–1972
(C) 1972–1973
(D) 1973–1974
(E) 1974–1975

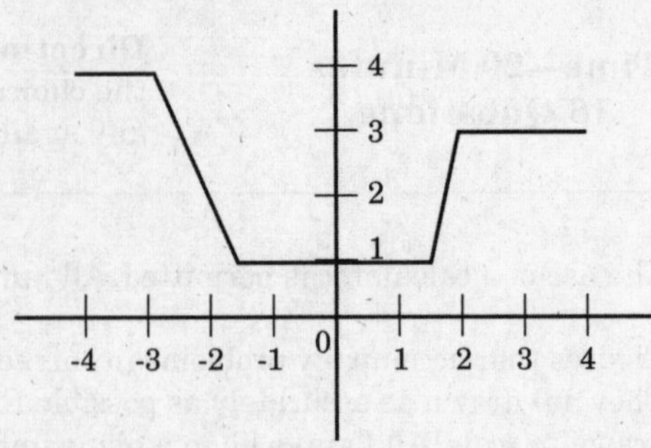

6. The figure above is represented by the equation $y = f(x)$. If $k = -2$, which of the following is a possible value for $f(k)$?

(A) –3
(B) –2
(C) 1
(D) 2
(E) 3

7. If x, y, and z are different positive integers and $(3^x)(3^y)(3^z) = 729$, then $x + y + z$ could equal which of the following?

(A) 0
(B) 6
(C) 7
(D) 27
(E) 37

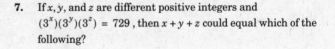

GO ON TO THE NEXT PAGE

SECTION 8

8. In an xy–plane, a square has a corner at coordinate (–3, –8). If the area of the square is 144, which of the following could be the coordinates of another corner of the same square?

(A) (9, 4)
(B) (–3, 9)
(C) (9, 8)
(D) (4, –8)
(E) (–3, 8)

9. A bookshelf can only hold books that are between 10 and 30 inches high. Which of the following inequalities can be used to determine whether a book with height h satisfies the regulation for this shelf?

(A) $|h - 1| < 5$
(B) $|h - 2| < 10$
(C) $|h - 5| < 5$
(D) $|h - 10| < 10$
(E) $|h - 10| < 20$

10. A rectangle has a height of 12, a width of 6, and an area of a. If another rectangle has a height of 2 and a width of 13, what is the area of this second rectangle in terms of a ?

(A) $\frac{a}{3}$
(B) $\frac{a}{2}$
(C) a
(D) $2a$
(E) $3a$

11. If p and q are integers, and $p{*}q = \frac{p}{q}$ if $p < q$ and p is odd, and $\frac{q}{p}$ if $p > q$ and q is odd, which of the following statements could be values for $p{*}q$?

I. $\frac{3}{4}$

II. $\frac{3}{2}$

III. $\frac{3}{7}$

(A) I only
(B) II only
(C) I and II
(D) I and III
(E) I, II, and III

12. The value of 6% of 10% of 8 is equal to what percent of 48 ?

(A) 1,000 percent
(B) 100 percent
(C) 10 percent
(D) 10th percent
(E) 1,000th percent

13. If x and y are distinct positive integers and $x + y < 11$, what is the greatest possible value for xy ?

(A) 25
(B) 24
(C) 22
(D) 21
(E) 20

GO ON TO THE NEXT PAGE

SECTION 8

14. If x is positive, which of the following must be true?

I. $3x > 2x$

II. $x^2 < x^3$

III. $x < \frac{x}{2}$

(A) I only
(B) II only
(C) I and II
(D) II and III
(E) I and III

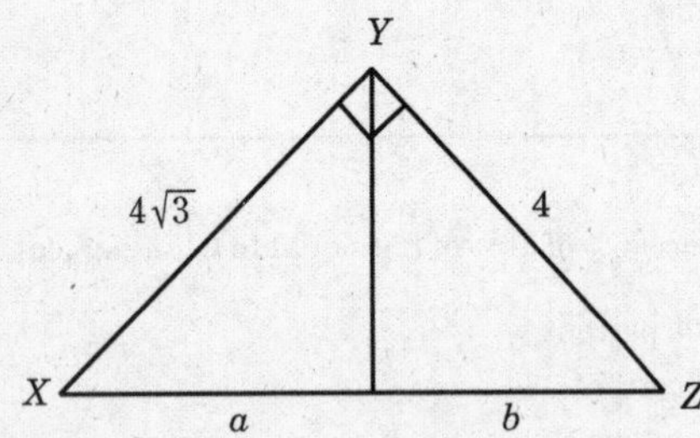

Note: Figure not drawn to scale.

15. In the figure above, what is the value of $2(a + b)$?

(A) 4
(B) $4\sqrt{3}$
(C) 8
(D) $8\sqrt{3}$
(E) 16

16. The figure above shows a cube with sides of length a. Each face of the cube is divided in half and painted as shown. What is the combined area of all the non-shaded triangles in terms of a?

(A) $6a^2$
(B) $3a^2$
(C) $\frac{3a^2}{2}$
(D) $\frac{a^2}{6}$
(E) $\frac{a^2}{36}$

S T O P

IF YOU FINISH BEFORE TIME IS CALLED, YOU MAY CHECK YOUR WORK ON THIS TEST ONLY. DO NOT TURN TO ANY OTHER SECTION IN THIS TEST.

SECTION 9

Turn to Section 9 of your answer sheet to answer the questions in this section.

Time—10 Minutes
14 Questions

Directions: For each question in this section, select the best answer from among the choices given.

The following sentences test correctness and effectiveness of expression. Part of each sentence or the entire sentence is underlined; beneath each sentence are five ways of phrasing the underlined material. Choice A repeats the original phrasing; the other four choices are different. If you think the original phrasing produces a better sentence than any of the alternatives, select choice A; if not, select one of the other choices.

In making your selection, follow the requirements of standard written English; that is, pay attention to grammar, choice of words, sentence construction, and punctuation. Your selection should result in the most effective sentence—clear and precise, without awkwardness or ambiguity.

Example:

In the poem "Ulysses" by Alfred, Lord Tennyson, the speaker says, "I cannot rest from travel," instead, he will live life to the fullest.

(A) "I cannot rest from travel," instead,
(B) "I cannot rest from travel"; instead,
(C) "I cannot rest from travel" instead,
(D) "I cannot rest from travel," upon which
(E) "I cannot rest from travel,"

1. On the deck of the USS *Missouri*, the Japanese and American governments signed a treaty that would have brought an end to the Second World War.

(A) would have brought an end to the Second World War
(B) brought an end to the Second World War
(C) would have ended the Second World War
(D) brings an end to the Second World War
(E) will bring an end to the Second World War

2. The new train line connecting Tokyo and Osaka, consisting of several hundred miles of perfectly straight track that even cuts through hillsides, and provides a very smooth ride.

(A) consisting of several hundred miles of perfectly straight track that even cuts through hillsides, and provides a very smooth ride
(B) and consists of several hundred miles of perfectly straight track that even cuts through hillsides, and provides a very smooth ride
(C) which consists of several hundred miles of perfectly straight track that even cuts through hillsides, and provides a very smooth ride
(D) consisting of several hundred miles of perfectly straight track that even cuts through hillsides, provides a very smooth ride
(E) consisting of several hundred miles of perfectly straight track that even cuts through hillsides, it provides a very smooth ride

3. Many people have heard about the dangers of exposing skin to too much sun, but they do not use this information to make them put on sunscreen daily and maintain this habit.

(A) daily and maintain this habit
(B) daily and maintain this habit each day
(C) by day and maintain this habit
(D) and maintain this day habit.
(E) and maintain this habit daily

4. No sooner had I gone all the way downstairs to exit my apartment but I realized it was raining and I had to go back upstairs to get my umbrella.

(A) but I realized it was raining and I had to go back upstairs to get my umbrella
(B) than I realized it was raining and my umbrella was gotten by me back upstairs
(C) but it was raining, I realized, and I had to go back upstairs to get my umbrella
(D) but I was realized it was raining and I had to go back upstairs for getting my umbrella
(E) than I realized it was raining and I had to go back upstairs to get my umbrella

GO ON TO THE NEXT PAGE

SECTION 9

5. During the 1990s, one reason that the female population was suspected of developing eating disorders, the abundance of food eliminated a fear of starvation.

(A) the abundance of food eliminated a fear of starvation
(B) was the abundance of food that had eliminated a fear of starvation
(C) the food abundance eliminated a fear of starvation
(D) the abundance of food had eliminated a fear of starvation
(E) abundant food eliminated a fear of starvation

6. In the end, Bill will not be remembered for his scandalous behavior any more than they will credit Daphne for bringing about an end to the strike.

(A) they will credit Daphne for bringing about an end to the strike
(B) Daphne is credited for bringing about an end to the strike
(C) Daphne will be credited for bringing about an end to the strike
(D) they will be crediting Daphne for bringing about an end to the strike
(E) they have credited Daphne for bringing about an end to the strike

7. The conductor, composer, and educator Leonard Bernstein was devoted to educating young children, because he believed that if you teach young children to love music they would secure an adult audience in the future.

(A) if you teach young children to love music they
(B) if you are going to teach young children to love music they
(C) with teaching young children to love music they
(D) teaching young children to love music
(E) by teaching young children to love music they

8. Many corporations now offer in-house day care centers, which provide child care for families and a stimulating environment for the child.

(A) , which provide child care for families
(B) and which provide child care for families
(C) ; it provide child care for families
(D) ; it provides child care for families
(E) they provide child care for families

9. One of the first businesses to benefit from the cross-country railroad, the lettuce industry, was based in California and sending fresh lettuce to the people in New York.

(A) the lettuce industry, was based in California and sending
(B) the lettuce industry, based in California, sent
(C) the lettuce industry, it was based in California and it sent
(D) the lettuce industry, was based in California and they sent
(E) the lettuce industry, which was based in California and sending

10. Until laws were passing to protect the friendly and playful animal, sea otters were on the brink of extinction.

(A) Until laws were passing to protect
(B) Before laws were passing to protect
(C) Until laws were passed to protect
(D) Up until the laws were passing to protect
(E) By the time the laws were passing to protect

11. Michelle married Andrew, even though we thought she would actually marry Mike, but she has steadfastly stated she is happy in her choice.

(A) but she has steadfastly stated she is happy in her choice
(B) but she is steadfastly stating she is happy in her choice
(C) however she has steadfastly stated she was happy with her choice
(D) and she has steadfastly stated she is happy in her choice
(E) so she has steadfastly stated she is happy in her choice

12. Challenging the old adage that one should not cast pearls before swine, the ability to ferret out pearls from other precious stones has been trained into Meredith's pet pig Myrtle.

(A) the ability to ferret out pearls from other precious stones has been trained into Meredith's pet pig Myrtle
(B) Meredith's pet pig Myrtle, ferreting out pearls from other precious stones has been trained into this ability
(C) the ferreting out of pearls from other precious stones has been trained into Meredith's pet pig Myrtle as an ability
(D) Myrtle, Meredith's pet pig, has been trained into the ability to ferret out pearls from other precious stones
(E) Meredith has trained her pet pig Myrtle to ferret out pearls from other precious stones

GO ON TO THE NEXT PAGE

13. The editors of the magazine recognized not only that they had a masterwork on their hands but also that the story's publication would have widespread ramifications within the genre of women's fiction.

(A) recognized not only that they had a masterwork on their hands
(B) recognized that they had a masterwork not only on their hands
(C) were cognizant not only that they were having a masterwork on their hands
(D) had recognized not only that a masterwork was on their hands
(E) recognized that a masterwork in essence was not only on their hands

14. One of the most popular jazz records of the 1960s was *Kind of Blue*, in which Miles Davis brought together an all-star group and was the pioneer of a distinctive modal jazz style.

(A) was the pioneer of a distinctive modal jazz style
(B) was pioneering a distinctive modal jazz style
(C) distinctively pioneered a modal jazz style
(D) was the pioneer, resulting in a distinctive modal jazz style
(E) pioneered a distinctive modal jazz style

S T O P

IF YOU FINISH BEFORE TIME IS CALLED, YOU MAY CHECK YOUR WORK ON THIS TEST ONLY.
DO NOT TURN TO ANY OTHER SECTION IN THIS TEST.

PRACTICE TEST 7 EXPLANATIONS

PRACTICE TEST 7 ANSWERS

Question Number	Answer	Right	Wrong	Question Number	Answer	Right	Wrong
Section 2				Section 4, continued			
1	A	___	___	8	D	___	___
2	D	___	___	9	C	___	___
3	A	___	___	10	D	___	___
4	E	___	___	11	A	___	___
5	C	___	___	12	B	___	___
6	B	___	___	13	E	___	___
7	E	___	___	14	B	___	___
8	A	___	___	15	D	___	___
9	E	___	___	16	A	___	___
10	E	___	___	17	C	___	___
11	A	___	___	18	D	___	___
12	C	___	___	19	C	___	___
13	B	___	___	20	B	___	___
14	E	___	___	21	B	___	___
15	D	___	___	22	A	___	___
16	A	___	___	23	C	___	___
17	D	___	___	24	E	___	___
18	D	___	___	Section 5			
19	C	___	___	1	D	___	___
20	A	___	___	2	D	___	___
21	E	___	___	3	A	___	___
22	B	___	___	4	C	___	___
23	E	___	___	5	B	___	___
24	D	___	___	6	B	___	___
Section 3				7	C	___	___
1	B	___	___	8	B	___	___
2	A	___	___	9	4	___	___
3	D	___	___	10	13	___	___
4	E	___	___	11	115	___	___
5	A	___	___	12	69	___	___
6	C	___	___	13	36	___	___
7	D	___	___	14	10	___	___
8	D	___	___	15	7/9	___	___
9	B	___	___	16	2	___	___
10	C	___	___	17	10/7	___	___
11	C	___	___	18	32	___	___
12	C	___	___	Section 6			
13	E	___	___	1	B	___	___
14	C	___	___	2	C	___	___
15	D	___	___	3	B	___	___
16	B	___	___	4	E	___	___
17	A	___	___	5	B	___	___
18	D	___	___	6	E	___	___
19	E	___	___	7	A	___	___
20	D	___	___	8	C	___	___
Section 4				9	D	___	___
1	B	___	___	10	D	___	___
2	E	___	___	11	C	___	___
3	A	___	___	12	A	___	___
4	B	___	___	13	B	___	___
5	B	___	___	14	A	___	___
6	E	___	___	15	D	___	___
7	C	___	___	16	A	___	___

Question Number	Answer	Right	Wrong
Section 6, continued			
17	A		
18	C		
19	B		
20	C		
21	B		
22	B		
23	E		
24	C		
25	D		
26	E		
27	D		
28	A		
29	E		
30	A		
31	E		
32	C		
33	B		
34	D		
35	E		
Section 7			
1	B		
2	A		
3	D		
4	E		
5	C		
6	B		
7	B		
8	A		
9	E		
10	A		
11	D		
12	C		
13	D		
14	B		
15	A		
16	C		

Question Number	Answer	Right	Wrong
Section 7, continued			
17	A		
18	D		
19	E		
Section 8			
1	D		
2	B		
3	B		
4	D		
5	B		
6	D		
7	B		
8	A		
9	E		
10	B		
11	D		
12	D		
13	B		
14	A		
15	E		
16	B		
Section 9			
1	B		
2	D		
3	E		
4	E		
5	B		
6	C		
7	D		
8	A		
9	B		
10	C		
11	A		
12	E		
13	A		
14	E		

CALCULATING YOUR SCORE

Writing Section Raw Score

A. Essay Score (from 1–6) ______ A

B. Section 6 Multiple Choice: ______ (no. correct) – (______ (no. incorrect) ÷ 4) = ______ B

C. Section 9 Multiple Choice: ______ (no. correct) – (______ (no. incorrect) ÷ 4) = ______ C

D. Unrounded Multiple-Choice Score (B + C) ______ D

E. Total Rounded Multiple-Choice Raw Score
(Rounded to the nearest whole number) ______ E

F. Writing Multiple-Choice Subscore
(See the Writing Multiple-Choice conversion table on the following pages) ______ Writing MC Score

G. Total Scaled Score
(See the Writing conversion table on the following pages) ______ SAT Writing Score

Math Section Raw Score

A. Section 3 Raw Score: ______ (no. correct) – (______ (no. incorrect) ÷ 4) = ______ Subtotal A

B. Section 5 Raw Score: ______ (no. correct) ______ Subtotal B

C. Section 8 Raw Score: ______ (no. correct) – (______ (no. incorrect) ÷ 4) = ______ Subtotal C

D. Total Unrounded Raw Score
(Total A + B + C) ______ D

E. Total Rounded Raw Score (Rounded to the nearest whole number) ______ E

F. Scaled Score
(See the conversion table on the following pages) ______ SAT Math Score

Critical Reading Section Raw Score

A. Section 2 Raw Score: ______ (no. correct) − (______ (no. incorrect) ÷ 4) = ______ A

B. Section 4 Raw Score: ______ (no. correct) − (______ (no. incorrect) ÷ 4) = ______ B

C. Section 7 Raw Score: ______ (no. correct) − (______ (no. incorrect) ÷ 4) = ______ C

D. Total Unrounded Raw Score
(Total A + B + C) ______ D

E. Total Rounded Raw Score
(Rounded to the nearest whole number) ______ E

F. Scaled Score
(See the conversion table on the next page) ______ SAT Critical Reading Score

CONVERTING YOUR RAW SCORES

Raw Score	Critical Reading Scaled Score	Math Scaled Score
67	800	
66	790	
65	770	
64	760	
63	750	
62	740	
61	720	
60	710	
59	700	
58	690	
57	680	
56	670	
55	670	
54	660	800
53	650	780
52	640	760
51	640	740
50	630	730
49	620	710
48	610	700
47	610	690
46	600	670
45	590	660
44	590	650
43	580	650
42	580	640
41	570	630
40	560	620
39	560	610
38	550	600
37	540	590
36	540	590
35	530	580
34	530	570
33	520	560
32	510	560
31	510	550
30	500	540
29	500	530
28	490	520
27	480	520
26	480	510
25	470	500
24	470	490
23	460	490
22	450	480
21	450	470
20	440	460
19	430	460

Raw Score	Critical Reading Scaled Score	Math Scaled Score
18	430	450
17	420	440
16	410	430
15	410	430
14	400	420
13	390	410
12	380	400
11	380	390
10	370	380
9	360	380
8	350	370
7	340	360
6	330	340
5	320	330
4	310	320
3	300	310
2	280	290
1	270	280
0	250	260
–1	250	250
–2	240	240
–3	230	230
–4	220	220
–5	210	210
–6	200	200

Writing Subscores

- **Essay Subscore:** Subtotal A from Writing Score (page 606)
- **Multiple-Choice Subscore:** Calculate by plugging in Subtotal E from your writing score (page 606) into the score conversion table below

Raw Score	Multiple-Choice Subscore	Raw Score	Multiple-Choice Subscore
49	80	30	59
48	79	29	58
47	77	28	57
46	76	27	56
45	75	26	55
44	74	25	54
43	72	24	53
42	71	23	52
41	70	22	51
40	69	21	51
39	68	20	50
38	67	19	49
37	66	18	48
36	65	17	47
35	64	16	46
34	63	15	45
33	62	14	44
32	61	13	43
31	60	12	42

Raw Score	Multiple-Choice Subscore	Raw Score	Multiple-Choice Subscore
11	41	2	32
10	40	1	30
9	39	0	29
8	38	–1	27
7	37	–2	25
6	36	–3	24
5	35	–4	23
4	34	–5	22
3	33	–6	21

Writing Scaled Score

MC raw score	Essay Score					
	6	5	4	3	2	1
49	800	790	780	770	720	700
48	790	780	760	730	700	680
47	780	770	750	720	690	670
46	770	760	740	710	680	660
45	770	750	740	700	670	650
44	760	750	730	690	660	640
43	750	740	710	680	650	630
42	750	730	700	670	640	620
41	740	730	690	660	630	610
40	740	720	690	650	620	600
39	740	710	680	640	610	590
38	730	700	670	630	610	590
37	720	690	660	630	600	580
36	710	680	650	620	590	570
35	710	680	640	610	580	560
34	700	670	640	600	570	550
33	690	660	630	590	560	540
32	680	650	620	580	560	540
31	670	640	610	580	550	530
30	660	630	600	570	540	520
29	650	630	590	560	530	510
28	640	620	590	550	520	510
27	640	610	580	540	510	490
26	630	600	570	530	500	490
25	620	590	560	520	500	480
24	610	580	550	510	490	470
23	600	570	540	510	480	460
22	590	570	530	500	470	450
21	590	570	530	500	470	450
20	580	560	520	490	460	440
19	570	550	520	480	450	430
18	570	540	520	470	440	420
17	560	530	510	460	430	420
16	550	520	500	450	430	410
15	540	510	490	450	420	400
14	530	500	480	440	410	390
13	520	500	470	430	400	380
12	510	490	460	420	390	370

Writing Scaled Score

MC raw score	Essay Score 6	5	4	3	2	1
11	510	480	450	410	380	360
10	500	470	450	400	370	350
9	490	460	440	390	360	350
8	480	450	430	390	360	340
7	470	440	420	380	350	330
6	460	430	410	370	340	320
5	450	430	400	360	330	310
4	450	420	390	350	320	300
3	440	410	390	340	310	290
2	430	400	380	330	300	280
1	420	380	370	320	290	270
0	400	370	350	310	280	260
−1	380	360	340	290	270	260
−2	370	340	320	270	260	250
−3	360	330	310	260	250	240
−4	350	320	290	250	240	230
−5	340	310	280	240	230	220
−6	340	310	280	240	220	210

SECTION 2: CRITICAL READING

Sentence Completions

1. **A** One-Word/One-Way *Easy*

The clues here are *who switch to* and *will not be able*. People who start engaging in healthy habits won't be able to "do something" to the effects of bad behavior committed earlier in life. A good guess would be a word that means "get rid or," or *counteract*, **A**.

2. **D** One-Word/One-Way *Easy*

The aristocracy in *The Marriage of Figaro* engages in *most unsavory and therefore unappealing behavior.* You can assume, therefore, that the aristocracy is not well treated by Mozart. A good guess for the blank would be a word that means "made fun of," or *mocked*, **D**.

3. **A** One-Word/One-Way *Medium*

Watch out for the twists and turns in this sentence. You are told that the government of country A *has apologized.* Despite this apology, however, *protests continue*. What does this mean? Clearly, the protests were not geared toward getting an apology from the government of country A. Instead, it's safe to assume that the protesters from country B are angry at their *own government*. A good guess for the blank would be something like "an indication of" or "reflecting." **A**, *testament to*, is the best answer.

4. **E** Two-Word/One-Way *Medium*

Karnatic music uses *many flourishes and arresting half-tones.* In other words, it is very "complicated." Eliminate **B** and **D**. As a result of this kind of complex musical structure, Karnatic music *may strike listeners accustomed to the tonality of Western music as* "something." A good guess would be a word like *difficult* or *ugly*, since karnatic music is in strong contrast to the *tonality* of Western music. Only **E** fits.

5. **C** Two-Word/One-Way *Difficult*
The word *numerous* tells you that the internet has "a lot of" *links, data-capturing devices, and complex, animated ads.* In other words, the internet has become very complicated: it is "full of" *links*, etc. So, what kinds of days are over? The days when a "casual" hobbyist could be hired to build a website for a company. The correct answer must be **C**.

Short Reading Passages

6. **B** Implied Information *Medium*
Here are the essential lines you need to answer this question: *Ellen Nussey, Charlotte's childhood friend, carefully saved every one of her friend's correspondences, directly against the wishes of Charlotte's husband. And while these letters are invaluable, they are frustrating to the literary detective, for they show quiet musings of a domestic nature.* Ellen saved letters, even though Charlotte's husband did not want her to do so. These letters are *quiet* and lack the ferocity of the one letter that we do have written to Mary. Thus the Ellen Nussey letters *show only one side* of Charlotte's character. Watch out for **D**: the passage expressly states that the family did not want Ellen to save these letters.

7. **E** Themes and Arguments *Medium*
Take a look at the line referenced: *As a result, we have the mistaken impression of Charlotte as a quiet woman whose passion was hidden and only expressed on occasion.* The author is referring to the fact that we do not have in our possession all of the letters written by Charlotte in her lifetime. We do, however, have the letters that Charlotte wrote to Ellen. The author then makes the point that these letters only give us one picture of Charlotte's nature. If we had Mary's letters, we would have a more complete picture of Charlotte as a person. In other words, the *mistaken impression* is our understanding of Charlotte's character.

8. **A** Implied Information *Difficult*
To answer this question, you need to have understood this line: *I worry, however, about the tendency to paint these people as virtuous simply as a result of their unfortunate position in society.* The word *virtuous* in this case means "possessing high virtue" or "possessing a character of high moral value." Another way of stating this is to say that minorities have sometimes been portrayed as being *perfect*, **A**.

9. **E** Words in Context *Medium*
The passage is written by a scholar examining how other scholars observe and write about minorities. The line in question is *if we are to truly examine the lives of minorities, we must do so with an open mind and paint them in all their garish colors and varying shades of virtuousness.* The word *paint* here is used metaphorically and does not really mean that the author intends to *paint* anyone in the literal sense of the word. Rather, he wishes to "describe" minorities in all their complexity.

Long Reading Passages

10. **E** Themes and Arguments *Medium*

Take a look at the lines surrounding the referenced line in the question: *He meant that when we look through a telescope, objects would appear even larger to us than they actually were. Certainly we are all now familiar with the concept of the speed of light, which, while very fast, is not so fast that objects viewed in distant galaxies are now in the same shape as they were when we spied them through a telescope. In other words, when we look at galaxies, we are looking at them in a past form—it takes light that long to reach us.* The author opens with the idea that what we see when we look through a telescope may not reflect reality. The line about the speed of light helps to support this concept.

11. **A** Implied Information *Easy*

The entire opening paragraph is devoted to introducing the idea that distant objects viewed through a telescope may be magnified by other heavenly bodies in the universe. This was a hypothesis put forward by Einstein, which, according to the author, has since been proven to be true. Watch out for **C**, which introduces the idea that Einstein didn't trust telescopes—nowhere is this stated in the passage. All we know is that Einstein thought that objects would be distorted by the universe. He didn't make any judgments about telescopes.

12. **C** Themes and Arguments *Medium*

Look at the following sentence: *When you look out at the night sky or even through the average telescope, the stars and galaxies are only a small part of what actually exists "out there."* This sentence contains an instruction: you are told to think about what you see when you look at the night sky, or **C**. Watch out for **A**. The author doesn't mention "stars" and "galaxies" at this point in the passage to help prove the existence of cosmic shear. That occurs later in the passage, not here.

13. **B** Technique *Medium*

In paragraph two, the author summarizes information about dark matter and dark energy that scientists have studied in the recent past. To contrast between these relatively recent studies, the author opens paragraph three with the phrase *Now comes word*. The author wants to demonstrate just how new the information regarding cosmic shear is: it is very new.

14. **E** Technique *Medium*

The author describes how cosmic shear works by using an analogy (the light bulb) and discussing the tools used by scientists. The author, however, remains very neutral. We don't know who he is, and he does not ever announce his presence. We do not, in other words, have a firsthand account.

15. **D** Themes and Arguments *Difficult*

You are looking for the fact that, if true, would undermine the discovery resulting from the study of the Sloan galaxies. Every single answer listed here is accounted for in the passage and helps to strengthen the author's point, except for **D**, which directly contradicts what is stated in the passage.

16. **A** Themes and Arguments *Easy*
The detail about the *brightness and color* of heavenly bodies is included to show how, despite a complication in studying quasars and galaxies, scientists can still determine the effect of cosmic shear. But paragraph 4 goes on to explain: *However, the light bending from galaxies may make a quasar "move" and appear to have a different density and placement in the sky. Scientists therefore need to examine a host of properties—brightness and color—to determine exactly how far away a quasar actually is and by how much it has been magnified.* **A** best restates this idea.

17. **D** Themes and Arguments *Easy*
Take a look at the following sentence: *The most abstract of ideas has always come into practical use much later—for example, Benjamin Franklin's dalliance with electricity seemed the hobby of an eccentric.* Here the author argues that a scientific discovery that may seem abstract at the time can have a practical use later on. Franklin's interest in electricity is one such scientific discovery.

18. **D** Words in Context *Easy*
Look at the sentence as it is used in context: *Benjamin Franklin's dalliance with electricity seemed the hobby of an eccentric.* Note the words *hobby* and *eccentric*. These are clues, which suggest that Franklin's interest in electricity was casual and not necessarily purposeful. A good prediction would be something along the lines of "slight interest," or *mild flirtation*.

19. **C** Main Idea *Medium*
The author spends almost the entire passage exploring what the Japanese consider beautiful, using the cherry blossom as an illustrative example. Watch out for **A**, which focuses on a detail contained in one paragraph, but not the entire passage. **E** is far too broad. Only **C** correctly encapsulates the scope of the passage.

20. **A** Words in Context *Easy*
Look at the sentence in which the word *transience* is used: *From such an awareness arises a deep sense of sadness that life, and therefore beauty, are impermanent. Nothing, according to the Japanese, better captures this sense of transience than the cherry blossom, which blooms for a short period of time before dying.* Note the clues: *impermanent, blooms for a short period.* A good prediction for *transience* would therefore be something that means "short-lived," or *fleeting*, **A**.

21. **E** Specific Information *Medium*
Look at the line describing the relevance of poems dedicated to cherry blossoms: *Literally thousands of poems have been written in praise of the cherry blossom in all its stages and all of its powers.* The author wants the reader to understand that cherry blossoms are viewed as having their own "power." **E** best restates this idea.

22. **B** Implied Information *Medium*
Here is what the author says about Western nature poetry: *Nature poetry exists in the West too, but it is different. Western poetry about nature is generally celebratory and generally focuses on the power of spring to express rejuvenation.* In other words, whereas the Japanese poets focus on the impermanence of beauty—and the poignant emotions elicited by this image—Western poets focus on nature's regenerative, springlike properties.

23. **E** Specific Information *Difficult*
The author says that *wabi-sabi* celebrates what is "imperfect" in nature. The correct answer will therefore be something similar to the word *imperfect*. **E** best restates "something that is not perfect"; all the other choices are mean "balanced" or "symmetrical."

24. **D** Themes and Arguments *Medium*
Remember, the correct answer to a Critical Reading question on the SAT is one that clearly restates an idea expressed in the passage. In the last paragraph, the author writes, *Certainly modern-day Japanese continue to reflect this cultural characteristic.* This characteristic refers to the Japanese love of cherry blossoms—and all that those blossoms represent. The author then goes on to describe how, using modern technology, contemporary Japanese continue to appreciate the singular powers of the cherry blossom. **D** best restates this idea. Watch out for **C** and **E**, which introduce ideas not covered in the passage.

SECTION 3: MATH

Multiple Choice

1. **B** Algebra: Solving Equations *Easy*
Simplify the expression and solve for a:

$$2a + 6 = 7a + 1$$
$$6 = 5a + 1$$
$$5 = 5a$$
$$1 = a$$

2. **A** Numbers & Operations: Sequences *Easy*
You need to determine how each subsequent number in the sequence was formed. Here's the sequence: 3, 8, 23, 68. With a little trial and error, you should notice that:

$$3 \times 3 = 9$$
$$9 - 1 = 8$$
$$8 \times 3 = 24$$
$$24 - 1 = 23$$

Now, the problem says that you will multiply by x, but subtract by y. In this case, x is equal to 3 and y is equal to 1. Note that you are asked to solve for y, not for x. Therefore, the answer is 1.

3. **D** Data Analysis, Statistics & Probability: Permutations and Combinations *Easy*
To find the total number of combinations possible, simply multiply the number of types of shoes by the number of types of jeans. There are 4 kinds of shoes and 4 kinds of jeans:

$$4 \times 4 = 16$$

4. **E** Algebra: Functions *Easy*

The only way that $f(-2)$ could ever be larger than $f(2)$ is if the function had a way to turn the negative number, –2, into a positive, while the positive number, 2, could become negative. Look at **E**, $f(x) = -2x^3$.

Now, see what happens when you plug in –2:

$$f(x) = -2x^3$$
$$f(-2) = -2(-2)^3$$
$$f(-2) = -2(-8)$$
$$f(-2) = 16$$

But look what happens when you plug in 2:

$$f(x) = -2x^3$$
$$f(2) = -2(2)63$$
$$f(2) = -2(8)$$
$$f(2) = -16$$

In this instance, $f(-2)$ is much larger than $f(2)$.

5. **A** Numbers & Operations: Ratios *Easy*

This is a proportion problem. To find the answer, you will need to set up a straightforward proportion. You are told that there are always 5 parts espresso for every 12 parts milk. You are then asked to find how much milk is necessary for 13 parts espresso. Set up the following proportion and solve:

$$\frac{5 \text{ espresso}}{12 \text{ milk}} = \frac{13 \text{ espresso}}{x \text{ milk}}$$
$$(12 \text{ milk})(13 \text{ espresso}) = 5 \text{ espresso}(x \text{ milk})$$
$$156 = 5x$$
$$31.2 = x$$

6. **C** Geometry: Angles and Lines *Easy*

If you have difficulty with this problem, try drawing a picture to make it more concrete.

You are told that line AC has a midpoint of B. The picture would look something like the following:

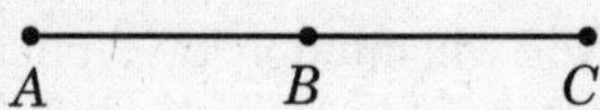

Now, take the statements one at a time. Is $AB = \frac{1}{2}AC$? Yes, because point B divides the line exactly in half. Eliminate **B**. Next take the second statement. Is $\frac{1}{2}AB = \frac{1}{2}BC$? Yes, because AB and BC are equal. Eliminate **A** and **D**. Finally, look at the third statement. Is $2BC = \frac{1}{2}AC$? No, definitely not. $2BC$ would equal the length of AC, not half of it. The answer must be **C**.

7. **D** Algebra: Substitution *Medium*

This problem is not as difficult as it seems if you work algebraically. Note that both equations have the term b in common. You can substitute $4b$ in the first equation with $12c$, then solve:

$$3a = 4b \text{ and } 4b = 12$$
$$3a = 12c$$
$$a = 4c$$

8. **D** Algebra: Substitution *Medium*

To answer this problem quickly, try plugging in numbers. Let's say there are 16 crates of strawberries total. There are 4 trucks, each of which can carry 5 crates. In other words, all together, the trucks could carry 20 crates, but with only 16 crates of strawberries, there will be 4 slots leftover—exactly what the problem calls for. Now, plugging in the above values for s, t, and c, see which equation will be true. Only **D** works:

$$s = tc - 4$$
$$16 = 4(5) - 4$$
$$16 = 20 - 4$$
$$16 = 16$$

9. **B** Algebra: Angles and Lines *Medium*

Remember, there are always 180 degrees in a straight line. Since one angle is marked 70 degrees, you can assume that the angle next to it is 110. Note that the 110-degree angle and the 30-degree angle form a triangle, which, in turn, will always have 180 degrees. The missing angle will thus be 40 degrees. Now your figure looks like this:

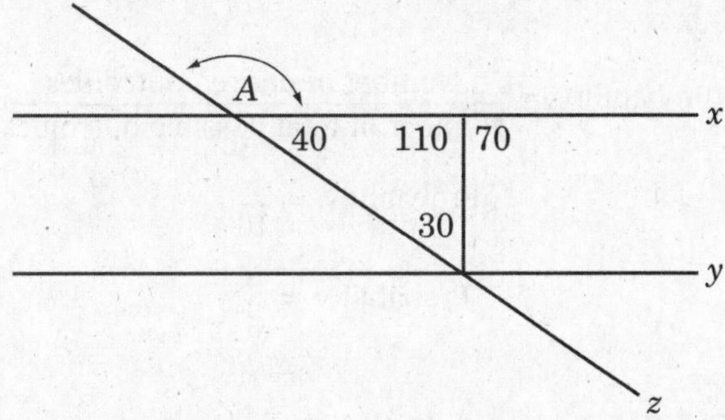

Again, since there are 180 degrees in a line, the angle next to the 40 degree angle will be 140. Since opposite angles are equal, angle A must be 140.

10. **C** Algebra: Absolute Value and Exponents *Medium*

This problem tests your understanding of number properties. The statement will only be true if x is equal to 0 or 1.

$$2x^3 = 2x^2$$
$$2(0)^3 = 2(0)^2$$
$$0 = 0$$

11. **C** Geometry: Circles *Medium*

This is a geometry question disguised as a word problem. You are comparing the diameters and circumferences of two circles. The diameter of the first log of sushi is one-third the diameter of the second log of sushi. Try plugging in numbers. Let's say that the diameter of the first log of sushi is 1 and the diameter of the second log of sushi is 3. Now, look at the circumferences.

Circumference of first log of sushi	Circumference of second log of sushi
$C = \pi d$	$C = \pi d$
$C = \pi 1$	$C = \pi 3$

Note that the circumference of the second log of sushi is three times the size of the circumference of the first log of sushi. This means that you will need a piece of seaweed that is three times as long as the first piece of seaweed in order to cover the entire circumference.

12. **C** Data Analysis, Statistics & Probability: Statistical Analysis *Medium*

The first ball is drawn and it is red. The probability of having drawn this ball is $\frac{5}{11}$.

Remember, the formula for probability is: $\frac{\text{Number of desired outcomes}}{\text{Number of total possible outcomes}}$

In the case of this problem:

$$\text{Probability} = \frac{\text{Number of red balls}}{\text{Number of total balls}} = \frac{5}{11}$$

So, there are 5 red balls, and originally there was a total of 11 balls. In other words, of the 11 original balls, 5 were red and 6 were blue. However, once the first ball is drawn and not replaced, you want to find the probability of drawing a blue ball. Note that now you only have 10 balls total:

$$\text{Probability} = \frac{\text{Number of desired outcomes}}{\text{Number of total possible outcomes}}$$

$$\text{Probability} = \frac{6}{10}$$

$$\text{Probability} = \frac{3}{5}$$

13. **E** Algebra: Binomials and Quadratics *Medium*

Plug in the values given, simplify, and solve:

$$C(x) = x^2 - 60x + k$$
$$300 = (30)^2 - (60)30 + k$$
$$300 = 900 - 1,800 + k$$
$$300 = -900 + k$$
$$1,200 = k$$

14. **C** Numbers & Operations: Inequalities *Medium*

The values must be positive and distinct—that is, they must be different from each other. Try the first two positive integers, 1 and 2:

$$3a + 2b \leq 8$$
$$3(1) + 2(2) \leq 8$$
$$3 + 4 \leq 8$$
$$7 \leq 8$$

Now, see what happens if you reverse the placements:

$$3(2) + 2(1) \leq 8$$
$$6 + 2 \leq 8$$
$$8 \leq 8$$

Next, try 1 and 3:

$$3a + 2b \leq 8$$
$$3(1) + 2(3) \leq 8$$
$$3 + 6 \leq 8$$

9 is not less than 8

There are only two possible pairs, **C**.

15. **D** Geometry: Triangles *Medium*

All the measurements of the sides of the triangles must be an integer value, according to the information given in the question. You are asked to find the greatest value by which the triangle *DEF* could be larger than triangle *ABC*. In other words, if you knew the smallest possible value for the perimeter for triangle *ABC*, you would then know the maximum amount by which the perimeter of triangle *DEF* could be larger. First, note that two of the angles in *DEF* measure 60; this means that all three angles measure 60 degrees, and that all sides are equal, or all are 6. The perimeter of the triangle *DEF* is therefore 18. Now, look at triangle *ABC*. You are given two sides, but not the third. At this point, you might be tempted to choose **A** as your answer, but you would be wrong. Remember: the sum of any two sides of a triangle must be larger than the third side. The smallest possible integer value for side *BC* is therefore 5. In this instance, the perimeter of triangle *ABC* would be 15. The perimeter of triangle *DEF* would therefore be 3 units larger.

16. **B** Numbers & Operations: Basic Operations *Medium*

Choosing the correct numbers will be the best way to solve this question. The first numbers that might come to mind are 2 and 4, but this pair will not help you solve the question. However, if you choose $a = 0$ and $b = 2$, then you can find the answer:

$$b^2 = (2)^2 = 4$$

Since **A** adds 1 to the even product of 2 and a, you know it will never be equal to b^2—which will always be even as well. Try **B**, $2a^2 + 2b$. Substitute:

$$2(0)^2 + 2(2)$$
$$0 + 4$$
$$4$$

17. **A** Geometry: Coordinate Geometry *Medium*

The x coordinate of the point of intersection will be $a + 1$. Your job, therefore, is to find the value of a, then add 1. Take a look at the first equation: $\frac{1}{3}x + y = c$. Rewritten, the equation is $y = -\frac{1}{3}x + c$. The line that passes through the origin is perpendicular to this line. A perpendicular line of one equation has the inverse, opposite slope of the previous equation. Since the slope of the first line is $-\frac{1}{3}$, you know that the slope of the second line is 3. Also, since the second line passes through the origin, you know that the x and y intercepts are both 0. Now, you are asked to find the point of intersection between the two lines, and you are told that they are consecutive numbers. Using the equation of the second line, set up an equation to solve for the consecutive points.

$$\begin{aligned} y &= 3x \\ a &= 3(a+1) \\ a &= 3a+3 \\ -2a &= 3 \\ a &= -\frac{3}{2} \\ a+1 &= -\frac{3}{2}+\frac{2}{2} \\ a+1 &= -\frac{1}{2} \end{aligned}$$

18. **D** Data Analysis, Statistics & Probability: Statistical Analysis *Medium*

The formula for average is $\frac{\text{sum of terms}}{\text{number of terms}}$.

There are 5 terms in the list a, b, c, d, and e. The letter d counts as the sum of three terms, $a + b + c$. To find the average, you will need to take twice the value of d, add this to e, and divide by 5. **D** expresses this information in algebraic form.

19. **E** Geometry: Circles *Difficult*

If point D bisects line AC, with point B touching the edge of the circle, then you know that drawing a line from B to D will give you the diameter of the circle. Note that line BD divides triangle ABC into two triangles—with angles measuring 30, 60, and 90 degrees—forming special triangles with sides measuring x, $x\sqrt{3}$, and $2x$. The diameter of the circle will be the side of each triangle opposite the 60-degree angle. If the hypotenuse of each triangle is 8, then the other sides will measure 4 and $4\sqrt{3}$. The diameter, therefore, measures $4\sqrt{3}$ and the radius $2\sqrt{3}$. Now, solve for the area of the circle:

$$\begin{aligned} A &= \pi r^2 \\ A &= \pi(2\sqrt{3})^2 \\ A &= \pi(4)(3) \\ A &= 12\pi \end{aligned}$$

20. **D** Numbers & Operations: Divisibility and Remainders *Difficult*

There are three values of a for which this statement is true: 2, 4, and 14. Add 1 to each of these numbers and divide each sum into 17. In each case, you will have a remainder of 2. There are no other possibilities.

SECTION 4: CRITICAL READING

Sentence Completions

1. **B** One-Word/One-Way *Easy*

Neither the bride nor the groom wants to force guests to wear something *fancy*. *Formal attire* is another way of saying *fancy* dress. How then should we consider *formal attire* in the context of this sentence? A good guess for the blank is something like "up to the guest," or *optional*, **B**.

2. **E** One-Word/One-Way *Easy*

The sentence tells you that *all parties* and *all branches . . . agree*. The beginning of the sentence tells you that there is *no* "something." If everyone is in agreement, you can assume that there is no "disagreement." **E**, *contention*, fits in with these clues.

3. **A** One-Word/One-Way *Easy*

The subject of this sentence is the *fruitful* business venture. The structural clue *as it is* tells you to look for a word that is in opposition to *individual vision and drive*. What is the opposite of *individual vision*? A good guess would be something that means "cooperation," or *collaboration*, **A**.

4. **B** One-Word/One-Way *Easy*

What kind of boss forces his employees to work all weekend and irritates them by singing bright and early on a Monday? A "bad" or "disliked" boss, or **B**. Be careful of **C**, *malevolent*: there's nothing here to indicate that the boss is particularly evil.

5. **B** Two-Word/One-Way *Medium*

How would an independent press feel about the *favoritism* that big name reviewers show to books published by *larger publishing houses*? An independent press would probably feel pretty "upset" about this. Eliminate **A** and **C**. Now, what would this kind of *favoritism* do to *new, emerging* authors? It would "silence" the *new* voices or at least "make it very difficult" for them to be heard. **B** is the correct answer.

6. **E** One-Word/Two-Way *Difficult*

The semicolon tells you that the word in the blank is defined by the clause that follows the blank. We then get a long clause describing what *does not* motivate the comedian, before finally learning that he takes *a delight in playful mockery*. This is your strongest clue: it tells you what the word in that blank must mean. A good guess would be something like "naughtiness" or "slight disrespect." If you were able to predict *irreverence*, **E**, then you might have found the answer even more easily.

7. **C** Two-Word/One-Way *Medium*

You are looking for two words to describe Charles Rennie Mackintosh's designs. Your clues are that his work consists of *charmingly coiled outlines of roses* and *fetching curls*. What kinds of words sum up this description? The word *charm* is a good guess for the first blank, based on the clue *charmingly coiled*. The word *fetching* is another good indication that you will want two positive-sounding words. Only **C** fits.

8. **D** Two-Word/Two-Way *Difficult*

The word *reconcile* tells you that this sentence will be divided into two contrasting halves. On the one hand, the sentence discusses *poverty and minimal personal accomplishment*. On the other hand, however, the sentence wonders why we as a society don't *celebrate acts* of "something" to *help the poor to elevate their circumstances*. What kind of an act would help the poor to *elevate their circumstances*? It must be some kind of act that is "helpful" or "kind." Eliminate **A** and **C**. Now, what is the opposite of a society that *celebrates acts of kindness to help the poor*? How would this "opposite" in society feel about the *stigma of poverty and minimal personal accomplishment*? They would feel "bad" about it or, to further define the missing word, they would feel "critical." **D** fits.

Paired Reading Passages

9. **C** Relating Two Passages *Easy*

Both of these passages are about travel. You are asked in this question to determine what point of view both authors share about travel. In the first passage, the author contrasts true *travelers* with "visitors." Travelers are those who are emotionally and personally affected by their time abroad. The author of the second passage describes the development of shorter trips abroad. He concludes: *this miniscule amount of time hardly allows one to adequately absorb the wisdom, age, and grace of these timeless cities—nor a chance to truly change as a result of travel.* In other words, both authors are very skeptical about the benefits of quick travel.

10. **D** Relating Two Passages *Medium*

Both authors are critical of travelers who do not take the time to adequately absorb the experience of foreign travel. However, the author of Passage 2, unlike the author of Passage 1, provides an explanation for *why* many people can't take the time to travel—most people the lack of vacation time.

11. **A** Relating Two Passages *Difficult*

Here is the line in question: *travel agencies are forced to put together tours that follow an aggressive schedule of sightseeing and pre-reserved dining.* You are looking for an example of this kind of forced, pre-planned, action-oriented traveling. In Passage 1, the author writes, *this kind of personality* [the true traveler] *is in direct opposition to the professional "visitor" who goes to a country with a checklist of foods to eat and sights to see, as though he were a bird watcher with a field guide, checking off which species he has spotted through his binoculars.* The checklist, in other words, is an example of an aggressive schedule. Watch out for **E**, which is there to trap test-takers who do not know a secondary definition of the word *aggressive*, and for **B** and **C**, which list items discussed in Passage 1 but are not logically connected to the question.

12. **B** Relating Two Passages *Medium*

Both authors are concerned with how travel is not necessarily conducted in a way that gives the traveler its full benefits. The author of Passage 1 draws a distinction between those who give themselves fully over to the process of traveling and those who drop into a country, then hop back home. The author of Passage 2 has more sympathy for people, pointing out that many are reduced to short trips due to poor vacation time. Still, the author of Passage 2 suggests that short trips don't adequately give travelers the chance to ingest and be altered by a culture. Both authors, therefore, are concerned with the way in which travel can have a transformative effect.

13. **E** Relating Two Passages *Easy*

Both authors are concerned with Wynton Marsalis, and both make mention of Marsalis's role in the creation of the Ken Burns jazz documentary. But while the first author is highly critical of Marsalis, the second author takes a more supportive position, pointing out all of the ways that Marsalis has helped spread jazz to a broad audience.

14. **B** Specific Information *Easy*

Look at the line in question: *Prior to this moment, the narrator of the documentary has informed the audience that, after 1963, jazz essentially died.*

15. **D** Themes and Arguments *Medium*

As usual, you need to look at the lines referenced: *Given the amount of influence Marsalis seems to have had on the documentary, this point of view is to be forgiven somewhat when we take into consideration that Ken Burns had not really listened to jazz in the six years before making the documentary.* The author's point in Passage 1 is that Marsalis has a skewed perspective on the history of jazz. The author introduces this point of view by showing how Marsalis has influenced Ken Burns, the documentary filmmaker. The author then shows that Burns was open to influence because he knew little about jazz, and he had to turn to an expert to help him. Watch out for **A**, which contradicts the passage: how could Burns naturally like some artists over others if he knew nothing about jazz?

16. **A** Implied Information *Medium*

To answer this question correctly, you need to be clear about the author's purpose in this particular paragraph. Note the author's words: *The 1960s and 1970s are generally classified in historical terms as a period of great social upheaval and change, and this restlessness is reflected in the music of these decades.* In other words, the music of the 1960s and 1970s mirrors the political problems of the times. The author then goes on to list a host of artists who reflect this upheaval, as in **A**. The other choices list information that may or may not have influenced Coltrane, but you are limiting your answer to what is explicitly stated in the passage.

17. **C** Words in Context *Medium*

With vocabulary-in-context questions, you must always answer the question based on how it is used in the sentence. Never try to guess from the question alone. Here is the second clause: *they became powerful spokespeople, commenting on the human condition and railing against injustice.* Words like *spokespeople* and *injustice* are your clues here. How would the jazz artists of the 1960s and 1970s feel about injustice? They would be "against" it, or they would "protest" it, **C**.

18. **D** Themes and Arguments *Medium*

The answer to this question is contained within the passage. The author says: *The birthplace is important—it was in this great southern city that many say jazz was born and still retains its classical roots.* The author of the second passage discusses Marsalis's important role in helping to spread jazz across the country. He acknowledges that Marsalis is a classicist and includes the detail about Marsalis's birthplace as part of an explanation for Marsalis's classical focus.

19. **C** Implied Information *Medium*

Here is the sentence in question: *Once again, audiences were able to listen to jazz music that was accessible, catchy, and uplifting.* The word *accessible* means "easily understood" or "having a broad appeal." The author is implying that, with Marsalis's album, people were able to listen to music that was "not difficult, but rather was *accessible*. Prior to this, we are to understand that music was *not accessible*—that is, it was "difficult" and appealed to few people.

20. **B** Themes and Arguments *Easy*

The word *predecessor* means "one who went before." You are told in both passages that both Marsalis and Davis play the trumpet. You should also infer, from the definition of *predecessor*, that Davis is older than Marsalis. However, **A** introduces information not explicitly stated in the passage: a predecessor may or may not die before a follower. A predecessor, however, has become expert in her or his field before a follower becomes similarly skilled.

21. **B** Implied Information *Medium*

Just before the line reference, the author discusses how Davis was more interested in musicians than in an audience. After that line, the author states, *For Marsalis, both are equally important, and this is a wise position to take when we consider that music cannot survive without an audience to support it.* The *both* referred to in this sentence means the *audience* and the *musicians*. The author is making the point that Marsalis is smart to court the audience, because music cannot survive without an audience to pay for and support its continued existence.

22. **A** Themes and Arguments *Medium*

In the third paragraph of Passage 2, the author praises Marsalis openly for his role as an educator and promoter of jazz: *Like Leonard Bernstein before him, Marsalis threw himself into the opportunity, reaching out to young people, bringing new jazz players into the fold, speaking sincerely to his audience, and generally working with tireless determination to ensure that the most American of musical art forms did not languish again.* Whether you have heard of Bernstein, it is clear that the author is using Bernstein as an example of a similar role to Marsalis's—that of educator and promoter.

23. **C** Relating Two Passages *Easy*

Both authors cover Marsalis. While the author of the first passage is critical of Marsalis's role in helping to shape the discussion of what jazz is and is not, the author of the second passage is more unabashedly supportive. Both, however, believe that Marsalis is a good musician with a strong base of knowledge. The author of Passage 1 states: *This criticism shows a surprising naiveté from someone who is as musically conscious and politically savvy as Marsalis.* This is clearly a compliment—perhaps a backhanded one, but nevertheless a compliment. The author of the second passage also compliments Marsalis throughout the passage: Marsalis has *near-flawless musicianship*; makes music that is *accessible*, *catchy*, and *uplifiting*; and, finally, *has done more to help ensure the survival of jazz than anyone else.*

24. **E** Relating Two Passages *Medium*

Of all these statements, the only one that is supported in both passages is **E**: *Jazz is truly the great American musical art form.* Passage 1 tells us: *great American art form* *of jazz*. Passage 2 claims: *the greatest of American of musical art forms.* **A** is wrong, because it is an attitude mostly supported by the author of Passage 2, who felt that music from the 1960s and 1970s was not *accessible*. **B** is wrong for similar reasons. **C** puts forward a view espoused only by the author of Passage 1, and the author of Passage 2 would most likely disagree. Finally, the attitude contained in **D** arises from the Ken Burns documentary.

SECTION 5: MATH

Multiple Choice

1. **D** Algebra: Solving Equations *Easy*

Simplify and solve:

$$x - 1 = 7$$
$$x = 8$$

$$x + 2 =$$
$$8 + 2 = 10$$

2. **D** Geometry: Solids *Easy*

If this figure is a cube, then you know that all sides along an edge are equal. However, note that line segment *AG* cuts through the center of the cube. It does not follow an edge of the cube. *AG*, or **D**, is therefore the answer.

3. **A** Data Analysis, Statistics & Probability: Graphs, Charts, and Tables *Easy*

This problem tests your ability to see information expressed in different kinds of graphs. The circle graph represents the following:

Boutique = 40 percent
Catalogue = 20 percent
Mall = 15 percent
Outlets = 7 percent
Internet = 18 percent

A shows the same information in bar graph form.

4. **C** Numbers & Operations: Fractions *Easy*

The fraction reduces to $\frac{1}{3}$, but, in the original fraction, the denominator is 8 more than the numerator. Take the original fraction and multiply the numerator and denominator by different integers until you find a fraction with the correct properties.

$$\frac{1}{3}$$

$$\times 2 \quad \frac{2}{6}$$

$$\times 3 \quad \frac{3}{9}$$

$$\times 4 \quad \frac{4}{12}$$

The fraction $\frac{4}{12}$ fulfills the requirements. You are asked to identify the numerator of the fraction, which is 4 (**C**).

5. **B** Geometry: Triangles *Medium*

The formula for the area of a triangle is:

$$A = \frac{bh}{2}$$

Plug in the values given and solve:

$$52 = \frac{4h}{2}$$
$$104 = 4h$$
$$h = 26$$

6. **B** Algebra: Absolute Value and Exponents *Medium*

Simplify and solve for $\sqrt{a}$:

$$5a^3b^2 = 125a^2$$
$$a^3b^2 = 25a^2$$
$$ab^2 = 25$$
$$a = \frac{25}{b^2}$$
$$\sqrt{a} = \frac{5}{b}$$

7. **C** Algebra: Absolute Value and Exponents *Medium*

The numbers 3 and 4 should immediately trigger the knowledge that you are dealing with a 3-4-5 triangle. Be careful that you do not choose **A** as your answer, however, because Jerry and Jimmy ride for 3 hours before the measurement is taken.

$$3 \times 3 = 9$$
$$3 \times 4 = 12$$
$$3 \times 5 = 15$$

8. **B** Geometry: Coordinate Geometry *Difficult*

Find the origin of the parabola. The vertex of the equation is located at the point:

$$\left(-\frac{b}{2a}, c - \frac{b^2}{4a}\right)$$

Use the equation to find the values:

$$y = ax^2 - bx + c$$
$$y = 3x^2 - 2x + 2$$

Since we now know that $x = -\frac{b}{2a}$, substitute the values to get $\frac{-(-2)}{(2)(3)}$. Reduce to $\frac{2}{6}$. Therefore, we know that the x-coordinate of the origin is $\frac{1}{3}$.

Next, solve for y, which we know is $c - \frac{b^2}{4a}$. Substitute in the values:

$$2 - \frac{(-2)^2}{(4)(3)} = 2 - \frac{4}{12} = \frac{24}{12} - \frac{4}{12} = \frac{20}{12}$$

Reduce to find that $\frac{5}{3}$ is the y-coordinate.

Since a is larger than 0, we know that the parabola must open upward. Eliminate **D** and **E**. Only **B** shows the parabola with the vertex at the properly plotted coordinates.

Grid-Ins

9. **4** Numbers & Operations: Factors and Multiples *Easy*

First, figure out how many cans of cat food total are needed. Each cat eats 2 cans per day. Since there are 2 cats, this works out to 4 cans per day for both of the cats. The family will be gone for 10 days, so they will need to buy a total of 40 cans of food. Now, the food is sold in "flats" of 12. Buying 3 flats is not quite enough, because that would only buy 36 cans of food. The family must by 4 flats for a total of 48 cans of food; 8 cans will be left over.

10. **13** Algebra: Absolute Value and Exponents *Easy*

This problem tests your knowledge of absolute value, which requires you to find the positive value—not the negative. Start with the second equation:

$$|a - 4| = 9$$
$$a - 4 = 9$$
$$a = 13$$

Now, check to see if this satisfies the first equation:

$$|2 - a| = 11$$
$$|2 - 13| = 11$$
$$|-11| = 11$$
$$11 = 11$$

11. **115** Geometry: Lines and Angles *Easy*

Add up all the known angles:

$$35 + 30 = 65$$

You know that there are always 180 degrees on a line. Subtract the value of known angles from 180 to find the value of X:

$$180 - 65 = 115$$

12. **69** Data Analysis, Statistics & Probability: Statistical Analysis *Medium*

This problem is actually much easier than it looks. The arithmetic mean in a list of integers is the "average." Furthermore, in a list containing an odd number of consecutive integers, the average number will be the middlemost term. (We've got an odd list here, since there are seven terms and 7 is an odd number.) All seven terms would therefore be:

$$69, 70, 71, 72, 73, 74, 75$$

The smallest term is 69.

13. **36** Algebra: Functions *Medium*

First, solve for $2f(c)$, then solve for $3f(c)$:

$$\begin{aligned} f(x) &= 2x+2 \\ 2f(c) &= 24 \\ 2f(c) &= 2(2x+2) \\ 24 &= 2(2x+2) \\ 24 &= 4x+4 \\ 20 &= 4x \\ 5 &= x \end{aligned}$$

Be careful. Make sure you plug 5 into the equation:

$$\begin{aligned} f(x) &= 2x+2 \\ 3f(c) &= 3(2x+2) \\ 3f(c) &= 3\{2(5)+2\} \\ 3f(c) &= 3(10+2) \\ 3f(c) &= 30+6 \\ 3f(c) &= 36 \end{aligned}$$

14. **10** Geometry: Lines and Angles *Medium*

A straight line always has 180 degrees. Note that the angle between the 70- and 50-degree angles must equal 60 degrees in order for the line to be 180. Also note that you have two out of the three angles in the triangle. Since two of the angles are 60, the third must also be 60 in order for all the angles to equal 180 degrees. Finally, angle x is part of another triangle. The angle next to the 60-degree angle must equal 120 in order for the straight line to equal 180 degrees. Adding 50 and 120 gives you 170. Since there must be 180 degrees in a triangle, x must equal 10 degrees.

15. **7/9** Numbers & Operations: Fractions *Medium*

Initially, $\frac{2}{3}$ is filled up with lilac. The remainder of the cup, or $\frac{1}{3}$, is empty. This $\frac{1}{3}$ must be filled with equal parts lilac, sandalwood, and honeysuckle—and this $\frac{1}{3}$ should be divided equally:

$$\frac{1}{3} \div 3 = \left(\frac{1}{3}\right)\left(\frac{1}{3}\right) = \frac{1}{9}$$

Now, add $\frac{2}{3}$ to $\frac{1}{9}$, and you'll get the total amount of lilac:

$$\frac{2}{3} + \frac{1}{9} = \frac{6}{9} + \frac{1}{9} = \frac{7}{9}$$

16. **2** Algebra: Solving Equations *Difficult*

Translate, simplify, and solve:

$$3x + 2y = (2)2x$$
$$3x + 2y = 4x$$
$$2y = x$$
$$2 = \frac{x}{y}$$

17. **10/7** Numbers & Operations: Divisibility and Remainders *Difficult*

There are fourteen even divisions between 0 and 2. Each division measures $\frac{1}{7}$. You can think of 2 as being $\frac{14}{7}$. The point x is located in the tenth spot on the number line. In fraction form, this would be $\frac{10}{7}$.

18. **32** Geometry: Triangles *Difficult*

The squares share a side with the right triangle *CDG*. You are told that the square *CEFG* has an area of 64.

$$\text{Area of square} = s^2$$
$$\text{Area of } 64 = s^2$$
$$s = 8$$

Now, you know that triangle *CDG* is a 45-45-90-degree triangle. Use this information to find side *CD*:

45	45	90
x	x	$x\sqrt{2}$
x	x	8
$\frac{8}{\sqrt{2}}$	$\frac{8}{\sqrt{2}}$	

Next plug this value into the formula for the area of a square to find the area of *ABCD*:

$$\text{Area of square} = s^2$$
$$\text{Area of square} = \left(\frac{8}{\sqrt{2}}\right)^2$$
$$\text{Area of square} = \frac{64}{2}$$
$$\text{Area of square} = 32$$

SECTION 6: WRITING

Improving Sentences

1. **B** Pronouns *Easy*

The subject, *Matt,* is already stated at the beginning of the sentence, so there is no reason to use the pronoun *he.* **B** corrects this error and also moves the modifying clause, *having already asked Sandy to go to the prom*, to the beginning of the sentence.

2. **C** Parallelism *Easy*

When comparing two or more items, the items must be in parallel form. The original wording of the sentence makes it sound as though *drenched* and *walking* are being compared, and yet they are not comparable characteristics or states. **C**, *as if they had walked*, fixes the problem.

3. **B** Subject-Verb Agreement *Medium*

This question tests your ability to recognize subject-verb agreement. Here, the subject is *properties*, which is plural, but the verb is *is*, which is singular. To be correct, the verb needs to be put in the plural form, which the solution in **B** accomplishes.

4. **E** Subject-Verb Agreement *Medium*

Every sentence must have a main verb and a main subject. In this sentence, the subject is clearly the word *crux*. There is no main verb, however; the original sentence was a fragment and was missing a verb. To be correct, the pronoun *which*, which is not necessary in the first place, must be removed.

5. **B** Subject-Verb Agreement *Medium*

This sentence lacks a main verb to go with its main subject, *airplane*. **B** changes the adjective *flying* to the verb *flew*, thus correcting the error.

6. **E** Run-Ons *Medium*

Here we have a run-on sentence: two complete sentences, or independent clauses, are joined together by a comma. To be correct, one of the sentences must be made dependent on the other and the two must be joined by a conjunction, the sentences must be separated by a semicolon, or the sentences must be separated by a period (and stand alone as two discrete sentences). **E** uses the dependent-independent solution.

7. **A** No Error *Medium*

This sentence uses a compound subject, *seasoning and use of real meat*. A compound subject like this, which is made up of more than one element, requires a plural verb. In the original sentence, the verb *give* is plural and is therefore correct.

8. **C** Misplaced Modifier *Medium*

The underlined portion of the sentence is a clause that should modify *Rick*. The sentence as it stands now is wordy and needlessly includes the phrase *as he does*. **C** changes the clause into a modifying phrase.

9. **D** Coordination and Subordination *Medium*

This sentence is flawed, because it does not correctly express causality. The word *although* sets the sentence up to have a contrast, but there is no contrast in the sentence. **D** includes the conjunction *because*, which correctly shows the relationship between the two halves of the sentence.

10. **D** Pronouns *Medium*

The verb *spent* needs a pronoun to anchor it and to help the reader to understand that the *song* spent time on *the charts*. **D** corrects this problem.

11. **C** Pronouns *Difficult*

Every pronoun must refer to a clear antecedent. In this case, the pronoun *they* refers to the word *game*. Notice, however, that *they* is plural while *game* is singular. Pronouns and antecedents must agree in number. The pronoun *they* must be changed to *it*, **C**.

Identifying Sentence Errors

12. **A** Subject-Verb Agreement *Easy*

The subject, *Amanda Siris,* is supposed to go with the verb *spending*. However, *spending* is an adjective here, not a verb. To be correct, *spending* needs to change to *spent*.

13. **B** Wordiness *Easy*

This sentence unnecessarily includes the pronoun *they* in the phrase *or were they*. Worse, it is not clear to what the pronoun *they* refers. To be correct, the phrase *or were they* should be shortened to *or*.

14. **A** Pronouns *Easy*

The pronoun *which* generally should only be used to refer to things. As it is used in this sentence, *which* refers to *students*. To be correct, the pronoun *which* must be changed to *who,* the pronoun that should be used to refer to people.

15. **D** Tense *Easy*

The verb phrase *had stayed* is in the incorrect form and should be changed to *having stayed*.

16. **A** Gerund *Easy*

The verb *maintaining* needs to be in the infinitive form, *to maintain*, when following the helping verb *was*.

17. **A** Adverbs and Adjectives *Easy*

This sentence has a problem with causality. One the one hand, we are told that *he is a very talented dancer*, but we are also told that he *lacks focus*. You need a word to demonstrate this contrast. The sentence would work better if *when* was replaced by *although*.

18. **C** Faulty Comparison *Easy*

It is redundant to use the words *more* and *clearer* together in a sentence. The word *clearer* is quite obviously making a comparison. You do not need to add *more* in front of *clearer*. To keep *more* in the sentence, the word *clearer* would need to be changed to *clear*. Otherwise, you would need to remove *more*.

19. **B** Subject-Verb Agreement *Easy*

The subject *people* is plural, but the verb *has* is singular. Since subjects and verbs must agree, the verb *has* needs to be changed to *have* to be correct.

20. **C** Pronouns *Easy*

A pronoun must always refer to one clear antecedent. However, in this case, it is not clear what the pronoun *they* refers to. It most likely refers back to food that contains *byproducts*, but, as the sentence reads now, it might refer back to *dogs* and is therefore unclear.

21. **B** Idioms *Medium*

The prepositional phrase *in the assistance with* is awkward. To be correct, it should be rephrased to *to assist with*.

22. **B** Tense *Medium*

The verb *to be interviewed* is in the incorrect form. It should be *being interviewed*.

23. **E** No Error *Medium*

There is no error here. All subjects and verbs agree and all idioms are correct.

24. **C** Run-Ons *Medium*

This sentence is a run-on. To be correct, a conjunction such as "but" or "although" should be inserted after the comma.

25. **D** Parallelism *Medium*

Items in a list must be in parallel form. Here, we have two items in a list: *the fresh ingredients* and *the way she pays special attention*. Notice that the first item in the list contains a noun, whereas the second item contains a subject and verb. In other words, the second item in the list is an entire clause, not just an item. To be correct, the entire clause *the way she pays* should be deleted.

26. **E** No Error *Medium*

In a sentence, subjects and verbs must always agree. In this sentence, the subject is the word *number*, which is singular, and the verb is *has calmed*, which is also singular. This sentence is therefore correct as it is written.

27. **D** Parallelism *Medium*

Items being compared must be in parallel form. In this sentence, two things are being compared: *the winner* and *in the presidential election*. Note that the second item is a prepositional phrase. To be correct, the second item needs to be changed to *the president* or *a presidential candidate*.

28. **A** Pronouns *Medium*

Every pronoun must have a clear antecedent. In this case, the pronoun *it* refers to *web magazines*. Notice, however, that while *it* is singular, *web magazines* is plural. To be correct, the pronoun *it* needs to be replaced by *they*, and the verb *is* should be replaced by *are*.

29. **E** No Error *Difficult*

When comparing more than two items, use the superlative case. This sentence compares several *sources of energy*. The phrase *the most exciting* is in the superlative form and is therefore correct.

Improving Paragraphs

30. **A** Essay Analysis *Medium*

The first sentence introduces an idea—turning a *sheep into a sweater*. The second sentence anticipates the reader's response to this slightly far-fetched idea by clarifying things; it is not the actual sheep that gets turned into a sweater but *its wool*. So, the second sentence *addresses the reader's skepticism*.

31. **E** Sentence Addition *Easy*

The original paragraph contains a jump in logic: the wool goes from being cleaned to being knitted. We need some kind of transitional sentence that shows how the wool goes from cleaning to becoming yarn.

32. **C** Sentence Revision *Easy*

Right now the sentences are rather choppy. It would be much smoother to connect the two sentences together, which **C** accomplishes. Watch out for **D** and **E**, which introduce conjunctions like *although* and *because* that indicate a causality or contrast not logically borne out by the sentence.

33. **B** Sentence Revision *Medium*

Sentence 6 sets up an idea, and sentence 7 provides an example of that idea. In order to clearly indicate this relationship, you need some kind of language. **B** provides that language.

34. **D** Essay Analysis *Easy*

Go through these answer choices one by one, eliminating anything that you have seen used in the passage. You should narrow down your answer choices to **D** alone, for the author never actually quotes someone directly.

35. **E** Sentence Revision *Medium*

As it stands, this sentence is a run-on. The revision in **E** corrects this error by joining the two independent clauses with a semicolon.

SECTION 7: CRITICAL READING

Sentence Completions

1. **B** Two-Word/One-Way *Easy*

Polio outbreaks are becoming more frequent in the world. What would world-wide health officials want to do in this case? They would want to stop these outbreaks from happening. A good prediction for the first blank is "support." Eliminate **A** and **E**. What would the health officials then want to see happen with immunization programs? They would want the programs to be "put into place." **B** must be the answer.

2. **A** One-Word/One-Way *Easy*

The sentence is chock-full of clues regarding when *the cat is asleep* and when it is awake. The cat, in fact, is awake during the night but sleeps during the day. The word that fits the blank would mean something like "awake" or "active at night," which is the definition of the word *nocturnal*, **A**. Watch out for **E**, which might seem like it fits but, given the clues, does not.

3. **D** Two-Word/One-Way *Medium*

The colon should tell you that the words that fit the blank are defined by the text that follows the blank. In fact, you are looking for words that mean *generous* and *positive*. In other words, you are looking for two positive words. Only **D** fits.

4. **E** One-Word/Two-Way *Medium*

You are looking for a word that is negative. You know this because you are told that some cultures *look down* on others for *pleasurable* activities. You should assume that *eating out* is another of these activities worth looking down on. You should assume, therefore, that eating out is something "bad." The word *debauchery*, **E**, fits.

5. **C** Two-Word/One-Way *Difficult*

What would neighboring countries do when faced with the prospect of another country developing *nuclear weapons*? They would certainly be unhappy, and you can assume that the word that fits the second blank will be something negative. Eliminate **A** and **E**. Now, try the remaining words in the first blank. Only **C** fits.

6. **B** One-Word/Two-Way *Difficult*

There are several clues here: you are told that a particular kind of medicine shows *no causal effect* on illness—that is, it doesn't actually do any good. However, the medicine makes people feel better. You are looking for a word that means "making you feel good, but not necessarily effective." The answer must be **B**, *panacea*.

Long Reading Passage

7. **B** Main Idea *Medium*

The entire passage is narrated by a person describing someone named only *she*. Along the way, we learn little bits about the narrator and her family, such as their brunch ritual and about the absence of parental influence on her friend. But, as a whole, the passage is concerned with describing this friend.

8. **A** Technique *Medium*

The first line of the passage states: *She had impeccable timing.* The author then goes on to describe all the ways in which the friend actually does not have good timing. You can assume, therefore, that this contrast between good and bad timing is an example of *irony*, or the use of words to mean something other than their literal meaning.

9. **E** Themes and Arguments *Medium*

The author opens the passage by telling us that while the character *she* has great timing, *she* also tends to show up consistently at the *wrong* time or when *she* is in need of help. The author also says, *This is what is so attractive about people who are always in trouble. All the commotion and hollering add up to drama.* From this, we get a sense that we will be introduced to a character who is difficult to pin down, but around whom drama swirls. In other words, *she* will be *unpredictable*, **E**.

10. **A** Themes and Arguments *Medium*

Here are the lines in question: *"Like, how is she wild?" I would ask. "Like, she just is," people would say. "Be careful." "Yes, but what does that mean?" I would persist. "You'll find out if you aren't careful."* Taken as a whole, these lines give the sense that the narrator is being *warned* against doing something—namely, becoming friends with the mysterious female character.

11. **D** Specific Information *Medium*

The author tells us, *As it turned out, Saturday turned out to be a pretty tame affair, lots of driving around and stopping to talk to boys who had parked by the beach, or by the park, or other areas where teens were known to congregate.* In other words, Saturday night is not really all that interesting, although the narrator is still drawn into the activities. She is certainly not bored, but she discovers that not much happens.

12. **C** Words in Context *Difficult*

Always answer vocabulary questions based on how they are used in context: *Going out on Saturdays was only a small part of her agenda. I blossomed under her attention. She showed up at my house on Sunday morning, and began to weed through my closet, throwing away anything that did not have style.* So, what is happening here? The female character is literally giving the narrator a "makeover." You can assume that an agenda is some sort of "blueprint" or *plan*, **C**.

13. **D** Specific Information *Medium*

Here is the full line reference: *Occasionally she would find something in my closet, and she would declare, "I don't understand why I've never seen you wear this."* This line occurs when the narrator is essentially being given a "makeover" by the mysterious female character. From this, we can assume that the female character felt that the narrator actually needed a makeover—that is, the narrator is not someone who is naturally comfortable with style or social situations.

14. **B** Themes and Arguments *Medium*

Take a look at the context of this sentence: *The teachers who told her she was not intelligent should have seen the fast and efficient way that she worked, running a continuous narrative the whole time. "You have to have a lot of shirts and sweaters. People don't notice when you repeat pants so much. But they notice new tops. You have to have a huge supply of tops."* First, the narrator tells us that the female character is very intelligent, despite the fact that the teachers in the school don't seem to think so. The lines that follow are meant, therefore, to illustrate in what ways the female character *is* intelligent.

15. **A** Themes and Arguments *Medium*

Here are the lines referenced: *I'll never forget the day she showed up at our house one morning, on another Sunday. I had sat down to eat brunch with my family—a tradition that we loved even if other families thought us old-fashioned and quaint—and suddenly there she was in her Mercedes in our driveway, sheepishly looking through the window. I felt awkward, caught between the soothing traditions of my wholesome family and her unregulated, untamed energy.* The narrator has just sat down to eat brunch, an activity she describes as a *tradition* and as being *quaint*. In contrast, the female friend is *unregulated* and has *untamed energy*. So, while the narrator may be happy to see her friend, she is concerned that her friend's energy is different from her family's. Be careful with **D**: nowhere does the passage state that the narrator wants to keep her friend away from her family. The same is true for **B**, which is too extreme to be correct.

16. **C** Implied Information *Medium*

Take a look at the lines in question: *I was a little jealous that I hadn't been invited, but by then I knew enough to realize that she would never invite me to something that she knew my parents would not approve of my participating in.* The narrator is slightly upset that she has not been invited to the party the night before. However, she is also not surprised, because she knows that there are limits to the kinds of activities in which she can participate.

17. **A** Themes and Arguments *Easy*

As with all Critical Reading passages, it is important to take a look not only at the line referenced, but those that surround it: *But hearing about the story this way—in which she was the active participant—my parents were amused. "Thank you for the pancakes," she thanked my father, like a pro. "I almost never get to eat this kind of stuff."* The friend has just told a story that might have been offensive to the parents, but which she manages to tell in such a way that the parents are charmed. Then, following this charming storytelling, the friend thanks the parents for the pancakes. This "thank you," therefore, is another example of the way in which the friend is able to charm adults. Watch out for **B** and **C**, which directly contradict the passage. **D** introduces information that isn't discussed at all.

18. **D** Themes and Arguments *Easy*
The friend is happy to eat pancakes and to entertain the parents. She also knows, as the narrator tells us, *how . . . to present the very best of herself to me, to my parents.* At the same time, the narrator has told us earlier in the passage that the friend has very little guidance from her parents. This revelation about the pancakes is yet another reference to the circumstances of the friend's home life, as well as another contrast between the friend's home life and the narrator's.

19. **E** Themes and Arguments *Medium*
The friend asks to use the shower. The narrator wants to know what the friend was doing the night before but does not receive an answer. So, on the one hand, the friend is asking for the support of friendship but, on the other hand, is remaining secretive. The narrator goes on to reiterate this conflict when she states, *I thought about how it was that she managed to present the very best of herself to me, to my parents, and to her parents, and how none of us really knew what her days and nights were really like.* In other words, there is a difference between how the friend seems on the outside to the rest of the world and how she really feels internally. Watch out for **B**, which directly contradicts the characterization of the two friends: the narrator's life is *not* fast-paced. We also don't really know if the narrator is happy with secrecy, **D**. While there is a difference between the friend's home life and the narrator's (**A**), this contrast is not what is illustrated at this point in the passage.

SECTION 8: MATH

Multiple Choice

1. **D** Numbers & Operations: Basic Operations *Easy*
One way to do this problem is to work backward. Look at **A**, or 3. The correct answer will be a number that is negative, odd, and less than 3. **A** is not negative and can therefore be eliminated. **B**, 2, is even. Eliminate **B**. **C** is odd, but it is not negative. Eliminate **C**. **D**, –1, is both odd and negative. It is also less than 3. This is your answer.

2. **B** Algebra: Absolute Value and Exponents *Easy*
Simplify and solve:

$$x^2 - 7 = 57$$
$$x^2 = 64$$
$$x = \sqrt{64}$$
$$x = 8$$

3. **B** Numbers & Operations: Fractions *Easy*
There are 45 doctors total. Exactly 25 doctors recommended medicine *Y*, and exactly 14 recommended medicine *Z*. That's a total of 39 doctors. Subtracting 39 from 45

gives you the number 6, or the number of doctors who recommended neither. Express this as a fraction and reduce:

$$\frac{6}{45} = \frac{2}{15}$$

4. **D** Geometry: Triangles *Easy*

There are 180 degrees in a triangle. In this diagram, you are shown two triangles, each of which has one angle of 45 degrees. Since you know that two triangles together would equal 360 (180 + 180 = 360), simply subtract the 45-degree angles from this value to find the sum of $A + B + C + D$:

$$360 - 45 - 45 = 270$$

5. **B** Data Analysis, Statistics & Probability: Graphs, Charts, and Tables *Easy*

Be careful here: you are looking for the year in which the number of inches *changed* the most. The question doesn't specify whether you are looking for an increase or decrease. You can approach this problem two ways: find the actual change in inches of rain from decade to decade, or look to see which two bars in the graph have the greatest disparity in height. Either way, you will find that the greatest change is between 1971 and 1972.

6. **D** Geometry: Coordinate Geometry *Medium*

You know that $f(x)$ represents the y-coordinate of the graph. In this case, you are asked to find the corresponding y coordinate when x is equal to –2. The graph shows that the y-coordinate would be 2.

7. **B** Numbers & Operations: Exponents *Medium*

Make sure you answer the actual question: you are trying to find the sum of the exponents themselves. To do this, you will first have to find the values of x, y, and z. Since you are dealing with a relatively low product, the values of the exponents will most likely be low too. Try plugging in numbers, keeping in mind that the values of x, y, and z must be distinct.

$$(3^x)(3^y)(3^z) = 729$$
$$(3^1)(3^2)(3^3) = 729$$
$$(3)(9)(27) = 729$$

In this case, the sum of the exponents would be:

$$1 + 2 + 3 = 6$$

8. **A** Geometry: Polygons *Medium*

If the square has an area of 144, then you know that one side measures 12. Draw a quick sketch of the square, making each side measure 12, with a corner at the coordinates (–3, –8). Note too that none of the coordinates listed in the answer choices features numbers that are extremely large, therefore the origin of the xy–coordinate will probably be inside the square.

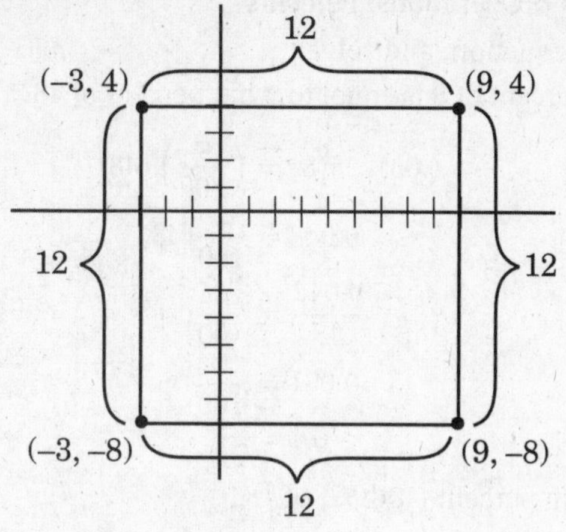

Only **A** (9, 4) could be the corner of this square.

9. **E** Algebra: Absolute Value *Medium*

For the book to fit on the shelf, it must be larger than 10 inches and less than 30. In whole number terms, this means that the first integer value the spine of the book could be is 11 inches, and the largest the spine could be is 29. The correct answer to this question will be the one where the numbers 11 and 29 will yield a true statement.

Take a look at **E**:

$$|h - 10| < 20$$
$$|29 - 10| < 20$$
$$19 < 20 \text{ True}$$

$$|11 - 10| < 20$$
$$1 < 20 \text{ True}$$

10. **B** Geometry: Polygon *Medium*

The area of the first rectangle is:

$$12 \times 6 = 72$$
$$a = 72$$

The area of the second rectangle is:

$$12 \times 3 = 36$$
$$36 = \frac{72}{2}$$
$$\frac{a}{2} = 36$$

11. **D** Algebra: Functions *Medium*

Take the values one at a time. Could $\frac{3}{4}$ possibly be a value for p^*q? Yes, if p is larger than q, which it would be in this case, and if p is odd, which it also would be. Eliminate **B**. Now, could $\frac{3}{2}$ equal p^*q. It doesn't fit the first possible definition of p^*q, because in the case of $\frac{3}{2}$, p is not smaller than q. It also doesn't fit the second case, because q, or 2, would not be odd. Eliminate **C** and **E**. Could $\frac{3}{7}$ equal p^*q? Yes, because q, or 3, would be odd, and p, or 7, would be larger than 3.

12. **D** Numbers & Operations: Percents *Medium*

Translate, set up an equation, and solve:

6 percent of 10 percent of 8 is equal to what percent of 48?

$$(.06)(.1)(8) = \left(\frac{x}{100}\right)(48)$$
$$0.048 = \frac{x}{100}(48)$$
$$\frac{0.048}{48} = \frac{x}{100}$$
$$0.001 = \frac{x}{100}$$
$$0.1 = x$$

So, 0.048 is one-tenth percent (10th%) of 48.

13. **B** Numbers & Operations: Basic Operations *Medium*

The best way to solve this problem is to pick numbers. When you add x and y, they must be less than 11. They must also be positive and distinct. Your initial impulse is probably to pick numbers as large as possible. Let's say that x is 9, and y is 1. The sum is less than 11, but the product is only 9. Is there any way to make the product larger? If x is equal to 6, and y is equal to 4, then the sum is less than 10, and the product is 24. No other pair of numbers will make the product larger.

14. **A** Algebra: Inequalities *Medium*

Take this problem a piece at a time. All you know about x is that it is positive. You don't know if it is a whole number or a fraction. Is $3x > 2x$ true? Yes, because three times something will always be larger than two times something, provided that the number is positive. Eliminate **B** and **D**. Next, is $x^2 < x^3$ true? Only if x is not a fraction. Eliminate **C**. Finally, is $x < \frac{x}{2}$? Not if x is an integer. Only I must be true, so the answer must be **A**.

15. **E** Geometry: Triangles *Difficult*

This problem is not as difficult as it initially seems. First, note that a and b add up to side XZ. You should note that angle Y is a right angle. Note too that side XY is $4\sqrt{3}$ and YZ is 4. These measurements should trigger in your mind the ratio of sides in a triangle whose angles measure 30, 60, and 90 degrees. This kind of a triangle has sides in a ratio of $x{:}x\sqrt{3}{:}2x$. You know, therefore, that XZ must be 8. Now, be careful answering the question here. You are asked to find *twice* the sum of a and b, or 16.

16. **B** Geometry: Triangles *Difficult*

The formula for area of a triangle is:

$$A = \frac{bh}{2}$$

The base and height of each triangle are both a, since the edge of one face of the cube is a. Plug this value into the equation to get the area of one triangle:

$$A = \frac{bh}{2}$$
$$A = \frac{(a)(a)}{2}$$
$$A = \frac{a^2}{2}$$

Now, remember, there are 6 sides to a cube. So, you must multiply the area by 6 to find the area of all the unshaded triangles:

$$\frac{6a^2}{2} = 3a^2$$

SECTION 9: WRITING

Improving Sentences

1. **B** Tense *Easy*

This question tests your understanding of verb tense. Note that the first part of the sentence is written in the simple past tense: *the Japanese and American governments signed.* The cause-and-effect nature of this sentence suggests that the following clause will also be in the past tense, but instead it is in the conditional: *would have brought*. To be correct, *would have brought* needs to be changed to *brought*, as in **B**.

2. **D** Subject-Verb Agreement *Easy*

Every sentence must have a main subject and a main verb. In this case, the subject of the sentence is *line*, and the verb is *provides*. However, the verb *provides* is preceded by the conjunction *and*. This would only make sense if the first half of the sentence were an independent clause. But it isn't: the verb *provides* is still part of the main clause and is connected to the main subject. To be correct, you need to either make the clause that starts with *consisting* independent or, as in **D**, remove the conjunction *and*.

3. **E** Wordiness *Medium*

With the adverb *daily* in its current position, the sentence sounds clumsy and redundant. To be correct, the adverb *daily* needs to follow the verb phrase *maintain this habit*.

4. **E** Idioms *Medium*

This sentence tests your familiarity with idiomatic expressions. The connector *no sooner* must always be paired with the word *than*. In this case, the conjunction, *but*, following *no sooner* is incorrect. Watch out for **B**, which correctly uses *than* but muddles the second half of the sentence. The correct answer is **E**.

5. **B** Subject-Verb Agreement *Medium*

Every subject must have a verb. In this case, the subject is *reason*, but the sentence is missing a verb. **B** corrects this problem.

6. **C** Parallelism *Medium*

This sentence tests your understanding of comparisons. When comparing two or more items, the items being compared must be placed in parallel form. In this sentence, the author is comparing *Bill will not be remembered* and *they will credit Daphne for bringing*. The second item being compared includes the pronoun *they*, which the first item does not. You need to bring the second item in line with the first, by making *Daphne* its subject and eliminating *they*. **C** accomplishes both fixes.

7. **D** Pronouns *Medium*

The wording of the original sentence introduces the unnecessary pronoun *you*—it is not *you* who believes in the importance of *teaching children*, but Bernstein himself. The correct answer choice will eliminate the pronoun *you* and simplify the rest of the clause. **D** does this. Watch out for **E**, which includes the preposition *by* and also retains the vague pronoun *they*.

8. **A** No Error *Medium*

This sentence is correct and contains no errors. All subjects and verbs agree. All clauses are complete. All verbs are in the proper tense.

9. **B** Tense *Medium*

The word *sending* should stand out, because it is in the wrong form. Both *sending* and—*was based* modify the subject *the lettuce industry*. **B** fixes the problem by changing *sending* to *sent*.

10. **C** Tense *Medium*

This question tests your ability to coordinate tense within a sentence. The verb phrase *were on the brink* tells you that the action has taken place in the past. Yet the first half of the sentence puts the verb in the present—*were passing*. To be correct, *were passing* would need to be turned into the past tense, or *were passed*, as is the case with **C**.

11. **A** No Error *Medium*

There are no errors in this sentence. All subjects and verbs agree, all pronouns are clear, and all verbs are in the correct tense.

12. **E** Misplaced Modifier *Medium*

This question is checking to see whether you are familiar with modifiers. Notice that the sentence opens with a modifying clause: *Challenging the old adage that one should not cast pearls before swine*. The sentence then continues with the noun *ability*. This is wrong, because it is not the *ability* that is *challenging* anything, but rather *Meredith*. To be correct, Meredith's name must appear just after *swine*, as it does with **B** and **E**. But while **B** is garbled and includes the passive voice, **E** cleanly rewrites the sentence so that the reader is clear as to who is performing each action.

13. **A** No Error *Medium*

There are no errors in this sentence. All subjects and verbs agree, all pronouns are clear, and all verbs are in the correct tense.

14. **E** Subject-Verb Agreement *Medium*

The second half of the sentence uses a subject, *Miles Davis*, and presents a compound verb, *brought* and *was*. Note that the second verb in the compound verb is in the passive voice, while the first verb is in the active voice. For the sentence to be correct, both verbs must be in the same voice. **E** corrects this problem by turning *was the pioneer* into an active verb, or *pioneered*.

SAT PRACTICE TEST 8

SAT* Reasoning Test—General Directions

Timing

- You will have 3 hours and 20 minutes to work on this test. (On the actual SAT, you would have 3 hours and 45 minutes to complete ten sections, one of which would be unscored and experimental.)
- There are nine separately timed sections:
  - ➤ One 25-minute essay
  - ➤ Five other 25-minute sections
  - ➤ Two 20-minute sections
  - ➤ One 10-minute section
- You may work on only one section at a time.
- The supervisor will tell you when to begin and end each section.
- If you finish a section before time is called, check your work on that section. You may NOT turn to any other section.
- Work as rapidly as you can without losing accuracy. Don't waste time on questions that seem too difficult for you.

Marking Answers

- Carefully mark only one answer for each question.
- Make sure each mark is dark and completely fills the circle.
- Do not make any stray marks on your answer sheet.
- If you erase, do so completely. Incomplete erasures may be scored as intended answers.
- Use only the answer spaces that correspond to the question numbers.
- Use the test book for scratchwork, but you will not receive credit for anything written there.
- After time has been called, you may not transfer answers to your answer sheet or fill in circles.
- You may not fold or remove pages or portions of a page from this book, or take the book or answer sheet from the testing room.

Scoring

- For each correct answer to a question, you receive one point.
- For questions you omit, you receive no points.
- For a wrong answer to a multiple-choice question, you lose one-fourth of a point.
  - ➤ If you can eliminate one or more of the answer choices as wrong, you increase your chances of choosing the correct answer and earning one point.
  - ➤ If you can't eliminate any choice, move on. You can return to the question later if there is time.
- For a wrong answer to a "grid-in" math question, you don't lose any points.
- The essay is scored on a 1 to 6 scale by two different readers. The total essay score is the sum of the two readers' scores.
- An off-topic or blank essay will receive a score of zero.

SAT PRACTICE TEST 8 ANSWER SHEET

SECTION 2

1. Ⓐ Ⓑ Ⓒ Ⓓ Ⓔ	7. Ⓐ Ⓑ Ⓒ Ⓓ Ⓔ	13. Ⓐ Ⓑ Ⓒ Ⓓ Ⓔ	19. Ⓐ Ⓑ Ⓒ Ⓓ Ⓔ
2. Ⓐ Ⓑ Ⓒ Ⓓ Ⓔ	8. Ⓐ Ⓑ Ⓒ Ⓓ Ⓔ	14. Ⓐ Ⓑ Ⓒ Ⓓ Ⓔ	20. Ⓐ Ⓑ Ⓒ Ⓓ Ⓔ
3. Ⓐ Ⓑ Ⓒ Ⓓ Ⓔ	9. Ⓐ Ⓑ Ⓒ Ⓓ Ⓔ	15. Ⓐ Ⓑ Ⓒ Ⓓ Ⓔ	21. Ⓐ Ⓑ Ⓒ Ⓓ Ⓔ
4. Ⓐ Ⓑ Ⓒ Ⓓ Ⓔ	10. Ⓐ Ⓑ Ⓒ Ⓓ Ⓔ	16. Ⓐ Ⓑ Ⓒ Ⓓ Ⓔ	22. Ⓐ Ⓑ Ⓒ Ⓓ Ⓔ
5. Ⓐ Ⓑ Ⓒ Ⓓ Ⓔ	11. Ⓐ Ⓑ Ⓒ Ⓓ Ⓔ	17. Ⓐ Ⓑ Ⓒ Ⓓ Ⓔ	23. Ⓐ Ⓑ Ⓒ Ⓓ Ⓔ
6. Ⓐ Ⓑ Ⓒ Ⓓ Ⓔ	12. Ⓐ Ⓑ Ⓒ Ⓓ Ⓔ	18. Ⓐ Ⓑ Ⓒ Ⓓ Ⓔ	24. Ⓐ Ⓑ Ⓒ Ⓓ Ⓔ

SECTION 3

1. Ⓐ Ⓑ Ⓒ Ⓓ Ⓔ	6. Ⓐ Ⓑ Ⓒ Ⓓ Ⓔ	11. Ⓐ Ⓑ Ⓒ Ⓓ Ⓔ	16. Ⓐ Ⓑ Ⓒ Ⓓ Ⓔ
2. Ⓐ Ⓑ Ⓒ Ⓓ Ⓔ	7. Ⓐ Ⓑ Ⓒ Ⓓ Ⓔ	12. Ⓐ Ⓑ Ⓒ Ⓓ Ⓔ	17. Ⓐ Ⓑ Ⓒ Ⓓ Ⓔ
3. Ⓐ Ⓑ Ⓒ Ⓓ Ⓔ	8. Ⓐ Ⓑ Ⓒ Ⓓ Ⓔ	13. Ⓐ Ⓑ Ⓒ Ⓓ Ⓔ	18. Ⓐ Ⓑ Ⓒ Ⓓ Ⓔ
4. Ⓐ Ⓑ Ⓒ Ⓓ Ⓔ	9. Ⓐ Ⓑ Ⓒ Ⓓ Ⓔ	14. Ⓐ Ⓑ Ⓒ Ⓓ Ⓔ	19. Ⓐ Ⓑ Ⓒ Ⓓ Ⓔ
5. Ⓐ Ⓑ Ⓒ Ⓓ Ⓔ	10. Ⓐ Ⓑ Ⓒ Ⓓ Ⓔ	15. Ⓐ Ⓑ Ⓒ Ⓓ Ⓔ	20. Ⓐ Ⓑ Ⓒ Ⓓ Ⓔ

SECTION 4

1. Ⓐ Ⓑ Ⓒ Ⓓ Ⓔ	7. Ⓐ Ⓑ Ⓒ Ⓓ Ⓔ	13. Ⓐ Ⓑ Ⓒ Ⓓ Ⓔ	19. Ⓐ Ⓑ Ⓒ Ⓓ Ⓔ
2. Ⓐ Ⓑ Ⓒ Ⓓ Ⓔ	8. Ⓐ Ⓑ Ⓒ Ⓓ Ⓔ	14. Ⓐ Ⓑ Ⓒ Ⓓ Ⓔ	20. Ⓐ Ⓑ Ⓒ Ⓓ Ⓔ
3. Ⓐ Ⓑ Ⓒ Ⓓ Ⓔ	9. Ⓐ Ⓑ Ⓒ Ⓓ Ⓔ	15. Ⓐ Ⓑ Ⓒ Ⓓ Ⓔ	21. Ⓐ Ⓑ Ⓒ Ⓓ Ⓔ
4. Ⓐ Ⓑ Ⓒ Ⓓ Ⓔ	10. Ⓐ Ⓑ Ⓒ Ⓓ Ⓔ	16. Ⓐ Ⓑ Ⓒ Ⓓ Ⓔ	22. Ⓐ Ⓑ Ⓒ Ⓓ Ⓔ
5. Ⓐ Ⓑ Ⓒ Ⓓ Ⓔ	11. Ⓐ Ⓑ Ⓒ Ⓓ Ⓔ	17. Ⓐ Ⓑ Ⓒ Ⓓ Ⓔ	23. Ⓐ Ⓑ Ⓒ Ⓓ Ⓔ
6. Ⓐ Ⓑ Ⓒ Ⓓ Ⓔ	12. Ⓐ Ⓑ Ⓒ Ⓓ Ⓔ	18. Ⓐ Ⓑ Ⓒ Ⓓ Ⓔ	24. Ⓐ Ⓑ Ⓒ Ⓓ Ⓔ

SECTION 5

1. Ⓐ Ⓑ Ⓒ Ⓓ Ⓔ	3. Ⓐ Ⓑ Ⓒ Ⓓ Ⓔ	5. Ⓐ Ⓑ Ⓒ Ⓓ Ⓔ	7. Ⓐ Ⓑ Ⓒ Ⓓ Ⓔ
2. Ⓐ Ⓑ Ⓒ Ⓓ Ⓔ	4. Ⓐ Ⓑ Ⓒ Ⓓ Ⓔ	6. Ⓐ Ⓑ Ⓒ Ⓓ Ⓔ	8. Ⓐ Ⓑ Ⓒ Ⓓ Ⓔ

9	10	11	12	13
⊘ . 0–9	⊘ . 0–9	⊘ . 0–9	⊘ . 0–9	⊘ . 0–9

14	15	16	17	18
⊘ . 0–9	⊘ . 0–9	⊘ . 0–9	⊘ . 0–9	⊘ . 0–9

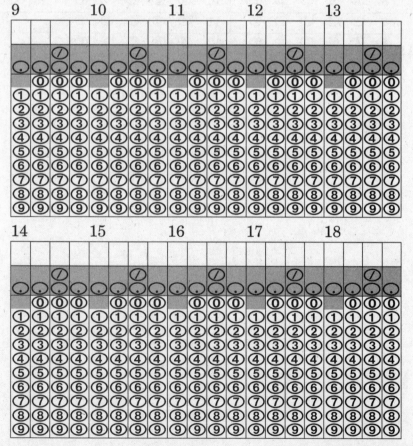

SAT PRACTICE TEST 8 ANSWER SHEET

SECTION 6

1. Ⓐ Ⓑ Ⓒ Ⓓ Ⓔ	10. Ⓐ Ⓑ Ⓒ Ⓓ Ⓔ	19. Ⓐ Ⓑ Ⓒ Ⓓ Ⓔ	28. Ⓐ Ⓑ Ⓒ Ⓓ Ⓔ
2. Ⓐ Ⓑ Ⓒ Ⓓ Ⓔ	11. Ⓐ Ⓑ Ⓒ Ⓓ Ⓔ	20. Ⓐ Ⓑ Ⓒ Ⓓ Ⓔ	29. Ⓐ Ⓑ Ⓒ Ⓓ Ⓔ
3. Ⓐ Ⓑ Ⓒ Ⓓ Ⓔ	12. Ⓐ Ⓑ Ⓒ Ⓓ Ⓔ	21. Ⓐ Ⓑ Ⓒ Ⓓ Ⓔ	30. Ⓐ Ⓑ Ⓒ Ⓓ Ⓔ
4. Ⓐ Ⓑ Ⓒ Ⓓ Ⓔ	13. Ⓐ Ⓑ Ⓒ Ⓓ Ⓔ	22. Ⓐ Ⓑ Ⓒ Ⓓ Ⓔ	31. Ⓐ Ⓑ Ⓒ Ⓓ Ⓔ
5. Ⓐ Ⓑ Ⓒ Ⓓ Ⓔ	14. Ⓐ Ⓑ Ⓒ Ⓓ Ⓔ	23. Ⓐ Ⓑ Ⓒ Ⓓ Ⓔ	32. Ⓐ Ⓑ Ⓒ Ⓓ Ⓔ
6. Ⓐ Ⓑ Ⓒ Ⓓ Ⓔ	15. Ⓐ Ⓑ Ⓒ Ⓓ Ⓔ	24. Ⓐ Ⓑ Ⓒ Ⓓ Ⓔ	33. Ⓐ Ⓑ Ⓒ Ⓓ Ⓔ
7. Ⓐ Ⓑ Ⓒ Ⓓ Ⓔ	16. Ⓐ Ⓑ Ⓒ Ⓓ Ⓔ	25. Ⓐ Ⓑ Ⓒ Ⓓ Ⓔ	34. Ⓐ Ⓑ Ⓒ Ⓓ Ⓔ
8. Ⓐ Ⓑ Ⓒ Ⓓ Ⓔ	17. Ⓐ Ⓑ Ⓒ Ⓓ Ⓔ	26. Ⓐ Ⓑ Ⓒ Ⓓ Ⓔ	35. Ⓐ Ⓑ Ⓒ Ⓓ Ⓔ
9. Ⓐ Ⓑ Ⓒ Ⓓ Ⓔ	18. Ⓐ Ⓑ Ⓒ Ⓓ Ⓔ	27. Ⓐ Ⓑ Ⓒ Ⓓ Ⓔ	

SECTION 7

1. Ⓐ Ⓑ Ⓒ Ⓓ Ⓔ	6. Ⓐ Ⓑ Ⓒ Ⓓ Ⓔ	11. Ⓐ Ⓑ Ⓒ Ⓓ Ⓔ	16. Ⓐ Ⓑ Ⓒ Ⓓ Ⓔ
2. Ⓐ Ⓑ Ⓒ Ⓓ Ⓔ	7. Ⓐ Ⓑ Ⓒ Ⓓ Ⓔ	12. Ⓐ Ⓑ Ⓒ Ⓓ Ⓔ	17. Ⓐ Ⓑ Ⓒ Ⓓ Ⓔ
3. Ⓐ Ⓑ Ⓒ Ⓓ Ⓔ	8. Ⓐ Ⓑ Ⓒ Ⓓ Ⓔ	13. Ⓐ Ⓑ Ⓒ Ⓓ Ⓔ	18. Ⓐ Ⓑ Ⓒ Ⓓ Ⓔ
4. Ⓐ Ⓑ Ⓒ Ⓓ Ⓔ	9. Ⓐ Ⓑ Ⓒ Ⓓ Ⓔ	14. Ⓐ Ⓑ Ⓒ Ⓓ Ⓔ	19. Ⓐ Ⓑ Ⓒ Ⓓ Ⓔ
5. Ⓐ Ⓑ Ⓒ Ⓓ Ⓔ	10. Ⓐ Ⓑ Ⓒ Ⓓ Ⓔ	15. Ⓐ Ⓑ Ⓒ Ⓓ Ⓔ	

SECTION 8

1. Ⓐ Ⓑ Ⓒ Ⓓ Ⓔ	5. Ⓐ Ⓑ Ⓒ Ⓓ Ⓔ	9. Ⓐ Ⓑ Ⓒ Ⓓ Ⓔ	13. Ⓐ Ⓑ Ⓒ Ⓓ Ⓔ
2. Ⓐ Ⓑ Ⓒ Ⓓ Ⓔ	6. Ⓐ Ⓑ Ⓒ Ⓓ Ⓔ	10. Ⓐ Ⓑ Ⓒ Ⓓ Ⓔ	14. Ⓐ Ⓑ Ⓒ Ⓓ Ⓔ
3. Ⓐ Ⓑ Ⓒ Ⓓ Ⓔ	7. Ⓐ Ⓑ Ⓒ Ⓓ Ⓔ	11. Ⓐ Ⓑ Ⓒ Ⓓ Ⓔ	15. Ⓐ Ⓑ Ⓒ Ⓓ Ⓔ
4. Ⓐ Ⓑ Ⓒ Ⓓ Ⓔ	8. Ⓐ Ⓑ Ⓒ Ⓓ Ⓔ	12. Ⓐ Ⓑ Ⓒ Ⓓ Ⓔ	16. Ⓐ Ⓑ Ⓒ Ⓓ Ⓔ

SECTION 9

1. Ⓐ Ⓑ Ⓒ Ⓓ Ⓔ	5. Ⓐ Ⓑ Ⓒ Ⓓ Ⓔ	9. Ⓐ Ⓑ Ⓒ Ⓓ Ⓔ	13. Ⓐ Ⓑ Ⓒ Ⓓ Ⓔ
2. Ⓐ Ⓑ Ⓒ Ⓓ Ⓔ	6. Ⓐ Ⓑ Ⓒ Ⓓ Ⓔ	10. Ⓐ Ⓑ Ⓒ Ⓓ Ⓔ	14. Ⓐ Ⓑ Ⓒ Ⓓ Ⓔ
3. Ⓐ Ⓑ Ⓒ Ⓓ Ⓔ	7. Ⓐ Ⓑ Ⓒ Ⓓ Ⓔ	11. Ⓐ Ⓑ Ⓒ Ⓓ Ⓔ	
4. Ⓐ Ⓑ Ⓒ Ⓓ Ⓔ	8. Ⓐ Ⓑ Ⓒ Ⓓ Ⓔ	12. Ⓐ Ⓑ Ⓒ Ⓓ Ⓔ	

SECTION 1
ESSAY

Time—25 minutes

The essay gives you an opportunity to show how effectively you can develop and express ideas. You should, therefore, take care to develop your point of view, present your ideas logically and clearly, and use language precisely.

Your essay must be written on the lines provided on your answer sheet—you will receive no other paper on which to write. You will have enough space if you write on every line, avoid wide margins, and keep your handwriting to a reasonable size. Remember that people who are not familiar with your handwriting will read what you write. Try to write or print so that what you are writing is legible to those readers.

You have twenty-five minutes to write an essay on the topic assigned below. DO NOT WRITE ON ANOTHER TOPIC. AN OFF-TOPIC ESSAY WILL RECEIVE A SCORE OF ZERO.

Think carefully about the issue presented in the following excerpt and the assignment below.

> Some scientists believe that knowledge is the most important resource for promoting human progress. Others argue that knowledge is constrained by our technology and skills, and that imagination is more important for human progress because it is unlimited. Scientists draw freely upon their imaginations much like artists do, and this process is crucial for enhancing progress.

Assignment: Is knowledge more important than imagination for promoting human progress? Plan and write an essay in which you develop your point of view on this issue. Support your position with reasoning and examples taken from your reading, studies, experience, or observations.

DO NOT WRITE YOUR ESSAY IN YOUR TEST BOOK. You will receive credit only for what you write on your answer sheet.

BEGIN WRITING YOUR ESSAY ON THE ANSWER SHEET.

IF YOU FINISH BEFORE TIME IS CALLED, YOU MAY CHECK YOUR WORK ON THIS SECTION ONLY.
DO NOT TURN TO ANY OTHER SECTION IN THE TEST.

SECTION 1—ESSAY

Time—25 minutes

SECTION 1—ESSAY

Time—25 minutes

SECTION 2

Turn to Section 2 of your answer sheet to answer the questions in this section.

Time—25 Minutes
24 Questions

Directions: For each question in this section, select the best answer from among the choices given and fill in the corresponding oval on the answer sheet.

Each sentence below has one or two blanks, each blank indicating that something has been omitted. Beneath the sentence are five words or sets of words labeled A through E. Choose the word or set of words that, when inserted in the sentence, best fits the meaning of the sentence as a whole.

Example:

Eliza felt ----- when her boss asked her to work seven weekends in a row but ----- when her work earned her a promotion.

(A) enervated . . weakened
(B) depressed . . intellectual
(C) advantageous . . salacious
(D) angry . . shopworn
(E) irate . . elated     ●

1. Sara's client instructed that none of the wedding colors should be too -----, so Sara made sure to include only pastels and other soft tones.

(A) neutral
(B) rigid
(C) bold
(D) light
(E) relaxed

2. The architectural team was ----- to learn that their plans were rejected by the zoning commission, since they had made painstaking efforts to adhere to every regulation.

(A) preoccupied
(B) undaunted
(C) gratified
(D) relieved
(E) astonished

3. Viewed by many as the most comprehensive research completed to date on the subject of the ocean floor, the professor's articles are ----- assigned as ----- reading for all marine biology students in the department.

(A) fastidiously . . elective
(B) rarely . . required
(C) frequently . . optional
(D) routinely . . compulsory
(E) rigorously . . alternative

4. Although Ricardo performed his back care exercises only -----, after three months he noticed an ----- of his back pain.

(A) sporadically . . amelioration
(B) perfunctorily . . extrication
(C) intermittently . . irritation
(D) diligently . . exacerbation
(E) precisely . . improvement

5. It is human nature for individuals to crave consistency and ----- in their lives; this explains how employees can maintain positions with the same companies for years in work environments that are ----- to their health.

(A) stability . . beneficial
(B) predictability . . deleterious
(C) excitement . . obdurate
(D) adventure . . calamitous
(E) discord . . disruptive

6. Chandler's speech lasted only minutes but made a ----- impression that was sure to be ----- for his career.

(A) repugnant . . edifying
(B) glowing . . regretful
(C) significant . . derogatory
(D) positive . . salutary
(E) fleeting . . conciliatory

GO ON TO THE NEXT PAGE

SECTION 2

7. After reviewing the defendant's history of repeated offenses, the judge determined that the defendant's ----- warranted a harsh sentence with no possibility of parole.

(A) recidivism
(B) pragmatism
(C) torpor
(D) veneration
(E) distention

8. Darrin's overly idealistic nature led him to espouse ----- plans built only on dreams, with no foundation for real-world success.

(A) hermeneutic
(B) lugubrious
(C) practicable
(D) duplicitous
(E) quixotic

GO ON TO THE NEXT PAGE

SECTION 2

Directions: Each passage below is followed by questions based on its content. Answer the questions on the basis of what is stated or implied in each passage and in any introductory material that may be provided.

Questions 9–10 are based on the following passage.

Swiss linguist Ferdinand de Saussure is known as "the father of modern linguistics." According to professor G. Ziegler, however, understanding Saussure's system of linguistics can often feel like "the mother of all battles." Saussure believed that all language was made up of what he referred to as *linguistic signs*. A linguistic sign, in Saussure's view, consists of two parts. The first part is the actual word or sound that we use to communicate an idea. This word or sound is known as a *signifier*. The second part of a linguistic sign is the concept, or mental idea, that comes to mind when we read or hear a word. This mental concept is known as the *signified*. As an example, the sound made by word "train" would be considered a signifier. The concept or idea of a train that we have in our minds would be the signified.

9. Lines 2–4 ("According to . . . battles") suggest that the author

(A) regards Saussure's system of linguistics as antiquated
(B) considers Saussure to be a valiant warrior as well as an accomplished scholar
(C) believes that Saussure's system of linguistics is difficult to understand
(D) is confident that Saussure's writings will be easily understood by students of his work
(E) rejects Saussure's arguments in favor of the views of other linguists

10. In line 11, the author mentions the word "train" in order to

(A) illustrate the ease with which multiple concepts can be held in a person's mind
(B) demonstrate the relevance of Saussure's system for understanding language
(C) provide an example of the two parts of a linguistic sign
(D) describe in detail the process through which a signifier evokes a signified
(E) critique Saussure's argument that all language is made up of linguistic signs

Questions 11–12 are based on the following passage.

In his work, Neill presents a comparison of urban development and city planning in two Russian cities: Tomsk, in western Siberia, and Vladivostok, in the Russian Far East. Neill views both cities as having experienced similar processes of development. He traces this development through three periods: before the Soviet Revolution, through the Soviet era, and after the Soviet decline. In the pre-Soviet era, Neill contends, both cities had a unique urban form. Tomsk possessed buildings made primarily of wood, while Vladivostok contained mostly brick structures. These building styles were part of the distinct heritage of each city and were largely neglected during the Soviet era, which focused primarily on developing infrastructure and housing to support rapid urban growth.

11. Which of the following would most likely be found at the beginning of Neill's study?

(A) A comparison of infrastructure development in Tomsk and Vladivostok after the Soviet decline
(B) A discussion of the distinctive building styles in Tomsk and Vladivostok before the Soviet Revolution
(C) A description of road and highway building undertaken in Russian cities during peak population surges
(D) An analysis of the brick-laying industry in Tomsk and the lumber industry in Vladivostok during the Soviet era
(E) An account of the urban development in non-Russian cities that took place during the Soviet era

12. The primary purpose of the passage is to

(A) analyze an historical document
(B) justify a policy decision
(C) refute a scientific argument
(D) describe a research study
(E) critique a theoretical approach

GO ON TO THE NEXT PAGE

SECTION 2

Directions: The passages below are followed by questions based on their content; questions following a pair of related passages may also be based on the relationship between the paired passages. Answer the questions on the basis of what is stated or implied in the passages and in any introductory material that may be provided.

Questions 13–24 are based on the following passages.

The narrator of Passage 1 describes the character of Thomas Gradgrind, a school teacher. This passage is adapted from the fiction work Hard Times, *by Charles Dickens, published in 1854. The second passage is an excerpt from a contemporary fictional essay in which a narrator describes a mother's relationship with her son.*

Passage 1

Thomas Gradgrind, sir. A man of realities. A man of fact and calculations. A man who proceeds upon the principle that two and two are four, and nothing over, and who is not to be talked into allowing for anything over. Thomas Gradgrind, sir—peremptorily Thomas—Thomas Gradgrind. With a rule and a pair of scales, and the multiplication table always in his pocket, sir, ready to weigh and measure any parcel of human nature, and tell you exactly what it comes to. It is a mere question of figures, a case of simple arithmetic. You might hope to get some other nonsensical belief into the head of George Gradgrind, or Augustus Gradgrind, or John Gradgrind, or Joseph Gradgrind (all suppositious, non-existent persons), but into the head of Thomas Gradgrind—no, sir!

In such terms Mr. Gradgrind always mentally introduced himself, whether to his private circle of acquaintance, or to the public in general. In such terms, no doubt, substituting the words "boys and girls" for "sir," Thomas Gradgrind now presented Thomas Gradgrind to the little pitchers before him, who were to be filled so full of facts.

Indeed, as he eagerly sparkled at them from the cellarage before mentioned, he seemed a kind of cannon loaded to the muzzle with facts, and prepared to blow them clean out of the regions of childhood at one discharge. He seemed a galvanizing apparatus, too, charged with a grim mechanical substitute for the tender young imaginations that were to be stormed away.

"Girl number twenty," said Mr. Gradgrind, squarely pointing with his square forefinger, "I don't know that girl. Who is that girl?"

"Sissy Jupe, sir," explained number twenty, blushing, standing up, and curtseying.

"Sissy is not a name," said Mr. Gradgrind. "Don't call yourself Sissy. Call yourself Cecilia."

"It's father as calls me Sissy, sir," returned the young girl in a trembling voice, and with another curtsey.

"Then he has no business to do it," said Mr. Gradgrind. "Tell him he mustn't. Cecilia Jupe. Let me see. What is your father?"

"He belongs to the horse-riding, if you please, sir."

Mr. Gradgrind frowned, and waved off the objectionable calling with his hand.

"We don't want to know anything about that, here. You mustn't tell us about that, here. Your father breaks horses, don't he?"

"If you please, sir, when they can get any to break, they do break horses in the ring, sir."

"You mustn't tell us about the ring, here. Very well, then. Describe your father as a horsebreaker. He doctors sick horses, I dare say?"

"Oh yes, sir."

"Very well, then. He is a veterinary surgeon, a farrier, and horsebreaker."

Passage 2

"That boy," Muriel said to her friend Sally, who was sitting across the table from her, diligently working on her needlepoint. "The stories he tells! Why, he has such a fanciful imagination—I don't know where he comes up with his tales."

Muriel recounted to Sally her experiencing of watching her son William perform as one of the actors in the Plantation Halloween Festival at Harrison Manor. William was part of the acting troupe that put on an annual multipart Halloween show for visitors to the manor in late October. He and twelve other actors created a series of storytelling stations at different points on the manor's grounds. Visitors would pay their admission fees and then be led by a guide to the various stations, each of which was set up as a different scene. William and his fellow actors put on a show for them at each station, telling frightening Halloween tales that had supposedly taken place at the manor long ago.

Muriel had been so proud of William as she stood there watching him speak. He took part in one of the barn scenes, at a station behind the manor. He grimaced and howled as he explained to cautious visitors how a werewolf had once haunted the fields nearby. William loved to entertain and had begun inventing wild tales when he was just a child. Muriel felt happy to see him now using his gifts professionally, in a part-time job that he loved.

"I bet you have a terrible time getting him to tell the truth when it really matters," Sally mused, listening to Muriel's story. "With an imagination like that, it must be hard to get straight facts out of the boy!"

"You would think," nodded Muriel, understanding how Sally might suspect such a thing. "But William really keeps his stories for entertainment. He can be very fanciful, but he also has a strong code of honor."

GO ON TO THE NEXT PAGE

She remembered a scene from William's childhood, when he'd broken a neighbor's window playing baseball with a group of friends. The neighbor had returned home to find the damage and combed the neighborhood, furious, knocking on doors to determine which children had been responsible. The other boys involved stayed mum, afraid to admit they had participated. William, on the other hand, came forward without even being asked. He heard Mr. Taylor knock on the door and ask in a grumbling voice about the accident. William came out of his room and told the truth on the spot, without Muriel having to say a word.

"I hit the ball through the window, Mr. Taylor," William said, his nine-year-old voice wavering. "I apologize. I'll do work around the yard to make it up to you," William offered. "Whatever it takes."

William never would divulge the names of the other boys he had been playing with that day. He simply took his punishment and made it up to Mr. Taylor, mowing the Taylors' lawn each week for the rest of the summer. He said that it didn't matter who the other boys were, as long as the damage was paid for. Muriel admired William's truthfulness and courage in the face of their neighbor's anger. She was proud of her son's sense of honor, which invariably led him to do the right thing.

13. The first three sentences of Passage 1 imply that Thomas Gradgrind

(A) is a straightforward individual who sticks to the facts
(B) comes from a background of British nobility
(C) is a specialist in mathematics
(D) is prone to stretching the truth to maintain appearances
(E) is an excellent storyteller

14. In line 39, "calling" most nearly means

(A) reply
(B) salutation
(C) name
(D) profession
(E) situation

15. In lines 31–36 ("Sissy . . . your father"), Mr. Gradgrind instructs Sissy to refer to herself as Cecilia because

(A) Sissy reminds him of another acquaintance who is called Cecilia
(B) he prefers to refer to his students by name and not by number
(C) Sissy's father calls her by the more traditional name Cecilia
(D) he finds Cecilia to be an easier name to remember
(E) he believes that the nickname "Sissy" is not an acceptable name

16. The statement in lines 17–19 ("Thomas Gradgrind . . . facts") suggests that Mr. Gradgrind

(A) found it frustrating that his students tended to forget what they learned in class
(B) believed it was important for him to impart facts and knowledge to his students
(C) viewed his students as unknowledgeable and unconcerned with learning
(D) saw his students as capable athletes who needed training in order to succeed
(E) was concerned that his students would rely too heavily on scientific facts

17. In Passage 2, Muriel's attitude toward her son William can best be described as

(A) fervent
(B) indifferent
(C) pleased
(D) disdainful
(E) boastful

18. In line 70, "wild" most nearly means

(A) uninhabited
(B) natural
(C) unruly
(D) outrageous
(E) uncivilized

19. In lines 81–103 ("She remembered . . . right thing"), Muriel describes William's boyhood incident with the broken window to illustrate that

(A) William's acting abilities have come in handy for helping him to escape trouble
(B) even though William is imaginative, he has a strong code of honor about telling the truth
(C) as a young boy, William was truthful to a fault, taking on responsibility for others' actions
(D) as a child, William's sense of honor about telling the truth was stronger than that of most boys
(E) William cannot be relied upon to respond truthfully in challenging situations

GO ON TO THE NEXT PAGE

SECTION 2

20. Which of the following best characterizes Mr. Taylor's reaction to the accident involving his window in Passage 2?

(A) Honesty
(B) Grief
(C) Embarrassment
(D) Outrage
(E) Indifference

21. In lines 85–89 ("The other boys . . . the accident"), the phrase "without even being asked" implies that

(A) William told the truth not because of outside pressure but because of his own moral code
(B) Mr. Taylor's facial expressions conveyed his questions even without words
(C) William's mother knew how to obtain answers from her son without asking him directly
(D) William anticipated Mr. Taylor's suspicion and chose to confess before he was accused
(E) Muriel could not find a comfortable way to ask her son about his role in the accident

22. William in Passage 2 differs most from Thomas Gradgrind in Passage 1 in that

(A) William lets his imagination run wild and lacks the ability to tell the truth, whereas Thomas Gradgrind focuses on facts and always emphasizes the reality of a situation
(B) William has an active imagination but, at heart, is truly honest, whereas Thomas Gradgrind thinks of himself as focusing on facts but actually stretches the truth to promote appearances
(C) William believes that it is important for him to share his knowledge with those around him, whereas Thomas Gradgrind prefers to entertain others by inventing fanciful stories
(D) William is prepared to take responsibility for his wrongdoings, but Thomas Gradgrind tends to blame others and to make excuses in order to escape punishment for his actions
(E) William spends most of his time in activities that take him away from reality, such as acting, whereas Thomas Gradgrind spends his efforts teaching his students how to cope with reality

23. Passage 1 and Passage 2 are similar in that

(A) both describe how their characters struggle to resolve challenging personal issues
(B) both involve central characters who turn out to be different from how they are initially presented
(C) both involve minor characters who ask questions that help to move the storyline forward
(D) both center around the themes of coming of age and learning to question authority
(E) both show how their characters come to terms with moral dilemmas by exercising certain virtues

24. William in Passage 2 would most likely advise Sissy in Passage 1 to

(A) take Mr. Gradgrind's suggestions seriously because he is more learned and clearly knows the facts
(B) behave as politely as possible in Mr. Gradgrind's class so as to avoid making him angry with her
(C) ignore the advice given to her by Mr. Gradgrind and tell the truth about her father's profession
(D) tell her father about Mr. Gradgrind's suggestion that he become a veterinary surgeon
(E) answer Mr. Gradgrind's questions with imaginative and untruthful responses

S T O P

IF YOU FINISH BEFORE TIME IS CALLED, YOU MAY CHECK YOUR WORK ON THIS TEST ONLY.
DO NOT TURN TO ANY OTHER SECTION IN THIS TEST.

SECTION 3

Turn to Section 3 of your answer sheet to answer the questions in this section.

Time—25 Minutes
20 Questions

Directions: For this section, solve each problem and decide which is the best of the choices given. Fill in the corresponding oval on the answer sheet. You may use any available space for scratchwork.

Notes:

1. The use of a calculator is permitted. All numbers used are real numbers.
2. Figures that accompany problems in this test are intended to provide information useful in solving the problems. They are drawn as accurately as possible EXCEPT when it is stated in a specific problem that the figure is not drawn to scale. All figures lie in a plane unless otherwise indicated.
3. Unless otherwise specified, the domain of any function f is assumed to be the set of all real numbers x for which $f(x)$ is a real number.

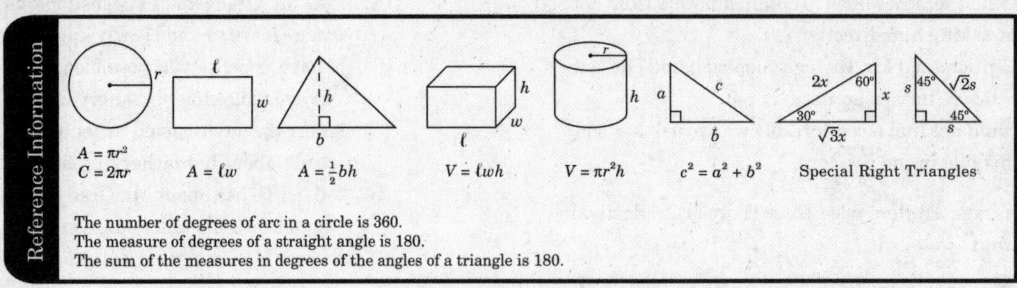

Reference Information
$A = \pi r^2$
$C = 2\pi r$
$A = \ell w$
$A = \frac{1}{2}bh$
$V = \ell wh$
$V = \pi r^2 h$
$c^2 = a^2 + b^2$
Special Right Triangles
The number of degrees of arc in a circle is 360.
The measure of degrees of a straight angle is 180.
The sum of the measures in degrees of the angles of a triangle is 180.

1. If $5n + 3 = 8$, what is the value of $2n + 7$?

(A) 1
(B) 5
(C) 9
(D) 11
(E) 15

2. A music collector has 7 cabinets of CDs. Each cabinet contains at least 135 CDs but not more than 180 CDs. Which of the following could be the number of CDs in this collection?

(A) 740
(B) 860
(C) 925
(D) 1,200
(E) 1,450

3. Which of the following describes the union of the set of integers less than $\sqrt{20}$ and the set of integers greater than $\sqrt{40}$?

(A) No integers
(B) Two integers
(C) Three integers
(D) All but two integers
(E) All integers

GO ON TO THE NEXT PAGE

SECTION 3

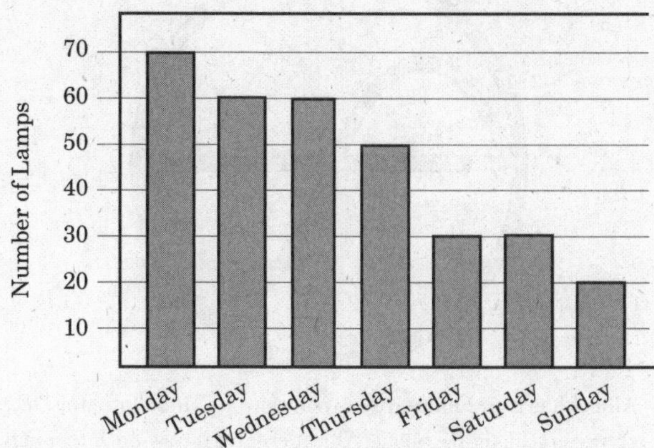

4. The graph above shows how the inventory of a lamp shop continued to decrease between Monday and Sunday of a certain week by indicating the total number of lamps in the shop inventory at the end of each day. The shop sold twenty lamps on the first day of an interior designer's convention in town. If the lamp shop did not receive any new lamps during the week, on what day did the convention begin?

(A) Tuesday
(B) Thursday
(C) Friday
(D) Saturday
(E) Sunday

---

5. The average (arithmetic mean) of a and b is 7 and the average of a, b, and c is 12. What is the value of c ?

(A) 22
(B) 21
(C) 12
(D) 10
(E) 4

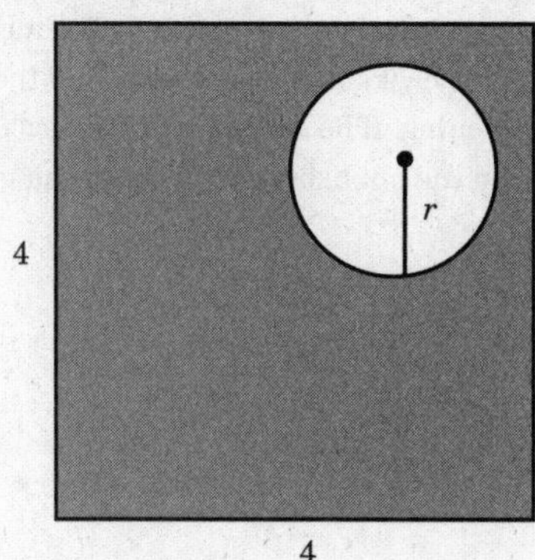

6. In the figure above, a small circle with radius r lies inside a larger square. What is the area, in terms of r, of the shaded region?

(A) $2\pi r - 8$
(B) $8 - r^2$
(C) $16 - 2\pi r$
(D) $\pi r^2 - 16$
(E) $16 - \pi r^2$

---

7. If $abcd = 1$ and $bced = 0$, which of the following must be true?

(A) $a < 1$

(B) $b < 1$

(C) $c > \frac{1}{2}$

(D) $e = 0$

(E) $d = 0$

GO ON TO THE NEXT PAGE

SECTION 3

8. During one day of a conference, a publisher sold one-fifth of his books in the morning, one-tenth of his books during lunch, three-fifths of his books in the afternoon, and the remaining books in the evening. If he sold a total of 50 books that day, how many books did the publisher sell in the evening?

(A) 5
(B) 10
(C) 15
(D) 20
(E) 30

9. If $4^{3a} = 16^{a+2}$, what is the value of a ?

(A) 0
(B) 1
(C) 2
(D) 4
(E) 6

10. If 5 more than 2 times a certain number is 7 less than the number, what is the number?

(A) −19
(B) −12
(C) 2
(D) 10
(E) 17

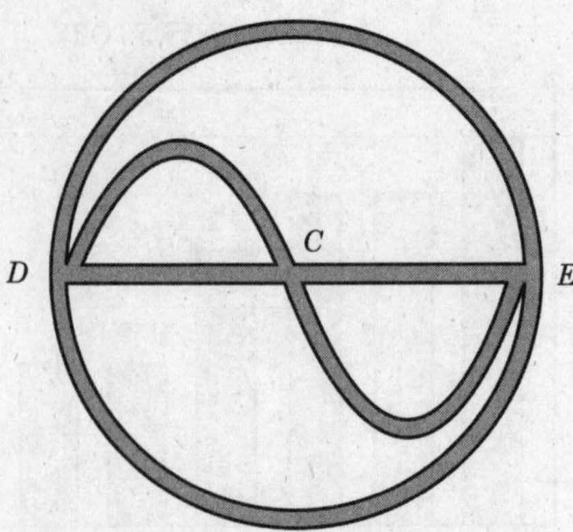

11. Albert has a circular garden with center C and diameter DE , as shown in the figure above. Albert creates a new path through his garden in the shape of two semicircles with diameters DC and CE. If the distance around the entire garden is 20π feet, how many feet does Albert walk by taking the curved path from D to E through C ?

(A) 10π
(B) 20
(C) 25π
(D) 40
(E) 100

2, 1, −1, . . .

12. The first term in the sequence of numbers shown above is 2. Each even numbered term is 1 less than the previous term and each odd-numbered term, after the first, is −1 times the previous term. For example, the second term is 2 − 1, and the third term is $(-1) \times 1$. What is the 63rd term of the sequence?

(A) −2
(B) −1
(C) 0
(D) 1
(E) 2

GO ON TO THE NEXT PAGE

x	$f(x)$
0	w
–1	17
–2	z

13. The table above shows some values for the function f. If f is a linear function, what is the value of $w + z$?

(A) 17
(B) 21
(C) 34
(D) 51
(E) It cannot be determined from the information given.

14. In the xy-plane, the equation of line j is $y = -3x - 1$. If line k is the reflection of line j across the x-axis, what is the equation of line k ?

(A) $y = 3x - 1$
(B) $y = 3x + 1$
(C) $y = -3x + 1$
(D) $y = \frac{1}{3}x + 1$
(E) $y = \frac{1}{3}x - 1$

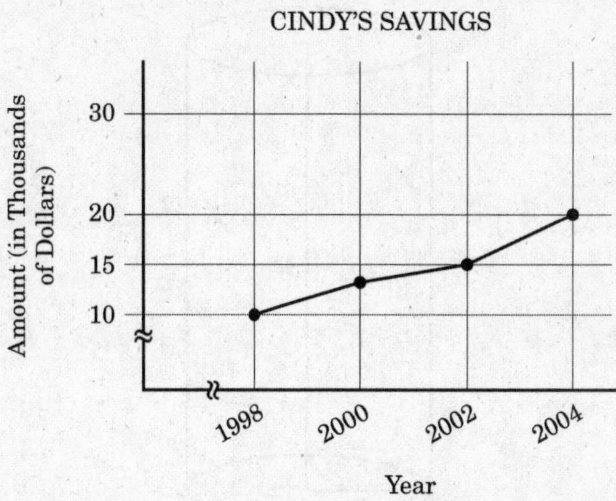

15. The graph above shows Cindy's savings in thousands of dollars from the year 1998 to the year 2004. The amount of Cindy's savings in 2004 was what percent greater than her savings in 2002?

(A) 1
(B) $16\frac{2}{3}$
(C) 25
(D) $33\frac{1}{3}$
(E) 50

GO ON TO THE NEXT PAGE

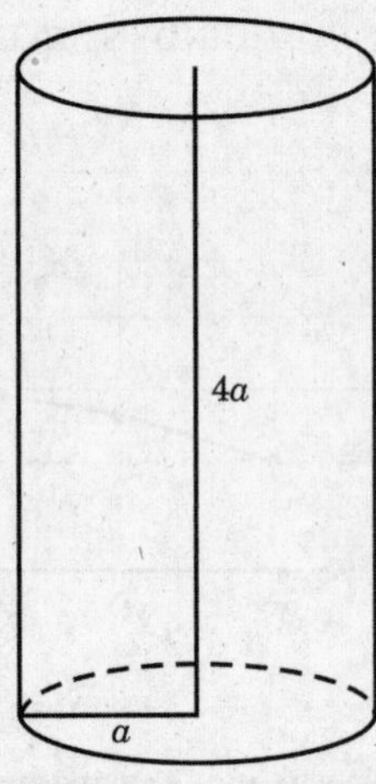

16. Which of the following has the same volume as the cylinder shown above with radius a and height $4a$?

(A) A cylinder with radius $4\pi a$ and height a
(B) A cube with edge $2\pi a$
(C) A cylinder with radius $4a$ and height a
(D) A rectangular solid with dimensions $2a$, $2a$, and πa
(E) A rectangular solid with dimensions $4a$, a, and π

17. If $t = \frac{(q+2)-p}{4}$, what is $q + 2$, in terms of t and p ?

(A) $4t$
(B) $4t + p$
(C) $t + p$
(D) $\frac{t+p}{2}$
(E) $\frac{t}{2p}$

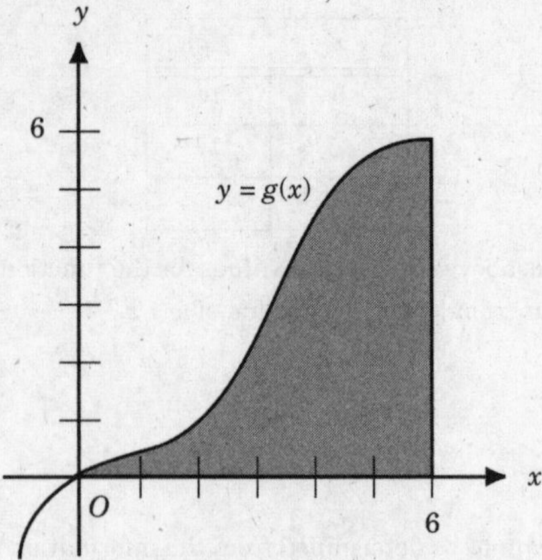

18. The shaded region in the figure above is bounded by the x-axis, the line $x = 6$, and the graph of $y = g(x)$. If the point (j, k) lies in the shaded region, which of the following must be true?

I. $k \le j$
II. $j \le 6$
III. $k \le g(j)$

(A) I only
(B) II only
(C) III only
(D) I and II only
(E) II and III only

GO ON TO THE NEXT PAGE

SECTION 3

19. At a toothpaste manufacturing plant, toothpaste tubes are filled by Machine #1 and packaged by Machine #2. Machine #2 accepts the tubes only if the net weight is between 169.95 and 170.05 grams. If Machine #2 accepts a tube containing g grams, which of the following describes all possible values of g ?

(A) $|g - 170| > 0.05$
(B) $|g + 170| < 0.05$
(C) $|g + 170| = 0.05$
(D) $|g - 170| < 0.05$
(E) $|g - 170| = 0.05$

20. The least integer in a set of consecutive integers is x. The greatest integer in the set is z. If the sum of these integers is y, which of the following represents the number of integers in this set?

(A) $z - x$
(B) $x - z + 1$
(C) $\frac{x + y}{z}$
(D) $y - x + z$
(E) $\frac{2y}{x + z}$

S T O P

IF YOU FINISH BEFORE TIME IS CALLED, YOU MAY CHECK YOUR WORK ON THIS TEST ONLY.
DO NOT TURN TO ANY OTHER SECTION IN THIS TEST.

SECTION 4

Turn to Section 4 of your answer sheet to answer the questions in this section.

Time—25 Minutes
24 Questions

Directions: For each question in this section, select the best answer from among the choices given and fill in the corresponding oval on the answer sheet.

Each sentence below has one or two blanks, each blank indicating that something has been omitted. Beneath the sentence are five words or sets of words labeled A through E. Choose the word or set of words that, when inserted in the sentence, best fits the meaning of the sentence as a whole.

Example:

Eliza felt ----- when her boss asked her to work seven weekends in a row but ----- when her work earned her a promotion.

(A) enervated . . weakened
(B) depressed . . intellectual
(C) advantageous . . salacious
(D) angry . . shopworn
(E) irate . . elated     ●

1. To ensure that the marchers would stop their loud protests, the constable paid them a visit and asked that they ----- from making any further noise.

(A) escape
(B) deprive
(C) isolate
(D) desist
(E) supplant

2. Llewellyn's high metabolism gave him a voracious ----- that was ----- only after several large helpings at each meal.

(A) condition . . alleviated
(B) appeal . . suppressed
(C) greed . . quelled
(D) hunger . . enhanced
(E) appetite . . satiated

3. Despite her fear of ----- from the school board, the principal presented her case against the superintendent with ----- determination, bolstering each accusation with concrete evidence.

(A) retaliation . . diffident
(B) recriminations . . stalwart
(C) adulation . . resolute
(D) opposition . . waning
(E) backlash . . faltering

4. Local residents thought of their neighbor as -----, but police investigations into his past revealed a long history of surreptitious behaviors.

(A) candid
(B) degenerate
(C) luminous
(D) choleric
(E) duplicitous

5. The professor's austere personality was poorly reflected by his ----- handwriting, which was often indecipherably -----.

(A) baroque . . simplistic
(B) nomadic . . extravagant
(C) florid . . ornate
(D) spartan . . prosaic
(E) stern . . modest

GO ON TO THE NEXT PAGE

SECTION 4

Directions: The passages below are followed by questions based on their content; questions following a pair of related passages may also be based on the relationship between the paired passages. Answer the questions on the basis of what is stated or implied in the passages and in any introductory material that may be provided.

Questions 6–9 are based on the following passages.

Passage 1

So often the temptation to cram more events into our days leads us to sacrifice a few hours of sleep in order to accomplish it all. This sacrifice may be more detrimental than we realize. A study on sleep conducted at the University of Pennsylvania revealed that chronic sleep deprivation can reduce our ability to concentrate and impair our thinking. The study examined subjects who slept only four to six hours every night during a two-week period. Participants in the study demonstrated a significant reduction in mental capacity, equivalent to going without any sleep at all for 72 hours. Participants had longer reaction times to different stimuli and made more mistakes when performing cognitive tasks. Overall, however, the study subjects did not realize that their functioning was impaired. Most reported feeling "only slightly sleepy."

Passage 2

Can too much sleep be damaging to our health? Recent research suggests that people who sleep too much are at an increased risk of heart disease. One study, conducted by Brigham and Women's Hospital in Boston, tracked sleep patterns and heart disease rates among 72,000 patients over a ten-year period. The study found that sleep-deprived individuals who got less than five hours of sleep per night were at a 50 percent increased risk of heart disease compared to those participants who averaged eight hours of sleep per night. Even those sleeping for six hours per night had a 20 percent higher risk. Interestingly, however, the study also found that those participants who regularly reported nine hours of sleep per night or more were also at a 38 percent higher risk of heart disease than the eight-hour group. This study suggests that balance in sleep patterns is key. While it's crucial to be sure to get enough sleep, it's important not to overdo it either.

6. The author of Passage 1 describes study results suggesting that

(A) excessive sleep can cause impairment of human memory
(B) adequate sleep is critical for effective human functioning
(C) the effects of sleep deprivation are difficult to quantify
(D) too little sleep can increase a person's risk of heart attack
(E) the cognitive effects of sleep deprivation are more serious than the health effects

7. Both passages address the

(A) health benefits of sleeping nine or more hours per night
(B) changing sleep needs of individuals as they age
(C) impact of sleep deprivation on concentration
(D) damaging results of too much sleep
(E) negative effects of incorrect amounts of sleep

8. The author of Passage 2 would most likely respond to the author of Passage 1 by

(A) acknowledging that people fail to notice their sleepiness
(B) questioning the methods used in the study cited
(C) agreeing that too little sleep can be harmful
(D) encouraging the author to interview study participants
(E) critiquing the notion that excess sleep carries risks

9. The two passages differ in their analysis of sleep in that

(A) Passage 1 utilizes research gathered from thousands of patients, while Passage 2 is based on a smaller number of study participants
(B) Passage 2 explains the connection between sleep disorders and diabetes, and Passage 1 focuses solely on how sleep disorders develop
(C) Passage 2 argues that recent research overemphasizes the risks associated with sleep deprivation, while Passage 1 presents evidence that documents these risks
(D) Passage 2 examines the relationship between sleep and risk for heart disease, but Passage 1 focuses on how sleep impairs our reflexes and thinking capacity
(E) Passage 2 looks only at the negative effects of too little sleep, while Passage 1 argues that both too little and too much sleep can be damaging

GO ON TO THE NEXT PAGE

SECTION 4

Directions: Each passage below is followed by questions based on its content. Answer the questions on the basis of what is stated or implied in each passage and in any introductory material that may be provided.

Questions 10–15 are based on the following passage.

In this passage, a theorist analyzes the comparative politics concept of political culture.

The concept of political culture is but one among the many frameworks utilized by political scientists in their studies of comparative politics. This concept has frequently been used to explain differences in the levels of political participation in societies. Introduced by theorist Gabriel Almond in 1956, the political culture theory represents a synthesis of ideas derived from the fields of psychology and sociology. In effect, the application of the concept may be compared to the psychoanalysis of a psychiatric patient. Examinations of political culture are used to explain why a political society behaves as it does, just as psychoanalysis evaluates the subconscious motivations behind human behavior.

Political culture is defined by James Bill and Robert Hardgrave as "the cultural milieu in which political behavior takes place and to which it is systematically related." Gabriel Almond and Sidney Verba further qualify this concept in *The Civic Culture*, describing political culture as different orientations toward the political system in general. This definition has enabled theorists to identify three basic types of political culture. The first is *parochial* political culture, in which individual participation is limited or nonexistent due to an absence of political awareness. The second type is *subject* political culture, in which individual political awareness is evident, but not strong enough to produce extensive societal participation. Finally, the third category is *participant* political culture, in which political awareness and activity levels are relatively high.

Theorists use the political culture concept by applying it to societies in two steps. The first step involves categorizing a society according to which type of culture dominates its political character. Although every political culture is, in reality, a mix of all three types—parochial, subject, and participant—each is nevertheless dominated by one particular type. The United States, for example, is a participatory political culture. Many Americans are politically active in some manner, whether through voting, volunteering for political campaigns, or even participating in political protests. According to theorist Alan Abramowitz, Americans participate because they basically feel confident in their ability to influence political decisions. Participation is also motivated by the sense of allegiance that pervades American culture. Although participation levels are admittedly difficult to generalize, because they vary over time, Americans have tended toward active political involvement, especially when compared to citizens of other societies.

After the type of culture has been identified, the second step in applying the framework of political culture involves examining the process of political socialization within a country. This requires analyzing why the society has become, and why it remains, the type of culture that it is. In the United States, the process of political socialization occurs through multiple channels, among them the educational system and the mass media. The educational system teaches cultural principles, while the mass media sheds positive light on national political values. These channels of communication with the general public ensure continued maintenance of American democratic ideals.

The concept of political culture does not present a "catch-all" method for evaluating political participation, however. There are several considerations that the concept fails to address. Perhaps the most important of these is the fact that the framework of political culture does not attempt to explain participation in terms of individual reactions to the performance of the political system. The framework takes into account only those attitudes toward the polity that have been shaped by socialization or cultivated by some type of early childhood experience. But what about the responses that occur in reaction to the performance of a political system? Allegiance is not just based on early socialization experiences—it can also be tempered by the actions of political institutions themselves. What happens to public support of institutions in America, for example, if the performance of these systems begins to decline? In general, as Abramowitz points out, it is not enough to assess how political culture affects the creation of political institutions. The institutions themselves can play a part in the shaping of political culture as well.

10. In the first sentence of the passage (lines 1–3) ("The concept . . . politics"), the author characterizes political culture as being

(A) introduced by comparative politics theorist Gabriel Almond in 1956
(B) one of multiple tools used by researchers who study comparative politics
(C) comparable to the psychoanalysis of a psychiatric patient
(D) developed primarily by scholars from other disciplines, such as anthropology
(E) defined as the cultural milieu in which political behavior takes place

GO ON TO THE NEXT PAGE

SECTION 4

11. The reference to "psychoanalysis" in lines 7–12 ("In effect . . . behavior") is included in order to

(A) provide an analogy that helps to explain how the concept of political culture is used
(B) convey the value of psychoanalysis as a tool for determining levels of political participation
(C) demonstrate that examinations of political culture can help evaluate subconscious motivations
(D) show that psychoanalysis represents a synthesis of ideas from the fields of psychology and sociology
(E) establish that psychoanalytic techniques can be applied on a national level to understand political behavior

12. The statement in lines 30–32 ("Although every . . . type") implies that

(A) participatory political cultures are characterized by low political awareness
(B) it is possible to classify countries in terms of one primary type of political culture
(C) most Western democratic countries qualify as participatory political cultures
(D) the concept of political culture can only be applied as a two-part process
(E) applying theoretical concepts is usually ineffective for studying societies

13. The reference to "allegiance" in line 39 is used to support the author's point that

(A) America is a subject political culture
(B) Americans are more politically oriented than citizens of other countries
(C) many Americans are politically active in some way
(D) Americans participate in politics by volunteering for campaigns
(E) political participation in America is difficult to generalize

14. According to the author, the second step in applying the concept of political culture involves

(A) identifying a "catch-all" method for evaluating political participation
(B) categorizing a society according to its dominant political culture
(C) determining a country's specific mix of political culture types
(D) encouraging a society's awareness of political corruption
(E) analyzing the process of political socialization within a country

15. In paragraph 5 (lines 55–72) ("The concept . . . well"), the author's tone in the passage shifts from

(A) encouraging to cautious
(B) explanatory to critical
(C) disinterested to engaged
(D) questioning to supportive
(E) concerned to alarmed

GO ON TO THE NEXT PAGE

Questions 16–24 are based on the following passage.

Unless you're out in nature, today it's hard to walk even a few feet without coming across a structure that uses electricity in some way. Electrical outlets and light switches are ordinary household fixtures that we now take for granted. Yet, it has required literally hundreds of years of research for electricity to evolve to the point of common household usage as we know it today. This indispensable modern convenience is the result of efforts by some of history's greatest scientists, inventors, and businessmen.

Most of us think of electricity as having been "discovered" by Benjamin Franklin. Franklin certainly had a great deal to do with our ability to harness the power of electricity in its current form; however, the phenomenon of electricity was acknowledged in Western culture as early as the year 600 B.C. At that time, a certain type of electrical charge was perceived by researchers who worked with the gemstone amber. When rubbed, the amber would attract light items, such as feathers, which would stick to the gemstone in a phenomenon that we now know as static electricity. This process was recorded in the writings of an ancient Greek philosopher, Thales of Miletus, but it took more than two centuries before the first scientific studies of the phenomenon were conducted by English physician William Gilbert in 1600. Gilbert coined the term *electricity* from the Greek word *elektron*, which means "amber."

Further research conducted in Europe in the 1700s produced an experimental device known as the Leyden jar. Developed in Leyden, Holland, by researcher Pieter van Musschenbroek, the Leyden jar was nothing more than a glass container filled with water and wrapped in metal foil. This simple device, however, was capable of storing static electricity and discharging it all at once. It therefore allowed researchers to carry out more in-depth investigations of the properties of static electricity. The most famous of these investigations was the one conducted by Benjamin Franklin, who used Leyden jars to prove that lightning was, in fact, a form of static electricity. In 1752, Franklin placed a key on the string of a kite and flew the kite just before a thunderstorm. Passing thunderclouds made the key spark, and this spark generated static electricity within Franklin's Leyden jars.

The Leyden jar was superseded in 1799 through the work of Italian scientist Allesandro Volta, who used metal disks and salt water to create an electric current that did not need to be charged like the Leyden jar. Because of Volta's success in generating electricity through a chemical process, the first battery was developed. Just twenty years after this invention, scientist Hans Christian Oersted of Denmark discovered that when electricity flows through a wire, it produces a magnetic field around the wire. This discovery, and further research into electromagnetism, led to the invention of the electric motor. The inventions of the telegraph, the telephone, and, of course, the ever-important lightbulb followed, all within a few years of one another in the late 1800s.

Our knowledge of electricity has come a long way since Thales of Miletus first recorded that mysterious charge produced when amber was rubbed. Today a total of 2,776 electric utility plants are currently operated in the United States alone, serving more than 130 million customers, according to the U.S. Energy Information Administration. About 51 percent of U.S. electricity is produced through coal plants, and 20 percent is powered by nuclear fuel. Another 17 percent is produced by natural gas. The amount of electricity sold in the U.S. has grown by more than 1,400 percent over the past 50 years, from 255 billion kilowatt hours in 1949 to 3,675 billion kilowatt hours in 2003. Clearly, the idea that was once just a gleam in a Greek philosopher's eye has become a necessity—indeed, a basic foundation—of contemporary society.

16. The primary purpose of the passage is to

(A) describe the history of electricity
(B) refute the principle of electromagnetism
(C) analyze statistics on electricity usage
(D) track the rising costs of electricity
(E) explain the invention of the lightbulb

17. The statement in lines 11–14 ("Franklin certainly . . . 600 B.C..") implies that

(A) Benjamin Franklin was the first Westerner to research electricity
(B) the ancient Greeks knew more about electricity than Benjamin Franklin
(C) Benjamin Franklin did not actually discover electricity
(D) Benjamin Franklin worked with electricity by conducting experiments on amber
(E) Benjamin Franklin performed his experiments on electricity in 600 B.C.

18. In line 17, "light" most nearly means

(A) sparkling
(B) floating
(C) faint
(D) weightless
(E) bright

GO ON TO THE NEXT PAGE

SECTION 4

19. In line 29, the author refers to "this simple device" to emphasize that

(A) because of its primitive design, the Leyden jar was incapable of storing static electricity
(B) although the Leyden jar was not elaborate, it served an important research function
(C) the Leyden jar was too simplistic to assist researchers in furthering their experiments
(D) scientists such as Benjamin Franklin had difficulty learning how to use the Leyden jar
(E) researchers in Holland during that time period tended to prefer simple devices to complex ones

20. According to the passage, Benjamin Franklin's kite experiment proved that

(A) electricity was in fact a viable scientific phenomenon
(B) static electricity could be generated and stored
(C) lightning tends to strike metal objects
(D) lightning was a type of static electricity
(E) kites could be flown even when weighted with metal objects

21. Which of the following inventions related to electricity is NOT discussed in the passage?

(A) The electric motor
(B) The elegraph
(C) The battery
(D) The lightbulb
(E) The television

22. In line 51, the author's use of the phrase "all within a few years of one another" suggests that

(A) the inventions of the telegraph, telephone, and lightbulb were delayed by problems with Oersted's research
(B) the invention of the electric motor was an important precursor to the establishment of power plants
(C) the discovery of electromagnetism was more important than the discovery of static electricity
(D) the invention of the lightbulb allowed researchers to continue their work during evening hours
(E) once scientists gained a certain level of knowledge about electricity, the progress of inventions proceeded very rapidly

23. In the last paragraph, lines 53–65 ("Our knowledge . . . society"), the author cites statistics on electricity usage to make the point that

(A) scientists today can harness the power of electricity without fully understanding the phenomenon
(B) our society would function more efficiently if we reduced our dependence on electricity
(C) our understanding of electricity has vastly increased since electricity was first discovered
(D) government leaders should make more of an effort to produce electricity through nuclear plants
(E) electricity consumption in the United States has now reached alarming proportions

24. According to the author, electricity has become

(A) a highly costly industrial resource
(B) an indispensable modern convenience
(C) an overdue technological innovation
(D) a menace to modern civilization
(E) a threat to the natural environment

S T O P

IF YOU FINISH BEFORE TIME IS CALLED, YOU MAY CHECK YOUR WORK ON THIS TEST ONLY. DO NOT TURN TO ANY OTHER SECTION IN THIS TEST.

SECTION 5

Turn to Section 5 of your answer sheet to answer the questions in this section.

Time—25 Minutes
18 Questions

Directions: For this section, solve each problem and decide which is the best of the choices given. Fill in the corresponding oval on the answer sheet. You may use any available space for scratchwork.

Notes:

1. The use of a calculator is permitted. All numbers used are real numbers.
2. Figures that accompany problems in this test are intended to provide information useful in solving the problems. They are drawn as accurately as possible EXCEPT when it is stated in a specific problem that the figure is not drawn to scale. All figures lie in a plane unless otherwise indicated.
3. Unless otherwise specified, the domain of any function f is assumed to be the set of all real numbers x for which $f(x)$ is a real number.

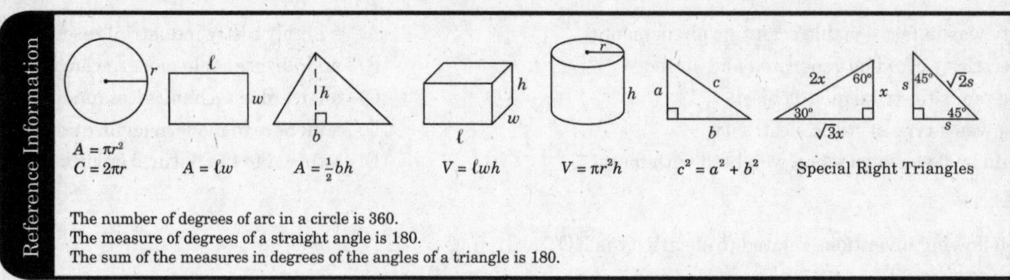

Reference Information
$A = \pi r^2$
$C = 2\pi r$
$A = \ell w$
$A = \frac{1}{2}bh$
$V = \ell wh$
$V = \pi r^2 h$
$c^2 = a^2 + b^2$
Special Right Triangles
The number of degrees of arc in a circle is 360.
The measure of degrees of a straight angle is 180.
The sum of the measures in degrees of the angles of a triangle is 180.

1. $\frac{7a - 2}{3} = 4$

What is the value of a ?

(A) 2
(B) 3
(C) 4
(D) 5
(E) 7

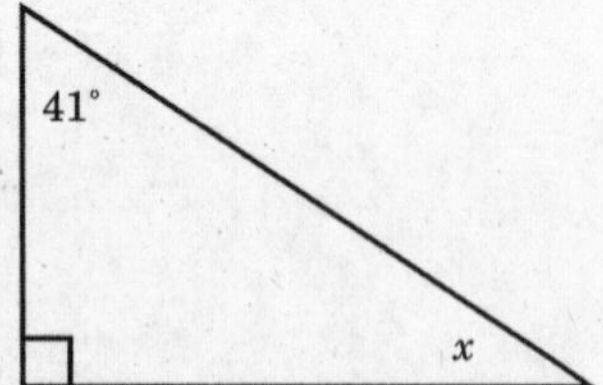
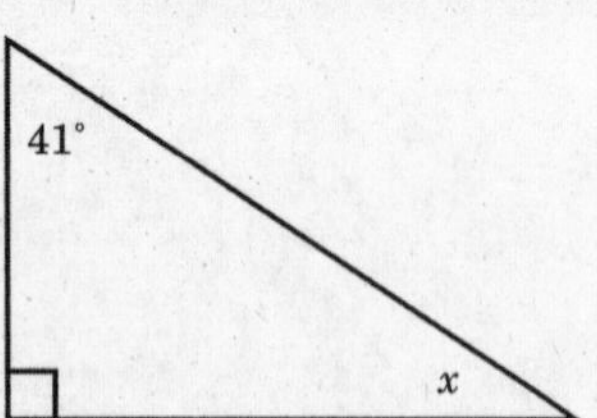

41°
x

2. In the right triangle above, what is the value of x ?

(A) 39°
(B) 41°
(C) 49°
(D) 90°
(E) 139°

3. A baker calculates the number of cups of flour, f, required to make a certain number of brownies, b, using the following equation: $f = 2b + 32$. If the baker wishes to bake 64 brownies, how many cups of flour must she use?

(A) 16
(B) 32
(C) 64
(D) 96
(E) 160

GO ON TO THE NEXT PAGE

SECTION 5

MUSEUM STORE INVENTORY

Greek	Egyptian	French
567	273	728

4. The table shown above represents three types of statues in a museum's collection. If the museum has a total of 1,903 statues in its collection, how many of its statues are neither Greek nor French?

(A) 273
(B) 335
(C) 608
(D) 1,001
(E) 1,295

All numbers that are divisible by both 3 and 9 are also divisible by 6.

5. Which of the following numbers can be used to show that the statement above is FALSE?

(A) 6
(B) 12
(C) 18
(D) 27
(E) 36

6. A bag of marbles contains only red and green marbles. The ratio of red to green marbles is 2:3. Which of the following could represent the number of marbles in the bag?

(A) 14
(B) 28
(C) 32
(D) 47
(E) 50

7. If $x = \frac{z}{y}$ and $\frac{z}{u} = wy$, then x is also equal to which of the following?

(A) uw
(B) $\frac{y}{z}$
(C) $\frac{u}{z}$
(D) $z + w$
(E) uwy

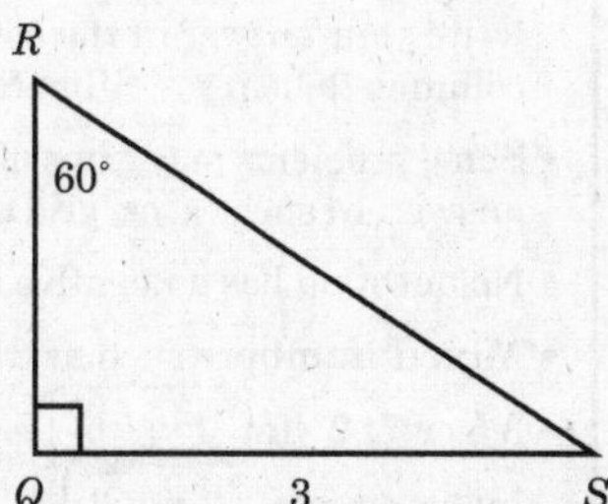

8. In the right triangle QRS shown above, what is the length of QR ?

(A) $\sqrt{3}$
(B) $3\sqrt{2}$
(C) $3\sqrt{3}$
(D) 6
(E) $9\sqrt{3}$

GO ON TO THE NEXT PAGE

SECTION 5

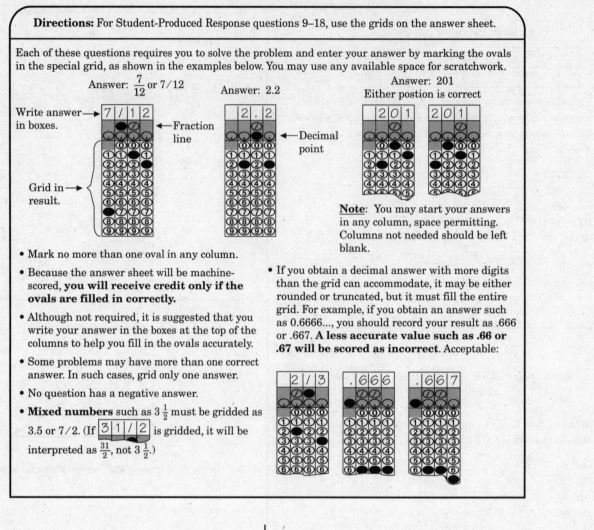

Directions: For Student-Produced Response questions 9–18, use the grids on the answer sheet.

Each of these questions requires you to solve the problem and enter your answer by marking the ovals in the special grid, as shown in the examples below. You may use any available space for scratchwork.

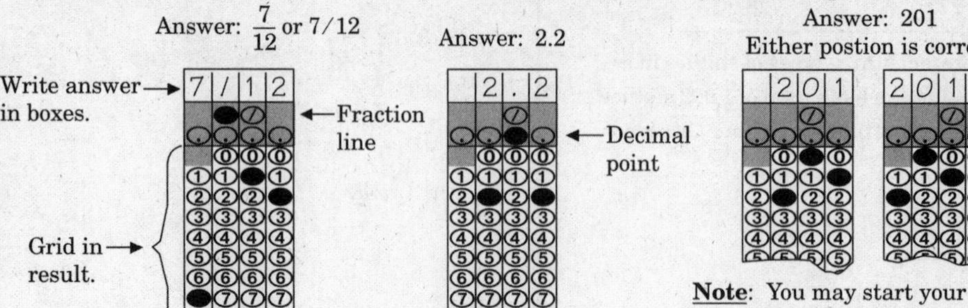

Note: You may start your answers in any column, space permitting. Columns not needed should be left blank.

- Mark no more than one oval in any column.
- Because the answer sheet will be machine-scored, **you will receive credit only if the ovals are filled in correctly.**
- Although not required, it is suggested that you write your answer in the boxes at the top of the columns to help you fill in the ovals accurately.
- Some problems may have more than one correct answer. In such cases, grid only one answer.
- No question has a negative answer.
- **Mixed numbers** such as $3\frac{1}{2}$ must be gridded as 3.5 or 7/2. (If 3 1 / 2 is gridded, it will be interpreted as $\frac{31}{2}$, not $3\frac{1}{2}$.)
- If you obtain a decimal answer with more digits than the grid can accommodate, it may be either rounded or truncated, but it must fill the entire grid. For example, if you obtain an answer such as 0.6666..., you should record your result as .666 or .667. **A less accurate value such as .66 or .67 will be scored as incorrect**. Acceptable:

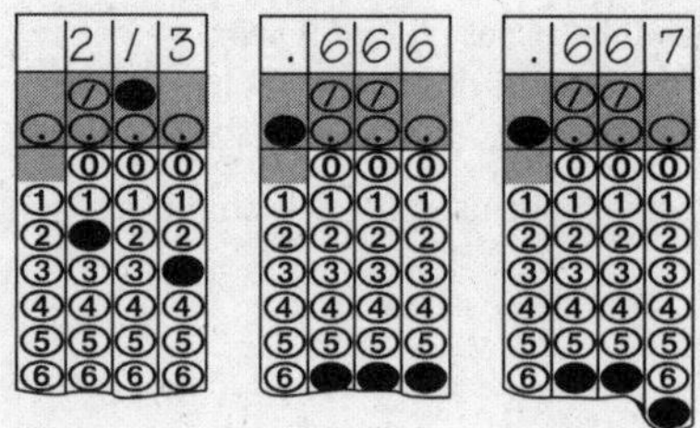

9. If $s^9 = 512$, what is the value of $\frac{s^9}{16}$?

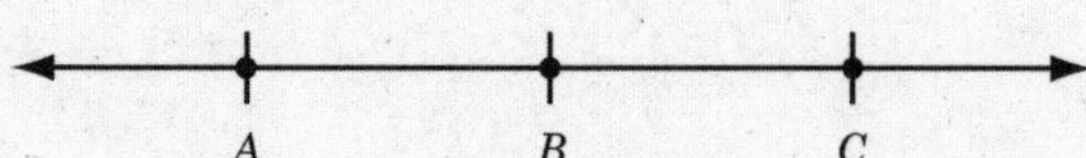

10. In the figure above, B is the midpoint of segment AC. If point A lies at –3 on the number line and point C lies at 4, what is the location of point B on the number line?

GO ON TO THE NEXT PAGE

SECTION 5

11. A square with sides of length 4 cm lies inside a square with sides of length 6 cm. What is the area, in square centimeters, of the part of the larger square that lies outside the smaller square?

12. The sum of 5 consecutive integers is 2,000. What is the value of the smallest of these integers?

13. The sides of triangle *EFG* have lengths 2, 5, and 8. Each angle of triangle *EFG* has the same measure as an angle in triangle *JKL*. If the length of one side of triangle *JKL* is 40, what is one possible perimeter of triangle *JKL* ?

14. If $x^2 - y^2 = 40$ and $x + y = 4$, then what is the value of x ?

GO ON TO THE NEXT PAGE

15. Let the operations $\oplus$ and $\otimes$ be defined for all real numbers m and n as follows:

$m \oplus n = m - 2n$

$m \otimes n = m - 7n$

If $3 \oplus (2x) = (2x) \otimes 3$, what is the value of x?

16. Let the function z be defined by $z(a) = 15 + \frac{a^2}{5}$.

If $z(5q) = 50q$, what is a positive value of q?

17. A fashion designer interviews eight models for a fashion show. Only three models can be chosen for the show. How many different combinations of three models can be chosen for the show?

18. A farmer drove to the market on Friday at an average speed of 60 miles per hour. He returned home on Sunday along the same route and averaged 40 miles per hour. If the farmer spent a total of two hours driving to and from the market, how many miles did the farmer drive to the market on Friday?

S T O P

IF YOU FINISH BEFORE TIME IS CALLED, YOU MAY CHECK YOUR WORK ON THIS TEST ONLY. DO NOT TURN TO ANY OTHER SECTION IN THIS TEST.

SECTION 6

Turn to Section 6 of your answer sheet to answer the questions in this section.

Time—25 Minutes
35 Questions

Directions: For each question in this section, select the best answer from among the choices given.

The following sentences test correctness and effectiveness of expression. Part of each sentence or the entire sentence is underlined; beneath each sentence are five ways of phrasing the underlined material. Choice A repeats the original phrasing; the other four choices are different. If you think the original phrasing produces a better sentence than any of the alternatives, select choice A; if not, select one of the other choices.

In making your selection, follow the requirements of standard written English; that is, pay attention to grammar, choice of words, sentence construction, and punctuation. Your selection should result in the most effective sentence—clear and precise, without awkwardness or ambiguity.

Example:

In the poem "Ulysses" by Alfred, Lord Tennyson, the speaker says, "I cannot rest from travel," instead, he will live life to the fullest.

(A) "I cannot rest from travel," instead,
(B) "I cannot rest from travel"; instead,
(C) "I cannot rest from travel" instead,
(D) "I cannot rest from travel," upon which
(E) "I cannot rest from travel,"

1. Cecelia had just boarded the plane and that was when she was told that her flight would be delayed.

(A) and that was when she was told
(B) and then they told her
(C) when it was learned by her
(D) and then she learned
(E) when she learned

2. Frustrated at being scratched twice by his frightened cat, Robert's attempt to restrain his pet was cautious.

(A) Robert's attempt to restrain his pet was cautious
(B) Robert's cautious attempt was to restrain his pet
(C) to restrain his pet was what Robert cautiously attempted
(D) to restrain his pet being what Robert cautiously attempted
(E) Robert attempted cautiously to restrain his pet

3. Linda, Charles, and Steven were skiing when, slipping on an ice patch, he collapsed in the snow.

(A) when, slipping on an ice patch, he collapsed in the snow
(B) and then he collapsed in the snow after he slipped on an ice patch
(C) when Steven collapsed in the snow after slipping on an ice patch
(D) when Steven collapsed in the snow, since he slipped on an ice patch
(E) and, since Steven has slipped on an ice patch, he collapsed in the snow

4. By trimming down the division's marketing budget, the training manager was able to hire many laid-off workers as independent contractors, this was an outcome many employees had hoped for.

(A) this was an outcome many employees had hoped for
(B) because many employees had hoped for this outcome
(C) the hope many workers had would be an outcome
(D) an outcome that many employees had hoped for
(E) it was hoped for by many workers as an outcome

5. A thriving business can be measured not only by the increases in its revenue but it has a growth of its net worth.

(A) it has a
(B) also the
(C) also by the
(D) in the way of having a
(E) as well in the

GO ON TO THE NEXT PAGE

SECTION 6

6. Today's students may rely primarily on calculators to solve complex math problems, but old-fashioned arithmetic still has value because it teaches students to execute basic operations.

(A) problems, but old-fashioned arithmetic still has value because it teaches
(B) problems, but old-fashioned arithmetic still would have value because of teaching
(C) problems; however, there is still value in old-fashioned arithmetic by teaching
(D) problems, old-fashioned arithmetic still having value because it teaches
(E) problems, but old-fashioned arithmetic still have value because it teaches

7. International politics research often involves case studies where they can assess the fit between a theory and historical fact.

(A) where they
(B) through which they
(C) and the political scientist
(D) through which the political scientist
(E) which they

8. The committee chairperson has argued that regular collection of dues from council members provides better cash flow for council activities than does occasional collection of member donations.

(A) provides better cash flow for council activities than does occasional collection of member donations
(B) provides better cash flow for council activities than member donations are collected occasionally
(C) providing better cash flow for council activities than does occasional collection of member donations
(D) do provide better cash flow for council activities than occasional collection of member donations do
(E) in contrast to occasional collection of member donations, provides better cash flow for council activities

9. The principal's term "unsavory characters" referring to the vandals who defaced the school by breaking several windows and spray painting graffiti on the main door.

(A) referring to the vandals who defaced the school
(B) referring to the school defacing that vandals committed
(C) which refers to the vandals' defacing of the school
(D) refers to the vandals who defaced the school
(E) is when it refers to vandals who defaced the school

10. Meteorologists predict weather patterns in the next month, they will be as erratic as were the weather patterns experienced over the past three months.

(A) month, they will be as erratic as were
(B) month, these will be as erratic as
(C) month; being as erratic as were
(D) month will be erratic as are
(E) month as erratic as

11. With thousands of pounds yet to be moved, some argue that fertilizer relocation efforts are too taxing on community resources.

(A) With thousands of pounds
(B) Because thousands of pounds of fertilizer are
(C) Because of fertilizer in thousands of pounds
(D) By considering that there are thousands of pounds
(E) Aware of the fertilizer in thousands of pounds

GO ON TO THE NEXT PAGE

SECTION 6

Directions: For each question in this section, select the best answer from among the choices given.

The following sentences test your ability to recognize grammar and usage errors. Each sentence contains either a single error or no error at all. No sentence contains more than one error. The error, if there is one, is underlined and lettered. If the sentence contains an error, select the one underlined part that must be changed to make the sentence correct. If the sentence is correct, select choice E. In choosing answers, follow the requirements of standard written English.

Example:

The other (A) delegates and him (B) immediately (C) accepted the resolution drafted by (D) the neutral states. No error (E)

12. Recognized (A) as a (B) very skilled teacher, Professor Lundstrom has motivated (C) many of his students to overcame (D) their fears about taking tests. No error (E)

13. The marketing department launched (A) a new campaign to (B) appeal to busy parents (C) by emphasizing snacks that (D) would combine convenience with healthy ingredients. No error (E)

14. Neither the actors or (A) the play's director could believe (B) the glowing reviews the show received, (C) so positive (D) was the critical response. No error (E)

15. Even though (A) Mariah was able to memorize only (B) part (C) of the Dickinson poem, she felt certain that eventually she will be able (D) to remember the entire piece. No error (E)

16. The investigators questioned (A) Mr. Rigby several times, (B) but he (C) remained silent throughout the entire investigation, refusing to say any thing. (D) No error (E)

17. Never believing that she can (A) win the writing contest, the author (B) was overjoyed to learn that her essay had been chosen (C) as the first-place entry. (D) No error (E)

18. Eyestrain can be caused (A) by many different factors, but by far (B) the most common cause among (C) students is overuse from long nights of studying, particularly around (D) exam time. No error (E)

19. Advised by (A) the best physical therapists in the city, the clinic director learned to admit, (B) treat, and to release (C) patients in a timely (D) and comprehensive manner. No error (E)

20. Hurricane Edna struck (A) the coast violently, demolishing (B) every solid structure in her path (C) and leaving behind a devastating (D) shoreline. No error (E)

21. Any person who (A) suffers from food allergies may find it difficult to control the emotional outbursts that they experience (B) after (C) eating (D) certain foods. No error (E)

22. Ricky noticed (A) that the processional was lagging behind (B) the music, and he realized (C) that the flower girl was stopping to picking up (D) each flower that she threw. No error (E)

23. Brandon researched (A) several law firms before he applied (B) to Brandt & Meyer, but after working there (C) for ten months he realized that (D) practicing law was not his passion. No error (E)

GO ON TO THE NEXT PAGE

SECTION 6

24. A manufacturing engineer typically works long shifts, because they are [A] responsible for overseeing [B] the production staff and [C] ensuring that [D] all company deadlines are met. No error [E]

25. The townspeople tended to keep their distance of [A] newcomers because [B] most of the [C] town inhabitants were suspicious [D] of strangers. No error [E]

26. After confirming [A] her plans with Russell and me [B], Sondra left to go waterskiing and [C] then waited for us [D] at the pier. No error [E]

27. Only shoppers [A] with [B] nine items or less [C] in their carts can check out through the express lanes [D]. No error [E]

28. When [A] considering whether to incorporate a business, the owner should evaluate the company's overall earnings [B] as well as it's [C] potential for [D] being sued. No error [E]

29. Crystal found [A] it frustrating to sit quiet [B] during the guest speaker's lectures; she [C] always wanted to fidget [D] or to leave the room. No error [E]

GO ON TO THE NEXT PAGE

SECTION 6

Directions: The following passage is an early draft of an essay. Some parts of the passage need to be rewritten.

Read the passage and select the best answers for the questions that follow. Some questions are about particular sentences or parts of sentences and ask you to improve sentence structure or word choice. Other questions ask you to consider organization and development. In choosing answers, follow the requirements of standard written English.

Questions 30–35 are based on the following passage, a response to an assignment to write about the novel *The Sorrows of Young Werther*.

(1) *In his novel* The Sorrows of Young Werther, *author Johann Wolfgang von Goethe uses several effective literary techniques to develop the primary theme: the conflict between reason and feeling.* **(2)** *One technique used by Goethe to develop it involves the structure of the novel itself.* **(3)** Werther *is an epistolary novel, meaning that it has been made up of a series of letters that Werther, the central character, has written to a friend.* **(4)** *Werther's letters are in diary form, and they describe the events that happen in his life.* **(5)** *The epistolary structure of the novel is particularly effective, because it allows the reader greater insight into Werther's character.* **(6)** *"Only the writer of the letters . . . can be truly known from within," writes critic Liselotte Dieckmann.*

(7) *As the story progresses, Werther's unsteady character is clearly revealed through the content of his letters.* **(8)** *Some of his letters are strictly factual and straightforward, they relate events without digression.* **(9)** *Other letters, however, are highly emotional and charged with passion; in these, Werther describes breathtaking idyllic scenes or detailed encounters with Lotte, the woman he loves.*

(10) *As critic Hans Reiss notes, this variation in Werther's writing shows his "strong emotional movement" and also gives shape to the tension between rationality and feeling that develops in his personality.* **(11)** *Werther's factual letters convey the logical side of his character.* **(12)** *His emotional letters show the passion that often envelops him; one style randomly interrupts the other.* **(13)** *Through this variation in structure, Goethe reveals the waves of reason and emotion that battle for possession of Werther throughout the novel.*

30. Considering its context, sentence 2 (reprinted below) can best be revised in what way?

> *One technique used by Goethe to develop it involves the structure of the novel itself.*

(A) Change "it" to "this theme".
(B) Delete "technique".
(C) Change "develop" to "developed".
(D) Delete "of the novel itself".
(E) Insert "changing" before "the structure".

31. Which is the best version of sentence 3 (reproduced below)?

> Werther *is an epistolary novel, meaning that it has been made up of a series of letters that Werther, the central character, has written to a friend.*

(A) (As it is now)
(B) *Werther* is an epistolary novel that you read as a series of letters written by Werther, the central character, to a friend.
(C) *Werther*, being an epistolary novel, is made up of a series of letters that were written by Werther, the central character, to a friend.
(D) *Werther* is an epistolary novel, composed of a series of letters that Werther, the central character, has written to a friend.
(E) *Werther* is an epistolary novel, comprising a series of letters of Werther's (the central character's) that he had written to a friend.

32. What should be done with sentence 7?

(A) (As it is now)
(B) Delete it.
(C) Change "unsteady" to "balanced".
(D) Change "is clearly revealed" to "was revealed".
(E) Change "content of his letters" to "content".

GO ON TO THE NEXT PAGE

SECTION 6

33. Which of the following is the best version of sentence 8 (reproduced below)?

Some of his letters are strictly factual and straightforward, they relate events without digression.

(A) (As it is now)
(B) Some of his letters are strictly factual and straightforward; they are the ones that relate events without digression.
(C) Some of his letters are strictly factual and straightforward, they were relating events without digression.
(D) Some of his letters are strictly factual and straightforward they relate events without digression.
(E) Some of his letters are strictly factual and straightforward, relating events without digression.

34. Which of the following is the best way to combine sentences 11 and 12 to improve the flow of ideas?

(A) Replace the period with a comma.
(B) Replace the period with a semicolon.
(C) Replace the period with a comma, followed by the word "while".
(D) Replace the period with the word "and".
(E) Replace the period with a comma, followed by the word "and".

35. If the author were to develop the essay further, which of the following would be the most suitable addition to the end of the current essay?

(A) A paragraph that discusses Goethe's use of imagery to create an emotional impact on the reader
(B) A paragraph that explains the observation made by Hans Reiss and mentioned in the essay's third paragraph
(C) A paragraph that describes yet another literary technique Goethe uses to develop the primary theme of *Werther*
(D) A paragraph that points out how *Werther* differs in structure from some of Goethe's other literary works
(E) A paragraph that examines Werther's character in greater detail

S T O P

IF YOU FINISH BEFORE TIME IS CALLED, YOU MAY CHECK YOUR WORK ON THIS TEST ONLY. DO NOT TURN TO ANY OTHER SECTION IN THIS TEST.

SECTION 7

Turn to Section 7 of your answer sheet to answer the questions in this section.

Time—20 Minutes
19 Questions

Directions: For each question in this section, select the best answer from among the choices given and fill in the corresponding oval on the answer sheet.

Each sentence below has one or two blanks, each blank indicating that something has been omitted. Beneath the sentence are five words or sets of words labeled A through E. Choose the word or set of words that, when inserted in the sentence, best fits the meaning of the sentence as a whole.

Example:

Eliza felt ----- when her boss asked her to work seven weekends in a row but ----- when her work earned her a promotion.

(A) enervated . . weakened
(B) depressed . . intellectual
(C) advantageous . . salacious
(D) angry . . shopworn
(E) irate . . elated   

1. Sheryl's sister admitted that she had ----- the entire story, making up each detail as she went along.

(A) fabricated
(B) derided
(C) narrated
(D) imitated
(E) endured

2. All of the contestants behaved ----- throughout the pageant, displaying a natural ----- that made them easy for the judges to like.

(A) cautiously . . abruptness
(B) ineptly . . clumsiness
(C) astutely . . beneficence
(D) agreeably . . decisiveness
(E) amiably . . congeniality

3. Though Wilbur developed the proposal with the intention of ----- his upset clients, his arrogant presentation instead served to further ----- them.

(A) convincing . . exasperate
(B) placating . . antagonize
(C) reassuring . . pacify
(D) dissuading . . indoctrinate
(E) alienating . . ingratiate

4. Harold Sorbie was known for his frequent ----- of groups with views opposed to his own, so it came as no surprise when he openly criticized the political caucus for failing to lobby for stricter regulations.

(A) contradiction
(B) dissolution
(C) discussion
(D) condemnation
(E) investigation

5. After receiving widespread ----- for producing its first set of bioengineering protocols, the company feared that it would not be able to repeat its initial successful performance.

(A) dominance
(B) disregard
(C) acclaim
(D) applause
(E) collusion

6. The museum had an ----- collection of well-preserved Assyrian artifacts spanning multiple centuries; its Babylonian holdings, by contrast, tended to be more ----- and limited to a single time period.

(A) evolved . . circumscribed
(B) antiquated . . venerable
(C) itinerant . . uniform
(D) unusual . . exotic
(E) eclectic . . homogenous

GO ON TO THE NEXT PAGE

SECTION 7

Directions: The passage below is followed by questions based on its content. Answer the questions on the basis of what is stated or implied in the passage and in any introductory material that may be provided.

Questions 7–19 are based on the following passage.

The following passage is adapted from the autobiography of John Stuart Mill, published in the early 1900s. In this excerpt, Mill discusses how he met his wife.

It was the period of my mental progress which I have now reached that I formed the friendship which has been the honor and chief blessing of my existence, as well as the source of a great part of all that I have attempted to do, or hope to effect hereafter, for human improvement. My first introduction to the lady who, after a friendship of twenty years, consented to become my wife, was in 1830, when I was in my twenty-fifth and she in her twenty-third year. With her husband's family it was the renewal of an old acquaintanceship. His grandfather lived in the next house to my father's in Newington Green, and I had sometimes when a boy been invited to play in the old gentleman's garden. He was a fine specimen of the old Scotch puritan; stern, severe, and powerful, but very kind to children, on whom such men make a lasting impression.

Although it was years after my introduction to Mrs. Taylor before my acquaintance with her became at all intimate or confidential, I very soon felt her to be the most admirable person I had ever known. It is not to be supposed that she was, or that anyone, at the age at which I first saw her, could be, all that she afterwards became. Least of all could this be true of her, with whom self-improvement, progress in the highest and in all senses, was a law of her nature. For Mrs. Taylor, self-improvement was a necessity that arose equally from the ardor with which she sought it, and from the spontaneous tendency of her faculties, which could not receive an impression without making it the source of an accession of wisdom.

Up to the time when I first saw her, her rich and powerful nature had chiefly unfolded itself according to the received type of feminine genius. To her outer circle she was a beauty and a wit, with an air of natural distinction, felt by all who approached her. To her inner circle, she was a woman of deep and strong feeling, of penetrating and intuitive intelligence, and of an eminently meditative and poetic nature. She was married at a very early age to a most upright, brave, and honorable man of liberal opinions and good education, but without the intellectual or artistic tastes which would have made him a companion for her. He was, though, a steady and affectionate friend, for whom she had true esteem and the strongest affection through life, and whom she most deeply lamented when dead.

Shut out by the social disabilities of women from any adequate exercise of her highest faculties in action on the world without, her life was one of inward meditation, varied by familiar interactions with a small circle of friends, of whom one only (long since deceased) was a person of genius, or of capacities of feeling or intellect kindred with her own. Nonetheless, all had more or less of an alliance with her in sentiments and opinions. Into this circle I had the good fortune to be admitted, and I soon perceived that she possessed, in combination, the qualities which in all other persons whom I had known I had been only too happy to find singly.

In her complete emancipation from every kind of superstition resulted not from the hard intellect, but from strength of noble and elevated feeling, and co-existed with a highly reverential nature. In general spiritual characteristics, as well as in temperament and organization, I have often compared her, as she was at this time, to Shelley. But in thought and intellect, Shelley, so far as his powers were developed in his short life, was but a child compared with what she ultimately became. Alike in the highest regions of speculation and in the smaller practical concerns of daily life, her mind was the same perfect instrument, piercing to the very heart and marrow of the matter; always seizing the essential idea or principle.

The same exactness and rapidity of operation, pervading as it did her sensitive as well as her mental faculties, would, with her gifts of feeling and imagination, have fitted her to be a consummate artist, as her fiery and tender soul and her vigorous eloquence would certainly have made her a great orator. Her profound knowledge of human nature and discernment in practical life, would, in the times when such a profession was open to women, have made her eminent among the rulers of mankind. Her intellectual gifts did but minister to a moral character at once the noblest and the best balanced which I have ever met with in life. Her unselfishness was not that of a taught system of duties, but of a heart which thoroughly identified itself with the feelings of others, and often went to excess in consideration for them by imaginatively investing their feelings with the intensity of its own.

The passion of justice might have been thought to be her strongest feeling, had it not been for her boundless generosity, and a lovingness ever ready to pour itself forth upon any or all human beings who were capable of giving the smallest feeling in return. The rest of her moral characteristics were such as naturally accompany these qualities of mind and heart: the most genuine modesty combined with the loftiest pride; a simplicity and sincerity which were absolute, towards all who were fit to receive them; the utmost scorn of whatever was mean and cowardly; and a burning indignation at everything brutal or tyrannical, faithless or dishonorable in conduct and character.

GO ON TO THE NEXT PAGE

7. In line 6, the term "friendship" refers to the relationship

(A) that the author had with his wife before they were married
(B) between Mrs. Taylor and her group of acquaintances
(C) between Mrs. Taylor and her husband's grandfather
(D) between the author and his wife's circle of friends
(E) that the author had with his wife's first husband

8. As used in line 22, "law" most nearly means

(A) legislation
(B) characteristic
(C) statement
(D) regulation
(E) judgment

9. The reference to "self-improvement" in lines 20–26 ("Least of all . . . wisdom") is used to emphasize Mrs. Taylor's

(A) commitment to helping her friends advance
(B) refusal to consider the advice of others
(C) dedication to pursuing personal growth
(D) habitual dependence on the flattery of others
(E) tendency to urge her husband to better himself

10. The author uses the term "inner circle" (line 31) in order to

(A) explain why Mrs. Taylor married her first husband at an early age
(B) illustrate that Mrs. Taylor participated in different activities with several groups of friends
(C) demonstrate that Mrs. Taylor was equally open with all who knew her, acquaintances and close friends alike
(D) emphasize that Mrs. Taylor was less appealing in person than she was to those who saw her from afar
(E) highlight the fact that Mrs. Taylor's close friends knew her better than her other acquaintances did

11. In line 45, the phrase "kindred with" most nearly means

(A) familiar to
(B) joined with
(C) related to
(D) similar to
(E) descendent from

12. In lines 45–46 ("Nonetheless, all . . . opinions"), the author points out that Mrs. Taylor's friends

(A) had trouble understanding her opinions
(B) basically agreed with her beliefs
(C) were highly emotional people
(D) were strategic thinkers
(E) tended to band together as a group

13. The author's attitude toward Mrs. Taylor can best be characterized as

(A) wistful
(B) intimidated
(C) admiring
(D) unforgiving
(E) critical

14. In paragraph 5 (lines 51–62) ("In her . . . principle"), the author uses which of the following techniques to make his point about Mrs. Taylor's personal qualities?

(A) Analogy
(B) Comparison and contrast
(C) Allegory
(D) Question and answer
(E) Flashback

15. In line 58, the author uses the word "child" to emphasize that

(A) Shelley's intellect was less developed than Mrs. Taylor's
(B) Shelley lived an unusually short life
(C) Shelley behaved like a child around Mrs. Taylor
(D) Shelley's talents were widely recognized at a young age
(E) Shelley's intellectual capacity far exceeded that of Mrs. Taylor

16. In lines 58–62 ("Alike in the . . . principle"), the author suggests that Mrs. Taylor

(A) tended to focus her concentration on learning about music and culture
(B) would have made a better scholar than most other women of her time period
(C) had difficulty implementing minor tasks and instead excelled at envisioning the larger perspective
(D) tended to approach intellectual issues with a seriousness that was uncharacteristic of her peers
(E) was equally capable of considering theoretical matters and handling mundane details

17. In line 64, "sensitive" is best understood to mean

(A) emotional
(B) thoughtful
(C) touchy
(D) painful
(E) delicate

GO ON TO THE NEXT PAGE

SECTION 7

18. Mrs. Taylor's "unselfishness" (line 73) was most likely based on

(A) her tendency to reject superstitious beliefs
(B) her ability to relate to the emotions experienced by others
(C) her formal education in ethics and philosophy
(D) her sense of unworthiness in comparison to others
(E) her commitment to behaving as she was taught to behave

19. The references to Mrs. Taylor's generosity and lovingness in lines 78–82 ("The passion . . . in return") serve to underscore the author's point that these qualities were

(A) expressed by Mrs. Taylor in a limited way
(B) overshadowed by Mrs. Taylor's hatred of cowardice
(C) less significant than her other moral characteristics
(D) expressed toward people who did not return them
(E) even stronger than Mrs. Taylor's intense passion for justice

S T O P

IF YOU FINISH BEFORE TIME IS CALLED, YOU MAY CHECK YOUR WORK ON THIS TEST ONLY. DO NOT TURN TO ANY OTHER SECTION IN THIS TEST.

SECTION 8

Turn to Section 8 of your answer sheet to answer the questions in this section.

Time—20 Minutes
16 Questions

Directions: For this section, solve each problem and decide which is the best of the choices given. Fill in the corresponding oval on the answer sheet. You may use any available space for scratchwork.

Notes:

1. The use of a calculator is permitted. All numbers used are real numbers.
2. Figures that accompany problems in this test are intended to provide information useful in solving the problems. They are drawn as accurately as possible EXCEPT when it is stated in a specific problem that the figure is not drawn to scale. All figures lie in a plane unless otherwise indicated.
3. Unless otherwise specified, the domain of any function f is assumed to be the set of all real numbers x for which $f(x)$ is a real number.

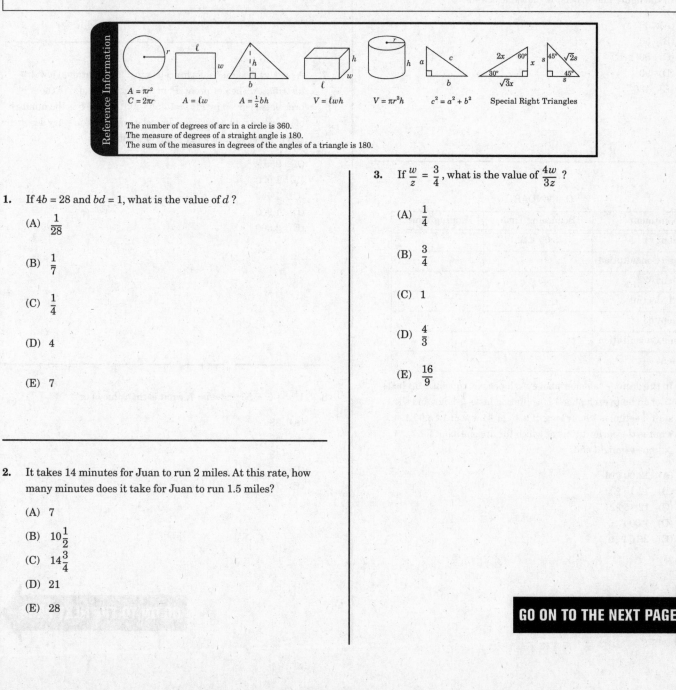

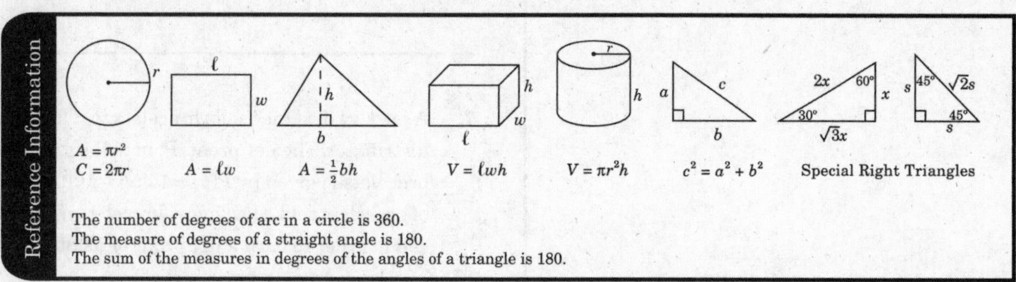
Reference Information
$A = \pi r^2$
$C = 2\pi r$
$A = \ell w$
$A = \frac{1}{2}bh$
$V = \ell wh$
$V = \pi r^2 h$
$c^2 = a^2 + b^2$
Special Right Triangles
The number of degrees of arc in a circle is 360.
The measure of degrees of a straight angle is 180.
The sum of the measures in degrees of the angles of a triangle is 180.

1. If $4b = 28$ and $bd = 1$, what is the value of d?

(A) $\frac{1}{28}$

(B) $\frac{1}{7}$

(C) $\frac{1}{4}$

(D) 4

(E) 7

2. It takes 14 minutes for Juan to run 2 miles. At this rate, how many minutes does it take for Juan to run 1.5 miles?

(A) 7

(B) $10\frac{1}{2}$

(C) $14\frac{3}{4}$

(D) 21

(E) 28

3. If $\frac{w}{z} = \frac{3}{4}$, what is the value of $\frac{4w}{3z}$?

(A) $\frac{1}{4}$

(B) $\frac{3}{4}$

(C) 1

(D) $\frac{4}{3}$

(E) $\frac{16}{9}$

GO ON TO THE NEXT PAGE

SECTION 8

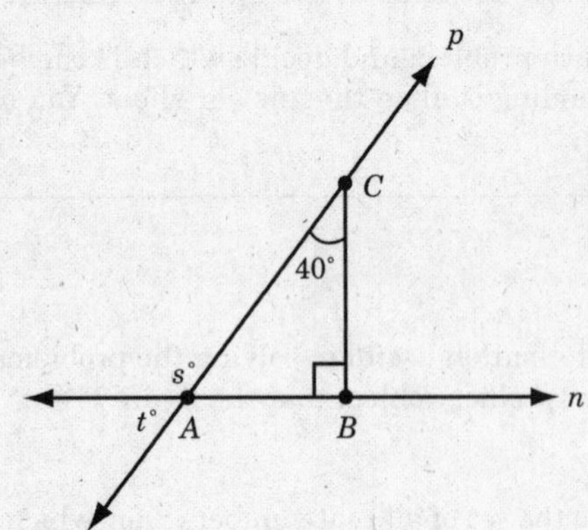

4. In the figure above, what is the value of $s - t$?

(A) 30°
(B) 50°
(C) 80°
(D) 90°
(E) 130°

CALENDAR

Appointment	Beginning Time	Ending Time
Patient #1	8:00 A.M.	
Phone Consultation		
Patient #2		
Staff Meeting		
Patient #3		
Phone Consultation		
Patient #4		?

5. In the doctor's calendar above, each patient appointment lasts $\frac{3}{4}$ of an hour, each phone consultation lasts $\frac{1}{2}$ hour, and the staff meeting is 1 hour long. If patient #1 is seen at 8:00 A.M., what is the earliest time at which the appointment for patient #4 might end?

(A) 12:00 P.M.
(B) 12:15 P.M.
(C) 12:45 P.M.
(D) 1:00 P.M.
(E) 2:15 P.M.

6. If $(2a - 1)$, $(a + 4)$, and $(4a - 7)$ all represent integers and $(a + 4)$ is the median of these integers, which of the following could be the value of a?

(A) 4
(B) 6
(C) 7
(D) 9
(E) 10

7. A jewelry designer sells bracelets to a large national jewelry distributor. The net profit, P, in dollars, from sales of the bracelets is given by $P(b) = 1.45b - 100$, where b is the number of bracelets sold. How many bracelets must the jewelry designer sell in order to earn a net profit of \$2,800?

(A) 950
(B) 1,000
(C) 1,450
(D) 1,900
(E) 2,000

8. If $a^2 + b^2 = 56$ and $ab = 7$, what is the value of $(a - b)^2$?

(A) 38
(B) 42
(C) 49
(D) 56
(E) 70

GO ON TO THE NEXT PAGE

SECTION 8

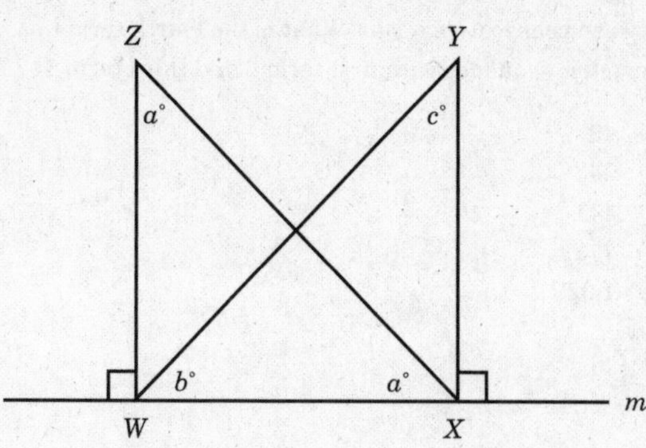

Note: Figure not drawn to scale.

9. In the figure above, $WZ = 1$ and $XY = \sqrt{3}$. What is the value of c?

(A) 15
(B) 18
(C) 24
(D) 30
(E) 36

---

10. If 45 percent of 50 percent of a positive number is equal to 25 percent of z percent of the same number, what is the value of z?

(A) 90
(B) 75
(C) 50
(D) 45
(E) 20

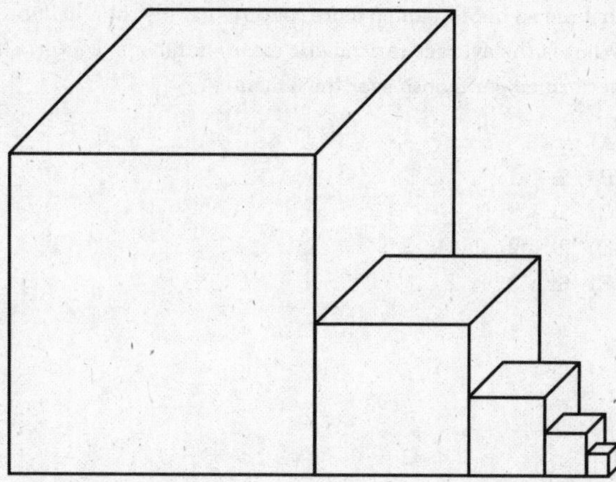

11. In the figure above, five cubes are lined up next to each other in decreasing order of size. The side length of each cube is half the length of the next largest cube directly to its left. The volume of the smallest cube is what fraction of the volume of the largest cube?

(A) $\frac{1}{32{,}768}$

(B) $\frac{1}{4{,}096}$

(C) $\frac{1}{513}$

(D) $\frac{1}{64}$

(E) $\frac{1}{8}$

---

12. If $3a < b < 0$, which of the following is greatest?

(A) $-3a$
(B) $-(3a + b)$
(C) $3a$
(D) 0
(E) $-b$

GO ON TO THE NEXT PAGE

SECTION 8

13. Clarence performed x concerts in May, 4 times as many concerts in June as in May, and 6 more concerts in July than in June. What is the average (arithmetic mean) number of concerts he performed per month over the 3 months?

(A) $x + 1$
(B) $2x - 2$
(C) $3x + 2$
(D) $2x + 2$
(E) $6x + 3$

14. If $(x-y)^{\frac{1}{2}} = (x+y)^{\frac{1}{2}}$, which of the following must be true?

(A) $x = 0$
(B) $x - y = 1$
(C) $x + y = 1$
(D) $x^2 - y^2 = 1$
(E) $x^2 + y^2 = 1$

15. In a geometric sequence of terms, there is a constant ratio between consecutive terms. What is the fourth term in a geometric sequence with first term 3 and third term 147 ?

(A) 49
(B) 343
(C) 441
(D) 772
(E) 1,029

16. Set R has r members and set S has s members. Set T consists of all unique members of set R and set S combined. If q represents the members common to both sets, which of the following represents the number of members in set T ?

(A) $q - rs$
(B) $r - s$
(C) $r + s + q$
(D) $r + s - q$
(E) $r + s - 2q$

S T O P

IF YOU FINISH BEFORE TIME IS CALLED, YOU MAY CHECK YOUR WORK ON THIS TEST ONLY.
DO NOT TURN TO ANY OTHER SECTION IN THIS TEST.

SECTION 9

Turn to Section 9 of your answer sheet to answer the questions in this section.

Time—10 Minutes
14 Questions

Directions: For each question in this section, select the best answer from among the choices given.

The following sentences test correctness and effectiveness of expression. Part of each sentence or the entire sentence is underlined; beneath each sentence are five ways of phrasing the underlined material. Choice A repeats the original phrasing; the other four choices are different. If you think the original phrasing produces a better sentence than any of the alternatives, select choice A; if not, select one of the other choices.

In making your selection, follow the requirements of standard written English; that is, pay attention to grammar, choice of words, sentence construction, and punctuation. Your selection should result in the most effective sentence—clear and precise, without awkwardness or ambiguity.

Example:

In the poem "Ulysses" by Alfred, Lord Tennyson, the speaker says, "I cannot rest from travel," instead, he will live life to the fullest.

(A) "I cannot rest from travel," instead,
(B) "I cannot rest from travel"; instead,
(C) "I cannot rest from travel" instead,
(D) "I cannot rest from travel," upon which
(E) "I cannot rest from travel,"

1. Some of Dr. Finkel's most important findings, from his discovery of certain artifacts to his confirmation of various hoaxes, resulting from experimental mistakes.

(A) resulting from
(B) they result from
(C) they have resulted from
(D) resulted from
(E) which resulted from

2. As shareholders, the directors of the company guarantee that you will be kept up to date on the progress of all major strategic negotiations.

(A) As shareholders, the directors of the company guarantee that you
(B) The guarantee of the company's directors about shareholders is that you
(C) You, as shareholders, are guaranteed by the company directors, and you
(D) The directors of the company, who guarantee that you, as shareholders
(E) The directors of the company guarantee that as shareholders, you

3. Coaching the swim team, focus on good sportsmanship was the tip Coach Riley gave his athletes.

(A) focus on good sportsmanship was the tip Coach Riley gave his athletes
(B) good sportsmanship was what Coach Riley instructed his athletes to focus on
(C) his athletes were advised by Coach Riley to focus on good sportsmanship
(D) good sportsmanship, instructed Coach Riley, was what his athletes should focus on
(E) Coach Riley instructed his athletes to focus on good sportsmanship

4. Frederick has scored higher grades on his history tests than the rest of the class because of being his favorite subject.

(A) the class because of being his favorite subject
(B) the class; this is the result of history being his favorite subject
(C) the class because history is his favorite subject
(D) the class as a result of history being his favorite subject
(E) the class since history is his favorite as a subject

GO ON TO THE NEXT PAGE

SECTION 9

5. Several clear road signs direct traffic to enter on the left side of the parking structure and exit on the right.

(A) to enter on the left side of the parking structure and exit
(B) to be entering on the left side of the parking structure and exiting
(C) that, having entered on the left side of the parking structure and exiting
(D) that entered on the left side of the parking structure and having exited
(E) to enter on the left side of the parking structure and exiting

6. Thomas, a budding athlete, could not learn to ride a bike until he can save enough money to purchase one.

(A) can save enough money to purchase one
(B) could save enough money to purchase one
(C) would be able to save enough money to purchase one
(D) can save enough money to purchase a bicycle
(E) could save enough money for the purchase of a bicycle

7. To ensure that flights can safely land at the airport, it is the air traffic controller who monitors the weather reports and evaluates landing conditions for each aircraft.

(A) it is the air traffic controller who monitors the weather reports and evaluates landing conditions for each aircraft
(B) the air traffic controller monitors the weather reports and evaluates landing conditions for each aircraft
(C) the weather reports being monitored by the air traffic controller, who evaluates landing conditions for each aircraft
(D) the air traffic controller—evaluating landing conditions for each aircraft—monitors the weather reports
(E) the air traffic controller is the one monitoring the weather reports and evaluating landing conditions for each aircraft

8. The automated system is faster, more efficient, and more accurate than the manual system, but the greater are its costs in maintenance.

(A) the greater are its costs in maintenance
(B) it has greater costs of maintenance
(C) in its maintenance costs it is greater
(D) there are the greater costs in maintenance
(E) its maintenance costs are greater

9. The state historical council regularly contributes donations to local library restoration funds—in some cities as much as ten thousand dollars annually.

(A) in some cities as much as ten thousand dollars annually
(B) in some cities having ten thousand dollars per year
(C) in some places donating about ten thousand dollars per year annually
(D) donating the equal of ten thousand dollars annually in some places
(E) which in some cities amounts to ten thousand dollars donated annually

10. Valued for their expertise, manufacturers will pay a high salary to trained specialists rather than settle for unskilled staff.

(A) Valued for their expertise, manufacturers will pay a high salary to trained specialists rather than settle for unskilled staff.
(B) Valued as experts, manufacturers will pay a high salary to trained specialists as opposed to settling for unskilled staff.
(C) Valued for their expertise, trained specialists command a high salary among manufacturers unwilling to settle for unskilled staff.
(D) As valued for expertise, trained specialists, receiving excellent pay, command a high salary for manufacturers unwilling to settle for unskilled staff.
(E) Trained specialists valued for their expertise by manufacturers who will pay a high salary but not to settle for unskilled staff.

11. Research on vitamins and supplements reveal that products produced by Brand X tend to be more effective than those produced by Brand Y.

(A) reveal that products produced by Brand X tend to be
(B) reveal products produced by Brand X that tend to be
(C) is revealing products produced by Brand X tending to be
(D) reveals that products produced by Brand X tend to be
(E) reveals that products produced by Brand X tends to be

12. Anna, Lacey, and Darlene always went everywhere together, so friends thought of them as the most inseparable trios in high school.

(A) thought of them as the most inseparable trios
(B) thought of them as the most inseparable trio
(C) were thinking of them as the most inseparable trios
(D) tended to think of them as the most inseparable trios
(E) were thinking of them as the most inseparable trio

GO ON TO THE NEXT PAGE

SECTION 9

13. Before eating breakfast, Mr. Peterson has a cup of coffee, Mrs. Peterson exercises first.

(A) Before eating breakfast, Mr. Peterson has a cup of coffee, Mrs. Peterson exercises first.
(B) Mr. Peterson has a cup of coffee before eating breakfast and Mrs. Peterson, she exercises first.
(C) Before eating breakfast, Mr. Peterson has a cup of coffee; Mrs. Peterson exercises first.
(D) Mrs. Peterson exercises first with Mr. Peterson having a cup of coffee before eating breakfast.
(E) Before eating breakfast, Mr. Peterson has a cup of coffee; Mrs. Peterson exercising first.

14. Philanthropist Hannah Striker is usually remembered for her contributions to medical research, and her well-known fundraising drive for Wild World Resources raised millions of dollars for environmental preservation.

(A) Philanthropist Hannah Striker is usually remembered for her contributions to medical research, and
(B) Philanthropist Hannah Striker is usually remembered for her contributions to medical research,
(C) Philanthropist Hannah Striker is usually remembered for her contributions to medical research, however
(D) Although philanthropist Hannah Striker is usually remembered for her contributions to medical research,
(E) Inasmuch as philanthropist Hannah Striker is usually remembered for her contributions to medical research,

S T O P

IF YOU FINISH BEFORE TIME IS CALLED, YOU MAY CHECK YOUR WORK ON THIS TEST ONLY.
DO NOT TURN TO ANY OTHER SECTION IN THIS TEST.

PRACTICE TEST 8

EXPLANATIONS

PRACTICE TEST 8 ANSWERS

Question Number	Answer	Right	Wrong
Section 2			
1	C		
2	E		
3	D		
4	A		
5	B		
6	D		
7	A		
8	E		
9	C		
10	C		
11	B		
12	D		
13	A		
14	D		
15	E		
16	B		
17	C		
18	D		
19	B		
20	D		
21	A		
22	B		
23	B		
24	C		
Section 3			
1	C		
2	D		
3	D		
4	C		
5	A		
6	E		
7	D		
8	A		
9	D		
10	B		
11	A		
12	B		
13	C		
14	B		
15	D		
16	D		
17	B		
18	E		
19	D		
20	E		
Section 4			
1	D		
2	E		
3	B		
4	A		
5	C		
6	B		
7	E		
Section 4, continued			
8	C		
9	D		
10	B		
11	A		
12	B		
13	C		
14	E		
15	B		
16	A		
17	C		
18	D		
19	B		
20	D		
21	E		
22	E		
23	C		
24	B		
Section 5			
1	A		
2	C		
3	E		
4	C		
5	D		
6	E		
7	A		
8	A		
9	32		
10	.5, 1/2		
11	20		
12	398		
13	75, 120, 300		
14	7		
15	4		
16	2		
17	56		
18	48		
Section 6			
1	E		
2	E		
3	C		
4	D		
5	C		
6	A		
7	D		
8	A		
9	D		
10	E		
11	B		
12	D		
13	E		
14	A		
15	D		

Question Number	Answer	Right	Wrong
Section 6, continued			
16	D	___	___
17	A	___	___
18	E	___	___
19	C	___	___
20	D	___	___
21	B	___	___
22	D	___	___
23	E	___	___
24	A	___	___
25	A	___	___
26	E	___	___
27	C	___	___
28	C	___	___
29	B	___	___
30	A	___	___
31	D	___	___
32	A	___	___
33	E	___	___
34	C	___	___
35	C	___	___
Section 7			
1	A	___	___
2	E	___	___
3	B	___	___
4	D	___	___
5	C	___	___
6	E	___	___
7	A	___	___
8	B	___	___
9	C	___	___
10	E	___	___
11	D	___	___
12	B	___	___
13	C	___	___
14	B	___	___
15	A	___	___

Question Number	Answer	Right	Wrong
Section 7, continued			
16	E	___	___
17	A	___	___
18	B	___	___
19	E	___	___
Section 8			
1	B	___	___
2	B	___	___
3	C	___	___
4	C	___	___
5	D	___	___
6	A	___	___
7	E	___	___
8	B	___	___
9	D	___	___
10	A	___	___
11	B	___	___
12	B	___	___
13	C	___	___
14	D	___	___
15	E	___	___
16	E	___	___
Section 9			
1	D	___	___
2	E	___	___
3	E	___	___
4	C	___	___
5	A	___	___
6	B	___	___
7	B	___	___
8	E	___	___
9	A	___	___
10	C	___	___
11	D	___	___
12	B	___	___
13	C	___	___
14	D	___	___

CALCULATING YOUR SCORE

Writing Section Raw Score

A. Essay Score (from 1–6) ______ A

B. Section 6 Multiple Choice: ______ no. correct − (______ no. incorrect ÷ 4) = ______ B

C. Section 9 Multiple Choice: ______ no. correct − (______ no. incorrect ÷ 4) = ______ C

D. Unrounded Multiple-Choice Score (B + C) ______ D

E. Total Rounded Multiple-Choice Raw Score
(Rounded to the nearest whole number) ______ E

F. Writing Multiple-Choice Subscore
(See the Writing Multiple-Choice conversion table on the following pages) ______ Writing MC Score

G. Total Scaled Score
(See the Writing conversion table on the following pages) ______ SAT Writing Score

Math Section Raw Score

A. Section 3 Raw Score: ______ no. correct − (______ no. incorrect ÷ 4) = ______ Subtotal A

B. Section 5 Raw Score: ______ no. correct ______ Subtotal B

C. Section 8 Raw Score: ______ no. correct − (______ no. incorrect ÷ 4) = ______ Subtotal C

D. Total Unrounded Raw Score
(Total A + B + C) ______ D

E. Total Rounded Raw Score (Rounded to the nearest whole number) ______ E

F. Scaled Score
(See the conversion table on the following pages) ______ SAT Math Score

Critical Reading Section Raw Score

A. Section 2 Raw Score: ______ (no. correct) − (______ (no. incorrect) ÷ 4) = ______ A

B. Section 4 Raw Score: ______ (no. correct) − (______ (no. incorrect) ÷ 4) = ______ B

C. Section 7 Raw Score: ______ (no. correct) − (______ (no. incorrect) ÷ 4) = ______ C

D. Total Unrounded Raw Score
(Total A + B + C) ______ D

E. Total Rounded Raw Score
(Rounded to the nearest whole number) ______ E

F. Scaled Score
(See the conversion table on the next page) ______ SAT Critical Reading Score

CONVERTING YOUR RAW SCORES

Raw Score	Critical Reading Scaled Score	Math Scaled Score
67	800	
66	790	
65	770	
64	760	
63	750	
62	740	
61	720	
60	710	
59	700	
58	690	
57	680	
56	670	
55	670	
54	660	800
53	650	780
52	640	760
51	640	740
50	630	730
49	620	710
48	610	700
47	610	690
46	600	670
45	590	660
44	590	650
43	580	650
42	580	640
41	570	630
40	560	620
39	560	610
38	550	600
37	540	590
36	540	590
35	530	580
34	530	570
33	520	560
32	510	560
31	510	550
30	500	540
29	500	530
28	490	520
27	480	520
26	480	510
25	470	500
24	470	490
23	460	490
22	450	480
21	450	470
20	440	460
19	430	460

Raw Score	Critical Reading Scaled Score	Math Scaled Score
18	430	450
17	420	440
16	410	430
15	410	430
14	400	420
13	390	410
12	380	400
11	380	390
10	370	380
9	360	380
8	350	370
7	340	360
6	330	340
5	320	330
4	310	320
3	300	310
2	280	290
1	270	280
0	250	260
−1	250	250
−2	240	240
−3	230	230
−4	220	220
−5	210	210
−6	200	200

Writing Subscores

- **Essay Subscore:** Subtotal A from Writing Score (page 694)
- **Multiple-Choice Subscore:** Calculate by plugging in Subtotal E from your writing score (page 694) into the score conversion table below

Raw Score	Multiple-Choice Subscore	Raw Score	Multiple-Choice Subscore
49	80	30	59
48	79	29	58
47	77	28	57
46	76	27	56
45	75	26	55
44	74	25	54
43	72	24	53
42	71	23	52
41	70	22	51
40	69	21	51
39	68	20	50
38	67	19	49
37	66	18	48
36	65	17	47
35	64	16	46
34	63	15	45
33	62	14	44
32	61	13	43
31	60	12	42

Raw Score	Multiple-Choice Subscore	Raw Score	Multiple-Choice Subscore
11	41	2	32
10	40	1	30
9	39	0	29
8	38	−1	27
7	37	−2	25
6	36	−3	24
5	35	−4	23
4	34	−5	22
3	33	−6	21

Writing Scaled Score

MC raw score	Essay Score					
	6	5	4	3	2	1
49	800	790	780	770	720	700
48	790	780	760	730	700	680
47	780	770	750	720	690	670
46	770	760	740	710	680	660
45	770	750	740	700	670	650
44	760	750	730	690	660	640
43	750	740	710	680	650	630
42	750	730	700	670	640	620
41	740	730	690	660	630	610
40	740	720	690	650	620	600
39	740	710	680	640	610	590
38	730	700	670	630	610	590
37	720	690	660	630	600	580
36	710	680	650	620	590	570
35	710	680	640	610	580	560
34	700	670	640	600	570	550
33	690	660	630	590	560	540
32	680	650	620	580	560	540
31	670	640	610	580	550	530
30	660	630	600	570	540	520
29	650	630	590	560	530	510
28	640	620	590	550	520	510
27	640	610	580	540	510	490
26	630	600	570	530	500	490
25	620	590	560	520	500	480
24	610	580	550	510	490	470
23	600	570	540	510	480	460
22	590	570	530	500	470	450
21	590	570	530	500	470	450
20	580	560	520	490	460	440
19	570	550	520	480	450	430
18	570	540	520	470	440	420
17	560	530	510	460	430	420
16	550	520	500	450	430	410
15	540	510	490	450	420	400
14	530	500	480	440	410	390
13	520	500	470	430	400	380
12	510	490	460	420	390	370

Writing Scaled Score

MC raw score	Essay Score 6	5	4	3	2	1
11	510	480	450	410	380	360
10	500	470	450	400	370	350
9	490	460	440	390	360	350
8	480	450	430	390	360	340
7	470	440	420	380	350	330
6	460	430	410	370	340	320
5	450	430	400	360	330	310
4	450	420	390	350	320	300
3	440	410	390	340	310	290
2	430	400	380	330	300	280
1	420	380	370	320	290	270
0	400	370	350	310	280	260
–1	380	360	340	290	270	260
–2	370	340	320	270	260	250
–3	360	330	310	260	250	240
–4	350	320	290	250	240	230
–5	340	310	280	240	230	220
–6	340	310	280	240	220	210

SECTION 2: CRITICAL READING

Sentence Completions

1. **C** One-Word/One-Way *Easy*

In following her client's instructions, Sara made sure that the wedding colors included *only pastels and other soft tones*. If Sara's client would accept pastels and soft colors, then the colors that the client did not want must be the opposite of *soft*. **C**, *bold*, fits best.

2. **E** One-Word/One-Way *Easy*

The architectural team made *painstaking*, or diligent, efforts to adhere to every zoning regulation. They were careful to follow the rules, so they most likely expected their plans to pass the zoning commission review. They must have been very surprised to learn that their plans had been rejected by the commission. **E**, *astonished*, expresses this surprise.

3. **D** Two-Word/One-Way *Medium*

The professor's articles are considered to be the *most comprehensive* research in his field. Therefore, it makes sense that the articles would be *required* or *compulsory* reading for students in the department. Eliminate **A**, **B**, and **E**. The articles are most likely assigned as required reading, so **C** doesn't work. **D** is correct.

4. **A** Two-Word/Two-Way *Difficult*

The word *although* at the start of this sentence signals a contrast in meaning. Either Ricardo practiced his exercises a great deal and noticed a worsening of his back pain, or he practiced his exercises infrequently but still noticed an improvement in his back pain. The word *only* suggests that Ricardo did not exercise very often. **A** is the only answer that provides an appropriate contrast. Ricardo practiced his exercises *sporadically*, but he still noticed an *amelioration* of his back pain—in other words, his back felt better.

5. **B** Two-Word/One-Way *Medium*

This sentence contains a semicolon but no connecting word immediately after it. This suggests that both blanks support the same meaning in the sentence. Start with the first blank. The word *and* suggests that the first blank will have a meaning similar to the word *consistency*. Eliminate **C**, **D**, and **E**. People crave stability, which explains why they might stay in work situations that are harmful to their health. The word *deleterious* is closest in meaning to harmful, so **B** is correct.

6. **D** Two-Word/One-Way *Medium*

Chandler's speech was short, but it made a certain type of impression. There are no contrast words between the two blanks in this sentence, which indicates that the two blanks will support the same idea. Look for a pair of words that reflects the same meaning, positive or negative. A positive impression would have a *salutary*, or "beneficial," effect on a person's career. **D** is correct.

7. **A** One-Word/One-Way *Difficult*

In this sentence, something about the defendant leads the judge to sentence him harshly. Note the clue given in the first part of the sentence: The defendant has a history of repeated crimes. The word *recidivism* means "a tendency to relapse." **A** is correct.

8. **E** One-Word/One-Way *Difficult*

The last part of this sentence explains the type of plans that Darrin makes: plans that lack the foundation for real-world success. In addition, the first part of the sentence gives a further clue about Darrin's personality: He is overly idealistic. The word *quixotic* means "foolish" or "impractical." **E** fits best.

Short Reading Passages

9. **C** Implied Information *Medium*

The author states that Saussure is considered to be the *father of modern linguistics*. Understanding his work, however, can feel like *the mother of all battles*. This reference to battles implies that it can be a huge struggle to understand Saussure's concepts. **C** is correct.

10. **C** Themes and Arguments *Easy*

The author mentions the word *train* in the last two lines of the passage to provide an example of a signifier and a signified. These concepts make up the two parts of a linguistic sign, so **C** is correct.

11. **B** Implied Information *Difficult*

Neill's study examines urban development and city planning in two Russian cities during three time periods. The first time period, according to the passage, is before the Soviet Revolution. During this time period, Neill contends, the two cities had very distinctive building styles. It is likely that he would discuss these building styles early on in his study.

12. **D** Main Idea *Easy*
In this passage, the author summarizes the findings of a research study completed by a scholar. The passage contains no reference to a particular historical document, so **A** can be eliminated. Neither does the author refute or criticize the findings of the study, so eliminate **C** and **E**. **D** fits best.

Paired Reading Passages

13. **A** Implied Information *Easy*
The first three sentences of Passage 1 describe Thomas Gradgrind in very certain terms: *Thomas Gradgrind, sir. A man of realities. A man of fact and calculations*. These sentences imply that Mr. Gradgrind is no-nonsense and focused on the facts. **A** is correct.

14. **D** Words in Context *Medium*
Mr. Gradgrind asks Sissy Jupe what her father does for his occupation. Sissy replies that her father *belongs to the horse-riding*, meaning that he rides horses for a living. Mr. Gradgrind *wave[s] off the objectionable calling* because he finds this profession to be unacceptable. In this context, the word *calling* refers to Sissy's father's job, so **D** is correct.

15. **E** Specific Information *Medium*
The correct answer to this question is stated directly in the passage. When Sissy tells Mr. Gradgrind her name, Mr. Gradgrind replies, *"Sissy is not a name. Don't call yourself Sissy. Call yourself Cecilia."* Mr. Gradgrind believes that the name Sissy is unacceptable for a young lady. **E** is correct.

16. **B** Implied Information *Medium*
The referenced lines point out that as Mr. Gradgrind introduced himself to his students, he saw them as *little pitchers before him, who were to be filled so full of facts*. This suggests that he believed it was important for him to fill his students' minds with facts and knowledge. **B** works best here.

17. **C** Attitude or Tone *Easy*
In Passage 2, Muriel describes her son in positive terms. The passage states twice that Muriel felt proud of William—first for his ability to use his storytelling gifts and later for his courageousness in responding to Mr. Taylor. The word *fervent* is too strong, so *pleased* is the best choice.

18. **D** Words in Context *Easy*
Passage 2 tells us that William was very imaginative and liked to tell stories. The referenced lines state that he started inventing *wild* tales when he was a young child. In this context, *wild* means "fantastic" or "hard to believe." **D** is correct.

19. **B** Themes and Arguments *Difficult*

In the second part of Passage 2, Muriel describes the incident with the broken window to illustrate a point to her friend Sally. Sally has just asked whether it is hard to get William to tell the truth when it really matters, since he has such an active imagination. Muriel replies that William has a strong sense of honor. She explains the story to make the point that even though William is imaginative, he is very truthful in important situations. **B** is correct. **C** can be eliminated because it was William himself who hit the ball through the window. **D** can be eliminated because although the story does show that William has a stronger code of honor than other boys in his neighborhood, this is not the point that Muriel is attempting to make by describing the event.

20. **D** Specific Information *Easy*

Passage 2 states that Mr. Taylor *combed the neighborhood, furious, knocking on doors to determine which children had been responsible* for the accident. He was definitely very angry, or *outraged.*

21. **A** Implied Information *Medium*

The following lines of the passage describe Mr. Taylor's appearance at the house and William's response: *William, on the other hand, came forward without even being asked. He heard Mr. Taylor knock on the door and ask in a grumbling voice about the accident. William came out of his room and told the truth on the spot, without Muriel having to say a word.* William was not pressured by Mr. Taylor or his mother to reply. Instead, he volunteered an answer because of his own willingness to tell the truth. **A** is correct.

22. **B** Relating Two Passages *Difficult*

In Passage 1, Thomas Gradgrind is first presented as very factually oriented and focused on reality. As the passage progresses, however, Mr. Gradgrind's true character is revealed through his interactions with Sissy Jupe. He is not willing to accept the truth about Sissy's name or even her father's occupation, and he counsels her to change her name and to lie about her father's profession to appear to be more "proper." William, in contrast, is first presented in Passage 2 as very fanciful, with an active imagination. Later in the passage, it becomes clear that William has a strong code of honor and is committed to telling the truth. **B** is correct.

23. **B** Relating Two Passages *Difficult*

Both passages present characters who appear to have certain characteristics on the surface but turn out to be different from how they first appear. Passage 1 presents Thomas Gradgrind as "a man of reality" who never bends the rules. This is a false image, however; Mr. Gradgrind is certainly willing to stretch the truth to help Sissy Jupe appear more "acceptable." The character of William goes through a similar transition in Passage 2. William's mother initially describes William as a wild storyteller but then explains that William is actually very honest.

24. **C** Relating Two Passages *Medium*

Mr. Gradgrind tells Sissy to describe her father's job as more sophisticated than it actually is. He counsels Sissy to say that her father is a veterinary surgeon, when in fact her father merely rides horses. William is an honest person at heart and would probably reject Mr. Gradgrind's advice that Sissy misrepresent her father's work. **C** is correct.

SECTION 3: MATH

Multiple Choice

1. **C** Algebra: Solving Equations *Easy*

Solve the first equation for n:

$$5n + 3 = 8$$
$$5n = 5$$
$$n = 1$$

Substitute 1 for n in the second equation:

$$2n + 7 = 2(1) + 7$$
$$2 + 7 = 9$$

2. **D** Numbers & Operations: Basic Operations *Easy*

Together, the CD cabinets contain at least $7 \times 135 = 945$ CDs. Eliminate **A**, **B**, and **C**. The cabinets don't contain more than $7 \times 180 = 1{,}260$ CDs. **D** is correct.

3. **D** Data Analysis, Statistics & Probability: Sets *Medium*

The union of two sets is the set that contains every member of *either* set. $\sqrt{20}$ is a fractional number between 4 and 5, and $\sqrt{40}$ is a fractional number between 6 and 7. Therefore, all integers *except* 5 and 6 are members of one set or the other. **D** is correct.

4. **C** Data Analysis, Statistics & Probability: Graphs, Charts, and Tables *Easy*

Friday's bar is the only bar that shows a decrease of 20 lamps from the previous day.

5. **A** Data Analysis, Statistics & Probability: Statistical Analysis *Medium*

Set up two equations using the information given in the question:

$$\frac{a+b}{2} = 7 \qquad \frac{a+b+c}{3} = 12$$

Cross multiply the first equation to determine that $a + b = 14$. Substitute 14 for the value of $a + b$ in the second equation, and solve for c:

$$\frac{a+b+c}{3} = 12$$
$$\frac{14+c}{3} = 12$$
$$14 + c = 36$$
$$c = 22$$

6. **E** Geometry: Circles *Easy*

Find the area of the circle: $A = \pi r^2$. Subtract this area from the area of the square, which is 4×4, or 16. The area of the shaded region equals the area of the square minus the area of the circle: $16 - \pi r^2$.

7. **D** Algebra: Solving Equations *Easy*

If a number is multiplied by 0, the result will be 0. The first equation is not equal to 0, so none of the variables in the first equation can be 0. Eliminate **E**. The second equation does equal 0. The only difference between the two equations is that the variable a in the first has been replaced by the variable e in the second. The new product equals 0, so e must be 0.

8. **A** Numbers & Operations: Fractions *Easy*

Calculate the books sold during the day. The publisher sold $\frac{1}{5}(50) = 10$ books, in the morning. He sold $\frac{1}{10}(50) = 5$ books, during lunch. He sold $\frac{3}{5}(50) = 30$ books, in the afternoon. That leaves $50 - 10 - 5 - 30 = 5$ books that must have been sold in the evening.

9. **D** Algebra: Absolute Value and Exponents *Medium*

Convert the number 16 to a base of 4 so that both sides of the equation will have the same base:

$$4^{3a} = 16^{a+2}$$
$$4^{3a} = (4^2)^{a+2}$$

To raise 4^2 to the "$a + 2$" power, multiply the exponents:

$$4^{3a} = (4^2)^{a+2}$$
$$4^{3a} = 4^{2(a+2)}$$
$$4^{3a} = 4^{2a+4}$$

Both sides of the equation now have the same base. Their exponents are therefore equal. Set them equal and solve for the value of a:

$$4^{3a} = 4^{2a+4}$$
$$3a = 2a + 4$$
$$a = 4$$

10. **B** Algebra: Solving Equations *Easy*

Set up an equation. Let the missing number equal x. Two times the number can be represented by $2x$. Five more than two times the number is $2x + 5$. This amount is equal to seven less than the number itself, or $x - 7$. Therefore, $2x + 5 = x - 7$. Solve for x:

$$2x + 5 = x - 7$$
$$x + 5 = -7$$
$$x = -12$$

11. **A** Geometry: Circles *Medium*

First, find the diameter of each semicircle. The circumference of the garden is 20π feet. The circumference of any circle equals $\pi \times$ diameter, so the diameter of the garden is 20 feet. The diameter of each semicircle is half of 20 feet, or 10 feet.

Next, find the circumference of each semicircle. Each semicircle has a diameter of 10 feet, so each has a circumference of $\frac{1}{2}(10\pi)$ feet, or 5π feet. To get from point D to point C, Albert walks 5π feet. He then walks another 5π feet to get from point C to point E. The total distance walked along the curved path is 10π feet.

12. **B** Numbers & Operations: Sequences *Medium*

Look for a pattern in the terms. Each even numbered term is 1 less than the previous term, and each odd numbered term is –1 times the previous term. Determine the first several terms until you come up with a pattern:

$$2, 1, -1, -2, 2, 1, -1, -2, \ldots$$

This pattern repeats itself after every four terms. The fourth term in the sequence is a –2, so the eighth term in the sequence will also be a –2. So will every fourth term after that, up until the sixtieth term. The sixty-first term will be a 2, the sixty-second term will be a 1, and the sixty-third term will be a –1.

13. **C** Algebra: Functions *Medium*

Based on the table, we know that $f(-1) = 17$. Both functions give us a sum of 34. If $f(x) = x + 18$, then $w = 0 + 18 = 18$, and $z = -2 + 18 = 16$. So $w + z = 34$. If $f(x) = -17x$, then $w = -17(0) = 0$, and $z = -17(-2) = 34$. So, again, $w + z = 34$.

14. **B** Geometry: Coordinate Geometry *Medium*

When a point is reflected across the x-axis, its x-coordinate remains the same, but its y-coordinate changes to its negative. Identify some points on the line $y = -3x - 1$. They are (–1, 2), (0, –1), (1, –4), and (2, –7). This line slants downward from left to right, with a slope of –3. It has a y-intercept of –1.

On line k, the y-coordinates of line j are reversed: (–1, –2), (0, 1), (1, 4), and (2, 7). This line slants upward from left to right and has a y-intercept of 1. Its slope exactly mirrors that of line j, so its slope is 3. Using the slope-intercept form of an equation, $y = mx + b$, we see that the equation of line k must be $y = 3x + 1$.

15. **D** Numbers & Operations: Percents *Medium*

First, find the amount of the increase. In 2002, Cindy had $15,000 in savings. By 2004, she had $20,000 in savings. During these two years, her savings grew by $5,000.

Next, find what percentage this increase represents of the original savings. Ask the question: $5,000 is what percent of $15,000? $5,000 is $\frac{1}{3}$, or $33\frac{1}{3}$ percent, of $15,000, so **D** is correct.

16. **D** Geometry: Solids *Medium*

Find the volume of the cylinder using the formula $V = \pi r^2 h$. Substitute a for r and $4a$ for h:

$$V = \pi r^2 h$$
$$V = \pi (a)^2 (4a)$$
$$V = 4\pi (a)^3$$

A rectangular solid has a volume of length × width × height. A rectangular solid with dimensions $2a$, $2a$, and πa would have a volume of $2a \times 2a \times \pi a$, or $4\pi a^3$.

17. **B** Algebra: Solving Equations *Medium*

Solve the equation to isolate $(q + 2)$:

$$t = \frac{(q+2) - p}{4}$$
$$4t = (q+2) - p$$
$$4t + p = (q+2)$$

18. **E** Geometry: Coordinate Geometry *Difficult*

The shaded region is bounded by the line $x = 6$. Therefore, any point in the shaded region must have an x-coordinate less than or equal to 6. Point (j, k) lies in the shaded region. Its x-coordinate, j, must be less than or equal to 6. Statement II must be true. Eliminate **A** and **C**.

Point (j, k) lies somewhere in the shaded region. Its coordinates could be (4, 5), for example. If the coordinates of (j, k) are (4, 5), then $k \leq j$ is not true, so statement I is not necessarily true. Eliminate **D**.

The shaded region in the figure is bounded by the line representing the function $y = g(x)$. The line is solid, which means that the points included in the shaded region satisfy the inequality $y \leq g(x)$. Substitute the coordinates given for point (j, k) into this inequality: $k \leq g(j)$. Statement III must be true, so **E** is the correct answer.

19. **D** Algebra: Absolute Value and Exponents *Difficult*

Machine #2 will accept the tube only if its net weight is between 169.95 and 170.05 grams. Therefore, the range of all possible values for g is $169.95 < g < 170.05$.

On the left side of the range, the value for g must be greater than 169.95, which is 170 – 0.05 grams. The left side of the range can therefore be written as follows:

$$169.95 < g$$
$$170 - 0.05 < g$$
$$-0.05 < g - 170$$

On the right side of the range, the value for g must be less than 170.05, or 170 + 0.05 grams. The right side of the range can therefore be written as follows:

$$g < 170.05$$
$$g < 170 + 0.05$$
$$g - 170 < 0.05$$

Combine the two inequalities to see that the range of values for g is $-0.05 < g - 170 < 0.05$. The absolute value of $g - 170$ will always be less than 0.05. **D** is correct.

20. **E** Numbers & Operations: Sequences *Difficult*

An arithmetic sequence is an ordered list of terms in which the difference between consecutive terms is constant. In this case, the sequence involves consecutive integers, so the difference between the terms is always 1.

The question tells you that the least integer of the sequence is x and the greatest integer is z. It also tells you that the sum of the integers in the sequence is y. You are asked to determine the number of integers in the set. Let's call this variable n.

In any arithmetic sequence of n terms, the sum of the first n terms can be found using this formula:

$$Sum = n \times \frac{\text{first term} + \text{last term}}{2}$$

Using what the question has told you, plug the values you know into this formula:

$$y = n \times \frac{x + z}{2}$$

Solve for n:

$$y = n \times \frac{x+z}{2}$$
$$2y = n(x+z)$$
$$\frac{2y}{x+z} = n$$

SECTION 4: CRITICAL READING

Sentence Completions

1. **D** One-Word/One-Way *Easy*

The constable wanted the protesters to stop making noise. The word *desist* means "to cease," so **D** fits here.

2. **E** Two-Word/One-Way *Medium*

Llewellyn's high metabolism gave him something that was *voracious*, which means "eager to consume." The first blank requires a word related to hunger in some way, so narrow the answers down to **D** and **E**. A voracious hunger would mostly likely be *satiated*, or satisfied, after a large meal, so **E** is correct.

3. **B** Two-Word/Two-Way *Difficult*

The word *despite* signals a contrast in the two parts of this sentence. The principal fears something from the school board. However, she still behaves with a certain type of determination. The second blank must be a word meaning "strong," so eliminate **A**, **D**, and **E**. The principle is most likely to fear *recriminations*, or countercharges brought against her. The correct answer is **B**.

4. **A** One-Word/Two-Way *Medium*

The word *but* indicates a contrast in the two parts of this sentence. Local residents viewed their neighbor one way, but it turns out that he had a history of *surreptitious*, or secretive, behaviors. The blank must contain a word that means the opposite of surreptitious. **A**, *candid*, means "frank," so **A** is correct.

5. **C** Two-Word/One-Way *Difficult*

The second part of this sentence contains two blanks that describe the professor's handwriting. These two blanks must contain words that are similar in meaning because the second blank elaborates upon the first. **A** and **B** contain words that are opposite in meaning, so these choices can be eliminated. The first part of the sentence reveals that the professor's handwriting is very different from his *austere*, or stern, personality. The word *florid* means "flowery or flamboyant," which is the opposite of *austere*. **C** is correct.

Paired Reading Passages

6. **B** Implied Information *Easy*

The answer to this question is implied in Passage 1. The author describes the results of a study that found that sleep deprivation impairs human functioning. It can be inferred from these results that adequate sleep is important for human functioning.

7. **E** Relating Two Passages *Medium*

Both passages address the subject of sleep but from slightly different perspectives. Passage 1 discusses the damage caused by too little sleep. Passage 2 notes the negative consequences of too little sleep but also emphasizes the risks faced by those who sleep too much. Both passages agree that the wrong amount of sleep is problematic, as **E** states.

8. **C** Relating Two Passages *Medium*

The author of Passage 2 claims that getting too much sleep can be as damaging as getting too little sleep. This author agrees that too little sleep can be harmful, so **C** is correct.

9. **D** Relating Two Passages *Medium*

These passages have two main differences. First, Passage 1 emphasizes the negative effects of too little sleep, while Passage 2 points out that both too little and too much sleep can be damaging. **E** reverses this difference, so it can be eliminated. The second main difference between the two passages concerns the effects addressed by each. Passage 1 discusses the relationship between sleep and cognitive functioning, while Passage 2 addresses the relationship between sleep and heart disease. **D** reflects this second difference.

Long Reading Passages

10. **B** Specific Information *Easy*

In the first sentence of the passage, the author states that *the concept of political culture is but one among the many frameworks utilized by political scientists in their studies of comparative politics*. **B** is therefore correct. **A**, **C**, and **E** can be eliminated because these descriptions are not mentioned until later in the passage.

11. **A** Themes and Arguments *Medium*

The author mentions psychoanalysis in paragraph 1 as part of an analogy. *In effect*, writes the author, *the application of the concept of political culture may be compared to the psychoanalysis of a psychiatric patient*. This comparison helps explain how the concept of political culture is used, an idea reflected by **A**.

12. **B** Implied Information *Medium*

The author acknowledges in paragraph 3 that *every political culture is, in reality, a mix of all three types—parochial, subject, and participant*. Even so, each society is *dominated by one particular type*. It is therefore possible to categorize societies according to a primary type.

13. **C** Themes and Arguments *Difficult*

The word *allegiance* is mentioned in the following sentence from paragraph 3: *participation is also motivated by the sense of allegiance that pervades American culture.* This statement provides one of two reasons that many Americans are politically active, according to the author. First, Americans *feel confident in their ability to influence political decisions*. Second, they have a strong sense of allegiance to their country. The reference to allegiance helps to explain the author's point that many Americans participate politically in some way.

14. **E** Specific Information *Easy*

The correct answer to this question is stated directly in paragraph 4. The first sentence of this paragraph states that *the second step in applying the framework of political culture involves examining the process of political socialization within a country.* **E** restates this exactly.

15. **B** Attitude and Tone *Medium*

In the first four paragraphs of the passage, the author uses an explanatory tone, describing the concept of political culture and how it is used. In the last paragraph, however, the author presents a critique of the political culture framework, pointing out that the framework overlooks the way in which political culture can be influenced by the actions of institutions. This last paragraph therefore takes on a more critical tone.

16. **A** Main Idea *Easy*

This passage starts by explaining that it has taken hundreds of years for electricity to evolve to the point of common usage that we know today. It then traces the evolution of electricity, from ancient times to the present. **A** fits best.

17. **C** Implied Information *Medium*

Paragraph 2 starts by acknowledging the widespread belief that electricity was discovered by Benjamin Franklin. It then explains that although Franklin's research did contribute to our understanding of electricity, the phenomenon of electricity was acknowledged in Western culture as early as the year 600 B.C., far before Franklin's time. Franklin researched electricity but was not the first to discover it.

18. **D** Words in Context *Medium*

The Greeks discovered that when amber was rubbed, it *would attract light items, such as feathers, which would stick to the gemstone* due to static electricity. A feather is an example of an item that weighs very little, so *weightless* fits best.

19. **B** Themes and Arguments *Medium*

The answer to this question can be found by rereading the lines around the referenced phrase. In paragraph 3, the author describes the Leyden jar as *nothing more than a glass container filled with water and wrapped in metal foil.* Despite its simple design, however, the Leyden jar had certain characteristics that allowed it to serve an important research function. *This simple device,* the author writes, *was capable of storing static electricity and discharging it all at once. It therefore allowed researchers to carry out more in-depth investigations of the properties of static electricity.* **B** is correct.

20. **D** Specific Information *Medium*

Paragraph 2 points out that, contrary to popular belief, Benjamin Franklin did not discover electricity. Other researchers worked with electricity long before Franklin's experiment. Eliminate **A**. Paragraph 3 states specifically that in his kite experiment, Franklin *used Leyden jars to prove that lightning was, in fact, a form of static electricity*. The correct answer must be **D**.

21. **E** Specific Information *Easy*

Paragraph 4 describes the inventions of the battery, the electric motor, the telegraph, and the lightbulb, which occurred during the 1800s. The invention of the television is not mentioned in the passage.

22. **E** Implied Information *Medium*

Paragraph 4 traces several inventions that occurred within a short period of time during the 1800s. After the discovery of electromagnetism, many new items were produced, practically all at once: the electric motor, the telegraph, the telephone, and the lightbulb. The author uses the phrase *all within a few years of one another* to highlight how rapidly these inventions were developed. The surge in inventions is most likely related to the fact that by that point, scientists knew enough about electricity to really make some progress. **E** is correct.

23. **C** Themes and Arguments *Medium*

Paragraph 5 starts with the point that *our knowledge of electricity has come a long way* since the ancient Greeks first experimented with amber. This point is then supported by statistics that show how widely electricity is now used. **C** is correct because it restates the point of the paragraph.

24. **B** Specific Information *Medium*

In the first paragraph of the passage, the author describes electrical fixtures as items *that we now take for granted*. In the last paragraph, the author again emphasizes how important and commonplace electricity has become. Electricity is portrayed as *a necessity—indeed, a basic foundation—of contemporary society*. Put simply, it is an indispensable modern convenience, as **B** states.

SECTION 5: MATH

Multiple Choice

1. **A** Algebra: Solving Equations *Easy*

Simplify to solve for a:

$$\begin{aligned} \frac{7a-2}{3} &= 4 \\ 7a-2 &= 4\times 3 \\ 7a-2 &= 12 \\ 7a &= 12+2 \\ 7a &= 14 \\ a &= 2 \end{aligned}$$

2. **C** Geometry: Angles and Lines *Easy*

The degree sum of the angles of any triangle is 180. This triangle has a right angle, which measures 90˚. Create an equation and substitute in the values you know to solve for x:

$$\begin{aligned} 90^\circ + 41^\circ + x &= 180^\circ \\ x &= 180^\circ - 90^\circ - 41^\circ \\ x &= 49^\circ \end{aligned}$$

3. **E** Algebra: Substitution *Easy*

Substitute 64 for b, the number of brownies. Then simplify and solve for f:

$$\begin{aligned} f &= 2b+32 \\ f &= 2(64)+32 \\ f &= 128+32 \\ f &= 160 \end{aligned}$$

4. **C** Data Analysis, Statistics & Probability: Graphs, Charts, and Tables *Easy*

The museum has a total of 1,903 statues. Add the given values to find the number of statues that are either Greek or French: 567 + 728 = 1,295. Don't stop here, however. The question asks for the number of statues that are *neither* Greek *nor* French. Subtract 1,295 from the total number of statues given: 1,903 – 1,295 = 608.

5. **D** Numbers & Operations: Factors and Multiples *Medium*

A and **B** are not divisible by both 3 and 9, so these choices can be eliminated. The numbers 18 and 36 are divisible by both 3 and 9, but they are also divisible by 6. Eliminate **C** and **E**. The number 27 is divisible by both 3 and 9, but it is not divisible by 6. **D** proves that the statement is false.

6. **E** Numbers & Operations: Ratios *Medium*

There are 2 red marbles for every 3 green marbles in the bag. This means that 2 out of every 5 marbles in the bag are red. The total number of marbles in the bag must always be a multiple of 5, because 2 + 3 = 5. **E** contains the only multiple of 5, so **E** must be correct.

7. **A** Algebra: Substitution *Medium*

Solve the second equation for z by multiplying both sides of the equation by u:

$$\frac{z}{u} = wy$$
$$z = uwy$$

Now substitute uwy for z in the first equation:

$$x = \frac{z}{y}$$
$$x = \frac{uwy}{y}$$
$$x = uw$$

8. **A** Geometry: Triangles *Difficult*

The figure shown is a 30-60-90 triangle. The sides of 30-60-90 triangles are in the ratio $x{:}x\sqrt{3}{:}x$. In this case, side QR is the side across from the 30° angle, so QR has the smallest length, x. Side QS lies across from the 60° angle, so QS is equal to $x\sqrt{3}$. The figure shows that QS measures 3. Use this value to set up an equation:

$$QS = x\sqrt{3}$$
$$3 = x\sqrt{3}$$
$$x = \frac{3}{\sqrt{3}}$$

To eliminate the square root in the denominator, multiply by $\frac{\sqrt{3}}{\sqrt{3}}$ (which is the same as multiplying by 1):

$$x = \frac{3}{\sqrt{3}}$$
$$x = \left(\frac{\sqrt{3}}{\sqrt{3}}\right)\left(\frac{3}{\sqrt{3}}\right)$$
$$x = \frac{(3\sqrt{3})}{(\sqrt{3} \times \sqrt{3})}$$
$$x = \frac{3\sqrt{3}}{3}$$
$$x = \sqrt{3}$$

Since x represents the length of the smallest side of the triangle, QR, this means that QR equals $\sqrt{3}$.

Grid-Ins

9. **32** Algebra: Absolute Value and Exponents *Easy*

This question looks difficult because of the exponent. Don't be fooled. The question tells you that $s^9 = 512$. To find the value of $\frac{s^9}{16}$, just substitute 512 for s^9:

$$\frac{s^9}{16} = \frac{512}{16}$$
$$= 32$$

10. **.5, 1/2** Geometry: Lines and Angles *Easy*

First, find the length of segment *AC*. Subtract –3 from 4:

$$4 - (-3) = 7$$

Next, find the length of segment *AB*. This segment is half the length of segment *AC*:

$$AB = \frac{7}{2} \text{ or } 3.5$$

The length of *AB* is 3.5, so point *B* lies 3.5 units to the right of point *A* on the number line. To find the location of point *B*, add 3.5 to –3:

$$3.5 + (-3) = 0.5$$

11. **20** Geometry: Polygons *Medium*

First, find the area of the larger square using the formula $A = s^2$. The area of the larger square is $6 \times 6 = 36 \text{ cm}^2$. Next, find the area of the smaller square: $4 \times 4 = 16 \text{ cm}^2$. The question asks for the area of the part of the larger square that lies outside the smaller square. Subtract the two areas to find their difference: $36 - 16 = 20 \text{ cm}^2$.

12. **398** Numbers & Operations: Basic Operations *Medium*

First, get a rough idea of the numbers by dividing 2,000 by 5. If the numbers were all identical, they would all be equal to 400. However, the question states that the numbers are consecutive integers. Which five integers close to 400 add up to 2,000? Along with 400, try the two numbers before 400 and the two numbers after it:

$$398 + 399 + 400 + 401 + 402 = 2{,}000$$

The smallest of these numbers is 398.

13. **75, 120, 300** Geometry: Triangles *Medium*

The perimeter of ΔEFG is 2 + 5 + 8, or 15. Each angle of ΔEFG has the same measure as an angle in *JKL*, so the two triangles are similar. This means that lengths of their sides are in the same ratio.

The question states that the length of one side of triangle *JKL* is 40. If this side is equivalent to the side from ΔEFG of length 8, then all of the legs of ΔJKL are five times larger than those of ΔEFG. In this case, the perimeter of ΔJKL would be $15 \times 5 = 75$. Any of the legs can be used, so two other correct responses would be 120 (8×15) and 300 (20×15).

14. **7** Algebra: Binomials and Quadratics *Medium*

The expression $x^2 - y^2$ can be factored into $(x - y)(x + y)$. The question tells you that $x^2 - y^2 = 40$, so $(x - y)(x + y) = 40$. The question also states that $x + y = 4$. Substitute this value into the equation and solve for $(x - y)$:

$$(x - y)(x + y) = 40$$
$$(x - y)(4) = 40$$
$$(x - y) = 10$$

Add the two equations to determine the value of x:

$$\begin{aligned} (x - y) &= 10 \\ + \ (x + y) &= 4 \\ \hline 2x &= 14 \\ x &= 7 \end{aligned}$$

15. **4** Algebra: Functions *Medium*

Don't worry—these symbols are made up. The question explains what the symbols mean. Whenever you see the function $m \oplus n$, for any two numbers m and n, perform the operation $m - 2n$. Whenever you see the function $m \otimes n$, perform the operation $m - 7n$.

Perform these operations on the two functions given in the question stem. First, take the function on the right side of the equation: $3 \oplus 2x$. In this case, the variable m is represented by 3 and the variable n is represented by $2x$. Perform the operation $m - 2n$:

$$\begin{aligned} 3 \oplus (2x) &= (2x) \otimes 3 \\ 3 - 2(2x) &= (2x) \otimes 3 \\ 3 - 4x &= (2x) \otimes 3 \end{aligned}$$

Now do the same for the function on the left side of the equation: $(2x) \otimes 3$. In this case, the variable m is represented by $2x$, and the variable n is represented by 3. Perform the operation $m - 7n$:

$$\begin{aligned} 3 \oplus (2x) &= (2x) \otimes 3 \\ 3 - 2(2x) &= 2x - 7(3) \\ 3 - 4x &= 2x - 21 \end{aligned}$$

Now you've got an equation you can work with. Solve for x:

$$\begin{aligned} 3 - 4x &= 2x - 21 \\ -4x &= 2x - 24 \\ -6x &= -24 \\ x &= 4 \end{aligned}$$

16. **2** Algebra: Functions *Difficult*

First, substitute into the equation the value you are given for a:

$$\begin{aligned} z(a) &= 15 + \frac{a^2}{5} \\ z(5q) &= 15 + \frac{(5q)^2}{5} \end{aligned}$$

Next, substitute the value you are given for $z(5q)$:

$$\begin{aligned} z(5q) &= 15 + \frac{(5q)^2}{5} \\ 50q &= 15 + \frac{(5q)^2}{5} \\ 50q &= 15 + \frac{25q^2}{5} \\ 50q &= 15 + 5q^2 \end{aligned}$$

Now, rewrite the equation in the general quadratic form $y = ax^2 + bx + c$:

$$50q = 15 + 5q^2$$
$$0 = 5q^2 - 50q + 15$$

Finally, factor the equation to find its roots:

$$0 = 5q^2 - 50q + 15$$
$$0 = 5(q^2 - 10q + 3)$$
$$0 = 5(q + 5)(q - 2)$$
$$q = -5 \text{ or } 2$$

17. **56** Data Analysis, Statistics & Probability: Permutations and Combinations *Difficult*

This is a combination question, because the order of the models in the show is not important. The question merely asks you to determine how many different combinations of 3 models can be selected from the 8 interviewees.

To determine the number of combinations, use the formula $\frac{n!}{r!(n-r)!}$, where n represents the total number of interviewees and r represents the number of models that can be chosen for the show.

$$\frac{n!}{(r!)(n-r)!} = \frac{8!}{(3!)(8-3)!}$$
$$= \frac{8!}{(3!)(5!)}$$
$$= \frac{8 \times 7 \times 6 \times 5 \times 4 \times 3 \times 2 \times 1}{(3 \times 2 \times 1)(5 \times 4 \times 3 \times 2 \times 1)}$$
$$= \frac{8 \times 7 \times 6}{(3 \times 2 \times 1)}$$
$$= 56$$

18. **48** Algebra: Systems of Equations *Difficult*

To answer this question, remember the distance formula: distance = rate × time. On Friday, the farmer traveled 60 miles per hour. Therefore, he traveled a distance of $d = 60t$.

On Sunday, the farmer traveled 40 miles per hour. You don't know how much time it took the farmer to return home; you only know that it took him 2 hours to make the entire trip. Since he traveled for t hours on Friday, on Sunday he traveled for $2 - t$ hours. His distance on Sunday equaled $d = 40(2 - t)$.

Both of the distances are the same, since he traveled the same route. Set the two distances expressed in terms of t equal to each other and solve for t:

$$60t = 40(2 - t)$$
$$60t = 80 - 40t$$
$$100t = 80$$
$$t = \frac{80}{100} \text{ or } \frac{4}{5}$$

Plug this value for t into the first equation and solve for d:

$$d = 60t$$
$$d = 60\left(\frac{4}{5}\right)$$
$$d = \frac{240}{5}$$
$$d = 48$$

SECTION 6: WRITING

Improving Sentences

1. **E** Conjunctions *Easy*

The underlined phrase is clumsy because the conjunction *and* is used ineffectively here. The conjunction *when* works better, and **E** is the most concise choice.

2. **E** Misplaced Modifiers *Easy*

This sentence makes it sound as though *Robert's attempt* was frustrated. In fact, Robert himself was frustrated. **E** corrects this error by placing *Robert* close to the modifying phrase at the beginning of the sentence. It also uses the active verb *attempted* and eliminates the passive voice.

3. **C** Coordination and Subordination *Easy*

The second part of this sentence doesn't make clear who collapsed in the snow. **C** corrects this error by mentioning Steven's name and using the conjunction *after* to explain the order of events.

4. **D** Run-Ons *Easy*

The underlined portion of this sentence is a run-on, an independent clause joined to another independent clause by a comma. **D** corrects the error by turning the clause into a dependent clause, which can be joined to the first part of the sentence with just a comma.

5. **C** Idioms *Medium*

The phrase *not only* should always be followed by the phrase *but also*. **C** adds this phrase correctly.

6. **A** No Error *Easy*

This sentence is correct as written. All subjects and verbs agree, and all phrases are in the proper form.

7. **D** Conjunctions *Medium*

The conjunction *where* is used incorrectly here, and the word *they* is vague. **D** uses the more effective conjunction *through which* and clarifies that *the political scientist* assesses the fit between theory and facts.

8. **A** No Error *Medium*

This sentence is correct as written. All subjects and verbs agree, and all phrases are in the proper form.

9. **D** Tenses *Easy*

The gerund *referring* is used incorrectly here. This sentence requires the present tense verb *refers*, which **D** provides.

10. **E** Run-Ons *Difficult*

This is a run-on sentence, in which two independent clauses are joined only by a comma. **E** corrects the run-on by deleting the comma and providing a concise phrase to describe the predicted weather patterns.

11. **B** Conjunctions *Medium*

The modifying phrase *with thousands of pounds yet to be moved* is vague because it doesn't clarify what remains to be moved. In addition, the conjunction *with* obscures the meaning of the sentence. In reality, some people are against the fertilization relocation program *because* there are so many pounds of fertilizer left to be moved. **B** rewrites the modifying phrase most clearly.

Identifying Sentence Errors

12. **D** Tense *Easy*

The verb *overcame* is used incorrectly here in the past tense. The infinitive form should be written with the word *to* followed by the present tense of the verb, *overcome*.

13. **E** No Error *Easy*

This sentence is correct as written. All subjects and verbs agree, and all phrases are written in their proper form.

14. **A** Idioms *Easy*

This sentence contains an idiom error. In a sentence, the word *neither* must always be followed by the word *nor*. To be correct, **A** should be written as *nor*.

15. **D** Tense *Easy*

The underlined verb in **D**, *will be able*, is in the wrong tense. The rest of the sentence takes place in the past, so this verb should be *would be able*.

16. **D** Idioms *Medium*

The two-word phrase *any thing* is used improperly here and should be replaced with the single word *anything*.

17. **A** Tense *Easy*

This sentence takes place in the past tense. Therefore, the verb *can* in **A** should be replaced by *could*.

18. **E** No Error *Difficult*

This sentence is correct as written. All subjects and verbs agree, all verbs are in the correct tense, and all words are in the correct format.

19. **C** Parallelism *Medium*

This sentence contains three terms that should be parallel: *admit, treat,* and *release.* **C**, *to release*, is not parallel in structure.

20. **D** Wrong Word *Medium*

The word *devastating* is used incorrectly here. The shoreline itself was not *devastating*. Instead, it was *devastated* by the hurricane.

21. **B** Pronouns *Easy*

The pronoun *they* in **B** is intended to modify the noun *person*. However, the noun *person* is singular and should therefore be modified by the pronoun phrase *he or she*. This singular pronoun will require a singular verb: *that he or she experiences*.

22. **D** Tense *Medium*

This sentence contains a verb tense error. The phrase *to picking up* should be written in the infinitive form, *to pick up*.

23. **E** No Error *Medium*

This sentence is written correctly. All subjects and verbs agree, all verbs are in the correct tense, and all words are in the correct format.

24. **A** Pronouns *Medium*

The pronoun *they* in **A** modifies the noun *manufacturing engineer*. Since *engineer* is singular, the plural pronoun *they* should be replaced with a singular pronoun, such as *he* or *she*, and followed by the singular verb *is*.

25. **A** Idioms *Medium*

The expression in **A** is written *keep their distance of*, but this expression should read *keep their distance from*.

26. **E** No Error *Medium*

This sentence is written correctly. The pronoun *I* is not the subject of the sentence, so the objective pronoun *me* is used instead.

27. **C** Wrong Word *Difficult*

The phrase *nine items or less* is incorrect in this sentence. It's common to see this expression in grocery stores, but it's incorrect there too. The word *less* should be used only for general amounts that cannot be counted, such as "less love" or "less water." The word *fewer* should be used for quantities that can be counted, such as "fewer gallons of water" or "fewer than nine grocery items."

28. **C** Pronouns *Medium*

The pronoun *its* should be used instead of the contraction *it's* (it is).

29. **B** Adverbs and Adjectives *Difficult*

The adjective *quiet* is used to modify the verb *sit*. *Quiet* should therefore be an adverb, not an adjective. The correct phrase is *to sit quietly*.

Improving Paragraphs

30. **A** Sentence Revision *Medium*

In sentence 2, the pronoun *it* is vague. It's difficult to tell what the pronoun *it* refers to. Reading back to sentence 1, you can determine that the pronoun *it* refers to the theme of the novel. **A** corrects the vague pronoun reference by substituting *this theme*.

31. **D** Sentence Revision *Easy*

The original version of sentence 3 contains some unnecessary wording. The revision in **D** eliminates this wordiness by replacing the phrase *meaning that it has been made up* with the single word *composed*.

32. **A** Sentence Revision *Medium*

This sentence is well written as it stands. It also performs an important function by restating the author's point at the beginning of paragraph 2. It should be left in the text as it is.

33. **E** Sentence Revision *Easy*

This sentence is a run-on sentence. It contains two independent clauses joined only by a comma. **B** joins the two sentences with a semicolon but adds unnecessary words after the semicolon, so it can be eliminated. **E** turns the second clause into a dependent clause and provides the best revision.

34. **C** Sentence Combination *Medium*

The two sentences point out a contrast among the letters. The word *while* serves as an effective signal that a contrasting idea lies just ahead.

35. **C** Essay Development *Difficult*

The essay's topic sentence (sentence 1) tells us that Goethe used several effective literary techniques to develop the theme of *Werther*. The first paragraph describes one such technique (the diary structure), while the second and third paragraphs describe a related, and more specific, technique (the contrasting content of Werther's letters to reveal his character). It would make sense for the essay to continue by discussing yet another such technique, as **C** indicates.

SECTION 7: CRITICAL READING

Sentence Completions

1. **A** One-Word/One-Way *Easy*

The description at the end of the sentence defines the meaning of the word in the blank. Sheryl's sister made up each detail of the story. The word *fabricate* means "to concoct or invent," so **A** is correct.

2. **E** Two-Word/One-Way *Medium*

The second blank in this sentence helps to describe the meaning of the first blank, so the two blanks will contain words that are similar in meaning. The last part of the sentence gives a clue to the meaning of the second blank: Something about the contestants *made them easy for the judges to like. Congeniality* means "friendly and sociable," and someone who behaves *amiably* is good-natured and likable, so **E** fits.

3. **B** Two-Word/Two-Way *Medium*

The word *though* signals a contrast in the two parts of this sentence. Wilbur intended to do one thing, but his presentation had the opposite result. An arrogant presentation would likely have a negative result, so the last blank should contain a word with a negative meaning. To *antagonize* means to "provoke hostility," whereas to *placate* means to "make less angry."

4. **D** One-Word/One-Way *Easy*

The word *so* indicates that the second part of this sentence follows from the first part of the sentence. It was not surprising that Harold Sorbie criticized the political caucus because he was known for a certain type of behavior toward groups with which he disagreed. To *condemn* means "to declare to be wrong," so *condemnation* works here.

5. **C** One-Word/One-Way *Medium*

The company's first performance was successful, so it must have received something positive for its accomplishments. The word *acclaim* means "praise or approval." Although *applause* is also positive, it doesn't make as much sense as *acclaim* in the context of the sentence. Therefore, **C** fits best.

6. **E** Two-Word/Two-Way *Difficult*

The phrase *by contrast* signals that the museum's Assyrian artifacts were different from its Babylonian relics. The correct answer will therefore contain two words that are opposite in meaning. **D** can be eliminated because *unusual* and *exotic* are fairly close in meaning. The word *eclectic* means "varied," while *homogenous* means "similar or uniform." These two words are opposites, and they fit the meaning of the sentence, so **E** is correct.

Long Reading Passage

7. **A** Implied Information *Medium*

The author states in the first paragraph that Mrs. Taylor consented to become his wife only *after a friendship of twenty years*. The word *friendship* therefore refers to the author's relationship with Mrs. Taylor before they were married.

8. **B** Words in Context *Easy*

In the second paragraph, the author describes self-improvement as a *law* of Mrs. Taylor's nature. By this he means that she was always focused on self-improvement. In this context, the word *law* means "characteristic" or "quality." **B** is correct.

9. **C** Themes and Arguments *Difficult*
The author describes the importance of self-improvement for Mrs. Taylor when he states that *self-improvement was a necessity that arose equally from the ardor with which she sought it, and from the spontaneous tendency of her faculties, which could not receive an impression without making it the source of an accession of wisdom.* The last part of this sentence reveals that Mrs. Taylor used every experience as an opportunity for personal growth. **C** is therefore correct.

10. **E** Themes and Arguments *Medium*
In paragraph 3, the author describes how Mrs. Taylor was known to various friends: *to her outer circle she was a beauty and a wit*, he states. However, *to her inner circle, she was a woman of deep and strong feeling, of penetrating and intuitive intelligence, and of an eminently meditative and poetic nature.* Mrs. Taylor's acquaintances saw certain of her qualities, but her close friends knew her deeper nature, as **E** reflects.

11. **D** Words in Context *Easy*
The author states that only one of Mrs. Taylor's friends had *capacities of feeling or intellect kindred with her own*. By this he means that only one of Mrs. Taylor's friends was as emotionally and intellectually developed as Mrs. Taylor was. In this context, therefore, the phrase *kindred with* most nearly means "similar to." **D** works best. Be careful not to confuse the word *kindred* with "kin," which means "relatives."

12. **B** Specific Information *Medium*
This statement from paragraph 4 comes just after the author notes that Mrs. Taylor's friends were not her intellectual equals. *Nonetheless,* he states, *all had more or less of an alliance with her in sentiments and opinions.* By this he means that Mrs. Taylor's friends basically shared her views and values, which **B** reflects.

13. **C** Attitude and Tone *Easy*
Throughout the passage, the author describes Mrs. Taylor in extremely positive terms. He even states in paragraph 2 that he found her to be the most admirable person he had ever known. **C** is correct.

14. **B** Technique *Medium*
In paragraph 5, the author describes Mrs. Taylor's characteristics by comparing and contrasting her to Shelley. **B** therefore fits best.

15. **A** Specific Information *Medium*
The author compares Mrs. Taylor to Shelley and ultimately concludes that Mrs. Taylor's intellect surpassed that of Shelley. The author states, *in thought and intellect, Shelley . . . was but a child compared with what she ultimately became.* As Mrs. Taylor's abilities grew, Shelley's intellectual talents seemed childlike by comparison. **A** is correct.

16. **E** Implied Information *Difficult*
The author states that Mrs. Taylor's mind *was the same perfect instrument*, whether it was dealing with *the highest regions of speculation* or *the smaller practical concerns of daily life*. He implies that she was equally capable of thinking theoretically or handling mundane (ordinary, day-to-day) details, as **E** states.

17. **A** Words in Context *Difficult*

In paragraph 6, where the term *sensitive* is used, the author states that *the same exactness and rapidity of operation, pervading as it did her sensitive as well as her mental faculties, would, with her gifts of feeling and imagination, have fitted her to be a consummate artist*. In other words, he believes that Mrs. Taylor would have been a great artist because the qualities of *exactness* and *rapidity of operation* were present in both her *sensitive* and *mental* faculties. **B** and **C** are tempting because a person who is sensitive is often thoughtful and may even be touchy, getting her feelings hurt easily. But these definitions don't make sense in the context of the sentence. Instead, the word *sensitive* here refers to Mrs. Taylor's emotional faculties—her ability to express deep feelings. **A** works best.

18. **B** Implied Information *Medium*

The passage tells us that Mrs. Taylor's unselfishness *was not that of a taught system of duties*, so eliminate **C** and **E**. Instead, writes the author, her unselfishness sprang from *a heart which thoroughly identified itself with the feelings of others*. This implies that Mrs. Taylor could relate to the emotions that others experienced, as **B** states.

19. **E** Themes and Arguments *Medium*

In the last paragraph, the author states that the *passion of justice might* have been considered to be Mrs. Taylor's *strongest feeling, had it not been for her boundless generosity, and a lovingness ever ready to pour itself forth*. Although Mrs. Taylor's passion for justice was very strong, the author believes that her generosity and lovingness were even stronger. This point is reflected in **E**.

SECTION 8: MATH

Multiple Choice

1. **B** Algebra: Solving Equations *Easy*

Solve the first equation for b:

$$4b = 28$$
$$b = 7$$

Substitute 7 for b in the second equation, and solve for d:

$$bd = 1$$
$$(7)d = 1$$
$$d = \frac{1}{7}$$

2. **B** Algebra: Ratios *Easy*

Set up a ratio, using x to represent the missing number of minutes:

$$\frac{14 \text{ minutes}}{2 \text{ miles}} = \frac{x \text{ minutes}}{1.5 \text{ miles}}$$

Cross multiply to solve for x:

$$2x = 14 \times 1.5$$
$$2x = 21$$
$$x = 10.5$$

3. **C** Algebra: Substitution *Easy*

Since $\frac{w}{z} = \frac{3}{4}$, let w equal 3 and z equal 4. Substitute these values into the second equation:

$$\frac{4w}{3z} = \frac{4(3)}{3(4)} = \frac{12}{12} = 1$$

4. **C** Geometry: Angles and Lines *Easy*

Determine the value of $\angle CAB$. The diagram shows that $\angle ACB$ measures 40°, so $\angle CAB$ measures 90° – 40°, or 50°. Angle t is vertical to $\angle CAB$, so t also measures 50°. Angle s is supplementary to t, so the measure of s is 180° – 50°, or 130°. Subtract the value of t from the value of s: 130° – 50° = 80°.

5. **D** Data Analysis, Statistics & Probability: Graphs, Charts, and Tables *Medium*

There are 4 patient appointments in the doctor's calendar, lasting a total of $4 \times 0.75 = 3$ hours. The calendar also lists 2 phone consultations, lasting a total of $2 \times 0.5 = 1$ hour. Including 1 hour for the staff meeting, the doctor has 5 hours of appointments scheduled. The appointment for Patient #4 should end no earlier than at 1 P.M.

6. **A** Data Analysis, Statistics & Probability: Statistical Analysis *Medium*

Start with **A** and substitute 4 for x in the three expressions provided:

$$2a - 1 = 2(4) - 1, \text{ or } 7$$
$$a + 4 = (4) + 4, \text{ or } 8$$
$$4a - 7 = 4(4) - 7, \text{ or } 9$$

When x equals 4, the expression $x + 4$ is the median or middle number of the three terms. All of the other answer choices produce sets of numbers such that $x + 4$ is the smallest number of the three terms.

7. **E** Algebra: Solving Equations *Medium*

Substitute \$2,800 for $P(b)$ in the equation and solve for b:

$$P(b) = 1.45b - 100$$
$$2,800 = 1.45b - 100$$
$$2,900 = 1.45b$$
$$b = \frac{2,900}{1.45}$$
$$b = 2,000$$

8. **B** Algebra: Binomials and Quadratics *Medium*

Multiply $(a - b)^2$ using the FOIL method:

$$(a-b)\times(a-b) = a^2 - 2ab + b^2$$

Substitute 56 for $a^2 + b^2$ and 7 for ab:

$$\begin{aligned} a^2 - 2ab + b^2 &= a^2 + b^2 - 2ab \\ &= 56 - 2(7) \\ &= 56 - 14 \\ &= 42 \end{aligned}$$

9. **D** Geometry: Triangles *Medium*

Triangle *WZX* contains a right angle and two angles with the same measurement, *a*. Therefore, ΔWZX is a 45-45-90 triangle. In a 45-45-90 triangle, the legs across from the congruent angles are equal in length. Since *WZ* measures 1, *XW* must measure 1 also.

Triangle *XYW* is a right triangle with one leg of length 1 and the other leg of length $\sqrt{3}$. Therefore, ΔXYW is a 30-60-90 triangle, with sides in the ratio $1:\sqrt{3}:2$. The angle opposite the smallest leg is the 30˚ angle. *WX*, which measures 1, is the smallest leg of ΔXYW, so *c* must measure 30˚.

10. **A** Numbers & Operations: Percents *Medium*

This question seems confusing but is fairly straightforward to solve once you decipher what it means. Write each percentage out as you go. The question mentions a "positive number" but doesn't say what the number is. So, let the positive unknown number be represented by *n*. The question asks for 45 percent of 50 percent of *n*. Fifty percent is the same as $0.50 \times n$, so write 50 percent of *n* as $(0.50)n$. Forty-five percent of that amount is $0.45(0.50)n$.

The question states that this value is equal to 25 percent of *z* percent of the same number. "The same number" just means the positive unknown number, *n*. Write *z* percent of *n* as, simply, *nz*. To write out 25 percent of this amount, multiply *nz* by 0.25. This produces $0.25nz$.

The question states that these two values are equal, so set up an equation:

$$0.45(0.50)n = 0.25nz$$

The question asks for the value of *z*, so it must be possible to isolate *z* on one side of the equation all by itself and come out with a whole number. Solve for *z*:

$$\begin{aligned} 0.45(0.50)n &= 0.25nz \\ \frac{0.45(0.50)n}{0.25n} &= z \\ z &= \frac{0.225}{0.25} \\ z &= .90 \text{ or } 90 \text{ percent} \end{aligned}$$

11. **B** Geometry: Solids *Difficult*

Let the side length of the largest cube be represented by *s*. Its volume is equal to $s \times s \times s$, or s^3. The side length of the second largest cube is half this length, or $\left(\frac{1}{2}\right)s$. The side length of the third largest cube is $\left(\frac{1}{2}\right)\left(\frac{1}{2}\right)s$, or $\left(\frac{1}{4}\right)s$. The side length of the fourth largest cube is $\left(\frac{1}{2}\right)\left(\frac{1}{4}\right)s$, or $\left(\frac{1}{8}\right)s$. The side length of the smallest cube is $\left(\frac{1}{2}\right)\left(\frac{1}{8}\right)s$, or $\left(\frac{1}{16}\right)s$.

Calculate the volume of the smallest cube:

$$\begin{aligned} V &= \left(\frac{1}{16}\right)s \times \left(\frac{1}{16}\right)s \times \left(\frac{1}{16}\right)s \\ &= \left(\frac{1}{4,096}\right)s^3 \end{aligned}$$

This volume is $\frac{1}{4{,}096}$ the volume of the largest cube, s^3.

12. **B** Numbers & Operations: Basic Operations *Medium*

The inequality shows that both $3a$ and b are less than 0. So, both are negative numbers. Any negative number multiplied by a negative will be positive. Therefore, **A**, **B**, and **E** will be positive numbers, while **C** is a negative number. Eliminate **C** and **D**.

Which of the remaining choices is greater? All three of them will be positive numbers. However, $-(3a + b)$ combined will be a larger positive number than either $-3a$ or $-b$ alone. Therefore, **B** is correct.

13. **C** Data Analysis, Statistics & Probability: Statistical Analysis *Medium*

This question tests your ability to translate words into an algebraic equation. Once you've translated the words into variables, you can solve for the average of the three numbers.

Clarence performed x concerts in May and 4 times as many in June. Therefore, he performed $4x$ concerts in June. In July, he then performed 6 more concerts than he had in June. The number of July concerts can be written as $4x + 6$. Use the three expressions to set up an equation:

$$\begin{aligned} \text{Average} &= \frac{\text{sum of terms}}{\text{number of terms}} \\ &= \frac{x + 4x + (4x + 6)}{3} \\ &= \frac{9x + 6}{3} \\ &= \frac{3(3x + 2)}{3} \\ &= 3x + 2 \end{aligned}$$

14. **D** Algebra: Absolute Value and Exponents *Difficult*

First, change the negative exponent to a positive exponent under a numerator of 1:

$$\begin{aligned} (x - y)^{\frac{1}{2}} &= (x + y)^{-\frac{1}{2}} \\ (x - y)^{\frac{1}{2}} &= \frac{1}{(x + y)^{\frac{1}{2}}} \end{aligned}$$

Raising a term to a fractional exponent is the same as taking the root of that term. (For example, $n^{\frac{a}{b}}$ is equivalent to $\sqrt[b]{n^a}$.) Thus, $(x - y)^{\frac{1}{2}}$ can be written as $\sqrt[2]{(x - y)^1}$.

Rewrite both sides of the equations using the square root notation:

$$(x-y)^{\frac{1}{2}} = \frac{1}{(x+y)^{\frac{1}{2}}}$$
$$\sqrt{(x-y)} = \frac{1}{\sqrt{(x+y)}}$$

Cross multiply to solve:

$$\left(\sqrt{(x-y)}\right)\left(\sqrt{(x+y)}\right) = 1$$

Remove the radicals by squaring both sides of the equation:

$$\left(\sqrt{(x-y)}\right)^2\left(\sqrt{(x+y)}\right)^2 = 1^2$$
$$(x-y)(x+y) = 1$$
$$x^2 + xy - xy - y^2 = 1$$
$$x^2 - y^2 = 1$$

15. **E** Algebra: Solving Equations *Difficult*

First, find the constant ratio (r) in the general equation $a \times r^{(n-1)} = T$. Let $T = 147$ and $n = 3$, and solve for r:

$$3 \times r^{(3-1)} = 147$$
$$3 \times r^2 = 147$$
$$r^2 = 49$$
$$r = 7$$

To find the fourth term in the sequence, multiply the third term (147) by the constant ratio (7): $147 \times 7 = 1,029$.

16. **E** Numbers & Operations: Sets *Difficult*

Draw a diagram to help visualize this problem. Let q represent the section where the two sets overlap:

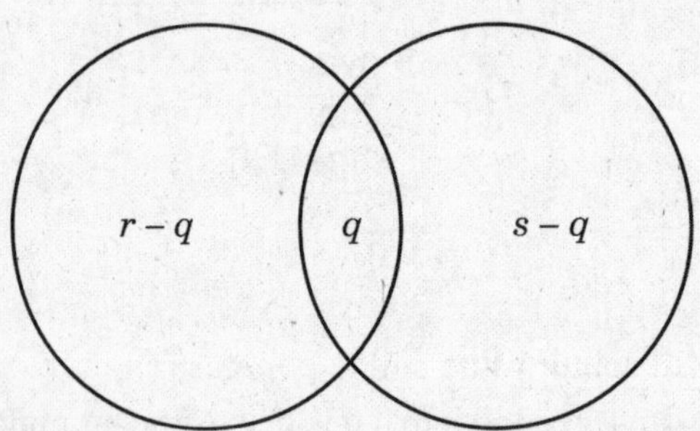

Set T equals the sum of set R and set S, minus the common members, q. Create an equation:

$$T = (r - q) + (s - q) = r + s - 2q$$

SECTION 9: WRITING

Improving Sentences

1. **D** Tenses *Easy*

This sentence has a verb tense error. The sentence should have a past tense verb, such as *resulted from*, as **D** provides.

2. **E** Misplaced Modifiers *Easy*

The original version of this sentence makes it sound as if the directors are the shareholders of the company. In fact, the directors are explaining their guarantee to the shareholders. The best revision of this sentence deletes the modifier *as shareholders* from the beginning of the sentence.

3. **E** Passive Voice *Easy*

This sentence uses the passive voice. It states that focusing on good sportsmanship *was* the tip that Coach Riley gave. The most effective revision deletes the passive verb *was* and rewrites the sentence using the active verb *instructed*.

4. **C** Coordination and Subordination *Easy*

The end of this sentence contains the phrase *because of being his favorite subject*, but it doesn't make clear which subject is Frederick's favorite. The revision in **C** clarifies, in the most concise way, that history is Frederick's favorite subject.

5. **A** No Error *Easy*

This sentence is correct as it is. All subjects and verbs agree, and other parts of speech are used correctly.

6. **B** Tenses *Easy*

This sentence starts with the verb *could* but ends with the incorrect tense *can*. **B** corrects this error.

7. **B** Wordiness *Easy*

This sentence is overly wordy. The phrase *it is* is unnecessary here. **B** revises the sentence in the most concise way.

8. **E** Parallelism *Medium*

The first part of this sentence states that the automated system *is faster, more efficient, and more accurate*. The second part of the sentence should maintain this parallel structure by using the phrase *are greater*.

9. **A** No Error *Medium*

This sentence is correct as written, so **A** is the best choice.

10. **C** Misplaced Modifier *Medium*

This sentence contains a misplaced modifier. The way the sentence reads originally, it sounds as though the *manufacturers* are valued for their expertise, when in fact it is the *trained specialists* who are the experts. **C** places the noun *trained specialists* close to the modifier *valued for their expertise* at the beginning of the sentence.

11. **D** Subject-Verb Agreement *Medium*

This sentence contains a problem with subject-verb agreement. The subject of the sentence, *research*, is singular. Therefore, the subject must be followed by the singular verb *reveals*.

12. **B** Other *Medium*

The verb tenses in this sentence are correct; the problem lies with the word *trios*. A single group of three people is referred to as a *trio* (singular). The word *trios* should only be used to describe two or more groups containing three people in each group.

13. **C** Run-Ons *Medium*

In this sentence, the phrase *Mrs. Peterson exercises first* is an independent clause. It can stand on its own as a complete sentence. Therefore, it must be joined to the first part of the sentence with a semicolon or a connecting word, such as *and* or *but*. **C** corrects the error by replacing the comma with a semicolon.

14. **D** Coordination and Subordination *Medium*

This sentence contains two independent clauses joined by the coordinating conjunction *and*. In fact, however, the first part of the sentence expresses an idea that contrasts with the idea in the second part of the sentence. To indicate this contrast, a conjunction, such as *although*, in **D**, should be used. **C** is incorrect because the word *however* should be preceded by a semicolon and followed by a comma. **E** is incorrect because the phrase *inasmuch as* is too wordy.

SAT PRACTICE TEST 9

SAT* Reasoning Test—General Directions

Timing

- You will have 3 hours and 20 minutes to work on this test. (On the actual SAT, you would have 3 hours and 45 minutes to complete ten sections, one of which would be unscored and experimental.)
- There are nine separately timed sections:
  - ➤ One 25-minute essay
  - ➤ Five other 25-minute sections
  - ➤ Two 20-minute sections
  - ➤ One 10-minute section
- You may work on only one section at a time.
- The supervisor will tell you when to begin and end each section.
- If you finish a section before time is called, check your work on that section. You may NOT turn to any other section.
- Work as rapidly as you can without losing accuracy. Don't waste time on questions that seem too difficult for you.

Marking Answers

- Carefully mark only one answer for each question.
- Make sure each mark is dark and completely fills the circle.
- Do not make any stray marks on your answer sheet.
- If you erase, do so completely. Incomplete erasures may be scored as intended answers.
- Use only the answer spaces that correspond to the question numbers.
- Use the test book for scratchwork, but you will not receive credit for anything written there.
- After time has been called, you may not transfer answers to your answer sheet or fill in circles.
- You may not fold or remove pages or portions of a page from this book, or take the book or answer sheet from the testing room.

Scoring

- For each correct answer to a question, you receive one point.
- For questions you omit, you receive no points.
- For a wrong answer to a multiple-choice question, you lose one-fourth of a point.
  - ➤ If you can eliminate one or more of the answer choices as wrong, you increase your chances of choosing the correct answer and earning one point.
  - ➤ If you can't eliminate any choice, move on. You can return to the question later if there is time.
- For a wrong answer to a "grid-in" math question, you don't lose any points.
- The essay is scored on a 1 to 6 scale by two different readers. The total essay score is the sum of the two readers' scores.
- An off-topic or blank essay will receive a score of zero.

---

* SAT test directions selected from the SAT Reasoning Test. Reprinted by permission of the College Board, the copyright owner.

SAT PRACTICE TEST 9 ANSWER SHEET

SECTION 2

1. Ⓐ Ⓑ Ⓒ Ⓓ Ⓔ	7. Ⓐ Ⓑ Ⓒ Ⓓ Ⓔ	13. Ⓐ Ⓑ Ⓒ Ⓓ Ⓔ	19. Ⓐ Ⓑ Ⓒ Ⓓ Ⓔ
2. Ⓐ Ⓑ Ⓒ Ⓓ Ⓔ	8. Ⓐ Ⓑ Ⓒ Ⓓ Ⓔ	14. Ⓐ Ⓑ Ⓒ Ⓓ Ⓔ	20. Ⓐ Ⓑ Ⓒ Ⓓ Ⓔ
3. Ⓐ Ⓑ Ⓒ Ⓓ Ⓔ	9. Ⓐ Ⓑ Ⓒ Ⓓ Ⓔ	15. Ⓐ Ⓑ Ⓒ Ⓓ Ⓔ	21. Ⓐ Ⓑ Ⓒ Ⓓ Ⓔ
4. Ⓐ Ⓑ Ⓒ Ⓓ Ⓔ	10. Ⓐ Ⓑ Ⓒ Ⓓ Ⓔ	16. Ⓐ Ⓑ Ⓒ Ⓓ Ⓔ	22. Ⓐ Ⓑ Ⓒ Ⓓ Ⓔ
5. Ⓐ Ⓑ Ⓒ Ⓓ Ⓔ	11. Ⓐ Ⓑ Ⓒ Ⓓ Ⓔ	17. Ⓐ Ⓑ Ⓒ Ⓓ Ⓔ	23. Ⓐ Ⓑ Ⓒ Ⓓ Ⓔ
6. Ⓐ Ⓑ Ⓒ Ⓓ Ⓔ	12. Ⓐ Ⓑ Ⓒ Ⓓ Ⓔ	18. Ⓐ Ⓑ Ⓒ Ⓓ Ⓔ	24. Ⓐ Ⓑ Ⓒ Ⓓ Ⓔ

SECTION 3

1. Ⓐ Ⓑ Ⓒ Ⓓ Ⓔ	6. Ⓐ Ⓑ Ⓒ Ⓓ Ⓔ	11. Ⓐ Ⓑ Ⓒ Ⓓ Ⓔ	16. Ⓐ Ⓑ Ⓒ Ⓓ Ⓔ
2. Ⓐ Ⓑ Ⓒ Ⓓ Ⓔ	7. Ⓐ Ⓑ Ⓒ Ⓓ Ⓔ	12. Ⓐ Ⓑ Ⓒ Ⓓ Ⓔ	17. Ⓐ Ⓑ Ⓒ Ⓓ Ⓔ
3. Ⓐ Ⓑ Ⓒ Ⓓ Ⓔ	8. Ⓐ Ⓑ Ⓒ Ⓓ Ⓔ	13. Ⓐ Ⓑ Ⓒ Ⓓ Ⓔ	18. Ⓐ Ⓑ Ⓒ Ⓓ Ⓔ
4. Ⓐ Ⓑ Ⓒ Ⓓ Ⓔ	9. Ⓐ Ⓑ Ⓒ Ⓓ Ⓔ	14. Ⓐ Ⓑ Ⓒ Ⓓ Ⓔ	19. Ⓐ Ⓑ Ⓒ Ⓓ Ⓔ
5. Ⓐ Ⓑ Ⓒ Ⓓ Ⓔ	10. Ⓐ Ⓑ Ⓒ Ⓓ Ⓔ	15. Ⓐ Ⓑ Ⓒ Ⓓ Ⓔ	20. Ⓐ Ⓑ Ⓒ Ⓓ Ⓔ

SECTION 4

1. Ⓐ Ⓑ Ⓒ Ⓓ Ⓔ	7. Ⓐ Ⓑ Ⓒ Ⓓ Ⓔ	13. Ⓐ Ⓑ Ⓒ Ⓓ Ⓔ	19. Ⓐ Ⓑ Ⓒ Ⓓ Ⓔ
2. Ⓐ Ⓑ Ⓒ Ⓓ Ⓔ	8. Ⓐ Ⓑ Ⓒ Ⓓ Ⓔ	14. Ⓐ Ⓑ Ⓒ Ⓓ Ⓔ	20. Ⓐ Ⓑ Ⓒ Ⓓ Ⓔ
3. Ⓐ Ⓑ Ⓒ Ⓓ Ⓔ	9. Ⓐ Ⓑ Ⓒ Ⓓ Ⓔ	15. Ⓐ Ⓑ Ⓒ Ⓓ Ⓔ	21. Ⓐ Ⓑ Ⓒ Ⓓ Ⓔ
4. Ⓐ Ⓑ Ⓒ Ⓓ Ⓔ	10. Ⓐ Ⓑ Ⓒ Ⓓ Ⓔ	16. Ⓐ Ⓑ Ⓒ Ⓓ Ⓔ	22. Ⓐ Ⓑ Ⓒ Ⓓ Ⓔ
5. Ⓐ Ⓑ Ⓒ Ⓓ Ⓔ	11. Ⓐ Ⓑ Ⓒ Ⓓ Ⓔ	17. Ⓐ Ⓑ Ⓒ Ⓓ Ⓔ	23. Ⓐ Ⓑ Ⓒ Ⓓ Ⓔ
6. Ⓐ Ⓑ Ⓒ Ⓓ Ⓔ	12. Ⓐ Ⓑ Ⓒ Ⓓ Ⓔ	18. Ⓐ Ⓑ Ⓒ Ⓓ Ⓔ	24. Ⓐ Ⓑ Ⓒ Ⓓ Ⓔ

SECTION 5

1. Ⓐ Ⓑ Ⓒ Ⓓ Ⓔ	3. Ⓐ Ⓑ Ⓒ Ⓓ Ⓔ	5. Ⓐ Ⓑ Ⓒ Ⓓ Ⓔ	7. Ⓐ Ⓑ Ⓒ Ⓓ Ⓔ
2. Ⓐ Ⓑ Ⓒ Ⓓ Ⓔ	4. Ⓐ Ⓑ Ⓒ Ⓓ Ⓔ	6. Ⓐ Ⓑ Ⓒ Ⓓ Ⓔ	8. Ⓐ Ⓑ Ⓒ Ⓓ Ⓔ

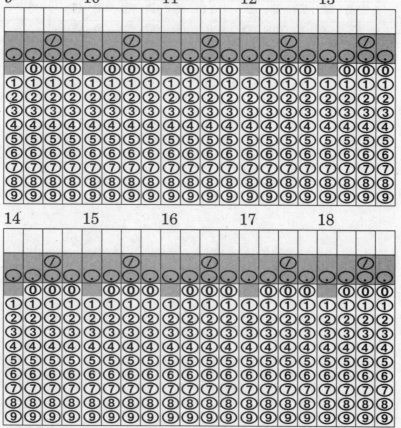

9 10 11 12 13

14 15 16 17 18

SAT PRACTICE TEST 9 ANSWER SHEET

SECTION 6			
1. Ⓐ Ⓑ Ⓒ Ⓓ Ⓔ	10. Ⓐ Ⓑ Ⓒ Ⓓ Ⓔ	19. Ⓐ Ⓑ Ⓒ Ⓓ Ⓔ	28. Ⓐ Ⓑ Ⓒ Ⓓ Ⓔ
2. Ⓐ Ⓑ Ⓒ Ⓓ Ⓔ	11. Ⓐ Ⓑ Ⓒ Ⓓ Ⓔ	20. Ⓐ Ⓑ Ⓒ Ⓓ Ⓔ	29. Ⓐ Ⓑ Ⓒ Ⓓ Ⓔ
3. Ⓐ Ⓑ Ⓒ Ⓓ Ⓔ	12. Ⓐ Ⓑ Ⓒ Ⓓ Ⓔ	21. Ⓐ Ⓑ Ⓒ Ⓓ Ⓔ	30. Ⓐ Ⓑ Ⓒ Ⓓ Ⓔ
4. Ⓐ Ⓑ Ⓒ Ⓓ Ⓔ	13. Ⓐ Ⓑ Ⓒ Ⓓ Ⓔ	22. Ⓐ Ⓑ Ⓒ Ⓓ Ⓔ	31. Ⓐ Ⓑ Ⓒ Ⓓ Ⓔ
5. Ⓐ Ⓑ Ⓒ Ⓓ Ⓔ	14. Ⓐ Ⓑ Ⓒ Ⓓ Ⓔ	23. Ⓐ Ⓑ Ⓒ Ⓓ Ⓔ	32. Ⓐ Ⓑ Ⓒ Ⓓ Ⓔ
6. Ⓐ Ⓑ Ⓒ Ⓓ Ⓔ	15. Ⓐ Ⓑ Ⓒ Ⓓ Ⓔ	24. Ⓐ Ⓑ Ⓒ Ⓓ Ⓔ	33. Ⓐ Ⓑ Ⓒ Ⓓ Ⓔ
7. Ⓐ Ⓑ Ⓒ Ⓓ Ⓔ	16. Ⓐ Ⓑ Ⓒ Ⓓ Ⓔ	25. Ⓐ Ⓑ Ⓒ Ⓓ Ⓔ	34. Ⓐ Ⓑ Ⓒ Ⓓ Ⓔ
8. Ⓐ Ⓑ Ⓒ Ⓓ Ⓔ	17. Ⓐ Ⓑ Ⓒ Ⓓ Ⓔ	26. Ⓐ Ⓑ Ⓒ Ⓓ Ⓔ	35. Ⓐ Ⓑ Ⓒ Ⓓ Ⓔ
9. Ⓐ Ⓑ Ⓒ Ⓓ Ⓔ	18. Ⓐ Ⓑ Ⓒ Ⓓ Ⓔ	27. Ⓐ Ⓑ Ⓒ Ⓓ Ⓔ	

SECTION 7			
1. Ⓐ Ⓑ Ⓒ Ⓓ Ⓔ	6. Ⓐ Ⓑ Ⓒ Ⓓ Ⓔ	11. Ⓐ Ⓑ Ⓒ Ⓓ Ⓔ	16. Ⓐ Ⓑ Ⓒ Ⓓ Ⓔ
2. Ⓐ Ⓑ Ⓒ Ⓓ Ⓔ	7. Ⓐ Ⓑ Ⓒ Ⓓ Ⓔ	12. Ⓐ Ⓑ Ⓒ Ⓓ Ⓔ	17. Ⓐ Ⓑ Ⓒ Ⓓ Ⓔ
3. Ⓐ Ⓑ Ⓒ Ⓓ Ⓔ	8. Ⓐ Ⓑ Ⓒ Ⓓ Ⓔ	13. Ⓐ Ⓑ Ⓒ Ⓓ Ⓔ	18. Ⓐ Ⓑ Ⓒ Ⓓ Ⓔ
4. Ⓐ Ⓑ Ⓒ Ⓓ Ⓔ	9. Ⓐ Ⓑ Ⓒ Ⓓ Ⓔ	14. Ⓐ Ⓑ Ⓒ Ⓓ Ⓔ	19. Ⓐ Ⓑ Ⓒ Ⓓ Ⓔ
5. Ⓐ Ⓑ Ⓒ Ⓓ Ⓔ	10. Ⓐ Ⓑ Ⓒ Ⓓ Ⓔ	15. Ⓐ Ⓑ Ⓒ Ⓓ Ⓔ	

SECTION 8			
1. Ⓐ Ⓑ Ⓒ Ⓓ Ⓔ	5. Ⓐ Ⓑ Ⓒ Ⓓ Ⓔ	9. Ⓐ Ⓑ Ⓒ Ⓓ Ⓔ	13. Ⓐ Ⓑ Ⓒ Ⓓ Ⓔ
2. Ⓐ Ⓑ Ⓒ Ⓓ Ⓔ	6. Ⓐ Ⓑ Ⓒ Ⓓ Ⓔ	10. Ⓐ Ⓑ Ⓒ Ⓓ Ⓔ	14. Ⓐ Ⓑ Ⓒ Ⓓ Ⓔ
3. Ⓐ Ⓑ Ⓒ Ⓓ Ⓔ	7. Ⓐ Ⓑ Ⓒ Ⓓ Ⓔ	11. Ⓐ Ⓑ Ⓒ Ⓓ Ⓔ	15. Ⓐ Ⓑ Ⓒ Ⓓ Ⓔ
4. Ⓐ Ⓑ Ⓒ Ⓓ Ⓔ	8. Ⓐ Ⓑ Ⓒ Ⓓ Ⓔ	12. Ⓐ Ⓑ Ⓒ Ⓓ Ⓔ	16. Ⓐ Ⓑ Ⓒ Ⓓ Ⓔ

SECTION 9			
1. Ⓐ Ⓑ Ⓒ Ⓓ Ⓔ	5. Ⓐ Ⓑ Ⓒ Ⓓ Ⓔ	9. Ⓐ Ⓑ Ⓒ Ⓓ Ⓔ	13. Ⓐ Ⓑ Ⓒ Ⓓ Ⓔ
2. Ⓐ Ⓑ Ⓒ Ⓓ Ⓔ	6. Ⓐ Ⓑ Ⓒ Ⓓ Ⓔ	10. Ⓐ Ⓑ Ⓒ Ⓓ Ⓔ	14. Ⓐ Ⓑ Ⓒ Ⓓ Ⓔ
3. Ⓐ Ⓑ Ⓒ Ⓓ Ⓔ	7. Ⓐ Ⓑ Ⓒ Ⓓ Ⓔ	11. Ⓐ Ⓑ Ⓒ Ⓓ Ⓔ	
4. Ⓐ Ⓑ Ⓒ Ⓓ Ⓔ	8. Ⓐ Ⓑ Ⓒ Ⓓ Ⓔ	12. Ⓐ Ⓑ Ⓒ Ⓓ Ⓔ	

SECTION 1

ESSAY

Time—25 minutes

The essay gives you an opportunity to show how effectively you can develop and express ideas. You should, therefore, take care to develop your point of view, present your ideas logically and clearly, and use language precisely.

Your essay must be written on the lines provided on your answer sheet—you will receive no other paper on which to write. You will have enough space if you write on every line, avoid wide margins, and keep your handwriting to a reasonable size. Remember that people who are not familiar with your handwriting will read what you write. Try to write or print so that what you are writing is legible to those readers.

You have twenty-five minutes to write an essay on the topic assigned below. DO NOT WRITE ON ANOTHER TOPIC. AN OFF-TOPIC ESSAY WILL RECEIVE A SCORE OF ZERO.

Think carefully about the issue presented in the following excerpt and the assignment below.

> In her book *A Room of One's Own*, author Virginia Woolf writes about the importance of privacy and solitude to artistic inspiration. Woolf believes that in order to develop their talents, all aspiring artists require a private sanctuary, in which they can think and work. Indeed, many artists produce their greatest masterpieces only after weeks, months, or years of dedicated solitary pursuit. Yet, other writers clearly prefer to work in public places, such as cafes and crowded city squares. These artists seem to thrive on the company of friends or even strangers, deriving much of their inspiration from interacting with and observing those around them.

Assignment: Is artistic inspiration more likely to be generated through solitude than through interaction with others? Plan and write an essay in which you develop your point of view on this issue. Support your position with reasoning and examples taken from your reading, studies, experience, or observations.

DO NOT WRITE YOUR ESSAY IN YOUR TEST BOOK. You will receive credit only for what you write on your answer sheet.

BEGIN WRITING YOUR ESSAY ON THE ANSWER SHEET.

IF YOU FINISH BEFORE TIME IS CALLED, YOU MAY CHECK YOUR WORK ON THIS SECTION ONLY.
DO NOT TURN TO ANY OTHER SECTION IN THE TEST.

SECTION 1—ESSAY

Time—25 minutes

SECTION 1—ESSAY

Time—25 minutes

SECTION 2

Turn to Section 2 of your answer sheet to answer the questions in this section.

Time—25 Minutes
24 Questions

Directions: For each question in this section, select the best answer from among the choices given and fill in the corresponding oval on the answer sheet.

Each sentence below has one or two blanks, each blank indicating that something has been omitted. Beneath the sentence are five words or sets of words labeled A through E. Choose the word or set of words that, when inserted in the sentence, best fits the meaning of the sentence as a whole.

Example:

Eliza felt ----- when her boss asked her to work seven weekends in a row but ----- when her work earned her a promotion.

(A) enervated . . weakened
(B) depressed . . intellectual
(C) advantageous . . salacious
(D) angry . . shopworn
(E) irate . . elated   

1. To avoid appearing -----, Doreen gave the bidders the impression that she had already made up her mind.

(A) biased
(B) determined
(C) subtle
(D) indecisive
(E) practical

2. Because it was so difficult for the board to act without specific plans, they chose to adopt a marketing strategy that was clearly -----.

(A) flexible
(B) vague
(C) defined
(D) available
(E) fluid

3. For many professionals, employment is a practical necessity that they may not ----- but are nevertheless willing to pursue for financial security.

(A) relish
(B) choose freely
(C) despise
(D) consider
(E) be qualified for

4. James was an extremely courageous soldier, naturally showing ----- and ----- in the most difficult situations.

(A) fearlessness . . circumspection
(B) fortitude . . valor
(C) timidity . . heroism
(D) creativity . . resilience
(E) intrepidity . . caution

5. Just as her mentors inspired her and encouraged her to succeed, Theresa always ----- her students and ----- them to live up to their potential.

(A) censured . . convinced
(B) taught . . educated
(C) motivated . . urged
(D) challenged . . limited
(E) rallied . . disheartened

6. The writer, renowned for his persuasiveness yet criticized for his dogmatism, often swayed readers with his ----- arguments by emphasizing the value of his ----- approach.

(A) potent . . dubious
(B) farfetched . . unyielding
(C) compelling . . doctrinaire
(D) eloquent . . ambiguous
(E) moving . . equivocal

GO ON TO THE NEXT PAGE

SECTION 2

7. The speaker was unsure about how to handle the ----- audience: he had never before encountered such a noisy and aggressively boisterous crowd.

(A) irascible
(B) assiduous
(C) reticent
(D) obstreperous
(E) taciturn

8. The reviews by music critic Kendall Close have been called -----, although most of them are not so derisive as to merit that label.

(A) vituperative
(B) garrulous
(C) juvenescent
(D) rapacious
(E) approbatory

GO ON TO THE NEXT PAGE

SECTION 2

Directions: Each passage below is followed by questions based on its content. Answer the questions on the basis of what is stated or implied in each passage and in any introductory material that may be provided.

Questions 9–10 are based on the following passage.

Our kidneys are remarkable organs that perform a function as crucial as any in the human body. According to ancient Chinese medicine, the kidneys store our vital energy and control the amount of fluid in the body. If the kidneys are out of balance, according to ancient Chinese wisdom, they can affect the functioning of many other bodily systems, especially the heart.

Western medicine also recognizes the vital role played by the kidneys in keeping our bodies healthy and operational. The primary function of the kidneys is to filter the blood, removing wastes and impurities. Each day, our kidneys process about fifty gallons of blood. They sift through the blood with the help of tiny filters, called nephrons, removing about two quarts of waste products and extra water daily. All this from two organs each no larger than the size of your fist!

9. The author's reference to ancient Chinese medicine primarily suggests that

(A) ailments of the kidneys are most effectively treated through acupuncture
(B) ancient Chinese views of the kidney are contradictory to the views of Western medicine
(C) the importance of the kidneys is acknowledged by disciplines outside of Western medical science
(D) the kidneys control the amount of fluid in the body by filtering the blood and removing wastes
(E) our kidneys are capable of processing fifty gallons of blood per day with the help of nephron filters

10. The author mentions the size of the kidneys in order to

(A) explain why kidney donors are able to function with only one kidney
(B) emphasize the significant amount of work completed by these small organs
(C) demonstrate that larger kidneys usually filter more blood each day
(D) compare the size of the kidneys to the size of a typical nephron
(E) explain the relationship between the kidneys and the heart

Questions 11–12 are based on the following passage.

Most of us are familiar with the popular story behind the discovery of gravity. According to legend, Sir Isaac Newton was sitting under an apple tree one day when he had the misfortune of being hit on the head by a falling apple. Misfortune turned into good fortune, however, for the enterprising Newton, who used the experience to help him understand how gravity operates.

How close is the story to actual reality? We can never know exactly what happened, but the truth is more likely that Newton discovered gravity by watching an apple's fall rather than experiencing the force of gravity personally. Newton noticed that the apple started to accelerate as it moved closer to the ground. This acceleration, he concluded, must be caused by a force that acts on the apple. As the apple neared the ground, the force seemed to grow stronger. Newton's observations helped him formulate his law of universal gravitation, which he believed to govern the gravitational relationships between any two objects in the universe.

11. The passage suggests that Sir Isaac Newton developed his understanding of gravity by

(A) studying gravitational theories of his era
(B) being hit on the head by a falling apple
(C) applying scientific laws of acceleration
(D) observing the stars while sitting under a tree
(E) watching an apple fall from a tree

12. The passage is primarily concerned with Sir Isaac Newton's

(A) biological research
(B) contributions to horticulture
(C) discovery of gravity
(D) memories of childhood
(E) understanding of chemistry

GO ON TO THE NEXT PAGE

SECTION 2

Directions: The passages below are followed by questions based on their content; questions following a pair of related passages may also be based on the relationship between the paired passages. Answer the questions on the basis of what is stated or implied in the passages and in any introductory material that may be provided.

Questions 13–24 are based on the following passages.

The author of Passage 1 describes the process of dispute resolution in Japan and explains some reasons behind the Japanese success with this approach. The author of Passage 2 evaluates whether alternative approaches to dispute resolution would be likely to succeed in the United States. Both passages are adapted from scholarly essays.

Passage 1

Extrajudicial reconciliation, with its modified form of conciliation that includes assistance by a third party, is the basic means of dispute settlement in Japan. This means of dispute settlement functions effectively in Japan in large part due to the cultural backdrop in this Far Eastern country. For one, group consciousness is deeply rooted in Japanese society, affecting every aspect of Japanese social structure. The well-known Japanese expression *uchi* (my house) refers to the place of work, office, school, or organization to which an individual belongs. This place of belonging is of overriding importance to the individual's life, oftentimes providing a holistic framework for the individual's entire social existence. This notion of communal belonging is firmly embedded in Japanese culture, which values harmonious living at all costs. The value placed on harmony is ingrained in Japanese mentalities, which explains in part why disputes are expected to be solved by mutual understanding.

Another factor that affects Japanese acceptance of extrajudicial dispute settlement concerns rank and social status. In Japanese society, social status is highly determined by the seniority that an individual possesses. In general, once seniority is established, it becomes fixed in the social order, driving and regulating all social relations in Japanese life. In Japan, awareness of rank is firmly embedded in social interaction—so much so that a person's individual qualities are superseded by his institutional position or title. In dispute situations, mediators who posses high social rank wield the authority necessary to secure negotiated settlements, merely by virtue of their accepted seniority.

In addition to cultural attributes that favor extrajudicial dispute settlement, the Japanese also have a historical legacy of amicable dispute resolution. According to law professor Yasuhei Taniguchi of Kyoto University, Japanese citizens have long been indoctrinated to view disputing as morally unacceptable. Historically, senior Japanese citizens were charged with the responsibility of keeping the peace within their circles of social influence. These authoritative members of society saw it as their duty to mediate any disputes that arose, making litigation the very last resort for resolving conflict. Even as the legal system was modernized in the late 1800s, the Japanese still upheld their tradition of mediation and felt a moral pressure to avoid litigation. This historical tradition continues to help the dispute resolution system function effectively in Japan.

Passage 2

In assessing the likely success of mediation systems in the United States, one must consider American culture and its values. Would people who believe that they have been harmed or unfairly disadvantaged in some fashion accept an informal treatment of their dispute? More specifically, would such persons agree to allow a random third party or board of conciliators to determine the outcomes of their disputes without legal representation? Considering American culture and its strong emphasis on individualism, it is doubtful that informal methods of dispute settlement could succeed in American society.

In American culture, a person's group membership in one particular organization or institution is only one aspect of his or her existence. The individual may posses other equally influential ties that affect his or her interactions in society. Even more important than communal ties for American citizens, however, is the value placed on individualism and personal accomplishment. Much of American history has been propelled and shaped by a belief in individual opportunity for economic triumph. Indeed, Americans are socially rewarded for merit, rather than for seniority. Systems of seniority do function within specific organizations, such as the military; otherwise, however merit systemically prevails as the predominant determinant of social status within American culture.

Because American society lacks an overriding emphasis upon harmonious community, it seems unlikely that minor disputes could be settled through an informal, extrajudicial mediation system. In mediation, disputes are settled through the efforts of a third-party mediator, who facilitates a mutual agreement between the conflicting parties. This type of system succeeds in other countries because third-party mediators are generally revered by disputants for their higher social rankings. While the mediators' suggestions have no binding power, in other countries the mediators generally have greater seniority than either of the disputants, so their authority is adequate for persuading parties to agree upon settlement. Since seniority does not carry much weight within American social structure, a third-party mediator would have less power to encourage disputants to restore a

GO ON TO THE NEXT PAGE

harmonious relationship. It seems unlikely that a mediator could command enough social authority to consistently induce binding agreements.

In order for an extrajudicial mediation system to succeed in the United States, several modifications to existing systems would be necessary. First, each establishing state authority could stipulate that all third-party mediators must be persons of high repute within the community, such as well-respected businesspersons or members of the clergy. Disputants would be instructed regarding the background of the mediator chosen for their case and asked to consent to respect the mediator's expertise in enabling the disputants to reach agreement. Second, if a mediator faced major difficulties in persuading the two disputants to reach a settlement, he or she would have the court's permission to seek further advice from other sources, including a member of the American Bar Association. These other sources would not be present in the mediation sessions, but their instructions would be explained to the two disputants during negotiations. This additional counsel would ideally enable both disputants to feel that their views had been appropriately considered, making reconciliation more plausible.

13. In the context of Passage 1, "extrajudicial" most nearly means

(A) opposed to the court system
(B) lacking justice
(C) outside the court system
(D) exceptionally fair
(E) carefully deliberated

14. Lines 12–14 ("This notion . . . costs") suggest that

(A) Japanese citizens place enormous importance on harmonious communal interactions
(B) Japanese students are taught to think outside the norms established by group consciousness
(C) most Japanese workers have individual offices within the organizations to which they belong
(D) the importance of group consciousness is a relatively new idea within Japanese society
(E) Japanese citizens tend to put their individual needs ahead of the greater needs of their communities

15. The author of Passage 1 considers seniority to be important within Japanese social structure (lines 19–28) because

(A) it can be easily adjusted based on an individual's professional accomplishments
(B) it regulates the Japanese economy more strictly than it controls familial ties
(C) it is a flexible indicator of social status, changing with political circumstances
(D) it enables a person's familial role to overshadow his or her professional role
(E) once it is established, it governs all social relations in Japanese life

16. All of the following are referred to in Passage 1 as reasons for the Japanese acceptance of extrajudicial dispute settlement EXCEPT

(A) the important role of rank and social status
(B) a historical legacy of amicable dispute resolution
(C) a tradition of moral pressure to avoid litigation
(D) the emphasis placed on personal accomplishment
(E) the overriding importance of an individual's place of belonging

17. Which statement about Japanese society, if true, would most directly weaken the view described in lines 29–42 ("In addition . . . Japan")?

(A) The greater the seniority of a Japanese mediator, the more effective that mediator tends to be in securing amicable dispute settlements.
(B) Japanese citizens value their historical traditions and tend to uphold those principles that have been passed down from generation to generation.
(C) During the 1800s, most senior members of Japanese society frowned on the use of litigation as a means of resolving conflict.
(D) With the modernization of the Japanese legal system came a torrent of new litigation, as Japanese citizens began to exercise their right to sue in court.
(E) Senior Japanese citizens generally view their mediation roles as honorable and willingly carry out the peacekeeping duties expected of them.

18. In line 46 "treatment" most nearly means

(A) authorization
(B) application
(C) cure
(D) resolution
(E) diagnosis

GO ON TO THE NEXT PAGE

SECTION 2

19. In Passage 2, the author's reference to "equally influential ties" (lines 55–56) suggests that

(A) Americans gravitate toward a single place of belonging, such as an office or a school, which provides a framework for their social existence
(B) systems of seniority are the most important organizing principles for specific American organizations, such as the military
(C) American citizens are socially rewarded for their personal accomplishments, rather than for their seniority
(D) Americans tend to downplay the importance of individualism because they feel such strong allegiances to particular institutions
(E) Americans tend to be influenced by memberships in multiple groups rather than by their affiliation with one primary organization

20. According to Passage 2, the likely failure of mediation systems in the United States results from which of the following?

(A) A moral imperative to avoid litigation
(B) A lack of qualified mediators
(C) The relative unimportance of seniority
(D) A lack of respect for individual rights
(E) The failure of the education system to stress cooperation

21. Which mediation scenario would best exemplify the modifications proposed in the last paragraph of Passage 2 (lines 83–100) ("In order . . . plausible")?

(A) A prominent businessman mediates a dispute and seeks an attorney's assistance in finalizing an equitable settlement.
(B) A college student serves as a mediator on a panel with several other students who jointly help to resolve a dispute.
(C) A member of a religious congregation is appointed by his peers to mediate a conflict between them.
(D) An attorney attempts to mediate a dispute but ultimately sides with one of the parties and advises his client to sue.
(E) A mediator fails to help disputants reach an amicable settlement and is denied permission to seek assistance from other sources.

22. Based on the information provided in both passages, which of the following would most likely characterize a Japanese citizen but not an American citizen?

(A) A belief that economic gain is achievable even for the poorest citizens
(B) An expectation that disputes will be resolved by mutual understanding
(C) A belief that individuals can triumph over adversity
(D) A belief that some personal and business disputes cannot be resolved
(E) A resistance to resolving disputes without legal representation

23. Passage 1 and Passage 2 share a general tone of

(A) reserved admiration
(B) academic rigor
(C) finely honed criticism
(D) marked concern
(E) scientific refutation

24. The information in Passage 2 supports which assumption about the dispute resolution process described in Passage 1?

(A) The individuals chosen as mediators for particular cases have greater seniority than the disputing parties in those cases.
(B) Third-party mediators are unable to command enough social power to consistently induce binding agreements.
(C) Japanese citizens view disputing as morally acceptable, although their legal history has long rejected litigation.
(D) Disputants who perceive themselves as unfairly disadvantaged are unlikely to accept the authority of a mediator.
(E) The Japanese emphasis on individualism stems originally from the belief that individual accomplishments could ensure economic gain.

S T O P

IF YOU FINISH BEFORE TIME IS CALLED, YOU MAY CHECK YOUR WORK ON THIS TEST ONLY.
DO NOT TURN TO ANY OTHER SECTION IN THIS TEST.

SECTION 3

Turn to Section 3 of your answer sheet to answer the questions in this section.

Time—25 Minutes
20 Questions

Directions: For this section, solve each problem and decide which is the best of the choices given. Fill in the corresponding oval on the answer sheet. You may use any available space for scratchwork.

Notes:

1. The use of a calculator is permitted. All numbers used are real numbers.
2. Figures that accompany problems in this test are intended to provide information useful in solving the problems. They are drawn as accurately as possible EXCEPT when it is stated in a specific problem that the figure is not drawn to scale. All figures lie in a plane unless otherwise indicated.
3. Unless otherwise specified, the domain of any function f is assumed to be the set of all real numbers x for which $f(x)$ is a real number.

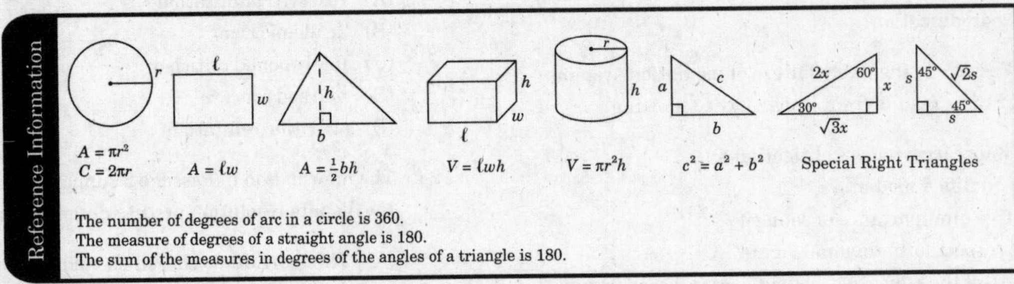
Reference Information
$A = \pi r^2$
$C = 2\pi r$
$A = \ell w$
$A = \frac{1}{2}bh$
$V = \ell wh$
$V = \pi r^2 h$
$c^2 = a^2 + b^2$
Special Right Triangles
The number of degrees of arc in a circle is 360.
The measure of degrees of a straight angle is 180.
The sum of the measures in degrees of the angles of a triangle is 180.

1. If $4a + 12 > 16$, which of the following cannot be the value of a ?

(A) 1
(B) 2
(C) 3
(D) 6
(E) 8

2. If $3^{3a} = 27$, then $a =$

(A) 1
(B) 3
(C) 9
(D) 10
(E) 11

3. How much greater than $s - 4$ is $s + 2$?

(A) 1
(B) 2
(C) 4
(D) 5
(E) 6

GO ON TO THE NEXT PAGE

SECTION 3

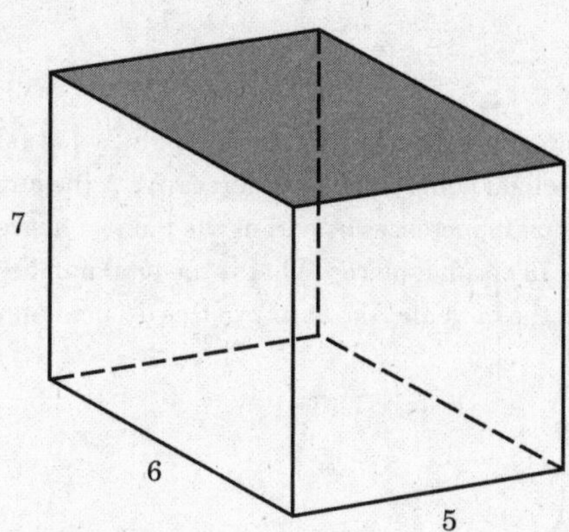

4. If the rectangular box with no lid shown above is cut along the vertical edges and flattened, which of the following figures best represents the result?

(A) 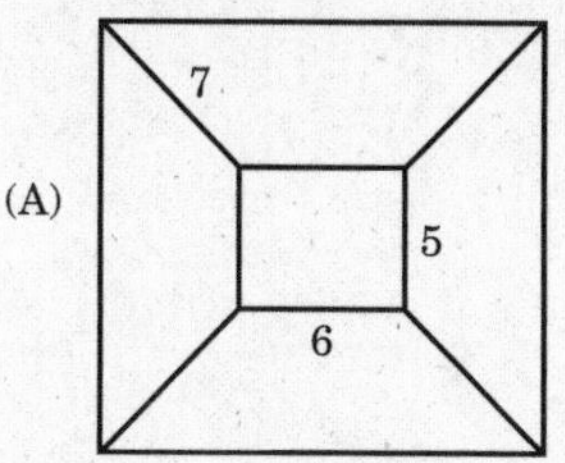

(B)

(C) 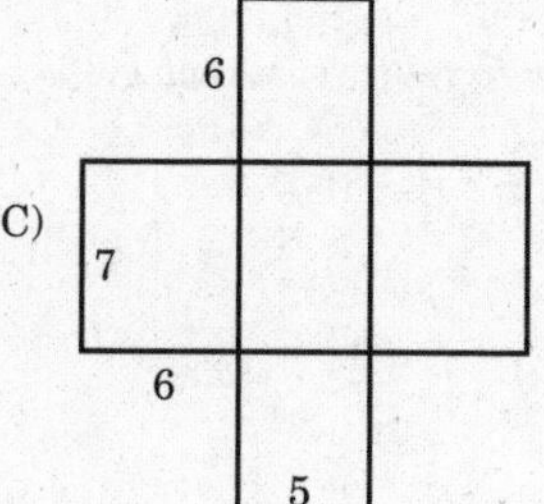

(D)

(E) 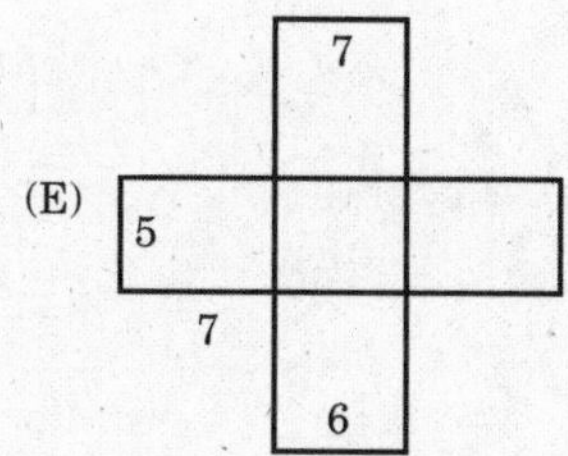

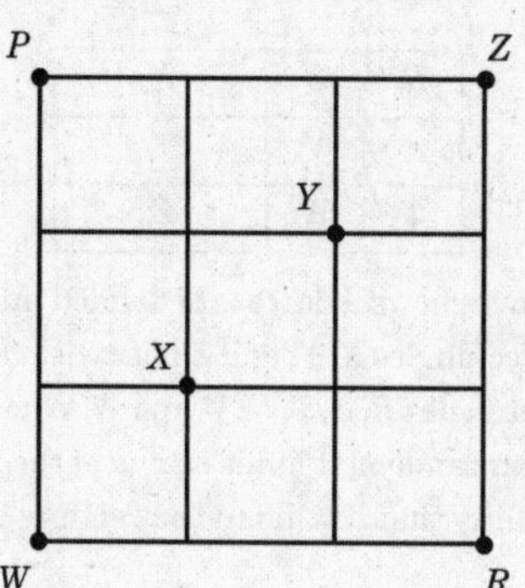

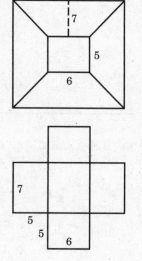

5. $PZRW$ in the figure above is a square divided into 9 congruent squares. If WR is 3 units in length, what is the unit length of WY?

(A) $\sqrt{2}$
(B) 2
(C) 3
(D) $2\sqrt{2}$
(E) $3\sqrt{2}$

6. If $\frac{4}{9}$ of x is 36, what is $\frac{7}{9}$ of x?

(A) 81
(B) 63
(C) 54
(D) 45
(E) 28

GO ON TO THE NEXT PAGE

SECTION 3

R	U	X
S	V	Y
T	W	Z

7. The table above shows a dartboard divided into nine rectangles. Each of the rectangles X, Y, and Z has twice the area of each of the equal rectangles R, S, T, U, V, and W. When a dart is thrown at the board at random, it lands on one of the rectangles. What is the probability that it will land on rectangle X?

(A) $\frac{1}{12}$

(B) $\frac{1}{9}$

(C) $\frac{2}{9}$

(D) $\frac{1}{6}$

(E) $\frac{1}{3}$

8. If c and d are even integers, which of the following must also be an even integer?

I. $(c + 1) - d$
II. $(c + 1)d$
III. $(c + 1) + d$

(A) I only
(B) II only
(C) III only
(D) I and II
(E) II and III

7.212112111211112 . . .

9. The decimal number above consists of only 2s and 1s to the right of the decimal point. After each successive 2, the number of continuous 1s increases by one, as the number above shows through 15 decimal places. What is the total number of 1s between the 56th and the 59th 2 in this decimal number?

(A) 104
(B) 113
(C) 115
(D) 171
(E) 230

10. If $g(n) = \frac{7 - 3n^2}{n}$ for all nonzero values of n, then $g(3) =$

(A) $-\frac{20}{3}$

(B) $-\frac{20}{7}$

(C) $-\frac{7}{3}$

(D) -2

(E) $-\frac{1}{7}$

GO ON TO THE NEXT PAGE

SECTION 3

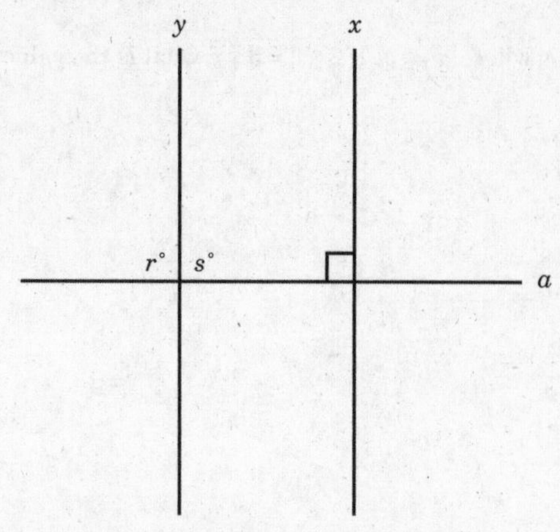

Note: Figure not drawn to scale.

11. In the figure above, $x \perp a$, and $s > 90$. Which of the following must be true?

(A) $r < 90$
(B) $r > 90$
(C) $r = 90$
(D) $a \perp y$
(E) $x \parallel y$

12. In the xy-plane, the line defined by the equation $y = 3x - 9$ crosses the x-axis at the point with coordinates (j, k). What is the value of j?

(A) –6
(B) 1
(C) 2
(D) 3
(E) 9

Box	Weight (kilograms)
1	34
2	19
3	15
4	w
5	42
6	28
7	23

13. The table above shows the weights of seven boxes designated 1 through 7. If the median weight of these boxes is 23 kilograms, then the weight of Box 4 could be any of the following EXCEPT

(A) 12 kg
(B) 18 kg
(C) 21 kg
(D) 23 kg
(E) 27 kg

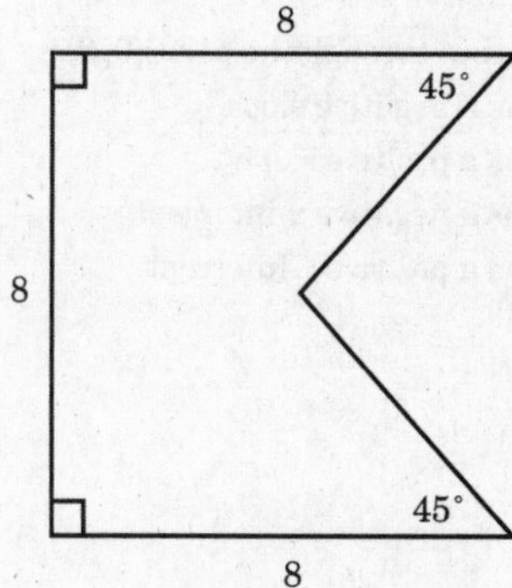

14. What is the perimeter of the figure above?

(A) $16\sqrt{2}$
(B) 24
(C) 32
(D) $24 + 8\sqrt{2}$
(E) $32\sqrt{2}$

GO ON TO THE NEXT PAGE

SECTION 3

15. If p is the greatest prime factor of 34 and q is the greatest prime factor of 60, what is the value of pq ?

(A) 10
(B) 68
(C) 85
(D) 120
(E) 170

16. Line m has a negative slope and passes through the point (0, 2). If line n is perpendicular to line m, which of the following must be true?

(A) Line n passes through the point (0, 2).
(B) Line n has a negative slope.
(C) Line n has a positive slope.
(D) Line n has a negative x-intercept.
(E) Line n has a positive y-intercept.

17. Let the operation ‡ be defined by $d \ddagger e = \frac{(d-e)}{(d+e)}$ for all numbers d and e, where $d \neq -e$. If $2 \ddagger 3 = 3 \ddagger f$, what is the value of f ?

(A) $\frac{9}{2}$
(B) 3
(C) $\frac{18}{5}$
(D) 15
(E) 18

18. During the busy season, a cabinet manufacturer can produce one cabinet for a cost of d dollars. Each additional cabinet the manufacturer makes costs m dollars less to produce than the first cabinet. For example, the cost of producing the second cabinet is $d - m$ dollars. Which of the following represents the cabinet manufacturer's cost, in dollars, for x cabinets made during the busy season?

(A) $d + (x-1)(d-m)$
(B) $d + x(d-m)$
(C) $x(d-m)$
(D) $\frac{d + (d-m)}{x}$
(E) $(d-m) + \frac{(d-m)}{x}$

GO ON TO THE NEXT PAGE

SECTION 3

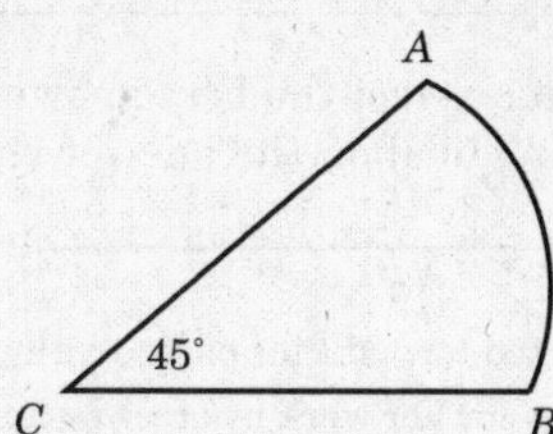

19. In the figure above, AB is the arc of a circle with center C. If the length of arc AB is 2π, what is the area of sector CAB ?

(A) 8π
(B) 12π
(C) 16π
(D) 32
(E) 64

20. There are 45 more cats than dogs living at Art's Animal Shelter, which houses only dogs and cats. If there are d dogs at the shelter, then, in terms of d, what *percent* of all animals at the shelter are dogs?

(A) $\dfrac{d}{d+45}$

(B) $\dfrac{d}{2d+45}$

(C) $\dfrac{d}{100(2d+45)}$

(D) $\dfrac{100d}{d+45}$

(E) $\dfrac{100d}{2d+45}$

S T O P

IF YOU FINISH BEFORE TIME IS CALLED, YOU MAY CHECK YOUR WORK ON THIS TEST ONLY.
DO NOT TURN TO ANY OTHER SECTION IN THIS TEST.

SECTION 4

Turn to Section 4 of your answer sheet to answer the questions in this section.

Time—25 Minutes
24 Questions

Directions: For each question in this section, select the best answer from among the choices given and fill in the corresponding oval on the answer sheet.

Each sentence below has one or two blanks, each blank indicating that something has been omitted. Beneath the sentence are five words or sets of words labeled A through E. Choose the word or set of words that, when inserted in the sentence, best fits the meaning of the sentence as a whole.

Example:

Eliza felt ----- when her boss asked her to work seven weekends in a row but ----- when her work earned her a promotion.

(A) enervated . . weakened
(B) depressed . . intellectual
(C) advantageous . . salacious
(D) angry . . shopworn
(E) irate . . elated    Ⓓ ●

1. Lawrence valued his solitude and preferred to live in -----, so he purchased a small cabin located in a remote area.

(A) freedom
(B) isolation
(C) connection
(D) privilege
(E) community

2. The administration's new policies upset students and faculty, causing an ----- on campus that was ----- only after an all-campus address by the college dean.

(A) investigation . . continued
(B) outcry . . encouraged
(C) agreement . . heightened
(D) uproar . . silenced
(E) order . . restored

3. After the respected town doctor passed away, the townspeople showed their ----- for her work by erecting a memorial in her honor.

(A) disregard
(B) predilection
(C) contempt
(D) equanimity
(E) veneration

4. The businesswoman ----- so frequently on her commitments that she developed a reputation for being -----.

(A) reneged . . capricious
(B) infringed . . dilatory
(C) acquiesced . . contentious
(D) withdrew . . veracious
(E) absconded . . conscientious

5. An adroit commander must be ----- strategist who uses inventiveness and cunning to defeat opponents, avoiding ----- approaches and conventional tactics.

(A) an adept . . vicarious
(B) a torpid . . ordinary
(C) a quiescent . . customary
(D) a skilled . . shrewd
(E) an ingenious . . hackneyed

GO ON TO THE NEXT PAGE

SECTION 4

Directions: The passages below are followed by questions based on their content; questions following a pair of related passages may also be based on the relationship between the paired passages. Answer the questions on the basis of what is stated or implied in the passages and in any introductory material that may be provided.

Questions 6–9 are based on the following passages.

The two passages below deal with the Peloponnesian War, fought between Sicily and Athens during the first century. The passages discuss the role of Athenian leaders in Athens's loss of the war.

Passage 1

The Sicilian expedition, at the end of the Peloponnesian War, was a series of battles that signaled the defeat of the Athenian army. Its outcome resulted in part from personal conflicts faced by the Athenian leaders, such as Nicias, a reluctant commander of the expedition.

Before the expedition, Nicias made a speech to the Athenians in which he revealed his conviction that Athens should avoid war with Sicily. When the Athenians rejected Nicias's advice and declared war on Sicily anyway, Nicias traveled to Sicily against his will. On the surface, he appeared to sacrifice his own interests for those of the state: instead of refusing to participate out of personal convictions, Nicias took on command of the expedition as a good soldier. Ultimately, however, his personal beliefs prohibited him from upholding his responsibility. Faced with what he viewed as certain defeat, Nicias became afraid to exercise his skills as a leader. He failed to raise morale or to regain Athens's position after several defeats, and he was unwilling to take charge of relief troops. Nicias allowed his personal beliefs to overshadow his commitment to serving Athens, and his inner conflict contributed to Athens's defeat.

Passage 2

The outcome of the Peloponnesian War was influenced in large part by the struggle of one Athenian leader, Alcibiades, who failed to subordinate his own personal interests to the interests of the state. Before the Sicilian expedition, Alcibiades clearly admitted that his personal interests were at stake for him in this journey. He wanted to gain the honor of victory, and he believed that Athens would be best served by gaining honor for herself also. He allowed his desire for conquest to lead Athens into battle.

During the expedition, however, Alcibiades betrayed the Athenians and chose to join forces with their enemies, the Spartans. Alcibiades selfishly placed his own interests above those of the state, revealing his personal weakness as a leader. Being so strongly motivated by his intense need to win, Alcibiades could not maintain loyalty to a goal greater than his own. He revealed Athenian strategies to the Spartans and transfered his loyalties to them for his own gain. Athens lost the war partly because of the trust that the Athenians placed in Alcibiades, a leader whose personal struggle for power led him to betray his own state.

6. Unlike Passage 2, Passage 1 is primarily concerned with the

(A) failure of Alcibiades to uphold leadership responsibility
(B) inability of Nicias to exercise his skills as a leader
(C) need of Alcibiades to achieve personal gain
(D) vulnerability that led Nicias to betray his country
(E) causes of the Athenian defeat in the Peloponnesian War

7. Both passages serve to emphasize the

(A) process through which leaders go in order to transfer their allegiances
(B) problems encountered by soldiers who enter losing battles
(C) strength of the loyalty most leaders feel for their states
(D) potential pitfalls that military leaders may face in the line of duty
(E) inaccuracy of historical accounts of past wars

8. Based on the two passages, which of the following would Alcibiades most likely assert in response to Nicias's conviction that Athens should avoid war with Sicily (lines 6–8) ("Before the . . . Sicily")?

(A) Athens should avoid war with Sicily, because Athens can achieve its strategic objectives without military confrontation.
(B) Athens should go to war with Sicily, because it is in the best interest of Athens to win the honor of victory.
(C) Nicias should be required to abstain from traveling to Sicily, because he does not support the war effort.
(D) Athens would be best served by avoiding war with Sicily, because Athens is not likely to win the war.
(E) Nicias should be required to lead Athens into battle to prove to himself that Athens can win the war.

9. Unlike Nicias in Passage 1, Alcibiades in Passage 2

(A) fails to raise the morale of his troops in Sicily
(B) travels to Sicily despite his personal lack of support for the war
(C) places the interests of the state above his own personal interests
(D) refuses to take charge of relief troops in Sicily
(E) betrays his country by revealing Athenian strategies to the Spartans

GO ON TO THE NEXT PAGE

SECTION 4

Directions: Each passage below is followed by questions based on its content. Answer the questions on the basis of what is stated or implied in each passage and in any introductory material that may be provided.

Questions 10–15 are based on the following passage.

In this passage, adapted from a fiction work published in the early 1900s, a businessman considers his relationship with one of his employees.

In one of the stateliest mansions on the lower Hudson, near New York, old Stanford Marvin, president of the Marvin Motors Company, dozed over his papers, while Owen, his confidential secretary, eyed him across the mahogany flat-topped desk. A soft purring sound floated in the open window and half-roused the aged manufacturer. It came from one of his own cars—six cylinders chanting in unison a litany of power to the great modern god of gasoline.

These things had been in Mr. Marvin's mind since the motor industry started. He had lived with them, wrestled with them during his meals, and taken them to his dreams at night. Now they formed a rhythm, and he heard them in his brain just before the fainting spells, which had come so frequently of late. He glanced at the secretary and noted Owen's gaze with something of a start.

"What are you thinking about, Raymond?" he queried of Owen, with his customary directness.

"Your health, sir," replied Owen, who, like all intelligent rascals, never lied when the truth would do equally well. As a matter of fact, Owen had wondered whether his employer would last a year or a month. He much preferred a month, for there was reason to believe that the Marvin will would contain a handsome bequest to "my faithful secretary."

"Oh, bosh!" said the old man. "You and Dr. Stevens would make a mummy of me before I'm dead."

"That reminds me, sir," said Owen, smoothly, "that the International Express Company has delivered a large crate addressed to you from Cairo, Egypt. I presume it is the mummy you bought on your last trip. Where shall I place it?"

Mr. Marvin's eye coursed around the walls of the handsome library, which had been his office since the doctor had forbidden him to visit his automobile works and steel-stamping mills.

"Take out that bust of Pallas Athene," he ordered, "and stand the mummy up in its place."

Owen nodded, poised his pencil and prompted: "You were just dictating about the new piston rings."

Mr. Marvin drew his hand across his eyes and looked out the window. Within the range of his vision was one of the most charming sights in the world—a handsome youth and a pretty girl, arrayed in white flannels, playing tennis.

"Never mind the letters. Tell Harry and Pauline I wish to see them."

Alone, the old man opened a drawer and took a dose of medicine, then he unfolded Dr. Stevens's letter and read its final paragraph, which prescribed a change of climate, together with complete and permanent rest, or, as Dr. Stevens had written, "I will not answer for the consequences."

There was little doubt that no prime mover in a great industry was better able to leave its helm than Stanford Marvin. His lieutenants were able, efficient, and contented. The factories would go on their own momentum for a year or two at least. Then his son, Harry, just out of college, should be able, perhaps, to help. His lieutenants had proved Marvin's unerring instinct in judging character. Not one single case came to the old employer's mind of a man who had failed to turn out exactly as he expected. Yet the most trusted man of all, Raymond Owen, the secretary, was disloyal and dishonest.

This one exception was easily enough explained. When Owen came to Marvin's attention, fifteen years before, he was a fine, honest, faithful man. At the age of forty, however, problems set in for Owen. They came in the form of insomnia. Loss of sleep will make any man irritable and unreasonable, but hardly dishonest. With the sleeplessness, however, came the temptation to take drugs to help him sleep. Owen shifted from one narcotic to another. Every physician knows that narcotic fiends become dishonest.

10. In lines 12–13 ("he heard . . . of late"), the narrator describes Mr. Marvin's fainting spells as

(A) recurring more frequently
(B) most common at mealtime
(C) prone to happening at night
(D) triggered by particular noises
(E) typically very mild

11. In the context of the passage, the phrase "never lied when the truth would do equally well" (line 19) suggests that Owen

(A) was prone to telling lies
(B) had difficulty keeping confidences
(C) was not particularly intelligent
(D) was an honest employee
(E) had difficulty discerning fact from fiction

GO ON TO THE NEXT PAGE

SECTION 4

12. The narrator's observation in lines 21–23 ("He much . . . secretary") suggests that

(A) Owen was not accustomed to accepting gifts from his employers and felt uncomfortable with the idea of receiving an inheritance from Mr. Marvin
(B) Owen had spoken privately with Mr. Marvin's doctor and learned the news that Mr. Marvin would probably die more quickly than expected
(C) Owen earned a reputation as Mr. Marvin's "faithful secretary," because of his honest dealings with Mr. Marvin's customers over the years
(D) Owen hoped that Mr. Marvin would pass away quickly so that Owen could receive the inheritance that he believed Mr. Marvin would leave him
(E) Owen disliked Mr. Marvin and looked forward to being relieved of his duties as Mr. Marvin's secretary once Mr. Marvin passed away

13. According to the passage, Mr. Marvin had been using his library as an office because

(A) he often felt ill and preferred to work at home in case he had a fainting spell
(B) his office at Marvin Motors Company was currently under construction
(C) his doctor would not allow him to visit his automobile company or steel mills
(D) the library was the only room in the house large enough to accommodate an office
(E) he preferred to work in his library, because he felt at home there

14. The description of Mr. Marvin's lieutenants (lines 49–50) primarily serves to suggest that

(A) Mr. Marvin perceived his managers as too strict with their employees
(B) Mr. Marvin was normally an excellent judge of character
(C) Mr. Marvin ran his company with militaristic discipline
(D) Mr. Marvin was disappointed in the progress of many of his workers
(E) Mr. Marvin had high expectations for his son, Harry, when Harry returned from military duty

15. The last paragraph of the passage indicates that Owen is

(A) an honest man who turned dishonest because of personal difficulties
(B) an eager employee who unfortunately lacked the skills for his position
(C) a dishonest individual who never earned Mr. Marvin's trust
(D) an honest man who made an exceptional employee
(E) a strong person who managed to triumph despite his personal struggles

GO ON TO THE NEXT PAGE

SECTION 4

Questions 16–24 are based on the following passage.

This passage discusses the founding of the International Atomic Energy Authority.

Ideas for the establishment of an International Atomic Energy Authority first came into play after the nuclear explosions over Japan in August 1945. World leaders decided at that time, however, that such an authority could be more effectively established only after cold war tensions had decreased, so efforts on the initiative were postponed. Successful action finally came in 1953, after President Eisenhower gave his "Atoms for Peace" speech to the United Nations. During the speech, Eisenhower recommended the development of an international atomic authority, and the International Atomic Energy Agency (IAEA) was launched in 1957.

The IAEA is based upon the principle of the peaceful use of atomic energy. Its purpose is to encourage international cooperation in the development and application of atomic energy, thereby ensuring the maintenance of international peace and security. The IAEA was established because world leaders believed that the peaceful use of nuclear energy could increase national economic capabilities and standards of living. This belief is reflected in the various resolutions and proposals created after World War II to encourage the establishment of the IAEA. It is also reflected in the Statute of the Agency itself. Article II of the statute, for instance, describes the agency's main objective as "to accelerate and enlarge the contribution of atomic energy to peace, health, and prosperity throughout the world."

Although the principle of peaceful cooperation reflects a great deal of international consensus on the purpose of the IAEA, many conflicts also affected the negotiation of agency agreements. For example, the Soviet Union strongly opposed the exclusion of Mainland China and the German Democratic Republic from the organization. The Soviet Union also objected when the organization Euratom was granted observer status in the agency. Although these objections pertained to membership issues, they nevertheless reflected the difficulties inherent in the establishment of international agreements regarding security concerns.

Over the years, the IAEA has remained dedicated to its main causes: the promotion of the peaceful use of atomic energy and the prevention of the spread of nuclear weapons. Yet, during this time, the agency has also undergone several changes in focus. The organization originally emphasized nuclear power until 1964, when it turned its attention to the technical problems of the design and construction of nuclear plants. The early 1970s saw an increased demand for nuclear power, but by the late 1970s this demand had slowed, and the IAEA once again shifted its emphasis to design and planning. Today, the agency facilitates international cooperation on the use of atomic energy through three main initiatives: promoting safeguards and verification, promoting the safety and security of nuclear resources, and promoting science and technology through technical assistance and research and development.

The IAEA has definitely experienced some setbacks. The organization is subject to internal constraints, such as the high turnover of staff and the inherent difficulties involved with managing many complex tasks. The agency is also plagued by external constraints, such as budgetary limitations that frequently restrain the organization's capabilities. A further external constraint lies in the fact that states accept IAEA inspections and safeguards only under certain conditions.

Despite these setbacks, however, the IAEA has had many significant achievements over its short duration. It has developed safeguard measures that have helped to build trust and confidence among member states, promoting international cooperation in an area usually characterized by high tensions. The agency has implemented successful initiatives to prevent the spread of nuclear weapons as well; these initiatives have been adopted in large part through the self-restraint and cooperation of member states. "In the twenty years of its existence," Kurt Waldhiem wrote in 1977, the IAEA "has proven an essential factor in the maintenance of international peace and security." This is still true of the organization today.

16. The author's purpose in the passage is to

(A) explain the causes of nuclear proliferation
(B) assess the value of atomic energy
(C) discuss uses of nuclear power
(D) critique efforts at international cooperation
(E) describe an international organization

17. As used in line 54, "plagued by" most nearly means

(A) overrun from
(B) dismantled by
(C) diseased by
(D) hindered by
(E) defeated by

GO ON TO THE NEXT PAGE

SECTION 4

18. The discussion of the establishment of the IAEA in the second paragraph (lines 12–24) primarily suggests that leaders

(A) believed that the peaceful use of nuclear energy could improve nations' economic status
(B) felt that the cold war environment was not conducive to creating an atomic energy authority
(C) viewed the IAEA as an important agency for research on nuclear weapons technology
(D) believed that a decrease in cold war tensions would improve international standards of living
(E) believed that the agency could help promote health and prosperity, but only in Western nations

19. The author refers to "international consensus" in line 26 to emphasize that

(A) discussions over membership in the IAEA were fraught with disagreement
(B) the Soviet Union strongly opposed the exclusion of two countries from the IAEA
(C) nations of the world generally agreed regarding the main principle of the IAEA
(D) world leaders presented many conflicting viewpoints over the fundamental role of the IAEA
(E) nations of the world had difficulty coming to agreement regarding the purpose of the IAEA

20. Which of the following assertions, if true, would detract LEAST from the author's argument in the third paragraph (lines 25–35)?

(A) Though conflicts over membership did arise during the IAEA negotiations, these conflicts were easily resolved.
(B) Membership issues were disputed only briefly during the IAEA negotiations, which progressed very smoothly overall.
(C) The Soviet Union was basically content with the IAEA membership and never presented its objections formally.
(D) The Soviet Union was easily appeased during membership negotiations, which helped to minimize its objections.
(E) Disagreements over membership posed some of the greatest threats to the process of establishing the IAEA.

21. The examples cited in the fourth paragraph (lines 36–50) are primarily drawn from

(A) a factual history of the IAEA's areas of emphasis
(B) an outline of provisions in the IAEA statute
(C) a theoretical discussion of possible areas of focus for the IAEA
(D) a critique that names issues overlooked by the IAEA
(E) a resolution that lists future IAEA action objectives

22. According to the passage, the establishment of the IAEA was delayed as a result of

(A) Eisenhower's "Atoms for Peace" speech
(B) disputes over membership requirements
(C) tensions arising from the cold war
(D) certain external budgetary limitations
(E) the nuclear explosions over Japan in 1945

23. Which of the following factors mentioned in the fifth paragraph best substantiates the claim that the IAEA has experienced "internal constraints" to its progress (line 52)?

(A) budgetary limitations
(B) high staff turnover
(C) the ease of managing complex tasks
(D) state restrictions on the acceptance of safeguards
(E) state willingness to undergo inspections

24. The reference to "safeguard measures" in line 61 extends the author's idea that

(A) the IAEA has implemented initiatives to prevent the spread of nuclear weapons
(B) the IAEA has had significant achievements since its creation
(C) IAEA member states have had difficulty establishing trust with one another
(D) the IAEA has experienced setbacks in many areas
(E) states typically agree to work with the IAEA only under certain conditions

S T O P

IF YOU FINISH BEFORE TIME IS CALLED, YOU MAY CHECK YOUR WORK ON THIS TEST ONLY.
DO NOT TURN TO ANY OTHER SECTION IN THIS TEST.

SECTION 5

Turn to Section 5 of your answer sheet to answer the questions in this section.

Time—25 Minutes
18 Questions

Directions: For this section, solve each problem and decide which is the best of the choices given. Fill in the corresponding oval on the answer sheet. You may use any available space for scratchwork.

Notes:

1. The use of a calculator is permitted. All numbers used are real numbers.
2. Figures that accompany problems in this test are intended to provide information useful in solving the problems. They are drawn as accurately as possible EXCEPT when it is stated in a specific problem that the figure is not drawn to scale. All figures lie in a plane unless otherwise indicated.
3. Unless otherwise specified, the domain of any function f is assumed to be the set of all real numbers x for which $f(x)$ is a real number.

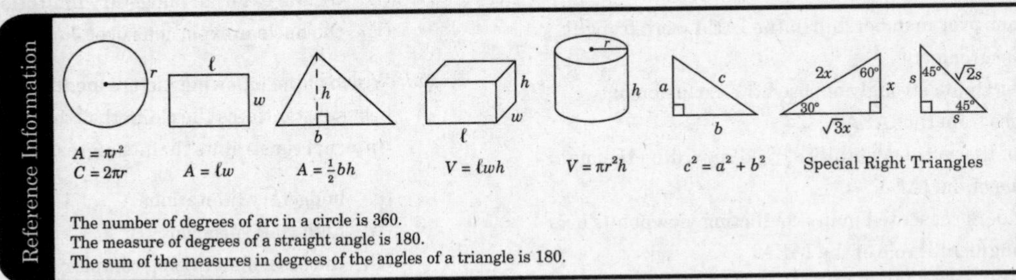

$$\frac{25 - \Omega}{4} = 4\frac{3}{4}$$

1. What number, when used in place of Ω above, makes the statement true?

(A) 1
(B) 3
(C) 4
(D) 6
(E) 7

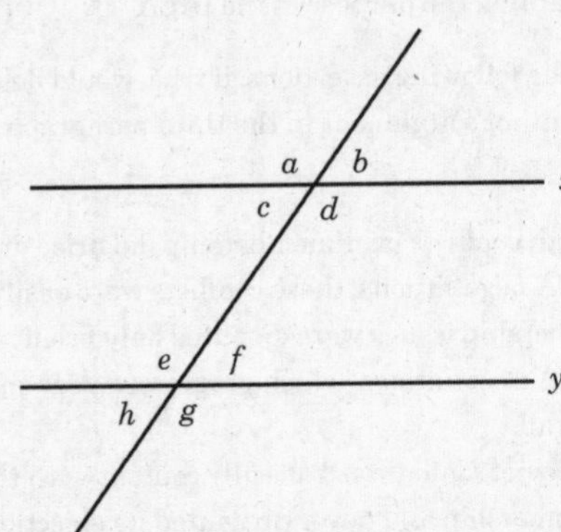

2. In the figure above, if $x \parallel y$, then the sum of the measures of angles a and d must equal the sum of the measures of which of the following pairs of angles?

(A) e and f
(B) f and h
(C) e and h
(D) e and g
(E) h and g

GO ON TO THE NEXT PAGE

SECTION 5

SCHOOL DISTRICT DONATED COMPUTERS

	Not Working	Working	Total
Laptops	32,000		
Desktops			38,750
Total	60,000		79,500

3. The table above, which describes computers donated to a school district, is partially filled in. Based on the information in the table, how many desktops donated to the school district are working?

(A) 7,500
(B) 10,000
(C) 12,500
(D) 13,625
(E) 10,750

4. Students in the ski club held a bake sale to raise money for their ski trip. The net amount, D, in dollars, raised by selling c cookies is given by the function $D(c) = 2c - 170$. If the group sold 200 cookies, what is the net amount they raised?

(A) \$30
(B) \$80
(C) \$140
(D) \$170
(E) \$230

5. If $mp = n$, $n = qp$, and $pn \neq 0$, which of the following is equal to q ?

(A) 1
(B) $\frac{1}{m}$
(C) $m - 1$
(D) m
(E) $m + 1$

6. All roses in a certain arrangement are either red or yellow. If the ratio of the number of red roses to the number of yellow roses is $\frac{1}{2}$, each of the following could be the number of roses in the arrangement EXCEPT

(A) 6
(B) 10
(C) 12
(D) 18
(E) 24

7. If $32\sqrt{32} = x\sqrt{y}$, where x and y are positive integers and $x > y$, which of the following could be the value of xy ?

(A) 32
(B) 64
(C) 256
(D) 512
(E) 1,024

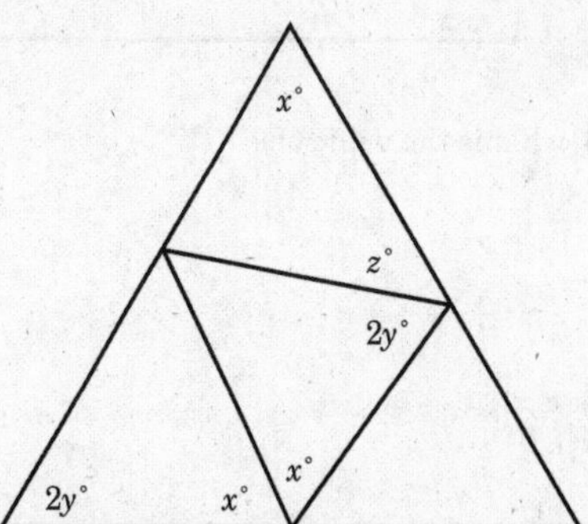

8. In the figure above, what is the value of z in terms of x and y ?

(A) $x + 4y - 180$
(B) $3x + 3y - 180$
(C) $180 - x - 2y$
(D) $360 - x - 2y$
(E) $360 - 3x - 4y$

GO ON TO THE NEXT PAGE

SECTION 5

Directions: For Student-Produced Response questions 9–18, use the grids on the answer sheet.

Each of these questions requires you to solve the problem and enter your answer by marking the ovals in the special grid, as shown in the examples below. You may use any available space for scratchwork.

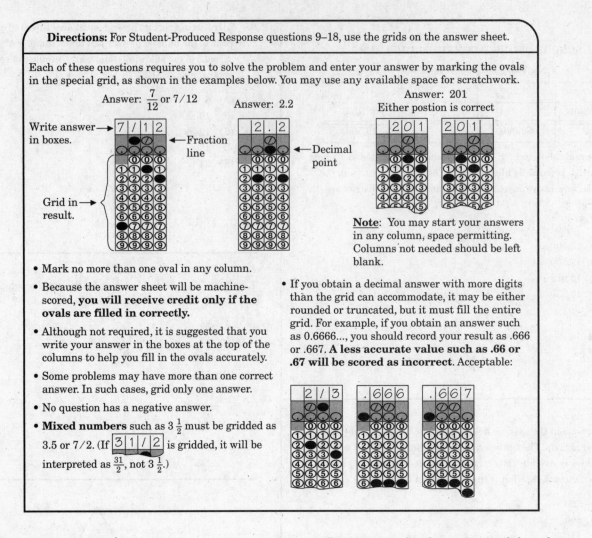

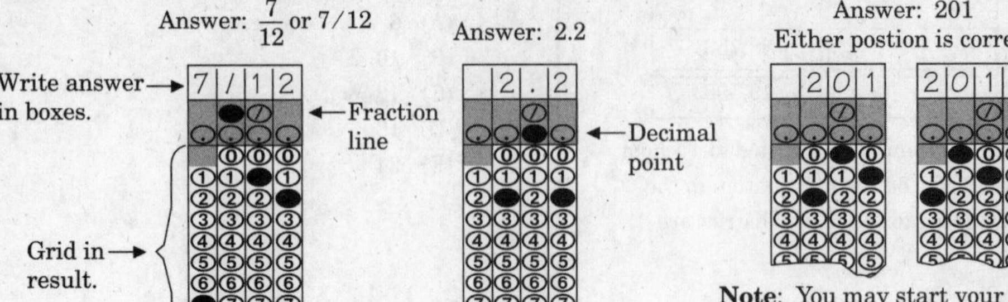

Note: You may start your answers in any column, space permitting. Columns not needed should be left blank.

- Mark no more than one oval in any column.
- Because the answer sheet will be machine-scored, **you will receive credit only if the ovals are filled in correctly.**
- Although not required, it is suggested that you write your answer in the boxes at the top of the columns to help you fill in the ovals accurately.
- Some problems may have more than one correct answer. In such cases, grid only one answer.
- No question has a negative answer.
- **Mixed numbers** such as $3\frac{1}{2}$ must be gridded as 3.5 or 7/2. (If 3 1 / 2 is gridded, it will be interpreted as $\frac{31}{2}$, not $3\frac{1}{2}$.)
- If you obtain a decimal answer with more digits than the grid can accommodate, it may be either rounded or truncated, but it must fill the entire grid. For example, if you obtain an answer such as 0.6666..., you should record your result as .666 or .667. **A less accurate value such as .66 or .67 will be scored as incorrect**. Acceptable:

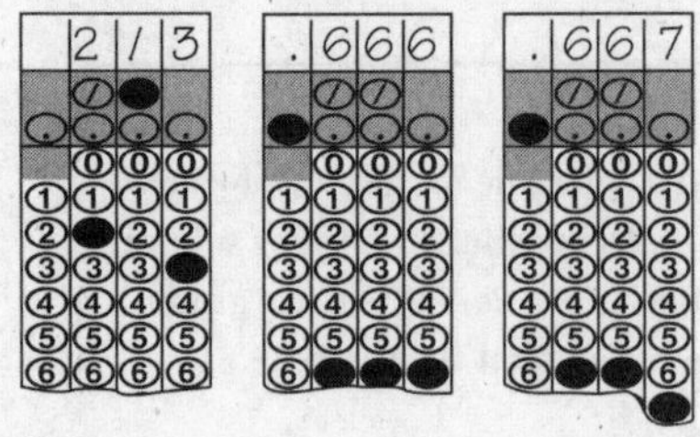

9. If $c^6 = 684$, what is the value of $9c^6$?

10. What is the coordinate of the point on a number line that is exactly halfway between the points with coordinates 69 and 76 ?

11. Two interior angles of a certain triangle have the same measure. If the lengths of two of the sides of the triangle are 40 and 65, what is the LEAST possible value for the perimeter of the triangle?

GO ON TO THE NEXT PAGE

SECTION 5

12. If $a^2 - b^2 = 60$ and $a - b = 6$, what is the value of a ?

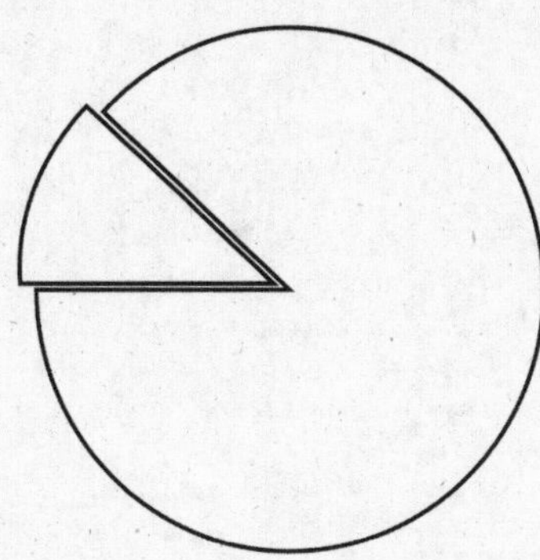

13. Rachelle cut a circular pie into wedge-shaped slices, one of which is shown above. The tip of each slice is at the center of the pie and the angle at the tip is always greater than 40°, but less than 60°. What is one possible value for the number of slices into which the pie is cut?

$2m, 8m, \ldots$

14. The first term in the sequence above is $2m$, and each term after the first is four times the preceding term. If the sum of the first 5 terms is 2,046, what is the value of m ?

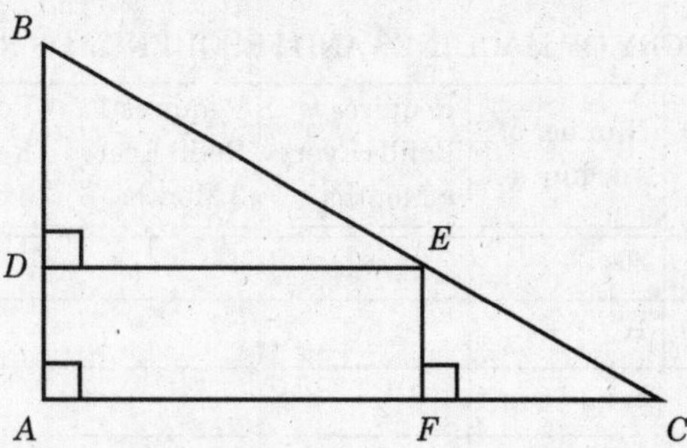

Note: Figure not drawn to scale.

15. In ΔABC above, $\frac{CF}{CA} = \frac{2}{5}$ and $\frac{AD}{AB} = \frac{1}{3}$. What is the value of the fraction $\frac{\text{area } \Delta DBE}{\text{area } \Delta ABC}$?

16. Let the function s be defined by $s(b) = \frac{15 + b^2}{9}$.

If $s(3c) = 8c$, what is one possible value of c ?

GO ON TO THE NEXT PAGE

SECTION 5

INVENTORY OF MACHINES AND FREQUENCY OF REFILLS

	Number of Machines	Requires n Refills Every n Months	Requires 1 Refill Every 3 Months	Requires 2 Refills Every 3 Months
Machine A	20	×		
Machine B	10			×
Machine C	5		×	
Machine D	3	×		
Machine E	12			×

17. A company uses three types of machines that require refills with normal use as indicated by the "× s" in the table above. If all of the machines start with fresh refills and are put to normal use, what is the total number of refills required by the inventory of machines in the six-month period from January through June?

18. If the four blocks shown above are placed in a row so that block B is never the first block, how many different arrangements are possible?

S T O P

IF YOU FINISH BEFORE TIME IS CALLED, YOU MAY CHECK YOUR WORK ON THIS TEST ONLY.
DO NOT TURN TO ANY OTHER SECTION IN THIS TEST.

SECTION 6

Turn to Section 6 of your answer sheet to answer the questions in this section.

Time—25 Minutes
35 Questions

Directions: For each question in this section, select the best answer from among the choices given.

The following sentences test correctness and effectiveness of expression. Part of each sentence or the entire sentence is underlined; beneath each sentence are five ways of phrasing the underlined material. Choice A repeats the original phrasing; the other four choices are different. If you think the original phrasing produces a better sentence than any of the alternatives, select choice A; if not, select one of the other choices.

In making your selection, follow the requirements of standard written English; that is, pay attention to grammar, choice of words, sentence construction, and punctuation. Your selection should result in the most effective sentence—clear and precise, without awkwardness or ambiguity.

<u>Example</u>:

In the poem "Ulysses" by Alfred, Lord Tennyson, the speaker says, <u>"I cannot rest from travel," instead,</u> he will live life to the fullest.

(A) "I cannot rest from travel," instead,
(B) "I cannot rest from travel"; instead,
(C) "I cannot rest from travel" instead,
(D) "I cannot rest from travel," upon which
(E) "I cannot rest from travel,"

1. In 2003, more students from St. Martin's High School vacationed in Florida than <u>they did in Georgia</u>.

   (A) they did in Georgia
   (B) Georgia did
   (C) compared to Georgia
   (D) Georgia vacations
   (E) in Georgia

2. D'Orelli, a marketing and public relations firm, is launching an advertising campaign for <u>Best Electric, it provides</u> commercial utilities in the metropolitan area.

   (A) Best Electric, it provides
   (B) Best Electric, which provides
   (C) Best Electric, providing
   (D) Best Electric, it is providing
   (E) Best Electric; for the provision of

3. The downtown ice-cream truck does not sell as much ice cream <u>as does our neighborhood</u>.

   (A) as does our neighborhood
   (B) as our neighborhood ice-cream truck
   (C) compared to the one in our neighborhood
   (D) like our neighborhood ice-cream truck does
   (E) like the one in our neighborhood does

4. During the strike, airline workers lined up with protest signs on the <u>runways, and they thereby delayed access to many flights</u>.

   (A) runways, and they thereby delayed access to many flights
   (B) runways and therefore delaying access to many flights
   (C) runways, by which many flights were delayed
   (D) runways, and therefore made many flights delayed
   (E) runways, thereby delaying many flights

5. Having grown accustomed to winning most of her arguments, <u>that Alan refused to accept her point of view annoyed Betty thoroughly</u>.

   (A) that Alan refused to accept her point of view annoyed Betty thoroughly
   (B) Betty's thorough annoyance resulted from Alan refusing to accept her point of view
   (C) Betty's annoyance at Alan's refusing to accept her point of view was thorough
   (D) Betty was thoroughly annoyed by Alan's refusal to accept her point of view
   (E) Alan's refusing to accept her point of view was a thorough annoyance to Betty

GO ON TO THE NEXT PAGE

SECTION 6

6. The main excuses Dr. Klein's patients give for neglecting to exercise is that they have very full schedules and find it difficult to stay motivated.

(A) is that they have very full schedules and find it difficult to
(B) are very full schedules and they find it difficult to
(C) are that they have very full schedules and that they find it difficult to
(D) is having very full schedules and finding it difficult to
(E) are very full schedules, in addition to finding it difficult to

7. The inhabitants of Fayetteville claim that their town library, which has 14,000 books and 1,200 magazines in its holdings, maintains the largest collection of printed material for 200 miles.

(A) which has 14,000 books and 1,200 magazines
(B) owning 14,000 books while having amassed 1,200 magazines
(C) with 14,000 books as well as magazines totaling 1,200 in number
(D) with 14,000 books, and it has 1,200 magazines
(E) having 14,000 books and 1,200 magazines counted from among those

8. Returning home from Europe after a year, Mandy's apartment seemed much larger to her than it had been when she was living there before her trip.

(A) Returning home from Europe after a year, Mandy's apartment seemed much larger to her
(B) Having returned home from Europe after a year, it seemed a much larger apartment to Mandy
(C) After Mandy returned home from Europe in a year, her apartment seems much larger
(D) Mandy returned home from Europe after a year, her apartment was seemingly much larger
(E) When Mandy returned home from Europe after a year, her apartment seemed much larger to her

9. Having skills at negotiation, mediation, as well as arbitration, Karen Shepherd was invited to moderate several important sessions of the disarmament proceedings.

(A) Having skills at negotiation, mediation, as well as arbitration
(B) Having skills at negotiation, mediation, and her arbitration background
(C) By having skills at both negotiation and mediation and also arbitration
(D) With her skills at negotiation and mediation and being an arbitrator
(E) Because of her negotiation, mediation, and arbitration skills

10. The engineer changed industries several times during his career, moving from electronics first he went into manufacturing, then eventually into laser optics from telecommunications.

(A) moving from electronics first he went into manufacturing, then eventually into laser optics from telecommunications
(B) the first move he made was from electronics to manufacturing and eventually from telecommunications to laser optics
(C) first from electronics to manufacturing and eventually from telecommunications to laser optics
(D) moving first from electronics, he worked in manufacturing and eventually in laser optics
(E) first from electronics to manufacturing and ended up in laser optics after leaving telecommunications

11. Though heavily reliant on her mentors for advice and inspiration while her backers provide the sculptor with financial support, as an artist she maintains complete creative control over her work.

(A) inspiration while her backers provide the sculptor with financial support, as an artist she maintains
(B) inspiration and on financial support by her backers, the sculptor, an artist who maintains
(C) inspiration and on her backers for financial support, the sculptor is an artist who maintains
(D) inspiration, her backers provide the sculptor with financial support, but she is an artist who maintains
(E) inspiration, her backers provide the sculptor with financial support, while she as an artist maintains

GO ON TO THE NEXT PAGE

SECTION 6

Directions: For each question in this section, select the best answer from among the choices given.

The following sentences test your ability to recognize grammar and usage errors. Each sentence contains either a single error or no error at all. No sentence contains more than one error. The error, if there is one, is underlined and lettered. If the sentence contains an error, select the one underlined part that must be changed to make the sentence correct. If the sentence is correct, select choice E. In choosing answers, follow the requirements of standard written English.

Example:

The other (A) delegates and him (B) immediately (C) accepted the resolution drafted by (D) the neutral states. No error (E)

Ⓐ ● Ⓒ Ⓓ Ⓔ

12. Thirty years after (A) the lawn shop was opened in Sturgeon Square, the business had to be shut down when (B) much of the inventory is demolished (C) by torrential rains and (D) flooding. No error (E)

13. The shoe manufacturer is releasing (A) a summer ad for sandals that (B) will encourage (C) new purchases and raise sales revenues (D) in July and August. No error (E)

14. Many authors are (A) inspired by either personal experiences and (B) current events, but some can (C) generate stories strictly from their imaginations (D). No error (E)

15. Although (A) only certain portions of Paul's homework had been (B) completed, these assignments were evaluated leniently by (C) Paul's teachers because it had been (D) so challenging for Paul to complete after his accident. No error (E)

16. The handmade watch that (A) Mr. Solomon purchased in Switzerland is (B) one of its kind (C), crafted diligently by a skilled Swiss watchmaker who hails (D) from a long line of jewelry artisans. No error (E)

17. Sarah Blaine Edwards, whose (A) poetry works have been lauded (B) by critics worldwide, tends to (C) end each piece passionately (D), with intense emotion. No error (E)

18. Because she is traveling (A) when her home was burglarized, Sandy is determined (B) to hire (C) someone to watch (D) her house when she leaves town on future business trips. No error (E)

19. In counseling training (A) programs in which (B) supervision is adequate, fewer ethical breaches occur and counseling students are rarely (C) involved in (D) lawsuits. No error (E)

20. Natural scientists have demonstrated that (A) light can appear (B) not only (C) in wave form but also as particle form (D), depending upon the conditions under which it is observed. No error (E)

21. The design Helen is presenting (A), a design developed jointly by she (B) and the fashion consultant, clearly meets the criteria (C) established by the judging panel (D) for originality and innovative style. No error (E)

22. It is often simpler (A) to finish a task oneself than explaining (B) to another exactly how (C) the task should be completed (D). No error (E)

23. Tia wanted, for the most part (A), to start her own business as a decorator (B), but sometimes she thought about (C) getting a job (D) with a successful company instead. No error (E)

GO ON TO THE NEXT PAGE

SECTION 6

24. Since some [A] people believe that [B] homeopathy, a system of treating illnesses with minute doses of remedies, is effective, but others criticize the approach as [C] simply quackery [D]. No error [E]

25. Her excuse of [A] giving Kevin the book was that she had forgotten [B] his birthday weeks ago, but Kevin knew that she really wanted him to read the book and was hoping [C] the gift would [D] encourage him. No error [E]

26. In recognition of [A] our value to the organization, Kendra invited Dawn and I [B] to a luncheon attended by [C] both of our departments and all of [D] the management staff. No error [E]

27. Equally appreciated [A] by Dr. Burnside's students was [B] his interesting assignments and his captivating lecture style [C], which helped students [D] understand complex concepts in an entertaining way. No error [E]

28. The success of acupuncture treatments is influenced [A] by how accurately [B] its [C] protocols can be applied [D] by highly skilled practitioners. No error [E]

29. The labor survey provides [A] evidence of a gradual [B] declining metropolitan unemployment rate that mirrors [C] the trend within the [D] city's outlying suburbs. No error [E]

GO ON TO THE NEXT PAGE

SECTION 6

Directions: The following passage is an early draft of an essay. Some parts of the passage need to be rewritten.

Read the passage and select the best answers for the questions that follow. Some questions are about particular sentences or parts of sentences and ask you to improve sentence structure or word choice. Other questions ask you to consider organization and development. In choosing answers, follow the requirements of standard written English.

Questions 30–35 are based on the following passage, a response to an assignment to write about the history or process of a musical composition.

(1) *The composition of the* Mass in B Minor *appears to have been a complex process that proceeded in stages.* **(2)** *From what we can interpret historically, it seems that Bach did not conceive of the mass as a whole work until the last few years of his life.* **(3)** *The piece was instead composed in separate sections that Bach eventually organized into the complete mass performed today.* **(4)** *The mass appears to have originated in 1733 with Bach's composition of the first section.* **(5)** *The first section was known as the Missa.* **(6)** *Early that year, the elector of Saxony died, and tradition held that all church music must stop until the elector's successor was crowned.* **(7)** *Bach's church music duties in Leipzig at the time were thus suspended, that gave him time to compose the Missa.*

(8) *Bach's setting of the Missa involved both new compositions as well as the reworking of earlier material from two of his previous cantatas and an instrumental concerto.* **(9)** *Bach presented the Missa to the new elector of Saxony in July of 1733, presumably in order to obtain the title of* court kapelle *in Dresden.* **(10)** *Bach was displeased with the lack of recognition that he was receiving in his position in Leipzig at the time.* **(11)** *Bach did finally receive his new title in 1736, although he never achieved the closer connection with the Dresden Court that he had hoped for.*

30. Which of the following, if inserted before sentence 1, would make a good introduction to the essay?

(A) J. S. Bach was a composer who lived during the 1700s and wrote many classical works.
(B) No overview of the music of J. S. Bach would be complete without analyzing the history behind his *Mass in B Minor*, one of his most significant works.
(C) Although J. S. Bach worked primarily as a composer and a musician, he was also very active in politics.
(D) During his lifetime, J. S. Bach developed an impressive portfolio of compositions, each one valued for its own specific features.
(E) J. S. Bach devoted much of his life to composing works that would ensure his promotions to musical positions of greater influence.

31. In context, which of the following is the best way to revise and combine sentences 4 and 5 (reproduced below)?

The mass appears to have originated in 1733 with Bach's composition of the first section. The first section was known as the Missa.

(A) The mass appears to have originated in 1733 with Bach's composition of the first section, known as the Missa.
(B) In 1733, the mass appears to have originated with Bach's composing of the first section, which was known as the Missa.
(C) The mass appears to have originated in 1733 with Bach's composition of the first section that was known as the Missa.
(D) The origination of the mass appears to have occurred with Bach's composition of the first section, known to have been called the Missa, in 1733.
(E) The first section of the mass was known as the Missa that appears to have originated in 1733 with Bach's composition.

32. Which of the following is the best replacement for the underlined portion of sentence 7 (reproduced below)?

Bach's church music duties in Leipzig at the time were thus <u>suspended, that gave</u> *him time to compose the Missa.*

(A) giving
(B) suspended, that resulted in giving
(C) suspended, that provided
(D) suspended and gave
(E) suspended, giving

GO ON TO THE NEXT PAGE

SECTION 6

33. Which of the following is the best version of sentence 9 (reproduced below)?

Bach presented the Missa to the new elector of Saxony in July of 1733, presumably in order to obtain the title of court kapelle *in Dresden.*

(A) (As it is now)
(B) Bach presented the Missa to the new elector of Saxony in July of 1733, which was in order to obtain the title of *court kapelle* in Dresden.
(C) To the new elector of Saxony in July of 1733, Bach presented the Missa in order to obtain the title of *court kapelle* in Dresden.
(D) Presumably to obtain the title of *court kapelle* in Dresden, Bach in July of 1733 presented the Missa to the new elector of Saxony.
(E) Bach, presenting the Missa to the new elector of Saxony in July of 1733, presumably in order to obtain the title of *court kapelle* in Dresden.

34. Which of the following sentences, if inserted before sentence 11, would best improve the second paragraph?

(A) His composition of the mass was strongly influenced by changes in musical styles during the eighteenth century.
(B) The mass was particularly significant for Bach, because it represented a personal statement of his devotion.
(C) He hoped through the Missa to win acknowledgement from Dresden and to widen his sphere of musical activity.
(D) Bach's efforts to expand the Missa into a full-scale mass began with his addition of the Sanctus section in D-major.
(E) His structural artistry in the mass is quite impressive considering the phenomenal proportions of this work.

35. Which of the following would make the most logical final sentence for the essay?

(A) The *Mass in B Minor* is widely considered to be one of J. S. Bach's greatest creations.
(B) Twelve years later, by 1748, Bach was also working on the last section of the mass, for which he again transcribed and revised several of his earlier compositions.
(C) The *Mass in B Minor* consists of four sections, as differentiated from the five sections of the Roman Catholic mass; these four sections are organized liturgically.
(D) The depth of Bach's conviction is revealed to us in the mass through his overwhelming effort of musical expression.
(E) Once the Missa was finalized, Bach composed the remaining sections of the mass between 1740 and 1749, finally tying together the masterpiece before he died.

S T O P

IF YOU FINISH BEFORE TIME IS CALLED, YOU MAY CHECK YOUR WORK ON THIS TEST ONLY. DO NOT TURN TO ANY OTHER SECTION IN THIS TEST.

SECTION 7

Turn to Section 7 of your answer sheet to answer the questions in this section.

Time—20 Minutes
19 Questions

Directions: For each question in this section, select the best answer from among the choices given and fill in the corresponding oval on the answer sheet.

Each sentence below has one or two blanks, each blank indicating that something has been omitted. Beneath the sentence are five words or sets of words labeled A through E. Choose the word or set of words that, when inserted in the sentence, best fits the meaning of the sentence as a whole.

Example:

Eliza felt ----- when her boss asked her to work seven weekends in a row but ----- when her work earned her a promotion.

(A) enervated . . weakened
(B) depressed . . intellectual
(C) advantageous . . salacious
(D) angry . . shopworn
(E) irate . . elated   

1. After several failed attempts at -----, the couple realized that they could not resolve their differences.

(A) adaptation
(B) coordination
(C) admiration
(D) reconciliation
(E) recuperation

2. As an entertainer, Gabriel Hall was able to use his ----- performing in a way that showcased his ----- to the fullest.

(A) skills at . . talents
(B) command of . . direction
(C) distaste for . . capabilities
(D) facility at . . accuracy
(E) mastery of . . learning

3. As ----- as the task of firing the production manager seemed to the CEO, that unpleasant experience nevertheless taught him some ----- lessons.

(A) demoralizing . . objective
(B) routine . . anticipated
(C) discouraging . . timely
(D) rewarding . . important
(E) distasteful . . valuable

4. Most of the hardened branches that fall from the trees in Halberton Glen are already dead: as the wood -----, it develops a stony texture.

(A) stabilizes
(B) revives
(C) emulsifies
(D) petrifies
(E) materializes

5. Barry and Michelle flew back home to join their families in celebrating the graduation of Barry's brother; this ----- occasion seemed like the perfect time for them to announce their wedding plans.

(A) auspicious
(B) inopportune
(C) inadvertent
(D) unpretentious
(E) amorphous

6. An athletic champion should never become so confident as to take his or her success for granted; victory is not a license for -----, nor does it ----- arrogance or vainglory.

(A) aplomb . . condone
(B) equanimity . . warrant
(C) conceit . . impugn
(D) complacency . . justify
(E) self-effacement . . eliminate

GO ON TO THE NEXT PAGE

SECTION 7

Directions: The passage below is followed by questions based on its content. Answer the questions on the basis of what is stated or implied in the passage and in any introductory material that may be provided.

Questions 7–19 are based on the following passage.

The following passage is adapted from an article printed in a scientific journal in the early 1900s. In this essay, an astronomy professor discusses several major advances in his field.

It is claimed by astronomers that their science is not only the oldest, but also the most highly developed of the sciences. Indeed it should be so, since no other science has ever received such support from royalty, from the government, and from private individuals. There is no doubt that in recent years astronomers have had granted to them greater opportunities for carrying on large pieces of work than have been entrusted to men in any other department of pure science. One might expect that the practical results of a science like physics would appeal to the man who has made a vast fortune through some of its applications. The telephone, the electric transmission of power, wireless telegraphy, and the submarine cable are instances of immense financial returns derived from the most abstruse principles of physics. Yet, there are scarcely any physics laboratories devoted to research, or endowed with independent funds for this object, except those supported by the government. By contrast, the endowment of astronomical observatories devoted to research, and not including that given for teaching, is estimated to amount to half a million dollars annually. Several of the larger observatories have an annual income of 50,000 dollars.

I once asked the wisest man I know the reason for this difference. He said that it was probably because astronomy appealed to the imagination. A practical man, who has spent all his life in his counting room or mill, is sometimes deeply impressed with the vast distances and grandeur of the problems of astronomy, and the very remoteness and difficulty of studying the stars attract him.

My object in calling your attention to this matter is the hope that what I have to say of the organization of astronomy may prove of use to those interested in other branches of science, and that it may lead to placing these branches on the footing they should hold. My arguments apply with almost equal force to physics, to chemistry, and, in fact, to almost every branch of physical or natural science in which knowledge may be advanced by observation or experiment.

The practical value of astronomy in the past is easily established. Without it, international commerce on a large scale would have been impossible. Without the aid of astronomy, accurate boundaries of large tracts of land could not have been defined, and standard time would have been impossible. The work of the early astronomers was eminently practical and appealed at once to everyone. This work has now been finished. We can compute the positions of the stars for years, almost for centuries, with all the accuracy needed for navigation, for determining time, or for approximating the boundaries of countries. The investigations now in progress at the greatest observatories have little, if any, value in dollars and cents. They appeal, however, to a far higher sense: the desire of the intellectual human being to determine the laws of nature, the construction of the material universe, and the properties of the heavenly bodies—of which those known to exist far outnumber those that can be seen.

The second great advance in astronomy originated in America and was in an entirely different direction: it concerned the application of photography to the study of the stars. The first photographic image of a star was obtained in 1850 by George P. Bond, with the assistance of Mr. J. A. Whipple, at the Harvard College Observatory. A daguerreotype plate was placed at the focus of the 15-inch equatorial, at that time one of the two largest refracting telescopes in the world. An image of Lyræ was thus obtained, and for this Mr. Bond received a gold medal at the first international exhibition at the Crystal Palace in London in 1851. In 1857, Mr. Bond again took up the matter with collodion wet plates, and in three masterly papers showed the advantages of photography in many ways. The lack of sensitivity of the wet plate was perhaps the only reason why its use progressed slowly. A quarter of a century later, with the introduction of the dry plate and gelatine film, a new start was made. These photographic plates were very sensitive and were easily handled. In addition, indefinitely long exposures could be made with them. As a result, photography has superseded visual observations in many departments of astronomy, and it is now carrying the discipline far beyond the limits that would have been deemed possible a few years ago.

The third great advance in astronomy is in photographing the spectra of the stars. The first photograph showing the lines in a stellar spectrum was obtained by Dr. Henry Draper of New York in 1872. Sir William Huggins in 1863 had obtained an image of the spectrum of Sirius on a photographic plate, but no lines were visible in the image. In 1876 Huggins again took up the subject and, by an early publication, preceded Dr. Draper. When we consider the attention the photography of stellar spectra is receiving at the present time in nearly all the great observatories in the world, this accomplishment may well be regarded as the third great advance in astronomy.

GO ON TO THE NEXT PAGE

SECTION 7

7. In the context of paragraph 1, the phrase "large pieces of work" (line 7) refers to

(A) significant legislative proposals
(B) major scientific research projects
(C) long academic papers
(D) sizable scholarly conferences
(E) major business ventures

8. As used in line 16, "supported" most nearly means

(A) documented
(B) financed
(C) validated
(D) encouraged
(E) endorsed

9. In the context of the passage, the author's reference to "the imagination" in line 23 suggests that astronomical research

(A) can be highly regimented, involving difficult scientific formulas
(B) requires more artistic skill than does research in other disciplines
(C) is best carried out by scientists who are highly creative and inventive
(D) is intriguing to business people, because it deals with the mysteries of space
(E) is of little interest to business investors compared to practical fields like physics

10. In lines 28–35 ("My object . . . experiment"), the author refers to other branches of science in order to

(A) reinforce his point that astronomy is the scientific discipline most deserving of advancement
(B) illustrate that other branches of science, such as physics or chemistry, are less advanced than astronomy
(C) highlight that the discipline of astronomy experienced a unique path of growth that cannot be replicated
(D) emphasize that his arguments can be applied to strengthen other scientific disciplines
(E) point out that other scientific disciplines may have practical value but are still less intriguing that astronomy

11. The phrase "international commerce" (line 37) is used to illustrate

(A) an example of experimental research
(B) a significant contribution of physics
(C) the practical value of astronomy
(D) an important astronomical observation
(E) the theoretical validity of science

12. Based on the information in paragraph 4 (lines 36–51) ("The practical . . . seen"), all of the following industries were directly affected by advances in astronomy EXCEPT

(A) architecture
(B) mapmaking
(C) timekeeping
(D) international business
(E) navigation

13. The author's attitude toward the contributions of astronomy can best be characterized as

(A) skeptical
(B) appreciative
(C) critical
(D) tentative
(E) rejecting

14. Which of the following techniques does the author use to describe each of the three main advances of astronomy?

(A) Critiquing a point of view and then providing an alternative perspective
(B) Raising a question and then providing an answer to that question
(C) Describing a hypothesis and then reviewing data to verify that hypothesis
(D) Presenting a theory and then conducting tests to evaluate that theory
(E) Asserting a point and then providing evidence to support that point

15. According to the passage, which of the following represents a great advance of astronomy?

(A) An understanding of the biochemistry of various planets
(B) The application of photography to the study of the stars
(C) The development of rocket propulsion capabilities
(D) The application of laser technology to improve telescope lenses
(E) The discovery of geologic processes on distant planets that resemble those on Earth

GO ON TO THE NEXT PAGE

SECTION 7

16. According to the passage, the use of collodion wet plates in photographing the stars was hindered by

(A) the fact that wet plates required such long exposure times
(B) the poor quality of research showing the advantages of wet plates
(C) the inaccuracy of photographs taken over long distances
(D) the slow development of photographic technology
(E) the lack of sensitivity of the wet plates

17. In paragraph 5, the comparison of wet plate and dry plate photographic technology suggests that

(A) wet plates were capable of indefinitely long exposures
(B) dry plates were more expensive to use than were wet plates
(C) dry plates were more difficult to handle than were wet plates
(D) wet plates were limited in the length of their exposure times
(E) dry plates were capable of producing sharper images than were wet plates

18. The "third great advance in astronomy" (line 74) is best summarized by which of the following statements?

(A) Before it was possible to photograph stellar spectra, many astronomers competed to be the first to develop this important technology.
(B) At the time the passage was written, the photography of stellar spectra was receiving a great deal of attention in observatories around the world.
(C) The first photograph showing the lines in a stellar spectrum was obtained in 1863 by a British scientist named Sir William Huggins.
(D) The first photograph showing the lines in a stellar spectrum was obtained through the use of a daguerreotype plate.
(E) At the time the passage was written, the use of photography to study the stars was much less popular than the use of visual observation.

19. In the last paragraph, the author's attitude toward the accomplishments of Dr. Henry Draper is primarily one of

(A) sympathetic respect
(B) humorous rivalry
(C) vague disinterest
(D) calculated disapproval
(E) overwhelming adulation

S T O P

IF YOU FINISH BEFORE TIME IS CALLED, YOU MAY CHECK YOUR WORK ON THIS TEST ONLY.
DO NOT TURN TO ANY OTHER SECTION IN THIS TEST.

SECTION 8

Turn to Section 8 of your answer sheet to answer the questions in this section.

Time—20 Minutes
16 Questions

Directions: For this section, solve each problem and decide which is the best of the choices given. Fill in the corresponding oval on the answer sheet. You may use any available space for scratchwork.

Notes:

1. The use of a calculator is permitted. All numbers used are real numbers.
2. Figures that accompany problems in this test are intended to provide information useful in solving the problems. They are drawn as accurately as possible EXCEPT when it is stated in a specific problem that the figure is not drawn to scale. All figures lie in a plane unless otherwise indicated.
3. Unless otherwise specified, the domain of any function *f* is assumed to be the set of all real numbers *x* for which *f*(*x*) is a real number.

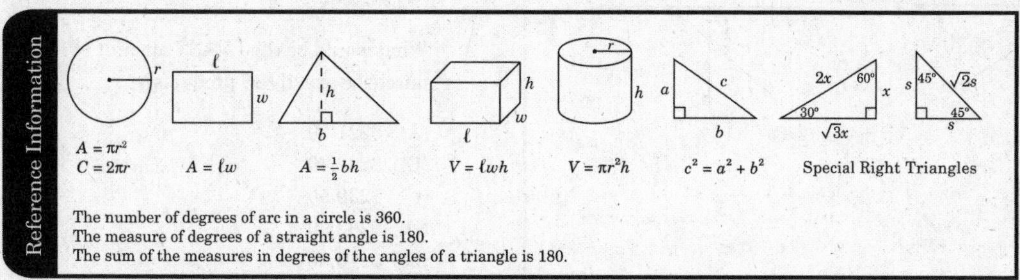
Reference Information
$A = \pi r^2$
$C = 2\pi r$
$A = \ell w$
$A = \frac{1}{2}bh$
$V = \ell wh$
$V = \pi r^2 h$
$c^2 = a^2 + b^2$
Special Right Triangles
The number of degrees of arc in a circle is 360.
The measure of degrees of a straight angle is 180.
The sum of the measures in degrees of the angles of a triangle is 180.

1. A certain sandwich truck departs on its delivery route, carrying the same number of turkey sandwiches as ham sandwiches. At the first stop, 18 turkey sandwiches but no ham sandwiches are sold. After the first stop, there are three times as many ham sandwiches as turkey sandwiches on the truck. How many ham sandwiches are on the truck?

(A) 3
(B) 8
(C) 9
(D) 10
(E) 14

GO ON TO THE NEXT PAGE

SECTION 8

2. Which of the following is the graph of a linear function with a positive slope and a negative y-intercept?

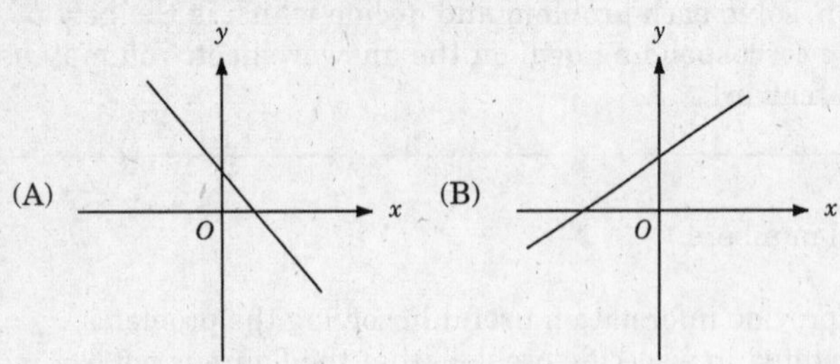

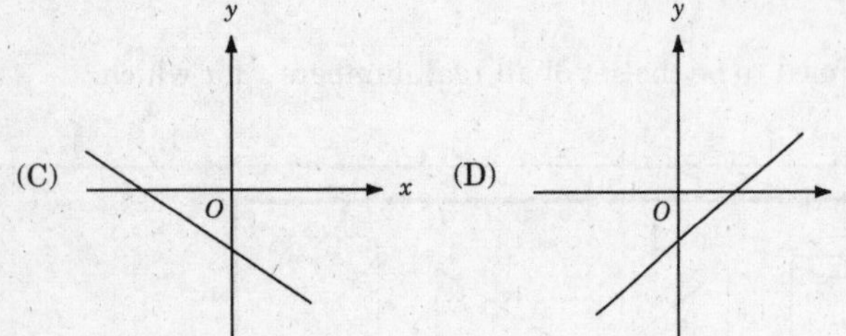

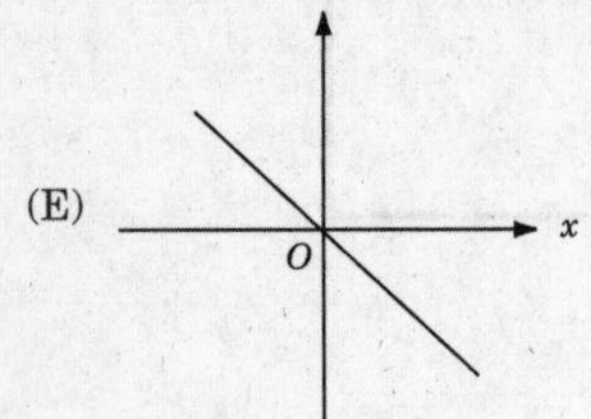

Questions 3–4 refer to the following price list.

Number of Products	Total Price
1	$15.00
Set of 5	$67.90
Set of 10	$110.50

3. Of the following, which is the closest approximation of the cost per product when one purchases a set of 5 ?

(A) $11.00
(B) $13.50
(C) $13.60
(D) $13.95
(E) $15.00

4. What would be the LEAST amount of money needed to purchase exactly 18 products?

(A) $221.00
(B) $223.40
(C) $230.50
(D) $262.90
(E) $270.00

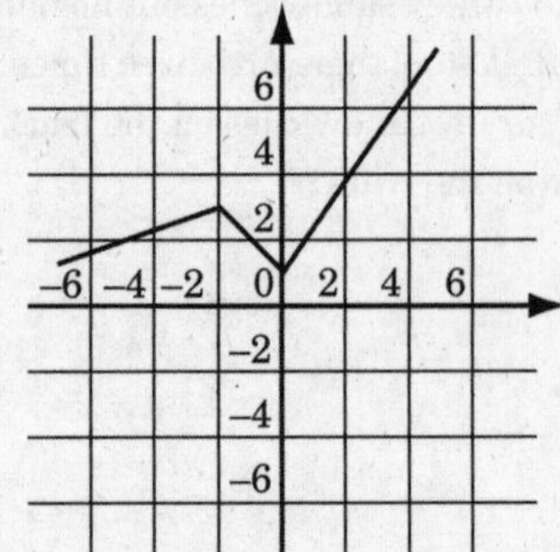

5. The figure above shows the graph of the function s. Which of the following is closest to $s(3)$?

(A) 1
(B) 3
(C) 5
(D) 6
(E) 7

GO ON TO THE NEXT PAGE

SECTION 8

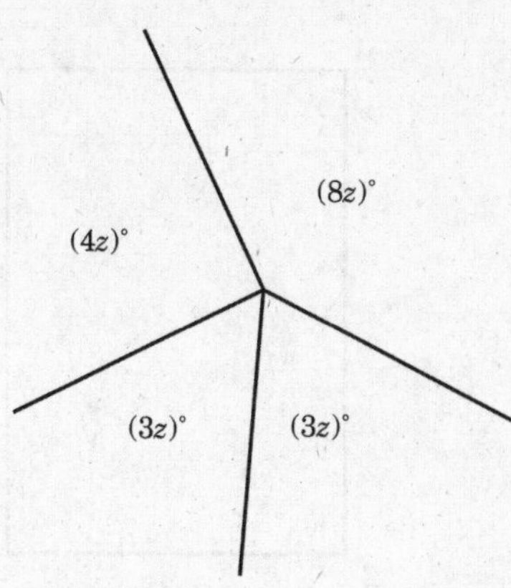

Note: Figure not drawn to scale.

6. In the figure above, four line segments meet at a point to form four angles. What is the value of z ?

(A) 15
(B) 18
(C) 20
(D) 36
(E) 40

7. Positive integers a, b, and c satisfy the equations $a^{-\frac{1}{2}} = \frac{1}{2}$ and $b^c = 81$. If $c > b$, what is the value of $a + c$?

(A) 3
(B) 4
(C) 7
(D) 8
(E) 11

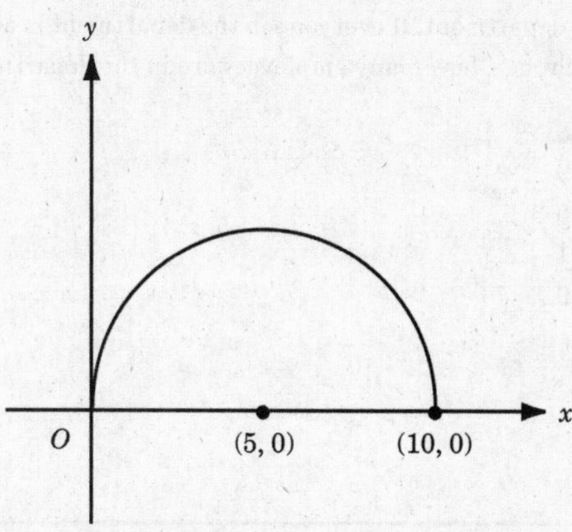

8. In the xy-plane above, all points on the semicircle are equidistant from the point (5, 0). Which of the following are x-coordinates of two points on this semicircle whose y-coordinates are equal?

(A) 1 and 7
(B) 2 and 9
(C) 3 and 7
(D) 3 and 9
(E) 4 and 7

9. If n is an integer and 4 is the remainder when $3n + 1$ is divided by 6, then n could equal

(A) 8
(B) 9
(C) 10
(D) 12
(E) 14

GO ON TO THE NEXT PAGE

SECTION 8

10. Erica is both the tenth-oldest and the tenth-youngest employee in her department. If everyone in the department is of a different age, how many employees are in the department?

(A) 18
(B) 19
(C) 20
(D) 21
(E) 30

11. The quadratic function f is given by $f(x) = ax^2 + bx + c$, where a and c are positive constants. Which of the following could be the graph of f?

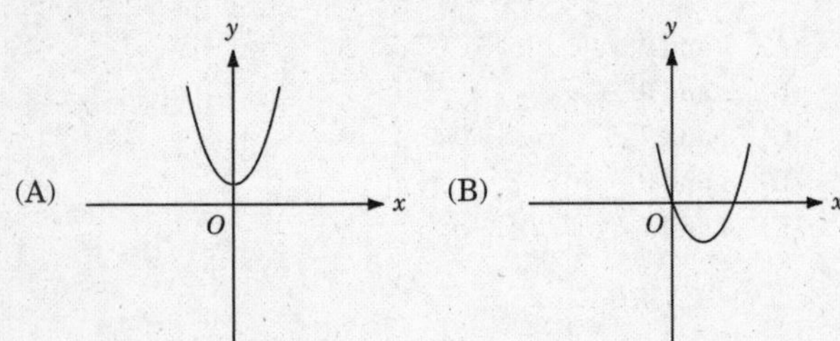

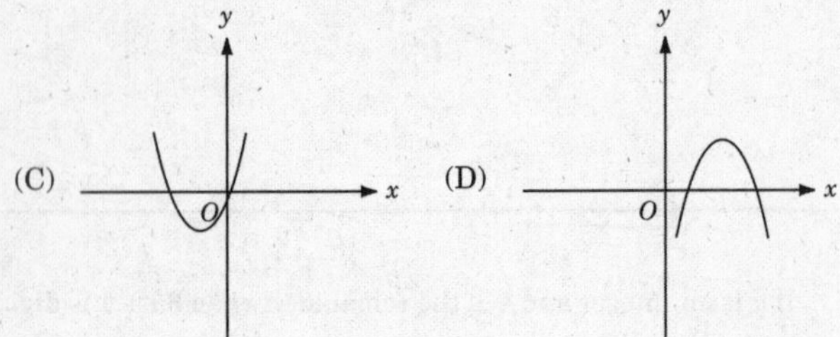

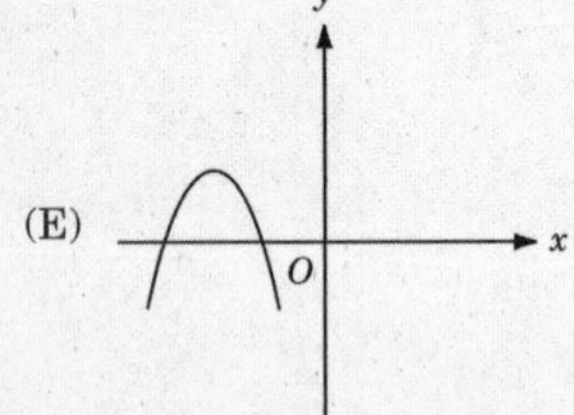

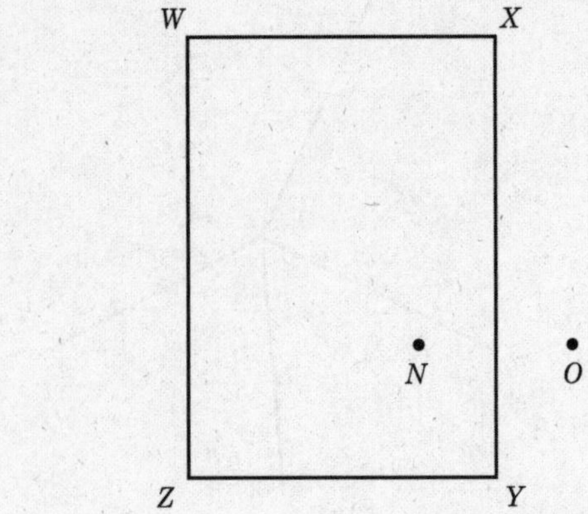

Note: Figure not drawn to scale.

12. In the figure above, $WXYZ$ is a rectangle with $WX = 8$ and $ZW = 15$. Points M, N, and O are different points on a line (not shown) that is parallel to ZY. Points M and N are symmetrical about line ZW and points N and O are symmetrical about line XY. What is the length of MO ?

(A) 15
(B) 16
(C) 23
(D) 30
(E) 46

13. The weight of a box of books was first increased by 30 percent and then the new weight was decreased by 55 percent. The final weight was what percent of the initial weight?

(A) 45 percent
(B) 52 percent
(C) 58.5 percent
(D) 75 percent
(E) 78.5 percent

GO ON TO THE NEXT PAGE

SECTION 8

14. When the number k is multiplied by 8, the result is the same as when 8 is added to k. What is the value of $7k$?

(A) $\frac{7}{8}$
(B) 1
(C) $\frac{8}{7}$
(D) 7
(E) 8

15. The lengths of the sides of a certain right triangle are consecutive odd integers, and the length of the hypotenuse is s. Which of the following equations could be used to find s ?

(A) $s - 3 + s - 1 = s$
(B) $(s - 3)^2 + (s - 1)^2 = s^2$
(C) $(s - 4)^2 + (s - 2)^2 = s^2$
(D) $s - 4 + s - 2 = s^2$
(E) $(s - 4)^2 = s(s - 2)$

16. If r is an integer greater than 1, and if $q = r + \frac{1}{r}$, which of the following must be true?

I. $q \neq r$
II. q is an integer
III. $rq > r^2$

(A) I only
(B) III only
(C) I and II only
(D) I and III only
(E) I, II, and III

S T O P

IF YOU FINISH BEFORE TIME IS CALLED, YOU MAY CHECK YOUR WORK ON THIS TEST ONLY. DO NOT TURN TO ANY OTHER SECTION IN THIS TEST.

SECTION 9

Turn to Section 9 of your answer sheet to answer the questions in this section.

Time—10 Minutes
14 Questions

Directions: For each question in this section, select the best answer from among the choices given.

The following sentences test correctness and effectiveness of expression. Part of each sentence or the entire sentence is underlined; beneath each sentence are five ways of phrasing the underlined material. Choice A repeats the original phrasing; the other four choices are different. If you think the original phrasing produces a better sentence than any of the alternatives, select choice A; if not, select one of the other choices.

In making your selection, follow the requirements of standard written English; that is, pay attention to grammar, choice of words, sentence construction, and punctuation. Your selection should result in the most effective sentence—clear and precise, without awkwardness or ambiguity.

Example:

In the poem "Ulysses" by Alfred, Lord Tennyson, the speaker says, "I cannot rest from travel," instead, he will live life to the fullest.

(A) "I cannot rest from travel," instead,
(B) "I cannot rest from travel"; instead,
(C) "I cannot rest from travel" instead,
(D) "I cannot rest from travel," upon which
(E) "I cannot rest from travel,"

1. In an unprecedented move arising largely out of the need to raise immediate funds, the laboratory's directors plan announcing to the public the results of the first round of experiments.

(A) plan announcing
(B) plan to announce
(C) plan they can announce
(D) have plans to announce
(E) are having plans of announcing

2. Amy Caldwell, one of the first women executives to join the company and take an active part in its governance, and eventually to hire and train her own top-notch operations staff.

(A) and eventually to hire and train her own top-notch operations staff
(B) eventually hired and trained her own top-notch operations staff
(C) she eventually hired and trained her own top-notch operations staff
(D) she eventually had her own top-notch operations staff that she hired and trained
(E) having eventually hired and trained her own top-notch operations staff

3. Talent is never a substitute for business savvy in achieving artistic success, for talent is usually commonplace in the arts while business savvy is not.

(A) for talent is usually commonplace in the arts while business savvy is not
(B) since you can usually find talent in the arts while the same is not true about business savvy
(C) for it is usually commonplace in the arts while the other is not
(D) because of its commonplace nature
(E) because the two differ regarding how common they are

4. Academic specialists should possess general knowledge of their disciplines but with their goal to demonstrate in-depth training regarding their particular areas of expertise.

(A) with their goal to demonstrate
(B) should also demonstrate
(C) aiming at the same time to demonstrate
(D) also trying to demonstrate
(E) its goal should also be in demonstrating

GO ON TO THE NEXT PAGE

5. The engineers evaluated the functionality of their filtering systems, created stringent tests, including one that assessed the volume of toxic chemicals still present in the test compound after three layers of filtration.

(A) systems, created
(B) systems creating
(C) systems; and created
(D) systems by creating
(E) systems with the creating of

6. The committee responsible for supervising the case workers asserted as to the justifiability of their decisions as moral and philosophical.

(A) as to the justifiability of their decisions as moral and philosophical
(B) as to their decisions and their justifiability on moral and philosophical grounds
(C) that their decisions, that is the case workers, are justifiable in moral terms as well as philosophy
(D) that in regards to justifiability their decisions are morally and philosophically justifiable
(E) that the decisions of the case workers are morally and philosophically justifiable

7. Richard Blockman was valued by Orchard Industries not only as a charismatic leader but also he conducted effectively the management of the company's three production departments.

(A) he conducted effectively the management
(B) having conducted the effective management
(C) conducting effectively the management
(D) being an effective manager
(E) as an effective manager

8. Although the After Hours Club in Lafayette is better known than the Golden Bell in Southtown, the designer of both clubs, Jan Grace Freidan, preferred the Golden Bell.

(A) Although the After Hours Club in Lafayette is better known than the Golden Bell in Southtown, the designer of both clubs, Jan Grace Freidan, preferred the Golden Bell.
(B) The After Hours Club in Lafayette being better known than the Golden Bell in Southtown, the designer of both, Jan Grace Freidan, preferred the latter.
(C) Although not as well known as the After Hours Club, Jan Grace Freidan, she designed both clubs, preferred the Golden Bell.
(D) The designer of both the After Hours Club and the Golden Bell was Jan Grace Freidan, she preferred the Golden Bell.
(E) Although more people know about Lafayette's After Hours Club than the Golden Bell in Southtown, Jan Grace Freidan, having designed both, has preferred the latter.

9. Because Summitville held its annual Labor Day parade and was surrounded by police barricades, this blocked almost all inbound traffic.

(A) barricades, this blocked almost all inbound traffic
(B) barricades, this accounts for it admitting almost no inbound traffic
(C) barricades is the reason why it admitted almost all no traffic
(D) barricades, almost no inbound traffic reached the city
(E) barricades, it blocks almost all inbound traffic from reaching the city

10. Lacking the proper equipment, my three attempts to construct a speaker cabinet from materials available in the shop were fruitless.

(A) my three attempts to construct a speaker cabinet from materials available in the shop were fruitless
(B) I made three fruitless attempts to construct a speaker cabinet from materials available in the shop
(C) there were fruitless results in the three attempts I made to construct a speaker cabinet from materials available in the shop
(D) I made three attempts to construct a speaker cabinet from materials available in the shop that were fruitless
(E) the three attempts I made at constructing a speaker cabinet from materials available in the shop were fruitless

11. It is ironic that some writers are so focused in conveying precise meanings and thus neglect to consider how their audiences might interpret their words.

(A) so focused in conveying precise meanings and thus
(B) focused about conveying precise meanings and therefore
(C) so focused on conveying precise meanings that they
(D) focused so much on conveying precise meanings that they
(E) too precise, and so they

12. By simply typing in key words related to the topic, a comprehensive search can be conducted on the internet for information on almost any conceivable subject matter.

(A) a comprehensive search can be conducted
(B) by conducting a comprehensive search
(C) they will submit your comprehensive search
(D) you can conduct a comprehensive search
(E) your comprehensive search can be conducted

GO ON TO THE NEXT PAGE

SECTION 9

13. Some futurists argue that one day <u>we will develop not only teleporting capability, but also telepathic communication will be learned</u>.

    (A) we will develop not only teleporting capability, but also telepathic communication will be learned
    (B) not only teleporting capability will be developed but also telepathic communication will be learned
    (C) we will not only develop teleporting capability but also learn telepathic communication
    (D) we will not only develop teleporting capability, but we will learn telepathic communication in addition
    (E) we will not only develop teleporting capability, but we will learn telepathic communication

14. The college is attended by many students who, although their admissions records show potential, <u>the course grades received do not match their high school achievements</u>.

    (A) the course grades received do not match their high school achievements
    (B) receiving course grades is failing to match their high school achievements
    (C) the grades received do not match their high school achievements for courses
    (D) receive course grades that do not match their high school achievements
    (E) they are receiving course grades not matching their high school achievements

S T O P

IF YOU FINISH BEFORE TIME IS CALLED, YOU MAY CHECK YOUR WORK ON THIS TEST ONLY. DO NOT TURN TO ANY OTHER SECTION IN THIS TEST.

PRACTICE TEST 9 EXPLANATIONS

PRACTICE TEST 9 ANSWERS

Question Number	Answer	Right	Wrong
Section 2			
1	D	___	___
2	C	___	___
3	A	___	___
4	B	___	___
5	C	___	___
6	C	___	___
7	D	___	___
8	A	___	___
9	C	___	___
10	B	___	___
11	E	___	___
12	C	___	___
13	C	___	___
14	A	___	___
15	E	___	___
16	D	___	___
17	D	___	___
18	D	___	___
19	E	___	___
20	C	___	___
21	A	___	___
22	B	___	___
23	B	___	___
24	A	___	___
Section 3			
1	A	___	___
2	A	___	___
3	E	___	___
4	E	___	___
5	D	___	___
6	B	___	___
7	D	___	___
8	B	___	___
9	D	___	___
10	A	___	___
11	A	___	___
12	D	___	___
13	E	___	___
14	D	___	___
15	C	___	___
16	C	___	___
17	A	___	___
18	A	___	___
19	A	___	___
20	E	___	___
Section 4			
1	B	___	___
2	D	___	___
3	E	___	___
4	A	___	___
5	E	___	___
6	B	___	___
7	D	___	___

Question Number	Answer	Right	Wrong
Section 4, continued			
8	B	___	___
9	E	___	___
10	A	___	___
11	A	___	___
12	D	___	___
13	C	___	___
14	B	___	___
15	A	___	___
16	E	___	___
17	D	___	___
18	A	___	___
19	C	___	___
20	E	___	___
21	A	___	___
22	C	___	___
23	B	___	___
24	B	___	___
Section 5			
1	D	___	___
2	D	___	___
3	E	___	___
4	E	___	___
5	D	___	___
6	B	___	___
7	C	___	___
8	E	___	___
9	6156	___	___
10	72.5	___	___
11	145	___	___
12	8	___	___
13	7, 8	___	___
14	3	___	___
15	2/5, 6/15	___	___
16	3, 5	___	___
17	236	___	___
18	18	___	___
Section 6			
1	E	___	___
2	B	___	___
3	B	___	___
4	E	___	___
5	D	___	___
6	C	___	___
7	A	___	___
8	E	___	___
9	E	___	___
10	C	___	___
11	C	___	___
12	C	___	___
13	E	___	___
14	B	___	___
15	D	___	___
16	C	___	___

Question Number	Answer	Right	Wrong
Section 6, continued			
17	E		
18	A		
19	E		
20	D		
21	B		
22	B		
23	E		
24	A		
25	A		
26	B		
27	B		
28	C		
29	B		
30	B		
31	A		
32	E		
33	A		
34	C		
35	E		
Section 7			
1	D		
2	A		
3	E		
4	D		
5	A		
6	D		
7	B		
8	B		
9	D		
10	D		
11	C		
12	A		
13	B		
14	E		
15	B		
16	E		
Section 7, continued			
17	D		
18	B		
19	A		
Section 8			
1	C		
2	D		
3	C		
4	B		
5	C		
6	C		
7	D		
8	C		
9	B		
10	B		
11	A		
12	B		
13	C		
14	E		
15	C		
16	D		
Section 9			
1	B		
2	B		
3	A		
4	B		
5	D		
6	E		
7	E		
8	A		
9	D		
10	B		
11	C		
12	D		
13	C		
14	D		

CALCULATING YOUR SCORE

Writing Section Raw Score

A. Essay Score (from 1–6) ______ A

B. Section 6 Multiple Choice: ______ no. correct – (______ no. incorrect ÷ 4) = ______ B

C. Section 9 Multiple Choice: ______ no. correct – (______ no. incorrect ÷ 4) = ______ C

D. Unrounded Multiple-Choice Score (B + C) ______ D

E. Total Rounded Multiple-Choice Raw Score
(Rounded to the nearest whole number) ______ E

F. Writing Multiple-Choice Subscore
(See the Writing Multiple-Choice conversion table on the following pages) ______ Writing MC Score

G. Total Scaled Score
(See the Writing conversion table on the following pages) ______ SAT Writing Score

Math Section Raw Score

A. Section 3 Raw Score: ______ no. correct – (______ no. incorrect ÷ 4) = ______ Subtotal A

B. Section 5 Raw Score: ______ no. correct ______ Subtotal B

C. Section 8 Raw Score: ______ no. correct – (______ no. incorrect ÷ 4) = ______ Subtotal C

D. Total Unrounded Raw Score
(Total A + B + C) ______ D

E. Total Rounded Raw Score (Rounded to the nearest whole number) ______ E

F. Scaled Score
(See the conversion table on the following pages) ______ SAT Math Score

Critical Reading Section Raw Score

A. Section 2 Raw Score: ________ (no. correct) – (________ (no. incorrect) ÷ 4) = ________ (A)

B. Section 4 Raw Score: ________ (no. correct) – (________ (no. incorrect) ÷ 4) = ________ (B)

C. Section 7 Raw Score: ________ (no. correct) – (________ (no. incorrect) ÷ 4) = ________ (C)

D. Total Unrounded Raw Score
(Total A + B + C) ________ (D)

E. Total Rounded Raw Score
(Rounded to the nearest whole number) ________ (E)

F. Scaled Score
(See the conversion table on the next page) ________ (SAT Critical Reading Score)

CONVERTING YOUR RAW SCORES

Raw Score	Critical Reading Scaled Score	Math Scaled Score
67	800	
66	790	
65	770	
64	760	
63	750	
62	740	
61	720	
60	710	
59	700	
58	690	
57	680	
56	670	
55	670	
54	660	800
53	650	780
52	640	760
51	640	740
50	630	730
49	620	710
48	610	700
47	610	690
46	600	670
45	590	660
44	590	650
43	580	650
42	580	640
41	570	630
40	560	620
39	560	610
38	550	600
37	540	590
36	540	590
35	530	580
34	530	570
33	520	560
32	510	560
31	510	550
30	500	540
29	500	530
28	490	520
27	480	520
26	480	510
25	470	500
24	470	490
23	460	490
22	450	480
21	450	470
20	440	460
19	430	460

Raw Score	Critical Reading Scaled Score	Math Scaled Score
18	430	450
17	420	440
16	410	430
15	410	430
14	400	420
13	390	410
12	380	400
11	380	390
10	370	380
9	360	380
8	350	370
7	340	360
6	330	340
5	320	330
4	310	320
3	300	310
2	280	290
1	270	280
0	250	260
−1	250	250
−2	240	240
−3	230	230
−4	220	220
−5	210	210
−6	200	200

Writing Subscores

- **Essay Subscore:** Subtotal A from Writing Score (page 780)
- **Multiple-Choice Subscore:** Calculate by plugging in Subtotal E from your writing score (page 780) into the score conversion table below

Raw Score	Multiple-Choice Subscore	Raw Score	Multiple-Choice Subscore
49	80	30	59
48	79	29	58
47	77	28	57
46	76	27	56
45	75	26	55
44	74	25	54
43	72	24	53
42	71	23	52
41	70	22	51
40	69	21	51
39	68	20	50
38	67	19	49
37	66	18	48
36	65	17	47
35	64	16	46
34	63	15	45
33	62	14	44
32	61	13	43
31	60	12	42

Raw Score	Multiple-Choice Subscore	Raw Score	Multiple-Choice Subscore
11	41	2	32
10	40	1	30
9	39	0	29
8	38	–1	27
7	37	–2	25
6	36	–3	24
5	35	–4	23
4	34	–5	22
3	33	–6	21

Writing Scaled Score

MC raw score	Essay Score					
	6	5	4	3	2	1
49	800	790	780	770	720	700
48	790	780	760	730	700	680
47	780	770	750	720	690	670
46	770	760	740	710	680	660
45	770	750	740	700	670	650
44	760	750	730	690	660	640
43	750	740	710	680	650	630
42	750	730	700	670	640	620
41	740	730	690	660	630	610
40	740	720	690	650	620	600
39	740	710	680	640	610	590
38	730	700	670	630	610	590
37	720	690	660	630	600	580
36	710	680	650	620	590	570
35	710	680	640	610	580	560
34	700	670	640	600	570	550
33	690	660	630	590	560	540
32	680	650	620	580	560	540
31	670	640	610	580	550	530
30	660	630	600	570	540	520
29	650	630	590	560	530	510
28	640	620	590	550	520	510
27	640	610	580	540	510	490
26	630	600	570	530	500	490
25	620	590	560	520	500	480
24	610	580	550	510	490	470
23	600	570	540	510	480	460
22	590	570	530	500	470	450
21	590	570	530	500	470	450
20	580	560	520	490	460	440
19	570	550	520	480	450	430
18	570	540	520	470	440	420
17	560	530	510	460	430	420
16	550	520	500	450	430	410
15	540	510	490	450	420	400
14	530	500	480	440	410	390
13	520	500	470	430	400	380
12	510	490	460	420	390	370

Writing Scaled Score

MC raw score	Essay Score					
	6	5	4	3	2	1
11	510	480	450	410	380	360
10	500	470	450	400	370	350
9	490	460	440	390	360	350
8	480	450	430	390	360	340
7	470	440	420	380	350	330
6	460	430	410	370	340	320
5	450	430	400	360	330	310
4	450	420	390	350	320	300
3	440	410	390	340	310	290
2	430	400	380	330	300	280
1	420	380	370	320	290	270
0	400	370	350	310	280	260
-1	380	360	340	290	270	260
-2	370	340	320	270	260	250
-3	360	330	310	260	250	240
-4	350	320	290	250	240	230
-5	340	310	280	240	230	220
-6	340	310	280	240	220	210

SECTION 2: CRITICAL READING

Sentence Completions

1. **D** One-Word/One-Way *Easy*

This sentence states that Doreen wished to *avoid appearing* a certain way, so she acted as if *she had already made up her mind*. In reality, she had not yet made up her mind. A person who has trouble making decisions would appear *indecisive*, so **D** is correct.

2. **C** One-Word/One-Way *Easy*

The first part of this sentence explains what kind of strategy the board needed: a strategy that contained very *specific plans*. A *defined* marketing strategy would contain specific plans, so **C** is correct.

3. **A** One-Word/One-Way *Medium*

The sentence indicates that professionals are willing to pursue employment for financial reasons despite something else about their jobs. You're looking for a positive word for this blank, such as "like." The word *relish*, which means "enjoy thoroughly," works best here, and so **A** is correcct.

4. **B** Two-Word/One-Way *Medium*

The first part of the sentence indicates that the two blanks should both be filled by words that mean something similar to *courageous*. One who displays *fortitude* endures adversity with courage, and one who displays *valor* shows courage or bravery. Therefore, **B** is correct.

5. **C** Two-Word/One-Way *Medium*

The phrase *just as* indicates that Theresa treated her students like her mentors had treated her. Theresa's mentors *inspired* her and *encouraged* her to succeed, so you're looking for two words that mean *inspired* and *encouraged*. **C** and **E** contain words similar to *inspired*, but only **C** contains a second word, *urged*, which means "encouraged."

6. **C** Two-Word/One-Way *Difficult*

The first part of the sentence indicates that the writer was well known for his *persuasiveness*. The first blank must contain a word similar to "persuasive," so eliminate **B**. The writer was also *criticized for his dogmatism*, or his tendency to stubbornly assert particular beliefs. The second blank must contain a word similar in meaning to "dogmatic." **C** is the only choice that fits.

7. **D** One-Word/One-Way *Difficult*

The last part of the sentence explains that the crowd was *noisy and aggressively boisterous*. You're looking for a word that means something like "loud and unruly." **D**, *obstreperous*, means "loud and stubbornly defiant," so **D** is correct.

8. **A** One-Word/Two-Way *Difficult*

The last part of this sentence indicates a contrast with the meaning of the word in the blank. Most of the reviews are not derisive enough to merit the label that is the missing word. The word *derisive* means "expressing contempt." Therefore, the missing word must mean something like "critical or derogatory." **A**, *vituperative*, means "harshly critical," so **A** is correct.

Short Reading Passages

9. **C** Implied Information *Difficult*

The author initially describes the ancient Chinese view of the kidneys and then introduces the second paragraph by stating that *Western medicine also recognizes the vital role played by the kidneys*. By including both Chinese and Western views on the kidney, the author implies that the importance of the kidneys is acknowledged within disciplines other than Western medical science. **C** is correct.

10. **B** Themes and Arguments *Medium*

The author mentions the size of the kidneys at the end of the second paragraph: *all this*, the author writes, *from two organs each no larger than the size of your fist!* This description comes directly after a discussion of the work performed by the kidneys on a daily basis. The kidneys aren't very large, the author points out, but they do a great deal of work. **B** fits best.

11. **E** Implied Information *Easy*

The first paragraph of the passage mentions the popular legend that Newton discovered gravity after being hit on the head by a falling apple. Paragraph 2 then asks: *how close is the story to actual reality?* The author concludes that we can't know for sure, but most likely Newton learned about gravity by watching an apple fall rather than by being hit on the head, so **E** is correct.

12. **C** Main Idea *Easy*

The passage discusses the process through which Newton discovered gravity, so **C** is correct.

Paired Reading Passages

13. **C** Words in Context *Medium*

Passage 1 discusses an alternative process that Japanese citizens use to resolve their disputes without going to court. **C**, *outside the court system*, therefore fits best.

14. **A** Implied Information *Easy*

The referenced lines explain that the *notion of communal belonging is firmly embedded in Japanese culture, which values harmonious living at all costs*. Since the Japanese value harmony so highly, this implies that they place enormous importance on harmonious interactions within their communities.

15. **E** Specific Information *Medium*

In paragraph 2 of Passage 1, the author demonstrates the importance of seniority by noting that *once seniority is established, it becomes fixed in the social order, driving and regulating all social relations in Japanese life*. This point is restated in **E**.

16. **D** Specific Information *Medium*

The importance of personal accomplishment is mentioned in paragraph 2 of Passage 2 as part of the American system of values. Personal accomplishment is not mentioned as a Japanese value in Passage 1.

17. **D** Themes and Arguments *Medium*

The last paragraph of Passage 1 states that even after their legal system was modernized, *the Japanese still . . . felt a moral pressure to avoid litigation*. **D** contradicts this point by claiming that Japanese litigation increased after the legal system was modernized. This claim most directly weakens the author's argument.

18. **D** Words in Context *Medium*

The first paragraph of Passage 2 raises the question of whether Americans would likely consent to having their legal disputes resolved without a formal trial. In this context, the phrase *informal treatment* of a dispute most nearly means "informal resolution" of the dispute.

19. **E** Implied Information *Medium*

The author of Passage 2 mentions *other influential ties* after making the point that *a person's group membership in one particular organization . . . is only one aspect of his or her existence*. The reference to *other ties* thus implies that Americans tend to be influenced by memberships in multiple groups, as **E** states.

20. **C** Specific Information *Easy*

The third paragraph of Passage 2 states that *since seniority does not carry much weight within American social structure*, a mediator would find it difficult to achieve binding agreements, so **C** is correct.

21. **A** Themes and Arguments *Medium*

The last paragraph of Passage 2 proposes two modifications to help U.S. mediators succeed. First, mediators would be required to have strong positive reputations within their communities. Second, mediators would be permitted to seek assistance from other sources to help with resolving difficult cases. Both of these modifications are exemplified by the scenario in **A**.

22. **B** Relating Two Passages *Medium*

The first paragraph of Passage 1 states that in Japan *disputes are expected to be solved by mutual understanding*. This expectation is never attributed to Americans in Passage 2, so **B** is correct.

23. **B** Relating Two Passages *Medium*

Both passages develop their arguments in a straightforward, academic manner, presenting evidence to uphold the points that are raised. The authors don't necessarily convey admiration or concern for their subjects, so **A** and **D** can be eliminated. The passages contain analyses rather than criticisms or rebuttals, so **C** and **E** are also incorrect. **B**, *academic rigor*, best describes the tone of each work.

24. **A** Relating Two Passages *Difficult*

Paragraph 3 of Passage 2 notes that third-party dispute resolution *succeeds in other countries because . . . mediators are generally revered by disputants for their higher social rankings*. Passage 1 indicates that third-party resolution is very successful in Japan and that *mediators who posses high social rank wield the authority necessary to secure negotiated settlements*. Therefore, the individuals chosen as mediators in Japan must have greater seniority than the disputing parties. **C** is incorrect because the author of Passage 1 indicates that the Japanese people regard disputing as morally *unacceptable*.

SECTION 3: MATH

Multiple Choice

1. **A** Algebra: Inequalities *Easy*

If $4a + 12 > 16$, then a must be greater than 1. This is because $4(1) + 12 = 16$. Only values of a that are greater than 1 can satisfy the inequality. **A** therefore cannot be the value of a.

2. **A** Numbers & Operations: Exponents *Easy*

Convert both sides of the equation to numbers with the same base. The number 27 equals $3 \times 3 \times 3$, or 3^3. Rewrite the equation:

$$3^{3a} = 27$$
$$3^{3a} = 3^3$$

The exponents are equal, which means that $3a = 3$. Therefore, $a = 1$.

3. **E** Algebra: Solving Equations *Easy*

Let x represent the unknown value. Now create an equation and solve for x:

$$s - 4 + x = s + 2$$
$$s + x - s = 2 + 4$$
$$x = 6$$

4. **E** Geometry: Geometric Visualizations *Medium*

When the rectangular box is cut along its vertical edges and flattened, it will have the shape of a cross. Eliminate **A** and **B**. Examine the remaining choices to see which diagram correctly reflects the length, width, and height of the box. The box is 6 units long, 5 units wide, and 7 units tall. Only **E** contains sides with heights of 7 inches.

5. **D** Geometry: Triangles *Medium*

Since *PZRW* is a square and side *WR* measures 3, then side *RZ* also measures 3. This makes *WRZ* a 45-45-90 triangle, so *WZ* measures $3\sqrt{2}$. *PZRW* is divided into 9 equal squares, so *WX* is equal to *XY* and *YZ*. Therefore, *WY* measures exactly $\frac{2}{3}$ of *WZ*, or $2\sqrt{2}$.

6. **B** Algebra: Solving Equations *Easy*

First, determine the value of x. Since $\frac{4}{9}$ of x equals 36, this means that $\frac{4}{9}x = 36$. Solve for x:

$$\frac{4}{9}x = 36$$
$$x = 36\left(\frac{9}{4}\right)$$
$$x = \frac{36 \times 9}{4}$$
$$x = \frac{9 \times 9}{1}$$
$$x = 81$$

Now, find $\frac{7}{9}$ of 81:

$$\frac{7}{9} \times 81 = \frac{81 \times 7}{9} = \frac{9 \times 7}{1} = 63$$

7. **D** Data Analysis, Statistics & Probability: Probability *Medium*

The dartboard appears to be divided into 9 rectangles. However, the rectangles are unequal in size: each of the rectangles *X*, *Y*, and *Z* has twice the area of each of the rectangles *R*, *S*, *T*, *U*, *V*, and *W*. If you drew a line directly down the middle of rectangles *X*, *Y*, and *Z*, the board would be divided into 12 rectangles of equal size.

The probability of the dart landing on rectangle *X* is therefore 2 out of 12, or $\frac{1}{6}$.

8. **B** Numbers & Operations: Basic Operations *Easy*

Choose two even numbers, such as 2 and 4. Plug them into the expressions to see which will produce an even result:

I. $(c + 1) - d = (2 + 1) - 4 = -1$
II. $(c + 1)d = (2 + 1)4 = 12$
III. $(c + 1) + d = (2 + 1) + 4 = 7$

II produces an even number, while I and III produce odd numbers, so **B** is correct.

9. **D** Numbers & Operations: Sequences *Difficult*

After the 56th number 2, there will be exactly 56 1s. After the 57th number 2, there will be 57 1s. After the 58th number 2, there will be 58 1s. Add these amounts together: 56 + 57 + 58 = 171.

10. **A** Algebra: Functions *Medium*

Substitute 3 for n in the function and solve:

$$g(n) = \frac{7 - 3n^2}{n}$$
$$g(3) = \frac{7 - 3(3)^2}{3}$$
$$g(3) = \frac{7 - 3(9)}{3}$$
$$g(3) = \frac{7 - 27}{3}$$
$$g(3) = \frac{-20}{3}$$

11. **A** Geometry: Angles and Lines *Easy*

The question mentions that angle s measures more than 90˚. Angle s is supplementary to angle r. The two angles lie on a straight line, so their measurements add up to 180˚. If s measures more than 90˚, then r must measure less than 90˚ in order for the two measurements to add up to 180˚.

12. **D** Geometry: Coordinate Geometry *Medium*

This question tells you that the line crosses the x-axis at the point (j, k). Whenever a line crosses the x-axis, its y-coordinate will be 0. Therefore, the line crosses the x-axis at the point $(j, 0)$.

To find the value of j, substitute 0 for k in the equation of the line:

$$y = 3x - 9$$
$$(k) = 3(j) - 9$$
$$(0) = 3j - 9$$
$$9 = 3j$$
$$3 = j$$

13. **E** Data Analysis, Statistics & Probability: Statistical Analysis *Medium*

The median of a set of numbers is the value that falls exactly in the middle of the set, when the numbers are ordered from smallest to largest. Order the weights of the boxes from smallest to largest:

15, 19, 23, 28, 34, 42

The question states that the median of the weights is 23 kg:

15, 19, <u>23</u>, 28, 34, 42

Therefore, the missing weight must fall somewhere to the *left* of the number 23 in this set. This would create three numbers *before* 23 and three numbers *after* it, placing 23 directly in the middle of the set.

Box 4 could weigh 23 kg or any amount less than 23 kg, but it could not weigh 27 kg. If Box 4 weighed 27 kg, then 27 would be the median of this set of numbers. **E** is correct.

14. **D** Geometry: Triangles *Medium*

This figure resembles a square with a triangular shape cut out of it. Draw in the missing side of the square:

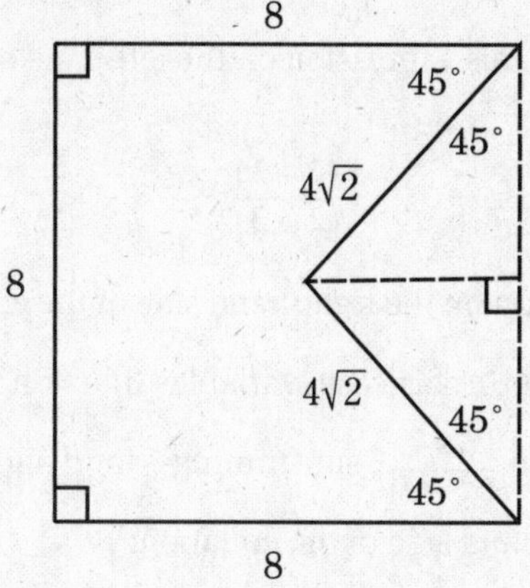

The missing side of the square is 8 units long. Draw a line from the apex of the triangle that divides the triangle in half, as shown. This line creates two congruent right triangles with legs measuring 4 units each. You need to find the length of the hypotenuse of each triangle.

Notice that both triangles are 45-45-90° triangles. A 45-45-90° triangle has sides in a ratio of $x:x:x\sqrt{2}$, with $x\sqrt{2}$ representing the length of the hypotenuse. Each right triangle in the diagram has legs of length 4. The hypotenuse of each triangle therefore measures $4\sqrt{2}$, as shown. Add these lengths to the lengths of the remaining sides to find the perimeter of the figure:

$$\begin{aligned} 8+8+8+4\sqrt{2}+4\sqrt{2} &= 24+4\sqrt{2}+4\sqrt{2} \\ &= 24+8\sqrt{2} \end{aligned}$$

15. **C** Numbers & Operations: Factors and Multiples *Medium*

Prime numbers are numbers whose sole factors are 1 and themselves. Factor 34 into its prime factors: $34 = 17 \times 2$. The greatest prime factor of 34 is 17. Therefore, p equals 17. Factor 60 into its prime factors: $60 = 5 \times 3 \times 2 \times 2$. The greatest prime factor of 60 is 5. Therefore, q equals 5. Multiply p by q: $17 \times 5 = 85$.

16. **C** Geometry: Coordinate Geometry *Easy*

Line m slants downward from left to right and crosses the y-axis at the point (0, 2). If line n is perpendicular to line m, then its slope is the negative reciprocal of the slope of line m. In this case, line m has a negative slope. The negative reciprocal of a negative slope will always be positive. Therefore, **C** must be true, and **B** must be false.

All that we know about line n is that it is perpendicular to line m. Line n could lie anywhere on the coordinate plane. It might cross the y-axis at the point (0, 2), or it might not. It might have a negative x-intercept, but it could also have a positive one—we don't know. The statements in **A**, **D**, and **E** cannot be determined from the information given, so these choices can be eliminated.

17. **A** Algebra: Solving Equations *Medium*

The symbol ‡ represents a specific function for all numbers d and e, where $d \neq -e$. When you see the notation d ‡ e, perform the operation $\frac{(d-e)}{(d+e)}$.

The equation in the question contains two operations with the ‡ symbol. One is on the left-hand side of the equation, and the other is on the right. On the left-hand side of the equation, you are given the function 2 ‡ 3. For this function, perform the operation $\frac{(2-3)}{(2+3)}$. Place this expression on the left-hand side of the equation:

$$\frac{(2-3)}{(2+3)} =$$

Now decipher the function on the right-hand side of the equation. This function also contains a variable: 3 ‡ *f*. In this case, variables function the same way as numbers do. Perform the operation $\frac{(d-e)}{(d+e)}$, substituting 3 for *d* and *f* for *e*: $\frac{(3-f)}{(3+f)}$. Place this expression on the right-hand side of the equation:

$$\frac{(2-3)}{(2+3)} = \frac{(3-f)}{(3+f)}$$

Now solve for *f*:

$$\begin{aligned}\frac{(2-3)}{(2+3)} &= \frac{(3-f)}{(3+f)}\\ -\frac{1}{5} &= \frac{(3-f)}{(3+f)}\\ -1(3+f) &= 5(3-f)\\ -3-f &= 15-5f\\ -f &= 18-5f\\ 4f &= 18\\ f &= \frac{18}{4} \text{ or } \frac{9}{2}\end{aligned}$$

18. **A** Algebra: Solving Equations *Difficult*

The question states that the first cabinet costs *d* dollars to produce. Each cabinet after the first costs *d* – *m* dollars to produce. If the cabinet manufacturer produced exactly two cabinets, the costs for these two would be equal to the cost for the first, *d*, plus the cost for the second, *d* – *m*. This expression could be written: $d + (d - m)$.

However, the question states that the cabinet manufacturer produces *x* number of cabinets all together. Remember that the first cabinet is already accounted for: it costs *d* dollars to make. Therefore, subtract this first cabinet from the total number of cabinets made: *x* – 1. Each cabinet after the first costs *d* – *m* dollars to make. Multiply $(x - 1)$ by $(d - m)$. All of the cabinets after the first cost $(x - 1)(d - m)$ dollars to make. Add this value to the cost of making the first cabinet: $d + (x - 1)(d - m)$.

19. **A** Geometry: Circles *Difficult*

This question asks you to determine the area of sector *CAB*. To determine the area, you must first know what portion this sector represents of the entire circle.

The sector conatains a central angle that measures 45°. There are 360° in a full circle, so the central angle of this sector represents $\frac{1}{8}$ of the entire circle. This also means that the area of the sector is $\frac{1}{8}$ the area of the entire circle. To solve the problem, then, you must find the *area* of the entire circle, and then find $\frac{1}{8}$ of that amount.

To determine the area of the circle, you must know the length of the radius. You aren't given the radius, but you are given the length of arc *AB*. You can use this knowledge to work backward and find the radius of the circle.

First, find the circumference of the entire circle. Arc *AB*, whose length is 2π, represents $\frac{1}{8}$ of the circumference. This means that the circumference equals 16π.

Now use this value to find the radius of the circle. The formula for the circumference of a circle is $C = 2\pi r$. We already know the value of the circumference (16π), so substitute this value into the formula and solve for:

$$C = 2\pi r$$
$$16\pi = 2\pi r$$
$$\frac{16}{2} \text{ or } 8 = r$$

Now that you know the radius, you can find the area of the entire circle:

$$A = \pi r^2$$
$$A = \pi(8)^2$$
$$A = 64\pi$$

Remember that the area of the sector is exactly $\frac{1}{8}$ the area of the entire circle. Therefore, the area of the sector is $\frac{1}{8} \times 64\pi$, or 8π.

20. **E** Numbers & Operations: Percents *Difficult*

The number of dogs at the shelter is represented by the letter *d*. There are 45 more cats than dogs at the shelter, so let the number of cats be represented by $d + 45$. The total number of dogs and cats at the shelter is therefore $d + (d + 45)$, or $2d + 45$.

Let *x* represent the percentage of animals at the shelter that are dogs. We know that the number of dogs at the shelter, *d*, is equal to *x* percent of the total number of animals at the shelter, $2d + 45$. Set up an equation:

$$d = \frac{d}{100}(2d+45)$$

Remember to place *x* over 100 in this equation because *x* represents a percent.

Now solve for *x*:

$$d = \frac{x}{100}(2d+45)$$
$$100d = x(2d+45)$$
$$\frac{100d}{2d+45} = x$$

SECTION 4: CRITICAL READING

Sentence Completions

1. **B** One-Word/One-Way *Easy*

Lawrence valued his solitude and chose to live in a small cabin in a remote area. He therefore preferred to live in *isolation*, or separate from others.

2. **D** Two-Word/Two-Way *Medium*

The new policies upset the students and faculty, so the students and faculty must have reacted in a negative way. Eliminate **A**, **C**, and **E**. The negative reaction must have been calmed by the dean's address, so **D** fits best.

3. **E** One-Word/One-Way *Difficult*

The townspeople respected the doctor so much that they erected a memorial in her honor. In doing so, they showed their *veneration*, or deep respect, for her work.

4. **A** Two-Word/One-Way *Difficult*

The businesswoman behaved in a certain way, and she developed a reputation based on her behavior. The two blanks in this sentence will therefore contain words with related meanings. Either the businesswoman "upheld" her commitments and developed a reputation for being "trustworthy," or she "backed out on" her commitments and developed a reputation for being "unreliable." The word *renege* means "to fail to carry out a commitment." A person who repeatedly reneges on her or his agreements would be considered *capricious*, or impulsive and unpredictable. **A** is correct.

5. **E** Two-Word/Two-Way *Difficult*

The first part of the sentence indicates that *an adroit commander must be* both *inventive and cunning*, so the word in the first blank must mean something like "imaginative" or "clever." Eliminate **B** and **C**. The second part of the sentence tells us that the commander must avoid approaches that are *conventional*, which means "ordinary or widely used," so the second blank must contain a word that carries a similar meaning. **E**, *hackneyed*, means "overused," so **E** works best.

Paired Reading Passages

6. **B** Relating Two Passages *Easy*

Passage 1 discusses the experience of Nicias, so eliminate **A** and **C**. Both passages discuss the causes of the Athenian defeat, so eliminate **E**. Passage 1 discusses how Nicias failed in his role as a leader, so **B** is correct.

7. **D** Relating Two Passages *Medium*

Both passages address the problems encountered by two Athenian leaders during the Sicilian expedition of the Peloponnesian War. **D** therefore fits best.

8. **B** Relating Two Passages *Medium*

According to Passage 2, Alcibiades believed that Athens should go to war with Sicily because the victory would bring honor to Athens. He would most likely respond to Nicias's statements by affirming the importance of gaining glory through victory.

9. **E** Relating Two Passages *Medium*

Passage 1 explains how Nicias failed to uphold his responsibilities as a leader because he did not believe in the Sicilian war effort. Passage 2 describes how Alcibiades betrayed his country by joining forces with the Spartans for his own personal gain, so **E** is correct.

Long Reading Passages

10. **A** Specific Information *Easy*

In paragraph 2, the narrator states that Mr. Marvin's fainting spells *had come so frequently of late*. **A** is correct.

11. **A** Implied Information *Medium*

When Mr. Marvin asks Owen what he is thinking about, Owen replies that he is thinking about Mr. Marvin's health. In reality, as paragraph 4 reveals, Owen is thinking about how long it will take before Mr. Marvin passes away. Owen tells a sort of "truth" to Mr. Marvin, but it is only a partial truth. The statement that he *never lied when the truth would do equally well* implies that Owen was prone to lying but would tell the truth if the whole truth or a partial truth would serve his agenda.

12. **D** Implied Information *Medium*

In paragraph 4, Owen wonders to himself whether Mr. Marvin will pass away quickly or within a longer time period, such as a year. The phrase *he much preferred a month* suggests that Owen hopes that Mr. Marvin will pass away quickly. The rest of the sentence then explains why: Owen had *reason to believe that the Marvin will would contain a handsome bequest to "my faithful secretary."* Owen believes that Mr. Marvin views him as "faithful" and will therefore leave him an inheritance. **D** is correct.

13. **C** Specific Information *Easy*

Paragraph 7 states that the library had been Mr. Marvin's office *since the doctor had forbidden him to visit his automobile works and steel-stamping mills*. **C** is correct.

14. **B** Implied Information *Medium*

Paragraph 13 describes Mr. Marvin's *lieutenants*, or company managers, *as able, efficient, and contented*. Mr. Marvin felt confident leaving the business in their hands. *His lieutenants had proved Marvin's unerring instinct in judging character*, the passage states, because all of them had turned out *exactly as he expected*. This description suggests that Mr. Marvin was generally a very good judge of character.

15. **A** Specific Information *Medium*

The last paragraph states that when Mr. Marvin first met Owen, Owen *was a fine, honest, faithful man*. Owen became dishonest, however, when he turned forty and faced a difficult personal struggle with insomnia. **A** is correct.

16. **E** Main Idea *Easy*

In the passage, the author describes the history of the IAEA, an international organization. **E** fits best.

17. **D** Words in Context *Easy*

In paragraph 5, the author describes the internal and external constraints faced by the IAEA. These constraints limit the progress of the organization, so the phrase *plagued by* most nearly means "hindered by."

18. **A** Implied Information *Easy*

In paragraph 2, the author writes that the IAEA was established *because world leaders believed that the peaceful use of nuclear energy could increase national economic capabilities and standards of living.* **A** is correct.

19. **C** Themes and Arguments *Medium*

The first sentence of paragraph 3 states that *the principle of peaceful cooperation reflects a great deal of international consensus on the purpose of the IAEA.* The author mentions *international consensus* to show that nations generally agreed that peaceful cooperation would be the main principle upon which the IAEA was based.

20. **E** Themes and Arguments *Difficult*

In paragraph 3, the author states that *many conflicts also affected the negotiation of agency agreements.* The author then describes Soviet objections over membership issues as examples of the conflicts that arose. **E** strengthens the author's argument by pointing out that membership conflicts posed some of the most serious threats to IAEA negotiations. The statements in the remaining choices all serve to weaken the author's argument, so **E** is correct.

21. **A** Technique *Easy*

Paragraph 4 lists historical examples that show how the IAEA has changed its focus over the years. These examples are drawn from the factual history of the IAEA, as **A** states.

22. **C** Specific Information *Medium*

According to paragraph 1, world leaders decided that the agency could be more effectively established only after cold war tensions had decreased. **C** is therefore correct.

23. **B** Themes and Arguments *Medium*

Paragraph 5 lists two types of constraints faced by the IAEA: internal constraints and external constraints. Two examples of internal constraints are provided: *the high turnover of staff and the inherent difficulties involved with managing many complex tasks.* **B**, *high staff turnover,* is one of the internal constraints mentioned in the passage.

24. **B** Themes and Arguments *Medium*

The author starts the sixth paragraph by noting that despite its setbacks, *the IAEA has had many significant achievements over its short duration.* The author then lists examples of the agency's achievements. The first example listed concerns safeguards: *it has developed safeguard measures that have helped to build trust and confidence among member states.* The reference to safeguards thus extends the author's idea that the IAEA has had many significant achievements.

SECTION 5: MATH

Multiple Choice

1. **D** Algebra: Solving Equations *Easy*

Treat Ω as a variable, and solve for Ω:

$$\frac{25-\Omega}{4}=4\frac{3}{4}$$
$$25-\Omega=4\left(4\frac{3}{4}\right)$$
$$25-\Omega=19$$
$$-\Omega=19-25$$
$$\Omega=25-19,\text{ or }6$$

2. **D** Geometry: Angles and Lines *Easy*

The diagram contains two parallel lines crossed by a transversal. In this figure, corresponding angles are congruent. This means that $a \cong e$ and $d \cong g$. Therefore, the sum $a + e$ is equal to the sum $e + g$.

3. **E** Data Analysis, Statistics & Probability: Graphs, Charts, and Tables *Easy*

First, determine the total number of desktops that are not working. There are 60,000 computers not working. Of these, 32,000 are laptops. The number of desktops not working is 60,000 – 32,000 = 28,000.

The table shows a total of 38,750 donated desktops. If 28,000 of these are not working, then 10,750 of them must be working.

4. **E** Algebra: Functions *Easy*

Substitute 200 for c in the function and solve for D, the net amount raised:

$$D(c)=2c-170$$
$$D(200)=2(200)-170$$
$$400-170=230$$

5. **D** Algebra: Solving Equations *Medium*

The question tells you that $mp = n$ and $n = qp$. Both mp and qp are equal to n, so they are also equal to each other:

$$mp = qp$$

None of the variables is equal to zero. Solve for q:

$$mp=qp$$
$$\frac{mp}{p}=q$$
$$m=q$$

6. **B** Numbers & Operations: Ratios *Medium*

There is one red rose for every two yellow roses in the arrangement. This means that one out of every three roses in the arrangement is red, and two out of every three roses are yellow. The total number of roses in the arrangement must always be a multiple of 3, because 1 + 2 = 3. The number 10, given in **B**, is not divisible by 3, so 10 cannot be the number of roses in the arrangement.

7. **C** Numbers & Operations: Roots and Radicals *Medium*

With roots and radicals questions, always look for ways to simplify the expression. Note that the expression $32\sqrt{32}$ can be simplified:

$$32\sqrt{32} = 32\sqrt{2 \times 16}$$
$$32\sqrt{2}\sqrt{16} = 32 \times 4 \times \sqrt{2}$$
$$= 128\sqrt{2}$$

The simplified expression meets the requirements listed in the question. Both 128 and 2 are positive integers, and 128 > 2. Therefore, 128 could equal x and 2 could equal y. Solve for xy:

$$xy = 128 \times 2$$
$$xy = 256$$

8. **E** Geometry: Triangles *Difficult*

In this diagram, the largest triangle contains angles measuring x° and $2y^\circ$. Let's call the missing angle a. There are two other triangles in the diagram that also contain angles measuring x° and $2y^\circ$. These two triangles are similar to the first triangle. Their missing angles can be labeled a also, as shown below:

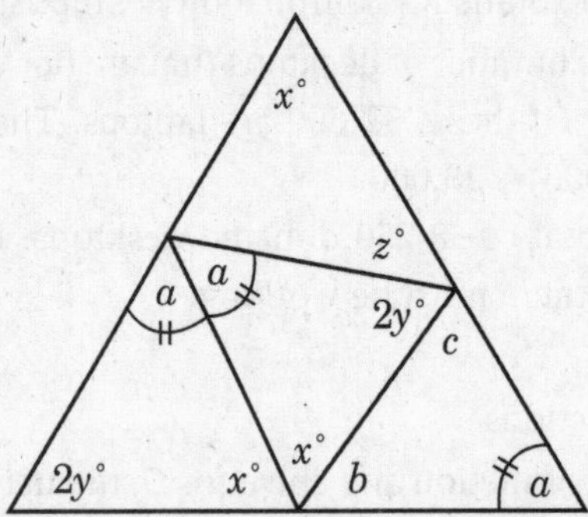

This diagram also contains labels for two of the remaining angles, b and c.

You're looking for the measurement of angle z in terms of x and y. Note that angle z lies on a straight line with angles $2y$ and c. The measures of these three angles add up to 180°: $z + 2y + c = 180$. Therefore, to find the value of z, subtract $2y$ and c from 180: $z = 180 - 2y - c$.

Now you've got to get rid of the c in that equation. You're asked for z in terms of $2y$ and x. How does c relate to x? Notice that $c + a + b = 180^\circ$. This means that $c = 180 - a - b$. So, based on the equation above, $z = 180 - 2y - (180 - a - b)$. This expression can be simplified to $180 - 2y - 180 + a + b$.

You can determine the values of a and b in terms of x and y by using what you know about the other parts of the figure. First, note that a makes up a triangle with angles x and $2y$. The measures of these angles add up to 180: $a + x + 2y = 180$. The value of a is therefore $180 - x - 2y$.

Second, note that b lies on a straight line with $x + x$. The measures of these angles also add up to 180: $b + x + x = 180$. The value of b is therefore $180 - x - x$.

This expression can be simplified to 180 – $2x$. Substitute the values you found for a and b into the equation for z, above:

$$z = 180 - 2y - 180 + a + b$$
$$z = 180 - 2y - 180 + (180 - x - 2y) + (180 - 2x)$$
$$z = 360 - 2y - x - 2y - 2x$$
$$z = 360 - 3x - 4y$$

Be especially careful about subtracting negative numbers when solving long equations like these.

Grid-Ins

9. **6156** Algebra: Solving Equations *Easy*
If $c^6 = 684$, then $9c^6$ equals $9 \times c^6$, or 9×684. The correct answer is 6,156.

10. **72.5** Numbers & Operations: Basic Operations *Easy*
First, find the distance between the two points. Subtract 69 from 76:

$$76 - 69 = 7$$

Next, find the distance between the first point, 69, and the midpoint. Take half of the total distance:

$$\frac{7}{2} = 3.5$$

Add this amount to the first point, 69:

$$69 + 3.5 = 72.5$$

11. **145** Geometry: Triangles *Medium*
The triangle has two angles that have the same measure. The sides opposite these angles are therefore equal in length. If two of the sides measure 40 and 65, the third side must be equal to one of these sides. It could measure 40 or 65. The smaller measure, 40, would produce the smallest perimeter: 40 + 40 + 65, or 145.

12. **8** Algebra: Binomials and Quadratics *Difficult*
Factor the equation $a^2 - b^2 = 60$:

$$a^2 - b^2 = 60$$
$$(a + b)(a - b) = 60$$

Substitute 6 for $(a - b)$ in the equation, and solve for $(a + b)$:

$$(a + b)(a - b) = 60$$
$$(a + b)(6) = 60$$
$$(a + b) = \frac{60}{6}$$
$$(a + b) = 10$$

Now you have two equations, $(a + b) = 10$ and $(a - b) = 6$. Combine these equations to solve for a:

$$\begin{aligned} (a + b) &= 10 \\ + (a - b) &= 6 \\ \hline 2a + 0 &= 16 \\ 2a &= 16 \\ a &= 8 \end{aligned}$$

13. **7, 8** Geometry: Circles *Medium*

The central angle of each pie slice always measures more than 40°. There are 360° in the entire circular pie, so the total number of 40° slices that could be cut from the pie is $\frac{360}{40} = 9$ slices. Therefore, the pie can never have 9 slices. It can have 8 slices at most.

The central angle of each pie slice always measures less than 60°. The total number of 60° slices that could be cut from the pie is $\frac{360}{60} = 6$ slices. Therefore, the pie can never have 6 slices. It can be cut into either 7 or 8 slices.

14. **3** Numbers & Operations: Sequences *Medium*

List the first five terms. Each term after the first is 4 times the preceding term, so the first five terms are: $2m$, $8m$, $32m$, $128m$, and $512m$.

Add the terms together. Their sum is 2,046:

$$2m + 8m + 32m + 128m + 512m = 2{,}046$$

Solve for m:

$$\begin{aligned} 682m &= 2{,}046 \\ m &= 3 \end{aligned}$$

15. **2/5, 6/15** Geometry: Triangles *Medium*

Label the diagram with the lengths of the sides, as indicated:

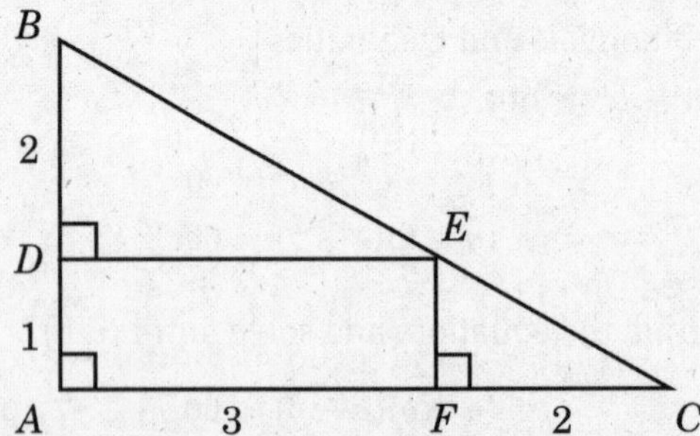

Note: Figure not drawn to scale.

The question states that $\frac{CF}{CA} = \frac{2}{5}$, so CF measures 2 and CA measures 5. This means that FA measures 5 – 2, or 3 units. The question also states that $\frac{AD}{AB} = \frac{1}{3}$. This means that AD measures 1 and AB measures 3. Therefore, DB measures 3 – 1, or 2 units.

Use these measures to calculate the areas of the two triangles. Triangle *DBE* has height 2. Its base, *DE*, is equal to the measure of *AF*. So, *DE* measures 3. Find the area of *DBE*:

$$A = \frac{1}{2}bh$$
$$A = \frac{1}{2}(3)(2)$$
$$A = \frac{6}{2} \text{ or } 3$$

Triangle *ABC* has base *AC*, which measures 5. Its height, *AB*, measures 3. Find the area of *ABC*:

$$A = \frac{1}{2}(5 \times 3)$$
$$A = \frac{1}{2}(15)$$
$$A = \frac{15}{2}$$

Find the value of the fraction $\frac{\text{area } \Delta DBE}{\text{area } \Delta ABC}$:

$$\frac{\text{area } \Delta DBE}{\text{area } \Delta ABC} = \frac{3}{15/2}$$
$$\frac{\text{area } \Delta DBE}{\text{area } \Delta ABC} = 3 \times \frac{2}{15}$$
$$\frac{\text{area } \Delta DBE}{\text{area } \Delta ABC} = \frac{6}{15}, \text{ or } \frac{2}{5}$$

16. **3, 5** Algebra: Binomials and Quadratics *Difficult*

First, substitute into the function the value you are given for *b*. In this case, the value of *b* is given as 3*c*:

$$s(b) = 15 + \frac{b^2}{9}$$
$$s(3c) = 15 + \frac{(3c)^2}{9}$$

Next, substitute the value you are given for $s(3c)$:

$$s(3c) = 15 + \frac{(3c)^2}{9}$$
$$8c = 15 + \frac{(3c)^2}{9}$$
$$8c = 15 + \frac{9c^2}{9}$$
$$8c = 15 + c^2$$

Now, rewrite the equation in the general form $y = ax^2 + bx + c$:

$$8c = 15 + c^2$$
$$0 = c^2 - 8c + 15$$

Finally, factor the quadratic equation to find its two roots:

$$0 = c^2 - 8c + 15$$
$$0 = (c - 3)(c - 5)$$
$$c = 3 \text{ or } 5$$

17. **236** Data Analysis, Statistics & Probability: Graphs, Charts, and Tables *Difficult*

Calculate the number of refills needed for each type of machine. Machine A requires n refills in n months. There are six months between January and June, so Machine A requires 6 refills during this time ($n = 6$). The inventory contains 20 machines of type A. These 20 machines require $20 \times 6 = 120$ refills during the six-month period.

Machine B requires 2 refills every three months. Over the six months between January and June, every Machine B requires $2 \times 2 = 4$ refills. The inventory contains 10 machines of type B. These 10 machines require $10 \times 4 = 40$ refills during the time period.

Machine C requires 1 refill every three months. Over the six months between January and June, each Machine C requires $2 \times 1 = 2$ refills. The inventory contains 5 machines of type C. These 5 machines require $5 \times 2 = 10$ refills during the time period.

Machine D requires n refills in n months. There are six months between January and June, so Machine D requires 6 refills during this time ($n = 6$). The inventory contains 3 machines of type D. These 3 machines require $3 \times 6 = 18$ refills during the six-month period.

Finally, Machine E requires 2 refills every 3 months. Over the six months between January and June, every Machine E requires $2 \times 2 = 4$ refills. The inventory contains 12 machines of type E. These 12 machines require $12 \times 4 = 48$ refills during the time period.

Add together the number of refills required by each type of machine:

$$120 + 40 + 10 + 18 + 48 = 236$$

18. **18** Data Analysis, Statistics & Probability: Permutations and Combinations *Difficult*

To answer this question, you could list out all of the possible arrangements one by one, or you could do your calculations using the faster way, as follows.

Block B can never be the first block. So, add up all of the possible combinations that could occur with block B in one of the *other* positions.

If block B is in the second position, there are 3 open positions. These 3 open positions can be filled by any of the remaining 3 blocks (A, C, and D). The number of possible orderings of these three blocks can be calculated using the factorial formula, $n!$, where n represents the number of items, 3. The number of possible orderings with block B always occupying the second position is $3!$, or $3 \times 2 \times 1$, which equals 6.

Perform the same calculation for block B in the third position. If block B is in position #3, the number of possible orderings of the remaining 3 blocks is $3!$, or 6.

Now find the number of possible orderings when block B is the fourth block. In this case, the number of possible orderings of the remaining 3 blocks is also $3!$, or 6.

Add the three sets of possible orderings together: $6 + 6 + 6 = 18$.

SECTION 6: WRITING

Improving Sentences

1. **E** Parallelism *Easy*

The phrase *they did in Georgia* at the end of this sentence is not parallel with the phrase *in Florida* earlier in the sentence. The two words *they did* should be omitted: *more students vacationed in Florida than in Georgia.*

2. **B** Run-Ons *Easy*

As it stands, this sentence is a run-on. The clause after the comma is an independent clause that can stand on its own, so it shouldn't be connected to the first part of the sentence with just a comma. **B** eliminates the run-on by turning the last phrase into a dependent clause, which can correctly be joined to the first part of the sentence with a comma.

3. **B** Other *Medium*

The second part of this sentence seems to suggest that *our neighborhood* sells more ice cream than the *downtown ice-cream truck*. This wording is confusing; the author really means that *our neighborhood ice-cream truck sells more ice cream*. **B** eliminates the ambiguity and makes the comparison clear.

4. **E** Wordiness *Easy*

The underlined portion of this sentence is overly wordy. **E** corrects this error in the most concise manner.

5. **D** Misplaced Modifiers *Medium*

The first part of this sentence contains the modifying phrase *having grown accustomed to winning most of her arguments*. This modifying phrase refers to Betty herself, so Betty should be the subject of the second part of the sentence. The name Betty should come directly after the comma to show that the modifying phrase refers to her. **B** and **C** can be eliminated because they both contain the subject *Betty's annoyance*. Only **D** contains Betty herself as the subject.

6. **C** Subject-Verb Agreement *Medium*

This sentence has an error in subject-verb agreement. The subject of the sentence is the plural word *excuses*. The verb of the sentence is the singular verb *is*. This verb should be in the plural form, *are*, to agree with its plural subject. **C** corrects the error and also makes the sentence parallel.

7. **A** No Error *Easy*

This sentence is correct as written. All subjects and verbs agree, and all phrases are in the proper form.

8. **E** Misplaced Modifiers *Medium*

This sentence makes it sound as if Mandy's apartment returned home from Europe after a year. That doesn't make sense; it must have been Mandy herself who returned from Europe. **E** clears up the confusion by revising the introductory phrase and still maintaining the meaning of the original sentence: *When Mandy returned home from Europe after a year, her apartment seemed much larger to her.*

9. **E** Coordination and Subordination *Medium*

The modifying phrase *having skills at* is awkward here. **E** corrects the problem by replacing *having skills at* with the more accurate conjunction *because*. **E** also eliminates the unparallel phrase *as well as*.

10. **C** Wordiness *Medium*

The second part of this sentence is overly wordy. **C** presents the most concise revision.

11. **C** Parallelism *Difficult*

The underlined portion of this sentence is not parallel with the first part of the sentence. The introductory phrase states that the sculptor is *reliant on her mentors for advice and inspiration*. To be parallel, the underlined part of the sentence must follow the same structure: reliant on ----- for -----. **C** corrects the error by making the entire phrase parallel. **C** describes the sculptor as *reliant on her mentors for advice and inspiration and on her backers for financial support*.

Identifying Sentence Errors

12. **C** Tense *Easy*

The action of this sentence takes place in the past, so the present tense verb phrase *is demolished* doesn't work here. This verb phrase should be *was demolished*, which is in the past tense.

13. **E** No Error *Easy*

This sentence is correct as written. All subjects and verbs agree, and all phrases are written in their proper form.

14. **B** Idioms *Easy*

This sentence contains an idiom error. In a sentence in which two items are referred to using the word *either*, the correct phrasing must also include the word *or*. To be correct, **B** should be written as *or*.

15. **D** Pronouns *Difficult*

The phrase *it had been* in **D** is used incorrectly to refer to the portions of Paul's homework that had been completed. The portions of homework are plural, so the plural pronoun *they* should be used here instead. The end of the sentence should read: *because they had been so challenging for Paul to complete after his accident*.

16. **C** Idioms *Medium*

C contains the incorrect phrase *one of its kind*. It is acceptable to say either that "the watch is the only one of its kind" or that "the watch is one of a kind." In this context, since the words *the only* are missing, we would say instead that the handmade watch is *one of a kind*.

17. **E** No Error *Medium*

This sentence is correct as written. All subjects and verbs agree, and all phrases are written in their proper form.

18. **A** Tense *Easy*

The first part of this sentence takes place in the past. Therefore, the phrase *is traveling* should be changed to *was traveling*. The first part of the sentence should make clear that Sandy *was traveling when her home was burglarized.*

19. **E** No Error *Easy*

This sentence is correct as written. All subjects and verbs agree, and all phrases are written in their proper form.

20. **D** Parallelism *Medium*

The phrase *as particle form* is not parallel with the earlier phrase *in wave form*. To be parallel, both of these phrases must contain the same preposition. The phrase *in wave form* is not underlined, so it must be correct. **D** should therefore be written as *in particle form*.

21. **B** Pronouns *Medium*

The pronoun *she* in **B** is used incorrectly here. If Helen had developed the design herself, it wouldn't sound correct to say that the design was developed by *she*. Instead, it would be correct to say that the design was developed by *her*. The same rule applies even if the design is developed by more than one person. The phrase should read: *a design developed jointly by her and the fashion consultant*.

22. **B** Parallelism *Medium*

The phrase *than explaining* in **B** is not parallel with the preceding phrase, *to finish*. To make the phrases parallel, *than explaining* must be rewritten as *than to explain*.

23. **E** No Error *Medium*

This sentence is written correctly. All subjects and verbs agree, all verbs are in the correct tense, and all words are in the correct format.

24. **A** Other *Medium*

As it stands, this sentence is a fragment. The word *since* in **A** turns the entire sentence into a dependent clause. The word *since* could be deleted to turn the fragment into a complete sentence consisting of two independent clauses joined correctly.

25. **A** Idioms *Medium*

The expression in **A** uses an incorrect idiom. Using *excuse of* is never correct. Instead, *excuse for* is used.

26. **B** Pronouns *Medium*

In this sentence, the pronoun *I* is used incorrectly. The pronoun *I* can be used only as the subject of a sentence. In this case, the pronoun *I* is not the subject of the sentence, so the objective pronoun *me* should be used instead.

27. **B** Subject-Verb Agreement *Easy*

The verb *was* is singular, but the subject of this verb is actually plural. Dr. Burnside's students appreciated two things about him: *his interesting assignments* and *his captivating lecture style*. Therefore, the verb *was* should be written in the plural form *were*.

28. **C** Pronouns *Medium*

The pronoun *its* in **C** is singular, but it refers to the noun *acupuncture treatments*. The word *treatments* is plural, so the correct pronoun is the plural pronoun *their*.

29. **B** Adverbs and Adjectives *Difficult*

The adjective *gradual* is used here to modify the adjective *declining*. In this case, however, *gradual* describes how the employment rate is declining, so *gradual* should be an adverb, not an adjective. The correct phrase is *gradually declining metropolitan unemployment rate*.

Improving Paragraphs

30. **B** Sentence Addition *Easy*

This question asks for a sentence that would serve as a good introduction to the essay. The essay discusses the history behind Bach's *Mass in B Minor*, and it explains how he composed the piece given the political circumstances of the time. **B** fits best.

31. **A** Sentence Combination *Medium*

These sentences can be combined most concisely by deleting the redundant phrase *the first section is* from the beginning of the second sentence.

32. **E** Sentence Revision *Medium*

As it stands, this sentence is a run-on. The revision in **E** corrects this error by turning the phrase after the comma into a dependent clause, which makes the sentence's meaning clear.

33. **A** Sentence Revision *Medium*

The original sentence presents the best version of sentence 9, so **A** is correct.

34. **C** Sentence Addition *Medium*

Sentence 10 states that *Bach was displeased with the lack of recognition that he was receiving in his position in Leipzig at the time.* **C** helps explain the relevance of sentence 10 by elaborating on Bach's hopes for the piece: He hoped that the Missa would secure him a new job in Dresden and increase his musical influence.

35. **E** Sentence Addition *Easy*

The passage introduces Bach's *Mass in B Minor* by noting that this complex work was composed in stages over a period of time and that it was finally completed only in the last few years of Bach's life. **E** recaps this point and thus works best as a concluding sentence for the passage.

SECTION 7: CRITICAL READING

Sentence Completions

1. **D** One-Word/One-Way *Easy*

The second part of the sentence gives clues to the meaning of the missing word. The couple *realized that they could not resolve their differences*, so the missing word must mean something like an "attempt to resolve differences." **D**, *reconciliation*, works best.

2. **A** Two-Word/One-Way *Medium*

Through performing, Gabriel Hall showcased the full potential of *something*, so he must have been a very accomplished performer. The first blank will therefore mean something like "abilities at." Eliminate **C**. Performing would most likely have enabled Hall to showcase his *talents* rather than his *direction*, *accuracy*, or *learning*. Therefore, **A** is correct.

3. **E** Two-Word/Two-Way *Medium*

The word *nevertheless* signals a contrast in the two parts of this sentence. Thus, the meaning of the second missing word will contrast with the meaning of the first missing word. The phrase *that unpleasant experience* indicates that the first blank contains a word with a negative meaning, so eliminate **B** and **D**. Of the remaining choices, only **E** contains two words that are roughly opposite in meaning. As *distasteful* as the task was, it still taught the CEO some *valuable* lessons.

4. **D** One-Word/One-Way *Medium*

Several clues in this sentence indicate the meaning of the missing word. The wood that falls from the trees is *hardened* and already *dead*; it also has a *stony texture*. *Petrified* wood is dead wood that has become stiff and stonelike, so **D** is correct.

5. **A** One-Word/One-Way *Medium*

Barry and Michelle chose to break the news of their engagement during a family celebration. This celebration honored Barry's brother's graduation, so it was a positive occasion—eliminate **B**, **C**, and **E**. The word *auspicious* means "marked by success," so **A** fits best.

6. **D** Two-Word/One-Way *Difficult*

The first part of this sentence gives clues to the meaning of the first missing word. That word must mean something similar to "overconfident" or "taking one's success for granted." The word *complacency* fits best here: Someone who is complacent is "content with no awareness of potential trouble." The word *justify* also fits the second blank: *success does not justify arrogance or vainglory*. **D** is correct.

Long Reading Passage

7. **B** Words in Context *Easy*

At the end of the first paragraph, the author makes the point that *the endowment of astronomical observatories devoted to research* is about *half a million dollars annually*. The entire paragraph helps to support the author's point that astronomy research receives more funding than any other type of scientific research. In this context, the phrase *large pieces of work* signifies major scientific research projects.

8. **B** Words in Context *Medium*

Paragraph 1 states that *there are scarcely any physics laboratories devoted to research, or endowed with independent funds for this object, except those supported by the government*. In this case, the word *supported* most nearly means "endowed with independent funds." Therefore, **B**, *financed*, fits best.

9. **D** Implied Information *Medium*

Paragraph 2 states that *a practical man, who has spent all his life in [business], is sometimes deeply impressed with the vast distances and grandeur of the problems of astronomy*. Such a person is attracted by *the very remoteness and difficulty of studying the stars*. This description implies that astronomy appeals to the imagination because it deals with the mysteries of outer space.

10. **D** Themes and Arguments *Medium*

The author makes the point in paragraph 3 that his arguments *apply with almost equal force* to other scientific disciplines. He expresses hope that his discussion of the organization of astronomy may lead to advancing other disciplines, or placing them *on the footing they should hold*. He emphasizes the potential application of his arguments to other scientific disciplines, so **D** is correct.

11. **C** Themes and Arguments *Easy*

The author starts the fourth paragraph by claiming that *the practical value of astronomy in the past is easily established*. To support this point, he states that without astronomy, *international commerce on a large scale would have been impossible*. The reference to *international commerce* therefore provides an example of the practical value of astronomy.

12. **A** Specific Information *Medium*

Paragraph 4 mentions that astronomy helped us learn to determine *the boundaries of countries*, so **B** can be eliminated. The paragraph also explains how astronomy helped to promote international commerce, navigation, and methods of determining time, so **C**, **D**, and **E** are incorrect. **A**, *architecture*, is never mentioned in paragraph 4 as a product of astronomy research.

13. **B** Attitude and Tone *Easy*

Throughout the passage, the author describes the contributions of astronomy in a positive light. **B**, *appreciative*, is the only answer choice that contains a positive attitude. **B** is correct.

14. **E** Technique *Medium*

The author discusses the three main advances of astronomy in the last three paragraphs of the passage. In each paragraph, the author presents a point and then provides evidence to support that point. The last paragraph, for example, begins with the point that *the third great advance in astronomy is in photographing the spectra of the stars*. The rest of the paragraph then explains this point in detail. This model is followed in the two previous paragraphs as well, so **E** fits best.

15. **B** Specific Information *Medium*

In paragraph 5, the author describes *the application of photography to the study of the stars* as *the second great advance in astronomy*. The author never mentions any of the other four advances listed as answer choices.

16. **E** Specific Information *Easy*

The answer to this question is stated directly in the passage. Wet plates are discussed in paragraph 5, in which the author notes that *the lack of sensitivity of the wet plate was perhaps the only reason why its use progressed slowly*. So, **E** is correct.

17. **D** Implied Information *Medium*

In paragraph 5, the author explains that dry plate photography was introduced twenty-five years after wet plate photography. He states that the dry photographic plates *were very sensitive and were easily handled. In addition*, the author points out, dry plates were capable of *indefinitely long exposures*. This statement suggests that wet plates had limited exposure times.

18. **B** Implied Information *Difficult*

In the last paragraph of the passage, the author describes *the third great advance in astronomy . . . photographing the spectra of the stars*. He concludes that this phenomenon may be regarded as the third great advance in part because of the attention that it has received: *When we consider the attention the photography of stellar spectra is receiving at the present time in nearly all the great observatories in the world*, he writes, *this accomplishment may well be regarded as the third great advance in astronomy.* Therefore **B** fits best.

19. **A** Attitude and Tone *Medium*

In the last paragraph, the author notes that Dr. Henry Draper was the first person to obtain a photograph showing the lines in a stellar spectrum. Even though Dr. Draper's photograph was taken first in 1872, Dr. Draper was not the first person to publicize his results. Instead, Sir William Huggins published his results first—despite the fact that his photograph was obtained four years *after* Dr. Draper's. The author seems sympathetic to Dr. Draper's circumstance and respectfully points out that even though Huggins had the first publication, Dr. Draper actually obtained the first photograph.

SECTION 8: MATH

Multiple Choice

1. **C** Algebra: Solving Equations *Medium*

Set up an equation representing the number of turkey sandwiches and the number of ham sandwiches after the first stop. Before the first stop, the number of turkey sandwiches, t, is equal to the number of ham sandwiches, h. After the first stop, the number of turkey sandwiches is reduced by 18. So, the number of turkey sandwiches after the first stop is $t - 18$. Since $t = h$, the expression $t - 18$ is equal to $h - 18$.

After the first stop, the number of ham sandwiches, h, is equal to three times the number of remaining turkey sandwiches, $h - 18$. Set up an equation:

$$h = 3(h - 18)$$

Solve for h:

$$\begin{aligned} h &= 3(h - 18) \\ h &= 3h - 54 \\ -2h &= -54 \\ h &= 27 \end{aligned}$$

2. **D** Geometry: Coordinate Geometry *Easy*

A line with a positive slope will slant upward from left to right. Eliminate **A**, **C**, and **E**. A line with a negative y-intercept will intersect the y-axis at a point where y has a negative value. **D** is correct.

3. **C** Data Analysis, Statistics & Probability: Graphs, Charts, and Tables *Easy*

A set of 5 products costs \$67.90. At this rate, the cost per product is $\$67.90 \div 5 = \$13.58$. This number is closest to **C**, \$13.60.

4. **B** Data Analysis, Statistics & Probability: Graphs, Charts, and Tables *Easy*

To purchase exactly 18 products in the least expensive way, you would buy one set of 10 products (\$110.50), plus one set of 5 products (\$67.90), plus three single products at \$15.00 each (\$45.00 total). Add these values together:

$$110.50 + 67.90 + 45.00 = \$223.40$$

5. **C** Geometry: Coordinate Geometry *Easy*

To find the value of $s(3)$ on the graph, look for the value of y when x equals 3. When x equals 3 on this graphed line, the value of y is about 5. **C** is correct.

6. **C** Geometry: Angles and Lines *Medium*

The four angles in the figure form a circle. A circle contains a total of 360°, so the sum of the measures of the four angles equals 360°.

Set up an equation using the values given for each angle, and solve for z:

$$\begin{aligned} 3z + 3z + 4z + 8z &= 360 \\ 18z &= 360 \\ z &= 20 \end{aligned}$$

7. **D** Numbers & Operations: Exponents *Difficult*

First, determine the value of a. The equation $a^{-\frac{1}{2}} = \frac{1}{2}$ contains a negative fractional exponent. Change the negative exponent to a positive exponent:

$$a^{-\frac{1}{2}} = \frac{1}{2}$$
$$\frac{1}{a^{\frac{1}{2}}} = \frac{1}{2}$$

Next, get rid of the fractional exponent. Any number x, raised to the fractional exponent $\frac{y}{z}$, can be converted by taking the root of that number:

$$x^{\frac{y}{z}} = \sqrt[z]{x^y}$$

Therefore, the term $a^{\frac{1}{2}}$ can be converted to $\sqrt[2]{a^1}$, which is the same as $\sqrt{a}$. Now, solve for a:

$$\frac{1}{a^{\frac{1}{2}}} = \frac{1}{2}$$
$$\frac{1}{\sqrt{a}} = \frac{1}{2}$$
$$\frac{1}{\sqrt{4}} = \frac{1}{2}$$
$$a = 4$$

Next, find the value of c. The question states that $b^c = 81$ and that $c > b$. Since $9^2 = 81$, these two numbers might work, but they don't fit the condition $c > b$. Try substituting 3 for b. In this case, $3 \times 3 \times 3 = 81$, which is the same as $3^4 = 81$. The numbers 3 and 4 do fit the condition $c > b$, so c must equal 4.

The value of $a + c$ is therefore $4 + 4 = 8$.

8. **C** Geometry: Coordinate Geometry *Easy*

The diameter of the semicircle starts at point (0, 0) and ends at point (10, 0). Among the five choices, find the pair of x-coordinates that are equidistant from each end of the diameter:

> The x-coordinates 1 and 9 each lie exactly 1 unit from the ends of the diameter.

However, none of the other four pairs fit the bill. **C** contains the only correct pair.

9. **B** Numbers & Operations: Divisibility and Remainders *Medium*

Try out each of the answer choices, starting with **A**. If $n = 8$, then $3n + 1 = 3(8) + 1$, or 25. When 25 is divided by 6, the result is 4 with a remainder of 1. Eliminate **A**.

Next, try **B**. If $n = 9$, then $3n + 1 = 3(9) + 1$, or 28. When 28 is divided by 6, the result is 4 with a remainder of 4. **B** is correct.

10. **B** Data Analysis, Statistics & Probability: Statistical Analysis *Easy*

Erica is both the tenth-oldest and the tenth-youngest employee in her department, so her age is the median age of the employees in the department. In other words, her age lies exactly in the middle of all the other ages. Nine of the employees are younger than Erica, and nine are older than her. Therefore, the department contains 9 younger employees, 9 older employees, and Erica, or 19 total employees.

11. **A** Algebra: Binomials and Quadratics *Medium*

When evaluating the graph of a quadratic equation $ax^2 + bx + c$, you can determine whether the parabola opens upward or downward by examining the value of a. If $a > 0$, then the parabola opens upward. If $a < 0$, then the parabola opens downward. The question states that a is a positive constant. So, in this case, $a > 0$ and the parabola opens upward. Eliminate **D** and **E**.

The question also states that c is a positive constant. Therefore, whenever x equals 0, the value of y will always be a positive number. Even if x is 0, the positive value of c will always produce a y-value that is greater than 0. This means that the parabola can never pass through the point (0, 0). **B** and **C** both contain parabolas that pass through the point (0, 0), so these choices can be eliminated. **A** must be correct.

12. **B** Geometry: Polygons *Difficult*

To make the figure easier to understand, draw line MO. Add points A and B where MO intersects the rectangle, as shown:

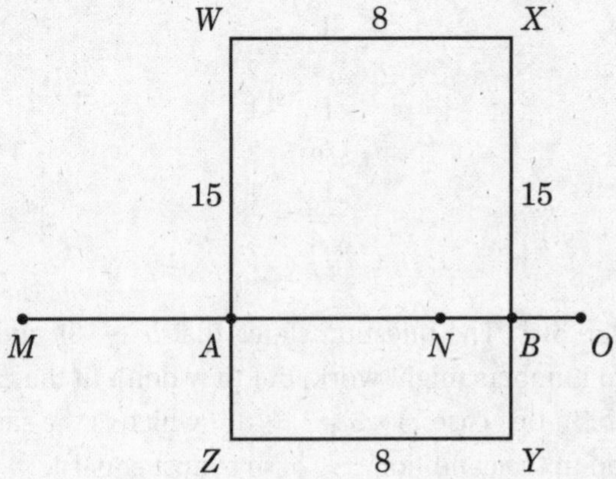

<u>Note:</u> Figure not drawn to scale.

Line MO is parallel to line ZY. Since ZY measures 8, AB must also measure 8. Now, determine the length of MO.

Segment AB is made up of two smaller segments, AN and NB. Since AB measures 8, you know that $AN + NB$ also measures 8. The question tells you that points M and N are symmetric about line ZW and points N and O are symmetric about line XY. This means that $AN = MA$ and $NB = BO$. Therefore, $AN + NB = MA + BO$.

You already know that the measure of $AN + NB$ is 8. So, $MA + BO$ must also equal 8. Add these four segments together to determine the length of MO:

$$MO = (AN + NB) + (MA + BO)$$
$$MO = (8) + (8)$$
$$MO = 16$$

13. **C** Numbers & Operations: Percents *Medium*

Let the original weight be represented by x. The weight of the box was first increased by 30 percent. After this increase, the new weight of the box was $x + 0.30x$.

The new weight of the box was then decreased by 55 percent. So, calculate 55 percent of the new weight: $0.55(x + 0.30x)$. Then subtract this amount from the new weight:

$$(x + 0.30x) - 0.55(x + 0.30x)$$

Solve for x:

$$x + 0.30x - 0.55(x + 0.30x) = x + 0.30x - 0.55x - 0.165x$$
$$= 0.585x$$

Multiply this amount by 100 to convert the decimal into a percentage: $0.585 \times 100 = 58.5$ percent. The final weight was 58.5 percent of the initial weight.

14. **E** Algebra: Solving Equations *Medium*

The question states that $8 \times k$ equals $k + 8$. Set up an equation and solve for k:

$$8k = k + 8$$
$$7k = 8$$
$$k = \frac{8}{7}$$

Now, substitute $\frac{8}{7}$ for k to determine the value of $7k$:

$$7k = 7\left(\frac{8}{7}\right)$$
$$k = 8$$

15. **C** Geometry: Triangles *Medium*

The sides of the triangle are consecutive odd integers. The length of the hypotenuse, the longest side, is s. Therefore, the lengths of the legs are $s - 2$ and $s - 4$.

Set up an equation using the Pythagorean theorem, $a^2 + b^2 = c^2$. Substitute s for c, $s - 2$ for b, and $s - 4$ for a:

$$a^2 + b^2 = c^2$$
$$(s - 4)^2 + (s - 2)^2 = s^2$$

16. **D** Algebra: Solving Equations *Difficult*

Pick a number for r that is an integer greater than 1. Try the number 2. Substitute 2 for r in the equation $q = r + \frac{1}{r}$, and solve for q:

$$q = r + \frac{1}{r}$$
$$q = (2) + \frac{1}{(2)}$$
$$q = 2\frac{1}{2}$$

Now, test out each of the statements using the values $r = 2$ and $q = 2\frac{1}{2}$. If r equals 2 and q equals $2\frac{1}{2}$, then I must be true. The value of q definitely does not equal r. For all positive integral values of r greater than 1, the value of q will always be a fraction, so q will never equal r. Eliminate **B**.

If r equals 2, then q is a fraction and not an integer. Statement II is false, so eliminate **C** and **E**.

Now test III. If r equals 2, then r^2 equals 4, and qr equals 2×2.5, or 5. In this case, rq is greater than r^2. For all positive integral values of r greater than 1, the value of rq will always be greater than the value of r^2. Statement III must be true, so **D** is correct.

SECTION 9: WRITING

Improving Sentences

1. **B** Tenses *Easy*

This sentence contains a verb tense error. The verb *plan announcing* should be in the infinitive form, *plan to announce*. Although **D** might be tempting, **B** is more concise and also uses the active form of the verb *plan*.

2. **B** Tenses *Easy*

The action of this sentence takes place in the past tense. Therefore, the verbs *hire* and *train* should be in the past tense, as **B** indicates. The conjunction *and* is unnecessary here.

3. **A** No Error *Medium*

This sentence is correct as it is. All subjects and verbs agree, and other parts of speech are used correctly.

4. **B** Parallelism *Easy*

The two verbs in this sentence are not parallel. The first verb is expressed as *should possess*. The second verb therefore must also be expressed in a parallel format: *should also demonstrate*.

5. **D** Conjunctions *Easy*

This sentence explains how the engineers tested the functionality of their filtration systems. The phrase *by creating* fits better here, because it connects the second part of the sentence to the first part. In this case, the comma is unnecessary.

6. **E** Wordiness *Easy*

This sentence is overly wordy. The phrase *as to the justifiability of* is awkward here. Also, the underlined part of the sentence is confusing: It's not clear whose decisions are being referred to. **E** revises the sentence in the most concise way, making clear that the case workers' decisions are being discussed.

7. **E** Parallelism *Easy*

This sentence contains an error in parallel structure. The first part of the sentence states that Blockman was valued *not only as a charismatic leader*. The second part of the sentence should retain this structure: *but also as an effective manager*.

8. **A** No Error *Medium*

This sentence is correct as written, so **A** is the best choice.

9. **D** Coordination and Subordination *Medium*

In the underlined portion of the sentence, the word *this* is confusing. It's not clear what *this* refers to—the parade or the barricades. **D** corrects this error by eliminating the word *this* and concisely clarifying that *almost no inbound traffic reached the city*.

10. **B** Misplaced Modifier *Medium*

The first part of this sentence contains the modifying phrase *lacking the proper equipment.* Who lacked the proper equipment? The original sentences makes it sound like *my attempts* lacked the proper equipment, which doesn't make any sense. Instead, the speaker of the sentence lacked the proper equipment. The pronoun *I* should come right after the comma to show that the first phrase modifies the speaker. **D** makes it sound as if the materials in the shop were fruitless, which also doesn't make sense, so **B** is correct.

11. **C** Conjunctions *Medium*

The phrase *and thus* doesn't work to connect the two parts of this sentence, and it sounds awkward. **C** corrects this error by replacing *and thus* with *that they*, which works much better as a connecting phrase. **C** also changes *focused in* to the correct idiomatic expression *focused on.*

12. **D** Misplaced Modifiers *Medium*

As it is written, this sentence makes it sound as if *a comprehensive search* itself is performing the action of *typing in key words.* That doesn't seem right. A person would be doing the typing, so this sentence needs to have an individual as its subject. **C** is incorrect because the plural pronoun *they* is confusing—it's not clear who "they" are. **D** works best: *By simply typing in key words, you can conduct a search.*

13. **C** Idioms *Medium*

This sentence uses the idiom *not only . . . but also.* Whenever this idiom is used, both parts of the phrase must have parallel structures. **C** uses the idiom correctly and also maintains the parallel structure within the sentence. It places the phrases in the following form: *We will not only develop* (verb) *teleporting capability* (object) *but also learn* (verb) *telepathic communication* (object).

14. **D** Fragments *Difficult*

As it stands, this sentence is a fragment. Granted, the sentence is a pretty complex fragment, but it's a fragment nonetheless. Notice how the subject *students* is introduced in the first part of the sentence, but no verb for *students* is ever provided. Instead, a phrase is added to describe the students. But we never see a verb that explains what the students do. **D** corrects this error by beginning the underlined part of the sentence with the verb *receive.* This clarifies the action carried out by the students: *The students at the college receive course grades that do not match their high school achievements.*

SAT PRACTICE TEST 10

SAT* Reasoning Test—General Directions

Timing

- You will have 3 hours and 20 minutes to work on this test. (On the actual SAT, you would have 3 hours and 45 minutes to complete ten sections, one of which would be unscored and experimental.)
- There are nine separately timed sections:
  - ➤ One 25-minute essay
  - ➤ Five other 25-minute sections
  - ➤ Two 20-minute sections
  - ➤ One 10-minute section
- You may work on only one section at a time.
- The supervisor will tell you when to begin and end each section.
- If you finish a section before time is called, check your work on that section. You may NOT turn to any other section.
- Work as rapidly as you can without losing accuracy. Don't waste time on questions that seem too difficult for you.

Marking Answers

- Carefully mark only one answer for each question.
- Make sure each mark is dark and completely fills the circle.
- Do not make any stray marks on your answer sheet.
- If you erase, do so completely. Incomplete erasures may be scored as intended answers.
- Use only the answer spaces that correspond to the question numbers.
- Use the test book for scratchwork, but you will not receive credit for anything written there.
- After time has been called, you may not transfer answers to your answer sheet or fill in circles.
- You may not fold or remove pages or portions of a page from this book, or take the book or answer sheet from the testing room.

Scoring

- For each correct answer to a question, you receive one point.
- For questions you omit, you receive no points.
- For a wrong answer to a multiple-choice question, you lose one-fourth of a point.
  - ➤ If you can eliminate one or more of the answer choices as wrong, you increase your chances of choosing the correct answer and earning one point.
  - ➤ If you can't eliminate any choice, move on. You can return to the question later if there is time.
- For a wrong answer to a "grid-in" math question, you don't lose any points.
- The essay is scored on a 1 to 6 scale by two different readers. The total essay score is the sum of the two readers' scores.
- An off-topic or blank essay will receive a score of zero.

---

* SAT test directions selected from the SAT Reasoning Test. Reprinted by permission of the College Board, the copyright owner.

SAT PRACTICE TEST 10 ANSWER SHEET

SECTION 2

1. Ⓐ Ⓑ Ⓒ Ⓓ Ⓔ	7. Ⓐ Ⓑ Ⓒ Ⓓ Ⓔ	13. Ⓐ Ⓑ Ⓒ Ⓓ Ⓔ	19. Ⓐ Ⓑ Ⓒ Ⓓ Ⓔ
2. Ⓐ Ⓑ Ⓒ Ⓓ Ⓔ	8. Ⓐ Ⓑ Ⓒ Ⓓ Ⓔ	14. Ⓐ Ⓑ Ⓒ Ⓓ Ⓔ	20. Ⓐ Ⓑ Ⓒ Ⓓ Ⓔ
3. Ⓐ Ⓑ Ⓒ Ⓓ Ⓔ	9. Ⓐ Ⓑ Ⓒ Ⓓ Ⓔ	15. Ⓐ Ⓑ Ⓒ Ⓓ Ⓔ	21. Ⓐ Ⓑ Ⓒ Ⓓ Ⓔ
4. Ⓐ Ⓑ Ⓒ Ⓓ Ⓔ	10. Ⓐ Ⓑ Ⓒ Ⓓ Ⓔ	16. Ⓐ Ⓑ Ⓒ Ⓓ Ⓔ	22. Ⓐ Ⓑ Ⓒ Ⓓ Ⓔ
5. Ⓐ Ⓑ Ⓒ Ⓓ Ⓔ	11. Ⓐ Ⓑ Ⓒ Ⓓ Ⓔ	17. Ⓐ Ⓑ Ⓒ Ⓓ Ⓔ	23. Ⓐ Ⓑ Ⓒ Ⓓ Ⓔ
6. Ⓐ Ⓑ Ⓒ Ⓓ Ⓔ	12. Ⓐ Ⓑ Ⓒ Ⓓ Ⓔ	18. Ⓐ Ⓑ Ⓒ Ⓓ Ⓔ	24. Ⓐ Ⓑ Ⓒ Ⓓ Ⓔ

SECTION 3

1. Ⓐ Ⓑ Ⓒ Ⓓ Ⓔ	6. Ⓐ Ⓑ Ⓒ Ⓓ Ⓔ	11. Ⓐ Ⓑ Ⓒ Ⓓ Ⓔ	16. Ⓐ Ⓑ Ⓒ Ⓓ Ⓔ
2. Ⓐ Ⓑ Ⓒ Ⓓ Ⓔ	7. Ⓐ Ⓑ Ⓒ Ⓓ Ⓔ	12. Ⓐ Ⓑ Ⓒ Ⓓ Ⓔ	17. Ⓐ Ⓑ Ⓒ Ⓓ Ⓔ
3. Ⓐ Ⓑ Ⓒ Ⓓ Ⓔ	8. Ⓐ Ⓑ Ⓒ Ⓓ Ⓔ	13. Ⓐ Ⓑ Ⓒ Ⓓ Ⓔ	18. Ⓐ Ⓑ Ⓒ Ⓓ Ⓔ
4. Ⓐ Ⓑ Ⓒ Ⓓ Ⓔ	9. Ⓐ Ⓑ Ⓒ Ⓓ Ⓔ	14. Ⓐ Ⓑ Ⓒ Ⓓ Ⓔ	19. Ⓐ Ⓑ Ⓒ Ⓓ Ⓔ
5. Ⓐ Ⓑ Ⓒ Ⓓ Ⓔ	10. Ⓐ Ⓑ Ⓒ Ⓓ Ⓔ	15. Ⓐ Ⓑ Ⓒ Ⓓ Ⓔ	20. Ⓐ Ⓑ Ⓒ Ⓓ Ⓔ

SECTION 4

1. Ⓐ Ⓑ Ⓒ Ⓓ Ⓔ	7. Ⓐ Ⓑ Ⓒ Ⓓ Ⓔ	13. Ⓐ Ⓑ Ⓒ Ⓓ Ⓔ	19. Ⓐ Ⓑ Ⓒ Ⓓ Ⓔ
2. Ⓐ Ⓑ Ⓒ Ⓓ Ⓔ	8. Ⓐ Ⓑ Ⓒ Ⓓ Ⓔ	14. Ⓐ Ⓑ Ⓒ Ⓓ Ⓔ	20. Ⓐ Ⓑ Ⓒ Ⓓ Ⓔ
3. Ⓐ Ⓑ Ⓒ Ⓓ Ⓔ	9. Ⓐ Ⓑ Ⓒ Ⓓ Ⓔ	15. Ⓐ Ⓑ Ⓒ Ⓓ Ⓔ	21. Ⓐ Ⓑ Ⓒ Ⓓ Ⓔ
4. Ⓐ Ⓑ Ⓒ Ⓓ Ⓔ	10. Ⓐ Ⓑ Ⓒ Ⓓ Ⓔ	16. Ⓐ Ⓑ Ⓒ Ⓓ Ⓔ	22. Ⓐ Ⓑ Ⓒ Ⓓ Ⓔ
5. Ⓐ Ⓑ Ⓒ Ⓓ Ⓔ	11. Ⓐ Ⓑ Ⓒ Ⓓ Ⓔ	17. Ⓐ Ⓑ Ⓒ Ⓓ Ⓔ	23. Ⓐ Ⓑ Ⓒ Ⓓ Ⓔ
6. Ⓐ Ⓑ Ⓒ Ⓓ Ⓔ	12. Ⓐ Ⓑ Ⓒ Ⓓ Ⓔ	18. Ⓐ Ⓑ Ⓒ Ⓓ Ⓔ	24. Ⓐ Ⓑ Ⓒ Ⓓ Ⓔ

SECTION 5

1. Ⓐ Ⓑ Ⓒ Ⓓ Ⓔ	3. Ⓐ Ⓑ Ⓒ Ⓓ Ⓔ	5. Ⓐ Ⓑ Ⓒ Ⓓ Ⓔ	7. Ⓐ Ⓑ Ⓒ Ⓓ Ⓔ
2. Ⓐ Ⓑ Ⓒ Ⓓ Ⓔ	4. Ⓐ Ⓑ Ⓒ Ⓓ Ⓔ	6. Ⓐ Ⓑ Ⓒ Ⓓ Ⓔ	8. Ⓐ Ⓑ Ⓒ Ⓓ Ⓔ

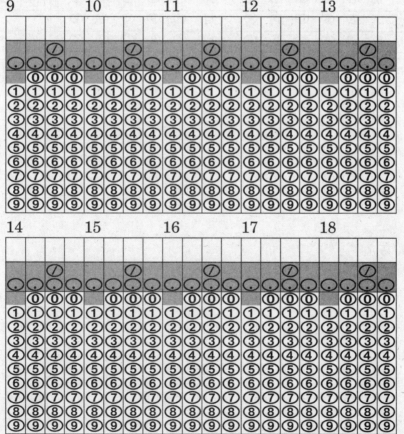

9 10 11 12 13

14 15 16 17 18

SAT PRACTICE TEST 10 ANSWER SHEET

SECTION 6			
1. Ⓐ Ⓑ Ⓒ Ⓓ Ⓔ	10. Ⓐ Ⓑ Ⓒ Ⓓ Ⓔ	19. Ⓐ Ⓑ Ⓒ Ⓓ Ⓔ	28. Ⓐ Ⓑ Ⓒ Ⓓ Ⓔ
2. Ⓐ Ⓑ Ⓒ Ⓓ Ⓔ	11. Ⓐ Ⓑ Ⓒ Ⓓ Ⓔ	20. Ⓐ Ⓑ Ⓒ Ⓓ Ⓔ	29. Ⓐ Ⓑ Ⓒ Ⓓ Ⓔ
3. Ⓐ Ⓑ Ⓒ Ⓓ Ⓔ	12. Ⓐ Ⓑ Ⓒ Ⓓ Ⓔ	21. Ⓐ Ⓑ Ⓒ Ⓓ Ⓔ	30. Ⓐ Ⓑ Ⓒ Ⓓ Ⓔ
4. Ⓐ Ⓑ Ⓒ Ⓓ Ⓔ	13. Ⓐ Ⓑ Ⓒ Ⓓ Ⓔ	22. Ⓐ Ⓑ Ⓒ Ⓓ Ⓔ	31. Ⓐ Ⓑ Ⓒ Ⓓ Ⓔ
5. Ⓐ Ⓑ Ⓒ Ⓓ Ⓔ	14. Ⓐ Ⓑ Ⓒ Ⓓ Ⓔ	23. Ⓐ Ⓑ Ⓒ Ⓓ Ⓔ	32. Ⓐ Ⓑ Ⓒ Ⓓ Ⓔ
6. Ⓐ Ⓑ Ⓒ Ⓓ Ⓔ	15. Ⓐ Ⓑ Ⓒ Ⓓ Ⓔ	24. Ⓐ Ⓑ Ⓒ Ⓓ Ⓔ	33. Ⓐ Ⓑ Ⓒ Ⓓ Ⓔ
7. Ⓐ Ⓑ Ⓒ Ⓓ Ⓔ	16. Ⓐ Ⓑ Ⓒ Ⓓ Ⓔ	25. Ⓐ Ⓑ Ⓒ Ⓓ Ⓔ	34. Ⓐ Ⓑ Ⓒ Ⓓ Ⓔ
8. Ⓐ Ⓑ Ⓒ Ⓓ Ⓔ	17. Ⓐ Ⓑ Ⓒ Ⓓ Ⓔ	26. Ⓐ Ⓑ Ⓒ Ⓓ Ⓔ	35. Ⓐ Ⓑ Ⓒ Ⓓ Ⓔ
9. Ⓐ Ⓑ Ⓒ Ⓓ Ⓔ	18. Ⓐ Ⓑ Ⓒ Ⓓ Ⓔ	27. Ⓐ Ⓑ Ⓒ Ⓓ Ⓔ	

SECTION 7			
1. Ⓐ Ⓑ Ⓒ Ⓓ Ⓔ	6. Ⓐ Ⓑ Ⓒ Ⓓ Ⓔ	11. Ⓐ Ⓑ Ⓒ Ⓓ Ⓔ	16. Ⓐ Ⓑ Ⓒ Ⓓ Ⓔ
2. Ⓐ Ⓑ Ⓒ Ⓓ Ⓔ	7. Ⓐ Ⓑ Ⓒ Ⓓ Ⓔ	12. Ⓐ Ⓑ Ⓒ Ⓓ Ⓔ	17. Ⓐ Ⓑ Ⓒ Ⓓ Ⓔ
3. Ⓐ Ⓑ Ⓒ Ⓓ Ⓔ	8. Ⓐ Ⓑ Ⓒ Ⓓ Ⓔ	13. Ⓐ Ⓑ Ⓒ Ⓓ Ⓔ	18. Ⓐ Ⓑ Ⓒ Ⓓ Ⓔ
4. Ⓐ Ⓑ Ⓒ Ⓓ Ⓔ	9. Ⓐ Ⓑ Ⓒ Ⓓ Ⓔ	14. Ⓐ Ⓑ Ⓒ Ⓓ Ⓔ	19. Ⓐ Ⓑ Ⓒ Ⓓ Ⓔ
5. Ⓐ Ⓑ Ⓒ Ⓓ Ⓔ	10. Ⓐ Ⓑ Ⓒ Ⓓ Ⓔ	15. Ⓐ Ⓑ Ⓒ Ⓓ Ⓔ	

SECTION 8			
1. Ⓐ Ⓑ Ⓒ Ⓓ Ⓔ	5. Ⓐ Ⓑ Ⓒ Ⓓ Ⓔ	9. Ⓐ Ⓑ Ⓒ Ⓓ Ⓔ	13. Ⓐ Ⓑ Ⓒ Ⓓ Ⓔ
2. Ⓐ Ⓑ Ⓒ Ⓓ Ⓔ	6. Ⓐ Ⓑ Ⓒ Ⓓ Ⓔ	10. Ⓐ Ⓑ Ⓒ Ⓓ Ⓔ	14. Ⓐ Ⓑ Ⓒ Ⓓ Ⓔ
3. Ⓐ Ⓑ Ⓒ Ⓓ Ⓔ	7. Ⓐ Ⓑ Ⓒ Ⓓ Ⓔ	11. Ⓐ Ⓑ Ⓒ Ⓓ Ⓔ	15. Ⓐ Ⓑ Ⓒ Ⓓ Ⓔ
4. Ⓐ Ⓑ Ⓒ Ⓓ Ⓔ	8. Ⓐ Ⓑ Ⓒ Ⓓ Ⓔ	12. Ⓐ Ⓑ Ⓒ Ⓓ Ⓔ	16. Ⓐ Ⓑ Ⓒ Ⓓ Ⓔ

SECTION 9			
1. Ⓐ Ⓑ Ⓒ Ⓓ Ⓔ	5. Ⓐ Ⓑ Ⓒ Ⓓ Ⓔ	9. Ⓐ Ⓑ Ⓒ Ⓓ Ⓔ	13. Ⓐ Ⓑ Ⓒ Ⓓ Ⓔ
2. Ⓐ Ⓑ Ⓒ Ⓓ Ⓔ	6. Ⓐ Ⓑ Ⓒ Ⓓ Ⓔ	10. Ⓐ Ⓑ Ⓒ Ⓓ Ⓔ	14. Ⓐ Ⓑ Ⓒ Ⓓ Ⓔ
3. Ⓐ Ⓑ Ⓒ Ⓓ Ⓔ	7. Ⓐ Ⓑ Ⓒ Ⓓ Ⓔ	11. Ⓐ Ⓑ Ⓒ Ⓓ Ⓔ	
4. Ⓐ Ⓑ Ⓒ Ⓓ Ⓔ	8. Ⓐ Ⓑ Ⓒ Ⓓ Ⓔ	12. Ⓐ Ⓑ Ⓒ Ⓓ Ⓔ	

SECTION 1

ESSAY

Time—25 minutes

The essay gives you an opportunity to show how effectively you can develop and express ideas. You should, therefore, take care to develop your point of view, present your ideas logically and clearly, and use language precisely.

Your essay must be written on the lines provided on your answer sheet—you will receive no other paper on which to write. You will have enough space if you write on every line, avoid wide margins, and keep your handwriting to a reasonable size. Remember that people who are not familiar with your handwriting will read what you write. Try to write or print so that what you are writing is legible to those readers.

You have twenty-five minutes to write an essay on the topic assigned below. DO NOT WRITE ON ANOTHER TOPIC. AN OFF-TOPIC ESSAY WILL RECEIVE A SCORE OF ZERO.

Think carefully about the issue presented in the following excerpt and the assignment below.

> Some people benefit from developing clear plans for their lives to help them achieve life goals. These individuals tend to map out specific paths for themselves and to follow these paths closely. They evaluate their level of fulfillment in life based on how successful they are in achieving pre-planned goals. Others prefer a more spontaneous approach, which leaves plenty of room to follow hunches and journey into unknown territory. These individuals believe that adventure is key to personal fulfillment and that a spontaneous life offers the possibility of even greater rewards than a person could plan for.

Assignment: Is planning more important than spontaneity for achieving fulfillment in life? Plan and write an essay in which you develop your point of view on this issue. Support your position with reasoning and examples taken from your reading, studies, experience, or observations.

DO NOT WRITE YOUR ESSAY IN YOUR TEST BOOK. You will receive credit only for what you write on your answer sheet.

BEGIN WRITING YOUR ESSAY ON THE ANSWER SHEET.

IF YOU FINISH BEFORE TIME IS CALLED, YOU MAY CHECK YOUR WORK ON THIS SECTION ONLY. DO NOT TURN TO ANY OTHER SECTION IN THE TEST.

SECTION 1—ESSAY

Time—25 minutes

SECTION 1—ESSAY

Time—25 minutes

SECTION 2

Turn to Section 2 of your answer sheet to answer the questions in this section.

Time—25 Minutes
24 Questions

Directions: For each question in this section, select the best answer from among the choices given and fill in the corresponding oval on the answer sheet.

Each sentence below has one or two blanks, each blank indicating that something has been omitted. Beneath the sentence are five words or sets of words labeled A through E. Choose the word or set of words that, when inserted in the sentence, best fits the meaning of the sentence as a whole.

Example:

Eliza felt ----- when her boss asked her to work seven weekends in a row but ----- when her work earned her a promotion.

(A) enervated . . weakened
(B) depressed . . intellectual
(C) advantageous . . salacious
(D) angry . . shopworn
(E) irate . . elated     ●

1. Decision-making during committee sessions occurred only through extensive -----, as committee members tended to argue their positions forcefully.

(A) indecision
(B) consensus
(C) judgment
(D) perception
(E) debate

2. Sharon urged Riley to stop being so -----; Riley always downplayed his sports achievements when in fact he was quite a skilled athlete.

(A) inappropriate
(B) humane
(C) talkative
(D) conceited
(E) modest

3. In business, success depends as much on a person's -----, or adherence to a code of ethics, as on financial savvy.

(A) reasoning
(B) consistency
(C) integrity
(D) separation
(E) identity

4. Using written materials to ----- complex concepts works best with learners who ----- strong reading comprehension skills.

(A) explain . . demonstrate
(B) approve . . exhibit
(C) review . . suggest
(D) illustrate . . lack
(E) confirm . . support

5. Many ----- of the realist view of international politics identify realism's belief that nations act in their own self-interest as the ----- reason why they adopt this theoretical approach.

(A) supporters . . pivotal
(B) critics . . central
(C) proponents . . questionable
(D) reviewers . . minor
(E) censors . . primary

6. The lobbyist's success came partly from his striking ability to ----- his colleagues; his leadership style raised awareness and spurred others to take action on important issues.

(A) reprehend
(B) exonerate
(C) galvanize
(D) cajole
(E) abase

GO ON TO THE NEXT PAGE

SECTION 2

7. The investigators described Harold's plan as ----- and -----, because it was secret and implemented slowly over time, in a very subtle manner.

(A) clandestine . . reproachful
(B) surreptitious . . insidious
(C) inexcusable . . unmistakable
(D) zealous . . persevering
(E) devious . . contemptible

8. Because the professor has been so overbearing in campus faculty meetings, it is difficult to reconcile this ----- behavior with her ----- in the classroom.

(A) vacuous . . temerity
(B) despotic . . peevishness
(C) imperious . . complaisance
(D) retiring . . evanescence
(E) haughty . . competence

GO ON TO THE NEXT PAGE

SECTION 2

Directions: Each passage below is followed by questions based on its content. Answer the questions on the basis of what is stated or implied in each passage and in any introductory material that may be provided.

Questions 9–10 are based on the following passage.

My messenger, sent to the mines, has returned with specimens of the gold; he dismounted in a sea of upturned faces. As he drew forth the yellow lumps from his pockets, and passed them around among the eager crowd, the doubts, which had lingered till now, fled. The excitement produced was intense, and many were soon busy in their hasty preparations for a departure to the gold mines. Husband and wife were both packing up; the blacksmith dropped his hammer, the carpenter his plane, the mason his trowel, the farmer his sickle, and the baker his loaf. All were off for the mines, some on horses, some on carts, and some on crutches. An American woman, who had recently established a boardinghouse here, pulled up stakes, and was off before her lodgers had even time to pay their bills.

9. Based on the information in the passage, the response to the messenger's specimens can best be described as

(A) totally outraged
(B) intensely excited
(C) vaguely interested
(D) moderately irritated
(E) coolly indifferent

10. In line 10, The reference to "some on crutches" serves to suggest the

(A) competitive nature of individuals who journeyed to the gold mines and were unwilling to help injured travelers
(B) degree of difficult terrain that individuals needed to cover on trips to the gold mines
(C) types of injuries that often occurred when individuals journeyed to reach the gold mines
(D) types of medical care that were available to individuals during their travels to the gold mines
(E) enthusiasm with which people took off for the gold mines, even if they could scarcely walk

Questions 11–12 are based on the following passage.

All of Shakespeare's plays abound with instances of his excellence in distinguishing characters. However, his merit in distinguishing characters appears most conspicuously by comparing two opposite characters who happen to be placed in similar circumstances. None of Shakespeare's characters seems to agree so much in situation, and to differ so much in disposition, as Richard III and Macbeth. Both are soldiers, and both are usurpers. Both attain the throne by the same means—treason and murder. Both lose the throne, too, in the same manner: in battle against the person claiming it as lawful heir. But Shakespeare ascribed opposite principles and motives to the same designs and actions of these characters. Richard and Macbeth, as represented by Shakespeare, agree in nothing but their fortunes.

11. The passage mentions the similarities between Richard III and Macbeth in order to emphasize the point that

(A) because of their similar personalities, these characters find themselves in similar circumstances
(B) because they are both created by Shakespeare, these characters share similar designs and actions
(C) despite their similar circumstances, these two characters have very different dispositions
(D) despite their similar fates in both losing their thrones, these characters manage to amass large fortunes
(E) because of their similar situations, these characters have identical principles and motives

12. Based on the information in the passage, the characters of Richard III and Macbeth share all of the following EXCEPT

(A) they are both soldiers
(B) both lost their thrones in battle
(C) both attained their thrones by treason
(D) both became kings
(E) both were consumed by jealousy

GO ON TO THE NEXT PAGE

SECTION 2

Directions: The passages below are followed by questions based on their content; questions following a pair of related passages may also be based on the relationship between the paired passages. Answer the questions on the basis of what is stated or implied in the passages and in any introductory material that may be provided.

Questions 13–24 are based on the following passages.

These two passages discuss scientific views regarding the relationship between metabolism and longevity. Both passages are adapted from scientific essays.

Passage 1

In a culture prone to idealizing the benefits of youth, it makes sense that scientific effort would be expended toward understanding factors that reverse the aging process and increase human longevity. Scientists who study *senescence*, the process of aging, have determined that one primary factor affecting longevity in organisms is the rate of the organism's metabolism.

According to University of Chicago scientists Leonid Gavrilov and Natalia Gavrilova, aging involves multiple processes that contribute to the deterioration of our health and, ultimately, to our deaths. As our cells age, they become less able to respond to stress, and they become more vulnerable to disease. This vulnerability increases with the rate of an organism's metabolism, claims biomedical researcher Denham Harmon, whose pioneering work formed the foundation for his "free radical" theory of aging.

Through his research, which began in the 1950s, Harmon theorized that certain harmful chemicals found in cells were responsible in part for the aging process. These chemicals are known as *free radicals* and are generated as byproducts when our cells perform routine metabolic functions, such as producing energy. Free radicals differ from normal molecules within the body because they have an incomplete number of electrons. Normal molecules contain negatively charged electrons that orbit in pairs around a positively charged nucleus. Free radicals have lost one of the electrons in one or more of their electron pairs. They literally "steal" electrons from other molecules in the body in order to restore their broken electron pairs.

Free radicals within our cells are very reactive and cause damage that can eventually kill the cell. The process through which a free radical steals electrons from other molecules is known as *oxidation*, and it produces a destructive chain reaction. Normal molecules lose their electrons to free radicals and then become free radicals themselves, in turn stealing electrons from other molecules in a vicious cycle. As free radical cell damage accumulates within the human body, according to Harmon, it accelerates the aging process.

Because free radicals are produced as part of the normal process of metabolism, Harmon hypothesized that organisms with faster metabolisms were more likely to age quickly. Organisms with fast or high metabolisms produce free radicals at a faster rate, thereby accumulating more free radicals within their cells. Thus, in this view, the *rate* of an organism's metabolism is responsible for the length of its life span.

This metabolic rate theory has several important implications. The most obvious of these is that a slower metabolism is important for increasing life span. Organisms with faster metabolisms produce higher levels of free radicals, which damage the cells and lead to disease. Organisms with slower metabolisms naturally produce lower levels of free radicals and are less subject to the stress caused by oxidation.

Another implication of the theory is the importance of reducing the levels of free radicals existing in an organism. Free radicals can be counteracted by anti-oxidant compounds, particularly the vitamins A, C, and E. Supplementation with these anti-oxidants can thus be important for promoting longevity and improving overall health.

Passage 2

The traditional theory on longevity and metabolism holds that longevity is most strongly affected by the rate of an organism's metabolism. Faster metabolic rates are believed to produce higher levels of free radicals in the system, which, in turn, accelerate aging. Recent discoveries, however, have revealed gaps in the theory that compel scientists to look for better explanations.

One researcher, Anja Brunet of the University of Minnesota, studies the relationship between metabolic rates and longevity in bats and shrews, a relative of bats. Author Jennifer Amie notes that Brunet's initial findings confirmed the hypothesis that shorter life spans are correlated with increased levels of free radicals. Brunet documented that shrews produce about twice as many free radicals as bats, and they live about one-tenth as long as bats do. However, as Amie points out, Brunet's research did not confirm the notion that longevity is correlated with metabolic rate. Both bats and shrews were determined to have approximately the same metabolic rates, despite the vast differences in their life spans.

Scientific studies conducted on mice in the United Kingdom further disprove the hypothesis that high metabolisms are linked to shorter life spans. Author Helen Pearson notes that, in 2004, a group of researchers led by John Speakman at the University of Aberdeen documented that mice with the highest metabolic rates lived more than 30 percent longer than mice with the slowest

GO ON TO THE NEXT PAGE

metabolisms in an experimental group. Speakman's team was surprised by the findings, which show that higher metabolisms can lead to longer lives, at least in one species.

These discoveries, and others like them, have led scientists to formulate alternative theories on longevity, such as the metabolic-stability theory. One of the most prominent proponents of the metabolic-stability hypothesis is Harvard evolutionary biologist Lloyd Demetrius. According to author Jonathan Shaw, Demetrius claims that longevity is determined not by how fast our metabolism operates, but rather by how stable our levels of free radicals are. Some levels of free radicals appear to be necessary within an organism to promote communication between cells. Demetrius proposes that keeping free radical levels stable (within an optimal range) may be more important for longevity than simply reducing these levels across the board.

13. Which of the following best reflects the main idea of Passage 1?

(A) The longevity of an organism is determined by the metabolic stability of that organism.
(B) Free radicals are highly reactive molecules that cause damage to our cells and accelerate aging.
(C) Bats and shrews have roughly equal metabolic rates, but, on average, bats live much longer than shrews.
(D) One major factor affecting the longevity of an organism is the organism's metabolic rate.
(E) Free radicals are produced as part of the normal metabolic process, so some free radicals in the body are beneficial.

14. Lines 7–10 ("According . . . deaths") suggest that

(A) aging in humans is brought about by several different biological phenomena
(B) free radicals in the body are responsible for slowing the aging process
(C) the aging process helps to protect our cells from vulnerability to disease
(D) human aging can be reversed through a process that boosts metabolism
(E) the aging process is most noticeable when it starts with a serious illness

15. In Passage 1, the reference to the "pioneering work" (line 14) of Denham Harmon is used to emphasize the

(A) importance of Denham's research for showing that higher metabolisms can lead to longer lives
(B) significance of Denham's research for developing a scientific definition of aging
(C) impact of Denham's efforts to disprove the hypothesis that metabolism is linked to life span
(D) significance of Denham's work in demonstrating that metabolic stability promotes longevity
(E) importance of Denham's contribution to developing the free radical theory of aging

16. According to the information in Passage 1, free radicals are

(A) similar to normal molecules in that they have an incomplete number of electrons
(B) generated as byproducts when our cells perform routine metabolic functions
(C) different from normal molecules because they contain positively charged nuclei
(D) created only during the division process of cancerous or other diseased cells
(E) signaling molecules that help cells to maintain equilibrium under stress

17. In Passage 1, the author suggests that free radicals produce a "destructive chain reaction" (line 31) because

(A) free radical activity impedes the oxidation process, which is vital to normal cell growth
(B) free radical cell damage can only be prevented by increasing the process of oxidation
(C) free radicals convert normal molecules into free radicals, thereby perpetuating destruction within the cell
(D) free radicals decompose during the oxidation process, leaving decaying matter within the cell wall
(E) free radicals multiply by stealing positively charged electrons from the nuclei of normal molecules

18. As it is used in line 50, the word "stress" most nearly means

(A) urgency
(B) anxiety
(C) damage
(D) pressure
(E) emphasis

19. Passage 2 mentions the metabolic rates of bats and shrews (lines 72–74) ("Both bats . . . spans") primarily in order to

(A) explain research that supports the theory that longevity is affected by metabolic stability
(B) describe evidence that refutes the notion that longevity is correlated with metabolic rate
(C) present data that confirms the hypothesis that longer life spans are correlated with increased levels of free radicals
(D) summarize findings that uphold the theory that high metabolisms are linked to longer life spans
(E) explain evidence that controverts the claim that free radicals are produced naturally within the cells

GO ON TO THE NEXT PAGE

SECTION 2

20. The author of Passage 2 implies that John Speakman's research team was "surprised by the findings" (line 82) of their research because

(A) their findings disproved the traditional hypothesis that high metabolisms produce shorter life spans
(B) their findings relied on innovative techniques for comparing metabolic rates in mice and bats
(C) the results of their experiments were inconclusive and shed no light on the factors affecting longevity
(D) the team used questionable procedures for measuring the metabolic rates in mice
(E) their findings documented that mice with slow metabolisms live longer than mice with high metabolisms

21. According to Passage 2, biologist Lloyd Demetrius supports which of the following as an important factor in affecting longevity?

(A) The stability of free radical levels within cells
(B) An organism's genetic predisposition to contract disease
(C) The rate at which a cell converts free radicals to normal molecules
(D) The speed of an organism's metabolism
(E) An individual's hereditary history

22. Based on the information provided in Passage 2, Lloyd Demetrius would most likely agree with which of the following statements?

(A) Reducing overall levels of free radicals is important for promoting longevity.
(B) It is impossible to determine the optimal range of free radicals within a cell.
(C) Anti-oxidant supplementation is important for keeping free radical levels stable.
(D) The rate of an organism's metabolism determines its life span.
(E) Free radicals have some beneficial biological functions.

23. Passage 1 is unlike Passage 2 in that Passage 1

(A) presents alternatives to the traditional theory on longevity and metabolism
(B) rejects the notion that harmful chemicals in the cells are responsible for aging
(C) explains flaws in the theory that longevity is determined by metabolic stability
(D) recommends anti-oxidant supplementation as a means of promoting longevity
(E) describes gaps in the theory that metabolic rate influences longevity

24. Which of the following scenarios would support the argument of Passage 2 but NOT Passage 1?

(A) A study finds that rats with the shortest life spans have the greatest incidence of obesity.
(B) Research conducted on human volunteers shows that individuals with fast metabolisms have an increased incidence of heart disease.
(C) A scientific experiment proves that vitamin A helps reduce levels of harmful free radicals in bats.
(D) A research study demonstrates that stable levels of free radicals are linked to longer life spans in laboratory mice.
(E) An experiment disproves the claim that bats and shrews have relatively equal metabolic rates.

S T O P

IF YOU FINISH BEFORE TIME IS CALLED, YOU MAY CHECK YOUR WORK ON THIS TEST ONLY. DO NOT TURN TO ANY OTHER SECTION IN THIS TEST.

SECTION 3

Turn to Section 3 of your answer sheet to answer the questions in this section.

Time—25 Minutes
20 Questions

Directions: For this section, solve each problem and decide which is the best of the choices given. Fill in the corresponding oval on the answer sheet. You may use any available space for scratchwork.

Notes:

1. The use of a calculator is permitted. All numbers used are real numbers.

2. Figures that accompany problems in this test are intended to provide information useful in solving the problems. They are drawn as accurately as possible EXCEPT when it is stated in a specific problem that the figure is not drawn to scale. All figures lie in a plane unless otherwise indicated.

3. Unless otherwise specified, the domain of any function f is assumed to be the set of all real numbers x for which $f(x)$ is a real number.

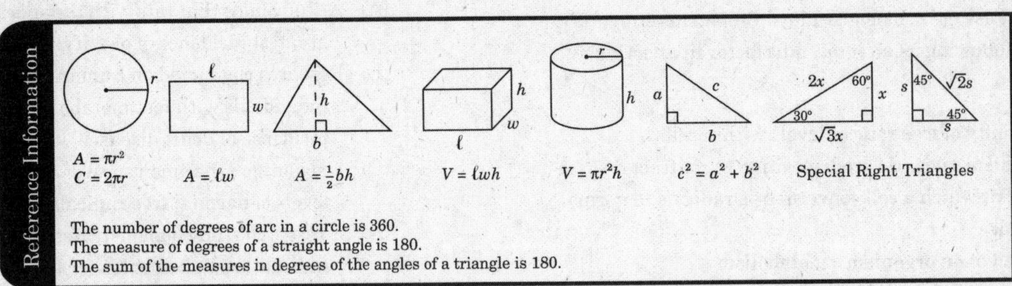

Reference Information
$A = \pi r^2$
$C = 2\pi r$
$A = \ell w$
$A = \frac{1}{2}bh$
$V = \ell wh$
$V = \pi r^2 h$
$c^2 = a^2 + b^2$
Special Right Triangles
The number of degrees of arc in a circle is 360.
The measure of degrees of a straight angle is 180.
The sum of the measures in degrees of the angles of a triangle is 180.

1. If $2r + 8 = 4r + 2$, what is the value of r?

(A) -1
(B) 0
(C) 2
(D) 3
(E) 6

1, 4, 13, 40, . . .

2. The first term in the sequence above is 1, and each term after the first is determined by multiplying the preceding term by n and then adding s. What is the value of n?

(A) 1
(B) 3
(C) 4
(D) 8
(E) 9

DOLLS

Hair Color	Clothing
Brown	Dress
Black	Jumpsuit
Blonde	Pajamas
Red	Jeans

3. The table above shows the different hair colors and types of clothing for dolls that are available at Laura's Doll Shop. How many different combinations of hair color and clothing are possible?

(A) 8
(B) 16
(C) 20
(D) 35
(E) 42

GO ON TO THE NEXT PAGE

SECTION 3

4. For which of the following functions is it true that $f(-5) > f(5)$?

(A) $f(x) = 6x^2$
(B) $f(x) = 6$
(C) $f(x) = \frac{6}{x}$
(D) $f(x) = 6 - x^3$
(E) $f(x) = x^4 + 6$

5. The amount of dog food required to feed a dog per day is proportional to the weight of the dog. If 87 grams of dog food is required to feed a dog that weighs 5 kilograms, what amount of dog food, in grams, is needed to feed a dog weighing 9 kilograms?

(A) 91
(B) 107
(C) 117.6
(D) 123
(E) 156.6

6. If B is the midpoint of line segment AC, which of the following must be true?

I. $BC = AC - AB$

II. $4AB = 2AC$

III. $BC = \frac{1}{2}AB$

(A) I only
(B) II only
(C) III only
(D) I and II
(E) I, II, and III

7. If $3n = 7p$ and $7p = 12q$, what does n equal in terms of q ?

(A) $\frac{36}{49}q$
(B) $\frac{12}{7}q$
(C) $4q$
(D) $21p$
(E) $84p$

8. A total of a attendees participated in a conference. Each of the r conference rooms that were used for the meetings contained a total of c chairs. If one conference room had 5 empty chairs while all chairs in the remaining conference rooms were filled, which of the following expresses the relationship among r, c, and a ?

(A) $rc - 5 = a$
(B) $rc + 5 = a$
(C) $r + c + 5 = a$
(D) $ra = c + 5$
(E) $ra = c - 5$

GO ON TO THE NEXT PAGE

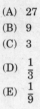

SECTION 3

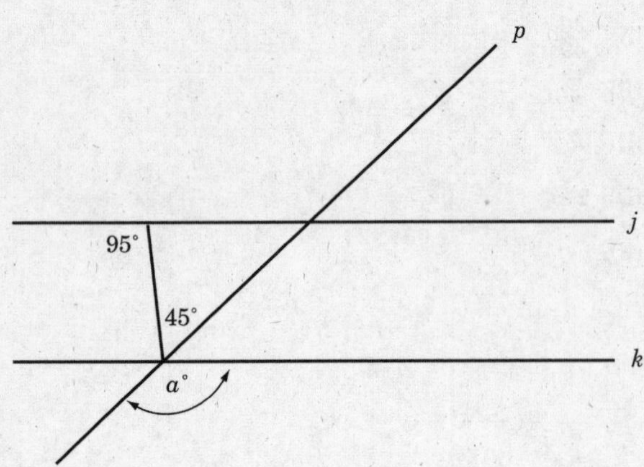

9. In the figure above, line j is parallel to line k. What is the value of a ?

(A) 140
(B) 135
(C) 130
(D) 115
(E) 50

$$4g^2 > (4g)^2$$

10. For what value of g is the statement above true?

(A) −2
(B) $\frac{1}{2}$
(C) 0
(D) 1
(E) For no value of g

11. Adam built a custom jeep with front wheels that have one-third the diameter of the back wheels. When Adam drives the car, how many revolutions does one of the front wheels make for each revolution made by one of the back wheels?

(A) 27
(B) 9
(C) 3
(D) $\frac{1}{3}$
(E) $\frac{1}{9}$

12. A set of integers contains e even numbers and o odd numbers. If a number is picked at random from this set, the probability that the number is even is $\frac{4}{7}$. What is the value of $\frac{o}{e}$?

(A) $\frac{4}{11}$
(B) $\frac{7}{11}$
(C) $\frac{3}{4}$
(D) $\frac{4}{3}$
(E) $\frac{11}{4}$

GO ON TO THE NEXT PAGE

SECTION 3

13. The total cost d, in dollars, of printing n copies of a certain technical manual is given by the function $d(n) = \frac{450n - 150}{n} + h$, where h is a constant and $n \le 200$.

If 30 copies of the technical manual are printed for a total cost of \$720, what is the value of h ?

(A) 160
(B) 275
(C) 305
(D) 445
(E) 700

14. For how many ordered pairs of positive integers (x, y) is $3x + 5y \le 16$?

(A) One
(B) Two
(C) Three
(D) Four
(E) Five

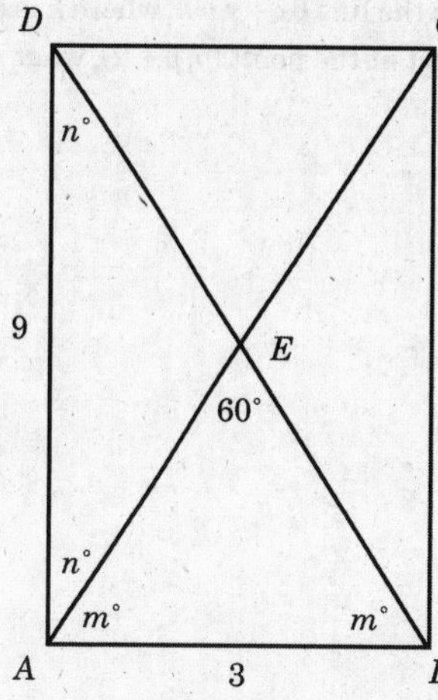

Note: Figure not drawn to scale.

15. In the figure above, $ABCD$ is a rectangle. How many units greater is the perimeter of ΔAED than the perimeter of ΔAEB ?

(A) 0
(B) 3
(C) 6
(D) 9
(E) 12

16. If a and b are positive consecutive even integers, where $b > a$, which of the following is equal to $a^2 + b^2$?

(A) $a^2 + 2$
(B) $a^2 + 2a$
(C) $a^2 + a + 2$
(D) $2(a^2 + 2a + 2)$
(E) $4(a^2 + a + 1)$

GO ON TO THE NEXT PAGE

SECTION 3

17. In the xy-plane, line m passes through the origin and is perpendicular to the line $6x + y = h$, where h is a constant. If the two lines intersect at the point $(p, p + 2)$, what is the value of p ?

(A) $-\frac{12}{5}$

(B) $-\frac{11}{5}$

(C) $\frac{5}{12}$

(D) $\frac{11}{7}$

(E) $\frac{12}{5}$

18. If the average (arithmetic mean) of a, b, and c is t, which of the following is the average of a, b, c, and d ?

(A) $\frac{3t+d}{4}$

(B) $\frac{3t+d}{3}$

(C) $\frac{t+d}{4}$

(D) $\frac{t+d}{3}$

(E) $\frac{3(t+d)}{4}$

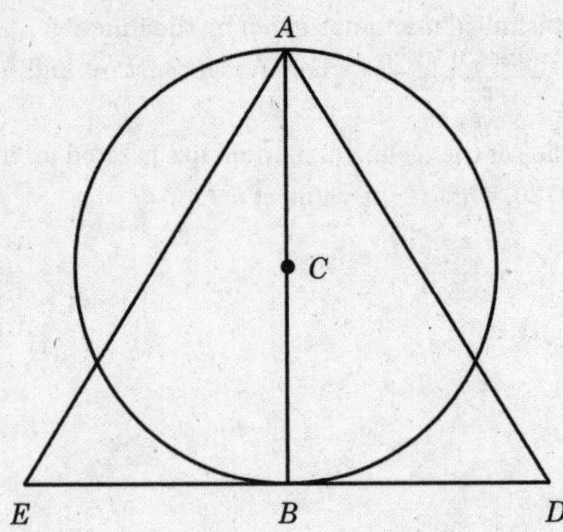

19. In the figure above, ΔADE is equilateral, with side of length $2\sqrt{3}$. If C is the center of the circle, then the area of the circle is

(A) $\frac{\sqrt{9}\pi}{4}$

(B) $\frac{2\pi}{3}$

(C) $\frac{9\pi}{4}$

(D) π

(E) $\frac{9\pi}{2}$

20. When 16 is divided by the positive integer m, the remainder is 4. How many different values of m are possible?

(A) One
(B) Two
(C) Three
(D) Four
(E) Five

S T O P

IF YOU FINISH BEFORE TIME IS CALLED, YOU MAY CHECK YOUR WORK ON THIS TEST ONLY. DO NOT TURN TO ANY OTHER SECTION IN THIS TEST.

SECTION 4

Turn to Section 4 of your answer sheet to answer the questions in this section.

Time—25 Minutes
24 Questions

Directions: For each question in this section, select the best answer from among the choices given and fill in the corresponding oval on the answer sheet.

Each sentence below has one or two blanks, each blank indicating that something has been omitted. Beneath the sentence are five words or sets of words labeled A through E. Choose the word or set of words that, when inserted in the sentence, best fits the meaning of the sentence as a whole.

Example:

Eliza felt ----- when her boss asked her to work seven weekends in a row but ----- when her work earned her a promotion.

(A) enervated . . weakened
(B) depressed . . intellectual
(C) advantageous . . salacious
(D) angry . . shopworn
(E) irate . . elated   

1. Over the summer, Karen had the impression that her co-workers agreed with her proposal for a fall park clean-up campaign; when September came, however, she realized that many ----- the idea.

(A) corrected
(B) prevented
(C) supported
(D) opposed
(E) accepted

2. In S. J. Forrester's novel *Talia*, the Italian heroine ----- her wealthy husband's family, admiring them to the point of blind devotion.

(A) overlooks
(B) educates
(C) distrusts
(D) idolizes
(E) scorns

3. The volume of fan mail that the talk show receives each week is a ----- the host's ability to connect with audiences and to make a real impact on viewers' lives.

(A) precursor to
(B) depiction of
(C) testament to
(D) revelation of
(E) rationale for

4. The engineering team found themselves paralyzed even though they knew that a systems failure was -----: multiple error alerts ----- the complete shutdown of the computer's circuitry within minutes.

(A) uncertain . . signaled
(B) unavoidable . . prevented
(C) imminent . . portended
(D) redundant . . disrupted
(E) possible . . accentuated

5. The defendant's history of miscreant behavior reflected such ----- motivations that even the most ----- judge would have refused to show him any leniency whatsoever.

(A) nefarious . . clement
(B) repugnant . . pernicious
(C) penitent . . propitious
(D) opprobrious . . abstemious
(E) unimpeachable . . reprehensible

GO ON TO THE NEXT PAGE

SECTION 4

Directions: The passages below are followed by questions based on their content; questions following a pair of related passages may also be based on the relationship between the paired passages. Answer the questions on the basis of what is stated or implied in the passages and in any introductory material that may be provided.

Questions 6–9 are based on the following passages.

Passage 1

In his best-known book, *Against Method*, philosopher of science Paul Feyerabend presents a keen attack on the notion that scientific progress can be furthered by one primary scientific method. Feyerabend's argument has been thought of as an "anything goes" approach. In reacting to the conventional view of scientific theory development, Feyerabend argues that human progress is much more likely to be promoted by scientific anarchy than by strict adherence to a single methodology. By "anarchy," Feyerabend does not mean a purely chaotic approach to science—far from it. Instead, he clarifies that knowledge can be best developed through combinations of different approaches that incorporate even seemingly irrational means. In Feyerabend's view, science cannot be advanced by adhering to a fixed set of rules or standards. He believes ultimately that "all methodologies, even the most obvious ones, have their limits."

Passage 2

Imre Lakatos was a Hungarian-born scholar whose work in the philosophy of science addressed, among other issues, the question of what constitutes effective *science*. How can we delineate scientific theories from nonscience approaches? This question was addressed first by Lakatos's predecessor, Karl Popper, who argued that theories could be classified as scientific only if they were capable of being disproved by evidence. If a theory could be formulated in such a way that experiments could be designed to disprove it, Popper believed, then that theory could be considered scientific.

Lakatos moved beyond Popper's view by arguing that one piece of contradictory evidence was not enough to prove an entire theory false. Certain aspects of the theory might still be viable. Lakatos proposed, therefore, that science should be comprised not of single theories but rather of sets of theories, or research programs, that continued to build upon an original core of knowledge. Only a *series* of theories could be evaluated as scientific or unscientific, in Lakatos's view, based on whether that set of theories met certain criteria.

6. Passage 1 and Passage 2 both address which of the following questions about science?

(A) How can human progress best be measured?
(B) What types of evidence can be used to disprove theories?
(C) What sorts of phenomena should science seek to explain?
(D) What types of approaches best promote scientific progress?
(E) How can scientific theories build up a core of basic knowledge?

7. Which of the following arguments about scientific theory is put forth in Passage 1 but not in Passage 2?

(A) Science cannot be advanced by adhering to a strict set of rules or standards.
(B) Theories can be classified as scientific only if they can be disproved by evidence.
(C) Scientific research programs should be built upon an original core of knowledge.
(D) Only a series of theories can be evaluated as scientific or unscientific.
(E) Human progress is most likely to be promoted by adherence to a single methodology.

8. The view of Karl Popper in Passage 2 differs from that of Paul Feyerabend in Passage 1 in that Popper believes that

(A) scientific theories cannot be delineated from nonscientific approaches
(B) one piece of contradictory evidence is not enough to prove an entire theory false
(C) science should be developed through a purely chaotic approach
(D) only specific types of theories can be classified as scientific
(E) scientific approaches should incorporate even seemingly irrational means

9. Imre Lakatos from Passage 2 would most likely respond to the argument of Paul Feyerabend from Passage 1 by

(A) accepting Feyerabend's argument on the grounds that all scientific methods should be considered acceptable
(B) rejecting Feyerabend's argument on the grounds that science should not adhere to a single methodology
(C) rejecting Feyerabend's argument on the grounds that science should be developed by an approach that emphasizes sets of theories
(D) accepting Feyerabend's argument on the grounds that his argument can easily be proven
(E) accepting Feyerabend's argument on the grounds that scientific progress is best promoted by an anarchic approach

GO ON TO THE NEXT PAGE

SECTION 4

Directions: Each passage below is followed by questions based on its content. Answer the questions on the basis of what is stated or implied in each passage and in any introductory material that may be provided.

Questions 10–15 are based on the following passage.

This passage is adapted from a work by a European author published during the late 1800s.

I was born in or near Paris, in the year 1844. My father was a fairly prosperous man of business—a general merchant, to be precise, who dealt largely in shoes; but when I was about ten years old, my mother, in consequence of certain domestic differences, took me to live with her at Montreux, and other places in Switzerland, where I was educated.

Boys soon begin to display their bent, and mine, curiously enough, was in the direction of geology. I was constantly bringing home pieces of stone and minerals picked up in the streets and on the mountains, and asking questions about their origin and history. My dear mother encouraged me in this, and later on I frequently went to Freiburg, in the Black Forest, to get a practical insight into smelting.* When I was about nineteen, however, a message arrived from my father, directing me to return to France and to report myself as a conscript**; but against this my mother resolutely set her face. I fancy my father wanted me to take up the army as a career, but, in deference to my mother's wishes, I remained with her in Switzerland for some time longer.

My mother and I had many talks about my future, and she at length advised me to take a trip to the East, and to see what the experience of travel would do for me. Neither of us had any definite project in view, but at length my mother gave me about 7,000 francs and I set out for Cairo, intending eventually to visit and make myself acquainted with the French possessions in the Far East. My idea was to visit such places as Tonkin, Cochin China, Madagascar, Mauritius, and Seychelles. My mother was of the opinion that if I saw a bit of the world in this way, I would be more inclined to settle down at home with her at the end of my wanderings.

The primary cause of my going away was a little love episode. Whilst at Montreux, I fell in love with a charming young lady at a boarding-school near my home. She was the daughter of some high personage in the court of Russia—but exactly what position he held I cannot say. My mother was quite charmed with the young lady and viewed our attachment with delight. But when my father heard of the matter, he raised a decided objection to it and ordered me to return to France and join the army. He had, as I have previously intimated, made his own plans for my future, even to the point of deciding upon a future wife for me, as is customary in France; but I resolutely declined to conform to his wishes in this respect, and my mother quite sided with me. I never quite knew how he got to hear of my love affair, but I conclude that my mother must have mentioned it to him. I only stayed a few days in the wonderful metropolis of Egypt; its noises, its cosmopolitanism, its crowds—these, and many other considerations, drove me from the city, and I set out for Singapore. I had not been many days in that place when I was casually introduced to a Dutch pearl-fisher named Peter Jensen. I am under the impression that Jensen told me he came from Copenhagen, but in those days the adjective "Dutchman" had a very wide application. If a man hailed from Holland, Sweden, Norway, or any neighboring country, he was always referred to as a Dutchman. This was in 1863. We grew quite friendly, Jensen and I, and he told me he had a small forty-ton schooner at Batavia, in which sturdy little craft he used to go on his pearling expeditions.

"I am now," he said, "about to organize a trip to some untouched pearling grounds off the south of New Guinea, but have not sufficient capital to defray the preliminary expenses."

This hint I took, and I offered to join him. He at once agreed, and we commenced our preparations without delay—in Batavia.

* The melting or fusing of ores to separate their metallic components

** One drafted into the armed services

10. The passage is primarily concerned with the narrator's

(A) study of stones and minerals
(B) work as a pearl fisher
(C) travels as a young adult
(D) first love affair
(E) first visit to Egypt

11. The narrator includes the phrase "against this my mother resolutely set her face" (lines 15–16) to emphasize the fact that the narrator's mother

(A) was resistant to loaning her son money for his travels
(B) was very opposed to having her son register for military service
(C) strongly discouraged the narrator's developing interest in geology
(D) was reluctant to allow her son to leave home to travel to the East
(E) was insistent that her son return to France and register for the draft

GO ON TO THE NEXT PAGE

SECTION 4

12. As used in line 16, "fancy" most nearly means

(A) desire
(B) embellish
(C) suppose
(D) adorn
(E) like

13. The narrator suggests that his mother ultimately supported his trip to the Far East because she

(A) wished to see her son separated from the young lady he had fallen in love with
(B) was convinced that her son would fare well as a pearl fisher
(C) believed that her son's travels would allow him to develop his interest in geology
(D) hoped that after her son saw the world, he would return home and settle down
(E) believed that her son could escape the draft by leaving the country undetected

14. The narrator's attitude toward his father's plans for his future (lines 37–41) ("He had . . . with me") can best be described as

(A) obediently conforming
(B) begrudgingly submissive
(C) thoroughly enraged
(D) sarcastically defiant
(E) steadfastly resistant

15. The narrator implies in the final paragraph that he

(A) helped enable Peter Jensen's pearling expedition to New Guinea by contributing money to pay for the trip
(B) chose not to join Peter Jensen on his pearl fishing trip because he was unsure of Jensen's expertise as a pearl fisher
(C) convinced Peter Jensen to change the location of his pearling trip from New Guinea to Batavia
(D) was unable to join Peter Jensen on his pearling voyage because he lacked the funds to pay for the trip
(E) offered to join Peter Jensen on his pearling expedition only after ensuring that Jensen's schooner was in fact safe

GO ON TO THE NEXT PAGE

SECTION 4

Questions 16–24 are based on the following passage.

The exhibit Masterworks in the Polaroid Collection, shown at the Clarence Kennedy Gallery, is a display of photographic excellence in its grandest sense. Of particular interest in the exhibit are two photographs that represent confrontations of human oppression. The first is Edward Weston's *William Edmonson, Sculptor*, taken in Nashville in 1941. This portrait is striking in its simplistic portrayal of Edmonson's life. Edmonson, a poor elderly black man, sits in tattered clothes upon a chair in front of his work area. He seems to be taking a rest from his work, and he confronts the camera with an almost indecipherable expression on his face. Is it a look of consternation? Or one of amusement?

Weston reveals Edmonson's social status to us directly—the clothing and ragged shoes are more than we need to understand how poor Edmonson has probably been all of his life, and how hard he has struggled to earn his living. But Edmonson's expression seems to tell us that he has removed himself from his situation somehow. Indeed, the imagery in the photograph implies Weston's intent to make us see that Edmonson *is* soon to leave his situation. The shadows in back of Edmonson's chair become a past that Edmonson, now sitting in light, may soon leave behind. Two stone carvings, one lying horizontally across Edmonson's workbench and the other standing upright next to it, seem reminiscent of tombstones—perhaps they are tombstones; we cannot tell. They lurk in the shadows behind Edmonson also. In front of them, to Edmonson's left, is a shroudlike covering. It is tacked to the roof of Edmonson's work place, almost waiting to be released.

Edmonson seems peaceful and somehow resigned to his fate. The ladder to his right, leading upward out of the picture frame, points to a life beyond in which Edmonson will be free of his suffering. Weston himself seems somewhat removed from Edmonson's plight, in that he places some distance between himself and his subject, but this is necessary if he is to reveal the surroundings that tell us so much about Edmonson. The portrait is so candid that we feel empathy for Edmonson despite Weston's distance.

Margaret Bourke-White's portrait *South African Diamond Miners* reminds us of where Edmonson's grandsons might be, almost twenty years later. Nearly two decades have passed, but have things really changed? Bourke-White's portrait is more than twice the size of Weston's, which makes her subjects almost lifelike. This photograph reveals two black miners, one standing in front of the other, both gazing intently at something that seems to be taking place near them. There is an ominous quality to the image—we're not sure of what has happened, and the men's reactions only confuse us. The second man appears disturbed, almost afraid. The first man seems to be more in control and self-possessed, for his expression is one of near amusement and complacency. We sense the power that the first man possesses, at least in relation to his fellow worker behind him. The whistle he wears around his neck signifies authority, particularly when contrasted to the scarf that is tied around the second man's neck.

Both men drip with sweat that covers them entirely. They've been working hard, and they are obviously strong and solid. Bourke-White's angle in the photograph is an extreme close-up shot from slightly below eye level, so that we are almost looking up at these men who fill the entire frame. Their muscular structures seem to symbolize a strength and a fearlessness that signals their removal from Edmonson's oppression. At the same time, the second man's disturbed expression contradicts the confident message of the miners' physicality. Bourke-White's portrayal of these men makes us question whether their status in 1957 is an improvement over that of Edmonson several decades before.

16. The author's attitude regarding the Masterworks in the Polaroid Collection exhibit can best be described as

(A) amused
(B) admiring
(C) disturbed
(D) confused
(E) disappointed

17. The author suggests in lines 8–11 ("He seems . . . amusement") that the expression of William Edmonson in his portrait

(A) is shrouded in shadow
(B) reveals Edmonson's confusion
(C) reflects an air of consternation
(D) is difficult to interpret
(E) shows Edmonson's sense of humor

18. Based on the information in the passage, William Edmonson is most likely

(A) out of touch with his feelings
(B) wealthy and successful
(C) prone to angry outbursts
(D) a well-known sculptor
(E) extremely poor

19. As used in line 28, the phrase "resigned to" most nearly means

(A) accepting of
(B) relinquishing of
(C) rejecting of
(D) dissatisfied with
(E) releasing of

GO ON TO THE NEXT PAGE

SECTION 4

20. The reference to Edmonson's grandsons (lines 38–39) ("reminds us . . . later") implies that

(A) by 1957 Edmonson's own grandsons might have been about the same age as the men in the photograph
(B) Margaret Bourke-White traveled from Nashville to South Africa to photograph Edmonson's grandsons
(C) Edmonson was originally from South Africa and had left relatives behind when he moved to Nashville
(D) Edmonson started his career in the family mining business but eventually left mining to work as a sculptor
(E) Edmonson's grandsons were able to pull their families out of poverty by working as diamond miners

21. In context, "intently" (line 43) most nearly means

(A) distractedly
(B) practically
(C) willingly
(D) attentively
(E) furtively

22. The author mentions the "ominous quality" of Bourke-White's photograph (line 44) in order to

(A) emphasize that Bourke-White purposely composed her photographs to convey a negative image to viewers
(B) contrast the foreboding tone of Bourke-White's work with the positive, uplifting tone of Weston's photographs
(C) demonstrate that Bourke-White is able to manipulate light in her photographs so as to convey particularly emotions
(D) explain why the two men in the photograph both have disturbed and confused looks on their faces
(E) emphasize that the subjects of the photograph appear to be reacting to an event that is unclear for the viewer

23. According to the passage, the muscular structures of the two men in Bourke-White's photograph (lines 57–59) ("Their muscular . . . oppression") seem to symbolize

(A) confusion and bewilderment
(B) disturbance and concern
(C) strength and fearlessness
(D) timidity and caution
(E) relief and exhilaration

24. In lines 59–61 ("At the same . . . physicality"), the author mentions the contradiction revealed in the second man's expression in order to emphasize the point that

(A) it is not clear from Weston's photograph exactly what the relationship is between Edmonson and the two miners portrayed by Bourke-White
(B) the men in Bourke-White's portrait are actually quite fearful, despite their outward appearance of strength and confidence
(C) it is not clear from Bourke-White's photograph whether the status of the miners has improved over that of Edmonson in Weston's portrait
(D) the first man in Bourke-White's photograph seems to be an authority of some sort in the mines
(E) the miners in Bourke-White's photograph have been hard at work, as is evidenced by the fact that they are both sweating

STOP

IF YOU FINISH BEFORE TIME IS CALLED, YOU MAY CHECK YOUR WORK ON THIS TEST ONLY. DO NOT TURN TO ANY OTHER SECTION IN THIS TEST.

SECTION 5

Turn to Section 5 of your answer sheet to answer the questions in this section.

Time—25 Minutes
18 Questions

Directions: For this section, solve each problem and decide which is the best of the choices given. Fill in the corresponding oval on the answer sheet. You may use any available space for scratchwork.

Notes:

1. The use of a calculator is permitted. All numbers used are real numbers.
2. Figures that accompany problems in this test are intended to provide information useful in solving the problems. They are drawn as accurately as possible EXCEPT when it is stated in a specific problem that the figure is not drawn to scale. All figures lie in a plane unless otherwise indicated.
3. Unless otherwise specified, the domain of any function f is assumed to be the set of all real numbers x for which $f(x)$ is a real number.

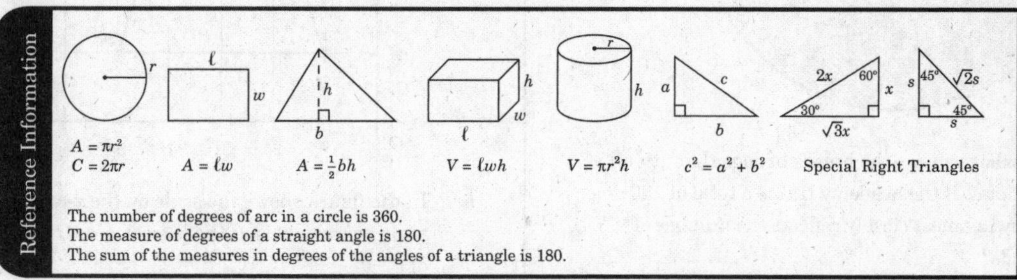

1. If $p - q = 5$, what is the value of $p - q - 7$?

(A) -2
(B) 0
(C) 1
(D) 2
(E) 3

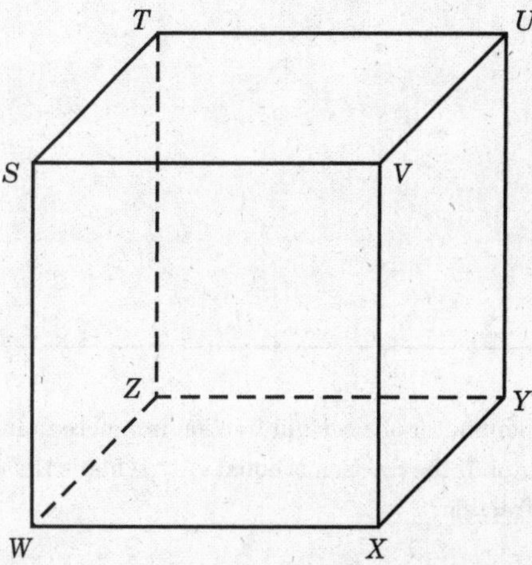

2. On the cube in the figure above, each of the following points is the same distance from S as it is from U EXCEPT

(A) T
(B) Z
(C) Y
(D) X
(E) V

GO ON TO THE NEXT PAGE

SECTION 5

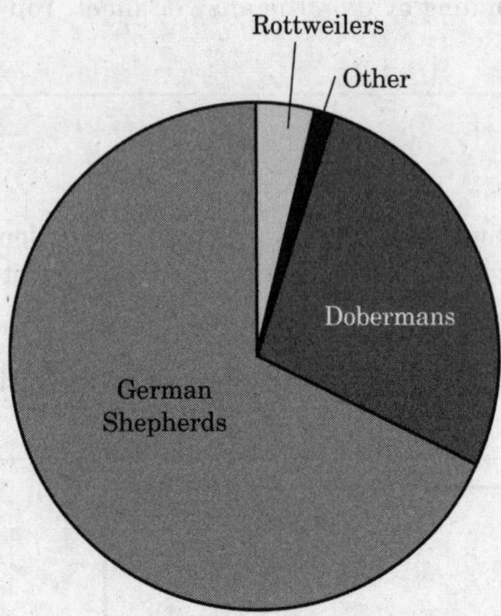

3. The circle graph above shows the breeds of dogs that attend a dog training academy. If the academy trains a total of 100 dogs, which of the following most closely reflects the number of German shepherds?

(A) 1
(B) 5
(C) 21
(D) 54
(E) 73

4. The denominator of a certain fraction is 5 more than the numerator. If the fraction is equal to $\frac{2}{3}$, what is the numerator of this fraction?

(A) 6
(B) 8
(C) 9
(D) 10
(E) 15

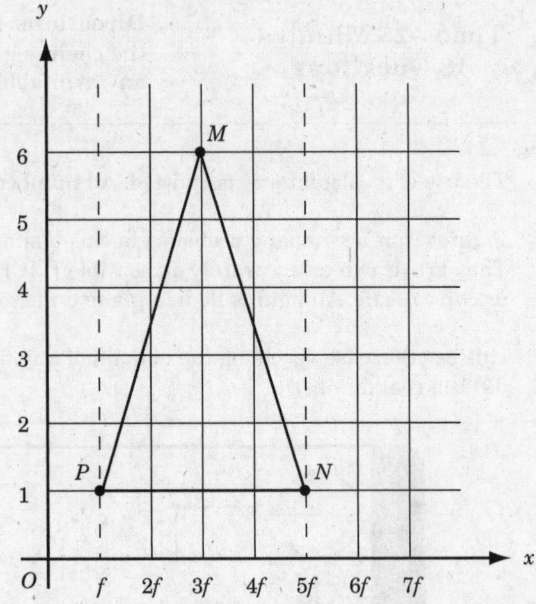

5. In the figure above, the scale on the x-axis is different from the scale on the y-axis. If the area of ΔMNP is 20, what is the value of f?

(A) $\frac{4}{9}$

(B) $\frac{4}{5}$

(C) $\frac{5}{4}$

(D) $\frac{3}{2}$

(E) 2

GO ON TO THE NEXT PAGE

SECTION 5

6. If x and y are positive and $9x^2y^{-1} = 81x$, what is x^{-1} in terms of y?

(A) $\frac{y}{9}$

(B) $\frac{y}{72}$

(C) $\frac{\sqrt{y}}{9}$

(D) $\frac{1}{9y}$

(E) $\frac{1}{72y}$

7. Priscilla and Gretchen leave the library at the same time and ride their bikes for 2 hours. Priscilla rides due west at the average rate of 5 miles per hour and Gretchen rides due south at the average rate of 12 miles per hour. What is the straight-line distance between them, in miles, at the end of the 2 hours?

(A) 2
(B) 10
(C) 13
(D) 24
(E) 26

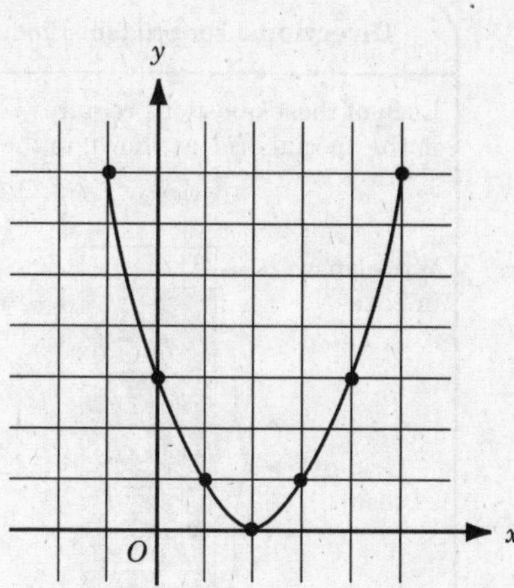

8. The figure above shows the graph of a quadratic function f that has a minimum value at the point (2, 0). If $f(s) = f(4)$, which of the following could be the value of s?

(A) −2
(B) −1
(C) 0
(D) 2
(E) 5

GO ON TO THE NEXT PAGE

SECTION 5

Directions: For Student-Produced Response questions 9–18, use the grids on the answer sheet.

Each of these questions requires you to solve the problem and enter your answer by marking the ovals in the special grid, as shown in the examples below. You may use any available space for scratchwork.

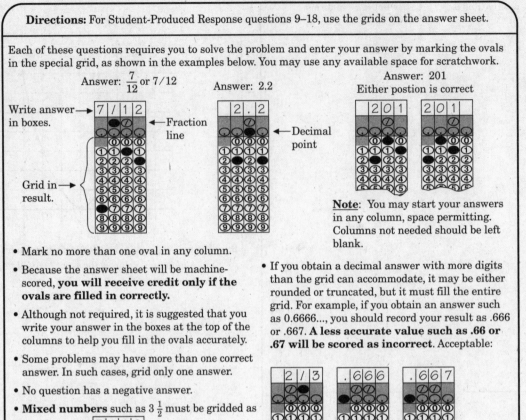

Answer: $\frac{7}{12}$ or 7/12

Answer: 2.2

Answer: 201
Either postion is correct

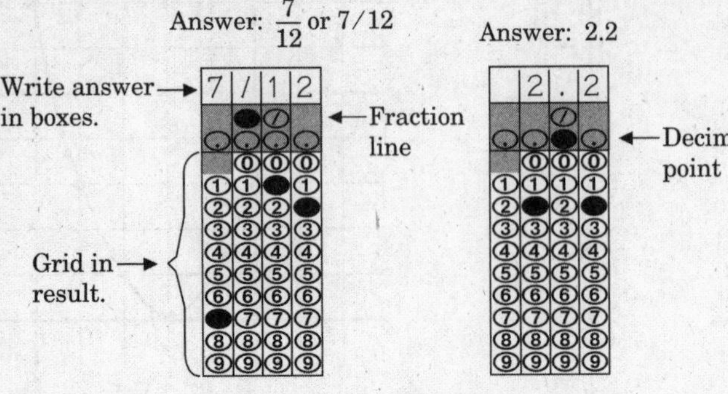

Note: You may start your answers in any column, space permitting. Columns not needed should be left blank.

- Mark no more than one oval in any column.
- Because the answer sheet will be machine-scored, **you will receive credit only if the ovals are filled in correctly.**
- Although not required, it is suggested that you write your answer in the boxes at the top of the columns to help you fill in the ovals accurately.
- Some problems may have more than one correct answer. In such cases, grid only one answer.
- No question has a negative answer.
- **Mixed numbers** such as $3\frac{1}{2}$ must be gridded as 3.5 or 7/2. (If 3 1 / 2 is gridded, it will be interpreted as $\frac{31}{2}$, not $3\frac{1}{2}$.)
- If you obtain a decimal answer with more digits than the grid can accommodate, it may be either rounded or truncated, but it must fill the entire grid. For example, if you obtain an answer such as 0.6666..., you should record your result as .666 or .667. **A less accurate value such as .66 or .67 will be scored as incorrect**. Acceptable:

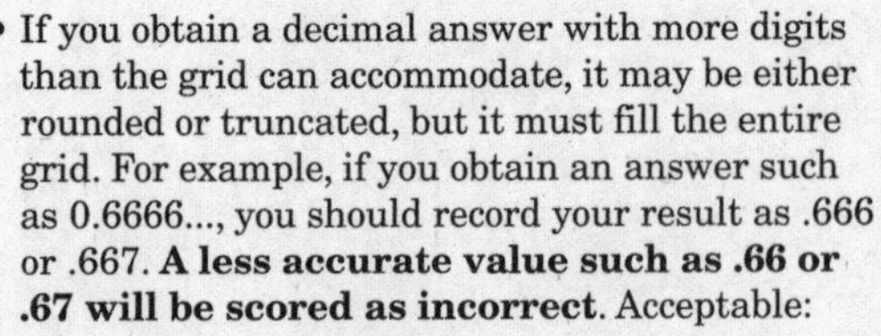

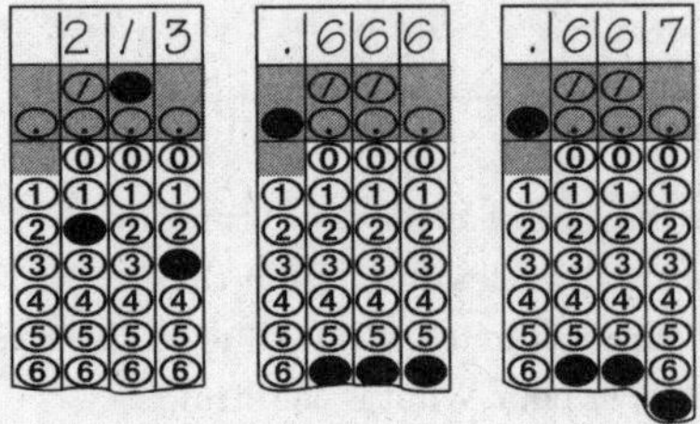

9. A class of 10 students is planning a 7-week experiment. Each student will need to use 5 sheets of graph paper per week to write up the results of the experiment. If the graph paper is sold only in 40-sheet packages, how many packages must the class buy for the experiment?

$$|10 - r| = 9$$
$$|r - 7| = 12$$

10. What is the value of r that satisfies both equations above?

GO ON TO THE NEXT PAGE

SECTION 5

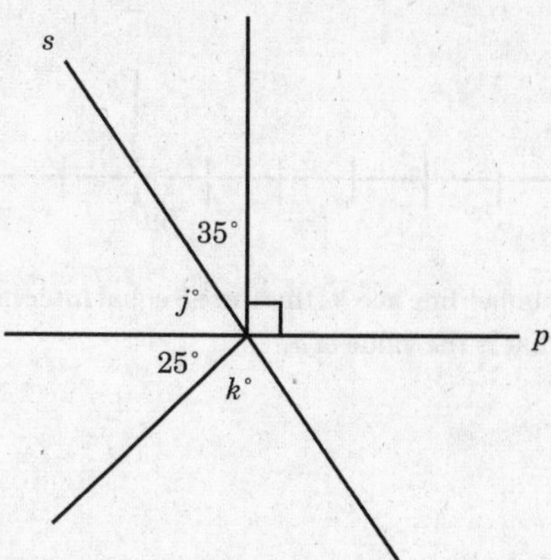

11. What is the value of k in the figure above?

12. The median of a set of 7 consecutive integers is 27. What is the smallest of these 7 integers?

13. Let the function f be defined by $f(x) = x - 3$. If $2f(s) = 10$, what is the value of $f(4s)$?

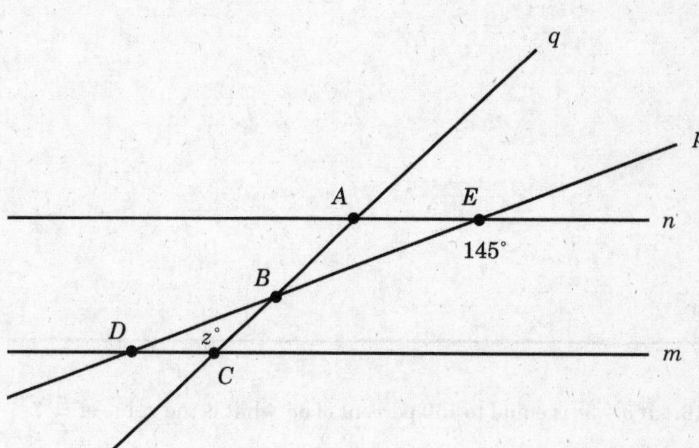

14. In the figure above, line n is parallel to line m. If the lengths of AE and AB are equal, what is the value of z ?

GO ON TO THE NEXT PAGE

SECTION 5

15. A bucket contains $\frac{1}{6}$ of a pound of blue-colored sand. It is then filled to a weight of 1 lb with a mixture that contains equal amounts of blue, red, and yellow sand. What fraction of the final mixture is blue sand?

16. If $p + 3r$ is equal to 150 percent of $6r$, what is the value of $\frac{p}{r}$?

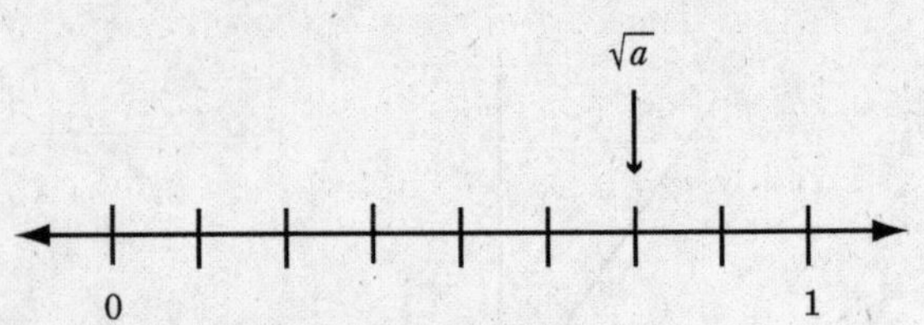

17. On the number line above, there are 8 equal intervals between 0 and 1. What is the value of a ?

18. In the xy-coordinate plane, the distance between point $M(9, 12)$ and point $N(x, 12)$ is 3. What is one possible value of x ?

S T O P

IF YOU FINISH BEFORE TIME IS CALLED, YOU MAY CHECK YOUR WORK ON THIS TEST ONLY. DO NOT TURN TO ANY OTHER SECTION IN THIS TEST.

SECTION 6

Turn to Section 6 of your answer sheet to answer the questions in this section.

Time—25 Minutes
35 Questions

Directions: For each question in this section, select the best answer from among the choices given.

The following sentences test correctness and effectiveness of expression. Part of each sentence or the entire sentence is underlined; beneath each sentence are five ways of phrasing the underlined material. Choice A repeats the original phrasing; the other four choices are different. If you think the original phrasing produces a better sentence than any of the alternatives, select choice A; if not, select one of the other choices.

In making your selection, follow the requirements of standard written English; that is, pay attention to grammar, choice of words, sentence construction, and punctuation. Your selection should result in the most effective sentence—clear and precise, without awkwardness or ambiguity.

Example:
In the poem "Ulysses" by Alfred, Lord Tennyson, the speaker says, "I cannot rest from travel," instead, he will live life to the fullest.

(A) "I cannot rest from travel," instead,
(B) "I cannot rest from travel"; instead,
(C) "I cannot rest from travel" instead,
(D) "I cannot rest from travel," upon which
(E) "I cannot rest from travel,"

1. The teacher working this hard to prepare for her class, she did not want her students to leave without learning something.

(A) The teacher working this hard to prepare for her class, she
(B) Working this hard to prepare for her class, the teacher felt she
(C) Having worked this hard to prepare for her class, the teacher
(D) To work this hard to prepare for her class, the teacher
(E) The teacher worked this hard to prepare for her class, so that she

2. After working all day in the scorching heat, the farm hands were as parched as if being stranded in the desert.

(A) if being
(B) having been
(C) if from being
(D) if they had been
(E) if they would have been

3. The beneficial effects of exercise, including lowering blood pressure and regulating body weight, has been widely recognized.

(A) has been widely recognized
(B) is being widely recognized
(C) have been widely recognized
(D) has been recognized in a widespread manner
(E) have been being recognized widely

4. The topic the focus group discussed, which was whether the organization's website proposal will adequately address all of the major issues of concern to members of the group.

(A) discussed, which was whether the organization's website proposal will adequately address
(B) discussed was if they would develop the website according to the proposal would this adequately address
(C) discussed was that the implementation of the website proposal would adequately address
(D) discussed was will developing the website based on the proposal mean the adequate addressing of
(E) discussed was whether the organization's website proposal would adequately address

GO ON TO THE NEXT PAGE

SECTION 6

5. University president Anne Banyon Quimby, the first woman to be elected to serve as head of the university's administration, achieving it just ten years after the first woman was elected as mayor of the city.

(A) Anne Banyon Quimby, the first woman to be elected to serve as head of the university's administration, achieving it
(B) Anne Banyon Quimby, the first woman to be elected to serve as head of the university's administration, and who achieved this
(C) Anne Banyon Quimby became the first woman to have been elected to serve as head of the university's administration and achieved it
(D) Anne Banyon Quimby was the first woman to be elected to serve as head of the university's administration, achieving this honor
(E) Anne Banyon Quimby was the first woman being elected to serve as head of the university's administration, the honor was achieved

6. Randy and Celeste will serve as co-chairs of the membership committee, their accomplishments in this having been extremely valuable to the organization's growth.

(A) committee, their accomplishments in this having been extremely valuable to the organization's growth
(B) committee; their accomplishments in this having been extremely valuable to the organization's growth
(C) committee, for their accomplishments in this have been extremely valuable to the organization's growth
(D) committee, for their accomplishments on the committee have been extremely valuable to the organization's growth
(E) committee; their accomplishments on the committee having been extremely valuable to the organization's growth

7. The song's intricate melody and its thought-provoking lyrics captivate the listener completely.

(A) captivate the listener completely
(B) captivate the one who is listening completely
(C) completely captivates the one who is listening
(D) captivate one who is listening to it
(E) captivates one in hearing it

8. Being as it is a refuge for homeless animals, the MaxFund Shelter houses more than fifty cats at any given time.

(A) Being as it is a refuge for homeless animals
(B) In being a refuge for homeless animals
(C) A refuge for homeless animals
(D) Although it is a refuge for homeless animals
(E) Being a refuge for animals that are homeless

9. Although the arbitrator Kevin Cooley never having facilitated arms negotiations, he viewed them as political charades that, despite their importance, lacked the potential to be skillfully resolved.

(A) Although the arbitrator Kevin Cooley never having facilitated arms negotiations, he viewed them
(B) The arbitrator Kevin Cooley never facilitated arms negotiations, he viewed them
(C) Never having facilitated arms negotiations, they were viewed by the arbitrator Kevin Cooley
(D) The arbitrator Kevin Cooley never facilitated arms negotiations; however, viewing them
(E) The arbitrator Kevin Cooley never facilitated arms negotiations because he viewed them

10. The intense rafting trip was already frightening and lasted two days, which duration made it seem absolutely terrifying.

(A) frightening and lasted two days, which duration made it seem
(B) frightening, and because of lasting two days, it made it seem
(C) frightening and lasted the duration of two days to make it to seem
(D) frightening, and its lasting two days made it seem
(E) frightening and, by lasting two days, making it seem

11. The reason computer software programs change so quickly is that it constantly draws on all the advances of technological innovation.

(A) that it constantly draws on
(B) that these programs constantly draw on
(C) because of these programs constantly drawing on
(D) because of them constantly drawing from
(E) their constant drawing upon

GO ON TO THE NEXT PAGE

SECTION 6

Directions: For each question in this section, select the best answer from among the choices given.

The following sentences test your ability to recognize grammar and usage errors. Each sentence contains either a single error or no error at all. No sentence contains more than one error. The error, if there is one, is underlined and lettered. If the sentence contains an error, select the one underlined part that must be changed to make the sentence correct. If the sentence is correct, select choice E. In choosing answers, follow the requirements of standard written English.

Example:

The other (A) delegates and him (B) immediately (C) accepted the resolution drafted by (D) the neutral states. No error (E)

Ⓐ ● Ⓒ Ⓓ Ⓔ

12. Written by a massage expert, the book *Healing Through Massage* revealing (A) how (B) massage techniques can relieve (C) muscle spasms that lead to chronic pain by loosening the muscles and keeping them (D) flexible. No error (E)

13. The issue of whether (A) homeopathic remedies actually cure illness or do they (B) simply reduce symptoms is (C) still being (D) investigated. No error (E)

14. People which believe (A) that retirement savings are important (B) typically devote (C) at least ten percent of their (D) earnings to a long-term interest-bearing account. No error (E)

15. The polygraph test administrator wondered what his subject meant (A) when he stated (B) that he was home at the time of the burglary, because (C) several eye witnesses have identified (D) him as part of the gang glimpsed fleeing the crime scene. No error (E)

16. One obstacle that many innovative entrepreneurs face is developing (A) competitive products while producing (B) them at a low enough cost to (C) maintain prices that will be viewed as affordable (D) by the general public. No error (E)

17. No one dares to (A) reject his offers of assistance, even though (B) he is known for making apparently generous offers and then (C) withdrawing them, when (D) he is a highly influential man. No error (E)

18. Just how (A) important an effective human resources department is to (B) the health of a business is never (C) more clearer (D) than it is after a major discrimination lawsuit. No error (E)

19. Critics of socialized medicine argue that (A) the benefits of the system is outweighed by (B) the fact that it places (C) a disproportionate financial burden on (D) the average taxpayer. No error (E)

20. Squids are mistakenly believed to be (A) unintelligent creatures because they (B) are portrayed (C) in movies as dumb and aggressive; in reality, however, they are highly intelligent and are aggressive only whenever (D) threatened. No error (E)

21. After listening to President Kinney's persuasive arguments for (A) an expanded scholarship program, some of the senior members of the academic board urged him in the reviewing of (B) the university's progress in implementing (C) its (D) fundraising plan. No error (E)

GO ON TO THE NEXT PAGE

SECTION 6

22. Although the librarian outwardly (A) seemed uninterested to develop (B) friendships with the other faculty members, inwardly she was simply shy and found it (C) difficult to strike up social conversations with others (D). No error (E)

23. Art critics tend to focus on (A) reviewing art that is created within their own cultures, whereas (B) art historians are more likely to evaluate works that are produced (C) during other time periods or by artists (D) from other cultures. No error (E)

24. Athletes Arthur Collins and Joseph Roth may have (A) very similar training backgrounds, but (B) Collins is the faster (C) runner and Roth the nimblest (D). No error (E)

25. The camp director's change in policy had (A) two effects: less freedom for (B) campers enrolled in the overnight program with an increase (C) in supervisory responsibilities for those counselors who chose (D) to renew their contracts. No error (E)

26. The number of phone calls received by (A) the police department after the recent string of bank robberies emphasize (B) the growing concerns (C) of neighborhood residents, who fear (D) for their personal safety. No error (E)

27. The novel *Puppet Cinema* by author James Beardly has been (A) more widely read within (B) literary circles and has received more positive reviews (C) by European critics than author Steven Watts' novels have (D). No error (E)

28. Until it (A) can be superceded by a more economical (B) and environmentally safe form of packaging, plastic bags will probably continue (C) to serve as the primary containers for transporting purchased items (D) home from grocery stores. No error (E)

29. Almost all (A) of the city council members concur (B) that of the two taxation proposals under consideration (C), the Laughton proposal is the more practical (D). No error (E)

GO ON TO THE NEXT PAGE

SECTION 6

Directions: The following passage is an early draft of an essay. Some parts of the passage need to be rewritten.

Read the passage and select the best answers for the questions that follow. Some questions are about particular sentences or parts of sentences and ask you to improve sentence structure or word choice. Other questions ask you to consider organization and development. In choosing answers, follow the requirements of standard written English.

Questions 30–35 are based on the following passage.

(1) *Everything around him was still mysterious in the pre-dawn darkness.* **(2)** *The coyotes were barking when the cook's triangle brought Dave from his blankets.* **(3)** *The shouting of the wranglers and the bells of the horses came musically, as if from a great distance.* **(4)** *Dave's friend Hart joined him the two young men walked out to the horses together.* **(5)** *On the previous night, each rider had placed a bell on the horse that he wanted, for he knew that in the morning it would be too dark to distinguish one bronco from another.* **(6)** *The animals were going round and round in a circle to escape from being roped.*

(7) *Dave rode in close and waited, rope ready, his ears attuned to the sound of his own bell.* **(8)** *A horse rushed jingling past.* **(9)** *The rope snaked out.* **(10)** *Tightening over the horse's neck.* **(11)** *Instantly the bronco surrendered, making no further attempt to escape.* **(12)** *Dave dropped his rope around the nose of the bronco, climbed up on its back, and rode back to camp.*

(13) *Once at camp, Dave saddled and then rode out upon the mesa.* **(14)** *There came an answering whinny, and presently out of the darkness a pony trotted.* **(15)** *The pony was a sleek and glossy little fellow named Chiquito, beautiful in action and gentle as a kitten.*

(16) *Dave took his head in his arms and patted the horse's soft, dainty nose as Chiquito nuzzled in his pocket for sugar.* **(17)** *Dave fed Chiquito a half-handful of the treat in his open palm, and then put Chiquito through the set of tricks that he had recently learned.*

30. Which is the best version of the underlined portion of sentence 4 (reproduced below)?

Dave's friend Hart joined <u>him the two young men</u> walked out to the horses together.

(A) (As it is now)
(B) him being that the two young men
(C) him insomuch as two young men
(D) him, although the two young men
(E) him, and the two young men

31. The logical flow of the first paragraph would be most improved by moving sentence 1 to which of the following locations?

(A) Between sentence 2 and sentence 3
(B) Between sentence 3 and sentence 4
(C) Between sentence 4 and sentence 5
(D) Between sentence 5 and sentence 6
(E) After sentence 6

32. Which is the best version of the underlined portions of sentences 9 and 10 (reproduced below)?

The rope <u>snaked out. Tightening</u> over the horse's neck.

(A) (As it is now)
(B) snaked out; tightening
(C) snaked out, which was tightening
(D) snaked out and tightened
(E) snaked out, in its tightening

33. Which of the following sentences would be most logical to insert before sentence 14?

(A) He whistled sharply.
(B) He had not ridden out to the mesa in quite some time.
(C) Dave rode quickly, shivering in the brisk wind.
(D) He had breakfast on his mind.
(E) Dave enjoyed his morning rides and looked forward to them.

34. In context, which is the best revision to make to sentence 16 (reproduced below)?

Dave took his head in his arms and patted the horse's soft, dainty nose as Chiquito nuzzled in his pocket for sugar.

(A) Insert "gently" after "his arms".
(B) Change "his head in his arms" to "Chiquito's head in his arms".
(C) Change "the horse's soft, dainty nose" to "his soft, dainty nose".
(D) Delete "for sugar".
(E) Insert "searching" after "nuzzled".

GO ON TO THE NEXT PAGE

SECTION 6

35. To which of the following assignments does this essay best respond?

(A) Describe an event using the first-person point of view.

(B) Describe a series of events from two distinct points of view.

(C) Provide a narrative description of an event from the third-person point of view

(D) Analyze a series of events that were important in your own life.

(E) Write an experimental essay in which imagery rather than events is central.

S T O P

IF YOU FINISH BEFORE TIME IS CALLED, YOU MAY CHECK YOUR WORK ON THIS TEST ONLY. DO NOT TURN TO ANY OTHER SECTION IN THIS TEST.

SECTION 7

Turn to Section 7 of your answer sheet to answer the questions in this section.

Time—20 Minutes
19 Questions

Directions: For each question in this section, select the best answer from among the choices given and fill in the corresponding oval on the answer sheet.

Each sentence below has one or two blanks, each blank indicating that something has been omitted. Beneath the sentence are five words or sets of words labeled A through E. Choose the word or set of words that, when inserted in the sentence, best fits the meaning of the sentence as a whole.

Example:

Eliza felt ----- when her boss asked her to work seven weekends in a row but ----- when her work earned her a promotion.

(A) enervated . . weakened
(B) depressed . . intellectual
(C) advantageous . . salacious
(D) angry . . shopworn
(E) irate . . elated

   Ⓓ ●

1. A choreographer who is troublesome to work with might find it ----- to obtain new jobs, because word of a person's reputation spreads so ----- in the entertainment industry.

(A) adventuresome . . starkly
(B) difficult . . quickly
(C) challenging . . abruptly
(D) appealing . . randomly
(E) simple . . easily

2. Leslie described Hal's chaotic and frenzied speeches to the group as an example of his frequent ----- behavior.

(A) rational
(B) maniacal
(C) belligerent
(D) untrustworthy
(E) intentional

3. The philanthropist was highly regarded for being both ----- and -----: liberal in sharing her resources and concerned about the needs of others.

(A) neighborly . . dedicated
(B) generous . . self-centered
(C) stingy . . compassionate
(D) benevolent . . considerate
(E) aloof . . humane

4. Though author Kip Singleton published several articles that mentioned his intense fear of flying, he emerged from his first flight at age 70 surprisingly ----- by the experience.

(A) intimidated
(B) bewildered
(C) undaunted
(D) traumatized
(E) ostracized

5. After enduring the senator's ----- speech for more than an hour, Ambassador Parcham could no longer fight his ----- and surprised all of the guests by excusing himself abruptly from the party.

(A) efficacious . . conscience
(B) scintillating . . surfeit
(C) soporific . . somnolence
(D) parsimonious . . repugnance
(E) penurious . . veracity

6. Always shy and retiring in the company of strangers, Johanna tended to ----- herself at parties to avoid drawing any attention her way.

(A) efface
(B) emblazon
(C) variegate
(D) evince
(E) promulgate

GO ON TO THE NEXT PAGE

SECTION 7

Directions: The passage below is followed by questions based on its content. Answer the questions on the basis of what is stated or implied in the passage and in any introductory material that may be provided.

Questions 7–19 are based on the following passage.

The following passage is excerpted from a scholarly essay that discusses the effect of World War I on the balance of power system in Europe.

Historians and political scientists alike frequently regard World War I as signaling the breakdown of the European balance of power system. This system, known as the classical balance of power, is believed to have existed in Europe during the period between the end of the Napoleonic Wars and the beginning of World War I. Did World War I actually represent a breakdown of Europe's classical balance of power system? A careful analysis of prewar and postwar Europe reveals great similarities between the two systems. Although World War I did affect the nature of international relations in several fundamental respects, the war did not bring about a collapse of the balance of power system existing among the European nations in the early 1900s. In fact, a multipolar balance of power continued to exist in Europe after World War I.

Theorist Edward Gulick defines the classical balance of power system as based upon four essential assumptions. First, the international system consists of a group of independent states possessing relatively equal power. Second, the balance of power system is a multipolar system that includes a minimum of three states, with no limit to its maximum as long as the system is workable. Third, all states in the system possess a relative cultural similarity. Finally, states have a rational means of estimating the power of other states within the system.

Gulick also defines the aims of states within a balance of power system as three-fold. States focus on preserving their survival and independence within the system. They also focus on preserving the international system itself. Finally, in a balance of power system, states work to ensure that no one state obtains hegemony, or a preponderance of power. If any one state appears to be gaining dominance within the system, the other states in the system will form alliances and band together to balance out the power of the dominant state.

In Gulick's view, the primary aim of the balance of power system is to maintain equilibrium of power among states. Peace is incidental to the system; it is not one of the system's primary aims. In this view, wars do not mark the failure of the balance of power system. On the contrary, wars may be necessary as a means for preserving the equilibrium between states and preventing a breakdown of the system.

Finally, Gulick describes nine major instruments of foreign policy that are used as the means of a balance of power system. These instruments are vigilance, alliance formation, intervention, policies of holding the balance, mobility of action, reciprocal compensation, moderation in dealing with other states, coalition building, and war.

According to Gulick's model of the balance of power system, a change in the system occurs when the assumptions, aims, and means of the system are altered in a fundamental way. Since peace is considered to be a secondary, rather than primary, aim of the system, the occurrence of war in itself cannot be considered to represent a breakdown of the system. Only if war causes a change in the essential structure of the system can a breakdown be said to have occurred.

Many scholars consider the several decades before World War I to have been the most successful era of balance of power politics. At that time, the multipolar system in Europe consisted of five major powers: Germany, France, Great Britain, Austria-Hungary, and Russia. Although this period saw many small conflicts and rivalries between the main powers, it still reflected relative peacefulness. All of the alliances between countries in the system remained flexible. It was not until 1914 that states in the system banded into solid coalitions, with France, Britain, and Russia grouping together to balance out the growing strength of Germany and Austria-Hungary, its ally.

After World War I, many historians believed that the balance of power in Europe had been destroyed. In fact, although the system did change slightly due to the war, overall the classical balance of power still remained in effect. First, the assumptions underlying the prewar balance still existed to a great degree after the war. The European state system was fundamentally intact, with all of the key states except Austria-Hungary still occupying their places in the system.

The aims and means of the classical balance of power also persisted after the war. States continued to interact in ways that ensured that no one state would gain preponderance within the system, using various means such as forming alliances and building coalitions. Germany looked for a balance as a way of escaping from the harsh peace imposed on it by the treaties that ended the war. France attempted to balance Germany by occupying the Ruhr basin to seize raw materials from Germany. England worked to balance France's drive for influence in the system and to protect Britain's interests in the Near East from Russian influence. Russia worked to ensure a balance favorable to its government, since it felt that world opinion had turned against it after the Socialist Revolution.

After World War I, then, the balance of power system continued to exist in a real sense, as postwar diplomacy used aims and means similar to those in place before the war. In reality, it

GO ON TO THE NEXT PAGE

SECTION 7

was World War II, and not World War I, that brought about the breakdown of the multipolar balance of power existing in Europe from 1815 to 1945. This war caused the transformation of the international system from a multipolar to a bipolar world, where only two states, the United States and the Soviet Union, predominated. It was not until World War II that the assumptions, aims, and means of the balance of power system were fundamentally changed.

7. The passage provides the most information about Gulick's

(A) criticism of the balance of power system
(B) argument regarding the history of Germany
(C) description of the outcome of World War II
(D) definition of the balance of power system
(E) explanation of the causes of World War I

8. In line 18, "relatively" most nearly means

(A) understandably
(B) moderately
(C) absolutely
(D) insufficiently
(E) approximately

9. Gulick would most likely agree with which of the following statements regarding balance of power systems?

(A) States in a balance of power system are culturally very distinct.
(B) A balance of power system is limited to a maximum of seven states.
(C) Within a balance of power system, states have two main aims.
(D) One of the aims of states within a balance of power system is to preserve the international system itself.
(E) A classical balance of power system consists of two states that balance each other's power equally.

10. The passage suggests that states form alliances in a balance of power system (lines 29–32) ("If any one . . . state") as a means of

(A) enhancing the power of a dominant state
(B) weakening the internal government of an enemy state
(C) preserving relationships with potential trade partners
(D) preventing any single state from becoming too powerful
(E) preserving peace within the system at all costs

11. The discussion of Gulick's views on war (lines 46–53) ("According to . . . occurred") implies that Gulick

(A) viewed military force as unnecessary within a balance of power system
(B) saw war as an acceptable method of preserving the balance of power
(C) viewed economic sanctions as far more effective than military force
(D) viewed war as the most important means of maintaining equilibrium between states
(E) saw war as an indication that the balance of power had failed

12. In lines 40–45 ("Finally, Gulick . . . war"), the author describes foreign policy strategies, such as vigilance, alliance formation, and intervention, in order to

(A) describe avenues through which governments can motivate their citizens to support a war
(B) stress that reciprocal compensation is the most difficult strategy for states to implement
(C) explain the major instruments used by states as the means of a balance of power system
(D) demonstrate why certain strategies are more effective for enabling states to achieve their objectives
(E) explain the primary means used by states to establish a preponderance of international power

13. The passage suggests that war constitutes a breakdown of the balance of power system (lines 51–53) ("Only if . . . occurred") if it

(A) causes a fundamental change in the assumptions, aims, and means of the system
(B) prevents states from accurately assessing whether other states have changed their military strategies
(C) enables states to preserve their survival and protect their independence
(D) serves to maintain the essential structure of the system as it existed before the war
(E) enables states to develop a rational means of estimating the power of other states in the system

GO ON TO THE NEXT PAGE

SECTION 7

14. The passage suggests that before World War I, the relationships between states in the international system were

(A) notably relaxed and devoid of conflict
(B) mostly hostile, with occasional periods of peace
(C) dominated for years by inflexible coalitions
(D) plagued by territorial battles between nations
(E) generally peaceful, despite many minor disputes

15. According to the passage, which of the following countries lost its place as a major international power after World War I?

(A) France
(B) Germany
(C) Austria-Hungary
(D) Great Britain
(E) Russia

16. According to the passage, France occupied the Ruhr basin (lines 79–80) after World War I in order to

(A) escape from the harsh peace imposed on it by the treaties that ended the war
(B) balance the power of Germany by seizing Germany's raw materials
(C) prevent Russia from ensuring a balance favorable to its new government
(D) protect its interests in the Near East from Russian influence
(E) balance Austria-Hungary's drive for influence in the international system

17. In lines 77–85 ("Germany looked for . . . Socialist Revolution"), the author describes the actions of various states after World War I in order to

(A) explain why the major powers were unsuccessful in preventing a second World War
(B) illustrate how different states allowed Germany to regain preponderance within the system
(C) provide evidence of the breakdown of the classical balance of power system after the war
(D) explain why the major powers decided to invest their resources in occupying foreign territories
(E) demonstrate that the aims and means of the classical balance of power persisted after the war

18. According to the author, the breakdown of the classical balance of power system in Europe was caused by

(A) the impact of World War II, which converted the system from a multipolar to a bipolar world
(B) the foreign policies of Russia after it refused to sign the treaties that ended World War I
(C) the decline of Austria-Hungary, which left a major gap in the leadership of the international system
(D) the strategies employed by Germany in attempting to ensure that the Socialist Revolution would not spread
(E) the impact of World War I, which replaced all of the major powers operating within the system

19. The primary purpose of the passage is to

(A) compare interpretations of a theoretical concept
(B) explain the results of historical case studies
(C) summarize the findings of a research experiment
(D) present an argument and support it with evidence
(E) draw conclusions based on statistical data

S T O P

IF YOU FINISH BEFORE TIME IS CALLED, YOU MAY CHECK YOUR WORK ON THIS TEST ONLY. DO NOT TURN TO ANY OTHER SECTION IN THIS TEST.

SECTION 8

Turn to Section 8 of your answer sheet to answer the questions in this section.

Time—20 Minutes
16 Questions

Directions: For this section, solve each problem and decide which is the best of the choices given. Fill in the corresponding oval on the answer sheet. You may use any available space for scratchwork.

Notes:

1. The use of a calculator is permitted. All numbers used are real numbers.
2. Figures that accompany problems in this test are intended to provide information useful in solving the problems. They are drawn as accurately as possible EXCEPT when it is stated in a specific problem that the figure is not drawn to scale. All figures lie in a plane unless otherwise indicated.
3. Unless otherwise specified, the domain of any function f is assumed to be the set of all real numbers x for which $f(x)$ is a real number.

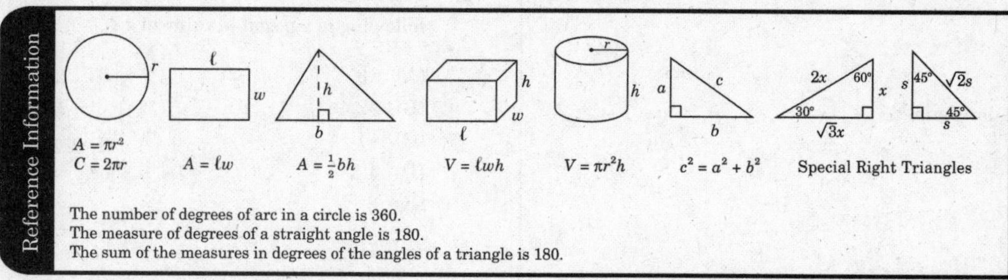
Reference Information
$A = \pi r^2$
$C = 2\pi r$
$A = \ell w$
$A = \frac{1}{2}bh$
$V = \ell wh$
$V = \pi r^2 h$
$c^2 = a^2 + b^2$
Special Right Triangles
The number of degrees of arc in a circle is 360.
The measure of degrees of a straight angle is 180.
The sum of the measures in degrees of the angles of a triangle is 180.

1. If O is the set of odd integers, P is the set of positive integers, and S is the set of integers less than 7, which of the following integers will be in all three sets?

(A) 7
(B) 5
(C) 2
(D) 0
(E) −1

2. If $9 + \sqrt{h} = 17$, then $h =$

(A) $\sqrt{8}$
(B) $\sqrt{26}$
(C) 8
(D) 64
(E) 676

3. In a survey, 21 people indicated that they liked Brand X toothpaste, 46 people indicated that they disliked Brand X toothpaste, and 3 people had not tried Brand X toothpaste. What fraction of those surveyed liked Brand X toothpaste?

(A) $\frac{3}{10}$
(B) $\frac{1}{3}$
(C) $\frac{5}{14}$
(D) $\frac{3}{7}$
(E) $\frac{7}{10}$

GO ON TO THE NEXT PAGE

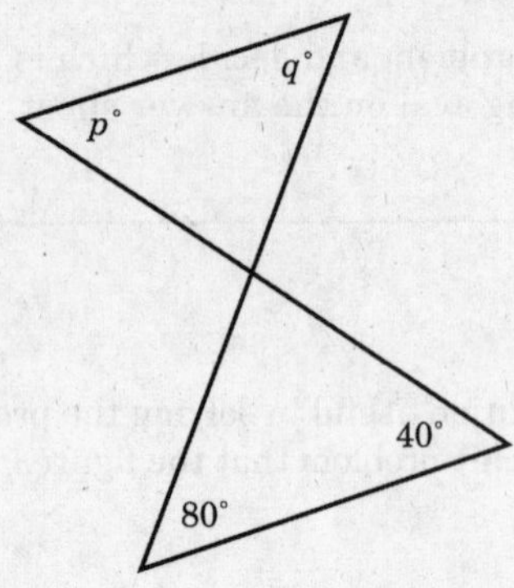

4. In the figure above, what is the value of $p + q$?

(A) 60
(B) 100
(C) 120
(D) 135
(E) It cannot be determined.

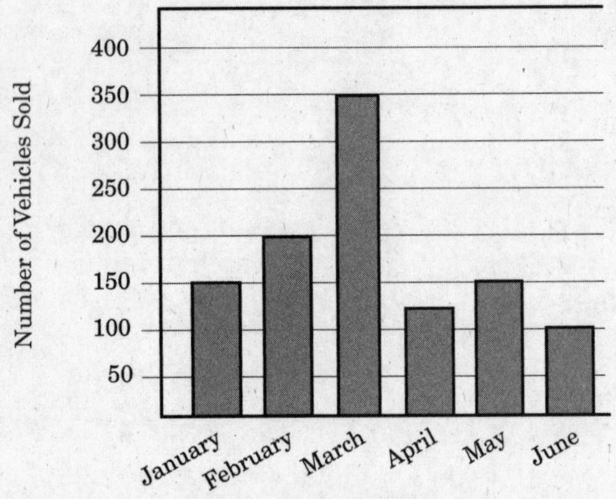

5. According to the graph above, between which two consecutive months was there the least change in the number of vehicles sold?

(A) January and February
(B) February and March
(C) March and April
(D) April and May
(E) May and June

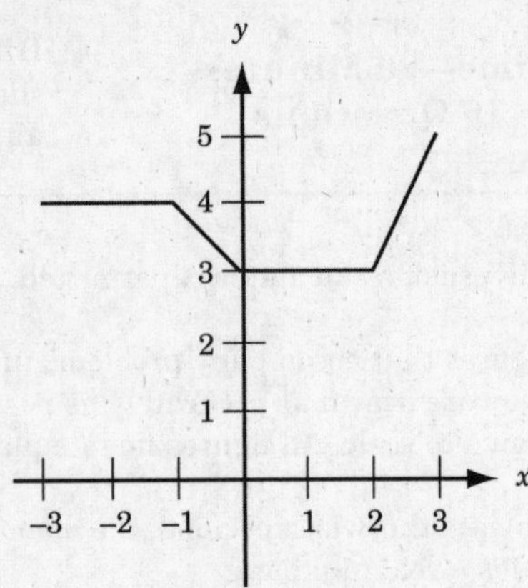

6. The graph of $y = h(x)$ is shown above. If $h(s) = 3$, which of the following is a possible value of s ?

(A) −3
(B) −2.5
(C) −1
(D) 1.5
(E) 3

7. If x, y, and z are consecutive positive integers and $3^x \times 3^y \times 3^z = 729$, then $3^x + 3^y + 3^z =$

(A) 39
(B) 42
(C) 47
(D) 54
(E) 58

GO ON TO THE NEXT PAGE

SECTION 8

8. In the xy-plane, the center of a circle has coordinates $(-1, 4)$. If one endpoint of a diameter of the circle is $(-4, 4)$, what are the coordinates of the other endpoint of this diameter?

(A) $(-7, 4)$
(B) $(-4, 2)$
(C) $(1, 2)$
(D) $(2, 2)$
(E) $(2, 4)$

9. A company uses an automated system to manufacture boxes. The automated system takes a minimum of 20 seconds to make each box with no printing. If a box requires printing, printing can add a maximum of 40 more seconds to the completion time. Which of the following inequalities best represents t, the time in seconds that it takes to manufacture one box?

(A) $t \leq 40$
(B) $20 < t < 40$
(C) $20 \leq t \leq 40$
(D) $20 < t < 60$
(E) $20 \leq t \leq 60$

10. A right circular cylinder with radius 4 and height 3 has volume v. In terms of v, what is the volume of a right circular cylinder with radius 4 and height 9 ?

(A) $v + 6$
(B) $3v$
(C) $4v$
(D) $6v$
(E) $9v$

11. If a, d, and g are integers, let $a \,§\, (d, g)$ be defined to be true only if $d > a > g$. If $3 \,§\, (7, g)$ is true, which of the following could be a possible value of g ?

I. -4
II. 2
III. 5

(A) I only
(B) II only
(C) I and II
(D) I and III
(E) II and III

12. If 35 percent of b equals 70 percent of d, which of the following expresses d in terms of b ?

(A) $d = 35$ percent of b
(B) $d = 50$ percent of b
(C) $d = 75$ percent of b
(D) $d = 105$ percent of b
(E) $d = 200$ percent of b

13. If a, b, and c are positive integers such that the value of $a + b$ is even and the value of $(a + b)^2 + a + c$ is even, which of the following CANNOT be true?

(A) The value of a is odd.
(B) The integer a is even and c is odd.
(C) The integers a, b, and c are all even.
(D) The value of ab is odd.
(E) The integers b and c are both odd.

GO ON TO THE NEXT PAGE

SECTION 8

14. If $-1 < z < 0$, which of the following statements must be true?

I. $z^3 > z^2$

II. $z < \frac{z}{4}$

III. $z > z^2$

(A) I only
(B) II only
(C) III only
(D) II and III only
(E) None of the above

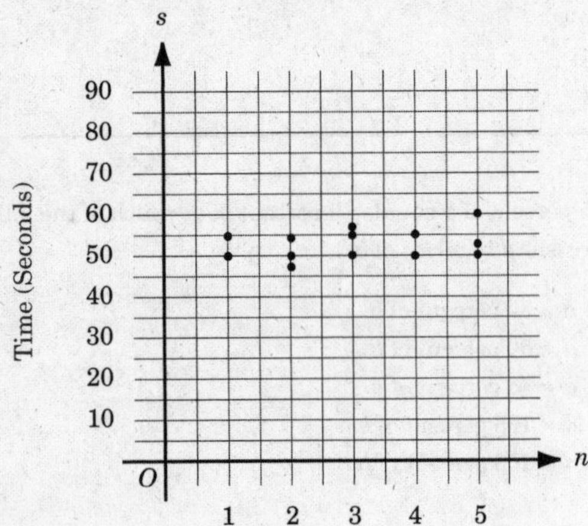

15. A track team prepared to enter 13 runners in a race by timing each runner's performance on a simulated course. Each runner completed at least one trial run before being timed. The scatterplot above shows the time each runner took to complete the simulated course and the corresponding number of trials that each runner completed. Based on the data, which of the following functions best models the relationship between s, the number of seconds to complete the simulated course, and n, the number of trials?

(A) $s(n) = 53$
(B) $s(n) = n$
(C) $s(n) = 53n$
(D) $s(n) = \frac{n}{53}$
(E) $s(n) = n + 53$

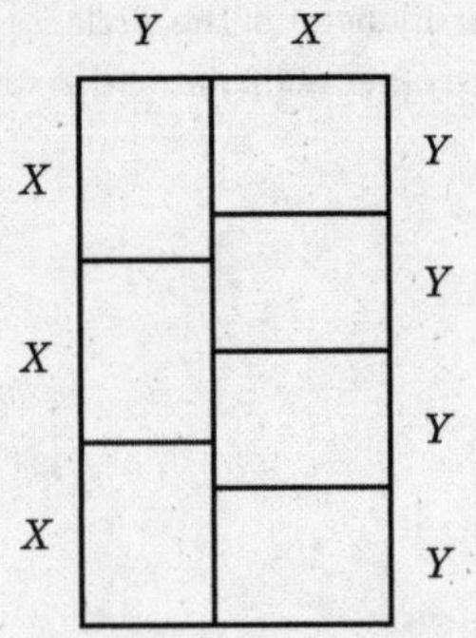

16. The pattern shown above is composed of rectangles, each one of dimensions X by Y. These rectangles are to be used repeatedly to completely cover a rectangular region $8X$ units long and $9X$ units wide. How many rectangles of dimension X by Y are needed?

(A) 32
(B) 36
(C) 54
(D) 72
(E) 96

S T O P

IF YOU FINISH BEFORE TIME IS CALLED, YOU MAY CHECK YOUR WORK ON THIS TEST ONLY.
DO NOT TURN TO ANY OTHER SECTION IN THIS TEST.

SECTION 9

Turn to Section 9 of your answer sheet to answer the questions in this section.

Time—10 Minutes
14 Questions

Directions: For each question in this section, select the best answer from among the choices given.

The following sentences test correctness and effectiveness of expression. Part of each sentence or the entire sentence is underlined; beneath each sentence are five ways of phrasing the underlined material. Choice A repeats the original phrasing; the other four choices are different. If you think the original phrasing produces a better sentence than any of the alternatives, select choice A; if not, select one of the other choices.

In making your selection, follow the requirements of standard written English; that is, pay attention to grammar, choice of words, sentence construction, and punctuation. Your selection should result in the most effective sentence—clear and precise, without awkwardness or ambiguity.

Example:

In the poem "Ulysses" by Alfred, Lord Tennyson, the speaker says, "I cannot rest from travel," instead, he will live life to the fullest.

(A) "I cannot rest from travel," instead,
(B) "I cannot rest from travel"; instead,
(C) "I cannot rest from travel" instead,
(D) "I cannot rest from travel," upon which
(E) "I cannot rest from travel,"

1. At Munich before World War II, the Allies believed they had negotiated an agreement that would have secured peace by appeasing Germany.

(A) would have secured peace by appeasing Germany
(B) would secure peace by appeasing Germany
(C) had secured peace by appeasing Germany
(D) will secure peace by appeasing Germany
(E) secures peace by appeasing Germany

2. The new atrium, constructed entirely from glass panels revealing a breathtaking view, and was made possible by a generous contribution from the Arboretum Fund.

(A) atrium, constructed entirely from glass panels revealing a breathtaking view, and was made possible by a generous contribution from the Arboretum Fund
(B) atrium is constructed entirely from glass panels revealing a breathtaking view, making possible a generous contribution from the Arboretum Fund
(C) atrium, constructed entirely from glass panels revealing a breathtaking view, was made possible by a generous contribution from the Arboretum Fund
(D) atrium that was constructed entirely from glass panels revealing a breathtaking view made possible by a generous contribution from the Arboretum Fund
(E) atrium, being constructed entirely from glass panels revealing a breathtaking view, it was made possible by a generous contribution from the Arboretum Fund

3. Even those who acknowledge the importance of quitting smoking often find it difficult to stop smoking permanently and stay smoke-free.

(A) permanently and stay smoke-free
(B) permanent and have them stay smoke-free
(C) and be able to stay quit permanently
(D) permanently as they remain smoke-free
(E) and stay smoke-free permanently

4. No sooner had Darius arrived in geology class to submit his midterm but he realized that he had forgotten his assignment at home.

(A) but he realized that he had forgotten
(B) but he had realized that he was forgetting
(C) than he was having the realization that he will forget
(D) but he realized his own forgetting of
(E) than he realized that he had forgotten

GO ON TO THE NEXT PAGE

SECTION 9

5. Guidance counselors often have specific training regarding how to assist high school students with their college and career decisions, which provides benefits to both the students and their parents.

(A) decisions, which provides benefits to both the students and
(B) decisions, which provide benefits to both the students and
(C) decisions, which provides both benefits to the students plus
(D) decisions; it provides benefits to both the students as well as
(E) decisions; this provides benefits both to the students and

6. Molly Sauder will not be acknowledged by her superiors for her contributions to the advertising campaign any more than they will acknowledge Molly's assistant, Joe Henderson, for his graphic and technical assistance on the project.

(A) any more than they will acknowledge Molly's assistant, Joe Henderson,
(B) as will Molly's assistant, Joe Henderson, not be acknowledged
(C) any more than Molly's assistant, Joe Henderson, will be acknowledged
(D) just as they will not acknowledge Molly's assistant, Joe Henderson,
(E) no more than Molly's assistant, Joe Henderson, will be acknowledged

7. Charlotte Jackson was interested in psychology because she believed that if you understood human motivations it could have a positive impact on reducing crime and promoting economic growth.

(A) if you understood human motivations it
(B) with the motivations of individuals understood they
(C) understanding the motivations that were affecting humans
(D) by understanding human motivations
(E) understanding human motivations

8. During his sophomore year in college, one reason why Daniel Brady's grades improved significantly, Daniel purchased a computer that helped him to complete his homework assignments more quickly.

(A) significantly, Daniel purchased a computer that helped him to complete his homework assignments more quickly
(B) significantly was relating to the fact that Daniel purchased a computer that helped him to complete his homework assignments more quickly
(C) significantly concerned the purchasing by Daniel of a computer that helped him to complete his homework assignments more quickly
(D) significantly, Daniel's completion of his homework was quicker due to his purchase of a computer
(E) significantly was because Daniel purchased a computer that helped him to complete his homework assignments more quickly

9. One of the first businesses in the area to adopt internet conferencing, Crown Teleco, was a fiber optic network developer, introducing the technology to its staff with great enthusiasm.

(A) Crown Teleco, was a fiber optic network developer, introducing
(B) Crown Teleco which was a fiber optic network developer and introduced
(C) Crown Teleco developed fiber optic networks that introduced
(D) Crown Teleco, a fiber optic network developer, introduced
(E) a fiber optic network developer, Crown Teleco, that introduced

10. Before being sold for their face value to another merchant in the plant shop's liquidation sale, the ficus tree was the centerpiece of the entire store, displayed proudly near the register for all to see.

(A) Before being sold for their
(B) Before it was being sold for its
(C) Up until they had been sold for their
(D) Before it was sold for its
(E) Until they started being sold for their

GO ON TO THE NEXT PAGE

SECTION 9

11. Tara moved to Minneapolis for a new job last year, and she has been living there in a lovely apartment ever since.

(A) and she has been living there in a lovely apartment ever since
(B) since that time has been living there in a lovely apartment
(C) where ever since she lives there in a lovely apartment
(D) she has been living there in a lovely apartment since then
(E) and since then is living there in a lovely apartment

12. Tempting all but the most reluctant of consumers to investigate the benefits of Kane Software Company's newest privacy control software, the effect of Stan Kovad's powerful sales pitch is to encourage even frugal customers to spend.

(A) the effect of Stan Kovad's powerful sales pitch is to encourage even frugal customers to spend
(B) Stan Kovad encourages even frugal customers to spend with his powerful sales pitch
(C) the effect of the sales pitch by Stan Kovad is to encourage even frugal customers to spend
(D) Stan Kovad has had the effect of encouraging even frugal customers to spend with his powerful sales pitch
(E) even frugal customers of Stan Kovad's are encouraged to spend by his powerful sales pitch

13. Most financial planners know not only that excessive spending on luxuries reduces savings, but also that it can lead to debt.

(A) know not only that excessive spending on luxuries reduces
(B) know that excessive spending on luxuries could be diminishing of
(C) are knowledgeable that excessive spending on luxuries not only reduces
(D) have known that excessive spending on luxuries reduces not only
(E) know that excessive spending on luxuries not only by itself can reduce

14. Cameron Theater's first performance was a variety show, in which Cameron's directors produced an interactive community showcase, and local artists were encouraged to share their talents.

(A) showcase, and local artists were encouraged to share their talents
(B) showcase and encouraging local artists to share their talents
(C) showcase, with the result being local artists sharing their talents
(D) showcase in where local artists share their talents
(E) showcase and encouraged local artists to share their talents

S T O P

IF YOU FINISH BEFORE TIME IS CALLED, YOU MAY CHECK YOUR WORK ON THIS TEST ONLY.
DO NOT TURN TO ANY OTHER SECTION IN THIS TEST.

PRACTICE TEST 10 EXPLANATIONS

PRACTICE TEST 10 ANSWERS

Question Number	Answer	Right	Wrong
Section 2			
1	E		
2	E		
3	C		
4	A		
5	A		
6	C		
7	B		
8	C		
9	B		
10	E		
11	C		
12	E		
13	D		
14	A		
15	E		
16	B		
17	C		
18	C		
19	B		
20	A		
21	A		
22	E		
23	D		
24	D		
Section 3			
1	D		
2	B		
3	B		
4	D		
5	E		
6	D		
7	C		
8	A		
9	C		
10	E		
11	C		
12	C		
13	B		
14	D		
15	C		
16	D		
17	A		
18	A		
19	C		
20	B		
Section 4			
1	D		
2	D		
3	C		
4	C		
5	A		
6	D		
7	A		
Section 4, continued			
8	D		
9	C		
10	C		
11	B		
12	C		
13	D		
14	E		
15	A		
16	B		
17	D		
18	E		
19	A		
20	A		
21	D		
22	E		
23	C		
24	C		
Section 5			
1	A		
2	C		
3	E		
4	D		
5	E		
6	D		
7	E		
8	C		
9	9		
10	19		
11	100		
12	24		
13	29		
14	110		
15	8/18, 4/9		
16	6		
17	9/16, .563		
18	6, 12		
Section 6			
1	C		
2	D		
3	C		
4	E		
5	D		
6	D		
7	A		
8	C		
9	E		
10	D		
11	B		
12	A		
13	B		
14	A		
15	D		

Question Number	Answer	Right	Wrong
Section 6, continued			
16	E		
17	D		
18	D		
19	B		
20	D		
21	B		
22	B		
23	E		
24	D		
25	C		
26	B		
27	E		
28	A		
29	E		
30	E		
31	A		
32	D		
33	A		
34	B		
35	C		
Section 7			
1	B		
2	B		
3	D		
4	C		
5	C		
6	A		
7	D		
8	E		
9	D		
10	D		
11	B		
12	C		
13	A		
14	E		
15	C		

Question Number	Answer	Right	Wrong
Section 7, continued			
16	B		
17	E		
18	A		
19	D		
Section 8			
1	B		
2	D		
3	A		
4	C		
5	D		
6	D		
7	A		
8	E		
9	E		
10	B		
11	C		
12	B		
13	B		
14	B		
15	A		
16	E		
Section 9			
1	B		
2	C		
3	E		
4	E		
5	A		
6	C		
7	E		
8	E		
9	D		
10	D		
11	A		
12	B		
13	A		
14	E		

CALCULATING YOUR SCORE

Writing Section Raw Score

A. Essay Score (from 1–6)

______ A

B. Section 6 Multiple Choice: ______ no. correct – (______ no. incorrect ÷ 4) = ______ B

C. Section 9 Multiple Choice: ______ no. correct – (______ no. incorrect ÷ 4) = ______ C

D. Unrounded Multiple-Choice Score (B + C)

______ D

E. Total Rounded Multiple-Choice Raw Score
(Rounded to the nearest whole number)

______ E

F. Writing Multiple-Choice Subscore
(See the Writing Multiple-Choice conversion table on the following pages)

______ Writing MC Score

G. Total Scaled Score
(See the Writing conversion table on the following pages)

______ SAT Writing Score

Math Section Raw Score

A. Section 3 Raw Score: ______ no. correct – (______ no. incorrect ÷ 4) = ______ Subtotal A

B. Section 5 Raw Score: ______ no. correct ______ Subtotal B

C. Section 8 Raw Score: ______ no. correct – (______ no. incorrect ÷ 4) = ______ Subtotal C

D. Total Unrounded Raw Score
(Total A + B + C)

______ D

E. Total Rounded Raw Score (Rounded to the nearest whole number)

______ E

F. Scaled Score
(See the conversion table on the following pages)

______ SAT Math Score

Critical Reading Section Raw Score

A. Section 2 Raw Score: ________ (no. correct) – (________ (no. incorrect) ÷ 4) = ________ A

B. Section 4 Raw Score: ________ (no. correct) – (________ (no. incorrect) ÷ 4) = ________ B

C. Section 7 Raw Score: ________ (no. correct) – (________ (no. incorrect) ÷ 4) = ________ C

D. Total Unrounded Raw Score
(Total A + B + C) ________ D

E. Total Rounded Raw Score
(Rounded to the nearest whole number) ________ E

F. Scaled Score
(See the conversion table on the next page) ________ SAT Critical Reading Score

CONVERTING YOUR RAW SCORES

Raw Score	Critical Reading Scaled Score	Math Scaled Score
67	800	
66	790	
65	770	
64	760	
63	750	
62	740	
61	720	
60	710	
59	700	
58	690	
57	680	
56	670	
55	670	
54	660	800
53	650	780
52	640	760
51	640	740
50	630	730
49	620	710
48	610	700
47	610	690
46	600	670
45	590	660
44	590	650
43	580	650
42	580	640
41	570	630
40	560	620
39	560	610
38	550	600
37	540	590
36	540	590
35	530	580
34	530	570
33	520	560
32	510	560
31	510	550
30	500	540
29	500	530
28	490	520
27	480	520
26	480	510
25	470	500
24	470	490
23	460	490
22	450	480
21	450	470
20	440	460
19	430	460

Writing Scaled Score

MC raw score	Essay Score					
	6	5	4	3	2	1
11	510	480	450	410	380	360
10	500	470	450	400	370	350
9	490	460	440	390	360	350
8	480	450	430	390	360	340
7	470	440	420	380	350	330
6	460	430	410	370	340	320
5	450	430	400	360	330	310
4	450	420	390	350	320	300
3	440	410	390	340	310	290
2	430	400	380	330	300	280
1	420	380	370	320	290	270
0	400	370	350	310	280	260
–1	380	360	340	290	270	260
–2	370	340	320	270	260	250
–3	360	330	310	260	250	240
–4	350	320	290	250	240	230
–5	340	310	280	240	230	220
–6	340	310	280	240	220	210

SECTION 2: CRITICAL READING

Sentence Completions

1. **E** One-Word/One-Way *Easy*

The last part of this sentence defines the meaning of the word in the blank. The committee members *tended to argue their positions forcefully*, so decision-making must have occurred through extensive *debate*.

2. **E** One-Word/One-Way *Easy*

The second part of the sentence helps explain the meaning of the word in the blank. You're looking for a word that means that Riley falsely downplays his skills or achievements. The word *modest* fits best.

3. **C** One-Word/One-Way *Easy*

The meaning of the missing word is defined by the phrase within the commas. You're looking for a word that means *adherence to a code of ethics*. **C**, *integrity*, works best.

4. **A** Two-Word/One-Way *Easy*

You would most likely use written materials to "explain," "review," or "illustrate" complex concepts, so eliminate **B** and **E**. Learners would most likely *demonstrate* reading comprehension skills rather than *suggest* them. **A** is correct.

5. **A** Two-Word/One-Way *Medium*

The last part of this sentence indicates that the individuals discussed in the sentence *adopt* the theoretical approach of realism. Therefore, they must be *supporters* or *proponents* of this view. Eliminate **B**, **D**, and **E**. The *belief that nations act in their own self-interest* appears to be the main reason why supporters adopt the realist approach. Only **A** contains a second word close in meaning to "main," so **A** is correct.

6. **C** One-Word/One-Way *Medium*

The lobbyist had some sort of effect on his colleagues. The precise type of effect is defined in the last part of the sentence: He *raised awareness* and *spurred [them] to take action*. The word *galvanize* means "to increase awareness or motivate action," so **C** is correct.

7. **B** Two-Word/One-Way *Difficult*

The last part of the sentence defines the meanings of the words in the blanks. The first missing word must mean something like *secret*, so eliminate **C** and **D**. The second missing word means *implemented slowly and subtly*. The word *insidious* means "spreading harmfully in a slow or stealthy manner," so **B** works best.

8. **C** Two-Word/Two-Way *Difficult*

The first part of the sentence explains that the professor is *overbearing in faculty meetings*, so the first blank will contain a word that means "arrogant" or "domineering." Eliminate **A** and **D**. It is difficult to reconcile the professor's overbearing behavior with her behavior in the classroom, so the second missing word must mean "relaxed" or "lenient." The word *complaisance* means "willingly complying with others," so **C** is correct.

Short Reading Passages

9. **B** Specific Information *Easy*

The passage states that when the messenger showed his gold specimens to the crowd, *the excitement produced was intense*. **B** is correct.

10. **E** Implied Information *Medium*

This passage discusses the intense reaction that occurred when one group of townspeople saw proof of gold at the mines. After seeing the evidence brought back by a messenger, individuals took off for the mines in droves, leaving behind their jobs and traveling any way they could. The reference to *some on crutches* serves to suggest the enthusiasm with which people made the trip, even if they had no transportation and could hardly walk.

11. **C** Themes and Arguments *Difficult*

The author's main point is contained in the third sentence of this passage: *None of Shakespeare's characters seem to agree so much in situation, and to differ so much in disposition, as Richard III and Macbeth.* The author points out the similarities between Richard III and Macbeth to emphasize the point that despite their similar circumstances, these characters have very different dispositions.

12. **E** Specific Information *Easy*

The passage states that both Richard III and Macbeth are soldiers, so **A** is true. The passage states that both attained the throne by treason and murder, so **C** and **D** are true. The passage also states that both leaders lost the throne *in battle*, so **B** is true. However, the passage never mentions that either was consumed by jealousy, so **E** is correct.

Paired Reading Passages

13. **D** Main Idea *Medium*

Passage 1 discusses metabolic rate theory, which states that longevity is affected by the rate of an organism's metabolism. **E** therefore fits best.

14. **A** Implied Information *Easy*

The referenced lines state that *aging involves multiple processes that contribute to the deterioration of our health*. The phrase *multiple processes* implies that aging is brought about by several different biological phenomena, so **A** is correct.

15. **E** Themes and Arguments *Medium*

Paragraph 2 of Passage 1 introduces Denham Harmon by explaining that his *pioneering work formed the foundation for his "free radical" theory of aging*. Denham's contribution was important for developing this theory, as **E** states.

16. **B** Specific Information *Medium*

The answer to this question is specifically stated in the passage. Paragraph 3 of Passage 1 defines free radicals as chemicals that *are generated as byproducts when our cells perform routine metabolic functions, such as producing energy*. **B** reiterates this definition from the passage.

17. **C** Implied Information *Difficult*

The *destructive chain reaction* caused by free radicals is explained in paragraph 4 of Passage 1. Here, the author states that free radicals steal electrons from normal molecules in a process known as *oxidation*. When normal molecules lose their electrons to free radicals, they *then become free radicals themselves, in turn stealing electrons from other molecules in a vicious cycle*. This implies that the destructive chain reaction occurs because of the fact that free radicals convert normal molecules into other free radicals.

18. **C** Words in Context *Medium*

Paragraph 4 of Passage 1 explains how oxidation produces a destructive chain reaction within the cells. During oxidation, free radicals steal electrons from other molecules, causing damage within the cells. Paragraph 6 notes that lower levels of free radicals cause less stress from oxidation. In this context, the word *stress* most nearly means *damage*, since oxidation damages the cells.

19. **B** Themes and Arguments *Difficult*

Paragraph 2 of Passage 2 explains how researcher Anja Brunet determined that bats and shrews have similar metabolic rates but have very different life spans. Bats live much longer than shrews, even though their metabolic rates are about the same. According to Passage 2, Brunet's research on bats and shrews served to refute *the notion that longevity is correlated with metabolic rate*. **B** is therefore correct.

20. **A** Implied Information *Medium*

Paragraph 3 of Passage 2 states that Speakman's team was surprised to discover that *at least in one species, higher metabolisms can lead to longer lives*. This discovery disconfirmed the traditional theory, described in paragraph 1, that faster metabolic rates lead to accelerated aging (and shorter life spans). Speakman's team was surprised that their research disproved this prevailing viewpoint, so **A** fits best.

21. **A** Specific Information *Easy*

The last paragraph of Passage 2 describes Lloyd Demetrius as *one of the most prominent proponents of the metabolic-stability hypothesis*. Specifically, Demetrius claims *that longevity is determined not by how fast our metabolism operates, but rather by how stable our levels of free radicals are*, as **A** states.

22. **E** Implied Information *Medium*

According to the last paragraph of Passage 2, Demetrius believes that *keeping free radical levels stable (within an optimal range) may be more important for longevity than simply reducing these levels across the board*. Demetrius does not support the reduction of free radical levels across the board, so eliminate **A**. He also appears to believe that an optimal range of free radical levels may be determined, so eliminate **B**. The paragraph notes that *some levels of free radicals appear to be necessary within an organism to promote communication between cells*. This statement helps explain Demetrius's view. He would therefore probably agree that free radicals have some positive biological functions.

23. **D** Relating Two Passages *Medium*

The last sentence of Passage 1 states that *supplementation with these anti-oxidants can be important for promoting longevity*. Passage 2 does not mention anti-oxidants or recommend any type of supplementation, so **D** is correct.

24. **D** Relating Two Passages *Medium*

The last paragraph of Passage 2 describes metabolic stability theory as one alternative to the metabolic rate theory of longevity. Metabolic stability theory claims that longevity is promoted by stable levels of free radicals. This view would be supported by a study that links stable free radical levels to long life spans in mice. Passage 1 does not address the metabolic stability theory, so **D** upholds the argument of Passage 2 only.

SECTION 3: MATH

Multiple Choice

1. **D** Algebra: Solving Equations *Easy*

Solve for r:

$$2r + 8 = 4r + 2$$
$$-2r = -6$$
$$r = 3$$

2. **B** Numbers & Operations: Sequences *Easy*

Each number in the sequence is determined by multiplying the preceding term by 3 and then adding 1:

$$1 \times 3 = 3 + 1 = 4$$
$$4 \times 3 = 12 + 1 = 13$$
$$13 \times 3 = 39 + 1 = 40$$

Therefore, the value of n is 3.

3. **B** Data Analysis, Statistics & Probability: Graphs, Charts, and Tables *Easy*

The dolls come in 4 different types of hair color and 4 different types of clothing. The total number of possible combinations is 4×4, or 16.

4. **D** Algebra: Functions *Medium*

The functions in **A** and **E** contain variables raised to an even power, which always produces an even result. The functions $f(-5)$ and $f(5)$ will produce the same result for **A** and **E**, so these can both be eliminated. The function in **B** produces a constant result of 6, so **B** can be eliminated as well. The function in **C** would produce a negative result for $f(-5)$ and a positive result for $f(5)$, so eliminate **C**. The function in **D** contains a variable raised to an odd power. Evaluate the function for $f(-5)$ and $f(5)$:

$$f(-5) = 6 - x^3 = 6 - (-5)^3 = 6 + 125, \text{ or } 131$$
$$f(5) = 6 - x^3 = 6 - (5)^3 = 6 - 125, \text{ or } -119$$

In this case, $f(-5) > f(5)$, so **D** is correct.

5. **E** Numbers & Operations: Ratios *Easy*

Let x represent the number of grams of dog food needed to feed a dog weighing 9 kilograms. Set up a ratio and solve for x:

$$\frac{87}{5} = \frac{x}{9}$$
$$5x = 87(9)$$
$$5x = 783$$
$$x = \frac{783}{5}$$
$$x = 156.6$$

6. **D** Geometry: Angles and Lines *Easy*

Draw the line segment to help you visualize the problem:

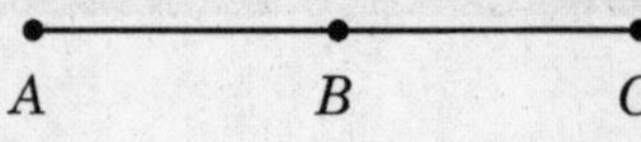

The point B lies on segment AC, so $AB + BC = AC$. This means that $BC = AC - AB$, so I is correct. Eliminate **B** and **C**. If B is the midpoint of AC, then $AB = \left(\frac{1}{2}\right)AC$. When both sides of this equation are multiplied by 4, this produces $4AB = 2AC$. Statement II is correct, so eliminate **A**.

If B is the midpoint of AC, then $BC = AB$. Statement III is incorrect, so **E** can be eliminated. **D** is the correct answer.

7. **C** Algebra: Solving Equations *Easy*

The question states that $3n = 7p$ and $7p = 12q$. Therefore, $3n = 12q$. Solve for n:

$$3n = 12q$$
$$n = \frac{12q}{3}$$
$$n = 4q$$

8. **A** Numbers & Operations: Basic Operations *Difficult*

The letter a represents the total number of filled chairs. One of the conference rooms had 5 empty chairs. The number of filled chairs in this room was therefore $c - 5$. The remaining conference rooms were all filled. There were r conference rooms total, so the remaining conference rooms can be represented by $r - 1$.

Each conference room had c chairs, so the number of attendees in the remaining conference rooms was $c(r - 1)$. Set up an equation:

$$a = c - 5 + c(r - 1)$$
$$a = c - 5 + cr - c$$
$$a = cr - 5$$

This equation can also be written as $rc - 5 = a$.

9. **C** Geometry: Angles and Lines *Medium*

This figure contains two parallel lines crossed by two transversals, as shown:

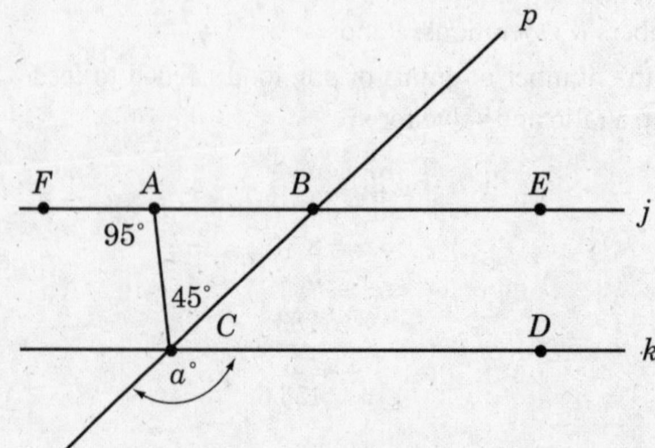

When two parallel lines are crossed by a transversal, opposite interior angles are congruent. This means that $m\angle FAC$ equals $m\angle ACD$. The measure of $\angle FAC$ is 95°, so $\angle ACD$ also measures 95°. Use this information to find the measure of $\angle BCD$:

$$m\angle ACB + m\angle BCD = \angle ACD$$
$$45° + m\angle BCD = 95°$$
$$m\angle BCD = 95° - 45°$$
$$m\angle BCD = 50°$$

Use the measure of $\angle BCD$ to determine the measure of $\angle a$. These angles are supplementary, so their measures add up to 180°:

$$m\angle BCD + m\angle a = 180°$$
$$50° + m\angle a = 180°$$
$$m\angle a = 180° - 50°$$
$$m\angle a = 130°$$

10. **E** Algebra: Inequalities *Medium*

The value of $4g^2$ will always be less than $(4g)^2$, unless g equals 1, 0, or –1. When g equals 1, 0, or –1, then $4g^2 = (4g)^2$. Otherwise, the product of $4g \times 4g$ will always be greater than the product of g^2 and 4. This might be easier to see if you break the expressions down into their component parts:

$$4g \times 4g > g^2 \times 4$$
$$4 \times g \times 4 \times g > g \times g \times 4$$
$$g \times g \times 4 \times 4 > g \times g \times 4$$
$$4(g \times g \times 4) > g \times g \times 4$$

There's an extra 4 on the left hand side of the inequality, so even for fractions and negative numbers, the left side will always be greater. **E** is correct.

11. **C** Geometry: Circles *Medium*

In order to make one revolution, a wheel must turn the entire distance of its circumference. Compare the circumferences of the front and back wheels. The circumference of a back wheel can be represented by $C = \pi d$. The circumference of a front wheel can be represented by $C = \left(\frac{1}{3}\right)\pi d$. The circumference of a back wheel is 3 times the circumference of a front wheel. So, a front wheel must make 3 revolutions for every 1 revolution made by a back wheel.

12. **C** Data Analysis, Statistics & Probability: Statistical Analysis *Medium*

If a number is picked at random from the set, the probability that the number is even is $\frac{4}{7}$. This means that there are 4 even numbers for every 7 numbers in the set. Therefore, for every 7 numbers, there must be 3 odd numbers. The ratio of odd to even numbers, $\frac{o}{e}$, must be $\frac{3}{4}$.

13. **B** Algebra: Functions *Medium*

Substitute the values you are given for d and n into the function and solve for h:

$$d(n) = \frac{450n - 150}{n} + h$$
$$720 = \frac{450(30) - 150}{30} + h$$
$$720 = \frac{13,500 - 150}{30} + h$$
$$720 = \frac{13,350}{30} + h$$
$$720 = 445 + h$$
$$275 = h$$

14. **D** Algebra: Inequalities *Medium*

The values in the ordered pairs must be positive, so start with the number 1. Substitute in the values (1, 1) for x and y:

$$3x + 5y \leq 16$$
$$3(1) + 5(1) \leq 16$$
$$3 + 5 \leq 16$$
$$8 \leq 16$$

The ordered pair (1, 1) works. Try the ordered pair (2, 2) as well:

$$3x + 5y \leq 16$$
$$3(2) + 5(2) \leq 16$$
$$6 + 10 \leq 16$$
$$16 \leq 16$$

The ordered pair (2, 2) also works. This means that the ordered pairs (1, 2) and (2, 1) will work as well. Therefore, **D** is correct.

15. **C** Geometry: Triangles *Medium*

The figure shows that $\angle AEB$ measures 60˚. Solve for the value of m:

$$m + m + 60° = 180°$$
$$2m + 60° = 180°$$
$$2m = 180° - 60°$$
$$2m = 120°$$
$$m = 60°$$

Triangle *AEB* is equilateral, so its perimeter is 3 + 3 + 3, or 9.

Now determine the perimeter of *AED*. Side *AE* is shared with *AEB*, so *AE* measures 3. This triangle has two congruent angles, n, so side *DE* also measures 3. The perimeter of *AED* is 3 + 3 + 9 = 15. Its perimeter is 6 units greater (15 – 9) than the perimeter of *AEB*.

16. **D** Algebra: Binomials and Quadratics *Medium*

If a and b are positive consecutive even integers and b is the larger of the two, this means that b equals $a + 2$. Substitute $a + 2$ into the equation $a^2 + b^2$ and solve:

$$\begin{aligned} a^2 + b^2 &= a^2 + (a+2)^2 \\ &= a^2 + (a+2)(a+2) \\ &= a^2 + (a^2 + 2a + 2a + 4) \\ &= 2a^2 + 4a + 4 \\ &= 2(a^2 + 2a + 2) \end{aligned}$$

17. **A** Geometry: Coordinate Geometry *Difficult*

Line m passes through the point (0, 0), so its y-intercept is 0. It is perpendicular to the line $6x + y = h$. Perpendicular lines have slopes that are negative reciprocals of each other. Determine the slope of $6x + y = h$ by first rewriting it in the general form $y = mx + b$:

$$\begin{aligned} 6x + y &= h \\ y &= -6x + h \end{aligned}$$

The slope of this line (b) is –6, so the slope of line m is $\frac{1}{6}$. The equation of line m is $y = \frac{1}{6}x$.

Line m passes through the point $(p, p + 2)$. Substitute these values into the equation for line m and solve for p:

$$\begin{aligned} y &= \frac{1}{6}x \\ (p+2) &= \frac{1}{6}(p) \\ 6(p+2) &= p \\ 6p + 12 &= p \\ 5p &= -12 \\ p &= -\frac{12}{5} \end{aligned}$$

18. **A** Data Analysis, Statistics & Probability: Statistical Analysis *Difficult*

Set up an equation based on the information given in the question:

$$\frac{a+b+c}{3} = t$$

Solve for the value of $a + b + c$:

$$a + b + c = 3t$$

The average of $a + b + c + d$ equals $\frac{a+b+c+d}{4}$. Substitute $3t$ for $a + b + c$:

$$\frac{a+b+c+d}{4} = \frac{3t+d}{4}$$

19. **C** Geometry: Triangles *Difficult*

Triangle ADE is equilateral, so $\angle E$ and $\angle D$ measure 60°. This means that $\angle EAB$ and $\angle DAB$ measure 30°. Therefore, EAB and DAB are both 30-60-90 triangles. Use this information to find the length of the diameter, AB.

The legs of a 30-60-90 triangle are in the ratio $x{:}x\sqrt{3}{:}2x$. The question states that AE measures $2\sqrt{3}$. Side AE is the hypotenuse of EAB, so its measurement is equivalent to $2x$, or 2 times the length of the shortest side. The shortest side, EB, therefore measures $\frac{1}{2}(2\sqrt{3})$, or $\sqrt{3}$. Side AB measures $x\sqrt{3}$, or $\sqrt{3} \times \sqrt{3}$, which is 3. These measurements are indicated in the sketch below:

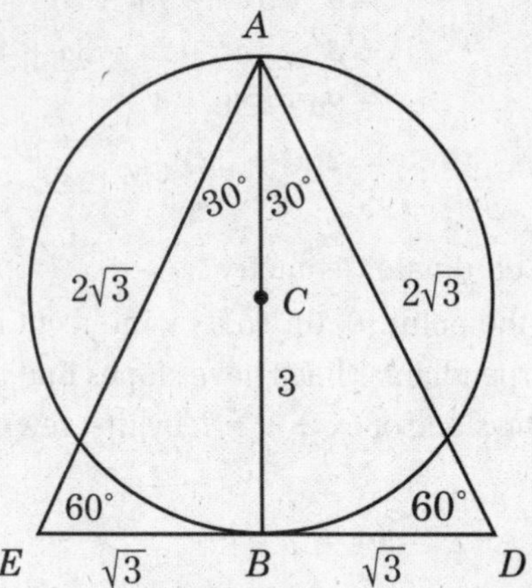

The diameter of the circle is 3. Therefore, the radius of the circle is $\frac{3}{2}$. The area of the circle is equal to πr^2, or $\pi\left(\frac{3}{2}\right)^2$. The area of the circle is $\frac{9}{4}\pi$.

20. **B** Numbers & Operations: Divisibility and Remainders *Medium*

If 16 is divided by a number m, the remainder produced is 4. This means that during the division process, m was multiplied by another whole number to produce 12. The product 12 was then subtracted from 16, leaving a remainder of 4.

Determine the integers smaller than 16 that are factors of 12: 1, 2, 3, 4, 6, and 12. Divide 16 by each of these numbers. The numbers 1, 2, and 4 divide evenly into 16, so these numbers can be eliminated. The number 3 can also be eliminated, because $16 \div 3$ equals 5 with a remainder of 1. The numbers 6 and 12 are the only two numbers that produce a remainder of 4 when divided into 16, so **B** is correct.

SECTION 4: CRITICAL READING

Sentence Completions

1. **D** One-Word/Two-Way *Easy*

Karen thought that her co-workers *agreed* with her idea, but it turns out that they did not. The word *oppose* means "to disagree with," so **D** is correct.

2. **D** One-Word/One-Way *Easy*

Talia admires her husband's family *to the point of blind devotion*, which is another way of saying that she *idolizes* them. **D** fits best here.

3. **C** One-Word/One-Way *Medium*

The fan mail is *evidence* of the host's ability to *connect with* [his] *audiences*. You're looking for a word that means something like "proof" or "evidence." The word *testament*, in **C**, means "to serve as tangible proof," so **C** works best.

4. **C** Two-Word/One-Way *Medium*

The colon (:) in this sentence indicates that the second part of the sentence serves to illustrate the first. Therefore, the two parts of the sentence are similar in meaning. *The engineering team found themselves paralyzed even though they knew that a systems failure was* "something." Look for words that mean "about to occur." **B**, **C**, and **E** look plausible, so eliminate **A** and **D**. If a systems failure was about to occur, then the error alerts must have "indicated" a shutdown. The word *portended* means "served as a warning of," so **C** is correct.

5. **A** Two-Word/One-Way *Difficult*

The defendant had a history of *miscreant*, or "villainous," behavior, so his motivations must have been negative. Look for answers with first words that are negative in meaning. The word *penitent* means "remorseful," so eliminate **C**. The word *unimpeachable* means "genuine," so eliminate **E** as well.

Even the most "something" *judge would have refused to show the defendant any leniency*. Look for an answer whose second word means "lenient." The word *clement* means "merciful," so **A** works best.

Paired Reading Passages

6. **D** Relating Two Passages *Medium*

Passage 1 presents Paul Feyerabend's argument that science should be developed through many different methodologies. Passage 2 presents the arguments of Popper and Lakatos, who each argue for a different scientific method. Both passages address the question of what types of approaches best promote scientific progress.

7. **A** Relating Two Passages *Medium*

In Passage 1, the argument of Paul Feyerabend is summarized: *In Feyerabend's view,* the passage states, *science cannot be advanced by adhering to a fixed set of rules or standards*. This viewpoint is not articulated in Passage 2, so **A** is correct.

8. **D** Relating Two Passages *Difficult*

According to Passage 2, Karl Popper believed that *theories could be classified as scientific only if they were capable of being disproved by evidence*. Popper's view differs from that of Feyerabend, who believed that science should be developed through combinations of different approaches—even seemingly irrational ones. Popper argued that only certain types of theories should be classified as scientific, whereas Feyerabend did not believe that science should adhere to strict criteria. **D** fits best.

9. **C** Relating Two Passages *Medium*

According to Passage 2, Lakatos believed that *science should be comprised not of single theories but rather of sets of theories, or research programs*. He would most likely reject Feyerabend's view, since Feyerabend did not believe in applying specific criteria to theories. Eliminate **A**, **D**, and **E**. Lakatos did argue that science should adhere to a particular methodology, so **B** can be eliminated. **C** is correct.

Long Reading Passages

10. **C** Main Idea *Easy*

The passage describes the narrator's travels during his early adult years, so **C** fits best.

11. **B** Themes and Arguments *Easy*

In paragraph 2, the narrator mentions that when he was nineteen, his father urged him to return to France and sign up for the draft. The narrator then states that *against this my mother resolutely set her face*. The narrator's mother was very opposed to the idea that the narrator should register for military service, so **B** is correct.

12. **C** Words in Context *Medium*

In paragraph 2, the narrator states, *I fancy my father wanted me to take up the army as a career*. Here he means that he "believes" or "supposes" that his father wanted him to serve in the army. **C** is the closest fit, and it is also the only definition that works when substituted into the sentence.

13. **D** Implied Information *Medium*

The narrator explains in paragraph 3 that his mother advised him to travel east, to see what the experience of travel would do for him. At the end of the paragraph, the narrator explains his mother's ulterior motive: *My mother was of the opinion that if I saw a bit of the world in this way, I would be more inclined to settle down at home with her at the end of my wanderings*.

14. **E** Attitude or Tone *Difficult*

The narrator states in paragraph 4 that his father had his own plans for the narrator's future: *He had, as I have previously intimated, made his own plans for my future, even to the point of deciding upon a future wife for me, as is customary in France*. The author reacts to his father's plans by *resolutely declining to conform to his father's wishes*. Although the author does defy his father's wishes, he does not react to his father with sarcasm, so **D** can be eliminated. The word *resolute* means "firm" or "determined," so **E** fits best. The author resisted his father's plans in a steadfast and determined way.

15. **A** Implied Information *Medium*

In the second to last paragraph, Peter Jensen tells the narrator that he would like to organize a pearling expedition to New Guinea but that he is lacking *sufficient capital to defray the preliminary expenses*. In other words, Jensen lacks the funds to pay for the trip. The narrator states in the last paragraph that he took Peter Jensen's hint and offered to join him on the voyage. The phrase *this hint I took* suggests that the narrator contributed funds to launch the expedition.

16. **B** Attitude or Tone *Easy*

The author describes the exhibit positively in paragraph 1 as *a display of photographic excellence in its grandest sense*. This description reflects an attitude of *admiration*, so **B** works best.

17. **D** Implied Information *Medium*

At the end of paragraph 1, the author notes that Edmonson has *an almost indecipherable expression on his face.* Is his look one of consternation (dismay), or is it one of amusement? The author cannot distinguish between these two possibilities, which suggests that Edmonson's expression is *difficult to interpret.*

18. **E** Implied Information *Medium*

Paragraph 2 states that Edmonson's *clothing and ragged shoes are more than we need to understand how poor Edmonson has probably been all of his life.* This implies that Edmonson is most likely extremely poor. **E** is correct.

19. **A** Words in Context *Medium*

Even though Edmonson appears to live in poverty, the author states that he *seems peaceful and somehow resigned to his fate.* In other words, Edmonson seems to accept his fate and to feel peaceful about it. In this case, *resigned to* most nearly means *accepting of.*

20. **A** Implied Information *Medium*

Paragraph 4 mentions Edmonson's grandsons, stating that Bourke-White's portrait reflects *where Edmonson's grandsons might be*, twenty years after Edmonson's photo was taken. Edmonson's photo was taken in 1941, and Bourke-White's photograph was taken in 1957. We can't know for sure whether Edmonson in fact had any grandchildren or any family at all—the passage doesn't mention his family. However, if Edmonson did have grandsons of his own, in the 16 years between these photographs, his grandsons would probably have grown up and started to work for a living. The phrase *might be* suggests not that Edmonson's actual grandchildren work in the mines but that by 1957 they might have been about the same age as the men in the photograph and could have had similar jobs. **A** works best.

21. **D** Words in Context *Easy*

In the fourth paragraph, the author states that the men in Bourke-White's photograph are both *gazing intently at something that seems to be taking place near them.* They have fixed their attention on this event, so they are looking at it *attentively.*

22. **E** Themes and Arguments *Difficult*

The *ominous quality* of Bourke-White's photograph is mentioned in paragraph 4, after the author notes that the men appear to be looking at some event that has taken place near them. The author claims that the image has an ominous (threatening) quality because as viewers *we're not sure of what has happened, and the men's reactions only confuse us.* The author uses the term *ominous* to emphasize that the men are reacting to something that the viewer is unclear about.

23. **C** Specific Information *Easy*

The passage explains in paragraph 5 that the muscular structures of the men in Bourke-White's photograph *seem to symbolize a strength and a fearlessness*, so **C** is correct here.

24. **C** Themes and Arguments *Medium*

At the end of paragraph 5, the author explains a contradiction apparent in the photograph. First, she notes, the muscular structures of both men *seem to symbolize a strength and a fearlessness that signals their removal from Edmonson's oppression.* In other words, both men appear physically very capable of moving beyond poverty into a better life. At the same time, however, the expression of the second man is disturbed and fearful. His expression contradicts the strength revealed in the photo. This contradiction is highlighted by the author to support the point raised in the last sentence of the paragraph: Bourke-White's conflicting portrayal of these men *makes us question whether their status in 1957 is an improvement over that of Edmonson* in America. **C** best summarizes this point.

SECTION 5: MATH

Multiple Choice

1. **A** Algebra: Solving Equations *Easy*

Substitute 5 for $p - q$ in the equation and solve:

$$p - q - 7 = 5 - 7 = -2$$

2. **C** Geometry: Solids *Easy*

Segment *SY* is a diagonal of the cube, so *SY* is longer than side *YU*. Point *Y* is closer to *U* than it is to point *S*, so **C** is correct.

3. **E** Data Analysis, Statistics & Probability: Graphs, Charts, and Tables *Easy*

The shaded section labeled German shepherds constitutes almost $\frac{3}{4}$ of the graph. German shepherds therefore make up almost 75 percent of the dogs at the training academy. The academy trains 100 dogs, so nearly 75 of these are German shepherds. **E** works best.

4. **D** Numbers & Operations: Fractions *Medium*

The denominator is 5 more than the numerator, so let the denominator be represented by $n + 5$. The fraction is equal to $\frac{2}{3}$, so set up an equation:

$$\frac{n}{n+5} = \frac{2}{3}$$
$$3n = 2(n+5)$$
$$3n = 2n + 10$$
$$n = 10$$

5. **E** Geometry: Triangles *Medium*

Judging from the graph, the triangle has a height of 5 units and a base of 4*f* units. The area of the triangle is given as 20. Substitute these values into the area formula and solve for *f*:

$$A = \frac{1}{2}bh$$
$$20 = \frac{1}{2}(4f)(5)$$
$$20 = \frac{1}{2}(20f)$$
$$20 = 10f$$
$$2 = f$$

6. **D** Algebra: Absolute Value and Exponents *Difficult*

Using the equation given in the question stem, first solve for *x*:

$$9x^2y^{-1} = 81x$$
$$\frac{9x^2}{y} = 81x$$
$$\frac{9x^2}{81x} = y$$
$$\frac{x}{9} = y$$
$$x = 9y$$

The value of x^{-1} is $\frac{1}{x}$. Therefore, $x^{-1} = \frac{1}{9y}$.

7. **E** Geometry: Triangles *Medium*

Draw a diagram to help you visualize the problem:

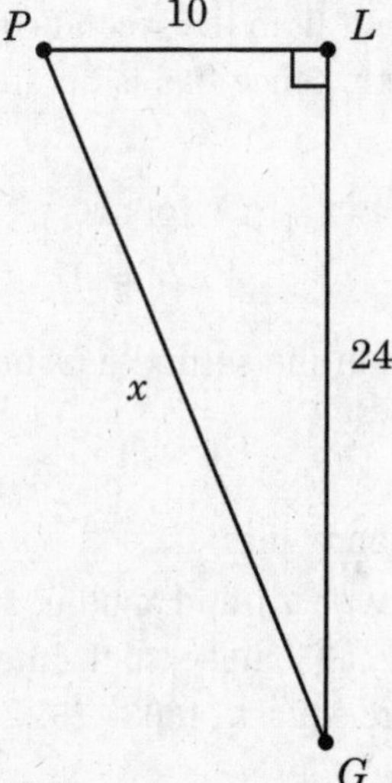

Priscilla and Gretchen start at the library, point *L*. Priscilla rides west at 5 mph for 2 hours, so she rides a total of 10 miles to point *P*. Gretchen rides south at 12 mph for 2 hours, so she rides a total of 24 miles to point *G*. Let *x* equal the length of *PG*. This triangle is a special right triangle, whose legs are in a ratio 5:12:13. Therefore, the length of *x* is 2×13, or 26 miles.

If you did not recognize this as a 5:12:13 triangle, you could also use the Pythagorean theorem to solve for x:

$$a^2 + b^2 = c^2$$
$$10^2 + 24^2 = x^2$$
$$100 + 576 = x^2$$
$$676 = x^2$$
$$\sqrt{676} = x$$
$$26 = x$$

8. **C** Algebra: Functions *Difficult*

This question tests your ability to interpret functional notation. It tells you that the function $f(s)$ is equal to the function $f(4)$. This means that the output, or y-value, of $f(4)$ is the same as the output, or y-value, of $f(s)$. The graph shows that the output, or y-value, of $f(4)$ is 3. The only other point on the parabola with a y-value of 3 is the point (0, 3). Therefore, in this case, $f(0) = f(4)$. The value of s could be 0.

Grid-Ins

9. **9** Algebra: Solving Equations *Easy*

Each of the 10 students will need to use 5 pieces of graph paper each week for 7 weeks. The total amount of graph paper needed is $10 \times 5 \times 7 = 350$ sheets. The graph paper is sold only in 40-sheet packages. Therefore, the class will need to buy 9 packages, or a total of 360 sheets, in order to have enough graph paper for the experiment.

10. **19** Numbers & Operations: Basic Operations *Easy*

Solve the first equation. One possible value for r in the first equation is 1: $10 - 1 = 9$. However, this value for r doesn't fit in the second equation: $1 - 7 \neq 12$. Try another value for r in the first equation. Since this is an absolute value equation, use the number 19:

$$|10 - 19| = 9$$
$$|-9| = 9$$

The value $r = 19$ also works in the second equation: $|19 - 7| = 12$. The correct answer is 19.

11. **100** Geometry: Angles and Lines *Medium*

Angle k lies on a straight line with $\angle j$ and another angle that measures 25°. Angle j is complementary to its adjacent 35° angle, so the measure of $\angle j$ is 90° – 35°, or 55°. The measure of $\angle k$ is therefore equal to 180° – 25° – 55°, or 100°.

12. **24** Data Analysis, Statistics & Probability: Statistical Analysis *Easy*

The question describes 27 as the median of a set of 7 integers, which means that when the numbers are placed in numerical order, 27 falls exactly in the middle of the set. The set therefore contains 3 integers smaller than 27 and three integers greater than 27. The integers are consecutive, so place 27 in the center and list out the numbers in order:

24, 25, 26, 27, 28, 29, 30

The smallest integer in the set is 24.

13. **29** Algebra: Functions *Medium*

The value of $2f(s) = 10$. This means that the value of $f(s) = \frac{10}{2}$, or 5. Use this information to create an equation and solve for s:

$$f(s) = s - 3$$
$$5 = s - 3$$
$$8 = s$$

Now, solve for $f(4s)$:

$$f(s) = s - 3$$
$$f(4s) = 4s - 3$$
$$29 = 4(8) - 3$$

14. **110** Geometry: Triangles *Medium*

When two parallel lines are crossed by a transversal, opposite interior angles are equal. Therefore, $m\angle z = m\angle EAB$. Use the information given in the diagram to determine the measure of $\angle EAB$.

Angle EAB is part of an isosceles triangle with two equal sides, AE and AB. These equal sides lie opposite two equal angles. One of these angles, $\angle AEB$, is supplementary to the angle marked 145°. Therefore, $\angle AEB$ measures 180° – 145°, or 35°.

Since $\angle AEB$ is equal to $\angle ABE$, you can now find the measure of $\angle EAB$:

$$m\angle AEB + m\angle ABE + m\angle EAB = 180°$$
$$35° + 35° + m\angle EAB = 180°$$
$$m\angle EAB = 180° - 35° - 35°$$
$$m\angle EAB = 110°$$

15. **8/18, 4/9** Numbers & Operations: Fractions *Medium*

The box starts with $\frac{1}{6}$ of a pound of blue sand. It is then filled to the 1-lb mark with a mixture of different colored sands. This added mixture weighs $1 - \frac{1}{6}$, or $\frac{5}{6}$ of a pound. In this $\frac{5}{6}$ of a pound are equal amounts of blue, red, and yellow sand. Each of these three types of sand thus weighs $\frac{1}{3} \times \frac{5}{6}$, or $\frac{5}{18}$ of a pound.

Add together the two portions of blue sand to get the total amount of blue sand:

$$\frac{1}{6} + \frac{5}{18} = \frac{3}{18} + \frac{5}{18}$$
$$= \frac{8}{18}, \text{ or } \frac{4}{9}$$

16. **6** Algebra: Solving Equations *Difficult*

Set up an equation and solve for $\frac{p}{r}$:

$$p + 3r = \frac{150}{100}(6r)$$
$$p + 3r = 1.5(6r)$$
$$p + 3r = 9r$$
$$p = 6r$$
$$\frac{p}{r} = 6$$

17. **9/16, .563** Numbers & Operations: Roots and Radicals *Difficult*

There are 8 intervals on the number line between 0 and 1. The variable $\sqrt{a}$ lies on the number line at $\frac{6}{8}$. This means that $\sqrt{a} = \frac{6}{8}$, or $\frac{3}{4}$.

Set up an equation and solve for a:

$$\sqrt{a} = \frac{3}{4}$$
$$(\sqrt{a})^2 = \left(\frac{3}{4}\right)^2$$
$$a = \frac{9}{16}$$

18. **6, 12** Algebra: Binomials and Quadratics *Difficult*

Substitute the values you are given into the distance formula:

$$d = \sqrt{(x_2 - x_1)^2 + (y_2 - y_1)^2}$$
$$3 = \sqrt{(x - 9)^2 + (12 - 12)^2}$$
$$3 = \sqrt{(x - 9)^2 + 0}$$
$$3 = \sqrt{(x - 9)(x - 9)}$$
$$3 = \sqrt{x^2 - 18x + 81}$$

Square both sides of the equation to eliminate the square root sign. Then, rewrite the equation in the general form $y = ax^2 + bx + c$, and find the two roots by factoring:

$$3^2 = x^2 - 18x + 81$$
$$9 = x^2 - 18x + 81$$
$$0 = x^2 - 18x + 72$$
$$0 = (x - 6)(x - 12)$$
$$x = 6 \text{ or } 12$$

SECTION 6: WRITING

Improving Sentences

1. **C** Coordination and Subordination *Easy*

The phrase *the teacher working this hard* uses the participle *working* incorrectly. The teacher's working took place in the past, which the phrase *having worked this hard* correctly expresses.

2. **D** Tenses *Easy*

This sentence takes place in the past, so the phrase *as if being stranded* should also reflect the past tense. **D** provides the correct revision with the past tense phrase *as if they had been stranded*.

3. **C** Subject-Verb Agreement *Medium*

This sentence has an error in subject-verb agreement. The subject of the sentence is the plural word *effects*. The verb of the sentence is the singular verb *has been widely recognized*. This verb should be in the plural form, *have been*, to agree with its plural subject.

4. **E** Coordination and Subordination *Medium*

The word *which* is unnecessary in the underlined portion of this sentence. As it stands, the sentence is a fragment. The revision in **E** corrects this error and also uses the correct tense of the verb *would*.

5. **D** Fragments *Medium*

As it stands, this sentence is a fragment. It has a subject, Anne Banyon Quimby, but it has no main verb. **D** corrects this problem by adding the verb *was*. **D** also replaces the ambiguous pronoun *it* with the more specific noun *this honor*.

6. **D** Conjunctions *Difficult*

The underlined portion of this sentence contains an unclear reference to *their accomplishments in this*, and it is also missing a conjunction. **D** corrects these errors by specifying that the accomplishments of Randy and Celeste have occurred *on the committee*. **D** also includes the conjunction *for* to indicate cause and effect.

7. **A** No Error *Medium*

This sentence is correct as written. All subjects and verbs agree, and all phrases are in the proper form.

8. **C** Wordiness *Medium*

The underlined portion of this sentence is wordy and contains the unnecessary phrase *being as it is*. **C** corrects this error most concisely.

9. **E** Coordination and Subordination *Difficult*

The underlined portion of this sentence starts with the conjunction *although*, but this conjunction doesn't work well with the verb phrase *never having facilitated*. **E** most effectively revises the underlined portion using the conjunction *because*, which expresses cause and effect. **E** also changes *having facilitated* to the simple past tense *never facilitated*.

10. **D** Wordiness *Difficult*

The underlined phrase *which duration made it seem* is wordy and awkward. This phrase is best corrected by the concise revision in **D**.

11. **B** Other *Medium*

The underlined portion of the sentence contains a pronoun error. The pronoun *it* refers to the noun *computer software programs*. However, the noun *programs* is plural and should therefore be referred to by a plural pronoun. **B** corrects this error by restating the noun *these programs*.

Identifying Sentence Errors

12. **A** Tense *Easy*

The word *revealing*, in **A**, is used incorrectly here. The simple present tense verb *reveals* should be used here instead.

13. **B** Parallelism *Easy*

The phrase *or do they* is not parallel with the earlier phrase *cure illness*. To be parallel, both of these phrases must contain the same verb form. The phrase *cure illness* is not underlined, so it must be correct. **B** should therefore be written as *or*, followed directly by the verb phrase *simply reduce*.

14. **A** Pronouns *Easy*

This sentence contains a pronoun error. The phrase *which believe* in **A** is used incorrectly to refer to *people*. The pronoun *who* should be used here instead.

15. **D** Tense *Medium*

The first part of this sentence takes place in the past. Therefore, the present-perfect phrase *have identified* in **D** should be changed to the past-perfect *had identified*. The second part of the sentence should state that *eye witnesses had identified him as part of the gang*.

16. **E** Tense *Medium*

The sentence is written correctly. All subjects and verbs agree, all verbs are in the correct tense, and all words are in the correct format.

17. **D** Conjunctions *Easy*

The word *when* is used incorrectly in **D** as the subordinating conjunction in this sentence. The conjunction *when* is normally used to indicate time. This sentence needs a conjunction that indicates cause and effect. The word *because* would work better here.

18. **D** Redundancy *Easy*

The phrase *more clearer* in **D** is redundant. The words *more* and *clearer* both signify comparison and thus should not be used together. The phrase *more clearer* should be replaced with either *more clear* or *clearer*.

19. **B** Subject-Verb Agreement *Easy*

This sentence uses the singular verb *is outweighed* incorrectly. The subject of this phrase is the plural noun *benefits*. The plural verb *are outweighed* should be after the plural noun.

20. **D** Pronouns *Medium*

The relative pronoun *whenever* is used incorrectly in **D**. The pronoun *when* should be used instead here.

21. **B** Tense *Medium*

The phrase *in the reviewing of* is used incorrectly here. The infinitive form of the verb *review* should be used instead: *The board members urged President Kinney to review the university's progress.*

22. **B** Easy *Easy*

This sentence contains an idiomatic error. The phrase *to develop* is used incorrectly after the word *uninterested*. The sentence should state that the librarian *seemed uninterested in developing friendships*.

23. **E** No Error *Medium*

This sentence is written correctly. All subjects and verbs agree, all verbs are in the correct tense, and all words are in the correct format.

24. **D** Adverbs and Adjectives *Medium*

This sentence compares two athletes. When comparing two persons or items, you should always use adjectives ending in *–er*. The phrase *the nimblest*, in **D**, should therefore be rewritten as *the nimbler*. Adjectives ending in *–est* should only be used to compare three or more persons or items.

25. **C** Other *Medium*

The conjunction *with* is used incorrectly in **C**. The sentence starts by stating that the change in policy had two effects. However, it's unclear whether the word *with* introduces a second effect or merely expands upon the first effect mentioned. To clearly delineate the two effects, the word *with* should be changed to the conjunction *and*.

26. **B** Subject-Verb Agreement *Medium*

The verb *emphasize* is plural, but the subject of this verb is actually singular. The subject is not the *phone calls* themselves, but rather the *number* of phone calls received. Therefore, the verb *emphasize* should be changed to the singular form *emphasizes*.

27. **E** No Error *Difficult*

The sentence is written correctly. It employs the present-perfect tense consistently and properly, and it draws a logical comparison between Beardly's novel (singular) and *Watts' novels* (plural).

28. **A** Pronouns *Difficult*

The pronoun *it* in **A** is singular, but it refers to the noun *plastic bags*. The word *bags* is plural, so the correct pronoun is the plural pronoun *they*.

29. **E** No Error *Difficult*

This sentence is written correctly. All subjects and verbs agree, all verbs are in the correct tense, and all words are in the correct format.

Improving Paragraphs

30. **E** Sentence Revision *Easy*

As it stands, this sentence is a run-on sentence. It consists of two independent clauses joined with no punctuation or conjunctions. The run-on is best corrected by the revision in **E**, which adds a comma and the conjunction *and* to join the two clauses.

31. **A** Essay Analysis *Difficult*

Sentence 1 refers to *him* (Dave). To make the pronoun reference clear, sentence 1 should immediately follow a sentence that mentions Dave by name. Sentence 2 fits the bill, so it would make sense to insert sentence 1 between sentences 2 and 3.

32. **D** Sentence Revision *Easy*

The original version of sentence 10 is a sentence fragment. It cannot stand alone as a complete sentence. This error is corrected by the revision in **D**, which joins sentences 9 and 10 by adding the conjunction *and*.

33. **A** Sentence Addition *Medium*

Sentence 14 starts out by stating that *there came an answering whinny*. However, the paragraph never mentions what the whinny came in answer to, so sentence 14 doesn't quite make sense. **A** makes it clear that the pony is responding to the sound of Dave's whistle.

34. **B** Sentence Revision *Medium*

Sentence 16 starts out by stating that *Dave took his head in his arms*, but it's not clear who the pronoun *his* refers to here. **B** corrects this problem by clarifying that *Dave took Chiquito's head in his arms*.

35. **C** Essay Analysis *Easy*

The author conveys a story by presenting it in narrative format, so **C** is correct.

SECTION 7: CRITICAL READING

Sentence Completions

1. **B** Two-Word/One-Way *Easy*

The first part of the sentence helps explain the meaning of the first blank. A person who is troublesome to work with might find it *hard* to obtain new jobs, so look for a word that means something like "hard." **B** and **C** are close, so eliminate **A**, **D**, and **E**. If a person's reputation makes it hard for him or her to find new jobs, then word of a person's reputation must spread *quickly* in the entertainment industry. **B** is correct.

2. **B** One-Word/One-Way *Medium*

A person who gives a speech in a *chaotic and frenzied* manner is exhibiting qualities of *maniacal* behavior. The word *maniacal* means "wildly disordered" or "displaying excessive enthusiasm," so **B** is correct.

3. **D** Two-Word/One-Way *Easy*

The second part of the sentence defines the meanings of the words in the blanks. The philanthropist was *liberal in sharing her resources* and *concerned about the needs of others*. A person who is liberal in sharing might properly be called either *generous* or *benevolent*. A person who cares about the needs of others is *considerate*, not *self-centered*. Therefore, **D** is correct.

4. **C** One-Word/Two-Way *Medium*

The word *though* at the beginning of this sentence signals that the last part of the sentence will contrast in meaning with the first part of the sentence. Singleton published articles mentioning his fear of flying, but his first flight must not have been terribly frightening for him after all. The word *undaunted* means "unshaken" or "maintaining courage," so **C** fits best.

5. **C** Two-Word/One-Way *Difficult*

This sentence contains no signals of contrast, so the first part of the sentence must be similar in meaning to the last part. The ambassador left the room abruptly during the senator's speech, so there must have been something about the speech that the ambassador did not like. Look for a first word with a negative meaning. **A** and **B** can be eliminated because *efficacious* and *scintillating* have positive meanings.

D and **E** can also be eliminated because *parsimonious* means "extremely frugal," and *penurious* means "stingy." A very long speech is excessive rather than frugal, so these words don't fit here. The word *soporific* means "sleep inducing," and the word *somnolence* means "sleepiness," so **C** makes sense.

6. **A** One-Word/One-Way *Difficult*

Johanna was shy around strangers, so she was probably very reserved at parties. The missing word must mean something similar to *withdraw*. The word *efface* means "to make invisible or inconspicuous," so **A** fits best.

Long Reading Passage

7. **D** Main Idea *Easy*

Paragraphs 2 through 6 discuss Gulick's definition of the classical balance of power system, so **D** fits best.

8. **E** Words in Context *Easy*

The word *relatively* is used in Paragraph 2 to describe *states possessing relatively equal power*. In other words, the power possessed by states is roughly, or *approximately*, equal.

9. **D** Implied Information *Difficult*

Paragraph 3 presents Gulick's views on the aims of states in a balance of power system. In this paragraph, Gulick argues that in addition to preserving their own survival, states also *focus on preserving the international system itself*. Gulick would therefore most likely agree with **D**.

10. **D** Implied Information *Medium*

In paragraph 3, the author notes that states in a balance of power system *work to ensure that no one state obtains hegemony, or a preponderance of power*. This implies that states form alliances to prevent any single state from becoming too strong.

11. **B** Implied Information *Medium*

Paragraph 4 points out that in Gulick's view, *wars may be necessary as a means for preserving the equilibrium between states*. This implies that Gulick saw war as an acceptable method of preserving the balance of power, so **B** is correct. **D** can be eliminated because it is too strong. The passage does not suggest that Gulick viewed war as the *most important* means of maintaining equilibrium but simply as a method that might be necessary under certain circumstances.

12. **C** Themes and Arguments *Medium*

The author mentions *vigilance, alliance formation, intervention* in paragraph 5. These strategies are listed among the *nine major instruments of foreign policy that are used as the means of a balance of power system*. **C** fits best.

13. **A** Implied Information *Medium*

The last sentence of paragraph 6 states that a war must cause *a change in the essential structure of the system* in order for the system to break down entirely. The first sentence of paragraph 6 explains that a change in the international system occurs only *when the assumptions, aims, and means of the system are altered in a fundamental way*. This phrase implies that in order for a war to cause a breakdown of the balance of power, it must cause a fundamental change in the assumptions, aims, and means of the system.

14. **E** Implied Information *Medium*

The author states in paragraph 7 that the decades before World War I *saw many small conflicts and rivalries between the main powers* but *still reflected relative peacefulness*. This implies that relationships between the states were generally peaceful, despite minor disputes.

15. **C** Specific Information *Medium*

The answer to this question can be found in paragraph 8. This paragraph notes that *after the war, the European state system was fundamentally intact, with all of the key states except Austria-Hungary still occupying their places in the system*.

16. **B** Specific Information *Easy*

Paragraph 9 states that after World War I, *France attempted to balance Germany by occupying the Ruhr basin to seize raw materials from Germany*. **B** is correct.

17. **E** Themes and Arguments *Medium*

Paragraph 9 starts by making the point that *the aims and means of the classical balance of power system also persisted after the war*. The actions of the major powers are described to support this point, so **E** works best.

18. **A** Specific Information *Medium*
The last paragraph of the passage argues that *it was World War II, and not World War I, that brought about the breakdown of the multipolar balance of power existing in Europe*. According to the passage, World War II transformed the international system *from a multipolar to a bipolar world*, as **A** indicates.

19. **D** Main Idea *Easy*
This passage starts out in paragraph 1 by stating its argument clearly. It claims that World War I *did not bring about a collapse of the balance of power system existing among the European nations in the early 1900s*. The rest of the passage provides evidence to support this argument, so **D** fits best.

SECTION 8: MATH

Multiple Choice

1. **B** Numbers & Operations: Basic Operations *Easy*
The correct answer must be an odd integer, so eliminate **C**. The correct answer must also be a positive integer, so eliminate **D** and **E**. Finally, the correct answer must be less than 7, so eliminate **A**. The number 5 is in all three sets.

2. **D** Algebra: Solving Equations *Easy*
Solve for h:

$$9+\sqrt{h}=17$$
$$\sqrt{h}=17-9$$
$$\sqrt{h}=8$$
$$h=8^2 \text{ or } 64$$

3. **A** Numbers & Operations: Fractions *Easy*
The total number of people surveyed was 21 + 46 + 3 = 70. Of these, $\frac{21}{70}$ liked Brand X toothpaste. The fraction $\frac{21}{70}$ can be reduced to $\frac{3}{10}$, so **A** is correct.

4. **C** Geometry: Triangles *Easy*
This figure contains two vertical angles, which are equal. In the lower triangle, the missing angle measures 180° – 80° – 40° = 60°. In the upper triangle, the missing angle also measures 60°. The value of $p + q$ equals 180 – 60°, or 120°.

5. **D** Data Analysis, Statistics & Probability: Graphs, Charts, and Tables *Easy*
According to the graph, the car dealership sold approximately 125 vehicles in April, and approximately 150 vehicles in May. This represents an increase of 25 vehicles from April to May, which is the least change shown on the graph from one month to the next.

6. **D** Geometry: Coordinate Geometry *Medium*
The function $h(s) = 3$ indicates that when some value, s, is plugged in as the x-variable of the function, the resulting y-variable is 3. Look on the graph to determine which

x-coordinates have y-coordinates of 3. The graph shows that all of the x-coordinates ranging from 0 to 2 have y-values of 3, so **D** is correct.

7. **A** Numbers & Operations: Exponents *Medium*

Try the numbers 1, 2, and 3 for x, y, and z:

$$\begin{aligned}3^x \times 3^y \times 3^z &= 3^1 \times 3^2 \times 3^3\\ &= 3 \times 9 \times 27\\ &= 729\end{aligned}$$

The numbers 1, 2, and 3 fit the first equation. Now, solve the second equation:

$$\begin{aligned}3^x + 3^y + 3^z &= 3^1 + 3^2 + 3^3\\ &= 3 + 9 + 27\\ &= 39\end{aligned}$$

8. **E** Geometry: Coordinate Geometry *Medium*

The diameter of the circle starts at the point (–4, 4) and runs through the center of the circle at point (–1, 4). The radius of the circle is thus 3 units long. The other endpoint of the diameter must be 3 units directly to the *right* of point (–1, 4). The coordinate located three units to the right of –1 on the x-axis is 2, so the other end of the diameter lies at (2, 4).

9. **E** Algebra: Inequalities *Medium*

Each box requires at least 20 seconds to make, without printing. Therefore, the minimum amount of time required to make each box is $t = 20$. If a box must be printed, the printing can add a maximum of 40 more seconds to the completion time. Therefore, the maximum amount of time that it could take to make and print one box is $20 + 40 = 60$ seconds. The range of time that it takes to complete a box is always somewhere from 20 seconds to 60 seconds. This range is best expressed by the inequality $20 \le t \le 60$.

10. **B** Geometry: Solids *Medium*

Determine the volume of the first cylinder:

$$\begin{aligned}V &= \pi r^2 h\\ &= \pi(4)^2(3)\\ &= \pi(16)(3)\\ &= 48\pi\end{aligned}$$

Now, determine the volume of the second cylinder:

$$\begin{aligned}V &= \pi r^2 h\\ &= \pi(4)^2(9)\\ &= \pi(16)(9)\\ &= 144\pi\end{aligned}$$

Since $144\pi \div 48\pi$ equals 3, this means that the volume of the second cylinder is three times larger than the volume of the first cylinder. The volume of the first cylinder is represented by v, so the volume of the second cylinder equals $3v$.

11. **C** Algebra: Inequalities *Medium*

The question states that a § (d, g) is true only if $d > a > g$. In the operation 3 § (7, g), a equals 3 and d equals 7. This operation can only be true if $7 > 3 > g$. Since g must be less than 3, it can equal either 2 or –4. **C** is correct.

12. **B** Numbers & Operations: Percents *Medium*

The question states that 35 percent of b equals 70 percent of d. Set up an equation and solve for d:

$$0.35b = 0.70d$$
$$\frac{0.35b}{0.70} = d$$
$$0.50b = d$$

Multiply 0.50 by 100 to determine the percentage: d is $0.50 \times 100 = 50$ percent of b.

13. **B** Numbers & Operations: Basic Operations *Difficult*

An even sum can only be produced by adding together two even numbers or two odd numbers. Therefore, a and b must be the same—either both even or both odd. The question states that the sum of $(a + b)^2 + a + c$ is also even. Since $a + b$ is even, this means that $(a + b)^2$ will also be even. The integers a and c must either both be odd or both be even to produce an even sum. **B** is correct.

14. **B** Algebra: Inequalities *Medium*

The variable z represents a negative fraction. When z is squared, the result will be a positive number. When z is cubed, the result will be a negative number. Therefore, I and II are both incorrect, and **A**, **C**, and **E** can be eliminated.

The negative fraction z will always be less (not greater) than $\frac{1}{4}(z)$, which will lie to the right of z on the real number line. Statement II must be true, so **B** is correct.

15. **A** Data Analysis, Statistics & Probability: Graphs, Charts, and Tables *Medium*

Notice that all but a few of the points on the scatterplot hover between 50 and 55 seconds. This means that the number of trials didn't really affect the runners' times much. Each runner had about the same time, between 50 and 55 seconds, regardless of how many trial runs he or she completed.

Add the values of the points to determine the average time for the 13 runners:

$$\frac{50 + 55 + 48 + 50 + 54 + 50 + 55 + 56 + 50 + 55 + 50 + 53 + 60}{13} = \frac{686}{13} = 52.77$$

On average, each runner completed the course in about 53 seconds, regardless of the number of trials. There was no variation in the results based on the number of trials. Therefore, the function $s(n)$ will be a constant, 53. For every input value of n, the output value $s(n)$ equals approximately 53. **A** best models this relationship.

16. **E** Geometry: Polygons *Difficult*

Determine the relationship between side length X and side length Y. The figure shows that 4 rectangles oriented horizontally can fit with the same height as three rectangles oriented vertically. Thus $4Y = 3X$. This means that $Y = \frac{3}{4}X$. Determine the area of one rectangle in terms of X:

$$A = XY$$
$$A = X\left(\frac{3}{4}x\right)$$
$$A = \frac{3}{4}X^2$$

The area of the rectangular region to be covered is $8X$ units long by $9X$ units wide, or $8X \times 9X$, which is $72X^2$. Divide this area by the area of one rectangle:

$$\frac{72X^2}{\frac{3}{4}X^2} = 72 \times \frac{4}{3}$$
$$= \frac{72 \times 4}{3}$$
$$= \frac{288}{3}, \text{ or } 96$$

SECTION 9: WRITING

Improving Sentences

1. **B** Tenses *Easy*

The first part of this sentence takes place in the past, and the second part of the sentence refers to an outcome that the Allies were hoping would happen. The verb phrase *would have secured peace* is incorrect here and should be replaced by the phrase *would secure peace*.

2. **C** Conjunctions *Easy*

The conjunction *and* is unnecessary in this sentence. **C** corrects this error by eliminating the unnecessary word.

3. **E** Other *Medium*

The underlined phrase is redundant as it stands. A person who stops smoking permanently naturally stays smoke-free. However, the act of stopping smoking is one thing—and the ability to remain smoke-free permanently is quite another. **E** revises the sentence to remove the redundancy and make the sentence clearer.

4. **E** Idioms *Medium*

The phrase *no sooner had* is always followed by the word *than*. By using the underlined word *but*, this sentence makes an idiomatic error. **E** corrects the error by replacing *but* with *than*.

5. **A** No Error *Medium*

This sentence is correct as written, so **A** is the best choice.

6. **C** Parallelism *Medium*

The underlined portion of this sentence is not parallel with the first part of the sentence. The sentence starts out by stating that *Molly Sauder will not be acknowledged*.

To be parallel, the sentence should finish with the phrase *any more than Molly's assistant, Joe Henderson, will be acknowledged.* **C** revises this sentence in an idiomatically correct way, maintaining parallel structure while also correctly using the phrase *will not be . . . any more than.*

7. **E** Wordiness *Medium*

The underlined phrase *if you understood human motivations it* is wordy and awkward. **E** corrects this error by rewriting the phrase most concisely.

8. **E** Fragments *Medium*

As it stands, this sentence is a fragment. **E** corrects this error by deleting the comma and adding the phrase *was because*.

9. **D** Tenses *Medium*

The word *introducing* is used incorrectly here. The action of this sentence takes place in the past, so *introducing* should be in the past tense form, *introduced.* **D** provides the most concise revision.

10. **D** Other *Medium*

The underlined portion of this sentence contains a pronoun error. The main subject of this sentence is *the ficus tree*. This subject is singular, so it should be referred to with the singular pronoun *its*.

11. **A** No Error *Medium*

This sentence is correct as written. All subjects and verbs agree, and all phrases are in the proper form.

12. **B** Misplaced Modifiers *Medium*

As it is written, this sentence makes it sound as if *the effect of Kovad's sales pitch* itself is performing the action of *tempting all but the most reluctant of consumers*. That doesn't seem right. **B** corrects this error by making it clear that Stan Kovad is actually doing the tempting.

13. **A** No Error *Medium*

This sentence is correct as written. All subjects and verbs agree, and all phrases are in the proper form.

14. **E** Passive Voice *Medium*

In the underlined portion of this sentence, the phrase *local artists were encouraged* is written in the passive voice. **E** corrects this error by using the active verb phrase *and encouraged local artists*.

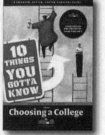